Preventing Tobacco Use Among Youth and Young Adults

A Report of the Surgeon General

2012

U.S. DEPARTMENT OF HEALTH AND HUMAN SERVICES
Public Health Service
Office of the Surgeon General
Rockville, MD

National Library of Medicine Cataloging in Publication

Preventing tobacco use among youth and young adults : a report of the Surgeon General. – Atlanta, GA. : Dept. of Health and Human Services, Centers for Disease Control and Prevention, National Center for Chronic Disease Prevention and Health Promotion, Office on Smoking and Health; Washington, D.C. : For sale by the Supt. of Docs., U.S. G.P.O., 2012.
p. 900
Includes bibliographical references.

1. Smoking – prevention & control. 2. Smoking – epidemiology. 3. Smoking – adverse effects. 4. Tobacco Industry. 5. Smoking Cessation. 6. Adolescent. 7. Young Adult. I. United States. Public Health Service. Office of the Surgeon General. II. National Center for Chronic Disease Prevention and Health Promotion (U.S.). Office on Smoking and Health.

HV 5745

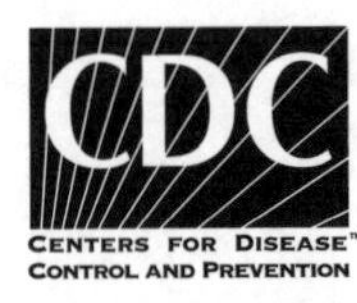

U.S. Department of Health and Human Services
Centers for Disease Control and Prevention
National Center for Chronic Disease Prevention and Health Promotion
Office on Smoking and Health

This publication is available on the World Wide Web at
http://www.surgeongeneral.gov/library

Suggested Citation

U.S. Department of Health and Human Services. *Preventing Tobacco Use Among Youth and Young Adults: A Report of the Surgeon General.* Atlanta, GA: U.S. Department of Health and Human Services, Centers for Disease Control and Prevention, National Center for Chronic Disease Prevention and Health Promotion, Office on Smoking and Health, 2012.

For sale by the Superintendent of Documents, U.S. Government Printing Office
Internet: bookstore.gpo.gov Phone: toll free (866) 512-1800; DC area (202) 512-1800
Fax: (202) 512-2104 Mail: Stop IDCC, Washington, DC 20402-0001

ISBN 978-0-16-090544-5

Message from Kathleen Sebelius

Secretary of Health and Human Services

Tobacco is the leading cause of preventable and premature death, killing an estimated 443,000 Americans each year. Cigarette smoking costs the nation $96 billion in direct medical costs and $97 billion in lost productivity annually. In addition to the billions in medical costs and lost productivity, tobacco is enacting a heavy toll on young people.

Each day in the United States, over 3,800 young people under 18 years of age smoke their first cigarette, and over 1,000 youth under age 18 become daily cigarette smokers. The vast majority of Americans who begin daily smoking during adolescence are addicted to nicotine by young adulthood. Despite the well-known health risks, youth and adult smoking rates that had been dropping for many years have stalled. When this Administration took office, we decided that if these numbers were not changing, we had to do something. We accelerated our efforts to fight tobacco by helping Americans stop smoking and protecting young people from starting to smoke.

The first step was the historic Family Smoking Prevention and Tobacco Control Act which gives the U.S. Food and Drug Administration the authority to regulate tobacco products to prevent use by minors and reduce the impact on public health. The law includes many vital provisions, including a ban on cigarettes with certain characterizing flavorings such as candy and fruit, restrictions on the sale of single cigarettes and the prohibition of marketing practices aimed at children. The Family Smoking Prevention and Tobacco Control Act also provides for graphic warning labels that make the danger of smoking abundantly clear.

Second, as part of the Recovery Act, the Department of Health and Human Services (HHS) invested $225 million to support tobacco prevention and control efforts in states. These investments were made in communities that have used evidence-based tobacco interventions and will eventually become models for the rest of the country.

The third step was the Affordable Care Act, which provides a new opportunity to transform how our nation addresses tobacco use through the Prevention and Public Health Fund. The law expands access to recommended treatment programs, such as tobacco use cessation, often at no additional cost. For the first time, Medicare and Medicaid will cover tobacco use cessation for all beneficiaries. The health care law also provides support for state 1-800 quitlines and implementation of innovative social media initiatives including text messaging and smart phone applications.

We are using the many tools at our disposal, from regulatory power to state and local investments, to end the tobacco epidemic. In November 2010, HHS announced the Department's first ever comprehensive tobacco control strategic action plan, titled Ending the Tobacco Epidemic, which will help us bring all of these strategies together to achieve our goals. An important component of our HHS plan focuses on preventing the initiation of tobacco use among young people, through hard-hitting mass media campaigns that will discourage our country's youth from starting to use tobacco products and motivate current tobacco users to quit. This key strategic action, combined with others in the plan, signify HHS's commitment to provide a clear roadmap for the future of tobacco prevention and control.

We have come a long way since the days of smoking on airplanes and in college classrooms, but we have a long way to go. We have the responsibility to act and do something to prevent our youth from smoking. The prosperity and health of our nation depend on it.

Message from Howard Koh

Assistant Secretary for Health

Tobacco use imposes enormous public health and financial costs on this nation—costs that are completely avoidable. Until we end tobacco use, more young people will become addicted, more people will become sick, and more families will be devastated by the loss of loved ones.

The simple fact is that we cannot end the tobacco epidemic without focusing our efforts on young people. Nearly 100% of adults who smoke every day started smoking when they were 26 or younger, so prevention is the key. The tobacco industry spends almost $10 billion a year to market its products, half of all movies for children under 13 contain scenes of tobacco use, and images and messages normalize tobacco use in magazines, on the Internet, and at retail stores frequented by youth. With a quarter of all high school seniors and a third of all young adults smoking, and with progress in reducing prevalence slowing dramatically, the time for action is now.

This Surgeon General's Report is an important addition to our base of knowledge on the prevalence, causes, effects, and implications of tobacco use by young people. It elucidates in powerful detail the factors that lead youth and young adults to initiate tobacco use, and the devastating health and economic impact of that decision on our nation as well as on individuals, their families, and their communities. This report also identifies proven, effective strategies that hold the potential of dramatically reducing tobacco use.

The Department's overall tobacco control strategy is to strengthen and fully implement these proven, effective strategies as part of a comprehensive approach that combines educational, clinical, regulatory, economic, and social initiatives. In November 2010, the Department released *Ending the Tobacco Epidemic: A Tobacco Control Strategic Action Plan for the U.S. Department of Health and Human Services* which provides a framework for coordinating this approach. The plan sets forth specific actions which HHS can implement to build on recent legislative milestones, respond to the changing market for tobacco products, and promote robust tobacco control programs at the federal, state, and community levels.

From 1997 to 2004 youth smoking fell rapidly. Since that time smoking among high school seniors has continued to fall, but slowly from 24.4% in 2003 to 18.7% in 2010 (daily smoking among youth has fallen from 16.8% in 1999 to 7.3% in 2009). Since 2003 prevalence among adults has fallen from 21.6 to 19.3% in 2010 The current problem is not that the evidence-based tools that drove the progress from 1997 to 2004 stopped working; it is that they have not been applied with sufficient effort or nationwide. That these tools still work is reflected in the fact that many states have seen significant reductions since 2005. Between 2005 and 2010 twenty states had declines of 20% or more.

Even with decades of progress and recent tobacco control initiatives, however, we must do more. We have ample evidence that comprehensive, multi-component interventions are effective at reducing tobacco use. But knowledge is not enough. We must also have commitment—the commitment to sustain comprehensive programs, to give our young people another perspective on tobacco, to create an environment that makes it harder for youth to smoke, to make cessation services accessible and affordable. It is within our grasp to make the next generation tobacco-free if we have the will to do so.

Foreword

Preventing smoking and smokeless tobacco use among young people is critical to ending the epidemic of tobacco use. Since the first Surgeon General's report on youth in 1994, the basis for concern about smoking during adolescence and young adulthood has expanded beyond the immediate health consequences for the young smoker to a deeper understanding of the implications for health across the life span from early use of tobacco. Cigarette smoking remains the leading cause of preventable death in the United States, accounting for approximately 443,000 deaths, or about 1 of every 5 deaths, in the United States each year.

Since 1994, there have been many legal and scientific developments that have curtailed somewhat the tobacco companies' ability to market to young people. The 1998 Master Settlement Agreement eliminated most cigarette billboard and transit advertising, print advertising directed to underage youth, and limited brand sponsorship. In addition, the Master Settlement Agreement resulted in the release of internal tobacco industry documents that have been analyzed by scientists. Furthermore, during this time, the prices of cigarettes and smokeless tobacco products also increased. These significant developments, among others, resulted in a sharp decrease in tobacco use among adults and youth. However, this progress has stalled in recent years.

More than 80% of adult smokers begin smoking by 18 years of age with 99% of first use by 26 years of age. In addition, adolescent smokeless tobacco users are more likely than nonusers to become adult cigarette smokers. Adolescents and young adults are uniquely susceptible to social and environmental influences to use tobacco, and tobacco companies spend billions of dollars on cigarette and smokeless tobacco marketing. The findings in this report provide evidence that coordinated, high-impact interventions including mass media campaigns, price increases, and community-level changes protecting people from secondhand smoke and norms are effective in reducing the initiation and prevalence of smoking among youth. However, many of these comprehensive tobacco control programs remain underfunded. Now more than ever, it is imperative that we continue investing in tobacco prevention and control. An increase in spending on sustained comprehensive tobacco control programs will result in reductions in youth and adult smoking rates and, ultimately, in health care costs.

Reducing tobacco use is a winnable battle. We have the science and, with additional effort and support for evidence-based, cost-effective strategies that we can implement now, we will improve on our nation's health and our children's future.

Thomas R. Frieden, M.D., M.P.H.
Director
Centers for Disease Control and Prevention
and
Administrator
Agency for Toxic Substances and Disease Registry

Preface

from the Surgeon General,
U.S. Department of Health and Human Services

Nearly all tobacco use begins during youth and young adulthood. These young individuals progress from smoking occasionally to smoking every day. Each day across the United States over 3,800 youth under 18 years of age start smoking. Although much progress has been made to reduce the prevalence of smoking since the first Surgeon General's report in 1964, today nearly one in four high school seniors and one in three young adults under age 26 smoke.

Of every three young smokers, only one will quit, and one of those remaining smokers will die from tobacco-related causes. Most of these young people never considered the long-term health consequences associated with tobacco use when they started smoking; and nicotine, a highly addictive drug, causes many to continue smoking well into adulthood, often with deadly consequences.

This Surgeon General's report examines in detail the epidemiology, health effects, and causes of tobacco use among youth ages 12 through 17 and young adults ages 18 through 25. For the first time tobacco data on young adults as a discrete population has been explored. This is because nearly all tobacco use begins in youth and young adulthood, and because young adults are a prime target for tobacco advertising and marketing activities. This report also highlights the efficacy of strategies to prevent young people from using tobacco.

After years of steady decrease following the Tobacco Master Settlement Agreement of 1998, declines in youth tobacco use have slowed for cigarette smoking and stalled for use of smokeless tobacco. The latest research shows that concurrent use of multiple tobacco products is common among young people, and suggest that smokeless tobacco use is increasing among White males.

An important element of this Surgeon General's report is the review of the health consequences of tobacco use by young people. Cigarette smoking by youth and young adults is proven to cause serious and potentially deadly health effects immediately and into adulthood. One of the most significant health effects is addiction to nicotine that keeps young people smoking longer, causing increased physical damage. Early abdominal aortic atherosclerosis has been found in young smokers which affects the flow of blood to vital organs such as the lungs. This leads to reduced lung growth that can increase the risk of chronic obstructive pulmonary disease later in life, and reduced lung function.

This report examines the social, environmental, advertising, and marketing influences that encourage youth and young adults to initiate and sustain tobacco use. Tobacco products are among the most heavily marketed consumer goods in the U.S. Much of the nearly $10 billion spent on marketing cigarettes each year goes to programs that reduce prices and make cigarettes more affordable; smokeless tobacco products are similarly promoted. Peer influences; imagery and messages that portray tobacco use as a desirable activity; and environmental cues, including those in both traditional and emerging media platforms, all encourage young people to use tobacco. These influences help attract youth to tobacco use and reinforce the perception that smoking and various forms of tobacco use are a social norm—a particularly strong message during adolescence and young adulthood.

Many initiatives have been put into place to help counter the influences that encourage young people to begin tobacco use. The Tobacco Master Settlement Agreement in 1998 curtailed much of the advertising that was particularly appealing to young people. With the passage of the 2009 legislation giving the U.S. Food and Drug Administration the authority to regulate tobacco products and tobacco advertising, we now have another important means of helping decrease the appeal of tobacco use to this population. Coordinated, multi-component interventions that include mass media campaigns, comprehensive community programs, comprehensive statewide tobacco control programs, price increases, and school-based policies have also proven effective in preventing onset and use of tobacco use among youth and young adults.

We know what works to prevent tobacco use among young people. The science contained in this and other Surgeon General's reports provides us with the information we need to prevent the needless suffering of premature disease caused by tobacco use, as well as save millions of lives. By strengthening and continuing to build upon effective policies and programs, we can help make our next generation tobacco free.

Regina Benjamin, M.D., M.B.A.
Surgeon General

Acknowledgments

This report was prepared by the U.S. Department of Health and Human Services under the general direction of the Centers for Disease Control and Prevention, National Center for Chronic Disease Prevention and Health Promotion, Office on Smoking and Health.

Vice Admiral Regina Benjamin, M.D., M.B.A., Surgeon General, U.S. Public Health Service, Office of the Assistant Secretary for Health, Office of the Surgeon General, Office of the Secretary, U.S. Department of Health and Human Services, Washington, D.C.

Howard K. Koh, M.D., M.P.H, Assistant Secretary for Health, U.S. Department of Health and Human Services, Washington, D.C.

Thomas R. Frieden, M.D., M.P.H., Director, Centers for Disease Control and Prevention, Atlanta, Georgia.

Ursula E. Bauer, Ph.D., M.P.H., Director, National Center for Chronic Disease Prevention and Health Promotion, Centers for Disease Control and Prevention, Atlanta, Georgia.

Barbara Bowman, Ph.D., Associate Director for Science, National Center for Chronic Disease Prevention and Health Promotion, Centers for Disease Control and Prevention, Atlanta, Georgia.

Tim A. McAfee, M.D., M.P.H., Director, Office on Smoking and Health, National Center for Chronic Disease Prevention and Health Promotion, Centers for Disease Control and Prevention, Atlanta, Georgia.

Terry F. Pechacek, Ph.D., Associate Director for Science, Office on Smoking and Health, National Center for Chronic Disease Prevention and Health Promotion, Centers for Disease Control and Prevention, Atlanta, Georgia.

The editors of the report were

Cheryl L. Perry, Ph.D., Senior Scientific Editor, Professor and Regional Dean, and Rockwell Distinguished Chair in Society and Health, Michael and Susan Dell Center for Healthy Living, School of Public Health, University of Texas, Austin, Texas.

Melissa H. Stigler, Ph.D., M.P.H., Senior Associate Editor, Assistant Professor, Division of Epidemiology, Human Genetics, and Environmental Sciences, Michael and Susan Dell Center for Healthy Living, School of Public Health, University of Texas, Austin, Texas.

Leslie Norman, M.B.A., Managing Editor, Office on Smoking and Health, National Center for Chronic Disease Prevention and Health Promotion, Centers for Disease Control and Prevention, Atlanta, Georgia.

Peter L. Taylor, M.B.A., Technical Editor, Fairfax, Virginia.

Contributing editors were

Frank J. Chaloupka, Ph.D., Director, Health Policy Center, Institute for Health Research and Policy, University of Illinois, Chicago, Illinois.

Brian R. Flay, D. Phil., Professor, Department of Public Health, Oregon State University, Corvallis, Oregon.

Jonathan M. Samet, M.D., M.S., Professor and Flora L. Thornton Chair, Department of Preventive Medicine, Keck School of Medicine, Director, Institute for Global Health, University of Southern California, Los Angeles, California.

Melissa H. Stigler, Ph.D., M.P.H., Assistant Professor, Division of Epidemiology, Human Genetics, and Environmental Sciences, Michael and Susan Dell Center for Healthy Living, School of Public Health, University of Texas, Austin, Texas.

Steve Sussman, Ph.D., Professor of Preventive Medicine and Psychology, Institute for Prevention Research, Keck School of Medicine, University of Southern California, Los Angeles, California.

Contributing authors were

Susan L. Ames, Ph.D., Associate Professor, School of Community and Global Health and Psychology, Claremont Graduate University, Claremont, California.

Deborah A. Burnette, Expert Consultant, ICF International, Atlanta, Georgia.

Frank J. Chaloupka, Ph.D., Director, Health Policy Center, Institute for Health Research and Policy, University of Illinois, Chicago, Illinois.

K. Michael Cummings, Ph.D., M.P.H., Senior Research Scientist, Chair, Department of Health Behavior, Division of Cancer Prevention and Population Sciences, Roswell Park Cancer Institute, Buffalo, New York.

Cristine Delnevo, Ph.D., M.P.H., Associate Professor, Director, Center for Tobacco Surveillance and Evaluation Research, University of Medicine and Dentistry of New Jersey, School of Public Health, New Brunswick, New Jersey.

Lori Dorfman, Dr.P.H., M.P.H., Director, Berkeley Media Studies Group, a project of the Public Health Institute, Berkeley, California.

Sarah J. Durkin, Ph.D., Senior Research Fellow, Centre for Behavioral Research in Cancer, Cancer Council Victoria, Melbourne, Australia.

Susan T. Ennett, Ph.D., Professor, Department of Health Behavior and Health Education, Gillings School of Global Public Health, University of North Carolina, Chapel Hill, North Carolina.

Michael Eriksen, Sc.D., Professor and Director, Institute of Public Health, Georgia State University, Atlanta, Georgia.

Ellen Feighery, R.N., M.S., Associate Director, International Research, Campaign for Tobacco-Free Kids, Washington, D.C.

Brian R. Flay, D. Phil., Professor, Department of Public Health, Oregon State University, Corvallis, Oregon.

Geoffrey Fong, Ph.D., Professor, Department of Psychology, University of Waterloo, Waterloo, Ontario, Canada, and Senior Investigator, Ontario Institute for Cancer Research, Toronto, Ontario, Canada.

Jean L. Forster, Ph.D., M.P.H., Professor, Division of Epidemiology and Community Health, School of Public Health, University of Minnesota, Minneapolis, Minnesota.

Samuel S. Gidding, M.D., Professor of Pediatrics, Thomas Jefferson University, Nemours Cardiac Center, A. I. duPont Hospital for Children, Wilmington, Delaware.

Gary A. Giovino, Ph.D., M.S., Professor and Chair, Department of Community Health and Health Behavior, School of Public Health and Health Professions, University at Buffalo, State University of New York, Buffalo, New York.

Stanton Glantz, Ph.D., Professor of Medicine, American Legacy Foundation Distinguished Professor in Tobacco Control, Department of Medicine, Division of Cardiology, University of California, San Francisco, California.

Diane R. Gold, M.D., M.P.H., Channing Laboratory, Brigham and Women's Hospital, Professor of Medicine, Harvard Medical School, and Associate Professor of Environmental Health, Harvard School of Public Health, Boston, Massachusetts.

Bonnie L. Halpern-Felsher, Ph.D., Professor of Pediatrics, Department of Pediatrics, Division of Adolescent Medicine, University of California, San Francisco, California.

David Hammond, Ph.D., Associate Professor, School of Public Health and Health Systems, University of Waterloo, Waterloo, Ontario, Canada.

Yvonne Hunt, Ph.D., M.P.H., Program Director, Tobacco Control Research Branch, Behavioral Research Program, Division of Cancer Control and Population Sciences, National Cancer Institute, National Institutes of Health, U.S. Department of Health and Human Services, Bethesda, Maryland.

Laura Kann, Ph.D., Branch Chief, Surveillance and Evaluation Research Branch, Division of Adolescent and School Health, National Center for Chronic Disease Prevention and Health Promotion, Centers for Disease Control and Prevention, Atlanta, Georgia.

Rachel Kaufmann, Ph.D., M.P.H., Deputy Associate Director for Science, Office on Smoking and Health, National Center for Chronic Disease Prevention and Health Promotion, Centers for Disease Control and Prevention, Atlanta, Georgia.

Steve Kinchen, Team Leader, Data Management and Analysis Team, Surveillance and Evaluation Research Branch, Division of Adolescent and School Health, National Center for Chronic Disease Prevention and Health Promotion, Centers for Disease Control and Prevention, Atlanta, Georgia.

Robert C. Klesges, Ph.D., Professor, Department of Preventive Medicine, University of Tennessee Health Science Center, and Member, Division of Epidemiology and Cancer Control, St. Jude Children's Research Hospital, Memphis, Tennessee.

Suchitira Krishnan-Sarin, Ph.D., Associate Professor, Department of Psychiatry, Yale University School of Medicine, New Haven, Connecticut.

Karol Kumpfer, Ph.D., Psychologist, Program Developer and Professor of Health Promotion and Education, Department of Health Promotion and Education, University of Utah, Salt Lake City, Utah.

Genelle Lamont, M.P.H., Doctoral Student, Division of Epidemiology and Community Health, School of Public Health, University of Minnesota, Minneapolis, Minnesota.

Christina N. Lessov-Schlaggar, Ph.D., Research Assistant Professor, Department of Psychiatry, School of Medicine, Washington University, St. Louis, Missouri.

Pamela Ling, M.D., M.P.H., Associate Professor of Medicine, Division of General Internal Medicine, Center for Tobacco Control Research and Education, University of California, San Francisco, California.

Patrick M. O'Malley, Ph.D., Research Professor, Survey Research Center, Institute for Social Research, University of Michigan, Ann Arbor, Michigan.

Terry F. Pechacek, Ph.D., Associate Director for Science, National Center for Chronic Disease Prevention and Health Promotion, Centers for Disease Control and Prevention, Atlanta, Georgia.

Cheryl L. Perry, Ph.D., Professor and Regional Dean, and Rockwell Distinguished Chair in Society and Health, Michael and Susan Dell Center for Healthy Living, School of Public Health, University of Texas, Austin, Texas.

Kurt M. Ribisl, Ph.D., Associate Professor, Department of Health Behavior and Health Education, Gillings School of Global Public Health, University of North Carolina, Chapel Hill, North Carolina.

Joni L. Rutter, Ph.D., Acting Director, Division of Basic Neuroscience and Behavioral Research, National Institute on Drug Abuse, National Institutes of Health, U.S. Department of Health and Human Services, Bethesda, Maryland.

Henry Saffer, Ph.D., Research Associate, National Bureau of Economic Research, New York, New York.

Jonathan M. Samet, M.D., M.S., Professor and Flora L. Thornton Chair, Department of Preventive Medicine, Keck School of Medicine, Director, Institute for Global Health, University of Southern California, Los Angeles, California.

James Sargent, M.D., Professor of Pediatrics, Dartmouth Medical School, Co-Director, Cancer Control Research Program, Norris Cotton Cancer Center, Lebanon, New Hampshire.

Herbert H. Severson, Ph.D., Senior Research Scientist, Oregon Research Institute, Eugene, Oregon.

Deborah Sherrill-Mittleman, Ph.D., Clinical Research Scientist, Division of Epidemiology and Cancer Control, St. Jude Children's Research Hospital, Memphis, Tennessee.

Anna V. Song, Ph.D., Assistant Professor, Health Psychology, School of Social Sciences, Humanities and Arts, Psychological Sciences, University of California, Merced, California.

Melissa H. Stigler, Ph.D., M.P.H., Assistant Professor, Division of Epidemiology, Human Genetics, and Environmental Sciences, Michael and Susan Dell Center for Healthy Living, School of Public Health, University of Texas, Austin, Texas.

Steve Sussman, Ph.D., Professor of Preventive Medicine and Psychology, Institute for Prevention Research, Keck School of Medicine, University of Southern California, Los Angeles, California.

John A. Tauras, Ph.D., Associate Professor, Department of Economics, and Research Associate, National Bureau of Economic Research, University of Illinois, Chicago, Illinois.

Jennifer B. Unger, Ph.D., Professor of Preventive Medicine, Keck School of Medicine, University of Southern California, Alhambra, California.

Mark Vander Weg, Ph.D., Associate Professor, Departments of Psychology and General Internal Medicine, University of Iowa, Iowa City, Iowa.

Melanie Wakefield, Ph.D., Director, Centre for Behavioural Research in Cancer, Cancer Council Victoria, Melbourne, Australia.

Rachel Widome, Ph.D, M.H.S., Core Investigator, Center for Chronic Disease Outcomes Research and Assistant Professor, Department of Medicine, University of Minnesota, Minneapolis, Minnesota.

Phillip W. Wilbur, M.A., Director, Tobacco Control and Health Programs, Danya International Inc., Silver Spring, Maryland.

Reviewers were

Cathy L. Backinger, Ph.D., M.P.H., Chief, Tobacco Control Research Branch, Behavioral Research Program, Division of Cancer Control and Population Sciences, National Cancer Institute, National Institutes of Health, Bethesda, Maryland.

Stephen W. Banspach, Ph.D., Associate Director for Science, Division of Adolescent and School Health, National Center for Chronic Disease Prevention and Health Promotion, Centers for Disease Control and Prevention, Atlanta, Georgia.

Neal Benowitz, M.D., Professor of Medicine and Bioengineering and Therapeutic Sciences, and Chief, Division of Clinical Pharmacology and Experimental Therapeutics, University of California, San Francisco, California.

Gerald S. Berenson, M.D., Research Professor, Department of Epidemiology, School of Public Health and Tropical Medicine, Tulane Center for Cardiovascular Health, New Orleans, Louisiana.

Stella A. Bialous, R.N., M.Sc.N., Dr.P.H., President, Tobacco Policy International, San Francisco, California.

Lois Biener, Ph.D., Senior Research Fellow, Center for Survey Research, University of Massachusetts, Boston, Massachusetts.

Anthony Biglan, Ph.D., Senior Scientist, Oregon Research Institute, Eugene, Oregon.

Mary Beth Bigley, Dr.P.H., M.S.N., A.N.P., Acting Director of the Office of Science and Communication, Office of the Surgeon General, Office of the Assistant Secretary for Health, Office of the Secretary, U.S. Department of Health and Human Services, Washington, D.C.

Michele Bloch, M.D., Ph.D., Medical Officer, Tobacco Control Research Branch, Behavioral Research Program, Division of Cancer Control and Population Sciences, National Cancer Institute, National Institutes of Health, Bethesda, Maryland.

Alan Blum, M.D., Director, The University of Alabama Center for the Study of Tobacco and Society, Tuscaloosa, Alabama.

David M. Burns, M.D., Professor Emeritus, Department of Family and Preventive Medicine, School of Medicine, University of California, San Diego, California.

Ralph S. Caraballo, Ph.D., M.P.H., Branch Chief, Epidemiology Branch, Office on Smoking and Health, National Center for Chronic Disease Prevention and Health Promotion, Centers for Disease Control and Prevention, Atlanta, Georgia.

Wilson M. Compton, M.D., M.P.E., Director, Division of Epidemiology, Services and Prevention Research, National Institute on Drug Abuse, Bethesda, Maryland.

Gregory N. Connolly, D.M.D., M.P.H., Professor, Department of Society, Human Development, and Health, Harvard School of Public Health, Harvard University, Boston, Massachusetts.

David Cowling, Ph.D., Chief, Evaluation Unit, California Department of Public Health, California Tobacco Control Program, Sacramento, California.

Jennifer Cullen, Ph.D., M.P.H., Director of Epidemiologic Research, Center for Prostate Disease Research, Research Assistant Professor, Department of Surgery, Uniformed Services University of the Health Sciences, Rockville, Maryland.

K. Michael Cummings, Ph.D., M.P.H., Senior Research Scientist, Chair, Department of Health Behavior, Division of Cancer Prevention and Population Sciences, Roswell Park Cancer Institute, Buffalo, New York.

Joseph DiFranza, M.D., Professor, Department of Family Medicine and Community Health, University of Massachusetts Medical School, Worcester, Massachusetts.

Timothy Dewhirst, Ph.D., Associate Professor, Department of Marketing and Consumer Studies, College of Management and Economics, University of Guelph, Guelph, Ontario, Canada.

Shanta R. Dube, Ph.D., M.P.H., Lead Health Scientist, Office on Smoking and Health, National Center for Chronic Disease Prevention and Health Promotion, Centers for Disease Control and Prevention, Atlanta, Georgia.

Sherry L. Emery, Ph.D., Senior Research Scientist, Institute for Health Research and Policy, University of Illinois, Chicago, Illinois.

Michael Eriksen, Sc.D., Professor and Director, Institute of Public Health, Georgia State University, Atlanta, Georgia.

Pebbles Fagan, Ph.D., M.P.H., Associate Professor and Program Director, Prevention and Control Program, University of Hawaii Cancer Center, Honolulu, Hawaii.

Jean L. Forster, Ph.D., M.P.H., Professor, Division of Epidemiology and Community Health, School of Public Health, University of Minnesota, Minneapolis, Minnesota.

Erika Fulmer, M.H.A., Health Scientist, Office on Smoking and Health, National Center for Chronic Disease Prevention and Health Promotion, Centers for Disease Control and Prevention, Atlanta, Georgia.

Elizabeth M. Ginexi, Ph.D., Program Director, Tobacco Control Research Branch, Division of Cancer Control and Population Sciences, National Cancer Institute, Bethesda, Maryland.

Stanton Glantz, Ph.D., Professor of Medicine, American Legacy Foundation Distinguished Professor in Tobacco Control, Department of Medicine, Division of Cardiology, University of California, San Francisco, California.

Thomas J. Glynn, Ph.D., Director, Cancer Science and Trends, and Director, International Cancer Control, American Cancer Society, Washington, D.C.

Marvin E. Goldberg, Ph.D., Emeritus Bard Professor of Marketing, Pennsylvania State University, and University Associate, Eller College of Management, University of Arizona, Tucson, Arizona.

Susan Marsiglia Gray, M.P.H., Coordinator, National Synar Program, Substance Abuse and Mental Health Services Administration/Center for Substance Abuse Prevention, Rockville, Maryland.

Gerard Hastings, Ph.D., OBE, Professor, Director, Institute for Social Marketing and Centre for Tobacco Control Research, University of Stirling and the Open University, Stirling, Scotland.

Dorothy Hatsukami, Ph.D., Forster Family Professor in Cancer Prevention, Professor of Psychiatry, Tobacco Research Programs, University of Minnesota, Minneapolis, Minnesota.

Lynne Haverkos, M.D., M.P.H., Program Director, Pediatric Behavior and Health Promotion, *Eunice Kennedy Shriver* National Institute of Child Health and Human Development, National Institutes of Health, Bethesda, Maryland.

Jack E. Henningfield, Ph.D., Vice President, Research and Health Policy, Pinney Associates, Bethesda, Maryland; and Professor, Adjunct, Department of Psychiatry and Behavioral Sciences, The Johns Hopkins University School of Medicine, Baltimore, Maryland.

Lisa Henriksen, Ph.D., Senior Research Scientist, Stanford Prevention Research Center, Stanford University School of Medicine, Palo Alto, California.

Yvonne M. Hunt, Ph.D., M.P.H., Program Director, Tobacco Control Research Branch, Behavioral Research Program, Division of Cancer Control and Population Sciences, National Cancer Institute, National Institutes of Health, Bethesda, Maryland.

Corinne Husten, M.D., M.P.H., Senior Medical Advisor, Center for Tobacco Products, Food and Drug Administration, Rockville, Maryland.

Andrew Hyland, Ph.D., Research Scientist, Department of Health Behavior, Division of Cancer Prevention and Population Sciences, Roswell Park Cancer Institute, Buffalo, New York.

Charles Irwin, Jr., M.D., Distinguished Professor of Pediatrics and Director of the Division of Adolescent Medicine, University of California San Francisco, California.

Rachel Kaufmann, Ph.D., M.P.H., Deputy Associate Director for Science, Office on Smoking and Health, National Center for Chronic Disease Prevention and Health Promotion, Centers for Disease Control and Prevention, Atlanta, Georgia.

Steven H. Kelder, M.P.H., Ph.D., Professor, Division of Epidemiology, Human Genetics, and Environmental Sciences, Co-Director, Michael and Susan Dell Center for Healthy Living, University of Texas School of Public Health, Austin, Texas.

Brian A. King, Ph.D., M.P.H., Epidemiologist, Office on Smoking and Health, National Center for Chronic Disease Prevention and Health Promotion, Centers for Disease Control and Prevention, Atlanta, Georgia.

Jonathan D. Klein, M.D., M.P.H., Professor of Pediatrics, Department of Pediatrics, University of Rochester School of Medicine and Dentistry, Rochester, New York, Associate Executive Director, and Director, Julius B. Richmond Center, American Academy of Pediatrics, Elk Grove Village, Illinois.

Katherine Kolor, Ph.D., M.S., Health Scientist, Office of Public Health Genomics, Centers for Disease Control and Prevention, Atlanta, Georgia.

Kelli A. Komro, M.P.H., Ph.D., Professor, Department of Health Outcomes and Policy, College of Medicine, Associate Director, Institute for Child Health Policy, University of Florida, Gainesville, Florida.

Nicole M. Kuiper, M.P.H., Health Scientist, Office on Smoking and Health, National Center for Chronic Disease Prevention and Health Promotion, Centers for Disease Control and Prevention, Atlanta, Georgia.

John Kulig, M.D., M.P.H., Director, Adolescent Medicine, Tufts Medical Center, Boston, Massachusetts.

Youn Ok Lee, Ph.D., Postdoctoral Fellow, Center for Tobacco Control Research and Education, University of California, San Francisco, California.

Pamela Ling, M.D, M.P.H., Associate Professor of Medicine, Division of General Internal Medicine, Center for Tobacco Control Research and Education, University of California, San Francisco, California.

Kathryn P. Mayhew, Ph.D., Associate Professor, Counselor Education and Educational Psychology, Saint Cloud State University, Saint Cloud, Minnesota.

Robin J. Mermelstein, Ph.D., Director, Institute for Health Research and Policy, Professor, Psychology Department, Clinical Professor, Community Health Sciences, School of Public Health, Institute for Health Research and Policy, University of Illinois, Chicago, Illinois.

Matthew L. Myers, J.D., President, Campaign for Tobacco-Free Kids, Washington, D.C.

Elizabeth Ozer, Ph.D., Associate Professor, Division of Adolescent Medicine, Department of Pediatrics, University of California, San Francisco, California.

Mark Parascandola, Ph.D., M.P.H., Epidemiologist, Tobacco Control Research Branch, Behavioral Research Program, Division of Cancer Control and Population Sciences, National Cancer Institute, Bethesda, Maryland.

John P. Pierce, Ph.D., Sam M. Walton Professor for Cancer Research, Department of Family and Preventive Medicine, and Associate Director for Population Sciences, Moores Cancer Center, University of California at San Diego, La Jolla, California.

John M. Pinney, President, Pinney Associates, Bethesda, Maryland.

Richard Pollay, Ph.D., Professor Emeritus, Marketing Division, and Curator, History of Advertising Archives, Sauder School of Business, University of British Columbia, Vancouver, British Columbia, Canada.

Gabbi Promoff, M.A., Issues Management Team Lead, Policy Unit, Office on Smoking and Health, National Center for Chronic Disease Prevention and Health Promotion, Centers for Disease Control and Prevention, Atlanta, Georgia.

William Riley, Ph.D., Program Director, Division of Cardiovascular Sciences, National Heart, Lung, and Blood Institute, Bethesda, Maryland.

Rosemary Rosso, J.D., Senior Attorney, Federal Trade Commission, Washington, D.C.

Joni L. Rutter, Ph.D., Acting Director, Division of Basic Neuroscience and Behavioral Research, National Institute on Drug Abuse, National Institutes of Health, U.S. Department of Health and Human Services, Bethesda, Maryland.

Yussuf Saloojee, Ph.D., Executive Director, National Council Against Smoking, Johannesburg, South Africa.

Dana Shelton, M.P.H., Associate Director for Policy, Planning, and Coordination, Office on Smoking and Health, National Center for Chronic Disease Prevention and Health Promotion, Centers for Disease Control and Prevention, Atlanta, Georgia.

Frank E. Speizer, M.D., Professor of Medicine, Channing Laboratory, Harvard Medical School, Professor of Environmental Science, Department of Environmental Health, Harvard School of Public Health, Harvard University, Boston, Massachusetts.

James F. Thrasher, Ph.D., M.S., M.A., Assistant Professor, Health Promotion, Education, and Behavior, Arnold School of Public Health, University of South Carolina, Columbia, South Carolina, and Visiting Professor and Researcher, Instituto Nacional de Salud Publica, Cuernavaca, Mexico.

Douglas Tipperman, M.S.W., Lead Public Health Advisor, Center for Substance Abuse Prevention, Substance Abuse and Mental Health Services Administration, Rockville, Maryland.

Donna Vallone, Ph.D., M.P.H., Senior Vice President, Research, American Legacy Foundation, Washington, D.C.

Kasisomayajula Viswanath, Ph.D., Associate Professor, Harvard School of Public Health, and Associate Professor of Medical Oncology, Dana-Farber Cancer Institute, Boston, Massachusetts.

Kenneth E. Warner, Ph.D., Avedis Donabedian Distinguished University Professor of Public Health, School of Public Health, University of Michigan, Ann Arbor, Michigan.

Jonathan P. Winickoff, M.D., M.P.H., Associate Professor of Pediatrics, Harvard University Medical School, Massachusetts General Hospital for Children, Boston, Massachusetts.

Other contributors were

René A. Arrazola, M.P.H., Epidemiologist, Office on Smoking and Health, National Center for Chronic Disease Prevention and Health Promotion, Centers for Disease Control and Prevention, Atlanta, Georgia.

David Chyen, M.S., Survey Statistician, Data Management and Analysis Team, Surveillance and Evaluation Research Branch, Division of Adolescent and School Health, National Center for Chronic Disease Prevention and Health Promotion, Centers for Disease Control and Prevention, Atlanta, Georgia.

James D. Colliver, Ph.D., Statistician (Retired), Division of Population Surveys, Substance Abuse and Mental Health Services Administration, Rockville, Maryland.

MeLisa R. Creamer, M.P.H., Doctoral Student and Dell Health Scholar, Michael and Susan Dell Center for Healthy Living, University of Texas School of Public Health, Austin, Texas.

Athena Foong, Research Writer/Research Assistant to Jonathan M. Samet, M.D., M.S., Department of Preventive Medicine, Keck School of Medicine, Institute for Global Health, University of Southern California, Los Angeles, California.

Joseph Gfroerer, Director, Division of Population Surveys, Center for Behavioral Health Statistics and Quality, Substance Abuse and Mental Health Service Administration, Rockville, Maryland.

Beth Han, M.D., Ph.D., M.P.H., Statistician, Center for Behavioral Health Statistics and Quality, Substance Abuse and Mental Health Service Administration, Rockville, Maryland.

William A. Harris, M.M., System Developer, Data Management and Analysis Team, Surveillance and Evaluation Research Branch, Division of Adolescent and School Health, National Center for Chronic Disease Prevention and Health Promotion, Centers for Disease Control and Prevention, Atlanta, Georgia.

Ghada Homsi, M.E., Research Economist, Public Health Policy Research, RTI international, Research Triangle Park, North Carolina.

Lynn A. Hughley, Health Communications Specialist, Office on Smoking and Health, National Center for Chronic Disease Prevention and Health Promotion, Centers for Disease Control and Prevention, Atlanta, Georgia.

Tim McManus, M.S., Survey Statistician, Data Management and Analysis Team, Surveillance and Evaluation Research Branch, Division of Adolescent and School Health, National Center for Chronic Disease Prevention and Health Promotion, Centers for Disease Control and Prevention, Atlanta, Georgia.

Luz M. Moncayo, Executive Assistant to Jonathan M. Samet, M.D., M.S., Department of Preventive Medicine, Keck School of Medicine, Institute for Global Health, University of Southern California, Los Angeles, California.

Emily Neusel, M.P.H., Doctoral Student, Michael and Susan Dell Center for Healthy Living, University of Texas School of Public Health, Austin Regional Campus, Austin, Texas.

Tariq Qureshi, M.D., M.P.H., Data Manager, Data Management and Analysis Team, Surveillance and Evaluation Research Branch, Division of Adolescent and School Health, National Center for Chronic Disease Prevention and Health Promotion, Centers for Disease Control and Prevention, Atlanta, Georgia.

Derek Smolenski, Ph.D., Research Associate, Division of Epidemiology and Community Health, School of Public Health, University of Minnesota, Minneapolis, Minnesota.

Kathryn Szynal, Editorial Assistant, Office on Smoking and Health, National Center for Chronic Disease Prevention and Health Promotion, Centers for Disease Control and Prevention, Atlanta, Georgia.

Angela Trosclair, M.S., Statistician, Office on Smoking and Health, National Center for Chronic Disease Prevention and Health Promotion, Centers for Disease Control and Prevention, Atlanta, Georgia.

Kimberly M. White, Executive Assistant to the Regional Dean, University of Texas School of Public Health, Austin, Texas.

Peggy Williams, M.S., Technical Writer-Editor, National Center for Chronic Disease Prevention and Health Promotion, Centers for Disease Control and Prevention, Atlanta, Georgia.

Preventing Tobacco Use Among Youth and Young Adults

Chapter 1
Introduction, Summary, and Conclusions

Introduction

Tobacco use is a global epidemic among young people. As with adults, it poses a serious health threat to youth and young adults in the United States and has significant implications for this nation's public and economic health in the future (Perry et al. 1994; Kessler 1995). The impact of cigarette smoking and other tobacco use on chronic disease, which accounts for 75% of American spending on health care (Anderson 2010), is well-documented and undeniable. Although progress has been made since the first Surgeon General's report on smoking and health in 1964 (U.S. Department of Health, Education, and Welfare [USDHEW] 1964), nearly one in four high school seniors is a current smoker. Most young smokers become adult smokers. One-half of adult smokers die prematurely from tobacco-related diseases (Fagerström 2002; Doll et al. 2004). Despite thousands of programs to reduce youth smoking and hundreds of thousands of media stories on the dangers of tobacco use, generation after generation continues to use these deadly products, and family after family continues to suffer the devastating consequences. Yet a robust science base exists on social, biological, and environmental factors that influence young people to use tobacco, the physiology of progression from experimentation to addiction, other health effects of tobacco use, the epidemiology of youth and young adult tobacco use, and evidence-based interventions that have proven effective at reducing both initiation and prevalence of tobacco use among young people. Those are precisely the issues examined in this report, which aims to support the application of this robust science base.

Nearly all tobacco use begins in childhood and adolescence (U.S. Department of Health and Human Services [USDHHS] 1994). In all, 88% of adult smokers who smoke daily report that they started smoking by the age of 18 years (see Chapter 3, "The Epidemiology of Tobacco Use Among Young People in the United States and Worldwide"). This is a time in life of great vulnerability to social influences (Steinberg 2004), such as those offered through the marketing of tobacco products and the modeling of smoking by attractive role models, as in movies (Dalton et al. 2009), which have especially strong effects on the young. This is also a time in life of heightened sensitivity to normative influences: as tobacco use is less tolerated in public areas and there are fewer social or regular users of tobacco, use decreases among youth (Alesci et al. 2003). And so, as we adults quit, we help protect our children.

Cigarettes are the only legal consumer products in the world that cause one-half of their long-term users to die prematurely (Fagerström 2002; Doll et al. 2004). As this epidemic continues to take its toll in the United States, it is also increasing in low- and middle-income countries that are least able to afford the resulting health and economic consequences (Peto and Lopez 2001; Reddy et al. 2006). It is past time to end this epidemic. To do so, primary prevention is required, for which our focus must be on youth and young adults. As noted in this report, we now have a set of proven tools and policies that can drastically lower youth initiation and use of tobacco products. Fully committing to using these tools and executing these policies consistently and aggressively is the most straight forward and effective to making future generations tobacco-free.

The 1994 Surgeon General's Report

This Surgeon General's report on tobacco is the second to focus solely on young people since these reports began in 1964. Its main purpose is to update the science of smoking among youth since the first comprehensive Surgeon General's report on tobacco use by youth, *Preventing Tobacco Use Among Young People*, was published in 1994 (USDHHS 1994). That report concluded that if young people can remain free of tobacco until 18 years of age, most will never start to smoke. The report documented the addiction process for young people and how the symptoms of addiction in youth are similar to those in adults. Tobacco was also presented as a gateway drug among young people, because its use generally precedes and increases the risk of using illicit drugs. Cigarette advertising and promotional activities were seen as a potent way to increase the risk of cigarette smoking among young people, while community-wide efforts were shown to have been successful in reducing tobacco use among youth. All of these conclusions remain important, relevant, and accurate, as documented in the current report, but there has been considerable research since 1994 that greatly expands our knowledge about tobacco use among youth, its prevention, and the dynamics of cessation among young people. Thus, there is a compelling need for the current report.

Tobacco Control Developments

Since 1994, multiple legal and scientific developments have altered the tobacco control environment and thus have affected smoking among youth. The states and the U.S. Department of Justice brought lawsuits against cigarette companies, with the result that many internal documents of the tobacco industry have been made public and have been analyzed and introduced into the science of tobacco control. Also, the 1998 Master Settlement Agreement with the tobacco companies resulted in the elimination of billboard and transit advertising as well as print advertising that directly targeted underage youth and limitations on the use of brand sponsorships (National Association of Attorneys General [NAAG] 1998). This settlement also created the American Legacy Foundation, which implemented a nationwide antismoking campaign targeting youth. In 2009, the U.S. Congress passed a law that gave the U.S. Food and Drug Administration authority to regulate tobacco products in order to promote the public's health (*Family Smoking Prevention and Tobacco Control Act* 2009). Certain tobacco companies are now subject to regulations limiting their ability to market to young people. In addition, they have had to reimburse state governments (through agreements made with some states and the Master Settlement Agreement) for some health care costs. Due in part to these changes, there was a decrease in tobacco use among adults and among youth following the Master Settlement Agreement, which is documented in this current report.

Recent Surgeon General Reports Addressing Youth Issues

Other reports of the Surgeon General since 1994 have also included major conclusions that relate to tobacco use among youth (Office of the Surgeon General 2010). In 1998, the report focused on tobacco use among U.S. racial/ethnic minority groups (USDHHS 1998) and noted that cigarette smoking among Black and Hispanic youth increased in the 1990s following declines among all racial/ethnic groups in the 1980s; this was particularly notable among Black youth, and culturally appropriate interventions were suggested. In 2000, the report focused on reducing tobacco use (USDHHS 2000b). A major conclusion of that report was that school-based interventions, when implemented with community- and media-based activities, could reduce or postpone the onset of smoking among adolescents by 20–40%. That report also noted that effective regulation of tobacco advertising and promotional activities directed at young people would very likely reduce the prevalence and onset of smoking. In 2001, the Surgeon General's report focused on women and smoking (USDHHS 2001). Besides reinforcing much of what was discussed in earlier reports, this report documented that girls were more affected than boys by the desire to smoke for the purpose of weight control. Given the ongoing obesity epidemic (Bonnie et al. 2007), the current report includes a more extensive review of research in this area.

The 2004 Surgeon General's report on the health consequences of smoking (USDHHS 2004) concluded that there is sufficient evidence to infer that a causal relationship exists between active smoking and (a) impaired lung growth during childhood and adolescence; (b) early onset of decline in lung function during late adolescence and early adulthood; (c) respiratory signs and symptoms in children and adolescents, including coughing, phlegm, wheezing, and dyspnea; and (d) asthma-related symptoms (e.g., wheezing) in childhood and adolescence. The 2004 Surgeon General's report further provided evidence that cigarette smoking in young people is associated with the development of atherosclerosis.

The 2010 Surgeon General's report on the biology of tobacco focused on the understanding of biological and behavioral mechanisms that might underlie the pathogenicity of tobacco smoke (USDHHS 2010). Although there are no specific conclusions in that report regarding adolescent addiction, it does describe evidence indicating that adolescents can become dependent at even low levels of consumption. Two studies (Adriani et al. 2003; Schochet et al. 2005) referenced in that report suggest that because the adolescent brain is still developing, it may be more susceptible and receptive to nicotine than the adult brain.

Scientific Reviews

Since 1994, several scientific reviews related to one or more aspects of tobacco use among youth have been undertaken that also serve as a foundation for the current report. The Institute of Medicine (IOM) (Lynch and Bonnie 1994) released *Growing Up Tobacco Free: Preventing Nicotine Addiction in Children and Youths,* a report that provided policy recommendations based on research to that date. In 1998, IOM provided a white paper, *Taking Action to Reduce Tobacco Use,* on strategies to reduce the increasing prevalence (at that time) of smoking among young people and adults. More recently, IOM (Bonnie et al. 2007) released a comprehensive report entitled *Ending the Tobacco Problem: A Blueprint for the Nation.* Although that report covered multiple potential approaches to tobacco control, not just those focused on youth, it characterized the overarching goal of reducing smoking as involving three distinct steps: "reducing the rate of initiation of smoking among youth (IOM [Lynch and Bonnie] 1994), reducing involuntary tobacco smoke exposure (National Research Council 1986), and helping people quit smoking" (p. 3). Thus, reducing onset was seen as one of the primary goals of tobacco control.

As part of USDHHS continuing efforts to assess the health of the nation, prevent disease, and promote health, the department released, in 2000, *Healthy People 2010* and, in 2010, *Healthy People 2020* (USDHHS 2000a, 2011). Healthy People provides science-based, 10-year national objectives for improving the health of all Americans. For 3 decades, Healthy People has established benchmarks and monitored progress over time in order to encourage collaborations across sectors, guide individuals toward making informed health decisions, and measure the impact of prevention activities. Each iteration of *Healthy People* serves as the nation's disease prevention and health promotion roadmap for the decade. Both *Healthy People 2010* and *Healthy People 2020* highlight "Tobacco Use" as one of the nation's "Leading Health Indicators," feature "Tobacco Use" as one of its topic areas, and identify specific measurable tobacco-related objectives and targets for the nation to strive for. *Healthy People 2010* and *Healthy People 2020* provide tobacco objectives based on the most current science and detailed population-based data to drive action, assess tobacco use among young people, and identify racial and ethnic disparities. Additionally, many of the *Healthy People 2010* and *2020* tobacco objectives address reductions of tobacco use among youth and target decreases in tobacco advertising in venues most often influencing young people. A complete list of the healthy people 2020 objectives can be found on their Web site (USDHHS 2011).

In addition, the National Cancer Institute (NCI) of the National Institutes of Health has published monographs pertinent to the topic of tobacco use among youth. In 2001, NCI published Monograph 14, *Changing Adolescent Smoking Prevalence*, which reviewed data on smoking among youth in the 1990s, highlighted important statewide intervention programs, presented data on the influence of marketing by the tobacco industry and the pricing of cigarettes, and examined differences in smoking by racial/ethnic subgroup (NCI 2001). In 2008, NCI published Monograph 19, *The Role of the Media in Promoting and Reducing Tobacco Use* (NCI 2008). Although young people were not the sole focus of this Monograph, the causal relationship between tobacco advertising and promotion and increased tobacco use, the impact on youth of depictions of smoking in movies, and the success of media campaigns in reducing youth tobacco use were highlighted as major conclusions of the report.

The Community Preventive Services Task Force (2011) provides evidence-based recommendations about community preventive services, programs, and policies on a range of topics including tobacco use prevention and cessation (Task Force on Community Preventive Services 2001, 2005). Evidence reviews addressing interventions to reduce tobacco use initiation and restricting minors' access to tobacco products were cited and used to inform the reviews in the current report. The Cochrane Collaboration (2010) has also substantially contributed to the review literature on youth and tobacco use by producing relevant systematic assessments of health-related programs and interventions. Relevant to this Surgeon General's report are Cochrane reviews on interventions using mass media (Sowden 1998), community interventions to prevent smoking (Sowden and Stead 2003), the effects of advertising and promotional activities on smoking among youth (Lovato et al. 2003, 2011), preventing tobacco sales to minors (Stead and Lancaster 2005), school-based programs (Thomas and Perara 2006), programs for young people to quit using tobacco (Grimshaw and Stanton 2006), and family programs for preventing smoking by youth (Thomas et al. 2007). These reviews have been cited throughout the current report when appropriate.

In summary, substantial new research has added to our knowledge and understanding of tobacco use and control as it relates to youth since the 1994 Surgeon General's report, including updates and new data in subsequent Surgeon General's reports, in IOM reports, in NCI Monographs, and in Cochrane Collaboration reviews, in addition to hundreds of peer-reviewed publications, book chapters, policy reports, and systematic reviews. Although this report is a follow-up to the 1994 report, other important reviews have been undertaken in the past 18 years and have served to fill the gap during an especially active and important time in research on tobacco control among youth.

Focus of the Report

Young People

This report focuses on "young people." In general, work was reviewed on the health consequences, epidemiology, etiology, reduction, and prevention of tobacco use for those in the young adolescent (11–14 years of age), adolescent (15–17 years of age), and young adult (18–25 years of age) age groups. When possible, an effort was made to be specific about the age group to which a particular analysis, study, or conclusion applies. Because hundreds of articles, books, and reports were reviewed, however, there are, unavoidably, inconsistencies in the terminology used. "Adolescents," "children," and "youth" are used mostly interchangeably throughout this report. In general, this group encompasses those 11–17 years of age, although "children" is a more general term that will include those younger than 11 years of age. Generally, those who are 18–25 years old are considered young adults (even though, developmentally, the period between 18–20 years of age is often labeled late adolescence), and those 26 years of age or older are considered adults.

In addition, it is important to note that the report is concerned with active smoking or use of smokeless tobacco on the part of the young person. The report does not consider young people's exposure to secondhand smoke, also referred to as involuntary or passive smoking, which was discussed in the 2006 report of the Surgeon General (USDHHS 2006). Additionally, the report does not discuss research on children younger than 11 years old; there is very little evidence of tobacco use in the United States by children younger than 11 years of age, and although there may be some predictors of later tobacco use in those younger years, the research on active tobacco use among youth has been focused on those 11 years of age and older.

Tobacco Use

Although cigarette smoking is the most common form of tobacco use in the United States, this report focuses on other forms as well, such as using smokeless tobacco (including chew and snuff) and smoking a product other than a cigarette, such as a pipe, cigar, or bidi (tobacco wrapped in tendu leaves). Because for young people the use of one form of tobacco has been associated with use of other tobacco products, it is particularly important to monitor all forms of tobacco use in this age group. The term "tobacco use" in this report indicates use of any tobacco product. When the word "smoking" is used alone, it refers to cigarette smoking.

Organization of the Report

This chapter begins by providing a short synopsis of other reports that have addressed smoking among youth and, after listing the major conclusions of this report, will end by presenting conclusions specific to each chapter. Chapter 2 of this report ("The Health Consequences of Tobacco Use Among Young People") focuses on the diseases caused by early tobacco use, the addiction process, the relation of body weight to smoking, respiratory and pulmonary problems associated with tobacco use, and cardiovascular effects. Chapter 3 ("The Epidemiology of Tobacco Use Among Young People in the United States and Worldwide") provides recent and long-term cross-sectional and longitudinal data on cigarette smoking, use of smokeless tobacco, and the use of other tobacco products by young people, by racial/ethnic group and gender, primarily in the United States, but including some worldwide data as well. Chapter 4 ("Social, Environmental, Cognitive, and Genetic Influences on the Use of Tobacco Among Youth") identifies the primary risk factors associated with tobacco use among youth at four levels, including the larger social and physical environments, smaller social groups, cognitive factors, and genetics and neurobiology. Chapter 5 ("The Tobacco Industry's Influences on the Use of Tobacco Among Youth") includes data on marketing expenditures for the tobacco industry over time and by category, the effects of cigarette advertising and promotional activities on young people's smoking, the effects of price and packaging on use, the use of the Internet and movies to market tobacco products, and an evaluation of efforts by the tobacco industry to prevent tobacco use among young people. Chapter 6 ("Efforts to Prevent and Reduce Tobacco Use Among Young People") provides evidence on the effectiveness of family-based, clinic-based, and school-based programs, mass media campaigns, regulatory and legislative approaches, increased cigarette prices, and community and statewide efforts in the fight against tobacco use among youth. Chapter 7 ("A Vision for Ending the Tobacco Epidemic") points to next steps in preventing and reducing tobacco use among young people.

Preparation of the Report

This report of the Surgeon General was prepared by the Office on Smoking and Health (OSH), National Center for Chronic Disease Prevention and Health Promotion, Centers for Disease Control and Prevention (CDC), USDHHS. In 2008, 18 external independent scientists reviewed the 1994 report and suggested areas to be added and updated. These scientists also suggested chapter editors and a senior scientific editor, who were contacted by OSH. Each chapter editor named external scientists who could contribute, and 33 content experts prepared draft sections. The draft sections were consolidated into chapters by the chapter editors and then reviewed by the senior scientific editor, with technical editing performed by CDC. The chapters were sent individually to 34 peer reviewers who are experts in the areas covered and who reviewed the chapters for scientific accuracy and comprehensiveness. The entire manuscript was then sent to more than 25 external senior scientists who reviewed the science of the entire document. After each review cycle, the drafts were revised by the chapter and senior scientific editor on the basis of the experts' comments. Subsequently, the report was reviewed by various agencies within USDHHS. Publication lags prevent up-to-the-minute inclusion of all recently published articles and data, and so some more recent publications may not be cited in this report.

Evaluation of the Evidence

Since the first Surgeon General's report in 1964 on smoking and health (USDHEW 1964), major conclusions concerning the conditions and diseases caused by cigarette smoking and the use of smokeless tobacco have been based on explicit criteria for causal inference (USDHHS 2004). Although a number of different criteria have been proposed for causal inference since the 1960s, this report focuses on the five commonly accepted criteria that were used in the original 1964 report and that are discussed in greater detail in the 2004 report on the health consequences of smoking (USDHHS 2004). The five criteria refer to the examination of the association between two variables, such as a risk factor (e.g., smoking) and an outcome (e.g., lung cancer). Causal inference between these variables is based on (1) the *consistency* of the association across multiple studies; this is the persistent finding of an association in different persons, places, circumstances, and times; (2) the degree of the *strength* of association, that is, the magnitude and statistical significance of the association in multiple studies; (3) the *specificity* of the association to clearly demonstrate that tobacco use is robustly associated with the condition, even if tobacco use has multiple effects and multiple causes exist for the condition; (4) the *temporal relationship* of the association so that tobacco use precedes disease onset; and (5) the *coherence* of the association, that is, the argument that the association makes scientific sense, given data from other sources and understanding of biological and psychosocial mechanisms (USDHHS 2004). Since the 2004 Surgeon General's report, The *Health Consequences of Smoking*, a four-level hierarchy (Table 1.1) has been used to assess the research data on associations discussed in these reports (USDHHS 2004). In general, this assessment was done by the chapter editors and then reviewed as appropriate by peer reviewers, senior scientists, and the scientific editors. For a relationship to be considered sufficient to be characterized as causal, multiple studies over time provided evidence in support of each criteria.

Table 1.1 Four-level hierarchy for classifying the strength of causal inferences based on available evidence

Level 1	Evidence is **sufficient** to infer a causal relationship.
Level 2	Evidence is **suggestive but not sufficient** to infer a causal relationship.
Level 3	Evidence is **inadequate** to infer the presence or absence of a causal relationship (which encompasses evidence that is sparse, of poor quality, or conflicting).
Level 4	Evidence is **suggestive of no causal relationship.**

When a causal association is presented in the chapter conclusions in this report, these four levels are used to describe the strength of the evidence of the association, from causal (1) to not causal (4). Within the report, other terms are used to discuss the evidence to date (i.e., mixed, limited, and equivocal evidence), which generally represent an inadequacy of data to inform a conclusion.

However, an assessment of a casual relationship is not utilized in presenting all of the report's conclusions. The major conclusions are written to be important summary statements that are easily understood by those reading the report. Some conclusions, particularly those found in Chapter 3 (epidemiology), provide observations and data related to tobacco use among young people, and are generally not examinations of causal relationships. For those conclusions that are written using the hierarchy above, a careful and extensive review of the literature has been undertaken for this report, based on the accepted causal criteria (USDHHS 2004). Evidence that was characterized as Level 1 or Level 2 was prioritized for inclusion as chapter conclusions.

In additional to causal inferences, statistical estimation and hypothesis testing of associations are presented. For example, confidence intervals have been added to the tables in the chapter on the epidemiology of youth tobacco use (see Chapter 3), and statistical testing has been conducted for that chapter when appropriate. The chapter on efforts to prevent tobacco use discusses the relative improvement in tobacco use rates when implementing one type of program (or policy) versus a control program. Statistical methods, including meta-analytic methods and longitudinal trajectory analyses, are also presented to ensure that the methods of evaluating data are up to date with the current cutting-edge research that has been reviewed. Regardless of the methods used to assess significance, the five causal criteria discussed above were applied in developing the conclusions of each chapter and the report.

Major Conclusions

1. Cigarette smoking by youth and young adults has immediate adverse health consequences, including addiction, and accelerates the development of chronic diseases across the full life course.

2. Prevention efforts must focus on both adolescents and young adults because among adults who become daily smokers, nearly all first use of cigarettes occurs by 18 years of age (88%), with 99% of first use by 26 years of age.

3. Advertising and promotional activities by tobacco companies have been shown to cause the onset and continuation of smoking among adolescents and young adults.

4. After years of steady progress, declines in the use of tobacco by youth and young adults have slowed for cigarette smoking and stalled for smokeless tobacco use.

5. Coordinated, multicomponent interventions that combine mass media campaigns, price increases including those that result from tax increases, school-based policies and programs, and statewide or community-wide changes in smoke-free policies and norms are effective in reducing the initiation, prevalence, and intensity of smoking among youth and young adults.

Chapter Conclusions

The following are the conclusions presented in the substantive chapters of this report.

Chapter 2. The Health Consequences of Tobacco Use Among Young People

1. The evidence is sufficient to conclude that there is a causal relationship between smoking and addiction to nicotine, beginning in adolescence and young adulthood.

2. The evidence is suggestive but not sufficient to conclude that smoking contributes to future use of marijuana and other illicit drugs.

3. The evidence is suggestive but not sufficient to conclude that smoking by adolescents and young adults is *not* associated with significant weight loss, contrary to young people's beliefs.

4. The evidence is sufficient to conclude that there is a causal relationship between active smoking and both reduced lung function and impaired lung growth during childhood and adolescence.

5. The evidence is sufficient to conclude that there is a causal relationship between active smoking and wheezing severe enough to be diagnosed as asthma in susceptible child and adolescent populations.

6. The evidence is sufficient to conclude that there is a causal relationship between smoking in adolescence and young adulthood and early abdominal aortic atherosclerosis in young adults.

7. The evidence is suggestive but not sufficient to conclude that there is a causal relationship between smoking in adolescence and young adulthood and coronary artery atherosclerosis in adulthood.

Chapter 3. The Epidemiology of Tobacco Use Among Young People in the United States and Worldwide

1. Among adults who become daily smokers, nearly all first use of cigarettes occurs by 18 years of age (88%), with 99% of first use by 26 years of age.

2. Almost one in four high school seniors is a current (in the past 30 days) cigarette smoker, compared with one in three young adults and one in five adults. About 1 in 10 high school senior males is a current smokeless tobacco user, and about 1 in 5 high school senior males is a current cigar smoker.

3. Among adolescents and young adults, cigarette smoking declined from the late 1990s, particularly after the Master Settlement Agreement in 1998. This decline has slowed in recent years, however.

4. Significant disparities in tobacco use remain among young people nationwide. The prevalence of cigarette smoking is highest among American Indians and Alaska Natives, followed by Whites and Hispanics, and then Asians and Blacks. The prevalence of cigarette smoking is also highest among lower socioeconomic status youth.

5. Use of smokeless tobacco and cigars declined in the late 1990s, but the declines appear to have stalled in the last 5 years. The latest data show the use of smokeless tobacco is increasing among White high school males, and cigar smoking may be increasing among Black high school females.

6. Concurrent use of multiple tobacco products is prevalent among youth. Among those who use tobacco, nearly one-third of high school females and more than one-half of high school males report using more than one tobacco product in the last 30 days.

7. Rates of tobacco use remain low among girls relative to boys in many developing countries, however, the gender gap between adolescent females and males is narrow in many countries around the globe.

Chapter 4. Social, Environmental, Cognitive, and Genetic Influences on the Use of Tobacco Among Youth

1. Given their developmental stage, adolescents and young adults are uniquely susceptible to social and environmental influences to use tobacco.

2. Socioeconomic factors and educational attainment influence the development of youth smoking behavior. The adolescents most likely to begin to use tobacco and progress to regular use are those who have lower academic achievement.

3. The evidence is sufficient to conclude that there is a causal relationship between peer group social influences and the initiation and maintenance of smoking behaviors during adolescence.

4. Affective processes play an important role in youth smoking behavior, with a strong association between youth smoking and negative affect.

5. The evidence is suggestive that tobacco use is a heritable trait, more so for regular use than for onset. The expression of genetic risk for smoking among young people may be moderated by small-group and larger social-environmental factors.

Chapter 5. The Tobacco Industry's Influences on the Use of Tobacco Among Youth

1. In 2008, tobacco companies spent $9.94 billion on the marketing of cigarettes and $547 million on the marketing of smokeless tobacco. Spending on cigarette marketing is 48% higher than in 1998, the year of the Master Settlement Agreement. Expenditures for marketing smokeless tobacco are 277% higher than in 1998.

2. Tobacco company expenditures have become increasingly concentrated on marketing efforts that reduce the prices of targeted tobacco products. Such expenditures accounted for approximately 84% of cigarette marketing and more than 77% of the marketing of smokeless tobacco products in 2008.

3. The evidence is sufficient to conclude that there is a causal relationship between advertising and promotional efforts of the tobacco companies and the initiation and progression of tobacco use among young people.

4. The evidence is suggestive but not sufficient to conclude that tobacco companies have changed the packaging and design of their products in ways that have increased these products' appeal to adolescents and young adults.

5. The tobacco companies' activities and programs for the prevention of youth smoking have not demonstrated an impact on the initiation or prevalence of smoking among young people.

6. The evidence is sufficient to conclude that there is a causal relationship between depictions of smoking in the movies and the initiation of smoking among young people.

Chapter 6. Efforts to Prevent and Reduce Tobacco Use Among Young People

1. The evidence is sufficient to conclude that mass media campaigns, comprehensive community programs, and comprehensive statewide tobacco control programs can prevent the initiation of tobacco use and reduce its prevalence among youth.

2. The evidence is sufficient to conclude that increases in cigarette prices reduce the initiation, prevalence, and intensity of smoking among youth and young adults.

3. The evidence is sufficient to conclude that school-based programs with evidence of effectiveness, containing specific components, can produce at least short-term effects and reduce the prevalence of tobacco use among school-aged youth.

References

Adriani W, Spijker S, Deroche-Gamonet V, Laviola G, Le Moal M, Smit AB, Piazza PV. Evidence for enhanced neurobehavioral vulnerability to nicotine during periadolescence in rats. *Journal of Neuroscience* 2003; 23(11):4712–6.

Alesci NL, Forster JL, Blaine T. Smoking visibility, perceived acceptability, and frequency in various locations among youth and adults. *Preventive Medicine* 2003;36(3):272–81.

Anderson G. *Chronic Care: Making the Case for Ongoing Care*. Princeton (NJ): Robert Wood Johnson Foundation, 2010; <http://www.rwjf.org/files/research/50968chronic.care.chartbook.pdf>; accessed: November 30, 2011.

Bonnie RJ, Stratton K, Wallace RB, editors. *Ending the Tobacco Problem: A Blueprint for the Nation*. Washington: National Academies Press, 2007.

Cochrane Collaboration. Home page, 2010; <http://www.cochrane.org/>; accessed: November 30, 2010.

Community Preventive Services Task Force. First Annual Report to Congress and to Agencies Related to the Work of the Task Force. Community Preventive Services Task Force, 2011; <http://www.thecommunityguide.org/library/ARC2011/congress-report-full.pdf>; accessed: January 9, 2012.

Dalton MA, Beach ML, Adachi-Mejia AM, Longacre MR, Matzkin AL, Sargent JD, Heatherton TF, Titus-Ernstoff L. Early exposure to movie smoking predicts established smoking by older teens and young adults. *Pediatrics* 2009;123(4):e551–e558.

Doll R, Peto R, Boreham J, Sutherland I. Mortality in relation to smoking: 50 years' observations on male British doctors. *BMJ (British Medical Journal)* 2004; 32:1519;doi: 10.1136/bmj.38142.554479.AE.

Fagerström K. The epidemiology of smoking: health consequences and benefits of cessation. *Drugs* 2002; 62(Suppl 2):1–9.

Family Smoking Prevention and Tobacco Control Act, Public Law 111-31, 123 *U.S. Statutes at Large* 1776 (2009).

Grimshaw G, Stanton A. Tobacco cessation interventions for young people. *Cochrane Database of Systematic Reviews* 2006, Issue 4. Art. No.: CD003289. DOI: 10.1002/14651858.CD003289.pub4.

Kessler DA. Nicotine addiction in young people. *New England Journal of Medicine* 1995;333(3):186–9.

Lovato C, Linn G, Stead LF, Best A. Impact of tobacco advertising and promotion on increasing adolescent smoking behaviours. *Cochrane Database of Systematic Reviews* 2003, Issue 4. Art. No.: CD003439. DOI: 10.1002/14651858.CD003439.

Lovato C, Watts A, Stead LF. Impact of tobacco advertising and promotion on increasing adolescent smoking behaviours. *Cochrane Database of Systematic Reviews* 2011;(10):CD003439. DOI: 10.1002/14651858.CD003439.pub2.

Lynch BS, Bonnie RJ, editors. *Growing Up Tobacco Free: Preventing Nicotine Addiction in Children and Youths*. Washington: National Academies Press, 1994.

National Association of Attorneys General. Master Settlement Agreement, 1998; <http://www.naag.org/backpages/naag/tobacco/msa/msa-pdf/MSA%20with%20Sig%20Pages%20and%20Exhibits.pdf/file_view>; accessed: June 9, 2011.

National Cancer Institute. *Changing Adolescent Smoking Prevalence*. Smoking and Tobacco Control Monograph No. 14. Bethesda (MD): U.S. Department of Health and Human Services, Public Health Service, National Institutes of Health, National Cancer Institute, 2001. NIH Publication. No. 02-5086.

National Cancer Institute. *The Role of the Media in Promoting and Reducing Tobacco Use*. Tobacco Control Monograph No. 19. Bethesda (MD): U.S. Department of Health and Human Services, National Institutes of Health, National Cancer Institute, 2008. NIH Publication No. 07-6242.

National Research Council. *Environmental Tobacco Smoke: Measuring Exposures and Assessing Health Effects*. Washington: National Academy Press, 1986.

Office of the Surgeon General. Reports of the Surgeon General, U.S. Public Health Service, 2010; <http://www.surgeongeneral.gov/library/reports/index.html>; accessed: November 30, 2010.

Perry CL, Eriksen M, Giovino G. Tobacco use: a pediatric epidemic [editorial]. *Tobacco Control* 1994;3(2):97–8.

Peto R, Lopez AD. Future worldwide health effects of current smoking patterns. In: Koop CE, Pearson CE, Schwarz MR, editors. *Critical Issues in Global Health*. San Francisco: Wiley (Jossey-Bass), 2001:154–61.

Reddy KS, Perry CL, Stigler MH, Arora M. Differences in tobacco use among young people in urban India by sex, socioeconomic status, age, and school grade: assessment of baseline survey data. *Lancet* 2006;367(9510):589–94.

Schochet TL, Kelley AE, Landry CF. Differential expression of arc mRNA and other plasticity-related genes induced by nicotine in adolescent rat forebrain. *Neuroscience* 2005;135(1):285–97.

Sowden AJ. Mass media interventions for preventing smoking in young people. *Cochrane Database of Systematic Reviews* 1998, Issue 4. Art. No.: CD001006. DOI: 10.1002/14651858.CD001006.

Sowden AJ, Stead LF. Community interventions for preventing smoking in young people. *Cochrane Database of Systematic Reviews* 2003, Issue 1. Art. No.: CD001291. DOI: 10.1002/14651858.CD001291.

Stead LF, Lancaster T. Interventions for preventing tobacco sales to minors. *Cochrane Database of Systematic Reviews* 2005, Issue 1. Art. No.: CD001497. DOI: 10.1002/14651858.CD001497.pub2.

Steinberg L. Risk taking in adolescence: what changes, and why? *Annals of the New York Academy of Sciences* 2004;1021:51–8.

Task Force on Community Preventive Services. Recommendations regarding interventions to reduce tobacco use and exposure to environmental tobacco smoke. *American Journal of Preventive Medicine* 2001;20(2 Suppl):S10–S15.

Task Force on Community Preventive Services. Tobacco. In: Zaza S, Briss PA, Harris KW, editors. *The Guide to Preventive Services: What Works to Promote Health?* New York: Oxford University Press, 2005:3–79. <http://www.thecommunityguide.org/tobacco/Tobacco.pdf>.

Thomas RE, Baker PRA, Lorenzetti D. Family-based programmes for preventing smoking by children and adolescents. *Cochrane Database of Systematic Reviews* 2007, Issue 1. Art. No.: CD004493. DOI: 10.1002/14651858.CD004493.pub2.

Thomas RE, Perera R. School-based programmes for preventing smoking. *Cochrane Database of Systematic Reviews* 2006, Issue 3. Art. No.: CD001293. DOI: 10.1002/14651858.CD001293.pub2.

U.S. Department of Health and Human Services. *Preventing Tobacco Use Among Young People. A Report of the Surgeon General*. Atlanta (GA): U.S. Department of Health and Human Services, Public Health Service, Centers for Disease Control and Prevention, National Center for Chronic Disease Prevention and Health Promotion, Office on Smoking and Health, 1994.

U.S. Department of Health and Human Services. *Tobacco Use Among U.S. Racial/Ethnic Minority Groups—African Americans, American Indians and Alaska Natives, Asian Americans and Pacific Islanders, and Hispanics. A Report of the Surgeon General.* Atlanta (GA): U.S. Department of Health and Human Services, Centers for Disease Control and Prevention, National Center for Chronic Disease Prevention and Health Promotion, Office on Smoking and Health, 1998.

U.S. Department of Health and Human Services. *Healthy People 2010: Understanding and Improving Health.* 2nd ed. Washington: U.S. Government Printing Office, 2000a.

U.S. Department of Health and Human Services. *Reducing Tobacco Use: A Report of the Surgeon General.* Atlanta (GA): U.S. Department of Health and Human Services, Centers for Disease Control and Prevention, National Center for Chronic Disease Prevention and Health Promotion, Office on Smoking and Health, 2000b.

U.S. Department of Health and Human Services. *Women and Smoking. A Report of the Surgeon General.* Rockville (MD): U.S. Department of Health and Human Services, Public Health Service, Office of the Surgeon General, 2001.

U.S. Department of Health and Human Services. *The Health Consequences of Smoking: A Report of the Surgeon General.* Atlanta (GA): U.S. Department of Health and Human Services, Centers for Disease Control and Prevention, National Center for Chronic Disease Prevention and Health Promotion, Office on Smoking and Health, 2004.

U.S. Department of Health and Human Services. *The Health Consequences of Involuntary Exposure to Tobacco Smoke: A Report of the Surgeon General.* Atlanta (GA): U.S. Department of Health and Human Services, Centers for Disease Control and Prevention, National Center for Chronic Disease Prevention and Health Promotion, Office on Smoking and Health, 2006.

U.S. Department of Health and Human Services. *How Tobacco Smoke Causes Disease—The Biology and Behavioral Basis for Tobacco-Attributable Disease: A Report of the Surgeon General*. Atlanta (GA): U.S. Department of Health and Human Services, Centers for Disease Control and Prevention, National Center for Chronic Disease Prevention and Health Promotion, Office on Smoking and Health, 2010.

U.S. Department of Health and Human Services, Office of Disease Prevention and Health Promotion. Healthy People 2020, 2011; <http://www.healthypeople.gov/2020/default.aspx>; accessed: November 1, 2011.

U.S. Department of Health, Education, and Welfare. *Smoking and Health: Report of the Advisory Committee to the Surgeon General of the Public Health Service*. Washington: U.S. Department of Health, Education, and Welfare, Public Health Service, Center for Disease Control, 1964. PHS Publication No. 1103.

Chapter 2
The Health Consequences of Tobacco Use Among Young People

Introduction

This chapter addresses the adverse health consequences of tobacco use by children and young adults. Although the chapter focuses primarily on childhood through young adulthood, it also briefly considers the prenatal period and examines the adverse effects of smoking before conception as well, even though that is not a main focus of this report. Previous Surgeon General's reports on tobacco use have covered the evidence on the increased risk of specific diseases and other adverse effects of active and involuntary smoking, with the most recent updates in the 2004, 2006, and 2010 reports (U.S. Department of Health and Human Services [USDHHS] 2004, 2006, 2010) discussing active smoking, exposure to secondhand smoke, and the biological basis of disease, respectively. Those reports covered the effects of maternal and paternal smoking on nearly all aspects of reproduction and on risk for congenital malformations as well as the increased risks from exposure to secondhand smoke for sudden infant death syndrome (SIDS), increased lower respiratory illnesses and respiratory symptoms, reduced lung growth, and asthma (see Tables 2.1a and 2.1b for the conclusions of the earlier reports).

This chapter complements those earlier reports by reviewing the health consequences of active smoking by adolescents and young adults, a topic last covered, in depth, in the 1994 report. That report reached several key conclusions on the adverse effects of smoking on young people related to their respiratory and cardiovascular health and, in regard to addiction, it noted that "among addictive behaviors, cigarette smoking is the one most likely to become established during adolescence. People who begin to smoke at an early age are more likely to develop severe levels of nicotine addiction than those who start at a later age" (USDHHS 1994, p. 41).

This chapter returns to the topic of the health consequences of smoking for young people who smoke, reviewing the substantial new evidence in detail and placing it within a life-course perspective. It also covers new information on the onset of nicotine addiction during adolescence and young adulthood, which includes prospectively collected data on trajectories of addiction from cohort studies. For young people, particularly females, considerations about weight play a role in the decision to start smoking and to continue this behavior; this issue, which is critical for efforts in prevention and cessation, is comprehensively reviewed in the present chapter. Information on the health consequences of smokeless tobacco use are documented in multiple prior publications (National Cancer Institute [NCI] 2012).

Table 2.1a Conclusions from previous Surgeon General's reports on the adverse effects of tobacco use and exposure to secondhand smoke in children and young adults

Preventing Tobacco Use Among Young People: A Report of the Surgeon General (1994, p. 9)

1. Cigarette smoking during childhood and adolescence produces significant health problems among young people, including cough and phlegm production, an increased number and severity of respiratory illnesses, decreased physical fitness, an unfavorable lipid profile, and potential retardation in the rate of lung growth and the level of maximum lung function.
2. Among addictive behaviors, cigarette smoking is the one most likely to become established during adolescence. People who begin to smoke at an early age are more likely to develop severe levels of nicotine addiction than are those who start at a later age.
3. Tobacco use is associated with alcohol and illicit drug use and is generally the first drug used by young people who enter a sequence of drug use that can include tobacco, alcohol, marijuana, and harder drugs.
4. Smokeless tobacco use by adolescents is associated with early indicators of periodontal degeneration and with lesions in the oral soft tissue. Adolescent smokeless tobacco users are more likely than nonusers to become cigarette smokers.

The Health Consequences of Smoking: A Report of the Surgeon General (2004, pp. 27–8)

Chronic Respiratory Diseases

1. The evidence is sufficient to infer a causal relationship between maternal smoking during pregnancy and a reduction of lung function in infants.
2. The evidence is suggestive but not sufficient to infer a causal relationship between maternal smoking during pregnancy and an increase in the frequency of lower respiratory tract illnesses during infancy.
3. The evidence is suggestive but not sufficient to infer a causal relationship between maternal smoking during pregnancy and an increased risk for impaired lung function in childhood and adulthood.
4. The evidence is sufficient to infer a causal relationship between active smoking and impaired lung growth during childhood and adolescence.
5. The evidence is sufficient to infer a causal relationship between active smoking and the early onset of lung function decline during late adolescence and early adulthood.
6. The evidence is sufficient to infer a causal relationship between active smoking and respiratory symptoms in children and adolescents, including coughing, phlegm, wheezing, and dyspnea.
7. The evidence is sufficient to infer a causal relationship between active smoking and asthma-related symptoms (i.e., wheezing) in childhood and adolescence.
8. The evidence is inadequate to infer the presence or absence of a causal relationship between active smoking and physician-diagnosed asthma in childhood and adolescence.
9. The evidence is suggestive but not sufficient to infer a causal relationship between active smoking and a poorer prognosis for children and adolescents with asthma.

Fertility

10. The evidence is inadequate to infer the presence or absence of a causal relationship between active smoking and sperm quality.
11. The evidence is sufficient to infer a causal relationship between smoking and reduced fertility in women.

Pregnancy and Pregnancy Outcomes

12. The evidence is suggestive but not sufficient to infer a causal relationship between maternal active smoking and ectopic pregnancy.
13. The evidence is suggestive but not sufficient to infer a causal relationship between maternal active smoking and spontaneous abortion.

Table 2.1a Continued

14. The evidence is sufficient to infer a causal relationship between maternal active smoking and premature rupture of the membranes, placenta previa, and placental abruption.
15. The evidence is sufficient to infer a causal relationship between maternal active smoking and a reduced risk for preeclampsia.
16. The evidence is sufficient to infer a causal relationship between maternal active smoking and preterm delivery and shortened gestation.
17. The evidence is sufficient to infer a causal relationship between maternal active smoking and fetal growth restriction and low birth weight.

Congenital Malformations, Infant Mortality, and Child Physical and Cognitive Development

18. The evidence is inadequate to infer the presence or absence of a causal relationship between maternal smoking and congenital malformations in general.
19. The evidence is suggestive but not sufficient to infer a causal relationship between maternal smoking and oral clefts.
20. The evidence is sufficient to infer a causal relationship between sudden infant death syndrome and maternal smoking during and after pregnancy.
21. The evidence is inadequate to infer the presence or absence of a causal relationship between maternal smoking and the physical growth and neurocognitive development of children.

The Health Consequences of Involuntary Exposure to Tobacco Smoke: A Report of the Surgeon General (2006, pp. 13–4)

Fertility

1. The evidence is inadequate to infer the presence or absence of a causal relationship between maternal exposure to secondhand smoke and female fertility or fecundability. No data were found on paternal exposure to secondhand smoke and male fertility or fecundability.

Pregnancy (Spontaneous Abortion and Perinatal Death)

2. The evidence is inadequate to infer the presence or absence of a causal relationship between maternal exposure to secondhand smoke during pregnancy and spontaneous abortion.

Infant Deaths

3. The evidence is inadequate to infer the presence or absence of a causal relationship between exposure to secondhand smoke and neonatal mortality.

Sudden Infant Death Syndrome

4. The evidence is sufficient to infer a causal relationship between exposure to secondhand smoke and sudden infant death syndrome.

Preterm Delivery

5. The evidence is suggestive but not sufficient to infer a causal relationship between maternal exposure to secondhand smoke during pregnancy and preterm delivery.

Low Birth Weight

6. The evidence is sufficient to infer a causal relationship between maternal exposure to secondhand smoke during pregnancy and a small reduction in birth weight.

Congenital Malformations

7. The evidence is inadequate to infer the presence or absence of a causal relationship between exposure to secondhand smoke and congenital malformations.

Table 2.1a Continued

Cognitive Development

8. The evidence is inadequate to infer the presence or absence of a causal relationship between exposure to secondhand smoke and cognitive functioning among children.

Behavioral Development

9. The evidence is inadequate to infer the presence or absence of a causal relationship between exposure to secondhand smoke and behavioral problems among children.

Height/Growth

10. The evidence is inadequate to infer the presence or absence of a causal relationship between exposure to secondhand smoke and children's height/growth.

Childhood Cancer

11. The evidence is suggestive but not sufficient to infer a causal relationship between prenatal and postnatal exposure to secondhand smoke and childhood cancer.
12. The evidence is inadequate to infer the presence or absence of a causal relationship between maternal exposure to secondhand smoke during pregnancy and childhood cancer.
13. The evidence is inadequate to infer the presence or absence of a causal relationship between exposure to secondhand smoke during infancy and childhood cancer.
14. The evidence is suggestive but not sufficient to infer a causal relationship between prenatal and postnatal exposure to secondhand smoke and childhood leukemias.
15. The evidence is suggestive but not sufficient to infer a causal relationship between prenatal and postnatal exposure to secondhand smoke and childhood lymphomas.
16. The evidence is suggestive but not sufficient to infer a causal relationship between prenatal and postnatal exposure to secondhand smoke and childhood brain tumors.
17. The evidence is inadequate to infer the presence or absence of a causal relationship between prenatal and postnatal exposure to secondhand smoke and other childhood cancer types.

Lower Respiratory Illnesses in Infancy and Early Childhood

18. The evidence is sufficient to infer a causal relationship between exposure to secondhand smoke from parental smoking and lower respiratory illnesses in infants and children.
19. The increased risk for lower respiratory illnesses is greater from smoking by the mother.

Middle Ear Disease and Adenotonsillectomy

20. The evidence is sufficient to infer a causal relationship between parental smoking and middle ear disease in children, including acute and recurrent otitis media and chronic middle ear effusion.
21. The evidence is suggestive but not sufficient to infer a causal relationship between parental smoking and the natural history of middle ear effusion.
22. The evidence is inadequate to infer the presence or absence of a causal relationship between parental smoking and an increase in the risk of adenoidectomy or tonsillectomy among children.

Respiratory Symptoms and Prevalent Asthma in School-Age Children

23. The evidence is sufficient to infer a causal relationship between parental smoking and cough, phlegm, wheeze, and breathlessness among children of school age.
24. The evidence is sufficient to infer a causal relationship between parental smoking and ever having asthma among children of school age.

Table 2.1a Continued

Childhood Asthma Onset

25. The evidence is sufficient to infer a causal relationship between exposure to secondhand smoke from parental smoking and the onset of wheeze illnesses in early childhood.

26. The evidence is suggestive but not sufficient to infer a causal relationship between exposure to secondhand smoke from parental smoking and the onset of childhood asthma.

Atopy

27. The evidence is inadequate to infer the presence or absence of a causal relationship between parental smoking and the risk of immunoglobulin E-mediated allergy in their children.

Lung Growth and Pulmonary Function

28. The evidence is sufficient to infer a causal relationship between maternal smoking during pregnancy and persistent adverse effects on lung function across childhood.

29. The evidence is sufficient to infer a causal relationship between exposure to secondhand smoke after birth and a lower level of lung function during childhood.

Source: U.S. Department of Health and Human Services 1994, 2004, 2006.

Table 2.1b Level of certainty of causality reported in the 2004 and 2006 Surgeon General's reports

	Sufficient	Suggestive	Undetermined or inadequately studied
Chronic respiratory diseases (USDHHS 2004)			
Maternal smoking in pregnancy			
Reduced lung function in infants	X		
Lower respiratory tract illnesses in infants		X	
Impaired lung function in childhood		X	
Active smoking			
Lung growth in childhood and adolescence	X		
Onset of decline in lung function	X		
Respiratory symptoms	X		
Asthma-type symptoms	X		
Physician-diagnosed asthma			X
Poor prognosis among asthmatics		X	
Fertility, pregnancy, and pregnancy outcomes and other effects on offspring (USDHHS 2004)			
Active smoking			
Relation to sperm quality			X
Reduced fertility among women	X		
Pregnancy and pregnancy outcomes			
Ectopic pregnancy		X	
Spontaneous abortion		X	
Premature rupture of the membranes, placenta previa, and placental abruption	X		
Reduced risk for preeclampsia	X		
Preterm delivery and shortened gestation	X		
Fetal growth restriction and low birth weight	X		
Congenital malformations, infant mortality, and child physical and cognitive development			
Congenital malformations in general			X
Oral clefts		X	
Sudden infant death syndrome and maternal smoking during and after pregnancy	X		
Physical growth and neurocognitive development of children			X
Maternal and paternal secondhand exposure (USDHHS 2006)			
Fertility and fecundability			
Maternal		X	
Paternal		X	
Spontaneous abortion		X	
Neonatal mortality		X	
Sudden infant death syndrome	X		
Preterm delivery		X	
Small reduction in birth weight	X		
Congenital malformations			X
Cognitive functioning among children			X
Behavioral problems among children			X
Children's height/growth			X

Table 2.1b Continued

	Sufficient	Suggestive	Undetermined or inadequately studied
Cancer			
Prenatal and postnatal exposure to secondhand smoke and childhood cancer		X	
Maternal exposure to secondhand smoke during pregnancy and childhood cancer			X
Exposure to secondhand smoke during infancy and childhood cancer			X
Prenatal and postnatal exposure to secondhand smoke and childhood leukemias		X	
Prenatal and postnatal exposure to secondhand smoke and childhood lymphomas		X	
Prenatal and postnatal exposure to secondhand smoke and childhood brain tumors		X	
Prenatal and postnatal exposure to secondhand smoke and other childhood cancer types			X
Respiratory effects			
Lower respiratory illnesses in infants and children	X		
Cough, phlegm, wheeze, and breathlessness among children of school age	X		
Ever having asthma among children of school age	X		
Onset of wheeze illnesses in early childhood	X		
Onset of childhood asthma		X	
Persistent adverse effects on lung function across childhood	X		
Lower level of lung function during childhood	X		

Source: U.S. Department of Health and Human Services 2004, 2006.

Smoking During Adolescence and Young Adulthood: A Critical Period for Health

Since the 1994 report, the basis for concern about smoking during adolescence and young adulthood has expanded beyond the immediate health consequences for the young smoker to a deeper understanding of the implications for health of exposure to tobacco smoke across the life course, including into the next generation. This broadened concern reflects the emergence of a body of evidence linking risk exposures in early life, even in the antenatal period, to risk for chronic disease in adulthood. The general hypothesis that has been constructed from this evidence is often called the "developmental origins of adult disease" hypothesis or the "Barker" hypothesis, in reference to David Barker, who documented associations between early-life nutrition and subsequent risk for cardiovascular disease (Barker 2004; de Boo and Harding 2006).

Research in humans that is relevant to this hypothesis has largely come from epidemiologic studies that have tied nutrition in early life to subsequent risk for hypertension and other cardiovascular diseases (Huxley et al. 2000; Barker et al. 2005; de Boo and Harding 2006). There is also relevant experimental research (Nuyt 2008). The proposed underlying mechanisms emphasize genetic and epigenetic changes that could have lasting implications across the life span (Young 2001; Gicquel et al. 2008).

Even before conception, the sperm and oocytes of future parents who smoke are exposed to the DNA-damaging constituents of tobacco smoke (USDHHS 2004); the fetus of a mother who smokes or who is exposed to secondhand smoke will be exposed to these damaging materials, resulting most often in reduced birth weight (USDHHS 2004, 2006). To date, however, there has been little investigation of the molecular changes as a result of these early-life exposures to tobacco smoke. One recent study, however, has demonstrated epigenetic changes in children with in utero exposure to maternal smoking

(Breton et al. 2009), a finding consistent with one proposed mechanism for long-term consequences of early-life exposures. Thus, given the numerous known carcinogens and toxins present in tobacco smoke and the known mechanism by which they cause disease, the developmental origins of adult disease is a critical concept to consider when addressing youth tobacco use.

For many of the chronic diseases caused by smoking, the risks increase with the duration and cumulative amount of this behavior. Consequently, the age of starting to smoke has consequences for the age at which the risks of smoking become manifest. In the United States, the age of starting to smoke regularly became increasingly younger late in the twentieth century (NCI 1997), first for males and then for females, but more recently, it has been stable (Figure 2.1). By the early 1990s, the mean age of first trying a cigarette was about 16 years for those who ever smoked (see Chapter 3, "The Epidemiology of Tobacco Use Among Young People in the United States and Worldwide"). In many other countries, the mean age of uptake is similarly young (see Chapter 3).

This earlier age of onset of smoking marks the beginning of exposure to the many harmful components of smoking. This is during an age range when growth is not complete and susceptibility to the damaging effects of tobacco smoke may be enhanced. In addition, an earlier age of initiation extends the potential duration of smoking throughout the lifespan. For the major chronic diseases caused by smoking, the epidemiologic evidence indicates that risk rises progressively with increasing duration of smoking; indeed, for lung cancer, the risk rises more steeply with duration of smoking than with number of cigarettes smoked per day (Doll and Peto 1978; Peto 1986; USDHHS 2004). For chronic obstructive pulmonary disease (COPD), risk varies directly with the total number of cigarettes consumed over a lifetime (USDHHS 2004), which would suggest greater risk for longer duration or higher intensity. There is little direct evidence, however, on whether the age of starting to smoke, by itself, modifies the risk of smoking-related disease later, that is, whether starting to smoke during adolescence versus young adulthood increases the subsequent risk for such disease (International Agency for Research on Cancer 2004).

Figure 2.1 Average age when a whole cigarette was smoked for the first time among 9th- to 12th-grade youth; Youth Risk Behavior Survey (YRBS) 1991–2009; United States

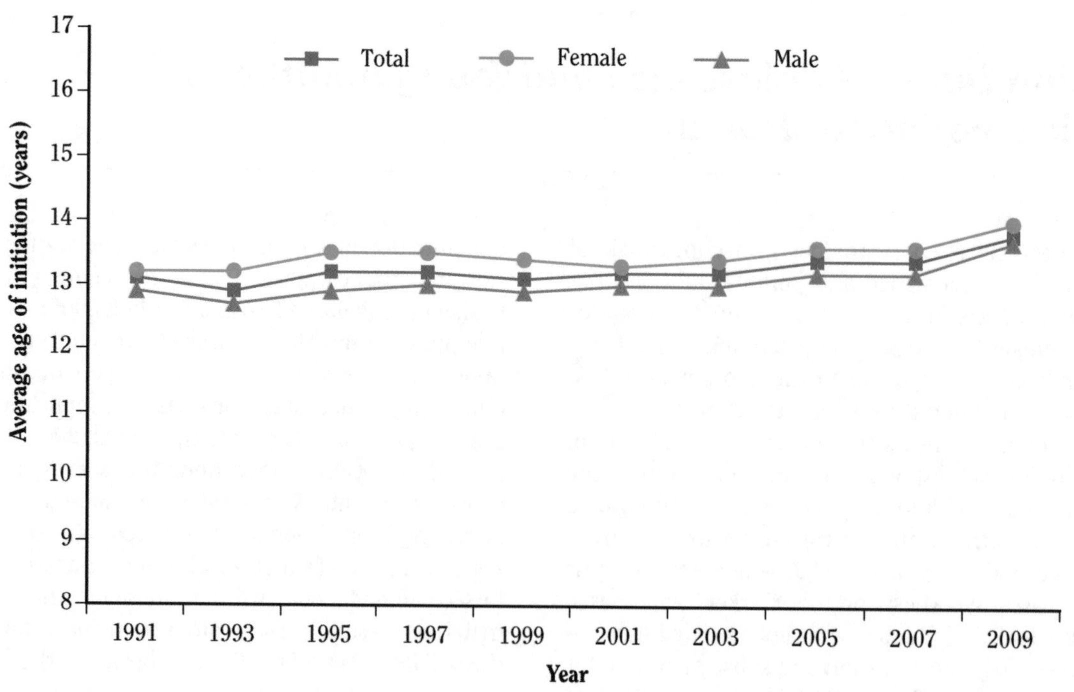

Source: 1991–2009 YRBS: Centers for Disease Control and Prevention, Division of Adolescent and School Health (unpublished data).

This chapter has four major sections which correspond to the principal health domains that are related to smoking during adolescence and young adulthood: factors related to initiation and continuation of smoking, including nicotine addiction, smoking and body weight, respiratory symptoms, and cardiovascular effects. Other adverse effects of smoking on adolescents and young adults have been covered in other reports during the last decade, including the effects of smoking on reproduction and on increasing risk for respiratory infections (USDHHS 2004).

This chapter was developed following the approach set out in the 2004 report of the Surgeon General (USDHHS 2004). The authors systematically searched for all relevant evidence that appeared in the scientific literature after earlier reviews on these topics; this evidence, along with the prior findings, was evaluated and classified as described in the 2004 report.

Nicotine Addiction

Introduction

The topic of nicotine and addiction to this substance has been covered in multiple Surgeon General's reports. The 1988 report concluded that "(1) Cigarettes and other forms of tobacco are addicting. (2) Nicotine is the identified drug in tobacco that causes addiction. (3) The pharmacologic and behavioral processes that determine tobacco addiction are similar to those that determine addiction to drugs such as heroin and cocaine" (USDHHS 1988, p. 78). The 2010 report, which covered the extensive advances in research on nicotine since the 1988 report (USDHHS 2010), reconfirmed nicotine's key role in causing addiction and concluded that genetic variations in responses to this drug contribute to determining patterns of smoking behavior and cessation.

This report summarizes the research on nicotine dependence among adolescents and young adults but does not address the mechanisms of addiction, which were covered in the 2010 report. It also does not cover the evidence related to maternal smoking during pregnancy and future risk for nicotine addiction; there is a substantial body of relevant experimental evidence as well as more limited observational research on this topic. The experimental studies provide coherent evidence that prenatal exposure to nicotine has lasting effects on the developing brain (Dwyer et al. 2008; Pauly and Slotkin 2008; Poorthuis et al. 2009). However, observational studies on whether maternal smoking during pregnancy increases risk for subsequent addiction of the child have provided mixed evidence (USDHHS 2010).

To meet the clinical diagnosis of nicotine dependence as defined by the American Psychiatric Association's *Diagnostic and Statistical Manual of Mental Disorders* 4th ed. (text rev.) (*DSM-IV-TR*) (American Psychiatric Association 2000), an adult must exhibit at least three of the primary symptoms of substance dependence, generally at any time during the same 12-month period. In addition to the two primary characteristics of withdrawal symptoms and unsuccessful quit attempts described below, criteria include tolerance to the aversive effects of nicotine (e.g., nausea and lightheadedness), limiting social or occupational activities because of prohibitions in place against smoking, continued use despite significant health concerns, and greater use than intended (American Psychiatric Association 2000; Fiore et al. 2008). Nicotine dependence among adult smokers is characterized by the emergence of withdrawal symptoms in response to abstinence and by unsuccessful attempts to reduce the use of tobacco or to quit altogether (Fiore et al. 2008). Withdrawal symptoms can occur as early as 4 to 6 hours after the last use of nicotine (USDHHS 1988; Hughes 2007); these early symptoms, which include depressed mood, insomnia, irritability, anxiety, difficulty concentrating, restlessness, increased appetite, and cravings for tobacco/nicotine, are almost immediately alleviated by using tobacco or nicotine. In adults, the severity of nicotine dependence is most commonly measured using the Fagerström Tolerance Questionnaire (FTQ) (Fagerström and Schneider 1989) or a modified version called the Fagerström Test for Nicotine Dependence (FTND) (Heatherton et al. 1991), both of which include inventories of tobacco-specific items.

Baker and colleagues (2009), in an NCI monograph on phenotypes and endophenotypes, characterize the *DSM-IV* and FTQ as directed at the "distal" phenotype of mature nicotine addiction (Baker et al. 2009). This monograph emphasizes the complexity and multidimensionality of nicotine dependence and its maturation from initial experimentation to addiction.

At present, the defining characteristics of nicotine dependence in adolescent smokers remain a topic of much debate, particularly as the inappropriateness of extending criteria developed for adults to youth smokers has been recognized. Evidence is conflicting as to whether adolescents meet some of the dependence criteria for adults described above, which are generally based on the premise that prolonged use is needed for dependence to be established. Indeed, until about 10 years ago, the dominant concept in the field proposed that adolescents could not be dependent on cigarettes because this population has short and often highly variable patterns of use. However, emerging evidence suggests that key symptoms of physical dependence on nicotine—such as withdrawal and tolerance—can be manifest following even minimal exposure to this substance. For example, DiFranza and colleagues (2000) prospectively followed occasional adolescent smokers and observed that a large proportion experienced at least one symptom of nicotine dependence upon quitting, even in the first 4 weeks after initiating monthly smoking (at least two cigarettes within a 2-month period). This finding, based on an instrument developed specifically for adolescents, suggests that adolescents can become dependent very shortly after initiating smoking. Similarly, a number of retrospective and prospective studies have found that adolescents experience subjective symptoms of withdrawal, such as craving, nervousness, restlessness, irritability, hunger, difficulty concentrating, sadness, and sleep disturbances, after stopping smoking (McNeil et al. 1986; Rojas et al. 1998; Killen et al. 2001; Prokhorov et al. 2005). In addition, Breslau and colleagues (1994) reported that nearly one-half of all young adults who smoked daily were nicotine dependent, a finding based on their having at least three of seven symptoms as ascertained by the National Institute of Mental Health Diagnostic Interview Schedule.

In addition to these reports, more recent preclinical and clinical evidence suggests that the qualitative experience of withdrawal may differ between adolescents and adults. For example, preclinical studies indicate that although adult rats display evidence of withdrawal, adolescent rats do not (O'Dell et al. 2004). Furthermore, in adolescent humans the nicotine patch may not prevent the development of withdrawal symptoms (Killen et al. 2001), and the treatment efficacy of this and other nicotine replacement therapies used in adults has not been established with adolescent smokers. The available studies in this area provide mixed evidence (Smith et al. 1996; Hurt et al. 2000; Hanson et al. 2003; Moolchan et al. 2005), drawing into question the utility of nicotine replacement in this age group. Furthermore, although adolescent smokers report having some withdrawal symptoms, these are generally minimal, with craving tobacco being the predominant symptom experienced during abstinence (Prokhorov et al. 2005; Bagot et al. 2007; Smith et al. 2008a,b). Finally, adolescents' patterns of tobacco use are likely more highly constrained than those of adults because they are influenced by environmental factors such as rules or regulations enacted by schools or rules in the home (Wiltshire et al. 2005), a difference that should be considered in examining the issue of addiction to nicotine among young people.

Interpretation of the relevant studies is complicated by the lack of adequate, validated measures of dependence for use in adolescent smokers (Colby et al. 2000). A number of measures have been developed to assess nicotine dependence among adolescents, including a modified FTQ (mFTQ) (Prokhorov et al. 1998, 2001). The Nicotine Dependence Syndrome Scale (NDSS) (Substance Abuse and Mental Health Services Administration 2002; Shiffman et al. 2004) measures important components of tobacco use behavior, including drive, priority, tolerance, stereotypy, and continuity. The Hooked on Nicotine Checklist (HONC) (DiFranza et al. 2000; O'Loughlin et al. 2003) measures loss of full autonomy over tobacco use; a *DSM-IV* checklist measures the physical and psychological consequences of tobacco use as well as tolerance and withdrawal (Kandel et al. 2005). However, most studies have found little if any concordance between results obtained using these scales. Evidence suggests that the *DSM-IV* scale and the mFTQ may measure different components of dependence (Kandel et al. 2005), that the HONC and mFTQ may be identifying adolescents at different points along the continuum of dependence (MacPherson et al. 2008), and that the NDSS complements information on tobacco use measured with the FTND (Clark et al. 2005). Moreover, classifications by many of the measures of nicotine dependence are strongly related to measures of the quantity/frequency of tobacco use and/or serum cotinine concentrations (Clark et al. 2005; Kandel et al. 2005; Rubinstein et al. 2007). This evidence has led researchers to propose that methods to assess the wide spectrum of use among adolescents, ranging from initiation and progression to maintenance, may be needed to understand nicotine dependence in this population (Strong et al. 2009).

From First Use to Addiction

This section will focus on multiple patterns of use, including experimentation, regular use of tobacco products, and use that is characterized by addiction. It also addresses the roles played by genetic determinants and mental disorders in the risk for addiction and the relationship of tobacco use to the use of other drugs and alcohol. External factors, including the social-environmental and the cultural, are covered in Chapter 4, "Social, Environmental, Cognitive, and Genetic Influences on the Use of Tobacco Among Youth."

Longitudinal Patterns of Tobacco Use in Adolescents

Mayhew and colleagues (2000) identified several stages of adolescent smoking, from not smoking at all to established smoking, as well as common and distinct predictors of the various stages. In addition, to characterize the course of adolescent smoking and to identify determinants of the trajectories of smoking across adolescence into adulthood, several cohort studies have been carried out that included appropriate statistical modeling. Chassin and colleagues (2000), who applied such models to data from a cohort study of smoking trajectories from adolescence to adulthood, identified four groups with different trajectories: early stable smokers, late stable smokers, experimenters, and quitters. Similarly, White and colleagues (2002) used growth mixture modeling to assess smoking behavior at five time points across 18 years, from early adolescence to adulthood (age 30). They identified three groups with different trajectories: heavy/regular users, occasional users/those maturing out of use, and nonsmokers/experimental smokers.

Colder and colleagues (2001), who used data from an annual assessment of adolescents 12–16 years of age, identified five kinds of smokers: early rapid escalators, late moderate escalators, late slow escalators, stable light smokers, and stable puffers. Similarly, Soldz and Cui (2002) examined the longitudinal patterns of smoking among adolescents, assessed on an annual basis from grades 6 to 12, and identified six clusters: nonsmokers, quitters, experimenters, early escalators, late escalators, and continuous smokers. Audrain-McGovern and colleagues (2004) used evidence from a longitudinal cohort study of 9th to 12th graders to identify four kinds of smokers by trajectory: never smokers, experimenters, earlier/faster smoking adopters, and later/slower smoking adopters. They also examined predictors of smoking behavior and found that early adopters, compared with never smokers, tended to be more novelty seeking, with poorer academic performance, more depressive symptoms, greater exposure to other smokers, and greater use of other substances. In another study, Robinson and colleagues (2004) reported that adolescents who initiated smoking early (before 14 years of age) had slower progression to daily smoking than those who initiated later and that earlier onset of daily smoking was associated with higher FTND scores. In contrast, in follow-ups of two prior studies (Hops et al. 2000; Swan et al. 2003), Lessov-Schlaggar and colleagues (2008) found that while higher levels of nicotine dependence among adolescents were associated with smoking trajectories marked by heavier smoking, there was no relationship between quantity/frequency of cigarette use during adolescence and lifetime levels of nicotine dependence. Thus, various studies point to heterogeneity in the onset and progression of smoking among adolescents (Schepis and Rao 2005).

Several predictors of being on a particular trajectory have been identified. For example, differences by race have been reported: in one study, African American adolescents initiated smoking and also became daily smokers an average of 1 year later than adolescents of other racial/ethnic groups (Robinson et al. 2004). Using similar trajectory analyses, Karp and coworkers (2005) found that among novice smokers (mean age = 13 years), only one-fourth reported rapid escalation toward patterns of heavier use; this escalation was predicted by male gender, poor academic performance, and having more than 50% of their friends smoke. A recent large, population-based cohort study found that the likelihood of being in a trajectory group defined by heavier use was enhanced by having parents who smoked, a greater number of friends who smoked, and a greater perception of the number of adults and adolescents who smoked. Conversely, negative perceptions of the tobacco industry, higher perceived difficulty regarding smoking in public places, and stricter home smoking policies were protective (Bernat et al. 2008). Finally, Riggs and colleagues (2007) evaluated the relationship between adolescent trajectories of tobacco use and nicotine dependence in early adulthood and found that adolescents who demonstrated early stable use of tobacco (two cigarettes per week by 12 years of age) were more likely to have greater nicotine dependence as young adults.

In summary, these results indicate that adolescent smoking patterns follow different trajectories from experimentation to addiction. Approaches using trajectory analyses allow researchers not only to account for variability in tobacco use behaviors, but also to extend the analyses to examine interindividual changes in smoking patterns across time and to assess the predictors of various trajectories. Several predictors of smoking trajectory have been identified through prospective cohort studies, and additional trajectory analyses from national data are shown in Chapter 3.

Genetic Influences

Emerging evidence indicates that addiction to tobacco smoking has a heritable component, with genetic factors contributing to all phases of the smoking trajectory, from initiation to dependence and cessation (for review, see NCI 2009; Bierut 2011). NCI's Monograph 20 addresses this topic in depth (NCI 2009). In addition, the mechanics of nicotine addiction and the role of genetics in determining addiction were addressed in the 2010 Surgeon General's report (USDHHS 2010). This is an active area of research, but the emphasis in this chapter is on genetic studies related to initiation and the trajectories of smoking across adolescence (see also Chapter 4). Recently, researchers have identified specific genetic markers as strongly associated with nicotine dependence (Li et al. 2008). Investigations into the specific genes that mediate cigarette smoking are complicated by different definitions of the nicotine dependence phenotype (Ho and Tyndale 2007). In fact, several components of the phenotype of nicotine dependence appear to be heritable, including tolerance, withdrawal, difficulty quitting, time to first cigarette in the morning, and number of cigarettes smoked per day (Lessov et al. 2004; Swan et al. 2009). The need for a broad framework for assessing the role of genetic factors in nicotine dependence is now well recognized (NCI 2009). It is clear that multiple genes may act through various pathways, and environmental factors also need consideration. For adolescents, the age of starting to smoke, trajectory of smoking, and persistence of smoking constitute the appropriate focus for genetic studies.

Reported investigations on the genetics of smoking now include some that have looked at the initiation and progression of smoking in adolescents (Haberstick et al. 2007). Laucht and colleagues (2008) found that among adolescent smokers, initiation was associated with allelic variation in the dopamine receptor D4 (*DRD4*) gene, and continuation of smoking and dependence were associated with the dopamine receptor D2 (*DRD2*) gene (Laucht et al. 2008). Another genetic influence on tobacco use and dependence has to do with the relative rate of nicotine metabolism (Malaiyandi et al. 2005); individuals with polymorphisms in genes encoding the enzymes primarily involved in nicotine metabolism (e.g., cytochrome P-450, family 2, subfamily A, polypeptide 6; *CYP2D6*) tend to smoke fewer cigarettes and are less likely to be current smokers. This finding could be driven by the fact that faster metabolizers smoke more cigarettes (Audrain-McGovern et al. 2007). Adolescents who metabolize nicotine normally have been found to progress to nicotine dependence more quickly than those with gene variants associated with slow metabolism (Audrain-McGovern et al. 2007). More recent evidence from a sample of young adult smokers suggests that polymorphisms in the genes encoding the neuronal cholinergic nicotinic subunit receptors, specifically in the genomic region containing the *CHRNA5/A3/B4* gene cluster, is a significant predictor of the age of initiation of cigarette smoking (Schlaepfer et al. 2008). In support, research from three independent samples of long-term smokers suggests that the *CHRNA5/A3/B4* gene cluster is associated with severity of nicotine dependence and daily smoking at or before 16 years of age (Weiss et al. 2008). This same gene cluster is associated with the transition from experimental to dependent smoking (Bierut et al. 2007; Saccone et al. 2007) and has been one of the most replicated findings in complex genetic studies; four separate meta-analyses have validated a strong association of this cluster with smoking phenotypes (Liu et al. 2010; Saccone et al. 2010; Thorgeirsson et al. 2010; Tobacco and Genetics Consortium 2010). Other studies show that this same cluster is associated with phenotypes that are known consequences of smoking later in life, such as COPD (Pillai et al. 2009), peripheral artery disease (Thorgeirsson et al. 2008), and lung cancer (Amos et al. 2008; Hung et al. 2008; Liu et al. 2008; Saccone et al. 2010; Thorgeirsson et al. 2008).

Summary

Longitudinal studies show differing trajectories of smoking across adolescence—the critical period of time when addiction begins for many young people. These trajectories reflect a range of rates of progression toward addiction, and they represent important phenotypes for researchers and possibly for prevention initiatives by offering an indication of which new smokers may be at greatest risk for addiction. Limited evidence suggests that these trajectories may differ across racial groups.

The documentation that adolescents follow different trajectories of the onset and progression of smoking has implications that extend beyond research to include prevention and intervention. Clearly, having several kinds of trajectories precludes being able to identify particular adolescents who are moving swiftly toward addiction. In addition, the trajectories are not necessarily linear, and the actual point of addiction is not clearly demarcated. Thus, practitioners cannot readily identify specific at-risk youth, and there is uncertainty as to how to tailor cessation initiatives for smokers at different points on these trajectories.

Identifying the determinants of particular trajectories, however, could help with early identification of high-risk adolescents. Some of the predictors that have been examined include the smoking behaviors and attitudes of parents and peers, the use of tobacco products for regulation of mood and affect, developmental changes in risk-taking behaviors, and genetic factors (see Chapter 4,) for discussion of these topics in greater depth). The newer evidence continues to show that peer influence is strongly associated with initiation and, in one study, with a trajectory of heavier use (Bernat et al. 2008). Several characteristics of adolescents are also relevant for predicting trajectories, including gender, impulsivity and risk taking, and affect. In addition, emerging evidence is suggesting that both risk for initiation and continuing to smoke may have genetic determinants. The findings to date indicate that the genes influencing dopaminergic reward pathways, nicotinic cholinergic receptors, and nicotine metabolism are relevant. However, the evidence on genetic determinants for adolescents and young adults is still too limited to make any suggestions concerning interventions based on genetic make-up.

Mental Health and Risk for Smoking

Introduction

Among adults, tobacco use is highly prevalent among people with psychiatric diagnoses over all and for such specific diagnoses as depression, schizophrenia, attention deficit hyperactivity disorder (ADHD), anxiety disorders, and substance abuse. For example, Lasser and colleagues (2000) found higher rates of tobacco use among those with psychiatric disorders (41%) or substance abuse (67%) than in the general population (21% at that time). In addition, adults with mental illness, broadly defined, were found to consume an estimated 44.3% of the cigarettes smoked in the United States (Upadhyaya et al. 2002), even though such adults constituted a far smaller percentage of the population. Explanations for the links between psychiatric disorders and cigarette use have emphasized the possible shared underlying predispositions for tobacco use and having a psychiatric disorder. There may be a genetic basis for this presumed shared predisposition that relates to neurologic pathways in the brain; individuals with serious mental illness, such as schizophrenia and depression, may be self-medicating and thus using nicotine to modulate symptoms related to their illness by influencing neurologic pathways (Ziedonis et al. 2008).

Adolescents

Although the links between tobacco use and both psychiatric comorbidities and disorders of substance abuse have been investigated in adults, they have not been rigorously examined in adolescents. In one study of youth, Kandel and colleagues (1997) examined the cross-sectional relationship between cigarette use and the use of other substances as well as with psychiatric disorders and found that daily cigarette smoking was associated with a 70% increase in the likelihood of diagnoses of anxiety and of disorders of mood and disruptive behavior. Later, a comprehensive review by Upadhyaya and colleagues (2002) found that psychiatric comorbidity is common in adolescent cigarette smokers, especially among those with disorders involving disruptive behavior (such as oppositional defiant disorder, conduct disorder, and ADHD), major depressive disorders, and drug and alcohol use. They concluded that anxiety disorders are modestly associated with cigarette smoking. They also found that early onset of cigarette smoking (before 13 years of age) and early onset of conduct problems were robust markers of increased psychopathology later in life, including substance abuse. Finally, a more recent case-control study found high rates of cigarette smoking in adolescents with bipolar disorder (Wilens et al. 2008).

A number of cross-sectional studies have found positive associations between depressive symptoms or a diagnosis of depression and tobacco use or nicotine dependence (Covey and Tam 1990; Brown et al. 1996; Nelson and Wittchen 1998; Acierno et al. 2000; Sonntag et al. 2000). Compared with their nondepressed peers, adolescents with depressive disorders have been found to be more likely to initiate experimental smoking, to become regular users (Patton et al. 1998), and to be nicotine dependent (Breslau et al. 1993). Furthermore, the presence of an affective disorder increases the likelihood of nicotine dependence by 10-fold in adolescents (Dierker et al. 2001). Evidence on the temporality of this relationship is somewhat equivocal, however. Some cohort studies have indicated that the presence of affective symptoms or the diagnosis of an affective disorder during adolescence leads to increased initiation and progression of smoking as well as to higher nicotine dependence (Kandel and Davies 1986; Fergusson et al. 1996); another cross-sectional study found a relationship between depressive symptoms and smoking among young adults in college (Kenney and Holahan 2008). In contrast, some cohort studies suggest that current smoking predicts depressive symptoms (Wu and Anthony 1999; Goodman and Capitman 2000) and not the other way around. Evidence from the National Longitudinal Alcohol Epidemiologic Survey indicated that onset of smoking before 13 years of age, when compared with onset after 17 years of age, was associated with earlier onset and more episodes of major depressive disorder (Hanna and Grant 1999). A more recent study conducted by Illomäki and colleagues (2008) examined the temporal nature of the relationship between onset of daily smoking and psychiatric disorders among hospitalized adolescents and found that substance use disorders, as well as psychotic and depressive disorders, follow the initiation of daily smoking, while conduct or oppositional defiant disorders appear to precede daily smoking.

Not surprisingly, evidence on the connection between smoking behavior and anxiety disorders is also equivocal. Adolescents with anxiety disorders have been found to have increased rates of smoking and nicotine dependence (Nelson and Wittchen 1998; Sonntag et al. 2000), and some studies indicate that anxiety predicts the initiation and progression of smoking (Patton et al. 1998).

Evidence for a link between nicotine use and ADHD is also somewhat equivocal. For example, a higher smoking prevalence among adolescents and adults diagnosed with ADHD has been reported (Pomerleau et al. 1995; Riggs et al. 1999; Ribeiro et al. 2008), but other studies have found no increased risk for smoking in association with ADHD (Dierker et al. 2001). One longitudinal study, however, found that an early diagnosis of ADHD was associated with an increased rate of later cigarette smoking (Chilcoat and Breslau 1999). It has been proposed that smokers with ADHD may be using nicotine as a way to improve their attention span by increasing the release of dopamine (Dani and Harris 2005); this self-medication hypothesis is supported by the finding that the nicotine transdermal patch improved performance on cognitive reaction tasks in both adult smokers and adult nonsmokers with ADHD (Conners et al. 1996; Levin et al. 1996). More recent evidence from a cohort study examining the temporal relationship between ADHD and conduct disorder in adolescence and smoking in adulthood suggests that the relationship between ADHD and cigarette smoking may be mediated by conduct disorders (Brook et al. 2008). In another study, Rodriguez and colleagues (2008) suggest that ADHD symptoms of inattention are associated with the progression of nicotine dependence in adolescence, while hyperactivity-impulsivity ADHD symptoms are associated with the progression of nicotine dependence in young adulthood.

Research has found an association between childhood oppositional disorder and subsequent daily smoking behavior. Individuals with conduct disorder were found to have increased rates of nicotine dependence (Donovan et al. 1988), and Dierker and colleagues (2001) found that nicotine dependence significantly increased the risk of oppositional defiant disorder. There may be a gender difference in the nature of this relationship: the time between initiation of smoking and childhood oppositional disorder was found to be shorter among girls than among boys (Illomäki et al. 2008).

It should be noted that more serious mental health problems, such as schizophrenia, have generally been studied among adults, even though the precursors to these problems are evident in adolescents. With the very high prevalence of smoking among those with schizophrenia (70–85%), it seems important to identify these precursors for early intervention with this population, given that the onset of smoking generally occurs before 18 years of age and before the onset of the disorder (Weiser et al. 2004; Ziedonis et al. 2008).

Summary

Evidence is emerging that smoking is associated with various developmental and mental health disorders that affect adolescents and young adults. The available evidence extends to mental health disorders, such as schizophrenia, anxiety, and depression, and to developmental disorders, such as ADHD and conduct disorder. One complication in interpreting the available evidence is the temporality of the associations of smoking with the various disorders; that is, do mental health disorders increase risk for starting to smoke or does smoking increase risk for mental health disorders? There also is the possibility that smoking and a mental health disorder are linked through a common predisposition, possibly genetic or environmental. Cohort studies (i.e., longitudinal studies) are needed to conclusively establish the temporal relationship between mental health and developmental disorders and smoking.

The Use of Tobacco and Risk for Using Other Substances

Introduction

Evidence from a number of studies indicates that cigarette smoking is strongly associated with the use of other substances. For example, adult smokers are twice as likely as nonsmokers to have ever used illicit drugs (Farrell and Marshall 2006). In adults, associations vary with the level of nicotine dependence, with dependent smokers at much greater risk for dependence on alcohol, cocaine, and marijuana than are nonsmokers and nondependent smokers. For example, based on 1989 data from a sample of 21- to 30-year-old members of a Michigan health maintenance organization, nicotine-dependent smokers had 12 times the risk for cocaine dependence as that of nonsmokers, but smokers who were not nicotine dependent had only 6.5 times the risk (Breslau 1995). This study used the *DSM-III-R* definition of nicotine dependence.

Evidence in Adolescents and Young Adults

Among adolescents, early initiation of tobacco use is associated with the use of other substances (Kandel and Yamaguchi 1993). In a cohort study of adolescents, reports of "ever" and "daily" smoking were associated with increased risks in the future of using marijuana and other illicit drugs as well as disorders involving the use of multiple drugs (Lewinsohn et al. 1999). In addition, early-onset smokers were found to be more likely to have substance use disorders than late-onset smokers or nonsmokers (Hanna and Grant 1999). In a study by Lewinsohn and colleagues (1999), lifetime smoking among older adolescents significantly increased the probability of future use of alcohol, marijuana, hard drugs, or multiple drugs during young adulthood. Having been a former smoker, however, did not reduce the risk of future substance abuse disorders, although having maintained smoking cessation for more than 12 months was associated with significantly lower rates of future alcohol abuse. In another study, early onset of smoking was the strongest predictor of high-risk behaviors among middle school students (DuRant et al. 1999). A Finnish study found that younger onset of daily smoking was significantly related to the subsequent incidence of substance use disorders (Illomäki et al. 2008).

The association of tobacco use with alcohol use is strong. Grant (1998), for example, found that early onset of smoking was associated with early onset of drinking as well as with an increased risk for developing alcohol use disorders. In addition, a cross-sectional study by Koopmans and colleagues (1997) found that adolescent and young adult smokers were more likely to drink than were their nonsmoking counterparts, and this relationship appeared to be mediated more by shared environmental factors than by genetic factors. Other authors have found a positive association between the incidence of alcohol use disorders and nicotine dependence (Nelson and Wittchen 1998; Sonntag et al. 2000). More recently, Weitzman and Chen (2005) found that among young adult college students, 98% of smokers drank alcohol and up to 59% of drinkers smoked tobacco; the risk for co-occurrence was highest among students with the highest alcohol consumption, problems with alcohol, and symptoms of alcohol abuse. However, while a positive relationship has been observed between smoking and drinking, the temporality of this relationship remains unclear (Istvan and Matarazzo 1984; Sutherland and Willner 1998). Still, smokers are more likely to drink alcohol than are nonsmokers, and drinkers are more likely to smoke than are nondrinkers. The evidence also indicates a dose-dependent relationship, with greater use of one substance being related to greater use of the other (Zacny 1990). As adolescents enter young adulthood, the risks for tobacco and alcohol use increase. For example, in one study, 22% of college students reported starting to engage in heavy drinking during their first semester in college (Wechsler et al. 1994), a behavior that also is associated with risk for smoking behaviors.

The comorbidity of alcohol and tobacco use in young adulthood may originate in adolescence, as teens' vulnerability to the use of other substances appears to be exacerbated by even experimental use of tobacco. For example, adolescent smokers are more likely to be heavier drinkers than are never smokers and have four times the risk of a comorbid alcohol use disorder; in fact, even those teens who only experiment with cigarettes are twice as likely to have an alcohol use disorder as are never smokers (Grucza and Bierut 2006). Studies of twins have implicated shared genetic factors as responsible for joint dependence on nicotine and alcohol (True et al. 1999).

Summary

Cohort studies show that smoking often antedates the use of other drugs in adolescents and is a risk factor for future use of drugs and alcohol (Kandel et al. 1992; Levine et al. 2011). In general, drugs of abuse such as smoking can cause neuroplastic changes in the brain that favor continued use (Benowitz 2010; Hong et al. 2010), and these changes may be more dynamic in the developing (e.g., adolescent) brain (Dwyer et al. 2008). Although smoking might increase risk for subsequent drug use through pharmacologic, environmental, developmental, and genetic factors (McQuown et al. 2007), vulnerability to drug use and future use likely relies on a variety of factors.

Smoking and Body Weight

Introduction

Weight control has been prominent in the marketing of cigarettes to females, influencing their decision making on the issues of starting to smoke and continuing to smoke (Suwarna 1985). This section addresses five key questions on smoking and weight for females and males in this age range:

- Do adolescents and young adults believe that smoking helps control body weight?
- Do adolescents and young adults use smoking in an attempt to control their body weight?
- Do concerns about body weight predict the initiation of smoking?
- Does concern about body weight affect the likelihood of smoking cessation?
- Does smoking *actually affect* body weight in adolescents and young adults?

The organization of this section is based on the mechanisms and pathways postulated as underlying the relationships between messages from the tobacco industry, other external influences, the perceptions of adolescents, and smoking behavior. First, the section addresses the use by industry of messages indicating that smoking is beneficial for weight control. These messages are hypothesized to have a direct impact on concern about weight gain and on the perceptions that cigarette smoking controls body weight and that initiation of cigarette smoking will reduce body weight. Those beliefs, in turn, may lead to the initiation of smoking, at least in certain susceptible groups (e.g., weight-conscious girls). Initiation can lead to nicotine addiction. This section concludes by addressing whether smoking cessation in young adults leads to weight gain and whether continued smoking has weight-control benefits in young adult smokers. Previous Surgeon General's reports (summarized below) concluded that there is a relationship between smoking and body weight in adults, but this report focuses more specifically on the relationship between smoking and body weight in adolescents and young adults. The chapter does not address the biological basis of an association of smoking with body weight (see Chiolero et al. 2008 for a review). In this section, the same study may provide information to address one or more of the questions above. Additional epidemiological data relevant to smoking and weight control can be found throughout Chapter 3 of this report, too.

Methods for the Evidence Review

Studies investigating beliefs about smoking and body weight, the use of smoking to control weight, and the impact of weight-related attitudes, beliefs, and concerns on smoking behavior were identified through computerized searches of the PubMed, PsycINFO, PsycARTICLES, and PsycCRITIQUES electronic databases. Search terms included Boolean combinations of "smoking" and "weight control" paired with terms used to identify age-appropriate persons, including "youth," "adolescent," and "young adult." To identify prospective studies examining the association between weight-related issues and changes in smoking behavior, the terms "initiation," "onset," and "cessation" were added to the searches. The references of identified articles were subsequently reviewed for additional studies that met inclusion criteria.

To address whether smoking affects body weight in younger people, relevant articles were identified through reviews of previous Surgeon General's reports, computerized searches in databases such as PubMed, PsycINFO, PsycARTICLES, and Google Scholar, and examination of reference lists in primary research and review articles. The search terms used in these computerized searches were variations of the term "smoking" (e.g., "tobacco use") paired with weight-related terms such as "body weight," "body composition," "BMI" (body mass index), and "weight control." To focus on adolescent and young adult populations, additional terms such as "adolescent" and "youth" were used. The research articles included were peer-reviewed English-language papers published from 1989 to 2008, and the search was completed in August 2008. Relevant articles that did not provide data on age and weight by smoking status were excluded.

Beliefs of Youth and Young Adults Concerning Smoking and Control of Body Weight

Emphasis on Weight Control in Tobacco Advertising

Numerous examples document how the tobacco companies have employed advertising to indicate a relationship between smoking and body weight. Indeed, messages extolling the weight-controlling "benefits" of smoking have been a common theme in cigarette marketing for many decades. In the 1920s, in an early attempt to capture the previously untapped market of female smokers, the American Tobacco Company launched a groundbreaking advertising campaign for its Lucky Strike cigarette brand. The advertisements, which urged women to "Reach for a Lucky Instead of a Sweet," promoted smoking as a weight-control strategy. Subsequent advertisements were even more direct in their messages ("To stay slender, reach for a Lucky, a most effective way of retaining a trim figure"; "To keep a slender figure no one can deny, reach for a Lucky instead of a sweet"). Other Lucky Strike advertisements employed scare tactics to prey on fears about weight gain by depicting exaggeratedly obese silhouettes in the form of shadows positioned next to trim female figures and featuring captions such as "Avoid that future shadow" or "Is this you five years from now?" (Amos and Haglund 2000; Ernster et al. 2000; USDHHS 2001). American Tobacco's strategy helped to firmly establish the link between smoking and weight control in the minds of the consumer, and within the first year, the company saw a sales increase of more than 300%, making Lucky Strike the top-ranked brand in the country and marking one of the most successful tobacco advertising campaigns in history (Howe 1984; Ernster 1985; Pierce and Gilpin 1995; USDHHS 2001). The Lucky Strike campaign, combined with concurrent efforts by the makers of the Chesterfield cigarette to market cigarettes directly to women, contributed significantly to the dramatic increase in cigarette smoking in the late 1920s among adolescent girls and young women (Pierce and Gilpin 1995; USDHHS 2001).

Since the highly successful Lucky Strike campaign, an implied association between smoking and weight control has been used countless times. Tobacco companies have commonly employed slender, attractive young models in an effort to generate an image of female smokers as thin, pretty, and glamorous (Krupka et al. 1990; Brown and Witherspoon 2002). Furthermore, several cigarettes have been specifically designed to strengthen the perceived association between cigarette smoking and a slender physique. For example, cigarettes with brand names containing descriptors such as "thins" and "slims" have been manufactured to be longer and slimmer than traditional cigarettes and to appeal directly to women, helping to reinforce the belief that the smoking of certain brands is an effective weight-control strategy (Davis 1987; Albright et al. 1988; Califano 1995). This notion was further strengthened by the inclusion of slogans emphasizing thinness (e.g., Misty's "Slim 'n Sassy" and Silva Thins' "I'm a thinner. Long and lean, that's the way I like things. I like my figure slim, my men trim, and my cigarette thin"). In addition, several brands, including Virginia Slims and Capri, have come out with "super slim" versions of their cigarettes that are even more slender in design. The marketing campaigns for these products further emphasized weight control in their captions (e.g., Capri: "There is no slimmer way to smoke"; Virginia Slims Superslims: "Fat smoke is history. It took Virginia Slims to create a great tasting ultra thin cigarette that gives you more than a sleek shape") and images. Furthermore, print advertisements for Virginia Slims Superslims in the early 1990s used images containing thin, elongated shapes and pictures of female models that appear to have been digitally "altered" to exaggerate their tall and lean appearance. As with Lucky Strike 40 years earlier, the introductory marketing of Virginia Slims in the late 1960s (which, in addition to glamour and thinness, famously emphasized autonomy and liberation through the theme "You've come a long way, baby") was tremendously successful and was associated with a dramatic increase in the initiation of smoking among adolescent girls (Pierce et al. 1994; Pierce and Gilpin 1995; USDHHS 2001).

Given the prohibitions against billboard advertising and restrictions on print advertisements that resulted from the 1998 Master Settlement Agreement and changing media environment, tobacco companies have changed their marketing strategies in an effort to reach their target audience. One approach used increasingly has been the Internet, but to date, relatively little attention has been given to the content and impact of tobacco advertising posted on protobacco, primarily non-tobacco-company, Web sites. In one of the few studies in this area, Hong and Cody (2002) randomly selected more than 300 such Web sites and found that tobacco advertising on the Internet was widespread. Furthermore, they found that many of the themes commonly seen earlier in print advertising were included in Web-based campaigns. These advertisements on the Web often glamorize smoking by using youthful and attractive female models.

Young People's Beliefs About the Impact of Smoking on Body Weight

Numerous studies, summarized in Table 2.2, have examined beliefs among youth about the utility of cigarette smoking as a weight-control strategy. Because of differences in methodology, sample characteristics, time period, and the methods through which beliefs were assessed, specific findings necessarily varied across studies. Regardless, this body of research indicates that a belief in the ability of cigarette smoking to help control body weight is quite pervasive among youth.

Most of the studies on the perceived impact of cigarette smoking on body weight have been conducted with samples of adolescents and young adults. Considering that adolescence and young adulthood are the developmental periods with the highest risk for initiation of smoking, a belief that smoking affects weight may have an especially potent effect in this age group. In an early study to examine perceptions about an association between smoking and body weight, Shor and colleagues (1981) surveyed 307 undergraduate students regarding their beliefs about the factors that motivate people to smoke cigarettes. Fifty-five percent reported the belief that smoking helps smokers avoid weight gain, with levels of agreement similar for smokers (59%) and nonsmokers (53%). Respondents were also asked whether they felt that smoking helped to control the quantity of food they ate, with 43% (smokers = 49%, nonsmokers = 41%) agreeing that this is a common characteristic of smoking.

In another early study, Charlton (1984) surveyed nearly 15,175 British students between the ages of 9 and 19 years regarding their smoking behavior and whether they agreed with the statement "Smoking keeps your weight down." Twenty-three percent agreed that smoking helps to control weight, with similar levels of endorsement in girls (24%) and boys (22%). Beliefs in the weight-controlling effects of smoking were positively associated with personal smoking history; those who had never smoked were least likely to agree (16.6%), while students who smoked at least six cigarettes per week were the most likely to agree (42.2%) that smoking reduces body weight.

Camp and colleagues (1993), who investigated the relationship between concerns about body weight and cigarette smoking in a sample of 659 high school students, asked participants to indicate their agreement with the statement "Smoking cigarettes can help you control your weight/appetite." Overall, 40.2% of adolescents agreed, with agreement considerably higher among smokers (67%) than among never smokers (37%). Differences were also noted across racial and gender subgroups. White girls were the most likely to believe that smoking helps to control weight (45.7%), followed by White boys (29.9%) and Black boys (13.5%). Among Black girls, only 10% endorsed this belief.

West and Hargreaves (1995) surveyed 117 female and 29 male nursing students (mean age = 24 years) in the United Kingdom in an effort to identify factors associated with smoking in this group. Overall, 34% of the participants were classified as current smokers. Participants rated their levels of agreement with 11 statements representing various beliefs about smoking, including its association with body weight ("Smoking helps with weight control"). Responses were on a five-point Likert scale ranging from "strongly disagree" to "strongly agree." Smokers were significantly more likely (38%) than either former smokers (26%) or never smokers (11%) to agree or strongly agree that smoking aids weight control. Even so, beliefs about the effect of smoking on weight were not significantly associated with the desire to quit smoking.

Klesges and colleagues (1997a) examined the associations between concerns about weight and smoking as a function of smoking status, race, and gender among a sample of 6,961 seventh-grade students enrolled in the Memphis Health Project. These adolescents were asked whether they believed that smoking cigarettes helps people control their weight; 39.4% endorsed this belief. Levels of agreement increased with smoking history, with daily and other regular smokers most likely to endorse this belief, followed by experimental smokers and never smokers. A significant race-by-gender interaction was also noted. As in Camp and colleagues (1993), White girls were most likely to endorse this belief, but in contrast to that earlier study, White boys were least likely to believe that smoking controls body weight; Black girls and Black boys fell in the middle.

George and Johnson (2001) investigated weight concerns and weight-loss behaviors among an ethnically diverse group of 1,852 college students, an estimated 57% of whom were Hispanic (the remainder classified themselves as White [18%] or "other" [24%]), and 62% were female. More than 90% of the sample were 17–24 years of age. Participants were recruited from two undergraduate classes and completed a 73-item survey assessing lifestyle behaviors, attitudes toward weight control, height and weight, and the 10-item version of the Dietary Restraint Scale (Herman and Mack 1975). Participants were also asked, "How do you think that smoking affects your weight?" Response options were "keeps it down," "no effect," "keeps it up," and "don't know." Overall, 24% of men and 17% of women reported that they smoked. Among current smokers, 22% of women and 16% of men said they thought that smoking helped keep their weight down. Forty-five percent of both male and female smokers responded that smoking had "no effect" on their weight,

Table 2.2 Studies assessing belief that smoking controls body weight

Study	Design/population	Measures	Percentage endorsing	Findings	Comments
Shor et al. 1981	307 undergraduates Age NR Cross-sectional questionnaire on benefits of smoking	"Smoking helps smokers avoid weight gains" "Smoking helps smokers control the quantity of food they eat" 5-point scale: "strongly agree" to "strongly disagree"	Smokers = 59% Never smokers = 53% Smokers = 49%* Never smokers = 41%* *Agreed or strongly agreed	• 19.9% classified as current smokers • 45.9% classified as never smokers • Remaining 34.2% (former smokers) excluded from analysis	Strengths: bipolar response scale with 0 as neutral point; respondents included both current smokers and never smokers
Loken 1982	178 female undergraduates Age NR Cross-sectional questionnaire about cigarette smoking	"My smoking cigarettes keeps (would keep) my weight down" Agreement and outcome evaluation (based on good-bad affective scale) measured using 7-point bipolar scales from -3 to +3	NR	• Strength of belief greater among heavy smokers than among light smokers or nonsmokers • Outcome evaluation regarding value of keeping one's weight down did not differ by smoking status	Strengths: female population is of interest to antismoking organizations; focus on both positive and negative consequences of smoking; findings are in line with other research Weaknesses: unable to compare findings by gender
Charlton 1984	15,175 students Age NR (range 9–19 years) Random sample stratified by age group and school type Cross-sectional questionnaire United Kingdom	"Smoking keeps your weight down" (yes, no, don't know)	**Girls:** Total = 24% Never smokers = 17.4% Experimenters = 23.4% Current smokers = 40.0% Former smokers = 26.8% **Boys:** Total = 22% Never smokers = 15.9% Experimenters = 21.7% Current smokers = 33.9% Former smokers = 27.8%	• Current smokers consuming ≥6 cigarettes/ week most likely to endorse • Under age 12, current smokers least likely to agree smoking controls weight; after age 12, current smokers most likely to agree	NR

Table 2.2 Continued

Study	Design/population	Measures	Percentage endorsing	Findings	Comments
Brandon and Baker 1991	547 undergraduates Mean 18.7 years of age (SD = 2.8; range 16–47 years) Cross-sectional questionnaire on smoking consequences	Smoking Consequences Questionnaire (SCQ): a multidimensional measure of the subjective expected utility (SEU) of smoking 5-item factor assesses expected effects of smoking on appetite and weight control Sample items: "Smoking helps me control my weight," "Smoking controls my appetite" Desirability of each consequence rated -5 to +5 and perceived probability rated 0 to 9 Cross-product of both ratings used to arrive at SEU	NR	• Daily smokers rated expected utility of smoking for weight control higher than did occasional smokers and never smokers • Daily smokers rated likelihood that smoking would control weight/appetite higher than did occasional smokers • Among former smokers, females gave higher ratings than did males on likelihood of smoking affecting weight control	Strengths: high internal consistency reliability of scales; target sample is at transitional stage of smoking so scale may be useful in predicting eventual smoking status Weaknesses: results cannot be generalized to adult population because of low smoking prevalence among sample
Camp et al. 1993	659 high school students Mean 16.3 years of age Cross-sectional questionnaire	"Smoking cigarettes can help you control your weight/appetite"	Total = 40.2% Smokers = 67% Never smokers = 36% Black boys = 13.5% Black girls = 10.0% White boys = 29.9% White girls = 45.7%	• Smokers were more likely to endorse than were never smokers • Belief that smoking helps control weight/appetite differed as a function of race and gender	Strengths: addresses several gaps in literature; racially diverse sample; use of variables supported by research; uses conservative statistical tests Weaknesses: cannot infer causality; results may not generalize to other areas or to nonparochial subjects; did not use bogus pipeline or biochemical methods
Li et al. 1994	585 Asian female airline cabin crew members Age NR (range 20–41 years; 87% <30) Cross-sectional questionnaire	Participants questioned regarding beliefs about various health risks of smoking, including that it will "help control body weight"	Total = 37% Never smokers = 34% Former smokers = 29% Current smokers = 48%	• Endorsement among current smokers greater than among never smokers and former smokers	Weaknesses: underreporting of smoking due to uncertainty of employer's views; inconsistent interpretation of various terms by subjects (i.e., "fit")

Table 2.2 Continued

Study	Design/population	Measures	Percentage endorsing	Findings	Comments
West and Hargreaves 1995	146 student nurses (80% female) Mean of age 24 years (SD = 5.42) Cross-sectional questionnaire United Kingdom	Participants completed questions regarding the perceived positive and negative effects of smoking including that "Smoking helps with weight control" 5-point scale: "strongly disagree" to "strongly agree"	Smokers = 38% Former smokers = 26% Never smokers = 11%	• Current smokers more likely to endorse belief that smoking helps control weight • Belief in weight-controlling effects of smoking not related to desire to quit	Weaknesses: limited generalizability; small sample size; possible underreporting of smoking
Klesges et al. 1997a	6,961 7th-grade students in Memphis public schools 13 years of age Cross-sectional questionnaire as part of Memphis Health Project Tennessee	Item asked whether participants endorsed belief that smoking cigarettes helps people control their weight	Total = 39.4%	• Endorsement increased with smoking exposure (daily smokers > regular [nondaily] smokers > experimental smokers > never smokers) • Race x gender interaction: White girls most likely and White boys least likely to endorse this belief • Among Black youth, boys more likely than girls to endorse this belief	Strengths: large sample size; high participation rate; ethnic and gender composition representative of Memphis schools; majority Black children in sample can add to literature about the behaviors and concerns of this population Weaknesses: limited generalizability outside of Memphis public schools; did not use bogus pipeline or biochemical procedures; possible response bias due to substance users missing school; lack of temporality
Wang et al. 1998	National sample of high school dropouts (weighted N = 492,352) Age NR (range 15–18 years) Cross-sectional computer-assisted telephone interview as part of the Teenage Attitudes and Practices Survey	"Smoking helps people keep their weight down"	NR	• Smoking rate among those who agreed smoking helps control body weight (69.1%) higher than for those who did not endorse this belief (54.6%)	Strengths: focuses on a rarely studied population of school dropouts

Table 2.2 Continued

Study	Design/population	Measures	Percentage endorsing	Findings	Comments
Cepeda-Benito and Ferrer 2000	212 Spanish smokers comprised of college students and university employees Mean 22.5 years of age (SD = 5.0) Cross-sectional questionnaire to test the validity of the SCQ when used on a Spanish population	SCQ-S, Spanish version of the SCQ Includes a 5-item subscale designed to assess expected effects of smoking on weight control	NR	• Female smokers endorsed higher expectancies than did male smokers for effect of smoking on body weight • SEU of smoking for weight control not related to nicotine dependence after Bonferroni adjustment for multiple comparisons	Strengths: good construct validity and internal consistency for instrument and scales Weaknesses: questionnaire may not generalize to other Spanish-speaking populations outside of Spain
Boles and Johnson 2001	1,200 adolescents Age NR (range 12–17 years) Cross-sectional telephone interview	"Do you think that smoking cigarettes helps you to control your weight"	Current smokers = 15% **Girls:** Total = 22.2% Aged 12–13 years = 0.0% Aged 14–15 years = 16.7% Aged 16–17 years = 28.6% **Boys:** Total = 9.9% Aged 12–13 years = 25.0% Aged 14–15 years = 16.7% Aged 16–17 years = 4.3%	• Question asked only of current smokers (n = 140) • Endorsement levels differed by gender and age • Agreement increased with age among female smokers and decreased with age among male smokers	Weaknesses: unable to make smoker-nonsmoker comparisons; did not collect height and weight data; small number of smokers in sample prohibited age comparisons; parents were interviewed during the same call as the adolescents
Budd and Preston 2001	172 undergraduates Mean 21.5 years of age (SD = 4.96; range 19–51 years) Cross-sectional questionnaire Pilot test of a newly developed instrument used to measure perceived consequences of smoking among young adults	Attitudes and Beliefs about Perceived Consequences of Smoking Scale: includes 3-item Body Image scale Sample items: "Smoking prevents weight gain," "Smoking keeps a person thin" 5-point scale: "strongly agree" to "strongly disagree"	NR	• Smokers endorsed stronger beliefs than did nonsmokers on the body-image-enhancing effects of smoking	Strengths: findings are in line with previous research; more precise measure of cigarette use compared to other studies Weaknesses: small number of male participants; convenience sample may not be representative of population

Table 2.2 Continued

Study	Design/population	Measures	Percentage endorsing	Findings	Comments
George and Johnson 2001	1,852 college students Age NR; >90%, 17–24 years of age Cross-sectional self-administered questionnaire	"How do you think smoking affects your weight?" (keeps it down, no effect, keeps it up, don't know)	22% of female smokers and 16% of male smokers believed smoking kept their weight down	• Male smokers more likely than nonsmokers to have dieted for weight loss during the past month • Female smokers more likely than nonsmokers to have used diet pills in the past month	Strengths: unique population of ethnically diverse university students Weaknesses: sample demographics and size; possible bias in self-reported weight and smoking status, question design, study design
Zucker et al. 2001	188 female undergraduates Mean 19.0 years of age (SD = 0.9; range 17–25 years) Cross-sectional-correlational Self-report questionnaire	"Smoking helps people control weight" 7-point scale: "do not agree at all" to "definitely agree"	NR	• Belief that smoking controls weight associated with greater odds of being a smoker	Weaknesses: generalizability limited because of highly selective sample; could not include ethnicity as a variable predicting smoking status
Cachelin et al. 2003	211 junior high and high school students Mean 16.3 years of age (SD = 1.3) Cross-sectional self-administered school-based questionnaire	Two items from Smoking Beliefs and Attitudes Scale: "Smoking keeps you from eating" "Smoking helps you control your weight"	NR	• Female dieters more likely than nondieters to believe smoking keeps one from eating • Among females, dieting status not related to belief that smoking helps control weight • Among males, dieting status not related to beliefs about smoking and eating or weight control	Strengths: ethnically diverse sample Weaknesses: small sample size of some groups (i.e., White and Hispanic dieters); self-report data; self-selection of sample; active consent may have resulted in a biased sample and underreported smoking levels

Table 2.2 Continued

Study	Design/population	Measures	Percentage endorsing	Findings	Comments
Copeland and Carney 2003	441 female undergraduates attending Louisiana State University Mean 19.9 years of age (SD = 1.6) Cross-sectional questionnaire; smoking status verified using carbon monoxide (CO) analysis	Appetite/Weight Control scale from SCQ	NR	• Expectancies for appetite and weight control a significant predictor of current smoking (vs. nonsmoking) • Among smokers, expectancies regarding appetite/weight control positively related to weekly smoking rate	Strengths: use of validated scales; use of CO analysis to verify smoking status Weaknesses: conclusions regarding mediation may not be warranted; naive sample of smokers; cannot compare results with older female smokers
Honjo and Siegel 2003	273 female adolescents who reported lifetime history of smoking ≤1 cigarettes Age NR (range 12–15 years at baseline) 4-year prospective cohort telephone-based survey Households chosen by random-digit dialing	"Do you believe that smoking helps people keep their weight down?"	Total = 20.0%		Strengths: first longitudinal study examining this relationship; included analysis of subjects lost to follow-up Weaknesses: small number of experimenters at baseline prohibited further analyses; 1-item measure of independent variable may be weak psychometrically; homogeneous sample prohibited comparison by gender or ethnicity
Facchini et al. 2005	144 female students Mean 20.0 years of age (SD = 1.74; range 18–27 years) Cross-sectional design, convenience sample, using a self-reported questionnaire Argentina	"Smoking helps to control weight" 5-point scale (anchors not reported)	NR	• Smokers endorsed higher levels of belief than did nonsmokers that smoking helps to control body weight	Strengths: first study of its kind in Argentina and with females older than 18; high level of participation Weaknesses: cross-sectional design; need for greater psychometric data on psychosocial items; convenience sample; self-reported weight and height

Table 2.2 Continued

Study	Design/population	Measures	Percentage endorsing	Findings	Comments
Cavallo et al. 2006	103 high school smokers who were interested in quitting Mean 16.5 years of age (range 14–18 years) Pilot study to determine which format of cognitive behavioral therapy is most effective when paired with a contingency management program 4-week school-based smoking cessation program	"How much do cigarettes help you control your weight?" and "How concerned are you about gaining weight as a result of quitting?" 5-point scale from "not at all" to "very much"	NR	• Female smokers reported stronger beliefs that smoking helps control weight than did males; females also expressed greater concerns about postcessation weight gain • Belief that smoking helps control weight positively associated with daily smoking rate and negatively related to years smoking • Among females, positive correlation between concerns about postcessation weight gain and daily smoking rate	Strengths: monetary incentives for contingency management Weaknesses: small sample size and high dropout rate; biochemical test cannot confirm smoking during entire follow-up period; infrequent assessment of abstinence posttreatment
McKee et al. 2006	40 female undergraduate smokers Mean 20.0 years of age (SD = 4.3) Participants viewed 30 slides of either nature scenes (neutral prime) or fashion models (body image prime) and rated their preference for each image Participants also completed a questionnaire on smoking outcomes and eating restraint	Appetite/Weight Control scale from SCQ	NR	• Restrained eaters exposed to a body image prime visual reported greater expectancies than did nonrestrained eaters that smoking helps to manage weight • Among participants exposed to a neutral (control) prime visual, expectancies regarding the effect of smoking on weight control did not differ according to dietary restraint	Strengths: confirmed smoking status by having subjects show their cigarettes Weaknesses: small sample size; limited generalizability; low level of nicotine dependence; no biochemical confirmation of smoking status; dietary restraint was measured after viewing images, which may have affected scores

Table 2.2 Continued

Study	Design/population	Measures	Percentage endorsing	Findings	Comments
Vidrine et al. 2006	350 female and 315 male high school students Age NR Secondary analysis of cross-sectional data gathered in a school-based survey Students listed 10 positive and 10 negative expected outcomes of smoking A questionnaire gathered information about self and peer smoking behavior	Participants asked to self-generate positive and negative expected outcomes from smoking	Proportion reporting weight-related outcome expectancies related to smoking: Girls = 23% Boys = 6%	• Girls more likely than boys to generate weight-control outcome expectancies for smoking • Weight-control outcome expectancies did not differ by smoking status	Strengths: good interrater agreement Weaknesses: cannot establish direction of relationship because of cross-sectional design; smoking rates have changed since data were collected in 1997, which limits generalizability of results
Copeland et al. 2007	742 students in grades 2–6 from 2 Catholic schools Mean 9.2 years of age (SD = 1.5; range 7–13 years) Aim of study was to develop a smoking expectancy measure for children Cross-sectional data Questionnaires were administered in group setting and were read to younger students	SCQ-Child, a revised version of the SCQ	"Smokers are thinner than nonsmokers" Total = 37.9% Aged 7–8 years = 38.9% Aged 9–10 years = 33.8% Aged 11–13 years = 43.1% "Smokers eat less than nonsmokers" Total = 52.2% Aged 7–8 years = 56.8% Aged 9–10 years = 48.2% Aged 11–13 years = 52.1%	• Scores on the Appetite/Weight Control scale lower among students who had a family member who smoked • Scores on the Appetite/Weight Control scale did not differ according to age, gender, peer smoking, perceived availability of cigarettes, ability to get cigarettes from friends, or whether students had ever tried cigarettes	Strengths: first smoking expectancy measure to be developed for use with children Weaknesses: low reliability of two scales; self-selected sample may have resulted in bias; homogeneous mainly White sample; low rate of smoking possibly due to religiosity; possible that young children did not understand questions

Table 2.2 Continued

Study	Design/population	Measures	Percentage endorsing	Findings	Comments
Kendzor et al. 2007	727 private school students in grades 2–6 were assigned to an environmental obesity prevention program or alcohol and tobacco prevention program Mean 9.2 years of age (SD = 1.5; range 7–13 years) Cross-sectional self-report questionnaire conducted in the classroom, measured height and weight	"Smokers are thinner than non-smokers" "Smokers eat less than non-smokers"	All Black students = 50.0% Black males = 46.5% Black females = 53.1% All White students = 36.6% White males = 37.7% White females 35.6% All Black students = 54.3% Black males = 53.5% Black females = 55.1% All White students = 52.4% White males = 52.3% White females 52.6%	• Black students more likely than Whites to believe smokers are thinner than nonsmokers • Black girls more likely than White girls to agree smokers are thinner than nonsmokers; differences among males not significant • No racial differences in belief that smokers eat less than nonsmokers	Strengths: elementary age sample; use of Eating Attitudes scale with internal reliability; included other factors related to weight concern and smoking in analyses Weaknesses: low smoking prevalence; racially homogeneous sample; convenience sample from Catholic schools may have introduced bias
Bean et al. 2008	730 rural high school students Mean 15.7 years of age (SD = 1.2; range 12–20 years) Part of Youth Tobacco Evaluation Project, which evaluates all Tobacco-Settlement-funded prevention programs Cross-sectional self-report questionnaire conducted in the classroom Virginia	Personal attitudes about link between smoking and body weight: "If I stay tobacco free, I will gain weight" 5-point scale: "strongly disagree" to "strongly agree" Perceptions of other people's weight-related reasons for smoking: composite score from 3 items: "People smoke because…" "…it helps them lose weight," "…it helps them stay thin," and "it makes them less hungry" 5-point scale: "definitely not" to "definitely yes"	NR	• Girls expressed greater agreement than did boys that people smoke for weight control • Boys endorsed stronger beliefs that remaining or becoming tobacco free would lead to weight gain • In multivariate models, smokers more likely than experimenters and nonsmokers to agree they will gain weight if they are tobacco free; in gender-stratified analyses, results were significant only for girls • Current smokers less likely than experimenters or nonsmokers to agree that people smoke for weight control	Strengths: first study to examine relationship between weight and smoking in a rural adolescent population; instrument composed of valid and reliable items; high participation rate Weaknesses: nested analyses not possible since school IDs were not recorded; possible bias due to self-reported data (i.e., height and weight); cross-sectional; limitations in how "smoker" is defined; use of single-item measures for some constructs; limited generalizability; considerable amount of missing data

Note: **NR** = not reported; SD = standard deviation.

and 34% of men and 27% of women who smoked were uncertain of the impact of smoking on their weight. Associations of smoking with three weight-loss behaviors (dieting, exercise, and use of diet pills) were also assessed. Male smokers were significantly more likely than their nonsmoking counterparts to report having dieted to lose weight during the past month. Among female students, no overall differences in dieting status were observed between smokers and nonsmokers, but smokers were significantly more likely than nonsmokers to have used diet pills in the past month in an effort to lose weight. Among male students, in contrast, use of diet pills did not differ between smokers and nonsmokers. Exercise for weight loss was not related to smoking status among either men or women.

Boles and Johnson (2001) examined associations between beliefs about weight and cigarette smoking in a sample of 1,200 adolescent boys and girls between the ages of 12 and 17 years. Smokers (n = 140), but not nonsmokers, were asked whether they thought that smoking helped them control their weight. Overall, 15% of smokers responded that it did, a rate lower than that observed in other studies reported in this review. Female smokers (22.2%) were significantly more likely to endorse this belief than were male smokers (9.9%). Agreement declined with age among males but increased with age among females.

Honjo and Siegel (2003) also investigated beliefs about the weight-controlling effects of smoking, in this case among adolescent girls 12–15 years of age who reported never smoking or smoking no more than one cigarette in their lifetime. Twenty percent of the girls responded affirmatively to the question "Do you believe that smoking helps people keep their weight down?"

Elsewhere, Vidrine and colleagues (2006) examined gender differences in expectations about the outcomes of smoking in a sample of 350 adolescent girls and 315 adolescent boys attending two same-gender high schools. Students were asked to come up with as many positive and negative expected outcomes from smoking as they could in 60 seconds, and they also completed measures of smoking behavior, susceptibility to smoking, and peer smoking. Overall, boys (6%) were less likely than girls (23%) to report expectations for smoking related to weight control (odds ratio [OR] = 0.22; 95% confidence interval [CI], 0.13–0.36, p <.001). Expectations did not differ significantly by smoking status for either gender.

Finally, few studies have examined whether younger children believe that smoking controls body weight. Kendzor and colleagues (2007), however, surveyed 727 children 7–13 years of age (mean age = 9.2 years) about their weight concerns and smoking history. In all, 38% of the children agreed that "smokers are thinner than nonsmokers." In contrast to the studies with older adolescents summarized above, agreement that smoking is related to weight control was greater in Black (50%) than in White (36.6%) children (p = .016). Endorsement of the belief that smokers are thinner than nonsmokers was highest in Black girls (53.1%), and it was lowest in White girls (35.6%), with Black and White boys in between.

The studies described above all involved elementary-age to college students. In contrast, Li and colleagues (1994) examined factors associated with cigarette smoking among a cohort of 585 Asian women 20–41 years of age who worked on airline cabin crews. The majority (87%) of these women were under 30 years of age, and 26% of the sample were current smokers. Participants were asked to rate the perceived probability of a series of potential positive and negative consequences of smoking, including weight control, on a scale from 0% to 100%. Thirty-seven percent of the total sample agreed that smoking helps to control body weight, with endorsement significantly higher among current smokers (48%) than for former smokers (29%) or never smokers (34%).

A few other studies have examined the association between the belief that smoking helps to control body weight and personal smoking status using items and scales devised to assess the perceived consequences of smoking or abstinence. Many of the studies have conducted comparisons according to smoking status or other characteristics without specifying an exact proportion of respondents who endorsed the belief that smoking promotes weight control. Loken (1982), for example, surveyed 178 college women regarding their beliefs about the health- and non-health-related consequences of cigarette smoking using seven-point bipolar scales ranging from -3 to +3. One of the beliefs examined was that "my smoking cigarettes keeps (would keep) my weight down." Heavy smokers endorsed significantly stronger beliefs than did either light smokers or nonsmokers. No differences were observed between the three groups, however, on an affective scale assessing the positive or negative impact of keeping one's weight down.

Brandon and Baker (1991) developed the widely used Smoking Consequences Questionnaire (SCQ) in an effort to assess the subjective expected utility (SEU) of cigarette smoking. Undergraduate college students 16–47 years of age (mean age = 18.7 years) rated the likelihood and desirability of some possible consequences of cigarette smoking listed on the SCQ. The cross-product of the likelihood and desirability ratings for each item was calculated to arrive at an index of subjective expected utility. On a factor of five items assessing the perceived impact of smoking on appetite/weight control, daily smokers scored significantly higher than either occasional smokers or never smokers. In addition, among former smokers, female students reported significantly greater expectations regarding the utility of smoking for helping to control weight and appetite than did males. Furthermore, daily smokers reported stronger expectations regarding the likelihood that smoking would aid weight control than did occasional smokers. Overall, comparisons with other categories of smoking status (former smoker, trier/experimenter, and never smoker) on the perceived likelihood that smoking would affect weight and appetite were not significant.

Cepeda-Benito and Ferrer (2000) developed a Spanish-language version of the SCQ (SCQ-S); as with the original questionnaire, the SCQ-S was designed to assess adults' positive and negative expectancies of cigarette smoking. A confirmatory factor analysis conducted among 212 Spanish-speaking smokers (65% of them female) who were either college students or university employees (mean age = 22.5 years) supported an 8-factor, 40-item model. Among the eight subscales was a five-item scale to assess expectancies related to the effect of smoking on weight control; overall, women reported significantly greater expectancies than did men. Although scores on the weight-control subscale were positively related to a measure of nicotine dependence ($\beta = .15$, $p = .033$), this effect was not significant after Bonferroni adjustments were made for multiple comparisons.

Copeland and Carney (2003) investigated expectancies regarding the perceived consequences of smoking as potential mediators of the association between (1) dietary restraint and disinhibition and (2) cigarette smoking among a sample of 441 undergraduate women. Outcome expectancies related to smoking were assessed using the appetite/weight-control factor from the SCQ. Smokers reported significantly higher expectancies than did nonsmokers relative to the impact of smoking on weight and appetite. In addition, expectancies for appetite and weight control were significantly associated with weekly smoking rate, with those consuming more cigarettes reporting greater expectations about the impact of smoking on weight/appetite.

In an effort to evaluate the subjective expected utility of smoking among children, Copeland and colleagues (2007) developed a revised version of the SCQ designed for children 7–12 years of age (SCQ-Child). The scale incorporated much of the original SCQ but was modified to account for reading level and the relevance of the items to make it more developmentally appropriate for the younger age group. In addition, items were modified from a Likert scale to a true/false format. Participants included 742 students in grades two to six who ranged in age from 7 to 13 years (mean age = 9.2 years). A confirmatory factor analysis was conducted to determine whether a one-, two-, three-, or four-factor solution was the most appropriate. Results indicated that a three-factor model (positive reinforcement, negative consequences/effects, appetite/weight control) comprised of 15 items provided the best fit with the data. The scale that assessed smoking-related expectations for appetite and weight control included two items: "Smokers are thinner than nonsmokers" and "Smokers eat less than nonsmokers." Overall, 37.9% of the sample agreed that smokers are thinner than nonsmokers, and 52.2% agreed that smokers eat less than nonsmokers. Students with a family member who smoked had significantly lower scores on the Appetite/Weight Control scale; however, these students were less likely to perceive smokers as thinner or that smokers ate less than nonsmokers. Scores on that scale did not differ significantly according to gender, age, peer smoking, perceived availability of cigarettes, whether participants could get cigarettes from friends, or history of ever trying cigarettes.

In the largest study to date to assess the perceived impact of smoking on body weight, Wang and coworkers (1998) investigated attitudes and beliefs about smoking among a representative national sample of high school dropouts between the ages of 15 and 18 years as part of the 1993 Teenage Attitudes and Practices Survey (weighted N = 492,352). Beliefs about the weight-controlling properties of smoking were assessed with the statement "Smoking helps people keep their weight down." The prevalence of smoking among those who agreed with this statement (69.1%) was significantly higher than among those who disagreed (54.6%).

In a study of young adults' attitudes and beliefs about the positive and negative consequences of smoking, Budd and Preston (2001) surveyed 172 undergraduate students 19–51 years of age (mean age = 21.5 years). Using a scale that measured the perceived impact of smoking on body image, a scale that included items reflecting the degree to which respondents believed that smoking prevents weight gain and helps to keep a person thin, smokers scored significantly higher than did nonsmokers. Thus, smokers were more likely than nonsmokers to believe that smoking helps enhance body image through weight control.

Zucker and colleagues (2001) investigated factors associated with cigarette smoking among 188 female undergraduate college students between the ages of 17 and 25 years (mean age = 19.0 years). Students were surveyed regarding their smoking status, attitudes toward thinness, exposure to media depicting thinness, level of skepticism toward tobacco advertisements, and degree of feminist consciousness. In addition, they were questioned on their beliefs about smoking and body weight using their response to the statement "Smoking helps people control their weight." Responses were on a seven-point Likert scale ranging from 1 (do not agree at all) to 7 (definitely agree). The belief that smoking helps to control body weight was positively correlated with measures of awareness of the societal emphasis on thinness as well as the degree to which respondents had internalized and accepted societal appearance standards. In addition, smokers endorsed significantly stronger beliefs than did nonsmokers regarding the weight-controlling effects of smoking. In a multivariate logistic regression model, those who considered that smoking is an effective strategy for weight control were significantly more likely to be current smokers.

Cachelin and coworkers (2003) examined the associations between dieting, smoking behaviors and attitudes, acculturation, and family environment in an ethnically diverse sample of 211 adolescent boys and girls (mean age = 16.3 years) recruited from junior and senior high schools. Fifty-seven percent of the youth were Asian, 16% Hispanic, and 27% White. Participants completed a survey assessing smoking behaviors, beliefs and attitudes toward smoking, family functioning, and acculturation. Smoking-related questions included two items from the Smoking Beliefs and Attitudes Questionnaire (Pederson and Lefcoe 1985) assessing beliefs about the impact of smoking on body weight: "Smoking keeps you from eating" and "Smoking helps you control your weight." In addition, the students were classified as dieters or nondieters depending on their responses to the 10-item Restraint Scale (Herman 1978). Overall, female dieters were more likely than nondieters to be current smokers; female dieters were also more likely to endorse the belief that smoking keeps one from eating. Dieting status was not, however, significantly related to the belief that smoking controls body weight. In addition, compared with nonsmokers, female smokers had significantly higher dietary restraint scores. No significant relationships were observed among male students between dieting and any of the smoking-related items.

In one of the few international studies located in the various searches described above that investigated young people's beliefs about the impact of smoking on body weight, Facchini and colleagues (2005) surveyed 144 female students in Argentina between the ages of 18 and 27 years (mean age = 20 years) who were attending a state-run school for nurses and preschool teachers. Participants completed items assessing smoking history and beliefs about smoking. With regard to beliefs, participants were asked to indicate their level of agreement with the statement "Smoking helps to control weight" on a five-point scale. In all, 47% of the students were cigarette smokers. Smokers expressed higher endorsement than did nonsmokers of the belief that smoking helps to control weight (mean score = 2.6 [1.16] vs. 1.9 [0.99], $p < 0.01$). In addition, in multiple logistic regression analyses, beliefs about the weight-controlling effects of smoking were a significant independent predictor of smoking status.

Cavallo and coworkers (2006) examined the extent to which adolescent smokers believed smoking helped to control their weight. Participants, who were 103 daily smokers between the ages of 14 and 18 years, were asked to respond to the question "How much do cigarettes help you control your weight?" using a Likert scale ranging from 1 (not at all) to 5 (very much). Females endorsed stronger beliefs than did males. The belief that smoking helps to control weight was positively associated with daily smoking rate and negatively associated with number of years of smoking. In addition, a significant interaction between gender and BMI was noted. For males, the belief that smoking controls body weight was positively associated with BMI ($p < 0.1$), but among females there was a nonsignificant inverse relationship between BMI and the perceived weight-controlling effects of smoking.

Recently, Bean and colleagues (2008) investigated attitudes toward smoking and weight control in a sample of 730 rural high school students 12–20 years of age (mean age = 15.7 years). In addition to being asked about smoking history and body weight, participants were questioned about the perceived consequences of abstaining from tobacco (e.g., weight gain) as well as their personal attitudes about the association between smoking and body weight. For the latter, a composite score was derived from students' levels of agreement with three items asking about weight-related reasons that people might smoke ("it helps them lose weight," "it helps them stay thin," and "it makes them less hungry"). Overall, girls scored significantly higher on the belief that people smoke to control weight (i.e., their composite score was significantly higher). Boys, for their part, endorsed stronger beliefs that remaining or becoming tobacco free would lead to weight gain. Interestingly, current smokers were significantly *less* likely than either experimental smokers or nonsmokers to believe that people smoke to control their weight. However, current smokers were more likely than both experimental smokers and nonsmokers to believe they would gain weight by being tobacco free. In stratified analyses by gender, however, this relationship remained significant only among girls.

Finally, McKee and associates (2006) investigated the associations between dietary restraint, primed visuals of body images, and expectations that smoking can control body weight among 40 undergraduate female smokers (mean age = 20.0 years). Participants were randomly assigned to view one of two sets of images representing either pictures of thin, attractive fashion models or landscape scenes. The former were intended to serve as primes for body image, and the latter were included as neutral control stimuli. Restrained eaters exposed to the body image primes scored significantly higher than those viewing the neutral images on the appetite/weight-control scale of the SCQ. They also scored higher than nonrestrained eaters exposed to either of the two types of primes. These findings suggest that beliefs about the impact of smoking on body weight among smokers may be modified by weight-related attitudes and behaviors as well as by media messages associated with body image.

Summary

These studies show that the belief that smoking helps to control body weight is not unusual among youth and young adults. Adding strength to this conclusion is the fact that the studies were carried out over several decades in diverse populations using varied methodologic approaches. Overall, belief in the weight-controlling effects of smoking tends to increase with smoking experience: current smokers and those having more extensive smoking histories typically endorse stronger beliefs than do nonsmokers. Studies that investigated gender differences regarding beliefs about the effect of smoking on body weight generally found greater endorsement among females, with some exceptions noted. Few studies compared beliefs about smoking and body weight by race or ethnicity (Camp et al. 1993; Klesges et al. 1997a; Kendzor et al. 2007).

Use of Smoking by Children and Young Adults to Control Weight

School and Population Surveys

The fact that many adolescents and young adults believe that cigarette smoking helps to control body weight does not necessarily mean that this belief actually influences smoking behavior. In several studies, however, youth have been questioned about the methods they use to control their weight and the reasons that they smoke in an effort to determine whether young people do, in fact, smoke cigarettes as a weight-control strategy. This section reviews the evidence that some adolescents and young adults smoke specifically for purposes of weight control (Table 2.3).

In an early study, Klesges and colleagues (1987) surveyed 204 male and female college students regarding the strategies they had used during the past 6 months to help them control their weight. In addition to reporting commonly used methods of restricting energy intake such as skipping meals, eating less, and controlling portions, a number of respondents indicated that they used cigarettes or caffeine as a weight-control strategy. Because smoking cigarettes and using caffeine were combined to make a single survey item, the authors could not determine the proportion of respondents who used each method. Overall, females (21%) were significantly more likely than males (4%) to endorse this combined item. Use of smoking/caffeine for purposes of weight control was also positively associated with body weight, with overweight males and females most likely to use this method (22%), followed by those who were normal weight (13%) and underweight (2%). Results were not reported by current smoking status.

In a follow-up study, Klesges and Klesges (1988) surveyed a sample of 1,076 university faculty, staff, and students 16–72 years of age (mean age = 21.7 years) about their use of smoking as a weight-control strategy. The prevalence of smoking among the sample was similar for males (21%) and females (18%). Overall, 32.5% of smokers reported using smoking as a weight-loss strategy. Although common in both genders, this practice was reported more frequently by female (39%) than by male (25%) smokers. The proportion of smokers using smoking to control weight did not differ significantly between overweight (34%) and normal-weight smokers (29%). Age appeared to make a difference, however, as smokers under the age of 25 years were significantly more likely than older smokers to use smoking as a weight-control strategy (38.0% vs. 23.4%). Ten percent of male smokers and 5% of female smokers reported that they started smoking specifically to help them lose weight or to maintain their weight. Although there were no main effects of gender or weight status on the proportion of respondents who initiated smoking for weight loss, a significant gender-by-body-weight interaction was found, with overweight women (20%) much more likely than other groups to report starting to smoke for this purpose.

Worsley and coworkers (1990) examined the weight-control practices of 809 15-year-old New Zealand youth, questioning participants about their current weight, perceptions of their ideal weight, monitoring of their body weight, intentions regarding weight control, and reasons for attempting weight loss. The youth were also surveyed about the weight-loss techniques they had used over the past year, including both healthy and unhealthy dietary practices and exercise. Significantly more girls (5%) than boys (2%) reported they had smoked cigarettes to control their weight.

Frank and colleagues (1991) investigated weight loss and disordered eating behaviors among 364 undergraduate female college freshmen (mean age = 18 years). Students completed a questionnaire that assessed use of purgatives (self-induced vomiting, laxatives, diuretics) and diet pills as well as other health behaviors such as cigarette smoking and use of alcohol and other psychoactive substances. Fourteen percent of participants reported being current smokers. Among those who smoked, 37% reported that one of the reasons they did so was to control their weight. Those in the study who reported currently

Table 2.3 Studies assessing use of smoking to control body weight (school and population surveys)

Study	Design/population	Measures	Percentage endorsing	Findings	Comments
Klesges et al. 1987	204 undergraduates Mean 19.9 years of age (SD = 3.4; range 17–40 years) Cross-sectional Self-reported questionnaires	Participants selected from among 21 weight-loss strategies they had used in past 6 months including "smoke cigarettes/use caffeine"	Females = 21% Males = 4%	• Overweight participants (22%) more likely than those of normal weight (13%) or underweight (2%) to endorse smoking/caffeine use for weight loss	NR
Klesges and Klesges 1988	1,076 university students, faculty, and staff Mean 21.7 years of age (SD = 6.5; range 16–72 years) Cross-sectional Self-reported questionnaires	Participants selected which of 6 dieting strategies (including smoking) they had used in past 6 months to lose weight Smokers indicated whether they initially started smoking to lose or maintain weight Reasons for relapse (including weight gain and increased appetite) also assessed	Use of smoking: Total smokers = 32.5% Female smokers = 39% Male smokers = 25% Nonsmokers = 0.5% Female smokers = 5% Male smokers = 10%	• Use of smoking to control weight did not differ between normal-weight and overweight smokers • Younger smokers (<25 years) more likely (38%) to endorse smoking as a weight-control strategy than were older smokers (23.4%) • Among females, overweight smokers more likely (20%) than normal-weight smokers (2%) to report starting to smoke to lose weight	Weaknesses: self-reported data
Worsley et al. 1990	809 adolescents Mean 15 years of age Cross-sectional study, part of the Dunedin Multidisciplinary Health and Development Study cohort New Zealand	Participants identified which weight-loss strategies they had used in past year, including cigarette smoking	Girls = 5% Boys = 2%	• Girls more likely than boys to report using smoking to control weight	NR
Frank et al. 1991	364 female college freshmen Mean 18 years of age Cross-sectional Self-reported questionnaire	Participants selected from among healthy and unhealthy strategies they had used for losing or maintaining their weight	37% of smokers reported 1 of the reasons they smoked was to control their weight	• Women currently endorsing methods of purging (self-induced vomiting, laxative, or diuretics use) more likely to smoke (44.4%) than were nonpurgers (10.7%)	Strengths: sample was not biased toward people in physical activity class Weaknesses: self-report; questions did not specify if diet pills were prescribed by a doctor or were over-the-counter

Table 2.3 Continued

Study	Design/population	Measures	Percentage endorsing	Findings	Comments
Camp et al. 1993	659 high school students Mean 16.3 years of age Cross-sectional questionnaire	Item asked smokers whether they had used smoking to control their weight	All female smokers = 39% Black females = 0% White females = 61% All male smokers = 12% Black males = 0% White males = 12%	• Among daily smokers, 100% of White females and 37.5% of White males reported smoking to control weight • Significant predictors of smoking for weight control included female gender, increasing age, and higher restrained eating scores	Strengths: addresses several gaps in literature; racially diverse sample; use of variables supported by research; uses conservative statistical tests Weaknesses: cannot infer causality; results may not generalize to other areas or to nonparochial subjects; did not use bogus pipeline or biochemical methods
Klesges et al. 1997a	6,961 7th-grade students enrolled in the Memphis Health Project Mean 13 years of age Cross-sectional questionnaire as part of Memphis Health Project Tennessee	Item asked smokers whether they had ever used smoking to control their weight	Total smokers = 12% All female smokers = 18% All male smokers = 8% All Black smokers = 9% Black girls = 11% Black boys = 7% All White smokers = 15% White girls = 27% White boys = 8%	• Female smokers more likely than male smokers to endorse smoking for weight control • Weight-control smoking did not differ between Black and White smokers	Strengths: large sample size; high participation rate; ethnic and gender composition representative of Memphis schools; majority Black children in sample can add to literature re: the behaviors and concerns of this population Weaknesses: limited generalizability outside of Memphis public schools; did not use bogus pipeline or biochemical procedures; possible response bias due to substance users missing school; lack of temporality
Robinson et al. 1997	6,967 7th-grade students enrolled in the Memphis Health Project Mean 13 years of age Cross-sectional questionnaire as part of Memphis Health Project Tennessee	Item asked smokers whether they had ever used smoking to control their weight	NR	• Students who endorsed smoking for weight control 3.34 times as likely to be regular (vs. experimental) smokers as those who did not smoke for weight control (Same sample as Klesges et al. 1997a)	Strengths: examined predictors of experimental and regular smokers Weaknesses: only two ethnic groups examined; did not measure some variables thought to be associated with cigarette smoking; cross-sectional

Table 2.3 Continued

Study	Design/population	Measures	Percentage endorsing	Findings	Comments
Jarry et al. 1998	220 female undergraduate college students Mean 27.0 years of age Cross-sectional retrospective questionnaire Canada	Never smokers were asked if they ever considered starting to smoke to avoid gaining or to lose weight 7-point scale: "never considered" to "seriously considered" Current and former smokers indicated agreement with the statements "I started smoking to avoid gaining weight or to lose weight" and "I smoke(d) to avoid gaining weight or to lose weight" 7-point scale: "totally disagree" to "totally agree"	NR	• Nonsmokers who were dieters marginally more likely than nondieters to report considering starting to smoke for weight control • Among current and former smokers, dieters agreed more than nondieters that they started smoking for weight control and continued smoking for this purpose • Current smokers more likely than former smokers to endorse starting and continuing to smoke to control weight	Strengths: focus on female population; direct measurement of subjects' self-perceived motivation to smoke as this relates to weight; assessment of self-reported postcessation weight gain among dieters and nondieters Weaknesses: retrospective nature of the design; subjects participated on a voluntary basis
Ryan et al. 1998	420 students Mean 15 years of age (range 14–17 years) Cross-sectional questionnaire Dublin, Ireland	Questionnaire assessing perceived body weight, weight concerns, and slimming practices including "beginning or continuing smoking"	Total sample: 13%	• Among those attempting to lose weight in the past, 19% reported beginning or continuing smoking as a weight-control strategy	NR
Crisp et al. 1999	2,768 female students from London (n = 1,936) and Ottawa (n = 832) Age NR (range 10–19 years) Cross-sectional questionnaire United Kingdom and Canada	Smokers identified reasons for smoking, including "instead of eating" and "makes you less hungry" Smokers indicated expected consequences of quitting smoking, including "eat more" and "put on weight"	**Reasons for smoking:** Instead of eating: London = 21%* Ottawa = 33%* Makes less hungry: London = 19%* Ottawa = 36%* **Expected consequences of quitting smoking:** Eat more: London = 30%* Ottawa = 34%* Put on weight: London = 31%* Ottawa = 33%* *Responded "yes, definitely"	• Smokers more likely than nonsmokers to report "proneness to overeating" and self-induced vomiting	Weaknesses: low response rate in Ottawa schools

Table 2.3 Continued

Study	Design/population	Measures	Percentage endorsing	Findings	Comments
Crocker et al. 2001	702 female 9th-grade students Age NR (range 14–15 years) Cross-sectional questionnaire Canada	Smoking Situations Questionnaire (SSQ) 6 items to measure use of smoking for weight control (sample items: "I continue to smoke so that I don't gain weight," "I smoke at the end of a meal so I won't eat so much")	19.4% of female smokers classified as smoking for weight control (defined based on scores of ≥2 on SSQ)	• Weight-control smokers reported higher levels of dietary restraint, lower levels of global self-esteem, and lower scores on measures reflecting self-perceived body attractiveness and physical condition	Strengths: incorporated a validated physical self-perception model and instrument; used a large regionalized sample of 9th-grade girls from various socioeconomic levels; included a measure of using smoking as a means to control weight Weaknesses: cross-sectional design; low prevalence of smoking and dietary restraint behavior; not assessing other weight control strategies; used self-reported data
George and Johnson 2001	1,852 college students Age NR (>90%, range 17–24 years) Cross-sectional self-administered questionnaire	Participants identified their primary reason for smoking	4% of female and 1% of male smokers cited weight control as primary reason for smoking	• Respondents allowed to identify only one primary reason for smoking	Strengths: unique population of ethnically diverse university students Weaknesses: sample demographics and size; possible bias in self-reported weight and smoking status, question design, study design
Granner et al. 2001	206 Black and White college students Mean 20.6 years of age (SD = 2.17) Cross-sectional ex post facto design	Weight Control Smoking Scale (WCSS) Eating Disorders Inventory-2 Sample item: "I smoke to keep from gaining weight"	58% endorsed at least one item regarding smoking for weight control 11.1% of Black smokers and 20.0% of White smokers scored above the cutoff (≥6) for being classified as a weight-control smoker	• Smokers scored higher on several subscales of the Eating Disorders Inventory-2 • Students at elevated risk for eating disorders more likely to smoke and scored significantly higher on the WCSS	Weaknesses: cross-sectional design and convenience sampling; some relatively small cell sizes may have limited the ability to fully test associations

Table 2.3 Continued

Study	Design/population	Measures	Percentage endorsing	Findings	Comments
Plummer et al. 2001	2,808 9th-grade students enrolled in a study of smoking, sun protection habits, and reduction in dietary fat Mean 15.2 years of age (SD = 0.6) Cross-sectional data from first intervention session Part of a larger study (n = 4,983)	2 items from the Temptation to Smoke measure for adolescents (Ding et al. 1994) that addressed temptations associated with weight control: "when I am afraid I might gain weight" and "when I want to get thinner"	NR	• Current smokers: temptations to smoke for weight control greater among those in the precontemplation (PC) stage than in the preparation (PR), action (AC), and maintenance (MN) stages; smokers in the contemplation (CN), PR, and AC stages reported stronger temptations related to weight control than those in MN stage • Nonsmokers: those in acquisition-PR stage had higher temptations to smoke related to weight control than those in acquisition-CN and acquisition-PC • Nonsmokers in acquisition-CN also reported higher temptations than those in acquisition-PC	Strengths: largest sample in which these theoretical constructs have been evaluated; provides basis for interventions based on the Transtheoretical Model (TTM), improved measurement model previously developed by Pallonen et al. (1998) (by including a Habit Strength factor and by using both smokers and nonsmokers in the development of the Weight Control subscale) Weaknesses: cross-sectional; sample not nationally representative
Zucker et al. 2001	188 female undergraduates Mean 19.0 years of age (SD = 0.9; range 14–17 years) Cross-sectional-correlational Self-reported questionnaire	WCSS	NR	• Acceptance of societal appearance standards toward thinness and belief that smoking helps control weight positively associated with smoking for weight control in a multivariate logistic regression model, while feminist consciousness was negatively related	Weaknesses: generalizability limited because of highly selective sample; could not include ethnicity as a variable predicting smoking status

Table 2.3 Continued

Study	Design/population	Measures	Percentage endorsing	Findings	Comments
Croll et al. 2002; Fulkerson and French 2003	Population-based sample of 81,247 9th- and 12th-grade public school students Age NR Cross-sectional from Minnesota Student Survey	"During the last 12 months, have you done any of the following to lose or control your weight? (mark all that apply)" Response choices included "smoking cigarettes"	**Female smokers (in past 30 days):** Total = 48.8% White = 48.6% Black = 32.6% Hispanic = 43.2% Asian American = 50.0% Native American = 49.4% Other/mixed = 55.0% **Male smokers (in past 30 days):** Total = 27.6% White = 26.5% Black = 27.8% Hispanic = 32.0% Asian American = 35.0% Native American = 38.2% Other/mixed = 31.3%	• Female smokers 2.5 (95% CI, 2.38–2.63) times as likely as male smokers to smoke for weight control • Among female smokers, Whites were more likely to smoke for weight control than were Black and less likely than those identifying themselves as multiracial • Among male smokers, Native Americans and Asian Americans were more likely than Whites to smoke to control their weight • In general, heavier smoking, perceiving oneself as overweight, and weight concerns correlated with weight-control smoking in both boys and girls	Strengths: examined ethnic-specific risk and protective factors for disordered eating across a large, statewide, population-based sample utilizing a range of socioenvironmental, personal, and behavioral measures (Croll et al. 2002) Weaknesses: caution needed when making inferences outside of Minnesota youth; socioeconomic status (SES) not directly assessed; nonspecific nature of the survey questions regarding disordered eating behaviors; not able to distinguish between youth with more severe, frequent disordered eating behaviors and those engaging in disordered eating behaviors less frequently (Croll et al. 2002) Weaknesses: staff-measured height and weight not feasible—unable to examine relationships among body mass index and perceptions of overweight, worrying about weight, and smoking to lose or control weight; SES data not collected; data do not include adolescents who are not enrolled in public school; cross-sectional (Fulkerson and French 2003)

Table 2.3 Continued

Study	Design/population	Measures	Percentage endorsing	Findings	Comments
Neumark-Sztainer et al. 2002	Population-based sample of 4,746 adolescents from urban public schools participating in Project EAT Mean 14.9 years of age (SD = 1.7) Cross-sectional questionnaire including height and weight measurements by staff; Project EAT surveys	Participants identified healthy, unhealthy, and extreme weight-control behaviors they had engaged in over the past year including "smoked more cigarettes"	**Girls:** Total = 9.2% White = 10.5% African American = 6.1% Hispanic = 9.3% Asian American = 7.1% Native American = 23.3% Other/mixed = 7.4% **Boys:** Total = 4.7% White = 4.1% African American = 2.8% Hispanic = 6.7% Asian American = 6.5% Native American = 8.7% Other/mixed = 6.7%	• Rates of smoking for weight control differed across race and ethnicity for both boys and girls	Strengths: large size and diverse nature of the study population; collection of actual height and weight measurements; assessment of a variety of weight-related concerns and behaviors Weaknesses: self-reported behaviors; generalizations to other populations need to be made cautiously
Forman and Morello 2003	2,524 8th- and 11th-grade students Age NR (range ≤13 to ≥18 years) Cross-sectional self-administered anonymous survey Argentina	Item and response indicative of weight control smoking: "Why did you first try cigarettes?" ("to avoid getting fat") "In what situations do you smoke?" ("to avoid eating when I am hungry") "Why do you smoke?" ("to maintain my weight")	 Female smokers = 11.3% Male smokers = 4.0% Female smokers = 22.3% Male smokers = 12.9% Female smokers = 16.0% Male smokers = 7.0%	• Participants endorsing smoking to avoid eating 2.84 (95% CI, 2.02–3.98) times as likely as those not endorsing this behavior to perceive difficulty in quitting (64.2% vs. 38.7%) • Participants reporting smoking to keep weight down 1.96 (95% CI, 1.32–2.90) times as likely as those not smoking to maintain weight to perceive difficulty in quitting (57.8% vs. 41.1%)	Strengths: use of profile analysis using generalized estimating equations to compare clustered groups of adolescents; large sample size; inclusion of specific survey questions regarding different types of weight concerns and perceived difficulty in quitting Weaknesses: inability to make causal inferences due to cross-sectional nature of the data; use of a single self-report questionnaire to assess the relationships among smoking, perceived difficulty in quitting, and weight concerns

Table 2.3 Continued

Study	Design/population	Measures	Percentage endorsing	Findings	Comments
Park et al. 2003	297 high school students who were current or former smokers Age NR Cross-sectional study; used TTM and structured self-report questionnaire Korea	Temptation to Smoke measure for adolescents (Ding et al. 1994)	NR	• Temptations to smoke for weight control differed significantly across students' stage of change; although weight-related temptations to smoke tended to decrease as readiness to change increased, none of the individual group comparisons was significant	NR
Dowdell and Santucci 2004	54 urban 7th-grade students Mean 11.9 years of age (range 11–13 years) Descriptive correlational study using a convenience sample; used Youth Risk Behavior Surveillance System (YRBSS) questionnaire	NR	62% of students who smoked indicated that controlling their weight was the reason they smoked	• Girls more likely than boys to endorse using smoking as their primary method of weight control (percentages not reported)	Strengths: YRBSS has a kappa statistic reliability of 61–80% or higher; alpha reliability of 0.79 determined for this sample of 54 students Weaknesses: small sample size; absence of information about parental health-related lifestyle behaviors and attitudes; absence of information about the subjects' access to health care providers and nurses; sample predominantly White children

Table 2.3 Continued

Study	Design/population	Measures	Percentage endorsing	Findings	Comments
Nichter et al. 2004	205 female 10th- and 11th-grade students interviewed during year 3 of a longitudinal study 10th grade (Mean 16.02 years of age; SD = 0.44) 11th grade (Mean 16.99 years of age; SD = 0.49) 178 surveyed again 5 years later Longitudinal study known as the Teen Lifestyle Project Qualitative and quantitative data collection	Various study-specific items assessing smoking for reasons related to weight control	**Year 3 (current smokers):** "Did you start smoking as a way to control your weight"? = 11% "I sometimes smoke so I'll be less hungry" = 25% of occasional and regular smokers **5-year follow-up (current and former smokers):** "Thinking back to when you first started smoking, would you say that you started smoking as a way to control your weight?" = 8% "Did you *ever smoke* as a way to control your weight?" = 15% "Do/did you ever smoke at the end of a meal so you wouldn't continue eating?" = 3% "Do you smoke at times so you'll be less hungry?" = 20%	• 20% of students endorsed the statement: "In general, I think people who smoke cigarettes are thinner than people who don't smoke" • Smokers and nonsmokers did not differ in the likelihood of trying to lose weight	Strengths: longitudinal span; use of ethnography to explore complex relationship between dieting and smoking; the rapport that was developed with informants over a period of years Weaknesses: sample of smokers is small and the response rate to the survey questionnaire mailed follow-up is low; findings may not be generalizable to other regions or girls of different ages

Table 2.3 Continued

Study	Design/population	Measures	Percentage endorsing	Findings	Comments
Facchini et al. 2005	144 female students Mean 20.0 years of age (SD = 1.74; range 18–27 years) Cross-sectional design, convenience sample, using a self-reported questionnaire Argentina	Participants selected from among various reasons for starting to smoke, currently smoking, anticipated consequences of quitting, and reasons for not quitting, several of which were related to eating and body weight	**Reasons for starting to smoke:** To avoid eating = 9% Because it makes them less hungry = 7% To control weight = 4% **Reasons for currently smoking:** Because it makes them less hungry = 27% Instead of snacking when bored = 24% At the end of a meal so they will not eat so much = 19% To avoid eating = 16% **Reasons for not quitting:** Eating more = 37% Putting on weight = 34%	• Restrained eaters who smoked scored higher on a measure of dietary restraint than did restrained eaters who were nonsmokers • Those endorsing at least one behavior indicating smoking for weight control scored higher on a measure of dietary restraint	Strengths: first study of its kind in Argentina and with females older than 18; high level of participation Weaknesses: cross-sectional design; greater psychometric data on psychosocial items; convenience sample; self-reported weight and height
Malinauskas et al. 2006	185 female undergraduate college students Mean 19.7 years of age (SD = 1.4; range 18–24 years) Quasi-experimental design; convenience sample; surveys and body composition assessment	Participants completed a dieting practices questionnaire (Calderon et al. 2004) that assessed the use of 15 different weight-loss behaviors	Total = 9% Normal weight = 8% Overweight = 14% Obese = 5%	NR	Weaknesses: cross-sectional study design—cannot determine if a causal relationship exists between dieting and weight control; only involved female students from 1 university

Table 2.3 Continued

Study	Design/population	Measures	Percentage endorsing	Findings	Comments
Jenks and Higgs 2007	30 female undergraduates Current dieters (n = 15) Nondieters (n = 15) Mean 20.5 years of age (SD = 1.6; range 18–24 years) Randomized intervention with participants randomized to session ordering by food cues Dieting status was used as an effect modifier	WCSS Participants also rated agreement with: "I started smoking to control my weight" and "I am concerned about weight gain upon smoking cessation" 100-mm visual analog scale: "totally disagree" to "totally agree"	NR	• Dieters scored higher than nondieters on measures of weight-control smoking and items assessing having started smoking to control weight and fear of weight gain upon cessation	Strengths: examined for the first time the relationship between weight-control smoking and smoking-related variables in young women and examined the effect of presentation of food cues on these responses Weaknesses: measurement of expired air carbon monoxide may not be sensitive enough to pick up small differences in the number of cigarettes smoked at low levels of daily smoking; self-report bias

Note: CI = confidence interval; mm = millimeter; NR = not reported; SD = standard deviation.

engaging in some form of purging behavior for weight control were four times as likely to smoke as those who did not engage in purging behaviors (44% vs. 11%).

In their study described earlier of the association between smoking and concerns about body weight among high school students, Camp and colleagues (1993) also investigated the use of smoking to control weight. Fifteen percent of the students were classified as regular smokers, defined here as smoking one or more times per week. Thirty-nine percent of all female regular smokers reported using smoking to control their weight versus 12% of male regular smokers. Notably, among regular smokers, 61% of White females and 12% of White males reported smoking for weight control, but no Black regular smoker endorsed smoking for this reason. Multivariate logistic regression analyses indicated that female gender, increasing age, and dietary restraint were all positively associated with smoking for weight control.

In the previously described Memphis Health Project, Klesges and colleagues (1997a) also questioned the 240 seventh graders with a history of active smoking about whether they had ever smoked to control their weight or to lose weight. Twelve percent of smokers reported this practice. As in other studies, among smokers, girls were more likely than boys to report smoking in an effort to control their weight (18% vs. 8% in this study). Differences between Black (9%) and White (15%) smokers were not significant. Consistent with findings of Camp and coworkers (1993), White female smokers (27%) were by far the most likely to report smoking for weight control. Eleven percent of Black females reported smoking to control their weight; rates were lower but generally similar for White (8%) and Black (7%) males.

In a subsequent set of analyses from the same data set (Memphis Health Project), Robinson and colleagues (1997) examined predictors of risk for different stages of smoking. The authors performed multivariate logistic regression analyses to identify demographic, social, environmental, proximal, and distal factors as well as weight-related variables that distinguished between different levels of smoking. Three groups were defined: (1) never smoker, (2) experimental smoker (<1 cigarette per week), and (3) regular smoker (≥1 cigarette per week). Use of smoking to control weight emerged as the single best predictor of regular versus experimental smoking. Specifically, students who reported smoking for weight control were 3.34 (95% CI; 1.60–6.95) times as likely to be regular smokers as those who did not report smoking for this reason. These findings suggest that smoking for weight control may be not only a factor in initial decisions to smoke but also a tool for distinguishing those who are more likely to progress to a heavier stage of smoking.

Ryan and colleagues (1998) investigated weight-loss strategies used by 420 female students 14–17 years of age (mean age = 15 years) in Dublin, Ireland; participants indicated whether they had used various weight-loss strategies including exercise, avoiding sugary foods, and several forms of dieting. Also included as strategies were unhealthy practices such as skipping meals, self-induced vomiting, taking laxatives, fasting, using diet pills or formula diets, and smoking. Overall, 13% of the participants reported smoking to control their weight. Among the 286 students who reported they had tried to lose weight in the past, 19% indicated they had smoked for this reason.

In a study of the associations between cigarette smoking and body weight, Crisp and associates (1998) surveyed 2,768 schoolgirls 10–19 years of age in Ottawa, Canada (N = 832), and London, England (N = 1,936). The questionnaire assessed current weight, history of weight change, dietary patterns, weight concerns, reasons for smoking, expected consequences of giving up cigarette smoking, and self-induced vomiting. Overall, 15% of the Ottawa students and 19% of the London students reported cigarette smoking (either occasional or regular, definitions not given). In both locations, girls who smoked were significantly more likely to report weight concerns, self-induced vomiting, and a "proneness for overeating." Regarding reasons for smoking, 33% of Ottawa students and 21% of students from London reported they smoked "instead of eating." The proportion of students in Ottawa and London who endorsed smoking because it "makes (them) less hungry" were 36% and 19%, respectively. Thirty-four percent of Ottawa students expected to eat more if they gave up smoking, and 33% anticipated gaining weight. Among London students, the proportions who anticipated these consequences of quitting smoking were 30% and 31%, respectively.

As noted earlier, George and Johnson (2001) investigated the association between weight concerns and lifestyle behaviors among 1,852 male and female college students; as part of the survey, participants were asked to identify their primary reason for smoking. Options included "control weight," "habit," "taste-feeling," and "friends." The most commonly endorsed reasons were habit (46% of men, 45% of women) and taste-feeling (43% of men, 37% of women). Weight control was cited the least, with just 4% of female smokers and 1% of male smokers identifying this as their primary motivation to smoke.

Crocker and colleagues (2001) examined associations between smoking, dietary restraint, and physical characteristics and self-perceptions in a sample of 702 ninth-grade girls 14–15 years of age. Participants completed a survey assessing physical characteristics, physical self-perceptions, dietary restraint, and smoking behavior, and they completed the Smoking Situations Questionnaire (SSQ; Weekley et al. 1992), a six-item scale designed to assess the use of smoking for purposes of weight control. In all, 19% of the students were classified as weight-control smokers on the basis of a score of less than 2 (out of 6) on the SSQ. BMI did not differ between those who reported and those who did not report smoking to control their weight. However, weight-control smokers demonstrated significantly higher levels of dietary restraint as well as lower scores on measures of global self-esteem, perceived body attractiveness, and physical condition.

Granner and coworkers (2001) investigated the associations between race, risk for eating disorders, use of alcohol, smoking, and motivations for alcohol and tobacco use in a sample of 206 Black and White undergraduate college students (mean age = 20.6 years). Participants were administered a survey that assessed smoking status, alcohol consumption, and reasons for smoking and drinking. In addition, participants completed the Eating Disorder Inventory-2 (EDI-2; Garner 1991) and the Weight Control Smoking Scale (WCSS; Pomerleau et al. 1993). In all, 34.0% of Whites and 8.7% of Blacks in the sample reported being current smokers (no specific definition provided). Twenty percent of White smokers and 11.1% of Black smokers were categorized as smokers for weight control on the basis of a score of ≥6 on the WCSS (χ^2 = 0.38, p = 0.54). Overall, 56% of Black smokers and 60% of White smokers endorsed at least one item regarding the use of smoking to control weight, appetite, or hunger. Smokers scored significantly higher than nonsmokers on several subscales of the EDI-2, including Body Dissatisfaction, Drive for Thinness, Ineffectiveness, and Social Insecurity. Finally, students classified as being at increased risk for an eating disorder on the basis of elevated scores on the Body Dissatisfaction and Drive for Thinness subscales of the EDI-2 were significantly more likely to smoke and scored significantly higher on the WCSS than those not identified as at risk.

Neumark-Sztainer and associates (2002) examined racial and ethnic differences in weight-related concerns and behaviors in a population-based sample of 4,746 adolescent boys and girls in grades 7–12 (mean age = 14.9 years). Participants were surveyed on their current and perceived weight status, weight concerns, and level of body satisfaction as well as on their use of healthy and unhealthy weight-control behaviors, including "smoked more cigarettes." Overall, 9.2% of girls and 4.7% of boys reported using cigarette smoking as a weight-management strategy. Among all females, Native Americans were most likely to report smoking for weight control (23.3%), followed by Whites (10.5%), Hispanics (9.3%), Asian Americans (7.1%), and African Americans (6.1%). Among all males, Native Americans were also the most likely to report smoking for weight control (8.7%); Hispanic (6.7%) and Asian American boys (6.5%) reported similar levels of smoking to manage their weight, followed by Whites (4.1%). Again, African Americans were least likely to report smoking for weight control (2.8%). These racial/ethnic group differences were statistically significant.

The Minnesota Student Survey, which is administered to middle and high school students in that state, is the largest study to date to examine smoking for weight control among adolescents (Croll et al. 2002; Fulkerson and French 2003). The 1998 survey, which included items to assess disordered eating behavior, was administered to 81,247 9th- and 12th-grade students. Students were asked to identify methods they had used to lose or control their weight during the past 12 months, with options including fasting or skipping meals, using diet pills or speed (methamphetamines), self-induced vomiting after eating, using laxatives, and cigarette smoking. Overall, among all students, 18.2% of girls and 9.8% of boys reported smoking for weight control, with this practice most common among Native Americans (females = 29.4%, males = 20.5%), followed by those identifying themselves as multiracial (females = 26.5%, males = 13.7%). Hispanic (females = 18.4%, males = 15.3%) and White (females = 18.2%, males = 9.8%) youth generally had intermediate rates (data not shown in Table 2.3). Among Asian Americans, the rates were 11.7% for girls and 10.7% for boys; they were lowest for Blacks: 6.6% for girls and 7.4% for boys. The authors did not formally test for heterogeneity by racial/ethnic group.

The 1998 survey also assessed smoking for weight control among students who reported smoking within the past 30 days. Rates of smoking to control weight among smokers (by gender) were as follows (females listed first): multiracial (55.0% and 31.3%), Asian American (50.0% and 35.0%), Native American (49.4% and 38.2%), White (48.6% and 26.5%), and Black (32.6% and 27.8%). Compared with White female smokers, adolescent girls who were multiracial were significantly more likely to smoke to control their weight (OR = 1.25; 95% CI, 1.07–1.48), and Black females were significantly less likely to do so (OR = 0.50; 95% CI, 0.35–0.70). Relative to White male smokers, Native American (OR = 1.62; 95% CI, 1.19–2.22) and Asian American (OR = 1.44; 95% CI, 1.15–1.80) boys were more likely to smoke for weight control. Weight concerns, perceiving oneself as overweight, and higher smoking rates were significantly associated with smoking for weight control, with the strength of these relationships varying across gender and racial/ethnic subgroups.

Forman and Morello (2003) investigated the relationships between weight concerns, smoking, and perceived difficulty in quitting among 2,524 Argentinean adolescents in the 8th and 11th grades. Smoking for weight control was determined by three separate items designed to identify those who (1) initially tried smoking to keep their weight down, (2) smoked to avoid eating when hungry, and (3) continued smoking to maintain their weight. Girls were more likely than boys to report each of these behaviors: tried smoking to keep weight down, 11.3% versus 4.0%; smoked to avoid eating, 22.3% versus 12.9%; and continued to smoke to keep weight down, 16.0% versus 7.0%. In addition, boys and girls who smoked and who reported that they smoked to avoid eating and continued to smoke to keep their weight down were significantly more likely to perceive difficulty in quitting than were those who did not report smoking for these reasons. Having initially tried smoking in an effort to manage weight was not associated with perceived difficulty in quitting for either boys or girls.

Dowdell and Santucci (2004) investigated the prevalence of health-risk behaviors related to nutrition, weight, physical activity, alcohol, and smoking in a seventh-grade class of 54 students in a parochial school, in a low-income neighborhood, by using items from the Youth Risk Behavior Surveillance System questionnaire. Overall, 70% of the students reported trying cigarettes during their lifetime, and 55% reported current daily smoking. Among those who smoked cigarettes, 62% reported that the main reason was to control their weight. The authors indicated that girls were more likely than boys to report smoking as their primary means of weight control, but data by gender were not reported.

Nichter and colleagues (2004) conducted a mixed-methods study that combined ethnographic interviews and quantitative surveys to examine the use of smoking as a weight-control strategy among adolescent girls and young women. The participants were students taking part in a longitudinal study of the relationships between body image, dieting, smoking, and advertising. The students took part in a semistructured interview and completed a questionnaire annually for 3 years, starting in the eighth or ninth grade. In the third year of the study, 205 students provided data on smoking for purposes of weight control. Five years later, 178 students were recontacted for a follow-up interview.

During the study's third year, when the participants were in the 10th or 11th grade (mean age = 16.02 and 16.99 years, respectively), 30% of the respondents were current smokers (either occasional or regular smokers). Eleven percent of current smokers responded affirmatively to the question "Did you start smoking as a way to control your weight?" An estimated 25% of current smokers endorsed the statement, "I sometimes smoke so I'll be less hungry," while 21% of regular smokers indicated they smoked instead of snacking "a lot of the time" and 33%

reported they did so "sometimes." Overall, an estimated 20% of students (i.e., nonsmokers, occasional smokers, plus regular smokers) agreed with the statement, "In general, I think people who smoke cigarettes are thinner than people who don't smoke." No differences in the proportion of students who were dieting were observed between smokers and nonsmokers.

At the 5-year follow-up interview (mean age = 21.67 years), 30% of the sample was classified as current smokers and 5% were former smokers. Eight percent of this subgroup of current and former smokers indicated they had initially started smoking to control their weight, while 15% reported smoking at some point to control their weight. Twenty percent of current and former smokers indicated they had sometimes smoked so they would be less hungry, and 3% reported they sometimes smoked at the end of a meal so they would not continue eating. When asked about concerns related to gaining weight if they quit smoking, 48% indicated they were "somewhat concerned," and 50% reported they were "not at all concerned."

Facchini and colleagues (2005), in their study of smoking and weight-control beliefs and behaviors among female Argentinean students described earlier, asked participants to indicate their motivations for initiating smoking, reasons they currently smoked, anticipated consequences of quitting smoking, and reasons for not quitting smoking. Included among the response options were reasons related to hunger, eating, and the perceived weight-related effects of smoking. In addition, participants were classified as restrained or unrestrained eaters based on their responses to the 10-item restrained eating subscale from the Dutch Eating Behavior Questionnaire (van Strien et al. 1986). Among the reasons chosen for initially starting smoking were "to avoid eating" (9%), "because it makes them less hungry" (7%), and to "control weight" (4%). Issues related to weight control were also commonly reported as reasons for continuing to smoke. For example, 27% reported "because it makes them less hungry," 24% "instead of snacking when bored," 19% "at the end of a meal so won't eat too much," and 16% "to avoid eating." In terms of consequences, nearly one-half (48%) expected to eat more if they quit smoking, and 34% believed they would gain weight if they stopped. Regarding reasons for not quitting, 37% reported concerns about eating more, and 34% identified fears of gaining weight. The researchers also found that smokers classified as restrained eaters scored higher on the restrained eating scale than did nonsmoking restrained eaters. Finally, those who reported smoking for weight control scored higher in dietary restraint than did smokers who did not smoke to control weight.

Malinauskas and colleagues (2006) compared the dieting practices of 113 normal-weight, 35 overweight, and 21 obese female college students between the ages of 18 and 24 years who completed a survey assessing perceptions about weight, perceived sources of pressure to control their weight, and level of physical activity. In addition, these students were asked to identify which of 15 different weight-management practices they currently followed. Such practices included both healthy behaviors (eating low-fat foods, exercise, self-monitoring of energy and kilocalories) and unhealthy behaviors (skipping meals, self-induced vomiting, use of laxatives, and cigarette smoking). Nine percent of the respondents reported that they smoked cigarettes to lose or control weight. This practice was reported most frequently by overweight students (14%), followed by those who were normal weight (8%) and students who were obese (5%).

Two studies (Plummer et al. 2001; Park et al. 2003) addressed associations between stage of change and temptations to smoke to control weight rather than actual smoking behavior. In the first study (Plummer et al. 2001), participants were 2,808 ninth-grade students enrolled in a 4-year study examining behaviors related to smoking, sun protection, and intake of dietary fat. Students completed measures of the stage of cessation (for current smokers) and onset (for nonsmokers) and a measure developed by Ding and colleagues (1994) of temptations to smoke (all participants); this last item assessed the degree to which respondents would feel tempted to smoke in various situations. Included in the measure of temptations were two items that assessed being tempted to smoke for purposes of weight control ("when I am afraid I might gain weight," "when I want to get thinner"). Among smokers, there was a linear relationship between stage of change and temptations to smoke to control weight, with those in the precontemplation stage reporting the highest temptation to smoke for this reason and those in the maintenance stage reporting the least. A similar linear trend was observed for nonsmokers. In that group, those in the acquisition-preparation phase reported significantly higher temptations to smoke for weight control than those in the acquisition-contemplation stage, who, in turn, expressed greater temptations to smoke that were related to weight control than did those in the acquisition-precontemplation stage.

In the second study, Park and colleagues (2003) investigated factors associated with stage of change among 297 male and female high school students in Korea who were current (n = 186) or former (n = 111) smokers. The students completed a survey assessing their smoking history, stage of change, processes of change, and decisional balance (a concept in which pros and cons combine to form a decisional balance sheet of comparative potential gains and losses). In addition, participants completed the measure of being tempted to smoke developed by Ding and coworkers (1994), which included the two items described above on temptation to smoke for weight control. Similar to the results reported by Plummer and colleagues (2001), overall temptations to smoke for purposes of weight control differed significantly as a function of stage of change. Although weight-related temptations to smoke generally decreased across the stages from precontemplation to maintenance, none of the post hoc comparisons between individual groups was statistically significant.

The studies summarized above investigated the prevalence of smoking for weight control among various groups; some other studies did not assess the proportion of the sample engaged in this practice but instead made comparisons between different groups of smokers and nonsmokers on measures of smoking for weight control in an effort to learn more about the mechanisms involved in this behavior. For example, Jarry and colleagues (1998) examined the associations between dieting, smoking status, weight gain, and smoking for purposes of weight control among 220 female undergraduate students. Never smokers (46.8% of the sample) were asked to indicate whether they had ever considered starting to smoke to avoid gaining or to lose weight. Current and former smokers (36.4% and 16.8% of the sample, respectively) were asked the extent to which they agreed with the statements "I started smoking to avoid gaining weight or to lose weight" and "I smoke(d) to avoid gaining weight or to lose weight." Dieting status was determined from scores on the Revised Restraint Scale (Polivy et al. 1988). Among never smokers, dieters were marginally more likely to agree that they had considered starting smoking to avoid gaining or to lose weight ($p = .08$). Among current and former smokers, dieters were significantly more likely to report they had started smoking to control their weight and that they continued to smoke for this reason. In addition, current smokers were significantly more likely than former smokers to report that they started to smoke and continued to smoke for purposes of weight control.

In a study described earlier, Zucker and colleagues (2001) also assessed the use of smoking for purposes of weight control among 75 female undergraduate students who reported cigarette smoking on a daily basis; smoking for weight control was assessed using the three-item WCSS (Pomerleau et al. 1993). In a multivariate logistic regression analysis to identify significant predictors of smoking for weight control, the belief that smoking helps people control their weight was associated with smoking for this purpose. Internalization of societal standards for thinness was also positively associated with smoking for purposes of weight control, and scores on a measure of feminist consciousness were negatively related to smoking for that purpose.

In a laboratory study, Jenks and Higgs (2007) examined the associations between dieting and smoking-related behaviors in 30 female smokers (mean age = 20 years), one-half of whom were currently dieting to lose weight. Participants completed a revised version of the WCSS (Pomerleau et al. 1993). Two items were included to assess the extent to which weight concerns influenced decisions to initiate smoking ("I started smoking to control my weight") and cessation ("I am concerned about weight gain upon smoking cessation"), both of which were scored on a visual analog scale ranging from "totally disagree" to "totally agree." In addition, participants attended two laboratory sessions; food cues (cookies) were present during one of the sessions but not at the other. Ratings of heart rate, expired carbon monoxide, and mood were obtained both before and after smoking a cigarette. Dieters were more likely than nondieters to report having initiated smoking to control their weight and expressed greater concerns about weight gain upon cessation. In addition, on the WCSS, dieters reported stronger motivation to smoke for purposes of weight control. Finally, dieters (but not nondieters) reported significantly greater urges to smoke during the session in which food cues were present.

Smoking for Weight Control in Clinical Studies

Several studies have demonstrated elevated rates of cigarette smoking among patients with eating disorders, particularly those with bulimia and/or other diagnostic categories containing binge/purge subtypes (Bulik et al. 1992; Anzengruber et al. 2006; Krug et al. 2008), as well as evidence of the use of cigarette smoking for purposes of weight control among patients with eating disorders. These studies are summarized below and presented in Table 2.4.

Welch and Fairburn (1998) investigated smoking rates and weight-related reasons for smoking and relapse among 102 female patients with bulimia nervosa (mean age = 23.7 years), a control group of 102 patients with anxiety or mood disorders who were matched for age and socioeconomic status (SES), and 204 age- and SES-matched healthy controls. Rates of current smoking were significantly higher among patients with bulimia (57%) than in psychiatric controls (29%) and healthy controls (24%). In addition, patients with bulimia reported substantially higher rates of smoking to avoid eating or to control their weight (73%) than did either psychiatric (19%) or healthy (13%) controls. Among current smokers who had ever achieved at least 6 months of abstinence from smoking,

Table 2.4 Studies assessing use of smoking to control body weight (clinical samples)

Study	Design/population	Measure	Percentage endorsing	Findings
Welch and Fairburn 1998	102 women with bulimia nervosa Mean 23.7 years of age (SD = 4.9) 102 women with mood or anxiety disorders matched by age and socioeconomic status (SES) 204 age- and SES-matched nonpsychiatric controls United Kingdom	NR	Ever smoked to avoid eating or to control weight (current and former smokers only): Bulimia = 73% Psychiatric controls = 19% Healthy controls = 13% Ever resumed smoking because of concerns about weight or shape (smokers who had achieved >6 months of abstinence only): Bulimia = 28% Psychiatric controls = 4% Healthy controls = 2%	• Patients with bulimia more likely (57%) than psychiatric controls (29%) or healthy controls (24%) to be current smokers • Bulimic patients more likely than members of either control group to report they started smoking to control weight and that they ever resumed smoking because of concerns about their weight or shape
Crisp et al. 1999	879 females with current or former history of eating disorders Age NR (range 17–40 years)	Participants answered questions assessing their reasons for smoking, including "instead of eating," "makes me less hungry," "when I feel like bingeing," and "to control my weight" Anticipated consequences of giving up smoking were also assessed, one of which was "put on weight"	Weight-related reasons for smoking:* Instead of eating = 70% Makes me less hungry = 52% When I feel like bingeing = 50% To control my weight = 48% Anticipated consequences of quitting smoking:* Put on weight = 40% *Responded "yes, definitely"	• All weight-control-related reasons for smoking were significantly associated with scores on the Interoceptive Awareness scale from the Eating Disorders Inventory (EDI) • Smokers scored higher than nonsmokers on the Bulimia subscale of the EDI but not on scales measuring drive for thinness or body dissatisfaction

Table 2.4 Continued

Study	Design/population	Measure	Percentage endorsing	Findings
Krug et al. 2008	Case-control study Mean 25.8 years of age (SD = 8.7) Eating disorders (n = 879) Healthy controls (n = 785) 5 European countries	Participants indicated whether they smoked cigarettes or took legal or illegal drugs and/or medicine to influence appetite or weight	Smoke cigarettes to control weight: **Current:** Total among patients with eating disorders = 26.8% Anorexia (restrictive type) = 11.0% Anorexia (bulimic and/or purging subtype) = 36.9% Bulimia = 39.4% Eating disorder not otherwise specified (NOS) = 21.1% Healthy controls = 9.1% **Lifetime:** Total among patients with eating disorders = 34.1% Anorexia (restrictive type) = 17.5% Anorexia (bulimic and/or purging subtype) = 43.6% Bulimia = 45.3% Eating disorder NOS = 31.5% Healthy controls = 9.2%	• Patients with eating disorders 3.7 times as likely as healthy controls to currently smoke to control appetite or weight and 5.1 times as likely to have a lifetime history of weight-control smoking • Lifetime (47.5% vs. 35.1%) and current (34.8% vs. 24.2%) rates of cigarette smoking significantly higher among patients with eating disorders than in healthy controls

Note: **NR** = not reported; **SD** = standard deviation.

28% of patients with bulimia indicated they had resumed smoking because of concerns about their weight or their shape. Corresponding rates for psychiatric and nonpsychiatric controls were 4% and 2%, respectively.

Crisp and colleagues (1999) investigated the associations between tobacco use, concerns about body weight, reasons for smoking, and anticipated consequences of giving up smoking in a sample of 879 females from the United Kingdom who were 17–40 years of age and either currently or formerly had an eating disorder. Participants were recruited from a nationwide support organization for eating disorders and were asked to complete a postal questionnaire addressing issues related to smoking and weight control along with the EDI (Garner and Olmsted 1984). Twenty-eight percent of the women were characterized as smokers. Overall, cigarette smokers scored significantly higher on the Bulimia, Interoceptive Awareness, and Maturity Fears subscales of the EDI (Garner et al. 1983) and were more likely to report self-induced vomiting. No differences between smokers and nonsmokers were observed on any of the other five subscales of the EDI, including Drive for Thinness. When questioned regarding their reasons for smoking, participants reported high levels of smoking for weight/appetite control purposes, including "instead of eating" (70%), "makes me less hungry" (52%), "when I feel like bingeing" (50%), and "to control my weight" (48%). In addition, 40% of smokers indicated they expected to experience weight gain as a consequence of giving up smoking.

More recently, Krug and coworkers (2008) compared current and lifetime substance use between patients with eating disorders and healthy controls as well as the use of smoking to influence appetite or weight. Participants included 879 patients with eating disorders (anorexia—restrictive subtype, anorexia—bulimic and/or purging subtype, bulimia, or eating disorder not otherwise specified [ED-NOS]; mean age = 27.2 years, 96.6% female) and 785 healthy controls (mean age = 24.3 years, 91.2% female) who were taking part in the Fifth European Framework Programme on Healthy Eating. Rates of both lifetime smoking (47.5% vs. 35.1%) and current smoking (34.8% vs. 24.2%) were significantly higher among patients with eating disorders than among healthy controls. Lifetime and current rates of smoking instead of eating to control appetite and weight were also significantly higher among patients with eating disorders than in healthy controls (lifetime: 34.1% vs. 9.2%; current: 26.8% vs. 9.1%). Within various subtypes of eating disorders, rates of overall smoking and smoking for weight control tended to be highest for patients with bulimia and anorexia—bulimic and/or purging subtype, followed by those with an ED-NOS and anorexia—restrictive subtype.

Summary

The findings reviewed above and summarized in Tables 2.2 and 2.3 indicate that a notable proportion of youth believe that smoking helps control body weight and that for some young smokers, this belief is an important factor in their decision to use tobacco. The data on use of smoking for weight control, however, are limited by being largely cross-sectional. Consequently, the direction of the associations between smoking and its use for weight control are uncertain. There are few longitudinal studies that examine the association of use of smoking to control body weight over time, particularly as body weight changes during adolescence and young adulthood.

Concerns About Body Weight and Risk for Smoking Initiation

Prior Reviews and Studies

Two earlier systematic reviews summarized the literature on the relationship between weight concerns and smoking in youth (French and Jeffery 1995; Potter et al. 2004); this section summarizes the primary findings from prospective studies included in the more recent review (Potter et al. 2004) of the association between concerns about weight and onset of smoking. It also updates research findings based on longitudinal studies published after the review by Potter et al. (2004) as a way of investigating the relationship between concerns about weight and smoking initiation.

In the first of the seven prospective studies of interest reviewed by Potter and coworkers (2004), French and colleagues (1994) examined the associations between concerns about weight, dieting, and initiation of smoking in a sample of 1,705 adolescents in grades 7–10. The students completed a questionnaire assessing smoking behavior and measures of concerns about weight, dietary restraint, symptoms of eating disorders, and dieting behavior at baseline and 1 year later. Girls with two or more symptoms of eating disorders, those who had tried to lose weight in the past year, and those who experienced constant thoughts about weight were all estimated to be twice as likely to start smoking within the subsequent year as girls not in these classifications. Dietary restraint, concerns about weight gain, and the desire to be thin were not associated with initiation of smoking. Among boys, none of the measures of weight concern and dieting behavior were related to the onset of smoking.

Killen and colleagues (1997) investigated risk factors for initiation of smoking among two cohorts of adolescents (N = 1,901) who were surveyed in the ninth grade and again 3 or 4 years later. A variety of potential predictors of smoking were assessed, including peer influences, alcohol use, temperament, BMI, and depressive symptoms. In addition, female participants completed the Drive for Thinness subscale from the EDI, which assesses level of preoccupation with body weight, concerns with dieting, and pursuit of thinness. Among girls who reported no history of smoking at baseline, levels of concern about weight, as measured by the Drive for Thinness subscale, were not related to initiation of smoking over time.

Patton and associates (1998) examined predictors of smoking initiation over a 3-year period among 2,032 14- and 15-year-old students in Australia. Participants reported their smoking history and cigarette consumption during the past 7 days. Dieting status was assessed using the Adolescent Dieting Scale (Patton et al. 1997), which was employed to place students in one of three categories (nondieter, intermediate dieter, severe dieter). At baseline, severe dieting was associated with reduced odds of any current smoking, with nondieters as the referent (OR = 0.4; 95% CI, 0.2–0.9), but it was not significantly related to current *daily* smoking. In prospective analyses, dieting status was not predictive of the progression to any current smoking or to daily smoking.

Austin and Gortmaker (2001) prospectively investigated the associations between dieting frequency and smoking initiation among 1,295 sixth- and seventh-grade girls and boys participating in an intervention study involving nutrition and physical activity. Students completed baseline measures of their smoking history and dieting frequency during the past month, and smoking status was assessed 2 years later. Initiation of smoking was defined as having reported no smoking at baseline but smoking within the past 30 days at follow-up. Among baseline nonsmokers, the frequency of dieting was a significant predictor of initiation; relative to those who reported no dieting at baseline and with the use of a multivariate logistic regression model, girls who dieted once a week or less were found to be 1.98 (95% CI, 1.12–3.50) times as likely to initiate smoking. For those who reported dieting more than once per week, the odds of initiating smoking were 3.9 (95% CI, 1.46–10.38) times as great as those for nondieters. Dieting frequency was not associated with the likelihood of smoking initiation among boys.

Field and colleagues (2002) investigated the temporal relationships between smoking initiation, beginning to binge eat and/or purge, and getting drunk for the first time in a sample of 11,358 boys and girls between the ages of 10 and 15 years. Students completed a survey assessing smoking history, alcohol use, binge eating, purging behaviors (use of laxatives, self-induced vomiting), and concerns about weight. Smoking was defined as having smoked during the previous 30 days. Assessments were conducted at baseline and 1 year later. During the follow-up period, 4.3% of girls and 3.6% of boys started smoking. Among girls who were nonsmokers at baseline, those who expressed high levels of concern about weight were significantly more likely to initiate smoking over the subsequent year (OR = 2.2; 95% CI, 1.5–3.2) than were those with lower levels of concern. The relationship between concerns about weight and initiation of smoking was somewhat weaker and only marginally significant among boys (OR = 1.7; 95% CI, 1.0–3.1). Neither binge eating nor purging was associated with starting to smoke for either girls or boys.

Voorhees and colleagues (2002) prospectively investigated predictors of initiating daily smoking among 1,213 Black and 1,116 White girls participating in the National Heart, Lung, and Blood Institute Growth and Health Study. Participants were assessed annually for 10 years. A variety of behavioral/personal, developmental, family/social environmental, and weight-related domains were assessed at baseline, when participants were 9 or 10 years old, and again 2 years later. These variables were used to predict smoking status during the 10th annual visit, at which time participants were 18 or 19 years old. For purposes of analysis, never smokers were compared with those who reported smoking on a daily basis during the past 30 days. Weight-related variables included percent overweight, currently trying to lose weight, ever trying to lose weight, level of body dissatisfaction, feelings of competence and acceptance related to physical appearance, and the Drive for Thinness subscale from EDI (Garner et al. 1983). Among Black girls, drive for thinness at 11 or 12 years of age (OR = 1.11; 95% CI, 1.05–1.17) and currently trying to lose weight at those ages (OR = 2.39; 95% CI, 1.25–4.75) were associated with initiation of daily smoking by 18 or 19 years of age in multivariate logistic regression models. For White girls, currently trying to lose weight at 11 or 12 years of age was significantly predictive of daily smoking by 18 or 19 years of age (OR = 1.51; 95% CI, 1.03–2.21). Drive for thinness also predicted later daily smoking among White girls, but only when trying to lose weight was removed from the model.

Lastly, Stice and Shaw (2003) prospectively examined the relationships between both body image and eating/affective disturbances and subsequent initiation of smoking among adolescent girls; participants included 496 girls 11–15 years of age (modal age = 13 years) upon entry into the study. Assessments were conducted at baseline (time 1) and 1 year later (time 2). Participants reported the frequency of cigarette use during the past year on a scale from 0 (never) to 6 (five to seven times per week). Those who reported never smoking during the previous year were classified as nonsmokers. Occasional (but nondaily) smokers were coded as experimenters, and those who reported smoking on a daily basis were considered regular smokers. Level of satisfaction with nine separate body parts was assessed using a modified version of the Satisfaction and Dissatisfaction with Body Parts Scale (Berscheid et al. 1973). Eating pathology was measured with the Eating Disorder Examination (Fairburn and Cooper 1993). Because of high correlation between these last two independent variables, they were collapsed to create a single body dissatisfaction-eating pathology composite score. In the time between baseline and 1-year follow-up, 6% of time 1 (baseline) nonsmokers became experimental smokers, and 5% became daily smokers. In a multivariate logistic regression model that controlled for negative effects, those with high levels of body dissatisfaction-eating pathology were more than four times as likely to initiate smoking (OR = 4.33; 95% CI, 1.71–10.95) as those who did not have high levels.

Most but not all evidence supports an association between concerns about weight and subsequent initiation of smoking. Notably, the three studies that included samples entirely of females found a significant relationship between concerns about weight and taking up smoking (French et al. 1994; Voorhees et al. 2002; Stice and Shaw 2003). Of the four studies that included both males and females, two failed to find a significant relationship between weight concerns and initiation of smoking in either girls or boys (Killen et al. 1997; Patton et al. 1998), and one (Austin and Gortmaker 2001) found dieting to be a significant predictor of starting to smoke for girls only. The remaining study (Field et al. 2002) found that weight concerns were significantly related to beginning to smoke in girls and marginally related in boys.

More Recent Evidence

Subsequent to the publication of the last of the prospective studies reviewed by Potter and colleagues (2004), eight papers have been published (representing seven different studies) on the topic of weight concerns and smoking. Two papers from the Memphis Health Project investigated the association between weight concerns and the onset and escalation of smoking (Blitstein et al. 2003; Robinson et al. 2006); as described above, the Memphis Health Project was designed to prospectively assess predictors of the onset of smoking in a large cohort of students surveyed annually from 7th to 12th grade. Potential risk factors for smoking initiation included a wide range of psychosocial variables: family and peer influences, the perceived functional utility of smoking, rebelliousness, social success, environmental factors, reactions to initial smoking experiences, and weight concerns. For the last item, students indicated the extent to which they believed smoking helps to reduce body weight and whether they had ever smoked to lose weight or control their weight. In addition, participants completed the six items comprising the "concern for dieting" factor from the Restraint Scale (Herman and Polivy 1980), which measures level of preoccupation with dietary control.

The paper by Blitstein and coworkers (2003) examined factors associated with the speed of transition through the stages of smoking among adolescents who were nonsmokers at the start of the study. Students who progressed from nonsmokers to regular smokers (at least weekly) over the course of 1 year (n = 98) were categorized as rapid progressors, and those who went from being nonsmokers to experimental smokers (less than weekly, n = 555) during this period were considered slow progressors. The belief that smoking controls body weight was not related to speed of progression for either boys or girls. However, girls who reported greater concerns with dieting were significantly more likely to progress rapidly from nonsmoking to regular smoking. Relative to those scoring at the median level on this scale, girls at the 75th and 90th percentiles were 1.90 (95% CI, 1.26–2.86) and 2.91 (95% CI, 1.47–5.75) times as likely, respectively, to be rapid progressors. Among boys, no association was observed between concerns with dieting and smoking progression.

In the paper by Robinson and associates (2006), the authors used data from the Memphis Health Project cohort to investigate racial differences in the potential risk factors (including weight concerns/behaviors) for onset and escalation of smoking. Multivariate regression models were used to identify predictors of several different levels of smoking (monthly smoking, weekly smoking, and daily smoking) in the 12th grade among Black and White adolescents who were never smokers at baseline (7th grade). None of the three measures of weight concerns or behaviors (the belief that smoking controls body weight, the use of smoking as a weight-control strategy, concern with dieting) was associated with onset of smoking.

Honjo and Siegel (2003) investigated associations (Table 2.2) between several measures of weight concerns or dieting behavior and initiation of smoking over a 3-year period among 273 girls between the ages of 12 and 15 years who reported having smoked no more than one cigarette in their lifetime at baseline. The belief that smoking controls weight was assessed by asking "Do you believe that smoking helps people keep their weight down?" Participants were also asked whether they considered themselves to be underweight, just about right, or overweight. The participants also indicated whether they were currently dieting. Finally, drive for thinness was assessed by having the girls rate the importance they gave to being slim or thin on an 11-point scale ranging from 0 (not at all important) to 10 (extremely important). Ratings of 0–4, 5–7, and 8–10 were classified as low, medium, and high concern, respectively.

Relative to those who gave a low rating to being thin, adolescents who gave a rating of medium (OR = 3.34; 95% CI, 1.04–10.94) or high (OR = 4.46; 95% CI, 1.40–16.69) were significantly more likely to progress to established smoking 3 years later, defined as having smoked 100 or more cigarettes in their lifetime by the follow-up assessment. Those who believed that smoking helps to control weight were slightly more likely to become established smokers (26.4%) than those who did not endorse this belief (23.1%), but these differences were not statistically significant. Onset of established smoking was slightly more common among those who considered their weight to be just about right (25.1%) than in those who reported being underweight or overweight (20% for both underweight and overweight groups; all differences between groups were not significant). Finally, those who had engaged in dieting and those who had not had nearly identical rates of smoking initiation over time (23.8% vs. 23.3%).

Using data from the 1997 cohort of the National Longitudinal Survey of Youth, Cawley and associates (2004) examined the relationship between self-perceived weight, attempting to lose weight, and smoking initiation over a 3-year period among 9,022 youth 12–16 years of age. Participants were given five options for describing their weight: very underweight, slightly underweight, about the right weight, slightly overweight, and very overweight. Responses were recoded into three categories: (1) overweight (slightly overweight or very overweight), (2) underweight (slightly underweight or very underweight), and (3) about the right weight. Two measures of smoking initiation were used: in the first, which used a more stringent definition, never smokers at baseline who indicated during one of the three follow-up interviews that they had smoked even a single cigarette were classified as smokers. The second definition required respondents to have smoked on at least 15 of the previous 30 days.

In analyses that included boys and girls together and boys and girls separately, perceiving oneself as underweight was associated with a reduced likelihood of smoking initiation according to the less stringent definition when "about the right weight" was the referent. When the more stringent criterion and the same referent were used, only girls who perceived themselves as underweight were significantly less likely to smoke. Girls who perceived themselves as overweight were significantly more likely than those in the "about the right weight" group to have smoked on the basis of the less stringent definition only. Perceptions of being overweight were not associated with initiation of smoking among boys when either definition was used. Attempting to lose weight was significantly associated with adoption of smoking on the basis of the less stringent definition when both genders were considered together and when girls were assessed separately. With the more stringent definition of smoking initiation, the association between attempted weight loss and initiation was significant only among girls in gender-stratified analyses.

Saules and colleagues (2004) investigated factors associated with the onset of smoking during college among 490 female undergraduate students. Smoking status was assessed during freshman orientation, after 9 months (end of the freshman year), and nearly 4 years after baseline (during the senior year). Disordered eating patterns/dieting concerns were measured using the Dieting and Bingeing Severity Scale (Krahn et al. 1992; Drewnowski et al. 1994). Among students who were nonsmokers at baseline, elevated concerns about dieting were a significant predictor of the onset of smoking during their college years.

Chesley and associates (2004) investigated the associations between intended behaviors about one's weight and the initiation and maintenance of smoking among 3,621 participants in the National Longitudinal Study of Adolescent Health. Participants were asked whether they were attempting to modify their weight (trying to lose weight, trying to gain weight, trying to maintain their weight, not trying to do anything about weight); smoking status was assessed during an initial interview and 1 year later. Among students who reported at baseline that they had never tried a cigarette, those who indicated they were attempting to lose weight were 1.8 (95% CI, 1.1–2.9) times as likely to initiate smoking during the following year as were those not trying to do anything with their weight. For those classified as smokers at baseline and who continued smoking during follow-up, the desire to maintain weight (but not the desire to lose or gain weight) was associated with a greater increase in the number of days smoked in the past month.

Wahl and colleagues (2005) investigated associations between expectancies for outcomes related to smoking and escalation of smoking in a sample of 8th and 10th graders enrolled in a prospective study of the natural progression of cigarette smoking. Participants included 273 students (54% female) who were classified as early experimenters because they had smoked between 2 and 100 cigarettes in their lifetimes. The majority of the sample (74%)

was White, with the remainder identifying themselves as Latino (16%), Black (3%), or other/biracial (6%). Expectancies related to smoking were assessed using a revised, 13-item version of the SCQ (Brandon and Baker 1991); the expectancy measure included three items related to weight control: "Smoking keeps my weight down," "Cigarettes keep me from eating more than I should," and "Smoking helps me control my weight." Responses were on a 4-point scale ranging from 1 (disagree) to 4 (agree). Assessments were conducted at baseline and at 6 months. Participants were placed in one of five groups (trier, escalator, rapid escalator, smoker, and quitter) according to their smoking behavior during the follow-up period. Girls had higher baseline expectancies related to weight control than did boys, but no differences in expectancies were noted by race or ethnicity. Significant differences in baseline smoking expectancies related to weight were noted by smoking behavior group. Specifically, escalators reported lower expectancies regarding the impact of smoking on weight and appetite control than did students who were smoking more regularly at baseline and continued as regular smokers. None of the other comparisons by group were significant.

Finally, in Ontario, Canada, Leatherdale and coworkers (2008) examined the association between self-perception of weight and susceptibility to smoking (susceptibility to smoking has been shown to be a reliable predictor of the future onset of smoking [Pierce et al. 1996, 2005; Choi et al. 2001]). Participants included 25,060 students in grades 9–12. In all, of the 14,795 participants who had never smoked cigarettes, 3,809 (25.8%) were classified as susceptible and 10,986 (74.2%) were categorized as nonsusceptible to future smoking from their responses to Pierce's Susceptibility Questionnaire (Pierce et al. 1996). Perception of body weight was assessed by asking students whether they considered themselves very underweight, slightly underweight, about the right weight, slightly overweight, or very overweight. Relative to those who thought they were at about the right weight, those who considered themselves either slightly overweight (OR = 1.21; 95% CI, 1.08–1.35) or slightly underweight (OR = 1.18; 95% CI, 1.05–1.33) were significantly more likely to be susceptible to future smoking. In contrast, self-perception as very overweight or very underweight was not associated with increased susceptibility. Relationships between perceptions of weight and susceptibility to smoking did not differ by gender.

Summary

The eight publications described above, which were based on seven studies published after the review by Potter and colleagues (2004), provide mixed findings regarding the association between concerns about weight and initiation of smoking. With the exception of one study, which did not find a significant relationship between concerns about weight and the onset and escalation of smoking among adolescents (Robinson et al. 2006), each of the studies found at least one association between weight concerns and initiation of smoking. However, methods of these studies differed according to the weight-related constructs assessed and the measures used. Associations between weight concerns and initiation were also frequently modified by gender, with relationships tending to be stronger among females than among males.

Because the associations between initiation of smoking and concerns about weight tend to differ according to how the concerns are conceptualized and assessed, the results are summarized below from all published studies, including those summarized in the 2004 review by Potter and colleagues, according to different dimensions of weight concerns. These include general weight concerns, perceived weight, dieting behaviors, and dispositional weight concerns/symptoms and attitudes relative to disordered eating. These categories were also used in two previous reviews (French and Jeffery 1995; Potter et al. 2004) as well.

General Weight Concerns

Five studies were identified that prospectively investigated the association between general weight concerns and initiation of smoking (French et al. 1994; Field et al. 2002; Honjo and Siegel 2003; Wahl et al. 2005; Robinson et al. 2006). Two of these studies investigated the use of smoking as a weight-control strategy, but neither demonstrated a significant relationship with the onset of smoking (Honjo and Siegel 2003; Robinson et al. 2006). However, Field and colleagues (2002) found that general weight concerns, as measured by the McKnight Risk Factor Survey (Shisslak et al. 1999), were a significant predictor of smoking initiation over 1 year among girls and a marginally significant predictor for boys. In another of the five studies, expectancies regarding the weight-controlling effects of smoking were a significant predictor of smoking trajectories over time (Wahl et al. 2005), with adolescents who increased their smoking over time reporting lower expectancies than those who were initially smoking more regularly and continued as regular smokers. In the remaining study (French et al. 1994), constant thoughts about weight, but not fears about weight gain, predicted smoking initiation during a 1-year period in girls. Neither measure was associated with initiation of smoking among boys.

Thus, general concerns about weight appear to be a modest predictor of the initiation of smoking in prospective studies. The limited evidence on gender differences suggests that this relationship is stronger among girls than boys. The small number of cohort studies and considerable variability in the ways in which weight concerns were conceptualized and measured, however, limit the conclusions that can be made about the nature and strength of this relationship.

Perceived Weight

Two studies were identified that used longitudinal designs to examine the relationship between self-perceived body weight and initiation of smoking (Honjo and Siegel 2003; Cawley et al. 2004), and one cross-sectional study was found that used susceptibility to smoking as a proxy for future initiation of smoking (Leatherdale et al. 2008). In one of the two longitudinal studies, perceptions about body weight were not significantly associated with starting to smoke among adolescent girls (Honjo and Siegel 2003), but in the second one (Cawley et al. 2004), self-perception of being underweight was associated with a reduced likelihood of initiation for both boys and girls on the basis of a liberal definition of smoking (any amount of smoking). When a definition of more regular use was used (smoking on ≥15 of the last 30 days), however, the relationship remained significant only among girls. Relative to those who considered their weight to be "just about right," adolescent girls who perceived themselves as overweight were significantly more likely to initiate smoking only by the definition of "any" use. Perceiving oneself as overweight did not predict the onset of smoking among boys when either definition was used. In the third study (Leatherdale et al. 2008), perceiving oneself as being slightly underweight or slightly overweight was associated with greater susceptibility to smoking in a sample of male and female adolescents. Those who perceived themselves as being very underweight or very overweight, however, were neither more nor less susceptible to smoking. The fact that these three studies used different designs and definitions of smoking may have contributed to the apparent discrepancies in their findings.

Dieting Behaviors

Seven studies (French et al. 1994; Patton et al. 1998; Austin and Gortmaker 2001; Voorhees et al. 2002; Honjo and Siegel 2003; Cawley et al. 2004; Chesley et al. 2004) prospectively investigated the association between dieting and the initiation of smoking among youth. The majority of findings supported a relatively strong association between dieting and the onset of smoking, particularly among females. In three studies, attempts to lose weight were predictive of smoking initiation among girls but not among boys (French et al. 1994; Austin and Gortmaker 2001; Cawley et al. 2004). In two of the other studies, which examined the association between dieting and onset of smoking in combined samples of males and females and did not stratify the analyses by gender, attempting to lose weight was a significant predictor of starting to smoke in one (Chesley et al. 2004) but not in the other (Patton et al. 1998). In the two remaining studies, both using exclusively female samples, trying to lose weight was a significant risk factor for initiation of smoking in one (Voorhees et al. 2002) but not the other (Honjo and Siegel 2003).

Dispositional Weight Concerns/Symptoms and Attitudes Relative to Disordered Eating

The term "dispositional weight concerns/symptoms" has been previously used in studies to mean individual differences in the tendency toward restrained eating and other extreme dieting behaviors. In total, eight studies have prospectively evaluated the associations between dispositional weight concerns or symptoms of/attitudes about disordered eating and initiation of smoking among adolescents and young adults (French et al. 1994; Killen et al. 1997; Voorhees et al. 2002; Blitstein et al. 2003; Honjo and Siegel 2003; Stice and Shaw 2003; Saules et al. 2004; Robinson et al. 2006). Similar to the results described above involving dieting behaviors, studies that included measures of dispositional weight concerns/disordered eating symptoms and attitudes have demonstrated a fairly consistent association with initiation of smoking, particularly among females. All four studies that included only females found responses to measures of dispositional weight concerns/symptoms and attitudes about disordered eating to be significant predictors of starting to smoke (Voorhees et al. 2002; Honjo and Siegel 2003; Stice and Shaw 2003; Saules et al. 2004). Although Killen and colleagues (1997) included both boys and girls, the Drive for Thinness subscale of the EDI (Garner et al. 1983) was administered only to the girls in the sample, for whom it was not a significant predictor of the onset of smoking. In a sixth study (French et al. 1994), having two or more symptoms of eating disorders predicted the uptake of smoking over 1 year among girls but not boys. Similarly, concern with dieting was a significant predictor of rapid progression from nonsmoking to regular cigarette smoking among girls but not for boys enrolled in the Memphis Health Study (Blitstein et al. 2003). However, in a subsequent set of analyses from the same cohort that examined predictors of the onset and escalation of smoking (Robinson et al. 2006), concern with dieting was not associated with initiation or progression of smoking in either gender.

Weight Concerns and Smoking Cessation in Adolescents and Young Adults

Review of the Evidence

This section examines the limited evidence available on the association between weight concerns and smoking cessation in youth. General concerns about weight and, more specifically, concerns about the weight gain that frequently accompanies smoking cessation have long been recognized as a potential barrier to cessation among adults. However, in contrast to the literature on adults, which includes several relevant studies (Klesges and Klesges 1988; French et al. 1992, 1995; Jeffery et al. 1997, 2000; Meyers et al. 1997), only two prospective studies were identified that investigated this issue in young smokers. In the first, Glasgow and colleagues (1999) focused on 506 female smokers (mean age = 24 years) attending Planned Parenthood clinics who were participating in a randomized clinical trial involving low-intensity interventions for quitting smoking. Participants completed the SSQ which, as noted earlier, is designed to assess the use of smoking for weight control (Weekley et al. 1992). Scores on the SSQ were not a significant predictor of successful cessation, attempts to quit smoking, changes in cigarette consumption, or changes in self-efficacy for quitting smoking.

The second prospective study (Wahl et al. 2005) examined the association between smoking-related outcome expectancies and cessation among 349 high school students enrolled in a cessation program (54% were female). The majority (75%) of the sample was White; 13% were Black; 5%, Latino; and 7% identified themselves as biracial/other. Participants ranged in age from 14 to 19 years (mean age = 16.4 years, SD = 1.1). Expectancies regarding the effect of smoking on weight control were assessed using a 13-item modified version of the SCQ (Brandon and Baker 1991). Participants were surveyed at baseline, end of treatment, and 6 months after baseline. Relative to males, female students reported greater expectancies about the impact of smoking on body weight. Furthermore, baseline expectancies about weight control related to smoking were significantly associated with the likelihood of being abstinent at the 6-month follow-up. Contrary to expectations, students who reported greater expectancies that smoking helps control weight were significantly more likely to successfully quit smoking (OR = 1.54; 95% CI, 1.05–2.24).

Summary

The relevant research is quite limited in scope. In the one study that prospectively investigated the relationship between weight concerns and smoking cessation in young smokers, use of smoking for weight control was not associated with any cessation-related outcome. A second study found that expectancies regarding the effect of smoking on body weight were associated with the likelihood of quitting smoking, but not in the predicted direction. Results from the literature on smoking among adults have been mixed regarding the issue of whether concerns about weight are inversely associated with quitting smoking. Although two studies (Klesges and Klesges 1988; Meyers et al. 1997) found that those with greater concerns about post-cessation weight gain were less likely to quit smoking, several others did not find this to be the case (French et al. 1992, 1995; Jeffery et al. 1997). One other study (Jeffery et al. 2000) found that elevated concerns about weight were associated with a reduced likelihood of quitting smoking in the bivariate analyses but not in multivariate models that controlled for demographics, nicotine dependence, and social factors. Thus, additional prospective studies are needed to clarify the impact of weight concerns on the likelihood of successful smoking cessation in adolescents and young adults.

Smoking and Reduction of Body Weight in Children and Young Adults

Overview and Methods

Two previous Surgeon General's reports (USDHHS 1988, 1990) evaluated the relationship between smoking and body weight. The 1988 report, which examined nicotine addiction as a health consequence of smoking, concluded from a review of 28 cross-sectional studies that, on average, smokers weighed 3.2 kilograms (kg) less than nonsmokers. In addition, from a review of 43 prospective studies, the report concluded that quitting smoking resulted in a weight gain of 2.8 kg. Similarly, in the 1990 report on the health benefits of smoking cessation, in which 15 prospective studies were reviewed, the average weight gain following cessation was 2.3 kg.

To evaluate the relationship between smoking and body weight in youth and young adults, all studies reporting a relationship between smoking and body weight subsequent to the 1990 Surgeon General's report were evaluated for the present report. To be included in the review, studies had to include smoking status, body weight or BMI, and sample size. Given the interest in the effects on younger smokers, body weight and smoking status needed to be specified by age group. Some studies reported extremely large age ranges and did not stratify by age (e.g., 18–70 years; Chiriboga et al. 2008; Fogarty et al. 2008) and thus were excluded because the impact of smoking on the body weights of younger versus older smokers could not be determined.

The inconsistent categorization of smoking status poses a potential limitation to interpreting this body of literature. Some studies differed in their definitions of cessation and of active smoking status (Townsend et al. 1991; Cooper et al. 2003; Stice and Martinez 2005; Carroll et al. 2006; Fidler et al. 2007; O'Loughlin et al. 2008), and others did not provide a definition of smoking status at all (Barrett-Connor and Khaw 1989; Freedman et al. 1997; Fulton and Shekelle 1997; Akbartabartoori et al. 2005; Jitnarin et al. 2006; Stavropoulos-Kalinoglou et al. 2008). Clearly, the duration and quantity of smoking status can markedly affect the amount of weight gain attributed to cessation. For example, Klesges and colleagues (1997a) evaluated the weight gain associated with cessation by using both point-prevalent (currently not smoking) and continuous abstinence (for 1 year) criteria for defining cessation. In a sample of 196 participants in a cessation program, the continuously abstinent participants gained 5.90 kg during 1 year, significantly more than those who were abstinent at a specific point (3.04 kg) or those who continuously smoked (1.09 kg).

The age of participants also affects the interpretation of findings, as definitions and categories of smokers typically vary between adolescents and adults. Most of the studies in adults define a smoker as someone who smokes every day (Marti et al. 1989; Shimokata et al. 1989; Molarius et al. 1997; Al-Riyami and Afifi 2003; Bamia et al. 2004; Sneve and Jorde 2008), but most studies of youth (e.g., aged <18 years) define a regular smoker as someone who smokes once a month or once a week (e.g., Townsend et al. 1991; Crawley and While 1995; Cooper et al. 2003). Given the potential difficulty of interpreting the overall findings, the few studies that define smoking among youth as daily smoking (e.g., Klesges et al. 1998a; Stice and Martinez 2005) will be discussed in more detail because these youth are likely to continue to smoke and with greater intensity.

After coding, studies were categorized by whether they addressed the major research questions, the first being whether there is a relationship between smoking and body weight in young people. Most of the studies addressing this issue were cross-sectional, but some cohort studies that had a report on the cross-sectional findings were also included. The second question was whether quitting smoking leads to a significant weight gain. Studies included here were longitudinal studies with participants who were smokers at one time point and had quit smoking at another time point. The final question was whether initiation of smoking is associated with weight loss in youth and young adults. The studies included here were longitudinal studies in which participants were nonsmokers at one time point and smokers at another time point.

Relationship Between Smoking and Body Weight in Youth and Young Adults

As concluded in previous Surgeon General's reports (USDHHS 1988, 1990), cross-sectional studies have shown a clear relationship between smoking and body weight. However, the majority of these investigations have involved adult samples. To evaluate the relationships between smoking and body weight in both younger and older smokers, studies were placed in one of three age groups: less than 25 years, 25 years and older, or 35 years and older. The results of these 25 studies are presented in Table 2.5.

On the basis of weighted means, the results indicated that among older persons the average BMI was lower for smokers than for nonsmokers. For example, in a large Greek cohort of more than 22,000 adults, the average BMI for smokers 45 years of age and older was 2.1 units (measured as kg of weight/square meters of height) lower than that of nonsmokers (Bamia et al. 2004). Similar results were reported for this age group in a Scottish cohort of more than 9,000 adults (Akbartabartoori et al. 2005). In contrast, in a study of 32,144 U.S. Air Force trainees (mean age = 19.8 years, SD = 2.1), daily smoking was not associated with body weight ($p > 0.05$) in females and was associated with only about a 1-kg difference in body weight in men (Klesges et al. 1998c). Moreover, in a study of 6,751 seventh graders, daily smokers had a significantly higher BMI than their nonsmoking peers (Klesges et al. 1998a).

Average BMI for smokers and nonsmokers in studies reported in Table 2.5 was weighted, averaged, and plotted for the same three age groups described above: less than 25 years, 25 years and older, and 35 years and older (Figure 2.2). Because reported age ranges varied a great deal, these three age groups were selected because most results of the relevant articles could be sorted into these categories. Individual study means that were not explicitly provided were calculated when data on weight and age by smoking status were provided. Study means were then weighted by sample size and averaged across studies.

BMI dramatically increased with age in both smokers and nonsmokers, but there was a discernible weight difference between smokers and nonsmokers among those

Table 2.5 Studies assessing association between smoking and body weight

Study	Design/population	Average age (years)	Age groups	Mean difference in body mass index (kg/m²)	Mean kg difference	Measures: Height/ weight	Measures: Smoking status	Comments
Barrett-Connor and Khaw 1989	Cross-sectional survey 1,933 adults Rancho Bernardo, California	NR	50–79 years[a] Smokers Nonsmokers	 24.0 25.2 -1.2	NR	Measured	Self-report	Smoking status not defined
Marti et al. 1989	Cross-sectional survey 15,281 adults Finland	NR	25–64 years[b] Smokers Nonsmokers	 25.6 26.5 -0.9	NR	Measured	Self-report	Smoker: daily use for 1 year
Shimokata et al. 1989	Cross-sectional analysis 3-year Baltimore Longitudinal Study of Aging 1,122 men Maryland	M = 51.7	19–44 years Smokers Nonsmokers ≥45 years[a] Smokers Nonsmokers	 24.5 25.2 -0.7 25.3 25.2 +0.1	NR	Measured	Self-report	Smoker: daily use; 19–44 years; not included in Figure 2.1
Townsend et al. 1991	Cross-sectional study 491 adolescents United Kingdom	NR	13–17 years[c] Smokers Nonsmokers	 23.1 20.6 +2.5	NR	Measured	Saliva cotinine	Smoker: ≥1 cigarette/ week
Lissner et al. 1992	Cross-sectional analysis Prospective population study (1974–1975) 1,291 women Sweden	NR	≥44 years[a] Smokers Nonsmokers	 23.8 25.1 -1.3	NR	Measured	NR	Smoking status not defined; smokers who quit ≥1 year classified as nonsmokers
Crawley and While 1995	Cross-sectional analysis 1970 longitudinal birth cohort 1,592 adolescents	NR	16–17 years[c] Smokers Nonsmokers	 21.4 21.1 +0.3	NR	Measured	Self-report	Smoker: >1 cigarette/ week
Elisaf et al. 1996	Cross-sectional study 590 female adolescents	M = 17	16–18 years[c] Smokers Nonsmokers	 21.2 22.6 -1.4	 57.0 60.0 -3.0	Measured	Self-report	Smoker: daily use

Table 2.5 Continued

Study	Design/population	Average age (years)	Age groups	Mean difference in body mass index (kg/m²)	Mean kg difference	Measures: Height/ weight	Measures: Smoking status	Comments
Freedman et al. 1997	Cross-sectional survey 160 Navajo adolescents	M = 16.2	12–19 years[c] Smokers Nonsmokers	 23.5 22.6 +0.9	NR	Measured	Self-report	Smoking status not defined
Fulton and Shekelle 1997	Cross-sectional analysis Chicago Western Electric Study 1,531 men	M = 48.6	40–59 years[a] Smokers Nonsmokers 20 years[c] Smokers Nonsmokers	 25.5 26.5 -1.0 22.2 22.2 0.0	 77.8 80.5 -2.7	Measured Self-reported weight for age 20	Self-report	Smoking status not defined Retrospective—participants were asked to recall weight at age 20
Molarius et al. 1997	Cross-sectional study WHO MONICA Project 67,981 adults 21 countries	NR	35–64 years Smokers Nonsmokers	 25.7 26.7 -1.0	NR	Measured	Self-report	Smoker: daily use; not included in Figure 2.1 (unable to weight nonsmoker mean)
Klesges et al. 1998a	Cross-sectional study 6,751 7th graders	M = 13	~13 years[c] Smokers Nonsmokers	 21.3 20.9 +0.4	NR	Self-report	Self-report	Smoker: daily use
Klesges et al. 1998b	Baseline 7-year prospective study CARDIA study 5,115 adults	M = 24.8	18–30 years Smokers Nonsmokers	NR	 69.6 72.2 -2.6	Measured	Baseline: Serum cotinine	Smoker: ≥5 cigarettes/ week; not included in Figure 2.1
Klesges et al. 1998c	Randomized controlled trial 32,144 recruits Lackland Air Force Base, Texas	M = 19.8	17–35 years Smokers Nonsmokers	NR	 71.56 72.52 -0.98	Self-report	Self-report	Smoker: ≥1 cigarette/ day; not included in Figure 2.1
Laaksonen et al. 1998	Cross-sectional surveys National Public Health Institute Finland	NR	≥25 years[b] Smokers Nonsmokers	 24.8 24.5 +0.3	NR	Self-report	Self-report	Smoker: use in past month

Table 2.5 Continued

Study	Design/population	Average age (years)	Age groups	Mean difference in body mass index (kg/m^2)	Mean kg difference	Measures: Height/ weight	Measures: Smoking status	Comments
Al-Riyami and Afifi 2003	Cross-sectional study 3,506 adult men Oman	M = 38.4	>20 years Smokers Nonsmokers	 24.7 25.2 -0.5	NR	Measured	Self-report	Smoker: daily use; not included in Figure 2.1
Copeland and Carney 2003	Cross-sectional study 441 female undergraduates Louisiana State University	M = 19.9 (SD = 1.6)	>25 years[c] Smokers Nonsmokers	 22.1 22.2 -0.1	NR	Self-report	Carbon monoxide analysis	Smoking status not defined
Bamia et al. 2004	Cross-sectional analysis Population-based cohort study 22,059 adults Greek EPIC cohort	NR	25–44 years[b] Smokers Nonsmokers ≥45 years Smokers Nonsmokers	 27.0 27.1 -0.1 27.9 30.0 -2.1	NR	Measured	Self-report	Smoker: daily use
Saarni et al. 2004	Cross-sectional study 4,521 twins Finland	M = 24.4	23–27 years Smokers Nonsmokers	 22.8 23.1 -0.3	NR	Self-report	Self-report	Smoker: daily use; not included in Figure 2.1
Akbartabartoori et al. 2005	Cross-sectional study Scottish Health Survey 9,047 adults Scotland	NR	16–24 years[c] Smokers Nonsmokers 25–44 years[b] Smokers Nonsmokers ≥45 years[a] Smokers Nonsmokers	 23.5 23.0 +0.5 25.1 26.1 -1.0 25.7 27.7 -2.0	NR	Measured	Self-report	Smoking status not defined; weights estimated from available data

Table 2.5 Continued

Study	Design/population	Average age (years)	Age groups	Mean difference in body mass index (kg/m^2)	Mean kg difference	Measures: Height/ weight	Measures: Smoking status	Comments
Carroll et al. 2006	Cross-sectional study 300 students University of Kansas	NR	18–24 years[c] Smokers Nonsmokers	 25.9 24.2 +1.7	NR	Measured	Self-report	Smoker: self-reported current smoker and smoked in past 30 days; nonsmokers include those who reported having ever smoked
Jitnarin et al. 2006	Cross-sectional study 1,027 adults Thailand	NR	>35 years Smokers Nonsmokers	 22.6 24.8 -2.2	NR	Measured	Self-report	Smoking status not defined
Fidler et al. 2007	Cross-sectional analysis 5-year longitudinal study 2,665 students HABITS South London, England	NR	15–16 years[c] Smokers Nonsmokers	 22.0 22.2 -0.2	NR	Measured	Saliva cotinine	Smoker: >6 cigarettes/ week; all nonsmokers at baseline
O'Loughlin et al. 2008	Cross-sectional analysis NDIT 755 students Montreal, Canada	NR	17–18 years[c] Smokers Nonsmokers	 22.8 22.4 +0.4	NR	Measured	Self-report	Smoker: ≥30 cigarettes/month; nonsmoker: <30 cigarettes/month
Sneve and Jorde 2008	Cross-sectional analysis 2001 Tromsø Study 5,102 adults Norway	M = 53.7	>29 years[b] Smokers Nonsmokers	 24.7 25.8 -1.1	NR	Measured	Self-report	Smoker: ≥1 cigarette/ day
Stavropoulos-Kalinoglou et al. 2008	Cross-sectional study 392 rheumatoid arthritis patients United Kingdom	Md = 63.1	>55 years[a] Smokers Nonsmokers	 26.0 27.5 -1.5	 70.0 72.5 -2.5	Measured	Self-report	Smoking status not defined

Note: **CARDIA** = Coronary Artery Risk Development in Young Adults; **EPIC** = European Prospective Investigation into Cancer and Nutrition; **HABITS** = Health and Behaviour in Teenagers Study; **kg** = kilograms; **m^2** = square meters; **M** = mean; **Md** = median; **NDIT** = Nicotine Dependence in Teens; **NR** = not reported; **WHO MONICA** = World Health Organization Multinational Monitoring of Trends and Determinants in Cardiovascular Disease.

[a]Categorized as ≥35 years.
[b]Categorized as ≥25 years.
[c]Categorized as <25 years.

Figure 2.2 Body mass index (BMI) differences among smokers and nonsmokers by age group

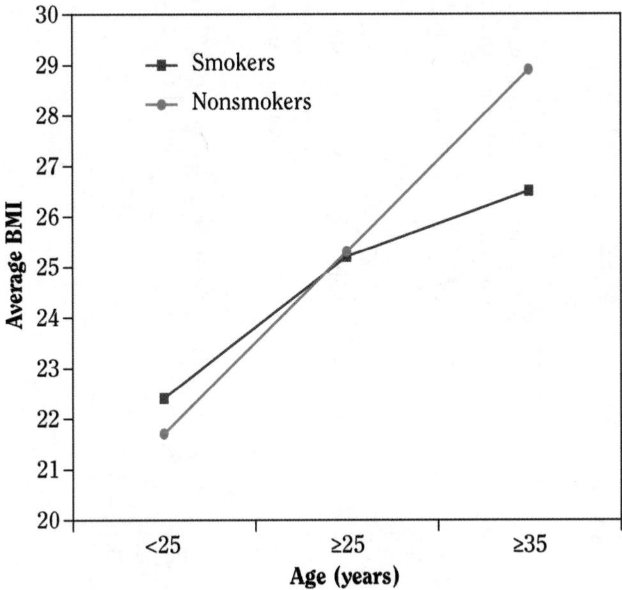

Source: Data from studies in Table 2.5: Barrett-Connor and Khaw 1989; Marti et al. 1989; Shimokata et al. 1989; and Townsend et al. 1991.

35 years of age and older. This difference was explained by the relatively lower gain in weight for smokers over time. The average BMI for smokers under 18 years of age appeared to be the same, if not slightly higher, than the average BMI for nonsmokers. Thus, these studies do not show a relationship between smoking and body weight in children and young adults.

Quitting Smoking and Weight Gain in Youth and Young Adults

Among smokers in general, cessation leads to weight gain (USDHHS 1988, 1990). Again, however, most of the investigations have reported this relationship in largely adult populations. To evaluate the relationships between cessation and weight change in both younger and older smokers, studies were examined by the age of the sample. Ages ranged from 11 to 15 years in one sample (Stice and Martinez 2005) to 46 years or older in another study (Janzon et al. 2004). The results of these 12 longitudinal studies, which extended from 6 weeks to 9 years, are summarized in Table 2.6.

Post-cessation weight gain appears to occur among young people and older adults alike. In one study, Klesges and colleagues (1998b) evaluated the relationship between cessation and weight change from baseline to a 7-year follow-up in a large biracial cohort, the Coronary Artery Risk Development in Young Adults (CARDIA) study; participants were 5,115 young adults 18–30 years of age at baseline. Over 7 years, all groups (smokers, nonsmokers, and former smokers) gained weight, but gains were the greatest among those who quit smoking during the study. Average weight gain attributable to cessation was 4.2 kg for Whites and 6.6 kg for African Americans. Similar findings were reported for 496 adolescent girls in the United Kingdom (Stice and Martinez 2005); in this 3-year prospective study, girls who quit smoking gained an average of 3.4 kg versus gains of 1.4 kg for smokers and 2.9 kg for nonsmokers. Finally, using the weighted means from six studies (Table 2.6) whose participants were adults 25 years of age or older, an average gain of 7.3 kg following cessation can be calculated (Klesges et al. 1997b; O'Hara et al. 1998; Nicklas et al. 1999; Janzon et al. 2004; Hutter et al. 2006; Pisinger and Jorgensen 2007). Thus, limited data suggest that quitting smoking among adolescents and young adults, just as for adults, appears to be associated with weight gain.

Initiation of Smoking and Weight Loss in Youth and Young Adults

Several previous reviews of the literature (USDHHS 1988, 1990; Klesges et al. 1989) concluded that, overall, people who start smoking lose weight. However, these reviews were based on adults and included a very small number of studies. To evaluate the relationship between initiation of smoking and changes in body weight in both younger and older smokers, available studies were coded by age of the sample. Ages ranged from 11 to 15 years (Stice and Martinez 2005) to 38 years of age and older (Lissner et al. 1992); the results of these studies are highlighted in Table 2.7.

Although nearly 20 years have passed since the last review in a Surgeon General's report, even now only a few studies have evaluated the relationship between initiation of smoking and body weight (Table 2.7). Overall, among older people who have participated in these studies, initiation of smoking has been associated with a smaller increase in weight than for nonsmokers (Sneve and Jorde 2008), including for women (Lissner et al. 1992). In the CARDIA study (Klesges et al. 1998b), those who were nonsmokers at baseline (age range of 18–30 years) and who reported smoking 7 years later were compared with other smoking groups (e.g., never smokers, former smokers, quitters, initiators, and intermittent smokers); all of the groups gained weight. Relative to the experience of never smokers and continuous smokers, initiation of smoking

Table 2.6 Studies assessing change in weight following smoking cessation

Study	Design/population	Average age (years)	Age groups	Mean body mass index change (kg/m^2)	Mean kg difference	Measures: Height/weight	Measures: Smoking status	Comments
Lissner et al. 1992	6-year Prospective Population Study of Women in Gothenburg (1968–1969) 1,291 women Sweden	NR	≥38 years Smokers Nonsmokers Quitters	 +0.5 +0.6 +1.4	NR	Measured	NR	Smoking status not defined; smokers quit ≥1 year classified as nonsmokers
Talcott et al. 1995	6-week longitudinal analysis 332 recruits Lackland Air Force Base, Texas	M = 20.4	Nonsmokers Quitters	NR	-0.89 -0.03	Measured	Self-report	Smoking status prior to basic military training not defined; age range NR
Klesges et al. 1997b	1-year longitudinal study 196 adult smokers Memphis, Tennessee	M = 44.6	Smokers Quitters	NR	+1.1 +5.9	Measured	CO	Smoker: CO ≥10 ppm; age range NR
Klesges et al. 1998b	7-year prospective study CARDIA study 5,115 adults	NR	18–30 years Smokers Nonsmokers Quitters	NR	 +5.7 +7.2 +10.9	Measured	Self-report	Smoker: ≥5 cigarettes/week
O'Hara et al. 1998	5-year longitudinal study Lung Health Study 5,887 adult smokers	M = 48.4	35–60 years Smokers Quitters	NR	 +1.5 +8.0	Measured	CO Salivary cotinine	Smoker: ≥10 cigarettes/day; weights estimated from available data
Nicklas et al. 1999	6-month longitudinal study 13 adult men Baltimore, Maryland	M = 63	>50 years Smokers Quitters	 NR +1.9	 NR +5.6	Measured	CO	Smoker: daily use
Janzon et al. 2004	9-year longitudinal study 3,391 women Sweden	M = 59.3	46–70 years Smokers Nonsmokers Quitters	NR	 +3.2 +3.7 +7.6	Measured	Self-report	Smoker: daily use at baseline, regular or occasional use at follow-up
Stice and Martinez 2005	3-year prospective study 496 females Southwestern United States	Md = 13	11–15 years Smokers Nonsmokers Quitters	 +0.2 +0.6 +1.0	 +1.4 +2.9 +3.4	Measured	Self-report	Smoker: 5–7 times/week and ≥1 cigarettes/day

Table 2.6 Continued

Study	Design/population	Average age (years)	Age groups	Mean body mass index change (kg/m²)	Mean kg difference	Measures: Height/ weight	Measures: Smoking status	Comments
Hutter et al. 2006	1-year longitudinal study 308 adult smokers Austria	Md = 40	33–46 years Smokers Quitters	 +0.3 +1.1	 +0.0 +4.0	NR	Self-report	Smoker: daily use
Fidler et al. 2007	5-year longitudinal study 2,665 students HABITS South London, England	NR	15–16 years Smokers Nonsmokers Quitters	 +2.3 +2.9 +3.0	NR	Measured	Saliva cotinine	Smoker: >6 cigarettes/ week; all nonsmokers at baseline
Pisinger and Jorgensen 2007	7-year longitudinal population study (Inter99) 1,343 adults Denmark	NR	30–60 years Smokers Nonsmokers Quitters	 +0.1 NR +1.4	 +0.3 NR +4.2	Measured	Cotinine	Smoking status not defined
Sneve and Jorde 2008	7-year longitudinal study 1994 and 2001 Tromsø Study 5,102 adults Norway	M = 53.7	>29 years Smokers Nonsmokers Quitters	 +0.7 +1.0 +2.0	NR	Measured	Self-report	Smoker: ≥1 cigarettes/day

Note: **CARDIA** = Coronary Artery Risk Development in Young Adults; **CO** = carbon monoxide; **HABITS** = Health and Behaviour in Teenagers Study; **kg** = kilogram; $\mathbf{m^2}$ = square meters; **M** = mean; **Md** = median; **NR** = not reported; **ppm** = parts per million.

Table 2.7 Studies assessing change in weight following smoking initiation

Study	Design/population	Average age (years)	Age groups	Mean body mass index change (kg/m²)	Mean kg difference	Measures: Height/ weight	Measures: Smoking status	Comments
Lissner et al. 1992	6-year Prospective Population Study of Women in Gothenburg (1968–1969) 1,291 women Sweden	NR	≥38 years Smokers Nonsmokers Initiators	 +0.5 +0.6 –0.4	NR	Measured	NR	Smoking status not defined; smokers quit ≥1 year classified as nonsmokers
Klesges et al. 1998b	7-year prospective study CARDIA study 5,115 adults	NR	18–30 years Smokers Nonsmokers Initiators	NR	 +5.7 +7.2 +5.1	Measured	Baseline: serum cotinine Follow-up: self-report	Smoker: ≥5 cigarettes/week
Stice and Martinez 2005	3-year prospective study 496 girls Southwestern United States	Md = 13	11–15 years Smokers Nonsmokers Initiators	 +0.2 +0.6 +0.2	 +1.4 +2.9 +1.8	Measured	Self-report	Smoker: 5 to 7 times/week and ≥1 cigarettes/day
Fidler et al. 2007	5-year longitudinal study 2,665 students HABITS South London, England	NR	15–16 years Nonsmokers Initiators	 +2.9 +2.3	NR	Measured	Saliva cotinine	Smoker: >6 cigarettes/week; all nonsmokers at baseline
Sneve and Jorde 2008	7-year longitudinal study 1994 and 2001 Tromsø Study 5,102 adults Norway	M = 53.7	>29 years Smokers Nonsmokers Initiators	 +0.7 +1.0 +0.1	NR	Measured	Self-report	Smoker: ≥1 cigarettes/day

Note: **CARDIA** = Coronary Artery Risk Development in Young Adults; **HABITS** = Health and Behaviour in Teenagers Study; **kg** = kilograms; **m²** = square meters; **M** = mean; **Md** = median; **NR** = not reported.

had no impact on body weight among Whites and only a small impact among African Americans (where weight gain was attenuated by 0.7 to 3.3 kg depending on the comparison group).

Among adolescent samples, initiation of smoking does not appear to have been associated with weight loss. Although some studies found a small attenuation of weight gain in adolescents (Stice and Martinez 2005; Fidler et al. 2007), one prospective study (Cooper et al. 2003) found an absolute weight gain for up to 3 years following initiation. The authors of this last study suggested that these smokers may have been relaxing their other weight-management strategies once they initiated smoking.

Summary

Overall, there is consistent evidence among youth that a substantial minority believe that smoking controls body weight. Moreover, using smoking as a weight-control strategy is not unusual in both youth and young adults. However, the evidence that concerns about body weight predicts either the onset or cessation of smoking is inconclusive. Overall, the results appear more consistently significant in females than in males, but this may in part be due to a greater proportion of females who are concerned about their body weight. Different definitions of concern about body weight and the heterogeneous populations studied may contribute to these conclusions. Finally, there is little evidence that smoking actually controls body weight in youth and young adults. There is evidence for a lowered weight among smokers than among nonsmokers after 35 years of age, but there is no relationship in smokers under 35 years of age. Some have speculated that (Klesges et al. 1998b) the weight-control effects of smoking appear to be very small and may take decades to accrue. The available evidence on the relationship between initiation of smoking and weight loss is mixed, but it suggests minimal, if any, effect of smoking initiation on weight loss in youth and young adults. However, youth and young adults who quit smoking also appear to gain weight. The evidence reviewed in this report, along with the reviews in prior reports, indicates a complicated relationship between initiation of smoking, continued smoking, and cessation over time. Interpretation of the evidence is further complicated by the concurrent secular trend of rising obesity.

Pulmonary Function and Respiratory Symptoms and Diseases

Introduction

This section addresses the consequences for respiratory health of active smoking during childhood, adolescence, and young adulthood. When the effects of active smoking were first investigated in adults, the early studies, in addition to examining the problem of lung cancer, assessed indicators of respiratory health. Questionnaires were used to measure the presence of symptoms, and spirometry, a test of ventilatory lung function, was used to measure damage to the lungs. These studies found strong associations between cigarette smoking and respiratory morbidity, including cough, production of phlegm, shortness of breath, and reduced lung function (U.S. Department of Health, Education, and Welfare [USDHEW] 1964). When these same methods were applied to adolescents and young adults who smoked, the findings were similar, indicating that respiratory morbidity was also increased in young smokers (Peters and Ferris 1967a,b; USDHHS 1994). In one of the first investigations of smoking in young adults, Peters and Ferris (1967b) surveyed male and female college students with a questionnaire on respiratory symptoms as well as a spirometry test; the smokers had more respiratory symptoms and lower lung function than did nonsmokers.

This section covers the principal respiratory consequences of active smoking in childhood, adolescence, and early adulthood: adverse effects on both the expected increase in lung function and its eventual decline as well as increased risk for chronic respiratory symptoms and disease. These topics were last covered specifically for children in the 1994 Surgeon General's report (USDHHS 1994). At that time, the evidence was characterized as limited and insufficient to support conclusions that active smoking was a cause of adverse respiratory consequences in this age group (USDHHS 1994). Subsequently, the body of relevant evidence enlarged substantially, particularly as follow-up has been extended in key cohort studies and results from more populations have become available. In addition, there is even more epidemiologic evidence on the effects of active smoking on adults (USDHHS 2004) and on the mechanisms by which smoking injures the respiratory tract (USDHHS 2010).

The 2004 Surgeon General's report (USDHHS 2004) comprehensively covered active smoking and respiratory health (Tables 2.1a and 2.1b). The evidence was found to be sufficient to infer that active smoking causes respiratory symptoms in childhood and adolescence. For this update of the 2004 report, the review on asthma is particularly comprehensive because evidence was limited at the time of the earlier review.

Methods for the Evidence Review

A systematic strategy was used to identify the evidence considered in this comprehensive literature review on the effects of smoking on lung function and on respiratory symptoms and asthma in children, adolescents, and young adults. In addition to reviewing prior Surgeon General's reports, a systematic search of the literature was conducted through PubMed with the following combinations of key words: cigarette smoking-adolescence-pulmonary function; adolescence-cigarette smoking-lung function growth; age of onset-cigarette smoking-lung function; smoking-allergy; adolescents-active cigarette smoking-allergy development; adolescents-active cigarette smoking; adolescence-cigarette smoking-asthma; adolescence-cigarette smoking-wheeze; and age of onset-cigarette smoking.

Lung Growth in Childhood, Adolescence, and Early Adulthood

Epidemiologic Evidence

Evidence reviewed in the 1994 and 2004 Surgeon General's reports (USDHHS 1994, 2004) demonstrated that active cigarette smoking during childhood and adolescence has the potential to slow the rate of lung growth and reduce the level of maximum lung function attained, thus increasing risk for development of chronic obstructive pulmonary disease (COPD) in adulthood. Results from six cohort studies of lung function in children and adolescents published from 1982 to 1992 were reviewed in the 1994 Surgeon General's report (USDHHS 1994), and two additional investigations were reviewed in the 2004 report (Sherrill et al. 1991; Gold et al. 1996). Two representative studies from the previous Surgeon General's reports are summarized here (see also Table 2.8) along with new evidence regarding (1) the effect of active smoking on growth of lung function and the maximum attained level of such function in females and males; (2) the effect of smoking on the early decline of lung function in adulthood; (3) the benefits of smoking cessation for limiting the early decline of lung function in young adults; and (4) the groups of children who may be particularly vulnerable to the effects of smoking on pulmonary function.

Evaluating smoking's effects on the growth of lung function in growing children and young adults requires an understanding of normative gender differences in growth patterns and in the age at which maximal lung function is attained. Attainment of maximum lung function follows the attainment of maximum height and occurs later for males than for females (Gold et al. 1996). Although females normally achieve peak lung function before 20 years of age, for males, peak height and subsequent peak lung function are reached several years later. Thus, while the effects of smoking on maximal obtained lung function can be studied in girls with follow-up to about 20 years of age, studies of males need to be extended to after 20 years of age to fully capture the effect of smoking on lung growth (Sherrill et al. 1992; Robbins et al. 1995). Because of the range of ages at which males and females reach the peak level of lung function, multiple repeated measures of lung function are needed to characterize whether smoking influences the age at which the peak lung function is reached and the length of the plateau phase after this peak. In the East Boston study, Tager and colleagues (1988) reported that asymptomatic nonsmoking male participants reached peak levels of forced expiratory volume in 1 second (FEV_1) at approximately 23–35 years of age, with a plateau phase that extended to age 45. Similarly, in their study of a Tucson, Arizona, population of young asymptomatic male and female nonsmokers, Sherrill and coworkers found that the age of reaching the peak FEV_1 level ranged between 17.4 and 25.9 years; the duration of the subsequent plateau phase was somewhat shorter, however, than for the East Boston cohort (Sherrill et al. 1992; Robbins et al. 1995). Both studies found that, on average, the plateau phase began earlier for females and lasted longer than for males. Because growth of lung function is not complete for males until after 20 years of age, this chapter considers reports of investigations that have tracked the effect of smoking in young adulthood as well as in adolescence.

As summarized in the 2004 Surgeon General's report, in a cohort study of 669 children and adolescents 5–19 years of age in East Boston, Massachusetts, Tager and colleagues (1985) found that among adolescents who started to smoke at 15 years of age and continued to smoke, the percentage of predicted FEV_1 level at 20 years of age was only 92% of the expected FEV_1 level for nonsmokers. Subsequently, Tager and associates (1988) analyzed follow-up data on 974 females and 913 males 5 years of age or older. For females, a linear increase in FEV_1 level

Table 2.8 Longitudinal studies on the association between smoking and maximum attained level of forced expiratory volume in one second (FEV_1), rates of growth, age of plateau in lung function, and age of onset of decline in lung function

Study	Population	Period of study/follow-up	Lung function outcome	Type of study/comments
Tager et al. 1985	669 children 5–19 years of age at baseline East Boston, Massachusetts	Baseline: 1974–1975 Follow-up: 8 annual examinations	Smoking led to decrease in rate of growth of FEV_1 ($p < 0.001$) and $FEF_{25–75}$	Longitudinal; 72.5% of original 411 families still under observation at conclusion of 8th annual examination
Tager et al. 1988	913 males and 974 females with at least one measurement of FEV_1 34% random sample of children 5–9 years of age and their families East Boston, Massachusetts	Baseline: 1974–1975 Follow-up: 10 annual examinations	**Males:** Maximal FEV_1 level same for smokers and nonsmokers but reached earlier for smokers Asymptomatic nonsmoking males demonstrated either a prolonged plateau phase or period of slow, continued FEV_1 growth from 23 to 35 years of age, followed by slow decline of -20–30 mL/year No plateau phase for smoking males; decline for smokers began earlier, in 1st part of 3rd decade at rate of 25–30 mL/year **Females:** Maximal FEV_1 level lower (2.9 vs. 3.1 L) and reached 1 year earlier for smokers compared with nonsmokers Female current smokers had more rapid rate of early decline than female nonsmokers	Longitudinal; approximately 70% of subjects still under observation at the 10th survey
Robbins et al. 1995	All male: 111 nonsmokers; 110 smokers Metal processing plant employees United States	Baseline: 1975 Follow-up: quarterly for up to 10 years Subjects selected if 5 or more observations at age 18–33 years with at least 1.5 years of follow-up Only tests up to 33 years of age included	As many as 40% of adult males 33 years of age or younger had significant slopes: either growth or decline in lung function, rather than a plateau A larger proportion of smokers had negative slopes (63%) than did nonsmokers (49%) ($p = 0.2$)	Longitudinal; working population of White men

Table 2.8 Continued

Study	Population	Period of study/follow-up	Lung function outcome	Type of study/comments
Gold et al. 1996	5,158 boys 4,902 girls Baseline: White children enrolled in the 1st–4th grades from 6 U.S. cities Study used data from children 10–18 years of age	Baseline: 1974–1979 Follow-up: annually through grade 12	Inverse association between amount smoked and level of FEV_1/FVC and FEF_{25-75} for boys and girls **Boys:** Rate of lung growth lower for smokers by 9 mL/year (95% CI, -6–24 mL/year) **Girls:** Rate of lung growth slower for smokers by 31 mL/year (95% CI, 16–46 mL/year) Maximal attained FEF_{25-75} lower for smokers than for nonsmokers (3.65 L/second vs. 3.80 L/second) At age 18, nonsmokers plateaued; smokers began early decline of FEV_1	Longitudinal; girls reached the maximal level of lung function between the ages of 16 and 18 years, a period when level of lung function was still increasing in boys
Twisk et al. 1998	78 males 89 females Mean age 13 years at baseline	Baseline: 1977 Follow-up: 6 follow-up measurements over 14 years, final measurement at age 27 years in 1991	Rate of growth of FVC and FEV_1 slower for smokers	Longitudinal; complete data for 14 years of follow-up available on 181 of 307 persons enrolled in 1977; 14 with asthma excluded from analyses
Doyle et al. 2003	60 consecutive extremely-low-birth-weight survivors	Baseline: 1977–1980 Follow-up at 20 years of age	Proportion with FEV_1/FVC <75% significantly higher in smokers than in nonsmokers (64% vs. 20%) Larger decrease in FEV_1/FVC ratio between the ages of 8 and 20 years in smokers (mean change -8.2%; 95% CI, -14.1 to 2.4)	Longitudinal; follow-up at age 20 years in 44 of the survivors (73%)
Wang et al. 2004	1,818 males 1,732 females 15–35 years of age The Netherlands	Baseline: Vlagtwedde, 1965–1967 Vlaardingen, 1969 Follow-up: every 3 years for 24 years	Inverse association between amount smoked and level of FEV_1/FVC and FEF_{25-75} for males and females For males, current and cumulative smoking predicted reduced maximal level of FEV_1 for males	Longitudinal

Note: **CI** = confidence interval; $\mathbf{FEF_{25-75}}$ = forced expiratory flow between 25% and 75% of forced vital capacity; **FVC** = forced vital capacity; **L** = liter; **mL** = milliliter.

was estimated to end 1 year earlier for current smokers (at 17 years of age, asymptomatic and symptomatic) than for nonsmokers without respiratory symptoms; the average maximal FEV_1 values were 2.9 liters (L) and 3.1 L, respectively. Female current smokers had a more rapid rate of early decline in FEV_1 than did nonsmoking females. For males, the estimated maximal FEV_1 was attained at an earlier age for current smokers (at 18 or 19 years of age) than for asymptomatic nonsmokers (20–34 years of age) or symptomatic nonsmokers (21 years of age). Also for males, smoothed estimates suggested similar maximum FEV_1 levels (4.1 L) for asymptomatic nonsmokers, symptomatic nonsmokers, and current smokers, but estimates suggested that the maximal FEV_1 level was slightly lower for smokers. In addition, while asymptomatic nonsmokers had a plateau phase over which lung function remained stable, smokers did not. Finally, in male smokers, FEV_1 began to decline almost 15 years earlier than in male nonsmokers.

In a cohort of 4,902 girls and 5,158 boys followed from 10 to 18 years of age and evaluated annually with spirometry, Gold and colleagues (1996) examined the effects of cigarette smoking on the level of lung function attained and the rate of growth in lung function (Figures 2.3 and 2.4). Among girls smoking five or more cigarettes per day, the rate of increase in FEV_1 level was slower by 31 milliliters (mL) per year (95% CI, 16–46 mL/year) than among girls who had never smoked. Although smoking five or more cigarettes per day slowed the rate of increase in FEV_1 level in boys, the magnitude of the effect (slower by 9 mL per year; 95% CI, -6.0 to 24.0 mL per year) was less than estimated in girls.

For both boys and girls, the amount smoked was inversely related to the level of FEV_1/FVC (forced vital capacity), as well as to the forced expiratory flow (FEF) [between 25% and 75% of the FVC (FEF_{25-75})] (Table 2.8). The girls reached their maximum level of lung function between the ages of 16 and 18 years, a period when lung function was still increasing in the boys. For girls at 18 years of age, maximally attained FEF_{25-75} was 3.80 L per second for girls who never smoked, compared with 3.65 L per second for those who smoked five or more cigarettes per day. At 17 and 18 years of age, FEV_1 levels began to decline among girls who smoked, but they plateaued among girls who did not smoke.

The Vlagtwedde/Vlaardingen study in The Netherlands followed 1,818 males and 1,732 females between the ages of 15 and 35 years at 3-year intervals (Wang et al. 2004). For females, FEV_1 reached a plateau by age 15, while in males, FEV_1 continued to rise until about age 20. However, on average, women had a longer plateau, such that their lung function began to decline at about the same age, 25 years, as in men. Both current and cumulative cigarette smoking were significant predictors of FEV_1 in males, with differences in the declines measuring -44 mL per pack per day for current smoking and -85 mL per 10 pack-years[1] for cumulative smoking.Athough no effect of smoking on maximum FEV_1 was found in females, gender differences in the effect of smoking were not significant, and the number of young female smokers was small. Smoking was associated with a lower level of FEV_1 in both males and females. The investigators observed that the magnitude of the smoking effect seen in this younger cohort was greater than that found in cohorts older than 35 years of age studied elsewhere.

In an analysis of data from 4,554 participants in the Vlagtwedde/Vlaardingen study who were 15–54 years of age at study onset (Xu et al. 1994), after 24 years of follow-up the data showed not only that sustained smoking was associated with the size of decline of FEV_1 in males and females but also that younger quitters (<45 years) benefited significantly more from smoking cessation than did older quitters (≥45 years).

In another Dutch study, quitting smoking was also associated with a smaller decline in FEV_1in a comparison with those who continued to smoke (Grol et al. 1999); the study included 199 people with allergic asthma who were recruited at 5–14 years of age and followed up at 22–32 and 32–42 years of age. The investigators described a "healthy smoker effect" (p. 1835) in this small cohort, however. Compared with those who had not taken up smoking, lung function was higher in childhood (presmoking) for those who took up smoking, and it remained higher into young adulthood. In the Amsterdam Growth and Health Study (Twisk et al. 1998) of 167 adolescents recruited at a mean age of 13 years, each with six repeated spirometry measurements during a 15-year period, smoking was associated with a decrease in FVC and FEV_1; the effects of smoking on maximum lung function and the impact of quitting smoking were not evaluated.

In the CARDIA longitudinal study of 5,115 African American and European American women and men 18–30 years of age, who were healthy at enrollment (Pletcher et al. 2006), the smoking of menthol cigarettes and nonmenthol cigarettes were associated with similar declines in lung function (excess decline of FEV_1: 84 mL; 95% CI, 32–137 mL for menthol cigarettes and 80 mL; 95% CI, 30–129 mL for nonmenthol cigarettes per 10-pack-year increase in exposure) relative to nonsmokers after adjustment for ethnicity and other factors. In addition, in a

[1]Pack-years = the number of years of smoking multiplied by the number of packs of cigarettes smoked per day.

Figure 2.3 Gender-specific effects of smoking on level of pulmonary function in youth 10–18 years of age

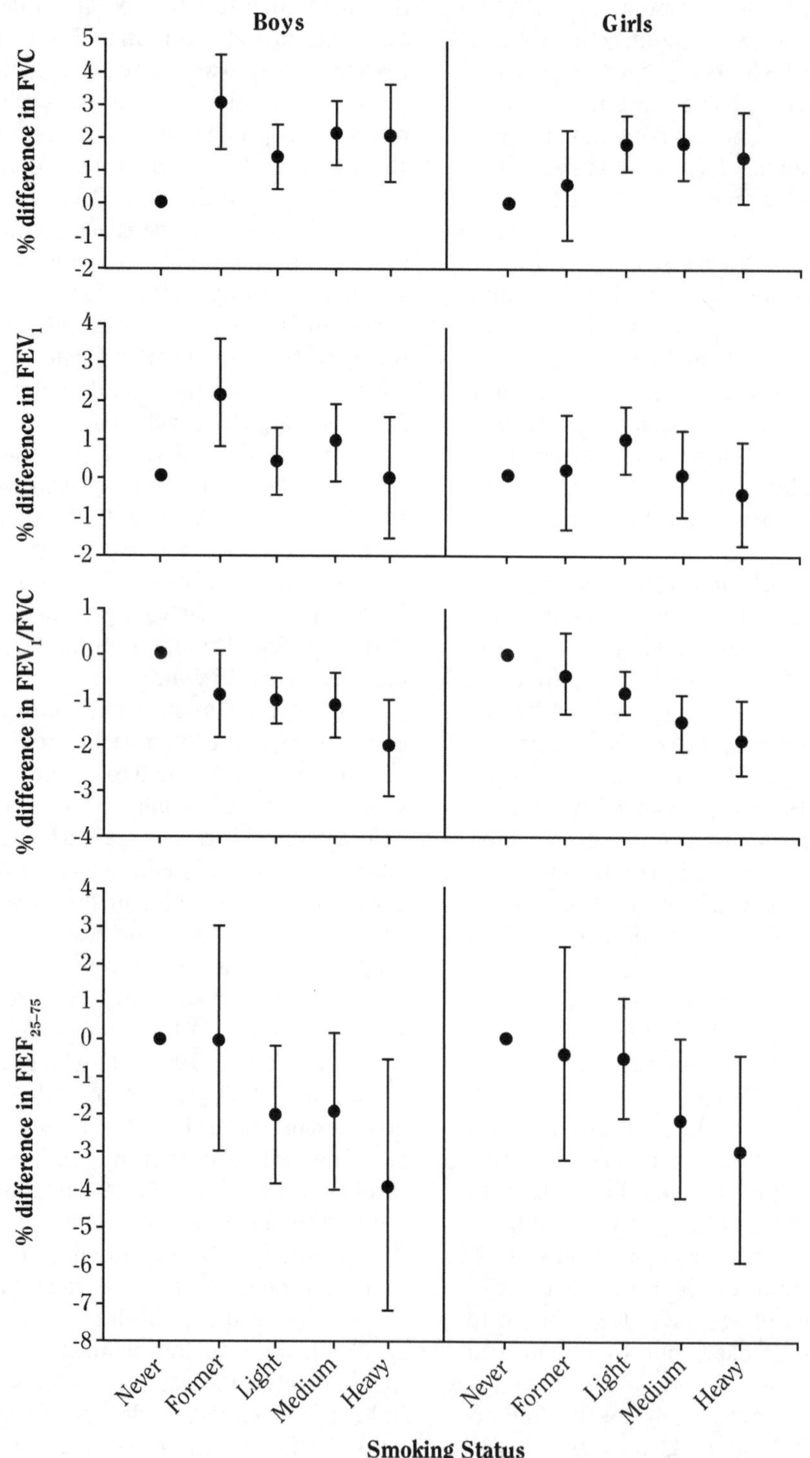

Source: Gold et al. 1996. Reprinted with permission from the Massachusetts Medical Society, ©1996.
Note: Percentage differences and 95% confidence intervals are plotted for groups of boys and girls with differing levels of smoking as compared with those of identical age and log height who had never smoked, with adjustment for age, log height at each age, residence, parental education, and maternal smoking status. "Never" denotes never having smoked; "Former," formerly having smoked; "Light," 1/2–4 cigarettes/day; "Medium," 5–14 cigarettes/day; and "Heavy," ≥15 cigarettes/day. **FEF_{25-75}** = forced expiratory flow between 25% and 75% of FVC; **FEV_1** = forced expiratory volume in 1 second; and **FVC** = forced vital capacity.

Figure 2.4 Mean rates of pulmonary function growth by age, gender, and category of smoking

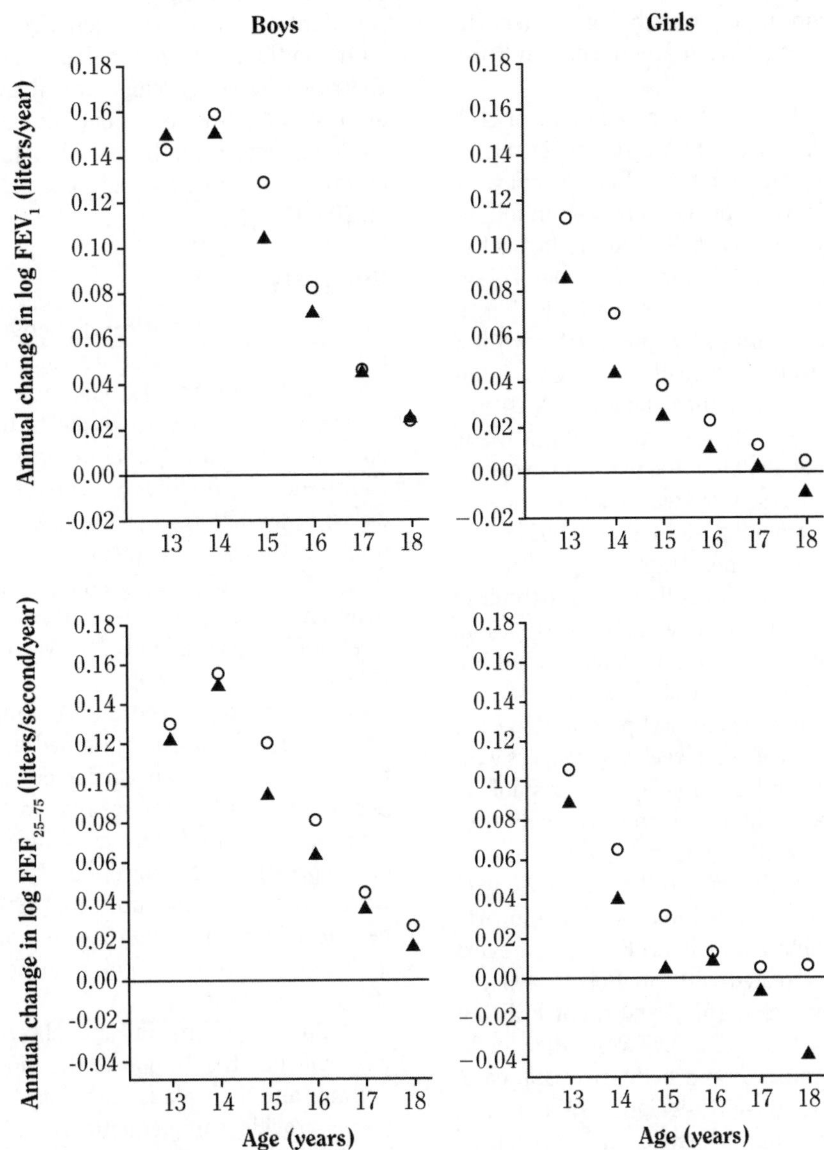

Source: Gold et al. 1996. Reprinted with permission from the Massachusetts Medical Society, ©1996.
Note: Mean rates of pulmonary-function growth according to age, gender, and category of smoking. The circles represent youth who had never smoked and the triangles those who smoked ≥5 cigarettes/day. There were fewer than 15 observations for smokers before the age of 13 years. The numbers of observations of FEV_1 in boys who smoked ≥5 cigarettes/day were 41 at age 13, 120 at age 14, 213 at age 15, 311 at age 16, 361 at age 17, and 151 at age 18. In girls who smoked ≥5 cigarettes/day, the numbers of observations of FEV_1 were 39 at age 13, 109 at age 14, 197 at age 15, 254 at age 16, 290 at age 17, and 90 at age 18. **FEF_{25-75}** = forced expiratory flow between 25% and 75% of the forced vital capacity; **FEV_1** = forced expiratory volume in 1 second.

comparison with smoking of nonmenthol cigarettes, the investigators found a significant increase in the risk of relapse among those who smoked menthol cigarettes. The results were similar among African Americans and European Americans.

More study is needed to define populations of children who are particularly susceptible to the effects of smoking on pulmonary function. In a Danish study, 85 asthmatic children 5–15 years of age were seen in follow-up 10 years after enrollment (Ulrik et al. 1995); active smoking was associated with a lower level of percentage of predicted FEV_1 for the 24 participants without allergic sensitization ("intrinsic asthma") but not for the 46 children with "extrinsic asthma." Rates of smoking were low in this small cohort, however. In the Scandinavian Asthma Genetic Study of asthmatic children, their siblings, and their parents (Bisgaard et al. 2007), the percentage of predicted FEV_1 level was inversely related to active smoking in comparison with not smoking (-3.5%; p = 0.0027).

Recent studies have demonstrated the relation of current cigarette smoking to difficult-to-treat asthma in young to middle-aged adults. In one such investigation, Chaudhuri and colleagues (2003) conducted a randomized, placebo-controlled, crossover study among participants 18–55 years of age by using oral prednisolone (40 milligrams daily) or a placebo for 2 weeks in smokers with asthma, former smokers with asthma, and never smokers with asthma. There was a significant improvement after prednisolone compared with a placebo in FEV_1, morning peak expiratory flow (PEF), and in the asthma control score for never smokers with asthma, but no improvement was seen in asthmatic smokers. Former smokers with asthma who were treated with prednisolone had a significant improvement in morning and night PEF but not in FEV_1. Tyc (2008) provides a review of other medically at-risk youth. Because of improving neonatal care, the population of very-low-birth-weight children has grown, but these children may be particularly susceptible to the effects of smoking, in part because of their early-life experience. These children frequently sustain lung injury as a consequence of the immaturity of their lungs at birth and the need for oxygen and mechanical ventilation. In an Australian study (Doyle 2000; Doyle et al. 2003), 60 consecutive extremely low-birth-weight (<1,000 grams [g]) children were followed longitudinally, with measurements of lung function obtained on 44 of them at a mean age of 20.2 years. The proportion with a clinically important reduction in the FEV_1/FVC ratio (to <75%) was significantly higher in smokers (64%) than in nonsmokers (20%). In addition, there was a larger decrease in the FEV_1/FVC ratio between the ages of 8 and 20 years in the smokers.

As detailed in the 2010 Surgeon General's report (USDHHS 2010), the past 15 years have seen a burgeoning of information on the genetics of pulmonary diseases, with additional understanding of genes that may modify the risk of early development of COPD, but researchers are just beginning to evaluate the genetic modification of smoking's effects on the growth of lung function, maximal attained lung function, and exercise tolerance (Harju et al. 2008).

Summary

Despite the logistical challenges of following cohorts from childhood into adolescence and then through young adulthood, a number of studies now provide a clear picture of how smoking adversely affects the growth and development of the lungs as children make the transition to adulthood. The findings are consistent for various studies of large populations. For example, in smokers, growth of lung function is slower during childhood and adolescence. In addition, there is a dose-response inverse relationship between smoking in adolescence and early adulthood and level of FEV_1/FVC and also between smoking and level of $FEF_{25–75}$.

For smokers, the growth of lung function ceases earlier, with lower maximal attained lung function, a briefer plateau phase, and an earlier decline in lung function. Active smoking may reduce maximal exercise tolerance in young adults. Smoking may reduce the beneficial effects of glucocorticoid therapy on lung function in young adults with asthma. Although quitting smoking at all ages can be beneficial, early quitting may be more valuable than later quitting because of its potential beneficial effect on the still-growing lung.

Both experimental and observational studies provide evidence that supports the biological basis of these findings and their plausibility. Studies of changes in lung tissue provide complementary evidence supporting the biological plausibility of the development of early airway changes in young adults who initiate smoking. Biological evidence presented in the 2010 Surgeon General's report shows that the inflammation, oxidative stress, and proteolytic responses to active cigarette smoking begin within minutes to hours after exposure. In lungs obtained at autopsy, Niewoehner and colleagues (1974) demonstrated pathologic changes in the peripheral airways of young cigarette smokers who were victims of sudden death occurring outside of the hospital. Compared with nonsmokers, the lungs of smokers showed significant increases in mural inflammatory cells, with changes consistent with respiratory bronchiolitis. In a Southern California study with 40 apparently healthy participants 20–49 years of age that included both smokers (of tobacco or marijuana) and nonsmokers, mucosal biopsies were evaluated for the presence of vascular hyperplasia, submucosal edema, inflammatory cell infiltrates, and goblet cell hyperplasia (Roth et al. 1998). Biopsies were positive for two of these criteria for 97% of smokers, and 72% were positive for three.

When the observational evidence is assessed against the accepted criteria for causality, there is strength and consistency among the studies, and the temporal relationship between smoking and its adverse effects (i.e., smoking precedes the effects) is well documented through cohort studies. In careful multivariate analyses, potential confounding factors have been considered and controlled, such as secondhand smoke exposure, reinforcing the specificity of the association. Injury has been demonstrated in the lungs of young smokers, and the mechanisms by which smoking injures the lung at any age have been well characterized and plausibility described.

Chronic Respiratory Symptoms and Diseases in Childhood

Overview

The 1994 and 2004 Surgeon General's reports, along with several other reports, have summarized the consistent evidence that the frequency of respiratory symptoms in children and adolescents is greater in current smokers than in nonsmokers or former smokers and that the duration and amount of smoking further increase the frequency of symptoms (USDHHS 1994, 2004; Arday et al. 1995; Larsson 1995; Lam et al. 1998; Withers et al. 1998). The 1994 Surgeon General's report concluded that "cigarette smoking during childhood and adolescence produces significant health problems among young people, including cough and phlegm production, an increased number and severity of respiratory illnesses, (and) decreased physical fitness" (USDHHS 1994, p. 41). The 2004 report further concluded that "the evidence is sufficient to infer a causal relationship between active smoking and respiratory symptoms in children and adolescents, including coughing, phlegm, wheezing, and dyspnea" (p. 27). This section includes representative evidence from the 2004 report and several additional investigations that have confirmed and extended the conclusions relevant to respiratory symptoms and disease in childhood and adolescence.

Wheeze and Asthma

Overview

As demonstrated in the 1994 and 2004 Surgeon General's reports (USDHHS 1994, 2004) and in more recent evidence presented below, studies have consistently documented that cigarette smoking among adolescents and young adults increases the incidence, persistence, and recurrence of wheeze symptoms in various populations. Although the 2004 Surgeon General's report concluded that "the evidence is inadequate to infer the presence or absence of a causal relationship between active smoking and physician-diagnosed asthma in childhood and adolescence," (p. 27) accumulating evidence suggests that in children who demonstrate early-life predisposition to wheeze before taking up smoking, starting to smoke cigarettes increases the risk of developing overt wheezing and variable airflow obstruction in adolescence, with symptoms persistent enough to be diagnosed as asthma (Yeatts et al. 2003). Cigarette smoking also increases the risk of apparent de novo development of wheeze in adolescence. Because many studies have only retrospective data on symptoms in early childhood, it often cannot be decided with certainty whether adolescents with de novo wheeze symptoms were without overt manifestations of a predisposition to disease—bronchial reactivity or allergic symptoms (wheeze, night cough, hay fever)—in earlier childhood before starting to smoke. Furthermore, whether the onset of wheezing in smokers constitutes asthma, as strictly defined, is not certain. The pathophysiological mechanism(s) by which smoking increases the risk of persistent wheeze may not be through an allergy-related pathway and, as data below suggest, may result in an asthmatic phenotype that is more refractory to glucocorticoids and other conventional therapy. Regardless, the data presented below strongly support the conclusion that without exposure to active smoking, a significantly higher proportion of adolescents and young adults with a predisposition to allergy and asthma would likely remain quiescent or with symptoms inadequately severe or recurrent to be called current or active asthma.

Asthma has been defined as

> 1. "a chronic inflammatory disease of the airways in which many cell types play a role—in particular, mast cells, eosinophils, and T-lymphocytes. In susceptible persons, the inflammation causes recurrent episodes of wheezing, breathlessness, chest tightness, and cough particularly at night and/or in the early morning. These symptoms are usually associated with widespread and variable airflow obstruction that is at least partly reversible either spontaneously or with treatment. The inflammation also causes an associated increase in airway responsiveness to a variety of stimuli" (USDHHS 2010, p. 439).

Although the debate continues as to whether asthma and chronic bronchitis/emphysema, or COPD, are distinct diseases (Bleecker 2004; Barnes 2006; Kraft 2006), the predisposition toward bronchial hyperresponsiveness is a characteristic phenotype shared by the two diseases (Bleecker 2004), with genetic as well as environmental origins that may also be shared. Both diseases manifest bronchial inflammation, but the cellular nature of the inflammation differs (USDHHS 2010). However, with exposure to active smoking superimposed on the predisposition to bronchial hyperreactivity and allergic inflammation, the nature of the bronchial inflammation in smokers may overlap more with that of COPD than with that of asthma and may result in more refractory asthmatic disease.

The evidence comes from diverse populations, with studies demonstrating the association of cigarette smoking with increased risk of wheeze in White and non-White and in non-U.S. or European teenagers.

Epidemiologic Evidence (Cross-Sectional and Case-Control Studies)

The evidence from cross-sectional studies is summarized in Table 2.9. In 1995 and again in 1998, children in 30 representative and randomly selected schools from throughout the Republic of Ireland took part in cross-sectional surveys of smoking behavior in secondary school children 13 and 14 years of age as part of the International Study of Asthma and Allergies in Childhood (ISAAC) survey (Manning et al. 2002). In 1995, 3,066 students, 634 (20.7%) of whom smoked cigarettes, completed a questionnaire, with significantly higher smoking rates among girls than among boys (23.3% vs. 17.6%). The investigators found that symptoms of bronchitis (cough and phlegm) were more commonly reported in active smokers than in nonsmokers, with an OR of 3.02 (95% CI, 2.34–3.88).

In a U.S. sample (1982–1989) of 26,504 high school seniors (Arday et al. 1995), regular cigarette smoking since ninth grade was associated with increased odds of at least one episode in the past 30 days of a coughing spell (OR = 2.1; 95% CI, 1.90–2.33), shortness of breath when not exercising (OR = 2.67; 95% CI, 2.38–2.99), and wheezing or gasping (OR = 2.58; 95% CI, 2.29–2.90), after adjusting for gender, use of marijuana and cocaine, parental education, and the year of the survey. A strong dose-response relationship was found between the amount smoked and most respiratory outcomes.

Between 1994 and 1995, Leung and colleagues (1997) studied 4,665 Hong Kong schoolchildren 13 and 14 years of age with the ISAAC protocol. In a comparison with epidemiologic data obtained in 1992, the prevalence of asthma and wheeze were found to have increased by 71% and 255%, respectively. In multiple logistic regression analyses, active smoking was associated with current wheeze (OR = 2.72; 95% CI, 1.38–2.89) and with severe wheeze that limited speech in the past 12 months (OR = 4.62; 95% CI, 2.43–8.75).

Also in Hong Kong, Lam and coworkers (1998) evaluated 6,304 mostly 12- to 15-year-old students from 172 classes in 61 schools and found a significant dose-response relationship between the amount smoked per week and risk for chronic cough (OR = 2.71; 95% CI, 1.95–4.69) for smoking more than six cigarettes per week versus never smoked, chronic phlegm (OR = 3.91; 95% CI, 2.77–5.53), wheeze in the past 3 months (OR = 2.91; 95% CI, 1.99–4.26), and use of asthma medicine in the past 2 days (OR = 3.07; 95% CI, 1.58–5.97). Ever having asthma, allergic rhinitis, or eczema diagnosed by a doctor was not significantly associated with smoking.

As part of the North Carolina School Asthma Survey of 128,568 seventh- and eighth-grade students primarily of African American, Native American, Mexican American, or White race/ethnicity who represented 99 of the state's 100 counties (Sotir et al. 2003), 33,534 children reported an episode of wheezing in the previous year. Of these, 17,358 reported experiencing at least one episode of wheezing triggered by a head cold (upper respiratory infection-triggered wheezing [URI-TW]). With adjustment for gender, race/ethnicity, SES, and urban/rural residence, there was a dose-response relationship between active smoking and URI-TW for those with a history of wheezing. In that same study (Sturm et al. 2004), relationships were found between smoking 2–10 cigarettes per day in the past 30 days and both active diagnosed asthma (OR = 1.24; 95% CI, 1.17–1.31) and wheezing in the past 12 months (OR = 1.27; 95% CI, 1.21–1.32) in comparisons with no smoking. Frequent wheezing not diagnosed as asthma was independently associated with current smoking (OR = 2.60; 95% CI, 2.43–2.79), after adjustment for gender, passive smoke, SES, allergies, and ethnicity (Yeatts et al. 2003).

Among 4,738 Chilean adolescents (mean age = 13 years) who responded to the ISAAC video questionnaire (Mallol et al. 2007), the prevalence of tobacco smoking in the last 12 months was 16.2%. Persistent smokers had higher rates of wheeze, wheeze with exercise, severe wheeze, and dry nocturnal cough than former smokers and nonsmokers. The investigators estimated that more than 27% of asthma symptoms in these adolescents were attributable to active smoking of tobacco.

Lewis and colleagues (1996) used data from two national British birth cohorts to compare the prevalence of wheezing illness (asthma and wheezy bronchitis) at 16 years of age between 1974 and 1986. The prevalence of asthma and/or wheezy bronchitis at 16 years of age

Table 2.9 Cross-sectional studies on the association of smoking with childhood cough, bronchitis symptoms, shortness of breath, wheeze, and asthma

Study	Population	Period of study	Findings	Definitions/comments
Arday et al. 1995	26,504 high school seniors United States	1982–1989	• 10.7% smoked • Regular smoking since 9th grade associated with: – Coughing spell in past 30 days: OR = 2.1; 95% CI, 1.90–2.33 – Shortness of breath when not exercising: OR = 2.67; 95% CI, 2.38–2.99 – Wheezing or gasping: OR = 2.58; 95% CI, 2.29–2.90	Dose-response relationship for most symptoms
Lewis et al. 1996	11,262 British children born in 1958, follow-up at age 16 United Kingdom 9,266 British children born in 1970, follow-up at age 16 United Kingdom	1974 and 1986	• Child smoking associated with increased odds of asthma and/or wheezy bronchitis (OR = 1.44; 95% CI, 1.14–1.82 for ≥40 cigarettes/week) • Smoking did not explain 70% increase in wheezy illnesses between 1974 and 1986	
Leung et al. 1997	4,665 schoolchildren 13–14 years of age Hong Kong	1994–1995	• Active smoking associated with: – Current wheeze: OR = 2.72; 95% CI, 1.38–2.89 – Severe wheeze limiting speech: OR = 4.62; 95% CI, 2.43–8.75	ISAAC protocol
Lam et al. 1998	6,304 students 12–15 years of age Hong Kong	1994	• Smoking >6 cigarettes/week associated with: – Chronic cough: OR = 2.71; 95% CI, 1.95–4.69 – Chronic phlegm: OR = 3.91; 95% CI, 2.77–5.53 – Wheeze in the past 3 months: OR = 2.91; 95% CI, 1.99–4.26 – Use of asthma medicine in the past 2 days: OR = 3.07; 95% CI, 1.58–5.97 • Ever asthma, allergic rhinitis, and eczema not associated significantly with smoking	Dose-response relationship for most symptoms
Manning et al. 2002	3,066 students 13–14 years of age Republic of Ireland	1995	• More girls smoked than boys (23.3% vs. 17.6%) • Active smoking associated with increased bronchitis symptoms: OR = 3.02; 95% CI, 2.34–3.88	ISAAC protocol

Table 2.9 Continued

Study	Population	Period of study	Findings	Definitions/comments
Sotir et al. 2003; Yeatts et al. 2003; Sturm et al. 2004	128,568 7th- and 8th-grade students primarily White, African American, Native American, or Mexican American North Carolina	1999–2000	• Smoking 1–10 cigarettes/day in past 30 days associated with wheeze triggered by upper respiratory infection (prevalence OR = 1.26; 95% CI, 1.9–1.34) • Smoking 2–10 cigarettes/day in past 30 days associated with: – Active diagnosed asthma (OR = 1.24; 95% CI, 1.17–1.31) – Wheezing in past 12 months (OR = 1.27; 95% CI, 1.21–1.32) • Current smoking associated with frequent wheezing not diagnosed as asthma (OR = 2.60; 95% CI, 2.43–2.79)	Dose-response relationship Dose-response relationship
Annesi-Maesano et al. 2004	14,578 adolescents France	1993–1994	• Active smoking >1 cigarette/day associated with increased odds of wheezing, current asthma, lifetime asthma, current rhinoconjunctivitis, lifetime hay fever, and current eczema after controlling for age, gender, geographic region, familial allergy, and passive smoking	ISAAC questionnaire
Zimlichman et al. 2004	38,047 young adult military conscripts Israel	Mid-1980s to 1990s	• Rates of smoking among asthmatic conscripts increased from 20–22% in the mid-1980s to an estimated 30% in the late 1990s	Cross-sectional study
Mallol et al. 2007	4,738 adolescents Mean age = 13 years Chile		• Persistent smokers had higher rates of wheeze, wheeze with exercise, severe wheeze, and dry nocturnal cough	ISAAC protocol

Note: **CI** = confidence interval; **ISAAC** = International Study of Asthma and Allergies in Childhood; **OR** = odds ratio.

increased from 3.8% to 6.5% during this 12-year period. Smoking by these young people was associated with increased odds of asthma and/or wheezy bronchitis, with an OR of 1.44 (95% CI, 1.14–1.82) associated with smoking at levels of 40 or more cigarettes per week (versus nonsmoking), but changes in smoking behavior did not explain the increase in asthma rates between 1974 and 1986.

In a sample of 14,578 French adolescents, active smoking of more than one cigarette per day (9.3% prevalence in this population) was associated with increased odds of wheezing, current asthma, lifetime asthma, current rhinoconjunctivitis, lifetime hay fever, and current eczema after controlling for age, gender, geographic region, familial allergy, and exposure to secondhand smoke (Annesi-Maesano et al. 2004).

A number of studies indicate that having asthma is often not a deterrent to active cigarette smoking (Tyc 2008). For example, in a study of 38,047 young adult military conscripts in Israel, whose mean age was 18.6 years at baseline (Zimlichman et al. 2004), the prevalence of smoking among those with asthma increased from 20% to 22% in the mid-1980s to an estimated 30% in the late 1990s. And in a French family-based, case-control study of 200 adult asthmatic cases, 265 nonasthmatic controls, and 586 relatives of asthmatics (147 with asthma), the investigators found that in cases with asthma, active smoking was associated with greater severity of that disorder (Siroux et al. 2000). In that study, having asthma in childhood was not associated with a reduced uptake of smoking, but persons with asthma who smoked quit more often than did controls. Adult-onset asthma was unrelated to ever having been a smoker, although as mentioned earlier in this chapter, retrospective data based on recall regarding childhood asthma may be limited. Finally among asthmatics, current smokers, compared with never smokers and former smokers, had more asthma symptoms, more frequent asthma attacks (OR = 2.39; 95% CI, 1.06–5.36), and higher asthma severity scores (Siroux et al. 2000).

Epidemiologic Evidence (Prospective Cohort Studies)

The relation of starting to smoke to the prevalence of asthma, wheezy bronchitis, or wheezing was studied in 18,559 people born March 3–9, 1958, in England, Scotland, or Wales, of whom 5,801 contributed information at 7, 11, 16, 23, and 33 years of age (Table 2.10; Strachan et al. 1996). Potential bias due to attrition was evaluated by using information obtained on 14,571 of the original 18,559 participants. Active cigarette smoking was associated with increased incidence of asthma or wheezing illness at 17–33 years of age (OR = 4.42; 95% CI, 3.31–5.92) in adjusted models. Moreover, relapse after prolonged remission of childhood wheezing was more common among current smokers than among nonsmokers. Further follow-up was reported at 42–45 years of age (Butland and Strachan 2007). The proportions of incident "asthma" and incident "wheeze without asthma" sensitivity associated with cigarette smoking, adjusted for gender and atopy (heightened sensitivity to allergic reactions), were estimated to be 13% (95% CI, 0–26) and 34% (95% CI, 27–40), respectively.

Also in the United Kingdom, in a case-control study of persons 39–45 years of age who were part of an Aberdeen, Scotland, community cohort of 2,056 asymptomatic children (originally studied in 1964) (Bodner et al. 1998), current smoking was associated with an increased risk of adult-onset wheeze (relative risk [RR] = 2.01; 95% CI, 1.08–3.74) in analyses adjusting for atopy, family history of atopy, education, and gender.

Withers and colleagues (1998), who followed a cohort of 2,289 children from Southampton, England, who were initially studied at 6–8 years of age, administered a repeat questionnaire when the participants were 14–16 years of age. Regular smoking by these adolescents (at least one cigarette per week during the past 12 months) was associated with current cough (OR = 1.71; 95% CI, 1.21–2.43), onset of cough between surveys (OR = 4.35; 95% CI, 1.12–3.25), persistent wheeze in boys (OR = 4.35; 95% CI = 1.20–3.25), and a new report of wheezing (OR = 1.65; 95% CI, 1.14–2.39). Regular smoking was not, however, associated with physician-diagnosed asthma.

In Germany, the incidence of asthma during adolescence was studied in a cohort study from two cities: Dresden and Munich (Genuneit et al. 2006). As part of ISAAC, the study population of 2,936 persons was studied in 1995–1996 at 9–11 years of age and then in 2002–2003 at 16–18 years of age. The adjusted incidence rate ratio (IRR) for incident wheeze for active smokers compared with nonsmokers was 2.30 (95% CI, 1.88–2.82). The adjusted IRRs were slightly higher for incident wheeze without having a cold (IRR = 2.76; 95% CI, 1.99–3.84) and for diagnosed asthma (IRR = 2.56; 95% CI, 1.55–4.21). Dose-dependent associations were demonstrated for all three problems when stratified by both duration of active smoking (in years) and intensity of smoking. In this same study, an observed inverse relationship between reduced physical activity and new onset of wheeze was explained by differences in active smoking (Vogelberg et al. 2007).

In Norway (Tollefsen et al. 2007), 2,300 adolescents were evaluated for wheeze and asthma at 13–15 years of age and in follow-up at 17–19 years of age. For those with no respiratory symptoms at baseline, current smoking predicted development of wheeze at follow-up, which was

Table 2.10 Longitudinal studies on the association of smoking with cough, bronchitis symptoms, shortness of breath, wheeze, and asthma in cohorts followed since childhood

Study	Population	Period of study	Findings	Definitions/comments
Strachan et al. 1996; Butland and Strachan 2007	18,550 people born March 3–9, 1958, in England, Scotland, or Wales 5,801 contributed information at 7, 11, 16, 23, and 33 years of age	1958–1991	• Active cigarette smoking was associated with incidence of asthma or wheezing illness from 17 to 33 years of age (OR = 4.42; 95% CI, 3.31–5.92) • Relapse after prolonged remission of childhood wheezing was more common among current smokers • At 42–45 years of age, the proportions of incident asthma and incident wheeze without asthma associated with cigarette smoking were estimated to be 13% (95% CI, 0–26) and 34% (95% CI, 27–40)	Attrition bias was evaluated using information on 14,571 subjects
Bodner et al. 1998	Study of subjects aged 39–45 years derived from an Aberdeen cohort of 2,056 asymptomatic children originally studied in 1964 117 cases with adult-onset wheeze 277 controls	1964–1995	• Current smoking was associated with increased risk of adult-onset wheeze (RR = 2.01; 95% CI, 1.08-3.74)	Case-control study nested in longitudinal follow-up study
Withers et al. 1998	2,289 children Baseline: 6–8 years of age Follow-up: 14–16 years of age Southampton, United Kingdom	Baseline: 1978–1980 Follow-up: 1987–1995	• Regular smoking of at least 1 cigarette/week during past 12 months was associated with: – Current cough (OR = 1.71; 95% CI, 1.21–2.43) – Onset of cough between surveys (OR = 4.35; 95% CI, 1.12–3.35) – Persistent wheeze in boys (OR = 4.35; 95% CI = 1.20–3.25) – New report of wheezing (OR = 1.65; 95% CI, 1.14–2.39) • Regular smoking was not associated with physician-diagnosed asthma	Dose-response relationships observed
Sears et al. 2003	1,037 children Birth cohort followed repeatedly from 9–26 years of age New Zealand	Baseline: 1972–1973	• Smoking at 21 years of age predicted persistence of wheeze from the study onset (adjusted OR = 1.84; 95% CI, 1.13–3.00). • Relapse of wheezing at 26 years of age after being wheeze free was significantly associated with smoking at 21 years of age in a univariate model (OR = 1.84; 95% CI, 1.11–3.04), but multivariate model controlling for bronchial hyperresponsiveness was not significant for relapse	Case-control study nested in longitudinal follow-up study

Table 2.10 Continued

Study	Population	Period of study	Findings	Definitions/comments
Genuneit et al. 2006; Vogelberg et al. 2007	2,936 children Dresden and Munich, Germany	Baseline: 1995–1996 Follow-up: 2002–2003	• For those with no respiratory symptoms at baseline, current smoking predicted development of wheeze at follow-up (OR = 2.8; 95% CI, 1.6–4.9 for girls; OR = 1.8; 95% CI, 0.9–3.9 for boys)	
Gilliland et al. 2006	2,609 children with no lifetime history of asthma or wheezing Baseline: 4th to 7th grades California	1993–2003	• Smoking 300 or more cigarettes/year was associated with increased risk of new-onset asthma (RR = 3.9; 95% CI, 1.7–8.5)	
Goksör et al. 2006	89 of 101 children hospitalized before the age of 2 years with wheezing Follow-up until 17–20 years of age	Baseline: 1984–1985	• Active smoking was associated with increased odds of current asthma (OR = 3.2; 95% CI, 1.2–8.4)	
Tollefsen et al. 2007	2,300 adolescents Baseline: 13–15 years of age Follow-up: 17–19 years of age	Baseline: 1995–1997 Follow-up: 2000–2001	• For those with no respiratory symptoms at baseline, current smoking predicted development of wheeze at follow-up, which was significant for girls (OR = 2.8; 95% CI, 1.6–4.9 for girls; OR = 1.8; 95% CI, 0.9–3.9 for boys)	

Note: **CI** = confidence interval; **OR** = odds ratio; **RR** = relative risk.

significant for girls (girls: OR = 2.8; 95% CI, 1.6–4.9; boys: OR = 1.8; 95% CI, 0.9–3.9).

In New Zealand, a cohort of 1,037 children born in 1972–1973 in the city of Dunedin (Sears et al. 2003) was followed repeatedly from 9 to 26 years of age. Study members with persistent or relapsing wheezing had higher prevalence rates of sensitivity to house dust, mites, and cat allergen, higher airway hyperresponsiveness, and lower lung-function measurements ($p < 0.001$ for all associations). The 613 participants with complete outcome data were found to be generally representative of the population. In univariate and multivariate models, smoking at 21 years of age predicted persistence of wheeze from the study's onset (adjusted OR = 1.84; 95% CI, 1.13–3.00). Relapse of wheezing at 26 years of age after being wheeze free was significantly associated with smoking at 21 years of age in a univariate model (OR = 1.84; 95% CI, 1.11–3.04), but the relationship with smoking was not significant in a multivariate model. In this case, however, smoking may have led to relapse of wheeze by increasing an intermediate phenotype, bronchial hyperresponsiveness (BHR). Therefore, adjustment for BHR in multivariate models may have led to the reduction of the estimate for the effects of smoking because BHR was in the causal pathway as a mediator rather than a confounder.

A Swedish study followed 89 of 101 children hospitalized with wheezing before the age of 2 years up to the ages of 17–20 years (Goksör et al. 2006). The study compared their risk of asthma with that of 401 age-matched, randomly selected controls; current asthma was increased in active smokers (OR = 3.2; 95% CI, 1.2–8.4) in the final multivariate model. This finding is notable because passive smoking, which was associated with active smoking, was included in the model.

Finally, in California, a prospective cohort study was conducted among 2,609 children with no lifetime history of asthma or wheezing who were recruited from fourth- and seventh-grade classrooms and followed annually in 12 Southern California communities (Gilliland et al. 2006). Smoking 300 or more cigarettes per year was associated with a RR for new-onset asthma of 3.9 (95% CI, 1.7–8.5) when no smoking was the referent. The increased risk of asthma associated with this level of smoking was greater in children with no history of allergies, but allergic sensitization was not evaluated (Table 2.10).

Summary

Since the 1994 and 2004 Surgeon General's reports on smoking and health, additional investigations have been published that confirm and extend the conclusions of those reports in demonstrating the association between starting to smoke and increased risk of the respiratory symptoms of cough, phlegm, and wheeze, as well as reduced exercise tolerance among children and young adults (Tables 2.9 and 2.10). Moreover, additional longitudinal data support the association of smoking with recurrence or persistence of childhood wheeze that preceded the start of smoking and with new-onset wheeze in adolescence and young adulthood.

Accumulating longitudinal evidence suggests that smoking contributes to incident asthma in susceptible children, adolescents, and young adults by increasing the already greater risk of recurrent, persistent, or new-onset persistent wheeze in children with underlying airway hyperreactivity and atopy. Although children who have allergic sensitization and chronic allergic airway inflammation may be particularly susceptible to the effects of smoking, the data do not consistently support the hypothesis that smoking increases atopy or allergic sensitization. Even so, the additional airway inflammation caused by smoking in atopic adolescents and young adults may be more resistant to conventional therapy for asthma. In addition, adolescents with atopy may be less likely to become smokers.

Cardiovascular Effects of Tobacco Use

Introduction

Atherosclerotic cardiovascular disease is a chronic process with origins in youth, and smoking is strongly and causally associated with cardiovascular morbidity and mortality (USDHHS 2004). The adverse cardiovascular effects of smoking begin with the fetus, which is exposed to components of tobacco smoke from active smoking by the mother or from her exposure to secondhand smoke. Permanent effects of smoking on the cardiovascular system have been found in children, adolescents, and young adults who smoke, and these effects are antecedents of incident cardiovascular disease in later adulthood. This section reviews findings of studies directed at the consequences of tobacco exposure for youth, extending from exposures in utero through young adulthood. The range of outcomes covered is diverse, and this section will review direct assessment of atherosclerosis, noninvasive imaging of subclinical atherosclerosis, assessment of endothelial cell function, and observations of physiological effects. The section also addresses the effects of smoking as they act in combination with other risk factors for cardiovascular disease.

The processes that lead to cardiovascular morbidity and mortality may be initiated by exposures during pregnancy, which act on the fetus, and by subsequent exposures across childhood and young adulthood (Napoli et al. 2006; McGill et al. 2008). Studies illustrating the fetal and childhood origins of cardiovascular diseases are considered here, as is the role of smoking across the life course.

Conclusions of Prior Surgeon General's Reports

Cardiovascular diseases have been considered in the Surgeon General's reports since the landmark report of 1964 (USDHEW 1964). Many of the subsequent reports have direct relevance to the present report, and cardiovascular diseases specifically were the topic of the 1983 report (USDHHS 1983). The 1994 report addressed the consequences of tobacco use in young people; effects on premature atherosclerosis, lipid profiles, physical fitness, left ventricular mass, and heart rate were described in that report (USDHHS 1994). At that time, however, the number of studies conducted in youth was still small.

The 2004 Surgeon General's report on the health consequences of smoking concluded that smoking does "adversely affect the homeostatic balance in the cardiovascular system, thus explaining the well-documented relationship between smoking and both subclinical and clinical manifestations of atherosclerosis" (USDHHS 2004, p. 371). "Research during the past decade has produced further evidence that tobacco smoking is causally related to all of the major clinical cardiovascular diseases" (USDHHS 2004, p. 397). The 2006 Surgeon General's report on involuntary exposure to secondhand smoke concluded that such exposure was associated with "increased risks of coronary heart disease morbidity and mortality among both men and women" and that accumulated evidence was suggestive but not conclusive in indicating a causal relationship between this exposure and both stroke and subclinical atherosclerosis (USDHHS 2006, p. 15).

The 2010 report of the Surgeon General reviewed the biological basis of the association between tobacco use and cardiovascular disease. Its findings are particularly relevant for the present report in documenting that smoking is linked to the early phases of cardiovascular injury, even before disease is evident. Additional conclusions not covered in the current report include (1) "cigarette smoking leads to endothelial injury and dysfunction in both coronary and peripheral arteries. There is consistent evidence that oxidizing chemicals and nicotine are responsible for endothelial dysfunction"; (2) "cigarette smoking produces a chronic inflammatory state"; (3) "cigarette smoking produces insulin resistance"; and (4) "cigarette smoking produces an atherogenic lipid profile, primarily due to an increase in triglycerides and a decrease in high-density lipoprotein cholesterol" (USDHHS 2010, pp. 10–11).

Atherosclerosis underlies much of adult cardiovascular morbidity and mortality, leading to the clinical consequences of angina pectoris and myocardial infarction, sudden death, stroke, abdominal aortic aneurysm, and symptomatic atherosclerotic peripheral vascular disease. The next section reviews the evidence on smoking and atherosclerosis in children, adolescents, and young adults, giving emphasis to findings since the 1994 report. The section addresses the links between the initiation of atherosclerosis and endothelial injury in youth and risk for disease during adulthood.

Mechanisms of Tobacco-Induced Vascular Injury in Children

Mechanisms of vascular injury related to tobacco exposure as reviewed in the 2004 and 2010 Surgeon General's reports include direct endothelial injury, induction of a prothrombotic state, promotion of inflammation, and the promotion of oxidative stress (USDHHS 2004, 2010). Some studies have addressed these mechanisms directly in fetuses, infants, children, and young adults, including the consequences of exposure to secondhand smoke and of active smoking.

Comparisons of schoolchildren exposed to tobacco smoke with an unexposed group showed increased oxidative stress and lower antioxidant levels among those who were exposed (Kosecik et al. 2005; Zalata et al. 2007). In a Korean study comparing 19 adolescent smokers with a mean duration of tobacco use of about 3 years with 19 nonsmoking adolescents, evidence of oxidative stress was obtained in assessments of multiple markers, as the researchers found lower selenium glutathione peroxidase activity, lower glutathione reductase, lower extracellular superoxide dismutase activity, and higher serum thiobarbituric acid-reactive substances (Kim et al. 2003). Thus, the available, but limited, evidence suggests that active smoking by youth is linked to oxidative stress.

There are as yet few studies on inflammatory markers and thrombosis in infants and children. In one population-based study, the authors did not show a relationship between the concentration of C-reactive protein and exposure to secondhand smoke (Cook et al. 2000). Thrombotic events in childhood are rare, and no studies have found a relationship between the risk for such events and use of tobacco or exposure to secondhand smoke. In adults, studies have linked both active tobacco use and exposure to secondhand smoke to prothrombotic effects and laboratory markers of endothelial injury (USDHHS 2004, 2006).

Methods for the Evidence Review

The evidence considered for this review was identified by a series of PubMed searches merging the terms "tobacco" or "smoking" with relevant subjects covered here, including atherosclerosis, endothelial dysfunction, vascular injury, and lipids. These searches were then further refined, adding the terms "children," "fetus," or "pregnancy" to the search string. Results were cross-checked with reference lists from prior relevant reports of the Surgeon General, including the 1994, 2004, 2006, and 2010 reports. Reference lists from review articles on atherosclerosis and tobacco-related morbidity in children were also used for cross-checking (e.g., McGill et al. 2008). Finally, references from articles identified in the search strategy described above and published since 2004 were reviewed to identify any articles not found with this approach.

Vascular Injury in the Fetus

Review of Evidence

Evidence of vascular injury in the fetus that was associated with tobacco use was first identified in studies of human umbilical artery specimens and other placental vascular structures (Asmussen and Kjeldsen 1975; Bylock et al. 1979; Asmussen 1982a,b; Pittilo 1990). Structural abnormalities were most commonly found in the endothelium of many different vascular structures; evidence of attempts at vascular repair was also found. Clinical support for the relevance of these experimental findings is suggested by an ultrasound study of resistance to blood flow in the umbilical artery—a measure of fetal well-being. Ultrasound studies performed at 20–24 weeks of gestation showed that fetuses exposed to tobacco smoke had evidence of increased vascular resistance (Kalinka et al. 2005). In utero exposure to tobacco smoke may also be associated with subclinical atherosclerosis. A recent study comparing neonates with and without intrauterine exposure to components of tobacco smoke from maternal smoking showed increased thickness of the aortic wall in those exposed to tobacco smoke (Gunes et al. 2007).

Animal studies confirm the vascular injury after exposure to secondhand smoke. A controlled study of fetal exposure of apolipoprotein E (Apo E) knockout mice—a genetic model of accelerated atherosclerosis—to secondhand smoke showed increased atherosclerosis in the exposed mice as adults, and the increase in atherosclerosis was linked to mitochondrial injury and oxidative stress (Yang et al. 2004). Specifically, exposed mice had increased formation of atherosclerotic lesions, damage to mitochondrial DNA, increased antioxidant activity, and increased oxidant load compared with controls. A similar controlled study in Apo E knockout mice showed that the pups of those exposed to tobacco smoke while pregnant had atherosclerotic changes after birth, but the unexposed did not (Gairola et al. 2001). Earlier animal studies of fetal exposure to secondhand smoke have shown abnormal vascular reactivity and endothelial dysfunction after birth. They also showed increased size of myocardial infarction after exposure to smoke, beginning in utero and extending up to 12 weeks after birth, when the infarction occurred (Zhu et al. 1997; Hutchison 1998).

In the past few years, there has been intense interest in markers of oxidative stress in relation to exposure to tobacco smoke. Several case-control studies have demonstrated oxidant stress in fetuses and infants exposed to tobacco smoke both in utero and postnatally (Aycicek et al. 2005; Noakes et al. 2007; Aycicek and Ipek 2008); these studies have included measurements of the oxidative stress index, total antioxidant capacity, lipid peroxidation, and F_2-isoprostane. Measurement of F_2-isoprostane was positively correlated with maternal cotinine levels in one study (Noakes et al. 2007).

Low Birth Weight

The association between maternal use of tobacco and low birth weight is well documented (USDHHS 2001, 2004). Low birth weight, in turn, is associated with future cardiovascular mortality, particularly in women. This association may reflect, among other risk factors, contributions of maternal smoking and of exposure to secondhand smoke during pregnancy (Davey Smith et al. 2007; Newnham and Ross 2009).

Summary

There is evidence that exposure of the fetus to tobacco smoke causes vascular injury; oxidative stress may be one of the mechanisms responsible for this effect. Because these exposures generally produce early grades of atherosclerosis that are reversible, this evidence does not imply that fetal exposure to components of tobacco smoke alone causes adult cardiovascular disease. Nonetheless, there is substantial evidence suggesting that early exposure to smoke is important in the context of lifelong exposure to cardiovascular risk factors in contemporary society. This evidence includes the following: (1) there is an association between low birth weight and future cardiovascular mortality (maternal use of tobacco lowers birth weight); (2) relationships between passive exposure to smoke and vascular injury are likely to continue postnatally with further exposure to passive smoke from parents who smoke; and (3) children of parents who smoke are more likely to smoke in the future. Thus, vascular injury of the fetus may be the first insult in a sequence of continuous exposures to risk factors.

Physiological Effects of Smoking

The relationship of left ventricular mass, an independent predictor of cardiovascular morbidity and mortality, to active use of tobacco has been assessed in several studies in young adults. In the CARDIA study, among young adults 23–35 years of age, smokers had greater left ventricular mass by 3 to 8 g, indexed to body size and depending on race/gender group (Gidding et al. 1995). In older individuals (mean age = 62 years) with left ventricular mass assessed by magnetic resonance imaging, in a comparison of active smokers with nonsmokers and after adjustment for body size, the smokers had greater mass (by 7.7 g) (Heckbert et al. 2006). In two studies of the relationship of left ventricular mass to hypertension, the recording of ambulatory blood pressure identified a relationship of higher left ventricular mass to smoking. This relationship was not found, however, when single daytime blood pressures were used to compare smokers with nonsmokers (Verdecchia et al. 1995; Majahalme et al. 1996). This difference in findings may be explained by the capturing through ambulatory monitoring of transient increases in blood pressure that are associated with smoking. A study of U.S. Army recruits involving measurement of left ventricular mass before and after an exercise intervention did not find an association between this measurement and smoking at baseline, but it showed a larger increase in left ventricular mass in those soldiers using tobacco during the intervention (Payne et al. 2006, 2007). Complementary findings were obtained in an animal study comparing smoke-exposed and unexposed rats with exposures of 2 and 6 months' duration. Increased left ventricular mass and greater left atrial size were found in the smoke-exposed group, and duration of exposure (2 vs.6 months) did not influence the magnitude of the effect (Castardeli et al. 2008).

A number of other physiological effects of smoking related to myocardial energetics, oxygen delivery, and exercise have been studied in children and young adults. In the CARDIA study, young adult smokers had increased resting heart rate, and those who were female had greater cardiac wall stress, both consistent with increased resting consumption of myocardial oxygen. In addition, young adult smokers had poorer endurance and lower peak heart rate with exercise compared with nonsmokers (Sidney et al. 1993). These findings could reflect an effect of smoking and/or a lower level of fitness among smokers. Finally, children exposed to secondhand smoke have abnormal concentrations of 2,3-diphosphoglycerate, an effect suggesting stressed delivery of oxygen to the tissues and increased risk for developing premature coronary heart disease (Moskowitz et al. 1990).

Atherosclerosis

Postmortem Studies

Three major studies have assessed atherosclerosis in young people at autopsy with the intent of characterizing the relationship of the presence and degree of atherosclerosis to cardiovascular risk factors, including smoking (Table 2.11). Descriptions of these studies follow.

In the Pathobiological Determinants of Atherosclerosis in Youth (PDAY) study, specimens of coronary arteries and the abdominal aorta were obtained from a group of almost 3,000 15- to 34-year-olds (Whites and Blacks) who had died of external causes (accidents, homicides, suicides) (McGill et al. 2008). The prevalence and severity of atherosclerosis were measured directly and quantified by the American Heart Association (AHA) grading system. Grades I and II reflect early lesions, including fatty streaks, that are considered reversible. Grade III reflects intermediate lesions, and grades IV and V reflect advanced lesions and plaque. Each 5-year increment in age from 15 to 34 years was associated with increased coverage of surface areas by atherosclerosis of the coronary arteries and aorta and also with increasing grade of atherosclerosis; 15- to 19-year-olds had mostly grade I and II lesions, while advanced lesions associated with cardiovascular risk factors were found in some 25- to 34-year-olds. In females, these changes occurred 5–10 years later than in males; thus, the vasculature of a 25- to 34-year-old woman resembled that of a 20-year-old man (McGill et al. 2008). Risk factors for atherosclerosis were measured in the postmortem period; tobacco use was defined by an elevated serum thiocyanate level (≥90 micromoles/L).

In the PDAY study, tobacco use was positively associated with the prevalence of the early lesions of

Table 2.11 Relationship between tobacco use and atherosclerosis or subclinical atherosclerosis

Study	Design/population	Atherosclerosis measure	Measure of tobacco use	Findings	Comments
Berenson et al. 1998	Autopsy study of a biracial cohort of children and young adults dying accidentally who previously participated in the Bogalusa Heart Study Includes 204 autopsies for which tobacco use history was available in 49 (15 smokers, 34 nonsmokers)	Pathologic study of the coronary arteries and the aorta; lesions classified according to American Heart Association (AHA) grading system	History of tobacco use from a questionnaire administered at 8 years of age and older	• Mean percentage of the abdominal aorta involved in fibrous plaque lesions (AHA grade 3–5) was higher in smokers (1.22% ± 0.62% vs. 0.12% ± 0.07%, p = 0.02) • Mean percentage of the coronary arteries involved with fatty streaks (AHA grade 1–2) was greater in smokers (8.27% ± 3.43% vs. 2.89% ± 0.83%, p = 0.04) • Increased number of risk factors increased the amount of atherosclerosis	Smoking is related to atherosclerosis in the coronary arteries and the abdominal aorta in those with a history of smoking
Kádár et al. 1999	Autopsy study of adolescents and young adults (aged 15–34 years) dying accidentally (n = 214) Cross-sectional analysis of the relationship of postmortem risk factors to measures of atherosclerosis Conducted in 5 countries: Cuba, Germany, Hungary, Mexico, and Sri Lanka	Pathologic study of the left anterior descending coronary artery, ascending aorta, and abdominal aorta; lesions classified according to AHA grading system	Data available on smoking status from 68 subjects in Hungary only (33 smokers)	• Prevalence of AHA grade 3–5 lesions higher in smokers than in nonsmokers (46% vs. 14%, p <0.02) • No effect seen in the coronary arteries	Smoking is related to advanced lesions in the abdominal aorta of young smokers
Zieske et al. 1999, 2005	As above, additional analyses of the proximal left anterior descending coronary artery (n = 1,128)	As above, except left anterior descending coronary artery studied	As above, adjustment for other cardiovascular risk factors	• Smoking was strongly associated with AHA grade lesion (p <0.0002) • Smoking was more likely to have any AHA lesion (OR = 1.34 [1.06–1.70]) • Smoking was associated with increased prevalence of grade 5 lesions (the most advanced) among those with grade 4 or 5 lesions (OR = 9.61 [2.34–39.57]) • In individuals with no other risk factors, grade 5 lesions were only present in smokers	Smoking increases atherosclerosis in the left anterior descending coronary artery and is associated with rapid progression of lesions to advanced AHA grade

Table 2.11 Continued

Study	Design/population	Atherosclerosis measure	Measure of tobacco use	Findings	Comments
McGill et al. 2000, 2008; McMahan et al. 2005, 2006	Autopsy study of adolescents and young adults (aged 15–34 years) dying accidentally (n = 1,110) Cross-sectional analysis of the relationship of postmortem risk factors to measures of atherosclerosis Conducted at multiple centers across the United States, cohort is biracial	Pathologic study of the right coronary artery and abdominal aorta; lesions classified according to AHA grading system	Postmortem thiocyanate level; tobacco use defined as level ≥90 micromole/L Other cardiovascular risk factors assessed as well	• In the abdominal aorta, fatty streaks are more extensive than in nonsmokers (p <0.05) • In the abdominal aorta, >20 years of age, smokers have more extensive involvement with raised lesions (p <0.03 [20–24 years] to <00001 [>25 years]) • No statistically significant effects in the right coronary artery • Increased number of risk factors increased the amount of atherosclerosis	Smoking is directly related to measurable atherosclerosis in the abdominal aorta and particularly to more advanced lesions, and it increases atherosclerosis in the presence of other risk factors
Raitakari et al. 2003	Relationship of carotid artery intima-media thickness measured 21 years after serial cardiovascular risk evaluation in youth 3–18 years of age (n = 2,229) Conducted in Finland	Carotid artery intima-media thickness	Smoking status defined as smoking at least weekly by history	• In a multivariable model including age, gender, body mass index, low-density lipoprotein cholesterol, and systolic blood pressure, adolescent smoking significantly predicted future carotid artery intima-media thickness (p <0.02) • Multiple risk factors increased carotid artery intima-media thickness	Smoking in youth predicts future carotid artery intima-media thickness
Loria et al. 2007	Relationship of coronary calcium measured by computed tomography (CT) scan at 33–45 years of age to risk factors measured beginning at 18–30 years of age and at intervals in between (n = 3,043) Conducted in a biracial cohort in the United States at 4 sites	Presence of coronary calcium	Smoking status defined by history, cigarettes smoked/day calculated	• In a multivariable model including all cardiovascular risk factors, tobacco use at 18–30 years of age predicted future coronary calcium after adjustment for smoking status at the time of the CT scan (OR = 1.5 [1.3–1.7] per 10 cigarettes smoked/day)	Smoking as a young adult is associated with the presence of coronary calcium 15 years later in a dose-dependent fashion

Note: **L** = liter; **OR** = odds ratio.

atherosclerosis (grades I and II) in the abdominal aorta in 15- to 19-year-olds and with all AHA grades of atherosclerosis in 30- to 34-year-olds (McGill et al. 2000b; McMahan et al. 2005, 2006). The abdominal aorta was more severely affected than were the coronary arteries by tobacco use. A case-control study of a subset of the PDAY cohort, comparing 50 smokers with 50 nonsmokers (randomly selected White men 25–34 years of age), found that smokers were twice as likely to have advanced lesions as were nonsmokers and that smokers had more advanced lesions than intermediate lesions (Zieske et al. 1999). A more complete analysis of atherosclerosis of the left anterior descending coronary artery found increased atherosclerosis in this vessel in smokers compared with nonsmokers, and it also found that smoking contributed to more rapid progression of lesions to advanced AHA grades (Zieske et al. 2005).

In the 1980s, the World Health Organization and the World Heart Federation initiated an international study in five countries in North America, Asia, and Europe that was comparable in design to the PDAY study (Kádár et al. 1999). Although this international study included 214 individuals, only 68, all from Hungary, provided information on tobacco use; a strong relationship between abdominal aortic atherosclerosis and smoking was found, with smokers more likely than nonsmokers to have advanced lesions in the descending aorta (46% vs. 14%, p <0.02).

From 1972 to 1992, the Bogalusa Heart Study collected population-based data on cardiovascular risk factors from a cohort of White and Black children living in Bogalusa, Louisiana (Berenson et al. 1998), at enrollment. Data on these risk factors, obtained at multiple follow-ups for most participants, was available beginning at 5 years of age and up to 38 years of age for some of the original participants. Smoking status was unknown for those without an assessment in late adolescence or young adulthood. Berenson and colleagues (1998) reported on an assessment at autopsy of atherosclerosis in original participants who died accidentally and for whom information on smoking was available; this sample included 49 of the 204 deceased participants, with 15 known smokers and 34 known nonsmokers. Compared with nonsmokers, involvement of the aortic surface area with fibrous plaque was greater in smokers (1.22% vs. 0.12%, p = 0.02), and fatty streaks in the surface area of the coronary arteries were more common in smokers (8.3% vs. 2.9%, p = 0.04).

The PDAY and Bogalusa studies also demonstrated that the presence of multiple cardiovascular risk factors accelerates atherosclerosis (Berenson et al. 1998; McMahan et al. 2005). With regard to smoking, the combination of tobacco use and other causal risk factors is associated with acceleration of progression from the earliest stages of atherosclerosis to more advanced lesions. Figure 2.5 shows the relationship of age and the number of cardio-

Figure 2.5 Relationship of age and the number of cardiovascular risk factors with severity of atherosclerosis in the right coronary artery in males in the Pathobiological Determinants of Atherosclerosis in Youth study

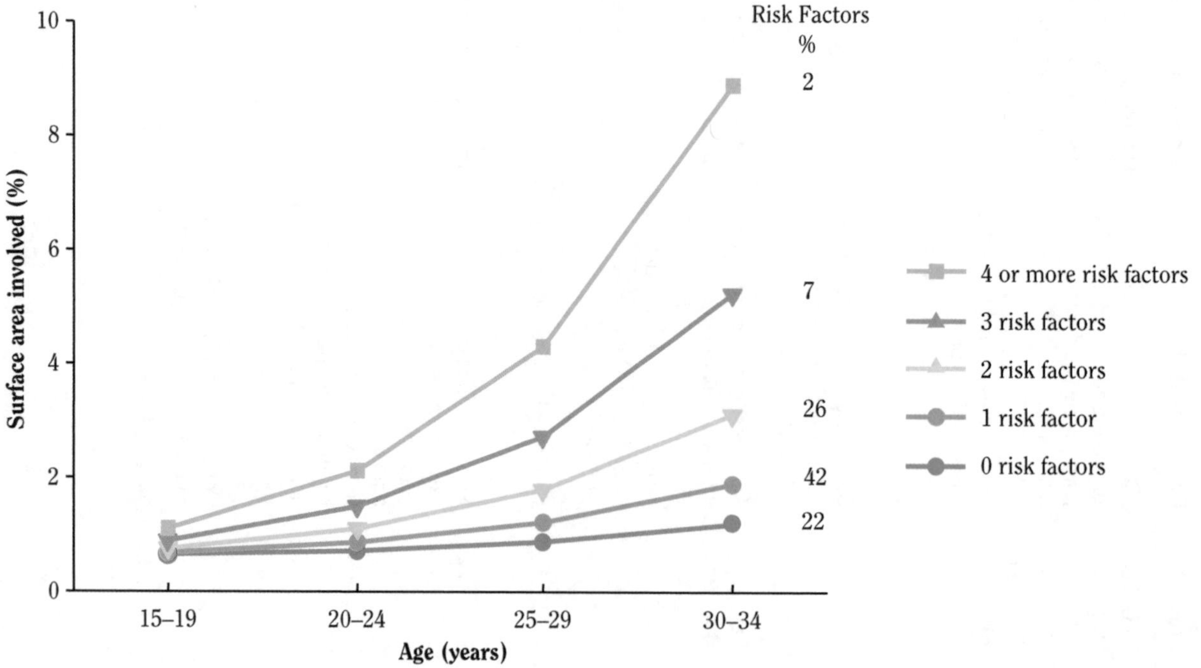

vascular risk factors to the severity of atherosclerosis in the right coronary artery among males in the PDAY study. The column on the right provides the percentage of the cohort with each level of risk. The slope of the rate of development of atherosclerosis is increased with the addition of each risk factor. Thus, each additional risk factor (including smoking) increases the amount of atherosclerosis at any given age; accordingly, a smoker with other risk factors will experience further acceleration of the damage from those risk factors. These changes in slope are consistent with independent actions of the major risk factors, including smoking, in promoting the development of atherosclerosis.

Summary

There are now three studies on the associations of atherosclerosis measured at postmortem examination in children and young adults who had had cardiovascular risk factors; two were based on postmortem measurement of risk factors, while the Bogalusa Heart Study used antemortem assessments of risk factors obtained at varying intervals before accidental death. These cohorts included Whites and Blacks in the United States and individuals from Hungary. Because atherosclerosis results from a chronic process and cardiovascular risk factors are known to track (or to be stable predictors over time) for individuals, the atherosclerotic lesions measured in these studies can be reasonably assumed to result from chronic exposure to tobacco smoke (McGill et al. 2008). Tobacco use and addiction to nicotine typically begin in adolescence, leading to the potential for lengthy exposure to tobacco smoke across the life course, and tobacco smoking has long been causally associated with atherosclerosis in adults (USDHHS 2004). The three studies show that smoking in adolescence and young adulthood contributes to the atherosclerotic process that manifests as incident cardiovascular disease in adults and that the association of smoking with atherosclerosis, so readily identified in adulthood, is also evident shortly after youth start to smoke. Over time, cigarette smoking is associated with a rapid acceleration of the atherosclerosis grade in both the abdominal aorta and left anterior descending coronary artery.

The evidence that tobacco use contributes to atherosclerosis, even in young adults, is striking. The early appearance of atherosclerosis suggests that vascular injury is initiated in association with the onset of smoking, with rapid acceleration to more advanced atherosclerotic lesions by 25 to 34 years of age. These preclinical observations in young adults parallel findings in older individuals with manifest disease. For example, the attributable risk of mortality from abdominal aortic aneurysm for tobacco use is more than 80%, and the association of smoking in youth with abdominal atherosclerosis at autopsy is strong. The findings of the PDAY study show that smoking advances the grade/severity of atherosclerosis when controlling for other risk factors (Zieske et al. 2005).

In these studies, smoking was associated at every age with atherosclerosis, and the results were consistent across all studies, particularly for abdominal aortic atherosclerosis. The mechanisms by which smoking causes atherosclerosis have been studied extensively, and multiple significant pathways for vascular injury have been documented (USDHHS 2010). Therefore, the relationship of tobacco use to abdominal aortic atherosclerosis can be considered causal. Only the PDAY study had sufficient statistical power to assess the relationship of tobacco use to atherosclerosis of the coronary arteries; these data show an association and are highly suggestive of a causal relationship as well.

Subclinical Atherosclerosis

Epidemiologic Studies

Measurements of coronary artery calcium by computed tomography (CT) scan and of the thickness of the carotid artery intima-media by ultrasound are established techniques to detect subclinical atherosclerotic disease that predict future clinical risk (Simon et al. 2007). Tobacco use in adults is associated with changes in these measures that are indicative of adverse effects from smoking (USDHHS 2004, 2010). The CARDIA and Cardiovascular Risk in Young Finns studies collected data on cardiovascular risk factors beginning in young adulthood and childhood, respectively. These data were examined as predictors of the extent of subclinical atherosclerosis on follow-up in young adulthood. Analyses in these two studies have compared profiles of risk factors measured at young ages with risk-factor profiles measured in adulthood with regard to the strength of association with the preclinical markers. These analyses provide an indication of the importance of early exposure to smoking for subsequent risk of disease (Table 2.11).

The CARDIA study measured cardiovascular risk factors at 18–30 years of age (baseline) in a cohort made up of African Americans and Whites, both male and female, and assessed coronary calcium by CT scanning 15 years later. The multivariate adjusted OR for the presence of coronary artery calcium at follow-up was 1.5 (95% CI, 1.3–1.7) per 10 cigarettes per day smoked at 18–30 years of age; this risk estimate was greater than the estimate for coronary calcium associated with cigarette use at the time of the scan (Loria et al. 2007). A second analysis of this data set used a risk score derived from the PDAY study (Gidding et al. 2006); this score incorporated the relative contributions of all risk factors, including tobacco use, into a single value. Gidding and associates (2006) found that the score was strongly associated with the presence of coronary calcium in CARDIA participants. The association was similar in strength to that obtained in the PDAY study data set, thereby showing comparability between effects estimated in the autopsy data and in data from young adults. In addition to documenting the relationship of risk factors measured early in life to subsequent risk for atherosclerosis, this analysis highlights the contribution of multiple risk factors and how each additional risk factor, such as initiating tobacco use, adds to the subsequent risk of coronary artery calcium (Gidding et al. 2006).

In the Cardiovascular Risk in Young Finns Study, which measured risk factors in adolescence and in young adulthood (24–39 years of age) (Raitakari et al. 2003; Juonala et al. 2005), thickness of the carotid intima-media was strongly associated with smoking status in adolescence, and this relationship persisted after adjustment for smoking status at the time of the ultrasound study to determine thickness. Elasticity of the carotid arteries—an index of carotid artery compliance measured in young adulthood—was more abnormal in individuals who had cardiovascular risk factors and smoked than in those with a similar cardiovascular risk factor profile who did not smoke.

Finally, in the Bogalusa Heart Study, determinants of carotid artery intima-media thickness were assessed among participants at 27–43 years of age (Bhuiyan et al. 2006). Active smoking was significantly and positively associated with this index of atherosclerosis.

Summary

In adults, a causal relationship of tobacco use with subclinical atherosclerosis has been established (USDHHS 2004). Both the CARDIA and Cardiovascular Risk in Young Finns studies have shown further that tobacco use at a younger age is associated with subclinical atherosclerosis later in life and that the response is time and dose dependent. The effects of tobacco use and other cardiovascular risk factors measured at a young age on subclinical atherosclerosis are stronger than the effect of tobacco use and other risk factors assessed at the same time as the measurement of subclinical atherosclerosis. This temporal profile of risk suggests that the effect of tobacco smoking begins at a young age and is cumulative. The effect of smoking is enhanced in individuals with more than one risk factor. The occurrence of demonstrable effects of smoking in young adults is consistent with the chronic nature of atherosclerosis and the current understanding of the underlying processes that produce this disease (USDHHS 2010) as well as with the observation that active smoking causes rapid acceleration of atherosclerosis grade because advanced lesions are thicker than early lesions and are more likely to incorporate calcium into plaques (McGill et al. 2008). Thus, tobacco use at a young age can be considered to be a cause of future subclinical atherosclerosis (USDHHS 2004, 2010).

Endothelial Dysfunction

Review of Evidence

Ultrasound assessment of vascular reactivity in the brachial artery provided the first documented evidence of a direct effect of tobacco exposure on the cardiovascular system in youth (Celermajer et al. 1993, 1996). Vascular reactivity, as assessed by this mechanism, is considered an index of endothelial health; that is, nitric-oxide-dependent vasodilation can occur. Adverse effects of both active and passive smoking have been demonstrated on measures of endothelial function. Endothelial dysfunction has been demonstrated in young current smokers with a dose-response relationship and also among young persons exposed to secondhand smoke (Table 2.12; Celermajer et al. 1993, 1996).

The initial observations discussed above in adolescents and young adults have been confirmed in other populations (Table 2.12). For example, young Chinese workers chronically exposed to tobacco smoke in the workplace had impaired endothelial function (Woo et al. 2000). A larger British study on the impact of low birth weight on endothelial function confirmed the association of active smoking with endothelial dysfunction at 20–28 years of age (Leeson et al. 2001). A comparison of smoking and nonsmoking young Chinese adults living in Hong Kong or the United States showed impaired flow-mediated dilation in smokers compared with nonsmokers in both locations (Thomas et al. 2008). In a study of young Australian adults exposed to secondhand smoke who were categorized as nonsmokers (no passive or active smoking), passive smokers, or former passive smokers, the former passive smokers had better endothelial function than did those with persistent current passive exposure (Raitakari et al. 1999). A study in young Japanese adults (mean age = 32 years) demonstrated endothelial dysfunction in response to exposure to active or passive smoking; both endothelial dysfunction and exposure to smoke were correlated with plasma levels of 8-isoprostane, a measure of oxidative stress (Kato et al. 2006). In Australia, pregnant women who smoked were found to have impaired flow-mediated dilation, and the degree of impairment

Table 2.12 Endothelial dysfunction in young smokers

Study	Design/population	Vascular function assessment technique	Findings	Comments
Celermajer et al. 1993	Case-control study with assessment of chronic exposure to tobacco (pack-years[a]) 200 English men and women 16–56 years of age with 80 nonsmokers, 40 former smokers, and 80 current smokers All subjects normotensive, cholesterol <240 mg/dl, nondiabetic, and no family history of cardiovascular disease Smoking status also assessed by cotinine levels	Brachial artery ultrasound and Doppler assessment of brachial artery flow at rest, after ischemia, and after sublingual glyceryl trinitrate	• Flow-mediated dilation (%): nonsmokers 10.0 ± 3.3, smokers 4.0 ± 3.9, former smokers 5.1 ± 3.8; p <0.0001 smokers vs. nonsmokers, p <0.07 smokers vs. former smokers • Flow-mediated dilation was dose dependent in a multivariate regression model including age, gender, cholesterol, cotinine, and pack-years; only pack-years significant, partial regression coefficient -0.33, p <0.05; cotinine nonsignificant • No difference among groups in response to glyceryl trinitrate	First demonstration of effect of tobacco use on endothelial function; tightly controlled study with large sample size; demonstrates both dose-dependent effects of tobacco exposure and residual chronic effects in former smokers
Celermajer et al. 1996	Case-control study comparing nonsmokers, those exposed to smoke passively (>1 hour/day for 3 years), and current smokers All subjects normotensive, cholesterol <240 mg/dl, nondiabetic, and no family history of cardiovascular disease 78 healthy men and women, 15–30 years of age, 26 nonsmokers, 26 smoke exposed, and 26 current smokers	Brachial artery ultrasound and Doppler assessment of brachial artery flow at rest, after ischemia, and after sublingual glyceral trinitrate	• Flow-mediated dilation (%): nonsmokers 8.2 ± 3.1, smokers 4.4 ± 3.1, smoke exposed 3.1 ± 2.7; p <0.0001 for smokers and smoke-exposed vs. nonsmokers • In those passively exposed, flow-mediated dilation was inversely related to smoke exposure (hours/day/year); r = 0.67, p <0.0001 • No difference among groups in response to glyceral trinitrate	First demonstration of effect of passive smoke exposure on endothelial function; effect similar to that of chronic exposure and also dose dependent
Leeson et al. 1997	Cross-sectional study of 333 British schoolchildren aged 9–11 years to assess the relationship of cardiovascular risk factors including low birth weight to endothelial dysfunction	Brachial artery ultrasound and Doppler assessment of brachial artery flow at rest and after ischemia Smoke exposure assessed by salivary cotinine	• No relationship between smoke-exposed and nonexposed children	Negative study; smoke exposure measure is cotinine as opposed to self-report of exposure history

Table 2.12 Continued

Study	Design/population	Vascular function assessment technique	Findings	Comments
Raitakari et al. 1999	Case-control study conducted in Australia comparing nonsmokers (passive or active), those exposed to smoke passively (>1 hour/day for 2 years), and former passive smokers All subjects normotensive, cholesterol <240 mg/dl, nondiabetic, and no family history of cardiovascular disease 60 healthy men and women, 15–39 years of age, 20 nonsmokers, 20 smoke exposed, and 20 former smoke exposed (average of 5 years since last exposure)	Brachial artery ultrasound and Doppler assessment of brachial artery flow at rest, after ischemia, and after sublingual glyceral trinitrate	• Flow-mediated dilation (%): nonsmokers 8.9 ± 3.2, passive smokers 2.3 ± 2.1, former smoke exposed 5.1 ± 4.1; $p < 0.01$ vs. nonsmokers for both groups, $p = 0.01$ for passive smokers vs. former passive smokers (ANOVA, Scheffe) • Flow-mediated dilation (%): subgroup comparison of those smoke exposed previously: >2 years 5.8 ± 4.0 vs. <2 years 1.2 ± 1.7; $p < 0.05$ • No difference among groups in response to glyceral trinitrate	Extends findings of Celermajer studies (1993, 1996) showing dose-dependent effect of passive smoke exposure; results are generally consistent for magnitude of effect across all 3 studies done by the same team
Woo et al. 2000	Case-control study comparing nonsmokers and those exposed to smoke passively in a casino Matched for other cardiovascular risk factors 20 men and women in each group, mean age 36.6 years Macao	Brachial artery ultrasound and Doppler assessment of brachial artery flow at rest, after ischemia, and after sublingual glyceral trinitrate	• Flow-mediated dilation (%): nonsmokers 10.6 ± 2.3, passive smokers 6.6 ± 3.4; $p < 0.0001$ • Passive smoking was the strongest predictor of flow-mediated dilation in multivariate analysis; beta = -0.59, $p < 0.0001$ for passive smoke exposure • No difference among groups in response to glyceral trinitrate	Confirmation of effect of passive smoke exposure on endothelial dysfunction in a work environment
Leeson et al. 2001	Cross-sectional study conducted in England to assess the relationship of cardiovascular risk factors, including low birth weight, to endothelial dysfunction 315 men and women 20–28 years of age	Brachial artery ultrasound and Doppler assessment of brachial artery flow at rest and after ischemia	• Smokers had lower flow-mediated dilation than did nonsmokers (mean difference 0.29); 95% CI, 0.07–0.51, $p = 0.009$ • There was an inverse relation between flow-mediated dilation and number of smoking pack-years; coefficient -0.4 pack-years, 95% CI, -0.004 to -0.07, $p = 0.03$	Findings consistent with prior studies
Levent et al. 2004	Case-control study of smoking and nonsmoking adolescents 30 in each group, mean age of 16 years, cohort 90% male Duration of smoking 3.4 years, higher passive smoke exposure in the smoking group Turkey	Aortic stiffness assessed by calculation of aortic strain, pressure strain, and normalized pressure strain elastic modulus using transthoracic echocardiography and peripheral blood pressure measurement	• Aortic strain: 0.262 ± 0.056 vs. 0.198 ± 0.042 (nonsmokers vs. smokers); $p < 0.0001$ • Elastic modulus: 152 ± 18 vs. 215 ± 17 (nonsmokers vs. smokers); $p < 0.0001$ • Elastic modulus normalized to aortic size: 2.2 ± 0.7 vs. 2.8 ± 0.4 (nonsmokers vs. smokers); $p < 0.001$	Findings suggest tobacco use increases stiffness in large conduit arteries

Table 2.12 Continued

Study	Design/population	Vascular function assessment technique	Findings	Comments
Kato et al. 2006	Case-control study comparing smoking and nonsmoking healthy males; nonsmokers were then exposed to tobacco smoke for 30 minutes, 15 in each group, mean age 32 years, matched for cardiovascular risk factors Japan	Brachial artery ultrasound and Doppler assessment of brachial artery flow at rest, after ischemia, and after sublingual glyceral trinitrate Plasma 8-isoprostane measured at baseline and 30 minutes after smoke exposure	• Flow-mediated dilation (%): nonsmokers 10.9 ± 3.1, smokers 4.3 ± 1.2; $p < 0.0001$ • Flow-mediated dilation after passive smoke exposure (%): nonsmokers 5.0 ± 1.9 (decreased), smokers 3.9 ± 1.0 (unchanged); $p < 0.003$ for decrease in nonsmokers • Plasma 8-isoprostane measured at baseline pg/mL: nonsmokers 26.9 ± 5.4, smokers 41.5 ± 5.8; $p < 0.001$ • Plasma 8-isoprostane measured 30 minutes after baseline pg/mL: nonsmokers 37.8 ± 9.6 (increased), smokers 39.2 ± 9.0 (unchanged); $p < 0.001$ for increase in nonsmokers • Flow-mediated dilation was negatively correlated with plasma 8-isoprostane; $r = -0.69$, $p < 0.001$	Confirms relationship of tobacco use and passive smoke exposure to flow-mediated dilation; correlates change in flow-mediated dilation with a measure of oxidative stress
Kallio et al. 2007	Longitudinal cohort study of boys and girls randomized to a low cholesterol/low saturated fat diet 402 children with cotinine measures from 8 to 11 years of age and stratified by cotinine concentration: nondetectable (n = 29), low (n = 134), top decile (n = 39) Finland	Brachial artery ultrasound and Doppler assessment of brachial artery flow at rest, after ischemia, and after sublingual glyceral trinitrate Annual cotinine measurements from 8 to 11 years of age (90% compliance in the cohort for the measurement) Controlled for cardiovascular risk factors and diet treatment group assignment	• Flow-mediated dilation decreased as cotinine level increased across the three groups: nondetectable 9.10 ± 3.88, low 8.57 ± 3.78, top decile 7.73 ± 3.85; $p < 0.02$ for trend ($p = 0.008$ for trend if analysis restricted to those with 4 cotinine measures)	Chronic passive smoke exposure contributes to endothelial dysfunction in children

Table 2.12 Continued

Study	Design/population	Vascular function assessment technique	Findings	Comments
Yufu et al. 2007	Case-control study comparing young adult men and women smokers and nonsmokers 26 smokers and 31 nonsmokers; mean age 30 years Japan	Brachial artery ultrasound and Doppler assessment of brachial artery flow at rest, after ischemia, and after sublingual glyceral trinitrate Pulse wave velocity assessed using a commercially available noninvasive automatic waveform analyzer	• Flow-mediated dilation (%): nonsmokers 16.1 ± 6.6, smokers 12.4 ± 5.8; $p < 0.03$ • Pulse wave velocity (cm/s): nonsmokers 1,201 ± 161, smokers 1,232 ± 160; not significant • In smokers only, flow-mediated dilation associated with pulse wave velocity; $F = 8.108$	Confirms effect of smoking on flow-mediated dilation in another country
Heiss et al. 2008	Nonsmokers exposed to tobacco smoke for 30 minutes and compared with clean air exposure 10 men and women, 30 years of age United States	Brachial artery ultrasound and Doppler assessment of brachial artery flow at rest, after ischemia Cotinine measured to confirm absence of tobacco use at baseline and amount of exposure Measurement of endothelial progenitor cells, plasma vascular endothelial growth factor, endothelial microparticles, and progenitor cell chemotaxis Plasma from smoke-exposed individuals used in in vitro experiments with unexposed endothelial progenitor cells	• Flow-mediated dilation decreased by 3% and returned to normal 2 hours after exposure; $p < 0.05$ compared with baseline state and clean air exposure for all findings presented • Increase in appearance of endothelial progenitor cells at 1 hour after exposure with sustained increase for 24 hours • Chemotaxis to vascular endothelial growth factor of endothelial progenitor cells abolished immediately after smoke exposure, effect persisted for 24 hours • Vascular endothelial growth factor concentrations increased immediately after exposure • Linear relationships between cotinine levels after exposure and measured biological parameters • Incubation of unexposed endothelial progenitor cells with exposed plasma leads to in vitro decreased nitric oxide production, decreased chemotaxis, and increased proliferation	Establishes a mechanistic link between decrease in endothelial function as assessed by brachial ultrasound after passive smoke exposure and endothelial cell dysfunction including nitric-oxide-mediated processes; effect seen in a relatively small sample

Table 2.12 Continued

Study	Design/population	Vascular function assessment technique	Findings	Comments
Quinton et al. 2008	Smoking (n = 21) and nonsmoking (n = 20) pregnant women compared for flow-mediated dilation Birth weight in the offspring of smoking women assessed and compared with flow-mediated dilation results	Brachial artery ultrasound and Doppler assessment of brachial artery flow at rest and a second time at 28–32 weeks gestation (after smoking in the smokers and after no intervention in the nonsmokers) Birth weight measured in g for all offspring	• Smokers had lower flow-mediated dilation compared with nonsmokers (4.0 ± 2.3 vs. 9.7 ± 4.0); p <0.001 • No change in flow-mediated dilation values after active smoking; no change in the nonsmokers; reproducibility of the test demonstrated • Smoking women had infants of lower birth weight (3,090 g ± 596 vs. 3,501 g ± 396); no small-for-gestational-age infants in the nonsmoking group; p = 0.014 • In all women, those with infants less than the 10th percentile for weight had lower flow-mediated dilation than those with normal birth weight infants (4.7 ± 2.2 vs. 7.3 ± 4.6); p <0.03	Confirms impact of tobacco use on endothelial function, confirms that regular smokers have chronic endothelial dysfunction (i.e., smoking an additional cigarette after a 9-hour abstinence does not change findings); relates endothelial dysfunction to poorer pregnancy outcome with respect to birth weight
Thomas et al. 2008	Total of 616 subjects from urban and rural sites Aged 18–75 years (152 smokers) China and United States	Brachial artery ultrasound and Doppler assessment of brachial artery flow at rest, after ischemia, and after sublingual glyceral trinitrate Measurement of carotid intima-media thickness and other cardiovascular risk factors	• Smokers had impaired flow-mediated dilation vs. nonsmokers (7.0 ± 2.3 vs. 8.2 ± 2.5%); p <0.001 • Additional factors related to flow-mediated dilation included urban location, triglycerides, age, diastolic blood pressure, and glucose; total $r^2 = 0.18$ • Smokers had higher carotid intima-media thickness vs. nonsmokers (0.61 ± 0.13 vs. 0.58 ± 0.12 mm); p = 0.25	Confirms findings in prior studies of individuals of Chinese ancestry, controlling for work environment, geographic location, and other cardiovascular risk factors

Note: **ANOVA** = analysis of variance; **cm/s** = centimeters per second; **dl** = deciliter; **g** = grams; **mg** = milligrams; **mL** = milliliters; **mm** = millimeters; **pg** = picograms.
[a]Pack-years = the number of years of smoking multiplied by the number of packs of cigarettes smoked per day.

was associated with risk for low birth weight of their babies (Quinton et al. 2008). In California, a controlled-exposure study in young nonsmoking adults (Heiss et al. 2008) demonstrated endothelial dysfunction after brief exposure to secondhand smoke. Following the exposure, increased numbers of dysfunctional endothelial progenitor cells appeared in the circulation. Because endothelial progenitor cells are involved in vascular repair after injury, Celermajer and Ng (2008) proposed that the effects of secondhand smoke on endothelial cells may contribute to cardiovascular risk.

One key finding on endothelial dysfunction and early exposure to tobacco smoke comes from a cohort study of cardiovascular risk in Finland that began at 6 months of age. Parental smoking history and children's cotinine levels were measured sequentially during 11 years of follow-up. Exposure to parental smoking, as assessed by cotinine levels, was associated with impairment in endothelial function at 11 years of age, and the response was dose dependent (Kallio et al. 2007). In another study, however, a large, population-based, cross-sectional assessment of 9- to 11-year-old boys and girls in which salivary cotinine was used as the biomarker for exposure to secondhand smoke, endothelial function, as assessed by brachial reactivity, was not associated with salivary cotinine level (Leeson et al. 1997).

Another noninvasive ultrasound vascular measure, aortic pulse wave velocity, is used to assess stiffness of the large vessels. Stiffer vessels (more rapid transmission of the pulse) are abnormal and are associated with cardiovascular mortality. In a Japanese study, endothelial dysfunction in smokers (mean age = 30.4 ± 5.7 years) was associated with increased arterial pulse wave velocity (Yufu et al. 2007). Aortic stiffness was also found to be increased in young Turkish smokers (Levent et al. 2004).

Li and colleagues (2005) examined a number of indicators of vascular function in Bogalusa Heart Study participants at a mean age of 36.3 years. Compliance of large and small arteries and systemic vascular resistance were assessed by noninvasively recorded radial artery waveforms. In a comparison of smokers with nonsmokers, compliance of small arteries was significantly lower and systemic vascular resistance significantly higher in smokers. The reduction in the compliance of small arteries was significantly associated with duration of smoking.

Summary

With regard to endothelial injury, the 2004 Surgeon General's report concluded: "A substantial body of laboratory and experimental evidence now demonstrates that cigarette smoking in general and some specific components of cigarette smoke affect a number of basic pathophysiological processes at the critical interface between circulating blood components and the inner arterial wall. Smoking leads to endothelial injury and cell dysfunction" (USDHHS 2004, p. 371). Some of the studies supporting this conclusion were performed in young people, and studies have now been conducted around the world in children and young adults showing associations of endothelial dysfunction with active and passive exposure to tobacco smoke. The association is stronger at higher doses. Active smokers have chronic endothelial dysfunction, which means that their function remains reduced after a period of abstinence and does not change after they smoke a cigarette. Nonsmokers develop acute endothelial dysfunction equivalent to that of a chronic smoker after exposure to secondhand smoke; the time course of recovery has not been well characterized but is probably 1 to 2 days.

Several studies have linked endothelial dysfunction to oxidative stress and injury to endothelial progenitor cells. The association between use of tobacco and endothelial dysfunction is supported by evidence from animal models in fetuses and pups. In these studies, vascular effects after exposure to smoke were examined. One study indicated a possible long-term effect of early involuntary exposure to smoke in childhood on endothelial dysfunction in late childhood (Kallio et al. 2007). A cross-sectional, population-based study did not confirm this finding, however (Leeson et al. 1997).

Interactions of Smoking with Other Cardiovascular Risk Factors

Lipids

The evidence for a connection between tobacco smoking and dyslipidemia covers both active and passive smoking. There are now several studies linking exposure to secondhand smoke to lipid abnormalities in children. A cohort study of twins (White and Black) found lower high-density lipoprotein (HDL) cholesterol in children with chronic exposure to secondhand smoke at baseline, and this difference persisted over time after controlling for other cardiovascular risk factors, overweight, and family history of heart disease (Moskowitz et al. 1990, 1999). A study of high school athletes that used measures of plasma cotinine as a marker of exposure to secondhand smoke found lower HDL cholesterol in those with a level indicative of exposure (Feldman et al. 1991). Similarly, in a cross-sectional study of 104 children, lower HDL cholesterol was associated with living in a household having at least one smoker (Neufeld et al. 1997). In a study of 194 children, exposure to secondhand smoke was associated with unfavorable lipid profiles, but this effect was attenuated by adjustment for SES (Işcan et al. 1996). A meta-analysis of data from seven studies on 8- to 19-year-olds comparing smokers with nonsmokers (N = >4,600 total subjects; the kinds of lipid measures obtained varied among studies) showed adverse lipid changes in smoking versus nonsmoking children, including higher triglycerides, lower HDL cholesterol, and higher low-density lipoprotein (LDL) cholesterol in children who smoked compared with those who did not (Craig et al. 1990).

Effects on lipids in the fetus have also been observed from maternal smoking during pregnancy. Two studies have shown more adverse lipid profiles in the cord blood of fetuses with mothers who smoked than in mothers who did not, including lower HDL cholesterol and a higher ratio of total cholesterol to HDL cholesterol (Adam et al. 1993; Işcan et al. 1997). Jaddoe and colleagues (2008) followed a cohort of 350 people enrolled at 5–19 years of age for at least 10 years with baseline and follow-up lipid measurements; participants with exposure to tobacco smoke in utero tended to have a higher rate of rise of total cholesterol over follow-up and a more adverse lipid profile.

Findings of two cohort studies have suggested a relationship between active smoking by youth and worsening lipid profiles. In the Bogalusa Heart Study, initiation of tobacco use was associated with higher LDL cholesterol, very-low-density lipoprotein (VLDL) cholesterol and lower HDL cholesterol in Whites, and higher VLDL cholesterol in Blacks (Clarke et al. 1986). In the Beaver County Lipid Study, individuals with higher cholesterol, at 11–14 years of age who did not become smokers were less likely than those who became smokers to have elevated cholesterol levels as adults (Stuhldreher et al. 1991).

Insulin Resistance

The relationship of tobacco use to insulin resistance has been of increasing interest in recent years (Weitzman et al. 2005; Chiolero et al. 2008). In the CARDIA study, tobacco use was associated with future glucose intolerance in a graded fashion: continuous tobacco use predicted the highest likelihood of future glucose intolerance, while prior smoking and exposure to secondhand smoke were associated with this risk but at a lower likelihood (Houston et al. 2006). Elsewhere, a meta-analysis of the relationship of smoking to diabetes, which included 1.2 million persons, confirmed a 60% increase in the likelihood of type 2 diabetes in heavy smokers, and lower but still significantly increased risk of type 2 diabetes in lighter smokers (Willi et al. 2007). These studies involved multiple ages (16–60 years at baseline), but no data were presented specifically for adolescents and young adults.

Summary

There are numerous adverse interactions between use of tobacco and other established cardiovascular risk factors. The evidence from studies of children and young adults is consistent with studies in adults showing a relationship between exposure to tobacco smoke in youth and worsening lipid profiles (USDHHS 2010). The possibility of confounding of the effect of smoking by other health behaviors needs to be considered in interpreting this evidence, however. There is also evidence for interactions of exposure to secondhand smoke with other cardiovascular risk factors in youth. These interactions could contribute to atherogenesis in youth or increased cardiovascular morbidity later in life.

In the development of this section on the cardiovascular effects of tobacco use, evidence for an association between exposure to tobacco in youth and cardiovascular morbidity has been reviewed. Studies in the fetus, child, adolescent, and young adult have been considered as well as animal studies of fetuses and pups. When relevant, studies in older individuals have been used. Evidence supporting the causal relationship of both passive and active exposure to tobacco smoke with the development of atherosclerosis and cardiovascular morbidity, beginning as early as fetal life, has been found in a wide array of studies, including those using direct measurement of atherosclerosis in humans and animals, noninvasive measurement of injury to cardiovascular end organs, and measurement of associations with biomarkers known to be associated with atherosclerosis and other forms of cardiovascular disease.

Evidence Summary

The evidence reviewed in this chapter covers how smoking adversely affects the health of children, adolescents, and young adults. Evidence reviewed in this report and in earlier reports shows that the adverse effects of smoking can begin before the onset of active smoking. For example, smoking by the mother during pregnancy is linked to vascular injury in the fetus, and exposure of youth to secondhand smoke is associated with an unfavorable lipid profile and endothelial dysfunction.

Smoking causes addiction to nicotine, and the evidence reviewed in this report shows that this addiction can begin in childhood and adolescence. Adolescents become addicted to nicotine along differing trajectories of increasing intensity of smoking. Peer and parental influences have been repeatedly identified as risk factors for initiating smoking, and emerging evidence now indicates a potential role for genetic factors as well (see Chapter 4). Adolescents and young adults who stop smoking experience withdrawal, although the symptoms are variable and not uniformly comparable to those of older smokers who quit.

One reason that some adolescents and young adults start to smoke is that the tobacco industry implies through its marketing that smoking is effective for weight control (see Chapter 5, "The Tobacco Industry's Influences on the Use of Tobacco Among Youth"). This long-used strategy continues to the present, and the belief that smoking is effective for weight control remains prevalent among adolescents and may contribute to the initiation of smoking. The evidence reviewed in this report, however, shows that smoking by adolescents and young adults has no weight-lowering effect. However, smoking cessation among adolescents and young adults is associated with weight gain, similar to adults.

Active smoking causes cancer, cardiovascular disease, COPD, and other diseases. The evidence reviewed in this chapter indicates that smoking by adolescents and young adults initiates the injurious processes that lead to cardiovascular disease and COPD. Smoking by the mother during pregnancy is associated with vascular injury to the fetus and a reduction in birth weight, a risk factor for future cardiovascular disease. Exposure to secondhand smoke across infancy and childhood has a well-documented harmful effect on lung growth, and research also indicates that exposure to secondhand smoke is associated with a less favorable lipid profile.

For COPD and cardiovascular disease, strong evidence demonstrates that active smoking across adolescence and young adulthood increases the development of atherosclerosis and limits lung growth while also accelerating the onset of decline in lung function. By early middle age, the more rapid progression of atherosclerosis and the rapid decline of lung function in some smokers lead to increasing occurrence of the corresponding clinical diseases: coronary heart disease and stroke, and COPD, respectively. These diseases are major contributors to the premature mortality of middle-aged and elderly smokers.

This chapter does not cover the various cancers caused by tobacco use; these cancers do not occur until adulthood. Epidemiologic studies, reviewed in earlier reports, indicate that duration of smoking, which reflects the age of starting to smoke, is a powerful determinant of risk for many of these cancers (USDHHS 1990, 2004). The mechanisms by which smoking causes cancer were reviewed in the 2010 report. Current understanding of these mechanisms indicates that they are first put in place with the initiation of active smoking, regardless of age.

Conclusions

1. The evidence is sufficient to conclude that there is a causal relationship between smoking and addiction to nicotine, beginning in adolescence and young adulthood.
2. The evidence is suggestive but not sufficient to conclude that smoking contributes to future use of marijuana and other illicit drugs.
3. The evidence is suggestive but not sufficient to conclude that smoking by adolescents and young adults is *not* associated with significant weight loss, contrary to young people's beliefs.
4. The evidence is sufficient to conclude that there is a causal relationship between active smoking and both reduced lung function and impaired lung growth during childhood and adolescence.
5. The evidence is sufficient to conclude that there is a causal relationship between active smoking and wheezing severe enough to be diagnosed as asthma in susceptible child and adolescent populations.
6. The evidence is sufficient to conclude that there is a causal relationship between smoking in adolescence and young adulthood and early abdominal aortic atherosclerosis in young adults.
7. The evidence is suggestive but not sufficient to conclude that there is a causal relationship between smoking in adolescence and young adulthood and coronary artery atherosclerosis in adulthood.

References

Acierno R, Kilpatrick DG, Resnick H, Saunders B, DeArellano M, Best C. Assault, PTSD, family substance use, and depression as risk factors for cigarette use in youth: findings from the National Survey of Adolescents. *Journal of Traumatic Stress* 2000;13(3):381–96.

Adam B, Cetinkaya F, Malatyalioglu E, Gürses N. Cigarette smoking and lipids and lipoproteins in cord plasma. *Japanese Heart Journal* 1993;34(6):759–62.

Akbartabartoori M, Lean MEJ, Hankey CR. Relationships between cigarette smoking, body size and body shape. *International Journal of Obesity* 2005;29(2):236–43.

Albright CL, Altman DG, Slater MD, Maccoby N. Cigarette advertisements in magazines: evidence for a differential focus on women's and youth magazines. *Health Education Quarterly* 1988;15(2):225–33.

Al-Riyami AA, Afifi MM. The relation of smoking to body mass index and central obesity among Omani male adults. *Saudi Medical Journal* 2003;24(8):875–80.

American Psychiatric Association. *Diagnostic and Statistical Manual of Mental Disorders,* 4th ed. (text rev.). Arlington (VA): American Psychiatric Association, 2000.

Amos A, Haglund M. From social taboo to "torch of freedom": the marketing of cigarettes to women. *Tobacco Control* 2000;9(1):3–8.

Amos CI, Wu X, Broderick P, Gorlov IP, Gu J, Eisen T, Ding Q, Zhang Q, Gu X, Vijayakrishnan J, et al. Genome-wide association scan of tag SNPs identifies a susceptibility locus for lung cancer at 15q25.1. *Nature Genetics* 2008;40(5):616–22.

Annesi-Maesano I, Oryszczyn MP, Raherison C, Kopferschmitt C, Pauli G, Taytard A, Tunon de Lara M, Vervloet D, Charpin D. Increased prevalence of asthma and allied diseases among active adolescent tobacco smokers after controlling for passive smoking exposure: a cause for concern? *Clinical and Experimental Allergy* 2004;34(7):1017–23.

Anzengruber D, Klump KL, Thorton L, Brandt H, Crawford S, Fichter MM, Halmi KA, Johnson C, Kaplan AS, LaVia M. Smoking in eating disorders. *Eating Behaviors* 2006;7(4):291–9.

Arday DR, Giovino GA, Schulman J, Nelson DE, Mowery P, Samet JM. Cigarette smoking and self-reported health problems among U.S. high school seniors, 1982–1989. *American Journal of Health Promotion* 1995;10(2):111–6.

Asmussen I. Ultrastructure of human umbilical arteries from newborn children of smoking and non-smoking mothers. *Acta Pathologica, Microbiologica, et Immunologica Scandinavica, Section A, Pathology* 1982a;90(5):375–83.

Asmussen I. Ultrastructure of the umbilical artery from a newborn delivered at term by a mother who smoked 80 cigarettes per day. *Acta Pathologica, Microbiologica, et Immunologica Scandinavica, Section A, Pathology* 1982b;90(6):397–404.

Asmussen I, Kjeldsen K. Intimal ultrastructure of human umbilical arteries: observations on arteries from newborn children of smoking and nonsmoking mothers. *Circulation Research* 1975;36(5):579–89.

Audrain-McGovern J, Al Koudsi N, Rodriguez D, Wileyto PE, Shields PG, Tyndale RF. The role of *CYP2A6* in the emergence of nicotine dependence in adolescents. *Pediatrics* 2007;119(1):e264–e274.

Audrain-McGovern J, Rodriguez D, Tercyak KP, Epstein LH, Goldman P, Wileyto EP. Applying a behavioral economic framework to understanding adolescent smoking. *Psychology of Addictive Behaviors* 2004; 18(1):64–73.

Austin SB, Gortmaker SL. Dieting and smoking initiation in early adolescent girls and boys: a prospective study. *American Journal of Public Health* 2001;91(3):446–50.

Aycicek A, Erel O, Kocyigit A. Decreased total antioxidant capacity and increased oxidative stress in passive smoker infants and their mothers. *Pediatrics International* 2005;47(6):635–9.

Aycicek A, Ipek A. Maternal active or passive smoking causes oxidative stress in cord blood. *European Journal of Pediatrics* 2008;167(1):81–5.

Bagot KS, Heishman SJ, Moolchan ET. Tobacco craving predicts lapse to smoking among adolescent smokers in cessation treatment. *Nicotine & Tobacco Research* 2007;9(6):647–52.

Baker TB, Conti DV, Moffit TE, Caspi A. The nicotine-dependence phenotype: translating theoretical perspectives and extant data into recommendations for genetic mapping. In: *Phenotypes and Endophenotypes: Foundations for Genetic Studies of Nicotine Use and Dependence*. Tobacco Control Monograph No. 20. Bethesda (MD): U.S. Department of Health and Human Services, National Institutes of Health, National Cancer Institute, 2009:73–131. NIH Publication No. 09-6366.

Bamia C, Trichopoulou A, Lenas D, Trichopoulos D. Tobacco smoking in relation to body fat mass and distribution in a general population sample. *International Journal of Obesity* 2004;28(8):1091–6.

Barker DJP. The developmental origins of adult disease. *Journal of the American College of Nutrition* 2004;23(6 Suppl):588S–595S.

Barker DJP, Osmond C, Forsén TJ, Kajantie E, Eriksson JG. Trajectories of growth among children who have coronary events as adults. *New England Journal of Medicine* 2005;353(17):1802–9.

Barnes PJ. Against the Dutch hypothesis: asthma and chronic obstructive pulmonary disease are distinct diseases. *American Journal of Respiratory and Critical Care Medicine* 2006;174(3):240–3.

Barrett-Connor E, Khaw KT. Cigarette smoking and increased central adiposity. *Annals of Internal Medicine* 1989;111(10):783–7.

Bean MK, Mitchell KS, Speizer IS, Wilson DB, Smith BN, Fries EA. Rural adolescent attitudes toward smoking and weight loss: relationship to smoking status. *Nicotine & Tobacco Research* 2008;10(2):279–86.

Benowitz NL. Mechanisms of disease: nicotine addiction. *New England Journal of Medicine* 2010;362(24):2295–03.

Berenson GS, Srinivasan SR, Bao W, Newman WP 3rd, Tracy RE, Wattigney WA. Association between multiple cardiovascular risk factors and atherosclerosis in children and young adults: the Bogalusa Heart Study. *New England Journal of Medicine* 1998;338(23):1650–6.

Bernat DH, Erickson DJ, Widome R, Perry CL, Forster JL. Adolescent smoking trajectories: results from a population-based cohort study. *Journal of Adolescent Health* 2008;43(4):334–40.

Berscheid E, Walster E, Bohrnstedt G. The happy American body: a survey report. *Psychology Today* 1973; 7(6):119–31.

Bhuiyan AR, Srinivasan SR, Chen W, Paul TK, Berenson GS. Correlates of vascular structure and function measures in asymptomatic young adults: the Bogalusa Heart Study. *Atherosclerosis* 2006;189(1):1–7.

Bierut LJ. Genetic vulnerability and susceptibility to substance dependence. *Neuron* 2011;69(4):618–27.

Bierut LJ, Madden PAF, Breslau N, Johnson EO, Hatsukami D, Pomerleau OF, Swan GE, Rutter J, Bertelsen S, Fox L, et al. Novel genes identified in a high-density genome wide association study for nicotine dependence. *Human Molecular Genetics* 2007;16(1):24–35.

Bisgaard H, Pedersen S, Anhøj J, Agertoft L, Hedlin G, Gulsvik A, Bjermer L, Carlsen KH, Nordvall L, Lundbäck B, et al. Determinants of lung function and airway hyperresponsiveness in asthmatic children. *Respiratory Medicine* 2007;101(7):1477–82.

Bleecker ER. Similarities and differences in asthma and COPD: the Dutch hypothesis. *Chest* 2004;126(2 Suppl):93S–95S.

Blitstein JL, Robinson LA, Murray DM, Klesges RC, Zbikowski SM. Rapid progression to regular cigarette smoking among nonsmoking adolescents: interactions with gender and ethnicity. *Preventive Medicine* 2003;36(4):455–63.

Bodner CH, Ross S, Little J, Douglas JG, Legge JS, Friend JAR, Godden DJ. Risk factors for adult onset wheeze: a case control study. *American Journal of Respiratory and Critical Care Medicine* 1998;157(1):35–42.

Boles SM, Johnson PB. Gender, weight concerns, and adolescent smoking. *Journal of Addictive Diseases* 2001;20(2):5–14.

Brandon TH, Baker TB. The Smoking Consequences Questionnaire: the subjective expected utility of smoking in college students. *Psychological Assessment* 1991;3(3):484–91.

Breslau N. Psychiatric comorbidity of smoking and nicotine dependence. *Behavior Genetics* 1995;25(2):95–101.

Breslau N, Fenn N, Peterson EL. Early smoking initiation and nicotine dependence in a cohort of young adults. *Drug and Alcohol Dependence* 1993;33(2):129–37.

Breslau N, Kilbey MM, Andreski P. DSM-III-R nicotine dependence in young adults: prevalence, correlates and associated psychiatric disorders. *Addiction* 1994;89(6):743–54.

Breton CV, Byun H-M, Wenten M, Pan F, Yang A, Gilliland FD. Prenatal tobacco smoke exposure affects global and gene-specific DNA methylation. *American Journal of Respiratory and Critical Care Medicine* 2009;180(5):462–7.

Brook JS, Duan T, Zhang C, Cohen PR, Brook DW. The association between attention deficit hyperactivity disorder in adolescence and smoking in adulthood. *American Journal on Addictions* 2008;17(1):54–9.

Brown JD, Witherspoon EM. The mass media and American adolescents' health. *Journal of Adolescent Health* 2002;31(6):153–70.

Brown RA, Lewinsohn PM, Seeley JR, Wagner EF. Cigarette smoking, major depression, and other psychiatric disorders among adolescents. *Journal of the American Academy of Child and Adolescent Psychiatry* 1996;35(12):1602–10.

Budd GM, Preston DB. College students' attitudes and beliefs about the consequences of smoking: development and normative scores of a new scale. *Journal of the American Academy of Nurse Practitioners* 2001;13(9):421–7.

Bulik CM, Sullivan PF, Epstein LH, McKee M, Kaye WH, Dahl RE, Weltzin TE. Drug use in women with anorexia and bulimia nervosa. *International Journal of Eating Disorders* 1992;11(3):213–25.

Butland BK, Strachan DP. Asthma onset and relapse in adult life: the British 1958 birth cohort study. *Annals of Allergy, Asthma & Immunology* 2007;98(4):337–43.

Bylock A, Bondjers G, Jansson I, Hansson HA. Surface ultrastructure of human arteries with special reference to the effects of smoking. *Acta Pathologica, Microbiologica, et Immunologica Scandinavica, Section A, Pathology* 1979;87A(3):201–9.

Cachelin FM, Weiss JW, Garbanati JA. Dieting and its relationship to smoking, acculturation, and family environment in Asian and Hispanic adolescents. *Eating Disorders* 2003;11(1):51–61.

Calderon LL, Yu CK, Jambazian P. Dieting practices in high school students. *Journal of the American Dietetic Association* 2004;104(9):1369–74.

Califano JA Jr. The wrong way to stay slim. *New England Journal of Medicine* 1995;333(18):1214–6.

Camp DE, Klesges RC, Relyea G. The relationship between body weight concerns and adolescent smoking. *Health Psychology*1993;12(1):24–32.

Carroll SL, Lee RE, Kaur H, Harris KJ, Strother ML, Huang TT-K. Smoking, weight loss intention and obesity-promoting behaviors in college students. *Journal of the American College of Nutrition* 2006;25(4):348–53.

Castardeli E, Duarte DR, Minicucci MF, Azevedo PS, Matsubara BB, Matsubara LS, Campana AO, Paiva SAR, Zornoff LA. Exposure time and ventricular remodeling induced by tobacco smoke exposure in rats. *Medical Science Monitor* 2008;14(3):BR62–BR66.

Cavallo DA, Duhig AM, McKee S, Krishnan-Sarin S. Gender and weight concerns in adolescent smokers. *Addictive Behaviors* 2006;31(11):2140–6.

Cawley J, Markowitz S, Tauras J. Lighting up and slimming down: the effects of body weight and cigarette prices on adolescent smoking initiation. *Journal of Health Economics* 2004;23(2):293–311.

Celermajer DS, Adams MR, Clarkson P, Robinson J, McCredie R, Donald A, Deanfield JE. Passive smoking and impaired endothelium-dependent arterial dilation in healthy young adults. *New England Journal of Medicine* 1996;334(3):150–4.

Celermajer DS, Ng MK. Where there's smoke.... *Journal of the American College of Cardiology* 2008;51(18): 1772–4.

Celermajer DS, Sorensen KE, Georgakopoulos D, Bull C, Thomas O, Robinson J, Deanfield JE. Cigarette smoking is associated with dose-related and potentially reversible impairment of endothelium-dependent dilation in healthy young adults. *Circulation* 1993;88(5 Pt 1):2149–55.

Cepeda-Benito A, Ferrer AR. Smoking Consequences Questionnaire—Spanish. *Psychology of Addictive Behaviors* 2000;14(3):219–30.

Charlton A. Smoking and weight control in teenagers. *Public Health* 1984;98(5):277–81.

Chassin L, Presson CC, Pitts SC, Sherman SJ. The natural history of cigarette smoking from adolescence to adulthood in a midwestern community sample: multiple trajectories and their psychosocial correlates. *Health Psychology* 2000;19(3):223–31.

Chaudhuri R, Livingston E, McMahon AD, Thomson L, Borland W, Thomson NC. Cigarette smoking impairs the therapeutic response to oral corticosteroids in chronic asthma. *American Journal of Respiratory and Critical Care Medicine* 2003;168(11):1308–11.

Chesley EB, Roberts TA, Auinger P, Kreipe RE, Klein JD. Longitudinal impact of weight-related intentions with the initiation and maintenance of smoking among adolescents. *Journal of Adolescent Health* 2004;34(2):130.

Chilcoat HD, Breslau N. Pathways from ADHD to early drug use. *Journal of the American Academy of Child and Adolescent Psychiatry* 1999;38(11):1347–54.

Chiolero A, Faeh D, Paccaud F, Cornuz J. Consequences of smoking for body weight, body fat distribution, and insulin resistance. *American Journal of Clinical Nutrition* 2008;87(4):801–9.

Chiriboga DE, Ma Y, Li W, Olendzki BC, Pagoto SL, Merriam PA, Matthews CE, Herbert JR, Ockene IS. Gender differences in predictors of body weight and body weight change in healthy adults. *Obesity* 2008;16(1):137–45.

Choi WS, Gilpin EA, Farkas AJ, Pierce JP. Determining the probability of future smoking among adolescents. *Addiction* 2001;96(2):313–23.

Clark DB, Wood DS, Martin CS, Cornelius JR, Lynch KG, Shiffman S. Multidimensional assessment of nicotine dependence in adolescents. *Drug and Alcohol Dependence* 2005;77(3):235–42.

Clarke WR, Srinivasan SR, Shear CL, Hunter SM, Croft J, Webber LS, Berenson GS. Cigarette smoking initiation and longitudinal changes in serum lipids and lipoproteins in early adulthood: the Bogalusa Heart Study. *American Journal of Epidemiology* 1986;124(2): 207–19.

Colby SM, Tiffany ST, Shiffman S, Niaura RS. Measuring nicotine dependence among youth: a review of available approaches and instruments. *Drug and Alcohol Dependence* 2000;59(Suppl 1):S23–S39.

Colder CR, Mehta P, Balanda K, Campbell RT, Mayhew KP, Stanton WR, Pentz MA, Flay BR. Identifying trajectories of adolescent smoking: an application of latent growth mixture modeling. *Health Psychology* 2001;20(2):127–35.

Conners CK, Levin ED, Sparrow E, Hinton SC, Erhardt D, Meck WH, Rose JE, March J. Nicotine and attention in adult attention deficit hyperactivity disorder (ADHD). *Psychopharmacology Bulletin* 1996;32(1):67–73.

Cook DG, Mendall MA, Whincup PH, Carey IM, Ballam L, Morris JE, Miller GJ, Strachan DP. C-reactive protein concentration in children: relationship to adiposity and other cardiovascular risk factors. *Atherosclerosis* 2000;149(1):139–50.

Cooper TV, Klesges RC, Robinson LA, Zbikowski SM. A prospective evaluation of the relationships between smoking dosage and body mass index in an adolescent, biracial cohort. *Addictive Behaviors* 2003;28(3): 501–12.

Copeland AL, Carney CE. Smoking expectancies as mediators between dietary restraint and disinhibition and smoking in college women. *Experimental and Clinical Psychopharmacology* 2003;11(3):247–51.

Copeland AL, Diefendorff JM, Kendzor DE, Rash CJ, Businelle MS, Patterson SM, Williamson DA. Measurement of smoking outcome expectancies in children: the Smoking Consequences Questionnaire-Child. *Psychology of Addictive Behaviors* 2007;21(4):469–77.

Covey LS, Tam D. Depressive mood, the single-parent home, and adolescent cigarette smoking. *American Journal of Public Health* 1990;80(11):1330–3.

Craig WY, Palomaki GE, Johnson AM, Haddow JE. Cigarette smoking-associated changes in blood lipid and lipoprotein levels in the 8- to 19-year-old age group: a meta-analysis. *Pediatrics* 1990;85(2):155–8.

Crawley HF, While D. The diet and body weight of British teenage smokers at 16–17 years. *European Journal of Clinical Nutrition* 1995;49(12):904–14.

Crisp A, Sedgwick P, Halek C, Joughin N, Humphrey H. Why may teenage girls persist in smoking? *Journal of Adolescence* 1999;22(5):657–72.

Crisp AH, Halek C, Sedgewick P, Stravraki C, Williams E, Kiossis I. Smoking and pursuit of thinness in schoolgirls in London and Ottawa. *Postgraduate Medical Journal* 1998;74(874):473–9.

Crocker P, Kowalski N, Kowalski K, Chad K, Humbert L, Forrester S. Smoking behaviour and dietary restraint in young adolescent women: the role of physical self-perceptions. *Canadian Journal of Public Health* 2001;92(6):428–32.

Croll J, Neumark-Sztainer D, Story M, Ireland M. Prevalence and risk and protective factors related to disordered eating behaviors among adolescents: relationship to gender and ethnicity. *Journal of Adolescent Health* 2002;31(2):166–75.

Dani JA, Harris RA. Nicotine addiction and comorbidity with alcohol abuse and mental illness. *Nature Neuroscience* 2005;8(11):1465–70.

Davey Smith G, Hyppönen E, Power C, Lawlor DA. Offspring birth weight and parental mortality: prospective observational study and meta-analysis. *American Journal of Epidemiology* 2007;166(2):160–9.

Davis RM. Current trends in cigarette advertising and marketing. *New England Journal of Medicine* 1987; 316(12):725–32.

de Boo HA, Harding JE. The developmental origins of adult disease (Barker) hypothesis. *Australian & New Zealand Journal of Obstetrics & Gynaecology* 2006;46(1):4–14.

Dierker LC, Avenevoli S, Merikangas KR, Flaherty BP, Stolar M. Association between psychiatric disorders and the progression of tobacco use behaviors. *Journal of the American Academy of Child and Adolescent Psychiatry* 2001;40(10):1159–67.

DiFranza JR, Rigotti NA, McNeill AD, Ockene JK, Savageau JA, St Cyr D, Coleman M. Initial symptoms of nicotine dependence in adolescents. *Tobacco Control* 2000;9(3):313–9.

Ding L, Pallonen UE, Migneault JP, Velicer WF. Development of a measure to assess adolescents' temptation to smoke [abstract]. *Annals of Behavioral Medicine* 1994; 16(Suppl):S175.

Doll R, Peto R. Cigarette smoking and bronchial carcinoma: dose and time relationships among regular smokers and lifelong non-smokers. *Journal of Epidemiology and Community Health* 1978;32(4):303–13.

Donovan JE, Jessor R, Costa FM. Syndrome of problem behavior in adolescence: a replication. *Journal of Consulting and Clinical Psychology* 1988;56(5):762–5.

Dowdell EB, Santucci ME. Health risk behavior assessment: nutrition, weight, and tobacco use in one urban seventh-grade class. *Public Health Nursing* 2004;21(2):128–36.

Doyle LW. Growth and respiratory health in adolescence of the extremely low-birth weight survivor. *Clinics in Perinatology* 2000;27(2):421–32.

Doyle LW, Olinsky A, Faber B, Callanan C. Adverse effects of smoking on respiratory function in young adults born weighing less than 1000 grams. *Pediatrics* 2003; 112(3):565–9.

Drewnowski A, Yee DK, Kurth CL, Krahn DD. Eating pathology and DSM-III-R bulimia nervosa: a continuum of behavior. *American Journal of Psychiatry* 1994;151(8):1217–9.

DuRant RH, Smith JA, Kreiter SR, Krowchuk DP. The relationship between early age of onset of initial substance use and engaging in multiple health risk behaviors among young adolescents. *Archives of Pediatrics & Adolescent Medicine* 1999;153(3):286–91.

Dwyer JB, Broide RS, Leslie FM. Nicotine and brain development. *Birth Defects Research Part C Embryo Today* 2008;84(1):30–44.

Elisaf M, Papanikolaou N, Letzaris G, Siamopoulos KC. Smoking habit in female students of northwestern Greece: relation to other cardiovascular risk factors.

Journal of the Royal Society for the Promotion of Health 1996;116(2):87–90.

Ernster VL. Mixed messages for women: a social history of cigarette smoking and advertising. *New York State Journal of Medicine* 1985;85(7):335–40.

Ernster V, Kaufman N, Nichter M, Samet J, Yoon SY. Women and tobacco: moving from policy to action. *Bulletin of the World Health Organization* 2000;78(7): 891–901.

Facchini M, Rozensztejn R, González C. Smoking and weight control behaviors. *Eating and Weight Disorders* 2005;10(1):1–7.

Fagerström KO, Schneider NG. Measuring nicotine dependence: a review of the Fagerström Tolerance Questionnaire. *Journal of Behavioral Medicine* 1989; 12(2):159–82.

Fairburn CG, Cooper Z. The eating disorder examination. In: Fairburn CG, Wilson GT, editors. *Binge Eating: Nature, Assessment, and Treatment*. New York: Guilford Press, 1993.

Farrell M, Marshall EJ. Epidemiology of tobacco, alcohol and drug use. *Psychiatry* 2006;5(12):427–30.

Feldman J, Shenker IR, Etzel RA, Spierto FW, Lilienfield DE, Nussbaum M, Jacobson MS. Passive smoking alters lipid profiles in adolescents. *Pediatrics* 1991;88(2): 259–64.

Fergusson DM, Lynskey MT, Horwood LJ. Comorbidity between depressive disorders and nicotine dependence in a cohort of 16-year-olds. *Archives of General Psychiatry* 1996;53(11):1043–7.

Fidler JA, West R, Van Jaarsveld CHM, Jarvis MJ, Wardle J. Does smoking in adolescence affect body mass index, waist or height: findings from a longitudinal study. *Addiction* 2007;102(9):1493–501.

Field AE, Austin SB, Frazier AL, Gillman MW, Camargo CA Jr, Colditz GA. Smoking, getting drunk, and engaging in bulimic behaviors: in which order are the behaviors adopted? *Journal of the American Academy of Child and Adolescent Psychiatry* 2002;41(7):846–53.

Fiore MC, Jaén CR, Baker TB, Bailey WC, Benowitz NL, Curry SJ, Dorfman SF, Froelicher ES, Goldstein MG, Healton CG, et al. *Treating Tobacco Use and Dependence: 2008 Update*. Clinical Practice Guideline. Rockville (MD): U.S. Department of Health and Human Services, Public Health Service, 2008.

Fogarty AW, Glancy C, Jones S, Lewis SA, McKeever TM, Britton JR. A prospective study of weight change and systemic inflammation over 9 y. *American Journal of Clinical Nutrition* 2008;87(1):30–5.

Forman VL, Morello P. Weight concerns, postexperimental smoking, and perceived difficulty in quitting in Argentinean adolescents. *Eating Behaviors* 2003;4(1):41–52.

Frank RE, Serdula MK, Adame D. Weight loss and bulimic eating behavior: changing patterns within a population of young adult women. *Southern Medical Journal* 1991;84(4):457–60.

Freedman DS, Serdula MK, Percy CA, Ballew C, White L. Obesity, levels of lipids and glucose, and smoking among Navajo adolescents. *Journal of Nutrition* 1997;127(10):2120S–2127S.

French SA, Jeffery RW. Weight concerns and smoking: a literature review. *Annals of Behavioral Medicine* 1995;17(3):234–44.

French SA, Jeffery RW, Klesges LM, Forster JL. Weight concerns and change in smoking behavior over two years in a working population. *American Journal of Public Health* 1995;85(5):720–2.

French SA, Jeffery RW, Pirie PL, McBride CM. Do weight concerns hinder smoking cessation efforts? *Addictive Behaviors* 1992;17(3):219–26.

French SA, Perry CL, Leon GR, Fulkerson JA. Weight concerns, dieting behavior, and smoking initiation among adolescents: a prospective study. *American Journal of Public Health* 1994;84(11):1818–20.

Fulkerson JA, French SA. Cigarette smoking for weight loss or control among adolescents: gender and racial/ethnic differences. *Journal of Adolescent Health* 2003; 32(4):306–13.

Fulton JE, Shekelle RB. Cigarette smoking, weight gain, and coronary mortality: results from the Chicago Western Electric Study. *Circulation* 1997;96(5):1438–44.

Gairola CG, Drawdy ML, Block AE, Daugherty A. Sidestream cigarette smoke accelerates atherogenesis in apolipoprotein E-/- mice. *Atherosclerosis* 2001;156(1):49–55.

Garner DM. *Eating Disorder Inventory-2: Professional Manual*. Odessa (FL): Psychological Assessment Resources, 1991.

Garner DM, Olmsted MP. *Manual for Eating Disorders Inventory (EDI)*. Odessa (FL): Psychological Assessment Resources, 1984.

Garner DM, Olmsted MP, Polivy J. Development and validation of a multidimensional eating disorder inventory for anorexia nervosa and bulimia. *International Journal of Eating Disorders* 1983;2(2):15–34.

Genuneit J, Weinmayr G, Radon K, Dressel H, Windstetter D, Rzehak P, Vogelberg C, Leupold W, Nowak D, von Mutius E, et al. Smoking and the incidence of asthma during adolescence: results of a large cohort study in Germany. *Thorax* 2006;61(7):572–8.

George VA, Johnson P. Weight loss behaviors and smoking in college students of diverse ethnicity. *American Journal of Health Behavior* 2001;25(2):115–24.

Gicquel C, El-Osta A, Le Bouc Y. Epigenetic regulation and fetal programming. *Best Practice & Research Clinical Endocrinology & Metabolism* 2008;22(1):1–16.

Gidding SS, McMahan CA, McGill HC, Colangelo LA, Schreiner PF, Williams OD, Liu K. Prediction of coronary artery calcium in young adults using the Pathobiological Determinants of Atherosclerosis in Youth (PDAY) risk score: the CARDIA study. *Archives of Internal Medicine* 2006:166(21):2341–7.

Gidding SS, Xie X, Liu K, Manolio T, Flack JM, Gardin JM. Cardiac function in smokers and nonsmokers: the CARDIA Study. *Journal of the American College of Cardiology* 1995;26(1):211–6.

Gilliland FD, Islam T, Berhane K, Gauderman WJ, McConnell R, Avol E, Peters JM. Regular smoking and asthma incidence in adolescents. *American Journal of Respiratory and Critical Care Medicine* 2006;174(10):1094–100.

Glasgow RE, Strycker LA, Eakin EG, Boles SM, Whitlock EP. Concern about weight gain associated with quitting smoking: prevalence and association with outcome in a sample of young female smokers. *Journal of Consulting and Clinical Psychology* 1999;67(6):1009–11.

Goksör E, Åmark M, Alm B, Gustafsson PM, Wennergren G. Asthma symptoms in early childhood—what happens then? *Acta Paediatrica* 2006;95(4):471–8.

Gold DR, Wang X, Wypij D, Speizer FE, Ware JH, Dockery DW. Effects of cigarette smoking on lung function in adolescent boys and girls. *New England Journal of Medicine* 1996;335(13):931–7.

Goodman E, Capitman J. Depressive symptoms and cigarette smoking among teens. *Pediatrics* 2000;106(4):748–55.

Granner ML, Abood DA, Black DR. Racial differences in eating disorder attitudes, cigarette, and alcohol use. *American Journal of Health Behavior* 2001;25(2):83–99.

Grant BF. Age at smoking onset and its association with alcohol consumption and DSM-IV alcohol abuse and dependence: results from the national longitudinal alcohol epidemiologic survey. *Journal of Substance Abuse* 1998;10(1):59–73.

Grol MH, Gerritsen J, Vonk JM, Schouten JP, Koëter GH, Rijcken B, Postma DS. Risk factors for growth and decline of lung function in asthmatic individuals up to age 42 years: a 30-year follow-up study. *American Journal of Respiratory and Critical Care Medicine* 1999;160(6):1830–7.

Grucza RA, Bierut LJ. Cigarette smoking and the risk for alcohol use disorders among adolescent drinkers. *Alcoholism, Clinical and Experimental Research* 2006;30(12):2046–54.

Gunes T, Koklu E, Yikilmaz A, Ozturk MA, Akcakus M, Kurtoglu S, Coskun A, Koklu S. Influence of maternal smoking on neonatal aortic intima-media thickness, serum IGF-I and IGFBP-3 levels. *European Journal of Pediatrics* 2007;166(10):1039–44.

Haberstick BC, Timberlake D, Ehringer MA, Lessem JM, Hopfer CJ, Smolen A, Hewitt JK. Genes, time to first cigarette and nicotine dependence in a general population sample of young adults. *Addiction* 2007;102(4):655–65.

Hanna EZ, Grant BF. Parallels to early onset alcohol use in the relationship of early onset smoking with drug use and DSM-IV drug and depressive disorders: findings from the National Longitudinal Epidemiologic Survey. *Alcoholism, Clinical and Experimental Research* 1999;23(3):513–22.

Hanson K, Allen S, Jensen S, Hatsukami D. Treatment of adolescent smokers with the nicotine patch. *Nicotine & Tobacco Research* 2003;5(4):515–26.

Harju T, Mazur W, Merikallio H, Soini Y, Kinnula VL. Glutathione-*S*-transferases in lung and sputum specimens, effects of smoking and COPD severity. *Respiratory Research* 2008;9:80.

Heatherton TF, Kozlowski LT, Frecker RC, Fagerström KO. The Fagerström Test for Nicotine Dependence: a revision of the Fagerström Tolerance Questionnaire. *British Journal of Addiction* 1991;86(9):1119–27.

Heckbert SR, Post W, Pearson GDN, Arnett DK, Gomes AS, Jerosch-Herold M, Hundley WG, Lima JA, Bluemke DA. Traditional cardiovascular risk factors in relation to left ventricular mass, volume, and systolic function by magnetic resonance imaging: the Multiethnic Study of Atherosclerosis. *Journal of the American College of Cardiology* 2006;48(11):2285–92.

Heiss C, Amabile N, Lee AC, Real WM, Schick SF, Lao D, Wong ML, Jahn S, Angeli FS, Minasi P, et al. Brief secondhand smoke exposure depresses endothelial progenitor cells activity and endothelial function: sustained vascular injury and blunted nitric oxide production. *Journal of the American College of Cardiology* 2008;51(18):1760–71.

Herman CP. Restrained eating. *Psychiatric Clinics of North America* 1978;1(3):593–607.

Herman CP, Mack D. Restrained and unrestrained eating. *Journal of Personality* 1975;43(4):647–60.

Herman CP, Polivy J. Restrained eating. In: Stunkard AJ, editor. *Obesity*. Philadelphia: Saunders, 1980.

Ho MK, Tyndale RF. Overview of the pharmacogenomics of cigarette smoking. *Pharmacogenomics Journal* 2007;7(2):81–98.

Hong LE, Hodgkinson CA, Yang Y, Sampath H, Ross TJ, Buchholz B, Salmeron BJ, Srivastava V, Thaker GK, Goldman D et. al. A genetically modulated, intrinsic cingulate circuit supports human nicotine addiction. *Proceedings of the National Academy of Sciences of the United States of America* 2010;107(30):13509–14.

Hong T, Cody MJ. Presence of pro-tobacco messages on the Web. *Journal of Health Communication* 2002; 7(4):273–307.

Honjo K, Siegel M. Perceived importance of being thin and smoking initiation among young girls. *Tobacco Control* 2003;12(3):289–95.

Hops H, Andrews JA, Duncan SC, Duncan TE, Tildesley E. Adolescent drug use development: a social interactional and contextual perspective. In: Sameroff AJ, Lewis M, Miller SM, editors. *Handbook of Developmental Psychopathology*. 2nd ed. New York: Kluwer Academic, 2000:589–605.

Houston TK, Person SD, Pletcher MJ, Liu K, Iribarren C, Kiefe CI. Active and passive smoking and development of glucose intolerance among young adults in a prospective cohort: CARDIA study. *BMJ (British Medical Journal)* 2006;332(7549):1064–9.

Howe H. An historical review of women, smoking and advertising. *Health Education* 1984;15(3):3–9.

Hughes JR. Effects of abstinence from tobacco: valid symptoms and time course. *Nicotine & Tobacco Research* 2007;9(3):315–27.

Hung RJ, McKay JD, Gaborieau V, Boffetta P, Hashibe M, Zaridze D, Mukeria A, Szeszenia-Dabrowska N, Lissowska J, Rudnai P, et al. A susceptibility locus for lung cancer maps to nicotine acetylcholine receptor subunit genes on 15q25. *Nature* 2008;452(7187):633–7.

Hurt RD, Croghan GA, Beede SD, Wolter TD, Croghan IT, Patten CA. Nicotine patch therapy in 101 adolescent smokers: efficacy, withdrawal symptom relief, and carbon monoxide and plasma cotinine levels. *Archives of Pediatrics & Adolescent Medicine* 2000;154(1):31–7.

Hutchison S. Smoking as a risk factor for endothelial dysfunction. *Canadian Journal of Cardiology* 1998;14(Suppl D):20D–22D.

Hutter HP, Moshammer H, Neuberger M. Smoking cessation at the workplace: 1 year success of short seminars. *International Archives of Occupational and Environmental Health* 2006;79(1):1432–46.

Huxley RR, Shiell AW, Law CM. The role of size at birth and postnatal catch-up growth in determining systolic blood pressure: a systematic review of the literature. *Journal of Hypertension* 2000;18(7):815–31.

Ilomäki R, Riala K, Hakko H, Lappalainen J, Ollinen T, Räsänen P, Timonen M, Study 70 Workgroup. Temporal association of onset of daily smoking with adolescent substance use and psychiatric morbidity. *European Psychiatry* 2008;23(2):85–91.

International Agency for Research on Cancer. *IARC Monographs on the Evaluation of Carcinogenic Risks to Humans: Tobacco Smoke and Involuntary Smoking*. Vol. 83. Lyon (France): International Agency for Research on Cancer, 2004.

Işcan A, Uyanik BS, Vurgun N, Ece A, Yiğitoğlu MR. Effects of passive exposure to tobacco, socioeconomic status and family history of essential hypertension on lipid profiles in children. *Japanese Heart Journal* 1996;37(6):917–23.

Işcan A, Yiğitoğlu MR, Ece A, Ari Z, Akyildiz M. The effect of cigarette smoking during pregnancy on cord blood lipid, lipoprotein and apolipoprotein levels. *Japanese Heart Journal* 1997;38(4):497–501.

Istvan J, Matarazzo JD. Tobacco, alcohol, and caffeine use: a review of their interrelationships. *Psychological Bulletin* 1984;95(2):301–26.

Jaddoe VWV, de Ridder MAJ, van den Elzen APM, Hofman A, Uiterwaal CSPM, Witteman JCM. Maternal smoking in pregnancy is associated with cholesterol development in the offspring: a 27-years follow-up study. *Atherosclerosis* 2008;196(1):42–8.

Janzon E, Hedblad B, Berglund G, Engström G. Changes in blood pressure and body weight following smoking cessation in women. *Journal of Internal Medicine* 2004;255(2):266–72.

Jarry JL, Coambs RB, Polivy J, Herman CP. Weight gain after smoking cessation in women: the impact of dieting status. *International Journal of Eating Disorders* 1998;24(1):53–64.

Jeffery RW, Boles SM, Strycker LA, Glasgow RE. Smoking-specific weight gain concerns and smoking cessation in a working population. *Health Psychology* 1997;16(5):487–9.

Jeffery RW, Hennrikus DJ, Lando HA, Murray DM, Liu JW. Reconciling conflicting findings regarding postcessation weight concerns and success in smoking cessation. *Health Psychology* 2000;19(3):242–6.

Jenks RA, Higgs S. Associations between dieting and smoking-related behaviors in young women. *Drug and Alcohol Dependence* 2007;88(2–3):291–9.

Jitnarin N, Kosulwat V, Boonpraderm A, Haddock CK, Booth KM, Berkel LA, Poston WS. The relationship between smoking, BMI and dietary intake [abstract]. *Journal of the American Dietetic Association* 2006; 106(8 Suppl 1):A39.

Juonala M, Järvisalo MJ, Mäki-Torkko N, Kähönen M, Viikari JSA, Raitakari OT. Risk factors identified in childhood and decreased carotid artery elasticity in adulthood: the Cardiovascular Risk in Young Finns Study. *Circulation* 2005;12(10):1486–93.

Kádár A, Mózes G, Illyés G, Schönefeld T, Kulka J, Sipos B, Glasz T, Tõkés AM, Szik A. World Health Organization (WHO) and the World Heart Federation (WHF) pathobiological determinants of atherosclerosis in youth study (WHO/WHF/PBDAY Study) 1986–1996: histomorphometry and histochemistry of atherosclerotic lesions in coronary arteries and the aorta in a young population. *Nutrition, Metabolism, and Cardiovascular Diseases* 1999;9(5):220–7.

Kalinka J, Hanke W, Sobala W. Impact of prenatal tobacco smoke exposure, as measured by midgestation serum cotinine levels, on fetal biometry and umbilical flow velocity waveforms. *American Journal of Perinatology* 2005;22(1):41–7.

Kallio K, Jokinen E, Raitakari OT, Hämäläinen M, Siltala M, Volanen I, Kaitosaari T, Viikari J, Rönnemaa T, Simell O. Tobacco smoke exposure is associated with attenuated endothelial function in 11-year-old healthy children. *Circulation* 2007;115(25):3205–12.

Kandel D, Schaffran C, Griesler P, Samuolis J, Davies M, Galanti R. On the measurement of nicotine dependence in adolescence: comparisons of the mFTQ and a DSM-IV-based scale. *Journal of Pediatric Psychology* 2005;30(4):319–32.

Kandel D, Yamaguchi K. From beer to crack: developmental patterns of drug involvement. *American Journal of Public Health* 1993;83(6):851–5.

Kandel DB, Davies M. Adult sequelae of adolescent depressive symptoms. *Archives of General Psychiatry* 1986;43(3):255–62.

Kandel DB, Johnson JG, Bird H, Canino G, Goodman SH, Lahey BB, Regier DA, Schwab-Stone M. Psychiatric disorders associated with substance use among children and adolescents: findings from the Methods for the Epidemiology of Child and Adolescent Mental Disorders (MECA) Study. *Journal of Abnormal Child Psychology* 1997;25(2):121–32.

Kandel DB, Yamaguchi K, Chen K. Stages of progression in drug involvement from adolescence to adulthood: further evidence for the gateway theory. *Journal of Studies on Alcohol* 1992;53(5):447–57.

Karp I, O'Loughlin J, Paradis G, Hanley J, DiFranza J. Smoking trajectories of adolescent novice smokers in a longitudinal study of tobacco use. *Annals of Epidemiology* 2005;15(6):445–52.

Kato T, Inoue T, Morooka T, Yoshimoto N, Node K. Short-term passive smoking causes endothelial dysfunction via oxidative stress in nonsmokers. *Canadian Journal of Physiology and Pharmacology* 2006;84(5):523–9.

Kendzor DE, Copeland AL, Stewart TM, Businelle MS, Williamson DA. Weight-related concerns associated with smoking in young children. *Addictive Behaviors* 2007;32(3):598–607.

Kenney BA, Holahan CJ. Depressive symptoms and cigarette smoking in a college sample. *Journal of American College Health* 2008;56(4):409–14.

Killen JD, Ammerman S, Rojas N, Varady J, Haydel F, Robinson TN. Do adolescent smokers experience withdrawal effects when deprived of nicotine? *Experimental and Clinical Psychopharmacology* 2001;9(2):176–82.

Killen JD, Robinson TN, Haydel KF, Hayward C, Wilson DM, Hammer LD, Litt IF, Taylor CB. Prospective study of risk factors for the initiation of cigarette smoking. *Journal of Consulting and Clinical Psychology* 1997;65(6):1011–6.

Kim SH, Kim JS, Shin HS, Keen CL. Influence of smoking on markers of oxidative stress and serum mineral concentrations in teenage girls in Korea. *Nutrition* 2003;19(3):240–3.

Klesges RC, Elliott VE, Robinson LA. Chronic dieting and the belief that smoking controls body weight in a biracial, population-based adolescent sample. *Tobacco Control* 1997a;6(2):89–94.

Klesges RC, Klesges LM. Cigarette smoking as a dieting strategy in a university population. *International Journal of Eating Disorders* 1988;7(3):413–9.

Klesges RC, Meyers AW, Klesges LM, LaVasque ME. Smoking, body weight, and their effects on smoking behavior: a comprehensive review of the literature. *Psychological Bulletin* 1989;106(2):204–30.

Klesges RC, Mizes JS, Klesges LM. Self-help dieting strategies in college males and females. *International Journal of Eating Disorders* 1987;6(3):409–17.

Klesges RC, Robinson LA, Zbikowski SM. Is smoking associated with lower body mass in adolescents: a large-scale biracial investigation. *Addictive Behaviors* 1998a;23(1):109–13.

Klesges RC, Ward KD, Ray JW, Cutter G, Jacobs DR Jr, Wagenknecht LE. The prospective relationships between smoking and weight in a young, biracial cohort: the Coronary Artery Risk Development in Young Adults Study. *Journal of Consulting and Clinical Psychology* 1998b;66(6):987–93.

Klesges RC, Winders SE, Meyers AW, Eck LH, Ward KD, Hultquist CM, Ray JW, Shadish WR. How much weight gain occurs following smoking cessation: a comparison of weight gain using both continuous and point prevalence abstinence. *Journal of Consulting and Clinical Psychology* 1997b;65(2):286–91.

Klesges RC, Zbikowski SM, Lando HA, Haddock CK, Talcott GW, Robinson LA. The relationship between smoking and body weight in a population of young military personnel. *Health Psychology* 1998c;17(5):454–8.

Koopmans J, vanDoornen LJP, Boomsma DI. Association between alcohol use and smoking in adolescent and young adult twins: a bivariate genetic analysis. *Alcoholism, Clinical and Experimental Research* 1997; 21(3):537–46.

Kosecik M, Erel O, Sevinc E, Selek S. Increased oxidative stress in children exposed to passive smoking. *International Journal of Cardiology* 2005;100(1):61–4.

Kraft M. Rebuttal by Dr. Kraft. *American Journal of Respiratory and Critical Care Medicine* 2006;174(3):243–4.

Krahn D, Kurth C, Demitrack M, Drewnowski A. The relationship of dieting severity and bulimic behaviors to alcohol and other drug use in young women. *Journal of Substance Abuse* 1992;4(4):341–53.

Krug I, Treasure J, Anderluh M, Bellodi L, Cellini E, di Bernardo M, Granero R, Karwautz A, Nacmias B, Penelo E, et al. Present and lifetime comorbidity of tobacco, alcohol and drug use in eating disorders: a European multicenter study. *Drug and Alcohol Dependence* 2008;97(1–2):169–79.

Krupka LR, Vener AM, Richmond G. Tobacco advertising in gender-oriented popular magazines. *Journal of Drug Education* 1990;20(1):15–29.

Laaksonen M, Rahkonen O, Prättälä R. Smoking status and relative weight by educational level in Finland, 1978–1995. *Preventive Medicine* 1998;27(3):431–7.

Lam TH, Chung SF, Betson CL, Wong CM, Hedley AJ. Respiratory symptoms due to active and passive smoking in junior secondary school students in Hong Kong. *International Journal of Epidemiology* 1998;27(1):41–8.

Larsson L. Incidence of asthma in Swedish teenagers: relation to sex and smoking habits. *Thorax* 1995;50(3):260–4.

Lasser K, Boyd JW, Woolhander S, Himmelstein DU, McCormick D, Bor DH. Smoking and mental illness: a population-based prevalence study. *JAMA: the Journal of the American Medical Association* 2000;284(20):2606–10.

Laucht M, Becker K, Frank J, Schmidt MH, Esser G, Treutlein J, Skowronek MH, Schumann G. Genetic variation in dopamine pathways differentially associated with smoking progression in adolescence. *Journal of the American Academy of Child and Adolescent Psychiatry* 2008;47(6):673–81.

Leatherdale ST, Wong SL, Manske SR, Colditz GA. Susceptibility to smoking and its association with physical activity, BMI, and weight concerns among youth. *Nicotine & Tobacco Research* 2008;10(3):499–505.

Leeson CPM, Kattenhorn M, Morley R, Lucas A, Deanfield JE. Impact of low birth weight and cardiovascular risk factors on endothelial function in early adult life. *Circulation* 2001;103(9):1264–8.

Leeson CPM, Whincup PH, Cook DG, Donald AE, Papacosta O, Lucas A, Deanfield JE. Flow-mediated dilation in 9- to 11-year-old children: the influence of intrauterine and childhood factors. *Circulation* 1997;96(7):2233–8.

Lessov CN, Swan GE, Ring HZ, Khroyan TV, Lerman C. Genetics and drug use as a complex phenotype. *Substance Use & Misuse* 2004;39(10–12):1515–69.

Lessov-Schlaggar CN, Hops H, Brigham J, Hudmon KS, Andrews JA, Tildesley E, McBride D, Jack LM, Javitz HS, Swan GE. Adolescent smoking trajectories and nicotine dependence. *Nicotine & Tobacco Research* 2008;10(2):341–51.

Leung R, Wong G, Lau J, Ho A, Chan JKW, Choy D, Douglass C, Lai CKW. Prevalence of asthma and allergy in Hong Kong schoolchildren: an ISAAC study. *European Respiratory Journal* 1997;10(2):354–60.

Levent E, Ozyürek AR, Ülger Z. Evaluation of aortic stiffness in tobacco-smoking adolescents. *Journal of Adolescent Health* 2004;34(4):339–43.

Levin ED, Conners CK, Sparrow E, Hinton SC, Erhardt D, Meck WH, Rose JE, March J. Nicotine effects on adults with attention-deficit/hyperactivity disorder. *Psychopharmacology* 1996;123(1):55–63.

Levine A, Huang Y, Drisaldi B, Griffin EA Jr, Pollak DD, Xu S, Yin D, Schaffran C, Kandel DB, Kandel ER. Molecular mechanism for a gateway drug: epigenetic changes initiated by nicotine prime gene expression by cocaine. *Science Translational Medicine* 2011;3(107):107ra109.

Lewinsohn P, Rohde P, Brown RA. Level of current and past adolescent cigarette smoking as predictors of future substance use disorders in young adulthood. *Addiction* 1999;94(6):913–21.

Lewis S, Butland B, Strachan D, Bynner J, Richards D, Butler N, Britton J. Study of the aetiology of wheezing illness at age 16 in two national British birth cohorts. *Thorax* 1996;51(7):670–6.

Li C, Fielding R, Marcoolyn G, Wong CM, Hedley A. Smoking behavior among female cabin crew from ten Asian countries. *Tobacco Control* 1994;3(1):21–9.

Li H, Srinivasan SR, Chen W, Xu J-H, Li S, Berenson GS. Vascular abnormalities in asymptomatic, healthy young adult smokers without other major cardiovascular risk factors: the Bogalusa Heart Study. *American Journal of Hypertension* 2005;18(3):319–24.

Li MD, Ma JZ, Payne TJ, Lou X-Y, Zhang D, Dupont RT, Elston RC. Genome-wide linkage scan for nicotine dependence in European Americans and its converging results with African Americans in the Mid-South Tobacco Family sample. *Molecular Psychiatry* 2008;13(4):407–16.

Lissner L, Bengtsson C, Lapidus L, Björkelund C. Smoking initiation and cessation in relation to body fat distribution based on data from a study of Swedish women. *American Journal of Public Health* 1992;82(2):273–5.

Liu JZ, Tozzi F, Waterworth DM, Pillai SG, Muglia P, Middleton L, Berrettini W, Knouff CW, Yuan X, Waeber G, et al. Meta-analysis and imputation refines the association of 15q25 with smoking quantity. *Nature Genetics* 2010;42(5):436–40.

Liu P, Vikis HG, Wang D, Lu Y, Wang Y, Schwartz AG, Pinney SM, Yang P, de Andrade M, Petersen GM, et al.

Familial aggregation of common sequence variants on 15q24-25.1 in lung cancer. *Journal of the National Cancer Institute* 2008;100(18):1326–30.

Loken B. Heavy smokers', light smokers', and nonsmokers' beliefs about cigarette smoking. *Journal of Applied Psychology* 1982;67(5):616–22.

Loria CM, Liu K, Lewis CE, Hulley SB, Sidney S, Schreiner PJ, Williams OD, Bild DE, Detrano R. Early adult risk factor levels and subsequent coronary artery calcification: the CARDIA Study. *Journal of the American College of Cardiology* 2007;49(20):2013–20.

MacPherson L, Strong DR, Myers MG. Using an item response model to examine the nicotine dependence construct characterized by the HONC and the mFTQ among adolescent smokers. *Addictive Behaviors* 2008; 33(7):880–94.

Majahalme S, Turjanmaa V, Weder A, Lu H, Tuomisto M, Virjo A, Uusitalo A. Blood pressure levels and variability, smoking, and left ventricular structure in normotension and in borderline and mild hypertension. *American Journal of Hypertension* 1996;9(11):1110–8.

Malaiyandi V, Sellers EM, Tyndale RF. Implications of *CYP2A6* genetic variation for smoking behaviors and nicotine dependence. *Clinical Pharmacology and Therapeutics* 2005;77(3):145–58.

Malinauskas BM, Raedeke TD, Aeby VG, Smith JL, Dallas MB. Dieting practices, weight perceptions, and body composition: a comparison of normal weight, overweight, and obese college females. *Nutrition Journal* 2006;5:11.

Mallol J, Castro-Rodriguez JA, Cortez E. Effects of active tobacco smoking on the prevalence of asthma-like symptoms in adolescents. *International Journal of Chronic Obstructive Pulmonary Disease* 2007;2(1): 65–9.

Manning P, Goodman P, Kinsella T, Lawlor M, Kirby B, Clancy L. Bronchitis symptoms in young teenagers who actively or passively smoke cigarettes. *Irish Medical Journal* 2002;95(7):202–4.

Marti B, Tuomilehto J, Korhonen HJ, Kartovaara L, Vartiainen E, Pietinen P, Puska P. Smoking and leanness: evidence for change in Finland. *BMJ (British Medical Journal)* 1989;298(6683):1287–90.

Mayhew KP, Flay BR, Mott JA. Stages in the development of adolescent smoking. *Drug and Alcohol Dependence* 2000;59(Suppl 1):S61–S81.

McGill HC Jr, McMahan CA, Gidding SS. Preventing heart disease in the 21st century: implications of the Pathobiological Determinants of Atherosclerosis in Youth (PDAY) Study. *Circulation* 2008;117(9):1216–27.

McGill HC Jr, McMahan CA, Herderick EE, Tracy RE, Malcom GT, Zieske AW, Strong JP, PDAY Research Group. Effects of coronary heart disease risk factors on atherosclerosis of selected regions of the aorta and right coronary artery. *Arteriosclerosis, Thrombosis, and Vascular Biology* 2000;20(3):836–45.

McKee SA, Nhean S, Hinson RE, Mase T. Smoking for weight control: effect of priming for body image in female restrained eaters. *Addictive Behaviors* 2006;31(12):2319–23.

McMahan CA, Gidding SS, Fayad ZA, Zieske AW, Malcom GT, Tracy RE, Strong JP, McGill HC Jr, Pathobiological Determinants of Atherosclerosis in Youth Research Group. Risk scores predict atherosclerotic lesions in young people. *Archives of Internal Medicine* 2005;165(8):883–90.

McMahan CA, Gidding SS, Malcom GT, Tracy RE, Strong JP, McGill HC, Pathobiological Determinants of Atherosclerosis in Youth Research Group. Pathobiological determinants of atherosclerosis in youth risk scores are associated with early and advanced atherosclerosis. *Pediatrics* 2006;118(4):1447–55.

McNeill AD, West RJ, Jarvis M, Jackson P, Bryant A. Cigarette withdrawal symptoms in adolescent smokers. *Psychopharmacology (Berlin)* 1986;90(4):533–6.

McQuown SC, Belluzzi JD, Leslie FM. Low dose nicotine treatment during early adolescence increases subsequent cocaine reward. *Neurotoxicology and Teratology* 2007;29(1):66–73.

Meyers AW, Klesges RC, Winders SE, Ward KD, Peterson BA, Eck LH. Are weight concerns predictive of smoking cessation: a prospective analysis. *Journal of Consulting and Clinical Psychology* 1997;65(3):448–52.

Molarius A, Seidell JC, Kuulasmaa K, Dobson AJ, Sans S. Smoking and relative body weight: an international perspective from the WHO MONICA Project. *Journal of Epidemiology and Community Health* 1997;51(3):252–60.

Moolchan ET, Robinson ML, Ernst M, Cadet JL, Pickworth WB, Heishman SJ, Schroeder JR. Safety and efficacy of the nicotine patch and gum for the treatment of adolescent tobacco addiction. *Pediatrics* 2005;115(4): e407–e414.

Moskowitz WB, Mosteller M, Schieken RM, Bossano R, Hewitt JK, Bodurtha JN, Segrest JP. Lipoprotein and oxygen transport alterations in passive smoking preadolescent children. The MCV Twin Study. *Circulation* 1990;81(2):586–92.

Moskowitz WB, Schwartz PF, Schieken RM. Childhood passive smoking, race, and coronary artery disease risk: the MCV Twin Study. *Archives of Pediatrics & Adolescent Medicine* 1999;153(5):446–53.

Napoli C, Lerman LO, de Nigris F, Gossl M, Balestrieri ML, Lerman A. Rethinking primary prevention of atherosclerosis-related diseases. *Circulation* 2006; 114(23):2517–27.

National Cancer Institute. *Changes in Cigarette-Related Disease Risks and Their Implications for Prevention and Control.* Smoking and Tobacco Control Monograph No. 8. Bethesda (MD): U.S. Department of Health and Human Services, National Institutes of Health, National Cancer Institute, 1997. NIH Publication No. 97-4213.

National Cancer Institute. *Phenotypes and Endophenotypes: Foundations for Genetic Studies of Nicotine Use and Dependence*. Tobacco Control Monograph No. 20. Bethesda (MD): U.S. Department of Health and Human Services, National Institutes of Health, National Cancer Institute, 2009. NIH Publication No. 09-6366.

National Cancer Institute. Smokeless tobacco, 2012; <http://www.cancer.gov/cancertopics/tobacco/smokeless-tobacco>; accessed: February 5, 2012.

Nelson CB, Wittchen H-U. Smoking and nicotine dependence: results from a sample of 14- to 24-year-olds in Germany. *European Addiction Research* 1998;4(1–2):42–9.

Neufeld EJ, Mietus-Snyder M, Beiser AS, Baker AL, Newburger JW. Passive cigarette smoking and reduced HDL cholesterol levels in children with high-risk lipid profiles. *Circulation* 1997;96(5):1403–7.

Neumark-Sztainer D, Croll J, Story M, Hannan PJ, French SA, Perry C. Ethnic/racial differences in weight-related concerns and behaviors among adolescent girls and boys: findings from Project EAT. *Journal of Psychosomatic Research* 2002;53(5):963–74.

Newnham JP, Ross MG, editors. *Early Life Origins of Human Health and Disease*. New York: Karger, 2009.

Nichter M, Nichter M, Vuckovic N, Tesler L, Adrian S, Ritenbaugh C. Smoking as a weight-control strategy among adolescent girls and young women: a reconsideration. *Medical Anthropology Quarterly* 2004;18(3):305–24.

Nicklas BJ, Tomoyasu N, Muir J, Goldberg AP. Effects of cigarette smoking and its cessation on body weight and plasma leptin levels. *Metabolism* 1999;48(6):804–8.

Niewoehner DE, Kleinerman J, Rice DB. Pathologic changes in the peripheral airways of young cigarette smokers. *New England Journal of Medicine* 1974; 291(15):755–8.

Noakes PS, Thomas R, Lane C, Mori TA, Barden AE, Devadason SG, Prescott SL. Association of maternal smoking with increased infant oxidative stress at 3 months of age. *Thorax* 2007;62(8):714–7.

Nuyt AM. Mechanisms underlying developmental programming of elevated blood pressure and vascular dysfunction: evidence from human studies and experimental animal models. *Clinical Science (London, England)* 2008;114(1):1–17.

O'Dell LE, Bruijnzeel AW, Ghozland S, Markou A, Koob GF. Nicotine withdrawal in adolescent and adult rats. *Annals of the New York Academy of Sciences* 2004; 1021:167–74.

O'Hara P, Connett JE, Lee WW, Nides M, Murray R, Wise R. Early and late weight gain following smoking cessation in the Lung Health Study. *American Journal of Epidemiology* 1998;148(9):821–30.

O'Loughlin J, DiFranza J, Tyndale RF, Meshefedjian G, McMillan-Davey E, Clarke PBS, Hanley J, Paradis G. Nicotine-dependence symptoms are associated with smoking frequency in adolescents. *American Journal of Preventive Medicine* 2003;25(3):219–25.

O'Loughlin J, Karp I, Henderson M, Gray-Donald K. Does cigarette use influence adiposity or height in adolescence? *Annals of Epidemiology* 2008;18(5):395–402.

Pallonen UE, Prochaska JO, Velicer WF, Prokhorov AV, Smith NF. Stages of acquisition and cessation for adolescent smoking: an empirical integration. *Addictive Behaviors* 1998;23(3):303–24.

Park NH, Kim JS, Lee YM. Factors associated with the stage of change of smoking cessation behavior in adolescents. *Taehan Kanho Hakhoe Chi* 2003;33(8): 1101–10.

Patton GC, Carlin JB, Coffey C, Wolfe R, Hibbert M, Bowes G. Depression, anxiety, and smoking initiation: a prospective study over 3 years. *American Journal of Public Health* 1998;88(10):1518–22.

Patton GC, Carlin JB, Shao Q, Hibbert ME, Rosier M, Selzer R, Bowes G. Adolescent dieting: healthy weight control or borderline eating disorder? *Journal of Child Psychology and Psychiatry, and Allied Disciplines* 1997;38(3):299–306.

Pauly JR, Slotkin TA. Maternal tobacco smoking, nicotine replacement and neurobehavioural development. *Acta Paediatrica* 2008;97(10):1331–7.

Payne JR, Eleftheriou KI, James LE, Hawe E, Mann J, Stronge A, Kotwinski P, World M, Humphries SE, Pennell DJ, et al. Left ventricular growth response to exercise and cigarette smoking: data from LARGE Heart. *Heart* 2006;92(12):1784–8.

Payne JR, James LE, Eleftheriou KI, Hawe E, Mann J, Stronge A, Banham K, World M, Humphries SE, Pennell DJ, et al. The association of left ventricular mass with blood pressure, cigarette smoking and alcohol consumption; data from the LARGE Heart Study. *International Journal of Cardiology* 2007;120(1):52–8.

Pederson LL, Lefcoe NM. Cross-sectional analysis of variables related to cigarette smoking in late adolescence. *Journal of Drug Education* 1985;15(3):225–40.

Peters JM, Ferris BG Jr. Smoking and morbidity in a college-age group. *American Review of Respiratory Disease* 1967a;95(5):783–9.

Peters JM, Ferris BG Jr. Smoking, pulmonary function, and respiratory symptoms in a college-age group. *American Review of Respiratory Disease* 1967b;95(5):774–82.

Peto R. Influence of dose and duration of smoking on lung cancer rates. *IARC Scientific Publications* 1986;(74):23–33.

Pierce JP, Choi WS, Gilpin EA, Farkas AJ, Merritt RK. Validation of susceptibility as a predictor of which adolescents take up smoking in the United States. *Health Psychology* 1996;15(5):355–61.

Pierce JP, Distefan JM, Kaplan RM, Gilpin EA. The role of curiosity in smoking initiation. *Addictive Behaviors* 2005;30(4):685–96.

Pierce JP, Gilpin EA. A historical analysis of tobacco marketing and the uptake of smoking by youth in the United States: 1890–1977. *Health Psychology* 1995;14(6):500–8.

Pierce JP, Lee L, Gilpin EA. Smoking initiation by adolescent girls, 1944 through 1988: an association with targeted advertising. *JAMA: the Journal of the American Medical Association* 1994;271(8):608–11.

Pillai SG, Ge D, Zhu G, Kong X, Shianna KV, Need AC, Feng S, Hersh CP, Bakke P, Gulsvik A, et al. A genome-wide association study in chronic obstructive pulmonary disease (COPD): identification of two major susceptibility loci. *PLoS Genetics* 2009;5(3):e1000421;doi:10.1371/journal/pgen.1000421.

Pisinger C, Jorgensen T. Waist circumference and weight following smoking cessation in a general population: the Inter99 Study. *Preventive Medicine* 2007;44(4):290–5.

Pittilo RM. Cigarette smoking and endothelial injury: a review. *Advances in Experimental Medicine and Biology* 1990;273:61–78.

Pletcher MJ, Hulley BJ, Houston T, Kiefe CI, Benowitz N, Sidney S. Menthol cigarettes, smoking cessation, atherosclerosis, and pulmonary function: the Coronary Artery Risk Development in Young Adults (CARDIA) Study. *Archives of Internal Medicine* 2006;166(17):1915–22.

Plummer BA, Velicer WF, Redding CA, Prochaska JO, Rossi JS, Pallonen UE, Meier KS. Stage of change, decisional balance, and temptations for smoking: measurement and validation in a large, school-based population of adolescents. *Addictive Behaviors* 2001;26(4):551–71.

Polivy J, Herman CP, Howard KI. Restraint scale: assessment of dieting. In: Hersen M, Bellack AS, editors. *Dictionary of Behavioral Assessment Techniques*. Pergamon General Psychology Series. New York: Pergamon Press, 1988:377–80.

Pomerleau CS, Ehrlich E, Tate JC, Marks JL, Flessland KA, Pomerleau OF. The female weight-control smoker: a profile. *Journal of Substance Abuse* 1993;5(4):391–400.

Pomerleau OF, Downey KK, Stelson FW, Pomerleau CS. Cigarette smoking in adult patients diagnosed with attention deficit hyperactivity disorder. *Journal of Substance Abuse* 1995;7(3):373–8.

Poorthuis RB, Goriounova NA, Couey JJ, Mansvelder HD. Nicotinic actions on neuronal networks for cognition: general principles and long-term consequences. *Biochemical Pharmacology* 2009;78(7):668–76.

Potter BK, Pederson LL, Chan SS, Aubut JA, Koval JJ. Does a relationship exist between body weight, concerns about weight, and smoking among adolescents: an integration of the literature with an emphasis on gender. *Nicotine & Tobacco Research* 2004;6(3): 397–425.

Prokhorov AV, Hudmon KS, Cinciripini PM, Marani S. "Withdrawal symptoms" in adolescents: a comparison of former smokers and never-smokers. *Nicotine & Tobacco Research* 2005;7(6):909–13.

Prokhorov AV, Hudmon KS, de Moor CA, Kelder SH, Conroy JL, Ordway N. Nicotine dependence, withdrawal symptoms, and adolescents' readiness to quit smoking. *Nicotine & Tobacco Research* 2001;3(2):151–5.

Prokhorov AV, Padgett DI, Wetter DW, Le TT, Kitsman HE. Spit tobacco intervention in dental practice: recommendations for clinicians. *Texas Dental Journal* 1998;115(6):59–63.

Quinton AE, Cook C-M, Peek MJ. The relationship between cigarette smoking, endothelial function and intrauterine growth restriction in human pregnancy. *BJOG* 2008;115(6):780–4.

Raitakari OT, Adams MR, McCredie RJ, Griffiths KA, Celermajer DS. Arterial endothelial dysfunction related to passive smoking is potentially reversible in healthy young adults. *Annals of Internal Medicine* 1999; 130(7):578–81.

Raitakari OT, Juonala M, Kähönen M, Taittonen L, Laitinen T, Mäki-Torkko N, Järvisalo MJ, Uhari M, Jokinen E, Rönnemaa T, et al. Cardiovascular risk factors in childhood and carotid artery intima-media thickness in adulthood: the Cardiovascular Risk in Young Finns Study. *JAMA: the Journal of the American Medical Association* 2003;290(17):2277–83.

Ribeiro SN, Jennen-Steinmetz C, Schmidt MH, Becker K. Nicotine and alcohol use in adolescent psychiatric inpatients: associations with diagnoses, psychosocial factors, gender and age. *Nordic Journal of Psychiatry* 2008;62(4):315–21.

Riggs NR, Chou CP, Li C, Pentz MA. Adolescent to emerging adulthood smoking trajectories: when do smoking trajectories diverge, and do they predict early adulthood nicotine dependence? *Nicotine & Tobacco Research* 2007;9(11):1147–54.

Riggs PD, Mikulich SK, Whitmore EA, Crowley TJ. Relationship of ADHD, depression, and non-tobacco substance use disorders to nicotine dependence in substance-dependent delinquents. *Drug and Alcohol Dependence* 1999;54(3):195–205.

Robbins DR, Enright PL, Sherrill DL. Lung function development in young adults: is there a plateau phase? *European Respiratory Journal* 1995;8(5):768–72.

Robinson LA, Klesges RC, Zbikowski SM, Glaser R. Predictors of risk for different stages of adolescent smoking in a biracial sample. *Journal of Consulting and Clinical Psychology* 1997;65(4):653–62.

Robinson LA, Murray DM, Alfano CM, Zbikowski SM, Blitstein JL, Klesges RC. Ethnic differences in predictors of adolescent smoking onset and escalation: a longitudinal study from 7th to 12th grade. *Nicotine & Tobacco Research* 2006;8(2):297–307.

Robinson ML, Berlin I, Moolchan ET. Tobacco smoking trajectory and associated ethnic differences among adolescent smokers seeking cessation treatment. *Journal of Adolescent Health* 2004;35(3):217–24.

Rodriguez D, Tercyak KP, Audrain-McGovern J. Effects of inattention and hyperactivity/impulsivity symptoms on development of nicotine dependence from mid adolescence to young adulthood. *Journal of Pediatric Psychology* 2008;33(6):563–75.

Rojas NL, Killen JD, Haydel KF, Robinson TN. Nicotine dependence among adolescent smokers. *Archives of Pediatrics & Adolescent Medicine* 1998;152(2):151–6.

Roth MD, Arora A, Barsky SH, Kleerup EC, Simmons M, Tashkin DP. Airway inflammation in young marijuana and tobacco smokers. *American Journal of Respiratory and Critical Care Medicine* 1998;157(3 Pt 1):928–37.

Rubinstein ML, Thompson PJ, Benowitz NL, Shiffman S, Moscicki AB. Cotinine levels in relation to smoking behavior and addiction in young adolescent smokers. *Nicotine & Tobacco Research* 2007;9(1):129–35.

Ryan YM, Gibney MJ, Flynn MA. The pursuit of thinness: a study of Dublin schoolgirls aged 15 y. *International Journal of Obesity and Related Metabolic Disorders* 1998;22(5):485–7.

Saarni SE, Silventoinen K, Rissanen A, Sarlio-Lähteenkorva S, Kaprio J. Intentional weight loss and smoking in young adults. *International Journal of Obesity* 2004;28(6):796–802.

Saccone NL, Culverhouse RC, Schwantes-An TH, Cannon DS, Chen X, Cichon S, Giegling I, Han S, Han Y, Keskitalo-Vuokko K, et al. Multiple independent loci at chromosome 15q25.1 affect smoking quantity: a meta-analysis and comparison with lung cancer and COPD. *PLoS Genetics* 2010;6(8):e1001053;doi:10.1371/journal/pgen.1001053.

Saccone SF, Hinrichs AL, Saccone NL, Chase GA, Konvicka K, Madden PAF, Breslau N, Johnson EO, Hatsukami D, Pomerleau O, et al. Cholinergic nicotinic receptor genes implicated in a nicotine dependence association study targeting 348 candidate genes with 3713 SNPs. *Human Molecular Genetics* 2007;16(1):36–49.

Saules KK, Pomerleau CS, Snedecor SM, Mehringer AM, Shadle MB, Kurth C, Krahn DD. Relationship of onset of cigarette smoking during college to alcohol use, dieting concerns, and depressed mood: results from the Young Women's Health Survey. *Addictive Behaviors* 2004;29(5):893–9.

Schepis TS, Rao U. Epidemiology and etiology of adolescent smoking. *Current Opinion in Pediatrics* 2005; 17(5):607–12.

Schlaepfer IR, Hoft NR, Collins AC, Corley RP, Hewitt JK, Hopfer CJ, Lessem JM, McQueen MB, Rhee SH, Ehringer MA. The CHRNA5/A3/B4 gene cluster variability as an important determinant of early alcohol and tobacco initiation in young adults. *Biological Psychiatry* 2008;63(11):1039–46.

Sears MR, Greene JM, Willan AR, Wiecek EM, Taylor DR, Flannery EM, Cowan JO, Herbison GP, Silva PA, Poulton R. A longitudinal, population-based, cohort study of childhood asthma followed to adulthood. *New England Journal of Medicine* 2003;349(15):1414–22.

Sherrill DL, Lebowitz MD, Knudson RJ, Burrows B. Smoking and symptom effects on the curves of lung function growth and decline. *American Review of Respiratory Disease* 1991;144(1):17–22.

Sherrill DL, Lebowitz MD, Knudson RJ, Burrows B. Continuous longitudinal regression equations for pulmonary function measures. *European Respiratory Journal* 1992;5(4):452–62.

Shiffman S, Paty JA, Gwaltney CJ, Dang Q. Immediate antecedents of cigarette smoking: an analysis of unrestricted smoking patterns. *Journal of Abnormal Psychology* 2004;113(1):166–71.

Shimokata H, Muller DC, Andres R. Studies in the distribution of body fat. III: effects of cigarette smoking. *JAMA: the Journal of the American Medical Association* 1989;261(8):1169–73.

Shisslak CM, Renger R, Sharpe T, Crago M, McKnight KM, Gray N, Bryson S, Estes LS, Parnaby OG, Killen J, et al. Development and evaluation of the McKnight Risk Factor Survey for assessing potential risk and protective factors for disordered eating in preadolescent and adolescent girls. *International Journal of Eating Disorders* 1999;25(2):195–214.

Shor RE, Williams DC, Canon LK, Latta RM, Shor MB. Beliefs of smokers and never smokers about the motives that underlie tobacco smoking. *Addictive Behaviors* 1981;6(4):317–24.

Sidney S, Sternfeld B, Gidding SS, Jacobs DR Jr, Bild DE, Oberman A, Haskell WL, Crow RS, Gardin JM. Cigarette smoking and submaximal exercise test duration in a biracial population of young adults: the CARDIA Study. *Medicine and Science in Sports and Exercise* 1993;25(8):911–6.

Simon A, Chironi G, Levenson J. Comparative performance of subclinical atherosclerosis tests in predicting coronary heart disease in asymptomatic individuals. *European Heart Journal* 2007;28(24):2967–71.

Siroux V, Pin I, Oryszczyn MP, Le Moual N, Kauffmann F. Relationships of active smoking to asthma and asthma severity in the EGEA study. *European Respiratory Journal* 2000;15(3):470–7.

Smith AE, Cavallo DA, Dahl T, Wu R, George TP, Krishnan-Sarin S. Effects of acute tobacco abstinence in adolescent smokers compared with nonsmokers. *Journal of Adolescent Health* 2008a;43(1):46–54.

Smith AE, Cavallo DA, McFetridge A, Liss T, Krishnan-Sarin S. Preliminary examination of tobacco withdrawal in adolescent smokers during smoking cessation treatment. *Nicotine & Tobacco Research* 2008b;10(7): 1253–9.

Smith TA, House RF Jr, Croghan IT, Gauvin TR, Colligan RC, Offord KP, Gomez-Dahl LC, Hurt RD. Nicotine patch therapy in adolescent smokers. *Pediatrics* 1996;98(4 Pt 1):659–67.

Sneve M, Jorde R. Cross-sectional study on the relationship between body mass index and smoking, and longitudinal changes in body mass index in relation to change in smoking status: The Tromso Study. *Scandinavian Journal of Public Health* 2008;36(4):397–407.

Soldz S, Cui X. Pathways through adolescent smoking: a 7-year longitudinal grouping analysis. *Health Psychology* 2002;21(5):495–504.

Sonntag H, Wittchen H-U, Höfler M, Kessler RC, Stein MB. Are social fears and DSM-IV social anxiety disorder associated with smoking and nicotine dependence in adolescents and young adults? *European Journal of Psychiatry* 2000;15(1):67–74.

Sotir M, Yeatts K, Shy C. Presence of asthma risk factors and environmental exposures related to upper respiratory infection-triggered wheezing in middle school-age children. *Environmental Health Perspectives* 2003;111(4):657–62.

Stavropoulos-Kalinoglou A, Metsios GS, Panoulas VF, Douglas KMJ, Nevill AM, Jamurtas AZ, Kita M, Koutedakis Y, Kitas GD. Cigarette smoking associates with body weight and muscle mass of patients with rheumatoid arthritis: a cross-sectional, observational study. *Arthritis Research & Therapy* 2008;10:R59; doi:10.1186/ar2429.

Stice E, Martinez EE. Cigarette smoking prospectively predicts retarded physical growth among female adolescents. *Journal of Adolescent Health* 2005;37(5): 363–70.

Stice E, Shaw H. Prospective relations of body image, eating, and affective disturbances to smoking onset in adolescent girls: how Virginia slims. *Journal of Consulting and Clinical Psychology* 2003;71(1):129–35.

Strachan DP, Butland BK, Anderson HR. Incidence and prognosis of asthma and wheezing illness from early childhood to age 33 in a national British cohort. *BMJ (British Medical Journal)* 1996;312(7040):1195–9.

Strong DR, Kahler CW, Colby SM, Griesler PC, Kandel D. Linking measures of adolescent nicotine dependence to a common latent continuum. *Drug and Alcohol Dependence* 2009;99(1–3):296–308.

Stuhldreher WL, Orchard TJ, Donahue RP, Kuller LH, Gloninger MF, Drash AL. Cholesterol screening in childhood: sixteen-year Beaver County Lipid Study experience. *Journal of Pediatrics* 1991;119(4):551–6.

Sturm JJ, Yeatts K, Loomis D. Effects of tobacco smoke exposure on asthma prevalence and medical care use in North Carolina middle school children. *American Journal of Public Health* 2004;94(2):308–13.

Substance Abuse and Mental Health Services Administration. *Results from the 2002 National Survey on Drug Use and Health: National Findings*. NHSDA Series H-22. Rockville (MD): U.S. Department of Health and Human Services, Substance Abuse and Mental Health Services Administration, Office of Applied Studies, 2002. DHHS Publication No. SMA 03–3836.

Sutherland I, Willner P. Patterns of alcohol, cigarette and illicit drug use in English adolescents. *Addiction* 1998;93(8):1199–208.

Suwarna L.Virginia Slims. 1985. Philip Morris Collection. Bates No. 2026305099. <http://legacy.library.ucsf.edu/tid/pov56b00>.

Swan GE, Hudmon KS, Jack LM, Hemberger K, Carmelli D, Khroyan TV, Ring HZ, Hops H, Andrews JA, Tildesley E, et al. Environmental and genetic determinants of tobacco use: methodology for a multidisciplinary, longitudinal family-based investigation. *Cancer Epidemiology, Biomarkers & Prevention* 2003;12(10): 994–1005.

Swan GE, Lessov-Schlagger CN, Bierut LJ, Shields AE, Bergen AW, Vanyukov M. Status of genetic studies of nicotine dependence. In: *Phenotypes and Endophenotypes: Foundations for Genetic Studies of Nicotine Use and Dependence*. Tobacco Control Monograph No. 20. Bethesda (MD): U.S. Department of Health and Human Services, National Institutes of Health, National Cancer Institute, 2009:19–69. NIH Publication No. 09-6366.

Tager IB, Muñoz A, Rosner B, Weiss ST, Carey V, Speizer FE. Effect of cigarette smoking on the pulmonary function of children and adolescents. *American Review of Respiratory Disease* 1985;131(5):752–9.

Tager IB, Segal MR, Speizer FE, Weiss ST. The natural history of forced expiratory volumes: effect of cigarette smoking and respiratory symptoms. *American Review of Respiratory Disease* 1988;138(4):837–49.

Talcott GW, Fiedler ER, Pascale RW, Klesges RC, Peterson AL, Johnson RS. Is weight gain after smoking cessation inevitable? *Journal of Consulting and Clinical Psychology* 1995;63(2):313–6.

Thomas GN, Chook P, Yip TWC, Kwong SK, Chan TYK, Qiao M, Huang XS, Guo DS, Feng JZ, Chan SW, et al. Smoking without exception adversely affects vascular structure and function in apparently healthy Chinese: implications in global atherosclerosis prevention. *International Journal of Cardiology* 2008;128(2):172–7.

Thorgeirsson TE, Geller F, Sulem P, Rafnar T, Wiste A, Magnusson KP, Manolescu A, Thorleifsson G, Stefansson H, Ingason A, et al. A variant associated with nicotine dependence, lung cancer and peripheral artery disease. *Nature* 2008;452(7187):638–42.

Thorgeirsson TE, Gudbjartsson DF, Surakka I, Vink JM, Amin N, Geller F, Sulem P, Rafnar T, Esko T, Walter S, et al. Sequence variants at *CHRNB3-CHRNA6* and *CYP2A6* affect smoking behavior. *Nature Genetics* 2010;42(5):448–53.

Tobacco and Genetics Consortium. Genome-wide meta-analyses identify multiple loci associated with smoking behavior. *Nature Genetics* 2010;42(5):441–7.

Tollefsen E, Langhammer A, Romundstad P, Bjermer L, Johnsen R, Holmen TL. Female gender is associated with higher incidence and more stable respiratory symptoms during adolescence. *Respiratory Medicine* 2007;101(5):896–902.

Townsend J, Wilkes H, Haines A, Jarvis M. Adolescent smokers seen in general practice: health, lifestyle, physical measurements, and response to antismoking advice. *BMJ (British Medical Journal)* 1991;303(6808):947–50.

True WR, Xian H, Scherrer JF, Madden PAF, Bucholz KK, Heath AC, Eisen SA, Lyons MJ, Goldberg J, Tsuang M. Common genetic vulnerability for nicotine and alcohol dependence in men. *Archives of General Psychiatry* 1999;56(7):655–61.

Twisk JW, Staal BJ, Brinkman MN, Kemper HC, van Mechelen W. Tracking of lung function parameters and the longitudinal relationship with lifestyle. *European Respiratory Journal* 1998;12(3):627–34.

Tyc VL. Introduction to the special issue: tobacco control strategies for medically at-risk youth. *Journal of Pediatric Psychology* 2008;33(2):113–8.

Ulrik CS, Backer V, Dirksen A, Pedersen M, Koch C. Extrinsic and intrinsic asthma from childhood to adult age: a 10-yr follow-up. *Respiratory Medicine* 1995;89(8):547–54.

Upadhyaya HP, Deas D, Brady KT, Kruesi M. Cigarette smoking and psychiatric comorbidity in children and adolescents. *Journal of the American Academy of Child and Adolescent Psychiatry* 2002;41(11):1294–305.

U.S. Department of Health and Human Services. *The Health Consequences of Smoking: Cardiovascular Disease. A Report of the Surgeon General*. Rockville (MD): U.S. Department of Health and Human Services, Public Health Service, Office on Smoking and Health, 1983. DHHS Publication No. (PHS) 84-50204.

U.S. Department of Health and Human Services. *The Health Consequences of Smoking: Nicotine Addiction. A Report of the Surgeon General*. Atlanta (GA): U.S. Department of Health and Human Services, Public Health Service, Centers for Disease Control, National Center for Chronic Disease Prevention and Health Promotion, Office on Smoking and Health, 1988. DHHS Publication No. (CDC) 88-8406.

U.S. Department of Health and Human Services. *The Health Benefits of Smoking Cessation. A Report of the Surgeon General*. Atlanta (GA): U.S. Department of Health and Human Services, Public Health Service, Centers for Disease Control, National Center for Chronic Disease Prevention and Health Promotion, Office on Smoking and Health, 1990. DHHS Publication No. (CDC) 90-8416.

U.S. Department of Health and Human Services. *Preventing Tobacco Use Among Young People. A Report of the Surgeon General*. Atlanta (GA): U.S. Department of Health and Human Services, Public Health Service, Centers for Disease Control and Prevention, National Center for Chronic Disease Prevention and Health Promotion, Office of Smoking and Health, 1994.

U.S. Department of Health and Human Services. *Women and Smoking. A Report of the Surgeon General*. Rockville (MD): U.S. Department of Health and Human Services, Public Health Service, Office of the Surgeon General, 2001.

U.S. Department of Health and Human Services. *The Health Consequences of Smoking: A Report of the Surgeon General*. Atlanta (GA): U.S. Department of Health and Human Services, Centers for Disease Control and Prevention, National Center for Chronic Disease Prevention and Health Promotion, Office on Smoking and Health, 2004.

U.S. Department of Health and Human Services. *The Health Consequences of Involuntary Exposure to Tobacco Smoke: A Report of the Surgeon General*. Atlanta (GA): U.S. Department of Health and Human

Services, Centers for Disease Control and Prevention, Coordinating Center for Health Promotion, National Center for Chronic Disease Prevention and Health Promotion, Office on Smoking and Health, 2006.

U.S. Department of Health and Human Services. *How Tobacco Smoke Causes Disease—The Biology and Behavioral Basis for Tobacco-Attributable Disease: A Report of the Surgeon General*. Atlanta (GA): U.S. Department of Health and Human Services, Centers for Disease Control and Prevention, National Center for Chronic Disease Prevention and Health Promotion, Office on Smoking and Health, 2010.

U.S. Department of Health, Education, and Welfare. *Smoking and Health. Report of the Advisory Committee to the Surgeon General of the Public Health Service*. Washington: U.S. Department of Health, Education, and Welfare, Public Health Service, Center for Disease Control, 1964. PHS Publication No. 1103.

van Strien T, Frijters JER, Bergers GPA, Defares PB. The Dutch Eating Behavior Questionnaire for assessment of restrained, emotional, and external eating behavior. *International Journal of Eating Disorders* 1986;5(2):295–315.

Verdecchia P, Schillaci G, Borgioni C, Ciucci A, Zampi I, Battistelli M, Gattogigio R, Sacchi N, Porcellati C. Cigarette smoking, ambulatory blood pressure and cardiac hypertrophy in essential hypertension. *Journal of Hypertension* 1995;13(10):1209–15.

Vidrine JI, Anderson CB, Pollak KI, Wetter DW. Gender differences in adolescent smoking: mediator and moderator effects of self-generated expected smoking outcomes. *American Journal of Health Promotion* 2006;20(6):383–7.

Vogelberg C, Hirsch T, Radon K, Dressel H, Windstetter D, Weinmayr G, Weiland SK, von Mutius E, Nowak D, Leupold W. Leisure time activity and new onset of wheezing during adolescence. *European Respiratory Journal* 2007;30(4):672–6.

Voorhees CC, Schreiber GB, Schumann BC, Biro F, Crawford PB. Early predictors of daily smoking in young women: the National Heart, Lung, and Blood Institute Growth and Health Study. *Preventive Medicine* 2002;34(6):616–24.

Wahl SK, Turner LR, Mermelstein RJ, Flay BR. Adolescents' smoking expectancies: psychometric properties and prediction of behavior change. *Nicotine & Tobacco Research* 2005;7(4):613–23.

Wang MQ, Fitzhugh EC, Eddy JM, Westerfield RC. School dropouts' attitudes and beliefs about smoking. *Psychological Reports* 1998;82(3 Pt 1):984–6.

Wang MQ, Fitzhugh EC, Eddy JM, Westerfield RC. School dropouts' attitudes and beliefs about smoking. *Psychological Reports* 1998;82(3 Pt 1):984–6.

Wang X, Mensinga TT, Schouten JP, Rijcken B, Weiss ST. Determinants of maximally attained level of pulmonary function. *American Journal of Respiratory and Critical Care Medicine* 2004;169(8):941–9.

Wechsler H, Davenport A, Dowdall G, Moeykens B, Castillo S. Health and behavioral consequences of binge drinking in college: a national survey of students at 140 campuses. *JAMA: the Journal of the American Medical Association* 1994;272(21):1672–7.

Weekley CK III, Klesges RC, Relyea G. Smoking as a weight-control strategy and its relationship to smoking status. *Addictive Behaviors* 1992;17(3):259–71.

Weiser M, Reichenberg A, Grotto I, Yasvitzky R, Rabinowitz J, Lubin G, Nahon D, Knobler HY, Davidson M. Higher rates of cigarette smoking in male adolescents before the onset of schizophrenia: a historical-prospective cohort study. *American Journal of Psychiatry* 2004;161(7):1219–23.

Weiss RB, Baker TB, Cannon DS, von Niederhausern A, Dunn DM, Matsunami N, Singh NA, Baird L, Coon H, McMahon WM, et al. A candidate gene approach identifies the CHRNA5-A3-B4 Region as a risk factor for age-dependent nicotine addiction. PLoS Genetics 2008;4(7):e1000125;doi:10.1371/journal/pgen.1000125.

Weitzman ER, Chen YY. The co-occurrence of smoking and drinking among young adults in college: national survey results from the United States. *Drug and Alcohol Dependence* 2005;80(3):377–86.

Weitzman M, Cook S, Auinger P, Florin TA, Daniels S, Nguyen M, Winickoff JP. Tobacco smoke exposure is associated with the metabolic syndrome in adolescents. *Circulation* 2005;112(6):862–9.

Welch SL, Fairburn CG. Smoking and bulimia nervosa. *International Journal of Eating Disorders* 1998; 23(4):433–7.

West R, Hargreaves M. Factors associated with smoking in student nurses. *Psychology & Health* 1995;10(3): 195–204.

White HR, Pandina RJ, Chen PH. Developmental trajectories of cigarette use from early adolescence into young adulthood. *Drug and Alcohol Dependence* 2002;65(2):167–78.

Wilens TE, Biederman J, Adamson JJ, Henin A, Sgambati S, Gignac M, Sawtelle R, Santry A, Monuteaux MC. Further evidence of an association between adolescent bipolar disorder with smoking and substance use disorders: a controlled study. *Drug and Alcohol Dependence* 2008;95(3):188–98.

Willi C, Bodenmann P, Ghali WA, Faris PD, Cornuz J. Active smoking and the risk of type 2 diabetes: a systematic review and meta-analysis. *JAMA: the Journal of the American Medical Association* 2007;298(22):2654–64.

Wiltshire S, Amos A, Haw S, McNeill A. Image, context and transition: smoking in mid-to-late adolescence. *Journal of Adolescence* 2005;28(5):603–17.

Withers NJ, Low L, Holgate ST, Clough JB. The natural history of respiratory symptoms in a cohort of adolescents. *American Journal of Respiratory and Critical Care Medicine* 1998;158(2):352–7.

Woo KS, Chook P, Leong HC, Huang XS, Celermajer DS. The impact of heavy passive smoking on arterial endothelial function in modernized Chinese. *Journal of the American College of Cardiology* 2000;36(4):1228–32.

Worsley A, Worsley AJ, McConnon S, Silva P. The weight control practices of 15 year old New Zealanders. *Journal of Paediatrics and Child Health* 1990;26(1):41–5.

Wu L-T, Anthony JC. Tobacco smoking and depressed mood in late childhood and early adolescence. *American Journal of Public Health* 1999;89(12):1837–40.

Xu X, Weiss ST, Rijcken B, Schouten JP. Smoking, changes in smoking habits, and rate of decline in FEV1: new insight into gender differences. *European Respiratory Journal* 1994;7(6):1056–61.

Yang Z, Knight CA, Mamerow MM, Vickers K, Penn A, Postlethwait EM, Ballinger SW. Prenatal environmental tobacco smoke exposure promotes adult atherogenesis and mitochondrial damage in apolipoprotein $E^{-/-}$ mice fed a chow diet. *Circulation* 2004;110(24):3715–20.

Yeatts K, Davis KJ, Sotir M, Herget C, Shy C. Who gets diagnosed with asthma: frequent wheeze among adolescents with and without a diagnosis of asthma. *Pediatrics* 2003;111(5 Pt 1):1046–54.

Young LE. Imprinting of genes and the Barker hypothesis. *Twin Research* 2001;4(5):307–17.

Yufu K, Takahashi N, Hara M, Saikawa T, Yoshimatsu H. Measurements of the brachial-ankle pulse wave velocity and flow-mediated dilatation in young, healthy smokers. *Hypertension Research* 2007;30(7):607–12.

Zacny JP. Behavioral aspects of alcohol-tobacco interactions. *Recent Developments in Alcoholism* 1990;8:205–19.

Zalata A, Yahia S, El-Bakary A, Elsheikha HM. Increased DNA damage in children caused by passive smoking as assessed by comet assay and oxidative stress. *Mutation Research* 2007;629(2):140–7.

Zhu B-Q, Sun Y-P, Sudhir K, Sievers RE, Browne AE, Gao L, Hutchison SJ, Chou TM, Deedwania PC, Chatterjee K, et al. Effects of second-hand smoke and gender on infarct size of young rats exposed in utero and in the neonatal to adolescent period. *Journal of the American College of Cardiology* 1997;30(7):1878–85.

Ziedonis D, Hitsman B, Beckham JC, Zvolensky M, Adler LE, Audrain-McGovern J, Breslau N, Brown RA, George TP, Williams J, et al. Tobacco use and cessation in psychiatric disorders: National Institute of Mental Health report. *Nicotine & Tobacco Research* 2008;10(12):1691–715.

Zieske AW, McMahan CA, McGill HC Jr, Homma S, Takei H, Malcolm GT, Tracy RE, Strong JP. Smoking is associated with advanced coronary atherosclerosis in youth. *Atherosclerosis* 2005;180(1):87–92.

Zieske AW, Takei H, Fallon KB, Strong JP. Smoking and atherosclerosis in youth. *Atherosclerosis* 1999;144(2):403–8.

Zimlichman E, Mandel D, Mimouni FB, Shochat T, Grotto I, Kreiss Y. Smoking habits in adolescents with mild to moderate asthma. *Pediatric Pulmonology* 2004;38(3):193–7.

Zucker AN, Harrell ZA, Miner-Rubino K, Stewart AJ, Pomerleau CS, Boyd CJ. Smoking in college women: the role of thinness pressures, media exposure, and critical consciousness. *Psychology of Women Quarterly* 2001;25(3):233–41.

Chapter 3
The Epidemiology of Tobacco Use Among Young People in the United States and Worldwide

Introduction

The purpose of this chapter is to document key patterns and trends in tobacco use among young people in the United States and worldwide, updating and expanding information presented in the 1994 report of the Surgeon General on preventing tobacco use among young people (U.S. Department of Health and Human Services [USDHHS] 1994). Effectively describing these key patterns and trends in tobacco use among young people is critical to the success of efforts designed to reduce the burden of tobacco-related morbidity and mortality. In addition to providing current information on tobacco use and influences on that behavior, this chapter includes information on new lines of research (e.g., transitions in tobacco use and trajectories of smoking behavior). This chapter can help readers assess the need for interventions designed to reduce tobacco use among young people, suggest appropriate target groups for interventions, and clarify when and where interventions should be implemented.

Data Sources

A variety of surveillance, research, and evaluation data collection systems related to youth and young adult tobacco use exist at national and subnational levels. Such data collections typically assess tobacco use behaviors and may also collect information on knowledge and attitudes, exposures to protobacco and antitobacco influences, effects of tobacco use, and other health risk behaviors (e.g., alcohol use), among other factors. Although each system or study serves a particular purpose, no individual survey is able to serve all purposes by comprehensively covering every relevant issue and reaching all relevant populations. Specific surveillance systems were selected to serve as primary data sources for this chapter by the salience of their content, the timeliness of their data, the completeness with which they cover the populations they are intended to represent, and the strength of their methodology.

The data presented include cross-sectional data from four national surveillance systems—the National Survey on Drug Use and Health (NSDUH), Monitoring the Future (MTF), the Youth Risk Behavior Surveillance System (YRBSS), and the National Youth Tobacco Survey (NYTS)—and one international surveillance system, the Global Youth Tobacco Survey (GYTS). Each of these surveys is population based and uses anonymous or confidential self-reported surveys, a methodology that provides valid youth tobacco use data (Brener et al. 2003). Table 3.1 provides basic information about these data sources, and they are discussed in detail in Appendix 3.2. Briefly, NYTS and the National Youth Risk Behavior Survey (YRBS), one component of the YRBSS, are based on probability samples of public and private school students with questionnaires administered anonymously in schools; NYTS includes students in grades 6–12 and YRBS includes students in grades 9–12 (CDC 2004, 2010a). MTF collects data from youth as well as college students and adults. The youth participants are from a probability sample of public and private students enrolled in 8th, 10th, or 12th grade within the 48 contiguous states; questionnaires are administered anonymously or confidentially at the schools. GYTS uses probability sampling of students enrolled in the grades typical for 13-, 14-, and 15-year-olds for a given country and usually includes both private and public schools. Again, questionnaires are administered anonymously in the school setting. NSDUH uses household-based sampling to represent the entire civilian noninstitutionalized population of the United States age 12 years and older. Questionnaires are completed confidentially in the home with computer-assisted interviewing (CAI), so that only the respondent is aware of the questions being asked.

These surveys provide comparable, but not identical, measures of tobacco use among youth. Because each survey provides some unique information, monitoring the results of all is necessary to fully understand behaviors and trends. GYTS is the only standardized source for comparable, population-based data on youth tobacco use internationally. Among the U.S. surveys, NSDUH and the YRBS are both used to track national progress toward the U.S. Healthy People goals for youth tobacco use (USDHHS 2011). Throughout this chapter, data from the national Youth Risk Behavior Survey (YRBS), one component of the YRBSS, are reported, unless otherwise indicated (e.g., in one case, state-level YRBS data are used).

Unless otherwise indicated, all YRBS data are from the 2009 survey. All NSDUH data are from the 2010 survey, MTF data from the 2009 survey, and NYTS data from the 2009 survey. GYTS data are from surveys conducted between 1999 and 2007. NSDUH is used to track initiation of tobacco use in adolescents as young as 12 years of age and provides comparable data for youth (12–17 years of age), young adults (18–25 years of age), and older adults (≥26 years of age). YRBS is used to track the prevalence of current use of tobacco and quit attempts among high school students. NYTS uses a sampling procedure identical to that of YRBS, but the surveys have important distinctions. NYTS includes middle school students and YRBS does not. Further, while YRBS monitors several categories

Table 3.1 Sources of national data on tobacco use among young people; United States and worldwide

	National Survey on Drug Use and Health (NSDUH)	Monitoring the Future (MTF)	Youth Risk Behavior Survey (YRBS)	National Health Interview Survey (NHIS)	Global Youth Tobacco Survey (GYTS)	National Youth Tobacco Survey (NYTS)	National Longitudinal Study of Adolescent Health (Add Health)
Sponsoring agency or organization	Substance Abuse and Mental Health Services Administration	National Institute on Drug Abuse; administered by the University of Michigan's Institute for Social Research	Centers for Disease Control and Prevention	National Center for Health Statistics	World Health Organization Tobacco Free Initiative	Centers for Disease Control and Prevention	*Eunice Kennedy Shriver* National Institute of Child Health and Human Development
Type of survey	Cross-sectional	Cross-sectional and longitudinal	Cross-sectional	Cross-sectional	Cross-sectional	Cross-sectional	Cross-sectional and longitudinal
Years	1971–2010[a]	1975–2009	1991, 1993, 1995, 1997, 1999, 2001, 2003, 2005, 2007, 2009	1965–2009 (various)	Varied by country: 1997–2009	1999, 2000, 2002, 2004, 2006, and 2009	Wave I: 1994–95 Wave II: 1996 Wave III: 2001–02 Wave IV: 2007–08
Mode of survey administration	Audio, computer-assisted self-interview	School-based, self-administered questionnaire	School-based, self-administered questionnaire	Audio, computer-assisted self-interview (since 1997)	School-based, self-administered questionnaire	School-based, self-administered questionnaire	School-based questionnaire; household, computer-administered interview
Response rate	2010: 88.8% for household screening; 74.7% for interviewing	2009: 88% of 8th graders, 89% of 10th graders, and 82% of 12th graders completed questionnaires; 54% of original schools responded; 98% response rate with replacements	2009: 81% for schools; 88% for students; 71% overall	2009: 82.2% household response rate; 65.4% adult survey response rate	Varied by country (see Appendix 3.1)	2009: 92.3% for schools; 91.9% for students; 84.8% overall	Wave I: 78.9% Wave II: 88.2% Wave III: 77.4%
Ages/grades	≥12 years	8th and 10th grades (since 1991) and 12th grade (since 1975); college students; young adults	9th–12th grades	All ages	Students aged 13–15 years	6th–12th grades	Wave I: 7th–12th grades Wave II: 8th–12th grades Wave III: 18–26 years of age
Sample size	2010: 68,487	2009: 46,097	2009: 16,410	2009: 33,856 households, for 34,640 families and 88,446 persons	Varied by country (see Appendix 3.1)	2009: 22,679	Wave I: 90,118 school based; 20,745 in home Wave II: 14,738 Wave III: 15,197

Table 3.1 Continued

	National Survey on Drug Use and Health (NSDUH)	Monitoring the Future (MTF)	Youth Risk Behavior Survey (YRBS)	National Health Interview Survey (NHIS)	Global Youth Tobacco Survey (GYTS)	National Youth Tobacco Survey (NYTS)	National Longitudinal Study of Adolescent Health (Add Health)
Type of tobacco use examined	Cigarettes, smokeless tobacco (chewing tobacco, snuff), cigars and pipe tobacco, blunts	Cigarettes and smokeless tobacco	Cigarettes, smokeless tobacco, cigars	Cigarettes	Cigarettes and smokeless tobacco	Cigarettes, smokeless tobacco, cigars, pipes, bidis, and kreteks	Cigarettes and smokeless tobacco

[a]The NSDUH survey has been administered annually since 1990. Previously, it was conducted every 2–3 years. Data in recent years are trendable only for 2002–2008, but for some variables there are discontinuities within that period.

of risk behaviors and has a limited focus on tobacco use, NYTS is dedicated to monitoring tobacco behaviors and is the most comprehensive source of nationally representative tobacco data among students. For example, NYTS includes information about exposure to protobacco and antitobacco influences, preferred brands, attitudes, and susceptibility to using tobacco, items that are not found in YRBS.

MTF has a unique strength in tracking trends because it was among the first of these surveys to be fielded in 1975. NSDUH began in 1971 but had a methodology change in 2002 that makes direct comparison to previous years' findings inadvisable (Substance Abuse and Mental Health Services Administration [SAMHSA] 2011b). Alone among these surveys, NSDUH covers the entire youth population, not just those enrolled in school; this is an important difference because tobacco use prevalence is higher among school dropouts than among enrolled youth (Kopstein 2001). Further, NSDUH is a lengthier survey that includes detailed questions about substance use, mental health issues, family socioeconomic status (SES), and other factors relevant to tobacco use.

Key Epidemiologic Measures

This chapter covers a variety of epidemiologic measures pertinent to the study of tobacco use among young people. Topics include age when cigarette smoking begins, current prevalence of cigarette smoking, trends in cigarette smoking over time, disparities in cigarette smoking and other tobacco use, current prevalence of smokeless tobacco use and cigar smoking, trends in smokeless tobacco use and cigar smoking over time, concurrent use of multiple tobacco products, and tobacco use among young people worldwide. This chapter also includes epidemiologic measures that support major conclusions of other chapters of this report: cigarette smoking and weight loss, related to Chapter 2, "The Health Consequences of Tobacco Use Among Young People"; tobacco use and academic achievement, related to Chapter 4, "Social, Environmental, Cognitive, and Genetic Influences on the Use of Tobacco Among Youth"; and tobacco brand preferences among young people, related to Chapter 5, "The Tobacco Industry's Influence on the Use of Tobacco Among Youth."

For each measure reviewed in this chapter, data from the survey or surveys best suited to address the issue are presented in the text and accompanying tables and figures. However, as noted above, more than one source is available to shed light on many of these issues, and examining data from multiple sources provides evidence of the range of effects as well as evidence that findings are valid or otherwise based on the consistency of those sources. Therefore, Appendix 3.1 provides a comprehensive, detailed review of the data and the measures provided from the four primary surveys as well as comparable findings gleaned from the National Longitudinal Study of Adolescent Health and the National Health Interview Survey (NHIS) of adults.

Appendix 3.1 also provides supplemental analyses on subtopics related to the major topics presented here, including intensity of cigarette smoking, transitions and trajectories in smoking, implications for smoking during adolescence for young adults, nicotine addiction in adolescence and young adulthood, attempts to quit smoking, trends in knowledge and attitudes about smoking, cigarette smoking and depression, patterns of cigar use, and patterns of use of emerging tobacco products.

Data Analysis

Using these data sources and relevant measures, population-weighted estimates with 95% confidence intervals were calculated using statistical software to account for the multistage probability sampling designs of the surveys. For some analyses, but not all, statistical tests were conducted to investigate differences in prevalence estimates by demographic factors of interest (e.g., age/grade, gender, race/ethnicity) and, when possible, in trends over time. Significance ($p < 0.05$) was determined by the use of two-sided t-tests, throughout.

Key Epidemiologic Findings

In this section, epidemiologic analyses that support the major conclusions of this chapter are considered. These analyses are selected from a more comprehensive set that is presented in Appendix 3.1. These findings reinforce and extend, as appropriate, conclusions that were first presented in the 1994 Surgeon General's report on preventing tobacco use among young people.

Age When Cigarette Smoking Begins

One of the most important—and widely cited—findings from the 1994 Surgeon General's report on smoking and health was that virtually all cigarette smoking begins before adulthood. Figure 3.1 and Table 3.2 illustrates and updates this finding, using the most recent data from NSDUH (2010) in an analysis parallel to that conducted for the 1994 Surgeon General's report. In this survey, adult smokers 30–39 years of age were asked about their first experience with cigarette smoking. Among adults who had ever tried a cigarette, 81.5% reported trying their first cigarette by the time they were 18 years of age, while an additional 16.5% did so by 26 years of age. Among adults who had ever smoked cigarettes daily, 88.2% reported trying their first cigarette by the time they were 18 years of age, while an additional 10.8% did so by 26 years of age. About two-thirds (65.1%) of adults who had ever smoked daily began smoking daily by 18 years of age, and almost one-third of these adults (31.1%) began smoking daily between 18 and 26 years of age. Therefore, virtually *no* initiation of cigarette smoking (<1–2%) and few transitions to daily smoking (<4%) actually occur in adulthood after 26 years of age. Moreover, it is important to note that the initiation of cigarette smoking can often occur quite early in adolescence, before 18 years of age. In this analysis of the 2010 NSDUH data, for example, more than one-third (36.7%) of adults who had ever smoked cigarettes reported trying their first cigarette by 14 years of age, which is the age when one typically enters high school in the U.S. (Table 3.2). This is one of the most critical epidemiologic findings of this report, underscoring again that adolescence and young adulthood represent a time of heightened vulnerability to tobacco use and the initiation of cigarette smoking. Additional analyses that investigate distinct developmental trajectories and transitions in cigarette smoking across adolescence through young adulthood are presented in Appendix 3.1 (e.g., see Figure 3.1.4 and Tables 3.1.16–3.1.20). It is important to note that these NSDUH estimates from adults represent smoking initiation that occurred during the late 1990s, at about the time of the Master Settlement Agreement, when the prevalence of youth tobacco use was beginning to decline (see "Trends in Cigarette Smoking Over Time" later in this chapter). To investigate more contemporary trends in tobacco use initiation, we turned to adolescent and young adult data from NSDUH in recent years (2006–2010). Initiation rates for cigarette smoking have been stable over the last 5 years. Comparing 2006 to 2010, the rate of initiation of cigarette smoking (number of persons who smoked cigarettes for the first time in the last 12

Figure 3.1 **Percentage of recalled age at which adult smokers first tried a cigarette and began smoking daily, among 30- to 39-year-old adult smokers, by smoking status; National Survey on Drug Use and Health (NSDUH) 2010; United States**

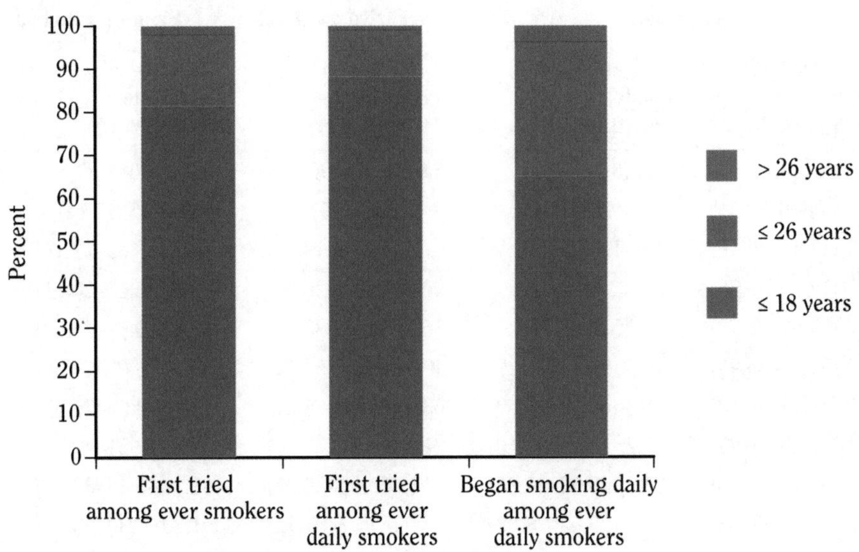

Source: 2010 NSDUH: Substance Abuse and Mental Health Services Administration (unpublished data).
Note: Based on responses to the following questions: "Have you ever smoked part or all of a cigarette?" "How old were you the first time you smoked part or all of a cigarette?" "Has there ever been a period in your life when you smoked cigarettes every day for at least 30 days?" "How old were you when you first started smoking cigarettes every day?" For further information, refer to Appendix 3.1, Table 3.1.12.

months divided by the number of persons who had never smoked in the last year) among adolescents (12–17 year of age) and young adults (18–25 years of age) did not change overall and for all subgroups (i.e., by gender and race/ethnicity) ($p > 0.05$) (Appendix 3.1, Table 3.1.30).

Current Prevalence of Cigarette Smoking

According to the 2009 NYTS, about 1 in 4 (23.2%) high school seniors is a current cigarette smoker (i.e., had smoked a cigarette in the last 30 days; see Appendix 3.3 for more detail on this definition). This figure is comparable to the prevalence of current cigarette smoking among adults (≥26 years of age), according to the 2010 NSDUH survey (22.8%) (SAMHSA 2011b). Young adults (18–25 years old) have the highest prevalence of current cigarette smoking of all age groups, at 34.2% (SAMHSA 2011b) (see Figure 3.1). By multiplying the current smoking prevalence in middle school (from the NYTS 2009) and the current smoking prevalence in high school (from the NYTS 2009) with the number of students enrolled in middle and high school, respectively (US Census Bureau 2009), this report finds that about 3.0 million (95% confidence interval [CI], 2,782,555–3,295,540) high school students and about 624,000 (95% CI, 515,957–731,939) middle school students are current cigarette smokers. Note, then, that the total number of current smokers is somewhat higher given out-of-school youth. By way of comparison, among young adults aged 18–25 years, about 11.7 million (95% CI, 11,352,000–11,980,000) are current cigarette smokers and about 14.7 million (95% CI, 14,343,000–15,005,000) have smoked a cigarette within the past year (SAMHSA 2011a). To achieve the national Healthy People objectives outlined for 2020, further reductions in cigarette smoking are necessary and will likely require renewed intervention efforts (see "Trends in Cigarette Smoking Over Time" later in this chapter). According to the 2009 YRBS, 19.5% of students in grades 9–12 currently smoke cigarettes. The target prevalence estimate referenced in *Healthy People 2020* for current smoking among adolescents (in grades 9–12) is 16% and among adults (≥18 years old) is 12% (USDHHS 2011). *Healthy People 2020* also references 2% reductions in smoking initiation (USDHHS 2011).

Table 3.2 Cumulative percentages of recalled age at which a respondent first used a cigarette and began smoking daily, by smoking status among 30- to 39-year-olds; National Survey on Drug Use and Health (NSDUH) 2010;[a] United States

	All persons		Persons who had ever tried a cigarette	Persons who had ever smoked daily	
Recalled age (years)	First tried a cigarette % (95% CI)	Began smoking daily % (95% CI)	First tried a cigarette % (95% CI)	First tried a cigarette % (95% CI)	Began smoking daily % (95% CI)
≤10	4.1 (3.54–4.77)	0.4 (0.24–0.61)	5.9 (5.12–6.90)	6.7 (5.60–8.09)	1.0 (0.65–1.64)
≤11	5.8 (5.16–6.58)	0.7 (0.48–1.01)	8.4 (7.47–9.51)	9.6 (8.25–11.14)	1.9 (1.29–2.70)
≤12	12.1 (11.13–13.19)	1.8 (1.40–2.23)	17.5 (16.14–19.02)	20.9 (18.85–23.14)	4.7 (3.75–5.93)
≤13	18.5 (17.36–19.78)	3.5 (2.95–4.07)	26.8 (25.18–28.53)	32.4 (30.15–34.71)	9.3 (7.93–10.82)
≤14	25.4 (24.02–26.78)	6.0 (5.30–6.72)	36.7 (34.89–38.56)	43.6 (41.17–46.09)	16.0 (14.31–17.81)
≤15	34.4 (32.94–35.93)	10.5 (9.57–11.52)	49.8 (47.87–51.72)	58.5 (56.03–61.00)	28.1 (25.89–30.46)
≤16	43.9 (42.31–45.42)	15.3 (14.22–16.39)	63.5 (61.59–65.27)	72.9 (70.55–75.07)	40.9 (38.53–43.26)
≤17	49.4 (47.76–50.95)	19.2 (18.08–20.40)	71.4 (69.64–73.10)	80.3 (78.21–82.27)	51.4 (49.09–53.74)
≤18	56.3 (54.75–57.90)	24.3 (23.03–25.66)	81.5 (79.91–82.98)	88.2 (86.45–89.81)	65.1 (62.67–67.41)
≤19	59.3 (57.72–60.86)	27.4 (26.06–28.88)	85.8 (84.37–87.10)	91.8 (90.30–93.11)	73.5 (71.14–75.65)
≤20	61.9 (60.38–63.41)	30.0 (28.55–31.44)	89.6 (88.33–90.68)	93.2 (91.75–94.38)	80.2 (78.11–82.16)
≤21	64.2 (62.67–65.72)	32.0 (30.53–33.50)	92.9 (91.81–93.86)	95.9 (94.78–96.77)	85.6 (83.82–87.27)
≤22	65.2 (63.72–66.75)	33.1 (31.63–34.61)	94.4 (93.40–95.25)	96.6 (95.61–97.43)	88.6 (86.92–90.08)
≤23	65.9 (64.39–67.39)	33.9 (32.40–35.40)	95.3 (94.45–96.11)	97.3 (96.34–98.00)	90.7 (89.13–92.02)
≤24	66.5 (65.03–68.02)	34.6 (33.09–36.12)	96.3 (95.42–96.97)	97.9 (97.02–98.50)	92.6 (91.14–93.78)
≤25	67.6 (66.11–69.04)	35.7 (34.22–37.27)	97.8 (97.14–98.30)	98.8 (98.23–99.23)	95.6 (94.56–96.49)
≤26	67.8 (66.28–69.20)	35.9 (34.43–37.47)	98.0 (97.39–98.53)	99.0 (98.39–99.36)	96.2 (95.18–96.96)
≤27	67.9 (66.44–69.36)	36.1 (34.62–37.68)	98.3 (97.64–98.73)	99.1 (98.46–99.42)	96.7 (95.74–97.44)
≤28	68.1 (66.61–69.52)	36.5 (34.98–38.04)	98.5 (97.90–98.94)	99.3 (98.75–99.60)	97.7 (96.90–98.27)
≤29	68.2 (66.69–69.59)	36.7 (35.14–38.20)	98.6 (98.01–99.03)	99.3 (98.81–99.64)	98.1 (97.39–98.63)
≤30	68.7 (67.28–70.14)	37.0 (35.50–38.56)	99.4 (98.98–99.69)	99.8 (99.44–99.93)	99.1 (98.50–99.43)
31–39	69.1 (67.68–70.53)	37.4 (35.85–38.91)	100.0	100.0	100.0
Never smoked	100.0	100.0	NA	NA	NA
Mean age (years)	15.9	17.9	15.9	15.1	17.9

Source: 2010 NSDUH: Substance Abuse and Mental Health Services Administration (unpublished data).
Note: **CI** = confidence interval; **NA** = not applicable.
[a]Based on responses to the following questions: "Have you ever smoked part or all of a cigarette?" "How old were you the first time you smoked part or all of a cigarette?" "Has there ever been a period in your life when you smoked cigarettes every day for at least 30 days?" "How old were you when you first started smoking cigarettes every day?"

Current Prevalence Among Adolescents

The prevalence of current cigarette smoking among high school and middle school students is provided in Table 3.3a and Appendix 3.1, Table 3.1.2. In the NYTS–high school survey, the prevalence of current cigarette smoking was higher for males than for females overall (19.6% vs. 14.8%, p <0.05), but no significant differences by gender were observed for YRBS (19.8% vs. 19.1%, p >0.05) or NYTS–middle school (5.6% vs. 4.7%, p >0.05). For NYTS–high school, White and Hispanic students had the highest prevalence of current cigarette smoking (19.2%), followed by Other youth (16.4%) and Blacks

Table 3.3a Percentage of high school students and middle school students who currently smoke cigarettes, by gender and race/ethnicity; National Youth Risk Behavior Survey (YRBS) 2009, and National Youth Tobacco Survey (NYTS) 2009; United States

	YRBS 9th–12th grades[a]		NYTS 9th–12 grades[a]		NYTS 6th–8th grades[a]	
Characteristic	**% (95% CI)**	**SN[b]**	**% (95% CI)**	**SN[b]**	**% (95% CI)**	**SN[b]**
Overall	19.5 (17.9–21.2)		17.2 (15.0–19.4)		5.2 (4.2–6.1)	
Gender						
Male	19.8 (17.8–21.9)	a	19.6 (16.6–22.5)	a	5.6 (4.3–6.9)	a
Female	19.1 (17.2–21.0)	a	14.8 (12.8–16.7)	b	4.7 (3.9–5.5)	a
Race/ethnicity						
White	22.5 (20.0–25.2)	a	19.2 (16.4–21.9)	a	4.3 (3.1–5.5)	a
Male	22.3 (18.9–26.0)		21.2 (18.0–24.5)		4.5 (3.0–5.9)	
Female	22.8 (20.3–25.5)		17.1 (14.5–19.8)		4.1 (2.7–5.6)	
Black or African American	9.5 (8.2–11.1)	b	7.5 (4.6–10.3)	b	5.1 (3.6–6.6)	a,b
Male	10.7 (8.4–13.5)		8.6 (3.6–13.6)		5.8 (3.6–8.0)	
Female	8.4 (6.5–10.9)		6.3 (3.0–9.6)		4.4 (2.7–6.1)	
Hispanic or Latino	18.0 (16.0–20.2)	c	19.2 (16.5–21.9)	a	6.7 (5.2–8.2)	b
Male	19.4 (16.7–22.5)		22.6 (19.9–25.4)		7.0 (5.3–8.7)	
Female	16.7 (14.4–19.2)		15.7 (12.0–19.4)		6.4 (4.5–8.3)	
Other[c]	16.5 (13.1–20.5)	c	16.4 (13.2–19.5)	a	7.2 (2.5–12.0)	a,b
Male	15.9 (12.4–20.2)		21.7 (16.6–26.8)		8.7 (0.2–17.2)	
Female	16.7 (12.5–21.9)		11.2 (6.7–15.8)		5.7 (3.0–8.5)	

Source: 2009 YRBS: Centers for Disease Control and Prevention (CDC 2011d); 2009 NYTS: CDC (unpublished data).
Note: **CI** = confidence interval; **SN** = statistical note.
[a]Estimates are based on responses to the question, "During the past 30 days, on how many days did you smoke cigarettes?" Respondents who reported that they had smoked on at least 1 or 2 days were classified as current smokers.
[b]This column represents the results of statistical tests that were run separately within each surveillance system (e.g., YRBS). These tests were performed to examine differences in estimates within specific demographic subgroups (e.g., gender). Estimates with the same letter (e.g., a and a) are not statistically significantly different from one another (p >0.05). Estimates with different letters (e.g., a and b) are, in contrast, statistically significantly different from one another (p <0.05).
[c]Includes Asians, American Indians or Alaska Natives, Native Hawaiians or Other Pacific Islanders, and persons of two or more races.

(7.5%; p <0.05 for all comparisons with Blacks). Note that students in the Other category include other racial/ethnic subgroups besides White, Black, and Hispanic (such as American Indian/Alaska Native and Asian). For YRBS, White students had the highest prevalence of current smoking (22.5%), compared to Hispanic (18.0%), Other (16.5%), and Black (9.5%) students (p <0.05 for all comparisons with White students). Differences between Hispanic and Other students were not significant for YRBS (p >0.05). For NYTS–middle school, Hispanic students had a higher prevalence of cigarette smoking than did White students (6.7% vs. 4.3%, p <0.05).

Current Prevalence Among Young Adults

The prevalence of current cigarette smoking among young adults (18–25 years old) is provided in Table 3.3b. In the 2010 NSDUH, the prevalence of current cigarette smoking was higher for young adult males than for females (38.1% vs. 30.3%). White youth had the highest prevalence (39.1%), followed by Hispanic (27.4%) and Black (23.3%) youth (SAMHSA 2011b). Of all age groups in the United States, young adults have the highest prevalence of current cigarette smoking (Figure 3.2), and this prevalence is especially high among young adults who are not college educated (Green et al. 2007). It should be noted that the tobacco industry targets young adults (18–

Table 3.3b Percentage of young adults (18–25 years old) who currently smoke cigarettes, by gender and race/ethnicity; National Survey on Drug Use and Health (NSDUH) 2010; United States

	NSDUH 18–25 years of age[a]	
Characteristic	**% (95% CI)**	**SN[b]**
Overall	34.2 (35.3–35.2)	
Gender		
Male	38.1 (36.8–39.4)	a
Female	30.3 (29.2–31.4)	b
Race/ethnicity		
White	39.1 (38.0–40.3)	a
Male	41.9 (40.3–43.5)	
Female	36.3 (34.9–37.8)	
Black or African American	26.3 (24.2–28.5)	b
Male	31.7 (28.5–35.0)	
Female	21.4 (19.0–24.1)	
Hispanic or Latino	27.4 (25.5–29.5)	b
Male	33.1 (30.2–36.1)	
Female	20.7 (18.1–23.6)	
Other[c]	27.2 (23.7–31.0)	b
Male	32.5 (27.8–37.5)	
Female	22.0 (18.0–26.5)	

Source: 2010 NSDUH: Substance Abuse and Mental Health Services Administration (unpublished data).
Note: **CI** = confidence interval; **SN** = statistical note.
[a]Based on responses to the question, "During the past 30 days, have you smoked part or all of a cigarette?" Respondents who chose "Yes" were classified as current smokers.
[b]This column represents the results of statistical tests that were run separately within each surveillance system (e.g., NSDUH). These tests were performed to examine differences in estimates within specific demographic subgroups (e.g., gender). Estimates with the same letter (e.g., a and a) are not statistically significantly different from one another (p >0.05). Estimates with different letters (e.g., a and b) are, in contrast, statistically significantly different from one another (p <0.05).
[c]Includes Asians, American Indians or Alaska Natives, Native Hawaiians or Other Pacific Islanders, and persons of two or more races.

25 years of age) through its advertising and promotional campaigns (Katz and Lavack 2002; Ling and Glantz 2002; Biener and Albers 2004). Therefore, cigarette smoking (and other tobacco use) among young adults should continue to be monitored closely. Data from NSDUH will be helpful in this regard, as this national surveillance system has a wide repertoire of tobacco use measures that can be compared across age groups, for adolescents (12–17 years old), young adults (18–25 years old), and adults (≥26 years old). Young adulthood may be a critical time in life for deciding whether cigarette smoking will become an established, lifelong behavior or will be rejected for a healthier lifestyle. Studies suggest that the number of individuals aged 18 and 19 years in the early stages of smoking initiation may be more than double that of established smokers aged 18 years (Ling and Glantz 2002; Biener and Albers 2004; Green et al. 2007). As illustrated in Figure 3.1 and Table 3.2, transitioning to daily smoking will not occur until young adulthood for about one-third of young smokers.

Trends in Cigarette Smoking Over Time

Trend data for cigarette smoking and other tobacco use among young people are available from four primary surveillance systems: YRBSS, NYTS, MTF, and NSDUH. Trends in the prevalence of current cigarette smoking and other tobacco use based on YRBS data are illustrated upfront in this chapter, (e.g., Figures 3.3a, 3.3b, 3.6a, 3.8a and 3.8b) and in Appendix 3.1 (e.g., Figures 3.1.6 onward). Trend data from MTF are also provided in Figure 3.6b and in Appendix 3.1 (e.g., Figures 3.1.5 onward). MTF data include prevalence estimates for ever and current cigarette smoking, as well as trends in knowledge and attitudes about cigarette smoking over time. Finally, trend data from NSDUH are also available here (Figures 3.5a and 3.5b) as well as in Appendix 3.1 (e.g., Figure 3.1.13 onward). This includes trends in the prevalence of current cigarette smoking among adolescents and young adults, as well as information on the initiation of tobacco use over time, among adolescents and young adults alike. To supplement these analyses, recent published manuscripts on trends in cigarette smoking over time are cited where appropriate (e.g. Nelson et al. 2008; CDC 2010a,d).

Trends in Cigarette Smoking Among Adolescents

Figures 3.3a and 3.3b illustrate trends in the prevalence of current cigarette smoking for students in 9th–12th grades since 1991, using YRBS. After a dramatic increase in the prevalence of current smoking in this population through the mid-1990s, the prevalence of current smoking dropped sharply. This inflection point (i.e., the point in time when the prevalence of cigarette smoking stopped increasing and began to decrease) coincided with

Figure 3.2 Percentage of middle school 8th graders, high school seniors, young adults (18–25 years of age), and adults (≥26 years of age) who currently smoke cigarettes; National Youth Tobacco Survey (NYTS)[a] 2009 and National Survey on Drug Use and Health (NSDUH)[b] 2010; United States

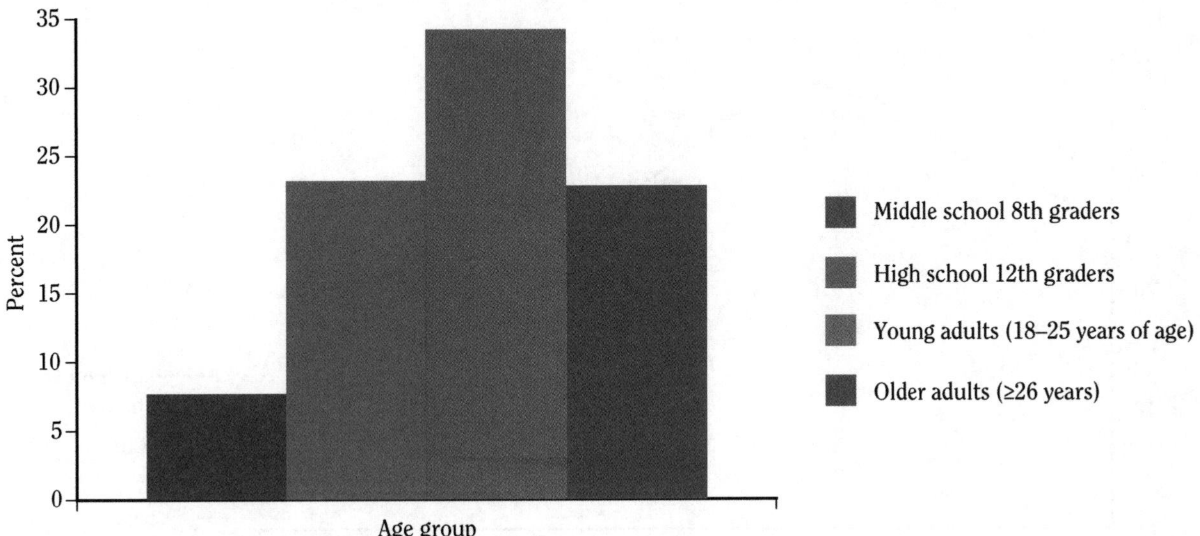

Source: Middle school and high school data, 2009 NYTS: Centers for Disease Control and Prevention (unpublished data). Young adult and older adult data, 2010 NSDUH: Substance Abuse and Mental Health Services Administration (published data). (For young adults, see SAMHSA 2011a, Table 2.24B.) (For adults ≥26 years, see SAMHSA 2011a, Table 2.25B.)
[a]Based on responses to the question, "During the past 30 days, on how many days did you smoke cigarettes?" Respondents who reported that they had smoked on at least 1 or 2 days were classified as current smokers.
[b]Based on responses to the question, "During the past 30 days, have you smoked part or all of a cigarette?" Respondents who chose "Yes" were classified as current smokers. For further information, refer to Appendix 3.1, Table 3.1.2.

the Master Settlement Agreement in 1998 when new initiatives to reduce youth tobacco use became widespread. Over time, however, this decline has decelerated, and for some subgroups, may have stopped altogether. YRBS data suggest the rates of decline in the prevalence of current smoking, ever smoking, and frequent smoking began to slow in 2003 (CDC 2010a). CDC estimates that if the decline in the prevalence of current smoking had continued from 2003 to 2009 at the same rate as had been seen from 1999 to 2003, 3 million fewer youth and young adults would have been current cigarette smokers by 2009 (Figure 3.4) (CDC unpublished data). Unfortunately, subgroup analyses suggest that the 1999–2003 rate of decline in the prevalence of current cigarette smoking only continued past 2003 for Black female students (CDC 2010a). For some subgroups of youth—White female students, Black male students, and younger students (9th–10th-grade students)—the decline in prevalence of current cigarette smoking began to slow in 2003 (CDC 2010a). The decline in current cigarette smoking stalled completely in 2003 for White males, Hispanic males, Hispanic females, and older students (11th–12th-grade students) (CDC 2010a). Data from MTF are consistent with the trends found using YRBS. According to MTF, the deceleration in ever smoking among students seems to have started in 2003, as well (Appendix 3.1, Figure 3.1.5), while the deceleration in current smoking among students may have started a year earlier or later, depending on the subgroup(s) involved (e.g., in 2002 for 12th-grade males and in 2004 for 8th-grade males and females; see Figure 3.1.8 in Appendix 3.1).

Detailed NSDUH data on trends in smoking prevalence among adolescents are not provided in this report, but are found elsewhere (SAMHSA 2009a,b; 2011b), with comparable surveillance data over time available from 2002. In contrast to YRBS and MTF, NSDUH, which includes both in-school and out-of-school youth, shows a consistent decline in the prevalence of cigarette smoking among adolescents overall (12–17 years old) from 2002 to 2008 (SAMHSA 2009b) and through 2010 (SAMHSA 2011b). However, when subgroup analyses were conducted, the decline in the prevalence of current cigarette

Figure 3.3 **Trends in the prevalence of current cigarette smoking over time among high school students, by gender and race/ethnicity; National Youth Risk Behavior Survey (YRBS) 1991–2009; United States**

A. Gender

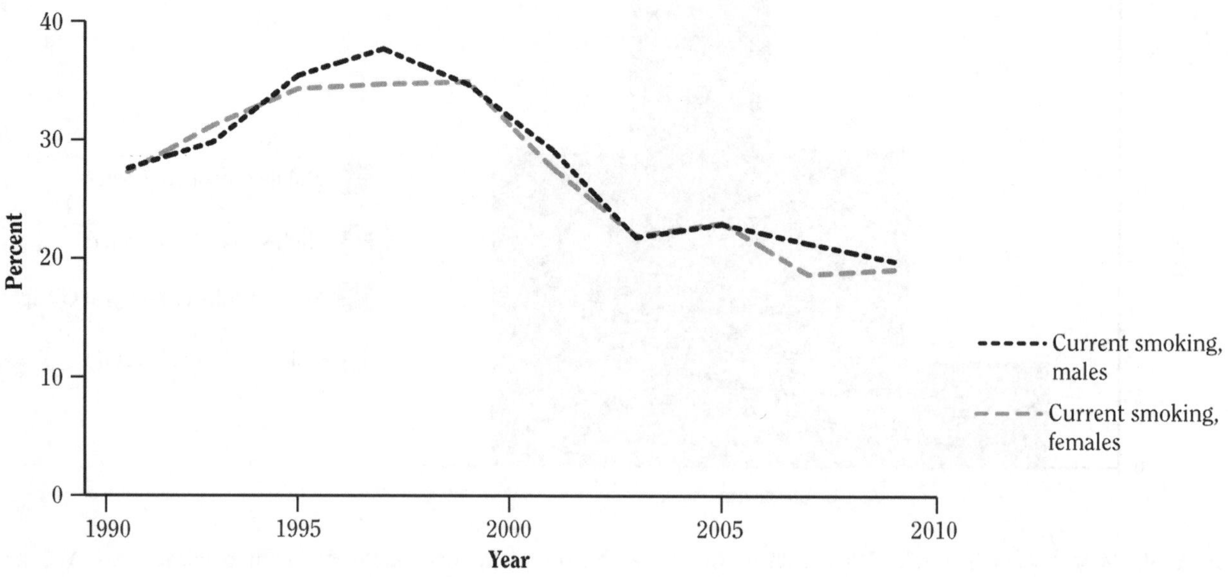

B. Race/ethnicity

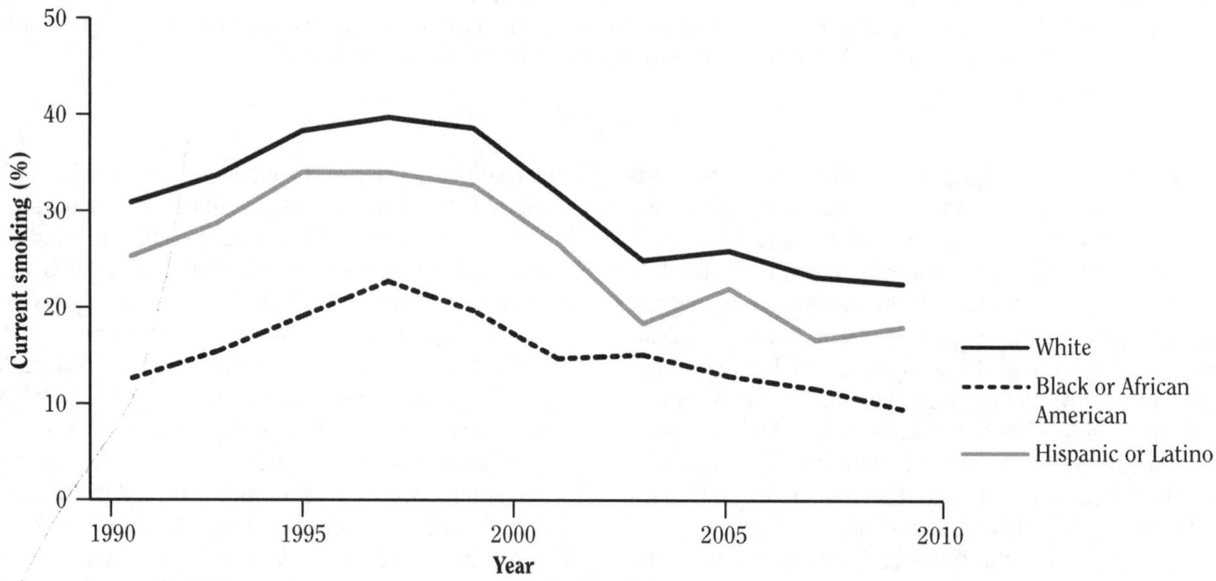

Source: 1991–2009 YRBS: Centers for Disease Control and Prevention (2011d).
Note: Based on responses to the question, "During the past 30 days, on how many days did you smoke cigarettes?" Respondents who reported that they had smoked on at least 1 or 2 days were classified as current smokers. Also see Appendix 3.1, Figures 3.1.7 and 3.1.9D.

Figure 3.4 Current high school cigarette smoking and projected rates if decline had continued; National Youth Risk Behavior Survey (YRBS); United States, 1991–2009

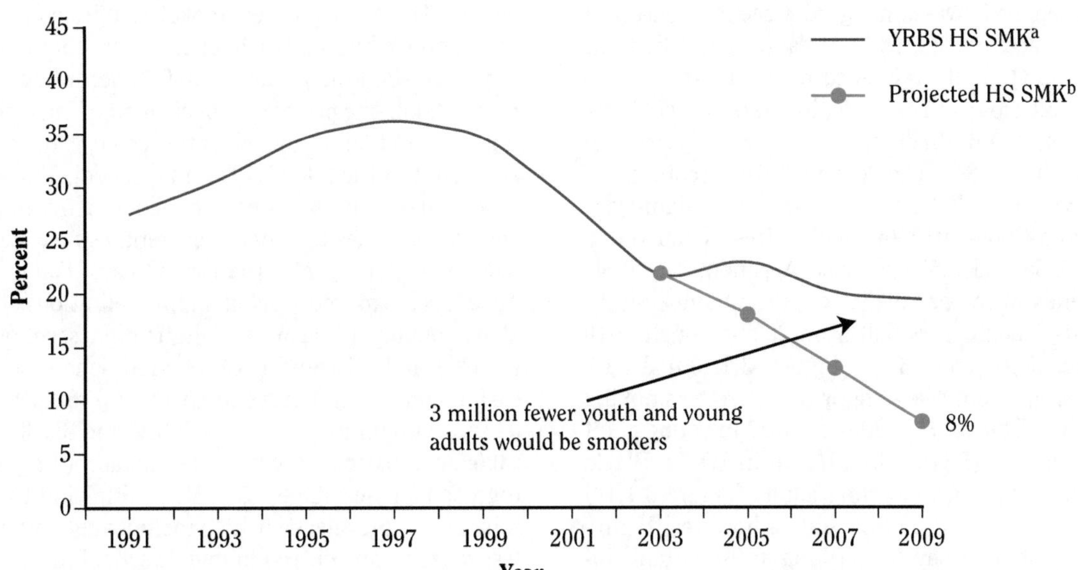

Source: 1991–2009 YRBS: Centers for Disease Control and Prevention, Division of Adolescent and School Health, Office on Smoking and Health (unpublished data).
Note: **HS SMK** = high school smokers. Based on responses to the question, "During the past 30 days, on how many days did you smoke cigarettes?" Respondents who reported that they had smoked on at least 1 or 2 days were classified as current smokers.
[a]High school students who smoked on 1 or more of the 30 days preceding the survey.
[b]Projected high school students who smoked on 1 or more days of the past 30 days if 1997–2003 decline had been maintained.

smoking between 2007 and 2008 appears to have been limited to White males and females only (SAMHSA 2009b), and between 2009 and 2010, the decline in the prevalence of current cigarette smoking was limited to White males only (SAMHSA 2001b). For all other subgroups, no significant differences in the prevalence of current cigarette smoking were observed between 2007 and 2008 (SAMHSA 2009b) or 2009 and 2010 (SAMSHA 2011b). This suggests the decline might have finally stalled for these subgroups at these time points, from NSDUH's perspective. However, the rate of initiation of cigarette smoking among adolescents (12–17 years old) declined overall from 2006–2010 (Appendix 3.1, Table 3.1.30) ($p < .05$), decreasing for females and Whites ($p < .05$) and unchanged for other groups.

These recent trends in the prevalence of current cigarette smoking among adolescents are difficult to fully reconcile, especially given subgroup differences both within and between surveillance systems. Nevertheless, it seems clear that progress in decreasing youth cigarette smoking has greatly slowed for some subgroups and halted altogether for others. Analyses of NYTS data through 2009 show that susceptibility to cigarette smoking (defined as the absence of a firm commitment not to smoke cigarettes or, conversely, a willingness to experiment with cigarette smoking) has remained unchanged since it was first measured in the 1999–2000 school year (Mowery et al. 2004; CDC 2010c).

Trends in Cigarette Smoking Among Young Adults

Trends in cigarette smoking among young adults from 1973 through 2005 have been reviewed elsewhere (Nelson et al. 2008) through an analysis of NHIS data. In this review, changes in the prevalence of current cigarette smoking among young adults (18–24 years old in this analysis) lagged a few years behind the changes for adolescents, providing evidence for a cohort effect (Lantz 2003; Nelson et al. 2008). After the increase in the prevalence of current smoking among adolescents in the mid-1990s, young adult smoking peaked at about the year 2000, a few years after the inflection point for adolescents, (i.e., the point when the prevalence of current cigarette smoking stopped increasing and began to decrease). Throughout this period, from the 1990s into the first part of the new millennium, the rise and fall of young adult smoking was never as steep as it was among adolescents (Nelson et al. 2008). In recent years, NSDUH data suggest that the decline in young adult prevalence may have stalled, too for certain subgroups. The initiation rate for cigarette smoking among young adults overall (18–25 years old) remained stable between 2006 and 2010, according to NSDUH (p >0.05). Still, for Whites, there was a significant decrease from 2006–2010 (p <0.05). This is illustrated in Figures 3.5a and 3.5b (see also Appendix 3.1, Table 3.1.31). Trends in the prevalence of current smoking for young adults (18–25 years old) from 2002 through 2010 are presented in Appendix 3.1, in Figures 3.1.13 to 3.1.15. As can be seen from these figures, cigarette smoking appears to have stalled from 2007 forward in young adult males and females (Figure 3.1.13) and in White, Black, and Hispanic subgroups of young adults (Figure 3.1.14) overall. When examined by SES status, however (Figure 3.1.15), this flat line may be masking an important difference: for young adults at or below the poverty line, the prevalence of current cigarette smoking actually began to increase in 2007, as it continued to decrease for those above the poverty line, albeit at a slower rate. No changes in current smoking for any of these subgroups occurred between 2009 and 2010, as reflected by either education level or employment status (trends by poverty level have not been publicly reported) (SAMHSA 2011b). The take-home message for young adults, then, is equally as worrisome as that for adolescents. As noted before (Figure 3.2), it must be emphasized that young adults have the highest prevalence of cigarette smoking of all age groups and may be uniquely situated, as they transition into older adulthood, to benefit from interventions, especially help with cessation, although research to date suggests few young adults avail themselves of these resources (see Chapter 6, "Efforts to Prevent and Reduce Tobacco Use Among Young People"). Continued surveillance of smoking and interventions to reduce smoking should be cognizant of critical differences in the prevalence of cigarette smoking among young adults by education level and SES status (Lantz 2003; Green et al. 2007).

Current Prevalence of Smokeless Tobacco Use and Cigar Smoking

According to the 2009 NYTS, about 1 in 10 high school males (11.6%) are current smokeless tobacco users (i.e., had used smokeless tobacco in the last 30 days [Table 3.4a; see Appendix 3.3 for more detail on this definition]), compared to about 1 in 100 high school females (1.8%), overall. The prevalence of smokeless tobacco use is highest among White high school students, compared to any other racial/ethnic group (p <0.05), according to NYTS–high school. The prevalence of cigar smoking is somewhat higher than that of smokeless tobacco use, overall. Again, according to the 2009 NYTS–high school, 15.0% of high school males and 6.7% of high school females (p <0.05, comparing males to females) currently smoke cigars (i.e., had smoked a cigar in the last 30 days; [Table 3.5a; see Appendix 3.3 for more detail on this definition]). The prevalence of current cigar smoking is highest among White (12.0%) and Hispanic (11.8%) high school students (p >0.05, comparing Whites to Hispanics), followed by students of Other race/ethnicities (8.0%) and Blacks (7.3%) (p >0.05, comparing Others to Blacks), according to NYTS–high school (see Table 3.5a). By multiplying the current tobacco use prevalence (which includes cigarettes, smokeless tobacco, and cigars) in middle school (from the NYTS 2009) and the current tobacco use prevalence in high school (from the NYTS 2009) with the number of students enrolled in middle and high school, respectively (US Census Bureau 2009), this report finds that approximately 4.3 million (95% CI, 3,699,710–4,399,235) high school students and about 985,000 (95% CI, 863,928–1,103,908) middle school students currently use a tobacco product (includes cigarettes, smokeless tobacco, and cigars). Similarly, NSDUH found that, among young adults aged 18–25 years in 2010, 13.9 million (95% CI, 13,582,000–14,228,000) used a tobacco product within the past month and 17.4 million (95% CI, 17,088,000–17,758,000) used a tobacco product within (includes cigarettes, smokeless tobacco, cigars) the past year.

The prevalence of current smokeless tobacco use among young adults (18–25 years old) is provided in Table 3.4b. In the 2010 NSDUH, the prevalence of current smokeless tobacco use was higher for young adult males than for females (12.0% vs. 0.7%; p <0.05). White (9.5%) youth had the highest prevalence, followed by Hispanic (2.2%) and Black (0.6%) youth (p <0.05 for all comparisons with Whites) (SAMHSA 2011b). The prevalence of current cigar smoking among young adults (18–25 years old) is provided in Table 3.5b. In the 2010 NSDUH, the prevalence of current cigar smoking was higher for young adult males than for females (16.6% vs. 5.6%; p <0.05). White (12.5%) and Black (11.5%) youth had the highest prevalence, followed by Hispanic (8.4%) youth (p <0.05 for all comparisons with Hispanics) (SAMHSA 2011b).

Figure 3.5 Trends in the initiation of cigarette smoking over time among young adults (18- to 25-year-olds), by gender and by race/ethnicity; National Survey on Drug Use and Health (NSDUH) 2006 and 2010; United States

A. Gender

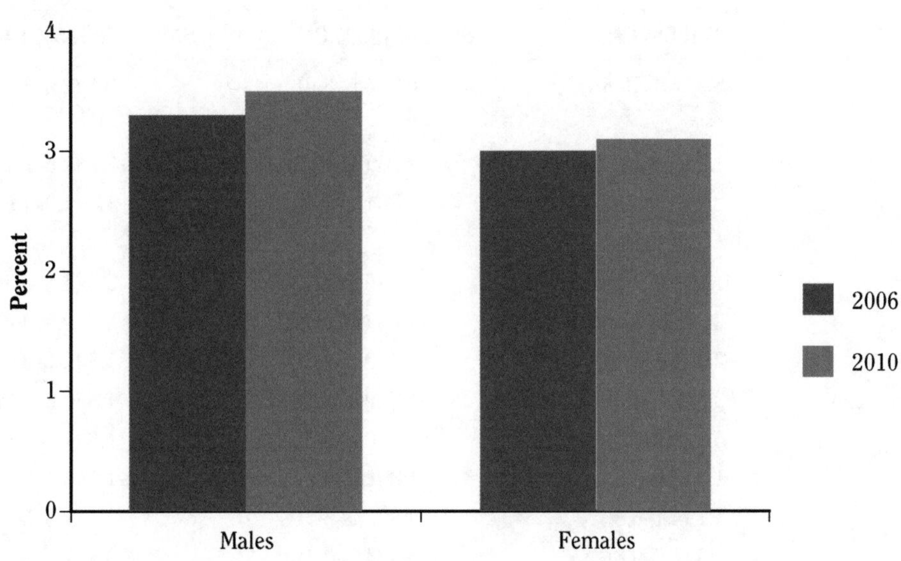

B. Race/ethnicity

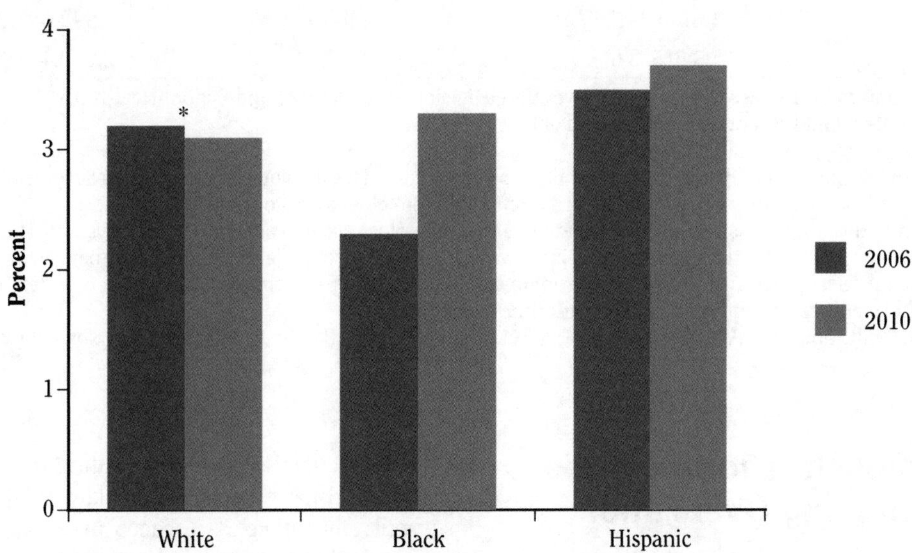

Source: 2006 and 2010 NSDUH: Substance Abuse and Mental Health Services Administration (unpublished data).
Note: For further information, refer to Appendix 3.1, Table 3.1.31. These data reflect initiation of cigarette smoking among all persons, not just those at–risk-for-initiation (i.e., those who did not use cigarettes in their lifetime or used cigarettes for the first time in the past year). Moreover, they reflect any initiation (i.e., smoked a cigarette for the first time). Difference between 2010 estimate and 2006 estimate is significant at the 0.05 level.
*Difference between 2010 estimate and 2006 estimate is significant at the 0.05 level.

Table 3.4a Percentage of high school students and middle school students who currently use smokeless tobacco, by gender and race/ethnicity and age/grade; Youth Risk Behavior Survey (YRBS) 2009, and National Youth Tobacco Survey (NYTS) 2009; United States

	YRBS 9th–12th grades[a]		NYTS 9th–12th grades[a]		NYTS 6th–8th grades[a]	
Characteristic	**% (95% CI)**	**SN[b]**	**% (95% CI)**	**SN[b]**	**% (95% CI)**	**SN[b]**
Overall	8.9 (7.3–10.8)		6.7 (4.5–8.9)		2.6 (2.0–3.2)	
Gender						
Male	15.0 (12.1–18.5)	a	11.6 (7.7–15.4)	a	3.7 (2.6-4.8)	a
Female	2.2 (1.8– 2.7)	b	1.8 (1.2–2.3)	b	1.4 (1.0–1.9)	b
Race/ethnicity						
White	11.9 (9.5–14.6)	a	8.7 (6.1–11.2)	a	2.5 (1.8–3.3)	a
Male	20.1 (15.8–25.4)		15.6 (11.2–20.0)		3.7 (2.5–4.8)	
Female	2.3 (1.7–3.2)		1.7 (0.8–2.6)		1.3 (0.7–2.0)	
Black or African American	3.3 (2.3–4.6)	b	1.7 (0.1–3.2)	b	1.5 (0.8–2.2)	b
Male	5.2 (3.7–7.4)		2.1 (0.4–3.7)		1.9 (1.1–2.8)	
Female	1.3 (0.8–2.3)		1.3 (0.3–4.8)		1.1 (0.1–2.1)	
Hispanic or Latino	5.1 (4.1–6.3)	c	4.8 (3.2–6.5)	c	2.5 (1.8–3.2)	a
Male	7.5 (5.7–9.8)		6.8 (4.2–9.5)		3.4 (2.3–4.6)	
Female	2.6 (1.9–3.5)		2.8 (1.4–4.3)		1.6 (0.7–2.5)	
Other[c]	5.7 (3.4–9.3)	b,c	5.3 (2.2–8.4)	c	5.1 (0.5–9.8)	a,b
Male	10.1 (6.3–15.7)		9.5 (4.0–15.0)		7.9 (2.6–21.8)	
Female	1.3 (0.5–3.6)		1.1 (0.0–2.2)		2.2 (0.4–3.9)	

Source: 2009 YRBS: Centers for Disease Control and Prevention, Division of Adolescent and School Health (CDC 2011d); 2009 NYTS: Centers for Disease Control and Prevention (unpublished data).
Note: **CI** = confidence interval; **SN** = statistical note.
[a]Based on responses to the question, "During the past 30 days, on how many days did you use chewing tobacco, snuff, or dip?" Respondents who chose 1 or 2 days or more were classified as current smokeless tobacco users.
[b]This column represents the results of statistical tests that were run separately within each surveillance system. These tests were performed to examine differences in estimates within specific demographic subgroups (e.g., gender). Estimates with the same letter (e.g., a and a) are not statistically significantly different from one another (p >0.05). Estimates with different letters (e.g., a and b) are, in contrast, statistically significantly different from one another (p <0.05).
[c]Includes Asians, American Indians or Alaska Natives, Native Hawaiians or Other Pacific Islanders, and persons of two or more races.

Trends in Smokeless Tobacco Use and Cigar Smoking Over Time

Trends in Smokeless Tobacco Use Among Adolescents and Young Adults

Trends in the prevalence of current smokeless tobacco use among adolescents are presented in Figures 3.6a and 3.6b, using data from YRBS (Figure 3.6a, 9th–12th-grade students) and MTF (Figure 3.6b, 12th-grade students only). As these data demonstrate, smokeless tobacco use occurs predominantly among White male students, as compared to other subgroups of students. Notably, for this particular subgroup, according to YRBS, following a sharp decline in use since the late 1990s, the prevalence of current smokeless tobacco use began to rise sharply again in 2003 and has continued to rise since. According to MTF, smokeless tobacco stalled for 12th- grade White male students from 2003 to 2007, after which it began to increase sharply again. For 8th- and 10th-grade White males, this recent increase was less sharp (Appendix 3.1, Figures 3.1.34a and 3.1.34b) but an increase nonetheless, following a similar stall from 2003 through 2008 (for 8th-grade students) and 2009 (for 10th-grade students). Since 2003, smokeless tobacco use among young adult (18–25 years old) White males has increased steadily according

Table 3.5a Percentage of high school students and middle school students who currently smoke cigars, by gender and race/ethnicity and age/grade; Youth Risk Behavior Survey (YRBS) 2009, and National Youth Tobacco Survey (NYTS) 2009; United States

	YRBS 9th–12th grades[a]		NYTS 9th–12 grades[a]		NYTS 6th–8th grades[a]	
Characteristic	**% (95% CI)**	**SN[b]**	**% (955 CI)**	**SN[b]**	**% (95% CI)**	**SN[b]**
Overall	14.0 (12.8–15.4)		10.9 (8.9–12.9)		3.9 (3.4–4.5)	
Gender						
Male	18.6 (17.0–20.5)	a	15.0 (12.1–18.0)	a	4.6 (3.8–5.5)	a
Female	8.8 (7.7–10.1)	b	6.7 (5.4–8.1)	b	3.2 (2.5–3.9)	b
Race/ethnicity						
White	14.9 (13.3–16.7)	a	12.0 (9.8–14.2)	a	2.9 (2.2–3.6)	a
Male	21.0 (18.7–23.4)		17.2 (14.1–20.3)		3.8 (2.6–4.9)	
Female	8.0 (6.8–9.3)		6.7 (5.0–8.3)		2.0 (1.2–2.8)	
Black or African American	12.8 (10.9–15.0)	a,b	7.3 (3.6–10.9)	b	4.5 (3.2–5.8)	b
Male	13.9 (11.6–16.5)		7.7 (2.6–12.8)		5.2 (3.4–7.0)	
Female	11.5 (8.8–14.8)		6.9 (3.4–10.3)		3.7 (1.8–5.7)	
Hispanic or Latino	12.7 (10.9–14.7)	a,b	11.8 (9.6–14.0)	a	6.2 (5.0–7.3)	c
Male	15.8 (13.1–19.1)		16.1 (13.4–18.7)		6.6 (5.2–8.0)	
Female	9.5 (7.6–11.9)		7.5 (5.5–9.4)		5.7 (3.6–7.8)	
Other[c]	11.1 (8.4–14.5)	b	8.0 (4.8–11.1)	b	4.6 (2.5–6.7)	a,b,c
Male	14.4 (10.9–18.9)		10.7 (6.2–15.2)		5.4 (2.0–8.9)	
Female	7.5 (4.8–11.7)		5.3 (2.1–8.4)		3.7 (1.6–5.9)	

Source: 2009 YRBS: Centers for Disease Control and Prevention, Division of Adolescent and School Health (unpublished data); 2009 NYTS: Centers for Disease Control and Prevention (unpublished data).
Note: **CI** = confidence interval; **SN** = statistical note.
[a]Based on responses to the question, "During the past 30 days, on how many days did you smoke cigars, cigarillos, or little cigars?" Respondents who reported that they had smoked cigars, cigarillos, or little cigars on 1 or 2 days or more were classified as current cigar smokers.
[b]This column represents the results of statistical tests that were run separately within each surveillance system (e.g., YRBS). These tests were performed to examine differences in estimates within specific demographic subgroups (e.g., gender). Estimates with the same letter (e.g., a and a) are not statistically significantly different from one another (p >0.05). Estimates with different letters (e.g., a and b) are, in contrast, statistically significantly different from one another (p <0.05).
[c]Includes Asians, American Indians or Alaska Natives, Native Hawaiians or Other Pacific Islanders, and persons of two or more races.

to NSDUH (see Appendix 3.1, Figures 3.1.30 and 3.1.31), with a sharp rise between 2008 and 2009. However from 2009 to 2010, the prevalence of current smokeless tobacco use did not change for this subgroup (SAMSHA 2011b).

According to YRBS and MTF, the decline in the prevalence of tobacco use began to slow or stall for adolescents, across separate measures of tobacco use (i.e., current cigarette smoking [see above] and smokeless tobacco use), in 2003. This is curious, worth noting, and may be useful to explore in future analyses that are beyond the scope of this chapter at present. The last published review of trends in smokeless tobacco use among adolescents and young adults was optimistic in tone, as trends up through 2003 were being described (Nelson et al. 2006). The review warned about the possible adverse effects of substantial reductions that had occurred in many states' antitobacco programs at that point in time (Schroeder 2004), and it may be that these adverse effects were, indeed, realized after 2003. Some subgroups have remained unaffected by these changes over time: the very low prevalence of smokeless tobacco use has remained unchanged among high school females and young adult females overall for the last decade (Figure 3.6a and Appendix 3.1, Figure 3.1.30). For other subgroups, such as Hispanic and Black 12th-grade males, trends in the prevalence of smokeless tobacco use over time have been more erratic, with

Table 3.4b Percentage of young adults (18–25 years old) who currently use smokeless tobacco, by gender and race/ethnicity; National Survey on Drug Use and Health (NSDUH) 2010; United States

Characteristic	NSDUH 18–25 years of age[a] % (95% CI)	SN[b]
Overall	6.4 (6.0–6.9)	
Gender		
Male	12.0 (11.1–12.8)	a
Female	0.7 (0.5–1.0)	b
Race/ethnicity		
White	9.5 (8.8–10.2)	a
Male	17.8 (16.6–19.1)	
Female	1.0 (0.7–1.5)	
Black or African American	0.6 (0.4–1.0)	b
Male	1.2 (0.8–2.0)	
Female	0.1 (0.0–0.6)	
Hispanic or Latino	2.2 (1.6–3.0)	c
Male	3.8 (2.8–5.2)	
Female	0.3 (0.1–0.7)	
Other[c]	3.6 (2.6–5.0)	d
Male	6.8 (4.9–9.4)	
Female	0.4 (0.2–1.0)	

Source: 2010 NSDUH: Substance Abuse and Mental Health Services Administration (unpublished data).
Note: **CI** = confidence interval; **SN** = statistical note.
[a]Based on responses to the question, "During the past 30 days, have you smoked part or all of a cigarette?" Respondents who chose "Yes" were classified as current smokers.
[b]This column represents the results of statistical tests that were run separately within each surveillance system (e.g., NSDUH). These tests were performed to examine differences in estimates within specific demographic subgroups (e.g., gender). Estimates with the same letter (e.g., a and a) are not statistically significantly different from one another ($p > 0.05$). Estimates with different letters (e.g., a and b) are, in contrast, statistically significantly different from one another ($p < 0.05$).
[c]Includes Asians, American Indians or Alaska Natives, Native Hawaiians or Other Pacific Islanders, and persons of two or more races.

Table 3.5b Percentage of young adults (18–25 years old) who currently smoke cigars, by gender and race/ethnicity; National Survey on Drug Use and Health (NSDUH) 2010; United States

Characteristic	NSDUH 18–25 years of age[a] % (95% CI)	SN[b]
Overall	11.2 (10.6–11.8)	
Gender		
Male	16.6 (15.7–17.6)	a
Female	5.6 (5.0–6.2)	b
Race/ethnicity		
White	12.5 (11.8–13.3)	a
Male	19.5 (18.3–20.8)	
Female	5.5 (4.8–6.2)	
Black or African American	11.5 (10.1–13.1)	a
Male	14.6 (12.3–17.3)	
Female	8.7 (7.1–10.5)	
Hispanic or Latino	8.4 (7.3–9.7)	b
Male	11.9 (10.1–14.0)	
Female	4.2 (3.2–5.6)	
Other[c]	6.6 (5.3–8.3)	b
Male	10.0 (7.5–13.2)	
Female	3.3 (2.1–5.2)	

Source: 2010 NSDUH: Substance Abuse and Mental Health Services Administration (unpublished data).
Note: **CI** = confidence interval; **SN** = statistical note.
[a]Based on responses to the question, "During the past 30 days, have you smoked part or all of a cigarette?" Respondents who chose "Yes" were classified as current smokers.
[b]This column represents the results of statistical tests that were run separately within each surveillance system (e.g., NSDUH). These tests were performed to examine differences in estimates within specific demographic subgroups (e.g., gender). Estimates with the same letter (e.g., a and a) are not statistically significantly different from one another ($p > 0.05$). Estimates with different letters (e.g., a and b) are, in contrast, statistically significantly different from one another ($p < 0.05$).
[c]Includes Asians, American Indians or Alaska Natives, Native Hawaiians or Other Pacific Islanders, and persons of two or more races.

Figure 3.6 Trends in the prevalence of current smokeless tobacco use over time among high school students (National Youth Risk Behavior Survey [YRBS]) and high school seniors (Monitoring the Future [MTF]), by gender and by race/ethnicity; YRBS 1995–2009 and MTF 1987 (or 1993)–2010; United States

A. Males and females, 9th–12th grades, YRBS[a]

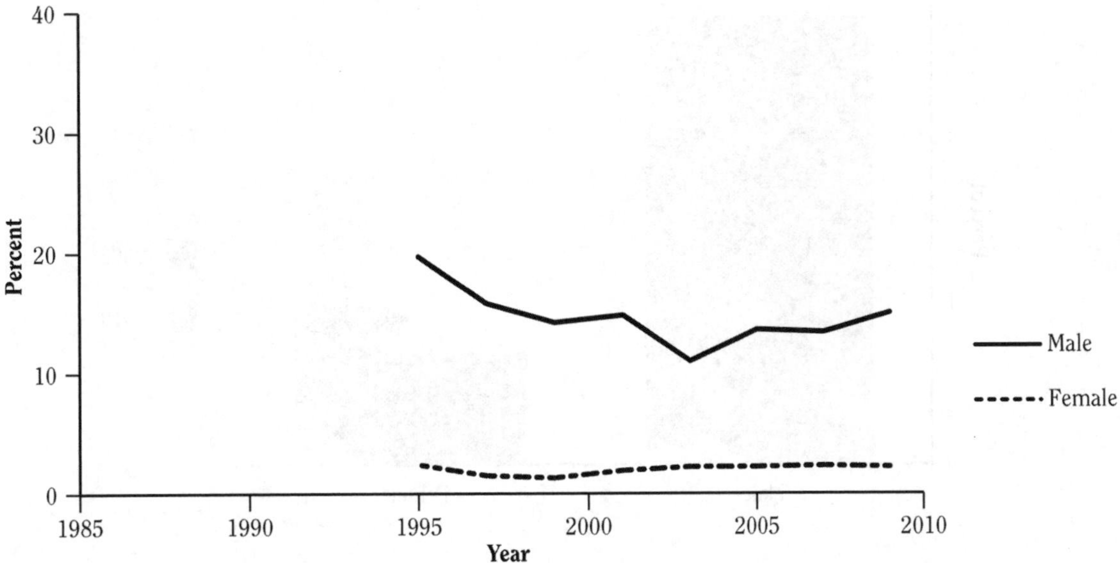

B. Males only, 12th grade, MTF[b]

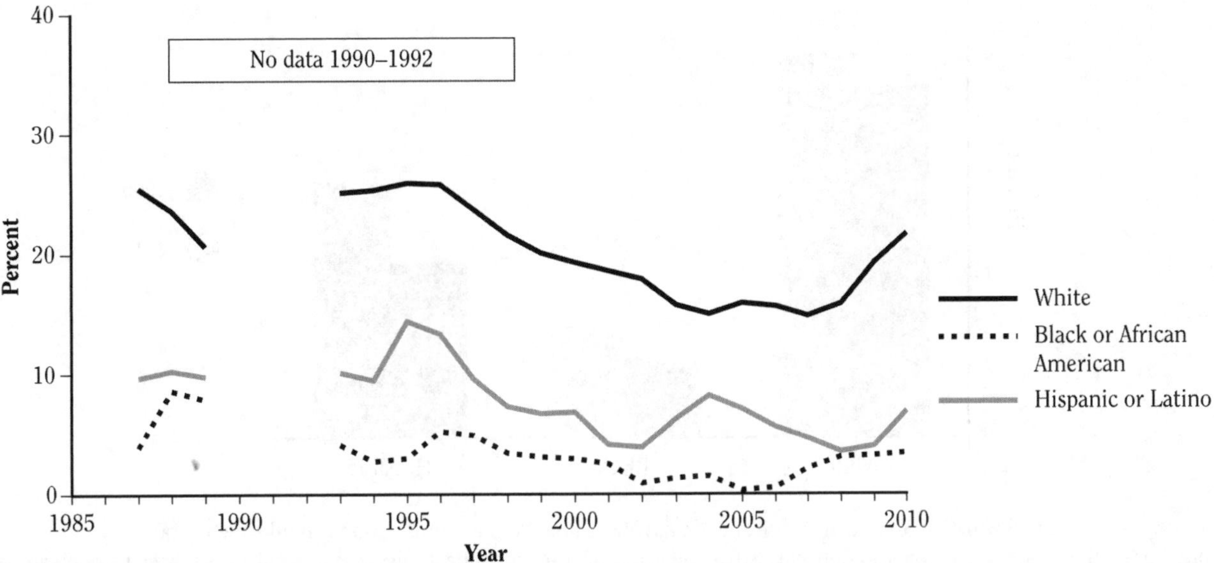

Source: 1995–2009 YRBS: Center for Disease Control and Prevention, Division of Adolescent and School Health (unpublished data); 1987 (or 1993)–2010 MTF: University of Michigan, Institute for Social Research (unpublished data).

[a]Based on responses to the question, "During the past 30 days, on how many days did you use chewing tobacco, snuff, or dip, such as Redman, Levi Garrett, Beechnut, Skoal, Skoal Bandits, or Copenhagen?" Respondents who reported that they had used chewing tobacco, snuff, or dip on 1 or 2 days or more were classified as current smokeless tobacco users.

[b]Based on responses to the question, "Have you ever taken or used smokeless tobacco (snuff, plug, dipping tobacco, chewing tobacco)?" Respondents who chose "regularly now" were classified as current users of smokeless tobacco. Also see Appendix 3.1, Figures 3.1.33C and 3.1.34.

Figure 3.7 **Trends in the initiation of smokeless tobacco use over time among young adults (18- to 25-year-olds), by gender and by race/ethnicity; National Survey on Drug Use and Health (NSDUH) 2006 and 2010; United States**

A. Gender

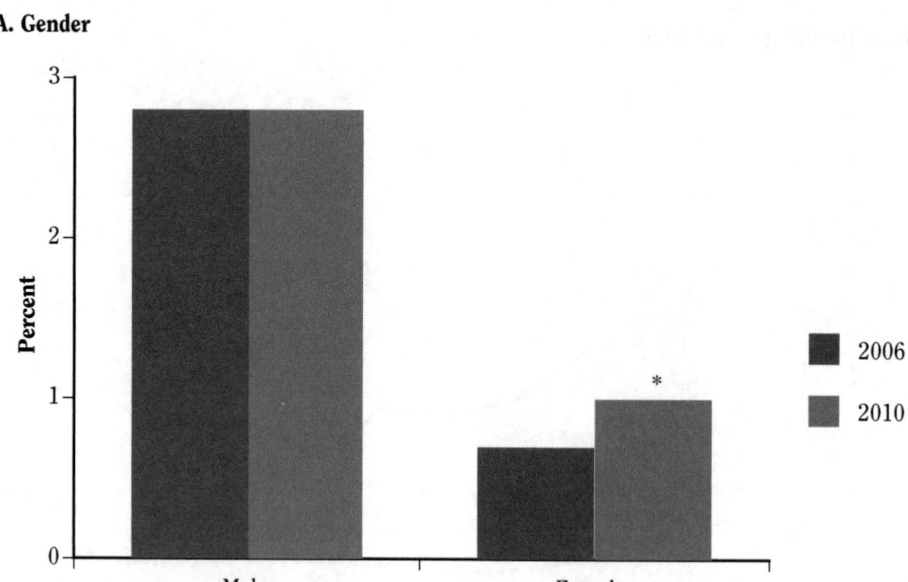

B. Race/ethnicity

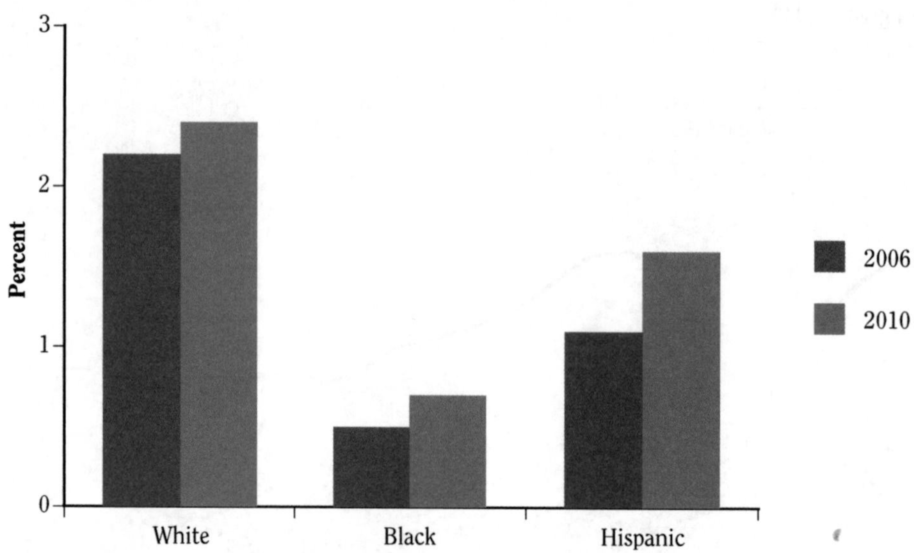

Source: 2006 and 2010 NSDUH: Substance Abuse and Mental Health Services Administration (unpublished data).
Note: For further information, refer to Appendix 3.1, Table 3.1.58. These data reflect initiation of smokeless tobacco among all persons, not just those at–risk-for-initiation (i.e., those who did not use smokeless in their lifetime or used smokeless for the first time in the past year). Moreover, they reflect any initiation (i.e., used smokeless for the first time).
*Difference between 2010 estimate and 2006 estimate is significant at the 0.05 level.

some evidence of an increase in the last few years. Among young adult males, the prevalence of smokeless tobacco use among Hispanics and Blacks has remained small and static, like that for females, over time (see Appendix 3.1, Figure 3.1.31). Unlike cigarette smoking, these trends do not appear to differ by SES status (Appendix 3.1, Figure 3.1.32).

Close monitoring of smokeless tobacco use among all subgroups of young people is warranted in the future, especially as the tobacco industry continues to diversify its portfolio of product offerings (see Chapter 5 in this report). According to NSDUH, from 2006 to 2010, the initiation of smokeless tobacco use did not increase significantly among adolescents (12–17 years old) or among young adults (18–25 year olds), overall ($p > 0.05$). However, for young adults, there was a significant increase in initiation for females during this period ($p < 0.05$). The young adult data are presented in Figures 3.7a and 3.7b (and Appendix 3.1, Table 3.1.58).

Trends in Cigar Smoking Among Adolescents and Young Adults

YRBS began collecting data on cigar smoking in 1997. Their measure includes the use of cigars, cigarillos, and little cigars. Trends in the prevalence of current cigar smoking among these students are presented in Figures 3.8a and 3.8b. Like the trends shown for current cigarette smoking, current cigar smoking declined in the late 1990s for high school males overall, then stalled from 2005 forward. For high school females overall, the prevalence of current cigar smoking has been low (although greater than that for smokeless tobacco use) and (like that for smokeless tobacco use) has decreased slowly over the last decade. From 2007 to 2009, although the prevalence of current cigar use among females overall has not increased ($p > 0.05$), the prevalence of current cigar smoking by Black females almost doubled (6.7% to 11.5%, $p < 0.05$) (CDC 2011d). MTF did not collect data on cigar smoking during this period, so the trend results from this surveillance system cannot be compared to YRBS. NYTS data did not show any changes in cigar smoking among any subgroup of middle or high school students, from 2006 to 2009 (6.8–6.5%, $p > 0.05$) (CDC 2010d), nor did NSDUH for adolescents (12–17 years old), from 2006 to 2010 (3.0–2.1%, $p > 0.05$) (SAMHSA 2011b).

NSDUH data show that the initiation of cigar smoking among adolescents (12–17 years old) decreased significantly, from 2006 to 2010, overall ($p < 0.05$), for males ($p < 0.05$), for females ($p < 0.05$), and for Whites ($p < 0.05$) (see Appendix 3.1, Table 3.1.61). For young adults (18–25 years old) over this same period, initiation of cigar smoking increased among Hispanics ($p < 0.05$) (Figure 3.9; Appendix 3.1, Table 3.1.60). For all other subgroups, initiation of cigar smoking remained unchanged over this period ($p < 0.05$). Trends in the prevalence of cigar smoking from 2002 to 2010 for young adults is displayed in Figures 3.1.37–3.1.39 in Appendix 3.1, using additional data from NSDUH. These trends suggest that current cigar smoking has remained relatively unchanged over this period for males and females, for all racial/ethnic subgroups, and for young adults above and below the poverty line. From 2009 to 2010, current cigar smoking decreased among all racial/ethnic subgroups of young adults (18–25 years old), except American Indians/Alaskan Natives overall (although this increase was not significant). The decline from 2009 to 2010 was also significant for young adult males overall ($p < 0.05$) (SAMHSA 2011b).

Disparities in Cigarette Smoking And Other Tobacco Use

Disparities in health outcomes and health behaviors, unfortunately, are not uncommon in the United States (CDC 2011b), and tobacco use among young people is no exception. Here, disparities in tobacco use are considered by race/ethnicity and SES among adolescents and young adults. Limited, if any, surveillance data exists for other demographic subgroups known to have higher rates of tobacco use (e.g., the lesbian, gay, bisexual, and transgender community; Lee et al. 2009), so are not explored. Geographic disparities are described in Appendix 3.1 (e.g., Figures 3.1.1–3.1.2).

Data from multiple NSDUH surveys (2008–2010) were combined to reliably estimate differences in the prevalence of current cigarette smoking among adolescents (12–17 years of age) and young adults (18–25 years of age), by race/ethnicity and within race/ethnicity, by gender. The results of these analyses are presented in Figures 3.10a and 3.10b (see also Appendix 3.1, Tables 3.1.3 and 3.1.4). For both age groups, American Indian/Alaskan Native males (14.3% adolescents; 50.0% young adults) and females (16.3% adolescents; 46.1% young adults) had the highest prevalence of cigarette smoking, followed by White males (10.0% adolescents; 43.0% young adults) and females (10.7% adolescents; 37.1% young adults). In young adults, the prevalence of cigarette smoking among Hispanic males (35.2%) was on par with that for White females. For both age groups, the prevalence of cigarette smoking was lowest for Black and Asian youth. Trend analyses using national YRBS and MTF data (Appendix 3.1, Figures 3.1.9A–D) show these differentials in current cigarette smoking have been relatively consistent over time, historically speaking, since the mid-1980s, at least

Figure 3.8 **Trends in the prevalence of current cigar smoking over time among high school students, by gender and by race/ethnicity; National Youth Risk Behavior Survey (YRBS) 1997–2009; United States**

A. Gender

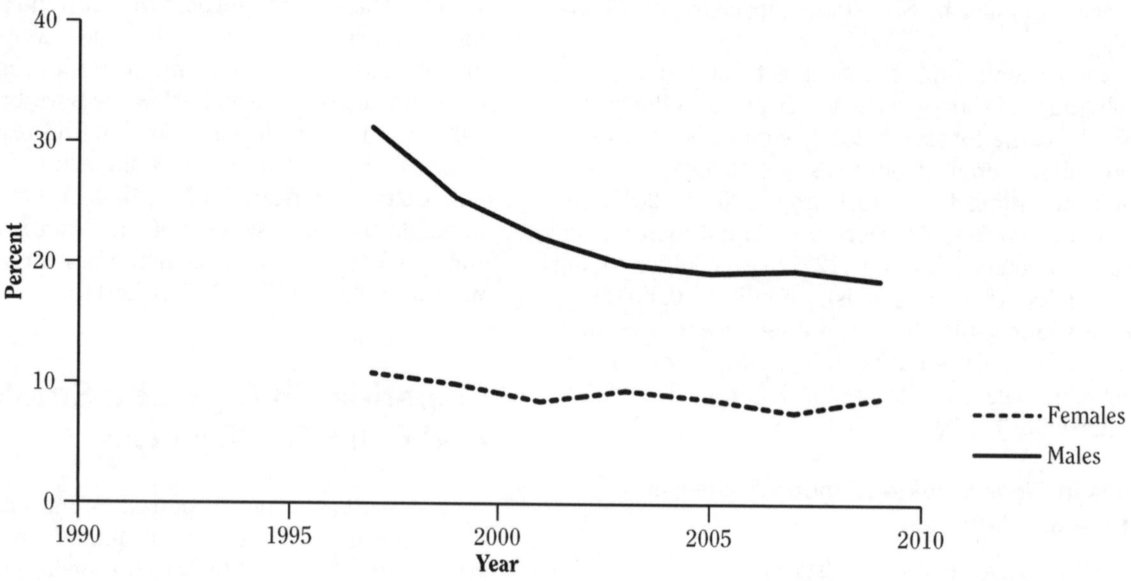

B. Race/ethnicity

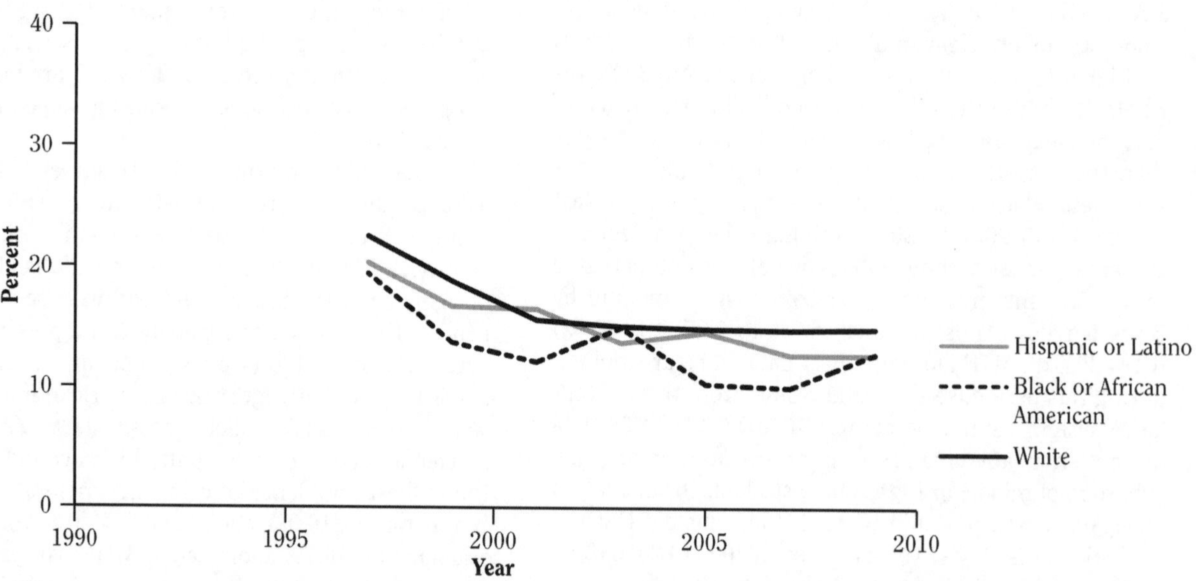

Source: 1997–2009 YRBS: Centers for Disease Control and Prevention, Division of Adolescent and School Health (unpublished data).
Note: Based on responses to the question, "During the past 30 days, on how many days did you smoke cigars, cigarillos, or little cigars?" Respondents who reported that they had smoked cigars, cigarillos, or little cigars on 1 or 2 days or more were classified as current cigar smokers. Also see Appendix 3.1, Figures 3.1.41A and 3.1.41B.

Figure 3.9 **Trends in the initiation of cigar smoking over time among young adults (18- to 25-year-olds), by gender and by race/ethnicity; National Survey on Drug Use and Health (NSDUH) 2006 and 2010; United States**

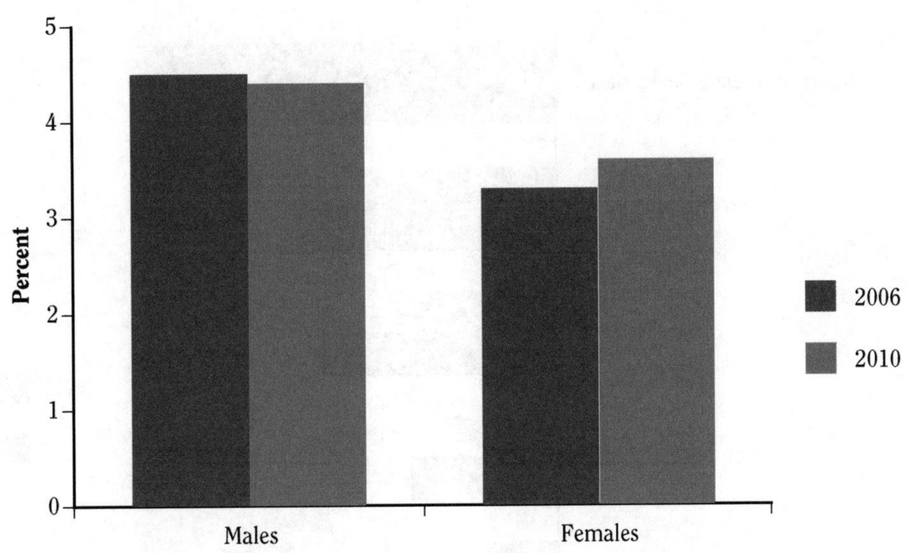

B. Race/ethnicity

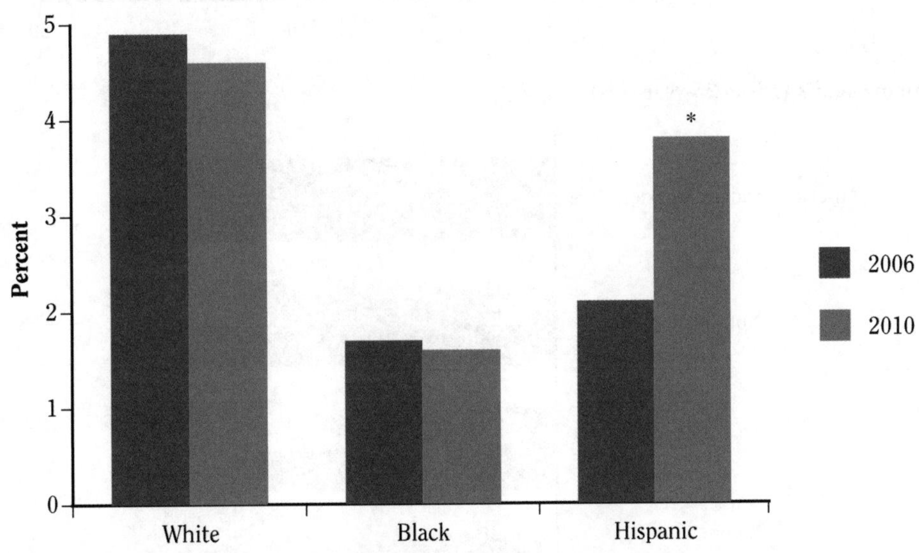

Source: 2006 and 2010 NSDUH: Substance Abuse and Mental Health Services Administration (unpublished data).
Note: For further information, refer to Appendix 3.1, Table 3.1.60. These data reflect initiation of cigar smoking among all persons, not just those at–risk-for-initiation (i.e., those who did not smoke cigars in their lifetime or smoked cigars for the first time in the past year). Moreover, they reflect any initiation (i.e., smoked cigars for the first time).
*Difference between 2010 estimate and 2006 estimate is significant at the 0.05 level.

Figure 3.10 Percentage of current cigarette smoking among adolescents (12- to 17-year-olds) and young adults (18- to 25-year-olds), by race/ethnicity and by gender; National Survey on Drug Use and Health (NSDUH) 2008–2010; United States

A. Adolescents (12- to 17-year-olds)

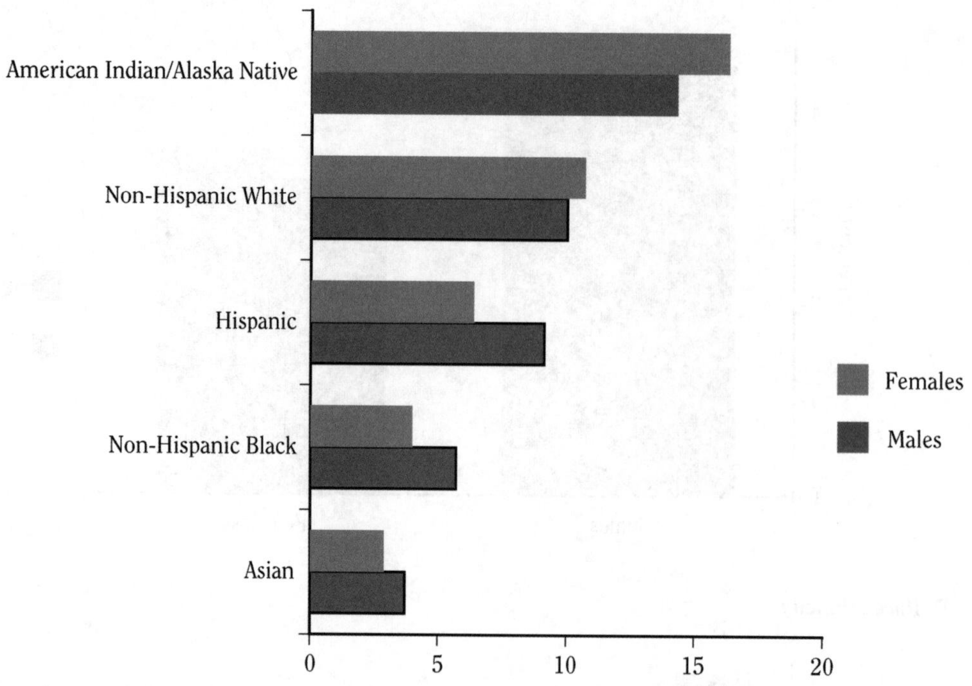

B. Young adults (18- to 25-year-olds)

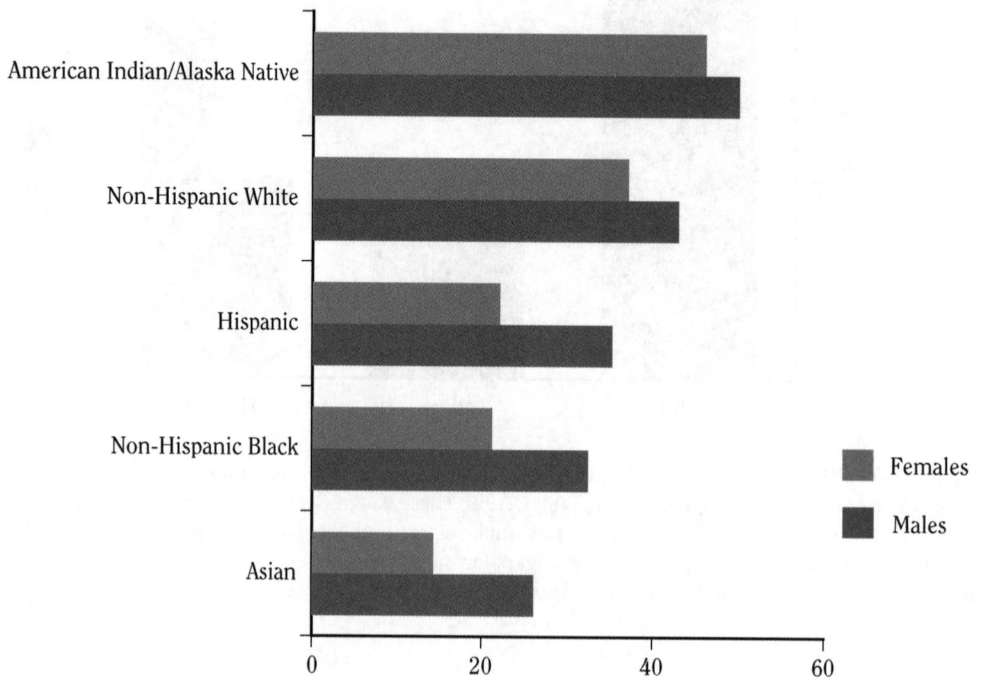

Source: 2008–2010 NSDUH: Substance Abuse and Mental Health Services Administration (unpublished data).
Note: Based on responses to the question, "During the past 30 days, have you smoked part or all of a cigarette?" Respondents who chose "Yes" were classified as current smokers. For further information, refer to Appendix 3.1, Tables 3.1.3 and 3.1.4.

for White, Hispanic, and Black students. Other analyses of NSDUH data (2002–2003 to 2007–2008) showed that American Indian/Alaskan Native youth have experienced especially sharp declines in current cigarette smoking in recent years, which suggests that some progress has been achieved in reducing disparities in cigarette smoking in this racial/ethnic group (Garrett et al. 2011). By adulthood, American Indian/Alaskan Native males and females will still have the highest prevalence of current cigarette smoking of all racial/ethnic subgroups.

Differences in tobacco use by SES can be somewhat challenging to determine, especially among adolescents, as reliable and widely accepted measures of SES are lacking, especially in surveillance data. Here, parental education is considered as a proxy for SES among 8th-, 10th-, and 12th-grade students, using MTF data collapsed across multiple years (2002–2007) (Figure 3.11). Education and employment levels are used as a proxy for SES among young adults using 2010 NSDUH data (Figure 3.12). The socioeconomic gradient in current cigarette smoking is clear and consistent in both analyses: youth of lower SES have a higher prevalence of current cigarette smoking than youth of a higher SES. The gradient among young adults is especially strong and mirrors other analyses of young adult data that suggest that the prevalence of current cigarette smoking for non-college-educated young adults is twice as high as that for their college-educated counterparts (Green et al. 2007). Although the socioeconomic gradient is strong here for adolescents, too, other analyses of MTF data suggest that differences in current cigarette smoking among adolescents by SES might be moderated by race/ethnicity (Bachman et al. 2010, 2011). In these studies, the effect of lower SES (as defined by parental education levels) on tobacco use is most pronounced among White and younger (e.g., eighth grade students) adolescents. The large proportion of Blacks and Hispanics in the lowest socioeconomic groups may mask SES disparities for these subpopulations that can be readily discerned among Whites.

The disparities noted here for cigarette smoking by SES extend to other tobacco products also (e.g., Bachman et al. 2010, 2011). Profiles for other tobacco

Figure 3.11 Percentage of current cigarette smoking among 8th, 10th, and 12th graders, by parental education (as a proxy for socioeconomic status) and grade level; Monitoring the Future (MTF) 2002–2007; United States

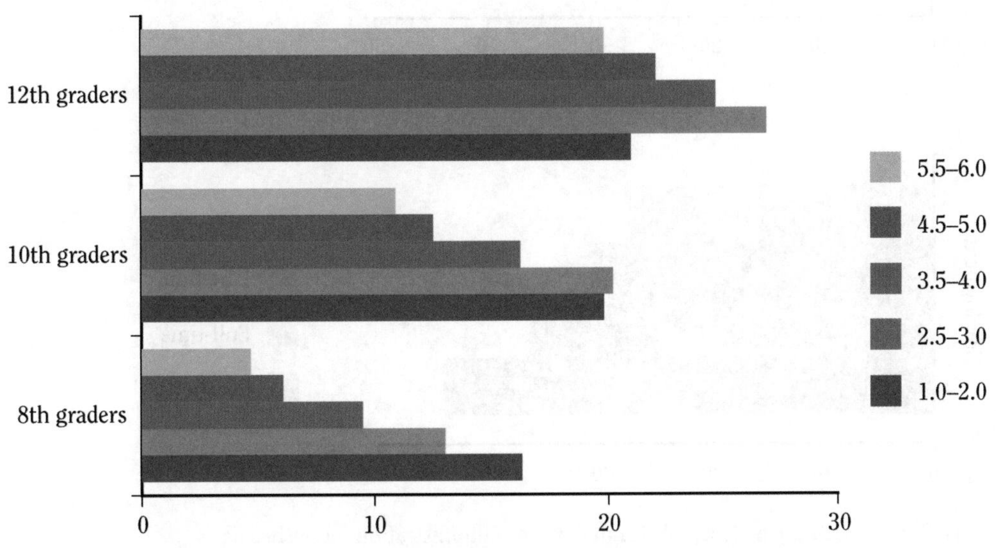

Source: 2002–2007 MTF: University of Michigan, Institute for Social Research (unpublished data).
Note: Parental education is measured as an average score of mother's education and father's education. Response categories are (1) completed some grade school or less, (2) some high school, (3) completed high school, (4) some college, (5) completed college, and (6) graduate or professional school after college. Based on responses to the question, "How frequently have you smoked cigarettes during the past 30 days?" Respondents who reported that they had smoked less than 1 cigarette per day or more were classified as current smokers. For further information, refer to Appendix 3.1, Table 3.1.5 (adolescents).

products by race/ethnicity, however, do differ and are discussed in Appendix 3.1. According to YRBS, the current use of smokeless tobacco, for example, is substantially more prevalent among adolescent males than among females ($p < 0.05$; Appendix 3.1, Table 3.1.41), and among Whites when compared to Other youth ($p < 0.05$, Appendix 3.1, Table 3.1.41). Current cigar smoking is also significantly more prevalent for males than females ($p < 0.05$ Appendix 3.1, Table 3.1.49), and among Whites when compared to Blacks, Hispanics and Other youth ($p < 0.05$ for all comparisons with Whites; Appendix 3.1, Table 3.1.49). From 2007 to 2009, however, the prevalence of cigar use by Black female high school students almost doubled (6.7–11.5%, $p < 0.05$) (CDC 2011b). However, NSDUH data for Black girls aged 12–17 years show the prevalence of cigar use remaining between 1.6% and 2.5% during 2007–2010.

Concurrent Use of Multiple Tobacco Products

This report finds that the concurrent use of two or more tobacco products (i.e., use of two or more tobacco products in the last 30 days) is common among some sub-

Figure 3.12 Percentage of current cigarette smoking among young adults (18- to 25-year-olds), by education and employment (as proxies for socioeconomic status); National Survey on Drug Use and Health (NSDUH) 2010; United States

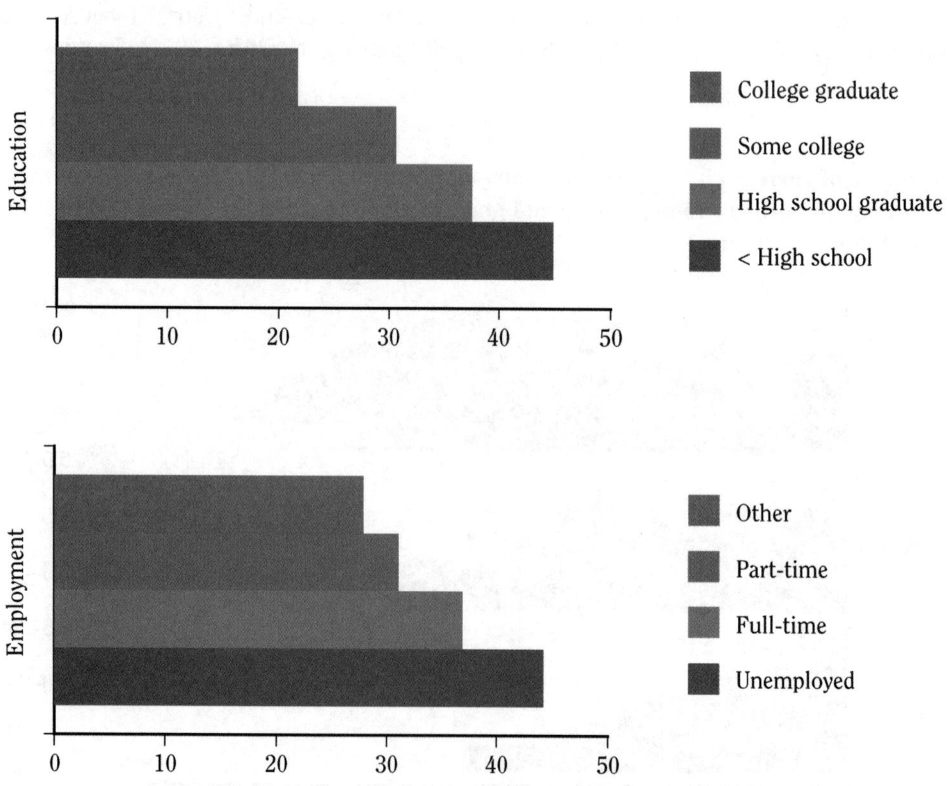

Source: 2010 NSDUH: Substance Abuse and Mental Health Services Administration (published data).
Note: Based on responses to the question, "During the past 30 days, have you smoked part or all of a cigarette?" Respondents who chose "Yes" were classified as current smokers. For young adults, see SAMHSA 2011a, Table 2.24B. "Other" includes all responses defined as not being in the labor force, including being a student, keeping house or caring for children full time, retired, disabled, or other miscellaneous work statuses. Respondents who reported that they did not have a job and did not want one also were classified as not being in the labor force. Similarly, respondents who reported not having a job and looking for work also were classified as not being in the labor force if they did not report making specific efforts to find work in the past 30 days. Those respondents who reported having no job and who provided no additional information could not have their labor force status determined and were therefore assigned to the "Other" employment category.

Figure 3.13 Prevalence of current use of multiple tobacco products among high school males who use tobacco; National Youth Risk Behavior Survey (YRBS) 2009; United States

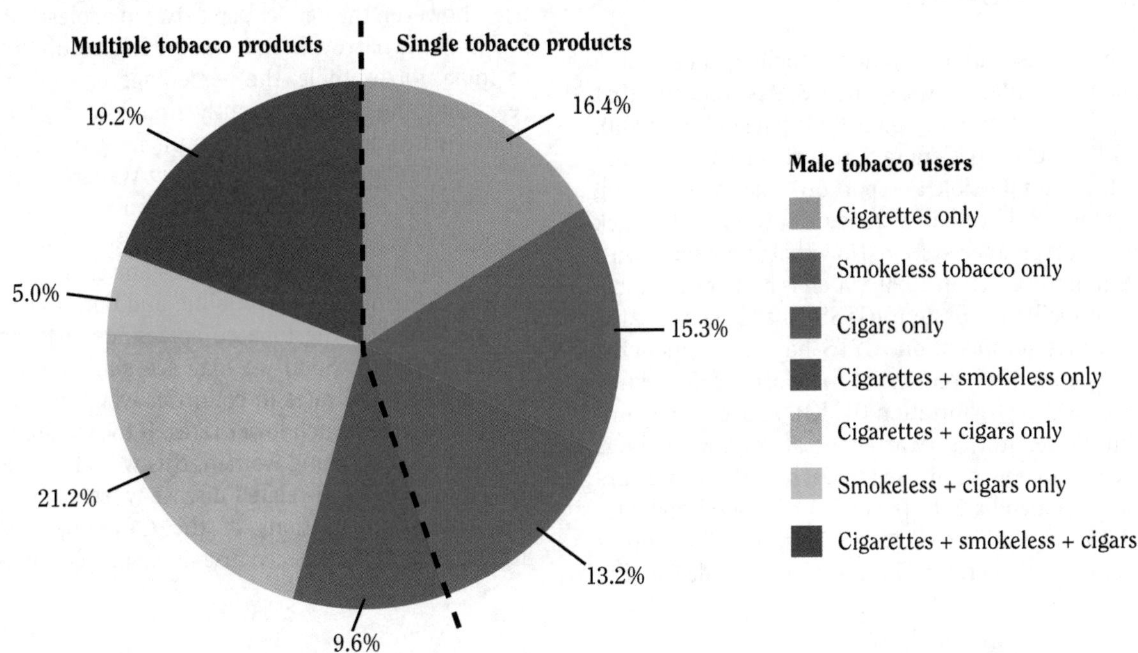

Source: 2009 YRBS: Centers for Disease Control and Prevention, Division of Adolescent and School Health (unpublished data).
Note: Based on responses to the questions, "During the past 30 days, on how many days did you smoke cigarettes?" and "During the past 30 days, on how many days did you use chewing tobacco, snuff, or dip, such as Redman, Levi Garrett, Beechnut, Skoal, Skoal Bandits, or Copenhagen?" and "During the past 30 days, on how many days did you smoke cigars, cigarillos, or little cigars?" For further information, refer to Appendix 3.1, Figure 3.1.43.

groups of youth. Based on data from the YRBS, the majority of high school males who currently use tobacco actually use more than one product concurrently (Figure 3.13). Concurrent cigarette and cigar smoking is most prevalent among high school male tobacco users (21.2%), followed closely by the concurrent use of cigarettes, cigars, and smokeless tobacco (19.2%). Less than one-half of all high school male tobacco users reported using a single product (i.e., cigarettes, cigars, or use of smokeless tobacco, alone), in the past 30 days, at 44.9%. The prevalence of the concurrent use of cigarettes, cigars, and/or smokeless tobacco has remained stable among high school male and female student tobacco users since 2001 (Appendix 3.1, Figure 3.1.44). In 2009, more than one-half of all White and Hispanic high school males who used tobacco reported using more than one tobacco product concurrently (Appendix 3.1, Figure 3.1.44). That same year, almost one-half of all Hispanic high school females who used tobacco reported the same, at a rate almost twice as high as their White and Black counterparts (Appendix 3.1, Figure 3.1.44). Thus, the concurrent use of multiple tobacco products among adolescents is not inconsequential and is cause for concern, especially for White male and Hispanic male and female high school students. It is noteworthy that the tobacco industry has diversified its portfolio in novel ways in recent years and now offers a variety of flavored (e.g., cigars, cigarillos, snus) and emerging (e.g., dissolvables, orbs) tobacco products that appeal to youth (see Chapter 5 of this report). Continued surveillance of the use of these new products is warranted. Measures specific to emerging tobacco products like these are being added to several surveillance system surveys, such as the NYTS, which will make them invaluable to future monitoring efforts. The 2011 NYTS, for example, includes measures of use of water pipes (hookahs), electronic cigarettes, roll-your-own cigarettes, dissolvables, snus, flavored little cigars, and clove cigars, allowing for more detailed examination of the use of these products alone or in combination. The sequence of initiation in regards to the use of multiple tobacco products (e.g., does cigarette smoking precede smokeless tobacco use – or, vice versa?) remains unclear and worthy of additional research in the future.

Tobacco Use Among Young People Worldwide

Tobacco use among young people is not just a phenomenon limited to the United States, but one that is widespread and growing globally (Shafey et al. 2009). In the 1994 Surgeon General's report on smoking and health, it was not possible to report on tobacco use among young people worldwide in a standard way, given the lack of a global surveillance system. Now that is possible, with the advent of the GYTS in 1999, which is part of the Global Tobacco Surveillance System (GTSS) that is coordinated by CDC. Since its inception, GYTS has been conducted at least once in all six regions of the world as defined by the World Health Organization (WHO), in over 140 countries and 11 territories (Warren et al. 2008). Findings from recent surveys conducted at each of these sites are provided in Appendix 3.1, Tables 3.1.63–3.1.66 and Figures 3.1.45–3.1.48. Here, Figure 3.14 shows differentials in tobacco use by gender for several rapidly developing countries, worldwide. Rates of tobacco use remain low among girls relative to boys in many developing countries; however, the gender gap between adolescent females and males is narrow in many countries around the globe. In India, for example, the percentage of adult males 15 years and older, who currently smoke tobacco is 24.3%, while this figure is 2.9% for adult females 15 years and older (Ministry of Health & Family Welfare 2010). Thus, the ratio in current smoking between males and females among adults (at 10:1) is much larger than the same ratio in current smoking between males and females for youth (at 2:1). This finding is troubling and does not bode well for the future of the tobacco epidemic worldwide (Warren et al. 2008). Soon we may see similar male/female adult tobacco use rates in countries where women previously smoked at much lower rates. If tobacco use rates do increase among young women, this would accelerate the epidemic of tobacco-related disease worldwide. Although repeated administrations of the GYTS have shown a decline in youth tobacco use in some countries (e.g.,

Figure 3.14 Percentage of youth 13–15 years of age who currently use any tobacco product, by gender; Global Youth Tobacco Survey (GYTS) (1999–2009); Brazil (Rio de Janeiro), China (Macao), India, Russian Federation, South Africa, and the Syrian Arab Republic

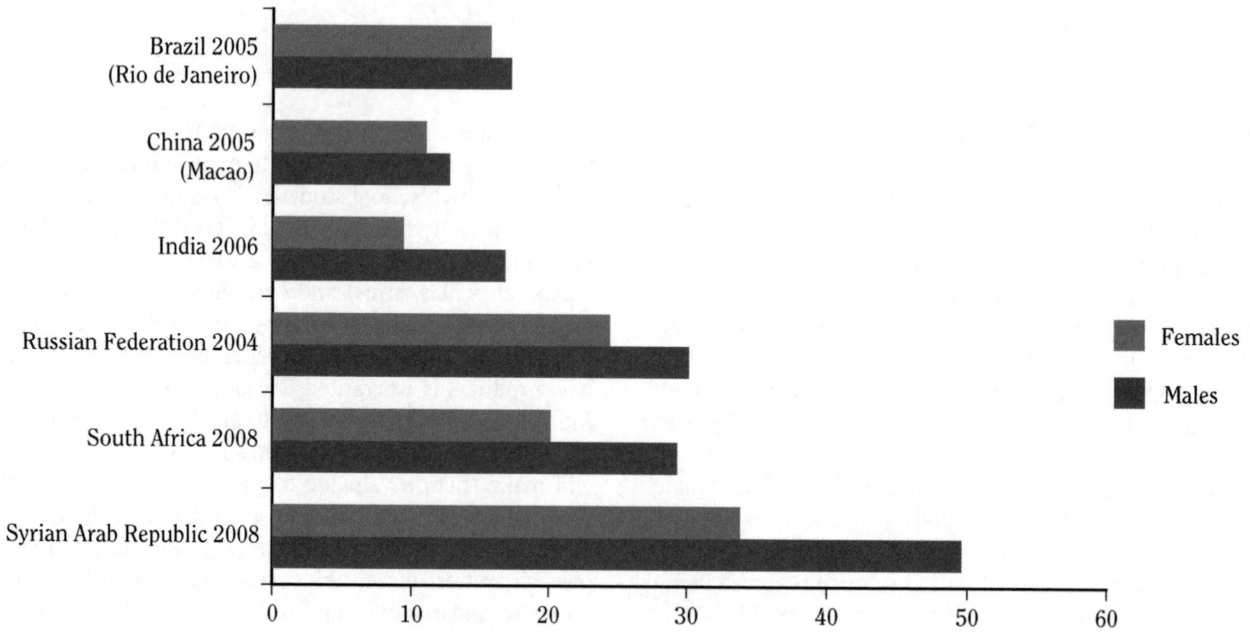

Source: 1999–2009 GYTS: Centers for Disease Control and Prevention 2010b.
Note: Brazil, China, India, Russian Federation, South Africa, and the Syrian Arab Republic are regional examples of (relatively) large, developing countries. Based on responses to the following questions: "During the past 30 days (one month), on how many days did you smoke cigarettes?" "During the past 30 days (one month), have you ever used any form of tobacco products other than cigarettes (e.g., chewing tobaccos, snuff, dip, cigars, cigarillos, little cigars, pipe)?" For further information, refer to Appendix 3.1, Table 3.1.66.

Panama, [CDC 2009a]), in others youth tobacco use has either remained consistent or increased over time, by comparison (e.g., Sri Lanka [CDC 2008]; India, [Sinha et al. 2008]). Continued monitoring of youth tobacco use worldwide is warranted and will help to assess progress in achieving tobacco-related goals. Awareness of tobacco advertising is high among males and females alike in many countries worldwide, and can be significantly higher among adolescents and young adults (15–24 years old) as compared to adults (≥25 years of age) (CDC 2010b). Figures 3.15a and 3.15b show the prevalence of current cigarette smoking by gender, among youth aged 13–15 year of age worldwide (see also Appendix 3.1, Figure 3.1.46).

Other Epidemiologic Findings

In this section, epidemiologic analyses that support major conclusions presented in other chapters of this report are considered here. These analyses are selected from a more comprehensive set presented in Appendix 3.1. The subheadings below are specific to conclusions in Chapters 2, 4, and 5 of this report.

Cigarette Smoking and Weight Loss

Chapter 2 also provides an extensive review of the literature specific to the relationship between cigarette smoking and weight loss. The chapter concludes that cigarette smoking by adolescents and young adults is not associated with statistically or clinically significant weight loss, although additional research may be necessary to confirm this (see Chapter 2 for additional information). Therefore, to explore this relationship further, additional analyses were conducted in this chapter to examine the relationship between cigarette smoking status and body mass index (BMI) in a nationally representative data set of young people. The analyses focused on high school seniors only and collapsed data from multiple rounds (2003–2009) of the YRBS to ensure that sample sizes were sufficient to detect differences, if any, in BMI by smoking status, by gender and race/ethnicity. Contrary to the belief held by many young people, the findings from these analyses show that cigarette smoking is not associated with a lower BMI. As shown in Figures 3.16a and 3.16b, never smokers had the smallest BMI, when compared to both current and former smokers. This was true for high school senior boys and girls and for high school senior Whites, Blacks, and Hispanics. Never smokers either had a statistically significantly smaller BMI than students in other smoking status categories ($p < 0.05$), or the differences in BMI between never smokers and certain smoking status categories (e.g., among Blacks, former daily smokers) were not statistically significantly different ($p > 0.05$) (Appendix 3.1, Table 3.1.38). The results of these analyses are consistent with other evidence presented in Chapter 2, which shows no relationship with a lower weight or BMI among smokers younger than 35 years of age.

YRBSS is a unique surveillance system. It can assess not only tobacco use among young people but also a wide range of other health risk behaviors and outcomes. In Appendix 3.1, Figures 3.1.27A–S, differences between current cigarette smokers and nonsmokers in these health risk behaviors are considered over time, from 1991 (or whenever the earliest data for a specific behavior were available) to 2009. The review presented in Chapter 2 suggests that the interpretation of evidence linking cigarette smoking to weight loss is complicated by the rising trend in obesity over the last decade. Additional YRBS analyses described here underscore this possibility. According to the YRBS in 1999, for example, the percentage of obese students (defined as ≥95th percentile for BMI, by age and gender) was significantly higher among nonsmokers when compared to current smokers (9.3% vs. 6.2%, $p < 0.05$; Appendix 3.1, Figure 3.1.27M). Across time, the situation reversed itself, such that one decade later, in 2009, 16.5% of current smokers were obese, compared to 12.3% of nonsmokers. By comparison, no significant differences between current smokers and nonsmokers in the percentage of overweight students (defined as ≥85th but <95th percentile for BMI, by age and gender) were observed either in 1999 or 2009 (both comparisons, $p > 0.05$; Appendix 3.1, Figure 3.1.27L). Interestingly, in these additional YRBS analyses, no differences between current smokers and nonsmokers in weight-related behaviors (television viewing, moderate-to-vigorous physical activity, fruit and vegetable intake, milk consumption) were observed over time, from 1999 to 2009 (see Appendix 3.1, Figures 3.1.27N–R), with one exception. Significantly more current cigarette smokers compared to nonsmokers were engaged in one or more unhealthy weight control behaviors (fasting; taking diet pills, powders, or liquids; or

Figure 3.15 Percentage of 13- to 15-year-olds who currently smoke cigarettes, by gender; Global Youth Tobacco Survey 1999–2007; worldwide

A. Boys

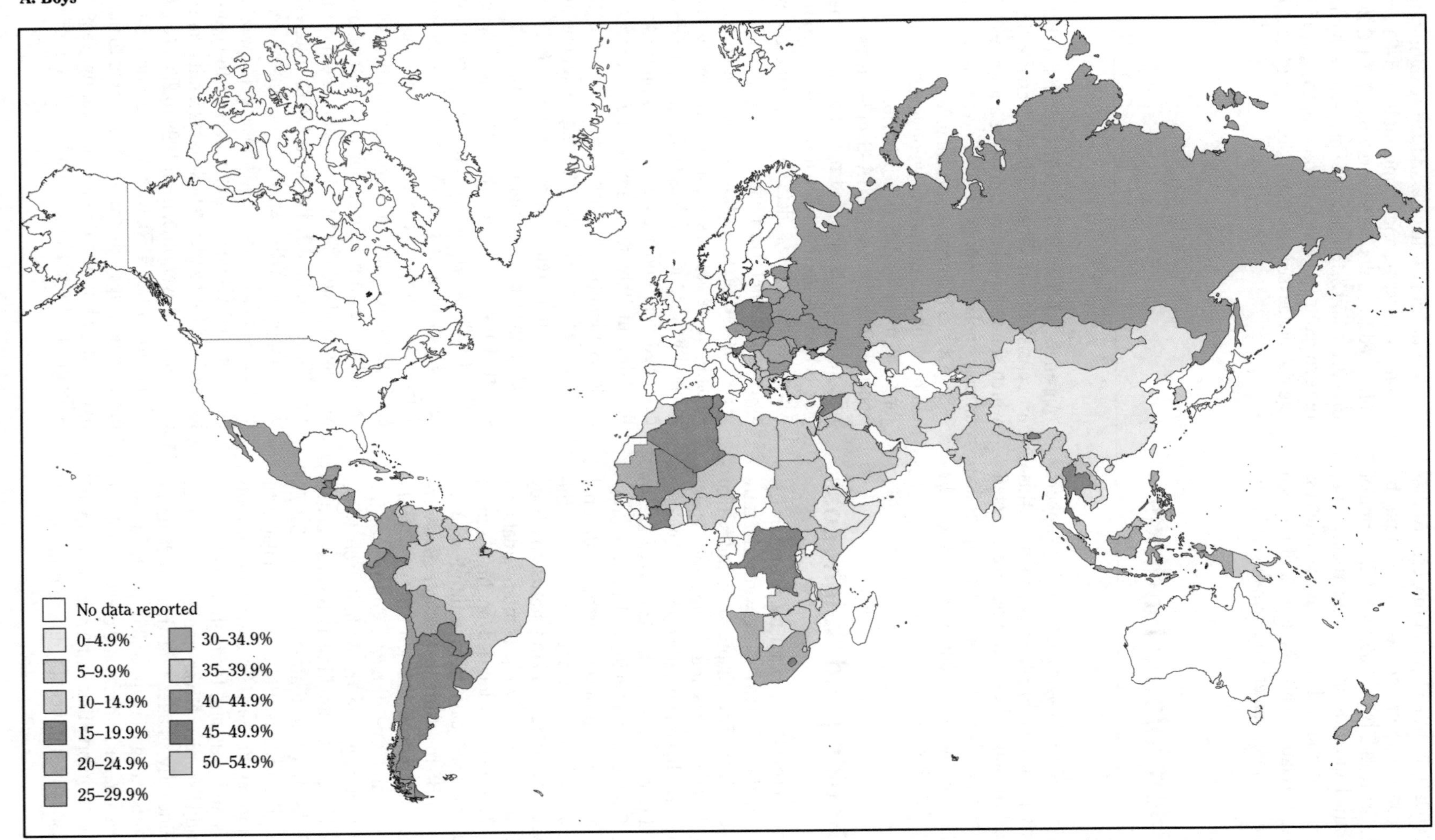

B. Girls

Source: Centers for Disease Control and Prevention 2010c.
Note: Based on responses to the question: "During the past 30 days (one month), on how many days did you smoke cigarettes?" Respondents who reported 1 or 2 days or more were classified as a current smoker.

Figure 3.16 Body mass index (BMI) by smoking status/frequency among high school seniors, by gender and race/ethnicity; National Youth Risk Behavior Survey (YRBS) 2003–2009; United States

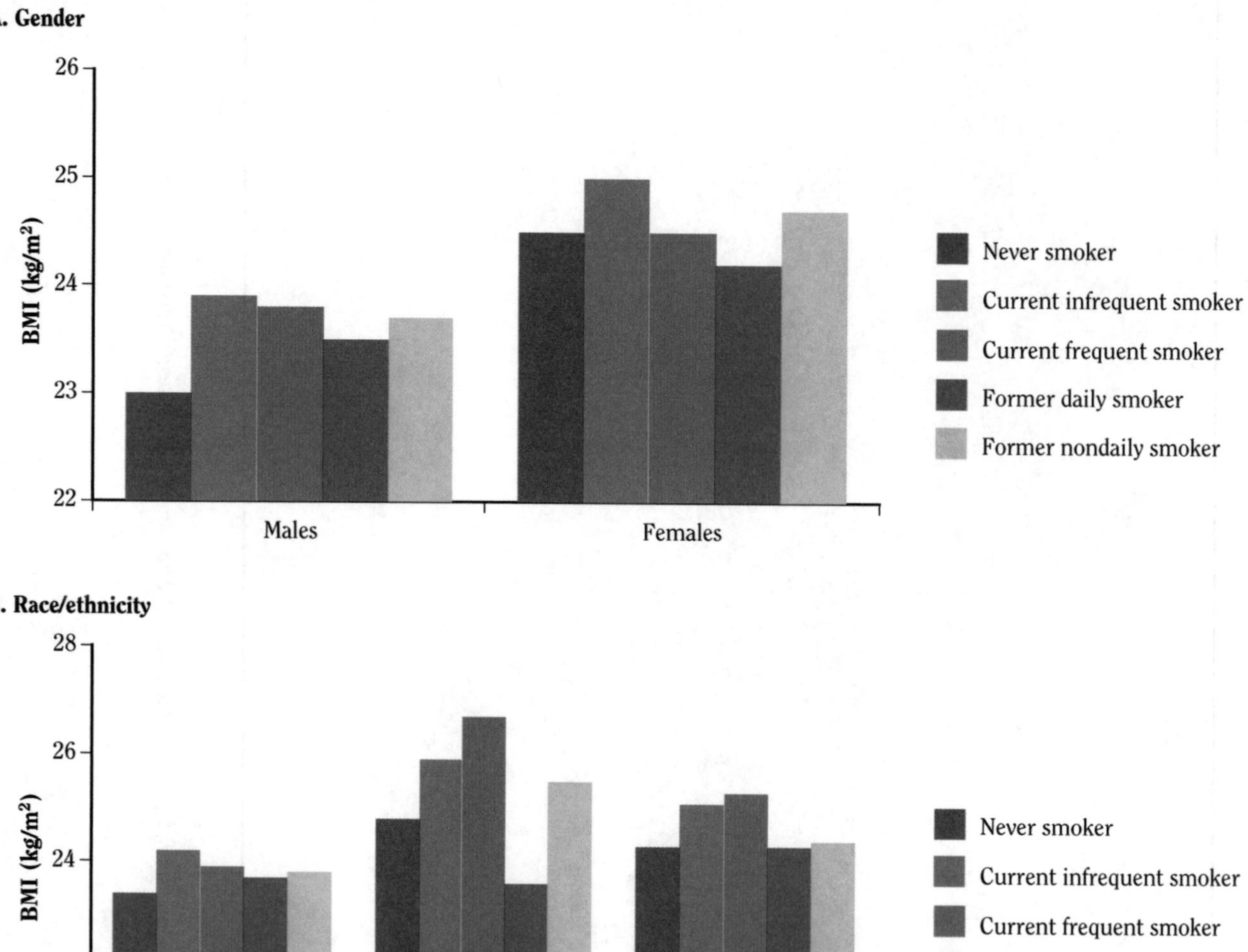

Source: 2003–2009 YRBS: Centers for Disease Control and Prevention, Division of Adolescent and School Health (unpublished data).
Note: Body mass index (kg/m2) (BMI) was calculated from self-reported height and weight. Definitions for these categories are as follows: Students who answered "no" to ever smoking were categorized as nonsmokers. Students who answered "yes" to ever smoke and "yes" to currently smoke were categorized as (a) current infrequent smokers for smoking 1–19 days during the base 30 days or (b) current frequent smokers for smoking >19 days during the past 30 days. Students who answered "yes" to ever smoke and "no" to currently smoke were categorized as (a) former daily smokers if they answered "yes" to daily or (b) former nondaily smokers if they answered "no" to daily. For further information, refer to Appendix 3.1, Table 3.1.38.

vomiting/taking laxatives to lose weight or to keep from gaining weight) over time, in both 1999 and 2009 (both comparisons, $p < 0.05$; Appendix 3.1, Figure 3.1.27S). Examination of the constellation of health risk behaviors that young cigarette smokers engage in may be helpful in further elucidating the causal relationship, if any, between cigarette smoking and weight loss among young people and adults.

Tobacco Use and Academic Achievement

Chapter 4 concludes that the adolescents most likely to begin using tobacco are those who have low academic achievement. Does tobacco use lead to lower grades, or does poor academic achievement predict tobacco use? Studies have lent support for both possibilities (e.g., Young and Rogers 1986; Hu et al. 1998; Bryant et al. 2000a,b; Bergen et al. 2005), suggesting that there is an ongoing reciprocal relationship between these two outcomes. The negative association between academic achievement and tobacco use, however, is undisputed and generalizes across developed and developing country contexts, including studies that have been conducted in Portugal (Azevedo et al. 1999), Canada (Leatherdale et al. 2008), Turkey (Yorulmaz et al. 2002), India (Mohan et al. 2005; Dhavan et al. 2010), China (Li et al. 1999), and the United States (Bryant et al. 2000a). Figures 3.17A and 3.17B show the results of analyses of MTF data collapsed over several years (2002–2007) to provide reliable estimates of the relationship between academic performance and tobacco use. Cigarette smoking and smokeless tobacco use are considered here, across three grade levels (8th, 10th, and 12th grades). For each grade level and for both tobacco products, tobacco use is lowest among students who typically get As in school and highest among students who typically get Ds in school. The dose-response relationship between academic performance and tobacco use is strong, with a monotonic increase in tobacco use, given lower academic performance. As this report considers school-based strategies to prevent tobacco use among young people, in Chapter 6, it is important to note that the implementation of evidence-based strategies does not deter from academic success. A primary goal of modern school health policies and programs is, in fact, to promote academic success (CDC 2011b). Comprehensive literature reviews of coordinated school health programs concluded that these programs can improve academic performance while reducing health risk behaviors, such as tobacco use (Zins et al. 2004; Murray et al. 2007).

Tobacco Brand Preferences Among Young People

Knowing what brands of cigarettes are preferred by young tobacco users can provide insight into the influence that the marketing practices of the tobacco industry and the design of its products may have on young people and, importantly, aid the development of interventions to prevent smoking (Cummings et al. 2002; Wayne and Connolly 2002; Carpenter et al. 2005; Klein et al. 2008; National Cancer Institute 2008). Additional information on the relationship between the marketing practices of the tobacco industry and tobacco use among young people can be found in Chapter 5 of this report. Here, Figure 3.18 (and in Appendix 3.1, Tables 3.1.10 and 3.1.11) provides evidence of which cigarette brands are preferred by adolescents (12–17 years of age) and young adults (18–25 years of age), using data that have been combined from multiple NSDUH surveys (2008–2010) to provide reliable estimates. The top six brands are displayed for each age group. Among adolescents, all 10 of the most commonly preferred brands of cigarettes (shown in Appendix 3.1, Table 3.1.10) were subbrands of Marlboro (46.2%), Newport (21.8%), or Camel (12.4%), making these 3 the preferred brands of 80.4% of adolescent smokers. Among young adults, 9 out of the 10 most commonly preferred brands (shown in Appendix 3.1, Table 3.1.11) were subbrands of Marlboro (46.1%), Newport (21.8%), or Camel (12.4%), making these 3 the preferred brands of 80.3% of young adult smokers. Marlboro full flavor (19.7%) was the most preferred brand overall among adolescents, while Marlboro Lights (22.7%) was the most preferred brand overall among young adults (Appendix 3.1, Tables 3.1.10 and 3.1.11). Among Blacks, Newport full flavor was preferred most often by adolescents (42.4%) and young adults (61.2%), followed by Newport Lights for adolescents (16.9%) and Newport Mediums for young adults (9.0%). Newport is a well-known brand of mentholated cigarettes. Mentholated cigarettes deserve special note and are discussed further in Appendix 3.1. They are also the subject of a recent report from the U.S. Food and Drug Administration's (FDA) Tobacco Product Scientific Advisory Committee (TPSAC 2011).

In comparing the overall market share that each brand secured in the United States in 2008, it can be seen that the market share data are aligned with the data for brand preference among adolescents and young adults in regard to the top three preferred brands. In 2008, Marlboro accounted for 41.0% of all cigarette sales in the United States, followed by Newport (9.7%), then Camel (6.7%) (Maxwell 2009). Other brands secured less than

Figure 3.17 Percentage of current cigarette smoking and smokeless tobacco use among 8th, 10th, and 12th graders, by grade level and academic performance; Monitoring the Future (MTF) 2002–2007; United States

A. Cigarette smoking[a]

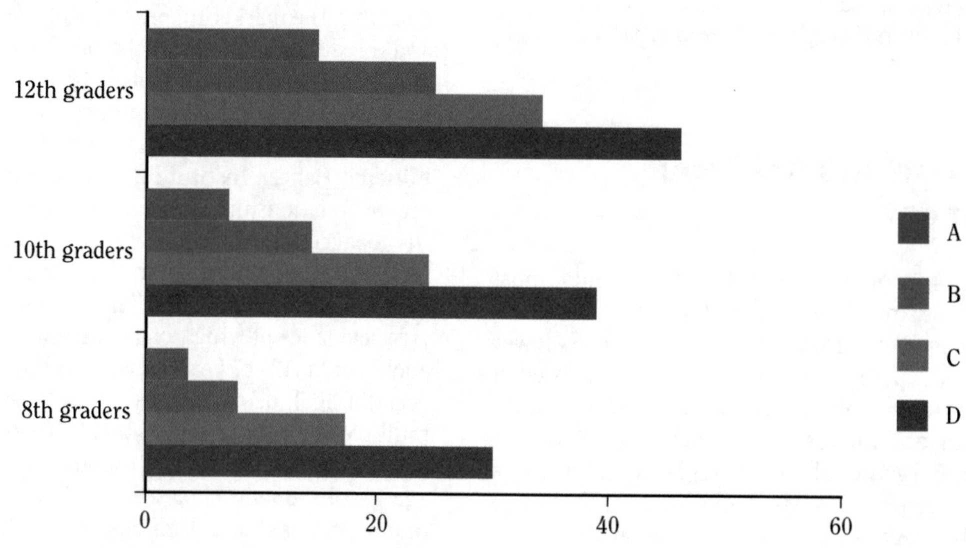

B. Smokeless tobacco use[b]

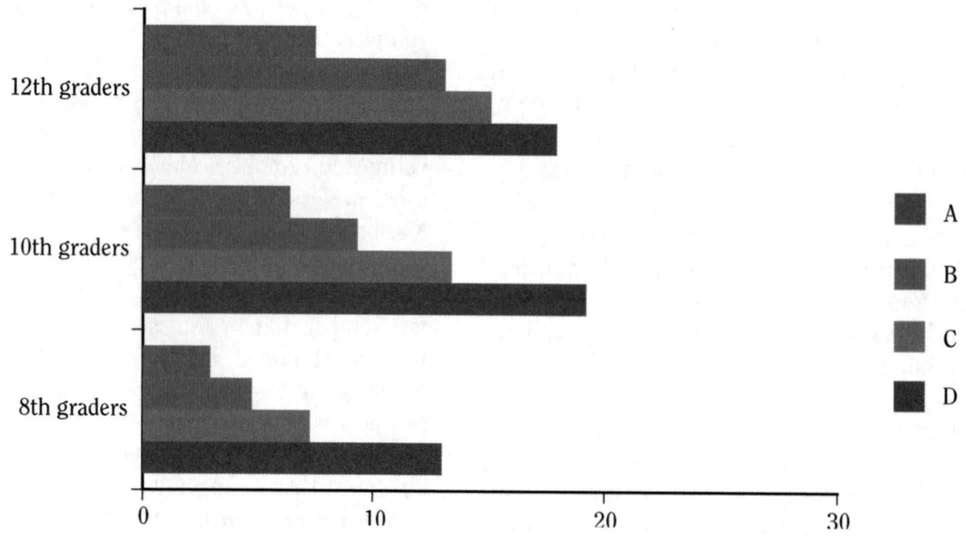

Source: 2002–2007 MTF: University of Michigan, Institute for Social Research (unpublished data).
Note: Note that the grades reported here are grades that students report typically getting in school.
[a]Based on responses to the question, "How frequently have you smoked cigarettes during the past 30 days?" Respondents who reported that they had smoked less than 1 cigarette per day or more were classified as current smokers.
[b]Based on responses to the question, "Have you ever taken or used smokeless tobacco (snuff, plug, dipping tobacco, chewing tobacco)?" Respondents who chose "regularly now" were classified as current users of smokeless tobacco. For further information, refer to Appendix 3.1, Table 3.1.5 (cigarette smoking) and Table 3.1.42 (smokeless tobacco use).

Figure 3.18 Percentage distribution of cigarette brands that adolescents (12- to 17-year-olds) and young adults (18- to 25-year-olds) who were current smokers preferred; National Survey on Drug Use and Health (NSDUH) 2008–2010; United States

A. Adolescents (12- to 17-year-olds)

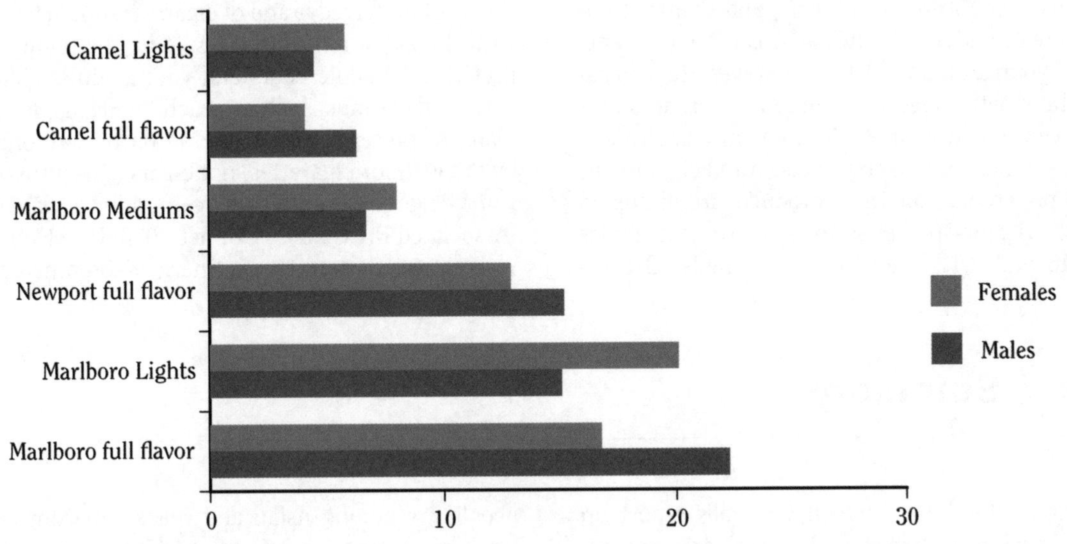

B. Young adults (18- to 25-year-olds)

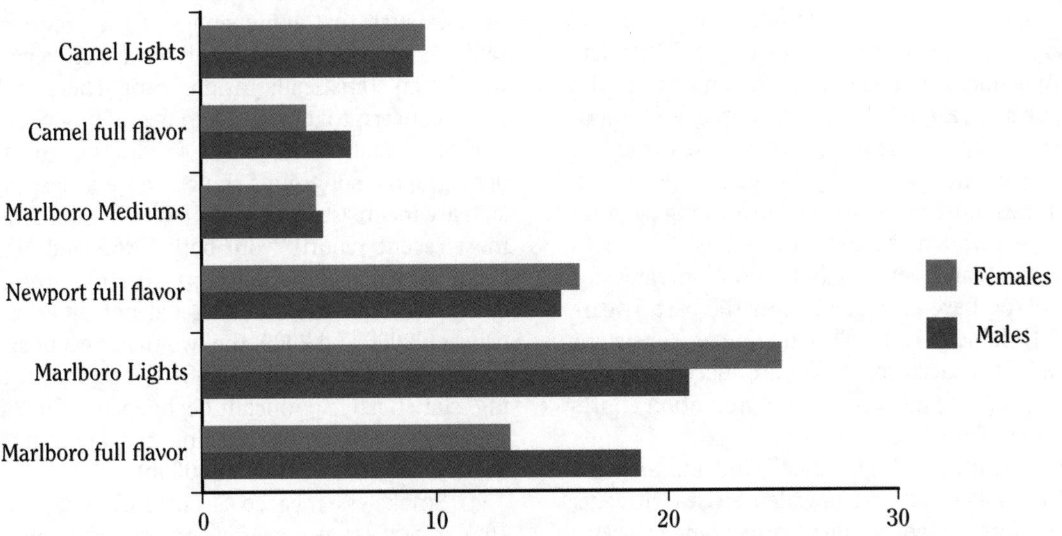

Source: 2008–2010 NSDUH: Substance Abuse and Mental Health Services Administration (unpublished data).
Note: Based on responses to the following questions: "During the past 30 days, what brand of cigarette did you smoke most often?" and "During the past 30 days, what type of cigarettes did you smoke most often?" For further information, refer to Appendix 3.1, Tables 3.1.9 and 3.1.10.

5% each of the total cigarette market (Maxwell 2009). It is important to note that market share is influenced primarily by the preferences of adults, not adolescents (given that market share represents cigarette sales, and many youth obtain their cigarettes through social, not commercial, sources). Therefore, these figures indicate that the combined share of Marlboro, Newport, and Camel is not as concentrated in adults (57.4%) as it is for adolescents (80.4%) and young adults (80.3%). However, the consistencies in these data suggest that brand preferences that develop early in the life course will extend into adulthood. This finding extends to smokeless tobacco and cigar use as well. Brand preferences for these products are discussed in Appendix 3.1 (for smokeless tobacco use, see Tables 3.1.44–3.1.45 and 3.1.47; for cigar use, Tables 3.1.50–3.1.52). Like that observed here, brand preference data for smokeless tobacco and cigars among young people are consistent with industry data for market share. Skoal and Grizzly are the most preferred brands of moist snuff (a type of smokeless tobacco that is preferred over chewing tobacco) among young people, while Black & Mild is the most preferred brand of cigars. It should be noted that with the exception of Black & Mild, the top cigar brands preferred by adolescents and young adults alike include various flavorings, such as peach, grape, apple, and chocolate. At present, characterizing flavors are only banned by the FDA for cigarettes, not cigars. Given this loophole, some flavored cigarettes are reemerging as flavored cigars (Associated Press 2009; CSPnet 2010; U.S. House of Representatives Committee on Energy & Commerce 2011).

Evidence Summary

Similar to the 1994 Surgeon General's report on smoking and health, this report finds that cigarette smoking virtually always begins in adolescence or young adulthood, as does the transition to daily smoking. In 2010, among adults aged 30–39 years, 81.5% of those who had ever tried a cigarette did so by the age of 18 years and 98.0% did so by the age of 26 years, based on NSDUH data (Table 3.2; Appendix 3.1, Table 3.1.9). Among those who had ever smoked cigarettes daily, the mean age of initiation was even younger; 88.2% first smoked by the age of 18 years and 99.0% first smoked by 26 years of age. Smoking initiation was most likely to occur in a young person's 15th or 16th year, which was also true in 1994 (USDHHS 2011). Adolescent and young adult initiation rates for cigarette smoking have been stable over the past 5 years (Appendix 3.1, Table 3.1.31). This finding is consistent with the idea that tobacco companies are successfully targeting young people in advertising and promotion efforts to attract new smokers (see Chapter 5).

Almost one-fifth of high school students are current cigarette smokers, and the prevalence rises with age; one-fourth of high school seniors are current cigarette smokers at present (Figure 3.3; Table 3.3a and Appendix 3.1, Table 3.1.2). Young adults have the highest smoking prevalence among all age groups (Figure 3.3). Males remain more likely than females to be current smokers in every age group except those aged 65 years and older (CDC 2011c). Similar to findings for adults (CDC 2011c), the prevalence of cigarette smoking among young people is highest for American Indians/Alaska Natives and Whites. The lowest prevalence of cigarette smoking among young people are among Asian and Blacks; in contrast, prevalence are lowest for Asians and Hispanics among adults (CDC 2011c). Since the late 1990s, smoking prevalence has decreased for both youth and young adults (CDC 2001, 2009b). Around 2003, however, the rate of decrease began to slow, such that any changes in the prevalence of current smoking from one iteration of a survey to the next were often statistically insignificant. These findings have led to concern that progress in decreasing youth smoking may have "stalled," or halted. Findings as to which youth demographic subgroups show a more or less pronounced stall are inconsistent across surveys. Overall, however, the most recent reports from both YRBS and MTF suggest a stall in particular subgroups. In NYTS, the prevalence of current cigarette smoking did not differ significantly between 2006 and 2009, the two most recent survey iterations (CDC 2010a). Only NSDUH has shown a continuing, statistically significant decline since 2002 in current smoking, although this decline may be limited to White youth since 2007 (SAMHSA 2009b).

Smokeless tobacco is currently used by less than 10% of adolescents overall, but this finding masks significant differences in patterns of use among youth subgroups. The prevalence of current use among females is less than 2% except in a few Western states (See section on current use of smokeless tobacco, Appendix 3.1). Further, White male students are far more likely than males in other racial/ethnic subgroups to use smokeless tobacco, with the prevalence of current use among white male high school students at around 20%, based on YRBS data (Table 3.4a). Recent data from YRBS and MTF indicate that smokeless tobacco use may have increased among young White males in the latter half of the last decade. The prevalence of current use of cigars (including little cigars and cigarillos) is more than 10% for high school students but is more common among White male youth than among other youth subgroups (Table 3.5a). However, there are a few states in which female cigar use prevalence is around 5% (Appendix 3.1), especially among Black females. The prevalence of cigar use among youth has been largely unchanged over the last few years with some evidence of an increase among Black females since 2007. Smokeless tobacco and cigars are often used by the same youth who smoke cigarettes. Indeed, more than one-half of White and Hispanic male high school students who use any tobacco product use more than one product, and just under one-half of Hispanic female high school students report the same. About 40% use both cigarettes and cigars; one-half of these youth use smokeless tobacco in addition. The prevalence of concurrent use of multiple tobacco products in the last 30 days among high school students has been stable for the past decade.

Globally, the prevalence of tobacco use and the predominant products used among youth vary broadly. Among the 140 countries and 11 territories, commonwealths, provinces, and regions that implemented the GYTS between 2000 and 2007, cigarettes were the predominant form of tobacco used by 13- to 15-year-old students in the Americas, Europe, and Western Pacific regions (Warren et al. 2008). In the Eastern Mediterranean and South-East Asia regions, other forms of tobacco (such as smokeless tobacco, water pipes, or bidis) were more commonly used (Warren et al. 2008). The prevalence of current cigarette smoking among 13- to 15-year-old students varied by region, from 4.0% in Africa to 9.3% in the Americas; however, even within a region, broad variations in prevalence were noted (Appendix 3.1, Table 3.1.64). Although boys were more likely than girls to be tobacco users and current smokers in the majority of countries, the gender gap was narrow or nonexistent in some places; for example, the gap in current use of any tobacco product was statistically indistinguishable in Brazil (Rio de Janeiro), China (Shanghai), and the Russian Federation (Warren et al. 2008). In Spain and some South American (e.g., Argentina, Brazil, Chile, Uruguay), ever cigarette smoking is more prevalent among girls than among boys.

Conclusions

1. Among adults who become daily smokers, nearly all first use of cigarettes occurs by 18 years of age (88%), with 99% of first use by 26 years of age.

2. Almost one in four high school seniors is a current (in the past 30 days) cigarette smoker, compared with one in three young adults and one in five adults. About 1 in 10 high school senior males is a current smokeless tobacco user, and about 1 in 5 high school senior males is a current cigar smoker.

3. Among adolescents and young adults, cigarette smoking declined from the late 1990s, particularly after the Master Settlement Agreement in 1998. This decline has slowed in recent years, however.

4. Significant disparities in tobacco use remain among young people nationwide. The prevalence of cigarette smoking is highest among American Indians and Alaska Natives, followed by Whites and Hispanics, and then Asians and Blacks. The prevalence of cigarette smoking is also highest among lower socioeconomic status youth.

5. Use of smokeless tobacco and cigars declined in the late 1990s, but the declines appear to have stalled in the last 5 years. The latest data show the use of smokeless tobacco is increasing among White high school males, and cigar smoking may be increasing among Black high school females.

6. Concurrent use of multiple tobacco products is prevalent among youth. Among those who use tobacco, nearly one-third of high school females and more than one-half of high school males report using more than one tobacco product in the last 30 days.

7. Rates of tobacco use remain low among girls relative to boys in many developing countries, however, the gender gap between adolescent females and males is narrow in many countries around the globe.

References

Associated Press. Importer tries to get around clove cigarette ban: will sell cigars with the flavored tobacco, which isn't covered in action, 2009; <http://www.msnbc.msn.com/id/32723154/ns/business-retail/>;accessed: December 5, 2011.

Azevedo A, Machado AP, Barros H. Tobacco smoking among Portuguese high-school students. *Bulletin of the World Health Organization* 1999;77(6):509–14.

Bachman JG, O'Malley PM, Johnston LD, Schulenberg JE. *Impacts of Parental Education on Substance Use: Differences Among White, African-American, and Hispanic Students in 8th, 10th, and 12th Grades (1999–2008).* Monitoring the Future Occasional Paper No. 70. Ann Arbor (MI): University of Michigan, Institute for Social Research, 2010.

Bachman JG, O'Malley PM, Johnston LD, Schulenberg JE, Wallace JM. Racial/ethnic differences in the relationship between parental education and substance use among U.S. 8th-, 10th-, and 12th-grade students: findings from the Monitoring the Future Project. *Journal of Studies on Alcohol and Drugs* 2011;72(2):279–85.

Bergen HA, Martin G, Roeger L, Allison S. Perceived academic performance and alcohol, tobacco and marijuana use: longitudinal relationships in young community adolescents. *Addictive Behaviors* 2005;30(8):1563–73.

Biener L, Albers AB. Young adults: vulnerable new targets of tobacco marketing. *American Journal of Public Health* 2004;94(2):326–30.

Brener ND, Billy JO, Grady WR. Assessment of factors affecting the validity of self-reported health-risk behavior among adolescents: evidence from the scientific literature. *Journal of Adolescent Health* 2003; 33(6):436–57.

Brener ND, Eaton DK, Kann L, Grunbaum JA, Gross LA, Kyle TM, Ross JG. The association of survey setting and mode with self-reported health risk behaviors among high school students. *Public Opinion Quarterly* 2006;70(3):354–74.

Bryant AL, Schulenberg J, Bachman JG, O'Malley PM, Johnston LD. *Acting Out and Lighting Up: Understanding the Links Among School Misbehavior, Academic Achievement, and Cigarette Use.* Monitoring the Future Occasional Paper No. 46. Ann Arbor (MI): University of Michigan, Institute for Social Research, 2000a.

Bryant AL, Schulenberg J, Bachman JG, O'Malley PM, Johnston LD. Understanding the links among school misbehavior, academic achievement, and cigarette use: a national panel study of adolescents. *Prevention Science* 2000b;1(2):71–87.

Carpenter CM, Wayne GF, Pauly JL, Koh HK, Connolly GN. New cigarette brands with flavors that appeal to youth: tobacco marketing strategies. *Health Affairs (Millwood)* 2005;24(6):1601–10.

Centers for Disease Control and Prevention. Cigarette smoking among adults—United States, 1999. *Morbidity and Mortality Weekly Report* 2001;50(40):869–73.

Centers for Disease Control and Prevention. Methodology of the youth risk behavior surveillance system. *Morbidity and Mortality Weekly Report* 2004;53(RR-12):1–13.

Centers for Disease Control and Prevention. Tobacco use among students aged 13–15 years—Sri Lanka, 1999–2007. *Morbidity and Mortality Weekly Report* 2008;57(20):545–9.

Centers for Disease Control and Prevention. Changes in tobacco use among youths aged 13–15 years—Panama, 2002 and 2008. *Morbidity and Mortality Weekly Report* 2009a;57(53):1416–9.

Centers for Disease Control and Prevention. Cigarette smoking among adults and trends in smoking cessation—United States, 2008. *Morbidity and Mortality Weekly Report* 2009b;58(44):1227–32.

Centers for Disease Control and Prevention. Cigarette use among high school students—United States, 1991–2009. *Morbidity and Mortality Weekly Report* 2010a; 59(26):797–801.

Centers for Disease Control and Prevention. Differences by sex in tobacco use and awareness of tobacco marketing—Bangladesh, Thailand, and Uruguay, 2009. *Morbidity and Mortality Weekly Report* 2010b;59(20):613–8.

Centers for Disease Control and Prevention. GTSS Data, 2010c; <http://apps.nccd.cdc.gov/GTSSData/Default/Default.aspx>; accessed: January 7, 2011

Centers for Disease Control and Prevention. Tobacco use among middle and high school students — United States, 2000–2009. *Morbidity and Mortality Weekly Report* 2010d;59:1063–8.

Centers for Disease Control and Prevention. CDC Health Disparities and Inequalities Report—United States, 2011. *Morbidity and Mortality Weekly Report* 2011a; 60(Suppl 4):1–161.

Centers for Disease Control and Prevention. *School Health Programs: Improving the Health of Our Nation's Youth.* Atlanta (GA): Centers for Disease Control and Prevention, National Center for Chronic Disease and Prevention, Division of Adolescent and School Health, 2011b; <http://www.cdc.gov/chronicdisease/resources/

publications/aag/pdf/2011/School_Health_AAG_WEB_PDF.pdf>; accessed: November 28, 2011.

Centers for Disease Control and Prevention. Vital signs: current cigarette smoking among adults aged ≥18 years—United States, 2005–2010. *Morbidity and Mortality Weekly Report* 2011c;60(35):1207–12.

Centers for Disease Control and Prevention. Youth Online: High School YRBS, 2011d; <http://apps.nccd.cdc.gov/youthonline/app/Default.aspx>; accessed: November 1, 2011.

CSPnet.com. Kretek drops cigar legal action, 2010; <http://www.cspnet.com/news/tobacco/articles/kretek-drops-cigar-legal-action>; accessed: December 5, 2011.

Cummings KM, Morley CP, Horan JK, Steger C, Leavell NR. Marketing to America's youth: evidence from corporate documents. *Tobacco Control* 2002;11(Suppl 1):I5–I17.

Dhavan P, Stigler MH, Perry CL, Arora M, Reddy KS. Is tobacco use associated with academic failure among government school students in urban India? *Journal of School Health* 2010;80(11):552–60.

Garrett BE, Dube SR, Trosclair A, Caraballo RS, Pechacek TF. Cigarette smoking—United States, 1965–2008. *Morbidity and Mortality Weekly Report Surveillance Summary* 2011;60(Suppl 1):109–13.

Green MP, McCausland KL, Xiao H, Duke JC, Vallone DM, Healton CG. A closer look at smoking among young adults: where tobacco control should focus its attention. *American Journal of Public Health* 2007;97(8):1427–33.

Hu TW, Lin Z, Keeler TE. Teenage smoking, attempts to quit, and school performance. *American Journal of Public Health* 1998;88(6):940–3.

Johnston LD, O'Malley PM, Bachman JG, Schulenberg JE. *Monitoring the Future National Results on Adolescent Drug Use: Overview of Key Findings, 2010.* Ann Arbor (MI): University of Michigan, Institute for Social Research, 2011.

Katz SK, Lavack AM. Tobacco related bar promotions: insights from tobacco industry documents. *Tobacco Control* 2002;11(Suppl 1):I92–I101.

Klein SM, Giovino GA, Barker DC, Tworek C, Cummings KM, O'Connor RJ. Use of flavored cigarettes among older adolescent and adult smokers: United States, 2004–2005. *Nicotine & Tobacco Research* 2008; 10(7):1209–14.

Kopstein A. *Tobacco Use in America: Findings from the 1999 National Household Survey on Drug Abuse.* Analytic Series A-15. Rockville (MD): U.S. Department of Health and Human Services, Substance Abuse and Mental Health Services Administration, Office of Applied Studies, 2001; <http://oas.samhsa.gov/nhsda/tobacco/tobacco.pdf>; accessed: November 28, 2011.

Lantz PM. Smoking on the rise among young adults: implications for research and policy. *Tobacco Control* 2003;12(Suppl 1):i60–i70.

Leatherdale ST, Hammond D, Ahmed R. Alcohol, marijuana, and tobacco use patterns among youth in Canada. *Cancer Causes & Control* 2008;19(4):361–9.

Lee JG, Griffin GK, Melvin CL. Tobacco use among sexual minorities in the USA, 1987 to May 2007: a systematic review. *Tobacco Control* 2009;18(4):275–82.

Li X, Fang X, Stanton B. Cigarette smoking among schoolboys in Beijing, China. *Journal of Adolescence* 1999;22(5):621–5.

Ling PM, Glantz SA. Why and how the tobacco industry sells cigarettes to young adults: evidence from industry documents. *American Journal of Public Health* 2002;92(6):908–16.

Maxwell JC Jr. *The Maxwell Report: Year End & Fourth Quarter 2008 Sales Estimates for the Cigarette Industry.* Richmond (VA): John C. Maxwell, Jr., 2009.

Ministry of Health & Family Welfare. *Global Adult Tobacco Survey, India 2009–2010.* New Delhi (India): Government of India, Ministry of Health & Family Welfare, 2010. <http://www.searo.who.int/linkfiles/regional_tobacco_surveillance_system_gats_india.pdf>; accessed: January 24, 2012.

Mohan S, Sankara Sarma P, Thankappan KR. Access to pocket money and low educational performance predict tobacco use among adolescent boys in Kerala, India. *Preventive Medicine* 2005;41(2):685–92.

Mowery PD, Farrelly MC, Haviland ML, Gable JM, Wells HE. Progression to established smoking among US youths. *American Journal of Public Health* 2004;94(2):331–7.

Murray NG, Low BJ, Hollis C, Cross AW, Davis SM. Coordinated school health programs and academic achievement: a systematic review of the literature. *Journal of School Health* 2007;77(9):589–600.

National Cancer Institute. *The Role of the Media in Promoting and Reducing Tobacco Use*. Tobacco Control Monograph No.19. Bethesda (MD): U.S. Department of Health and Human Services, National Institutes of Health, National Cancer Institute, 2008. NIH Publication No. 07-6242.

Nelson DE, Mowery P, Tomar S, Marcus S, Giovino G, Zhao L. Trends in smokeless tobacco use among adults and adolescents in the United States. *American Journal of Public Health* 2006;96(5):897–905.

Nelson DE, Mowery P, Asman K, Pederson LL, O'Malley PM, Malarcher A, Maibach EW, Pechacek TF. Long-term trends in adolescent and young adult smoking in the United States: metapatterns and implications. *American Journal of Public Health* 2008;98(5):905–15.

Ogden CL, Carroll MD, Curtin LR, Lamb MM, Flegal KM. Prevalence of high body mass index in US children and adolescents, 2007–2008. *JAMA: the Journal of the American Medical Association* 2010;303(3):242–9.

Schroeder SA. Tobacco control in the wake of the 1998 master settlement agreement. *New England Journal of Medicine* 2004;350(3):293–301.

Shafey O, Eriksen M, Ross H, Mackay J. *The Tobacco Atlas*. 3rd ed. Atlanta (GA): American Cancer Society, 2009.

Sinha DN, Gupta PC, Reddy KS, Prasad VM, Rahman K, Warren CW, Jnoes NR, Asma S, et al. Linking Global Youth Tobacco Survey 2003 and 2006 data to tobacco control policy in India. *Journal of School Health* 2008;78(7):368–73.

Substance Abuse and Mental Health Services Administration. *Results from the 2008 National Survey on Drug Use and Health: National Findings*. NSDUH Series H-36. Rockville (MD): U.S. Department of Health and Human Services, Substance Abuse and Mental Health Services Administration, 2009a. DHHSPublication No. SMA 09-4443.

Substance Abuse and Mental Health Services Administration. *The NSDUH Report: Trends in Tobacco Use Among Adolescents: 2002 to 2008*. NSDUH Series H-36. Rockville (MD): U.S. Department of Health and Human Services, Substance Abuse and Mental Health Services Administration, Office of Applied Studies, 2009b. HHSPublication No. SMA 09-4343.

Substance Abuse and Mental Health Services Administration. Results from the 2010 National Survey on Drug Use and Health: detailed tables, 2011a; <http://www.samhsa.gov/data/NSDUH/2k10ResultsTables/Web/HTML/LOTSect2pe.htm#TopOfPage>; accessed: December 14, 2011.

Substance Abuse and Mental Health Services Administration. *Results from the 2010 National Survey on Drug Use and Health: Summary of National Findings*. NSDUH Series H-41. Rockville (MD): U.S. Department of Health and Human Services, Substance Abuse and Mental Health Services Administration, 2011b. HHS Publication No. (SMA) 11-4658.

Tobacco Products Scientific Advisory Committee. Menthol cigarettes and public health: Review of the scientific evidence and recommendations, 2011; http://www.fda.gov/downloads/AdvisoryCommitttees/CommitteesMeetingMaterials/TobaccoProductsScientificAdvisoryCommittee/UCM247689.pdf>; accessed: November 28, 2011.

U.S. Census Bureau. Profile America Facts for Features, 2009; <http://www.census.gov/newsroom/releases/archives/facts_for_features_special_editions/cb11-ff15.html>; accessed: February 3, 2012.

U.S. Department of Health and Human Services. *Preventing Tobacco Use Among Young People. A Report of the Surgeon General.* Atlanta (GA): U.S. Department of Health and Human Services, Centers for Disease Control and Prevention, National Center for Chronic Disease Prevention and Health Promotion, Office on Smoking and Health, 1994.

U.S. Department of Health and Human Services, Office of Disease Prevention and Health Promotion. Healthy People 2020, 2011; <http://www.healthypeople.gov/2020/default.aspx>; accessed: November 1, 2011.

U.S. House of Representatives Committee on Energy & Commerce. Rep. Walxam urges FDA to ban clove-flavored cigars, 2011; <http://democrats.energycommerce.house.gov/index.php?q=news/rep-waxman-urges-fda-to-ban-clove-flavored-cigars>; accessed: December 5, 2011.

Warren CW, Jones NR, Peruga A, Chauvin J, Baptiste JP, Costa de Silva V, el Awa F, Tsouros A, Rahman K, Fishburn B, et al. Global youth tobacco surveillance, 2000–2007. *Morbidity and Mortality Weekly Report* 2008;57(SS-1):1–28.

Wayne GF, Connolly GN. How cigarette design can affect youth initiation into smoking: Camel cigarettes 1983–93. *Tobacco Control* 2002;11(Suppl 1):I32–I39.

Yorulmaz F, Akturk Z, Dagdeviren N, Dalkilic A. Smoking among adolescents: relation to school success, socioeconomic status nutrition and self-esteem. *Swiss Medical Weekly* 2002;132(31–32):449–54.

Young TL, Rogers KD. School performance characteristics preceding onset of smoking in high school students. *American Journal of Diseases of Children* 1986;140(3):257–9.

Zins JE, Weissberg R, Wang MC, Walberg HJ, editors. *Building Academic Success on Social and Emotional Learning: What Does the Research Say?* New York: Teachers College Press, 2004.

Chapter 3 Appendices
The Epidemiology of Tobacco Use Among Young People in the United States and Worldwide

The Use of Other Tobacco Products Among Young People in the United States *199*

Tobacco Use Among Young People Worldwide *209*

Appendix 3.2. Sources of Data *210*

Appendix 3.1. Additional Analyses

This appendix provides additional analyses that describe the epidemiology of tobacco use among young people in the United States and worldwide. It starts with cigarette smoking and then describes the epidemiology of other forms of tobacco use (e.g., smokeless tobacco, cigars, and other emerging products) in this population and concludes with new information on tobacco use among young people worldwide. When possible, appropriate statistical tests have been conducted to determine differences in tobacco use between groups of young people. The results of these tests are presented in tables and text. The results of these analyses should be generalizable to the populations represented (e.g., U.S. youth), given that the surveillance systems from which these data are drawn are based on nationally representative samples. Across surveillance systems, the analyses were purposely restricted to particular age ranges and/or grade levels to ensure as much consistency in analyses and results as possible.

Cigarette Smoking Among Young People in the United States

Recent Patterns of Cigarette Smoking

Ever Smoking a Cigarette

The prevalence of ever smoking a cigarette (see varied definitions in "Ever Smoking," Appendix 3.3) among youth living in the United States is presented in Table 3.1.1. Overall, estimates suggest that almost one-third (28.2%, National Survey on Drug Use and Health [NSDUH]; 30.9%, Monitoring the Future [MTF]) to somewhat less than one-half (42.7%, National Youth Tobacco Survey [NYTS] (high school); 46.3%, Youth Risk Behavior Surveys [YRBS]) of high school students have ever smoked part or all of a cigarette. Per the younger NYTS sample (6th–8th grades), about one-fifth of middle school students have ever smoked a cigarette (18.2%). Among all measures of tobacco use considered in this report, the discrepancies between surveillance systems presented here are the largest. Possible explanations include differences in the composition of the study samples and variability in the question posed by the surveys. Because the prevalence of having ever smoked increases with age (see discussion below), the estimates reported for YRBS and NYTS–high school might be higher than those reported in MTF and NSDUH. The NYTS–middle school estimates are lower because this survey represents a younger population. In addition, the question that YRBS and NYTS ask ("Have you ever tried cigarette smoking, even one or two puffs?") may have been more likely to draw an affirmative response than the questions for MTF ("Have you ever smoked cigarettes?") and NSDUH ("Have you ever smoked part or all of a cigarette?"). Appendices 3.2 and 3.3 further discuss how the four surveillance systems and their measures of smoking might differ. Overall, patterns and trends in other measures of tobacco use, as revealed in the remainder of this Appendix and chapter, are more similar.

The prevalence of ever smoking a cigarette was higher for males than for females in MTF (32.2% vs. 29.3%, $p < 0.05$), NSDUH (29.6% vs. 26.7%, $p < 0.05$), and NYTS (middle school: 19.4% vs. 16.9%, $p < 0.05$; high school: 44.4% vs. 41.1%, $p < 0.05$), but no differences by gender were detected in YRBS (46.3% vs. 46.1%, $p > 0.05$). According to these surveys, the prevalence of ever smoking a cigarette increased significantly with each increase in age (NSDUH) or grade level (MTF, YRBS, NYTS) ($p < 0.05$ for each increase in age or grade in all surveys) except between 11th and 12th grades for NYTS–high school ($p > 0.05$). By 18 years of age or the 12th grade, about one-half of adolescents had ever smoked (44.0%, NSDUH; 42.2%, MTF; 55.5%, YRBS; 52.1%, NYTS-high school).

Differences in ever smoking across racial and ethnic subgroups varied between surveillance systems. Generally speaking, the prevalence of ever smoking was highest among White and Hispanic youth and lowest among Black youth and youth in the Other category. Note that Other includes Asians, American Indians or Alaska Natives, Native Hawaiians or Other Pacific Islanders, and persons of two or more races/ethnicities, which likely mask important differences between these groups. Data from multiple years must be combined to provide reliable estimates for each of these subgroups (see Table 3.1.3). For NSDUH, Whites and Hispanics had the highest prevalence of ever smoking (30.3% vs. 28.4%, respectively, $p > 0.05$), and both were significantly higher than those for Blacks and Other youth (22.1% vs. 23.1%, respectively, $p > 0.05$)

($p < 0.05$ for all White and Hispanic comparisons with Black and Other youth). For MTF, Hispanic and White students had the highest prevalence of ever smoking (32.9% vs. 31.3%, respectively; $p > 0.05$), significantly higher than Other students and Black students (26.4% vs. 24.8%, respectively; $p > 0.05$) ($p < 0.05$ for all White and Hispanic comparisons with Black and Other students). For YRBS, Hispanic and White students again had the highest prevalence of ever smoking (51.0% vs. 46.1%, respectively), followed by Black and Other students (43.5% vs. 39.4%, respectively) ($p < 0.05$ for all Hispanic comparisons with Black and Other students; $p > 0.05$ for all White comparisons with Black and Other students). For NYTS, among middle school students, Whites had the lowest prevalence of ever smoking (14.3%, $p < 0.05$ for all racial/ethnic comparisons with Whites), while among high school students, the prevalence of ever smoking was highest among Hispanics (50.3%, $p < 0.05$ for all racial/ethnic comparisons with Hispanics). Differences between other racial groups for high school and middle school students were not significant for NYTS.

The prevalence of ever cigarette smoking was generally highest in the South and Midwest regions of the United States. In NSDUH, youth living in the South had the highest prevalence of ever cigarette smoking (29.7%) and those living in the Northeast had the lowest prevalence (26.6%) ($p < 0.05$ for comparison between South and Northeast). For MTF, ever use was highest in the South (34.6%) and lowest in the Northeast (27.5%) and West (27.1%) ($p < 0.05$ for comparison of South with Northeast and West). For YRBS, the prevalence of ever smoking among youth was also highest in the South (51.3%) and lowest in the West (41.7%) ($p < 0.05$ for comparison between South and West).

Current Cigarette Smoking

The prevalence of current cigarette smoking (i.e., having smoked a cigarette in the last 30 days; see Appendix 3.3 for further detail on this definition) among youth living in the United States is presented in Table 3.1.2. These estimates suggest that as many as one in five adolescents in the United States overall are current cigarette smokers.

The prevalence of current cigarette smoking was higher for males than for females for MTF (14.2% vs. 11.2%, $p < 0.05$), NSDUH (13.9% vs. 12.4%, $p < 0.05$), and NYTS–high school (19.6% vs. 14.8%, $p < 0.05$), but no differences by gender were detected in YRBS (19.8% vs. 19.1%, $p > 0.05$) or NYTS–middle school (5.6% vs. 4.7%, $p > 0.05$). As with ever cigarette smoking, current cigarette smoking also increased as either age (NSDUH) or grade level (MTF, YRBS, and NYTS) increased. The differences between each subsequent age or grade level were significant for MTF, NSDUH, and YRBS ($p < 0.05$ for each increase in age or grade in all three surveys) and between most grade levels for NYTS. By 18 years of age or the 12th grade, approximately one-quarter of adolescents were current smokers (23.5%, NSDUH; 19.2%, MTF; 25.2%, YRBS; 23.2%, NYTS).

As was the case with ever smoking, differences across racial/ethnic subgroups varied between surveillance systems, but here the variation was not as great. For NSDUH, White youth had the highest prevalence of current smoking (15.2%), which was significantly higher than that of Hispanic youth (12.2%), Other youth (9.9%), and Black youth (8.2%) ($p < 0.05$ for all racial/ethnic comparisons with Whites). For NSDUH, the prevalence of current smoking among Black youth was also significantly lower than among Hispanic youth ($p < 0.05$). For MTF, White students again had the highest prevalence of current smoking (14.4%), which was significantly higher than the prevalence among Other students (11.1%), Hispanic students (11.0%), and Black students (7.0%) ($p < 0.05$ for all racial/ethnic comparisons with White students). Again, the prevalence among Black students was significantly lower than among other racial/ethnic groups ($p < 0.05$ for all racial/ethnic comparisons with Black students). For YRBS, White students had the highest prevalence of current smoking (22.5%) as well, which was significantly higher than the prevalence for Hispanic students (18.0%), Other students (16.5%), and Black students (9.5%) ($p < 0.05$ for all racial/ethnic comparisons with White students). For NYTS–middle school, White students had the lowest prevalence of current smoking (4.3%), and Other students had the highest prevalence (7.2%), but this difference was not statistically significantly different ($p > 0.05$). For NYTS–high school, White and Hispanic students had the highest prevalence of current smoking (19.2%, each), and Black students had the lowest prevalence (7.5%; $p < 0.05$ for all racial/ethnic comparisons with Black students).

Tables 3.1.3 and 3.1.4 provide estimates on current smoking for more specific racial/ethnic subgroups from NSDUH data collapsed for multiple years (2008–2010); these estimates are provided for adolescents (Table 3.1.3) and young adults (Table 3.1.4) separately. Among both adolescents and young adults, American Indians/Alaska Natives had the highest prevalence of current smoking (15.2% and 47.9%, respectively). Although significance testing was not performed for these data, the confidence intervals indicate that the prevalence of current smoking among American Indian/Alaska Native adolescents was significantly higher than among all other racial/ethnic subgroups, except Cuban adolescents. For young adults, the prevalence among American Indians/Alaska Natives was significantly higher than all other racial/ethnic subgroups. Both tables show variability within the Asian and Hispanic subcategories that also should be noted. The numbers of racial/ethnic minorities in other surveys (YRBS, NYTS, MTF) were too small to conduct similar, meaningful analyses.

The prevalence of current cigarette smoking across the United States is reported by region in Table 3.1.2 and illustrated by state in Figures 3.1.1 and 3.1.2. In each survey with available data, the prevalence of current cigarette smoking was highest in the Midwest or the South. For NSDUH, the Midwest had the highest prevalence of current smoking (14.7%), which was significantly higher than the prevalence in the Northeast (12.1%) and West (12.5%) ($p <0.05$ for comparisons with the Northeast and West). For MTF, the Midwest (14.3%) and South (14.3%) had the highest prevalence, which was significantly higher than in the Northeast (11.6%; $p <0.05$ for comparisons with Midwest and South) and West (9.7%; $p <0.05$ for comparisons with Midwest and South). For YRBS, the prevalence of current smoking was highest in the South (22.0%), and Midwest (20.2%) and this was significantly higher than in the West only (15.5%) ($p <0.05$). The maps provided in Figures 3.1.1 and 3.1.2 illustrate by state the prevalence of current cigarette smoking by age (Figure 3.1.1) and by gender and age (Figure 3.1.2) from NSDUH data collapsed over multiple years (2006–2010). Among youth, current cigarette smoking was lowest in Utah (5.4%) and California (6.8%) and highest in Wyoming (15.8%) and Kentucky (14.1%). For young adults, current cigarette smoking was lowest in Utah (20.6%) and California (28.6%) and highest in Kentucky (46.7%) and West Virginia (46.7%). For persons 26 years of age or older, prevalence was lowest in Utah (14.4%) and Massachusetts (18.0%) and highest in West Virginia (31.3%). Using NSDUH data from 2008–2010, Figure 3.1.3 illustrates the association between the prevalence of current smoking among older adults (≥26 years of age) and the prevalence of current smoking among youth (12–17 years of age) nationwide. This strong relationship ($\beta = 0.41$, $p <0.05$) suggests that current smoking among youth resembled that of adults across the nation during this time period.

Data from MTF (Table 3.1.5) show that current cigarette smoking in 2002–2007 was more prevalent in rural areas (i.e., not part of a metropolitan statistical area [MSA]) than in large MSAs (e.g., among 12th-grade students, 27.8% vs. 20.9%, $p <0.05$). In addition, current cigarette smoking was less prevalent in large MSAs than in smaller MSAs ("Other MSA") (e.g., among 12th-grade students, 20.9% vs. 23.5%, $p <0.05$). Table 3.1.5 also presents the prevalence of current cigarette smoking by other sociodemographic risk factors. Among 8th-grade students, current cigarette smoking was strongly and inversely related to the level of parental education (e.g., low vs. high, 16.3% vs. 4.7%, $p <0.05$). This relationship was weaker among older students (e.g., among those in the 12th grade, the difference between high and low was no longer significant: 21.0% vs. 19.8%, $p >0.05$). These data also show that across all grade levels, current cigarette smoking was inversely related to students' academic performance. Prevalence was highest among those with the poorest grades (e.g., among 12th-grade students, D vs. A, 46.1% vs. 14.9%, $p <0.05$). These differences were most pronounced in 8th grade (prevalence ratio of 8 to 1) and least pronounced in 12th grade (prevalence ratio of 3 to 1). Across all grade levels, students who lived alone had a higher prevalence of current smoking than did students with other arrangements (e.g., for 12th grade, 41.3% for those living alone vs. 22.1% for those living with both parents, $p <0.05$). Current cigarette smoking was least prevalent among youth for whom religion was very important (e.g., among 12th-grade students, 15.0% vs. 30.8% among those for whom religion was not important or only somewhat important; $p <0.05$). This observation was consistent across all grade levels. More information and research regarding sociodemographic risk factors for cigarette smoking can be found in Chapter 4 ("Social, Environmental, Cognitive, and Genetic Influences on the Use of Tobacco Among Youth"), which focuses on the etiology of tobacco use.

Frequency and Intensity of Cigarette Smoking

The prevalence of frequent cigarette smoking (having smoked on ≥ 20 of the previous 30 days; see Appendix 3.3) among youth living in the United States is presented in Table 3.1.6, and the prevalence of heavy cigarette smoking (smoking at least one-half pack a day; see Appendix 3.3) is presented in Table 3.1.7. For both measures of smoking intensity, estimates were similar across data sources. Overall, these estimates suggest that up to 7% of adolescents are frequent cigarette smokers and up to 3% are heavy cigarette smokers.

Frequent cigarette smoking was more prevalent among males than females for NSDUH (6.2% vs. 5.3%, $p <0.05$), YRBS (8.0% vs. 6.4%, $p <0.05$), and NYTS (middle school: 2.0% vs. 0.8%, $p <0.05$; high school: 7.4% vs. 5.1%, $p <0.05$). Heavy cigarette smoking was more prevalent among males than females for NSDUH (2.9% vs. 2.2%, $p >0.05$), MTF (3.0% vs. 1.9%, $p <0.05$), and NYTS–high school (2.5% vs. 1.0%, $p <0.05$). For all surveys except NYTS–middle school, the prevalence of frequent and heavy cigarette smoking was higher with each increase in age (NSDUH) or grade level (MTF, YRBS, NYTS–high school). By 18 years of age or the 12th grade, up to 12% of adolescents were frequent smokers (Table 3.1.6: 11.5%, NSDUH; 11.2%, YRBS; 10.0%, NYTS) and up to 6% of adolescents were smoking at least one-half pack per day (Table 3.1.7: 5.4%, NSDUH; 4.7%, MTF; 3.0%, NYTS).

For all surveillance systems except NYTS, the prevalence of frequent and heavy cigarette smoking was highest among White youth, followed by Other, Hispanic, and Black youth. For NSDUH, the prevalence of frequent smoking (Table 3.1.6) was significantly higher among White youth (7.4%) than among Other (4.6%), Hispanic (3.5%), and Black (2.9%) youth (p <0.05 for all racial/ethnic comparisons with Whites). None of the other racial/ethnic comparisons in NSDUH were significant. For YRBS, the prevalence of frequent smoking (Table 3.1.6) was significantly higher among White students (9.5%) than among Other (5.7%), Hispanic (4.2%), and Black (2.1%) students (p <0.05 for all racial/ethnic comparisons with White students). For NSDUH, the prevalence of heavy smoking (Table 3.1.7) was significantly higher among White youth (3.7%) than among Black (1.0%), Hispanic (0.9%), and Other (0.8%) youth (p <0.05 for all racial/ethnic comparisons with Whites). None of the other racial/ethnic comparisons for NSDUH were significant. For MTF, the prevalence of heavy smoking (Table 3.1.7) was higher among White students (3.2%) than among Other (2.0%), Black (1.3%) and Hispanic (1.1%) students (p <0.05 for all racial/ethnic comparisons with White students). For NYTS–middle school, there were no significant racial/ethnic differences for frequent or heavy cigarette smoking. For NYTS–high school, White students (7.9%) and Other students (6.2%) had the highest prevalence of frequent cigarette smoking (Table 3.1.6), and both were significantly greater than that for Black students (1.8%, p <0.05 for comparisons of Black with White and Other students). For heavy cigarette smoking (Table 3.1.7) for NYTS–high school, the only significant racial/ethnic difference was between White (1.9%) and Black (1.0%) students (p <0.05).

The prevalence of frequent and heavy cigarette smoking was generally highest in the Midwest and lowest in the West. For NSDUH, the prevalence of frequent smoking was highest in the Midwest (7.2%), followed by the South (6.0%) and the Northeast (5.5%), and lowest in the West (4.2%; p <0.05 for all regional comparisons with the Midwest and the West). For YRBS, the prevalence of frequent cigarette smoking was highest in the Northeast (8.7%), South (8.5%), and Midwest (8.3%), and lowest in the West (3.5%) (p <0.05 for all regional comparisons with the West). For NSDUH, the prevalence of heavy cigarette smoking was highest in the Midwest (3.6%) followed by the South (2.6%) and the Northeast (2.6%), and was lowest in the West (1.6%) (p <0.05 for all regional comparisons with the Midwest and with the West). For MTF, heavy smoking was most prevalent in the South (3.1%), Midwest (3.0%), and Northeast (2.4%), and was least prevalent in the West (1.2%) (p <0.05 for all regional comparisons with the West).

Table 3.1.8 uses data from YRBS to describe the intensity of cigarette smoking among adolescents. Here, the frequency of cigarette smoking (the number of days in the last 30 days that a person smoked a cigarette) is cross-tabulated with the number of cigarettes smoked per day. Although significance testing for these data was not performed, nonoverlapping confidence intervals suggest daily smokers (smoked a cigarette on all 30 preceding days) were more likely to smoke more than one-half pack per day (i.e., 11–20 and >20 cigarettes per day in Table 3.1.8) than all other categories of smoking frequency. Among these daily smokers, 26.0% smoked more than one-half pack per day, 34.1% smoked 6–10 cigarettes per day, and 35.8% smoked 2–5 cigarettes per day. Nondaily smokers (smoked on 1–29 of the 30 preceding days) were the lightest smokers. Most of the nondaily smokers smoked 2–5 cigarettes per day; this was the range for 76.5% of those who smoked on 20–29 days, 62.8% of those who smoked on 10–19 days, and 52.2% of those who smoked on 6–9 days (in the last 30 days). Further information about the intensity of smoking among daily smokers can be found in Caraballo and associates (2009), which confirms these findings.

Research on other patterns of cigarette smoking among young people, such as intermittent smoking (smoking on "some days," or less than daily or frequently), has become more common in recent years. An analysis of a nationally representative sample of persons 15–25 years of age suggested that almost one-fourth of current smokers (23.7%) could be classified as "some day" smokers (i.e., intermittent smokers) (Hassmiller et al. 2003). On average in that analysis, intermittent smokers smoked cigarettes on 15 days and a total of 102 cigarettes per month (vs. 30 days and 566 cigarettes per month among daily smokers) (Hassmiller et al. 2003).

In the United States, nondaily smoking (smoking on some days but not every day) is increasing overall at the same time that daily smoking is decreasing (Schane et al. 2009). To date, however, there has been no consensus on how to define and study nondaily smoking, although it is a distinct pattern that falls under the broader category of light (i.e., low-volume) or intermittent smoking (Husten 2009). The phenomenon of light or intermittent smoking is more clearly defined among adults and may be a stable behavior in some. Studies of adolescents and young adults, in contrast, suggest this phenomenon may be quite different in earlier years of the life span and much less stable than it is in older men and women (White et al. 2009). For example, those who are light and intermittent smokers in the 12th grade are more likely to end up heavy smokers 2 years later, in young adulthood, than they are to remain light and intermittent smokers (White et al. 2009). A special issue of *Nicotine & Tobacco Research* was focused entirely on this topic (Fagan and Rigotti 2009); the reader is directed there for further information, which is beyond the scope of this report.

Cigarette Smoking Among Young Adults

Increasingly, attention is being focused on cigarette smoking behaviors among young adults (18–25 years of age), as this age group has the highest prevalence of cigarette smoking of any age group in the United States (Green et al. 2007; Lawrence et al. 2007; Ling et al. 2009) and because the tobacco industry targets young adult consumers (Katz and Lavack, 2002; Ling and Glantz, 2002). Analyses suggest that 20% (Green et al. 2007) and 22.7% (Table 3.1.9) of adult smokers became regular and daily smokers, respectively, during young adulthood. Separate analyses of the Tobacco Use Supplement to the Current Population Survey in 1998–1999 and 2003 demonstrate that the prevalence of current cigarette smoking is highest among non-college-educated young adults (Green et al. 2007) and blue-collar and service workers (Lawrence et al. 2007). In these groups, the prevalence of current cigarette smoking is twice that of college-educated and white-collar workers (Green et al. 2007; Lawrence et al. 2007). As among adolescents, the prevalence of current cigarette smoking among young adults is highest among American Indians/Alaska Natives and Whites (Green et al. 2007; Lawrence et al. 2007). More young adult males are current cigarette smokers than are young adult females (Green et al. 2007; Lawrence et al. 2007). About one-third of young adults fall into each of the light smoker (<10 cigarettes per day), moderate smoker (10–19 cigarettes per day), and heavy smoker (≥20 cigarettes per day) categories (Lawrence et al. 2007). To date, however, few interventions for preventing or quitting tobacco use have been directed at young adults, particularly among non-college-educated young adults, and young adults are not consumers of evidence-based cessation treatments (Curry et al. 2007, Solberg et al. 2007). Additional studies of predictors of tobacco use in this subpopulation will be required to develop effective interventions for this age group.

Preferences for Particular Cigarette Brands

Knowing what brands of cigarettes are preferred by adolescent and young adult smokers can provide insight into the influence that the marketing practices of the tobacco industry and the design of its products may have on young people and, importantly, aid the development of programs to prevent smoking (Cummings et al. 2002; Wayne and Connolly 2002; Carpenter et al. 2005; Klein et al. 2008; National Cancer Institute [NCI] 2008). More information on the relationship between the marketing practices of the tobacco industry and tobacco use among young people can be found in Chapter 5 ("The Tobacco Industy's Influences on the Use of Tobacco Among Youth") of this report. Here, Tables 3.1.10 and 3.1.11 provide evidence of which cigarette brands were preferred most often by adolescents (12–17 years of age) and young adults (18–25 years of age) in 2008–2010, by drawing on data from recent NSDUH surveys stratified by important demographic variables. These analyses are restricted to current smokers—that is, adolescents and young adults who smoked in the last 30 days.

Among adolescents, all 10 of the most commonly preferred brands of cigarettes were subbrands of Marlboro (46.2%), Newport (21.8%), or Camel (12.4%), making these the preferred brands of 80.4% of adolescent smokers. Marlboro full flavor (19.7%) was the most preferred brand overall, followed by Marlboro Lights (17.5%). Other Marlboro subbrands in the top 10 included Marlboro Mediums (7.3%) and Marlboro Ultra Lights (1.7%). Subbrands of Newport, a menthol cigarette, in the top 10 included Newport full flavor (14.1%), Newport Lights (5.0%), and Newport Mediums (2.7%). Subbrands of Camel in the top 10 included Camel full flavor (5.2%), Camel Lights (5.1%), and Camel Mediums (2.1%). Among the five most preferred brands overall, boys ranked Newport full flavor (15.2%) over Marlboro Lights (15.1%), and girls ranked Marlboro Lights (20.1%) over Marlboro full flavor (16.8%). Among Whites and Other adolescents, the top two choices were the same as in the overall rankings. Among Hispanics, Marlboro Lights ranked first. Among Blacks, Newport full flavor (42.4%) was preferred most often, followed by Newport Lights (16.9%). Among older (15–17 years of age) adolescents, the top three choices were the same as the overall choices. Younger adolescents (12–14 years of age) preferred Marlboro Light most often (18.4%) followed by Marlboro full flavor (13.8%) and Marlboro Mediums (10.2%). There was some regional variation in brand preference. Newport full flavor, for example, was the most preferred brand in the Northeast (25.0%). Marlboro Lights ranked first in the South (20.9%), with Marlboro full flavor (18.1%) next. Marlboro full flavor (23.0%), Marlboro Mediums (10.4%), Camel full flavor (8.6%), Camel Lights (7.3%) and Camel Mediums (4.2%) were more commonly preferred in the West compared with other regions, while Newport full flavor (4.0%) was much less commonly preferred in the West than in other regions.

There were differences between adolescents and young adults in the brands they preferred. Among young adults, 9 of the 10 most commonly preferred brands (Table 3.1.11) were subbrands of Marlboro (46.1%), Newport (19.5%), or Camel (14.9%). Marlboro Lights (22.7%) was, by a large margin, the most preferred brand. Other Marlboro subbrands in the top 10 for young adults included Marlboro full flavor (16.3%), Marlboro Mediums (5.0%), and Marlboro Ultra Lights (2.1%). Newport full flavor (15.7%) was the third most preferred brand overall, and Newport Lights (2.2%) and Newport Medium (1.6%) were also in the top 10. Camel Lights (9.3%) was preferred by more young adults than was Camel full flavor (5.6%). Parliament Lights (2.6%) was also included in the 10 most preferred brands among young adults. These preferences were largely consistent across gender, with one major exception being that females preferred Newport full flavor (16.2%) over Marlboro full flavor (13.2%), while males did not. Preferences were also generally consistent among young adults for Whites, Hispanics, and Other. Among Black young adults, Newport full flavor (61.2%) was by far the most preferred brand, followed by Newport Mediums (9.0%) and Newport Lights (8.1%). Among the younger (18–20 years) group of young adults, Malboro full flavor (19.8%) was preferred over Marlboro Lights (19.1%). The older (21–25 years of age) group preferred Newport full flavor (15.5%) over Marlboro full flavor (14.2%). Regional differences were minimal. In the West, Newport full flavor (5.0%) was preferred much less commonly than in the other regions, and Camel full flavor (9.7%) was preferred more commonly than in the other regions.

It is helpful to look at the overall market share that each brand of cigarettes secured in the United States in 2008, the first year of the NSDUH data presented in Tables 3.1.10 and 3.1.11, to compare this market share with brand preferences of adolescents and young adults (Maxwell 2009c). Market share, noted as a percentage, represents the portion of total cigarette sales that a certain brand accounted for in the United States. This information was not available for subbrands of cigarettes (e.g., Marlboro Lights) but was available for major brands (e.g., Marlboro overall). The market share data were closely aligned with the data for brand preference among both adolescents (Table 3.1.10) and young adults (Table 3.1.11). In 2008, Marlboro accounted for 41.0% of cigarette sales in the United States, followed by Newport (9.7%) and Camel (6.7%) (Maxwell 2009c). As noted earlier, these three brands were the ones most preferred by adolescents and young adults. These three brands accounted for 57.4% of overall market share, which is influenced mostly by the preferences of adults and not adolescents. These figures indicate that the combined share of Marlboro, Newport, and Camel is not as concentrated among adults overall as it is among adolescents (80.4%) and young adults (80.5%). Overall, other brands each secured less than 5% of the total cigarette market (Maxwell 2009c), which is consistent with the findings from the NSDUH surveys of youth.

Mentholated cigarettes deserve special note in this section and are the focus of a report by the U.S. Food and Drug Administration's (FDA's) Tobacco Product Scientific Advisory Committee (TPSAC 2011). Menthol is an additive in cigarettes; those brands (e.g., Newport) that are marketed as a menthol cigarette contain sufficient levels of menthol to warrant describing them as having a "characterizing flavor" (USFDA 2011). Some studies suggest that mentholated cigarettes increase the addictive potential of smoking among youth (Wackowski and Delnovo, 2007; Hersey et al. 2010). Furthermore, because mentholation can improve the taste of cigarettes for smokers, this additive may facilitate initiation or inhibit quitting (Giovino et al. 2004). Adolescent and young adult smokers smoke menthol cigarettes at a higher percentage than any other age group (Substance Abuse and Mental Health Services Administration [SAMHSA] 2009d; Lawrence et al. 2010; TPSAC 2011). In the 2006 NYTS, 51.7% (95% confidence interval [CI], 45.8–57.5%) of middle school smokers and 43.1% (95% CI, 37.0–49.1%) of high school smokers usually smoked a menthol brand of cigarettes (Hersey et al. 2010). (Note these percentages are much higher than the preference data reported in Table 3.1.10 [21.8%] of 12- to 17-year-olds preferred menthol brand cigarettes–Newports. The reason for this discrepancy is not clear). In the NYTS data, the prevalence of smoking menthol cigarettes was higher among established smokers in middle school (i.e., those who had been smoking for 1 year or more) than among those who had just initiated smoking (Hersey et al. 2010). Consistent with the data on preferences for Newport cigarettes among Black adolescents, mentholated cigarettes are especially popular among Black smokers generally (Lawrence et al. 2010). Continued surveillance of this type of cigarette product is warranted. At present, cigarettes with characterizing flavors are banned, except those with menthol flavoring. Studies indicate that mentholated cigarettes are as dangerous as nonmentholated ones (Giovino et al. 2004) though other studies suggest lower risk of lung cancer (TPSAC 2011). Further information on mentholated cigarettes can be found in a special supplement published in 2010 (see Ahijevych and Garret, 2010; Foulds et al. 2010; Gardiner and Clark 2010; Hersey et al. 2010).

Summary

About one-third to one-half of all adolescents in the United States have ever smoked part or all of a cigarette. One in four (25%) high school seniors and one in three (33%) young adults are current cigarette smokers. The prevalence of current cigarette smoking is highest among American Indian/Alaska Native adolescents, followed by

White and Hispanic adolescents and Asian and Black adolescents. Among American Indian/Alaskan Native, White, and Asian adolescents, the prevalence of current smoking is essentially the same for boys as for girls. Among Hispanics and Blacks, it is higher for boys than girls. By the end of 12th grade, more than 10% of current smokers are smoking at least 20 days per month (i.e., they can be classified as frequent smokers), and more than 5% are smoking at least a half-pack of cigarettes or more per day (i.e., they can be categorized as heavy smokers). The prevalence of frequent and heavy smoking is highest among White adolescents in high school (American Indians/Alaska Natives were not considered here), while racial/ethnic differences are less prominent among middle school youth. Marlboro, Camel, and Newport are the most preferred brands of cigarettes for adolescents and young adults alike. Newport, a menthol cigarette brand, is particularly preferred by Blacks (note that Newport Red, a new brand of Newports, is nonmentholated). Continued surveillance of menthol cigarettes is warranted.

Developmental Patterns of Cigarette Smoking

Adolescence and young adulthood represent a time of heightened vulnerability for both the initiation of tobacco use and the development of nicotine dependence (see Chapter 2 "The Health Consequences of Tobacco Use Among Young People"). Identifying factors that distinguish between young people who experiment with smoking and desist after relatively few trials and those who experiment, escalate, and become dependent smokers can inform the design of interventions. This section describes developmental patterns that would be relevant to these etiologic studies, especially during adolescence. Young adulthood should not be overlooked, however, as recent data suggest at least 20% of smokers begin smoking regularly in young adulthood (Green et al. 2007) and the average consumption per smoker increases in the decade following adolescence (Hammond 2005).

Age or Grade When Smoking Begins

The initiation of cigarette smoking at a young age increases the risk of later heavy smoking and of subsequent smoking-attributable mortality (Tailoi and Wynder 1991; Escobedo et al. 1993; Everett et al. 1999, Lando et al. 1999). Initiation is a complex process that can occur over a number of weeks or years. This section of the chapter focuses on two points in the process of uptake and progression: the age a young person first tries a cigarette and the age at which a young person begins to smoke cigarettes daily. In addition, it considers susceptibility to start smoking cigarettes among never smokers. Susceptibility is defined as the absence of a firm decision to not start smoking.

Table 3.1.12 uses data from recent NSDUH surveys (2008–2010) to estimate the percentage of nonsmoking adolescents who were susceptible to starting to smoke in those years. Susceptibility to smoking, which is a strong predictor of the onset of smoking (Evans et al. 1995; Pierce et al. 1996), was measured with two questions: (1) "If one of your best friends offered you a cigarette, would you smoke it?" and (2) "At any time during the next 12 months, do you think that you will smoke a cigarette?" Those answering "definitely not" to both questions were categorized as not susceptible. Overall, 19.9% of nonsmoking adolescents were classified as susceptible, with boys (20.4%) slightly more susceptible than girls (19.3%). Hispanics had the highest prevalence of susceptibility (24.2%), which was significantly higher than among Blacks (19.4%), Whites (19.0%), and Asians (15.1%) (95% confidence intervals do not overlap).

Because initiation can occur after the adolescent years, this section continues with data from adults in the 2010 NSDUH (Table 3.1.9). The analysis was restricted to adults 30–39 years of age because virtually all initiation ultimately occurs before the age of 30 years (USDHHS 1994), and because in the United States, the majority of the increased mortality that results from cigarette smoking occurs after the age of 40 years (Lopez et al. 1994). Because the recalled age of initiation is often 10 or more years less than the age of the adult respondent at the time of the survey, recall bias may affect the reliability of these estimates. Moreover, these estimates represent initiation that occurred up to 30 years earlier (i.e., from the early 1980s onward). According to the 2010 NSDUH, more than one-half (56.3%) of adults 30–39 years of age (including those who had smoked and those who had not) had first tried a cigarette while they were an adolescent or child (≤18 years of age). Of all adults 30–39 years of age who had ever tried a cigarette, 81.5% tried their first cigarette during adolescence or earlier, with 15.9 years the mean age of first trying a cigarette. Among all adults 30–39 years of age, 24.3% became daily smokers while they were under 18 years of age. Of those who had ever smoked daily, 88.2% tried their first cigarette by 18 years of age, and two-thirds (65.1%) started smoking daily by the time they were 18 years old. The mean age of becoming a daily smoker was 17.9 years. Some initiation does occur in young adulthood (19–26 years of age), and the estimate in this survey was that 11.5% of all persons 30–39 years of age (ever smokers or not) tried their first cigarette as a young adult. Of all adults 30–39 years of age who had ever tried a cigarette, 16.5% tried their first cigarette in young adulthood. In all, 11.6% of adults (30–39 years of age) became daily smokers when in young adulthood. Of those who had ever smoked daily, 10.8% tried their first cigarette as a young adult and 31.1% started smoking daily in young adulthood.

Surveys conducted in 2009 and 2010 among youth (Table 3.1.13), although lacking information on post-adolescent initiation, provide information on more recent patterns of initiation (i.e., from the mid-1990s onward). Among all 12th-grade students (mostly 17–19 years of age), estimates were that 16.0% (MTF), 19.0% (YRBS), and 18.4% (NYTS) first tried a cigarette by 14 years of age or by the end of 8th grade. Per the NSDUH survey, among 17- and 18-year-olds who had completed the 11th grade, 16.2% first tried a cigarette by the age of 14 years. In all, the estimated percentages of young people who had tried smoking were 43.9% for NSDUH (17 or 18 years of age and completed 11th grade), 39.0% for MTF (12th-grade students), 45.1% for YRBS (12th-grade students), and 41.5% for NYTS (12th-grade students). Daily cigarette use (Table 3.1.14) began by the age of 16 years (or the 10th grade) for 7.4% of 12th-grade students, per MTF, and for 9.3% of those 17 years of age, per NSDUH. Among these youth, by 17 years of age or 10th grade, 13.2% (NSDUH) and 11.7% (MTF) were smoking daily.

Transitions and Trajectories in Smoking

Tobacco use among adolescents and young adults, including use specific to cigarette smoking, is increasingly being conceptualized as a developmental pathway(s) characterized by "transitions and trajectories … from no use to dependence" (Clayton et al. 2000, p. S1). Fortunately, the analysis of these more sophisticated models of smoking onset and progression is now possible because of advances in statistical theory and techniques (Collins and Sayer 2001). A more extensive review of these types of studies is provided in Chapters 2 and 4. In the present chapter, a brief overview of these new analytic approaches is provided, followed by the presentation of data from Add Health, a nationally representative longitudinal study of adolescents and young adults. These data are used to describe "transitions and trajectories" of tobacco use in youth.

Trajectories of Cigarette Smoking

Most research to date describes the natural history of cigarette smoking as a process that begins in adolescence, increases as an adolescent ages and grows into a young adult, then peaks and either stabilizes or declines with time (Chen and Kandel 1995). This conceptualization of the onset and progression of cigarette smoking, however, is limited. It describes only a single trajectory of age-related changes in smoking behavior over time, averaged across all adolescents, and thus it obscures any heterogeneity in this process that is likely to exist.

By using sophisticated statistical procedures, such as growth mixture modeling, recent studies have started to empirically identify multiple trajectories of cigarette smoking behavior. Some have focused only on cigarette smoking in adolescence (e.g., Bernat et al. 2008), while others have described cigarette smoking in young adulthood (e.g., Colder et al. 2006), and still others have characterized cigarette smoking from adolescence through young adulthood (e.g., Chassin et al. 2000). In addition, some studies have considered special populations such as Blacks (e.g., Fergus et al. 2005). In each study, multiple subgroups of youth have been identified who shared a common pathway(s) with regard to the onset and progression of smoking over time; subgroups have usually been defined by measures of the frequency and/or quantity of cigarette smoking across time. Chassin and colleagues (2000), for example, identified six subgroups: (1) abstainers, (2) experimenters, (3) early stable smokers, (4) late stable smokers, (5) quitters, and (6) erratics. These subgroups differed by the intensity of smoking and by the age at which the intensity of cigarette smoking increased or decreased as respondents aged across time. In addition, Chassin and coworkers (2000) used key correlates of tobacco use to differentiate these subgroups in adolescence or young adulthood.

In this chapter, one of several ways to characterize trajectories of cigarette smoking is presented. Multiple trajectories of cigarette smoking are identified using data from Add Health (University of North Carolina [UNC], 2009). These trajectories describe different developmental pathways specific to the onset and progression of smoking from early adolescence through young adulthood. In Add Health, data were collected from a nationally representative sample of youth in three waves. Wave I was collected in 1994–1995, when students were in the 7th–12th grades (11–17 years of age); Wave II in 1996, when students were in the 8th–12th grades (12–18 years of age); and Wave III in 2001–2002, when the youth were young adults (18–26 years of age). At the time this chapter was being developed, data from Wave IV (2007–2008; 24–32 years of age) were not yet available for analysis. The present analysis makes use of only those who participated in Wave I and Wave III. The analysis uses a single measure: "During the past 30 days, on how many days did you smoke cigarettes?" These data were combined through the use of a cohort sequential design to map developmental pathways of smoking from 11 to 26 years of age. Age was included as the only covariate in all models.

Overall, four distinct trajectories were identified in these analyses: (1) nonsmokers, (2) early establishers, (3) late establishers, and (4) quitters (Figure 3.1.4). Nonsmokers had no past-month cigarette use at any time point from adolescence through young adulthood; 48.3% fit this description. Early establishers had an early onset of smoking (ages of 12 or 13 years), which escalated quickly to daily use (smoking on all 30 days before the survey) by age 17 years and remained there throughout young adulthood; 14.5% could be characterized as early establishers. Late establishers had a later onset of smoking, at 15 or 16 years of age, escalating to intermittent use (smoking on no more than 20 of the 30 days before the survey) by the age of 21 years, peaking at 23 years of age, and then falling through the age of 26 years; 25.0% fit this description. Quitters had the earliest onset of smoking, before the age of 11 years, which escalated to less than daily use by 16 years of age then fell throughout the rest of adolescence and young adulthood to the lowest levels among those who reported smoking in the last 30 days; 12.0% of the sample could be characterized in this way. Nonsmokers could be identified by a linear model, early and late establishers with a quadratic model, and quitters by a cubic model.

Some of these trajectories varied by gender and race/ethnicity (Table 3.1.15). Boys, for example, were significantly more likely than girls to be late establishers (odds ratio [OR] = 1.87, 95% CI = 1.55–2.25). Boys and girls were equally likely, however, to belong to the early establisher group and to be quitters. Blacks were significantly less likely than Whites to be members of the late establisher, early establisher, or quitter groups (e.g., for late establishers, OR = 0.55, 95% CI = 0.42–0.72). Comparisons of Hispanics versus Whites yielded similar results (e.g., for late establishers, OR = 0.62, 95% CI = 0.45–0.85).

Levels of nicotine dependence in young adulthood (Wave III), as measured by a modified version of the Fagerström Tolerance Questionnaire (Payne et al. 1994), were highest for early establishers (scale score = 4.04), followed by late establishers (2.94), and then quitters (1.18) (Table 3.1.16). The differences in scale scores between all of these smoking trajectory groups were significant, according to the 95% confidence intervals. A scale score above 4.0 is typically used to identify adults who are dependent on nicotine (Breslau and Johnson 2000). The score on the Fagerström scale was significantly and positively correlated with being an early establisher and being a late establisher ($p < 0.05$), and it was significantly and negatively correlated with being a quitter and being a nonsmoker ($p < 0.05$).

These findings suggest that early—and sustained—intervention throughout adolescence is critical. This includes prevention and cessation initiatives. In Add Health, for example, those who became daily smokers in late adolescence (i.e., early establishers), started smoking before the age of 13 years, on average. Once they became daily smokers, at the age of 18 years, on average, they remained daily smokers throughout young adulthood (26 years of age). The escalation in smoking for early establishers occurred during early adolescence (i.e., as they transitioned from middle school to high school, then throughout high school), while the escalation in smoking for late establishers occurred in late adolescence (i.e., during the latter years of high school, to the transition into college, or to other pursuits of young adulthood). Efforts to prevent the onset of tobacco use and progression to regular use/established smoking, therefore, should begin early in adolescence (e.g., middle school) and be sustained over time (e.g., through young adulthood), to maximize their impact.

Transitions in Cigarette Smoking

The 1994 Surgeon General's report on preventing tobacco use among young people described the continuum of smoking behavior as one that has five stages: (1) preparation, (2) trying, (3) experimentation, (4) regular use, and (5) dependence (USDHHS 1994). To date, however, these stages are still based mostly on theory (Flay 1993), with limited empirical evidence to validate them. Not all young people advance through these stages, but those who become smokers as adults appear to experience similar steps in the onset and progression of cigarette smoking (Caraballo et al. 2009).

Several models of the stages of smoking onset and progression have been proposed; the model presented in the 1994 Surgeon General's report is based on the work of Flay and colleagues (1983). Adolescents begin to develop positive attitudes and beliefs about smoking in the preparation stage, although they have yet to try a single puff of a cigarette. That occurs in the second stage, trying, and can progress to experimentation, the third stage, depending on the physiological effects of initial attempts and social reinforcements. In this model, experimentation is defined by repeated, but irregular, use of cigarettes over an extended period of time. Young people advance to the fourth stage, regular use, when they begin to smoke more often—at least weekly across a variety of personal and social situations. The final stage, dependence, is defined by the physiological need for nicotine. Other models of the onset and progression of smoking include the stages of change (the Transtheoretical Model) (Prochaska and DiClemente 1983), which has been adapted for use with adolescents (Pallonen et al. 1998); and a model specific to susceptibility to smoking (Pierce et al. 1996). These two models have been combined into a single model (Prokhorov et al. 2002) that further subdivides the preparation stage, above, according to one's susceptibility.

In this chapter, the stages of smoking onset and progression were identified using data from Add Health (UNC 2009). As with the presentation on trajectories (above), data for this analysis included data collected in Wave I (1994–1995, when students were 11–17 years of age) and Wave III (2001–2002, when they were 18–26 years of age), but not Wave II. The two groups of youth considered for the present analysis were those 12–14 years of age at Wave I and those 15–18 years of age at Wave I. These analyses, which included a latent class analysis (LCA) and latent transition analysis (LTA), used four measures: (1) "Have you ever tried cigarette smoking, even one or two puffs?" (2) "During the past 30 days, on how many days did you smoke cigarettes?" (3) "During the past 30 days, on the days you smoked, how many cigarettes did you smoke each day?" and (4) "During the past 6 months, have you tried to quit smoking cigarettes?" LCA and LTA, which are advanced statistical techniques useful in furthering the study of stage-sequential behavior, allow one to empirically identify stages of behavioral change (LCA) and examine movement through them sequentially (LTA) (Lanza et al. 2007).

Data for the younger cohort (12–14 years of age in Wave I) are provided in Tables 3.1.17 and 3.1.19. In this cohort, three statuses, or stages, of cigarette smoking/smokers were empirically identified in the analysis: (1) never smokers, (2) current smokers, and (3) former smokers (Table 3.1.17). Never smokers were those who reported never trying to smoke a cigarette, no cigarette smoking in the past 30 days, and no quit attempts in the last 6 months. Current smokers were those who reported having ever tried to smoke a cigarette and some cigarette smoking in the past 30 days. Some current smokers reported a quit attempt in the last 6 months, while others did not. Former smokers were most likely to report having ever tried a cigarette but reported no use in the last 30 days.

At Wave I (12–14 years of age), 84.8% of these adolescents were never smokers, 12.2% were current smokers, and 3.1% were former smokers. At Wave III (when they were 19–21 years of age), 53.4% of these young adults were never smokers, 38.3% were current smokers, and 8.3% were former smokers. Differences by gender were minimal in Wave I, but at Wave III, substantially more women (57.4%) than men (48.5%) were never smokers, and more men (44.1%) than women were current smokers (33.7%). At Wave I, more Blacks (95.2%) were never smokers than were White (86.2%), Hispanic (85.1%), and Other youth (80.3%). At Wave III, Blacks (76.8%) were also more often never smokers than were White (57.1%), Hispanic (51.9%), or Other youth (44.0%).

Table 3.1.18 presents the probabilities of transitioning from one stage to another time from Wave I (12–14 years of age) to Wave III (19–21 years of age). Estimates in the diagonals (noted in bold) represent stability, or the proportion of young people who stayed in the same stage over time. Estimates in the off-diagonals (noted in plain text) represent change, or the proportion of young people in one stage who moved to a different stage over time. Overall, for example, 63% of those who were never smokers at Wave I remained never smokers at Wave III, while 31% of them had become current smokers. Another 6%, in turn, were former smokers at Wave III, having become current smokers at some point between Wave I and Wave III. Of those who were current smokers at Wave I, 79% remained current smokers at Wave III, and 21% had become former smokers. Of those who had been former smokers at Wave I, only 20% remained in this category at Wave III, and the rest (80%) had become current smokers (again) by Wave III. Differences in transitions across time by gender and race/ethnicity are also presented in Table 3.1.18.

Data for the older cohort (15–18 years of age at Wave I) are provided in Tables 3.1.19 and 3.1.20. In this cohort, four classes, or stages, of smoking/smokers were empirically identified (1) never smokers, (2) former smokers, (3) nondaily smokers, and (4) daily smokers (Table 3.1.19). Never smokers were those who reported never trying to smoke a cigarette, no smoking in the past 30 days, and no quit attempts in the last 6 months. Former smokers reported having ever tried a cigarette but no smoking in the past 30 days. Nondaily smokers reported having ever tried to smoke a cigarette and smoking on 1–29 of the past 30 days. Some nondaily smokers reported a quit attempt in the last 6 months, while others did not. Daily smokers reported having ever tried to smoke a cigarette and smoking on all of the past 30 days. Some daily smokers reported a quit attempt in the last 6 months, but others did not.

At Wave I (15–18 years of age), 63.3% of these adolescents were never smokers; 5.5%, former smokers; 20.3%, nondaily smokers; and 11.0%, daily smokers. At Wave III (22–25 years of age), 48.9% of these adolescents were never smokers; 11.1%, former smokers; 16.7%, nondaily smokers; and 23.3%, daily smokers. Differences by gender were small at Wave I, but at Wave III, more women (53.6%) than men (44.0%) were never smokers, as more men than women fell into the nondaily and daily smoker categories at Wave III (e.g., nondaily smokers, 19.0% of men and 14.8% of women). At Wave I, more Blacks (82.4%) were never smokers than were Whites (70.0%), Hispanics (70.4%), or Other youth (50.9%). More Blacks (61.2%) were never smokers at Wave III, as well, than were Whites (53.8%), Hispanics (58.6%), or Other youth (36.4%).

Table 3.1.20 presents the probabilities of transitioning from one stage to another from Wave I (15–18 years of age) to Wave III (22–25 years of age). As in Table 3.1.18, estimates in the diagonals (in bold) represent stability, or the proportion of young people who stayed in the same stage over time. Estimates in the off-diagonals (plain text) represent change, or the proportion of young people in one stage who moved to a different stage over time. Overall, for example, 77% of those who were never smokers at Wave I remained never smokers at Wave III; 10% of these earlier never smokers had become nondaily smokers by Wave III, and 8% had become daily smokers. Another 4% were former smokers at Wave III, having been current smokers at some point between Wave I and Wave III. Of those who were nondaily smokers at Wave I, 38% remained nondaily smokers at Wave III, while another 38% became daily smokers and 24% became former smokers. Of those who were daily smokers at Wave I, 82% remained daily smokers at Wave III, while 6% became nondaily smokers and 12% became former smokers. Of those who were former smokers at Wave I, only 37% remained in this category at Wave III, while 34% became nondaily smokers and 29% became daily smokers. Differences by gender and race/ethnicity are also shown in Table 3.1.20.

Measures of cigarette smoking related to early stages of use (e.g., preparation and/or susceptibility) were not available for this study as these measures were not used in Add Health. Having such measures would have allowed for empirical identification of these early stages in theoretical models designed to describe the onset and progression of smoking over time during adolescence. In using the measures available, however, the current analysis does depict the variability inherent in this process, reinforcing the concept of other "stages" of smoking reflected elsewhere in this chapter (e.g., current smoking, frequent smoking, and former smoking). The findings presented here again underscore the need for early intervention, prior to onset, if possible. In the younger cohort, for example, 79% of current smokers at Wave I remained current smokers at Wave III. In the older cohort, 38% of nondaily smokers at Wave I were nondaily smokers at Wave III, and 38% of them became daily smokers. Less than 25% of either of these groups (current smokers at Wave I in the younger cohort, nondaily smokers at Wave I in the older cohort) moved backwards to become former smokers by Wave III. Furthermore, in the older cohort, only 12% of the daily smokers had quit and become former smokers by Wave III.

Implications of Smoking During Adolescence for Young Adults

Some notable findings from MTF regarding young people's expectations to smoke, or to abstain from smoking, are presented in Tables 3.1.21–3.1.24, which use data from students originally surveyed in 1996–2001 as high school seniors. In their senior year, respondents were asked, "Do you think you will be smoking cigarettes five years from now?" In all, an estimated 1.4% of the seniors reported that they would definitely be smoking in 5 years, 11.4% probably would, 24.3% probably would not, and 62.9% definitely would not (Table 3.1.21). This distribution varied by the intensity of smoking. Almost all (98.2%) of those who were not smoking at the time reported that they would probably or definitely not be smoking in 5 years. Among those who were smoking one to five cigarettes per day as a high school senior, two-thirds (67.1%) said they would not be smoking ("probably not" or "definitely not") in 5 years. Just over one-half (53.3%) of the half-pack per day smokers said they would probably or definitely not be smoking in 5 years, and somewhat more than one-third (36.8%) of those smoking one or more packs per day said they would probably or definitely not be smoking at that point. As with any forecasts based on personal predictions, the percentages must be viewed cautiously but are still illustrative of intention.

This group of high school seniors was followed and then surveyed 5–6 years later in 2001–2007 (Table 3.1.22). Of students who were not smoking in their senior year, 86.1% were still not smoking 5–6 years later (Table 3.1.22), well below the predicted 98.2% for this group (probably or definitely not smoking in 5 years) (Table 3.1.21). Among those who were smoking one to five cigarettes a day as a senior, only 30.1% were not smoking 5–6 years later, less than one-half of the prediction of 67.1% for this group (again, "probably or definitely not") in 5 years (Table 3.1.21). As young adults, 21.3% of those who had smoked one to five cigarettes per day as seniors were still smoking one to five cigarettes per day, and 31.0% had begun to smoke a half-pack or more per day (Table 3.1.22). Among those who were smoking one-half pack of cigarettes as a senior, just 22.7% were not smoking 5–6 years later. This, again, was well below the prediction for this group (53.3% for probably or definitely not smoking in 5 years) (Table 3.1.21). In young adulthood, 26.5% were smoking at the same intensity level, and 25.1% had begun to smoke one pack or more each day (Table 3.1.22). Among those who were smoking one pack or more as a senior, only 15.2% were not smoking 5–6 years later (Table 3.1.22), far below the prediction of 36.8% for this group (Table 3.1.21). Almost one-half (48.3%) were still smoking one pack or more a day, and over one-third (36.6%) were still smoking cigarettes but less frequently. This change over time is also summarized in Table 3.1.23.

When earlier smoking behavior was controlled statistically in the analysis, seniors' expectations about quitting ("Will not smoke" in the table) had very limited power to predict their subsequent smoking behavior

(Table 3.1.24). For seniors who smoked one pack per day, for example, only 27.2% of those in the "Will not smoke" classification were not smoking 5–6 years later. The same phenomenon was true for those seniors who smoked one-half pack daily (only 13.3% were not smoking) and those smoking one to five cigarettes per day in high school (just 26.2% were not smoking). In fact, only slightly more than one-half (55.8%) of those who smoked less than one cigarette per day as a senior and were in the "Will not smoke" group were not smokers at follow-up.

Thus, the expectation to avoid smoking seemed to have some impact among those who were nonsmokers and very light smokers in high school, but very few seniors in these two groups had an expectation to smoke. However, among light, moderate, and heavy daily smokers, the expectation to abstain from smoking in the future was not realized in young adulthood. One key implication of these results is that young people should be made aware of the strongly addictive nature of nicotine and its ability to cast aside good expectations about the future. Clearly, prevention is a key goal, but encouraging tobacco cessation is also critically important for adolescents and young adults at all stages.

Nicotine Addiction in Adolescence and Young Adulthood

To date, our understanding of the pathways and processes of nicotine addiction among young people is limited, especially when compared to the findings from decades of research on nicotine addiction among adults (USDHHS 2010). Compared with adults, adolescents appear to display evidence of addiction at much lower levels of cigarette consumption (USDHHS 2010), and thus, attempts to quit smoking may be more difficult for young people. More information about nicotine dependence is provided in Chapter 2. This section presents data from NSDUH that is relevant to nicotine dependence among youth.

Understanding the patterns of addiction among current smokers can inform studies of its etiology and guide interventions to help young smokers quit. As discussed more fully in Chapter 2, indicators of dependence can appear early in the uptake process (CDC 1994; DiFranza et al. 2002, 2007; O'Loughlin et al. 2003). Tables 3.1.25–3.1.27 present data for three indicators of dependence for 12- to 17-year-olds (adolescents), 18- to 25-year-olds (young adults), and older smokers (26 years of age or older), respectively, using data from multiple NSDUH surveys (2007–2010). The first indicator, the percentage of smokers who smoke more than 15 cigarettes per day, is used because the number of cigarettes smoked per day predicts quitting, with heavier smoking associated with lower prevalence of cessation (USDHHS 1988; Hymowitz et al. 1997). The second indicator, the percentage of smokers who smoke their first cigarette within 30 minutes of awakening, is used because time to first cigarette also predicts quitting, with earlier smoking associated with fewer successful quit attempts (Hymowitz et al. 1997; West 2004; Baker et al. 2007). The third indicator is SAMHSA's adaptation of the Nicotine Dependence Syndrome Scale (NDSS) (Shiffman et al. 2004), which uses multiple items to assess dependence on nicotine (for further explanation of these items, see SAMHSA 2009b).

As shown in Tables 3.1.25–3.1.27, all three indicators varied significantly with age of first use ("first puffed" in tables) and age of first daily use, with younger age of first puffing and younger age of first daily smoking associated with increased likelihood of dependence (significance based on 95% confidence intervals). Among 12- to 17-year-olds (Table 3.1.25), the duration (in years) of transitioning from first cigarette use to first daily smoking was not significantly associated with smoking more than 15 cigarettes per day, time to first cigarette or NDSS score (significance based on 95% confidence intervals). For 18- to 25-year-old smokers (Table 3.1.26) and older smokers (Table 3.1.27), there was an inverse relationship between the duration of the transition from first use to first daily smoking and all three indicators of dependence, with a rapid transition from initial trial to daily smoking associated with a higher probability of dependence in later years. The relationship between current smoking behavior and nicotine dependence was strong as well. For the 12- to 17-year-old (Table 3.1.25) and 18- to 25-year-old smokers (Table 3.1.26), the average NDSS score and the percentage who had their first cigarette within 30 minutes of waking increased significantly as the frequency and heaviness of smoking increased. Dependence also varied as a function of use of alcohol, marijuana, or other illicit substances. For example, among 12- to 17-year-olds (Table 3.1.25), the three indicators of dependence were significantly more prevalent or higher among persons who had used alcohol or engaged in binge drinking on 11 or more of the previous 30 days compared to those who engaged in these behaviors on 1–10 of the previous 30 days (significance based on 95% confidence intervals). The same was observed for past month marijuana use (≥11 days vs. 1–10 days and ≥11 days vs. never used) and past month illicit drug use other than marijuana (used in past month vs. never used). Among 18- to 25-year-olds (Table 3.1.26), the prevalence or mean of all three indicators of dependence was significantly higher among persons who smoked marijuana on 11 or more days during the previous month compared to persons who had smoked marijuana on 1–10 days during the previous month or who had never used marijuana (significance based on 95% confidence intervals). In this age group, dependence was also significantly more likely among persons who used any illicit substances other than marijuana during the previous month compared to never users. The situation with alcohol, however, was different. Two of the three indicators (first cigarette within 30 minutes and the NDSS) were especially high among persons who had previously used alcohol but had not done so during the previous month, while these two indicators were relatively low for the most frequent users of alcohol. For the other indicator (smoke >15 cigarettes per day), the prevalence was significantly higher for the most frequent alcohol users and binge drinkers when compared to the less frequent and never alcohol users and binge drinkers.

Summary

Initiation of cigarette smoking usually occurs during adolescence, although initiating cigarette smoking as a young adult is not uncommon. Among U.S. adults (30–39 years old) who have ever smoked daily, 88.2% did so as an adolescent (≤18 years old), while 10.8% tried their first cigarette in young adulthood (19–26 years old). Moreover, 65% began smoking daily in adolescence, while 31% began smoking daily as a young adult. There is heterogeneity in the developmental pathways that characterize the onset and progression of cigarette smoking during adolescence and young adulthood. For example, some young people begin smoking in early adolescence (12–13 years old), progress to daily smoking in late adolescence (17 years old), and stay daily smokers throughout young adulthood (18–26 years old), while others begin smoking later in adolescence (15–16 years old) and escalate to less than daily use in young adulthood (21 years old). Compared with adults, adolescents appear to display evidence of nicotine addiction at much lower levels of consumption, making quit attempts potentially more difficult for them (USDHHS 2010). Many young smokers have strong expectations of discontinuing use in the near future, but relatively few are able to do so.

Trends in Cigarette Smoking

This section describes trends in the prevalence and initiation of cigarette smoking among young people over time. Again, it relies primarily on data from MTF, YRBS, and NSDUH. Long-term trends in the prevalence of cigarette smoking among adolescents and young adults alike have been nonlinear during the last two decades, particularly since the publication in 1994 of the last Surgeon General's report focused on tobacco use among young people (USDHHS 1994; Nelson et al. 2008; CDC 2010a). In the early 1990s, the prevalence of cigarette smoking began increasing until it hit a peak in the late 1990s, at the time of the Master Settlement Agreement (1998), when it began to decline for both adolescents (Nelson et al. 2008; CDC 2010a) and young adults (Nelson et al. 2008). Since 2003, however, the decline in the prevalence of cigarette smoking among young people overall has slowed considerably, and may have stopped altogether for some subgroups. Between 2003 and 2009, for example, the prevalence of current cigarette use declined more slowly than it did between 1997 and 2003 among female and Black high school students, while it remained stable (i.e., did not decline at all) among male, White, and Hispanic high school students, overall (CDC 2010e). Data from NYTS show that there has been no change between 2000 and 2009 in the percentage of middle and high school students who are susceptible to initiate smoking (CDC 2010e). Those who are susceptible to begin smoking are defined as never smokers who report being willing to try smoking cigarettes. Trends in susceptibility are not discussed in detail in this section; however, cross-sectional data are presented earlier in the chapter. Further details on these more recent trends in cigarette smoking over time are provided below. To achieve the national health objectives outlined for 2020, further reductions in cigarette smoking are necessary and will require sustained support. The target referenced in *Healthy People 2020* for current smoking among adolescents (9th–12th grades) is 16% (USDHHS 2000); in 2009, YRBS indicated that 19.5% of these students were current smokers (Table 3.1.2).

Ever Smoking a Cigarette

Trends over time in the prevalence of ever smoking a cigarette are provided in Figures 3.1.5–3.1.7 using data from MTF (Figures 3.1.5 and 3.1.6A–C) and YRBS (Figures 3.1.6D and 3.1.7). These figures present trends by grade level, gender, and race/ethnicity.

Figure 3.1.5A presents data from MTF that are stratified by grade level (8th, 10th, and 12th grades) and gender. Among 12th-grade students, the prevalence of ever smoking decreased from 1977 to 1992 by an average of about 1% per year (0.9% boys; 1.0%, girls). Then, from 1992 to 1997, it increased by an average of 0.7 % per year (0.5%, boys; 0.8%, girls). From 1997 to 2010, it decreased again, but at a much higher average rate of about 2% per year (1.6%, boys; 2.0%, girls). In 1976, approximately three-quarters (75.6%, boys; 74.8%, girls) of 12th-grade students had ever smoked a cigarette, but by 1992, this figure had fallen to about five-eighths (63.5%, boys; 60.2%, girls). After increasing to 65.9% for boys and 64.4% for girls in 1997, the prevalence of ever smoking fell to less than one-half (44.8%, boys; 38.9%, girls) of 12th-grade students in 2010. Among 10th-grade students (Figure 3.1.5C), from 1991 to 1996, ever smoking increased by an average of 1.2% (1.2%, boys; 1.3%, girls) per year. It then declined by an average of 2.5% per year (2.4%, boys; 2.5%, girls) from 1996 to 2008, and increased (overall) by 1.3% between 2008 and 2010 (1.9%, boys; 0.7%, girls). In 1991, more than one-half (55.5%, boys; 54.8%, girls) of all 10th-grade students were ever cigarette smokers. In 1996, this figure peaked (60.3%, boys; 60.3%, girls), then fell to about one-third (32.3%, boys; 31.0%, girls) in 2008, after which it rose slightly for boys to 34.2% in 2010 while reaching 31.8% for girls in that year. Among 8th-grade students (Figure 3.1.5B), from 1991 to 1996, ever smoking increased more steeply for girls (1.4% per year) than for boys (0.7% per year). The decline from 1996 to 2008, however, was the same for both genders, at 2.4% per year on average. Between 2008 and 2010, the decline in ever smoking among 8th-grade students stalled at about 21% for males and about 20% for females. In 1991, in 8th grade, 46.1% of boys and 41.7% of girls were ever smokers. After peaking in 1996 (49.5%, boys; 48.5%, girls), this figure also declined through 2008, when essentially one in five (20.8%, boys; 19.9%, girls) 8th-grade students had ever smoked. This decline in ever smoking stalled between 2008 and 2010, however, and remained at about 20% for both boys and girls.

Figure 3.1.6 presents data from MTF but this time stratified by grade level and race/ethnicity. Among 12th-grade students (Figure 3.1.6C), the decline in the prevalence of ever smoking from 1976 to 1990 was highest among Black students (2.0% per year), while the prevalence among White and Hispanic students decreased more slowly during this period (0.6% per year). From 1991 to 1997, the prevalence of ever smoking remained essentially flat for Black and Hispanic students but increased among White students (0.6% per year). From 1998 to 2010, prevalence decreased at similar rates for all three of the groups (per year: 1.5%, Blacks; 1.6%, Hispanics; 2.1%, Whites). In 1976, Black students had the highest prevalence of ever smoking among 12th-grade students (76.4% vs. 75.2% for White students and 70.1% for Hispanic students), but in 2010, they had the lowest prevalence (30.6% vs. 42.6% for Hispanic students and 44.5% for White students). Among 10th-grade students (Figure 3.1.6B), the annual increase from 1991 to 1996 in ever smoking was largest among Hispanic students (1.6 percentage points), followed by White (1.2 percentage points) and Black students (0.4 percentage points). Among Black 10th-grader students, the prevalence decreased by an average of 1.7% per year between 1997 and 2009, then increased by 1.2% in 2010. White and Hispanic students decreased at a faster annual rate during 1996 to 2007 (2.6% and 2.5%, respectively). Between 2008 and 2010, White students increased their rate and Hispanic students stalled. In 1991, among 10th-grade students, Black students had the lowest prevalence of ever cigarette smoking (42.7% vs. 57.8% for Whites and 55.1% for Hispanics); in 2010, Black students continued to have the lowest prevalence (25.7% vs. 33.4% for Whites and 36.9% for Hispanics). For 8th-grade students (Figure 3.1.6A), the average increase in ever smoking from 1991 to 1997 was larger for Blacks (1.4% per year) than for Whites (0.7% per year), with the prevalence among Hispanic students remaining essentially flat during this period. From 1997 to 2010, annual declines were similar among White (2.3%) and Hispanic students (2.2%), with Black students at 1.8% per year. In 1991, among 8th-grade students, Blacks had the lowest prevalence of ever smoking (34.7% vs. 44.5% for White students and 50.8% for Hispanic students), but in 2010, White students had the lowest prevalence of ever smoking (19.2% vs. 19.5% for Black students and 21.6% for Hispanic students). Between 2008 and 2010, the rate of decline in ever cigarette smoking appears to have slowed in certain racial/ethnic subgroups and may have begun to increase again in others, such as White and Hispanic 10th-grade students.

YRBS data for high school students (9th–12th grade) shows that for ever smoked cigarettes, the prevalence did not change from 1991 (70.1%) to 1999 (70.4%), declined to 58.4% in 2003, and then declined more gradually, to 46.3% in 2009. Figure 3.1.7 presents YRBS data stratified by gender. In 1991, 70.6% of boys and 69.5% of girls had ever smoked cigarettes. The prevalence did not change through 1999 but then declined so that by 2009, less than one-half of high school students (46.3% of boys; 46.1% of girls) were ever smokers. Figure 3.1.6D also presents data from the YRBS, this time stratified by race/ethnicity. In 1991, Hispanic students had the highest prevalence of ever smoking cigarettes (75.3% vs. 67.2% for Black and 70.4% for White students). The prevalence of students who had ever smoked cigarettes did not change through 1999 among White and Black students, but then declined so that in 2009, 46.1% of White students and 43.5% of Black students were ever smokers. The prevalence of ever smoking cigarettes among Hispanic students did not change from 1991 to 1995, and then declined to 51.0% in 2009. In 2009, the prevalence of ever smoking cigarettes was still higher among Hispanic students than Black students, but there were no longer any statistically significant differences between Hispanic students and White students.

Current Cigarette Smoking

Trends in current cigarette smoking over time are presented separately here for adolescents and young adults. As with ever cigarette smoking, trends in current smoking have been nonlinear over time.

Adolescents

Trends in the prevalence of current cigarette smoking over the last three decades are provided in Figures 3.1.7–3.1.10, again using data from MTF (Figures 3.1.8 and 3.1.9) and YRBS (Figures 3.1.7, 3.1.9, and 3.1.10). These four figures present trends by several important demographic subgroups, including grade level, gender, race/ethnicity, and/or geographic region.

Figure 3.1.8 presents data from MTF that are stratified by grade level (8th, 10th, and 12th grades) and gender. In 1976, among 12th-grade students (Figure 3.1.8D), the prevalence of current cigarette smoking was somewhat higher for girls (39.1%) than for boys (37.7%). Among both male and female 12th-grade students, current smoking declined sharply through the remainder of the 1970s. In 1980, this decline stopped for boys and slowed considerably for girls. Across the 1980s, current cigarette smoking continued its decline among girls, but the prevalence began to rise slowly among boys, such that by 1990, male and female 12th-grade students were smoking at the same prevalence (29.1%). Then, in the early 1990s, current cigarette smoking began to escalate rapidly among both male and female 12th-grade students. This upturn peaked in 1997, when boys (37.3%) were smoking slightly more than girls (35.2%). Since 1997, current cigarette smoking has declined in both groups. In 2010, male 12th-grade students (21.9%) were more likely to smoke than were female 12th-grade students (15.7%). Trend data for current cigarette smoking among 8th and 10th-grade students are available only from 1991 onward; trends in these grade levels paralleled those of the 12th-grade students until 2008. In brief, the prevalence of current cigarette smoking in these groups also rose rapidly in the early- to mid-1990s, at which time it began to fall. Current smoking increased among 10th-grade male students (Figure 3.1.8C) from 2008 to 2010 and among 8th-grade students overall between 2009 and 2010. In 2010, 10th-grade male students (15.0%) were smoking at a higher prevalence than female students (12.1%), and male 8th-grade students (7.4%) (Figure 3.1.8B) were smoking at a slightly higher prevalence than were female 8th-grade students (6.8%). Like many of the trends in ever smoking reported above, the prevalence of current cigarette smoking from 2007 to 2010 in certain subgroups appears to have leveled off completely (e.g., female 10th-grade students and male 12th-grade students).

Figure 3.1.9 presents data from MTF, this time stratified by grade level and race/ethnicity. Among 12th-grade students (Figure 3.1.9C), the prevalence of current smoking declined sharply among all racial/ethnic groups from 1976 to 1980. For Black students, this decline continued for more than a decade, until 1992 (8.7%). For White students, the prevalence remained almost level throughout the 1980s and into the early 1990s. The prevalence of current cigarette smoking among Hispanic 12th-grade students, in contrast, remained steady through the mid-1980s, then declined until 1989. Although the prevalence of current smoking was relatively similar across 12th-grade students groups in 1976 (33.1.7%, Hispanics; 38.3%, Whites; 39.7%, Blacks), by the early 1990s, the three groups differed considerably. In 1990, Black students had the lowest prevalence of current smoking (12.0%), well below that of Hispanic students (23.2%) or White students (32.5%). The differences remained through much of the 1990s, and by 1999, the highest post-1990 values had been reached for all three ethnic groups. From 1999 to 2010, the prevalence of current smoking dropped particularly precipitously among White and Hispanic 12th-grade students—from 39.1% to 22.2% for Whites and from 29.6% to 14.4% for Hispanics. In contrast, among Black 12th-grade students, the prevalence of current smoking leveled out between 2004 and 2010. Among 8th (Figure 3.1.9A) and 10th-grade students (Figure 3.1.9B), the prevalence of current smoking declined from the mid- to late-1990s until about 2007, particularly among White and Hispanic students. Between 2007 and 2010, the decline slowed. In 2010, among 10th-grade students, 7.0% of Blacks, 12.3% of Hispanics, and 14.8% of Whites were current smokers. For Black and Hispanic students, these represented increases since 2007, when 5.8% of Black students and 10.1% of Hispanic students were current smokers. Among 8th-grade students Hispanics and Whites were much more closely aligned over time than they were for the other grade levels. In 2010, among 8th-grade students, 4.0% of Blacks, 7.0% of Hispanics, and 7.9% of Whites were current smokers. For White and Hispanic students, these represented slight increases from 2008.

Further information regarding trends in the prevalence of current cigarette smoking among 9th–12th-grade students by state is provided in Figure 3.1.10 using data from the state YRBS's (1991–2009). Figures 3.1.7 and 3.1.9D also present trend data from YRBS that are stratified by gender (Figure 3.1.7) and race/ethnicity (Figure 3.1.9D). Both figures underscore the trends observed in the MTF data, specifically the increase in current smoking from 1991 to 1997, followed by a substantial decline across strata of gender and race/ethnicity. In 1991, just over one-quarter (27.6% of boys, 27.3% of girls) of these high school students were current smokers (Figure 3.1.7).

In 1997, this figure had increased to more than one-third (37.7%, boys; 34.7%, girls). Among girls, current smoking decreased to 21.9% in 2003 and then continued to decline, but more slowly, to 19.1% in 2009. Among boys, current smoking decreased to 21.8% in 2003 and then remained stable through 2009 when 19.8% of boys were current smokers (CDC 2010a). In 1991, 12.6% of Black, 25.3% of Hispanic, and 30.9% of White students were current smokers (Figure 3.9D). Among Black students, current smoking increased from 1991 to 22.7% in 1997, declined to 15.1% in 2003, and then continued to decline, but more gradually, to 9.5% in 2009. Among Hispanic students, current smoking increased from 25.3% in 1991 to 34.0% in 1995, declined to 18.4% in 2003, and then remained stable through 2009 so that in 2009, 18.0% of Hispanic students were current smokers. Among White students, current smoking increased from 1991 to 39.7% in 1997, declined to 24.9% in 2003, and then remained stable so that in 2009, 22.5% of White students were current smokers (CDC 2010a).

Table 3.1.28 combines data from MTF across multiple years to provide reliable estimates of the prevalence of current smoking over time, from 1976 to 2007, for the three racial/ethnic groups described above among boys and girls separately (high school seniors only). These data mimic trends (for older age groups shown) in Figures 3.1.11 and 3.1.12. Among high school senior boys, the prevalence of current cigarette smoking among Black students was highest in 1976–1979 (33.1%) and lowest in 1990–1994 (11.6%). For White senior boys, current smoking peaked at 39.7% in 1995–1999 and reached its nadir in 1980–1984 (27.5%). Current smoking among Hispanic boys was highest in 1976–1979 (30.3%) and lowest in 2000–2007 (21.2%). Among high school senior girls, the prevalence of current smoking among Blacks was highest in 1976–1979 (33.6%) and lowest in 1990–1994 (8.6%) and 2000–2004 (8.8%). For White girls, current smoking peaked in 1995–1999 (39.5%), then fell to its lowest level, 28.5%, in 2000–2007. Current smoking among Hispanic girls was highest in 1976–1979 (31.4%) and lowest in 2000–2007 (15.9%).

As shown in Tables 3.1.2 and 3.1.3, among the three groups described above, the most recent estimates showed that the prevalence of current cigarette smoking among adolescents is generally lowest among Blacks, intermediate among Hispanics, and highest among Whites. Among adults in 2006 and 2007, the prevalence of cigarette smoking was statistically similar among Whites and Blacks and lower among Hispanics (CDC 2008a). Historically, the age of initiation has been slightly older in Black youth than among White youth (CDC 1991; Geronimus et al. 1993; USDHHS 1998; Moon-Howard 2003; Trinidad et al. 2004), raising the issue of whether the gains made in reducing the prevalence of smoking among Black youth in the 1970s and 1980s could have been lost as they matured into young adulthood (NCI 2001). The 1998 Surgeon General's report on tobacco use among U.S. racial/ethnic minority groups presented data from NHIS for Black and White adults aged 20–24 years, 25–29 years, and 30–34 years that covered 1978–1980 to 1994–1995 (USDHHS 1998); the analyses there indicated that the prevalence of current smoking among those in the age ranges of 20–24 years, 25–29 years, and 30–34 years declined more for Blacks, regardless of gender, than for Whites, from 1978–1980 to 1994–1995. Here, Figures 3.1.11A–E and 3.1.12A–C and Table 3.1.29 update the previous analyses to 2009 and expand them to include Hispanics and persons 35–39 years of age and 40–44 years of age.

As revealed in Figures 3.1.11A–E, in 1978–1980, among persons in all five age groups (i.e., from 20–24 years up through 40–44 years), the prevalence of smoking was at least as high among Blacks as among Whites. Among 20- to 24-year-olds, prevalence among Blacks dropped below that of Whites by 1983–1985. In addition, prevalence among Blacks dropped below that of Whites by 1990–1992 for 25- to 29-year-olds, by 1997–1998 among 30- to 34-year-olds, and by 1999–2001 among 35- to 39-year-olds. Among 40- to 44-year-olds, prevalence was higher among Blacks than among Whites during 1990–1995, but it dropped to be marginally lower than that of Whites in 2005–2009. The trend lines for Blacks in all five age groups are presented in Figure 3.1.12B, which suggests that the drops observed among Black high school seniors during the 1970s and 1980s (Figure 3.1.9C) persisted as these seniors matured into young adulthood and even through the ages of 35–39 years.

Jemal and colleagues (2009) charted gender-specific incidence and mortality rates for lung cancer during 1992–2006 among 20- to 39-year-old Blacks and Whites. Although incidence and mortality decreased significantly for male and female Blacks and Whites, prevalence decreased more rapidly among Blacks of both genders. For example, from 1992–1994 to 2004–2006, the Black/White mortality rate ratio (with 95% CI) decreased from 2.16 (1.90–2.44) to 1.28 (1.05–1.55) among men and from 1.47 (1.25–1.71) to 0.97 (0.78–1.19) among women. The authors concluded that the steeper declines in incidence of lung cancer and related mortality rates among young Blacks were due primarily to the steeper decline in smoking prevalence among Black adolescents and young adults.

Similar patterning of trends among young adults on the basis of trends for 12th-grade students was not observed for Hispanics (Figure 3.1.12A) or for Whites (Figure 3.1.12C). For example, the sharp decline in prevalence among Hispanic 12th-grade students observed after 2000 (Figure 3.1.9C) was not reflected in NHIS data for

20- to 24-year-old Hispanics in 2002–2004 or 2005–2006 (Figures 3.1.11A and 3.1.12A). In addition, the sharp increase observed among White 12th-grade students during 1992–1998 (Figure 3.1.9C) was not observed among 20- to 24-year-old Whites (Figure 3.1.11A). The slight increase in prevalence among 20- to 24-year-old Whites that began in 1987–1988 and ended in 1997–1998 might have been influenced during 1994–1998 by trends in cigarette smoking among White 12th-grade students (NCI 2008). However, the increase in the prevalence among White 12th-grade students during this time period (1997–1998) did not then transfer to higher prevalence estimates among 20- to 24-year-olds subsequent to 1998, as might be expected.

Because trends in current cigarette smoking over time by socioeconomic status are difficult to distinguish for adolescents, they are not shown here. Recent publications from the MTF group (Bachman et al. 2010, 2011) suggest that differences in current cigarette smoking (and the use of smokeless tobacco and cigars, as well) by socioeconomic status are modified by race/ethnicity. The effect of lower socioeconomic status (as defined by parental education levels) on tobacco use among adolescents is most pronounced among White and younger (8th and 10th grades) adolescents (Bachman et al. 2010, 2011). However, the large proportions of Blacks and Hispanics in the lowest socioeconomic group may mask effects for these subpopulations that can be readily discerned among Whites.

Young Adults

The trends over time in current cigarette smoking among adolescents described above are consistent with the trends among young adults reported recently by Nelson and colleagues (2008). In that report, Nelson and coworkers described long-term trends in current cigarette smoking among adolescents and young adults by using data from MTF and NHIS, respectively. The analysis of the NHIS data considered young adults 18–24 years of age and used responses from NHIS (an annual survey) for 1974 to 2005. Overall, the long-term trends in current smoking for young adults were similar to the trends described above for adolescents. Notably, changes in the prevalence of current smoking among young adults lagged a few years behind the changes for adolescents, providing evidence for a cohort effect (Nelson et al. 2008). This might also reflect changes in patterns of smoking behavior among young adults, as the percentage of ever smokers who become regular smokers between the ages of 19 and 21 has increased since the last Surgeon General's report in 1994 (Lantz 2003).

During much of the period of interest, the gender gap in cigarette smoking was wider for young adults than for adolescents (Nelson et al. 2008). In 1974, the prevalence of current cigarette smoking was higher for young adult men than for young adult women. Throughout the rest of the 1970s, into the mid-1980s, the prevalence rate remained steady among young adult women but declined for young adult men. As a result, through much of the 1980s, the prevalence of current cigarette smoking was about the same for young adult women and their male counterparts. Toward the end of the 1980s, however, the prevalence of current smoking began to decline at a faster speed for young adult women than for young adult men. In the 1990s, most of the increase in the prevalence of current smoking among young adults occurred in men; because of this increase, the prevalence of current cigarette smoking was about 5% higher among young adult men than in their female counterparts from the mid-1990s to 2005 (Nelson et al. 2008).

The trends in current cigarette smoking among young adults during the period researched by Nelson and colleagues (2008) differed by race/ethnicity as well. Figures 3.1.13 and 3.1.14 update the study by Nelson and colleagues (2008). Using NSDUH data, the prevalence of current cigarette smoking was plotted from 2002 to 2010 by gender (Figure 3.1.13) and race/ethnicity (Figure 3.1.14). Declines in current cigarette smoking began to stall among young adult males in 2006 and young adult females in 2007, but these declines continued between 2009 and 2010. The estimated prevalence of current cigarette smoking among young adult males in 2010 was significantly lower than the estimate in 2009 ($p < 0.05$). Similarly, for young adult females, the prevalence of current cigarette smoking in 2010 was significantly lower than the prevalence estimate in 2009 ($p < 0.05$). These phenomena are also reflected in Figure 3.1.14. Decreases among Whites, Blacks, and Hispanics between 2009 and 2010 were not significant. Although no statistical tests were applied across the entire 2002–2010 period, prevalence may have decreased among Blacks and may be increasing, by comparison, among Hispanics, after what may have been a significant drop for that group from 2003 to 2006. Figure 3.1.15 also presents data from NSDUH that show differences in current cigarette smoking from 2005 to 2010 by socioeconomic status. Across all time points, smoking was least prevalent in the highest socioeconomic group (defined as 200% or more of the poverty level).

Table 3.1.29 provides estimates of 20- to 44-year-olds who identified themselves as current smoker from 1978–2009. For Whites, the prevalence of current smoking among young adults was consistent from the late 1970s through the early 1980s; from there, it declined slightly over time through the early 1990s, when it began to rise slowly through the late 1990s before decreasing slightly through 2005. For Blacks, current cigarette smoking declined precipitously from the early 1980s through the mid-1990s, then increased through the late 1990s, after which it began to decline again to 2005. For Hispanics, the prevalence of current cigarette smoking declined rapidly from the late 1970s through the late 1980s; from there, it remained steady through the 1990s, then began to decline again to 2005. In 2005, the prevalence of current cigarette smoking was highest for Whites and very similar for Blacks and Hispanics (Nelson et al. 2008).

The differences by educational level in current cigarette smoking over time (Nelson et al. 2008) among young adults are striking. Compared with those having at least a high school education, current cigarette smoking among those with less than a high school education has declined more rapidly over time, and this decline has been consistent since the early 1980s. In addition, the increases in the prevalence of current cigarette smoking for young adults in the late 1990s were observed only among those subgroups with at least a high school diploma. In 2005, current cigarette smoking was least prevalent among young adults with more than a high school diploma, and the prevalence was reasonably similar between young adults with just a high school diploma and those who had not graduated from high school. By contrast, in 1974 the prevalence of current cigarette smoking was approximately 15% higher among those with less than a high school diploma than among those who had graduated from high school (Nelson et al. 2008).

Intensity of Cigarette Smoking

Trends in the intensity of smoking among high school seniors, as derived from MTF data, indicate that all levels of smoking have declined since 1976 (Figure 3.1.16). The drop in heavy smoking (one-half pack or more of cigarettes per day in the last 30 days) has been steepest. In 1976, 19.2% of seniors were heavy smokers, but in 2010, only 4.7% were. The decreases in light smoking (<1 cigarette per day in the last 30 days) and intermittent smoking (1–5 cigarettes per day in the last 30 days) have been more subtle. In 1976, 10.0% of seniors were light smokers, and in 2010, 8.5% were. In 1976, 9.6% of seniors were intermittent smokers; in 2010, 6.1% were. The proportion of seniors who were ever smokers but had not smoked in the past 30 days declined from 36.5% in 1976 to 23.0% in 2010.

Preferences for Particular Cigarette Brands

Trends in preferences for cigarette brands over time, from 2002 to 2010, are illustrated in Figure 3.1.17 for current smokers 12–17 years of age and in Figure 3.1.18 for current smokers 18–25 years of age; the data are stratified by gender and based on NSDUH. These data are based on responses to a question about the brand that interviewees smoked most often. Over this period, Marlboro, Newport, and Camel, respectively, were the three brands of cigarettes preferred by adolescents and young adults alike. Marlboro was preferred by about 50% of adolescent smokers, while approximately 25% preferred Newport and 10% Camel. Among young adults, Marlboro was also preferred by about 50% of smokers, while about 20% preferred Newport and about 15% preferred Camel. From 2008 to 2010, preference for Newports increased among adolescent females, while preference for Camels decreased slightly and for Marlboros by a somewhat larger amount. Among adolescent males during the same time period, preference for Marlboros increased slightly, while preference for Camels declined.

There is evidence to suggest that the use of mentholated brands of cigarettes has increased in recent years. For example, according to a recent report from SAMHSA (2009d), the prevalence of smoking menthol cigarettes among current smokers aged 12 and older increased from 31.0% in 2004 to 33.9% in 2008. The most pronounced increases were among adolescents aged 12–17 years and young adults aged 18–25 years. In 2008, 47.7% of current adolescent smokers smoked menthol cigarettes, as did 40.8% of young adult smokers (SAMHSA 2009d). Among adolescent smokers, this was an 11% increase over the prevalence in 2004, a statistically significant increase. This increase was driven exclusively by a jump in the use of mentholated cigarettes among White adolescents and young adults. Importantly, this study also showed that past-month smoking of mentholated cigarettes was more prevalent among recent initiates than among longer-term smokers. This is in contrast to findings from a prior analysis of 2006 NYTS data (Hersey et al. 2010).

Age or Grade When Smoking Begins

Tracking the initiation of cigarette smoking over time can provide helpful information to policymakers and researchers alike, as these trends reveal emerging patterns of tobacco use. In turn, these patterns can be used to drive the development of appropriate policies and programs focused on reducing tobacco use among youth. Historical data suggest that, over the last century (the 1900s), young people living in the United States started to smoke at progressively younger ages. By 1955–1966, women, especially, were smoking at younger ages (USDHHS 1994). This report focuses on trends in the initiation of smoking during the twenty-first century.

Tables 3.1.30 and 3.1.31 provide estimates of the initiation of cigarette smoking using data from NSDUH (2006–2010). Here, initiates are defined as those who started smoking cigarettes in the 12 months before the survey. Estimates for each year were produced separately using data obtained from the survey conducted that year. This approach minimizes recall bias and provides particularly timely information on the incidence of smoking among youth. Table 3.1.30 focuses on adolescents only; overall, the prevalence of initiation in this group decreased over time, between 2006 and 2010 ($p < 0.05$). In 2006, 6.9% of girls began smoking cigarettes, compared with 6.3% of boys. In 2010, the prevalence of initiation was 5.7% for boys and 6.0% for girls. The decrease among girls was statistically significant ($p < 0.05$) as was the decrease among Whites overall. Table 3.1.31 focuses on young adults only; overall, the prevalence of initiation in this group was steady over time, with no significant differences from 2006 to 2010 ($p > 0.05$). In 2006, 8.7% of young adults began to smoke cigarettes, and in 2010, this figure was 7.9%.

Although the percentage of Black initiates among adolescents and young adults was smaller than that for Whites and Hispanics, other data show that smoking remains a problem among Black adults (Table 3.1.29). Although Table 3.1.30 reveals a lower rate of initiation among Black youth than among their White counterparts, Black adults (especially men) have a prevalence of smoking that is similar to that for White adults, experience a higher burden of tobacco-related disease (e.g., lung cancer), and quit smoking less successfully (USDHHS 1998).

Attempts to Quit Smoking

According to multiple surveys of high school seniors conducted by MTF over time, a substantial percentage of seniors who smoked wanted to stop immediately ("now" in the survey) (Table 3.1.32). In 1990–1994, 42.7% and 45.5% of high school seniors who were current and daily smokers, respectively, wanted to stop smoking cigarettes immediately. For 2000–2004, those figures were 44.8% and 47.4%, respectively, but for 2005–2009, they decreased significantly to 34.4% and 37.7% (significance determined by 95% confidence intervals). In 1990–1994, just under one-third (31.7%) of students who were current smokers had tried at least once to stop smoking; for 2005–2009, this estimate was 26.5%. In 1990–1994, 44.4% of students who were daily smokers had tried at least once to stop smoking, but failed; in 2005–2009, this figure was down to 38.9%. Trends in the percentage of high school seniors who at some time had smoked regularly but had not smoked during the preceding 30 days (i.e., were former smokers) have been erratic over time (Figure 3.1.19), but generally speaking, they have followed trends in the prevalence of current smoking over time. In the 1970s, as the percentage of current smokers declined, the percentage of former smokers went up, in turn. Over the aggregate period of 1980 to 1990, both figures did not change much. In the early 1990s, the percentage of former smokers decreased as the percentage of current smokers increased. By the mid- to late 1990s, however, the percentage of former smokers again began to increase as current smoking, in turn, decreased. The differential in these trends by gender (male vs. female) seems to have been negligible (Figure 3.1.19). In 2010, more females than males were classified as former smokers.

Summary

Declines in cigarette smoking among young people since the Master Settlement Agreement have slowed and may have begun to stall. This is true for adolescents and young adults alike. Since the last Surgeon General's report on tobacco use among young people (USDHHS 1994) was published, the prevalence of cigarette smoking among adolescents has remained highest among Whites, followed by Hispanics and then Blacks (some racial subgroups such as American Indian/Alaskan Native are not large enough to provide reliable estimates and trend data for comparison). Overall, the prevalence of smoking has been reasonably similar for boys and girls during this time period. Differences over time in the prevalence of cigarette smoking by gender within racial/ethnic subgroups were not considered in this chapter. The rates for initiation of cigarette smoking have remained essentially flat among adolescents and young adults in recent years (2006–2010). Interest in quitting smoking among adolescents has fallen. Marlboro, Camel, and Newport have consistently been the most preferred brands of cigarettes for adolescents and young adults in recent years (2002–2010). The order of preference of these three brands has remained consistent over this time period as well.

Trends in Knowledge and Attitudes About Smoking

Trends in the Perceived Health Risks of Cigarette Smoking

Data from MTF allow trends in beliefs about the health risks associated with cigarette smoking to be compared with trends in actual smoking behavior. As illustrated in Figure 3.1.20, during the last three and one-half decades, these trends mirrored each other among high school seniors. From 1976 to 2010, the overall decline in the prevalence of ever smoking (defined here as having smoked a cigarette at least once or twice during one's lifetime) was accompanied by an increase in the percentage of high school seniors who believed that smoking cigarettes was a serious health risk. This trend was observed for both male and female students and for White, Black, and Hispanic students (MTF, unpublished data). The proportion of seniors who believed that cigarette smoking entails a great risk to health increased from 56.4% in 1976 to 75.0% in 2010; during the same period, the percentage of high school seniors who had ever smoked a cigarette fell from 75.4% to 42.2%. Regardless, as the figures for 2010 show, almost one-fourth of seniors in that year still did not believe that cigarette smoking presented a great risk to health.

Trends in Perceptions of Cigarette Smoking

According to MTF surveys, the percentage of high school students who considered smoking a "dirty habit" increased slightly, but steadily, over time, from 1991 to 2010. As shown in Figure 3.1.21, differences in perceptions across grade levels (8th, 10th, and 12th) were negligible over time. In 2010, 72.4% of 8th-grade students, 71.7% of 10th-grade students, and 73.1% of 12th-grade students believed that cigarette smoking is a "dirty habit," up from 71.4%, 70.7%, and 71.6%, respectively, in 1991.

Throughout the 1980s, the proportion of high school seniors who believed that their close friends would disapprove of their smoking heavily remained quite steady (Figure 3.1.22). This figure declined in the first half of the 1990s, however, as smoking climbed. Then, from 1997 it increased, peaking in 2008, after which it declined slightly to 2010. In 1980, 74.4% of seniors believed their friends would not approve of their smoking one pack or more of cigarettes; in 2008, this figure was 82.5% (and in 2010, it was 81.4%).

Trends in Perceptions of Cigarette Smokers

Data from MTF indicate that most high school seniors prefer to date nonsmokers. Over time, the trends in this preference have inversely paralleled those for cigarette smoking (Figure 3.1.23). In 1990, the proportion of high school seniors who preferred to date nonsmokers was somewhat higher than it was in 1980, but this figure dropped in the early 1990s as smoking became more prevalent, and it increased in the late 1990s as smoking began its decline. After about 1988, the differences between male and female students were quite modest (Figure 3.1.23). In 1981, 61.9% of female students and 71.6% of male students preferred to date nonsmokers; this discrepancy narrowed over time (fairly rapidly in the 1980s) while the overall prevalence of this preference increased, such that by 2007, 76.0% of female students and 77.5% of male students preferred to date nonsmokers. In 2010, these figures had dropped slightly to 73.7% of female students and 73.5% of male students. These trends were also consistent across racial/ethnic categories (Figure 3.1.24), although the data from these annual surveys for Black and Hispanic students indicated much more variability for these groups than for White students. In 1981, 67.4% of White students, 61.4% of Black students, and 61.1% of Hispanic students preferred to date nonsmokers; in 2007, these proportions had increased to 76.9%, 73.5%, and 77.9%, respectively. In 2010, these figures decreased slightly again to 74.0% of White students, 69.7% of Black students, and 73.2% of Hispanic students. Recalling the results above for perceived health risks of cigarette smoking, in 2010, about one-fourth of seniors were willing to date smokers.

In 2010, about two-thirds of adolescents were concerned about other people smoking around them, while about one-third were not (Figure 3.1.25). Trends in the proportion of high school students who did not mind being around others who smoked also paralleled those of cigarette smoking over time. For example, as smoking increased in the 1990s, young people's tolerance of others smoking around them did, too. When smoking began its decline around 1997, so, also, did students' willingness to be around others who smoked (Figure 3.1.25). These trends were similar across grade levels over time, with students in higher grades (10th or 12th) appearing to be more tolerant of other smokers than were students in 8th-grade students. According to the 2010 MTF, 27.1% of 8th-grade students, 30.3% of 10th-grade students, and 32.4% of 12th-grade students did not mind being around other people who smoked.

Summary

The percentages of high school seniors who believe that (a) cigarette smoking is a serious health risk and (b) their close friends would disapprove of their heavy smoking of cigarettes have consistently increased since the publication of the last Surgeon General's report on tobacco use among young people, in 1994. The percentages of high school seniors who (a) believe that smoking is a "dirty habit" and (b) prefer to date nonsmokers have also increased since 1994, although not to the same degree as the other two attitudes.

Cigarette Smoking, Smokeless Tobacco Use, and the Use of Other Drugs

In this part of the chapter, detailed information on high school seniors' usage patterns for cigarettes, smokeless tobacco, and other drugs (i.e. alcohol, marijuana, cocaine, and inhalants) is provided. As noted in the 1994 Surgeon General's report on preventing tobacco use among young people, the use of these substances often covaries among youth (USDHHS 1994). In addition, cigarette smoking is often considered a "gateway drug" and can precede smokeless tobacco use and other types of drug use (USDHHS 1994). The prevalence of past-month use of each substance will be considered in this section, and the ages at first use of each substance (based on self-reports) will be compared. Data from MTF are presented in Tables 3.1.33–3.1.37.

Prevalence of Cigarette Smoking, Smokeless Tobacco Use, and the Use of Other Drugs

Among high school senior males in 2002–2007, smoking was quite common among smokeless tobacco users and users of other licit and illicit drugs (Table 3.1.33). In all, 41.6% of male students who were alcohol users were also cigarette smokers, while 56.6%, 59.9%, and 64.0% of those who smoked marijuana, used smokeless tobacco, and used inhalants, respectively, were cigarette smokers as well. Three-quarters of those who used cocaine (75.7%) also smoked cigarettes. The prevalence of cigarette smoking was 2.6 (for inhalants) to 5.2 (for alcohol) times as high among users of these drugs as among nonusers.

Although more than one-half of high school senior male drinkers (58.4%) did not smoke, the great majority (83.9%) of smokers in this population were drinkers (Table 3.1.33). Just over one-half (53.0%) of cigarette smokers were marijuana smokers, 8.2% were cocaine users, 4.7% used inhalants, and 29.3% used smokeless tobacco (see also "Co-occurrence of Tobacco Use Behaviors" later in this chapter). The prevalence of other drug use was from 2.2 (for alcohol use) to 9.1 (for cocaine use) times as high among cigarette smokers as among nonsmokers.

Patterns were very similar among high school senior females (Table 3.1.34). Two of every five (39.7%) senior girls who drank alcohol smoked cigarettes, and 60.6%, 78.0%, and 62.3% of those who smoked marijuana, used cocaine, and used inhalants, respectively, were cigarette smokers as well (Table 3.1.34). The prevalence of cigarette smoking was 2.9 (for inhalants) to 4.8 (for alcohol) times as high among users of these drugs as among nonusers. Although three-fifths of female students who drank (60.3%) did not smoke cigarettes, four out of five female students who smoked cigarettes (78.8%) drank alcohol. An estimated 45.4% of cigarette smokers were marijuana users, 6.2% were cocaine users, and 3.3% used inhalants (see also "Co-occurrence of Tobacco Use Behaviors" later in this chapter). Among female high school seniors, the prevalence of other drug use was from 2.3 (for alcohol use) to 12.4 (for cocaine use) times as high among cigarette smokers as among nonsmokers (Table 3.1.34).

Grade When Cigarette Smoking, Smokeless Tobacco Use, and Other Drug Use Begins

Data from several recent MTF surveys were merged to provide reliable estimates of the grade at which seniors tried cigarettes, smokeless tobacco, alcohol, marijuana, and cocaine for the first time (Figure 3.1.26). Among those who had ever smoked a cigarette, 22.1% had tried one by the sixth grade and 52.4% by the eighth grade. Among those who had ever used smokeless tobacco, 10.7% had done so by the sixth grade and 28.5% by the eighth grade. Compared with cigarettes, proportionately fewer users of alcohol and marijuana initiated use before the ninth grade. Similarly, proportionately fewer cocaine users than users of smokeless tobacco had initiated use this early.

Per data from the MTF, by the 12th grade, 19.8% of high school seniors had not tried cigarettes or alcohol, 48.4% had tried both, 1.2% had tried cigarettes but not alcohol, and 30.6% had tried alcohol but not cigarettes (Table 3.1.35). Of those students who had tried both cigarettes and alcohol by 12th grade, 40.8% had tried cigarettes before trying alcohol, while 36.4% had tried alcohol and cigarettes at about the same time. In all, 44.8% of these high school seniors had not tried cigarettes or marijuana by the 12th grade (Table 3.1.36), 35.2% had tried both, 12.5% had tried cigarettes but not marijuana, and 7.5% had tried marijuana but not cigarettes. Of those who had tried both by the 12th grade, more than one-half (53.6%) had tried cigarettes before marijuana, and 35.3% had tried marijuana and cigarettes at about the same time. Overall, 52.3% had not tried cigarettes or cocaine, 6.7% had tried both, 40.7% had tried cigarettes but not cocaine, and 0.3% had tried cocaine but not cigarettes (Table 3.1.37). Of those who had tried both by 12th grade, 84.9% tried cigarettes before trying cocaine, and 12.5% tried the two about the same time. These data support the contention that the use of tobacco occurs early in the sequence of drug use for young adolescents and may be considered a "gateway" drug.

Summary

Cigarettes are often considered a "gateway drug," and smoking cigarettes frequently precedes the use of smokeless tobacco and other types of drugs. Use of cigarettes, at a minimum, often covaries with smokeless tobacco and the use of other drugs. Among high school male cigarette smokers, for example, an estimated 84% also drink alcohol, 53% smoke marijuana, 29% use smokeless tobacco, 8% use cocaine, and 5% use inhalants. These percentages are much higher than the percentages of smokeless tobacco use and other types of drug use among male nonsmokers attending high school. Similar differences are observed among high school girls. Although cigarette smoking and the use of alcohol are initiated at a similar age, the initiation of cigarette smoking typically precedes the use of marijuana or cocaine.

Cigarette Smoking, Other Health-Related Behaviors, and Obesity

Research suggests that health-compromising behaviors co-occur among adolescents (Brener and Collins 1998; Weden and Zabin 2005). Incorporating data collected from repeated surveys by YRBS of high school seniors from 1991 to 2009, Figure 3.1.27 illustrates how some of these health-compromising behaviors covary with cigarette smoking. Here, behaviors are considered that relate to (1) drug use (i.e., use of alcohol, marijuana, cocaine), (2) smokeless tobacco and cigar use, (3) sexual activity, (4) suicidal ideation (i.e, seriously contemplating suicide), (5) violence (i.e., carrying a weapon, engaging in a physical fight), and (6) weight and weight-related behaviors. The prevalence of each behavior is mapped over time to compare current smokers with nonsmokers. Here, current smokers were defined as those who smoked on at least 1 or 2 days during the past 30 days and nonsmokers are defined as those who did not smoking during the past 30 days. Statistical tests of the trends across time are reported below, as are statistical tests at the earliest (i.e., 1991) and latest (i.e., 2009) survey points, so as to compare the two groups of interest. Covariation in health risk behaviors can have important implications for designing interventions.

Some evidence suggests that adolescent cigarette smokers have "hardened"—or become more prone to deviant behaviors, like alcohol use—over the last few decades (Chassin et al. 2007; Curry et al. 2009). For example, in a study comparing adolescent smokers in 1980 with adolescent smokers in 2001, Chassin and colleagues (2007) found some evidence to suggest that adolescent smokers were more "deviance prone" in 2001 than in 1980. This finding was especially strong for regular smokers in middle school who, over this period of time, showed the largest increase in tolerance of deviance and significant decreases in positive beliefs about academics, positive parental influences, and positive peer relations (Chassin et al. 2007). With the decreasing prevalence of smoking in the population as a whole, particularly among adolescents, youth who smoke today may be more committed to smoking than were adolescents in previous decades. They might also be more dependent on nicotine and have more difficulty in quitting smoking (Curry et al. 2009).

Drug Use

As shown in Figure 3.1.27, the prevalence of current alcohol use among high school seniors from 1991 to 2009 remained consistent over time for both current smokers and nonsmokers, with the prevalence of current alcohol use much higher for current smokers than for nonsmokers. In 1991, the prevalence of current alcohol use was 87.7% among current smokers but only 46.9% among nonsmokers ($p < 0.05$ for comparison between current smokers and nonsmokers); in 2009, the corresponding figures were 85.0% and 39.4% ($p < 0.05$ for comparison between current smokers and nonsmokers). By comparison, the percentage of students who ever rode with a driver who had been drinking alcohol among high school seniors declined from 1991 to 2009 for both current smokers ($p < 0.05$, linear trend) and nonsmokers ($p < 0.05$, linear trend). Again, in each year, the prevalence of riding with a driver who had been drinking alcohol among high school seniors was higher for current smokers than for nonsmokers. In 1991, just over two-thirds (69.9%) of current smokers had ever ridden with someone who had been drinking alcohol among high school seniors versus just under one-third (32.7%) of nonsmokers who had done so ($p < 0.05$ for comparison between current smokers and nonsmokers). By 2009, the figures had declined to essentially one-half (50.4%) of current smokers and 19.7% of nonsmokers ($p < 0.05$ for comparison between current smokers and nonsmokers).

The prevalence of current marijuana use among high school seniors increased over time from 1991 to 2009 for both current cigarette smokers ($p < 0.05$, linear trend; $p < 0.05$, quadratic trend) and nonsmokers ($p < 0.05$, linear trend; $p < 0.05$, quadratic trend). As with the first two behaviors discussed above, in each year the prevalence of current marijuana use among high school seniors was higher for current smokers than for nonsmokers. In 1991, the prevalence of current marijuana use among high school seniors was 41.9% for current smokers and 7.1% among nonsmokers ($p < 0.05$ for comparison between current smokers and nonsmokers); in 2009, these rates were

45.0% and 11.8%, respectively ($p < 0.05$ for comparison between current smokers and nonsmokers). By comparison, from 1991 to 2009 the prevalence of current cocaine use among high school seniors stayed flat among nonsmokers, but it increased and then declined somewhat for current smokers ($p < 0.05$, linear trend; $p < 0.05$, quadratic trend). In each year, the prevalence of current cocaine use among high school seniors was higher among current smokers than among nonsmokers. For example, in 1991, among high school seniors an estimated 5.2% of current cigarette smokers currently used cocaine, compared with 0.7% of nonsmokers ($p < 0.05$ for comparison between current smokers and nonsmokers). By 2009, the prevalence of cocaine use among high school seniors had risen to 9.5% among current smokers, but among nonsmokers it was 0.4% ($p < 0.05$ for comparison between current smokers and nonsmokers).

Smokeless Tobacco and Cigar Use

From 1995 to 2009, the prevalence of smokeless tobacco use among high school seniors remained generally steady among nonsmokers, with a slight decrease in 2003 ($p < 0.05$, quadratic trend); among current smokers, it declined in the late 1990s but then began to increase in the early 2000s ($p < 0.05$, quadratic trend). At each survey, the prevalence of smokeless tobacco use was higher among current smokers than among nonsmokers. In 1995, 20.8% of current smokers used smokeless tobacco versus 5.0% of nonsmokers ($p < 0.05$ for comparison between current smokers and nonsmokers); in 2009, these values were 24.9% and 4.2%, respectively ($p < 0.05$ for comparison between current smokers and nonsmokers). From 1997 to 2009, the prevalence of cigar smoking did not change significantly for either current smokers or nonsmokers, with prevalence always higher for current smokers. In 1997, the prevalence of cigar smoking was 42.3% among current cigarette smokers compared with 11.6% among nonsmokers ($p < 0.05$ for comparison between current smokers and nonsmokers); in 2009, these figures were 46.8% and 7.5%, respectively ($p < 0.05$ for comparison between current smokers and nonsmokers).

Sexual Activity

Just as other tobacco use and many forms of other drug use are more common among young cigarette smokers than among nonsmokers, so, too, is sexual activity more common among young smokers. The percentage of high school seniors who had ever had sexual intercourse decreased through the mid-1990s among current smokers and nonsmokers alike, but for both groups there was a significant increase from 2001 to 2009 ($p < 0.05$, linear trends; $p < 0.05$, quadratic trends). At each survey, sexual activity among high school seniors was more prevalent among current smokers. In 1991, 83.2% of current cigarette smokers had ever had intercourse versus 59.3% of nonsmokers ($p < 0.05$ for comparison between current smokers and nonsmokers); these figures dipped to 75.9% and 50.7%, respectively, in 1997. In 2009, the percentages were 85.5% of current smokers and 53.1% of nonsmokers ($p < 0.05$ for comparison between current smokers and nonsmokers). Use of a condom at last intercourse increased significantly from 1991 to 2009 for both current smokers ($p < 0.05$, linear trend; $p < 0.05$, quadratic trend) and nonsmokers ($p < 0.05$, linear trend), with use of a condom always more prevalent among those who did not smoke. In 1991, 44.8% of nonsmokers had used a condom at last intercourse compared with 35.9% of current cigarette smokers ($p < 0.05$ for comparison between current smokers and nonsmokers); in 2009, these figures were statistically similar at 56.6% and 50.9%, respectively ($p < 0.05$).

Suicide Ideation and Violence

From 1991 to 2009, suicidal ideation among high school seniors (defined as seriously considering attempting suicide) decreased significantly among both nonsmokers ($p < 0.05$, linear trend; $p < 0.05$, quadratic trend) and current smokers ($p < 0.05$, linear trend). At each survey, suicidal ideation was more prevalent among current smokers than among nonsmokers. In 1991, about one in every three (35.6%) current cigarette smokers had seriously considered attempting suicide in the last year, compared with one in five (21.5%) nonsmokers ($p < 0.05$ for comparison between current smokers and nonsmokers); in 2009, these figures were 17.4% and 10.1%, respectively ($p < 0.05$ for comparison between current smokers and nonsmokers). The prevalence of carrying a weapon fluctuated from 1991 to 2009 for both current smokers ($p < 0.05$, linear trend; $p < 0.05$, quadratic trend) and nonsmokers ($p < 0.05$, quadratic trend). In addition, the prevalence of engaging in a physical fight changed from 1991 to 2009 for both current smokers ($p < 0.05$, linear trend; $p < 0.05$) and nonsmokers ($p < 0.05$, quadratic trend). In 1991, among high school seniors 31.3% of current smokers had carried a weapon and 44.6% had engaged in a physical fight over the last 12 months versus 16.7% and 28.4% of nonsmokers, respectively ($p < 0.05$ for comparisons between current smokers and nonsmokers). In 1997, these percentages were 19.9% and 34.3%, respectively, for current smokers; in 1999, they were down to 10.8% and 20.9% for nonsmokers. In 2009, prevalence of the two behaviors had increased to 28.4% and 42.1% for current smokers, but there was relatively little change for nonsmokers, as shown by their prevalence of 12.1% and 17.8%, respectively ($p < 0.05$ for comparisons between current smokers and nonsmokers).

Obesity and Weight-Related Behaviors

The prevalence of obesity (defined as ≥95th percentile for body mass index (BMI; weight in kilograms divided by height in meters squared) by age and gender among high school senior current smokers and nonsmokers is considered over time from 1999 to 2009, in Figure 3.1.27M. At the first survey, obesity was significantly more prevalent among nonsmokers than among current smokers, but this situation had reversed itself by 2009. In 1999, 6.2% of current smokers and 9.3% of nonsmokers were categorized as obese ($p < 0.05$ for comparison between current smokers and nonsmokers), but by 2009, the prevalence of obesity had risen to 16.5% among current smokers compared with 12.3% of nonsmokers (difference not significant). During the same 8-year period, the prevalence of overweight (defined as ≥85th but <95th percentile for BMI, by age and gender) did not change significantly for either nonsmokers or current smokers. Furthermore, there were no significant differences between these two groups at either the first or last survey. In 1999, 13.4% of current smokers were categorized as overweight versus 15.0% of nonsmokers; in 2009, the figures were 14.1% and 15.1%, respectively.

Also from 1999 to 2009, the percentage high school seniors who watched television for 3 or more hours per day was similar for both current smokers and nonsmokers, and there were no significant changes over time for either group. At each survey, a higher percentage of nonsmokers than current smokers engaged in this amount of TV watching, but the differences at each survey were not significant. In 1999, 34.8% of nonsmokers watched television 3 or more hours per day versus 29.7% of current smokers; in 2009, these figures were 30.5% and 27.1%, respectively. Over this same period, differences were seen between current smokers and nonsmokers in the percentage who had not engaged in any moderate-to-vigorous intensity physical activity (MVPA) over the last week (defined as any kind of physical activity that increases the heart rate and makes one breathe hard). Among nonsmokers, the prevalence of no MVPA rose from 1999 to 2003, then dropped from 2003 to 2009 ($p < 0.05$, quadratic trend). Among current smokers, in contrast, the prevalence of no MVPA increased from 1999 to 2007, then decreased substantially in 2009 ($p < 0.05$, quadratic trend). In 1999, 31.7% of current smokers and 33.0% of nonsmokers had not participated in any MVPA over the last week; by 2009, this behavior had become more prevalent among current smokers (33.2%) than among nonsmokers (31.8%). The differences between current smokers and nonsmokers in both of these years were not significant.

From 1999 to 2009, at each survey, the percentage of high school seniors who did not eat fruits and vegetables five or more times a day did not differ significantly between current smokers and nonsmokers. In 1999, 21.8% of current smokers and 24.7% of nonsmokers did not eat fruits and vegetables five or more times a day; in 2009, these figures were 20.7% and 20.3%, respectively. During the same time period, the percentage of high school seniors who drank three or more glasses of milk per day did not change significantly for either current smokers or nonsmokers. In addition, at each survey, the prevalence of this behavior did not differ significantly between current smokers and nonsmokers. In 1999, 13.7% of current smokers and 13.5% of nonsmokers drank three or more glasses of milk each day; in 2009, the figures for this healthy behavior were 14.4% and 12.7%, respectively.

From 1991 to 2009, the percentage of students who were trying to lose weight increased significantly among nonsmokers, although there was a small dip from 2001 to 2003 ($p < 0.05$, linear trend; $p < 0.05$, quadratic trend). Among current smokers, there was a decrease between 1991 and 1999 and then an increase from 1999 to 2009 in this percentage ($p < 0.05$, linear trend). In 1991, significantly more current smokers (49.9%) than nonsmokers (36.7%) were trying to lose weight ($p < 0.05$ for comparison between current smokers and nonsmokers), but by 2009, the difference between current smokers (49.3%) and nonsmokers (45.9%) was not significant. Finally, from 1999 to 2009 the percentage of nonsmokers who engaged in unhealthy weight-control behaviors (defined as fasting, taking diet pills, powders, or liquids, or vomiting/taking laxatives to lose weight or to keep from gaining weight) decreased significantly ($p < 0.05$, quadratic trend); in contrast, among current smokers the percentage of students who engaged in these behaviors rose from 1999 to 2003, then decreased from 2003 to 2009 ($p < 0.05$, linear trend). At each survey, the prevalence of this unhealthy behavior was higher among current smokers than among nonsmokers. In 1999, 22.7% of current smokers and 16.4% of nonsmokers engaged in unhealthy weight-control behaviors ($p < 0.05$ for comparison between current smokers and nonsmokers); in 2009, these figures were 24.0% and 10.5%, respectively ($p < 0.05$ for comparison between current smokers and nonsmokers).

Summary

Cigarette smoking often covaries with other health-risk behaviors. In addition to alcohol use, other tobacco use, and other drug use, the percentage of high school seniors who have ever engaged in sexual intercourse is higher among current smokers than among nonsmokers, although the use of a condom at last intercourse does not differ between these two groups. Suicidal ideation is more prevalent among current smokers than nonsmokers, as is the prevalence of carrying a weapon and engaging in a physical fight. When behaviors related to weight and weight management are considered, few differences between current smokers and their nonsmoking peers are observed. The percentage of high school seniors who are overweight or obese does not vary between current smokers and nonsmokers, nor does the percentage who watch television 3 or more hours per day, engage in *no* physical activity of moderate to vigorous intensity, eat five or more fruits or vegetables per day, or consume three or more glasses of milk a day. The percentage of high school seniors who are trying to lose weight does not differ between current smokers and nonsmokers, although the percentage who engages in unhealthy weight control behaviors is significantly higher among current smokers than nonsmokers. The findings cited here have been consistent since the publication of the last Surgeon General's report on tobacco use among young people (USDHHS 1994).

Cigarette Smoking, Body Mass Index, and Depression

Cigarette Smoking and Body Mass Index

BMI, a measure of relative adiposity (i.e., body fat), is often used in epidemiologic studies to identify individuals as underweight, normal weight, overweight, or obese, often by using age- and gender-specific cutpoints (e.g., Cole et al. 2000, 2007). A higher BMI usually indicates more adiposity. Having a higher BMI has been linked to increased morbidity and mortality in adults, including a higher prevalence of heart disease, diabetes, and cancer, among other diseases (National Institutes of Health 1998).

Among adults, the inverse relationship between cigarette smoking and BMI is strong and reliable across studies; adult smokers typically weigh less and have less body fat (i.e., have a lower BMI) than do nonsmokers. In an analysis of the second National Health and Nutrition Examination Survey (1976–1980) data, BMI decreased with the duration of smoking but not with the intensity of smoking after adjustment for age and gender (Albanes et al. 1987). Later, in an analysis of 2005 NHIS data, current cigarette smoking was more prevalent among adults who were of normal weight (22.0%, men; 15.3%, women) than among overweight (16.2%, men; 13.2%, women) or obese (15.7%, men; 11.3%, women) adults (Kruger et al. 2009). In that study, after adjustment for demographic factors and other behavioral variables, current cigarette smokers were significantly less likely to be overweight ($p < 0.05$) or obese ($p < 0.05$) than were nonsmokers (Kruger et al. 2009). In contrast, among men, former smokers were significantly more likely to be overweight ($p < 0.05$) or obese ($p < 0.05$) than were nonsmokers (Kruger et al. 2009). Such a relationship was not significant for women (Kruger et al. 2009).

Among adolescents, the association between cigarette smoking and BMI is less clear. In a gender-focused review of 19 related studies, Potter and colleagues (2004) concluded that while some of the studies supported a positive correlation (i.e., as cigarette smoking increases, so does BMI), some did not. For example, in three of the U.S. studies, BMI was higher among both male and female smokers compared to nonsmokers. Another study found this relationship among males only, and four others observed no relationship between smoking and BMI among either males or females. The study outcomes appeared to depend upon ethnicity, age, and/or how smoking was defined in the study (Potter et al. 2004). The findings of research conducted since that review have been more consistent and seem to suggest that adolescent smokers, in contrast to adults, weigh more and have more body fat than do their nonsmoking counterparts. Findings from an analysis of repeated YRBS surveys (1999–2005) indicate that BMI was higher for smokers than for nonsmokers (Seo et al. 2009), and the evidence from this analysis indicates that this association has grown stronger with each (more recent) cohort of youth. Cooper and colleagues (2003) found that adolescents' weight increased for 2 years after initiation of smoking, but they found no difference in BMI between smokers and nonsmokers at the 3-year mark.

Table 3.1.38, using data from YRBS collapsed across the 2003, 2005, 2007, and 2009 surveys, illustrates the relationship between cigarette smoking and mean BMI among high school seniors according to smoking status by gender and race/ethnicity. Among female students, there were no differences in BMI by smoking status; among male students, never smokers had a significantly lower BMI than current infrequent smokers, current frequent smokers, and former nondaily smokers ($p < 0.05$, all comparisons with never smokers). Among Whites, BMI was significantly lower among never smokers than among current infrequent smokers ($p < 0.05$), but there were no other significant differences among White students. Among Black students, the mean BMI of former daily smokers and never smokers was significantly lower than current infrequent smokers, current frequent smokers, and former nondaily smokers ($p < 0.05$ for comparisons between these three groups and former daily smokers/never smokers). Among Hispanic students, former nondaily smokers and never smokers had a significantly lower mean BMI than current infrequent smokers ($p < 0.05$ for both comparisons); all other comparisons by smoking status among Hispanic students were not significant.

Cigarette Smoking and Depression

Adolescents who show symptoms of depression are at higher risk of starting to smoke than are nondepressed adolescents. In an analysis of the Teenage Attitudes and Practices Survey (1989–1993), adolescent never smokers, male and female ($p < 0.05$ for both), were more likely to begin smoking at follow-up if they had symptoms of depression at baseline (Escobedo et al. 1998). Adolescents who smoke are also more likely to develop symptoms of depression than are adolescents who do not smoke. Similarly, Choi and colleagues (1997) found that nondepressed nonsmokers were more likely to become depressed if they started smoking. Later, in an analysis of Add Health data (1995–1996), Steuber and Danner (2006) found that adolescents who were current smokers or former smokers at baseline were 1.5–2.0 times as likely to show symptoms of depression at follow-up as were nonsmokers. These analyses (Steuber and Danner 2006) controlled for depression at baseline. For females in this study, depression increased at the onset of smoking and decreased during a quit attempt, but these findings were not observed among males.

Other research supports a bidirectional relationship between cigarette smoking and depression. In a longitudinal study of adolescents, Brown and colleagues (1996) found that lifetime prevalence of a major depressive disorder (MDD) predicted smoking uptake at 1-year follow-up. In addition, adolescents who smoked at baseline were twice as likely as nonsmokers to have an MDD episode in the next 12 months. These analyses also controlled for depression at baseline. In their cross-sectional analysis, in contrast, the authors found no significant relationship between smoking status and MDD after adjusting for other psychiatric disorders. The authors, therefore, hypothesized that a "*specific* relationship between smoking and MDD exists only in smokers who are nicotine-dependent" (Brown et al. 1996, p. 1607). This may explain why a stronger relationship between smoking and depression has been observed in adults, who are more likely to be addicted to nicotine than are adolescents (Breslau et al. 1991, 1993).

Table 3.1.39 uses NSDUH data to illustrate the relationship between cigarette smoking and a major depressive episode among adolescents and young adults. Here, the prevalence of a major depressive episode is presented by smoking status, stratified by gender as well as race/ethnicity. Across all strata, the prevalence of a major depressive episode was lowest for adolescents and young adults who had never smoked a cigarette (never smokers). This result was significant for male and female adolescents and for female young adults, as well as for White adolescents and Hispanic young adults ($p < 0.05$ for all comparisons of never smokers with other smoking statuses within these subgroups). Among adolescents, the prevalence of a major depressive episode was highest among current infrequent smokers across all strata except Blacks. Among young adults, the highest prevalence was among current frequent smokers across all strata. Across age, gender, and race/ethnicity, however, differences in the prevalence of a major depressive episode between classes of ever smokers (former, current infrequent, current frequent) were often small and not always significant. Among adolescent boys, the prevalence of a major depressive episode was about 2 times as high for current infrequent smokers as for never smokers; among adolescent girls, it was about 3 times as high. Among young adult males, it was about 1 times as high for current frequent smokers as for never smokers, and among young adult females it was about 2 times as high.

Summary

Chapter 2 considers the relationship between cigarette smoking and weight status among adolescents. Here, the relationship between cigarette smoking and BMI using a nationally representative sample has been considered. Few differences in BMI by smoking status were observed. Among Whites, BMI was lowest among adolescents who had never smoked, while among Blacks and Hispanics, former daily smokers and never smokers tied for the lowest BMI.

Chapter 2 also considers the relationship between cigarette smoking and depression. In the present chapter, the association between cigarette smoking and a major depressive episode has been considered using representative samples of adolescents (12–17 years old) and young adults (18–25 years old). Across age, gender, and race/ethnicity, the prevalence of a major depressive episode was lowest among those who had never smoked a cigarette. There was often little difference between the other three types of smokers (former, current infrequent, current frequent) in the prevalence of a major depressive episode.

The Use of Other Tobacco Products Among Young People in the United States

Cigarettes remain the most popular form of tobacco among adults and youth in the United States and most industrialized nations, but the use of other tobacco products, such as cigars and smokeless tobacco, is still common. The U.S. Department of Agriculture (USDA) and industry trade data indicate that although the consumption of cigarettes has declined substantially, consumption and sales of smokeless tobacco, specifically moist snuff and cigars has risen (USDA 2007; Maxwell 2009a,b). Although cigars and smokeless tobacco are predominantly featured in this section, it should be noted that other emerging forms of tobacco, such as bidis, kreteks, and hookahs, have been shown in some local and state surveys to be popular with youth (Soldz et al. 2003a; Hrywna et al. 2004; Primack et al. 2009). Measures of the use of other emerging tobacco products like snus and dissolvables were not available on surveys that had been implemented before production of this chapter was complete, so these products are not addressed here.

The use of smokeless tobacco has been linked to both localized oral health consequences at the site of tobacco placement and systemic effects. Smokeless tobacco contains at least 28 carcinogens (International Agency for Research on Cancer [IARC] 2007), and there is strong evidence to show that users have an increased risk of developing leukoplakia, a precancerous lesion on oral soft tissue, as well as oral cancers (IARC 1998, 2007; Walsh and Epstein 2000). Other undesirable oral health outcomes that have been linked to smokeless tobacco use include gingival recession, periodontal disease, and tooth decay (USDHHS 1986; Walsh and Epstein 2000; Fisher et al. 2005). Less serious outcomes include staining of teeth and halitosis (Christen et al. 1982; Walsh and Epstein 2000).

The systemic effects of using smokeless tobacco include nicotine addiction and dependence (NCI 1992; IARC 2007) and acute cardiovascular effects like an elevated heart rate and high blood pressure (Westman 1995; Winn 1997). Use of smokeless tobacco may also be related to long-term cardiovascular effects and mortality, although the evidence on such associations is mixed (Winn 1997; Gupta et al. 2004). A recent meta-analysis found heightened relative risks for fatal myocardial infarction (MI) and fatal stroke from ever using smokeless tobacco, while the risk estimates for nonfatal MI and stroke were not as large (Boffetta and Straif 2009). One large longitudinal study in Sweden found an elevated prevalence of hypertension among users of oral snuff compared with nonusers and a greater risk of death from cardiovascular disease (Bolinder 1997). Other studies have found no associations with cardiovascular variables, as was the case in Siegel and colleagues' (1992) study of cardiovascular risk factors among professional baseball players. Although there is some discussion in the medical literature on whether the harmful consequences of using smokeless tobacco are as severe as those from smoking, the literature confirms both short- and long-term negative consequences for using smokeless tobacco. The majority of these studies have focused on health outcomes occurring in adulthood.

Recent Patterns of Smokeless Tobacco Use

Ever Use of Smokeless Tobacco

Overall, national estimates for adolescents for ever trying smokeless tobacco were 10.2% for youth 13–18 years of age in the 2010 NSDUH, 14.5% for 8th, 10th, and 12th-grade students in the 2010 MTF, 6.1% for 6th–8th-grade students in the 2009 NYTS, and 14.1% for 9th–12th-grade students in the 2009 NYTS (Table 3.1.40). In all surveys, males were significantly more likely than females to have ever tried smokeless tobacco ($p < 0.05$ for comparisons between genders in all surveys). White males had the highest prevalence of any subgroup in NSDUH, MTF, and NYTS–high school, with ever use exceeding 20% in all three surveys. In NYTS–middle school, Other male students had the highest prevalence (13.7%). In NSDUH, MTF, and NYTS–middle school, Black youth had the lowest prevalence of ever using smokeless tobacco among the four racial/ethnic categories ($p < 0.05$ for all racial/ethnic comparisons with Blacks in these three surveys). In NSDUH, the percentage of ever use rose significantly with increasing age; those 13 and 14 years of age (3.9%) were significantly less likely to be ever users than were those 15 and 16 years of age (9.7%; $p < 0.05$), and 15- and 16-year-olds were significantly less likely to be ever users than were 17- and 18-year-olds (16.1%; $p < 0.05$). In MTF, 8th-grade students (9.8%) were significantly less likely than 10th-grade (16.8%; $p < 0.05$) and 12th-grade (17.6%; $p < 0.05$) students to be ever users of smokeless tobacco. In NYTS, ever use increased significantly between 7th and 8th grade (5.0% vs. 8.3%, $p < 0.05$) and 10th and 11th grade (13.2% vs. 17.5%, p <0.05). The prevalence of ever using smokeless tobacco varied by regions. Significantly higher percentages were noted in the Midwest and South than in the Northeast and West in both NSDUH and MTF (p <0.05 for comparisons between Midwest and South vs. Northeast and West).

Current Use of Smokeless Tobacco

Overall, national estimates for current use of smokeless tobacco were 3.7% for youth 13–18 years of age in the 2010 NSDUH; 6.5% for 8th, 10th, and 12th-grade students in the 2010 MTF; 8.9% for 9th–12th-grade students in the 2009 YRBS; 6.7% for 9th–12th-grade students in the 2009 NYTS; and 2.6% for 6th–8th-grade students in the 2009 NYTS (Table 3.1.41). Patterns of current use were fairly consistent with those previously described for ever use. Current use was significantly more prevalent among males than among females: 6.3% versus 0.8% in NSDUH (p <0.05), 11.3% versus 1.9% in MTF (p <0.05), 15.0% versus 2.2% in YRBS (p <0.05), 11.6% versus 1.8% in NYTS–high school (p <0.05), and 3.7% versus 1.4% in NYTS–middle school (p <0.05). The prevalence of current use of smokeless tobacco was significantly higher among White than Black, Hispanic, or Other youth in all surveys (p <0.05 for all racial/ethnic comparisons with Whites in NSDUH, MTF, YRBS, and NYTS–high school). The percentage of youth who were current users of smokeless tobacco increased significantly between each age level in NSDUH (p <0.05 for all comparisons between age levels), but significant between-grade increases were not consistent in MTF, YRBS, and NYTS. In MTF, 8th-grade students were significantly less likely than 10th (p <0.05) and 12th-grade students (p <0.05) to currently use smokeless tobacco. In YRBS, 9th-grade students were significantly less likely to use smokeless tobacco than were 11th and 12th-grade students (p <0.05 for both comparisons). In NYTS–high school, 9th-grade students were significantly less likely to use smokeless tobacco than were 10th, 11th, and 12th-grade students (p <0.05 for comparisons with 9th-grade students). These findings perhaps suggest that most initiation of smokeless tobacco use occurs in the earlier high school years. As with ever use of smokeless tobacco, current use varied by region, with the highest prevalence in NSDUH seen in the South and Midwest, and the highest prevalence in YRBS and MTF found in the South, Midwest, and Northeast. In all three surveys, the West had the lowest prevalence (p <0.05 when compared with the South and Midwest).

Given the regional variations noted, it is not surprising that there was considerable variation at the state level in current use of smokeless tobacco. Figure 3.1.28 illustrates the percentages of youth (12–17), young adults (18–25), and adults (26 years of age and older) who were current users of smokeless tobacco by state, from 2006 to 2010. Figure 3.1.29 shows similar data for the same time period, further separated by gender within each of the age groups. Based on NSDUH data from 2006 to 2010, the prevalence ranged from 0.4% to 6.9% for those 12–17 years of age, from 1.7% to 16.1% for the 18- to 25-year-olds, and from 0.6% to 9.5% for those 26 years of age and older. The states with the highest prevalence among youth were Wyoming (6.9%), Kentucky (6.4%), West Virginia (6.0%), Montana (5.4%), and Tennessee (5.0%), while the states with the lowest prevalence (all at or below 1.0%) were Maryland, California, Arizona, Hawaii, and Rhode Island (the District of Columbia [DC], also had a prevalence below 1.0%). Among young adults, Wyoming (15.8%) and Montana (16.1%) had the highest prevalence of smokeless tobacco use, while the states with the lowest prevalence (all below 3.0%) included Hawaii, California, Rhode Island, and New Jersey (DC, also had a prevalence below 3.0%).

The use of smokeless tobacco is predominantly a male behavior, but in some states the use of smokeless by young girls is not inconsequential. For example, the prevalence of current smokeless tobacco use among girls 12–17 years of age was notable in Alaska (3.1%), Montana (2.5%), Wyoming (2.0%), New Mexico (1.5%) and South Dakota (1.3%) (Figure 3.1.29). It is particularly striking that use of smokeless tobacco by young girls in Alaska exceeded use among young boys in 12 states and DC, in 2006–2010. The high percentages among girls in the states listed above may be partially attributable to their racial/ethnic composition. American Indians and Alaska Natives are known to have a high prevalence of smokeless tobacco use, even among females, compared with the general population (Kaplan et al. 1997), and Alaska, Montana, and South Dakota are among the top five states with respect to the proportion of American Indians and Alaska Natives in their populations (U.S. Census Bureau 2009).

Data pooled from the years 2002–2007 from MTF surveys suggest that current use of smokeless tobacco among male youth varies by several sociodemographic risk factors (Table 3.1.42). Among 8th-grade males, current use of smokeless tobacco increased as parental education decreased. Although fewer significant differences can be seen for 10th- and 12th-grade students and the incremental effects are less pronounced, those males whose parents had the highest level of education had the lowest prevalence of using smokeless tobacco. The prevalence of current use of smokeless tobacco was significantly highest among 8th- and 10th-grade boys who lived alone (37.4% and 31.7%, respectively) than among those with any other household structure (p <0.05 for all comparisons with other household structures). In addition, use of smokeless tobacco was significantly higher among 8th-grade boys living in father-only households (10.2%) than in boys who lived with both parents (4.7%, $p < 0.05$) or in a mother-only household (3.8%, $p < 0.05$). The lowest prevalence by household structure was noted for 8th-, 10th-, and 12th-grade male students living in mother-only households. Among 12th-grade males, those who lived in such households had a significantly lower prevalence of current smokeless tobacco use (8.6%) than those living with both parents (12.9%, $p < 0.05$) or other relatives (15.5%, $p < 0.05$).

By residence, living in rural (non-MSA) areas was associated with the highest prevalence of using smokeless tobacco and living in a large MSA was associated with the lowest prevalence of smokeless tobacco use; this was significant for all three grades ($p < 0.05$ for all comparisons between population densities). In addition, the percentage of males who currently used smokeless tobacco was negatively associated with academic performance (based on self-rated performance by participants) in both the 8th and 10th grades. In those two grades, the prevalence of current smokeless tobacco use differed significantly between each level of academic performance ($p < 0.05$ for all comparisons). In the 12th grade, while the pattern was similar, only students with the highest levels of performance (A, 7.5%) differed significantly from other levels (B, 13.1%; C, 15.1%; D, 17.9%; $p < 0.05$ for all comparisons with A). The perceived importance of religion was not associated with the prevalence of use among 8th-grade students, but among 10th-grade students, those viewing religion as very important had significantly lower usage (8.2%) than those believing it was not/somewhat important (11.3%, $p < 0.05$) or important (12.7%, $p < 0.05$). Among 12th-grade males, those viewing religion as important were significantly more likely to use smokeless tobacco (15.7%) than those believing religion was very important (10.7%, $p < 0.05$) or not/somewhat important (13.0%, $p < 0.05$).

When the Use of Smokeless Tobacco Begins

MTF data from 2002 through 2007 were merged to observe the grade at which 12th-grade students reported trying tobacco, including smokeless tobacco, and other drugs (Figure 3.1.26). According to these data, 10.7% of ever users of smokeless tobacco had done so by the 6th grade, 43.5% by the 9th grade, and 85% by 11th grade (Figure 3.1.26). This pattern differed notably from that for cigarettes, where initiation occurred in earlier grades; more than two-thirds of those who ever used cigarettes had tried them by 9th grade. The findings for smokeless tobacco are replicated in the 2009 NYTS; there, among 12th-grade students who ever used smokeless tobacco, 16.2% first tried it before 13 years of age, 23.2% at 13 or 14 years of age, 35.2% at the age of 15 or 16 years, and 25.4% at the age of 17 years or older (Table 3.1.43). Whether the use of smokeless tobacco serves as a gateway to using cigarettes has been debated in the research literature (Kozlowski et al. 2003; Tomar 2003; O'Connor et al. 2005). Cigarettes, however, may serve as a gateway for smokeless tobacco use, too (SAMSHA 2009b). It is interesting to note that statewide prevalence data from the 2009 Behavioral Risk Factor Surveillance System (BRFSS) show that use of smokeless tobacco is more common among young adults (ages 18–24) than among other adults (CDC 2010d).

Preferences for Particular Brands of Smokeless Tobacco

In the United States, smokeless tobacco is usually consumed in one of two forms: chewing tobacco or moist snuff. Chewing tobacco is made up of long strands of tobacco, and snuff tobacco is a fine-grain product that comes in a moist blend (used orally) as well as in dry varieties (the latter are taken through the nostrils). Moist snuff is the most popular of all of today's smokeless tobacco products (Maxwell 2009b). The different types of smokeless tobacco as well as the specific brands within each type vary widely in the amount of nicotine and carcinogens (primarily tobacco-specific nitrosamines) they contain (Henningfield et al. 1995; Richter and Spierto 2003; McNeill et al. 2006; Stepanov et al. 2006; Alpert et al. 2008; Richter et al. 2008). As shown in Table 3.1.44, youth 12–17 years of age greatly prefer moist snuff brands to chewing tobacco (about 80.0% for moist snuff vs. about 9.0% for chew), and this is consistent with the preference for moist snuff revealed in overall U.S. market share (all ages) as shown in Table 3.1.45 (Maxwell 2009b). Skoal, which was the most popular brand of smokeless tobacco among young people per the 1994 Surgeon General's report, is now the second most popular brand (24.1%) among young people (Table 3.1.44), with Grizzly (32.1%) first and Copenhagen (15.8%) third; Red Man is the most popular chewing tobacco (5.3%).

Considerable variation in the smokeless brands preferred by youth can be seen by region (Table 3.1.44). Youth in the Northeast overwhelmingly favor Skoal (50.1%), while youth in the Midwest and South prefer Grizzly (36.7% and 38.1%, respectively) over any other single brand, and youth in the West choose Copenhagen (29.2%) more than other brands. Among young adults (18–25 years of age), Skoal (30.1%) is the most popular smokeless brand, followed by Grizzly (28.6%) and Copenhagen (17.9%); again, Red Man is the most popular chewing tobacco (4.5%) (Table 3.1.46). Regional patterns for young adults (18–25 years of age) are similar to those for youth 12–17 years of age; Skoal is the preferred brand in the Northeast (52.9%). In the Midwest and South, Grizzly and Skoal are the top choices (see Table 3.1.47), while in the West, Copenhagen and Skoal rank very close together as the top choices (31.4% and 28.6%, respectively) (Table 3.1.47).

It is worth noting that Grizzly, introduced by the American Snuff Company in 2002, is a fairly new brand and is known as a deep-discount or subvalue item. Deep-discount brands retail at less than $2 per can, while premium brands, such as Skoal and Copenhagen, average closer to $5 per can (Covino 2006). Previous research has demonstrated that youth, particularly males, are price sensitive to smokeless tobacco (Ohsfeldt and Boyle 1994; Ohsfeldt et al. 1997). The growth in deep-discount brands like Grizzly in the last few years is disturbing. Clearly, making smokeless tobacco products available more cheaply could promote their use among price-sensitive youth. In addition, disparities in tobacco taxation (i.e., higher taxes for cigarettes than for smokeless tobacco) could result in a switch to smokeless tobacco among young males (Ohsfeldt and Boyle 1994; Ohsfeldt et al. 1997).

Trends Over Time in the Use of Smokeless Tobacco

Using NSDUH data, the prevalence of current use of smokeless tobacco was plotted for young adults (18–25 years of age) from 2002 to 2010 by gender (Figure 3.1.30) and race/ethnicity (Figure 3.1.31). From 2002 to 2008, current use of smokeless tobacco remained stable among young adult females and then increased significantly from 0.4% in 2008 to 0.8% in 2009 ($p < 0.05$), and remained stable at 0.7% in 2010 ($p > 0.05$ vs 2009). Among young adult males, current use of smokeless tobacco increased from 8.9% in 2003 to 10.3% in 2008 ($p < 0.05$), with an additional significant jump from 10.3% in 2008 to 11.4% in 2009 ($p < 0.05$), then stabilized at 12.0% in 2010 ($p > 0.05$ vs. 2009). As will be seen among adolescents (Figures 3.1.33–34), the jump between 2008 and 2009 was particularly notable for White young adults (Figure 3.1.31). Figure 3.1.32 presents additional data from NSDUH that examine differences in current use of smokeless tobacco from 2005 to 2010 by socioeconomic status. Across all points of time, use of smokeless tobacco was most prevalent in the highest socioeconomic group (defined as ≥200% of the poverty level). Increases in the use of smokeless tobacco from 2005 to 2010, however, were not limited to this group, as they also occurred in the lowest (below the poverty level) and middle (100–199% or more of the poverty level) socioeconomic groups (Figure 3.1.32).

Trends in the prevalence of current use of smokeless tobacco among adolescents (12–17 years of age) indicate that, for males, use in the past month rose in the early 1990s, peaked around 1995, and then declined in the late 1990s (Figure 3.1.33). Per MTF, progress in reducing use among male students slowed considerably between 2000 and 2008, and current use increased among 10th- and 12th-grade students overall between 2008 and 2010. Per YRBS, the increase in current use of smokeless tobacco among male students began in 2003 and continued through 2009 (Figure 3.1.33C). The prevalence of current use of smokeless tobacco among females, on the other hand, has remained low and constant (between 1% and 3%) since 1995 (Figure 3.1.33C). Use of smokeless tobacco among males over time has differed by race/ethnicity, with White male students in the 8th, 10th, and 12th grades having a consistently higher prevalence of use than their Hispanic and Black counterparts (Figure 3.1.34). Historically, young Black males have had a low prevalence of use, and the contrast with young White male students is particularly striking among 12th-grade students. Especially noteworthy are the increases in the current use of smokeless tobacco among White and Hispanic 12th-grade males between 2008 and 2010 and among White 10th-grade males from 2009 to 2010.

The MTF surveys have monitored perceptions of risk concerning smokeless tobacco since 1986. Overall, in 2010, 41.2% of 12th-grade students believed there is great risk of harm associated with the regular use of smokeless tobacco (Figure 3.1.35). Previous research suggests that perceptions that smokeless tobacco is a serious health risk vary by gender and race/ethnicity, with females more likely than males and Blacks more likely than Whites to hold this opinion (USDHHS 1994; Tomar and Hatsukami 2007). Since 1986, there was a gradual but substantial increase in the proportion of 12th-grade students believing that there is a great risk in using smokeless tobacco regularly (Figure 3.1.35), but the increasing trend stalled after 1999, with the percentage holding this perception essentially the same in 1999 and 2010. The smokeless tobacco industry has participated in the debate about reducing harm by switching from cigarettes to smokeless, and subtle marketing of its products that may suggest they are safer than cigarettes (Myers 2003; Alpert et al. 2008) could have contributed to the stagnant levels of risk perception. Per the MTF surveys, when the overall percentage of 12th-grade students who believed that great risk is associated with use of smokeless tobacco is plotted against the percentage of 12th-grade students who have ever used the product, the trends are inversely related (Figure 3.1.35).

Prevalence of the Use of Smokeless Tobacco, Cigarette Smoking, and Other Drugs

According to the 2002–2007 MTF surveys, the majority of male 12th-grade students who used alcohol, marijuana, or cocaine did not use smokeless tobacco as well (Table 3.1.46). Regardless, use of smokeless tobacco was from 2.2 (for marijuana) to 6.1 times (for alcohol) as high among users of these drugs as among nonusers. Similarly, the prevalence of other drug use was higher among users of smokeless tobacco than among those who did not use smokeless tobacco. Most notably, 85.4% of smokeless users were also alcohol drinkers, 39.3% used marijuana, and 6.5% used cocaine; three-fifths (59.9%) smoked cigarettes. The prevalence of other drug use was from 1.9 (for marijuana) to 3.0 times (for cigarettes) as great among users of smokeless tobacco as among nonusers. Similar trends were observed in the same analyses by NSDUH (Table 3.1.46).

Summary

The prevalence of smokeless tobacco use is highest among males, Whites, and older youth, and lowest among females and Blacks. At present, about 1 out of 5 high school males has ever used smokeless tobacco, and about 1 out of 8 currently uses smokeless tobacco. There is considerable regional variation in use, with those residing in rural areas using smokeless more frequently than those living in large urban areas. Initiation of smokeless tobacco use appears to occur somewhat later in adolescence than does cigarette smoking. Over time, use among female adolescents and young adults has remained constant, but it has increased among male adolescents and young adults since 2003, particularly in older age groups and among Whites. Moist snuff is the most popular type of smokeless tobacco among youth, and discount brands like Grizzly have become popular among young people in recent years.

Recent Patterns of Cigar Use

Historically, cigar smoking in the United States has been a behavior of older men, but the industry's increased marketing of cigars during the 1990s to targeted groups increased the prevalence of use among adolescents (NCI 1998). Thus, the rise in the prevalence of cigar use during the mid-1990s was not limited to adults; instead, as documented by numerous local, state, and national surveys, cigar use and experimentation with this product have been widespread among both male and female adolescents (CDC 1997; Rigotti et al. 2000; Delnevo et al. 2002; Marshall et al. 2006). By definition, large cigars are any roll of tobacco wrapped in leaf tobacco or in any substance containing tobacco and weighing more than 3 pounds per 1,000 cigars; whereas little or small cigars weigh no more than 3 pounds per 1,000 cigars. Little or small cigars have other characteristics that set them apart from large cigars and make them similar to cigarettes, such as shape, size, filters, and packing (i.e., 20 sticks to a pack). In recent years, marketing strategies have blurred the line between cigarettes and little cigars (Delnevo and Hrywna 2007).

Ever Use of Cigars

According to the 2010 NSDUH, an estimated 16.7% of youth 13–18 years of age have ever tried a cigar. In the 2009 NYTS, 10.1% of 6th–8th grade students and 28.6% of 9th–12th-grade students were ever cigar smokers (Table 3.1.48). Per both surveys, males were much more likely than females to have ever smoked a cigar ($p < 0.05$). In NSDUH, White youth (19.5%) had a significantly higher prevalence than Hispanic (14.9%), Black (11.3%), or Other youth (9.9%) ($p < 0.05$ for all comparisons with White youth). In NYTS–high school, White (32.5%) and Hispanic (29.2%) students had a significantly higher prevalence of ever smoking a cigar than Other youth (22.0%) and Black students (16.3%) ($p < 0.05$ for each comparison with White and Hispanic students). In NYTS–middle school, prevalence was lowest among White students (8.1%) ($p < 0.05$ for comparisons with Black and Hispanic students) and highest among Hispanic students (14.9%) ($p < 0.05$ for comparisons with White and Black students). The percentage of youth who had ever used a cigar rose significantly with increasing age in NSDUH ($p < 0.05$, for all age comparisons) and with increasing grade level in NYTS ($p < 0.05$ for all grade comparisons) except between 11th and 12th grades ($p > 0.05$). In NSDUH, 28.1% of 17- and 18-year-olds had ever used a cigar, and 37.4% of 12th-grade students had done so per NYTS. The prevalence of ever use did not notably vary by region.

Current Use of Cigars

Per 2010 NSDUH, 5.6% of 13- to 18-year-olds currently smoked cigars, while 14.0% of 9th–12th-grade students did so per the 2009 YRBS, 3.9% of 6th–8th-grade students did so according to the 2009 NYTS, and 10.9% of 9th–12th-grade students were current cigar smokers per the 2009 NYTS (Table 3.1.49). Current cigar use differed significantly by gender ($p < 0.05$) and was approximately 1.5 times more common for males as for females students per NYTS–middle school and 2.5 times greater for males as for females according to the other surveys. In the 2010 NSDUH, White youth 13–18 years of age had a significantly higher prevalence of current cigar use (6.6%) than did Blacks (4.6%), Hispanics (9.4%), and Other youth (3.0%) ($p < 0.05$ for all comparisons with White youth).

In the 2009 YRBS, White students (14.9%) had a significantly higher prevalence of current use than did students in the Other group (11.1%, $p < 0.05$ vs. White students). The NYTS–middle school survey found that Hispanic students (6.2%) had the highest prevalence of current cigar use, which was significantly greater than the prevalence among White (2.9%) and Black (4.5%) ($p <0.05$) but not Other students (4.6%, $p > 0.05$). The NYTS–high school survey found that prevalence was significantly higher among White (12.0%) and Hispanic (11.8%) students than among Black (7.3%) or Other (8.0%) ($p <0.05$ for the comparisons with White and Hispanic students). It is important to note here that recently, some have questioned whether the prevalence of cigar use among adolescents may be underestimated, particularly among Black youth; research suggests that some cigar users know their product only by its brand name and may not even consider it a cigar or tobacco (Malone et al. 2001; Page and Evans 2004; Delnevo and Hrywna 2006; Terchek et al. 2009). Moreover, there is a paradoxical finding regarding the use of blunts (hollowed-out cigars filled with marijuana), with Black youth having the highest prevalence of current blunt use but the lowest prevalence of current cigar use (Delnevo and Hrywna 2006).

White males had the highest prevalence of any racial/ethnic subgroup in terms of current cigar use in NSDUH (9.1%), YRBS (21.0%), and NYTS–high school (17.2%). In fact, the prevalence of current cigar use by White male students according to YRBS (21.0%), did not differ appreciably from their prevalence of current cigarette smoking (22.3%) (Table 3.1.2). Moreover, in some states, current cigar use among adolescent males actually exceeds the prevalence of current cigarette smoking in this population (Delnevo et al. 2005; Eaton et al. 2010). Although males have a higher prevalence of cigar use, the use of cigars by females is not insubstantial. In stark contrast to what has been found for cigarettes, the prevalence of cigar use among adolescent females has been found to exceed that of adult women nationally (Delnevo et al. 2002). Not surprisingly, the percentage of current cigar users rose with increasing age. Per the 2010 NSDUH, each 2-year age group through 17–18 years of age differed significantly from the one below it ($p <0.05$). Similarly, in the 2009 YRBS, 9th-grade students had a significantly lower rate of use than did 10th-, 11th-, or 12th-grade students, and 10th- and 11th-grade students had significantly lower use than did 12th-grade students ($p <0.05$). A similar relationship was noted in NYTS. In the 2010 NSDUH and 2009 YRBS, the highest prevalence of current cigar use was in the Midwest region. In NSDUH, the prevalence in the Midwest was significantly higher than in the Northeast only ($p <0.05$), while in YRBS, the prevalence in the Midwest was significantly higher than the prevalence in the Northeast and West ($p <0.05$) but not in the South ($p >0.05$).

The prevalence of current cigar use at the state level varied considerably, with prevalence rates ranging from 1.8% to 6.7% for 12- to 17-year-olds (Figure 3.1.36A), from 6.3% to 15.8% for 18- to 25-year-olds (Figure 3.1.36B), and from 2.1% to 6.1% for adults 26 years of age or older (Figure 3.1.36C). The states with the highest cigar use among youth (12–17 years of age) were Wyoming (6.7%), Colorado (6.1%), Montana (5.8%), Ohio (5.6%), and Indiana (5.6%) while the states with the lowest prevalence were Utah (1.8%), Hawaii (2.5%), and California (2.7%) (Figure 3.1.36A). The states with the highest use among young adults (18–25 years of age) were Ohio (15.8%), Kansas (15.7%), Missouri (14.9%), Indiana (14.5%), and Kentucky (14.5%); the lowest prevalence was again found in Utah (6.3%) and Hawaii (7.7%) (Figure 3.1.36B).

Using NSDUH data, the prevalence of current cigar smoking was plotted over time for young adults (18–25 years of age) from 2002 to 2010 by gender (Figure 3.1.37) and race/ethnicity (Figure 3.1.38). Over the period, current cigar smoking remained stable among young adult females. Among young adult males, in contrast, current cigar smoking was little different at the end of the period and the beginning, but it rose from 2002 to 2004, when it peaked. The prevalence of current cigar smoking was stable among Whites across the period but showed somewhat more variability for Blacks and Hispanics (Figure 3.1.38). Figure 3.1.39 also presents data from NSDUH that illustrate differences in cigar smoking from 2005 to 2010 by socioeconomic status. During 2006–2008, cigar smoking was most prevalent in the highest socioeconomic group (defined as 200% or more of the poverty level) (Figure 3.1.39). In the lowest socioeconomic group (below poverty level) and the middle group (100–199% of poverty level), cigar smoking increased from 2008 to 2009 after a slight decline from 2006 to 2008 (Figure 3.1.39). In 2009, cigar smoking was equally prevalent among the three socioeconomic groups represented here. In 2010, cigar smoking increased among the lowest socioeconomic group only and was most prevalent in this group compared to the other two for the first since 2005.

Current cigar use is predominantly a male behavior; as noted previously, among youth, male cigar use overall is approximately 2.5 times that of females. However, some states had a notable prevalence of cigar use by young girls (12–17 years of age), such as Kansas (4.8%) (Figure 3.1.40B). This prevalence exceeded that for cigar use by young males in 12 states, including Kansas (4.6% for males) (Figure 3.1.40A). As noted earlier, the prevalence of cigar use among adolescent females has been found to exceed that among adult females (Delnevo et al.

2002). Indeed, the NSDUH data indicate that, with the exception of Idaho, Louisiana, Mississippi, Oklahoma and the District of Columbia (DC), current cigar use by 12- to 17-year-old girls exceeded cigar use by adult women (≥26 years of age or older) in their respective states and DC (Figures 3.1.40B and 3.1.40F). In general, however, this pattern did not hold for males; in most states, cigar use was higher among adult men (≥26 years of age) than for adolescent boys 12–17 years of age (Figures 3.1.40A, 3.1.40C, 3.1.40E). In all states, young adults 18–25 years of age (both genders) had the highest prevalence of current cigar use (Figures 3.1.40C and 3.1.40D).

Preferences for Particular Cigar Brands

There are many different types of cigars, including large premium cigars, cigarillos, and small or little cigars; the last type is the same size as cigarettes and often includes a filter. Despite the wide variety of cigar products, however, there is no universally accepted classification system (Baker et al. 2000). As shown in Table 3.1.50, among current cigar smokers, the most popular brand of cigars among young people 12–17 years of age, as reported in the 2008–2010 NSDUH, was Black & Mild (42.9%). These cigars were somewhat more popular among girls (48.8%) than among boys (40.3%), and were overwhelmingly preferred by Black youth (58.4%), a finding consistent with previous reports (Yerger et al. 2001; Soldz et al. 2003b; Page and Evans 2004). Consistent with industry data for market share (Table 3.1.51), other popular brands among youth in 2008–2010 were Swisher Sweets (20.3%), Phillies (5.6%), White Owl (3.7%), and Dutch Masters (3.1%) (Table 3.1.50). In all regions, Black & Mild was the most preferred brand. Swisher Sweets was next in all regions except the Northeast, where Dutch Masters ranked second in adolescent preferences. Data for market share for all ages (Table 3.1.51) showed that Swisher Sweets (29.7%) was the leader, followed by Dutch Masters (11.1%) and Phillies (8.4%) (Maxwell 2009c). Preferences by demographic characteristics among 18- to 25-year-olds (Table 3.1.52) were similar to those for adolescents, but it is interesting to note that preference for Black & Mild diminished somewhat with increasing age (35.6% for this group vs. 42.9% for the younger group). With the exception of Black & Mild, the top brands for both age groups include various flavorings, such as peach, grape, apple, and chocolate. In addition, they are commonly sold as a single stick, often for around $1.00 (Delnevo 2007). The use of such flavors in cigarettes has raised much concern in the public health and tobacco control community for fear that these products may be especially appealing to youth (Klein et al. 2008). Clearly, these concerns should extend to cigars, as these products are even more commonly flavored. Notably, the *Family Smoking Prevention and Control Act* banned cigarettes with characterizing flavors in 2009, and some products subsequently became flavored cigars. For example. Djarum clove cigarettes re-emerged in the market as clove flavored cigars, and Sweet Dreams flavored cigarettes re-emerged as Sweet Dreams flavored cigars (Purple Haze 2011). Finally, it bears noting that some of these brands, such as Dutch Masters, White Owl, and Phillies, are particularly known for their use as blunts (Sifaneck et al. 2005), and as such, the popularity of such brands may be associated with marijuana use. This practice reinforces that the use of tobacco products co-occurs with other substances.

Trends Over Time in the Use of Cigars

As shown in Figure 3.1.41 (data from YRBS), current cigar use declined in the late 1990s for young male students, but appears to have stalled since 2003. Among young female students, slight declines in current use can be seen in Figure 3.1.41A during the 1997–2007 period, but there was an increase between 2007 and 2009. Current use among all racial/ethnic groups, as noted in Figure 3.1.41B, declined from 1997 to 2007, but there appears to have been a flattening among White students and, among Black students, a sharp increase between 2007 and 2009.

Prevalence of the Use of Cigars, Other Tobacco Products, and Other Drugs

According to the 2010 NSDUH, adolescents who used other drugs, such as alcohol, marijuana, and inhalants, had a much higher prevalence of cigar use than did nonusers of those products (Table 3.1.53). Similarly, current cigar use was higher among users of other tobacco products, such as cigarettes and smokeless tobacco, than among those who did not use those products. Current blunt users had a considerably higher usage of cigars than did nonusers, but because those cigars may be used as a device for delivering marijuana, it is surprising that the estimate for cigar use was not even higher (30.1% among users of blunts, 24.1% among users of marijuana) (Table 3.1.53). Some argue, however, that use of a blunt does not constitute cigar use because much of the cigar's content is discarded during preparation of the blunt, while others note that smoking a blunt is an important form of the initiation and regular use of tobacco (Soldz et al. 2003b; Sifaneck et al. 2005; Delnevo and Hrywna 2006). Regardless, the estimate for use of cigars by blunt users must be treated with caution, given the real possibility of underreporting. Not surprisingly, the prevalence of other drug use was higher among cigar users than among nonusers. Most notably, 65.3% of cigar users were also alcohol drinkers, 55.3% used marijuana, and 39.7% used blunts. Concurrent use of cigarettes and smokeless tobacco was noted for 60.8% and 19.1% of cigar users, respectively.

Summary

Nearly one of three high school seniors has ever tried smoking a cigar. Like smokeless tobacco, the prevalence of cigar smoking is highest among males, Whites, and older youth. The prevalence of cigar use among adolescent females is substantial and especially troubling, with estimates exceeding the prevalence of cigar smoking among adult women in some states. From 2007 to 2009, however cigar use increased significantly among female Black students, according to YRBS. From 2002 to 2010, current cigar smoking has remained stable among young adult females, overall. Likewise, among young adult males, current cigar smoking has remained stable across this period, after peaking in 2004. Cigar use appears to covary with use of other substances, such as cigarettes, smokeless tobacco, alcohol, marijuana, and blunts. The cigar data in this chapter reflect the use of large cigars, little cigars, and cigarillos.

Recent Patterns of Emerging Tobacco Products Use

Since the last Surgeon General's report on tobacco use among youth was issued, other emerging forms of tobacco, such as bidis, kreteks, and hookah, have been shown to be popular with youth in local and state surveys (CDC 1999; Taylor and Biener 2001; Soldz et al. 2003a; Hrywna et al. 2004; Primack et al. 2009). In general, documented prevalence of the use of bidis and kreteks is low (Soldz et al. 2003a; Hrywna et al. 2004; CDC 2005; Eissenberg et al. 2008; Barnett et al. 2009; Primack et al. 2009), while the use of hookahs appears to be more prevalent. Unfortunately, data collection on these emerging tobacco products has been limited to date (i.e., through 2010).

Ever Use of Specialty Cigarettes: Bidis and Kreteks

Bidis, manufactured primarily in Southeast Asia, are small brown cigarettes that are hand rolled and unfiltered; they consist of tobacco flakes rolled in a tendu leaf. According to the 2009 NYTS (Table 3.1.54), 3.1% of students in middle school (6th–8th grades) and 5.1% of students in high school (9th–12th grades) have ever smoked bidis. Male students were significantly more likely than female students to be ever users in middle school (3.8% vs. 2.3%; $p < 0.05$) and high school (5.9% vs. 4.3%; $p < 0.05$). The highest prevalence of ever use of bidis was among Hispanic students in both middle school (5.1%) and high school (7.4%), and the lowest prevalence was among White students (2.1%, middle school; 4.3%, high school) ($p < 0.05$ for Hispanic vs. White comparisons).

Kreteks were slightly less likely to have ever been used than were bidis. According to the 2009 NYTS, 1.8% of middle school students and 4.6% of high school students had ever smoked kreteks. Again, male students had a significantly higher prevalence of ever use than female students in middle school (2.4% vs. 1.2%; $p < 0.05$) and high school (5.8% vs. 3.4%; $p < 0.05$). Differences between racial/ethnic sub-groups in ever kretek use were small and generally nonsignificant ($p > 0.05$) in middle school and high school.

Current Use of Specialty Cigarettes: Bidis and Kreteks

According to the 2009 NYTS, 1.6% of middle school students (6th–8th grades) and 2.4% of high school students (9th–12th grades) were current smokers of bidis, with male students more likely than female students to be current users in both middle school (2.0% vs. 1.2%%; $p < 0.10$ and high school (2.7% vs. 2.1%; $p < 0.05$) (Table 3.1.54). Differences by race/ethnicity were small and generally nonsignificant ($p > 0.05$) in middle school and high school.

Patterns for current use of kreteks (or clove cigarettes) were similar to those for bidis (Table 3.1.54). According to the 2009 NYTS, 1.2% of middle school students and 2.4% of high school students were current users of kreteks, with males more likely than females to be users in both middle school (1.6% vs. 0.7%; $p < 0.05$) and high school (2.9% vs. 1.9%; $p < 0.10$). Differences by race/ethnicity were small and generally nonsignificant ($p > 0.05$) in middle school and high school.

Current Use of Water Pipes (Hookahs)

The use of water pipes, also known as hookahs, originated in the Middle East/ancient Persia and is an emerging trend in the twenty-first century. The MTF survey for 12th-grade students first included a question about hookah use in 2010 and found that 17% of high school seniors in the United States had used hookahs in the past year (data not shown in tables) (Johnston et al. 2011). This rate was slightly higher among boys (19%) than girls (15%) (Johnston et al. 2011). According to the 2007 Florida Youth Tobacco Survey, 4% of middle school students and 11% of high school students in that state had ever used water pipes (Barnett et al. 2009). In Florida, the prevalence of water pipe use was significantly higher for boys and for students who were ever or current smokers. Other small-scale studies on young adults indicate that the use of a water pipe is more prevalent among university students in the United States, with estimates for past-year use ranging from 22% to 40% (Primack et al. 2008; Dugas et al. 2010).

Although research on the health effects of using a hookah is limited, studies have shown that hookah smoke contains many of the same harmful components found in cigarette smoke, such as nicotine, tar, and heavy metals (Shihadeh 2003). Moreover, the heat sources used to burn hookah tobacco release other dangerous substances, including carbon monoxide and metals, that may impart additional risks to the user (World Health Organization [WHO] 2005; American Lung Association [ALA] 2007). In a typical 1-hour hookah smoking session, users may inhale 100–200 times the amount of smoke they would inhale from a single cigarette (WHO 2005). In addition, in a single water pipe session, users are exposed to up to 9 times the carbon monoxide and 1.7 times the nicotine of a single cigarette (Eissenberg and Shihadeh 2009; Maziak et al. 2009). Accordingly, over time, hookah users may be exposed to higher concentrations of toxins than are cigarette smokers. Existing studies also indicate that hookah smoking is linked to many of the same adverse health effects as cigarette smoking, including lung, oral, and bladder cancers, low birth weight in offspring, and heart disease (Knishkowy and Amitai 2005; WHO 2005; ALA 2007).

Trends Over Time in Use of Bidis and Kreteks

National trend data for the use of bidis and kreteks are available only since 1999 via NYTS. As shown in Figure 3.1.42A–H, current use of bidis and kreteks among middle school students remained relatively constant between 1999 and 2009. Current use of bidis and kreteks among high school students declined between 1999 and 2002, and then progress stalled, with no significant changes overall between 2002 and 2009. Few differences in these trends by gender or race/ethnicity were observed during this time period. Notably, the *Family Smoking Prevention and Tobacco Control Act* (2009) gave FDA the authority to regulate tobacco products and included a ban on cigarettes with characterizing flavorings. However, in anticipation of FDA regulation, some of these products, kreteks in particular, have reappeared in the marketplace as "little cigars."

Summary

The prevalence of bidi and kretek use is low and has declined over the last decade, while hookah use is higher. Surveillance data on these products are limited, however. Among middle school students, an estimated 3.1% have ever used bidis and 1.6% currently use bidis. Estimates for ever use and current use of kreteks among middle school students are slightly less (1.8% and 1.2%). Five percent of high school students have ever used bidis or kreteks, and an estimated 2% are currently using these products. Among high school seniors, 17% have smoked a hookah in the past year (Johnston et al. 2011). Other emerging tobacco products, like snus, e-cigarettes, and dissolvables, are not considered in this chapter, as nationally representative surveillance data were unavailable when this report was prepared.

Co-occurrence of Tobacco Use Behaviors

Concurrent Use of Multiple Tobacco Products

A relatively small, but not inconsequential, number of American youth use cigarettes and smokeless tobacco concurrently. According to the 2010 NSDUH, 2.0% of all youth 13–18 years of age were current users of both cigarettes and smokeless tobacco (Table 3.1.55). Per the 2009 YRBS, 5.1% of 9th- to 12th-grade students were concurrent users of these two products, and according to the 2010 MTF, 3.6% of those in 8th, 10th, and 12th grade combined. Per the 2009 NYTS, 1.3% of 6th–8th grade students and 3.8% of 9th–12th-grade students were current users of both cigarettes and smokeless tobacco (Table 3.1.55). According to the NSDUH, YRBS, MTF, and NYTS–high school, males were significantly more likely than females ($p < 0.05$) to use the products concurrently; the gender difference in NYTS–middle school was not significant. According to NSDUH, MTF, YRBS, and NYTS–high school, concurrent use of cigarettes and smokeless tobacco was highest among White students; differences between White students and other classifications were always significant in NSDUH, MTF, and YRBS ($p < 0.05$, for all comparisons between White and other racial/ethnic subgroups of students) but not in NYTS–high school. As was the case in YRBS, according to NSDUH, White youth (3.1%) were more likely to be concurrent users than were Other (0.9%), Hispanic (0.7%), or Black youth (0.2%) ($p < 0.05$ for all comparisons with White students). According to MTF, the estimates were 4.8%, White; 2.3%, Other; 2.0%, Hispanic; and 1.0%, Black ($p < 0.05$ for all comparisons with White students). In NYTS–high school, White students had the highest prevalence of concurrent use (4.7%), and this was significantly greater than the prevalence among Black (1.2%, $p < 0.05$) but not among Hispanic (3.3%) or Other students (3.3%) ($p > 0.05$). Concurrent use increased with greater age in NSDUH ($p < 0.05$

for all age comparisons). In MTF, 8th-grade students (2.1%) were significantly less likely to be concurrent users than were 10th-grade students (3.9%, $p < 0.05$ vs. 8th-grade students) or 12th-grade students (5.2%, $p < 0.05$ vs. 8th-grade students). In YRBS, concurrent use was significantly greater among 11th-grade (6.2%, $p < 0.05$ vs. 9th-grade students) and 12th-grade students (5.2%, $p < 0.05$ vs. 9th-grade students) than among 9th-grade students (3.4%). According to NYTS–middle school, there were no significant differences by age, but per NYTS–high school, 9th-grade students (2.4%) were significantly less likely to use both products than were 10th- (3.6%), 11th- (4.8%), and 12th-grade students (4.5%) ($p < 0.05$ for all comparisons). Regional variations were found in all surveys; the highest prevalence of concurrent use was in the Midwest and South per NSDUH, YRBS, and MTF, and the prevalence in these regions was significantly higher than in the other regions in all three surveys ($p < 0.05$).

The previous Surgeon General's report on preventing tobacco use among youth suggested that adolescents who use smokeless tobacco are more likely to become cigarette smokers (USDHHS 1994). Since that time there has been much debate on whether using smokeless tobacco serves as a gateway to later cigarette use (Kozlowski et al. 2003; Tomar 2003; O'Connor et al. 2005); data from MTF on grade of first use of cigarettes and smokeless tobacco among male high school seniors are presented in Table 3.1.56. By the 12th grade, 47.7% of seniors had not tried cigarettes or smokeless tobacco, 24.2% had tried both, 24.3% had tried cigarettes but not smokeless tobacco, and 3.8% had tried smokeless tobacco but not cigarettes. Of those students who had tried both cigarettes and smokeless tobacco by 12th grade, 50.5% had tried cigarettes before trying smokeless tobacco, 35.0% had tried both smokeless tobacco and cigarettes at about the same time, and 14.6% had tried smokeless first.

The use of multiple tobacco products is fairly common among adolescent males, as illustrated in Figure 3.1.43. Overall, 29.9% of high school male students for YRBS and 19.4% of high school males for NSDUH were current users of at least one type of tobacco product. Among males of high school age who were users of at least one tobacco product, use of cigarettes alone was more common than any other combination of tobacco products for NSDUH (39.3%), and combined use of cigarettes and cigars was the most common combination for YRBS (21.2%). Although few male student users of tobacco solely combined cigars and smokeless products (5.0%) or cigarettes and smokeless products (9.6%) for YRBS, a considerable percentage combined use of cigarettes, cigars, and smokeless tobacco (19.2%).

Figure 3.1.44 illustrates trends in the percentage of high school students who were current users (i.e., in the past 30 days) of two or more different types of tobacco products (dual use or concurrent use) between 1997 and 2009 according to YRBS. Among students who used at least one type of tobacco product, males were about twice as likely as females to be concurrent users in each year from 1997 to 2009 (Figure 3.1.44A). Among male tobacco users, Blacks had a lower prevalence of at least dual use during this time period than White or Hispanic males (Figure 3.1.44B). In the same time period among female tobacco users, Hispanics had the highest prevalence, followed by Black and then White females (Figure 3.1.44C). In 2009, 58.0% of Hispanic male tobacco users and 55.8% of White male tobacco users were concurrent users, as were 43.4% of Hispanic female tobacco users, according to YRBS.

Tables 3.1.57 and 3.1.58 illustrate the initiation of smokeless tobacco use among 12- to 17-year-olds (Table 3.1.57) and 18- to 25-year-olds (Table 3.1.58) between 2006 and 2010. The percentage of adolescents who were initiates remained stable at 2.4% from 2006 to 2010. The percentage of young adults who were initiates also remained stable from 2.1% in 2006 to 2.3%. While the market for moist snuff overall grew by 18% between 2005 and 2007, the "value" and deep-discount brands sold grew by 70% (Delnevo et al. 2009; Maxwell 2009b). Moreover, although deep-discount brands were responsible for 81% of the growth in moist snuff overall, one brand, Grizzly, accounted for 55% of the overall growth in consumption of moist snuff between 2005 and 2007.

Data for cigars over the same 5-year period (2006–2010) show a higher rate of initiation, roughly 4–5% per year for youth 12–17 years of age (Table 3.1.59) and 6% per year for young adults 18–25 years of age (Table 3.1.60). The percentage of initiates declined significantly between 2006 and 2010 among adolescents overall, and among male and White adolescents ($p < 0.05$); among females, it rose significantly ($p < 0.05$). The difference among young adults between 2006 and 2010 was only significant for Hispanics ($p < 0.05$); this was an increase. Taken together, the number of adolescents and young adults who began using cigars in 2010 was about 2.3 million. Perhaps the most disconcerting trend in cigar use initiation is that, among youth, girls made up roughly 40% of the initiates every year.

The number of initiates of "any tobacco product" can be seen to be less than the number of initiates of cigarettes, cigars, and smokeless tobacco combined, suggesting that when youth and young adults initiate tobacco use, some do so with more than one product, or they quickly switch to another product. Among youth, initiation of any tobacco product fluctuated between 7.3% and 7.9% during 2006 to 2010. In 2010, an estimated 1.48 million youth 12–17 years of age tried at least one tobacco product for the first time (Table 3.1.61). The initiation rate for any tobacco products among young adults was higher than that for youth (Table 3.1.62). The rate for young adults remained stable during the 5-year period from 2006 to 2010 ($p > 0.05$) overall.

Summary

Among adolescent and young adult tobacco users, concurrent use of cigarettes, smokeless tobacco, and/or cigars is common. Males, Whites, Hispanics, and older youth are most likely to use these products concurrently, and Blacks are the least likely. In 2009, among tobacco users, more than 50% of high school White males and Hispanic males were concurrent users, as were more than 40% of high school Hispanic females. The data are mixed as to whether users of smokeless tobacco are more likely to begin smoking cigarettes than are nonusers of smokeless tobacco. The initiation rates of smokeless tobacco among adolescents and young adults did not increase significantly between 2006 and 2010. Initiation of cigar use decreased significantly among adolescents during this time and remained constant among young adults. For all tobacco products combined (cigarettes, smokeless tobacco, and cigars), White youth had the highest rates of initiation except in 2009, when Hispanic youth reported rates of initiation similar to Whites. The rate of initiation of any tobacco product during this time period was considerably higher among adolescents than for young adults.

Tobacco Use Among Young People Worldwide

Global Youth Tobacco Survey

This section of Chapter 3 focuses on tobacco use among adolescents worldwide. Since the 1994 Surgeon General's report on reducing tobacco use among young people, a new global surveillance system, the Global Youth Tobacco Survey (GYTS), developed by CDC and WHO at the end of 1998, has become available. GYTS is part of the Global Tobacco Surveillance System (GTSS), which monitors tobacco use among various populations (e.g., youth, school personnel, adults, health professionals) worldwide. Since 1999, GYTS has been conducted at least once in all six of the WHO regions, across more than 140 countries and 11 territories (Warren et al. 2008). All participating countries can repeat the survey once every 4–5 years (Warren et al. 2008). A core questionnaire is used across all sites, as is a common survey methodology. The survey is administered to 13- to 15-year-old students enrolled in a random sample of schools drawn from the sampling frame.

The data presented in this chapter update and/or complement data presented in previous publications from GYTS (e.g., CDC 2006; Warren et al. 2008). The data presented below focus on cigarette smoking and the use of other tobacco products (e.g., smokeless tobacco, bidis). Estimates are presented for each site that participated in the survey (i.e., each country, territory). Weighted aggregate estimates are also provided for each of the six WHO regions: Africa (AFRO), the Americas (PAHO), the Eastern Mediterranean (EMRO), Europe (EURO), South-East Asia (SEARO), and the Western Pacific (WPRO). These data are presented in Tables 3.1.63–3.1.66 (also see Figures 3.1.45–3.1.48).

Cigarette Smoking

Overall, per the 1999–2009 GYTS, about one in four (27.3%) students aged 13–15 years had ever smoked a cigarette (Table 3.1.63). The prevalence of ever smoking was highest in EURO (39.7%) and lowest in AFRO (11.5%). In general, the proportion of students who had ever smoked a cigarette was higher among boys (34.2%) than girls (18.2%). This pattern was observed in all six regions, with the differential ranging from 6.0 percentage points in PAHO to 21.1 percentage points in WPRO. Almost one in every four (23.2%) ever smokers had tried their first cigarette before the age of 10 years. Early initiation (<10 years of age) was most prevalent in EURO (26.8%) and least prevalent in PAHO (16.1%). The proportion of ever smokers who tried their first cigarette before the age of 10 years was higher for boys in all regions, except for SEARO, where it was higher for girls. Among students who had never smoked, one in six (17.6%) was susceptible (i.e., had no firm decision not to smoke) to initiating the smoking of cigarettes in the next year. The prevalence of susceptibility was highest in EURO (25.1%) and lowest in AFRO (10.1%). Boys were more susceptible to starting to smoke in AFRO, EMRO, and PAHO, while girls were more susceptible in SEARO, EURO, and WPRO.

Overall, 7.1% of youth (9.3% of boys and 4.0% of girls) currently smoked cigarettes (Table 3.1.64). The prevalence of current smoking was highest in WPRO

(13.7%) and lowest in AFRO (4.0%). Frequent smoking was highest in EURO (1.9%) and lowest in EMRO and AFRO (0.6%). The proportion of current smokers who smoked frequently was higher for boys in all six regions.

Overall, 9.6% of current smokers either always had or felt like having a cigarette the first thing in the morning (Table 3.1.65); this measure can be used as an indicator of nicotine dependence (Chapter 2). This prevalence was highest in EMRO (10.5%) and lowest in PAHO (4.6%). It was higher among boys than for girls in all regions except for AFRO. Three-quarters (75.6%) of current smokers wanted to quit smoking, and 74.7% of current smokers had tried to quit smoking at least once in the past year.

Other Tobacco Products

Overall, 7.1% of the 13- to 15-year-old students were current users of a tobacco product other than a cigarette (e.g., pipes, smokeless tobacco, bidis) (Table 3.1.66). This prevalence was highest in EMRO (16.5%) and lowest in EURO (4.9%). The proportion of students who currently used a tobacco product other than cigarettes was higher among boys than girls in all six regions, although this differential was relatively small in all of the regions. Current use of other tobacco products was more common than use of cigarettes in AFRO, EMRO, and SEARO, while in EURO, WPRO, and PAHO, cigarette use was more common (Tables 3.1.64, 3.1.66).

European School Survey Project on Alcohol and Other Drugs

At present, the only part of the world that GYTS does not cover comprehensively is Western Europe, where other surveillance systems are used. The European School Survey Project on Alcohol and Other Drugs (ESPAD), which is coordinated by the Swedish Council for Information on Alcohol and Other Drugs, is one example. Data were first collected on this project from 16-year-olds in 1995, and subsequent data collections have been made every fourth year. The overarching goal of ESPAD is to study substance use among adolescents throughout Europe by using a standardized epidemiological survey to compare these data between countries. Data from ESPAD are provided in Table 3.1.67. In contrast to GYTS, which surveys youth 13–15 years of age, ESPAD surveys youth at 16 years of age only. Thus, the estimates presented below for current cigarette smoking would be expected to exceed those presented above from GYTS.

The latest survey available from ESPAD is for 2007 (Hibell et al. 2009); with a few exceptions, the prevalence of current (i.e., past 30 days) cigarette smoking exceeded 20% across the countries included in the survey. Prevalence was highest in Austria (45%) and several Eastern European countries (Czech Republic, 41%; Latvia, 41%; Bulgaria, 40%) and lowest in Armenia (7%). The other countries with low levels were in the north (Iceland, 16%; Norway, 19%; Sweden, 21%) and in Portugal (19%) and Poland (21%). In 13 countries, current smoking was higher among boys (e.g., in Russia, 41% of boys and 29% of girls were current smokers), and in 21 countries, current smoking was higher among girls (e.g., in Ireland, 27% of girls and 19% of boys were current smokers).

Appendix 3.2. Sources of Data

Global Youth Tobacco Survey

The World Health Organization (WHO), the Centers for Disease Control and Prevention (CDC), and the Canadian Public Health Association developed the Global Tobacco Surveillance System (GTSS) to assist countries in establishing tobacco control surveillance and monitoring programs (CDC 2010b). GTSS includes the collection of data through four surveys: the Global Youth Tobacco Survey (GYTS), the Global School Personnel Survey, the Global Health Professions Students Survey, and the Global Adult Tobacco Survey. This report of the Surgeon General uses data from GYTS that countries rely on to enhance their capacity to monitor tobacco use among youth and to guide national programs in preventing and controlling tobacco use; the data are also used to facilitate comparison of tobacco-related data at the national, regional, and global levels. Since 1999, GYTS has been conducted in 140 countries and 11 territories across all six WHO regions and has become the most comprehensive system for youth tobacco surveillance ever developed and implemented (Warren et al. 2008).

The target population for a GYTS can be national or regional, or the survey can focus on specific urban or rural areas, depending on data requirements, resources, and safety considerations. The standard GYTS uses a two-stage cluster sample design that produces samples of students enrolled in the grades that students 13–15 years of age typically attend. Each sampling frame includes all schools (usually both public and private) in a geographically defined area that contain any of the identified grades. In the first sampling stage, schools are selected with a probability that matches their enrollment in the identified grades. In the second sampling stage, classes within the selected schools are randomly selected. All students in selected classes who are enrolled the day the survey is administered are eligible to participate. Schools that decline to participate in the original sample are not replaced. The standard GYTS sample design is tailored to meet the needs of participating countries, territories, and regions. All data are weighted to produce estimates representative of students in each country, territory, or region (Warren et al. 2008).

GYTS questionnaires are translated into local languages as needed and back-translated to check them for accuracy. Country coordinators for GYTS conduct focus groups of students 13–15 years of age to further test the accuracy of the translation and the students' comprehension of the questions. Trained personnel administer the questionnaires to students in their classrooms. Students complete self-administered paper-and-pencil questionnaires and record their responses on computer-scannable answer sheets; participation is voluntary and anonymous (Warren et al. 2008).

The sample sizes for students aged 13–15 years among the 170 GYTS sites included in this report of the Surgeon General ranged from 129 to 15,420. Student response rates ranged from 53.2% to 100.0%, class response rates ranged from 53.0% to 100.0%, school response rates ranged from 50.0% to 100.0%, and the overall response rate (the product of the rates for students, classes, and schools) ranged from 32.3% to 100.0% (median: 84.9%). GYTS data from 1999 to 2008 are available by registering at the CDC Web site (CDC 2009a).

Monitoring the Future Study

Monitoring the Future (MTF): A Continuing Study of American Youth is a study of American adolescents, college students, and adults through the age of 45 years. The purpose of this study is to monitor changes in the beliefs, attitudes, and behavior of young people in the United States that are relevant to drug use and other health and social issues. Self-administered paper-and-pencil questionnaires are used to survey nationally representative samples of 12th-grade students in public and private schools in 48 of the 50 states (all but Alaska and Hawaii). Follow-up surveys using self-administered paper-and-pencil questionnaires mailed to the residence of a randomly selected subsample of the respondents in each 12th-grade sample are conducted biennially through 30 years of age and then every 5 years through 45 years of age. Since 1991, self-administered paper-and-pencil questionnaires also have been used to survey separate nationally representative samples of 8th- and 10th-grade students in public and private schools (Johnston et al. 2007). The MTF study, ongoing on an annual basis since its inception in 1975, is conducted by the University of Michigan's Institute for Social Research and supported through grants from the National Institute on Drug Abuse (Johnston et al. 2008).

The 12th-grade surveys and follow-up surveys in MTF have always used confidential questionnaires. From 1991 to 1997, the 8th- and 10th-grade surveys also used confidential questionnaires, but in 1998, one-half of the 8th- and 10th-grade samples used confidential questionnaires (name provided but confidentiality assured) and the remaining half used anonymous questionnaires. Since 1999, the 8th- and 10th-grade surveys have used anonymous questionnaires. A study of the 1998 split-sample results revealed no effect of the change in methods among 10th-grade students and a modest effect on self-reported substance use among 8th-grade students (i.e., prevalence was slightly higher for anonymous surveys) (Johnston et al. 2007).

For the 8th-, 10th-, and 12th-grade samples, a three-stage cluster sample design is used to select (1) geographic areas within the 48 contiguous states, (2) schools with a probability proportional to their enrollment, and (3) students. Students are selected either randomly by classroom or by some other unbiased random method. Schools are invited to participate in the study for a 2-year period. To maintain an adequate sample size, for each school that declines to participate in the original school sample a similar school (in terms of gender, geographic area, level of urbanization, and other demographic characteristics) is recruited as a replacement for that slot (Johnston et al. 2007). Schools are provided $1,000 each year to increase their incentive to participate (Bachman et al. 2006).

In 2009, 15,509 8th-grade students, 16,320 10th-grade students, and 14,268 12th-grade students participated in the MTF study. In all, 389 schools participated: 145, 119, and 125 in the 8th-, 10th-, and 12th-grade surveys, respectively. Response rates for the students were 88%, 89%, and 82% for the 8th, 10th, and 12th grades, respectively (Johnston et al. 2010). In the MTF design, one slot is identified for each selected sample unit. For each slot, 55% of originally selected 8th-grade schools,

52% of originally selected 10th-grade schools, and 55% of originally selected 12th-grade schools agreed to participate in the survey; for those slots where originally selected schools did not participate, a replacement school was selected such that of the school slots for grades 8, 10, and 12, 97%, 99%, and 99%, respectively, were filled (personal communication, Patrick O'Malley, MTF, July 2010). MTF study data from the cross-sectional in-school surveys conducted from 1976 to 2008 are available at the Substance Abuse & Mental Health Data Archive (University of Michigan 2012).

National Health Interview Survey

The National Health Interview Survey (NHIS) is a multipurpose survey conducted by the National Center for Health Statistics of the CDC and is the principal source of information on the health of the civilian, noninstitutionalized population of the United States. NHIS has been conducted continuously since 1957. Questions on smoking have been included in selected survey years only since 1965, and detailed items allowing classification by race and ethnicity have been included only since 1978. Face-to-face interviews are used to collect confidential data from a representative sample of the population at their place of residence (National Center for Health Statistics 2008).

The sampling plan follows a multistage area probability design that permits the representative sampling of households and noninstitutional group quarters (e.g., college dormitories) in all 50 states and the District of Columbia (DC). African American or Black, Hispanic or Latino, and Asian persons are oversampled. For each family in NHIS, one sample child (<18 years of age) and one sample adult are randomly selected, and information on each is collected. For children and those adults not at home during the interview, information is provided by a knowledgeable adult family member. Since 1974, only self-reports of cigarette smoking and use of other tobacco products have been employed. Thus, no proxy data have been used since 1974 on questions of import to this report. NHIS is conducted using computer-assisted personal interviewing by interviewers from the U.S. Census Bureau; sampling and interviewing are continuous throughout each year (National Center for Health Statistics 2008).

The interviewed sample for the 2009 NHIS consisted of 33,856 households, which yielded 88,446 persons in 34,640 families. The 2009 NHIS obtained data on health behaviors for 27,731 sampled adults. These data were collected by an interview administered in person to this group of adults, who constitute a nationally representative sample of the noninstitutionalized U.S. civilian population 18 years of age or older. The total household response rate was 82.2%, and the overall survey response rate for the adult component of the NHIS survey, which was used here, was 65.4%. NHIS data from 1978 to 2009 are available at the CDC Web site (CDC 2009b).

National Longitudinal Study of Adolescent Health

The National Longitudinal Study of Adolescent Health (Add Health) is a nationally representative study that explores the causes of health-related behaviors of adolescents in grades 7–12 and the outcomes of these behaviors in young adulthood. Add Health examines how social contexts (families, friends, peers, schools, neighborhoods, and communities) influence adolescents' health and risk behaviors. The study was designed and continues to be conducted by the Carolina Population Center at the University of North Carolina at Chapel Hill and is funded by a grant from the *Eunice Kennedy Shriver* National Institute of Child Health and Human Development. The study also receives funding from 17 other federal agencies (University of North Carolina 2009).

Add Health uses a longitudinal design; data were collected at baseline (Wave I, conducted during 1994 and 1995), for a second time at a 1-year interval (Wave II, conducted during 1996), and for a third time at a 6-year interval (Wave III, conducted during 2001 and 2002). The study includes in-school and in-home questionnaires for students and questionnaires for parents and school administrators (University of North Carolina 2009).

Wave I, Stage 1: A stratified random sample of 80 U.S. high schools was selected to participate in Stage 1 of Wave I. A school was eligible for the sample if it included an 11th grade and had a minimum of 30 students. More than 70% of the originally sampled high schools participated. Each school that declined to participate was replaced by a school within the stratum. A feeder school—a school that sent graduates to the high school and that included a 7th grade—was also recruited from the community. Because some high schools spanned grades 7–12, they functioned as their own feeder school, and the "pair" was in fact a single school. In total, 132 schools participated in Wave I. Students and school administrators both completed confidential computer-scannable questionnaires that were self-administered and used paper and pencil.

Wave I, Stage 2: An in-home sample of 27,000 adolescents was selected for Stage 2, Wave I, consisting of a core sample from each school plus selected special oversamples. Oversamples were drawn to explore additional study questions such as examining the influence of genetic factors on adolescent health. Eligibility for oversamples was determined by an adolescent's responses on the in-school questionnaire. Adolescents could qualify for more than one oversample. In the analyses reported here, information from only the core sample of adolescents was used, not the oversamples. Data collected in the home from adolescents were recorded on laptop computers. For less sensitive sections, trained interviewers read the questions and entered the adolescent's answers. For more sensitive sections, such as tobacco use, the adolescent listened to prerecorded questions through earphones and entered the answers directly using ACASI (audio computer-assisted self-interviewing). In addition, parents were asked to complete an interviewer-assisted, computer-scannable questionnaire.

Wave II: The in-home sample for Wave II was the same group included in the Wave I in-home sample, with a few exceptions. The mode of data collection also was the same. In addition, school administrators were contacted by telephone to update information on their schools.

Wave III: The in-home Wave III sample consisted of 15,170 Wave I respondents who could be located and reinterviewed 6 years later. A sample of 1,507 partners of the original respondents were also interviewed. Release forms to obtain high school transcripts as well as samples of urine and saliva were collected during Wave III.

National Survey on Drug Use and Health

The National Survey on Drug Use and Health (NSDUH) is an annual survey of the civilian, noninstitutionalized population of the United States 12 years of age or older. Before 2002, this survey, which has been conducted by the federal government since 1971, was called the National Household Survey on Drug Abuse. NSDUH is the primary source of statistical information on the use of illegal drugs by the U.S. population; face-to-face interviews are used to collect confidential data from a representative sample of the population at their place of residence. The survey is sponsored by the Substance Abuse and Mental Health Services Administration (SAMHSA) of the U.S. Department of Health and Human Services and is planned and managed by SAMHSA's Office of Applied Studies (SAMHSA 2009b).

Since 1999, SAMHSA has implemented major improvements in the methods used in this survey (SAMHSA 2009a). Because of changes in the survey instrument, recent trends over time are available only from 2002 to 2010 (SAMHSA 2010). Data are collected using computer-assisted interviewing (CAI), and respondents are given a US$30 incentive payment for participation. The total targeted sample size of 67,500 for each year is equally allocated across three age groups: 12–17 years, 18–25 years, and 26 years of age or older. The 2010 NSDUH sampling frame included residents of noninstitutional group quarters (e.g., shelters, rooming houses, dormitories, and group homes), residents of Alaska and Hawaii as well as those in the other 48 states plus DC, and civilians living on military bases. Persons excluded from the 2010 universe were those with no fixed household address (e.g., homeless transients not in shelters) and residents of institutional group quarters (e.g., jails and hospitals). The 2010 NSDUH employed a state-based design with an independent, multistage area probability sample within each state and DC. The eight states with the largest population (which together account for about one-half of the total U.S. population 12 years old or older) were designated as large-sample states (California, Florida, Illinois, Michigan, New York, Ohio, Pennsylvania, and Texas) and had a sample size of about 3,600 each. For the remaining 42 states and DC, the sample size was about 900 per state (SAMHSA 2010). However, combining data over multiple survey years allows direct estimates for all states. The 2010 NSDUH was conducted from January to December of that year. The overall weighted response rate in 2010, defined as the product of the weighted screening response rate, was 88.8%, and the weighted interview response rate, 74.7%, was 66.3%. A total of 68,487 persons were included in the main sample. The NSDUH public use microdata files from 2002 to 2010 are available for download and online analysis (University of Michigan 2012).

National Youth Tobacco Survey

The National Youth Tobacco Survey (NYTS) was developed by CDC to assist with the evaluation of the national tobacco prevention and control program (TCP) and state TCPs. The NYTS provides nationally representative data on tobacco-related behaviors among middle school (grades 6–8) and high school (grades 9–12) students. NYTS was first conducted in the fall of 1999 and has since been conducted in 2000, 2002, 2004, 2006, and 2009. The NYTS sampling frame consists of all students enrolled in public, Catholic, and other private middle schools and high schools (grades 6–12) in the 50 states and DC. In the 2009 NYTS, Black and Hispanic students were oversampled. The survey uses a three-stage cluster sample design, with units in the first stage stratified by racial composition and urban/rural classification. In the first sampling stage, primary sampling units (PSUs), defined as a county, a group of smaller counties, or a portion of a very large county, within each stratum are randomly sampled without replacement, with probability proportional to the total number of eligible students enrolled in all eligible schools within the PSU. In the second stage, schools within each selected PSU are randomly selected with probability proportional to the number of eligible students enrolled in the school. In the third and final stage, classes within each selected school are randomly selected. All students in the chosen classes are eligible to participate in the survey, although participation is voluntary and anonymous. Participants complete a self-administered paper-and-pencil questionnaire and record their responses on a computer-scannable questionnaire booklet (CDC 2009d).

In the 2009 NYTS, 205 of the 222 selected schools participated (92.3% school response rate) and 22,679 of the 24,666 selected students participated (91.9% student response rate), resulting in an overall response rate of 84.8% (CDC 2009d).

Youth Risk Behavior Surveillance System

The Youth Risk Behavior Surveillance System (YRBSS) monitors six categories of priority health-risk behaviors among adolescents in the United States: (1) behaviors that contribute to unintentional injuries and violence; (2) tobacco use; (3) alcohol and other drug use; (4) sexual behaviors that result in unintended pregnancy and sexually transmitted infections, including HIV; (5) unhealthy dietary behaviors; and (6) physical inactivity. In addition, YRBSS monitors the prevalence of asthma and obesity and overweight calculated from self-reported height and weight (CDC 2004). YRBSS consists of Youth Risk Behavior Surveys (YRBSs) conducted by state, local, territorial, and tribal health and education agencies and a national YRBS conducted by CDC. CDC developed YRBSS in 1990 and provides cooperative agreement funding and technical assistance for the state, local, territorial, and tribal surveys (CDC 2004). The current report includes data from the national YRBS and the state YRBSs.

The sampling frame for the national YRBS is all public and private school students in grades 9–12 in the 50 states and DC. A three-stage cluster sample design is used to sample (1) large-sized counties or groups of smaller adjacent counties, (2) public and private schools with a probability proportional to the schools' enrollment, and (3) one or two randomly selected classes in each grade. Examples of classes include homerooms, classes of a required discipline (e.g., English or social studies), and all classes meeting during a required period (e.g., second period). All students in a sampled class are eligible to participate. Oversampling is used to achieve sufficiently large subsamples of Black or African American and Hispanic or Latino students to enable separate analyses of these subgroups. Schools that decline to participate in the original sample are not replaced (CDC 2004).

The target population for the state YRBSs comprises all public school students in grades 9–12 in all but a few participating states. A two-stage cluster sample design is used to produce representative samples of students in grades 9–12 in each jurisdiction. In the first sampling stage in all but a few states, schools are selected with probability proportional to school enrollment or size. In the second sampling stage, intact classes of a required subject or intact classes during a required period (e.g., second period) are selected randomly. All students in sampled classes are eligible to participate. Certain states modify these procedures to meet their individual needs, such as selecting all schools rather than a sample of schools to participate (CDC 2004).

For both the national and state surveys, students complete self-administered paper-and-pencil questionnaires and record their answers directly on the questionnaire booklet or a separate computer-scannable answer sheet (CDC 2004). Local procedures to obtain the permission of parents are followed. Trained personnel administer the questionnaires to students in their classrooms for the national survey and most state surveys. The participation of students is both voluntary and anonymous (CDC 2004). The national YRBS and most state YRBSs are conducted during the spring of odd-numbered years (CDC 2004).

In 2009, 16,410 students in grades 9–12 from 158 schools participated in the national YRBS. The student response rate was 88%, the school response rate was 81%, and the overall response rate (the product of the student and school response rates) was 71%. National YRBS data from 1991 to 2009 are available at CDC's Web site (CDC 2010c). The number of states conducting a YRBS has varied each cycle, from a low of 26 in 1991 to a high of 47 in 2009 (Eaton et al. 2010). States must meet three criteria (a scientifically selected sample at the school and student levels, appropriate documentation, and an overall response rate of 60% or more) before their data are weighted to be representative of all students in grades 9–12 attending public schools in their jurisdiction (CDC 2004). In 2009, 42 states (and 20 local municipalities) conducted a YRBS that met the criteria for weighting and were included in an analyses reported here. The size of the student samples across these surveys ranged from 965 to 14,870. Student response rates ranged from 61% to 94%, the response rate for schools ranged from 73% to 100%, and overall response rates ranged from 60% to 94% (Eaton et al. 2010). Additional information about YRBS is available at at CDC's Web site (CDC 2010b).

Appendix 3.3. Measures of Tobacco Use

Validity of Measures of Tobacco Use

All of the data on tobacco use among youth that are presented in this report are based on retrospective self-reported responses to questionnaires. Because of the retrospective nature of data collection, and because tobacco use is viewed by many as a socially undesirable behavior, there is a risk of inaccurate or dishonest responses. Because it was not feasible to verify the self-reported data included here, it is important for researchers to interpret these data with some caution and an understanding of possible sources of inaccuracy. Many factors can affect the validity of self-reported data—factors that can be categorized as cognitive or situational. Cognitive processes that affect responses include comprehension of the question, retrieval of relevant information from memory, decision making about the adequacy of the information retrieved, and the generation of a response (Brener et al. 2003). Each of these processes can contribute to errors in responses and, subsequently, to problems with validity.

Situational factors that affect the validity of self-reported data refer to characteristics of the external environment in which the survey is being conducted. These include the setting (i.e., school or home based), the method (i.e., self-administered questionnaire or in-person interview), the social desirability of the behavior being reported, and the perception of privacy and/or confidentiality of responses (U.S. Department of Health and Human Services [USDHHS] 1994; Brener et al. 2003). Many studies have found that youth report a higher number of sensitive behaviors when a survey is completed in a school setting rather than in their homes (Gfroerer et al. 1997; Hedges and Jarvis 1998; Kann et al. 2002). One study in particular compared the school-based national Youth Risk Behavior Survey (YRBS) with the household-based YRBS supplement to the National Health Interview Survey (NHIS). That study found that the school-based survey produced a significantly higher reporting of many sensitive behaviors, such as driving after drinking alcohol, binge drinking, and current use of marijuana and cocaine (Kann et al. 2002). Four measures of various stages of the smoking uptake process were higher in the school-based survey, but current cigarette use and frequent cigarette use, while elevated in the school-based survey, were not significantly different from estimates generated in the household-based survey. Few differences in nonsensitive behaviors were observed. Two other studies indicate that while self-reported estimates of current use of alcohol and illicit drugs were higher in school-based versus household-based surveys, estimates of current cigarette smoking were quite similar across settings (Gfroerer et al. 1997; Brener et al. 2006). It is noteworthy that all three of these studies used self- rather than interviewer-administered interviews/questionnaires. Nevertheless, the provision of privacy that school surveys provide is important, especially if smoking becomes more socially unacceptable over time. However, household-based surveys are more likely to include youth who drop out of school or are frequently absent from school, and these groups are more likely to smoke.

Self-administered methods of data collection have generally produced higher reporting of sensitive behaviors, including tobacco use, than have interviewer-administered methods (Turner et al. 1992; Aquilino 1994; Brittingham et al. 1998). For example, Turner and colleagues (1992) found that the prevalence of current smoking among 12- to 17-year-olds reported on the self-administered version of the National Household Survey on Drug Abuse (NSDUH) home-based survey was considerably higher (by 10–30%) than on the interviewer-administered version. The absence of personal interaction with an interviewer on self-administered surveys may reduce the reporting biases associated with perceived privacy and the social desirability of a behavior (Brener et al. 2003).

Another situational influence is the use of the "bogus pipeline" (Brener et al. 2003). This method has been used to improve the validity of self-reported measures of smoking, especially in school-based surveys. Respondents are told that a biochemical test will be used to accurately evaluate their smoking behavior after the questionnaire is completed, although in fact such a test will not be employed. This method has been associated with higher reported smoking prevalence (Aguinis et al. 1993). None of the surveys used in this report make use of the bogus pipeline, but each survey has taken alternate steps to ensure that the survey setting is private and that the data collected are at least confidential if not anonymous.

In conclusion, the factors described above may affect the point estimate of smoking prevalence. However, if these factors remain stable over the years, they should not affect the trends seen over time.

Measures of Cigarette Smoking

Information on the measures of cigarette smoking used in this report is provided below and in Appendix Table 3.3.1.

Ever Smoking

The definitions for ever smoking vary slightly in the four surveys used in this report. In the NSDUH, an ever smoker is defined as someone who has ever smoked "part or all of a cigarette." In Monitoring the Future (MTF), respondents who report having smoked cigarettes at least "once or twice" are considered ever users. In the YRBSS and the National Youth Tobacco Survey (NYTS), an ever smoker is one who has "ever tried cigarette smoking, even one or two puffs."

Current Smoking

Five surveys—NSDUH, the Global Youth Tobacco Survey (GYTS), NYTS, MTF, and YRBSS—define current smoking as having smoked cigarettes during the 30 days preceding the survey. NSDUH asks whether the respondent has smoked "part or all of a cigarette" in the past 30 days to determine current usage. GYTS and NYTS regard current smokers as those who smoked cigarettes on 1 or more of the past 30 days. MTF asks how frequently students have smoked cigarettes during the past 30 days, and the choices range from "not at all" to "two packs or more per day." A response other than "not at all" categorizes that respondent as a current smoker. For YRBS, a student who reports having smoked on at least 1 or 2 days during the past 30 days is considered a current smoker.

Intensity of Smoking

Intensity of smoking is characterized by the frequency and heaviness of cigarette smoking. NSDUH, YRBS, and NYTS include separate measures for these two factors, while MTF measures only heaviness. In this Surgeon General's report, frequent smoking is defined as smoking on at least 20 of the 30 days preceding the survey. For NSDUH, respondents are asked to enter the total number of days smoked (Appendix Table 3.3.1). In YRBS and NYTS, students are asked to report how many days they smoked during the past 30 days; they are considered frequent smokers if they choose either "20 to 29 days" or "all 30 days."

In this report, heavy smoking is generally defined as smoking at least one-half of a pack of cigarettes per day during the past 30 days. NSDUH asks for the average number of cigarettes smoked per day on the days smoked, and respondents who choose "6 to 15 cigarettes (about ½ pack)" or above fall into the heavy smoker category. For YRBS and NYTS, students are asked: "During the past 30 days, on the days you smoked, how many cigarettes did you smoke per day?" Students who choose 11 or more cigarettes per day are considered heavy smokers. MTF asks how "frequently" students have smoked during the past 30 days. Students who answer with at least "about one-half pack per day" are categorized as heavy smokers (Appendix Table 3.2.1).

Initiation of Smoking

This report provides information about the initiation of cigarette smoking from five surveys—NSDUH, MTF, YRBS, NYTS, and NHIS—three of which use age. The age of initiation is measured in NSDUH as when a participant first smoked "part or all of a cigarette," in YRBSS and NYTS it is when the subject first smoked a whole cigarette, and in NHIS it is when the person first started to "smoke fairly regularly." MTF asks for the school grade in which a student (1) first smoked a cigarette and (2) began to smoke "on a daily basis."

Brand Preference

In NSDUH, participants are asked to select the brand of cigarettes smoked most often during the past 30 days. They are given a list of 25 common brands, with the additional option of "A brand not on this list." They are also asked to select the type of cigarettes most often smoked, either lights, ultra lights, mediums, or full flavor. These two responses were combined to determine the most popular subbrands among young people.

Attempts to Quit Smoking

Attempts to quit smoking are measured by MTF and YRBS. MTF asks participants: "Have you ever tried to stop smoking and found that you could not?" and "How many times (if any) have you tried to stop smoking?" YRBS asks: "During the past 12 months, did you ever try to quit smoking cigarettes?"

Measures of the Use of Smokeless Tobacco

Ever Use of Smokeless Tobacco

The definitions for ever use of smokeless tobacco vary slightly in the three surveys used in this report. For NSDUH, two questions are asked that address chewing tobacco and moist snuff separately; an ever user of smokeless tobacco is defined as someone who reports having "ever used snuff, even once" and/or has "ever used chewing tobacco, even once." For MTF and NYTS, one survey question is used. Respondents on MTF who report ever having taken or used smokeless tobacco (defined for the participant as "chewing tobacco, plug, dipping tobacco, snuff") at least "Once or twice" are considered ever users. For NYTS, a similar question is used, but smokeless tobacco is defined as "chewing tobacco, snuff, or dip, such as Redman, Levi Garrett, Beechnut, Skoal, Skoal Bandits, or Copenhagen."

Current Use of Smokeless Tobacco

NSDUH, MTF, YRBSS, and NYTS each define current use of smokeless tobacco as having used it during the 30 days preceding the survey. NSDUH asks whether the respondent has "used snuff, even once" and/or "used chewing tobacco, even once" in the past 30 days to determine current usage. An affirmative answer to either question categorizes that respondent as a current user. MTF asks how often students have taken smokeless tobacco during the past 30 days; a response other than "Not at all" categorizes that respondent as a current user. For YRBSS and NYTS, a student who reports having used chewing tobacco, snuff, or dip on at least 1 or 2 days during the past 30 days is considered a current user.

Initiation of Smokeless Tobacco

This report provides information about the initiation of smokeless tobacco use from four surveys: NSDUH, MTF, NYTS, and GYTS. The age of initiation is measured as the age when a participant first used "chewing tobacco" and/or "snuff" (NSDUH) or, similarly, used chewing tobacco, snuff, or dip for the first time (NYTS and GYTS). MTF asks for the school grade in which a student first tried smokeless tobacco.

Brand Preference

In NSDUH, participants are asked to select the brand of snuff and/or the brand of chewing tobacco they used most often during the past 30 days. They are given a list of 13 common moist snuff brands and 11 chewing tobacco brands with the additional option of "A brand not on this list."

Measures of Cigar Use

Ever Use of Cigars

The NSDUH and NYTS surveys are used to report ever use of cigars. In NSDUH, an ever user is defined as someone who reports having "smoked part or all of any type of cigar." Respondents are instructed to consider big cigars, cigarillos, and little cigars that look like cigarettes. In NYTS, an ever user is one who reports having "tried smoking cigars, cigarillos, or little cigars, even one or two puffs."

Current Cigar Use

NSDUH, YRBSS, and NYTS each define current cigar use as having smoked cigars during the 30 days preceding the survey. NSDUH asks whether the respondent has "smoked part or all of any type of cigar" in the past 30 days to determine current usage. An affirmative answer categorizes that respondent as a current cigar smoker. For YRBSS and NYTS, a student who reports having smoked cigars, cigarillos, or little cigars on at least 1 or 2 of the past 30 days is considered a current cigar smoker.

Initiation of Cigars

This report provides information about the initiation of cigar use from NSDUH, NYTS, and GYTS. The age of initiation in NSDUH is the age when a participant first smoked part or all of any type of cigar; in NYTS and GYTS, it is when the participant smoked a cigar, cigarillo, or little cigar for the first time.

Brand Preference

In NSDUH, participants are asked to select the brand of cigars used most often during the past 30 days; they are given a list of 28 common brands, with the additional option of "A brand not on this list."

Measures of Bidi and Kretek Use

The NYTS is used to provide information about ever and current use of bidis and kreteks. For each product, an ever user is defined as someone who reports having ever tried smoking bidis or kreteks. A student who reports having smoked bidis on at least 1 or 2 of the past 30 days is considered a current bidi smoker. The product is defined for participants as "small brown cigarettes from India made of tobacco wrapped in a leaf tied with a thread." For kreteks, current smoking is defined in the same manner as for bidis: at least 1 or 2 days during the past 30 days. The product is defined for participants as "clove cigarettes or cigarettes containing tobacco and clove extract."

References

Aguinis H, Pierce CA, Quigley BM. Conditions under which a bogus pipeline procedure enhances the validity of self-reported cigarette smoking: a meta-analytic review. *Journal of Applied Social Psychology* 1993;23(5):352–73.

Ahijevych K, Garrett BE. The role of menthol in cigarettes as a reinforcer of smoking behavior. *Nicotine & Tobacco Research* 2010;12(Suppl 2):S110–S116.

Albanes D, Jones DY, Micozzi MS, Mattson ME. Associations between smoking and body weight in the US population: analysis of NHANES II. *American Journal of Public Health* 1987;77(4):439–44.

Alpert HR, Koh H, Connolly GN. Free nicotine content and strategic marketing of moist snuff tobacco products in the United States: 2000–2006. *Tobacco Control* 2008;17(5):332–8.

American Lung Association. *American Lung Association Tobacco Policy Trend Alert: An Emerging Deadly Trend: Waterpipe Tobacco Use, 2007;* <http://www.lungusa2.org/embargo/slati/Trendalert_Waterpipes.pdf.>; accessed: May 19, 2011.

Aquilino WS. Interview mode effects in surveys of drug and alcohol use: a field experiment. *Public Opinion Quarterly* 1994;58(2):210–40.

Bachman JG, Johnston LD, O'Malley PM, Schulenberg JE. *The Monitoring the Future Project After Thirty-two Years: Design and Procedures.* Ann Arbor (MI): University of Michigan, Institute for Social Research, 2006. Monitoring the Future Occasional Paper No. 64.

Bachman JG, O'Malley PM, Johnston LD, Schulenberg JE. *Impact of Parental Education on Substance Use: Differences among White, African-American, and Hispanic Students in 8th, 10th, and 12th Grades (1999–2008).* Monitoring the Future Occasional Paper No. 70. Ann Arbor (MI): University of Michigan, Institute for Social Research, 2010.

Bachman JG, O'Malley PM, Johnston LD, Schulenberg JE, Wallace JM Jr. Racial/ethnic differences in the relationship between parental education and substance use among U.S. 8th-, 10th-, and 12th-grade students: findings from the Monitoring the Future Project. *Journal of Studies on Alcohol and Drugs* 2011;72(2):279–85.

Baker F, Ainsworth SR, Dye JT, Crammer C, Thun MJ, Hoffmann D, Repace JL, Henningfield JE, Slade J, Pinney J, et al. Health risks associated with cigar smoking. *JAMA: the Journal of the American Medical Association* 2000;284(6):735–40.

Baker TB, Piper ME, McCarthy DE, Bolt DM, Smith SS, Kim SY, Colby S, Conti D, Giovino GA, Hatsukami D, et al. Time to first cigarette in the morning as an index of ability to quit smoking: implications for nicotine dependence. *Tobacco Control* 2007;9(Suppl 4): S555–S570.

Barnett TE, Curbow BA, Weitz JR, Johnson TM, Smith-Simone SY. Water pipe tobacco smoking among middle and high school students. *American Journal of Public Health* 2009;99(11):2014–9.

Bernat DH, Erickson DJ, Widome R, Perry CL, Forster JL. Adolescent smoking trajectories: results from a population-based cohort study. *Journal of Adolescent Health* 2008;43(4):334–40.

Boffetta P, Straif K. Use of smokeless tobacco and risk of myocardial infarction and stroke: systematic review with meta-analysis. *BMJ (British Medical Journal)* 2009;339:b3060. doi: 10.1136/bmj.b3060.

Bolinder G. Kunskapsöversikt om hälsoeffekter av rökfri tobak. Ökad kardiovaskulär sjukdom och död av snus [Overview of knowledge of health effects of smokeless tobacco: increased risk of cardiovascular diseases and mortality because of snuff]. *Lakartidningen* 1997;94(42):3725–31.

Brener ND, Billy JO, Grady WR. Assessment of factors affecting the validity of self-reported health-risk behavior among adolescents: evidence from the scientific literature. *Journal of Adolescent Health* 2003;33(6):436–57.

Brener ND, Collins JL. Co-occurrence of health-risk behaviors among adolescents in the United States. *Journal of Adolescent Health* 1998;22(3):209–13.

Brener ND, Eaton DK, Kann L, Grunbaum JA, Gross LA, Kyle TM, Ross JG. The association of survey setting and mode with self-reported health risk behaviors among high school students. *Public Opinion Quarterly* 2006;70(3):354–74.

Breslau N, Johnson EO. Predicting smoking cessation and major depression in nicotine-dependent smokers. *American Journal of Public Health* 2000;90(7):1122–7.

Breslau N, Kilbey MM, Andreski P. Nicotine dependence, major depression, and anxiety in young adults. *Archives of General Psychiatry* 1991;48(12):1069–74.

Breslau N, Kilbey MM, Andreski P. Nicotine dependence and major depression: new evidence from a prospective investigation. *Archives of General Psychiatry* 1993; 50(1):31–5.

Brittingham A, Tourangeau R, Kay W. Reports of smoking in a national survey: data from screening and detailed interviews, and from self- and interviewer-administered questions. *Annals of Epidemiology* 1998;8(6):393–401.

Brown RA, Lewinsohn PM, Seeley JR, Wagner EF. Cigarette smoking, major depression, and other psychiatric disorders among adolescents. *Journal of the American Academy of Child and Adolescent Psychiatry* 1996; 35(12):1602–10.

Caraballo RS, Novak SP, Asman K. Linking quantity and frequency profiles of cigarette smoking to the presence of nicotine dependence symptoms among adolescent smokers: findings from the 2004 National Youth Tobacco Survey. *Nicotine & Tobacco Research* 2009;11(1):49–57.

Carpenter CM, Wayne GF, Pauly JL, Koh HK, Connolly GN. New cigarette brands with flavors that appeal to youth: tobacco marketing strategies. *Health Affairs (Millwood)* 2005;24(6):1601–10.

Centers for Disease Control and Prevention. Differences in the age of smoking initiation between blacks and whites—United States. *Morbidity and Mortality Weekly Report* 1991;40(44):754–7.

Centers for Disease Control and Prevention. Reasons for tobacco use and symptoms of nicotine withdrawal among adolescent and young adult tobacco users—United States, 1993. *Morbidity and Mortality Weekly Report* 1994;43(41):745–50.

Centers for Disease Control and Prevention. Cigar smoking among teenagers—United States, Massachusetts, and New York, 1996. *Morbidity and Mortality Weekly Report* 1997;46(20):433–40.

Centers for Disease Control and Prevention. Bidi use among urban youth—Massachusetts, March–April 1999. *Morbidity and Mortality Weekly Report* 1999; 48(36):796–9.

Centers for Disease Control and Prevention. Methodology of the youth risk behavior surveillance system. *Morbidity and Mortality Weekly Report* 2004;53(RR–12):1–13.

Centers for Disease Control and Prevention. Tobacco use, access, and exposure to tobacco in media among middle and high school students—United States, 2004. *Morbidity and Mortality Weekly Report* 2005;54(12): 297–301.

Centers for Disease Control and Prevention. Use of cigarettes and other tobacco products among students aged 13–15 years—worldwide, 1999–2005. *Morbidity and Mortality Weekly Report* 2006;55(20):553–6.

Centers for Disease Control and Prevention. Cigarette smoking among adults—United States, 2007. *Morbidity and Mortality Weekly Report* 2008a;57(45):1221–6.

Centers for Disease Control and Prevention. Cigarette use among high school students—United States, 1991–2007. *Morbidity and Mortality Weekly Report* 2008b;57(25):686–8.

Centers for Disease Control and Prevention. Core questions: Global Youth Tobacco Survey (GYTS) 2008c; <http://apps.nccd.cdc.gov/gtssdata/Ancillary/Documentation.aspx?SUID=1&DOCT=1>; accessed: July 25, 2011.

Centers for Disease Control and Prevention. GYTS Introduction, 2009a; <http://www.cdc.gov/TOBACCO/global/gyts/intro.htm>; accessed: December 11, 2009.

Centers for Disease Control and Prevention. National Health Interview Survey, 2009b; <http://www.cdc.gov/nchs/nhis.htm>; accessed: December 11, 2009.

Centers for Disease Control and Prevention. 2009 National Youth Risk Behavior Survey, 2009c; <http://www.cdc.gov/healthyyouth/yrbs/pdf/questionnaire/2009_national_questionnaire.pdf >; accessed: July 25, 2011.

Centers for Disease Control and Prevention. NYTS Methodology Report, 2009d;<http://www.cdc.gov/tobacco/data_statistics/surveys/nyts/>; accessed: December 12, 2011.

Centers for Disease Control and Prevention. Cigarette use among high school students—United States, 1991–2009. *Morbidity and Mortality Weekly Report* 2010a; 59(26):797–801.

Centers for Disease Control and Prevention. GTSS Data, 2010b; <http://apps.nccd.cdc.gov/GTSSData/Default/Default.aspx>; accessed: January 7, 2011.

Centers for Disease Control and Prevention. Healthy Youth, 2010c; <http://www.cdc.gov/HealthyYouth/yrbs/index.htm>; accessed: March 29, 1010.

Centers for Disease Control and Prevention. State-specific prevalence of cigarette smoking and smokeless tobacco use among adults—United States, 2009. *Morbidity and Mortality Weekly Report* 2010d;59(43):1400–6.

Centers for Disease Control and Prevention. Tobacco use among middle and high school students—United States, 2000–2009. *Morbidity and Mortality Weekly Report* 2010e;59(33):1063–8.

Centers for Disease Control and Prevention. Youth Online: High School YRBS, 2011a; <http://apps.nccd.cdc.gov/youthonline/app/default.aspx>; accessed: October 19, 2011.

Centers for Disease Control and Prevention. Youth Risk Behavior Surveillance System (YRBSS), 2011b; <http://cdc.gov/HealthyYouth/yrbs/index.htm>; accessed: November 4, 2011

Chassin L, Presson C, Morgan-Lopez A, Sherman SJ. "Deviance proneness" and adolescent smoking 1980 versus 2001: has there been a "hardening" of adolescent smoking? *Journal of Applied Developmental Psychology* 2007;28(3):264–76.

Chassin L, Presson CC, Pitts SC, Sherman SJ. The natural history of cigarette smoking from adolescence to adulthood in a midwestern community sample: multiple trajectories and their psychosocial correlates. *Health Psychology* 2000;19(3):223–31.

Chen K, Kandel DB. The natural history of drug use from adolescence to the mid-thirties in a general population sample. *American Journal of Public Health* 1995;85(1):41–7.

Choi WS, Patten CA, Gillin JC, Kaplan RM, Pierce JP. Cigarette smoking predicts development of depressive symptoms among U.S. adolescents. *Annals of Behavioral Medicine* 1997;19(1):42–50.

Christen AG, Swanson BZ, Glover ED, Henderson AH. Smokeless tobacco: the folklore and social history of snuffing, sneezing, dipping, and chewing. *Journal of the American Dental Association* 1982;105(5):821–9.

Clayton RR, Ries Merkangas K, Abrams DB. Introduction to tobacco, nicotine, and youth: the tobacco etiology research network [editorial]. *Drug and Alcohol Dependence* 2000;59(Suppl 1):S1–S4.

Colder CR, Lloyd-Richardson EE, Flaherty BP, Hedeker D, Segawa E, Flay BR, Tobacco Etiology Research Network. The natural history of college smoking: trajectories of daily smoking during the freshman year. *Addictive Behaviors* 2006;31(12):2212–22.

Cole TJ, Bellizzi MC, Flegal KM, Dietz WH. Establishing a standard definition for child overweight and obesity worldwide: international survey. *BMJ (British Medical Journal)* 2000;320(7244):1240–3.

Cole TJ, Flegal KM, Nicholls D, Jackson AA. Body mass index cut offs to define thinness in children and adolescents: international survey. *BMJ (British Medical Journal)* 2007;335(7612):194.

Collins LM, Sayer AG, editors. *New Methods for the Analysis of Change*. Washington: American Psychological Association, 2001.

Cooper TV, Klesges RC, Robinson LA, Zbikowski SM. A prospective evaluation of the relationships between smoking dosage and body mass index in an adolescent, biracial cohort. *Addictive Behaviors* 2003;28(3): 501–12.

Covino RM. Smokeless is smokin' hot, July/August, 2006; <http://web.archive.org/web/20061124123641/www.tobonline.com/ArticlePages/ArticlePagesVol94/vol94p46.htm>; accessed: December 3, 2009.

Cummings KM, Morley CP, Horan JK, Steger C, Leavell NR. Marketing to America's youth: evidence from corporate documents. *Tobacco Control* 2002;11(Suppl 1): i5–i17.

Curry SJ, Mermelstein RJ, Sporer AK. Therapy for specific problems: youth tobacco cessation. *Annual Review of Psychology* 2009;60:229–55.

Curry SJ, Sporer AK, Pugach O, Campbell RT, Emery S. Use of tobacco cessation treatments among young adult smokers: 2005 National Health Interview Survey. *American Journal of Public Health* 2007;97(8):1464–9.

Delnevo CD. Under our radar: increases in cigar consumption in the United States [abstract]. In: Society for Research on Nicotine and Tobacco annual meeting, Feb. 21–24, 2007:8; <http://www.srnt.org/meeting/2007/pdf/onsite/2007/SRNTAbstracts-FINAL.pdf>; accessed: December 9, 2009.

Delnevo CD, Foulds J, Hrywna M. Trading tobacco: are youths choosing cigars over cigarettes? [letter]. *American Journal of Public Health* 2005;95(12):2123.

Delnevo CD, Gundersen D, Hrywna M. Examining market trends in smokeless tobacco use, 2005-2007. Poster presented at the National Conference on Tobacco or Health; June 10–12, 2009; Phoenix (AZ).

Delnevo CD, Hrywna M. The relationship of cigars, marijuana, and blunts to adolescent bidi use. *Public Health Reports* 2006;121(5):603–8.

Delnevo CD, Hrywna M. "A whole 'nother smoke" or a cigarette in disguise: how RJ Reynolds reframed the image of little cigars. *American Journal of Public Health* 2007;97(8):1368–75.

Delnevo CD, Pevzner ES, Steinberg MB, Warren CW, Slade J. Cigar use in New Jersey among adolescents and adults. *American Journal of Public Health* 2002;92(6):943–5.

DiFranza JR, Savageau JA, Fletcher K, O'Loughlin J, Pbert L, Ockene JK, McNeill AD, Hazelton J, Friedman K, Dussault G, et al. Symptoms of tobacco dependence after brief intermittent use: the Development and Assessment of Nicotine Dependence in Youth-2 study. *Archives of Pediatrics & Adolescent Medicine* 2007;161(7):704–10.

DiFranza JR, Savageau JA, Rigotti NA, Fletcher K, Ockene JK, McNeill AD, Coleman M, Wood C. Development of symptoms of tobacco dependence in youths: 30 month follow up data from the DANDY study. *Tobacco Control* 2002;11(3):228–35.

Dugas E, Tremblay M, Low NC, Cournoyer D, O'Loughlin J. Water-pipe smoking among North American youths. *Pediatrics* 2010;125(6):1184–9.

Eaton DK, Kann L, Kinchen S, Shanklin S, Ross J, Hawkins J, Harris WA, Lowry R, McManus T, Chyen D, et al. Youth risk behavior surveillance—United States, 2007. *Morbidity and Mortality Weekly Report* 2008;57(SS-4): 1–131.

Eaton DK, Kann L, Kinchen S, Shanklin S, Ross J, Hawkins J, Harris WA, Lowry R, McManus T, Chyen D, et al. Youth risk behavior surveillance—United States 2009. *Morbidity and Mortality Weekly Report* 2010;59(SS-5): 1–142.

Eissenberg T, Shihadeh A. Waterpipe tobacco and cigarette smoking: direct comparison of toxicant exposure. *American Journal of Preventive Medicine* 2009; 37(6):518–23.

Eissenberg T, Ward KD, Smith-Simone S, Maziak W. Waterpipe tobacco smoking on a U.S. college campus: prevalence and correlates. *Journal of Adolescent Health* 2008;42(5):526–9.

Escobedo LG, Marcus SE, Holtzman D, Giovino GA. Sports participation, age at smoking initiation, and the risk of smoking among US high school students. *JAMA: the Journal of the American Medical Association* 1993;269(11):1391–5.

Escobedo LG, Reddy M, Giovino GA. The relationship between depressive symptoms and cigarette smoking in US adolescents. *Addiction* 1998;93(3):433–40.

Evans N, Farkas A, Gilpin E, Berry C, Pierce JP. Influence of tobacco marketing and exposure to smokers on adolescent susceptibility to smoking. *Journal of the National Cancer Institute* 1995;87(20):1538–45.

Everett SA, Warren CW, Sharp D, Kann L, Husten CG, Crossett LS. Initiation of cigarette smoking and subsequent smoking behavior among U.S. high school students. *Preventive Medicine* 1999;29(5):327–33.

Fagan P, Rigotti NA. Light and intermittent smoking: the road less traveled. *Nicotine & Tobacco Research* 2009;11(2):107–10.

Family Smoking Prevention and Tobacco Control Act, Public Law 111-13, 123 *U.S. Statutes at Large* 1776 (2009).

Fergus S, Zimmerman MA, Caldwell CH. Psychosocial correlates of smoking trajectories among urban African American adolescents. *Journal of Adolescent Research* 2005;20(4):423–52.

Fisher MA, Taylor GW, Tilashalski KR. Smokeless tobacco and severe active periodontal disease, NHANES III. *Journal of Dental Research* 2005;84(8):705–10.

Flay BR. Youth tobacco use: risks, patterns, and control. In: Orleans CT, Slade J, editors. *Nicotine Addiction: Principles and Management*. New York: Oxford University Press, 1993:365–84.

Flay BR, d'Avernas JR, Best JA, Kersell MW, Ryan KB. Cigarette smoking: why young people do it and ways of preventing it. In: McGrath PJ, Firestone P, editors. *Pediatric and Adolescent Behavioral Medicine*. New York: Springer-Verlag, 1983:132–83.

Foulds J, Hooper MW, Pletcher MJ, Okuyemi KS. Do smokers of menthol cigarettes find it harder to quit smoking? *Nicotine & Tobacco Research* 2010;12(Suppl 2):S102–S109.

Gardiner P, Clark PI. Menthol cigarettes: moving toward a broader definition of harm. *Nicotine & Tobacco Research* 2010;12(Suppl 2):S85–S93.

Geronimus AT, Neidert LJ, Bound J. Age patterns of smoking in US black and white women of childbearing age. *American Journal of Public Health* 1993;83(9): 1258–64.

Gfroerer J, Wright D, Kopstein A. Prevalence of youth substance use: the impact of methodological differences between two national surveys. *Drug and Alcohol Dependence* 1997;47(1):19–30.

Giovino GA, Sidney S, Gfroerer JC, O'Malley PM, Allen JA, Richter PA, Cummings KM. Epidemiology of menthol cigarette use. *Nicotine & Tobacco Research* 2004;6(Suppl 1):S67–S81.

Green MP, McCausland KL, Xiao H, Duke JC, Vallone DM, Healton CG. A closer look at smoking among young adults: where tobacco control should focus its attention. *American Journal of Public Health* 2007; 97(8):1427–33.

Gupta R, Gurm H, Bartholomew JR. Smokeless tobacco and cardiovascular risk. *Archives of Internal Medicine* 2004;164(17):1845–9.

Hammond D. Smoking behaviour among young adults: beyond youth prevention. *Tobacco Control* 2005; 14(3):181–5.

Hassmiller KM, Warner KE, Mendez D, Levy DT, Romano E. Nondaily smokers: who are they? *American Journal of Public Health* 2003;93(8):1321–7.

Hedges B, Jarvis M. Cigarette smoking. In: Prescott-Clark P, Primatesta P, editors. *Health Survey for England: The Health of Young People, '95–97*. London: The Stationery Office, 1998:191–221.

Henningfield JE, Radzius A, Cone EJ. Estimation of available nicotine content of six smokeless tobacco products. *Tobacco Control* 1995;4(1):57–61.

Hersey JC, Nonnemaker JM, Homsi G. Menthol cigarettes contribute to the appeal and addiction potential of smoking for youth. *Nicotine & Tobacco Research* 2010;12(Suppl 2):S136–S146.

Hibell B, Guttormsson U, Ahlström S, Balakireva O, Bjarnason T, Kokkevi A, Kraus L. *The 2007 ESPAD Report: Substance Use Among Students in 35 European Countries*. Stockholm: The Swedish Council for Information on Alcohol and Other Drugs, 2009.

Hrywna M, Delnevo CD, Pevzner ES, Abatemarco DJ. Correlates of bidi use among youth. *American Journal of Health Behavior* 2004;28(2):173–9.

Husten CG. How should we define light or intermittent smoking: does it matter? *Nicotine & Tobacco Research* 2009;11(2):111–21.

Hymowitz N, Cummings KM, Hyland A, Lynn WR, Pechacek TF, Hartwell TD. Predictors of smoking cessation in a cohort of adult smokers followed for five years. *Tobacco Control* 1997;6(Suppl 2):S57–S62.

International Agency for Research on Cancer. *IARC Monographs on the Evaluation of Carcinogenic Risks to Humans: Tobacco Habits Other Than Smoking; Betel-Quid and Areca-Nut Chewing; and Some Related Nitrosamines.* Vol. 37. Lyon (France): World Health Organization, 1985 [updated April 21, 1998]. <http://monographs.iarc.fr/ENG/Monographs/vol37/volume37.pdf>; accessed: May 31, 2011.

International Agency for Research on Cancer. *IARC Monographs on the Evaluation of Carcinogenic Risks to Humans: Smokeless Tobacco and Some Tobacco-specific* N-*Nitrosamines.* Vol. 89. Lyon (France): International Agency for Research on Cancer, 2007.

Jemal A, Center MM, Ward E. The convergence of lung cancer rates between blacks and whites under the age of 40, United States. *Cancer Epidemiology, Biomarkers & Prevention* 2009;18(12):3349–52.

Johnston LD, O'Malley PM, Bachman JG, Schulenberg JE. *Monitoring the Future National Survey Results on Drug Use, 1975–2006: Volume I, Secondary School Students.* Bethesda (MD): U.S. Department of Health and Human Services, National Institutes of Health, National Institute on Drug Abuse, 2007. NIH Publication No. 07-6205.

Johnston LD, O'Malley PM, Bachman JG, Schulenberg JE. *Monitoring the Future National Survey Results on Drug Use, 1975–2007: Volume I, Secondary School Students.* Bethesda (MD): U.S. Department of Health and Human Services, National Institutes of Health, National Institute on Drug Abuse, 2008. NIH Publication No. 08-6418A.

Johnston LD, O'Malley PM, Bachman JG, Schulenberg JE. *Monitoring the Future National Survey Results on Drug Use, 1975–2009: Volume I, Secondary School Students.* Bethesda (MD): U.S. Department of Health and Human Services, National Institutes of Health, National Institute on Drug Abuse, 2010. NIH Publication No. 10-7584.

Johnston LD, O'Malley PM, Bachman JG, Schulenberg JE. *Monitoring the Future National Results on Adolescent Drug Use: Overview of Key Findings, 2010.* Ann Arbor (MI): The University of Michigan, Institute for Social Research, 2011.

Kann L, Brener ND, Warren CW, Collins JL, Giovino GA. An assessment of the effect of data collection setting on the prevalence of health risk behaviors among adolescents. *Journal of Adolescent Health* 2002;31(4):327–35.

Kaplan SD, Lanier AP, Merritt RK, Siegel PZ. Prevalence of tobacco use among Alaska Natives: a review. *Preventive Medicine* 1997;26(4):460–5.

Katz SK, Lavack AM. Tobacco related bar promotions: insights from tobacco industry documents. *Tobacco Control* 2002;11(Suppl 1):I92-I101.

Klein SM, Giovino GA, Barker DC, Tworek C, Cummings KM, O'Connor RJ. Use of flavored cigarettes among older adolescent and adult smokers: United States, 2004–2005. *Nicotine & Tobacco Research* 2008; 10(7):1209–14.

Knishkowy B, Amitai Y. Water-pipe (narghile) smoking: an emerging health risk behavior. *Pediatrics* 2005; 116(1):e113–e119.

Kozlowski LT, O'Connor RJ, Edwards BQ, Flaherty BP. Most smokeless tobacco use is not a causal gateway to cigarettes: using order of product use to evaluate causation in a national US sample. *Addiction* 2003;98(8):1077–85.

Kruger J, Ham SA, Prohaska TR. Behavioral risk factors associated with overweight and obesity among older adults: the 2005 National Health Interview Survey. *Preventing Chronic Disease* 2009;6(1); <http://www.cdc.gov/pcd/issues/2009/jan/07_0183.htm>; accessed: December 22, 2010.

Lando HA, Thai DT, Murray DM, Robinson LA, Jeffery RW, Sherwood NE, Hennrikus DJ. Age of initiation, smoking patterns, and risk in a population of working adults. *Preventive Medicine* 1999;29(6 Pt 1):590–8.

Lantz PM. Smoking on the rise among young adults: implications for research and policy. *Tobacco Control* 2003;12(Suppl 1):i60–i70.

Lanza ST, Collins LM, Lemmon DR, Schafer JL. PROC LCA: a SAS procedure for latent class analysis. *Structural Equation Modeling* 2007;14(4):671–94.

Lawrence D, Fagan P, Backinger CL, Gibson JT, Hartman A. Cigarette smoking patterns among young adults aged 18–24 years in the United States. *Nicotine & Tobacco Research* 2007;9(6):687–97.

Lawrence D, Rose A, Fagan P, Moolchan ET, Gibson JT, Backinger CL. National patterns and correlates of mentholated cigarette use in the United States. *Addiction* 2010;105(Suppl 1):13–31.

Ling PM, Glantz SA. Why and how the tobacco industry sells cigarettes to young adults: evidence from industry documents. *American Journal of Public Health* 2002;92(6):908–16.

Ling PM, Neilands TB, Glantz SA. Young adult smoking behavior: a national survey. *American Journal of Preventive Medicine* 2009;36(5):389–94.

Lopez AD, Collishaw NE, Piha T. A descriptive model of the cigarette epidemic in developed countries. *Tobacco Control* 1994;3(3):242–7.

Malone RE, Yerger V, Pearson C. Cigar risk perceptions in focus groups of urban African American youth. *Journal of Substance Abuse* 2001;13(4):549–61.

Marshall L, Schooley M, Ryan H, Cox P, Easton A, Healton C, Jackson K, Davis KC, Nomsi G. Youth tobacco surveillance—United States, 2001–2002. *Morbidity and Mortality Weekly Report* 2006;55(SS-3):1–56.

Maxwell JC. *The Maxwell Report: CIGAR INDUSTRY in 2008.* Richmond (VA): John C. Maxwell, Jr., 2009a.

Maxwell JC. *The Maxwell Report: The SMOKELESS TOBACCO INDUSTRY in 2008.* Richmond (VA): John C. Maxwell, Jr., 2009b.

Maxwell JC. *The Maxwell Report: YEAR END & FOURTH QUARTER 2008 SALES ESTIMATES FOR THE CIGARETTE INDUSTRY.* Richmond (VA): John C. Maxwell Jr., 2009c.

Maziak W, Rastam S, Ibrahim I, Ward KD, Shihadeh A, Eissenberg T. CO exposure, puff topography, and subjective effects in waterpipe tobacco smokers. *Nicotine & Tobacco Research* 2009;11(7):806–11.

McNeill A, Bedi R, Islam S, Alkhatib MN, West R. Levels of toxins in oral tobacco products in the UK. *Tobacco Control* 2006;15(1):64–7.

Moon-Howard J. African American women and smoking: starting later. *American Journal of Public Health* 2003;93(3):418–20.

Myers M. Beware the rooster: smokeless tobacco companies who claim they want to help. *Tobacco Control* 2003;12(4):342.

National Cancer Institute. *Smokeless Tobacco or Health: An International Perspective.* Smoking and Tobacco Control Monograph No. 2. Bethesda (MD): U.S. Department of Health and Human Services, Public Health Service, National Institutes of Health, National Cancer Institute, 1992. NIH Publication. No. 92-3461.

National Cancer Institute. *Cigars: Health Effects and Trends*. Smoking and Tobacco Control Monograph No. 9. Bethesda (MD): U.S. Department of Health and Human Services, Public Health Service, National Institutes of Health, National Cancer Institute, 1998. NIH Publication No. 98-4302.

National Cancer Institute. *Changing Adolescent Smoking Prevalence.* Smoking and Tobacco Control Monograph No. 14. Bethesda (MD): U.S. Department of Health and Human Services, Public Health Service, National Institutes of Health, National Cancer Institute, 2001. NIH Publication No. 02-5086.

National Cancer Institute. *The Role of the Media in Promoting and Reducing Tobacco Use.* Tobacco Control Monograph No. 19. Bethesda (MD): U.S. Department of Health and Human Services, National Institutes of Health, National Cancer Institute, 2008. NIH Publication No. 07-6242.

National Center for Health Statistics. *2007 National Health Interview Survey (NHIS): Public Use Data Release: NHIS Survey Description.* Hyattsville (MD): U.S. Department of Health and Human Services, Centers for Disease Control and Prevention, National Center for Health Statistics, 2008.

National Institutes of Health. Clinical guidelines on the identification, evaluation, and treatment of overweight and obesity in adults—the Evidence Report. *Obesity Research* 1998;6(Suppl 12): 51S–209S.

Nelson DE, Mowery P, Asman K, Pederson LL, O'Malley PM, Malarcher A, Maibach EW, Pechacek TF. Long-term trends in adolescent and young adult smoking in the United States: metapatterns and implications. *American Journal of Public Health* 2008;98(5):905–15.

O'Connor RJ, Kozlowski LT, Flaherty BP, Edwards BQ. Most smokeless tobacco use does not cause cigarette smoking: results from the 2000 National Household Survey on Drug Abuse. *Addictive Behaviors* 2005; 30(2):325–36.

Ohsfeldt RL, Boyle RG. Tobacco excise taxes and rates of smokeless tobacco use in the US: an exploratory ecological analysis. *Tobacco Control* 1994;3(4):316–23.

Ohsfeldt RL, Boyle RG, Capilouto E. Effects of tobacco excise taxes on the use of smokeless tobacco products in the USA. *Health Economics* 1997;6(5):525–31.

O'Loughlin J, DiFranza J, Tyndale RF, Meshefedjian G, McMillan-Davey E, Clarke PBS, Hanley J, Paradis G. Nicotine-dependence symptoms are associated with smoking frequency in adolescents. *American Journal of Preventive Medicine* 2003;25(3):219–25.

Page JB, Evans S. Cigars, cigarillos, and youth: emergent patterns in subcultural complexes. *Journal of Ethnicity in Substance Abuse* 2004;2(4):63–76.

Pallonen UE, Prochaska JO, Velicer WF, Prokhorov AV, Smith NF. Stages of acquisition and cessation for adolescent smoking: an empirical integration. *Addictive Behaviors* 1998;23(3):303–24.

Payne TJ, Smith PO, McCracken LM, McSherry WC, Antony MM. Assessing nicotine dependence: a comparison of the Fagerström Tolerance Questionnaire (FTQ) with the Fagerström Test for Nicotine Dependence (FTND) in a clinical sample. *Addictive Behaviors* 1994;19(3):307–17.

Pierce JP, Choi WS, Gilpin EA, Farkas AJ, Merritt RK. Validation of susceptibility as a predictor of which adolescents take up smoking in the United States. *Health Psychology* 1996;15(5):355–61.

Potter BK, Pederson LL, Chan SS, Aubut JA, Koval JJ. Does a relationship exist between body weight, concerns about weight, and smoking among adolescents: an integration of the literature with an emphasis on gender. *Nicotine & Tobacco Research* 2004;6(3): 397–425.

Primack BA, Sidani J, Agarwal AA, Shadel WG, Donny EC, Eissenberg TE. Prevalence of and associations with waterpipe tobacco smoking among U.S. university students. *Annals of Behavioral Medicine* 2008;36(1):81–6.

Primack BA, Walsh M, Bryce C, Eissenberg T. Water-pipe tobacco smoking among middle and high school students in Arizona. *Pediatrics* 2009;123(2):e282–e288.

Prochaska JO, DiClemente CC. Stages and processes of self-change of smoking: toward an integrative model of change. *Journal of Consulting and Clinical Psychology* 1983;51(3):390–5.

Prokhorov AV, de Moor CA, Hudmon KS, Hu S, Kelder SH, Gritz ER. Predicting initiation of smoking in adolescents: evidence for integrating the stages of change and susceptibility to smoking constructs. *Addictive Behaviors* 2002;27(5):697–712.

Purple Haze. Cigarettes & Cigars, 2011; <http://shoppurplehaze.com/shop/index.php?main_page=index&cPath=3_28>; accessed: October 24, 2011.

Richter P, Hodge K, Stanfill S, Zhang L, Watson C. Surveillance of moist snuff: total nicotine, moisture, pH, un-ionized nicotine, and tobacco-specific nitrosamines. *Nicotine & Tobacco Research* 2008;10(11):1645–52.

Richter P, Spierto FW. Surveillance of smokeless tobacco nicotine, pH, moisture, and unprotonated nicotine content. *Nicotine & Tobacco Research* 2003;5(6):885–9.

Rigotti NA, Lee JE, Wechsler H. US college students' use of tobacco products: results of a national survey. *JAMA: the Journal of the American Medical Association* 2000;284(6):699–705.

RTI International. 2009 National Survey On Drug Use And Health, CAI Specifications for Programming English Version, 2009; <http://oas.samhsa.gov/nsduh/2k9MRB/2k9Q.pdf>; accessed: July 25, 2011.

Schane RE, Glantz SA, Ling PM. Nondaily and social smoking: an increasingly prevalent pattern. *Archives of Internal Medicine* 2009;169(19):1742–4.

Seo DC, Jiang N, Kolbe LJ. Association of smoking with body weight in US high school students, 1999–2005. *American Journal of Health Behavior* 2009;33(2):202–12.

Shiffman S, Waters A, Hickcox M. The nicotine dependence syndrome scale: a multidimensional measure of nicotine dependence. *Nicotine & Tobacco Research* 2004;6(2):327–48.

Shihadeh A. Investigation of mainstream smoke aerosol of the argileh water pipe. *Food and Chemical Toxicology* 2003;41(1):143–52.

Siegel D, Benowitz N, Ernster VL, Grady DG, Hauck WW. Smokeless tobacco, cardiovascular risk factors, and nicotine and cotinine levels in professional baseball players. *American Journal of Public Health* 1992;82(3):417–21.

Sifaneck SJ, Johnson BD, Dunlap E. Cigars-for-blunts: choice of tobacco products by blunt smokers. *Journal of Ethnicity in Substance Abuse* 2005;4(3–4):23–42.

Solberg LI, Boyle RG, McCarty M, Asche SE, Thoele MJ. Young adult smokers: are they different? *American Journal of Managed Care* 2007;13(11):626–32.

Soldz S, Huyser DJ, Dorsey E. Characteristics of users of cigars, bidis, and kreteks and the relationship to cigarette use. *Preventive Medicine* 2003a;37(3):250–58.

Soldz S, Huyser DJ, Dorsey E. Youth preferences for cigar brands: rates of use and characteristics of users. *Tobacco Control* 2003b;12(2):155–60.

Stepanov I, Jensen J, Hatsukami D, Hecht SS. Tobacco-specific nitrosamines in new tobacco products. *Nicotine & Tobacco Research* 2006;8(2):309–13.

Steuber TL, Danner F. Adolescent smoking and depression: which comes first? *Addictive Behaviors* 2006;31(1):133–6.

Substance Abuse and Mental Health Services Administration. Appendix A: description of the survey. In: *Results from the 2008 National Survey on Drug Use and Health: National Findings.* NSDUH Series H-36. Rockville (MD): U.S. Department of Health and Human Services, Substance Abuse and Mental Health Services Administration, Office of Applied Studies, 2009a:115–23. DHHS Publication No. SMA 09-4434.

Substance Abuse and Mental Health Services Administration. *Results from the 2008 National Survey on Drug Use and Health: National Findings.* NSDUH Series H-36. Rockville (MD): U.S. Department of Health and Human Services, Substance Abuse and Mental Health Services Administration, Office of Applied Studies, 2009b. DHHS Publication No. SMA 09-4434.

Substance Abuse and Mental Health Services Administration. *The NSDUH Report: Smokeless Tobacco Use, Initiation and Relationship to Cigarette Smoking: 2002 to 2007.* Rockville (MD): U.S. Department of Health and Human Services, Substance Abuse and Mental Health Services Administration, Office of Applied Studies, 2009c.

Substance Abuse and Mental Health Services Administration. The NSDUH Report: use of menthol cigarettes. Rockville (MD): U.S. Department of Health and Human Services, Substance Abuse and Mental Health Services Administration, Office of Applied Studies, 2009d; <http://www.oas.samhsa.gov/2k9/134/134MentholCigarettes.htm>; accessed: May 31, 2011.

Substance Abuse and Mental Health Services Administration. *Results from the 2010 National Survey on Drug Use and Health: Summary of National Findings.* NSDUH Series H-41. Rockville (MD): U.S. Department of Health and Human Services, Substance Abuse and Mental Health Services Administration, 2011. HHS Publication No. (SMA) 11-4658.

Taioli E, Wynder EL. Effect of the age at which smoking begins on frequency of smoking in adulthood. *New England Journal of Medicine* 1991;325(13):968–9.

Taylor TM, Biener L. Bidi smoking among Massachusetts teenagers. *Preventive Medicine* 2001;32(1):89–92.

Terchek JJ, Larkin EM, Male ML, Frank SH. Measuring cigar use in adolescents: inclusion of a brand-specific item. *Nicotine & Tobacco Research* 2009;11(7):842–6.

Tobacco Products Scientific Advisory Committee. Menthol cigarettes and public health: Review of the scientific evidence and recommendations, 2011; http://www.fda.gov/downloads/AdvisoryCommitttees/Committees-MeetingMaterials/TobaccoProductsScientificAdvisory-Committee/UCM247689.pdf>; accessed: November 28, 2011.

Tomar SL. Is use of smokeless tobacco a risk factor for cigarette smoking: the U.S. experience. *Nicotine & Tobacco Research* 2003;5(4):561–9.

Tomar SL, Hatsukami DK. Perceived risk of harm from cigarettes or smokeless tobacco among U.S. high school seniors. *Nicotine & Tobacco Research* 2007;9(11):1191–6.

Trinidad DR, Gilpin EA, Lee L, Pierce JP. Has there been a delay in the age of regular smoking onset among African Americans? *Annals of Behavioral Medicine* 2004;28(3):152–7.

Turner CF, Lessler JT, Devore J. Effects of mode of administration and wording on reporting of drug use. In: Turner CF, Lessler JT, Gfroerer JD, editors. *Survey Measurement of Drug Use: Methodological Studies*. Rockville (MD): U.S. Department of Health and Human Services, Public Health Service, Substance Abuse and Mental Health Services Administration, 1992. DHHS Publication No. (ADM) 92-1929.

University of Michigan. Substance Abuse and Mental Health Data Archive, 2012; <http://www.icpsr.umich.edu/icpsrweb/SAMHDA>; accessed: February 2, 2012.

University of North Carolina. Add Health, 2009; <http://www.cpc.unc.edu/projects/addhealth>; accessed: December 11, 2009.

U.S. Census Bureau. 2005–2007 Table GCT0203: Percent of the Total Population Who Are American Indian and Alaska Native Alone, 2009; <http://factfinder.census.gov/servlet/GCTTable?_bm=y&-state=gct&-ds_name=ACS_2007_3YR_G00_&-_box_head_nbr=GCT0203&-mt_name=&-redoLog=true&-_caller=geoselect&-geo_id=&-format=US-9T&-_lang=en>; accessed: December 9, 2009.

U.S. Department of Agriculture. *Tobacco Outlook*. Washington: U.S. Department of Agriculture, Economics Research Service, 2007. TBS-263.

U.S. Department of Health and Human Services. *The Health Consequences of Using Smokeless Tobacco. A Report of the Advisory Committee to the Surgeon General of the Public Health Service*. Bethesda (MD): U.S. Department of Health and Human Services, Public Health Service, 1986. NIH Publication No. 86-2874.

U.S. Department of Health and Human Services. *The Health Consequences of Smoking: Nicotine Addiction. A Report of the Surgeon General*. Atlanta (GA): U.S. Department of Health and Human Services, Public Health Service, Centers for Disease Control, National Center for Chronic Disease Prevention and Health Promotion, Office on Smoking and Health, 1988. DHHS Publication No. (CDC) 88-8406.

U.S. Department of Health and Human Services. *Preventing Tobacco Use Among Young People. A Report of the Surgeon General*. Atlanta (GA): U.S. Department of Health and Human Services, Public Health Service, Centers for Disease Control and Prevention, National Center for Chronic Disease Prevention and Health Promotion, Office on Smoking and Health, 1994.

U.S. Department of Health and Human Services. *Tobacco Use Among U.S. Racial/Ethnic Minority Groups—African Americans, American Indians and Alaska Natives, Asian Americans and Pacific Islanders, and Hispanics. A Report of the Surgeon General*. Atlanta (GA): U.S. Department of Health and Human Services, Centers for Disease Control and Prevention, National Center for Chronic Disease Prevention and Health Promotion, Office on Smoking and Health, 1998.

U.S. Department of Health and Human Services. *Healthy People 2010: Understanding and Improving Health*. 2nd ed. Washington: U.S. Government Printing Office, 2000.

U.S. Department of Health and Human Services. *How Tobacco Smoke Causes Disease—The Biology and Behavioral Basis for Tobacco-Attributable Disease. A Report of the Surgeon General*. Atlanta (GA): U.S. Department of Health and Human Services, Centers for Disease Control and Prevention, National Center for Chronic Disease Prevention and Health Promotion, Office on Smoking and Health, 2010.

Wackowski O, Delnevo CD. Menthol cigarettes and indicators of tobacco dependence among adolescents. *Addictive Behaviors* 2007;32(9):1964–9.

Walsh PM, Epstein JB. The oral effects of smokeless tobacco. *Journal of the Canadian Dental Association* 2000;66(1):22–5.

Warren CW, Jones NR, Peruga A, Chauvin J, Baptiste JP, Costa de Silva V, El Awa F, Tsouros A, Rahman K, Fishburn B, et al. Global youth tobacco surveillance, 2000–2007. *Morbidity and Mortality Weekly Report* 2008;57(SS-1):1–28.

Wayne GF, Connolly GN. How cigarette design can affect youth initiation into smoking: Camel cigarettes 1983–93. *Tobacco Control* 2002;11(Suppl 1):i32–i39.

Weden MM, Zabin LS. Gender and ethnic differences in the co-occurrence of adolescent risk behaviors. *Ethnicity & Health* 2005;10(3):213–34.

West R. Assessment of dependence and motivation to stop smoking. *BMJ (British Medical Journal)* 2004; 328(7435):338–9.

Westman EC. Does smokeless tobacco cause hypertension? *Southern Medical Journal* 1995;88(7):716–20.

White HR, Bray BC, Fleming CB, Catalano RF. Transitions into and out of light and intermittent smoking during emerging adulthood. *Nicotine & Tobacco Research* 2009;11(2):211–9.

Winn DM. Epidemiology of cancer and other systemic effects associated with the use of smokeless tobacco. *Advances in Dental Research* 1997;11(3):313–21.

World Health Organization. Tobacco Regulation Advisory Note. *Waterpipe Tobacco Smoking: Health Effects, Research Needs and Recommended Actions by Regulators.* Geneva (Switzerland): World Health Organization, Tobacco Free Initiative, 2005.

Yerger V, Pearson C, Malone RE. When is a cigar not a cigar: African American youths' understanding of "cigar" use [letter]. *American Journal of Public Health* 2001;91(2):316–7.

Table 3.1.1 Percentage of young people who have ever smoked cigarettes, by gender, race/ethnicity, age/grade, and region; National Survey on Drug Use and Health (NSDUH) 2010, Monitoring the Future (MTF) 2010, National Youth Risk Behavior Survey (YRBS) 2009, and National Youth Tobacco Survey (NYTS) 2009; United States

	NSDUH 13–18 years of age[a]		MTF 8th, 10th, and 12th grades[b]		YRBS 9th–12th grades[c]		NYTS 9th–12th grades[d]		NYTS 6th–8th grades[d]	
Characteristic	**% (95% CI)**	**SN[e]**	**% (95% CI)**	**SN[e]**	**% (95% CI)**	**SN[e]**	**% (95% CI)**	**SN[e]**	**% (95% CI)**	**SN[e]**
Overall	28.2 (27.32–29.10)		30.9 (28.8–32.9)		46.3 (43.7–48.9)		42.7 (39.4–46.1)		18.2 (16.0–20.4)	
Gender										
Male	29.6 (28.39–30.83)	a	32.2 (29.9–34.5)	a	46.3 (42.6–50.0)	a	44.4 (40.6–48.2)	a	19.4 (16.7–22.0)	a
Female	26.7 (25.51–27.96)	b	29.3 (27.0–31.5)	b	46.1 (43.7–48.6)	a	41.1 (37.8–44.3)	b	16.9 (14.8–19.1)	b
Race/ethnicity										
White	30.3 (29.16–31.42)	a	31.3 (28.7–33.9)	a	46.1 (42.3–50.0)	a,b	43.2 (38.3–48.1)	a	14.3 (11.7–16.9)	a
Male	30.6 (29.07–32.17)		32.3 (29.2–35.5)		45.2 (39.7–50.9)		44.4 (39.2–49.7)		15.1 (12.1–18.0)	
Female	29.9 (28.37–31.56)		30.2 (27.4–32.9)		47.2 (43.9–50.5)		41.9 (37.0–48.8)		13.5 (10.6–16.4)	
Black or African American	22.1 (20.13–24.17)	b	24.8 (21.7–27.9)	b	43.5 (39.0–48.0)	a	34.6 (27.2–42.0)	a	24.5 (21.4–27.6)	b
Male	25.5 (22.58–28.72)		27.6 (23.4–31.9)		43.5 (39.2–47.9)		35.3 (23.8–46.9)		26.6 (22.0–31.1)	
Female	18.5 (16.09–21.14)		22.4 (18.9–25.9)		43.4 (37.3–49.7)		33.8 (29.2–38.3)		22.5 (18.9–26.1)	
Hispanic or Latino	28.4 (26.42–30.53)	a	32.9 (30.1–35.7)	a	51.0 (47.4–54.6)	b	50.3 (46.0–54.5)	b	24.2 (20.9–27.4)	b
Male	31.6 (29.02–34.33)		36.0 (32.2–39.7)		54.5 (50.4–58.6)		51.8 (47.3–56.2)		26.5 (22.5–30.6)	
Female	24.8 (22.00–27.84)		30.3 (27.0–33.7)		47.6 (43.4–51.8)		48.9 (42.9–54.9)		21.8 (18.5–25.2)	
Other[f]	23.1 (20.09–26.33)	b	26.4 (19.3–33.6)	b	39.4 (32.9–46.3)	a	38.6 (33.4–43.8)	a	20.9 (15.4–26.5)	b
Male	23.6 (19.40–28.49)		28.0 (20.2–35.8)		39.9 (34.2–45.8)		45.0 (37.8–52.2)		21.2 (12.3–30.1)	
Female	22.5 (18.49–26.98)		24.6 (16.7–32.5)		38.7 (30.2–48.0)		32.3 (26.7–37.8)		20.6 (16.0–25.2	
Age (in years)/grade										
13–14	11.8 (10.87–12.84)	a	NA		NA		NA		NA	
15–16	26.8 (25.49–28.18)	b	NA		NA		NA		NA	
17–18	44.0 (42.31–45.70)	c	NA		NA		NA		NA	
6th	NA		NA		NA		NA		11.6 (9.2–13.9)	a
7th	NA		NA		NA		NA		16.2 (13.8–18.6)	b
8th	NA		20.0 (18.3–21.8)	a	NA		NA		26.8 (23.6–30.1)	c
9th	NA		NA		37.7 (34.6–40.8)	a	32.4 (26.3–38.5)	a	NA	
10th	NA		33.0 (30.7–35.2)	b	44.0 (39.9–48.3)	b	40.3 (36.9–43.8)	b	NA	
11th	NA		NA		50.0 (46.2–53.8)	c	48.8 (45.7–51.8)	c	NA	
12th	NA		42.2 (40.2–44.3)	c	55.5 (52.0–58.9)	d	52.1 (48.9–55.3)	c	NA	

Table 3.1.1 Continued

	NSDUH 13–18 years of age[a]		MTF 8th, 10th, and 12th grades[b]		YRBS 9th–12th grades[c]		NYTS 9th–12th grades[d]		NYTS 6th–8th grades[d]	
Characteristic	**% (95% CI)**	**SN[e]**	**% (95% CI)**	**SN[e]**	**% (95% CI)**	**SN[e]**	**% (95% CI)**	**SN[e]**	**% (95% CI)**	**SN[e]**
Region										
Northeast	26.6 (24.85–28.32)	a	27.5 (23.3–31.7)	a	45.7 (38.5–53.1)	a,b	NA		NA	
Midwest	28.1 (26.65–29.55)	b	31.2 (27.5–35.0)	a,b	44.2 (38.1–50.5)	a,b	NA		NA	
South	29.7 (28.17–31.23)	b	34.6 (31.8–37.5)	b	51.3 (47.8–54.8)	a	NA		NA	
West	27.2 (25.24–29.31)	a	27.1 (21.7–32.6)	a	41.7 (37.0–46.7)	b	NA		NA	

Source: 2010 NSDUH, Substance Abuse and Mental Health Services Administration (unpublished data); 2010 MTF: University of Michigan, Institute for Social Research (unpublished data); 2009 YRBS: Centers for Disease Control and Prevention (CDC 2011a); 2009 NYTS: CDC (unpublished data).
Note: **CI** = confidence interval; **NA** = not applicable; **SN** = statistical note.
[a]Based on responses to the question, "Have you ever smoked part or all of a cigarette?" Respondents who chose "Yes" were classified as ever smokers.
[b]Based on responses to the question, "Have you ever smoked cigarettes?" Respondents who reported that they had smoked "Once or twice," "Occasionally but not regularly," or "Regularly in the past" were classified as ever smokers.
[c]Based on responses to the question, "Have you ever tried cigarette smoking, even one or two puffs?" Respondents who chose "Yes" were classified as ever smokers.
[d]Estimates are based on responses to the question, "Have you ever tried cigarette smoking, even one or two puffs?"
[e]This column represents the results of statistical tests that were run separately within each surveillance system (e.g., NSDUH). These tests were performed to examine differences in estimates within specific demographic subgroups (e.g., gender). Estimates with the same letter (e.g., a and a) are not statistically significantly different from one another ($p > 0.05$). Estimates with different letters (e.g., a and b) are, in contrast, statistically significantly different from one another ($p < 0.05$).
[f]Includes Asians, American Indians or Alaska Natives, Native Hawaiians or Other Pacific Islanders, and persons of two or more races.

Table 3.1.2 Percentage of young people who currently smoke cigarettes, by gender, race/ethnicity, age/grade, and region; National Survey on Drug Use and Health (NSDUH) 2010, Monitoring the Future (MTF) 2010, National Youth Risk Behavior Survey (YRBS) 2009, and National Youth Tobacco Survey (NYTS) 2009; United States

	NSDUH 13–18 years of age[a]		MTF 8th, 10th, and 12th grades[b]		YRBS 9th–12th grades[c]		NYTS 9th–12 grades[d]		NYTS 6th–8th grades[d]	
Characteristic	**% (95% CI)**	**SN[e]**	**% (95% CI)**	**SN[e]**	**% (95% CI)**	**SN[e]**	**% (95% CI)**	**SN[e]**	**% (95% CI)**	**SN[e]**
Overall	13.2 (12.57–13.87)		12.8 (11.6–14.0)		19.5 (17.9–21.2)		17.2 (15.0–19.4)		5.2 (4.2–6.1)	
Gender										
Male	13.9 (13.05–14.90)	a	14.2 12.7–15.7)	a	19.8 (17.8–21.9)	a	19.6 (16.6–22.5)	a	5.6 (4.3–6.9)	a
Female	12.4 (11.53–13.37)	b	11.2 (9.8–12.5)	b	19.1 (17.2–21.0)	a	14.8 (12.8–16.7)	b	4.7 (3.9–5.5)	a
Race/ethnicity										
White	15.2 (14.38–16.14)	a	14.4 (12.9–15.8)	a	22.5 (20.0–25.2)	a	19.2 (16.4–21.9)	a	4.3 (3.1–5.5)	a
Male	15.3 (14.16–16.57)		15.4 (13.6–17.3)		22.3 (18.9–26.0)		21.2 (18.0–24.5)		4.5 (3.0–5.9)	
Female	15.1 (13.92–16.45)		13.2 (11.5–14.8)		22.8 (20.3–25.5)		17.1 (14.5–19.8)		4.1 (2.7–5.6)	
Black or African American	8.2 (6.99–9.53)	b	7.0 (5.3–8.7)	b	9.5 (8.2–11.1)	b	7.5 (4.6–10.3)	b	5.1 (3.6–6.6)	a,b
Male	10.4 (8.59–12.57)		9.2 (6.5–11.9)		10.7 (8.4–13.5)		8.6 (3.6–13.6)		5.8 (3.6–8.0)	
Female	5.8 (4.46–7.57)		4.7 (3.2–6.3)		8.4 (6.5–10.9)		6.3 (3.0–9.6)		4.4 (2.7–6.1)	
Hispanic or Latino	12.2 (10.75–13.73)	c	11.0 (9.3–12.7)	c	18.0 (16.0–20.2)	c	19.2 (16.5–21.9)	a	6.7 (5.2–8.2)	b
Male	14.2 (12.15–16.50)		13.5 (10.9–16.0)		19.4 (16.7–22.5)		22.6 (19.9–25.4)		7.0 (5.3–8.7)	
Female	9.8 (8.06–11.97)		8.8 (6.9–10.8)		16.7 (14.4–19.2)		15.7 (12.0–19.4)		6.4 (4.5–8.3)	
Other[f]	9.9 (7.83–12.38)	c	11.1 (7.0–15.1)	c	16.5 (13.1–20.5)	c	16.4 (13.2–19.5)	a	7.2 (2.5–12.0)	a,b
Male	9.1 (6.67–12.21)		12.6 (7.3–17.8)		15.9 (12.4–20.2)		21.7 (16.6–26.8)		8.7 (0.2–17.2)	
Female	10.7 (7.89–14.41)		9.4 (5.4–13.3)		16.7 (12.5–21.9)		11.2 (6.7–15.8)		5.7 (3.0–8.5)	
Age (in years)/grade										
13–14	4.0 (3.44–4.68)	a	NA		NA		NA		NA	
15–16	10.9 (9.94–11.84)	b	NA		NA		NA		NA	
17–18	23.5 (22.21–24.91)	c	NA		NA		NA		NA	
6th	NA		NA		NA		NA		3.3 (2.1–4.5)	a
7th	NA		NA		NA		NA		4.5 (3.4–5.6)	a
8th	NA		7.1 (6.1–8.1)	a	NA		NA		7.7 (6.1–9.3)	b
9th	NA		NA		13.5 (12.0–15.3)	a	11.1 (8.1–14.1)	a	NA	
10th	NA		13.6 (12.4–14.8)	b	18.3 (15.9–21.0)	b	15.3 (13.0–17.6)	b	NA	
11th	NA		NA		22.3 (19.6–25.2)	c	20.7 (18.2–23.3)	c	NA	
12th	NA		19.2 (17.7–20.7)	c	25.2 (22.5–28.1)	d	23.2 (19.2–27.1)	c	NA	

Table 3.1.2 Continued

	NSDUH 13–18 years of age[a]		MTF 8th, 10th, and 12th grades[b]		YRBS 9th–12th grades[c]		NYTS 9th–12 grades[d]		NYTS 6th–8th grades[d]	
Characteristic	**% (95% CI)**	**SN[e]**	**% (95% CI)**	**SN[e]**	**% (95% CI)**	**SN[e]**	**% (95% CI)**	**SN[e]**	**% (95% CI)**	**SN[e]**
Region										
Northeast	12.1 (10.81–13.49)	a	11.6 (8.9–14.3)	a	19.6 (15.1–25.1)	a,b	NA		NA	
Midwest	14.7 (13.68–15.88)	b	14.3 (12.1–16.5)	b	20.2 (16.7–24.2)	a,b	NA		NA	
South	13.2 (12.14–14.44)	a	14.3 (12.4–16.3)	b	22.0 (19.4–24.8)	a	NA		NA	
West	12.5 (11.08–14.17)	a	9.7 (7.4–12.1)	a	15.5 (12.9–18.5)	b	NA		NA	

Source: 2010 NSDUH: Substance Abuse and Mental Health Services Administration (unpublished data); 2010 MTF: University of Michigan, Institute for Social Research (unpublished data); 2009 YRBS: Centers for Disease Control and Prevention (CDC 2011a); 2009 NYTS: CDC (unpublished data).

Note: **CI** = confidence interval; **NA** = not applicable; **SN** = statistical note.

[a]Based on responses to the question, "During the past 30 days, have you smoked part or all of a cigarette?" Respondents who chose "Yes" were classified as current smokers.

[b]Based on responses to the question, "How frequently have you smoked cigarettes during the past 30 days?" Respondents who reported that they had smoked less than 1 cigarette per day or more were classified as current smokers.

[c]Based on responses to the question, "During the past 30 days, on how many days did you smoke cigarettes?" Respondents who reported that they had smoked on at least 1 or 2 days were classified as current smokers.

[d]Estimates are based on responses to the question, "During the past 30 days, on how many days did you smoke cigarettes?" The estimates are compared and matched the ones reported by CDC (2010e).

[e]This column represents the results of statistical tests that were run separately within each surveillance system (e.g., NSDUH). These tests were performed to examine differences in estimates within specific demographic subgroups (e.g., gender). Estimates with the same letter (e.g., a and a) are not statistically significantly different from one another ($p > 0.05$). Estimates with different letters (e.g., a and b) are, in contrast, statistically significantly different from one another ($p < 0.05$).

[f]Includes Asians, American Indians or Alaska Natives, Native Hawaiians or Other Pacific Islanders, and persons of two or more races.

Table 3.1.3 Percentage of current cigarette use among 12- to 17-year-olds, by race/ethnicity and gender; National Survey on Drug Use and Health (NSDUH) 2008–2010;[a] United States

Race/ethnicity	Total % (95% CI)	Males % (95% CI)	Females % (95% CI)
Overall	8.8 (8.5–9.1)	8.9 (8.5–9.3)	8.6 (8.2–9.0)
All non-Hispanic	9.0 (8.7–9.3)	8.9 (8.5–9.3)	9.2 (8.7–9.6)
White	10.3 (10.0–10.7)	10.0 (9.5–10.5)	10.7 (10.2–11.3)
Black or African American	4.9 (4.3–5.4)	5.7 (4.9–6.6)	4.0 (3.4–4.8)
American Indian/Alaska Native	15.2 (12.6–18.2)	14.3 (10.9–18.4)	16.3 (11.9–22.1)
Hawaiian or Other Pacific Islander	8.6 (4.3–16.6)	NR	NR
Asian	3.3 (2.3–4.6)	3.7 (2.3–5.9)	2.9 (1.8–4.6)
Chinese	0.6 (0.2–2.0)	1.0 (0.2–4.0)	0.3 (0.1–1.4)
Filipino	4.4 (2.3–8.5)	3.7 (1.2–11.1)	5.3 (2.5–10.9)
Japanese	NR	NR	NR
Asian Indian	3.6 (1.7–7.6)	3.9 (1.3–10.9)	3.3 (1.2–9.0)
Korean	3.0 (1.0–8.4)	NR	NR
Vietnamese	5.5 (2.2–13.1)	NR	NR
Hispanic	7.8 (7.1–8.5)	9.1 (8.1–10.2)	6.4 (5.6–7.4)
Mexican	7.7 (6.9–8.6)	9.5 (8.3–10.9)	5.8 (4.8–6.9)
Puerto Rican	8.6 (6.7–10.9)	8.8 (6.2–12.3)	8.3 (5.8–11.8)
Central or South American	6.6 (5.1–8.7)	6.7 (4.6–9.6)	6.6 (4.4–9.8)
Cuban	10.3 (6.6–15.8)	12.2 (7.2–19.9)	8.4 (4.0–16.7)

Source: 2008–2010 NSDUH: Substance Abuse and Mental Health Services Administration (unpublished data).
Note: **CI** = confidence interval; **NR** = low precision, no estimate reported.
[a]Based on responses to the question, "During the past 30 days, have you smoked part or all of a cigarette?" Respondents who chose "Yes" were classified as current smokers.

Table 3.1.4 Percentage of current cigarette use among 18- to 25-year-olds, by race/ethnicity and gender; National Survey on Drug Use and Health (NSDUH) 2008–2010;[a] United States

Race/ethnicity	Total % (95% CI)	Male % (95% CI)	Female % (95% CI)
Overall	35.2 (34.7–35.8)	39.3 (38.6–40.1)	31.1 (30.4–31.8)
All non-Hispanic	36.6 (36.0–37.2)	40.3 (39.5–41.1)	33.0 (32.3–33.7)
White	40.1 (39.4–40.7)	43.0 (42.0–43.9)	37.1 (36.3–37.9)
Black or African American	26.5 (25.2–27.9)	32.4 (30.5–34.4)	21.2 (19.7–22.8)
American Indian/Alaska Native	47.9 (42.2–53.7)	50.0 (41.9–58.0)	46.1 (38.5–53.8)
Hawaiian or Other Pacific Islander	37.7 (29.7–46.5)	41.1 (30.4–52.6)	NR
Asian	20.2 (18.1–22.5)	26.0 (22.9–29.4)	14.3 (11.7–17.2)
Chinese	13.0 (9.9–17.0)	18.9 (14.1–25.0)	6.0 (3.5–10.2)
Filipino	24.7 (19.5–30.7)	28.1 (20.1–37.6)	21.8 (15.0–30.6)
Japanese	21.4 (15.0–29.5)	NR	NR
Asian Indian	15.0 (11.7–19.1)	23.3 (17.9–29.6)	6.9 (4.0–11.4)
Korean	30.0 (22.7–38.4)	NR	28.4 (19.8–38.9)
Vietnamese	20.2 (13.4–29.1)	NR	NR
Hispanic	29.1 (27.9–30.3)	35.2 (33.4–37.1)	22.1 (20.6–23.8)
Mexican	28.5 (27.0–30.0)	36.0 (33.8–38.3)	20.2 (18.4–22.2)
Puerto Rican	34.1 (30.5–37.9)	36.3 (30.8–42.2)	32.0 (27.2–37.1)
Central or South American	24.3 (21.1–27.9)	28.1 (23.8–32.8)	19.0 (14.8–24.0)
Cuban	29.3 (24.2–34.9)	35.3 (27.8–43.7)	22.5 (15.9–30.8)

Source: 2008–2010 NSDUH: Substance Abuse and Mental Health Services Administration (unpublished data).
Note: **CI** = confidence interval; **NR** = low precision, no estimate reported.
[a]Based on responses to the question, "During the past 30 days, have you smoked part or all of a cigarette?" Respondents who chose "Yes" were classified as current smokers.

Table 3.1.5 Percentage of current cigarette smoking, by various sociodemographic risk factors among 8th, 10th, and 12th graders; Monitoring the Future (MTF) 2002–2007;[a] United States

	8th graders		10th graders		12th graders	
Sociodemographic risk factor	**% (95% CI)**	**SN[b]**	**% (95% CI)**	**SN[b]**	**% (95% CI)**	**SN[b]**
Population density						
Large MSA	6.8 (6.0–7.5)	a	12.4 (11.2–13.5)	a	20.9 (19.2–22.6)	a
Other MSA	9.2 (7.3–11.1)	b	15.4 (13.4–17.4)	b	23.5 (20.7–26.3)	b
Non-MSA	12.3 (10.1–14.6)	c	20.8 (18.2–23.3)	c	27.8 (25.6–30.0)	c
Parental education[c]						
1.0–2.0 (low)	16.3 (13.6–18.9)	a	19.8 (15.7–23.8)	a	21.0 (18.3–23.7)	a
2.5–3.0	13.0 (11.7–14.2)	b	20.2 (18.7–21.8)	a	26.9 (24.8–29.0)	b,c
3.5–4.0	9.5 (8.6–10.3)	c	16.2 (15.1–17.3)	b	24.7 (22.8–26.6)	c
4.5–5.0	6.1 (5.3–6.8)	d	12.5 (11.6–13.4)	c	22.1 (20.8–23.3)	d
5.5–6.0 (high)	4.7 (4.0–5.4)	e	10.9 (9.5–12.2)	d	19.8 (18.6–21.0)	a,c
Academic performance						
A	3.6 (2.9–4.2)	a	7.1 (6.2–8.0)	a	14.9 (13.7–16.1)	a
B	7.9 (7.0–8.7)	b	14.4 (13.0–15.8)	b	25.0 (23.1–27.0)	b
C	17.3 (15.5–19.1)	c	24.5 (21.5–27.4)	c	34.2 (30.8–37.5)	c
D	30.1 (26.9–33.3)	d	38.9 (33.8–43.9)	d	46.1 (40.7–51.5)	d
Household structure						
Lives with both parents	7.6 (6.4–8.6)	a	14.1 (12.7–15.5)	a	22.1 (20.4–23.7)	a
Lives with father only	15.9 (14.5–17.3)	b	24.4 (22.4–26.5)	b	30.8 (28.2–33.3)	b
Lives with mother only	11.7 (10.4–13.0)	c	17.1 (15.2–19.0)	c	23.9 (22.1–25.8)	c
Lives alone	27.1 (21.3–32.9)	d	33.2 (26.2–40.3)	d	41.3 (36.8–45.7)	d
Other	17.7 (15.0–20.3)	b	24.6 (22.7–26.6)	b	31.4 (28.8–33.9)	b
Importance of religion						
Very important	5.8 (5.0–6.5)	a	9.4 (8.3–10.4)	a	15.0 (13.5–16.4)	a
Important	8.6 (7.3–9.8)	b	15.8 (14.4–17.2)	b	24.8 (23.0–26.6)	b
Not/somewhat important	13.8 (12.2–15.3)	c	22.2 (20.2–24.2)	c	30.8 (29.3–32.2)	c

Source: 2002–2007 MTF: University of Michigan, Institute for Social Research (unpublished data).
Note: **CI** = confidence interval; **MSA** = metropolitan statistical area; **SN** = statistical note.
[a]Based on responses to the question, "How frequently have you smoked cigarettes during the past 30 days?" Respondents who reported that they had smoked less than 1 cigarette per day or more were classified as current smokers.
[b]This column represents the results of statistical tests that were performed to examine differences in estimates within specific demographic subgroups (e.g., gender). Estimates with the same letter (e.g., a and a) are not statistically significantly different from one another ($p > 0.05$). Estimates with different letters (e.g., a and b) are, in contrast, statistically significantly different from one another ($p < 0.05$).
[c]Parental education is an average score of mother's education and father's education. Response categories are (1) completed some grade school or less, (2) some high school, (3) completed high school, (4) some college, (5) completed college, and (6) graduate or professional school after college.

Table 3.1.6 Percentage of frequent cigarette smoking, by gender, race/ethnicity, age/grade, and region; National Survey on Drug Use and Health (NSDUH) 2010, National Youth Risk Behavior Survey (YRBS) 2009, and National Youth Tobacco Survey (NYTS) 2009; United States

	NSDUH 13–18 years of age[a]		YRBS 9th–12th grades[b]		NYTS 9th–12th grades[c]		NYTS 6th–8th grades[c]	
Characteristic	**% (95% CI)**	**SN[d]**	**% (95% CI)**	**SN[d]**	**% (95% CI)**	**SN[d]**	**% (95% CI)**	**SN[d]**
Overall	5.8 (5.37–6.23)		7.3 (6.4–8.3)		6.2 (4.9–7.6)		1.4 (0.9–1.9)	
Gender								
Male	6.2 (5.63–6.90)	a	8.0 (7.1–9.0)	a	7.4 (5.8–8.9)	a	2.0 (1.1–3.0)	a
Female	5.3 (4.74–5.91)	a	6.4 (5.4–7.6)	b	5.1 (3.7–6.4)	b	0.8 (0.5–1.1)	b
Race/ethnicity								
White	7.4 (6.85–8.06)	a	9.5 (8.2–11.1)	a	7.9 (6.3–9.4)	a	1.2 (0.7–1.6)	a
Male	7.7 (6.89–8.65)		10.0 (8.5–11.8)		9.1 (7.2–10.9)		1.4 (0.7–2.2)	
Female	7.1 (6.30–8.03)		9.0 (7.5–10.8)		6.7 (5.0–8.3)		0.9 (0.4–1.4)	
Black or African American	2.9 (2.11–4.03)	b	2.1 (1.4–3.2)	b	1.8 (0.4–3.2)	b	0.8 (0.3–2.2)	a
Male	3.5 (2.26–5.29)		2.9 (1.8–4.6)		1.9 (0.4–3.5)		1.0 (0.0-2.0)	
Female	2.3 (1.42–3.86)		1.4 (0.7–2.5)		1.6 (0.5–4.6)		0.6 (0.2-2.5)	
Hispanic or Latino	3.5 (2.80–4.42)	b,c	4.2 (3.3–5.3)	c	4.7 (3.7–5.6)	c	1.4 (0.8–1.9)	a
Male	4.5 (3.42–5.98)		5.2 (3.8–7.0)		5.8 (4.4–7.2)		2.2 (1.2–3.2)	
Female	2.4 (1.66–3.37)		3.2 (2.4–4.3)		3.5 (2.5–4.5)		0.6 (0.2–0.9)	
Other[e]	4.6 (3.28–6.40)	c	5.7 (3.7–8.8)	c	6.2 (4.4–7.9)	a,c	4.0 (1.2–12.2)	a
Male	4.7 (3.10–7.14)		6.9 (4.3–11.0)		8.5 (5.4–11.5)		6.2 (1.5–22.8)	
Female	4.5 (2.79–7.07)		4.5 (2.6–7.7)		3.9 (1.8–5.9)		1.6 (0.5–4.4)	
Age (in years)/grade								
13–14	0.9 (0.65–1.19)	a	NA		NA		NA	
15–16	4.3 (3.72–4.92)	b	NA		NA		NA	
17–18	11.5 (10.57–12.55)	c	NA		NA		NA	
6th	NA		NA		NA		1.2 (0.2–2.1)	a
7th	NA		NA		NA		1.1 (0.5–1.8)	a
8th	NA		NA		NA		2.0 (1.3–2.7)	a
9th	NA		4.7 (3.7–5.9)	a	3.0 (2.0–4.0)	a	NA	
10th	NA		5.7 (4.7–7.0)	a	5.7 (4.2–7.3)	b	NA	
11th	NA		8.3 (7.0–9.8)	b	7.0 (4.9–9.1)	b	NA	
12th	NA		11.2 (9.5–13.2)	c	10.0 (7.2–12.8)	c	NA	

Table 3.1.6 Continued

	NSDUH 13–18 years of age[a]		YRBS 9th–12th grades[b]		NYTS 9th–12th grades[c]		NYTS 6th–8th grades[c]	
Characteristic	**% (95% CI)**	**SN[d]**	**% (95% CI)**	**SN[d]**	**% (95% CI)**	**SN[d]**	**% (95% CI)**	**SN[d]**
Region					NA		NA	
Northeast	5.5 (4.64–6.56)	a,b	8.7 (5.8–12.8)	a	NA		NA	
Midwest	7.2 (6.41–8.12)	a	8.3 (6.7–10.2)	a	NA		NA	
South	6.0 (5.29–6.87)	b	8.5 (6.8–10.5)	a	NA		NA	
West	4.2 (3.47–5.18)	c	3.5 (2.4–5.1)	b	NA		NA	

Source: 2010 NSDUH: Substance Abuse and Mental Health Services Administration (unpublished data); 2009 YRBS: Centers for Disease Control and Prevention (CDC 2011a); 2009 NYTS: CDC (unpublished data).
Note: **CI** = confidence interval; **NA** = not applicable; **SN** = statistical note.
[a]Based on responses to the question, "During the past 30 days… on how many days did you smoke part or all of a cigarette?" Respondents who reported that they had smoked on at least 20 days were classified as frequent smokers.
[b]Based on responses to the question, "During the past 30 days, on how many days did you smoke cigarettes?" Respondents who reported that they had smoked on "20 to 29 days" or "all 30 days" were classified as frequent smokers.
[c]Estimates are based on responding "20 to 29 days" or "all 30 days" to the question, "During the past 30 days, on how many days did you smoke cigarettes?" Nonsmokers are counted in the denominator of the reported percentages.
[d]This column represents the results of statistical tests that were run separately within each surveillance system (e.g., NSDUH). These tests were performed to examine differences in estimates within specific demographic subgroups (e.g., gender). Estimates with the same letter (e.g., a and a) are not statistically significantly different from one another ($p > 0.05$). Estimates with different letters (e.g., a and b) are, in contrast, statistically significantly different from one another ($p < 0.05$).
[e]Includes Asians, American Indians or Alaska Natives, Native Hawaiians or Other Pacific Islanders, and persons of two or more races.

Table 3.1.7 Percentage of heavy cigarette smoking, by gender, race/ethnicity, age/grade, and region; National Survey on Drug Use and Health (NSDUH) 2010, Monitoring the Future (MTF) 2010, and National Youth Tobacco Survey (NYTS) 2009; United States

	NSDUH 13–18 years of age[a]		MTF 8th, 10th, and 12th grades[b]		NYTS 9th–12th grades[c]		NYTS 6th–8th grades[c]	
Characteristic	**% (95% CI)**	**SN[d]**	**% (95% CI)**	**SN[d]**	**% (95% CI)**	**SN[d]**	**% (95% CI)**	**SN[d]**
Overall	2.6 (2.29–2.85)		2.5 (2.1–3.0)		1.8 (1.2–2.3)		0.7 (0.3–1.2)	
Gender								
Male	2.9 (2.48–3.36)	a	3.0 (2.4–3.6)	a	2.5 (1.7–3.3)	a	1.2 (0.3–2.1)	a
Female	2.2 (1.86–2.59)	a	1.9 (1.4–2.4)	b	1.0 (0.5–1.4)	b	0.3 (0.1–0.5)	a
Race/ethnicity								
White	3.7 (3.33–4.21)	a	3.2 (2.6–3.8)	a	1.9 (1.2–2.6)	a	0.3 (0.1–0.6)	a
Male	4.1 (3.51–4.83)		3.6 (2.8–4.4)		2.7 (1.5–3.9)		0.6 (0.2–1.1)	
Female	3.3 (2.82–3.97)		2.7 (2.0–3.4)		1.1 (0.6–1.6)		0.0002 (0.0–0.002)	
Black or African American	1.0 (0.51–1.81)	b	1.3 (0.7–1.9)	b,c	1.0 (0.1–1.9)	b	0.6 (0.1–2.3)	a
Male	1.4 (0.65–2.88)		1.7 (0.8–2.7)		0.7 (0.1–1.3)		0.6 (0.2–2.4)	
Female	0.5 (0.15–1.80)		0.7 (0.1–1.2)		1.3 (0.4–4.4)		0.5 (0.0–2.7)	
Hispanic or Latino	0.9 (0.56–1.43)	b	1.1 (0.5–1.6)	b	1.6 (1.0–2.1)	a,b	0.7 (0.2–1.1)	a
Male	1.2 (0.64–2.16)		1.7 (0.7–2.8)		2.4 (1.5–3.3)		1.1 (0.4–1.9)	
Female	0.6 (0.30–1.07)		0.5 (0.0–1.0)		0.8 (0.2–1.3)		0.3 (0.0–0.5)	
Other[e]	0.8 (0.45–1.33)	c	2.0 (0.7–3.4)	c	2.5 (0.8–4.1)	a,b	3.3 (0.8–12.7)	a
Male	0.9 (0.48–1.65)		2.5 (0.7–4.3)		4.7 (1.5–7.9)		5.2 (0.9–24.4)	
Female	0.6 (0.30–1.38)		1.5 (0.0–2.9)		0.3 (-0.3–1.0)		1.4 (0.4–4.5)	
Age (in years)/grade								
13–14	0.3 (0.20–0.50)	a	NA					
15–16	1.6 (1.28–1.97)	b	NA					
17–18	5.4 (4.79–6.16)	c	NA					
6th	NA						0.9 (0.3–2.5)	a
7th	NA						0.6 (0.1–1.1)	a
8th	NA		0.9 (0.7–1.1)	a			0.7 (0.3–1.2)	a
9th	NA		NA		0.7 (0.3–1.2)	a		
10th	NA		2.4 (2.0–2.9)	b	1.7 (0.9–2.5)	b		
11th	NA		NA		1.8 (1.1–2.5)	b,c		
12th	NA		4.7 (3.9–5.5)	c	3.0 (1.8–4.3)	c		

Table 3.1.7 Continued

Characteristic	NSDUH 13–18 years of age[a] % (95% CI)	SN[d]	MTF 8th, 10th, and 12th grades[b] % (95% CI)	SN[d]	NYTS 9th–12th grades[c] % (95% CI)	SN[d]	NYTS 6th–8th grades[c] % (95% CI)	SN[d]
Region								
Northeast	2.6 (2.06–3.35)	a	2.4 (1.3–3.4)	a				
Midwest	3.6 (2.99–4.21)	a	3.0 (2.3–3.7)	a				
South	2.6 (2.10–3.10)	a	3.1 (2.2–4.0)	a				
West	1.6 (1.08–2.29)	b	1.2 (0.5–1.8)	b				

Source: 2010 NSDUH: Substance Abuse and Mental Health Services Administration (unpublished data); 2010 MTF: University of Michigan, Institute for Social Research (unpublished data); 2009 NYTS: Centers for Disease Control and Prevention (unpublished data).
Note: **CI** = confidence interval; **NA** = not applicable; **SN** = statistical note.
[a]Based on responses to the question, "On the [number of] days you smoked cigarettes during the past 30 days, how many cigarettes did you smoke per day, on average?" Respondents who reported smoking "6 to 15 cigarettes per day (about ½ pack)" or more were classified as heavy smokers.
[b]Based on responses to the question, "How frequently have you smoked cigarettes during the past 30 days?" Respondents who reported smoking at least "about one-half pack per day" were classified as heavy smokers.
[c]Estimates are based on responding "11 to 20 cigarettes per day" or "more than 20 cigarettes per day" to the question, "During the past 30 days, on the days you smoked, how many cigarettes did you smoke per day?" Current smokers who usually smoked Marlboro were considered to be heavy smokers even if they reported 11–20 cigarettes per day. Nonsmokers are counted in the denominator of the reported percentages.
[d]This column represents the results of statistical tests that were run separately within each surveillance system (e.g., NSDUH). These tests were performed to examine differences in estimates within specific demographic subgroups (e.g., gender). Estimates with the same letter (e.g., a and a) are not statistically significantly different from one another (p >0.05). Estimates with different letters (e.g., a and b) are, in contrast, statistically significantly different from one another (p <0.05).
[e]Includes Asians, American Indians or Alaska Natives, Native Hawaiians or Other Pacific Islanders, and persons of two or more races.

Table 3.1.8 Percentage distribution of smoking intensity among 9th–12th graders, by the number of cigarettes smoked per day during the 30 days preceding the survey; National Youth Risk Behavior Survey (YRBS) 2009;[a] United States

Number of days	<1 cigarette smoked per day % (95% CI)	1 cigarette smoked per day % (95% CI)	2–5 cigarettes smoked per day % (95% CI)	6–10 cigarettes smoked per day % (95% CI)	11–20 cigarettes smoked per day % (95% CI)	>20 cigarettes smoked per day % (95% CI)
1–2	52.2 (48.2–56.2)	31.9 (28.5–35.5)	14.4 (12.0–17.2)	1.3 (0.5–2.9)	0.0	0.3 (0.1–1.0)
3–5	22.6 (17.7-28.5)	33.8 (27.1–41.4)	40.5 (35.2–46.0)	2.3 (1.1–5.0)	0.4 (0.1–2.1)	0.3 (0.0–2.4)
6–9	17.6 (12.0–25.2)	23.3 (17.8–29.8)	52.2 (43.9–60.4)	6.0 (3.2-11.0)	0.8 (0.1–4.8)	0.1 (0.0–0.4)
10–19	6.8 (4.5–10.2)	21.4 (16.3–27.5)	62.8 (55.6–69.5)	7.8 (5.1–11.7)	1.2 (0.5–3.1)	0.0
20–29	0.5 (0.1–2.1)	8.9 (4.8–15.8)	76.5 (68.8–82.8)	12.5 (8.3–18.6)	1.5 (0.5–4.6)	0.0
All 30	0.3 (0.1–1.3)	3.8 (2.4–6.0)	35.8 (32.1–39.7)	34.1 (30.1–38.4)	15.3 (12.8–18.1)	10.7 (7.4–15.2)
All current smokers	20.0 (18.4–21.8)	20.1 (18.3–22.0)	39.3 (37.2–41.5)	12.8 (11.1–14.8)	4.7 (3.8–5.7)	3.1 (2.2–4.2)

Source: 2009 YRBS: Centers for Disease Control and Prevention, Division of Adolescent and School Health (unpublished data).
Note: **CI** = confidence interval.
[a]Based on responses to the questions, "During the past 30 days, on how many days did you smoke cigarettes?" and "During the past 30 days, on the days you smoked, how many cigarettes did you smoke per day?"

Table 3.1.9 Cumulative percentages of recalled age at which a respondent first used a cigarette and began smoking daily, by smoking status among 30- to 39-year-olds; National Survey on Drug Use and Health (NSDUH) 2010;[a] United States

	All persons		Persons who had ever tried a cigarette	Persons who had ever smoked daily	
Recalled age (years)	First tried a cigarette % (95% CI)	Began smoking daily % (95% CI)	First tried a cigarette % (95% CI)	First tried a cigarette % (95% CI)	Began smoking daily % (95% CI)
≤10	4.1 (3.54–4.77)	0.4 (0.24–0.61)	5.9 (5.12–6.90)	6.7 (5.60–8.09)	1.0 (0.65–1.64)
≤11	5.8 (5.16–6.58)	0.7 (0.48–1.01)	8.4 (7.47–9.51)	9.6 (8.25–11.14)	1.9 (1.29–2.70)
≤12	12.1 (11.13–13.19)	1.8 (1.40–2.23)	17.5 (16.14–19.02)	20.9 (18.85–23.14)	4.7 (3.75–5.93)
≤13	18.5 (17.36–19.78)	3.5 (2.95–4.07)	26.8 (25.18–28.53)	32.4 (30.15–34.71)	9.3 (7.93–10.82)
≤14	25.4 (24.02–26.78)	6.0 (5.30–6.72)	36.7 (34.89–38.56)	43.6 (41.17–46.09)	16.0 (14.31–17.81)
≤15	34.4 (32.94–35.93)	10.5 (9.57–11.52)	49.8 (47.87–51.72)	58.5 (56.03–61.00)	28.1 (25.89–30.46)
≤16	43.9 (42.31–45.42)	15.3 (14.22–16.39)	63.5 (61.59–65.27)	72.9 (70.55–75.07)	40.9 (38.53–43.26)
≤17	49.4 (47.76–50.95)	19.2 (18.08–20.40)	71.4 (69.64–73.10)	80.3 (78.21–82.27)	51.4 (49.09–53.74)
≤18	56.3 (54.75–57.90)	24.3 (23.03–25.66)	81.5 (79.91–82.98)	88.2 (86.45–89.81)	65.1 (62.67–67.41)
≤19	59.3 (57.72–60.86)	27.4 (26.06–28.88)	85.8 (84.37–87.10)	91.8 (90.30–93.11)	73.5 (71.14–75.65)
≤20	61.9 (60.38–63.41)	30.0 (28.55–31.44)	89.6 (88.33–90.68)	93.2 (91.75–94.38)	80.2 (78.11–82.16)
≤21	64.2 (62.67–65.72)	32.0 (30.53–33.50)	92.9 (91.81–93.86)	95.9 (94.78–96.77)	85.6 (83.82–87.27)
≤22	65.2 (63.72–66.75)	33.1 (31.63–34.61)	94.4 (93.40–95.25)	96.6 (95.61–97.43)	88.6 (86.92–90.08)
≤23	65.9 (64.39–67.39)	33.9 (32.40–35.40)	95.3 (94.45–96.11)	97.3 (96.34–98.00)	90.7 (89.13–92.02)
≤24	66.5 (65.03–68.02)	34.6 (33.09–36.12)	96.3 (95.42–96.97)	97.9 (97.02–98.50)	92.6 (91.14–93.78)
≤25	67.6 (66.11–69.04)	35.7 (34.22–37.27)	97.8 (97.14–98.30)	98.8 (98.23–99.23)	95.6 (94.56–96.49)
≤26	67.8 (66.28–69.20)	35.9 (34.43–37.47)	98.0 (97.39–98.53)	99.0 (98.39–99.36)	96.2 (95.18–96.96)
≤27	67.9 (66.44–69.36)	36.1 (34.62–37.68)	98.3 (97.64–98.73)	99.1 (98.46–99.42)	96.7 (95.74–97.44)
≤28	68.1 (66.61–69.52)	36.5 (34.98–38.04)	98.5 (97.90–98.94)	99.3 (98.75–99.60)	97.7 (96.90–98.27)
≤29	68.2 (66.69–69.59)	36.7 (35.14–38.20)	98.6 (98.01–99.03)	99.3 (98.81–99.64)	98.1 (97.39–98.63)
≤30	68.7 (67.28–70.14)	37.0 (35.50–38.56)	99.4 (98.98–99.69)	99.8 (99.44–99.93)	99.1 (98.50–99.43)
31–39	69.1 (67.68–70.53)	37.4 (35.85–38.91)	100.0	100.0	100.0
Never smoked	100.0	100.0	NA	NA	NA
Mean age (years)	15.9	17.9	15.9	15.1	17.9

Source: 2010 NSDUH: Substance Abuse and Mental Health Services Administration (unpublished data).
Note: **CI** = confidence interval; **NA** = not applicable.
[a]Based on responses to the following questions: "Have you ever smoked part or all of a cigarette?" "How old were you the first time you smoked part or all of a cigarette?" "Has there ever been a period in your life when you smoked cigarettes every day for at least 30 days?" "How old were you when you first started smoking cigarettes every day?"

Table 3.1.10 Percentage distribution of cigarette brands that 12- to 17-year-olds who were current smokers preferred, by gender, race/ethnicity, age, and region; National Survey on Drug Use and Health (NSDUH) 2008–2010;[a] United States

Characteristic	Marlboro full flavor % (95% CI)	Marlboro Lights % (95% CI)	Newport full flavor % (95% CI)	Marlboro Mediums % (95% CI)	Camel full flavor % (95% CI)	Camel Lights % (95% CI)
Overall	19.7 (18.3–21.0)	17.5 (16.3–18.9)	14.1 (13.0–15.3)	7.3 (6.5–8.2)	5.2 (4.6–5.9)	5.1 (4.4–6.0)
Gender						
Male	22.3 (20.4–24.2)	15.1 (13.4–17.1)	15.2 (13.6–16.9)	6.7 (5.6–7.9)	6.3 (5.3–7.4)	4.5 (3.6–5.5)
Female	16.8 (15.1–18.7)	20.1 (18.4–22.0)	12.9 (11.5–14.6)	8.0 (6.9–9.3)	4.1 (3.3–5.0)	5.8 (4.6–7.3)
Race/ethnicity						
White	22.9 (21.2–24.6)	18.0 (16.6–19.5)	11.2 (10.0–12.6)	8.0 (7.1–9.1)	5.7 (4.9–6.6)	5.8 (4.9–6.8)
Male	26.5 (24.2–29.0)	14.4 (12.5–16.6)	12.0 (10.3–13.8)	7.3 (6.1–8.8)	7.2 (5.9–8.7)	5.3 (4.3–6.6)
Female	19.3 (17.2–21.6)	21.5 (19.4–23.8)	10.5 (9.0–12.2)	8.7 (7.3–10.4)	4.3 (3.4–5.4)	6.3 (4.9–8.0)
Black or African American	1.7 (0.8–3.6)	4.3 (2.1–8.3)	42.4 (36.8–48.1)	0.7 (0.2–1.9)	0.8 (0.3–2.3)	0.5 (0.2–1.5)
Male	1.4 (0.5–3.7)	5.1 (2.0–12.2)	44.2 (37.2–51.4)	0.3 (0.0–2.0)	NR	NR
Female	2.3 (0.8–6.5)	3.1 (1.3–7.0)	39.8 (31.6–48.7)	1.2 (0.4–4.0)	1.4 (0.4–4.5)	1.3 (0.5–3.6)
Hispanic or Latino	15.6 (12.7–19.0)	21.6 (17.9–25.7)	12.5 (9.9–15.8)	7.2 (5.3–9.6)	5.1 (3.7–7.1)	5.4 (3.6–8.1)
Male	18.8 (14.8–23.6)	21.0 (16.4–26.5)	12.9 (9.4–17.5)	7.5 (5.1–10.9)	6.1 (4.2–8.8)	4.6 (2.6–7.9)
Female	10.9 (7.5–15.5)	22.4 (16.6–29.6)	12.0 (8.3–17.0)	6.7 (4.1–10.6)	3.7 (1.8–7.5)	6.6 (3.5–12.3)
Other[b]	19.3 (13.9–26.0)	19.2 (13.6–26.4)	12.5 (8.3–18.3)	8.7 (5.6–13.3)	5.8 (3.6–9.2)	3.0 (1.6–5.8)
Male	19.3 (11.9–29.6)	NR	11.8 (6.5–20.3)	6.7 (3.7–11.8)	6.9 (3.6–12.7)	1.9 (0.5–6.4)
Female	19.3 (12.3–28.9)	18.4 (13.0–25.3)	13.0 (7.4–21.9)	10.5 (5.7–18.4)	4.9 (2.4–9.6)	4.0 (1.9–8.5)
Age (years)						
12–14	13.8 (11.2–16.8)	18.4 (15.3–22.1)	9.4 (7.2–12.0)	10.2 (7.9–13.1)	3.6 (2.4–5.3)	4.1 (2.7–6.0)
15–17	20.8 (19.3–22.3)	17.4 (16.0–18.8)	15.0 (13.8–16.4)	6.8 (6.0–7.7)	5.5 (4.8–6.3)	5.3 (4.5–6.3)
Region						
Northeast	14.9 (12.4–17.7)	13.8 (11.2–16.7)	25.0 (21.8–28.6)	4.9 (3.6–6.7)	3.3 (2.3–4.9)	3.6 (2.5–5.2)
Midwest	22.0 (19.9–24.2)	14.8 (13.0–16.7)	16.4 (14.5–18.5)	8.0 (6.7–9.6)	5.0 (4.0–6.2)	4.7 (3.7–5.9)
South	18.1 (15.9–20.5)	20.9 (18.7–23.3)	13.8 (11.8–16.0)	6.0 (4.9–7.4)	4.2 (3.2–5.4)	4.8 (3.7–6.4)
West	23.0 (19.6–26.8)	18.0 (14.9–21.4)	4.0 (2.7–5.9)	10.4 (8.3–13.1)	8.6 (6.9–10.7)	7.3 (5.3–9.8)

Table 3.1.10 Continued

Characteristic	Newport Lights % (95% CI)	Newport Mediums % (95% CI)	Camel Mediums % (95% CI)	Marlboro Ultra Lights % (95% CI)	All other brands/ types % (95% CI)	Unknown brand % (95% CI)
Overall	5.0 (4.4–5.8)	2.7 (2.2–3.3)	2.1 (1.6–2.7)	1.7 (1.3–2.1)	16.0 (14.9–17.3)	3.5 (2.9–4.2)
Gender						
Male	4.6 (3.8–5.7)	2.7 (2.0–3.6)	1.9 (1.3–2.8)	1.4 (1.0–2.0)	15.4 (13.8–17.2)	3.9 (3.1–4.9)
Female	5.5 (4.5–6.6)	2.7 (2.0–3.6)	2.3 (1.7–3.1)	1.9 (1.3–2.7)	16.7 (15.0–18.5)	3.1 (2.4–4.0)
Race/ethnicity						
White	3.5 (2.9–4.2)	1.3 (0.9–1.8)	2.4 (1.8–3.1)	1.7 (1.3–2.2)	16.6 (15.2–18.1)	3.0 (2.4–3.7)
Male	2.6 (1.8–3.7)	1.4 (0.8–2.3)	2.3 (1.5–3.6)	1.6 (1.1–2.4)	15.9 (14.0–18.1)	3.4 (2.6–4.5)
Female	4.4 (3.4–5.6)	1.2 (0.7–1.8)	2.4 (1.7–3.4)	1.7 (1.1–2.5)	17.2 (15.3–19.4)	2.5 (1.9–3.5)
Black or African American	16.9 (13.2–21.4)	10.3 (7.6–13.9)	NR	0.3 (0.0–1.8)	16.8 (12.3–22.3)	4.3 (2.4–7.8)
Male	17.4 (12.5–23.7)	8.7 (5.6–13.1)	NR	NR	17.4 (12.0–24.6)	3.2 (1.4–6.9)
Female	16.1 (11.1–22.7)	12.6 (7.9–19.6)	0.3 (0.0–2.1)	NR	15.8 (9.7–24.7)	6.0 (2.6–13.4)
Hispanic or Latino	6.4 (4.6–9.0)	4.4 (2.8–6.9)	1.4 (0.8–2.6)	1.9 (1.0–3.5)	13.3 (10.7–16.5)	5.0 (3.4–7.4)
Male	6.3 (4.1–9.5)	3.6 (2.0–6.6)	0.8 (0.3–2.5)	1.4 (0.7–3.0)	12.3 (8.9–16.6)	4.7 (2.6–8.2)
Female	6.7 (4.1–10.7)	5.6 (2.9–10.7)	2.3 (1.1–5.0)	2.6 (1.1–6.3)	14.9 (10.9–20.0)	5.5 (3.2–9.2)
Other[b]	2.4 (1.3–4.6)	3.5 (1.6–7.2)	2.5 (1.0–6.0)	2.7 (0.9–7.7)	16.3 (12.3–21.3)	4.1 (1.8–8.9)
Male	1.5 (0.4–5.1)	4.8 (1.9–11.6)	NR	0.1 (0.0–0.6)	17.3 (11.7–24.7)	NR
Female	3.2 (1.5–6.7)	NR	3.4 (1.2–9.2)	NR	15.5 (10.2–22.9)	0.5 (0.1–2.0)
Age (years)						
12–14	7.5 (5.6–9.9)	3.4 (2.0–5.6)	1.6 (0.8–3.3)	2.4 (1.5–3.8)	19.2 (16.3–22.4)	6.6 (4.7–9.3)
15–17	4.6 (3.9–5.4)	2.5 (2.0–3.2)	2.2 (1.7–2.9)	1.5 (1.1–2.0)	15.4 (14.2–16.8)	2.9 (2.4–3.6)
Region						
Northeast	9.0 (7.2–11.3)	4.0 (2.5–6.4)	1.0 (0.4–2.4)	1.9 (1.1–3.5)	15.2 (12.5–18.4)	3.2 (2.1–4.7)
Midwest	5.3 (4.2–6.8)	3.5 (2.7–4.5)	1.5 (1.0–2.3)	1.4 (0.9–2.2)	14.7 (12.9–16.8)	2.7 (2.0–3.7)
South	5.1 (4.0–6.4)	2.5 (1.7–3.6)	1.7 (1.0–2.8)	1.6 (1.1–2.4)	17.5 (15.6–19.7)	3.8 (2.8–5.1)
West	1.7 (0.7–4.3)	1.1 (0.5–2.4)	4.2 (2.9–6.2)	1.8 (1.0–3.3)	15.6 (13.0–18.7)	4.2 (2.9–6.1)

Source: 2008–2010 NSDUH: Substance Abuse and Mental Health Services Administration (unpublished data).
Note: **CI** = confidence interval; **NR** = low precision, no estimate reported.
[a]Based on responses to the questions, "During the past 30 days, what brand of cigarettes did you smoke most often?" and "During the past 30 days, what type of cigarettes did you smoke most often?"
[b]Includes Asians, American Indians or Alaska Natives, Native Hawaiians or Other Pacific Islanders, and persons of two or more races.

Table 3.1.11 Percentage distribution of cigarette brands that young adults 18–25 years of age who were current smokers preferred, by gender, race/ethnicity, age, and region; National Survey on Drug Use and Health (NSDUH) 2008–2010;[a] United States

Characteristic	Marlboro Lights % (95% CI)	Marlboro full flavor % (95% CI)	Newport full flavor % (95% CI)	Camel Lights % (95% CI)	Camel full flavor % (95% CI)	Marlboro Mediums % (95% CI)
Overall	22.7 (21.9–23.4)	16.3 (15.7–17.0)	15.7 (15.0–16.4)	9.3 (8.8–9.8)	5.6 (5.2–6.0)	5.0 (4.7–5.4)
Gender						
Male	20.9 (20.0–22.0)	18.8 (17.9–19.7)	15.4 (14.5–16.2)	9.1 (8.5–9.8)	6.4 (5.9–7.0)	5.2 (4.7–5.7)
Female	24.9 (23.8–26.0)	13.2 (12.4–14.0)	16.2 (15.2–17.2)	9.6 (8.9–10.4)	4.5 (4.0–5.1)	4.9 (4.4–5.5)
Race/ethnicity						
White	24.1 (23.3–25.0)	18.5 (17.7–19.3)	9.1 (8.5–9.7)	11.3 (10.7–11.9)	6.8 (6.3–7.3)	5.7 (5.3–6.2)
Male	21.6 (20.4–22.8)	21.4 (20.3–22.6)	8.8 (8.0–9.5)	11.3 (10.5–12.2)	7.9 (7.2–8.6)	6.1 (5.5–6.7)
Female	27.1 (25.9–28.4)	15.0 (14.1–16.0)	9.5 (8.7–10.4)	11.2 (10.4–12.2)	5.5 (4.8–6.2)	5.4 (4.7–6.0)
Black or African American	3.7 (2.7–5.1)	2.1 (1.5–3.0)	61.2 (58.5–63.8)	1.3 (0.8–2.0)	0.3 (0.2–0.5)	1.1 (0.6–1.7)
Male	3.7 (2.5–5.4)	2.2 (1.4–3.4)	59.8 (56.4–63.2)	1.3 (0.7–2.3)	0.3 (0.2–0.7)	0.8 (0.4–1.5)
Female	3.7 (2.2–6.3)	2.1 (1.2–3.5)	63.0 (58.8–67.1)	1.2 (0.6–2.4)	0.3 (0.1–0.6)	1.4 (0.7–3.0)
Hispanic or Latino	28.2 (26.0–30.5)	17.5 (15.7–19.5)	14.2 (12.6–16.0)	6.9 (5.7–8.3)	4.2 (3.3–5.4)	4.7 (3.7–5.9)
Male	28.4 (25.6–31.4)	20.3 (17.9–23.1)	13.2 (11.3–15.3)	6.2 (4.9–8.0)	4.9 (3.7–6.4)	4.3 (3.2–5.8)
Female	27.6 (24.1–31.5)	12.5 (10.2–15.3)	16.1 (13.3–19.3)	8.0 (5.9–10.8)	3.0 (1.8–5.1)	5.4 (3.8–7.6)
Other[b]	26.4 (23.3–29.8)	13.9 (11.9–16.2)	13.8 (11.1–17.0)	7.4 (5.7–9.5)	5.0 (3.6–6.8)	5.0 (3.9–6.4)
Male	24.2 (20.4–28.5)	16.1 (13.2–19.6)	12.5 (9.6–16.1)	7.1 (5.1–9.8)	6.0 (4.1–8.8)	5.4 (3.9–7.5)
Female	29.7 (24.7–35.2)	10.6 (8.2–13.6)	15.7 (11.7–20.6)	7.7 (5.1–11.6)	3.5 (2.0–6.0)	4.4 (2.9–6.6)
Age (years)						
18–20	19.1 (18.0–20.2)	19.8 (18.7–21.0)	16.1 (15.1–17.2)	8.3 (7.6–9.1)	6.9 (6.2–7.6)	5.7 (5.2–6.4)
21–25	24.8 (23.9–25.7)	14.2 (13.5–15.0)	15.5 (14.7–16.3)	9.9 (9.3–10.6)	4.8 (4.4–5.3)	4.6 (4.2–5.1)
Region						
Northeast	19.7 (18.1–21.4)	14.9 (13.6–16.4)	24.6 (22.6–26.7)	6.8 (5.8–7.9)	3.5 (3.0–4.2)	4.1 (3.5–4.9)
Midwest	22.7 (21.5–24.0)	16.8 (15.8–17.9)	14.5 (13.5–15.5)	11.1 (10.3–12.1)	5.6 (5.0–6.3)	4.9 (4.4–5.6)
South	25.4 (24.1–26.8)	14.9 (13.8–16.1)	18.3 (17.0–19.6)	8.2 (7.4–9.2)	4.2 (3.7–4.9)	4.5 (4.0–5.2)
West	20.4 (18.7–22.2)	19.5 (17.9–21.2)	5.0 (4.0–6.2)	11.3 (10.0–12.7)	9.7 (8.5–10.9)	6.8 (5.8–8.1)

Table 3.1.11 Continued

Characteristic	Parliament Lights % (95% CI)	Newport Lights % (95% CI)	Marlboro Ultra Lights % (95% CI)	Newport Mediums % (95% CI)	All other brands/ types % (95% CI)	Unknown brands % (95% CI)
Overall	2.6 (2.3–2.9)	2.2 (2.0–2.5)	2.1 (1.9–2.4)	1.6 (1.3–1.8)	15.2 (14.6–15.8)	1.6 (1.4–1.9)
Gender						
Male	2.3 (2.0–2.7)	2.2 (1.9–2.6)	1.7 (1.4–2.1)	1.7 (1.4–2.1)	14.5 (13.8–15.3)	1.7 (1.5–2.0)
Female	2.9 (2.4–3.5)	2.2 (1.8–2.6)	2.6 (2.3–3.0)	1.3 (1.1–1.7)	16.1 (15.3–17.0)	1.5 (1.2–1.9)
Race/ethnicity						
White	3.2 (2.8–3.7)	0.9 (0.8–1.1)	2.2 (2.0–2.6)	0.5 (0.3–0.6)	16.2 (15.5–17.0)	1.4 (1.2–1.7)
Male	3.0 (2.6–3.5)	0.8 (0.6–1.1)	1.6 (1.3–2.0)	0.5 (0.3–0.7)	15.4 (14.5–16.4)	1.6 (1.3–2.0)
Female	3.5 (2.9–4.2)	1.0 (0.8–1.3)	3.0 (2.5–3.5)	0.4 (0.3–0.6)	17.2 (16.1–18.3)	1.2 (0.9–1.6)
Black or African American	0.2 (0.1–0.4)	8.1 (6.8–9.6)	0.7 (0.3–1.5)	9.0 (7.6–10.8)	10.4 (8.9–12.0)	2.1 (1.5–2.9)
Male	0.2 (0.1–0.7)	7.9 (6.2–10.1)	0.6 (0.2–1.8)	9.9 (7.8–12.4)	10.8 (8.9–13.0)	2.5 (1.7–3.6)
Female	0.1 (0.0–0.5)	8.3 (6.1–11.0)	0.9 (0.4–1.8)	7.9 (5.9–10.4)	9.8 (7.8–12.2)	1.5 (0.7–3.0)
Hispanic or Latino	1.2 (0.7–2.0)	3.7 (2.8–4.8)	2.5 (1.8–3.5)	1.5 (1.1–2.1)	12.9 (11.4–14.7)	2.5 (1.8–3.4)
Male	0.7 (0.3–1.3)	3.8 (2.7–5.2)	2.8 (1.8–4.3)	1.5 (1.0–2.4)	12.0 (10.1–14.2)	1.9 (1.2–2.9)
Female	2.0 (1.0–4.2)	3.5 (2.3–5.3)	2.1 (1.4–3.2)	1.4 (0.8–2.6)	14.7 (12.2–17.6)	3.7 (2.4–5.6)
Other[b]	2.9 (1.9–4.3)	2.6 (1.6–4.3)	2.5 (1.5–4.2)	0.9 (0.4–1.9)	18.7 (16.2–21.5)	1.0 (0.6–1.7)
Male	3.0 (1.7–5.0)	2.5 (1.3–4.8)	2.3 (1.1–4.7)	1.0 (0.4–2.4)	19.0 (15.8–22.7)	0.9 (0.4–2.2)
Female	2.7 (1.4–5.3)	2.8 (1.3–5.7)	2.7 (1.3–5.8)	0.8 (0.2–3.2)	18.4 (14.7–22.7)	1.1 (0.6–1.9)
Age (years)						
18–20	1.3 (1.0–1.7)	2.9 (2.4–3.4)	1.5 (1.2–1.9)	1.7 (1.4–2.1)	14.7 (13.8–15.7)	1.9 (1.5–2.4)
21–25	3.3 (2.9–3.8)	1.8 (1.5–2.1)	2.5 (2.2–2.9)	1.5 (1.2–1.8)	15.5 (14.8–16.3)	1.5 (1.2–1.8)
Region						
Northeast	5.3 (4.4–6.3)	3.7 (3.0–4.5)	1.8 (1.4–2.5)	1.6 (1.1–2.2)	12.5 (11.3–13.8)	1.5 (1.1–2.1)
Midwest	2.4 (2.0–2.9)	1.5 (1.2–1.8)	2.2 (1.8–2.8)	1.3 (1.1–1.6)	15.6 (14.7–16.6)	1.2 (0.9–1.5)
South	1.3 (0.9–1.7)	2.2 (1.8–2.7)	2.3 (1.8–2.8)	2.1 (1.7–2.6)	15.0 (14.0–16.1)	1.6 (1.3–2.0)
West	2.8 (2.0–3.8)	1.7 (1.2–2.3)	2.0 (1.5–2.8)	0.9 (0.6–1.6)	17.5 (16.0–19.2)	2.4 (1.8–3.2)

Source: 2008–2010 NSDUH: Substance Abuse and Mental Health Services Administration (unpublished data).
Note: **CI** = confidence interval.
[a]Based on responses to the questions, "During the past 30 days, what brand of cigarettes did you smoke most often?" and "During the past 30 days, what type of cigarettes did you smoke most often?"
[b]Includes Asians, American Indians or Alaska Natives, Native Hawaiians or Other Pacific Islanders, and persons of two or more races.

Table 3.1.12 Percentage of 12- to 17-year-olds who had never smoked but were susceptible to starting to smoke cigarettes, by race/ethnicity and gender; National Survey on Drug Use and Health (NSDUH) 2008–2010;[a] United States

Race/ethnicity	Total % (95% CI)	Males % (95% CI)	Females % (95% CI)
Overall	19.9 (19.5–20.4)	20.4 (19.8–21.1)	19.3 (18.7–20.0)
All non-Hispanic	18.9 (18.4–19.3)	19.6 (18.9–20.3)	18.1 (17.4–18.8)
White	19.0 (18.4–19.6)	19.7 (18.9–20.5)	18.2 (17.4–19.1)
Black or African American	19.4 (18.5–20.5)	20.3 (18.8–21.9)	18.6 (17.2–20.2)
American Indian/Alaska Native	19.7 (14.8–25.7)	18.9 (12.5–27.6)	20.7 (14.6–28.4)
Hawaiian or Other Pacific Islander	16.0 (10.3–24.0)	NR	NR
Asian	15.1 (12.9–17.6)	15.3 (12.2–18.9)	15.0 (12.0–18.5)
Chinese	11.7 (8.2–16.5)	12.3 (7.6–19.4)	11.2 (7.1–17.2)
Filipino	18.6 (13.5–25.0)	16.6 (9.9–26.4)	21.0 (13.1–32.0)
Japanese	NR	NR	NR
Asian Indian	12.8 (9.3–17.3)	11.1 (7.2–16.6)	14.5 (9.3–22.0)
Korean	NR	NR	NR
Vietnamese	15.8 (9.5–24.9)	NR	NR
Hispanic	24.2 (22.9–25.5)	24.1 (22.4–25.9)	24.3 (22.6–26.1)
Mexican	25.8 (24.1–27.5)	26.1 (23.9–28.4)	25.5 (23.3–27.8)
Puerto Rican	18.3 (15.3–21.8)	15.7 (12.0–20.3)	20.7 (16.3–25.9)
Central or South American	22.1 (18.9–25.7)	23.2 (18.4–28.8)	21.0 (17.0–25.7)
Cuban	22.0 (16.9–28.1)	21.1 (14.2–30.3)	22.9 (15.1–33.0)

Source: 2008–2010 NSDUH: Substance Abuse and Mental Health Services Administration (unpublished data).
Note: **CI** = confidence interval; **NR** = low precision, no estimate reported.
[a]Susceptibility to starting to smoke among self-reported nonsmokers was determined by the following 2 questions: "If one of your best friends offered you a cigarette, would you smoke it?" and "At any time during the next 12 months do you think you will smoke a cigarette?" Possible answers were "definitely not," "probably not," "probably yes," and "definitely yes." Those who answered "definitely not" to both questions were classified as nonsusceptible to starting to smoke; respondents who had unknown information for both susceptibility questions were excluded from the analysis. Those who answered with any other combination of responses were classified as susceptible to starting to smoke.

Table 3.1.13 Age or grade when respondents first used a cigarette, among those aged 17–18 years who had completed 11th grade, National Survey on Drug Use and Health (NSDUH) 2010; and among 12th graders, Monitoring the Future (MTF) 2010, National Youth Risk Behavior Survey (YRBS) 2009, and National Youth Tobacco Survey (NYTS) 2009; United States

Age or grade	NSDUH[a] % (95% CI)	MTF[b] % (95% CI)	YRBS[c] % (95% CI)	NYTS[d] % (95% CI)
≤12 years or ≤ grade 6	7.2 (6.3–8.1)	5.9 (5.0–6.9)	8.6 (6.9–10.6)	7.1 (5.0–9.2)
13–14 years or grades 7–8	9.0 (7.9–10.1)	10.1 (9.0–11.1)	10.4 (9.0–11.9)	11.3 (9.9–12.7)
15–16 years or grades 9–10	17.3 (16.0–18.7)	13.8 (12.4–15.2)	16.1 (14.6–17.8)	15.0 (12.9–17.2)
≥17 years or > grade 10	10.4 (9.3–11.6)	9.2 (8.2–10.2)	10.1 (8.6–11.7)	8.0 (6.3–9.8)
Never smoked	56.1 (54.2–58.1)	61.0 (58.4–63.7)	54.9 (51.1–58.6)	58.5 (55.4–61.6)

Source: 2010 NSDUH: Substance Abuse and Mental Health Services Administration (unpublished data); 2010 MTF: University of Michigan, Institute for Social Research (unpublished data); 2009 YRBS: Centers for Disease Control and Prevention, Division of Adolescent and School Health (unpublished data); 2009 NYTS: Centers for Disease Control and Prevention (unpublished data).
Note: **CI** = confidence interval.
[a]Based on responses to the question, "How old were you the first time you smoked part or all of a cigarette?"
[b]Based on responses to the question, "When (if ever) did you first do each of the following things?...Smoke your first cigarette." Data based on one questionnaire form only, which explains any inconsistency between the "never smoked" category above and the results from the question on smoking in lifetime.
[c]Based on responses to the question, "How old were you when you smoked a whole cigarette for the first time?"
[d]Estimates are based on responses to the question "How old were you when you smoked a whole cigarette for the first time?" Analyses are restricted among youth who reported being in 12th grade.

Table 3.1.14 Age or grade when respondents first began smoking daily, among 17- to 18-year-olds who had completed 11th grade, National Survey on Drug Use and Health (NSDUH) 2010; and among 12th graders, Monitoring the Future (MTF) 2010; United States

Age (in years) or grade	NSDUH[a] % (95% CI)	MTF[b] % (95% CI)
≤12 years or ≤ grade 6	0.8 (0.5–1.3)	0.9 (0.6–1.2)
13–14 years or grades 7–8	2.1 (1.7–2.6)	2.1 (1.7–2.6)
15–16 years or grades 9–10	6.4 (5.5–7.5)	4.4 (3.5–5.2)
≥17 years or > grade 10	3.9 (3.2–4.7)	4.3 (3.6–4.9)
Never smoked daily	30.7 (28.8–32.6)	88.3 (86.8–89.9)
Never smoked	56.1 (54.2–58.1)	NA

Sources: 2010 NSDUH: Substance Abuse and Mental Health Services Administration (unpublished data); 2010 MTF: University of Michigan, Institute for Social Research (unpublished data).
Note: **CI** = confidence interval; **NA** = not available.
[a]Based on responses to the question, "How old were you when you first started smoking cigarettes every day?"
[b]Based on responses to the question, "When (if ever) did you FIRST do each of the following things?...Smoke cigarettes on a daily basis."

Table 3.1.15 Distribution of developmental trajectories of cigarette smoking across adolescence and young adulthood, 11–26 years of age, by gender and race/ethnicity; National Longitudinal Study of Adolescent Health (Add Health) 1994–2002; United States

	Nonsmokers (48.5% overall) versus			
Demographic	**Quitters (12.0% overall) OR (95% CI)[a]**	**Late established (25.0% overall) OR (95% CI)**	**Early established (14.5% overall) OR (95% CI)**	χ^2
By gender[b]				
Male	0.83 (0.67–1.04)	1.87 (1.55–2.25)*	1.06 (0.86–1.31)	38.49*
By race/ethnicity[c]				
Black	0.13 (0.06–0.28)*	0.55 (0.42–0.72)*	0.06 (0.03–0.13)*	41.64*
Other[d]	0.61 (0.38–0.95)*	0.87 (0.63–1.22)	0.40 (0.27–0.59)*	9.78*
Hispanic	0.48 (0.31–0.74)*	0.62 (0.45–0.85)*	0.22 (0.14–0.32)*	17.44*

Source: 1994–2002 Add Health: *Eunice Kennedy Shriver* National Institute of Child Health and Human Development (unpublished data).
Note: **CI** = confidence interval; **OR** = odds ratio.
[a]Generalized logit model using nonsmokers as the reference group.
[b]Females are the reference group.
[c]Whites are the reference group.
[d]Includes Asians, American Indians or Alaska Natives, Native Hawaiians or Other Pacific Islanders, and persons of two or more races.
*p <0.05 (statistically significant).

Table 3.1.16 Distribution of developmental trajectories of cigarette smoking across adolescence and young adulthood, 11–26 years of age, by level of nicotine dependence (Fagerström scale); National Longitudinal Study of Adolescent Health (Add Health) 1994–2002; United States

	Smoking trajectory groups			
Fagerström scale	**Nonsmokers**	**Quitters**	**Late established**	**Early established**
Pearson correlation coefficient	-0.63*	-0.05*	0.31*	0.51*
Average scale score (95% CI)	0.05 (0.03–0.08)	1.18 (0.90–1.46)	2.94 (2.78–3.1)	4.04 (3.87–4.21)

Source: 1994–2002 Add Health: *Eunice Kennedy Shriver* National Institute of Child Health and Human Development (unpublished data).
Note: **CI** = confidence interval.
*p <0.01 (statistically significant).

Table 3.1.17 Percentage of young people (12–14 years of age at Wave I and 19–21 years of age at Wave III) who were characterized as never smokers, current smokers, or former smokers, by gender and race/ ethnicity; National Longitudinal Study of Adolescent Health (Add Health) 1994–2002; United States

Stage of smoking (type of smoker)	Wave I (12–14 years of age) %	Wave III (19–21 years of age) %
Overall		
Never	84.8	53.4
Former	3.1	8.3
Current	12.2	38.3
Male		
Never	85.8	48.5
Former	2.7	7.5
Current	11.5	44.1
Female		
Never	84.0	57.4
Former	3.3	8.9
Current	12.7	33.7
Hispanic		
Never	85.1	51.9
Former	3.7	15.3
Current	11.2	32.8
White		
Never	86.2	57.1
Former	2.0	8.5
Current	11.9	34.5
Black		
Never	95.2	76.8
Former	1.2	4.2
Current	3.6	19.0
Other[a]		
Never	80.3	44.0
Former	3.8	8.7
Current	15.9	47.3

Source: 1994–2002 Add Health: *Eunice Kennedy Shriver* National Institute of Child Health and Human Development (unpublished data).
[a]Includes Asians, American Indians or Alaska Natives, Native Hawaiians or Other Pacific Islanders, and persons of two or more races.

Table 3.1.18 Probability of transitioning from one stage of cigarette smoking to another, from Wave I (12–14 years of age) to Wave III (19–21 years of age); National Longitudinal Study of Adolescent Health (Add Health) 1994–2002; United States

	Stage of smoking at Wave III		
Stage of smoking (type of smoker) at Wave I	Never smoker	Former smoker	Current smoker
Overall			
Never	**0.63**	0.06	0.31
Former	0.00	**0.20**	0.80
Current	0.00	0.21	**0.79**
Male			
Never	**0.56**	0.06	0.37
Former	0.00	**0.11**	0.89
Current	0.00	0.16	**0.84**
Female			
Never	**0.68**	0.06	0.26
Former	0.00	**0.26**	0.74
Current	0.00	0.25	**0.75**
Hispanic			
Never	**0.61**	0.11	0.28
Former	0.00	**0.38**	0.63
Current	0.00	0.38	**0.62**
White			
Never	**0.66**	0.06	0.28
Former	0.00	**0.50**	0.50
Current	0.00	0.23	**0.77**
Black			
Never	**0.81**	0.03	0.16
Former	0.00	**0.29**	0.71
Current	0.00	0.27	**0.73**
Other[a]			
Never	**0.55**	0.07	0.39
Former	0.00	0.15	0.85
Current	0.00	**0.18**	**0.82**

Source: 1994–2002 Add Health: *Eunice Kennedy Shriver* National Institute of Child Health and Human Development (unpublished data).
Note: Estimates in the diagonals (noted in bold) represent stability or the proportion of young people who stayed in the same stage over time.
[a]Includes Asians, American Indians or Alaska Natives, Native Hawaiians or Other Pacific Islanders, and persons of two or more races.

Table 3.1.19 Percentage of young people (15–18 years of age at Wave I and 22–25 years of age at Wave III) who were characterized as never smokers, former smokers, nondaily smokers, or daily smokers, by gender and race/ethnicity; National Longitudinal Study of Adolescent Health (Add Health) 1994–2002; United States

Stage of smoking (type of smoker)	Wave I (15–18 years of age) %	Wave III (22–25 years of age) %
Overall		
Never	63.3	48.9
Former	5.5	11.1
Nondaily	20.3	16.7
Daily	11.0	23.3
Male		
Never	63.3	44.0
Former	5.2	11.7
Nondaily	21.2	19.0
Daily	10.4	25.3
Female		
Never	63.2	53.6
Former	5.7	10.5
Nondaily	19.0	14.8
Daily	12.0	21.2
Hispanic		
Never	70.4	58.6
Former	5.1	11.2
Nondaily	19.0	19.6
Daily	5.5	10.7
White		
Never	70.0	53.8
Former	4.4	10.6
Nondaily	15.7	14.8
Daily	9.8	20.8
Black		
Never	82.4	61.2
Former	2.6	6.4
Nondaily	4.4	10.6
Daily	10.6	21.9
Other[a]		
Never	50.9	36.4
Former	6.8	13.0
Nondaily	25.6	17.0
Daily	16.7	33.6

Source: 1994–2002 Add Health: *Eunice Kennedy Shriver* National Institute of Child Health and Human Development (unpublished data).
[a]Includes Asians, American Indians or Alaska Natives, Native Hawaiians or Other Pacific Islanders, and persons of two or more races.

Table 3.1.20 Probability of transitioning from one stage of cigarette smoking to another, from Wave I (15–18 years of age) to Wave III (22–25 years of age); National Longitudinal Study of Adolescent Health (Add Health) 1994–2002; United States

	Stage of smoking at Wave III			
Stage of smoking (type of smoker) at Wave I	**Never smoker**	**Former smoker**	**Nondaily smoker**	**Daily smoker**
Overall				
Never	**0.77**	0.04	0.10	0.08
Former	0.00	**0.37**	0.34	0.29
Nondaily	0.00	0.24	**0.38**	0.38
Daily	0.00	0.12	0.06	**0.82**
Male				
Never	**0.70**	0.06	0.15	0.09
Former	0.00	**0.40**	0.28	0.31
Nondaily	0.00	0.23	**0.34**	0.44
Daily	0.00	0.12	0.06	**0.82**
Female				
Never	**0.85**	0.03	0.06	0.05
Former	0.00	**0.35**	0.37	0.28
Nondaily	0.00	0.26	**0.40**	0.33
Daily	0.00	0.12	0.07	**0.81**
Hispanic				
Never	**0.83**	0.04	0.09	0.04
Former	0.00	**0.48**	0.47	0.05
Nondaily	0.00	0.26	**0.56**	0.18
Daily	0.00	0.14	0.05	**0.81**
White				
Never	**0.77**	0.06	0.08	0.09
Former	0.00	**0.39**	0.27	0.34
Nondaily	0.00	0.25	**0.47**	0.28
Daily	0.00	0.09	0.05	**0.86**
Black				
Never	**0.73**	0.03	0.12	0.12
Former	0.00	**0.21**	0.00	0.79
Nondaily	0.28	0.02	**0.07**	0.63
Daily	0.00	0.29	0.00	**0.71**
Other[a]				
Never	**0.72**	0.05	0.11	0.13
Former	0.00	**0.38**	0.30	0.32
Nondaily	0.00	0.23	**0.32**	**0.46**
Daily	0.00	0.13	0.08	0.80

Source: 1994–2002 Add Health: *Eunice Kennedy Shriver* National Institute of Child Health and Human Development (unpublished data).
Note: Estimates in the diagonals (noted in bold) represent stability or the proportion of young people who stayed in the same stage over time.
[a]Includes Asians, American Indians or Alaska Natives, Native Hawaiians or Other Pacific Islanders, and persons of two or more races.

Table 3.1.21 Predicted likelihood (%) of smoking in young adulthood (5 years later), by intensity of smoking among 1996–2001 high school seniors; Monitoring the Future (MTF) 1996–2007;[a] United States

					Total	
Intensity of smoking	**Definitely will % (95% CI)**	**Probably will % (95% CI)**	**Probably will not % (95% CI)**	**Definitely will not % (95% CI)**	**%**	**Weighted number**
Not smoking	0.3 (0.2–0.4)	1.5 (1.2–1.8)	15.6 (14.6–16.6)	82.6 (81.5–83.7)	66.2	9,388
<1 cigarette per day	1.1 (0.4–1.8)	13.5 (10.7–16.3)	49.2 (46.4–52.0)	36.2 (33.1–39.4)	11.5	1,637
1–5 cigarettes per day	1.2 (0.6–1.9)	31.6 (28.3–35.0)	45.1 (41.9–48.3)	22.0 (19.2–24.9)	9.5	1,349
About ½ pack per day	3.5 (2.2–4.8)	43.2 (39.2–47.2)	39.0 (35.9–42.0)	14.3 (11.3–17.3)	6.9	973
≥1 pack per day	11.0 (8.9–13.1)	52.2 (47.3–57.1)	25.0 (21.0–29.1)	11.8 (8.9–14.8)	5.8	827
Total	1.4 (1.2–1.6)	11.4 (10.5–12.2)	24.3 (23.4–25.2)	62.9 (61.5–64.4)	100.0	14,175

Source: 1996–2007 MTF: University of Michigan, Institute for Social Research (unpublished data).
Note: **CI** = confidence interval.
[a]Based on responses to the questions, "How frequently have you smoked cigarettes during the past 30 days?" and "Do you think you will be smoking cigarettes five years from now?"

Table 3.1.22 Intensity of smoking (%) in young adulthood (5–6 years later), by intensity of smoking among 1996–2001 high school seniors; Monitoring the Future (MTF) 1996–2007;[a] United States

Intensity of smoking	**Not smoking % (95% CI)**	**<1 cigarette per day % (95% CI)**	**1–5 cigarettes per day % (95% CI)**	**About ½ pack per day % (95% CI)**	**≥1 pack per day % (95% CI)**	**Total %**
Not smoking	86.1 (85.0–87.1)	6.5 (5.7–7.2)	3.2 (2.7–3.8)	2.4 (1.9–2.8)	1.9 (1.5–2.3)	66.9
<1 cigarette per day	56.5 (52.9–60.0)	17.5 (14.9–20.2)	12.2 (9.8–14.6)	8.7 (6.8–10.7)	5.1 (3.6–6.6)	11.4
1–5 cigarettes per day	30.1 (26.6–33.6)	17.6 (14.8–20.4)	21.3 (18.2–24.5)	19.4 (16.3–22.5)	11.6 (9.1–14.1)	9.5
About ½ pack per day	22.7 (18.6–26.8)	8.6 (6.0–11.2)	17.1 (13.6–20.5)	26.5 (22.4–30.7)	25.1 (20.8–29.5)	6.5
≥1 pack per day	15.2 (11.3–19.2)	7.4 (4.7–10.0)	8.2 (5.4–11.0)	21.0 (16.3–25.6)	48.3 (42.8–53.7)	5.8
Total	69.2 (67.9–70.5)	9.0 (8.2–9.7)	7.2 (6.5–7.8)	7.3 (6.6–8.1)	7.4 (6.6–8.1)	100.0

Source: 1996–2007 MTF: University of Michigan, Institute for Social Research (unpublished data).
Note: **CI** = confidence interval.
[a]Based on responses to the questions, "How frequently have you smoked cigarettes during the past 30 days?" and "How frequently have you smoked cigarettes during the past 30 days?"

Table 3.1.23 Percentage change in the direction of intensity of smoking between senior year of high school and young adulthood (5–6 years later), among 1996–2001 high school seniors; Monitoring the Future (MTF) 1996–2007;[a] United States

Intensity of smoking	Quit % (95% CI)	Less use % (95% CI)	Same level % (95% CI)	More use % (95% CI)	Total %
Not smoking	NA	NA	86.1 (85.0–87.1)	13.9 (12.9–15.0)	66.9
<1 cigarette per day	56.5 (52.9–60.0)	NA	17.5 (14.9–20.2)	26.0 (22.8–29.2)	11.4
1–5 cigarettes per day	30.1 (26.6–33.6)	17.6 (14.8–20.4)	21.3 (18.2–24.5)	31.0 (27.2–34.8)	9.5
About ½ pack per day	22.7 (18.6–26.8)	25.7 (21.3–30.0)	26.5 (22.4–30.7)	25.1 (20.8–29.5)	6.5
≥1 pack per day	15.2 (11.3–19.2)	44.4 (38.8–50.0)	29.9 (25.3–34.5)	10.5 (7.2–13.8)	5.8
Total	11.6 (10.8–12.4)	5.9 (5.3–6.5)	65.0 (63.6–66.4)	17.5 (16.4–18.5)	100.0

Source: 1996–2007 MTF: University of Michigan, Institute for Social Research (unpublished data).
Note: **CI** = confidence interval; **NA** = not applicable.
[a]Based on responses to the questions, "How frequently have you smoked cigarettes during the past 30 days?" and "How frequently have you smoked cigarettes during the past 30 days?"

Table 3.1.24 Intensity of smoking in young adulthood (5–6 years later), by intensity of smoking in senior year of high school and expectation to smoke within 5 years, among 1996–2001 high school seniors; Monitoring the Future (MTF) 1996–2007;[a] United States

Intensity of smoking and expectation to smoke within 5 years	Not smoking % (95% CI)	<1 cigarette per day % (95% CI)	1–5 cigarettes per day % (95% CI)	About ½ pack per day % (95% CI)	≥1 pack per day % (95% CI)	Total %
Not smoking						
Will smoke	85.4 (59.1–100.0)	14.6 (0.0–40.9)	0.0 (0.0–0.0)	0.0 (0.0–0.0)	0.0 (0.0–0.0)	1.1
Will not smoke	84.6 (82.0–87.2)	8.4 (6.2–10.6)	3.0 (1.7–4.3)	2.4 (1.3–3.6)	1.6 (0.6–2.5)	98.9
Total	84.6 (82.1–87.2)	8.5 (6.3–10.7)	3.0 (1.7–4.2)	2.4 (1.2–3.6)	1.5 (0.6–2.5)	67.1
<1 cigarette per day						
Will smoke	36.0 (11.1–61.0)	14.0 (0.0–34.6)	21.3 (0.0–42.5)	9.6 (0.0–27.7)	19.1 (0.0–43.0)	9.6
Will not smoke	55.8 (46.1–65.5)	16.5 (9.2–23.7)	10.7 (4.5–16.8)	10.6 (5.1–16.1)	6.4 (1.7–11.2)	90.4
Total	53.9 (44.8–63.0)	16.2 (9.2–23.2)	11.7 (5.7–17.7)	10.5 (5.3–15.7)	7.6 (2.9–12.4)	13.2
1–5 cigarettes per day						
Will smoke	27.5 (9.9–45.1)	8.7 (0.0–20.4)	35.9 (16.8–55.0)	22.3 (4.2–40.4)	5.6 (0.0–13.8)	34.4
Will not smoke	26.2 (13.9–38.5)	23.0 (10.1–36.0)	18.4 (6.4–30.4)	18.5 (6.8–30.2)	13.8 (4.2–23.5)	65.6
Total	26.6 (16.7–36.6)	18.1 (8.5–27.7)	24.4 (14.0–34.9)	19.8 (9.8–29.8)	11.0 (4.0–18.0)	8.1
About ½ pack per day						
Will smoke	26.0 (8.5–43.5)	16.9 (2.8–31.0)	15.5 (0.9–30.1)	24.1 (7.2–40.9)	17.6 (0.1–35.0)	43.9
Will not smoke	13.3 (1.3–25.2)	14.4 (3.1–25.6)	17.1 (4.4–29.8)	20.0 (4.9–35.1)	35.2 (18.7–51.8)	56.1
Total	18.8 (8.6–29.1)	15.5 (6.9–24.1)	16.4 (6.8–25.9)	21.8 (9.9–33.7)	27.5 (14.4–40.6)	6.2
≥1 pack per day						
Will smoke	6.5 (0.0–13.0)	16.3 (0.0–33.2)	10.4 (0.0–21.1)	11.6 (0.6–22.5)	55.3 (34.4–76.2)	55.6
Will not smoke	27.2 (6.6–47.7)	1.9 (0.0–5.7)	16.4 (0.0–34.9)	17.3 (1.5–33.1)	37.3 (14.4–60.1)	44.4
Total	15.7 (4.5–26.9)	9.9 (0.0–19.9)	13.0 (2.7–23.4)	14.1 (4.8–23.4)	47.3 (31.1–63.4)	5.4
Total	68.1 (65.1–71.1)	10.8 (8.6–13.0)	7.2 (5.6–8.8)	6.7 (4.9–8.5)	7.2 (5.4–9.0)	100.0

Source: 1996–2007 MTF: University of Michigan, Institute for Social Research (unpublished data).
Note: **CI** = confidence interval.
[a]Based on responses to the questions, "How frequently have you smoked cigarettes during the past 30 days?" and "Do you think you will be smoking cigarettes 5 years from now?"

Table 3.1.25 Indicators of cigarette smoking and nicotine dependence among 12- to 17-year-olds smoking cigarettes during the previous 30 days; National Survey on Drug Use and Health (NSDUH) 2007–2010; United States

	Percentage by category % (95% CI)	Smoke >15 cigarettes per day[a] % (95% CI)	First cigarette within 30 minutes of waking % (95% CI)	Nicotine Dependence Syndrome Scale Mean % (95% CI)
Overall	100.0	5.5 (4.9–6.1)	29.7 (28.4–31.1)	2.29 (2.27–2.30)
Gender				
Male	51.8 (50.5–53.2)	6.6 (5.7–7.6)	30.3 (28.5–32.2)	2.28 (2.25–2.30)
Female	48.2 (46.8–49.5)	4.3 (3.6–5.2)	29.1 (27.2–31.0)	2.30 (2.27–2.32)
Race/ethnicity				
White	70.2 (68.8–71.6)	6.6 (5.9–7.5)	31.6 (30.1–33.2)	2.33 (2.31–2.35)
Black or African American	8.6 (7.8–9.5)	1.3 (0.7–2.4)	34.3 (29.4–39.5)	2.18 (2.13–2.23)
Hispanic	16.0 (14.9–17.3)	2.9 (1.8–4.7)	19.9 (16.8–23.3)	2.18 (2.13–2.22)
Other[b]	5.1 (4.5–5.8)	4.8 (2.7–8.3)	26.2 (21.0–32.2)	2.24 (2.18–2.30)
Age first puffed (years)				
<12	20.4 (19.3–21.4)	10.0 (8.4–11.9)	42.7 (39.6–45.9)	2.49 (2.45–2.53)
12–14	51.8 (50.4–53.2)	5.5 (4.7–6.5)	29.6 (27.8–31.5)	2.31 (2.28–2.33)
15–17	27.8 (26.6–29.1)	2.1 (1.5–3.0)	20.1 (17.8–22.6)	2.10 (2.08–2.13)
Age first smoked daily (years)				
<15	55.2 (53.1–57.2)	13.9 (12.2–15.9)	56.2 (53.5–58.9)	2.76 (2.73–2.79)
15–17	44.8 (42.8–46.9)	9.0 (7.4–11.1)	40.8 (37.8–43.9)	2.57 (2.54–2.61)
Transition (in years) from first cigarette to daily smoking				
≤1	55.8 (53.8–57.9)	10.8 (9.2–12.5)	51.0 (48.3–53.8)	2.68 (2.64–2.71)
2–3	31.1 (29.2–33.1)	12.9 (10.6–15.7)	46.1 (42.3–50.0)	2.68 (2.64–2.73)
≥4	13.1 (11.8–14.5)	13.2 (10.0–17.2)	49.1 (43.4–54.8)	2.65 (2.59–2.71)
Number of days smoked in past month				
<10	47.1 (45.7–48.4)	1.0 (0.7–1.5)	12.1 (10.7–13.6)	1.95 (1.94–1.97)
10–19	14.6 (13.6–15.6)	2.1 (1.3–3.3)	18.4 (15.9–21.3)	2.17 (2.13–2.20)
20–29	14.7 (13.7–15.7)	3.1 (2.2–4.4)	30.4 (27.4–33.7)	2.44 (2.40–2.47)
30	23.7 (22.6–24.8)	18.0 (15.9–20.2)	65.2 (62.6–67.7)	2.92 (2.89–2.95)
Average number of cigarettes smoked on days smoked				
≤1	46.8 (45.5–48.1)	NA	11.7 (10.3–13.3)	1.97 (1.95–1.98)
2–5	34.1 (32.8–35.4)	NA	28.7 (26.7–30.8)	2.35 (2.32–2.38)
6–15	13.6 (12.7–14.5)	NA	65.7 (62.1–69.1)	2.89 (2.85–2.93)
16–25	4.3 (3.8–4.8)	100.0	79.8 (74.5–84.3)	3.14 (3.06–3.22)
≥26	NR	100.0	NR	2.99 (2.82–3.16)

Table 3.1.25 Continued

	Percentage by category % (95% CI)	Smoke >15 cigarettes per day[a] % (95% CI)	First cigarette within 30 minutes of waking % (95% CI)	Nicotine Dependence Syndrome Scale Mean % (95% CI)
Use of alcohol (past month)				
Never used alcohol	8.7 (8.0–9.5)	4.8 (3.1–7.4)	28.0 (23.4–33.1)	2.20 (2.16–2.25)
Lifetime alcohol use (but not in past month)	30.9 (29.6–32.2)	4.2 (3.4–5.2)	30.0 (27.7–32.4)	2.28 (2.26–2.31)
1–10 days	50.3 (48.9–51.7)	5.4 (4.6–6.3)	28.1 (26.4–30.0)	2.27 (2.24–2.29)
≥11 days	10.1 (9.3–10.9)	10.6 (8.3–13.6)	38.0 (33.7–42.5)	2.45 (2.40–2.51)
Binge drinking (past month)				
Never used alcohol	8.7 (8.0–9.5)	4.8 (3.1–7.4)	28.0 (23.4–33.1)	2.20 (2.16–2.25)
Lifetime alcohol use (but not in past month)	30.9 (29.6–32.2)	4.2 (3.4–5.2)	30.0 (27.7–32.4)	2.28 (2.26–2.31)
Used alcohol in past month (no binge drinking)	12.5 (11.6–13.5)	3.9 (2.6–5.6)	25.3 (21.7–29.2)	2.21 (2.16–2.27)
1–10 days	44.0 (42.6–45.4)	6.1 (5.1–7.1)	29.6 (27.8–31.6)	2.30 (2.28–2.33)
≥11 days	3.9 (3.4–4.5)	15.8 (11.4–21.6)	45.5 (38.4–52.9)	2.56 (2.47–2.64)
Marijuana use (past month)				
Never used marijuana	24.6 (23.4–25.7)	3.2 (2.3–4.4)	22.5 (20.0–25.1)	2.12 (2.10–2.15)
Lifetime marijuana use (but not in past month)	31.1 (29.9–32.4)	5.8 (4.7–7.1)	30.4 (28.0–32.9)	2.32 (2.29–2.36)
1–10 days	24.0 (22.8–25.3)	3.7 (2.9–4.8)	26.8 (24.2–29.5)	2.24 (2.21–2.27)
≥11 days	20.2 (19.2–21.4)	10.0 (8.4–11.8)	39.9 (36.8–43.1)	2.48 (2.44–2.52)
Illicit drug use other than marijuana (past month)				
Never used any other illicit drug	43.0 (41.7–44.4)	4.0 (3.3–4.9)	25.1 (23.2–27.2)	2.16 (2.14–2.18)
Lifetime illicit drug use (but not in past month)	36.0 (34.6–37.3)	5.5 (4.5–6.6)	31.1 (29.0–33.2)	2.34 (2.31–2.36)
Used in past month	21.0 (19.9–22.1)	8.5 (7.1–10.2)	36.3 (33.5–39.1)	2.46 (2.42–2.50)

Source: 2008–2010 NSDUH: Substance Abuse and Mental Health Services Administration (unpublished data).
Note: **CI** = confidence interval; **NA** = not applicable; **NR** = low precision, no estimate reported.
[a]Cigarettes per day on days smoked; n = 9,500.
[b]Includes Asians, American Indians or Alaska Natives, Native Hawaiians or Other Pacific Islanders, and persons of two or more races.

Table 3.1.26 Indicators of cigarette smoking and nicotine dependence among 18- to 25-year-olds smoking cigarettes during the previous 30 days; National Survey on Drug Use and Health (NSDUH) 2007–2010; United States

	Percentage by category % (95% CI)	Smoke >15 cigarettes per day[a] % (95% CI)	First cigarette within 30 minutes of waking % (95% CI)	Nicotine Dependence Syndrome Scale Mean % (95% CI)
Overall	100.0	16.1 (15.6–16.6)	35.4 (34.7–36.2)	2.43 (2.42–2.44)
Gender				
Male	56.3 (55.6–57.1)	18.6 (17.9–19.4)	35.8 (34.8–36.8)	2.40 (2.39–2.42)
Female	43.7 (42.9–44.4)	12.8 (12.2–13.5)	34.9 (33.9–36.0)	2.46 (2.44–2.47)
Race/ethnicity				
White	69.1 (68.2–70.0)	20.3 (19.6–20.9)	37.7 (36.7–38.6)	2.48 (2.47–2.50)
Black or African American	10.5 (10.0–11.1)	6.4 (5.5–7.6)	44.9 (42.6–47.2)	2.39 (2.36–2.42)
Hispanic	15.0 (14.3–15.7)	6.1 (5.2–7.3)	19.4 (17.6–21.2)	2.22 (2.19–2.24)
Other[b]	5.4 (5.0–5.7)	9.1 (7.6–10.9)	31.5 (28.7–34.5)	2.35 (2.32–2.39)
Education (years)				
<12	23.3 (22.6–24.0)	21.2 (20.0–22.3)	50.3 (48.8–51.9)	2.63 (2.61–2.65)
12	38.1 (37.3–38.9)	18.6 (17.7–19.4)	39.6 (38.5–40.8)	2.48 (2.47–2.50)
≥13	38.6 (37.7–39.6)	10.6 (9.9–11.3)	22.1 (21.1–23.2)	2.25 (2.23–2.27)
Age first puffed (years)				
<12	9.6 (9.2–10.0)	30.0 (28.2–31.9)	52.5 (50.3–54.7)	2.72 (2.69–2.75)
12–14	31.5 (30.8–32.2)	21.5 (20.6–22.5)	42.1 (40.7–43.5)	2.56 (2.55–2.58)
15–17	38.8 (38.1–39.5)	12.7 (12.0–13.5)	31.7 (30.7–32.9)	2.36 (2.35–2.38)
≥18	20.1 (19.5–20.7)	7.4 (6.5–8.3)	23.3 (21.9–24.7)	2.20 (2.18–2.22)
Age first smoked daily (years)				
<15	16.3 (15.7–17.0)	37.7 (35.9–39.6)	64.2 (62.2–66.1)	2.93 (2.90–2.95)
15–17	44.5 (43.6–45.4)	24.4 (23.4–25.4)	49.9 (48.7–51.2)	2.70 (2.69–2.72)
≥18	39.2 (38.3–40.0)	14.6 (13.6–15.6)	34.2 (32.9–35.5)	2.49 (2.48–2.51)
Transition (in years) from first cigarette to daily smoking: first tried at ≤16 years				
≤1	34.0 (33.2–34.7)	28.6 (27.4–29.8)	55.8 (54.4–57.2)	2.78 (2.76–2.80)
2–3	36.7 (35.9–37.5)	25.5 (24.4–26.7)	46.8 (45.5–48.2)	2.69 (2.67–2.71)
≥4	29.4 (28.6–30.2)	22.0 (20.8–23.4)	40.5 (39.0–42.1)	2.58 (2.56–2.60)
Transition (in years) from first cigarette to daily smoking: first tried at >16 years				
≤1	76.5 (75.1–77.9)	17.3 (16.0–18.8)	41.4 (39.6–43.1)	2.57 (2.55–2.59)
2–3	19.5 (18.3–20.8)	10.2 (8.2–12.6)	31.2 (28.0–34.7)	2.42 (2.38–2.46)
≥4	3.9 (3.2–4.7)	6.7 (3.4–12.6)	21.8 (15.2–30.2)	2.37 (2.27–2.46)
Number of days smoked in past month				
<10	28.7 (28.0–29.5)	1.9 (1.6–2.3)	11.1 (10.2–12.0)	1.90 (1.89–1.91)
10–19	10.8 (10.4–11.3)	2.6 (2.0–3.4)	14.6 (13.0–16.4)	2.02 (2.00–2.04)
20–29	13.2 (12.7–13.7)	5.4 (4.6–6.3)	22.9 (21.3–24.7)	2.30 (2.28–2.32)
30	47.3 (46.5–48.1)	30.7 (29.8–31.7)	56.9 (55.8–57.9)	2.87 (2.86–2.88)

Table 3.1.26 Continued

	Percentage by category % (95% CI)	Smoke >15 cigarettes per day[a] % (95% CI)	First cigarette within 30 minutes of waking % (95% CI)	Nicotine Dependence Syndrome Scale Mean % (95% CI)
Average number of cigarettes smoked on days smoked				
≤1	27.4 (26.8–28.1)	NA	9.0 (8.2–10.0)	1.91 (1.90–1.92)
2–5	31.4 (30.7–32.1)	NA	20.8 (19.8–21.9)	2.23 (2.22–2.25)
6–15	25.0 (24.4–25.7)	NA	53.7 (52.3–55.1)	2.79 (2.77–2.80)
16–25	13.5 (13.1–14.0)	100.0	74.6 (73.0–76.1)	3.10 (3.08–3.12)
≥26	2.6 (2.4–2.8)	100.0	81.9 (78.5–84.8)	3.23 (3.19–3.28)
Alcohol use (past month)				
Never used alcohol	3.7 (3.4–4.0)	14.3 (11.8–17.2)	42.8 (39.0–46.7)	2.43 (2.39–2.48)
Lifetime alcohol use (but not in past month)	17.4 (16.8–18.0)	17.9 (16.7–19.1)	44.3 (42.7–46.0)	2.60 (2.58–2.62)
1–10 days	55.3 (54.6–56.0)	14.6 (14.0–15.3)	33.5 (32.5–34.5)	2.39 (2.38–2.40)
≥11 days	23.6 (22.9–24.3)	18.5 (17.4–19.7)	32.1 (30.6–33.7)	2.38 (2.36–2.40)
Binge drinking (past month)				
Never used alcohol	3.7 (3.4–4.0)	14.3 (11.8–17.2)	42.8 (39.0–46.7)	2.43 (2.39–2.48)
Lifetime alcohol use (but not in past month)	17.4 (16.8–18.0)	17.9 (16.7–19.1)	44.3 (42.7–46.0)	2.60 (2.58–2.62)
Used alcohol in past month (no binge drinking)	15.8 (15.3–16.3)	13.5 (12.3–14.7)	34.4 (32.7–36.1)	2.42 (2.40–2.44)
1–10 days	54.4 (53.6–55.1)	15.3 (14.6–16.0)	32.2 (31.2–33.2)	2.37 (2.36–2.38)
≥11 days	8.7 (8.3–9.2)	23.3 (21.2–25.4)	36.3 (33.8–38.9)	2.46 (2.42–2.50)
Marijuana use (past month)				
Never used marijuana	22.2 (21.6–22.9)	12.9 (12.0–13.9)	33.6 (32.2–35.0)	2.33 (2.31–2.35)
Lifetime marijuana use (but not in past month)	44.1 (43.4–44.8)	16.6 (15.9–17.4)	35.1 (34.1–36.2)	2.46 (2.45–2.48)
1–10 days	15.1 (14.6–15.7)	13.0 (11.9–14.3)	30.5 (28.7–32.3)	2.33 (2.30–2.35)
≥11 days	18.6 (18.0–19.2)	21.0 (19.7–22.4)	42.2 (40.4–44.0)	2.54 (2.52–2.56)
Illicit drug use other than marijuana (past month)				
Never used any other illicit drug	40.3 (39.5–41.0)	12.2 (11.6–12.9)	31.8 (30.7–32.9)	2.32 (2.31–2.33)
Lifetime illicit drug use (but not in past month)	43.5 (42.8–44.2)	17.5 (16.7–18.3)	36.8 (35.7–37.9)	2.49 (2.47–2.51)
Used in past month	16.3 (15.7–16.8)	22.1 (20.7–23.5)	40.6 (38.7–42.6)	2.53 (2.50–2.55)

Source: 2008–2010 NSDUH: Substance Abuse and Mental Health Services Administration (unpublished data).
Note: **CI** = confidence interval; **NA** = not applicable.
[a]Cigarettes per day on days smoked; n = 34,400.
[b]Includes Asians, American Indians or Alaska Natives, Native Hawaiians or Other Pacific Islanders, and persons of two or more races.

Table 3.1.27 Indicators of cigarette use and nicotine dependence among adults 26 years of age or older smoking cigarettes during the previous 30 days; National Survey on Drug Use and Health (NSDUH) 2007–2010; United States

	Percentage by category % (95% CI)	Smoke >15 cigarettes per day[a] % (95% CI)	First cigarette within 30 minutes of waking % (95% CI)	Nicotine Dependence Syndrome Scale Mean % (95% CI)
Overall	100.0	37.9 (37.1–38.8)	53.0 (52.0–53.9)	2.66 (2.65–2.67)
Age first puffed (years)				
<12	9.3 (8.8–9.9)	50.0 (47.3–52.8)	63.2 (60.4–65.9)	2.85 (2.81–2.89)
12–14	29.4 (28.6–30.2)	44.9 (43.4–46.4)	57.6 (56.1–59.1)	2.76 (2.74–2.78)
15–17	34.7 (33.9–35.6)	37.3 (35.8–38.7)	53.3 (51.8–54.9)	2.65 (2.63–2.67)
≥18	26.5 (25.7–27.3)	26.8 (25.2–28.4)	43.8 (41.9–45.6)	2.50 (2.48–2.52)
Age first smoked daily (years)				
<15	15.1 (14.4–15.7)	58.7 (56.5–60.9)	73.9 (71.8–75.9)	3.02 (2.99–3.05)
15–17	33.6 (32.7–34.6)	49.4 (47.9–51.0)	65.2 (63.7–66.7)	2.84 (2.82–2.86)
≥18	51.3 (50.3–52.2)	33.0 (31.8–34.2)	48.1 (46.7–49.4)	2.61 (2.59–2.63)
Transition (in years) from first cigarette to daily smoking: First tried at ≤16 years				
≤1	38.3 (37.4–39.2)	54.1 (52.6–55.6)	70.1 (68.6–71.6)	2.92 (2.90–2.94)
2–3	26.9 (26.1–27.8)	48.7 (46.9–50.6)	59.9 (58.0–61.7)	2.84 (2.81–2.86)
≥4	34.8 (33.9–35.7)	38.5 (37.0–40.1)	49.7 (48.1–51.3)	2.66 (2.64–2.68)
Transition (in years) from first cigarette to daily smoking: First tried at >16 years				
≤1	63.9 (62.3–65.4)	38.8 (36.9–40.8)	56.9 (55.0–58.8)	2.68 (2.65–2.70)
2–3	16.5 (15.4–17.6)	30.2 (27.1–33.6)	49.3 (45.6–53.0)	2.61 (2.57–2.65)
≥4	19.6 (18.4–21.0)	21.0 (18.2–24.1)	38.8 (35.2–42.5)	2.51 (2.47–2.55)

Source: 2008–2010 NSDUH: Substance Abuse and Mental Health Services Administration (unpublished data).
Note: **CI** = confidence interval.
[a]Cigarettes per day on days smoked; n = 25,400.

Table 3.1.28 Percentage of high school seniors who were smokers during the previous month, by gender and race/ethnicity; Monitoring the Future (MTF) 1976–2007;[a] United States

Gender and race/ethnicity	1976–1979 % (95% CI)	1980–1984 % (95% CI)	1985–1989 % (95% CI)	1990–1994 % (95% CI)	1995–1999 % (95% CI)	2000–2007 % (95% CI)
Male	34.9 (32.8–37.0)	26.8 (24.9–28.7)	27.8 (26.1–29.4)	30.1 (28.1–32.2)	35.7 (33.4–38.0)	26.3 (24.7–27.9)
Black or African American	33.1 (28.6–37.6)	19.4 (17.5–21.4)	15.6 (12.3–19.0)	11.6 (8.5–14.8)	19.3 (17.4–21.2)	14.0 (10.9–17.0)
White	35.0 (32.8–37.2)	27.5 (25.5–29.5)	29.8 (28.3–31.4)	33.4 (31.6–35.1)	39.7 (37.6–41.8)	29.5 (27.7–31.3)
Hispanic	30.3 (26.6–33.9)	23.8 (20.0–27.6)	23.3 (20.7–25.8)	28.0 (21.9–34.0)	28.8 (26.2–31.3)	21.2 (19.2–23.2)
American Indian and Alaska Native[b]	NA	NA	NA	NA	NA	NA
Asian American and Pacific Islander[c]	NA	NA	NA	NA	NA	NA
Female	38.4 (36.0–40.8)	32.3 (30.0–34.5)	30.3 (27.5–33.0)	28.1 (25.4–30.8)	33.3 (30.6–36.0)	23.6 (21.8–25.5)
Black or African American	33.6 (29.3–37.9)	22.8 (20.2–25.4)	13.3 (10.7–15.9)	8.6 (6.2–11.0)	10.8 (8.9–12.7)	8.8 (7.3–10.3)
White	39.1 (36.6–41.5)	34.3 (32.1–36.4)	34.0 (31.9–36.1)	33.1 (31.4–34.9)	39.5 (37.3–41.7)	28.5 (26.9–30.1)
Hispanic	31.4 (26.4–36.4)	25.1 (21.8–28.4)	20.6 (15.4–25.7)	19.9 (15.7–24.0)	24.4 (21.1–27.7)	15.9 (14.2–17.6)
American Indian and Alaska Native[b]	55.3 (50.5–60.0)	50.0 (42.6–57.4)	43.6 (36.2–50.9)	39.4 (32.7–46.0)	51.7 (43.6–59.8)	35.5 (30.9–40.0)
Asian American and Pacific Islander[c]	24.3 (18.5–30.1)	16.2 (12.5–19.9)	14.3 (11.6–17.0)	13.8 (9.4–18.3)	17.5 (13.6–21.5)	12.8 (10.6–15.1)

Source: 1976–2007 MTF: University of Michigan, Institute for Social Research (unpublished data).
Note: **CI** = confidence interval; **NA** = not applicable.
[a]Based on responses to the question, "How frequently have you smoked cigarettes during the past 30 days?" Respondents who reported that they had smoked less than 1 cigarette per day or more were classified as previous-month smokers.
[b]Response categories did not include "Alaska Native" before 2005. For years before 2005, data are based on responses for "American Indian" only.
[c]Response categories did not include "Pacific Islander" before 2005. For years before 2005, data are based on responses for "Asian American" only.

Table 3.1.29 Percentage of 20- to 44-year-olds who identified themselves as current smokers, by age group, race/ethnicity, and gender; National Health Interview Surveys (NHIS) 1978–2009; United States

Age group, race/ethnicity, gender	1978–1980 % (95% CI)	1983–1985 % (95% CI)	1987–1988 % (95% CI)	1990–1992 % (95% CI)	1993–1995 % (95% CI)
20–24 years					
Black or African American: total	37.0 (32.4–41.5)	32.9 (29.0–36.7)	24.7 (21.6–27.9)	16.0 (12.4–19.5)	14.1 (10.9–17.2)
Male	44.5 (37.6–51.4)	32.9 (26.7–39.1)	26.0 (20.8–31.1)	20.2 (14.3–26.2)	20.3 (14.0–26.5)
Female	31.4 (26.4–36.6)	32.8 (28.7–37.0)	23.8 (19.8–27.7)	12.5 (9.5–15.6)	9.0 (6.5–11.4)
Hispanic: total	33.1 (28.2–38.0)	25.4 (22.1–28.7)	23.4 (19.1–27.7)	16.6 (13.5–19.6)	20.9 (17.2–24.6)
Male	36.7 (29.9–43.5)	30.4 (24.8–36.0)	28.9 (21.7–36.1)	19.1 (15.6–22.6)	26.2 (20.2–32.2)
Female	29.8 (23.6–35.9)	20.2 (16.1–24.4)	18.4 (13.2–23.6)	14.3 (10.1–18.4)	15.0 (11.2–18.9)
White: total	35.7 (33.8–37.5)	35.9 (34.6–37.2)	30.7 (29.1–32.3)	31.1 (29.2–33.1)	32.5 (30.5–34.6)
Male	37.5 (35.0–40.1)	34.5 (32.4–36.6)	31.0 (28.4–33.6)	31.1 (28.4–33.8)	33.4 (30.5–36.4)
Female	33.8 (31.7–36.0)	37.2 (35.0–39.4)	30.4 (28.5–32.4)	31.1 (28.8–33.5)	31.7 (28.9–34.4)
25–29 years					
Black or African American: total	43.3 (38.4–48.1)	38.6 (34.9–42.3)	38.9 (35.0–42.7)	26.4 (23.1–29.8)	20.9 (17.5–24.3)
Male	49.1 (42.3–55.9)	40.9 (34.5–47.4)	43.8 (36.9–50.6)	28.7 (22.7–34.7)	21.8 (15.5–28.2)
Female	38.6 (32.4–44.9)	36.6 (32.4–40.7)	34.8 (31.3–38.3)	24.5 (20.8–28.2)	20.1 (15.9–24.3)
Hispanic: total	31.2 (25.8–36.6)	28.8 (24.4–33.3)	23.7 (20.6–26.8)	24.4 (21.4–27.4)	18.7 (14.8–22.7)
Male	38.5 (30.2–46.8)	33.1 (24.7–41.5)	26.9 (22.1–31.8)	29.1 (24.0–34.1)	26.1 (19.5–32.7)
Female	24.6 (19.2–30.1)	24.8 (21.0–28.7)	20.8 (16.4–25.3)	20.5 (16.3–24.6)	11.1 (7.8–14.3)
White: total	38.3 (36.6–40.0)	36.3 (35.1–37.4)	35.0 (33.7–36.3)	31.5 (30.0–33.0)	31.6 (29.8–33.3)
Male	41.7 (39.1–44.3)	38.5 (36.4–40.6)	34.4 (32.4–36.5)	32.5 (30.6–34.4)	31.6 (28.8–34.3)
Female	34.9 (32.8–37.0)	34.1 (31.9–36.3)	35.6 (33.9–37.2)	30.6 (28.6–32.6)	31.6 (29.4–33.7)
30–34 years					
Black or African American: total	42.5 (36.8–48.2)	41.0 (36.8–45.2)	40.8 (37.4–44.2)	35.8 (32.6–39.0)	32.1 (28.2–35.9)
Male	50.7 (42.0–59.3)	45.2 (37.7–52.7)	44.2 (38.8–49.6)	38.6 (33.3–43.9)	33.7 (28.1–39.4)
Female	36.2 (28.7–43.6)	37.7 (33.3–42.1)	37.9 (34.3–41.5)	33.5 (29.5–37.5)	30.7 (25.7–35.7)
Hispanic: total	38.5 (31.5–45.5)	29.8 (23.9–35.7)	27.1 (23.6–30.6)	24.2 (21.0–27.4)	24.0 (20.8–27.3)
Male	51.4 (42.2–60.7)	38.9 (27.8–49.9)	31.9 (25.4–38.4)	29.9 (24.7–35.1)	28.6 (23.7–33.5)
Female	25.1 (17.3–32.9)	22.1 (17.7–26.4)	22.5 (18.1–26.9)	18.3 (15.0–21.6)	19.1 (14.8–23.3)
White: total	38.2 (36.2–40.2)	34.6 (33.1–36.0)	32.7 (31.4–34.0)	32.9 (31.6–34.3)	30.8 (29.3–32.3)
Male	42.9 (40.5–45.3)	37.5 (35.1–39.9)	35.4 (33.4–37.3)	33.5 (31.5–35.5)	31.5 (29.5–33.6)
Female	33.6 (30.7–36.5)	31.7 (30.0–33.5)	30.1 (28.4–31.8)	32.3 (30.6–34.1)	30.0 (28.1–32.0)
35–39 years					
Black or African American: total	47.9 (41.5–54.2)	40.2 (35.7–44.7)	38.7 (35.1–42.3)	28.1 (25.2–30.9)	20.0 (17.5–22.5)
Male	54.9 (46.1–63.8)	46.0 (38.4–53.6)	44.6 (38.7–50.5)	29.0 (24.7–33.3)	22.2 (18.2–26.3)
Female	42.8 (34.8–50.8)	36.0 (31.5–40.5)	33.8 (30.1–37.4)	27.4 (23.6–31.1)	18.3 (15.5–21.2)
Hispanic: total	31.1 (26.1–36.1)	29.2 (24.6–33.8)	27.0 (23.3–30.7)	19.9 (17.9–21.9)	17.3 (15.4–19.2)
Male	40.5 (34.0–47.0)	36.1 (25.0–47.1)	33.3 (27.3–39.3)	25.7 (22.4–29.0)	23.8 (20.5–27.0)
Female	22.9 (15.9–29.9)	23.6 (18.3–28.9)	21.0 (17.3–24.8)	14.0 (11.6–16.4)	10.4 (8.2–12.5)
White: total	40.4 (38.5–42.4)	35.8 (34.1–37.2)	31.6 (30.3–32.9)	29.0 (27.8–30.2)	26.8 (25.5–28.2)
Male	44.0 (41.2–46.8)	38.7 (36.6–40.8)	34.8 (32.8–36.8)	28.7 (26.9–30.5)	29.2 (27.2–31.2)
Female	37.0 (34.5–39.5)	32.9 (30.8–35.1)	28.5 (27.0–30.1)	29.3 (27.6–31.0)	24.6 (22.9–26.2)

Table 3.1.29 Continued

Age group, race/ethnicity, gender	1978–1980 % (95% CI)	1983–1985 % (95% CI)	1987–1988 % (95% CI)	1990–1992 % (95% CI)	1993–1995 % (95% CI)
40–44 years					
Black or African American: total	38.8 (33.9–43.7)	41.5 (36.2–46.8)	36.7 (32.4–41.1)	31.0 (27.9–34.1)	27.9 (25.2–30.6)
Male	44.3 (34.9–53.7)	45.4 (39.0–51.8)	42.9 (35.6–50.1)	34.8 (30.2–39.4)	30.5 (25.9–35.1)
Female	34.7 (29.0–40.5)	38.1 (30.9–45.2)	32.0 (27.0–37.1)	27.6 (24.0–31.2)	25.8 (22.6–28.9)
Hispanic: total	31.5 (25.6–37.4)	32.0 (27.5–36.5)	25.5 (21.8–29.2)	19.7 (17.6–21.8)	20.4 (17.8–23.0)
Male	39.6 (29.6–49.7)	38.2 (32.3–44.2)	35.8 (28.3–43.3)	25.1 (21.8–28.4)	25.7 (21.9–29.5)
Female	24.5 (15.1–33.8)	25.9 (18.7–33.1)	17.5 (12.4–22.5)	14.3 (11.7–16.9)	15.0 (12.2–17.8)
White: total	38.1 (35.9–40.3)	36.3 (34.5–38.1)	34.6 (33.1–36.2)	28.9 (27.6–30.3)	28.3 (26.9–29.6)
Male	38.6 (35.5–41.8)	38.9 (36.9–40.9)	38.0 (35.6–40.4)	30.5 (28.6–32.4)	29.0 (27.1–31.0)
Female	37.6 (34.8–40.3)	33.9 (30.8–36.9)	31.3 (29.4–33.2)	27.4 (25.8–28.9)	27.6 (25.8–29.3)

Age group, race/ethnicity, gender	1997–1998 % (95% CI)	1999–2001 % (95% CI)	2002–2004 % (95% CI)	2005–2006 % (95% CI)	2007–2009 % (95% CI)
20–24 years					
Black or African American: total	15.2 (12.4–17.9)	19.1 (16.3–21.9)	18.9 (16.2–21.5)	22.4 (18–26.8)	16.3 (12.8–19.7)
Male	22.4 (17.0–27.8)	24.8 (19.7–29.8)	24.0 (18.6–29.4)	28.2 (20.6–35.8)	20.7 (14.4–27.1)
Female	9.9 (7.0–12.7)	14.5 (11.5–17.6)	14.8 (12.2–17.4)	17.5 (12.8–22.2)	12.8 (9.1–16.5)
Hispanic: total	22.4 (19.3–25.5)	18.9 (16.6–21.1)	16.7 (14.6–18.8)	16.6 (14.1–19.1)	14.1 (11.1–17.2)
Male	30.4 (25.5–35.4)	24.5 (20.7–28.2)	24.0 (20.6–27.3)	23.6 (19.2–28.0)	19.9 (14.8–24.9)
Female	13.6 (10.5–16.6)	13.2 (10.5–15.8)	8.9 (7.0–10.8)	9.4 (6.8–11.9)	8.0 (5.7–10.3)
White: total	35.2 (33.1–37.3)	32.9 (31.2–34.7)	32.2 (30.2–34.3)	31.0 (28.7–33.4)	27.9 (25.2–30.7)
Male	38.7 (35.5–41.9)	34.5 (32.1–36.9)	34.6 (31.9–37.3)	35.4 (31.5–39.3)	32.8 (28.7–36.9)
Female	31.7 (29.0–34.3)	31.4 (29.1–33.7)	29.8 (27.5–32.2)	26.7 (23.8–29.7)	23.0 (19.9–26.1)
25–29 years					
Black or African American: total	21.3 (18.3–24.2)	18.4 (16.1–20.7)	20.6 (17.6–23.5)	24.7 (21.0–28.5)	24.5 (20.6–28.4)
Male	25.8 (20.8–30.9)	20.8 (16.9–24.7)	25.7 (20.1–31.4)	32.5 (26.1–38.9)	34.4 (27.0–41.8)
Female	17.9 (14.4–21.4)	16.4 (13.1–19.7)	16.5 (13.6–19.4)	18.4 (14.6–22.1)	16.1 (12.6–19.7)
Hispanic: total	18.7 (16.7–20.7)	18.2 (16.1–20.2)	15.4 (13.5–17.3)	14.7 (12.2–17.1)	15.2 (12.4–17.9)
Male	24.7 (21.4–28.1)	23.7 (20.1–27.2)	20.2 (17.2–23.2)	19.7 (15.9–23.5)	20.6 (16.1–25.1)
Female	11.9 (9.7–14.0)	12.7 (10.5–14.9)	9.9 (7.9–11.9)	8.6 (5.8–11.4)	8.3 (5.7–11.0)
White: total	30.6 (28.9–32.2)	30.5 (29.0–32.0)	30.1 (28.6–31.7)	30.7 (28.5–33.0)	31.9 (29.0–34.7)
Male	31.9 (29.6–34.2)	32.8 (30.6–34.9)	31.5 (29.2–33.8)	33.2 (29.7–36.6)	34.3 (30.1–38.4)
Female	29.3 (27.0–31.6)	28.3 (26.4–30.1)	28.8 (26.8–30.7)	28.3 (25.4–31.2)	29.5 (26.1–32.9)

Table 3.1.29 Continued

Age group, race/ethnicity, gender	1997–1998 % (95% CI)	1999–2001 % (95% CI)	2002–2004 % (95% CI)	2005–2006 % (95% CI)	2007–2009 % (95% CI)
30–34 years					
Black or African American: total	27.5 (24.2–30.8)	21.1 (18.0–24.1)	21.0 (18.5–23.6)	19.0 (15.3–22.8)	20.9 (16.9–24.9)
Male	29.9 (24.4–35.3)	25.7 (20.9–30.4)	27.1 (22.9–31.4)	24.9 (18.0–31.8)	23.0 (17.8–28.2)
Female	25.4 (21.4–29.4)	17.3 (14.5–20.2)	16.0 (12.9–19.1)	14.0 (10.7–17.3)	19.2 (14.1–24.2)
Hispanic: total	20.6 (18.4–22.9)	17.8 (15.8–19.8)	15.4 (13.7–17.1)	15.9 (13.3–18.5)	13.6 (11.3–15.9)
Male	27.0 (23.2–30.9)	23.1 (19.8–26.4)	21.4 (18.4–24.3)	20.8 (16.9–24.7)	17.7 (13.9–21.6)
Female	13.3 (10.6–16.0)	12.4 (10.5–14.3)	8.9 (7.2–10.6)	10.1 (7.6–12.7)	8.9 (6.0–11.7)
White: total	28.3 (26.9–29.8)	27.8 (26.5–29.0)	26.1 (24.7–27.6)	26.7 (24.8–28.7)	26.0 (24.0–27.9)
Male	29.1 (27.0–31.2)	29.0 (27.1–30.9)	28.2 (26.1–30.2)	27.1 (24.2–30.1)	29.3 (26.3–32.3)
Female	27.6 (25.6–29.5)	26.5 (24.9–28.2)	24.1 (22.4–25.9)	26.4 (23.7–29.1)	22.7 (20.2–25.1)
35–39 years					
Black or African American: total	18.9 (15.7–22.2)	28.1 (25.2–30.9)	20.0 (17.5–22.5)	18.9 (15.7–22.2)	17.7 (13.9–21.6)
Male	22.8 (16.9–28.8)	29.0 (24.7–33.3)	22.2 (18.2–26.3)	22.8 (16.9–28.8)	18.7 (13.1–24.3)
Female	15.4 (11.7–19.2)	27.4 (23.6–31.1)	18.3 (15.5–21.2)	15.4 (11.7–19.2)	17.0 (12.2–21.8)
Hispanic: total	19.4 (16.7–22.2)	19.9 (17.9–21.9)	17.3 (15.4–19.2)	19.4 (16.7–22.2)	15.4 (12.2–18.5)
Male	25.2 (21.0–29.4)	25.7 (22.4–29.0)	23.8 (20.5–27.0)	25.2 (21.0–29.4)	19.5 (14.3–24.7)
Female	12.5 (9.4–15.6)	14.0 (11.6–16.4)	10.4 (8.2–12.5)	12.5 (9.4–15.6)	10.5 (7.2–13.7)
White: total	24.4 (22.6–26.3)	29.0 (27.8–30.2)	26.8 (25.5–28.2)	24.4 (22.6–26.3)	25.6 (23.7–27.5)
Male	25.7 (23.1–28.2)	28.7 (26.9–30.5)	29.2 (27.2–31.2)	25.7 (23.1–28.2)	25.8 (22.9–28.7)
Female	23.2 (20.6–25.8)	29.3 (27.6–31.0)	24.6 (22.9–26.2)	23.2 (20.6–25.8)	25.4 (22.5–28.4)
40–44 years					
Black or African American: total	24.2 (20.9–27.5)	31.0 (27.9–34.1)	27.9 (25.2–30.6)	24.2 (20.9–27.5)	22.2 (18.5–25.9)
Male	24.0 (18.6–29.4)	34.8 (30.2–39.4)	30.5 (25.9–35.1)	24.0 (18.6–29.4)	23.8 (18.2–29.5)
Female	24.3 (20.1–28.5)	27.6 (24.0–31.2)	25.8 (22.6–28.9)	24.3 (20.1–28.5)	20.9 (15.8–26.0)
Hispanic: total	15.9 (13.3–18.6)	19.7 (17.6–21.8)	20.4 (17.8–23.0)	15.9 (13.3–18.6)	15.9 (12.9–18.9)
Male	18.1 (14.2–22.1)	25.1 (21.8–28.4)	25.7 (21.9–29.5)	18.1 (14.2–22.1)	21.7 (16.8–26.7)
Female	13.8 (10.5–17.1)	14.3 (11.7–16.9)	15.0 (12.2–17.8)	13.8 (10.5–17.1)	9.8 (7.0–12.6)
White: total	25.7 (23.9–27.5)	28.9 (27.6–30.3)	28.3 (26.9–29.6)	25.7 (23.9–27.5)	25.2 (22.9–27.4)
Male	27.4 (24.9–29.9)	30.5 (28.6–32.4)	29.0 (27.1–31.0)	27.4 (24.9–29.9)	27.0 (24.0–30.0)
Female	24.1 (21.7–26.5)	27.4 (25.8–28.9)	27.6 (25.8–29.3)	24.1 (21.7–26.5)	23.4 (20.5–26.3)

Source: 1978–2009 NHIS: Centers for Disease Control and Prevention, National Center for Health Statistics (unpublished data).

Table 3.1.30 Trends in the initiation of cigarette smoking over time among 12- to 17-year-olds at risk for initiation—number (in thousands) and percentage of initiates—by gender and race/ethnicity; National Survey on Drug Use and Health (NSDUH) 2006–2010; United States

	2006		2007		2008		2009		2010	
Gender and race/ ethnicity	N	% (95% CI)	N	% (95% CI)	N	% (95% CI)	N	% (955 CI)	N	% (95% CI)
Overall	1,328	6.6 (6.1–7.1)	1,197	5.9 (5.4–6.3)	1,268	6.2 (5.7–6.7)	1,259	6.2 (5.7–6.7)	1,196	5.5 (5.4–6.3)
Gender										
Male	644	6.3 (5.7–6.9)	592	5.7 (5.2–6.4)	592	5.7 (5.1–6.3)	642	6.2 (5.6–6.9)	592	5.7 (5.1–6.3)
Female	685	6.9 (6.3–7.6)	606	6.0 (5.3–6.7)	676	6.7 (6.0–7.5)	617	6.1 (5.5–6.8)	604	6.0 (5.4–6.6)
Race/ethnicity										
White	879	7.5 (6.9–8.1)	819	6.9 (6.3–7.6)	819	6.9 (6.3–7.5)	770	6.6 (6.0–7.2)	751	6.4 (5.8–7.0)
Black or African American	149	4.6 (3.7–5.7)	121	3.7 (2.9–4.7)	138	4.3 (3.4–5.5)	127	4.0 (3.0–5.3)	107	3.5 (2.7–4.5)
Hispanic or Latino	250	6.8 (5.6–8.1)	213	5.4 (4.5–6.6)	243	6.2 (5.1–7.5)	303	7.6 (6.4–9.0)	265	6.4 (5.3–7.6)

Source: 2006–2010 NSDUH: Substance Abuse and Mental Health Services Administration (unpublished data).
Note: At risk for initiation is defined as persons who did not use the substance(s) in their lifetime or used the substance(s) for the first time in the past year. **CI** = confidence interval; **N** = number (in 1,000s).

Table 3.1.31 Trends in the initiation of cigarette smoking over time among 18- to 25-year-olds at risk for initiation—number (in thousands) and percentage of initiates—by gender and race/ethnicity; National Survey on Drug Use and Health (NSDUH) 2006–2010; United States

	2006		2007		2008		2009		2010	
Gender and race/ethnicity	N	% (95% CI)	N	% (95% CI)	N	% (95% CI)	N	% (95% CI)	N	% (95% CI)
Overall	1,038	8.7 (7.9–9.5)	989	7.9 (7.2–8.7)	1,062	8.3 (7.4–9.2)	1,144	8.6 (7.8–9.5)	1,110	7.9 (7.2–8.7)
Gender										
Male	544	9.6 (8.4–11.0)	497	8.7 (7.6–9.9)	584	9.7 (8.4–11.1)	595	9.9 (8.7–11.2)	597	9.3 (8.1–10.6)
Female	495	7.8 (6.8–8.9)	492	7.2 (6.3–8.2)	478	7.0 (6.0–8.1)	549	7.5 (6.5–8.7)	513	6.8 (5.9–7.7)
Race/ethnicity										
White	650	10.7 (9.6–12.0)	601	9.0 (8.0–10.1)	657	9.7 (8.6–10.9)	728	10.4 (9.2–11.8)	634	8.8 (7.9–9.9)
Black or African American	103	4.5 (3.4–6.0)	127	5.5 (4.2–7.0)	122	4.7 (3.6–6.3)	138	5.3 (4.0–7.0)	161	5.8 (4.5–7.3)
Hispanic or Latino	203	7.9 (6.0–10.3)	173	6.9 (5.3–8.8)	217	9.1 (6.9–11.7)	216	8.3 (6.3–10.7)	245	8.4 (6.8–10.4)

Source: 2006–2010 NSDUH: Substance Abuse and Mental Health Services Administration (unpublished data).
Note: At risk for initiation is defined as persons who did not use the substance(s) in their lifetime or used the substance(s) for the first time in the past year. **CI** = confidence interval; **N** = number (in 1,000s).

Table 3.1.32 Percentage of high school senior smokers who answered "yes" to questions about interest in quitting smoking and attempts to quit smoking, by frequency of smoking during the past 30 days; Monitoring the Future (MTF) 1990–2009; United States

Question and frequency of smoking	1990–1994 % (95% CI)	1995–1999 % (95% CI)	2000–2004 % (95% CI)	2005–2009 % (95% CI)
Do you want to stop smoking now?				
Among those who smoked at all during the past 30 days	42.7 (40.9–44.5)	42.3 (40.0–44.7)	44.8 (41.4–48.1)	34.4 (30.9–37.9)
Among those who smoked ≥1 cigarette per day during the past 30 days	45.5 (43.1–48.0)	43.1 (40.4–45.7)	47.4 (43.8–50.9)	37.7 (33.7–41.8)
Have you ever tried to stop smoking and found that you could not?				
Among those who smoked at all during the past 30 days	31.7 (29.4–34.0)	31.3 (29.1–33.4)	33.6 (30.6–36.7)	26.5 (23.4–29.6)
Among those who smoked ≥1 cigarette per day during the past 30 days	44.4 (41.9–47.0)	43.1 (40.9–45.3)	46.2 (43.0–49.4)	38.9 (35.3–42.5)

Source: 1990–2009 MTF: University of Michigan, Institute for Social Research (unpublished data).
Note: **CI** = confidence interval.

Table 3.1.33 Prevalence of cigarette smoking among users of smokeless tobacco and among users of drugs (e.g., alcohol, marijuana, cocaine, and inhalants) and prevalence of other drug use among cigarette smokers, among male high school seniors; Monitoring the Future (MTF) 2002–2007; United States

Other drug	Prevalence of cigarette smoking among users of smokeless tobacco and users of drugs % (95% CI)	Prevalence of cigarette smoking among nonusers of smokeless tobacco and nonusers of drugs % (95% CI)	Prevalence of smokeless tobacco use and drug use among cigarette smokers % (95% CI)	Prevalence of smokeless tobacco use and drug use among cigarette nonsmokers % (95% CI)
Alcohol	41.6 (39.5–43.7)	8.0 (7.0–8.9)	83.9 (82.3–85.4)	38.8 (36.5–41.1)
Marijuana	56.6 (53.4–59.9)	15.0 (13.6–16.4)	53.0 (50.0–56.0)	13.3 (11.8–14.7)
Cocaine	75.7 (71.2–80.1)	23.3 (21.6–24.9)	8.2 (7.2–9.2)	0.9 (0.7–1.0)
Inhalants	64.0 (59.4–68.7)	24.5 (22.7–26.3)	4.7 (4.0–5.5)	0.9 (0.7–1.1)
Smokeless tobacco	59.9 (57.2–62.6)	19.7 (18.3–21.1)	29.3 (26.4–32.3)	6.4 (5.0–7.7)

Source: 2002–2007 MTF: University of Michigan, Institute for Social Research (unpublished data).
Note: **CI** = confidence interval.

Table 3.1.34 Prevalence of cigarette smoking among users of other drugs (e.g., alcohol, marijuana, cocaine, and inhalants) and prevalence of other drug use among cigarette smokers, among female high school seniors; Monitoring the Future (MTF) 2002–2007; United States

Other drug	Prevalence of cigarette smoking among users of other drugs % (95% CI)	Prevalence of cigarette smoking among nonusers of other drugs % (95% CI)	Prevalence of drug use among cigarette smokers % (95% CI)	Prevalence of drug use among cigarette nonsmokers % (95% CI)
Alcohol	39.7 (37.2–42.1)	8.3 (7.3–9.2)	78.8 (77.0–80.6)	33.7 (31.9–35.5)
Marijuana	60.6 (56.9–64.2)	14.3 (12.9–15.6)	45.4 (43.2–47.7)	8.3 (7.2–9.3)
Cocaine	78.0 (74.2–81.7)	20.9 (19.1–22.7)	6.2 (5.2–7.1)	0.5 (0.4–0.6)
Inhalants	62.3 (53.2–71.4)	21.6 (19.9–23.2)	3.3 (2.6–4.0)	0.6 (0.5–0.7)

Source: 2002–2007 MTF: University of Michigan, Institute for Social Research (unpublished data).
Note: **CI** = confidence interval.

Table 3.1.35 Percentage distribution of grade in which high school seniors first (if ever) used cigarettes or alcohol, or both; Monitoring the Future (MTF) 2002–2007; United States

Grade first (if ever) used cigarettes	First used alcohol in ≤6th grade (%)	First used alcohol in 7th or 8th grade (%)	First used alcohol in 9th grade (%)	First used alcohol in 10th grade (%)	First used alcohol in 11th grade (%)	First used alcohol in 12th grade (%)	Never used alcohol (%)
≤6th	3.13	4.50	1.92	0.81	0.90	0.43	0.30
7th or 8th	1.22	7.12	3.91	2.04	0.85	0.55	0.34
9th	0.27	1.86	3.38	1.45	0.75	0.39	0.10
10th	0.18	0.77	1.77	1.86	0.71	0.22	0.10
11th	0.17	0.57	0.89	1.17	1.46	0.33	0.21
12th	0.07	0.34	0.51	0.57	0.66	0.70	0.11
Never used cigarettes	1.68	4.62	6.04	6.44	6.90	4.92	19.82

Source: 2002–2007 MTF: University of Michigan, Institute for Social Research (unpublished data).
Note: Yellow = tried both cigarettes and alcohol in the same grade; light green = tried both, cigarettes first; pink = tried both, alcohol first; dark green = tried only cigarettes; light orange = tried only alcohol; blue = tried neither.

Table 3.1.36 Percentage distribution of grade in which high school seniors first (if ever) used cigarettes or marijuana, or both; Monitoring the Future (MTF) 2002–2007; United States

Grade first (if ever) used cigarettes	First used marijuana in ≤6th grade (%)	First used marijuana in 7th or 8th grade (%)	First used marijuana in 9th grade (%)	First used marijuana in 10th grade (%)	First used marijuana in 11th grade (%)	First used marijuana in 12th grade (%)	Never used marijuana (%)
≤6th	1.55	3.80	1.63	0.83	0.71	0.42	2.58
7th or 8th	0.23	4.51	3.74	2.06	1.01	0.43	3.50
9th	0.09	0.81	2.61	1.41	0.69	0.38	1.89
10th	0.06	0.26	0.56	1.85	0.85	0.38	1.37
11th	0.02	0.25	0.27	0.56	1.26	0.53	1.74
12th	0.02	0.14	0.18	0.19	0.27	0.65	1.37
Never used cigarettes	0.17	0.98	1.38	1.62	1.96	1.43	44.83

Source: 2002–2007 MTF: University of Michigan, Institute for Social Research (unpublished data).
Note: Yellow = tried both cigarettes and marijuana in the same grade; light green = tried both, cigarettes first; pink = tried both, marijuana first; dark green = tried only cigarettes; light orange = tried only marijuana; blue = tried neither.

Table 3.1.37 Percentage distribution of grade in which high school seniors first (if ever) used cigarettes or cocaine, or both; Monitoring the Future (MTF) 2002–2007; United States

Grade first (if ever) used cigarettes	First used cocaine in ≤6th grade (%)	First used cocaine in 7th or 8th grade (%)	First used cocaine in 9th grade (%)	First used cocaine in 10th grade (%)	First used cocaine in 11th grade (%)	First used cocaine in 12th grade (%)	Never used cocaine (%)
≤6th	0.15	0.32	0.46	0.57	0.49	0.51	8.93
7th or 8th	0.01	0.25	0.23	0.52	0.64	0.45	13.05
9th	0.02	0.02	0.16	0.25	0.40	0.36	6.71
10th	0.00	0.00	0.01	0.10	0.16	0.17	4.91
11th	0.00	0.00	0.02	0.04	0.11	0.16	4.30
12th	0.00	0.00	0.01	0.03	0.01	0.07	2.77
Never used cigarettes	0.03	0.02	0.06	0.06	0.05	0.09	52.34

Source: 2002–2007 MTF: University of Michigan, Institute for Social Research (unpublished data).
Note: Yellow = tried both cigarettes and cocaine in the same grade; light green = tried both, cigarettes first; pink = tried both, cocaine first; dark green = tried only cigarettes; light orange = tried only cocaine; blue = tried neither.

Table 3.1.38 Body mass index by smoking status/frequency among high school seniors, by gender and race/ethnicity; National Youth Risk Behavior Survey (YRBS) 2003–2009; United States

	Males		Females		White		Black or African American		Hispanic or Latino	
Smoking status/frequency[a]	**Mean (95% CI)**	**SN[b]**	**Mean (95% CI)**	**SN[b]**	**Mean (95% CI)**	**SN[b]**	**Mean (95% CI)**	**SN[b]**	**Mean (95% CI)**	**SN[b]**
Never smoker	23.0 (22.8–23.2)	a	24.5 (24.0–24.9)	a	23.4 (23.0–23.8)	a	24.8 (24.4–25.2)	a	24.3 (24.0–24.7)	a
Current infrequent smoker	23.9 (23.5–24.3)	b	25.0 (24.6–25.4)	a	24.2 (23.8–24.6)	b	25.9 (25.0–26.9)	b	25.1 (24.6–25.7)	b
Current frequent smoker	23.8 (23.3–24.4)	b	24.5 (23.8–25.1)	a	23.9 (23.4–24.4)	a,b	26.7 (25.5–27.9)	b	25.3 (24.1–26.6)	a,b
Former daily smoker	23.5 (22.6–24.4)	a,b	24.2 (22.9–25.4)	a	23.7 (22.8–24.5)	a,b	23.6 (22.1–25.2)	a	24.3 (23.2–25.3)	a,b
Former nondaily smoker	23.7 (23.4–23.9)	b	24.7 (24.4–24.9)	a	23.8 (23.5–24.1)	a,b	25.5 (25.0–25.9)	b	24.4 (24.0–24.8)	a

Source: 2003–2009 YRBS: Centers for Disease Control and Prevention, Division of Adolescent and School Health (unpublished data).
Note: **CI** = confidence interval; **SN** = statistical note.
[a]Definitions for these categories are as follows: Students who answered "no" to ever smoke were categorized as nonsmokers. Students who answered "yes" to ever smoke and "yes" to currently smoke were categorized as (a) current infrequent smokers for smoking 1–19 days during the past 30 days or (b) current frequent smokers for smoking >19 days during the past 30 days. Students who answered "yes" to ever smoke and "no" to currently smoke were categorized as (a) former daily smokers if they answered "yes" to daily or (b) former nondaily smokers if they answered "no" to daily.
[b]These tests were performed to examine differences in estimates within specific demographic subgroups (e.g., gender). Estimates with the same letter (e.g., a and a) are not statistically significantly different from one another (p >0.05). Estimates with different letters (e.g., a and b) are, in contrast, statistically significantly different from one another (p <0.05).

Table 3.1.39 Percentage of 12- to 17-year-olds and 18- to 25-year-olds who have experienced a major depressive episode, by smoking status/frequency, gender, and race/ethnicity; National Survey on Drug Use and Health (NSDUH) 2009–2010; United States

Smoking status/ frequency among youth 12–17 years old	Males % (95% CI)	SN[a]	Females % (95% CI)	SN[a]	White % (95% CI)	SN[a]	Black or African American % (95% CI)	SN[a]	Hispanic or Latino % (95% CI)	SN[a]
Never smoker[b]	3.6 (3.3–4.0)	a	8.7 (8.2–9.3)	a	6.2 (5.8–6.7)	a	6.3 (5.4–7.3)	a	6.1 (5.4–7.0)	a
Former smoker[c]	7.4 (6.1–8.9)	b	23.4 (21.3–25.6)	b,c	15.6 (14.0–17.3)	b	12.9 (10.1–16.5)	b	13.8 (11.2–16.9)	b
Current infrequent smoker[d]	8.7 (6.8–11.0)	c	26.3 (23.0–29.8)	b	18.6 (16.3–21.1)	c	10.8 (6.4–17.6)	a,b	14.6 (10.8–19.4)	b
Current frequent smoker[e]	7.8 (6.0–10.0)	b,c	19.2 (16.1–22.9)	c	13.2 (11.2–15.5)	b	NR		10.3 (5.9–17.6)	a,b

Smoking status/ frequency among young adults 18–25 years old	Males % (95% CI)	SN[a]	Females % (95% CI)	SN[a]	White % (95% CI)	SN[a]	Black or African American % (95% CI)	SN[a]	Hispanic or Latino % (95% CI)	SN[a]
Never smoker[b]	4.0 (3.4–4.6)	a	7.9 (7.2–8.6)	a	7.0 (6.4–7.7)	a	5.6 (4.7–6.8)	a	4.8 (3.9–5.9)	a
Former smoker[c]	4.7 (4.1–5.5)	a	10.2 (9.3–11.2)	b	7.7 (7.0–8.4)	a	7.3 (5.7–9.2)	b	7.5 (6.1–9.1)	b
Current infrequent smoker[d]	6.2 (5.2–7.5)	b	14.9 (13.1–16.8)	b	9.8 (8.7–11.2)	a	6.1 (4.3–8.7)	a,b	10.3 (8.0–13.2)	b,c
Current frequent smoker[e]	7.2 (6.3–8.2)	b	16.3 (14.9–17.7)	c	11.4 (10.4–12.4)	b	10.6 (8.1–13.9)	b	10.8 (8.4–13.8)	c

Source: 2009–2010 NSDUH: Substance Abuse and Mental Health Services Administration (unpublished data).
Note: For "depressive episode," see SAMHSA 2005. **CI** = confidence interval; **NR** = low precision, no estimate reported; **SN** = statistical note.
[a]This column represents the results of statistical tests that were run within NSDUH. These tests were performed to examine differences in estimates within specific demographic subgroups (e.g., gender). Estimates with the same letter (e.g., a and a) are not statistically significantly different from one another ($p > 0.05$). Estimates with different letters (e.g., a and b) are, in contrast, statistically significantly different from one another ($p < 0.05$).
[b]Never smoker: reported no use of cigarettes in his or her lifetime.
[c]Former smoker: reported cigarette use in his or her lifetime but no cigarette use in the past month.
[d]Current infrequent smoker: reported smoking fewer than 20 cigarettes in the past 30 days.
[e]Current frequent smoker: reported smoking 20 or more cigarettes in the past 30 days.

Table 3.1.40 Percentage of young people who have ever used smokeless tobacco, by gender, race/ethnicity, age/grade, and region; National Survey on Drug Use and Health (NSDUH) 2010, Monitoring the Future (MTF) 2010, and National Youth Tobacco Survey (NYTS) 2009; United States

	NSDUH 13–18 years of age		MTF 8th, 10th, and 12th grades		NYTS 9th–12 grades[a]		NYTS 6th–8th grades[a]	
Characteristic	**% (95% CI)**	**SN[b]**	**% (95% CI)**	**SN[b]**	**% (95% CI)**	**SN[b]**	**% (95% CI)**	**SN[b]**
Overall	10.2 (9.61–10.74)		14.5 (12.2–16.8)		14.1 (10.7–17.5)		6.1 (5.2–7.1)	
Gender						a		
Male	15.8 (14.91–16.80)	a	23.2 (19.5–26.8)	a	22.5 (16.6–28.3)	b	8.5 (7.0–10.1)	a
Female	4.1 (3.63–4.65)	b	6.1 (4.7–7.6)	b	5.7 (4.3–7.0)		3.5 (2.8–4.3)	b
Race/ethnicity						a		
White	14.3 (13.53–15.19)	a	18.6 (15.7–21.5)	a	17.8 (13.7–21.8)		6.2 (4.8–7.6)	a
Male	22.7 (21.39–24.08)		29.3 (24.8–33.7)		28.7 (22.3–35.2)		9.0 (6.9–11.1)	
Female	5.5 (4.83–6.35)		7.8 (5.8–9.9)		6.7 (4.7–8.8)	b	3.2 (2.0–4.3)	
Black or African American	2.4 (1.82–3.17)	b	5.7 (3.3–8.1)	b	7.7 (5.3–10.1)		3.8 (2.4–5.2)	b
Male	3.3 (2.40–4.52)		9.1 (5.1–13.2)		10.3 (5.1–15.5)		4.9 (2.9–6.9)	
Female	1.5 (0.84–2.54)		2.4 (0.5–4.4)		5.1 (0.9–9.4)	b	2.7 (1.4–3.9)	
Hispanic or Latino	5.3 (4.46–6.32)	c	8.4 (5.1–11.6)	c	9.4 (6.8–11.9)		6.0 (5.0–6.9)	a
Male	8.2 (6.72–9.96)		13.7 (8.4–19.0)		14.2 (10.9–17.5)		8.1 (6.2–9.9)	
Female	2.0 (1.32–3.13)		3.8 (1.9–5.6)		4.5 (2.2–6.8)	b	3.9 (2.6–5.2)	
Other[c]	5.6 (4.36–7.25)	c	10.7 (4.0–17.3)	c	9.5 (4.6–14.3)		10.5 (5.3–15.6)	a
Male	7.6 (5.50–10.51)		16.4 (6.1–26.7)		16.7 (8.5–25.0)		13.7 (4.5–23.0)	
Female	3.5 (2.47–5.02)		5.2 (1.0–9.0)		2.3 (0.5–4.0)		7.0 (4.1–9.9)	
Age (in years)/grade								
13–14	3.9 (3.38–4.60)	a	NA		NA		NA	
15–16	9.7 (8.90–10.60)	b	NA		NA		NA	
17–18	16.1 (14.98–17.26)	c	NA		NA		NA	
6th	NA		NA		NA		5.1 (3.8–6.5)	a
7th	NA		NA		NA		5.0 (3.8–6.2)	a
8th	NA		9.9 (8.1–11.8)	a	NA	a	8.3 (6.6–10.1)	b
9th	NA		NA		10.3 (7.2–13.4)	a	NA	
10th	NA		16.8 (14.4–19.2)	b	13.2 (9.6–16.8)	b	NA	
11th	NA		NA		17.5 (12.8–22.3)	a,b	NA	
12th	NA		17.6 (14.9–20.4)	b	16.3 (10.7–22.0)		NA	

Table 3.1.40 Continued

	NSDUH 13–18 years of age		MTF 8th, 10th, and 12th grades		NYTS 9th–12 grades[a]		NYTS 6th–8th grades[a]	
Characteristic	**% (95% CI)**	**SN[b]**	**% (95% CI)**	**SN[b]**	**% (95% CI)**	**SN[b]**	**% (95% CI)**	**SN[b]**
Region								
Northeast	8.5 (7.50–9.61)	a	12.0 (7.6–16.3)	a	NA		NA	
Midwest	11.8 (10.88–12.85)	b	18.9 (13.8–24.1)	b	NA		NA	
South	11.7 (10.60–12.82)	b	16.0 (11.9–20.0)	b	NA		NA	
West	7.5 (6.46–8.70)	a	9.7 (6.4–13.0)	a	NA		NA	

Source: 2010 NSDUH: Substance Abuse and Mental Health Services Administration (unpublished data); 2010 MTF: University of Michigan, Institute for Social Research (unpublished data); 2009 NYTS: Centers for Disease Control and Prevention (unpublished data).
Note: **CI** = confidence interval; **NA** = not applicable; **SN** = statistical note.
[a]Estimates are based on responses to the question, "Have you ever used chewing tobacco, snuff, or dip, such as Redman, Levi Garrett, Beechnut, Skoal Bandits, or Copenhagen?"
[b]This column represents the results of statistical tests that were run separately within each surveillance system (e.g., NSDUH). These tests were performed to examine differences in estimates within specific demographic subgroups (e.g., gender). Estimates with the same letter (e.g., a and a) are not statistically significantly different from one another ($p > 0.05$). Estimates with different letters (e.g., a and b) are, in contrast, statistically significantly different from one another ($p < 0.05$).
[c]Includes Asians, American Indians or Alaska Natives, Native Hawaiians or Other Pacific Islanders, and persons of two or more races.

Table 3.1.41 Percentage of young people who currently use smokeless tobacco, by gender, race/ethnicity, age/grade, and region; National Survey on Drug Use and Health (NSDUH) 2010, Monitoring the Future (MTF) 2010, National Youth Risk Behavior Survey (YRBS) 2009, and National Youth Tobacco Survey (NYTS) 2009; United States

	NSDUH 13–18 years of age		MTF 8th, 10th, and 12th grades		YRBS 9th–12th grades		NYTS 9th–12th grades[a]		NYTS 6th–8th grades[a]	
Characteristic	**% (95% CI)**	**SN[b]**	**% (95% CI)**	**SN[b]**	**% (95% CI)**	**SN[b]**	**% (95% CI)**	**SN[b]**	**% (95% CI)**	**SN[b]**
Overall	3.7 (3.33–4.03)		6.5 (5.2–7.8)		8.9 (7.3–10.8)		6.7 (4.5–8.9)		2.6 (2.0–3.2)	
Gender										
Male	6.3 (5.73–6.96)	a	11.3 (9.0–13.6)	a	15.0 (12.1–18.5)	a	11.6 (7.7–15.4)	a	3.7 (2.6-4.8)	a
Female	0.8 (0.56–1.22)	b	1.9 (1.2–2.6)	b	2.2 (1.8– 2.7)	b	1.8 (1.2–2.3)	b	1.4 (1.0–1.9)	b
Race/ethnicity										
White	5.5 (5.01–6.09)	a	8.7 (6.9–10.4)	a	11.9 (9.5–14.6)	a	8.7 (6.1–11.2)	a	2.5 (1.8–3.3)	a
Male	9.6 (8.74–10.61)		15.0 (11.9–18.1)		20.1 (15.8–25.4)		15.6 (11.2–20.0)		3.7 (2.5–4.8)	
Female	1.2 (0.80–1.84)		2.3 (1.3–3.4)		2.3 (1.7–3.2)		1.7 (0.8–2.6)		1.3 (0.7–2.0)	
Black or African American	0.4 (0.25–0.77)	b	2.1 (0.9–3.3)	b	3.3 (2.3–4.6)	b	1.7 (0.1–3.2)	b	1.5 (0.8–2.2)	b
Male	0.7 (0.36–1.20)		3.2 (1.1–5.4)		5.2 (3.7–7.4)		2.1 (0.4–3.7)		1.9 (1.1–2.8)	
Female	0.2 (0.06–0.81)		0.9 (0.0–1.9)		1.3 (0.8–2.3)		1.3 (0.3–4.8)		1.1 (0.1–2.1)	
Hispanic or Latino	1.3 (0.90–1.83)	c	3.2 (1.4–5.0)	b,c	5.1 (4.1–6.3)	c	4.8 (3.2–6.5)	c	2.5 (1.8–3.2)	a
Male	2.1 (1.44–3.10)		5.3 (2.2–8.3)		7.5 (5.7–9.8)		6.8 (4.2–9.5)		3.4 (2.3–4.6)	
Female	0.3 (0.15–0.80)		1.5 (0.3–2.7)		2.6 (1.9–3.5)		2.8 (1.4–4.3)		1.6 (0.7–2.5)	
Other[c]	1.7 (1.04–2.93)	c	4.0 (0.9–7.1)	c	5.7 (3.4–9.3)	b,c	5.3 (2.2–8.4)	c	5.1 (0.5–9.8)	a,b
Male	3.2 (1.81–5.47)		7.0 (1.0–13.0)		10.1 (6.3–15.7)		9.5 (4.0–15.0)		7.9 (2.6–21.8)	
Female	0.3 (0.12–0.57)		1.2 (0.0–2.9)		1.3 (0.5–3.6)		1.1 (0.0–2.2)		2.2 (0.4–3.9)	
Age (in years)/grade							NA		NA	
13–14	1.2 (0.89–1.57)	a	NA		NA		NA		NA	
15–16	3.1 (2.69–3.64)	b	NA		NA		NA		NA	
17–18	6.4 (5.58–7.22)	c	NA		NA		NA		NA	
6th	NA		NA		NA		NA		2.4 (1.4–3.4)	a
7th	NA		NA		NA		NA		2.2 (1.5–3.0)	a
8th	NA		4.1 (3.0–5.1)	a	NA		NA		3.1 (2.1–4.1)	a
9th	NA		NA		7.2 (5.7–9.0)	a	4.3 (2.2–6.3)	a	NA	
10th	NA		7.5 (6.2–8.9)	b	8.1 (6.3–10.5)	a,c	7.2 (4.9–9.5)	b	NA	
11th	NA		NA		10.7 (8.7– 13.1)	b	7.8 (5.3–10.4)	b	NA	
12th	NA		8.5 (6.9–10.1)	b	10.0 (7.6–13.1)	b,c	8.0 (4.7–11.3)	b	NA	

Table 3.1.41 Continued

	NSDUH 13–18 years of age		MTF 8th, 10th, and 12th grades		YRBS 9th–12th grades		NYTS 9th–12th grades[a]		NYTS 6th–8th grades[a]	
Characteristic	**% (95% CI)**	**SN[b]**	**% (95% CI)**	**SN[b]**	**% (95% CI)**	**SN[b]**	**% (95% CI)**	**SN[b]**	**% (95% CI)**	**SN[b]**
Region										
Northeast	3.3 (2.67–3.98)	a	5.9 (2.7–9.2)	a,c	10.7 (5.3–20.4)	a,b	NA		NA	
Midwest	4.0 (3.38–4.61)	b	8.4 (5.7–11.1)	b	9.3 (7.5–11.5)	b	NA		NA	
South	4.2 (3.56–4.89)	b	7.2 (4.9–9.5)	a,b	10.7 (8.5–13.4)	b	NA		NA	
West	2.9 (2.22–3.77)	a	4.0 (2.0–6.0)	c	4.6 (3.1–6.7)	a	NA		NA	

Source: 2010 NSDUH: Substance Abuse and Mental Health Services Administration (unpublished data); 2010 MTF: University of Michigan, Institute for Social Research (unpublished data); 2009 YRBS: Centers for Disease Control and Prevention, Division of Adolescent and School Health (CDC 2011a); 2009 NYTS: Centers for Disease Control and Prevention (unpublished data).
Note: **CI** = confidence interval; **NA** = not applicable; **SN** = statistical note.
[a]Estimates are based on responses to the question, "During the past 30 days, on how many days did you use chewing tobacco, snuff, or dip?" The estimates were compared and matched the ones reported by CDC (2010e).
[b]This column represents the results of statistical tests that were run separately within each surveillance system (e.g., NSDUH). These tests were performed to examine differences in estimates within specific demographic subgroups (e.g., gender). Estimates with the same letter (e.g., a and a) are not statistically significantly different from one another ($p > 0.05$). Estimates with different letters (e.g., a and b) are, in contrast, statistically significantly different from one another ($p < 0.05$).
[c]Includes Asians, American Indians or Alaska Natives, Native Hawaiians or Other Pacific Islanders, and persons of two or more races.

Table 3.1.42 Prevalence of 8th-, 10th-, and 12th-grade males who currently use smokeless tobacco, by various sociodemographic risk factors; Monitoring the Future (MTF) 2002–2007; United States

	8th graders		10th graders		12th graders	
Sociodemographic risk factors	**% (95% CI)**	**SN[a]**	**% (95% CI)**	**SN[a]**	**% (95% CI)**	**SN[a]**
Parental education[b]						
1.0–2.0 (low)	8.4 (3.5–13.3)	a	9.6 (5.5–13.7)	a,c	10.4 (6.1–14.6)	a,b
2.5–3.0	6.7 (5.0–8.4)	a,b	13.1 (11.2–15.0)	b	15.4 (12.2–18.6)	a,b
3.5–4.0	5.4 (3.8–7.0)	b,c	10.4 (8.7–12.2)	a	12.0 (10.1–13.9)	a
4.0–5.0	4.2 (2.9–5.5)	c	9.4 (7.9–10.9)	a,c	12.9 (10.0–15.8)	b
5.5–6.0 (high)	3.9 (2.3–5.4)	c	7.8 (5.8–9.7)	c	8.4 (5.9–10.8)	a,b
Household structure						
Lives with both parents	4.7 (3.1–6.3)	a,d	9.8 (8.3–11.3)	a	12.9 (10.9–14.9)	a
Lives with father only	10.2 (5.6–14.9)	b	12.4 (9.3–15.5)	a	10.8 (6.4–15.2)	a,b
Lives with mother only	3.8 (2.8–4.8)	a	9.2 (6.9–11.5)	a	8.6 (6.4–10.7)	b
Lives alone	37.4 (18.1–56.7)	c	31.7 (21.9–41.4)	b	12.3 (3.6–20.9)	a,b
Other relations	7.8 (4.1–11.5)	b,d	12.0 (7.7–16.3)	a	15.5 (9.6–21.3)	a
Population density						
Large MSA	2.3 (1.8–2.7)	a	6.8 (5.2–8.3)	a	7.5 (5.2–9.9)	a
Other MSA	4.3 (2.8–5.8)	b	9.3 (7.8–10.8)	b	10.9 (8.2–13.6)	b
Non-MSA	10.6 (5.5–15.8)	c	16.4 (11.8–21.0)	c	20.3 (17.8–22.8)	c
Academic performance						
A	2.9 (1.7–4.0)	a	6.4 (5.2–7.6)	a	7.5 (5.5–9.5)	a
B	4.7 (3.4–6.0)	b	9.3 (7.9–10.7)	b	13.1 (11.3–14.9)	b
C	7.3 (5.0–9.6)	c	13.4 (10.7–16.1)	c	15.1 (11.9–18.4)	b
D	13.0 (8.5–17.5)	d	19.2 (10.7–27.7)	d	17.9 (6.8–28.9)	b
Importance of religion						
Very important	5.9 (3.7–8.0)	a	8.2 (6.0–10.4)	a	10.7 (8.1–13.3)	a
Important	5.2 (3.2–7.2)	a	12.7 (10.2–15.2)	b	15.7 (13.5–17.8)	b
Not/somewhat important	5.4 (3.9–6.8)	a	11.3 (9.7–12.9)	b	13.0 (11.2–14.8)	a

Source: 2002–2007 MTF: University of Michigan, Institute for Social Research (unpublished data).
Note: **CI** = confidence interval; **MSA** = metropolitan statistical area; **SN** = statistical note.
[a]These tests were performed to examine differences in estimates within specific demographic subgroups (e.g., parental education). Estimates with the same letter (e.g., a and a) are not statistically significantly different from one another (p >0.05). Estimates with different letters (e.g., a and b) are, in contrast, statistically significantly different from one another (p <0.05).
[b]Parental education is an average score of mother's education and father's education. Response categories are (1) completed some grade school or less, (2) some high school, (3) completed high school, (4) some college, (5) completed college, and (6) graduate or professional school after college.

Table 3.1.43 Age at which high school senior respondents first used smokeless tobacco or cigars; National Youth Tobacco Survey (NYTS) 2009; United States

Age (years)[a]	Smokeless tobacco[b] % (95% CI)	Cigars[b] % (95% CI)
≤12	16.2 (7.5–24.9)	13.2 (10.0–16.4)
13–14	23.2 (14.8–31.5)	12.8 (10.0–15.6)
15–16	35.2 (26.4–44.0)	40.0 (35.5–44.6)
≥17	25.4 (17.8–33.0)	34.0 (29.7–38.3)

Source: 2009 NYTS, Centers for Disease Control and Prevention (unpublished data).
Note: **CI** = confidence interval.
[a]Estimates for age when first used smokeless tobacco are based on responding to the question, "How old were you when you used chewing tobacco, snuff, or dip for the first time?" The estimates for age when first smoked a cigar are based on responding to the question "How old were you when you smoked a cigar, cigarillo, or little cigars for the first time?" Those who reported never having used the relevant tobacco product were excluded from the denominator.
[b]Percentages calculated from those who reported ever having used smokeless tobacco or cigars.

Table 3.1.44 Percentage distribution of smokeless tobacco brands that youth 12–17 years of age who were current users of smokeless tobacco preferred, by gender, race/ethnicity, age, and region; National Survey on Drug Use and Health (NSDUH) 2006–2010; United States

Characteristic	Grizzly (MS) % (95% CI)	Skoal (MS) % (95% CI)	Copenhagen (MS) % (95% CI)	Red Man (Chew) % (95% CI)	Red Seal (MS) % (95% CI)	Levi Garrett (Chew) % (95% CI)
Overall	32.1 (29.9–34.3)	24.1 (22.2–26.2)	15.8 (14.3–17.5)	5.3 (4.3–6.6)	2.7 (2.0–3.7)	2.4 (1.7–3.3)
Gender						
Male	33.2 (30.9–35.6)	24.3 (22.2–26.5)	15.9 (14.2–17.7)	5.6 (4.5–6.9)	3.0 (2.2–4.0)	2.6 (1.8–3.6)
Female	22.1 (16.6–28.8)	22.5 (17.4–28.5)	15.7 (11.7–20.7)	2.8 (1.0–7.8)	0.7 (0.2–2.9)	0.9 (0.3–2.9)
Race/ethnicity						
White	33.2 (30.9–35.6)	24.7 (22.6–26.9)	16.1 (14.4–17.9)	4.9 (3.9–6.1)	3.0 (2.2–4.0)	2.6 (1.9–3.6)
Male	34.1 (31.6–36.6)	24.8 (22.7–27.2)	16.3 (14.5–18.3)	5.1 (4.1–6.4)	3.2 (2.3–4.3)	2.7 (1.9–3.9)
Female	24.3 (17.8–32.2)	22.8 (16.9–30.0)	13.7 (9.3–19.5)	NR	0.8 (0.2–3.6)	1.1 (0.3–3.6)
Black or African American	NR	NR	NR	NR	NR	NR
Male	NR	NR	NR	NR	NR	NR
Female	NR	NR	NR	NR	NR	NR
Hispanic or Latino	23.6 (15.9–33.7)	22.1 (15.0–31.4)	14.5 (9.0–22.6)	NR	1.3 (0.4–4.1)	1.1 (0.3–3.8)
Male	26.5 (17.5–38.0)	23.4 (15.5–33.9)	11.0 (6.2–18.8)	NR	1.5 (0.5–4.9)	1.4 (0.4–4.6)
Female	NR	NR	NR	NR	NR	NR
Other[a]	16.9 (10.7–25.7)	28.5 (20.1–38.7)	NR	9.4 (4.4–19.0)	1.1 (0.3–3.6)	NR
Male	16.4 (10.6–24.4)	NR	NR	9.1 (4.2–18.5)	1.6 (0.5–5.1)	NR
Female	NR	NR	NR	NR	NR	NR
Age (years)						
12–14	29.0 (24.1–34.5)	20.3 (16.3–25.1)	12.9 (9.5–17.3)	6.9 (4.6–10.3)	3.1 (1.9–5.2)	2.9 (1.0–7.7)
15–17	32.7 (30.4–35.2)	24.9 (22.7–27.2)	16.5 (14.7–18.4)	5.0 (3.9–6.3)	2.7 (1.9–3.8)	2.3 (1.7–3.1)
Region						
Northeast	14.6 (11.4–18.6)	50.1 (43.9–56.4)	11.5 (8.3–15.7)	5.8 (3.3–10.1)	1.1 (0.5–2.4)	0.6 (0.2–1.8)
Midwest	36.7 (32.8–40.8)	26.2 (22.9–29.8)	11.2 (8.9–14.0)	5.3 (3.8–7.4)	1.1 (0.4–2.7)	1.5 (0.7–3.1)
South	38.1 (34.6–41.7)	17.1 (14.5–20.2)	15.0 (12.6–17.7)	3.8 (2.6–5.5)	5.0 (3.6–7.0)	3.2 (2.1–4.9)
West	22.7 (17.7–28.7)	18.8 (14.6–23.8)	29.2 (24.1–34.8)	9.2 (5.9–14.0)	NR	2.9 (1.3–6.2)

Table 3.1.44 Continued

Characteristic	Timber Wolf (MS) % (95% CI)	Beech–Nut (MS) % (95% CI)	Camel–Snus (Chew) % (95% CI)	Kodiak (MS) % (95% CI)	All other brands % (95% CI)	Unknown % (95% CI)
Overall	1.8 (1.3–2.5)	1.4 (1.0–2.1)	1.4 (0.9–2.2)	1.3 (1.0–1.9)	6.0 (5.0–7.3)	5.5 (4.4–6.8)
Gender						
Male	1.9 (1.3–2.6)	1.3 (0.9–2.0)	1.1 (0.7–1.6)	1.4 (1.0–1.9)	5.3 (4.3–6.6)	4.6 (3.6–6.0)
Female	1.2 (0.4–3.4)	2.7 (0.9–8.2)	NR	1.2 (0.4–3.4)	12.6 (8.2–18.9)	13.2 (9.1–18.8)
Race/ethnicity						
White	2.0 (1.5–2.7)	1.4 (0.9–2.2)	1.5 (0.9–2.4)	1.4 (1.0–2.0)	5.1 (4.1–6.3)	4.1 (3.4–5.1)
Male	2.0 (1.5–2.8)	1.2 (0.8–1.9)	1.1 (0.7–1.7)	1.4 (1.0–2.1)	4.8 (3.8–6.0)	3.1 (2.5–4.0)
Female	1.6 (0.6–4.3)	3.3 (1.0–10.3)	NR	1.5 (0.5–4.3)	8.7 (5.2–14.4)	14.3 (9.5–21.0)
Black or African American	NR	NR	NR	NR	NR	NR
Male	NR	NR	NR	NR	NR	NR
Female	NR	NR	NR	NR	NR	NR
Hispanic or Latino	0.3 (0.0–2.2)	NR	0.8 (0.2–3.4)	0.6 (0.1–3.2)	NR	NR
Male	0.4 (0.1–2.6)	NR	NR	NR	6.0 (2.3–14.5)	NR
Female	NR	NR	NR	NR	NR	NR
Other[a]	0.2 (0.0–1.6)	5.1 (1.9–12.9)	1.6 (0.4–6.2)	0.9 (0.2–3.9)	12.6 (6.7–22.5)	4.0 (1.8–8.6)
Male	NR	NR	NR	NR	NR	4.6 (1.8–11.2)
Female	NR	NR	NR	NR	NR	NR
Age (years)						
12–14	2.0 (1.0–4.0)	1.4 (0.4–4.3)	0.7 (0.2–2.0)	1.6 (0.5–4.4)	9.0 (6.3–12.6)	10.3 (6.5–15.9)
15–17	1.8 (1.2–2.5)	1.5 (1.0–2.2)	1.5 (0.9–2.5)	1.3 (0.9–1.9)	5.4 (4.3–6.8)	4.5 (3.5–5.7)
Region						
Northeast	1.6 (0.8–3.2)	1.0 (0.4–2.7)	1.1 (0.4–3.2)	1.8 (0.8–3.8)	5.1 (3.1–8.4)	5.6 (3.2–9.6)
Midwest	0.6 (0.2–1.4)	1.2 (0.5–2.7)	2.5 (1.4–4.4)	1.5 (0.8–2.6)	6.5 (4.7–9.1)	5.7 (4.1–7.8)
South	3.0 (2.1–4.3)	1.3 (0.7–2.4)	1.1 (0.4–3.0)	1.3 (0.8–2.3)	6.3 (4.8–8.4)	4.7 (3.1–7.1)
West	0.4 (0.1–1.2)	2.5 (1.1–5.6)	0.9 (0.4–2.0)	0.8 (0.3–2.3)	5.2 (2.8–9.3)	7.5 (4.9–11.5)

Source: 2006–2010 NSDUH: Substance Abuse and Mental Health Services Administration (unpublished data).
Note: ***CI*** = confidence interval; **MS** = moist snuff; **NR** = low precision, no estimate reported.
[a]Includes Asians, American Indians or Alaska Natives, Native Hawaiians or Other Pacific Islanders, and persons of two or more races.

Table 3.1.45 Share of the smokeless tobacco market in 2008 by type and brand; the Maxwell Report; United States

Type/brand	Market share (%)
Moist snuff	
Skoal	25.0
Copenhagen	24.0
Grizzly	24.0
Red Seal	7.0
Timber Wolf	6.0
Longhorn	5.0
Kodiak	4.0
Other	5.0
Total	100.0
Chew	
Red Man	34.0
Levi Garrett	18.0
Stoker's chew	11.0
Other	37.0
Total	100.0

Source: Adapted from Maxwell 2009b with permission from John C. Maxwell, Jr., ©2009.
[a]Represents market share within type of product (i.e., moist snuff or chew).

Table 3.1.46 Prevalence of smokeless tobacco use among cigarette smokers and users of drugs and prevalence of cigarette smoking and drug use among users of smokeless tobacco in the past 30 days, among male high school seniors; Monitoring the Future (MTF) 2002–2007 and National Survey on Drug Use and Health (NSDUH) 2010; United States

Other drugs	Prevalence of smokeless tobacco use among cigarette smokers and users of drugs % (95% CI)	Prevalence of smokeless tobacco use among cigarette nonsmokers and nonusers of drugs % (95% CI)	Prevalence of cigarette smoking and drug use among smokeless tobacco users % (95% CI)	Prevalence of cigarette smoking and drug use among smokeless tobacco nonusers % (95% CI)
MTF				
Alcohol	20.7 (17.9–23.6)	3.4 (2.2–4.6)	85.4 (80.4–90.4)	44.0 (41.6–46.4)
Marijuana	20.4 (17.3–23.4)	9.4 (7.6–11.2)	39.3 (34.3–44.4)	20.8 (19.1–22.4)
Cocaine	26.3 (18.4–34.1)	11.7 (9.7–13.6)	6.5 (4.5–8.5)	2.5 (2.0–3.0)
Cigarettes	29.3 (26.4–32.3)	6.4 (5.0–7.7)	59.9 (57.0–62.6)	19.7 (18.3–21.1)
NSDUH[a]				
Alcohol	21.8 (17.5–26.7)	4.1 (2.9–5.8)	70.7 (61.2–78.7)	27.3 (24.3–30.4)
Marijuana	18.2 (13.3–24.6)	7.5 (6.0–9.4)	38.1 (28.9–48.2)	18.3 (15.7–21.2)
Cocaine	NR	9.6 (7.9–11.5)	1.9 (0.6–6.1)	0.3 (0.1–1.4)
Inhalants	NR	9.7 (8.0–11.7)	NR	0.8 (0.3–1.8)
Cigarettes	25.6 (20.3–31.8)	5.6 (4.1–7.5)	54.4 (44.7–63.9)	17.0 (14.5–19.7)

Source: 2002–2007 MTF: University of Michigan, Institute for Social Research (unpublished data); 2010 NSDUH: Substance Abuse and Mental Health Services Administration (unpublished data).
Note: **CI** = confidence interval; **NR** = low precision, no estimate reported.
[a]Excluded male respondents who reported being currently enrolled in 12th grade but were older than 19 years of age.

Table 3.1.47 Percentage distribution of smokeless tobacco brands that young adults 18–25 years of age who were current users of smokeless preferred, by gender, race/ethnicity, age, and region; National Survey on Drug Use and Health (NSDUH) 2006–2010; United States

Characteristic	Skoal (MS) % (95% CI)	Grizzly (MS) % (95% CI)	Copenhagen (MS) % (95% CI)	Red Man (Chew) % (95% CI)	Kodiak (MS) % (95% CI)	Red Seal (Chew) % (95% CI)
Overall	30.1 (28.7–31.5)	28.6 (27.0–30.2)	17.9 (16.7–19.1)	4.5 (3.9–5.2)	2.6 (2.2–3.1)	2.4 (2.0–2.9)
Gender						
Male	30.2 (28.7–31.7)	28.8 (27.2–30.4)	18.0 (16.8–19.3)	4.5 (3.9–5.2)	2.5 (2.1–3.0)	2.6 (2.1–3.1)
Female	27.9 (22.0–34.7)	24.2 (18.6–30.9)	14.9 (11.1–19.8)	5.2 (2.4–10.6)	3.5 (1.8–6.6)	0.2 (0.0–1.3)
Race/ethnicity						
White	29.8 (28.4–31.3)	29.9 (28.3–31.6)	17.6 (16.4–18.8)	4.5 (3.9–5.3)	2.6 (2.1–3.1)	2.6 (2.1–3.1)
Male	30.1 (28.6–31.6)	30.1 (28.4–31.8)	17.7 (16.5–19.0)	4.5 (3.8–5.2)	2.5 (2.1–3.1)	2.7 (2.2–3.3)
Female	25.1 (19.5–31.6)	27.5 (21.2–34.8)	15.0 (10.8–20.3)	5.8 (2.7–12.2)	3.3 (1.6–6.6)	0.2 (0.0–1.5)
Black or African American	NR	NR	NR	NR	NR	NR
Male	NR	NR	NR	NR	NR	NR
Female	NR	NR	NR	NR	NR	NR
Hispanic or Latino	33.0 (26.1–40.7)	12.0 (8.1–17.6)	22.8 (17.2–29.5)	4.9 (2.6–9.0)	2.3 (1.0–5.5)	1.3 (0.4–4.1)
Male	32.5 (25.5–40.3)	12.7 (8.5–18.7)	23.7 (17.8–30.9)	5.3 (2.8–9.6)	2.5 (1.0–5.9)	1.4 (0.4–4.4)
Female	NR	NR	NR	NR	NR	NR
Other[a]	34.6 (27.2–42.7)	20.7 (14.4–28.8)	21.5 (16.2–27.9)	3.9 (2.3–6.5)	2.8 (1.3–5.9)	1.5 (0.6–3.3)
Male	32.6 (25.4–40.6)	22.3 (15.5–31.0)	21.2 (15.8–27.9)	4.1 (2.4–7.0)	2.7 (1.2–6.0)	1.6 (0.7–3.6)
Female	NR	NR	NR	NR	NR	NR
Age (years)						
18–20	27.3 (25.3–29.5)	32.0 (29.7–34.4)	17.0 (15.2–19.0)	5.8 (4.8–7.0)	1.8 (1.3–2.5)	2.5 (1.9–3.3)
21–25	32.3 (30.4–34.2)	25.8 (23.8–27.9)	18.5 (17.1–20.1)	3.5 (2.9–4.3)	3.2 (2.6–3.9)	2.4 (1.9–3.1)
Region						
Northeast	52.9 (49.0–56.6)	13.9 (11.5–16.7)	12.9 (10.5–15.7)	2.9 (2.0–4.2)	2.7 (1.8–4.2)	1.5 (1.0–2.4)
Midwest	27.7 (25.5–30.0)	36.5 (34.0–39.1)	9.8 (8.5–11.2)	5.7 (4.6–7.1)	3.7 (2.9–4.7)	0.7 (0.4–1.3)
South	24.2 (22.0–26.5)	31.8 (28.7–34.9)	19.0 (16.8–21.3)	4.1 (3.2–5.4)	1.8 (1.2–2.7)	5.2 (4.2–6.4)
West	28.6 (25.0–32.5)	21.2 (18.0–24.9)	31.4 (28.1–34.8)	4.8 (3.3–6.9)	2.3 (1.4–3.7)	0.2 (0.0–0.6)

Table 3.1.47 Continued

Characteristic	Camel–Snus (Chew) % (95% CI)	Timber Wolf (MS) % (95% CI)	Levi Garrett (Chew) % (95% CI)	Beech-Nut (MS) % (95% CI)	All other brands % (95% CI)	Unknown % (95% CI)
Overall	2.2 (1.8–2.7)	2.1 (1.6–2.6)	2.0 (1.6–2.4)	0.9 (0.6–1.2)	4.9 (4.3–5.6)	1.9 (1.6–2.4)
Gender						
Male	2.1 (1.7–2.6)	2.1 (1.7–2.7)	2.1 (1.7–2.5)	0.9 (0.7–1.2)	4.6 (4.0–5.3)	1.7 (1.3–2.2)
Female	4.9 (2.9–8.2)	0.8 (0.3–2.6)	0.4 (0.1–1.5)	0.3 (0.1–1.2)	11.2 (7.2–17.1)	6.5 (4.2–9.9)
Race/ethnicity						
White	2.2 (1.8–2.7)	2.2 (1.7–2.8)	2.0 (1.6–2.6)	0.7 (0.5–1.0)	4.3 (3.7–5.0)	1.6 (1.2–2.0)
Male	2.0 (1.6–2.5)	2.3 (1.8–2.8)	2.1 (1.7–2.7)	0.7 (0.5–1.0)	4.0 (3.4–4.7)	1.4 (1.0–1.8)
Female	5.7 (3.3–9.6)	1.0 (0.3–3.1)	0.5 (0.1–1.8)	0.2 (0.0–1.7)	10.1 (6.8–14.8)	5.7 (3.4–9.5)
Black or African American	NR	NR	NR	NR	NR	NR
Male	NR	NR	NR	NR	NR	NR
Female	NR	NR	NR	NR	NR	NR
Hispanic or Latino	2.7 (1.4–5.2)	0.6 (0.2–1.8)	1.4 (0.5–4.0)	2.2 (0.7–6.6)	9.7 (5.4–16.8)	7.0 (3.9–12.3)
Male	2.9 (1.5–5.5)	0.7 (0.2–1.9)	1.5 (0.5–4.3)	2.3 (0.7–7.0)	8.2 (4.5–14.5)	6.3 (3.3–12.0)
Female	NR	NR	NR	NR	NR	NR
Other[a]	2.3 (0.7–6.9)	1.4 (0.4–5.5)	1.6 (0.6–4.2)	1.3 (0.6–3.0)	6.5 (3.9–10.7)	2.0 (1.1–3.7)
Male	2.5 (0.8–7.5)	1.6 (0.4–6.0)	1.8 (0.7–4.6)	1.3 (0.5–3.2)	6.5 (3.7–11.1)	1.9 (1.0–3.8)
Female	NR	NR	NR	NR	NR	NR
Age (years)						
18–20	1.6 (1.1–2.2)	1.7 (1.2–2.4)	2.4 (1.8–3.2)	1.0 (0.6–1.5)	4.8 (3.9–5.9)	2.1 (1.5–2.9)
21–25	2.7 (2.1–3.5)	2.4 (1.8–3.1)	1.6 (1.2–2.2)	0.8 (0.5–1.2)	5.0 (4.1–5.9)	1.8 (1.4–2.4)
Region						
Northeast	2.3 (1.3–3.8)	0.9 (0.5–1.6)	1.4 (0.8–2.4)	1.0 (0.5–1.9)	5.0 (3.4–7.3)	2.7 (1.7–4.1)
Midwest	3.4 (2.6–4.3)	2.4 (1.5–3.7)	1.8 (1.2–2.6)	1.0 (0.6–1.6)	5.6 (4.4–7.0)	1.9 (1.4–2.6)
South	1.4 (0.8–2.3)	3.2 (2.5–4.3)	2.4 (1.7–3.3)	0.6 (0.3–1.1)	4.7 (3.8–5.8)	1.6 (1.1–2.6)
West	2.1 (1.3–3.5)	0.1 (0.0–0.5)	1.9 (1.2–3.2)	1.2 (0.6–2.1)	4.2 (2.9–6.1)	2.1 (1.4–3.2)

Source: 2006–2010 NSDUH: Substance Abuse and Mental Health Services Administration (unpublished data).
Note: **CI** = confidence interval; **MS** = moist snuff; **NR** = low precision, no estimate reported.
[a]Includes Asians, American Indians or Alaska Natives, Native Hawaiians or Other Pacific Islanders, and persons of two or more races.

Table 3.1.48 Percentage of young people who have ever smoked cigars, by gender, race/ethnicity, age/grade, and region; National Survey on Drug Use and Health (NSDUH) 2010 and National Youth Tobacco Survey (NYTS) 2009; United States

	NSDUH 13–18 years of age		NYTS 9th–12th grades[a]		NYTS 6th–8th grades[a]	
Characteristic	**% (95% CI)**	**SN[b]**	**% (95% CI)**	**SN[b]**	**% (95% CI)**	**SN[b]**
Overall	16.7 (16.04–17.41)		28.6 (25.4–31.8)		10.1 (9.2–11.1)	
Gender						
Male	20.7 (19.64–21.76)	a	35.4 (30.7–40.0)	a	12.4 (11.1–13.8)	a
Female	12.5 (11.62–13.40)	b	21.8 (19.2–24.4)	b	7.7 (6.6–8.7)	b
Race/ethnicity						
White	19.5 (18.62–20.51)	a	32.5 (29.4–35.5)	a	8.1 (6.9–9.3)	a
Male	24.4 (23.03–25.74)		40.4 (36.7–44.2)		10.6 (8.8–12.4)	
Female	14.5 (13.32–15.74)		24.4 (21.3–27.5)		5.4 (4.3–6.6)	
Black or African American	11.3 (9.75–12.99)	b	16.3 (10.1–22.4)	b	11.6 (10.0–13.3)	b
Male	14.1 (11.69–16.81)		20.4 (11.7–29.1)		14.6 (12.1–17.0)	
Female	8.3 (6.73–10.31)		12.3 (6.4–18.2)		8.6 (6.1–11.2)	
Hispanic or Latino	14.9 (13.44–16.42)	c	29.2 (26.5–31.8)	a	14.9 (13.0–16.8)	c
Male	18.1 (15.87–20.50)		33.5 (29.1–37.8)		16.9 (14.4–19.3)	
Female	11.2 (9.27–13.51)		24.9 (21.3–28.5)		12.9 (9.8–16.1)	
Other[c]	9.9 (7.96–12.16)	b	22.0 (16.9–27.0)	c	10.1 (7.1–13.0)	a,b
Male	11.7 (8.95–15.15)		28.7 (21.7–35.7)		11.8 (7.6–15.9)	
Female	7.9 (5.74–10.86)		15.5 (11.6–19.3)		8.2 (5.5–11.0)	
Age (in years)/grade						
13–14	5.3 (4.65–6.02)	a	NA		NA	
15–16	15.4 (14.39–16.43)	b	NA		NA	
17–18	28.1 (26.64–29.55)	c	NA		NA	
6th	NA		NA		6.1 (4.8–7.5)	a
7th	NA		NA		9.8 (8.3–11.3)	b
8th	NA		NA		14.5 (13.0–16.0)	c
9th	NA		18.8 (14.4–23.2)	a	NA	
10th	NA		26.9 (23.9–30.0)	b	NA	
11th	NA		33.8 (29.2–38.3)	c	NA	
12th	NA		37.4 (32.5–42.3)	c	NA	
Region						
Northeast	16.7 (15.22–18.24)	a	NA		NA	
Midwest	18.2 (17.03–19.35)	b	NA		NA	
South	16.1 (14.92–17.29)	a	NA		NA	
West	16.4 (14.88–18.10)	a	NA		NA	

Source: 2010 NSDUH: Substance Abuse and Mental Health Services Administration (unpublished data); 2009 NYTS: Centers for Disease Control and Prevention (unpublished data).
Note: **CI** = confidence interval; **NA** = not applicable; **SN** = statistical note.
[a]Estimates are based on responses to the question, "Have you ever tried smoking cigars, cigarillos, or little cigars, even one or two puffs?"
[b]These tests were performed to examine differences in estimates within specific demographic subgroups (e.g., gender). Estimates with the same letter (e.g., a and a) are not statistically significantly different from one another (p >0.05). Estimates with different letters (e.g., a and b) are, in contrast, statistically significantly different from one another (p <0.05).
[c]Includes Asians, American Indians or Alaska Natives, Native Hawaiians or Other Pacific Islanders, and persons of two or more races.

Table 3.1.49 Percentage of young people and young adults 18–25 years of age who currently smoke cigars, by gender, race/ethnicity, age/grade, and region; National Survey on Drug Use and Health (NSDUH) 2010, National Youth Risk Behavior Survey (YRBS) 2009, and National Youth Tobacco Survey (NYTS) 2009; United States

	NSDUH 13–18 years of age		YRBS 9th–12th grades		NSDUH 18–25 years of age		NYTS 6th–8th grades[a]		NYTS 9th–12 grades[a]	
Characteristic	**% (95% CI)**	**SN[b]**	**% (95% CI)**	**SN[b]**	**% (95% CI)**	**SN[b]**	**% (95% CI)**	**SN[b]**	**% (955 CI)**	**SN[b]**
Overall	5.6 (5.20–6.03)		14.0 (12.8–15.4)		11.2 (10.63–11.79)		3.9 (3.4–4.5)		10.9 (8.9–12.9)	
Gender										
Male	7.6 (6.93–8.28)	a	18.6 (17.0–20.5)	a	16.6 (15.72–17.63)	a	4.6 (3.8–5.5)	a	15.0 (12.1–18.0)	a
Female	3.5 (3.07–3.96)	b	8.8 (7.7–10.1)	b	5.6 (5.04–6.19)	b	3.2 (2.5–3.9)	b	6.7 (5.4–8.1)	b
Race/ethnicity										
White	6.6 (6.01–7.16)	a	14.9 (13.3–16.7)	a	12.5 (11.78–13.34)	a	2.9 (2.2–3.6)	a	12.0 (9.8–14.2)	a
Male	9.1 (8.24–10.11)		21.0 (18.7–23.4)		19.5 (18.26–20.80)		3.8 (2.6–4.9)		17.2 (14.1–20.3)	
Female	3.9 (3.31–4.50)		8.0 (6.8–9.3)		5.5 (4.80–6.22)		2.0 (1.2–2.8)		6.7 (5.0–8.3)	
Black or African American	4.6 (3.74–5.68)	b	12.8 (10.9–15.0)	a,b	11.5 (10.10–13.08)	b	4.5 (3.2–5.8)	b	7.3 (3.6–10.9)	b
Male	5.7 (4.34–7.52)		13.9 (11.6–16.5)		14.6 (12.27–17.33)		5.2 (3.4–7.0)		7.7 (2.6–12.8)	
Female	3.5 (2.48–4.79)		11.5 (8.8–14.8)		8.7 (7.12–10.54)		3.7 (1.8–5.7)		6.9 (3.4–10.3)	
Hispanic or Latino	4.4 (3.64–5.32)	b	12.7 (10.9–14.7)	a,b	8.4 (7.30–9.67)	c	6.2 (5.0–7.3)	c	11.8 (9.6–14.0)	a
Male	5.9 (4.64–7.44)		15.8 (13.1–19.1)		11.9 (10.13–14.00)		6.6 (5.2–8.0)		16.1 (13.4–18.7)	
Female	2.7 (2.00–3.68)		9.5 (7.6–11.9)		4.2 (3.22–5.57)		5.7 (3.6–7.8)		7.5 (5.5–9.4)	
Other[c]	3.0 (2.05–4.45)	b	11.1 (8.4–14.5)	b	6.6 (5.26–8.35)	c	4.6 (2.5–6.7)	a,b,c	8.0 (4.8–11.1)	b
Male	3.5 (2.25–5.39)		14.4 (10.9–18.9)		10.0 (7.51–13.19)		5.4 (2.0–8.9)		10.7 (6.2–15.2)	
Female	2.5 (1.39–4.59)		7.5 (4.8–11.7)		3.3 (2.08–5.16)		3.7 (1.6–5.9)		5.3 (2.1–8.4)	
Age (in years)/grade										
13–14	1.2 (0.88–1.54)	a	NA		NA		NA		NA	
15–16	4.4 (3.83–4.98)	b	NA		NA		NA		NA	
17–18	10.7 (9.74–11.66)	c	NA		NA		NA		NA	
18-20	NA		NA		12.8 (11.93–13.73)	a	NA		NA	
21-25	NA		NA		10.1 (9.43–10.86)	b	NA		NA	
6th	NA		NA		NA		2.8 (2.1–3.5)	a	NA	
7th	NA		NA		NA		3.4 (2.5–4.2)	a	NA	
8th	NA		NA		NA		5.7 (4.7–6.7)	b	NA	
9th	NA		9.6 (8.3–11.2)	a	NA		NA		6.2 (4.3–8.1)	a
10th	NA		13.2 (11.4–15.3)	b	NA		NA		10.8 (8.4–13.2)	b
11th	NA		15.8 (13.6–18.2)	b	NA		NA		13.0 (10.2–15.9)	b,c
12th	NA		18.5 (15.5–21.8)	c	NA		NA		14.6 (11.3–18.0)	c

Table 3.1.49 Continued

Characteristic	NSDUH 13–18 years of age		YRBS 9th–12th grades		NSDUH 18–25 years of age		NYTS 6th–8th grades[a]		NYTS 9th–12 grades[a]	
	% (95% CI)	SN[b]	% (95% CI)	SN[b]	% (95% CI)	SN[b]	% (95% CI)	SN[b]	% (955 CI)	SN[b]
Region										
Northeast	5.1 (4.38–6.04)	a	11.5 (8.6–15.2)	a	10.5 (9.41–11.80)	a	NA		NA	
Midwest	6.4 (5.74–7.18)	b	16.3 (14.0–18.9)	b	13.8 (12.72–14.89)	b	NA		NA	
South	5.5 (4.80–6.28)	a	15.9 (14.3–17.6)	b	11.5 (10.41–12.71)	a	NA		NA	
West	5.3 (4.53–6.26)	a	11.5 (9.5–13.7)	a	8.8 (7.81–9.96)	a	NA		NA	

Source: 2010 NSDUH: Substance Abuse and Mental Health Services Administration (unpublished data); 2009 YRBS: Centers for Disease Control and Prevention, Division of Adolescent and School Health (unpublished data); 2009 NYTS: Centers for Disease Control and Prevention (unpublished data).
Note: **CI** = confidence interval; **NA** = not applicable; **SN** = statistical note.
[a]Estimates are based on responses to the question, "During the past 30 days, on how many days did you smoke cigars, cigarillos, or little cigars?"
[b]This column represents the results of statistical tests that were run separately within each surveillance system (e.g., NSDUH). These tests were performed to examine differences in estimates within specific demographic subgroups (e.g., gender). Estimates with the same letter (e.g., a and a) are not statistically significantly different from one another ($p > 0.05$). Estimates with different letters (e.g., a and b) are, in contrast, statistically significantly different from one another ($p < 0.05$).
[c]Includes Asians, American Indians or Alaska Natives, Native Hawaiians or Other Pacific Islanders, and persons of two or more races.

Table 3.1.50 Percentage distribution of cigar brands that youth 12–17 years of age who currently smoke cigars preferred, by gender, race/ethnicity, age, and region; National Survey on Drug Use and Health (NSDUH) 2008–2010; United States

Characteristic	Black & Mild % (95% CI)	Swisher Sweets % (95% CI)	Phillies % (95% CI)	White Owl % (95% CI)	Dutch Masters % (95% CI)	Al Capone % (95% CI)
Overall	42.9 (40.3–45.6)	20.3 (18.3–22.4)	5.6 (4.5–6.8)	3.7 (2.8–4.8)	3.1 (2.4–4.1)	2.0 (1.4–2.8)
Gender						
Male	40.3 (37.0–43.7)	22.7 (20.2–25.3)	6.5 (5.1–8.1)	4.5 (3.3–6.0)	3.9 (2.9–5.2)	1.8 (1.2–2.7)
Female	48.8 (44.3–53.2)	14.9 (12.0–18.3)	3.6 (2.2–5.8)	1.8 (1.0–3.5)	1.5 (0.7–3.0)	2.3 (1.3–4.2)
Race/ethnicity						
White	39.4 (36.5–42.4)	22.8 (20.4–25.5)	5.5 (4.3–7.0)	3.8 (2.9–5.0)	2.8 (2.0–3.8)	2.2 (1.4–3.4)
Male	37.1 (33.6–40.8)	24.9 (21.9–28.2)	6.4 (4.9–8.2)	4.9 (3.6–6.5)	3.4 (2.4–4.7)	2.1 (1.3–3.3)
Female	45.1 (39.8–50.4)	17.6 (13.8–22.3)	3.2 (1.8–5.9)	1.3 (0.6–2.8)	1.3 (0.5–3.5)	2.4 (1.1–5.3)
Black or African American	58.4 (50.3–66.1)	16.7 (12.1–22.5)	4.3 (2.3–8.0)	6.0 (2.7–13.0)	5.5 (2.9–10.3)	0.9 (0.3–2.2)
Male	54.1 (43.8–64.1)	18.9 (13.0–26.6)	5.0 (2.4–10.1)	NR	6.3 (2.8–13.4)	1.2 (0.4–3.4)
Female	NR	12.9 (7.1–22.4)	NR	1.8 (0.5–7.0)	4.2 (1.5–11.4)	0.4 (0.1–1.6)
Hispanic or Latino	46.8 (39.1–54.6)	12.8 (9.2–17.6)	6.8 (4.0–11.3)	0.4 (0.1–1.4)	2.4 (1.0–6.1)	1.9 (0.8–4.6)
Male	46.6 (37.1–56.3)	14.5 (9.7–21.2)	7.0 (3.7–12.8)	0.2 (0.0–1.4)	3.4 (1.3–8.8)	1.4 (0.4–5.0)
Female	NR	9.1 (5.0–16.1)	NR	NR	0.4 (0.1–1.8)	NR
Other[a]	NR	19.2 (12.3–28.7)	5.7 (2.4–12.8)	NR	NR	1.9 (0.5–6.4)
Male	NR	NR	NR	NR	NR	0.3 (0.1–1.1)
Female	NR	NR	NR	NR	NR	NR
Age (years)						
12–14	44.1 (36.9–51.6)	12.4 (8.8–17.3)	2.6 (1.2–5.4)	1.3 (0.5–3.2)	1.7 (0.8–3.6)	2.2 (1.0–5.0)
15–17	42.7 (40.0–45.5)	21.5 (19.4–23.8)	6.0 (4.9–7.5)	4.0 (3.1–5.3)	3.4 (2.5–4.5)	1.9 (1.3–2.8)
Region						
Northeast	36.8 (30.2–43.9)	10.0 (7.4–13.3)	8.9 (6.1–12.8)	3.7 (2.0–6.8)	11.9 (8.5–16.5)	2.9 (1.4–5.8)
Midwest	41.2 (37.3–45.1)	27.4 (23.6–31.5)	5.2 (3.6–7.4)	5.3 (3.7–7.6)	0.7 (0.3–1.6)	1.0 (0.5–1.9)
South	52.6 (47.9–57.3)	15.0 (12.2–18.2)	6.2 (4.3–8.9)	4.1 (2.5–6.6)	2.6 (1.5–4.4)	1.7 (1.0–3.1)
West	33.7 (27.5–40.6)	28.1 (22.8–34.1)	2.5 (1.4–4.4)	0.9 (0.3–2.6)	0.3 (0.1–2.0)	2.9 (1.4–5.7)

Table 3.1.50 Continued

Characteristic	Prime Time Little Cigars % (95% CI)	Backwoods % (95% CI)	Garcia y Vega % (95% CI)	Cohiba % (95% CI)	All other brands % (95% CI)	Unknown % (95% CI)
Overall	1.5 (1.0–2.1)	1.2 (0.8–1.8)	0.6 (0.4–1.1)	0.6 (0.2–1.5)	6.9 (5.7–8.2)	11.7 (10.1–13.6)
Gender						
Male	1.1 (0.7–1.9)	1.4 (0.9–2.3)	0.6 (0.3–1.2)	0.8 (0.3–2.1)	6.4 (5.1–8.0)	9.9 (8.1–12.2)
Female	2.2 (1.3–3.7)	0.7 (0.3–1.6)	0.6 (0.2–1.8)	NR	7.9 (5.9–10.5)	15.7 (12.8–19.2)
Race/ethnicity						
White	1.1 (0.6–1.8)	1.3 (0.8–2.2)	0.7 (0.3–1.3)	0.8 (0.3–2.2)	7.2 (5.8–8.8)	12.4 (10.6–14.5)
Male	0.7 (0.3–1.5)	1.7 (1.0–2.9)	0.6 (0.2–1.3)	1.2 (0.4–3.0)	7.3 (5.7–9.3)	9.9 (7.9–12.3)
Female	2.0 (1.1–3.8)	0.3 (0.1–1.9)	1.0 (0.3–2.8)	NR	6.9 (4.8–9.8)	18.8 (14.9–23.4)
Black or African American	NR	1.7 (0.7–3.9)	1.4 (0.4–4.2)	NR	3.4 (1.6–7.2)	1.1 (0.4–3.0)
Male	NR	1.0 (0.3–3.6)	2.2 (0.7–6.5)	NR	1.6 (0.4–5.8)	1.4 (0.4–4.2)
Female	NR	2.9 (1.0–8.5)	NR	NR	6.6 (2.7–15.6)	NR
Hispanic or Latino	3.1 (1.7–5.5)	0.5 (0.1–2.1)	NR	0.1 (0.0–0.7)	8.5 (5.5–12.8)	16.6 (11.5–23.6)
Male	3.5 (1.7–7.0)	0.8 (0.2–3.1)	NR	0.2 (0.0–1.1)	6.6 (3.6–11.8)	15.9 (9.7–24.9)
Female	2.2 (1.0–4.8)	0.1 (0.0–0.5)	NR	NR	12.6 (6.8–22.0)	NR
Other[a]	NR	0.8 (0.2–2.5)	NR	NR	5.1 (2.0–12.3)	11.4 (5.9–21.0)
Male	NR	0.9 (0.2–3.9)	0.0 (0.0–0.1)	NR	3.0 (1.1–7.7)	NR
Female	NR	NR	NR	NR	NR	NR
Age (years)						
12–14	2.3 (1.0–4.8)	1.3 (0.5–3.4)	0.8 (0.2–3.1)	0.6 (0.2–2.5)	9.4 (6.3–14.0)	21.2 (16.0–27.7)
15–17	1.3 (0.9–2.0)	1.2 (0.8–1.9)	0.6 (0.3–1.1)	0.6 (0.2–1.7)	6.4 (5.3–7.9)	10.2 (8.6–12.1)
Region						
Northeast	NR	3.5 (1.9–6.6)	1.2 (0.4–3.4)	0.2 (0.0–1.0)	8.5 (6.1–11.8)	12.3 (8.4–17.9)
Midwest	0.1 (0.0–0.4)	0.8 (0.3–1.9)	0.4 (0.1–1.3)	0.5 (0.2–1.5)	6.7 (5.0–9.0)	10.8 (8.6–13.5)
South	0.3 (0.1–1.2)	0.6 (0.3–1.6)	0.9 (0.4–2.1)	1.1 (0.3–4.0)	5.7 (4.0–8.2)	9.1 (6.8–11.9)
West	6.3 (4.2–9.2)	0.9 (0.4–1.9)	NR	0.1 (0.0–0.6)	7.6 (5.1–11.1)	16.8 (12.3–22.4)

Source: 2008–2010 NSDUH: Substance Abuse and Mental Health Services Administration (unpublished data).
Note: **CI** = confidence interval; **NR** = low precision, no estimate reported.
[a]Includes Asians, American Indians or Alaska Natives, Native Hawaiians or Other Pacific Islanders, and persons of two or more races.

Table 3.1.51 Share of cigar market in 2008, by brand; the Maxwell Report; United States

Brand	Market share (%)[a]
Swisher Sweets[b]	29.7
Phillies	8.4
Dutch Masters	11.1
White Owl	5.1
Backwoods	4.6
Other little or large cigars	41.1

Source: Adapted from Maxwell 2009a with permission from John C. Maxwell, Jr., ©2009.
Note: By definition, large cigars are any roll of tobacco wrapped in leaf tobacco or in any substance containing tobacco and weighing more than 3 pounds per 1,000 cigars, whereas little or small cigars weigh no more than 3 pounds per 1,000 cigars. Little or small cigars have other characteristics that set them apart from large cigars, most notably characteristics common to cigarettes, such as shape, size, filters, and packaging (i.e., 20 sticks to a pack).
[a]Represents market share within type of product (i.e., moist snuff or chew).
[b]Brand available in both large and small cigars.

Table 3.1.52 Percentage distribution of cigar brands that young adults, 18–25 years of age who currently smoke cigars preferred, by gender, race/ethnicity, age, and region; National Survey on Drug Use and Health (NSDUH) 2008–2010; United States

Characteristic	Black & Mild % (95% CI)	Swisher Sweets % (95% CI)	Dutch Masters % (95% CI)	Phillies % (95% CI)	White Owl % (95% CI)	Romeo y Julieta % (95% CI)
Overall	35.6 (34.2–37.0)	18.4 (17.3–19.6)	5.1 (4.5–5.8)	5.0 (4.4–5.6)	3.7 (3.2–4.3)	3.0 (2.6–3.6)
Gender						
Male	33.4 (31.8–35.0)	17.2 (15.9–18.5)	5.2 (4.5–6.1)	5.4 (4.7–6.2)	3.8 (3.2–4.5)	3.7 (3.1–4.4)
Female	42.8 (40.1–45.6)	22.4 (20.1–24.9)	4.7 (3.6–6.1)	3.7 (2.8–4.8)	3.4 (2.6–4.5)	0.9 (0.5–1.6)
Race/ethnicity						
White	30.7 (29.2–32.4)	18.9 (17.5–20.3)	4.6 (3.9–5.5)	5.3 (4.6–6.0)	4.6 (3.9–5.3)	3.5 (2.9–4.2)
Male	28.7 (27.0–30.5)	17.5 (16.0–19.1)	5.0 (4.2–6.0)	5.7 (4.8–6.6)	4.7 (4.0–5.5)	4.2 (3.5–5.0)
Female	38.5 (35.0–42.0)	24.0 (21.0–27.3)	3.1 (2.0–4.8)	3.8 (2.8–5.2)	4.0 (2.9–5.6)	1.1 (0.5–2.2)
Black or African American	62.6 (58.8–66.3)	16.7 (14.0–19.9)	8.2 (6.1–10.8)	2.3 (1.4–3.9)	2.9 (1.9–4.5)	0.2 (0.0–1.2)
Male	64.7 (59.7–69.5)	15.3 (11.9–19.5)	7.9 (5.3–11.7)	1.6 (0.8–2.9)	2.6 (1.3–4.9)	0.3 (0.0–1.9)
Female	59.0 (53.1–64.6)	19.2 (15.1–24.1)	8.6 (5.4–13.4)	3.6 (1.7–7.6)	3.6 (2.1–6.0)	NR
Hispanic or Latino	31.9 (28.1–36.0)	17.5 (14.4–21.2)	5.0 (3.5–7.2)	6.1 (4.4–8.4)	1.3 (0.6–2.9)	3.5 (2.1–5.8)
Male	30.2 (25.9–34.9)	16.7 (13.1–21.0)	4.8 (3.2–7.2)	7.3 (5.1–10.3)	1.3 (0.5–3.5)	4.3 (2.5–7.3)
Female	37.4 (29.8–45.7)	20.4 (14.1–28.5)	5.7 (2.8–11.3)	2.2 (0.9–5.3)	1.5 (0.5–3.9)	* (* –*)
Other[a]	36.5 (30.3–43.2)	19.8 (14.7–26.1)	2.6 (1.3–5.2)	5.8 (3.6–9.2)	1.1 (0.5–2.8)	3.3 (1.6–6.9)
Male	35.4 (28.1–43.4)	18.5 (13.1–25.4)	2.2 (1.0–4.8)	5.6 (3.1–9.7)	1.2 (0.4–3.1)	3.6 (1.6–7.8)
Female	NR	NR	NR	6.5 (2.8–14.4)	NR	NR
Age (years)						
18–20	39.5 (37.5–41.5)	20.8 (19.1–22.6)	4.9 (3.9–6.0)	5.5 (4.7–6.5)	4.1 (3.4–4.9)	2.2 (1.7–2.9)
21–25	32.3 (30.5–34.1)	16.3 (14.9–17.9)	5.3 (4.5–6.3)	4.5 (3.8–5.4)	3.4 (2.8–4.2)	3.8 (3.0–4.7)
Region						
Northeast	27.7 (24.8–30.8)	5.9 (4.6–7.4)	16.3 (13.7–19.3)	5.8 (4.4–7.5)	3.9 (2.9–5.3)	5.0 (3.5–7.0)
Midwest	33.5 (31.3–35.7)	24.7 (22.8–26.6)	1.2 (0.7–2.2)	6.2 (5.1–7.5)	4.9 (4.0–5.9)	2.3 (1.7–3.1)
South	43.9 (41.5–46.5)	15.5 (13.7–17.5)	5.2 (4.1–6.6)	4.8 (3.8–5.9)	4.0 (3.2–5.1)	3.0 (2.3–4.1)
West	29.8 (26.2–33.6)	26.0 (22.6–29.6)	0.7 (0.3–1.7)	3.2 (2.2–4.7)	1.5 (0.8–2.6)	2.4 (1.5–3.9)

Table 3.1.52 Continued

	Backwoods % (95% CI)	Cohiba % (95% CI)	Al Capone % (95% CI)	Garcia y Vega % (95% CI)	All other brands % (95% CI)	Unknown % (95% CI)
Overall	2.3 (1.9–2.8)	2.3 (1.9–2.8)	2.2 (1.9–2.7)	1.4 (1.1–1.8)	12.7 (11.7–13.8)	8.1 (7.3–8.9)
Gender						
Male	2.8 (2.3–3.4)	2.9 (2.4–3.5)	2.6 (2.1–3.1)	1.7 (1.3–2.1)	14.2 (13.0–15.4)	7.2 (6.3–8.1)
Female	0.7 (0.4–1.2)	0.4 (0.2–1.0)	1.1 (0.7–1.9)	0.7 (0.4–1.2)	8.1 (6.7–9.8)	11.0 (9.3–13.1)
Race/ethnicity						
White	2.9 (2.4–3.5)	2.6 (2.1–3.2)	2.4 (2.0–3.0)	1.6 (1.2–2.1)	15.2 (14.0–16.5)	7.8 (6.9–8.7)
Male	3.4 (2.8–4.2)	3.2 (2.6–3.9)	2.8 (2.2–3.5)	1.8 (1.4–2.4)	16.8 (15.4–18.4)	6.2 (5.4–7.1)
Female	0.7 (0.4–1.4)	0.4 (0.1–1.2)	1.1 (0.6–2.1)	0.6 (0.3–1.4)	9.0 (7.3–11.2)	13.7 (11.3–16.4)
Black or African American	1.3 (0.6–2.6)	0.3 (0.1–0.7)	0.9 (0.5–1.5)	0.9 (0.5–1.7)	1.7 (1.0–2.7)	2.1 (1.2–3.4)
Male	1.4 (0.6–3.6)	0.2 (0.1–0.8)	1.2 (0.7–2.3)	0.9 (0.4–2.0)	1.7 (0.9–3.2)	2.1 (1.1–3.8)
Female	1.0 (0.4–2.7)	0.3 (0.0–1.9)	0.2 (0.0–0.8)	0.9 (0.3–2.5)	1.5 (0.6–3.7)	2.1 (0.9–4.7)
Hispanic or Latino	1.0 (0.4–2.2)	3.1 (1.8–5.1)	2.7 (1.7–4.1)	1.0 (0.4–2.0)	13.2 (10.4–16.6)	13.8 (10.8–17.4)
Male	1.2 (0.5–2.8)	3.7 (2.2–6.3)	2.8 (1.7–4.4)	1.2 (0.5–2.6)	12.8 (9.7–16.8)	13.7 (10.4–17.8)
Female	0.1 (0.0–1.0)	NR	2.4 (0.9–6.4)	0.3 (0.0–1.8)	14.4 (9.4–21.5)	14.1 (8.7–22.0)
Other[a]	1.2 (0.5–3.0)	2.1 (1.0–4.3)	2.3 (1.0–5.0)	2.4 (1.0–5.8)	9.0 (6.2–12.8)	13.8 (9.4–19.8)
Male	1.6 (0.6–4.0)	2.9 (1.4–5.9)	2.2 (0.8–5.7)	2.7 (1.0–7.3)	9.1 (5.9–13.8)	15.1 (9.7–22.7)
Female	0.1 (0.0–1.1)	NR	NR	NR	8.5 (3.9–17.4)	NR
Age (years)						
18–20	2.3 (1.8–3.1)	1.2 (0.8–1.8)	2.2 (1.6–2.9)	1.0 (0.7–1.4)	9.6 (8.4–10.9)	6.7 (5.8–7.8)
21–25	2.3 (1.8–2.9)	3.2 (2.6–4.1)	2.3 (1.8–3.0)	1.8 (1.3–2.5)	15.5 (14.1–17.0)	9.3 (8.1–10.5)
Region						
Northeast	2.6 (1.9–3.6)	2.7 (1.8–4.1)	1.5 (1.0–2.4)	3.1 (2.1–4.6)	15.9 (13.5–18.6)	9.6 (7.9–11.5)
Midwest	3.2 (2.4–4.2)	1.8 (1.3–2.6)	2.5 (1.8–3.5)	1.5 (1.0–2.4)	11.9 (10.5–13.5)	6.3 (5.3–7.4)
South	1.2 (0.8–1.9)	2.4 (1.7–3.3)	2.4 (1.8–3.3)	1.0 (0.6–1.6)	9.6 (8.2–11.3)	6.9 (5.7–8.2)
West	3.0 (1.9–4.5)	2.4 (1.4–4.1)	2.2 (1.5–3.2)	0.6 (0.3–1.3)	16.9 (14.1–20.0)	11.4 (9.1–14.3)

Source: 2008–2010 NSDUH: Substance Abuse and Mental Health Services Administration (unpublished data).
Note: **CI** = confidence interval; **NR** = low precision, no estimate reported.
[a]Includes Asians, American Indians or Alaska Natives, Native Hawaiians or Other Pacific Islanders, and persons reporting two or more races.

Table 3.1.53 Prevalence of cigar use among users of other tobacco products and drugs and prevalence of other tobacco products and drug use among cigar users, among youth 12–17 years of age; National Survey on Drug Use and Health (NSDUH) 2010; United States

Other drugs	Cigar use among users of other tobacco products and drugs % (95% CI)	Cigar use among nonusers of other tobacco products and drugs % (95% CI)	Other tobacco product and drug use among cigar users % (95% CI)	Other tobacco product and drug use among cigar nonusers % (95% CI)
Alcohol	15.4 (13.9–17.1)	1.3 (1.1–1.5)	65.3 (60.7–69.5)	11.9 (11.3–12.5)
Marijuana	24.1 (21.6–26.8)	1.6 (1.4–1.8)	55.3 (50.7–59.8)	5.8 (5.3–6.3)
Cocaine	NR	3.1 (2.9–3.4)	2.8 (1.7–4.5)	0.2 (0.1–0.3)
Inhalants	12.3 (7.7–19.2)	3.1 (2.8–3.4)	4.1 (2.5–6.8)	1.0 (0.8–1.2)
Cigarettes	23.4 (21.0–26.0)	1.4 (1.2–1.6)	60.8 (56.3–65.1)	6.6 (6.1–7.1)
Smokeless	26.6 (22.2–31.6)	2.7 (2.4–2.9)	19.1 (15.9–22.8)	1.7 (1.5–2.0)
Blunt	30.1 (26.4–34.0)	2.0 (1.8–2.3)	39.7 (35.3–44.3)	3.1 (2.7–3.4)

Source: 2010 NSDUH: Substance Abuse and Mental Health Services Administration (unpublished data).
Note: **CI** = confidence interval; **NR** = low precision, no estimate reported.

Table 3.1.54 Prevalence of the use of bidis and kreteks among youth in grades 6–12, by gender and race/ethnicity; National Youth Tobacco Survey (NYTS) 2009; United States

	Bidis 6th–8th grades		Bidis 9th–12th grades		Kreteks 6th–8th grades		Kreteks 9th–12th grades	
Characteristic	**% (95% CI)**	**SN**	**% (95% CI)**	**SN**	**% (95% CI)**	**SN**	**% (95% CI)**	**SN**
Ever use								
Overall	3.1 (2.6–3.6)		5.1 (4.4–5.8)		1.8 (1.5–2.2)		4.6 (3.7–5.5)	
Gender								
Male	3.8 (3.0–4.7)	a	5.9 (5.1–6.8)	a	2.4 (1.8–3.1)	a	5.8 (4.8–6.8)	a
Female	2.3 (1.7–2.9)	b	4.3 (3.4–5.2)	b	1.2 (0.8–1.6)	b	3.4 (2.3–4.6)	b
Race/ethnicity								
White	2.1 (1.5–2.6)	a	4.3 (3.3–5.2)	a	1.4 (1.1–1.8)	a	5.0 (3.8–6.3)	a
Black or African American	3.4 (2.3–4.6)	b	5.4 (3.2–7.7)	a,b	1.8 (1.0–2.5)	a,b	3.0 (1.4–4.5)	a
Hispanic or Latino	5.1 (4.1–6.1)	c	7.4 (5.3–9.4)	b	2.5 (1.7–3.3)	b	4.7 (3.3–6.1)	a
Other[a]	4.0 (1.9–6.1)	a,b,c	5.9 (3.4–8.5)	a,b	2.8 (0.8–4.9)	a,b	4.5 (2.3–6.6)	a
Current use								
Overall	1.6 (1.2–2.0)		2.4 (1.9–2.9)		1.2 (0.8–1.5)		2.4 (2.0–2.9)	
Gender								
Male	2.0 (1.4–2.6)	a	2.7 (2.0–3.4)	a	1.6 (1.1–2.1)	a	2.9 (2.3–3.6)	a
Female	1.2 (0.7–1.7)	b	2.1 (1.6–2.6)	a	0.7 (0.3–1.0)	b	1.9 (1.1–2.7)	a
Race/ethnicity								
White	1.0 (0.6–1.4)	a	1.7 (1.1–2.2)	a	0.8 (0.5–1.1)	a	2.4 (1.9–3.0)	a
Black or African American	1.7 (0.8–2.5)	a,b	3.8 (1.6–5.9)	a,b	1.2 (0.6–1.9)	a,b	1.8 (0.8–2.8)	a
Hispanic or Latino	2.6 (1.8–3.5)	b	3.7 (2.5–4.8)	b	1.8 (1.0–2.5)	b	2.9 (1.9–3.9)	a
Other[a]	3.3 (1.3–5.3)	b	2.6 (0.5–4.6)	a,b	1.9 (0.0–3.7)	a,b	2.4 (1.0–3.9)	a

Source: 2009 NYTS, Centers for Disease Control and Prevention (unpublished data).
Note: **CI** = confidence interval.
[a]These tests were performed to examine differences in estimates within specific demographic subgroups (e.g., gender). Estimates with the same letter (e.g., a and a) are not statistically significantly different from one another ($p > 0.05$). Estimates with different letters (e.g., a and b) are, in contrast, statistically significantly different from one another ($p < 0.05$).
[b]Includes Asians, American Indians or Alaska Natives, Native Hawaiians or Other Pacific Islanders, and persons of two or more races.

Table 3.1.55 Percentage of young people currently using both cigarettes and smokeless tobacco, by gender, race/ethnicity, age/grade, and region; National Survey on Drug Use and Health (NSDUH) 2010, Monitoring the Future (MTF) 2010, National Youth Risk Behavior Survey (YRBS) 2009, and National Youth Tobacco Survey (NYTS) 2009; United States

	NSDUH 13–18 years of age		MTF 8th, 10th, and 12th grades		YRBS 9th–12th grades		NYTS 9th–12 grades[a]		NYTS 6th–8th grades[a]	
Characteristic	**% (95% CI)**	**SN[b]**	**% (95% CI)**	**SN[b]**	**% (95% CI)**	**SN[b]**	**% (95% CI)**	**SN[b]**	**% (95% CI)**	**SN[b]**
Overall	2.0 (1.77–2.34)		3.6 (2.8–4.4)		5.1 (4.2–6.1)		3.8 (2.5–5.0)		1.3 (0.7–1.8)	
Gender										
Male	3.3 (2.90–3.86)	a	5.9 (4.5–7.3)	a	8.4 (6.8–10.3)	a	6.5 (4.3–8.6)	a	1.7 (0.7–2.7)	a
Female	0.6 (0.39–1.02)	b	1.3 (0.8–1.9)	b	1.5 (1.1–2.0)	b	1.0 (0.6–1.4)	b	0.8 (0.4–1.1)	a
Race/ethnicity										
White	3.1 (2.68–3.57)	a	4.8 (3.7–5.9)	a	6.6 (5.2–8.2)	a	4.7 (3.2–6.1)	a	1.1 (0.7–1.5)	a
Male	5.1 (4.39–5.88)		7.7 (5.8–9.7)		10.9 (8.4–14.1)		8.4 (5.9–10.9)		1.4 (0.8–2.0)	
Female	1.0 (0.61–1.63)		1.7 (0.9–2.6)		1.6 (1.1–2.4)		0.8 (0.2–1.5)		0.7 (0.3–1.2)	
Black or African American	0.2 (0.09–0.38)	b	1.0 (0.1–1.9)	b	1.6 (1.0–2.6)	b	1.2 (0.4–3.7)	b	0.8 (0.1–1.4)	a
Male	0.4 (0.18–0.74)		1.6 (0.0–3.3)		3.0 (1.8–4.8)		1.3 (0.5–3.6)		0.7 (0.1–1.3)	
Female	NR		0.4 (0.0–1.1)		0.4 (0.2–0.8)		1.0 (0.2–4.7)		0.8 (0.3–2.5)	
Hispanic or Latino	0.7 (0.44–1.16)	c	2.0 (0.7–3.2)	c	3.4 (2.5–4.5)	c	3.3 (2.3–4.2)	a	1.0 (0.6–1.5)	a
Male	1.2 (0.68–1.96)		3.0 (0.8–5.1)		4.8 (3.4–6.7)		4.8 (2.7–6.8)		1.5 (0.8–2.1)	
Female	0.2 (0.06–0.66)		1.1 (0.0–2.2)		2.0 (1.3–3.1)		1.7 (0.6–2.8)		0.6 (0.1–1.0)	
Other[c]	0.9 (0.42–2.02)	c	2.3 (0.4–4.3)	c	3.1 (1.8–5.2)	b,c	3.3 (1.2–5.3)	a,b	3.9 (1.2–12.2)	a
Male	1.7 (0.76–3.86)		3.6 (0.0–7.1)		5.5 (3.3–9.1)		5.5 (1.8–9.2)		5.7 (1.2–23.0)	
Female	0.1 (0.02–0.37)		1.1 (0.0–2.8)		0.8 (0.3–2.1)		1.0 (0.4–2.8)		1.9 (0.2–3.6)	
Age (in years)/grade										
13–14	0.6 (0.40–0.97)	a	NA		NA		NA		NA	
15–16	1.3 (1.06–1.66)	b	NA		NA		NA		NA	
17–18	3.9 (3.32–4.69)	c	NA		NA		NA		NA	
6th	NA		NA		NA		NA		1.2 (0.3–2.2)	a
7th	NA		NA		NA		NA		1.1 (0.5–1.6)	a
8th	NA		2.1 (1.5–2.7)	a	NA		NA		1.5 (0.8–2.1)	a
9th	NA		NA		3.4 (2.6–4.3)	a	2.4 (1.3–3.6)	a	NA	
10th	NA		3.9 (3.2–4.7)	b	4.8 (3.7–6.3)	a,c	3.6 (2.1–5.1)	b	NA	
11th	NA		NA		6.2 (5.1–7.6)	b	4.8 (3.2–6.4)	b	NA	
12th	NA		5.2 (4.0–6.3)	b	6.2 (4.6–8.4)	b,c	4.5 (2.5–6.5)	b	NA	

Table 3.1.55 Continued

Characteristic	NSDUH 13–18 years of age		MTF 8th, 10th, and 12th grades		YRBS 9th–12th grades		NYTS 9th–12 grades[a]		NYTS 6th–8th grades[a]	
	% (95% CI)	SN[b]	% (95% CI)	SN[b]	% (95% CI)	SN[b]	% (95% CI)	SN[b]	% (95% CI)	SN[b]
Region										
Northeast	1.7 (1.28–2.27)	a	3.1 (1.3–5.0	a,c	5.3 (2.7–10.3)	a,b	NA		NA	
Midwest	2.4 (1.95–2.92)	b	4.6 (3.0–6.2)	b	5.7 (4.3–7.4)	a	NA		NA	
South	2.3 (1.86–2.92)	c	4.1 (2.6–5.5)	a,b	6.3 (5.0–7.8)	a	NA		NA	
West	1.5 (0.98–2.26)	a,c	2.3 (0.7–3.9)	c	2.8 (1.9–4.0)	b	NA		NA	

Source: 2010 NSDUH: Substance Abuse and Mental Health Services Administration (unpublished data); 2010 MTF: University of Michigan, Institute for Social Research (unpublished data); 2009 YRBS: Centers for Disease Control and Prevention, Division of Adolescent and School Health (unpublished data); 2009 NYTS: Centers for Disease Control and Prevention (unpublished data).

Note: **CI** = confidence interval; **NA** = not applicable; **NR** = low precision, no estimate reported; **SN** = statistical note.

[a]Estimates are based on responses to the questions, "During the past 30 days, on the days you smoked, how many cigarettes did you smoke per day?" and "During the past 30 days, on how many days did you use chewing tobacco, snuff, or dip?"

[b]This column represents the results of statistical tests that were run separately within each surveillance system (e.g., NSDUH). These tests were performed to examine differences in estimates within specific demographic subgroups (e.g., gender). Estimates with the same letter (e.g., a and a) are not statistically significantly different from one another ($p > 0.05$). Estimates with different letters (e.g., a and b) are, in contrast, significantly different from one another ($p < 0.05$).

[c]Includes Asians, American Indians or Alaska Natives, Native Hawaiians or Other Pacific Islanders, and persons of two or more races.

Table 3.1.56 Percentage distribution of grade in which male high school seniors first (if ever) used smokeless tobacco and cigarettes; Monitoring the Future (MTF) 2002–2007; United States

Grade in which first (if ever) tried cigarette	First tried smokeless tobacco in ≤6th grade (%)	First tried smokeless tobacco in 7th or 8th grade (%)	First tried smokeless tobacco in 9th grade (%)	First tried smokeless tobacco in 10th grade (%)	First tried smokeless tobacco in 11th grade (%)	First tried smokeless tobacco in 12th grade (%)	Never used smokeless tobacco (%)
≤6th	2.20	1.66	0.80	0.93	0.62	0.43	5.25
7th or 8th	0.76	2.73	1.88	1.28	0.92	0.49	7.05
9th	0.26	0.42	1.47	0.85	0.60	0.39	3.82
10th	0.10	0.16	0.57	0.90	0.60	0.34	3.13
11th	0.08	0.08	0.20	0.41	0.66	0.43	2.91
12th	0.01	0.02	0.11	0.08	0.27	0.51	2.16
Never used cigarettes	0.33	0.51	0.64	0.68	0.90	0.76	47.65

Source: 2002–2007 MTF: University of Michigan, Institute for Social Research (unpublished data).
Note: Yellow = tried both cigarettes and smokeless tobacco in the same grade; light green = tried both, cigarettes first; pink = tried both, smokeless tobacco first; dark green = tried only cigarettes; light orange = tried only smokeless tobacco; blue = tried neither cigarettes nor smokeless tobacco.

Table 3.1.57 Trends in the initiation of smokeless tobacco use over time among youth 12–17 years of age at risk for initiation—number (in thousands) and percentage of initiates—by gender and race/ethnicity; National Survey on Drug Use and Health (NSDUH) 2006–2010; United States

	2006		2007		2008		2009		2010	
Gender and race/ethnicity	**N**	**% (95% CI)**	**N**	**% (95% CI)**	**N**	**% (95% CI)**	**N**	**% (95% CI)**	**N**	**% (95% CI)**
Overall	589	2.4 (2.2–2.7)	619	2.6 (2.3–2.9)	603	2.5 (2.3–2.8)	654	2.8 (2.5–3.1)	566	2.4 (2.2–2.7)
Gender										
Male	473	3.9 (3.5–4.4)	474	4.0 (3.5–4.6)	462	3.9 (3.5–4.4)	516	4.4 (4.0–5.0)	430	3.7 (3.3–4.3)
Female	116	1.0 (0.8–1.2)	146	1.2 (1.0–1.5)	146	1.2 (1.0–1.5)	137	1.2 (1.0–1.4)	136	1.2 (0.9–1.5)
Race/ethnicity										
White	474	3.3 (3.0–3.7)	519	3.7 (3.3–4.2)	495	3.6 (3.2–4.1)	519	3.9 (3.5–4.3)	4731	3.6 (3.2–4.1)
Black or African American	23	0.6 (0.3–1.2)	21	0.6 (0.3–1.2)	31	0.8 (0.5–1.5)	15	0.4 (0.2–0.9)	20	0.4 (0.3–1.0)
Hispanic or Latino	68	1.5 (1.1–2.2)	66	1.4 (0.9–2.2)	56	1.2 (0.8–1.8)	94	2.0 (1.4–2.8)	61	1.3 (0.9–1.8)

Source: 2006–2010 NSDUH: Substance Abuse and Mental Health Services Administration (unpublished data).
Note: At risk for initiation is defined as persons who did not use the substance(s) in their lifetime or used the substance(s) for the first time in the past year. **CI** = confidence interval; **N** = number (in 1,000s).

Table 3.1.58 Trends in the initiation of smokeless tobacco use over time among young adults 18–25 years of age at risk for initiation—number (in thousands) and percentage of initiates—by gender and race/ethnicity; National Survey on Drug Use and Health (NSDUH) 2006–2010; United States

	2006		2007		2008		2009		2010	
Gender and race/ethnicity	**N**	**% (95% CI)**	**N**	**% (95% CI)**	**N**	**% (95% CI)**	**N**	**% (95% CI)**	**N**	**% (95% CI)**
Overall	567	2.1 (1.8–2.4)	597	2.2 (2.0–2.5)	577	2.2 (1.9–2.5)	658	2.4 (2.1–2.7)	645	2.3 (2.1–2.6)
Gender										
Male	456	3.9 (3.4–4.6)	457	3.9 (3.4–4.6)	435	3.8 (3.2–4.4)	487	4.2 (3.6–4.8)	480	4.0 (3.5–4.7)
Female	111	0.7 (0.6–1.0)	140	0.9 (0.7–1.2)	142	0.9 (0.7–1.2)	172	1.1 (0.9–1.4)	164	1.1 (0.8–1.3)
Race/ethnicity										
White	434	2.9 (2.5–3.3)	484	3.2 (2.8–3.7)	459	3.0 (2.6–3.5)	506	3.4 (2.9–3.9)	493	3.3 (2.9–3.8)
Black or African American	22	0.5 (0.3–0.9)	15	0.3 (0.2–0.7)	38	0.8 (0.5–1.5)	17	0.4 (0.2–0.7)	33	0.7 (0.4–1.2)
Hispanic or Latino	66	1.2 (0.7–2.0)	77	1.4 (1.0–2.1)	61	1.2 (0.8–1.8)	91	1.6 (1.1–2.4)	105	1.8 (1.2–2.5)

Source: 2006–2010 NSDUH: Substance Abuse and Mental Health Services Administration (unpublished data).
Note: At risk for initiation is defined as persons who did not use the substance(s) in their lifetime or used the substance(s) for the first time in the past year. **CI** = confidence interval; **N** = number (in 1,000s).

Table 3.1.59 Trends in the initiation of cigar smoking over time among youth 12–17 years of age at risk for initiation—number (in thousands) and percentage of initiates—by gender and race/ethnicity; National Survey on Drug Use and Health (NSDUH) 2006–2010; United States

	2006		2007		2008		2009		2010	
Gender and race/ethnicity	**N**	**% (95% CI)**	**N**	**% (95% CI)**	**N**	**% (95% CI)**	**N**	**% (95% CI)**	**N**	**% (95% CI)**
Overall	1,212	5.2 (4.9–5.6)	1,144	5.0 (4.6–5.3)	1,108	4.8 (4.5–5.2)	1,076	4.8 (4.4–5.1)	933	4.1 (3.8–4.5)
Gender										
Male	711	6.2 (5.7–6.8)	705	6.2 (5.6–6.8)	645	5.6 (5.1–6.2)	686	6.1 (5.5–6.7)	538	4.8 (4.2–5.3)
Female	501	4.3 (3.8–4.8)	440	3.8 (3.3–4.3)	464	4.0 (3.6–4.6)	390	3.4 (3.0–3.9)	395	3.5 (3.1–4.0)
Race/ethnicity										
White	915	6.7 (6.2–7.2)	865	6.4 (5.9–6.9)	786	5.9 (5.4–6.4)	735	5.6 (5.1–6.2)	655	5.1 (4.6–5.6)
Black or African merican	89	2.5 (1.8–3.3)	80	2.2 (1.6–3.0)	99	2.8 (2.1–3.7)	77	2.2 (1.6–3.0)	88	2.6 (1.9–3.5)
Hispanic or Latino	163	3.9 (3.1–4.9)	153	3.6 (2.9–4.4)	180	4.1 (3.3–5.2)	214	4.8 (4.0–5.8)	161	3.5 (2.9–4.4)

Source: 2006–2010 NSDUH: Substance Abuse and Mental Health Services Administration (unpublished data).
Note: At risk for initiation is defined as persons who did not use the substance(s) in their lifetime or used the substance(s) for the first time in the past year.
CI = confidence interval; **N** = number (in 1,000s).

Table 3.1.60 Trends in the initiation of cigar smoking over time among young adults, 18–25 years of age at risk for initiation—number (in thousands) and percentage of initiates—by gender and race/ethnicity; National Survey on Drug Use and Health (NSDUH) 2006–2010; United States

	2006		2007		2008		2009		2010	
Gender and race/ethnicity	**N**	**% (95% CI)**	**N**	**% (95% CI)**	**N**	**% (95% CI)**	**N**	**% (95% CI)**	**N**	**% (95% CI)**
Overall	1,279	6.4 (5.9–7.0)	1,376	6.8 (6.3–7.4)	1,261	6.1 (5.6–6.7)	1,406	6.7 (6.2–7.3)	1,371	6.4 (5.8–7.0)
Gender										
Male	747	9.2 (8.2–10.2)	784	9.5 (8.5–10.5)	751	8.8 (7.9–9.8)	832	9.6 (8.7–10.7)	769	8.5 (7.5–9.7)
Female	532	4.5 (4.0–5.1)	591	4.9 (4.4–5.6)	510	4.2 (3.7–4.8)	574	4.7 (4.0–5.4)	602	4.8 (4.2–5.5)
Race/ethnicity										
White	995	9.3 (8.5–10.1)	965	8.7 (7.9–9.5)	911	8.1 (7.4–8.9)	984	8.7 (7.9–9.6)	934	8.2 (7.4–9.0)
Black or African American	77	2.3 (1.7–3.1)	104	3.0 (2.2–4.0)	102	2.8 (2.1–3.8)	135	3.6 (2.8–4.7)	79	2.1 (1.4–3.0)
Hispanic or Latino	121	2.9 (2.1–3.9)	202	5.0 (3.9–6.2)	162	4.0 (3.0–5.3)	183	4.2 (3.3–5.4)	250	5.4 (4.2–6.8)

Source: 2006–2010 NSDUH: Substance Abuse and Mental Health Services Administration (unpublished data).
Note: At risk for initiation is defined as persons who did not use the substance(s) in their lifetime or used the substance(s) for the first time in the past year.
CI = confidence interval; **N** = number (in 1,000s).

Table 3.1.61 Trends in the initiation of cigarettes, smokeless tobacco, and cigars over time among youth 12–17 years of age at risk for initiation—number (in thousands) and percentage of initiates—by gender and race/ethnicity; National Survey on Drug Use and Health (NSDUH) 2006–2010; United States

	2006		2007		2008		2009		2010	
Gender and race/ethnicity	**N**	**% (95% CI)**	**N**	**% (95% CI)**	**N**	**% (95% CI)**	**N**	**% (95% CI)**	**N**	**% (95% CI)**
Overall	1,495	7.7 (7.2–8.2)	1,445	7.3 (6.8–7.9)	1,519	7.7 (7.2–8.3)	1,551	7.9 (7.4–8.5)	1,475	7.5 (7.0–8.0)
Gender										
Male	771	8.0 (7.3–8.7)	785	8.1 (7.3–8.9)	757	7.7 (7.0–8.4)	886	9.2 (8.4–10.0)	798	8.1 (7.4–8.9)
Female	724	7.5 (6.8–8.3)	660	6.7 (6.0–7.4)	762	7.8 (7.0–8.6)	665	6.8 (6.1–7.4)	677	6.8 (6.2–7.6)
Race/ethnicity										
White	1,013	9.0 (8.4–9.7)	993	8.8 (8.1–9.5)	988	8.7 (8.1–9.5)	996	8.9 (8.3–9.7)	962	8.6 (7.9–9.3)
Black or African American	171	5.4 (4.4–6.6)	150	4.7 (3.8–5.9)	176	5.6 (4.6–7.0)	146	4.7 (3.7–6.1)	156	5.2 (4.1–6.5)
Hispanic or Latino	250	7.0 (5.9–8.4)	252	6.6 (5.5–7.9)	278	7.3 (6.0–8.8)	337	8.7 (7.4–10.3)	283	7.0 (5.9–8.2)

Source: 2006–2010 NSDUH: Substance Abuse and Mental Health Services Administration (unpublished data).
Note: At risk for initiation is defined as persons who did not use the substance(s) in their lifetime or used the substance(s) for the first time in the past year.
CI = confidence interval; **N** = number (in 1,000s).

Table 3.1.62 Trends in the initiation of cigarettes, smokeless tobacco, or cigars over time among young adults 18–25 years of age at risk for initiation—number (in thousands) and percentage of initiates—by gender and race/ethnicity; National Survey on Drug Use and Health (NSDUH) 2006–2010; United States

	2006		2007		2008		2009		2010	
Gender and race/ethnicity	**N**	**% (95% CI)**	**N**	**% (95% CI)**	**N**	**% (95% CI)**	**N**	**% (95% CI)**	**N**	**% (95% CI)**
Overall	1,136	11.0 (10.0–12.0)	1,103	10.2 (9.3–11.2)	1,199	10.9 (9.9–11.9)	1,223	10.7 (9.7–11.7)	1,212	10.2 (9.3–11.1)
Gender										
Male	587	13.2 (11.6–15.0)	550	12.3 (10.7–14.0)	654	13.8 (12.2–15.6)	625	13.2 (11.6–14.9)	651	13.1 (11.6–14.8)
Female	549	9.3 (8.1–10.5)	553	8.7 (7.7–9.9)	545	8.7 (7.6–9.9)	599	8.9 (7.8–10.2)	561	8.1 (7.1–9.1)
Race/ethnicity										
White	741	15.0 (13.6–16.6)	685	12.6 (11.2–14.0)	765	13.8 (12.4–15.4)	739	13.0 (11.6–14.6)	714	12.4 (11.1–13.9)
Black or African American	118	5.7 (4.3–7.6)	135	6.3 (4.9–8.1)	124	5.4 (4.1–7.2)	156	6.6 (5.2–8.5)	182	7.3 (5.7–9.2)
Hispanic or Latino	188	7.9 (6.0–10.3)	190	8.1 (6.4–10.3)	221	10.0 (7.8–12.8)	243	10.1 (7.9–12.8)	238	9.0 (7.3–11.2)

Source: 2006–2010 NSDUH: Substance Abuse and Mental Health Services Administration (unpublished data).
Note: At risk for initiation is defined as persons who did not use the substance(s) in their lifetime or used the substance(s) for the first time in the past year.
CI = confidence interval; **N** = number (in 1,000s).

Table 3.1.63 Percentage of youth 13–15 years of age who have ever smoked cigarettes, who first tried smoking when younger than 10 years of age, and among never smokers who are susceptible to starting to smoke within the next year, by gender; Global Youth Tobacco Survey 1999–2009; worldwide

WHO region and WHO member state, territory, or special administrative region, and year	% Ever smoked cigarettes (ever smokers)			% Ever smokers who first tried smoking at <10 years of age			% Never smokers susceptible to starting to smoke within the next year		
	Total % (95% CI)	Males % (95% CI)	Females % (95% CI)	Total % (95% CI)	Males % (95% CI)	Females % (95% CI)	Total % (95% CI)	Males % (95% CI)	Females % (95% CI)
Africa	11.5 (11.0–11.9)	16.6 (15.9–17.2)	7.8 (7.4–8.3)	26.8 (26.7–27.9)	28.3 (27.1–29.5)	27.7 (25.6–29.8)	10.1 (9.7–10.6)	11.8 (11.2–12.4)	9.2 (8.7–9.7)
Algeria, 2007 (Constantine)	20.2 (16.4–24.5)	40.2 (34.4–46.3)	6.2 (3.8–10.1)	32.8 (29.2–36.7)	31.5 (27.5–35.8)	42.4 (28.1–58.1)	14.9 (12.8–17.3)	22.7 (17.4–29.0)	11.5 (9.5–13.8)
Benin, 2003 (Atlantique Littoral)	15.4 (12.0–19.6)	22.8 (17.6–29.0)	5.3 (2.8–9.6)	18.9 (11.0–30.5)	21.9 (13.7–33.2)	4.4 (0.6–27.2)	13.1 (10.3–16.6)	12.4 (9.6–15.8)	13.7 (9.7–18.9)
Botswana, 2008	15.5 (12.2–19.6)	21.3 (16.7–26.8)	11.1 (7.6–15.9)	32.4 (26.9–38.5)	30.8 (23.6–39.1)	36.7 (25.2–50.0)	27.1 (22.8–32.0)	33.3 (28.1–38.9)	22.5 (18.0–27.8)
Burkina Faso, 2006 (Ouagadougou)	18.8 (16.7–21.2)	29.5 (25.1–34.3)	8.1 (6.3–10.2)	18.0 (13.1–24.3)	16.5 (11.9–22.4)	25.2 (12.7–43.8)	9.4 (6.8–12.7)	15.0 (10.7–20.6)	5.1 (3.5–7.4)
Burundi, 2008	19.1 (14.6–24.5)	23.9 (18.4–30.3)	14.1 (10.3–19.0)	53.3 (41.2–65.1)	47.9 (31.2–65.0)	65.1 (46.1–80.2)	17.8 (12.2–25.1)	20.1 (14.5–27.1)	16.2 (10.3–24.6)
Cameroon, 2008 (Yaoude)	15.0 (11.9–18.7)	21.7 (17.9–26.0)	10.1 (6.4–15.5)	33.1 (27.8–38.8)	31.4 (24.7–39.0)	35.9 (28.1–44.6)	10.2 (8.0–12.8)	13.0 (9.9–16.9)	7.9 (5.9–10.5)
Cape Verde, 2007	10.2 (7.5–13.7)	12.3 (8.4–17.6)	7.8 (5.2–11.7)	31.5 (21.9–43.1)	38.6 (24.5–54.9)	24.9 (13.9–40.6)	15.3 (12.4–18.8)	16.4 (12.1–21.9)	14.6 (11.6–18.3)
Central African Republic, 2008 (Bangui)	27.6 (12.6–50.1)	23.8 (19.1–29.4)	30.4 (8.4–67.6)	14.1 (8.2–23.1)	17.3 (9.3–29.8)	NR	17.0 (13.0–22.1)	16.1 (11.7–21.8)	18.3 (12.6–25.8)
Comoros, 2007	26.5 (21.9–31.7)	39.3 (28.5–51.3)	17.2 (13.8–21.3)	25.0 (17.9–33.8)	24.9 (16.8–35.2)	22.7 (14.4–33.9)	9.9 (6.8–14.2)	11.3 (6.3–19.4)	9.5 (6.1–14.4)
Congo, 2006	22.0 (17.3–27.5)	26.6 (20.6–33.6)	17.2 (12.1–23.8)	20.9 (15.1–28.1)	20.4 (13.1–30.3)	23.8 (14.7–36.1)	15.1 (12.0–18.8)	17.7 (12.7–24.0)	12.9 (9.4–17.3)
Côte D'Ivoire, 2003 (Abidjan)	35.4 (31.8–39.1)	50.0 (45.1–54.9)	18.5 (16.5–20.6)	12.0 (8.6–16.4)	11.4 (7.5–16.9)	13.6 (8.6–20.9)	11.2 (9.3–13.4)	13.0 (9.9–16.9)	9.9 (7.8–12.4)
Democratic Republic of the Congo, 2008 (Kinshasa)	19.5 (15.4–24.5)	27.3 (19.5–36.8)	9.1 (6.4–12.8)	27.9 (18.1–40.3)	29.0 (16.5–45.6)	NR	30.1 (17.6–46.5)	35.3 (19.3–55.4)	25.2 (14.6–39.8)
Equatorial Guinea, 2008	15.9 (13.2–19.1)	20.5 (16.6–25.1)	10.5 (7.1–15.4)	23.8 (17.5–31.5)	17.4 (10.7–27.1)	36.3 (21.9–53.8)	16.1 (11.1–22.8)	17.2 (12.1–23.8)	15.4 (9.9–23.2)

Table 3.1.63 Continued

WHO region and WHO member state, territory, or special administrative region, and year	% Ever smoked cigarettes (ever smokers)			% Ever smokers who first tried smoking at <10 years of age			% Never smokers susceptible to starting to smoke within the next year		
	Total % (95% CI)	Males % (95% CI)	Females % (95% CI)	Total % (95% CI)	Males % (95% CI)	Females % (95% CI)	Total % (95% CI)	Males % (95% CI)	Females % (95% CI)
Eritrea, 2006	3.3 (2.5–4.3)	4.3 (3.2–5.7)	1.4 (0.8–2.5)	21.4 (11.3–36.9)	19.2 (9.9–34.2)	37.2 (20.1–58.2)	12.8 (11.1–14.8)	15.1 (12.9–17.7)	9.5 (7.7–11.7)
Ethiopia, 2003 (Addis Ababa)	7.6 (4.4–12.8)	10.8 (5.4–20.4)	4.6 (3.0–7.1)	12.7 (4.6–30.7)	6.3 (1.3–26.0) NR	28.9 (8.4–64.3)	12.0 (10.0–14.3)	12.8 (10.1–16.0)	11.0 (8.8–13.6)
Gambia, 2008 (Banjul)	24.5 (19.4–30.5)	28.1 (22.1–34.9)	20.3 (14.6–27.5)	46.4 (38.3–54.8)	44.0 (34.2–54.3)	44.8 (30.9–59.5)	21.5 (18.0–25.4)	21.4 (17.2–26.4)	19.7 (15.9–24.3)
Ghana, 2006	9.2 (7.8–10.9)	9.4 (7.5–11.7)	8.0 (6.1–10.3)	44.4 (34.0–55.2)	35.1 (25.9–45.6)	55.9 (37.3–72.9)	14.2 (11.1–18.1)	13.8 (10.5–17.9)	14.1 (11.1–17.8)
Guinea, 2008	13.3 (10.0–17.5)	19.1 (13.6–26.1)	6.4 (4.4–9.1)	31.2 (20.0–45.3)	29.0 (17.5–43.9)	NR	16.5 (13.3–20.2)	15.4 (11.7–19.9)	17.1 (12.9–22.4)
Guinea-Bissau, 2008 (Bissau)	5.4 (4.4–6.6)	7.7 (6.0–9.9)	3.0 (1.8–5.0)	6.0 (1.5–20.6)	3.5 (0.8–14.8)	NR	24.5 (20.0–29.6)	25.4 (20.7–30.7)	23.7 (18.1–30.5)
Kenya, 2007	21.2 (15.5–28.4)	29.5 (22.2–38.1)	13.5 (10.5–17.2)	38.4 (32.6–44.5)	36.7 (34.0–39.4)	43.0 (28.5–58.8)	19.5 (16.0–23.5)	19.8 (13.9–27.5)	19.1 (14.6–24.8)
Lesotho, 2008	22.3 (18.5–26.6)	29.0 (24.7–33.7)	16.7 (12.3–22.1)	31.8 (24.9–39.6)	20.7 (12.0–33.4)	41.0 (25.7–58.2)	33.7 (27.4–40.6)	33.7 (25.6–43.0)	33.1 (26.4–40.5)
Liberia, 2008 (Monrovia)	8.3 (5.6–12.0)	8.4 (5.7–12.3)	7.3 (4.3–12.3)	NR	NR	NR	4.8 (2.4–9.3)	6.4 (2.7–14.1)	3.4 (1.8–6.5)
Madagascar, 2008	27.6 (21.4–34.7)	42.3 (32.3–53.0)	15.6 (10.8–22.1)	14.6 (11.0–19.1)	13.4 (8.8–19.9)	17.1 (8.5–31.5)	12.5 (8.7–17.7)	12.3 (7.3–20.0)	12.5 (8.0–19.2)
Malawi, 2005	7.8 (5.4–11.0)	10.2 (7.4–13.8)	5.6 (3.2–9.6)	55.3 (34.1–74.7)	54.7 (38.2–70.2)	56.4 (25.8–82.8)	2.8 (2.0–3.9)	3.6 (2.2–5.7)	2.1 (1.1–3.8)
Mali, 2008	29.0 (24.0–34.6)	44.6 (36.0–53.6)	10.1 (6.6–15.2)	22.9 (15.3–32.9)	24.3 (16.0–35.0)	12.6 (4.7–29.6)	5.6 (3.4–9.1)	8.6 (4.5–15.9)	3.4 (1.9–6.2)
Mauritania, 2006	29.2 (25.1–33.7)	32.4 (28.2–36.9)	24.9 (19.5–31.2)	43.7 (35.9–51.9)	44.7 (37.4–52.1)	43.4 (32.5–54.9)	19.9 (16.8–23.4)	18.8 (15.6–22.5)	20.6 (16.2–26.0)
Mauritius, 2008	28.4 (22.7–34.7)	37.7 (29.5–46.6)	19.9 (14.4–26.9)	13.4 (8.9–19.8)	12.4 (7.3–20.1)	15.0 (7.3–28.3)	11.2 (8.8–14.3)	12.1 (9.2–15.8)	10.7 (6.3–17.6)
Mozambique, 2007 (Maputo City)	6.3 (4.8–8.2)	9.0 (6.1–13.1)	3.6 (2.2–5.7)	51.2 (33.8–68.4)	58.2 (39.5–74.8)	NR	22.9 (19.5–26.8)	24.1 (19.6–29.2)	21.5 (16.7–27.1)
Namibia, 2004	38.3 (34.2–42.5)	42.3 (37.6–47.2)	34.9 (30.2–40.0)	23.0 (20.3–26.0)	23.1 (19.6–27.1)	23.1 (18.2–28.8)	36.4 (32.2–40.7)	37.4 (31.3–44.0)	35.5 (30.8–40.5)

Table 3.1.63 Continued

WHO region and WHO member state, territory, or special administrative region, and year	% Ever smoked cigarettes (ever smokers)			% Ever smokers who first tried smoking at <10 years of age			% Never smokers susceptible to starting to smoke within the next year		
	Total % (95% CI)	Males % (95% CI)	Females % (95% CI)	Total % (95% CI)	Males % (95% CI)	Females % (95% CI)	Total % (95% CI)	Males % (95% CI)	Females % (95% CI)
Niger, 2006	14.9 (12.0–18.5)	26.2 (20.6–32.6)	4.0 (2.4–6.7)	18.8 (10.8–30.6)	16.0 (7.8–29.9)	48.7 (19.6–78.7)	11.5 (6.7–19.0)	15.6 (8.3–27.3)	8.1 (5.0–13.0)
Nigeria, 2008 (Cross River State)	13.4 (8.4–20.7)	13.9 (7.8–23.6)	9.9 (5.6–16.9)	NR	NR	NR	10.4 (6.1–17.3)	12.9 (6.6–23.7)	8.7 (3.7–18.9)
Rwanda, 2008	16.3 (12.7–20.6)	23.5 (19.0–28.6)	9.5 (6.6–13.3)	40.9 (30.1–52.8)	40.5 (29.8–52.2)	NR	10.0 (7.5–13.3)	12.0 (8.6–16.5)	7.8 (5.3–11.4)
Senegal, 2007	12.8 (8.5–18.9)	20.7 (13.8–29.9)	5.2 (3.1–8.7)	25.9 (18.3–35.2)	24.3 (18.2–31.5)	38.9 (19.6–62.4)	31.0 (20.0–44.6)	37.2 (24.4–52.2)	27.7 (17.6–40.8)
Seychelles, 2007	48.4 (42.4–54.4)	54.1 (46.8–61.3)	42.4 (35.2–49.9)	19.4 (15.1–24.6)	18.9 (14.1–24.9)	20.5 (14.7–27.9)	15.4 (12.1–19.4)	14.4 (9.5–21.2)	16.2 (12.4–20.9)
Sierra Leone, 2008 (Western Area)	15.5 (11.7–20.2)	19.4 (13.4–27.2)	11.9 (7.9–17.6)	32.1 (18.5–49.6)	19.0 (8.0–38.8)	48.3 (32.9–64.1)	15.5 (12.0–19.8)	17.5 (10.7–27.2)	13.6 (11.1–16.6)
South Africa, 2008	30.7 (27.1–34.6)	38.2 (34.3–42.3)	25.3 (21.1–30.1)	19.2 (15.4–23.7)	20.3 (15.3–26.4)	18.0 (13.5–23.6)	15.4 (13.3–17.7)	17.4 (14.5–20.7)	14.3 (11.8–17.2)
Swaziland, 2005	13.3 (11.9–14.9)	19.8 (17.4–22.3)	9.0 (7.7–10.5)	33.4 (30.4–36.6)	36.1 (31.2–41.3)	29.1 (24.0–34.9)	8.0 (7.0–9.0)	9.1 (7.4–11.0)	7.4 (6.5–8.3)
Togo, 2007	12.6 (9.4–16.8)	17.4 (12.3–24.0)	5.4 (3.7–7.9)	33.3 (24.2–43.9)	31.2 (21.4–43.1)	NR	9.1 (6.7–12.2)	9.6 (6.6–13.6)	8.2 (5.9–11.2)
Uganda, 2007	15.6 (13.1–18.4)	19.2 (15.7–23.3)	11.2 (9.3–13.6)	43.4 (36.9–50.2)	42.7 (35.1–50.8)	44.7 (33.2–56.9)	6.7 (5.4–8.3)	8.1 (6.3–10.4)	5.1 (3.5–7.5)
United Republic of Tanzania, 2008 (Arusha)	6.2 (3.6–10.6)	7.5 (3.9–13.9)	4.9 (2.5–9.1)	31.2 (17.5–49.2)	NR	NR	3.0 (2.0–4.5)	3.3 (2.3–4.7)	2.8 (1.4–5.8)
Zambia, 2007 (Lusaka)	22.3 (17.0–28.8)	25.3 (19.9–31.5)	20.4 (14.4–28.0)	43.7 (34.9–53.0)	48.2 (37.8–58.7)	39.5 (26.7–54.0)	22.6 (17.7–28.3)	21.1 (15.3–28.3)	23.4 (17.7–30.3)
Zimbabwe, 2008 (Harare)	10.8 (8.4–13.8)	13.2 (9.3–18.4)	8.1 (5.5–11.7)	32.3 (20.1–47.5)	40.1 (29.7–51.5)	NR	30.0 (24.8–35.8)	29.5 (26.0–33.4)	30.4 (22.7–39.5)
The Americas	34.3 (33.7–35.0)	37.6 (36.8–38.5)	31.6 (30.8– 2.4)	16.1 (15.4–16.8)	18.2 (17.2–19.2)	12.9 (12.0–13.8)	17.0 (16.5–17.6)	17.1 (16.3–17.8)	16.5 (15.9–17.2)
Antigua & Barbuda, 2004	19.2 (16.5–22.2)	20.4 (16.4–25.0)	17.6 (14.0–21.8)	26.0 (20.2–32.7)	25.6 (17.6–35.7)	25.8 (17.1–36.8)	11.5 (9.5–13.9)	12.6 (9.4–16.7)	9.6 (7.5–12.1)
Argentina, 2007	52.0 (49.5–54.5)	48.9 (45.6–52.2)	54.8 (50.6–58.9)	8.7 (6.9–10.8)	10.9 (7.9–14.8)	6.8 (5.4–8.7)	28.1 (25.2–31.1)	24.3 (20.8–28.1)	31.6 (28.3–35.0)

Table 3.1.63 Continued

WHO region and WHO member state, territory, or special administrative region, and year	% Ever smoked cigarettes (ever smokers)			% Ever smokers who first tried smoking at <10 years of age			% Never smokers susceptible to starting to smoke within the next year		
	Total % (95% CI)	Males % (95% CI)	Females % (95% CI)	Total % (95% CI)	Males % (95% CI)	Females % (95% CI)	Total % (95% CI)	Males % (95% CI)	Females % (95% CI)
Bahamas, 2004	25.3 (21.2–29.9)	27.7 (22.5–33.5)	23.0 (17.1–30.1)	34.3 (27.3–42.2)	37.5 (27.7–48.5)	30.8 (20.4–43.7)	20.2 (16.9–23.9)	21.1 (16.2–27.1)	19.1 (13.7–25.9)
Barbados, 2007	32.4 (28.3–36.9)	40.2 (34.8–45.8)	25.3 (19.7–31.9)	32.0 (26.1–38.5)	33.1 (25.1–42.2)	29.3 (21.8–38.1)	21.5 (18.0–25.5)	20.4 (15.7–26.0)	22.4 (17.4–28.2)
Belize, 2008	26.6 (22.1–31.7)	36.2 (28.8–44.3)	18.6 (15.4–22.4)	22.1 (16.3–29.3)	24.2 (17.4–32.7)	18.6 (10.1–31.6)	21.3 (18.6–24.3)	25.1 (20.6–30.2)	18.8 (14.5–23.9)
Bolivia, 2003 (La Paz)	41.3 (37.7–45.1)	46.5 (41.6–51.4)	35.8 (32.6–39.3)	15.4 (13.4–17.6)	15.1 (12.9–17.7)	15.6 (12.0–20.1)	25.0 (22.0–28.3)	27.0 (22.6–31.9)	23.2 (18.8–28.2)
Brazil, 2005 (Rio de Janeiro)	34.5 (30.9–38.3)	29.5 (23.7–36.2)	36.5 (30.9–42.4)	14.2 (10.1–19.7)	14.5 (9.5–21.6)	13.5 (7.5–23.2)	17.9 (15.2–21.0)	11.0 (7.9–15.0)	22.7 (19.7–26.0)
British Virgin Islands, 2001[a]	21.9 (16.2–28.8)	26.2 (18.3–35.9)	18.2 (12.5–25.9)	27.1 (17.2–39.9)	23.3 (10.9–42.9)	31.3 (18.3–48.0)	9.9 (6.8–14.0)	9.1 (4.7–17.0)	10.1 (6.5–15.3)
Chile, 2008 (Santiago)	66.2 (62.6–69.7)	60.2 (55.4–64.8)	72.2 (68.4–75.6)	16.9 (15.1–18.8)	19.1 (16.4–22.1)	15.0 (12.3–18.0)	28.5 (25.6–31.6)	27.3 (23.1–31.9)	30.0 (26.0–34.4)
Colombia, 2007 (Bogota)	57.1 (52.3–61.7)	58.7 (54.1–63.1)	55.6 (48.1–62.8)	13.5 (10.4–17.4)	17.2 (11.0–25.8)	10.5 (7.0–15.3)	32.0 (28.7–35.5)	31.9 (25.9–38.6)	31.8 (27.5–36.5)
Costa Rica, 2008	26.4 (23.0–30.1)	26.5 (22.5–30.8)	26.2 (22.2–30.7)	13.2 (10.4–16.7)	15.5 (11.5–20.5)	10.8 (7.8–14.7)	17.4 (15.4–19.5)	16.5 (14.0–19.3)	18.3 (15.2–21.8)
Cuba, 2004 (Havana)	25.5 (20.7–30.9)	27.2 (21.7–33.4)	23.6 (18.5–29.7)	11.3 (7.0–17.7)	16.0 (9.5–25.7)	6.2 (3.3–11.3)	9.5 (7.1–12.6)	7.3 (4.8–10.8)	11.7 (8.5–16.0)
Dominica, 2004	32.4 (27.9–37.3)	36.8 (30.2–44.0)	26.2 (21.7–31.3)	27.7 (22.2–33.9)	29.0 (21.3–38.1)	25.8 (18.6–34.5)	13.8 (11.3–16.7)	15.8 (11.9–20.7)	11.5 (8.5–15.4)
Dominican Republic, 2004	21.4 (18.5–24.6)	22.3 (19.3–25.7)	20.4 (16.8–24.4)	24.9 (18.4–32.7)	24.7 (16.9–34.5)	24.4 (18.3–31.7)	14.1 (11.0–17.9)	14.4 (11.2–18.3)	13.8 (10.2–18.4)
Ecuador, 2007 (Quito)	56.0 (50.1–61.7)	62.6 (57.0–67.9)	50.2 (41.2–59.3)	16.6 (13.4–20.4)	18.4 (13.4–24.7)	14.7 (12.3–17.5)	28.0 (23.4–33.2)	26.1 (21.7–31.1)	28.8 (22.6–36.0)
El Salvador, 2003	34.5 (25.9–44.3)	44.4 (33.5–55.8)	27.5 (19.7–36.9)	17.1 (13.2–21.7)	19.3 (15.6–23.7)	14.6 (9.4–22.0)	10.7 (6.3–17.5)	11.8 (6.1–21.8)	10.0 (6.0–16.4)
Grenada, 2004	33.5 (29.3–38.0)	36.5 (30.6–42.9)	30.8 (26.6–35.3)	32.8 (26.9–39.3)	36.4 (28.6–45.0)	28.4 (21.2–36.9)	10.9 (8.6–13.6)	11.7 (8.4–16.1)	10.2 (7.5–13.8)
Guatemala, 2008	32.8 (28.9–37.1)	39.2 (33.4–45.2)	26.4 (22.6–30.6)	16.8 (14.6–19.3)	17.6 (15.2–20.4)	15.2 (10.7–21.2)	14.8 (12.3–17.6)	16.4 (13.3–20.1)	13.7 (11.1–16.7)

Table 3.1.63 Continued

WHO region and WHO member state, territory, or special administrative region, and year	% Ever smoked cigarettes (ever smokers)			% Ever smokers who first tried smoking at <10 years of age			% Never smokers susceptible to starting to smoke within the next year		
	Total % (95% CI)	Males % (95% CI)	Females % (95% CI)	Total % (95% CI)	Males % (95% CI)	Females % (95% CI)	Total % (95% CI)	Males % (95% CI)	Females % (95% CI)
Guyana, 2004	27.7 (23.8–31.9)	34.7 (28.8–41.2)	20.4 (15.1–27.0)	33.8 (26.4–42.0)	32.2 (24.0–41.6)	36.7 (22.8–53.3)	9.9 (7.2–13.4)	11.5 (7.3–17.7)	8.9 (5.8–13.5)
Haiti, 2005 (Port au Prince)	30.9 (27.1–35.1)	34.2 (31.5–37.0)	27.9 (21.8–35.1)	19.3 (14.4–25.5)	13.7 (9.7–18.9)	23.6 (14.5–36.0)	24.9 (16.7–35.3)	23.7 (14.1–37.1)	26.8 (19.2–36.0)
Honduras, 2003 (Tegucigalpa)	46.3 (39.7–53.0)	47.3 (39.1–55.6)	44.8 (38.4–51.3)	16.5 (13.8–19.8)	19.7 (14.1–26.9)	14.5 (10.3–20.0)	25.9 (20.8–31.6)	19.7 (13.6–27.7)	30.7 (23.1–39.6)
Jamaica, 2006	35.1 (29.4–41.2)	40.8 (33.5–48.5)	29.7 (23.4–36.7)	29.5 (23.4–36.5)	25.6 (18.8–33.9)	34.8 (25.2–45.8)	18.7 (14.4–23.8)	21.8 (15.7–29.4)	16.3 (12.5–21.0)
Mexico, 2006 (Mexico City)	60.2 (56.8–63.6)	61.7 (57.8–65.4)	58.2 (54.0–62.3)	NA	NA	NA	31.5 (28.2–35.1)	31.5 (26.6–36.8)	29.6 (24.5–35.2)
Montserrat, 2000[a]	20.6	20.7	18.5	36.4 NR	44.4 NR	36.4 NR	13.1	15.6	11.3
Nicaragua, 2003 (Centro Managua)	51.2 (44.6–57.8)	55.9 (48.2–63.3)	47.4 (39.2–55.7)	19.5 (14.7–25.5)	21.5 (16.0–28.2)	17.4 (10.6–27.1)	21.3 (17.0–26.3)	27.0 (20.1–35.3)	17.1 (12.3–23.4)
Panama, 2008	17.1 (14.5–20.0)	21.7 (18.4–25.4)	13.0 (9.8–16.9)	16.2 (12.7–20.4)	15.9 (10.9–22.7)	17.0 (12.1–23.4)	10.0 (8.8–11.4)	12.3 (10.6–14.3)	8.3 (6.5–10.4)
Paraguay, 2008	21.6 (19.2–24.3)	26.0 (22.5–30.0)	17.6 (14.7–20.8)	17.1 (12.9–22.4)	17.5 (12.3–24.4)	16.5 (12.2–22.0)	14.2 (12.1–16.7)	15.4 (12.4–18.9)	13.3 (11.3–15.7)
Peru, 2007 (Lima)	45.9 (40.6–51.2)	44.6 (37.2–52.2)	46.1 (41.0–51.3)	9.2 (6.2–13.4)	10.1 (5.7–17.3)	8.7 (5.2–14.2)	26.2 (22.2–30.7)	27.6 (22.7–33.1)	25.2 (20.7–30.3)
Puerto Rico, 2004[b]	24.0 (18.9–30.1)	23.1 (16.2–31.8)	24.9 (14.5–39.4)	NA	NA	NA	24.2 (19.3–29.9)	25.6 (19.6–32.5)	23.2 (17.7–30.0)
Saint Kitts & Nevis, 2002	17.3 (14.1–21.2)	24.7 (18.7–31.8)	11.5 (8.4–15.5)	39.3 (28.8–51.0)	36.5 (23.8–51.5)	37.8 (20.0–59.7)	15.6 (12.5–19.3)	19.2 (13.8–25.9)	12.8 (9.7–16.6)
Saint Lucia, 2007	33.5 (29.6–37.7)	44.6 (37.4–52.0)	25.5 (21.7–29.7)	24.9 (18.9–32.0)	22.9 (14.9–33.5)	26.7 (19.7–35.1)	16.8 (13.6–20.7)	17.1 (11.8–24.2)	16.1 (12.4–20.7)
Saint Vincent & the Grenadines, 2007	32.4 (27.7–37.4)	37.7 (30.4–45.6)	27.9 (23.1–33.3)	28.8 (22.6–36.0)	31.9 (23.7–41.4)	25.4 (18.4–33.8)	19.7 (16.8–23.0)	22.8 (17.9–28.6)	17.4 (14.2–21.2)
Suriname, 2004	37.4 (33.8–41.1)	47.8 (42.0–53.7)	27.8 (23.0–33.2)	27.5 (20.6–35.6)	26.0 (18.5–35.2)	30.3 (20.5–42.2)	18.7 (14.8–23.4)	18.8 (13.0–26.5)	18.7 (14.9–23.3)
Trinidad & Tobago, 2007	34.4 (28.9–40.4)	37.3 (30.4–44.6)	29.9 (23.5–37.1)	26.3 (22.4–30.5)	26.0 (21.1–31.4)	24.9 (18.4–32.8)	14.4 (11.6–17.7)	11.9 (8.5–16.3)	15.8 (11.9–20.6)

Table 3.1.63 Continued

WHO region and WHO member state, territory, or special administrative region, and year	% Ever smoked cigarettes (ever smokers)			% Ever smokers who first tried smoking at <10 years of age			% Never smokers susceptible to starting to smoke within the next year		
	Total % (95% CI)	Males % (95% CI)	Females % (95% CI)	Total % (95% CI)	Males % (95% CI)	Females % (95% CI)	Total % (95% CI)	Males % (95% CI)	Females % (95% CI)
U.S. Virgin Islands, 2004[b]	25.0 (22.0–28.1)	23.3 (19.8–27.2)	26.2 (22.1–30.9)	NA	NA	NA	19.3 (16.6–22.2)	22.2 (18.6–26.2)	16.2 (12.8–20.5)
Uruguay, 2007	48.9 (45.9–51.8)	45.0 (41.1–48.9)	51.9 (48.1–55.6)	8.8 (7.1–11.0)	12.0 (8.7–16.2)	6.7 (4.8–9.4)	25.8 (23.0–28.8)	17.8 (15.0–21.0)	33.0 (28.9–37.5)
Venezuela, 1999	21.9 (18.8–25.4)	24.1 (19.5–29.4)	20.3 (17.5–23.5)	12.1 (8.7–16.4)	13.2 (8.7–19.6)	11.2 (7.6–16.3)	12.5 (10.5–14.8)	10.9 (8.4–14.0)	13.6 (10.7–17.1)
Eastern Mediterranean	17.8 (16.9–18.7)	25.5 (24.4–26.5)	10.4 (9.7–11.1)	24.4 (23.3–25.6)	24.0 (22.8–25.2	22.9 (20.8–25.1)	15.3 (14.7–15.8)	16.6 (15.8–17.4)	14.4 (13.7–15.1)
Afghanistan, 2004 (Kabul)	22.7 (14.3–34.1)	27.4 (17.1–40.9)	15.5 (6.0–34.8)	23.3 (12.6–39.2)	20.7 (10.2–37.5)	37.6 (7.8–81.0)	8.8 (5.6–13.6)	9.0 (4.8–16.2)	8.9 (5.0–15.4)
Bahrain, 2002	23.9 (19.5–29.1)	34.2 (28.7–40.1)	13.7 (9.9–18.7)	20.4 (15.8–25.9)	22.0 (16.5–28.6)	15.3 (9.1–24.7)	23.1 (19.6–27.1)	26.0 (19.7–33.4)	20.9 (17.5–24.7)
Djibouti, 2003	12.5 (9.0–17.1)	16.7 (11.9–23.1)	6.8 (3.9–11.5)	20.1 (12.3–31.1)	17.6 (10.7–27.8)	28.8 (13.1–52.1)	19.7 (16.6–23.2)	22.3 (17.9–27.4)	16.7 (12.4–22.1)
Egypt, 2005	13.3 (9.8–17.9)	19.0 (14.6–24.5)	5.6 (4.2–7.3)	29.8 (24.6–35.5)	28.2 (23.1–33.9)	41.7 (31.6–52.5)	18.3 (15.7–21.3)	22.3 (18.7–26.5)	14.1 (10.9–18.0)
Gaza Strip, 2008[c]	14.2 (9.8–20.1)	20.9 (14.8–28.5)	6.8 (5.3–8.8)	35.0 (27.8–43.0)	32.9 (26.5–39.9)	NR	12.9 (9.3–17.7)	14.7 (10.2–20.8)	10.1 (6.8–14.8)
Iran, 2007	17.5 (12.8–23.4)	23.7 (16.1–33.5)	11.0 (7.2–16.3)	36.1 (27.1–46.1)	40.7 (32.7–49.3)	27.0 (15.1–43.5)	8.7 (7.0–10.6)	10.3 (7.9–13.4)	7.0 (4.9–9.9)
Iraq, 2008 (Baghdad)	7.4 (5.2–10.6)	7.4 (5.1–10.7)	6.8 (3.6–12.3)	23.3 (12.6–39.2)	23.8 (10.9–44.4)	21.8 (10.9–38.7)	13.0 (10.1–16.5)	13.7 (10.0–18.5)	11.8 (9.3–14.8)
Jordan, 2008[c]	32.6 (23.5–43.3)	43.9 (34.4–53.8)	20.0 (14.9–26.4)	18.5 (13.2–25.3)	16.2 (10.4–24.3)	19.5 (12.9–28.4)	18.3 (15.3–21.7)	19.4 (12.9–28.1)	16.8 (15.2–18.6)
Kuwait, 2005	25.9 (21.0–31.6)	36.7 (32.0–41.8)	16.3 (13.4–19.8)	21.5 (18.3–25.0)	18.6 (15.9–21.7)	24.1 (17.4–32.4)	17.3 (15.3–19.4)	19.5 (16.2–23.2)	15.9 (13.8–18.3)
Lebanon, 2008[c]	22.1 (15.8–29.9)	33.0 (26.8–39.9)	12.9 (8.7–18.8)	20.9 (13.4–31.0)	21.7 (12.9–34.2)	19.0 (11.0–30.7)	15.6 (12.6–19.2)	18.2 (13.6–24.0)	13.8 (10.2–18.5)
Libya, 2007	13.1 (9.7–17.4)	19.9 (14.4–26.8)	5.8 (3.5–9.4)	36.9 (25.6–49.7)	37.9 (23.8–54.5)	32.7 (13.1–61.1)	18.5 (15.2–22.3)	22.1 (18.0–26.9)	15.0 (11.5–19.3)
Morocco, 2006	9.5 (7.3–12.2)	13.6 (10.4–17.5)	4.6 (2.9–7.2)	27.3 (18.0–39.2)	27.3 (17.1–40.5)	28.5 (14.1–49.2)	NA	NA	NA

Table 3.1.63 Continued

WHO region and WHO member state, territory, or special administrative region, and year	% Ever smoked cigarettes (ever smokers)			% Ever smokers who first tried smoking at <10 years of age			% Never smokers susceptible to starting to smoke within the next year		
	Total % (95% CI)	Males % (95% CI)	Females % (95% CI)	Total % (95% CI)	Males % (95% CI)	Females % (95% CI)	Total % (95% CI)	Males % (95% CI)	Females % (95% CI)
Oman, 2007	10.0 (6.7–14.6)	14.5 (9.5–21.5)	5.7 (3.3–9.4)	32.5 (19.3–49.3)	28.8 (18.3–42.2)	41.5 (14.5–74.8)	12.5 (9.3–16.5)	14.2 (10.6–18.7)	10.7 (6.6–16.7)
Pakistan, 2003 (Islamabad)	7.1 (4.5–10.9)	10.8 (6.9–16.6)	3.8 (1.7–8.2)	35.9 (27.1–45.7)	35.6 (27.4–44.9)	32.1 (11.7–62.9)	9.2 (6.7–12.5)	13.3 (9.5–18.4)	5.9 (3.5–9.8)
Qatar, 2007	20.7 (17.2–24.7)	29.9 (24.3–36.2)	15.5 (11.5–20.6)	20.9 (14.8–28.8)	18.7 (11.6–28.9)	22.2 (14.5–32.5)	13.1 (10.4–16.4)	19.0 (12.5–27.8)	10.4 (7.8–13.9)
Saudi Arabia, 2007	26.1 (22.9–29.7)	35.8 (30.2–41.8)	16.1 (12.8–20.1)	21.6 (17.9–25.9)	24.3 (19.8–29.4)	16.5 (11.7–22.7)	19.2 (17.1–21.5)	19.9 (17.4–22.7)	17.3 (14.1–20.9)
Somalia, 2007 (Somaliland)	12.6 (9.5–16.6)	11.0 (8.3–14.4)	10.4 (5.1–20.0)	46.2 (20.1–74.5)	46.8 (17.0–79.1)	29.4 (6.2–72.3)NR	24.1 (17.8–31.8)	25.1 (18.1–33.8)	22.2 (15.4–30.8)
Sudan, 2005	19.3 (13.7–26.6)	26.5 (19.5–34.9)	12.6 (8.9–17.6)	37.3 (32.5–42.5)	32.6 (28.0–37.6)	49.3 (37.5–61.2)	13.9 (10.5–18.3)	14.4 (12.4–16.7)	13.2 (8.4–20.3)
Syrian Arab Republic, 2008[c]	29.6 (23.3–36.7)	39.5 (33.0–46.5)	18.5 (12.7–26.1)	17.1 (12.9–22.4)	18.4 (13.7–24.2)	15.1 (8.7–24.8)	20.7 (16.9–25.1)	21.7 (16.0–28.8)	19.7 (16.1–23.8)
Tunisia, 2007	24.6 (21.4–28.1)	39.8 (33.4–46.5)	9.5 (6.8–13.3)	24.3 (18.6–31.0)	25.2 (19.5–31.7)	16.8 (7.8–32.5)	19.9 (16.5–23.9)	26.7 (21.9–32.1)	15.5 (11.8–20.3)
United Arab Emirates, 2005	22.6 (20.1–25.3)	30.7 (27.9–33.7)	14.2 (12.2–16.6)	28.0 (25.4–30.8)	26.5 (23.5–29.6)	31.4 (25.8–37.6)	12.5 (11.4–13.7)	14.3 (13.1–15.7)	11.1 (9.6–12.8)
West Bank, 2008[c]	41.1 (30.2–53.0)	58.5 (52.9–63.9)	27.6 (22.5–33.5)	22.1 (16.7–28.7)	23.7 (18.8–29.4)	17.5 (12.4–24.1)	19.9 (14.8–26.0)	20.1 (12.0–31.8)	19.8 (14.3–26.6)
Yemen, 2008	14.0 (10.2–18.9)	15.3 (10.0–22.5)	9.6 (6.1–14.8)	28.8 (13.8–50.5)	NR	NR	24.1 (19.2–29.8)	22.1 (14.6–32.1)	27.4 (21.1–34.7)
Europe	39.7 (40.2.9)	50.2 (49. 5–50.8)	31.3 (30.7–31.9)	26.8 (26.2–27.4)	33.1 (32.3–33.8)	20.3 (19.5–21.0)	25.1 (24.8–25.4)	26.3 (25.8–26.8	44.5 (44.1–44.9)
Albania, 2004	31.3 (27.7–35.1)	40.6 (35.8–45.5)	23.9 (20.5–27.6)	25.3 (21.2–29.9)	28.5 (23.8–33.8)	20.9 (14.1–29.9)	14.0 (11.4–17.1)	15.5 (12.2–19.3)	13.1 (10.3–16.6)
Armenia, 2004	23.9 (20.0–28.4)	41.0 (34.0–48.3)	10.4 (7.6–14.1)	46.5 (40.7–52.4)	44.3 (37.7–51.1)	53.4 (36.1–70.0)	98.2 (96.2–99.1)	97.7 (93.6–99.2)	98.4 (97.1–99.1)
Belarus, 2004	62.5 (59.2–65.7)	70.2 (66.1–73.9)	54.8 (50.7–58.9)	30.3 (27.6–33.1)	38.0 (34.5–41.6)	20.4 (16.7–24.7)	48.9 (43.7–54.2)	43.4 (36.5–50.6)	52.6 (47.1–57.9)
Bosnia & Herzegovina, 2008	42.2 (39.1–45.3)	47.9 (44.4–51.3)	36.9 (33.4–40.5)	39.2 (35.9–42.6)	42.5 (39.1–46.0)	35.6 (31.1–40.4)	27.5 (25.0–30.0)	25.3 (22.4–28.5)	28.8 (26.2–31.6)

Table 3.1.63 Continued

WHO region and WHO member state, territory, or special administrative region, and year	% Ever smoked cigarettes (ever smokers)			% Ever smokers who first tried smoking at <10 years of age			% Never smokers susceptible to starting to smoke within the next year		
	Total % (95% CI)	Males % (95% CI)	Females % (95% CI)	Total % (95% CI)	Males % (95% CI)	Females % (95% CI)	Total % (95% CI)	Males % (95% CI)	Females % (95% CI)
Bulgaria, 2008	58.8 (53.3–64.1)	56.1 (49.8–62.2)	61.3 (54.5–67.7)	21.2 (19.4–23.2)	26.6 (23.9–29.4)	16.3 (14.2–18.7)	31.2 (28.8–33.7)	27.0 (24.3–29.9)	36.4 (31.2–42.0)
Croatia, 2007	67.1 (63.3–70.6)	66.3 (61.9–70.4)	67.4 (62.8–71.7)	31.1 (27.5–35.0)	35.2 (30.2–40.6)	26.9 (22.7–31.5)	19.7 (16.4–23.6)	15.3 (12.2–18.9)	24.7 (19.5–30.9)
Cyprus, 2005	30.6 (29.7–31.4)	35.5 (34.3–36.8)	25.7 (24.6–26.8)	17.6 (16.3–18.9)	20.4 (18.6–22.3)	13.6 (11.9–15.5)	15.3 (14.6–16.1)	15.0 (13.9–16.2)	15.5 (14.5–16.6)
Czech Republic, 2007	71.2 (66.9–75.1)	72.2 (67.4–76.4)	70.0 (65.4–74.3)	23.6 (20.4–27.0)	28.0 (24.8–31.5)	18.2 (14.3–22.8)	26.8 (23.0–31.0)	18.4 (14.3–23.4)	35.9 (30.1–42.2)
Estonia, 2007	78.0 (74.3–81.4)	83.0 (79.5–86.0)	73.0 (67.3–78.0)	37.3 (34.4–40.3)	45.6 (41.3–49.9)	27.9 (24.4–31.6)	30.8 (25.5–36.6)	25.3 (20.0–31.4)	34.3 (27.4–41.9)
Georgia, 2008	28.2 (18.9–39.9)	41.3 (28.0–55.9)	16.4 (10.2–25.4)	41.1 (29.1–54.3)	46.0 (32.7–59.9)	27.5 (13.4–48.1)	26.4 (18.0–36.8)	33.1 (22.6–45.7)	22.0 (13.9–33.1)
Greece, 2005	32.1 (29.4–35.0)	34.6 (30.8–38.7)	28.9 (26.4–31.5)	23.3 (20.2–26.6)	25.5 (21.8–29.5)	21.4 (17.1–26.5)	19.5 (17.5–21.7)	19.4 (17.1–22.0)	19.4 (17.0–22.1)
Hungary, 2008	57.9 (52.8–62.9)	56.5 (50.2–62.6)	58.4 (54.1–62.7)	18.0 (15.8–20.3)	19.7 (16.1–23.9)	15.7 (12.3–19.8)	18.5 (16.4–20.9)	16.2 (13.4–19.4)	21.0 (16.7–26.0)
Kazakhstan, 2004	28.5 (24.5–32.8)	36.6 (32.1–41.3)	21.8 (17.9–26.3)	34.8 (32.5–37.3)	41.1 (38.4–43.9)	25.3 (21.7–29.2)	36.5 (31.5–41.9)	33.8 (29.0–39.0)	38.6 (33.2–44.3)
Kosovo, 2004[d]	27.4 (22.9–32.4)	35.5 (29.6–41.8)	19.9 (15.2–25.5)	23.9 (18.6–30.2)	26.8 (20.5–34.2)	19.2 (12.8–27.8)	11.2 (8.1–15.2)	12.0 (8.6–16.6)	10.7 (7.2–15.5)
Kyrgyzstan, 2008	17.7 (15.3–20.4)	25.7 (20.9–31.1)	10.6 (8.0–13.9)	28.7 (23.7–34.2)	35.5 (28.3–43.5)	12.6 (7.1–21.4)	70.1 (64.6–75.0)	64.6 (57.0–71.6)	74.2 (68.0–79.5)
Latvia, 2007	80.6 (77.3–83.6)	82.8 (79.8–85.4)	78.8 (73.9–83.0)	32.4 (29.0–36.0)	39.6 (33.8–45.7)	26.0 (21.4–31.2)	22.3 (16.0–30.2)	25.8 (17.0–37.2)	20.0 (13.9–27.8)
Lithuania, 2005	72.3 (68.4–75.9)	80.0 (76.4–83.1)	65.6 (60.0–70.8)	32.8 (28.7–37.1)	41.5 (36.1–47.2)	23.5 (18.9–28.9)	18.2 (14.2–23.0)	18.3 (11.3–28.4)	18.1 (14.0–22.9)
Macedonia, former Yugoslav Republic of, 2008	26.0 (21.6–30.8)	27.7 (23.3–32.5)	24.2 (19.2–29.9)	16.3 (12.8–20.5)	19.7 (14.7–25.7)	12.6 (8.9–17.5)	16.7 (15.0–18.5)	15.4 (13.4–17.7)	17.9 (15.5–20.5)
Moldova, Republic of, 2008	39.2 (34.6–43.9)	57.7 (51.6–63.6)	24.3 (19.7–29.5)	49.2 (45.3–53.2)	54.1 (50.2–57.9)	40.5 (32.8–48.6)	18.7 (15.8–22.0)	19.7 (15.6–24.5)	18.1 (14.7–22.1)
Montenegro, 2008	31.3 (27.3–35.7)	30.7 (27.1–34.7)	31.9 (25.7–38.7)	39.6 (34.6–44.9)	40.6 (34.4–47.0)	38.8 (32.9–45.0)	16.0 (14.1–18.2)	15.7 (12.3–19.9)	16.5 (13.9–19.4)

Table 3.1.63 Continued

WHO region and WHO member state, territory, or special administrative region, and year	% Ever smoked cigarettes (ever smokers)			% Ever smokers who first tried smoking at <10 years of age			% Never smokers susceptible to starting to smoke within the next year		
	Total % (95% CI)	Males % (95% CI)	Females % (95% CI)	Total % (95% CI)	Males % (95% CI)	Females % (95% CI)	Total % (95% CI)	Males % (95% CI)	Females % (95% CI)
Poland, 2003	54.0 (49.7–58.2)	58.6 (53.8–63.2)	49.6 (44.1–55.0)	27.4 (23.5–31.8)	31.4 (26.9–36.4)	22.8 (18.3–28.1)	24.0 (20.6–27.6)	20.6 (16.5–25.4)	26.6 (22.2–31.5)
Romania, 2004	49.9 (44.3–55.4)	60.2 (54.7–65.5)	40.7 (33.9–47.8)	29.9 (26.2–33.8)	35.7 (31.0–40.7)	22.1 (17.3–27.9)	28.5 (19.4–39.7)	19.7 (12.9–28.9)	33.7 (22.6–46.9)
Russian Federation, 2004	55.0 (53.2–56.7)	61.5 (57.1–65.8)	48.1 (44.1–52.3)	30.9 (28.1–33.8)	40.7 (36.5–45.0)	17.8 (16.1–19.7)	46.8 (42.3–51.3)	42.3 (36.0–48.8)	50.3 (43.7–57.0)
Serbia, 2008	42.7 (37.8–47.7)	41.4 (35.6–47.4)	43.3 (38.5–48.2)	36.8 (32.4–41.4)	43.5 (36.3–50.9)	32.8 (26.9–39.3)	19.0 (16.8–21.4)	16.2 (12.8–20.3)	20.9 (18.1–24.0)
Slovakia, 2007	64.4 (61.5–67.2)	68.7 (65.4–71.9)	60.2 (56.4–63.8)	28.8 (26.4–31.2)	34.9 (31.5–38.5)	21.8 (19.1–24.8)	24.5 (21.4–27.9)	17.7 (14.6–21.4)	29.5 (24.8–34.6)
Slovenia, 2007	57.3 (52.1–62.4)	56.1 (48.0–64.0)	56.7 (51.5–61.8)	23.9 (20.1–28.2)	27.8 (22.8–33.4)	19.8 (14.8–26.0)	20.6 (17.1–24.6)	17.2 (12.0–24.0)	24.1 (20.7–27.9)
Tajikistan, 2004	7.1 (5.2–9.6)	9.8 (7.0–13.7)	3.6 (2.3–5.6)	45.2 (29.3–62.2)	44.9 (29.4–61.5)	39.0 (16.9–66.7)	77.6 (65.8–86.1)	75.8 (62.8–85.4)	79.8 (68.8–87.7)
Turkey, 2003	26.3 (24.3–28.4)	31.7 (29.0–34.5)	19.7 (17.6–22.0)	30.7 (28.0–33.4)	34.9 (32.4–37.4)	23.7 (19.5–28.5)	7.0 (6.5–7.5)	8.2 (7.3–9.2)	5.3 (4.6–6.1)
Ukraine, 2005	57.5 (54.6–60.3)	64.5 (60.9–68.0)	50.6 (47.1–54.2)	31.8 (28.4–35.5)	40.4 (35.7–45.2)	21.4 (17.9–25.4)	61.6 (56.5–66.4)	55.1 (47.9–62.1)	66.0 (60.1–71.5)
Uzbekistan, 2008 (Tashkent)	7.7 (4.6–12.5)	10.4 (5.6–18.5)	5.0 (2.5–9.7)	17.1 (7.4–34.5)	25.2 (11.5–46.8)	NR	45.1 (40.0–50.4)	46.0 (40.8–51.2)	45.9 (39.2–52.8)
South East Asia	15.6 (14.4 – 16.8)	19.2 (17.8 – 20.5)	8.1 (7.0 – 9,3)	23.3 (24.2 – 28.5)	22.0 (20.0 – 23.9)	28.8 (25.1 – 32.5)	16.8 (16.0 – 17.6)	12.0 (11.2 – 12.8)	23.7 (22.7 – 24.7)
Bangladesh, 2007	9.3 (6.2–13.6)	15.8 (10.6–23.0)	4.8 (2.4–9.3)	38.6 (25.4–53.6)	47.6 (34.6–60.9)	23.5 (5.0–64.0)	13.2 (10.7–16.2)	13.4 (9.8–17.9)	12.9 (9.3–17.7)
Bhutan, 2006 (country)	22.0 (18.3–26.2)	33.0 (26.0–40.8)	12.2 (9.3–15.7)	31.1 (21.6–42.5)	33.5 (24.4–44.0)	28.0 (12.2–52.2)	11.0 (8.4–14.1)	15.2 (11.1–20.6)	7.8 (4.9–12.2)
East Timor, 2006	41.5 (34.3–49.0)	59.9 (50.5–68.6)	26.0 (19.1–34.3)	20.1 (12.6–30.4)	16.7 (8.4–30.6)	25.6 (15.6–38.9)	48.8 (41.4–56.1)	51.3 (40.5–62.0)	47.2 (39.4–55.2)
India, 2006	12.0 (9.1–15.7)	14.4 (11.4–18.1)	8.7 (5.4–13.9)	36.9 (31.8–42.3)	32.1 (26.9–37.9)	55.1 (43.6–66.1)	15.1 (13.1–17.4)	16.4 (13.8–19.3)	13.5 (10.7–16.8)
Indonesia, 2006	37.7 (32.8–42.8)	62.9 (54.6–70.5)	15.6 (11.5–20.9)	30.0 (25.8–34.6)	27.1 (23.4–31.1)	41.1 (28.6–54.8)	95.1 (88.8–97.9)	93.9 (80.8–98.3)	95.5 (90.7–97.9)

Table 3.1.63 Continued

WHO region and WHO member state, territory, or special administrative region, and year	% Ever smoked cigarettes (ever smokers)			% Ever smokers who first tried smoking at <10 years of age			% Never smokers susceptible to starting to smoke within the next year		
	Total % (95% CI)	Males % (95% CI)	Females % (95% CI)	Total % (95% CI)	Males % (95% CI)	Females % (95% CI)	Total % (95% CI)	Males % (95% CI)	Females % (95% CI)
Maldives, 2007	16.0 (12.6–20.0)	8.1 (6.2–10.5)	24.5 (18.6–31.6)	30.5 (24.7–37.0)	31.3 (14.7–54.6)	29.0 (22.8–36.1)	6.7 (5.2–8.6)	3.8 (2.5–5.6)	10.6 (7.8–14.1)
Myanmar, 2007	14.7 (11.5–18.6)	23.4 (17.9–30.1)	6.3 (4.8–8.2)	19.0 (12.6–27.7)	14.0 (7.6–24.4)	47.1 (33.3–61.3)	11.4 (9.4–13.8)	15.9 (12.5–20.0)	8.1 (6.2–10.6)
Nepal, 2007	7.9 (5.9–10.4)	11.4 (8.6–15.1)	3.8 (2.2–6.4)	37.1 (27.5–47.9)	31.8 (21.9–43.8)	57.0 (40.4–72.1)	7.5 (5.7–9.8)	8.6 (5.4–13.3)	6.3 (4.2–9.2)
Sri Lanka, 2007	5.1 (2.9–9.0)	6.9 (3.5–12.9)	3.4 (1.6–7.4)	39.5 (21.6–60.8)	31.7 (16.1–52.7)NR	58.3 (25.2–85.3)	3.7 (2.4–5.6)	5.2 (3.1–8.7)	2.2 (1.2–4.3)
Thailand, 2005	26.7 (23.5–30.2)	37.9 (34.6–41.3)	15.1 (11.7–19.2)	16.9 (13.8–20.6)	15.7 (13.4–18.4)	15.6 (11.0–21.7)	10.0 (5.5–17.3)	8.7 (7.6–9.9)	10.0 (4.0–23.0)
Western Pacific	37.3 (36.7–37.9)	44.6 (43.8–45.4)	23.5 (22.9–24.1)	22.8 (22.0–23.6)	24.0 (22.9–25.1)	22.5 (21.2–23.8)	17.6 (17.4–17.8)	17.8 (17.5–18.0)	23.1 (22.8–3.3)
American Samoa, 2005[b]	40.7 (36.5–45.0)	44.7 (39.2–50.4)	37.0 (32.1–42.1)	NA	NA	NA	23.7 (19.6–28.3)	29.6 (23.7–36.1)	19.2 (14.7–24.6)
Cambodia, 2003	3.2 (1.7–6.0)	5.8 (3.2–10.4)	0.4 (0.1–1.9)	33.2 (11.9–64.7)NR	33.2 (11.9–64.7)NR	NA NR	7.1 (5.4–9.2)	10.3 (7.5–14.0)	3.9 (2.1–7.1)
China, 2005[e] (Macau)	31.2 (27.2–35.6)	33.8 (29.6–38.3)	28.3 (22.4–35.1)	35.6 (30.5–41.0)	40.8 (33.6–48.4)	28.2 (23.1–34.0)	15.1 (12.6–18.0)	14.0 (11.2–17.3)	16.3 (11.7–22.2)
China, 2005 (Shanghai)	17.5 (13.9–21.9)	23.1 (17.0–30.6)	12.4 (9.3–16.3)	43.8 (34.1–53.9)	43.4 (31.8–55.8)	44.5 (28.7–61.3)	4.9 (3.4–7.0)	7.0 (4.9–9.9)	3.2 (2.0–5.0)
Cook Islands, 2008	60.5 (59.3–61.7)	59.0 (57.2–60.7)	61.5 (59.9–63.1)	38.0 (36.5–39.6)	42.7 (40.4–45.0)	33.9 (31.8–36.0)	20.8 (19.3–22.4)	22.8 (20.5–25.3)	18.9 (16.9–21.1)
Fiji, 2005	17.3 (10.6–26.9)	22.4 (12.9–36.0)	11.7 (7.0–18.7)	14.2 (8.9–21.9)	17.5 (11.0–26.9)	9.2 (4.5–18.1)	16.9 (11.1–25.0)	16.9 (8.5–30.7)	17.0 (13.1–21.8)
Guam, 2002[b]	61.6 (58.1–65.0)	62.9 (58.7–66.9)	60.2 (55.2–64.9)	NA	NA	NA	26.8 (22.8–31.3)	26.9 (21.9–32.7)	26.6 (21.2–32.7)
Lao People's Democratic Republic, 2007 (Vientiane Capital)	6.9 (4.9–9.6)	11.9 (7.5–18.4)	2.6 (1.6–4.3)	12.7 (6.3–24.1)	12.8 (6.4–24.1)	NR	4.8 (3.7–6.1)	6.5 (4.6–9.2)	3.5 (2.2–5.5)
Malaysia, 2003	33.1 (29.1–37.3)	54.6 (48.5–60.5)	11.5 (9.3–14.1)	16.4 (12.7–20.9)	14.1 (10.6–18.5)	28.8 (20.2–39.3)	15.5 (13.0–18.2)	21.4 (17.2–26.3)	12.4 (10.0–15.2)
Micronesia, 2007	45.6 (41.4–49.8)	56.2 (49.7–62.6)	34.7 (29.9–39.7)	24.3 (21.0–28.0)	26.3 (21.8–31.3)	20.5 (14.9–27.5)	30.1 (26.3–34.3)	34.1 (25.9–43.5)	27.4 (23.9–31.3)

Table 3.1.63 Continued

WHO region and WHO member state, territory, or special administrative region, and year	% Ever smoked cigarettes (ever smokers)			% Ever smokers who first tried smoking at <10 years of age			% Never smokers susceptible to starting to smoke within the next year		
	Total % (95% CI)	Males % (95% CI)	Females % (95% CI)	Total % (95% CI)	Males % (95% CI)	Females % (95% CI)	Total % (95% CI)	Males % (95% CI)	Females % (95% CI)
Mongolia, 2007	23.4 (15.7–33.3)	35.2 (25.3–46.7)	13.3 (7.2–23.1)	15.6 (10.7–22.1)	18.3 (12.1–26.8)	9.1 (4.3–18.2)	8.1 (5.9–11.2)	8.8 (5.5–13.7)	7.8 (4.6–12.8)
New Zealand, 2008	39.7 (32.1–47.8)	40.0 (31.7–48.9)	39.4 (31.0–48.5)	27.0 (14.8–44.2)	31.2 (16.0–51.9)	22.5 (11.8–38.7)	26.5 (18.0–37.3)	21.4 (14.4–30.5)	31.8 (21.8–43.8)
Northern Mariana Islands, 2004[f]	70.1 (67.3–72.9)	68.2 (64.7–71.6)	72.0 (68.2–75.5)	NA	NA	NA	22.3 (18.3–27.0)	23.7 (18.2–30.3)	20.5 (15.7–26.5)
Palau, 2005	64.7 (61.3–68.0)	68.3 (63.4–72.9)	61.2 (56.5–65.8)	NA	NA	NA	20.0 (15.4–25.6)	22.4 (16.2–30.1)	18.3 (12.7–25.7)
Papua New Guinea, 2007	55.3 (50.7–59.9)	64.4 (59.7–68.8)	47.0 (40.6–53.5)	8.7 (6.6–11.5)	10.6 (7.0–15.8)	6.6 (4.2–10.3)	16.0 (12.2–20.8)	17.8 (12.1–25.5)	14.8 (10.4–20.8)
Philippines, 2007	39.5 (36.1–43.1)	51.2 (47.4–55.0)	29.9 (25.7–34.4)	13.6 (10.9–16.8)	11.7 (8.6–15.7)	15.4 (11.6–20.1)	12.9 (11.1–15.0)	15.0 (12.0–18.7)	11.6 (9.6–13.9)
Republic of Korea (South), 2008	26.1 (24.0–28.5)	31.3 (28.6–34.0)	20.3 (17.9–22.9)	14.5 (12.5–16.8)	15.5 (13.1–18.3)	12.9 (9.2–17.7)	20.1 (18.6–21.6)	20.3 (18.5–22.2)	19.8 (17.4–22.4)
Samoa, 2007	21.9 (16.6–28.3)	25.9 (17.4–36.6)	17.0 (12.1–23.2)	25.9 (16.9–37.4)	35.3 (22.6–50.3)	15.0 (6.4–31.2)	26.9 (22.3–32.0)	28.6 (21.8–36.5)	24.6 (18.5–31.9)
Singapore, 2000	21.5 (20.1–23.0)	23.9 (21.5–26.5)	18.8 (16.7–21.2)	22.7 (20.8–24.6)	24.1 (21.5–26.9)	21.0 (17.8–24.6)	8.9 (8.1–9.8)	9.2 (7.8–10.8)	8.6 (7.5–9.7)
Solomon Islands, 2008	41.2 (36.8–45.8)	42.8 (37.9–47.8)	39.1 (31.3–47.5)	12.8 (9.4–17.1)	9.3 (5.0–16.7)	16.1 (9.7–25.5)	25.6 (19.9–32.3)	24.6 (13.5–40.5)	27.1 (19.0–37.0)
Tuvalu, 2006	36.5 (36.3–36.7)	45.1 (44.8–45.5)	30.4 (30.1–30.7)	19.6 (19.3–19.9)	26.9 (26.4–27.4)	13.9 (13.5–14.3)	14.6 (14.4–14.8)	18.4 (18.0–18.7)	12.8 (12.6–13.1)
Vanuatu, 2007	27.1 (25.8–28.5)	39.3 (37.0–41.6)	18.6 (17.1–20.2)	15.2 (13.0–17.7)	16.0 (13.3–19.2)	13.9 (10.5–18.2)	38.7 (37.0–40.4)	42.7 (39.8–45.6)	36.4 (34.3–38.5)
Viet Nam, 2007 (Hanoi)	9.7 (6.9–13.5)	13.4 (9.7–18.1)	6.2 (3.5–10.6)	35.4 (22.9–50.3)	27.5 (17.6–40.2)	55.1 (28.3–79.3)	6.8 (5.4–8.6)	10.0 (7.5–13.2)	4.0 (2.6–6.2)

Source: CDC 2010b.
Note: **CI** = confidence interval; **NA** = question not asked; **NR** = cell size less than 35; **WHO** = World Health Organization.
[a]Territory of United Kingdom
[b]Territory of United States
[c]United Nations Relief and Works Agency
[d]United Nations Administered Province
[e]Special Administrative Region of China
[f]Commonwealth in political union with the United States

Table 3.1.64 Percentage of youth 13–15 years of age who have smoked cigarettes on 1 or more days during the past 30 days, and of those who have smoked cigarettes on 20 or more of the past 30 days, by gender; Global Youth Tobacco Survey 1999–2009; worldwide

	% Smoked cigarettes on ≥1 days of the past 30 days (current smokers)			% Smoked cigarettes on ≥20 days of the past 30 days		
WHO region and WHO member state, territory, or special administrative region, and year	**Total % (95% CI)**	**Males % (95% CI)**	**Females % (95% CI)**	**Total % (95% CI)**	**Males % (95% CI)**	**Females % (95% CI)**
Africa	4.0 (3.8–4.3)	6.2 (5.8–6.6)	2.7 (2.4–3.0)	0.6 (0.5–0.7)	0.9 (0.7–1.1)	0.4 (0.2–0.5)
Algeria, 2007 (Constantine)	8.3 (6.4–10.7)	18.3 (14.1–23.5)	1.5 (0.6–3.6)	1.5 (0.8–2.8)	2.9 (1.5–5.5)	0.5 (0.1–1.8)
Benin, 2003 (Atlantique Littoral)	7.2 (5.1–10.1)	11.2 (7.4–16.5)	1.8 (0.9–3.6)	0.3 (0.1–0.9)	0.5 (0.1–1.7)	0.0
Botswana, 2008	14.3 (11.2–18.1)	18.1 (13.4–23.9)	10.9 (7.8–15.0)	4.2 (2.7–6.5)	4.5 (2.8–6.9)	3.7 (2.1–6.5)
Burkina Faso, 2006 (Ouagadougou)	8.4 (6.3–11.1)	14.1 (10.4–18.7)	2.4 (1.3–4.3)	0.4 (0.2–0.9)	0.8 (0.3–2.0)	0.0
Burundi, 2008	4.6 (2.6–7.9)	5.8 (2.8–11.8)	3.2 (1.6–6.4)	0.5 (0.2–1.3)	0.3 (0.0–2.5)	0.5 (0.1–1.8)
Cameroon, 2008 (Yaoude)	4.8 (3.4–6.8)	7.6 (5.5–10.5)	2.8 (1.5–5.2)	0.6 (0.3–1.1)	0.9 (0.4–1.7)	0.5 (0.1–2.0)
Cape Verde, 2007	3.5 (2.6–4.8)	3.7 (2.2–6.1)	3.1 (1.8–5.4)	0.3 (0.1–0.8)	0.4 (0.1–1.7)	0.0
Central African Republic, 2008 (Bangui)	8.1 (5.9–11.0)	10.4 (6.7–15.7)	4.3 (2.2–8.3)	0.1 (0.0–1.0)	0.0	0.3 (0.0–2.1)
Comoros, 2007	9.6 (6.8–13.4)	13.5 (8.3–21.3)	6.9 (3.7–12.6)	0.6 (0.2–2.0)	1.0 (0.2–4.4)	0.4 (0.1–1.9)
Congo, 2006	11.4 (7.7–16.6)	15.0 (9.8–22.2)	8.1 (4.3–14.7)	0.0 (0.0–0.3)	0.1 (0.0–0.7)	0.0
Côte D'Ivoire, 2003 (Abidjan)	13.6 (11.4–16.2)	19.3 (16.1–23.0)	7.1 (5.1–9.9)	0.8 (0.5–1.2)	1.3 (0.8–2.2)	0.2 (0.0–1.0)
Democratic Republic of the Congo, 2008 (Kinshasa)	8.1 (6.0–10.9)	11.5 (8.1–16.1)	3.7 (2.8–4.7)	0.6 (0.3–1.2)	0.7 (0.4–1.3)	0.2 (0.0–1.5)
Equatorial Guinea, 2008	7.0 (4.8–10.1)	9.9 (6.2–15.4)	3.4 (2.0–5.5)	0.1 (0.0–0.8)	0.2 (0.0–1.6)	0.0
Eritrea, 2006	1.6 (1.2–2.0)	2.0 (1.5–2.7)	0.6 (0.2–1.4)	0.3 (0.2–0.5)	0.3 (0.1–0.7)	0.1 (0.0–0.5)
Ethiopia, 2003 (Addis Ababa)	1.9 (0.8–4.3)	2.5 (1.1–5.3)	0.7 (0.2–2.4)	0.4 (0.2–0.9)	0.3 (0.0–2.2)	0.2 (0.0–1.8)

Table 3.1.64 Continued

WHO region and WHO member state, territory, or special administrative region, and year	% Smoked cigarettes on ≥1 days of the past 30 days (current smokers)			% Smoked cigarettes on ≥20 days of the past 30 days		
	Total % (95% CI)	Males % (95% CI)	Females % (95% CI)	Total % (95% CI)	Males % (95% CI)	Females % (95% CI)
Gambia, 2008 (Banjul)	10.8 (8.5–13.6)	12.7 (9.6–16.5)	8.6 (5.8–12.6)	2.8 (1.8–4.3)	3.3 (2.2–5.0)	2.3 (1.1–4.8)
Ghana, 2006	2.7 (1.9–4.0)	2.8 (1.7–4.7)	2.3 (1.4–3.5)	0.9 (0.5–1.4)	0.8 (0.4–1.6)	0.8 (0.5–1.4)
Guinea, 2008	7.1 (4.8–10.4)	11.6 (7.9–16.7)	1.6 (0.7–3.7)	0.8 (0.4–1.6)	1.2 (0.5–3.0)	0.2 (0.0–1.3)
Guinea-Bissau, 2008 (Bissau)	5.1 (4.1–6.3)	7.2 (5.5–9.5)	3.0 (1.7–5.1)	0.0	0.0	0.0
Kenya, 2007	8.2 (6.1–11.1)	11.2 (8.9–14.0)	5.2 (3.5–7.6)	1.2 (0.6–2.0)	0.7 (0.4–1.5)	1.3 (0.6–2.5)
Lesotho, 2008	10.1 (6.9–14.4)	11.8 (7.0–19.3)	7.5 (4.9–11.2)	3.3 (1.8–5.8)	3.8 (1.6–8.6)	2.2 (1.4–3.4)
Liberia, 2008 (Monrovia)	2.1 (1.1–4.1)	2.0 (0.7–5.5)	1.2 (0.3–4.3)	0.1 (0.0–1.3)	0.3 (0.0–2.9)	0.0
Madagascar, 2008	19.3 (15.0–24.6)	30.7 (23.0–39.7)	10.2 (5.9–17.0)	1.7 (0.4–6.5)	3.9 (1.0–13.9)	0.0
Malawi, 2005	2.9 (1.8–4.7)	3.8 (2.2–6.4)	2.2 (1.3–3.6)	0.3 (0.1–1.1)	0.7 (0.2–2.3)	0.0 (0.0–0.2)
Mali, 2008	10.4 (7.3–14.6)	17.4 (12.2–24.3)	2.5 (1.4–4.5)	1.0 (0.6–1.6)	1.4 (0.8–2.4)	0.4 (0.1–1.9)
Mauritania, 2006	19.5 (16.3–23.2)	20.3 (17.5–23.4)	18.3 (13.4–24.5)	3.0 (2.1–4.4)	3.5 (2.5–4.8)	2.5 (1.3–4.7)
Mauritius, 2008	13.7 (9.3–19.8)	20.3 (13.9–28.6)	7.7 (4.1–14.0)	3.1 (1.7–5.6)	5.6 (3.0–10.1)	0.7 (0.4–1.5)
Mozambique, 2007 (Maputo City)	2.7 (1.6–4.7)	4.5 (2.6–7.9)	1.2 (0.4–3.5)	0.1 (0.0–0.7)	0.2 (0.0–1.4)	0.0
Namibia, 2004	18.8 (16.5–21.4)	21.9 (18.9–25.2)	16.1 (13.3–19.3)	5.3 (4.2–6.7)	6.2 (4.4–8.6)	4.3 (3.3–5.7)
Niger, 2006	6.3 (4.2–9.2)	11.7 (7.6–17.4)	1.1 (0.3–3.9)	0.4 (0.2–1.2)	0.7 (0.2–2.3)	0.2 (0.0–1.6)
Nigeria, 2008 (Cross River State)	4.1 (1.4–11.1)	6.8 (2.4–17.7)	1.2 (0.2–6.4)	0.6 (0.1–2.9)	0.7 (0.1–5.9)	0.6 (0.1–5.7)

Table 3.1.64 Continued

WHO region and WHO member state, territory, or special administrative region, and year	% Smoked cigarettes on ≥1 days of the past 30 days (current smokers)			% Smoked cigarettes on ≥20 days of the past 30 days		
	Total % (95% CI)	Males % (95% CI)	Females % (95% CI)	Total % (95% CI)	Males % (95% CI)	Females % (95% CI)
Rwanda, 2008	1.8 (1.0–3.4)	3.0 (1.7–5.2)	0.9 (0.2–3.0)	0.2 (0.0–1.3)	0.0	0.3 (0.0–2.5)
Senegal, 2007	7.5 (4.6–12.1)	12.1 (7.6–18.9)	2.7 (1.3–5.4)	1.5 (0.5–4.1)	1.9 (0.7–5.0)	0.0
Seychelles, 2007	21.5 (16.7–27.2)	23.2 (17.4–30.2)	20.0 (15.0–26.2)	0.5 (0.2–1.6)	0.4 (0.1–2.6)	0.6 (0.1–2.6)
Sierra Leone, 2008 (Western Area)	5.8 (3.7–9.1)	6.6 (3.8–11.3)	5.0 (3.0–8.0)	1.8 (0.8–4.0)	1.8 (0.8–4.1)	1.3 (0.4–4.1)
South Africa, 2008	13.6 (11.6–16.0)	17.9 (15.2–21.0)	10.6 (8.0–13.8)	3.0 (2.1–4.1)	4.2 (3.0–6.0)	2.0 (1.4–3.0)
Swaziland, 2005	5.6 (4.9–6.4)	8.9 (7.8–10.2)	3.2 (2.5–4.2)	0.8 (0.6–1.0)	1.2 (0.8–1.6)	0.4 (0.3–0.6)
Togo, 2007	6.2 (3.6–10.2)	9.1 (5.1–15.6)	1.7 (1.1–2.6)	0.4 (0.1–1.6)	0.5 (0.2–1.9)	0.0
Uganda, 2007	5.5 (4.2–7.1)	6.6 (5.2–8.5)	4.0 (2.7–5.8)	1.0 (0.5–1.8)	1.1 (0.4–2.5)	0.6 (0.2–1.8)
United Republic of Tanzania, 2008 (Arusha)	1.7 (0.9–3.5)	2.2 (0.9–5.5)	1.1 (0.3–3.6)	0.0	0.0	0.0
Zambia, 2007 (Lusaka)	6.8 (4.3–10.5)	6.7 (4.0–11.1)	6.8 (4.0–11.3)	2.1 (0.9–4.6)	1.7 (0.5–5.7)	2.3 (1.0–5.4)
Zimbabwe, 2008 (Harare)	3.2 (1.7–5.7)	4.8 (2.6–9.0)	1.5 (0.5–4.6)	0.1 (0.0–1.3)	0.3 (0.0–2.7)	0.0
The Americas	9.3 (8.9–9.7)	10.1 (9.5–10.7)	8.8 (8.3–9.3)	0.7 (0.6–0.8)	1.0 (0.8–1.2)	0.3 (0.2–0.3)
Antigua & Barbuda, 2004	3.6 (2.4–5.4)	2.7 (1.7–4.3)	4.4 (2.3–8.2)	0.1 (0.0–0.7)	0.2 (0.0–1.5)	0.0
Argentina, 2007	24.5 (22.2–27.0)	21.1 (18.5–23.8)	27.3 (23.4–31.6)	5.6 (4.2–7.4)	4.9 (3.8–6.4)	6.0 (3.7–9.5)
Bahamas, 2004	5.2 (4.0–6.7)	6.2 (3.8–10.1)	3.7 (2.1–6.6)	0.5 (0.2–1.4)	0.4 (0.1–1.9)	0.3 (0.1–1.5)
Barbados, 2007	11.6 (8.9–15.0)	14.3 (10.4–19.3)	9.3 (6.4–13.2)	0.3 (0.1–1.0)	0.4 (0.1–1.5)	0.2 (0.0–1.2)

Table 3.1.64 Continued

WHO region and WHO member state, territory, or special administrative region, and year	% Smoked cigarettes on ≥1 days of the past 30 days (current smokers)			% Smoked cigarettes on ≥20 days of the past 30 days		
	Total % (95% CI)	Males % (95% CI)	Females % (95% CI)	Total % (95% CI)	Males % (95% CI)	Females % (95% CI)
Belize, 2008	7.7 (5.7–10.4)	11.7 (8.3–16.2)	4.4 (2.6–7.5)	0.4 (0.1–1.1)	0.8 (0.3–2.4)	0.0
Bolivia, 2003 (La Paz)	16.3 (13.4–19.6)	20.3 (16.5–24.7)	12.0 (9.3–15.3)	0.9 (0.6–1.5)	1.3 (0.7–2.6)	0.5 (0.2–1.2)
Brazil, 2005 (Rio de Janeiro)	12.3 (10.0–15.1)	9.1 (6.5–12.5)	12.9 (9.6–17.1)	1.0 (0.5–2.2)	0.5 (0.2–1.3)	1.1 (0.5–2.4)
British Virgin Islands, 2001[a]	3.5 (2.0–5.9)	4.1 (1.7–9.2)	2.8 (1.1–6.7)	0.3 (0.0–1.9)	0.0	0.4 (0.1–3.0)
Chile, 2008 (Santiago)	34.2 (31.3–37.3)	28.0 (24.3–32.0)	39.9 (36.0–43.9)	7.6 (6.0–9.6)	6.4 (4.8–8.4)	8.9 (6.8–11.7)
Colombia, 2007 (Bogota)	26.2 (22.5–30.3)	25.4 (21.0–30.3)	26.6 (20.9–33.1)	2.1 (1.4–3.2)	2.9 (1.7–4.8)	1.3 (0.6–3.0)
Costa Rica, 2008	9.6 (7.9–11.7)	9.4 (7.2–12.0)	9.7 (7.8–12.1)	1.0 (0.7–1.6)	1.1 (0.6–1.8)	1.0 (0.6–1.5)
Cuba, 2004 (Havana)	10.0 (7.6–13.1)	11.2 (8.3–15.1)	8.8 (6.5–11.9)	1.1 (0.7–1.8)	1.3 (0.6–2.8)	0.8 (0.5–1.4)
Dominica, 2004	11.5 (9.0–14.7)	11.8 (8.1–16.9)	9.6 (7.0–13.0)	1.1 (0.6–2.0)	1.3 (0.5–2.9)	0.7 (0.3–1.9)
Dominican Republic, 2004	6.6 (5.4–7.9)	7.3 (5.9–9.0)	5.8 (4.0–8.2)	0.4 (0.2–0.8)	0.4 (0.1–1.2)	0.4 (0.2–1.0)
Ecuador, 2007 (Quito)	20.5 (15.6–26.6)	23.2 (19.4–27.6)	18.1 (11.1–28.0)	0.9 (0.4–1.9)	0.9 (0.4–2.3)	0.8 (0.2–2.9)
El Salvador, 2003	14.0 (9.7–19.7)	18.4 (13.4–24.8)	10.9 (6.8–17.1)	2.0 (1.0–3.8)	4.1 (2.2–7.6)	0.5 (0.1–2.6)
Grenada, 2004	10.2 (8.2–12.8)	10.9 (7.4–15.8)	9.5 (7.4–12.2)	0.5 (0.2–1.2)	0.4 (0.1–1.6)	0.6 (0.2–1.8)
Guatemala, 2008	11.4 (9.5–13.6)	13.7 (10.9–17.0)	9.1 (7.0–11.6)	1.0 (0.7–1.3)	1.1 (0.7–1.7)	0.9 (0.5–1.5)
Guyana, 2004	8.1 (5.3–12.3)	11.0 (7.4–16.0)	5.4 (3.1–9.3)	0.6 (0.2–1.9)	0.3 (0.0–2.1)	0.8 (0.2–3.5)
Haiti, 2005 (Port au Prince)	17.6 (13.6–22.6)	17.2 (12.4–23.5)	17.7 (13.3–23.0)	1.9 (0.8–4.3)	2.9 (1.1–7.6)	0.8 (0.2–3.1)

Table 3.1.64 Continued

WHO region and WHO member state, territory, or special administrative region, and year	% Smoked cigarettes on ≥1 days of the past 30 days (current smokers)			% Smoked cigarettes on ≥20 days of the past 30 days		
	Total % (95% CI)	Males % (95% CI)	Females % (95% CI)	Total % (95% CI)	Males % (95% CI)	Females % (95% CI)
Honduras, 2003 (Tegucigalpa)	14.2 (10.6–18.8)	14.4 (10.9–18.8)	14.1 (9.8–19.9)	1.8 (0.9–3.6)	2.3 (1.1–4.7)	1.5 (0.6–3.6)
Jamaica, 2006	15.4 (10.2–22.6)	20.6 (14.1–29.3)	10.9 (6.5–17.7)	1.2 (0.8–1.9)	1.7 (1.0–3.1)	0.7 (0.3–1.7)
Mexico, 2006 (Mexico City)	27.1 (23.8–30.8)	26.3 (22.0–31.0)	27.1 (23.7–30.8)	2.3 (1.5–3.4)	2.8 (1.5–4.9)	1.5 (0.7–3.0)
Montserrat, 2000[a]	5.6	3.5	6.3	0.0	0.0	0.0
Nicaragua, 2003 (Centro Managua)	21.2 (17.2–25.8)	25.6 (21.4–30.3)	17.4 (12.6–23.6)	1.6 (0.9–2.8)	2.7 (1.2–6.1)	0.6 (0.2–2.0)
Panama, 2008	4.3 (3.0–6.2)	5.9 (4.0–8.5)	2.8 (1.7–4.6)	0.4 (0.2–0.9)	0.6 (0.2–1.5)	0.3 (0.1–1.0)
Paraguay, 2008	8.3 (6.9–9.9)	11.3 (9.3–13.6)	5.5 (3.7–8.2)	0.4 (0.2–0.7)	0.7 (0.3–1.5)	0.1 (0.1–0.2)
Peru, 2007 (Lima)	16.5 (13.0–20.7)	16.7 (12.8–21.6)	15.2 (11.0–20.7)	1.9 (1.0–3.6)	1.5 (0.7–3.3)	2.3 (1.1–4.7)
Puerto Rico, 2004[b]	7.3 (4.2–12.4)	5.7 (2.8–11.2)	9.0 (4.9–16.0)	1.0 (0.3–3.4)	1.7 (0.6–4.3)	0.4 (0.0–4.4)
Saint Kitts & Nevis, 2002	4.6 (3.0–7.0)	7.0 (4.2–11.3)	1.9 (0.9–4.1)	1.0 (0.5–2.2)	1.4 (0.5–3.9)	0.3 (0.1–1.2)
Saint Lucia, 2007	12.7 (10.4–15.3)	17.0 (12.2–23.1)	9.6 (7.4–12.4)	0.8 (0.3–1.7)	1.2 (0.5–3.2)	0.4 (0.1–1.9)
Saint Vincent & The Grenadines, 2007	12.0 (9.0–15.9)	14.8 (9.8–21.7)	9.5 (6.6–13.4)	0.6 (0.3–1.1)	1.3 (0.7–2.4)	0.0
Suriname, 2004	6.9 (5.2–9.1)	9.3 (6.3–13.5)	4.7 (2.7–8.2)	0.5 (0.2–1.6)	0.8 (0.2–2.9)	0.3 (0.0–2.2)
Trinidad & Tobago, 2007	12.9 (9.9–16.7)	14.7 (10.9–19.6)	10.3 (6.9–15.1)	1.2 (0.6–2.3)	1.3 (0.6–2.6)	0.8 (0.3–2.8)
U.S. Virgin Islands, 2004[b]	3.4 (2.5–4.6)	3.1 (2.0–4.7)	3.5 (2.4–5.2)	0.1 (0.0–0.5)	0.1 (0.0–1.0)	0.1 (0.0–1.0)
Uruguay, 2007	20.2 (18.0–22.6)	16.4 (13.5–19.8)	22.9 (20.1–26.0)	5.4 (3.9–7.4)	4.3 (2.7–6.8)	6.2 (4.3–8.9)

Table 3.1.64 Continued

WHO region and WHO member state, territory, or special administrative region, and year	% Smoked cigarettes on ≥1 days of the past 30 days (current smokers)			% Smoked cigarettes on ≥20 days of the past 30 days		
	Total % (95% CI)	Males % (95% CI)	Females % (95% CI)	Total % (95% CI)	Males % (95% CI)	Females % (95% CI)
Venezuela, 1999	7.4 (5.8–9.3)	6.0 (4.3–8.4)	8.4 (6.6–10.7)	0.5 (0.3–0.8)	0.1 (0.0–1.1)	0.8 (0.5–1.3)
Eastern Mediterranean	5.6 (5.1 – 6.0)	8.9 (8.2 – 9.5)	2.5 (2.2 – 2.9)	0.6 (0.5 – 0.7)	1.2 (0.9 – 1.4)	0.3 (0.1 – 0.4)
Afghanistan, 2004 (Kabul)	4.8 (2.7–8.6)	7.6 (4.5–12.7)	0.0	0.0	0.0	0.0
Bahrain, 2002	10.6 (8.3–13.4)	17.5 (14.5–20.8)	3.9 (2.2–6.7)	2.2 (1.3–3.5)	3.3 (2.0–5.5)	0.9 (0.3–2.4)
Djibouti, 2003	6.1 (4.0–9.0)	8.6 (5.3–13.6)	2.6 (1.3–5.4)	1.9 (1.0–3.6)	2.9 (1.5–5.7)	0.7 (0.1–3.1)
Egypt, 2005	4.0 (2.7–5.8)	5.9 (4.4–7.9)	1.4 (0.9–2.3)	0.2 (0.1–0.5)	0.4 (0.2–0.9)	0.0
Gaza Strip, 2008[c]	5.7 (4.1–7.8)	8.0 (5.9–10.9)	2.8 (1.6–4.9)	0.8 (0.3–2.5)	1.1 (0.3–4.0)	0.1 (0.0–1.0)
Iran, 2007	3.0 (1.7–5.5)	5.1 (2.8–9.1)	0.9 (0.4–1.9)	0.6 (0.2–1.3)	1.1 (0.5–2.6)	0.0
Iraq, 2008 (Baghdad)	3.2 (2.1–4.8)	3.3 (1.9–5.7)	2.7 (1.5–4.8)	0.3 (0.1–1.0)	0.4 (0.1–1.6)	0.1 (0.0–0.6)
Jordan, 2008[c]	12.7 (7.6–20.4)	18.9 (12.1–28.2)	5.8 (3.7–9.0)	2.5 (0.9–6.9)	3.9 (1.6–9.5)	0.9 (0.3–3.0)
Kuwait, 2005	10.8 (7.7–15.1)	17.7 (14.2–21.7)	4.5 (3.0–6.9)	2.2 (1.3–3.9)	3.6 (2.4–5.4)	0.8 (0.4–1.6)
Lebanon, 2008[c]	10.6 (7.0–15.6)	16.6 (11.1–24.0)	5.5 (3.3–9.0)	1.2 (0.6–2.2)	2.2 (1.2–4.1)	0.2 (0.0–2.0)
Libya, 2007	4.6 (2.9–7.2)	7.7 (4.9–11.9)	0.9 (0.3–2.5)	0.4 (0.1–1.1)	0.5 (0.1–2.2)	0.1 (0.0–1.0)
Morocco, 2006	3.5 (2.7–4.6)	4.3 (2.9–6.4)	2.1 (1.1–3.9)	0.3 (0.1–0.9)	0.5 (0.2–1.6)	0.0
Oman, 2007	2.3 (1.1–4.8)	3.5 (1.8–6.6)	1.2 (0.3–4.1)	0.3 (0.0–2.5)	0.4 (0.0–2.8)	0.2 (0.0–2.3)
Pakistan, 2003 (Islamabad)	1.4 (0.6–3.3)	2.3 (0.9–5.4)	0.6 (0.2–1.9)	0.2 (0.1–0.7)	0.3 (0.1–1.5)	0.0

Table 3.1.64 Continued

WHO region and WHO member state, territory, or special administrative region, and year	% Smoked cigarettes on ≥1 days of the past 30 days (current smokers)			% Smoked cigarettes on ≥20 days of the past 30 days		
	Total % (95% CI)	Males % (95% CI)	Females % (95% CI)	Total % (95% CI)	Males % (95% CI)	Females % (95% CI)
Qatar, 2007	6.5 (4.7–8.9)	13.4 (9.5–18.7)	2.3 (1.0–5.1)	0.7 (0.3–1.8)	1.6 (0.5–4.5)	0.2 (0.0–1.8)
Saudi Arabia, 2007	6.7 (5.2–8.7)	10.2 (7.9–13.2)	2.6 (1.3–5.4)	1.4 (0.9–2.2)	2.2 (1.4–3.6)	0.2 (0.1–0.7)
Somalia, 2007 (Somaliland)	5.8 (4.0–8.4)	4.9 (3.2–7.4)	4.5 (1.6–11.8)	1.4 (0.4–5.1)	0.7 (0.1–5.6)	2.5 (0.5–10.9)
Sudan, 2005	6.0 (3.6–10.0)	10.2 (6.6–15.5)	2.1 (1.4–3.2)	0.5 (0.2–1.3)	0.2 (0.0–0.8)	0.7 (0.2–2.5)
Syrian Arab Republic, 2008[c]	13.3 (9.6–18.0)	19.6 (15.7–24.2)	6.3 (4.1–9.6)	1.4 (0.7–2.6)	2.3 (1.3–3.9)	0.3 (0.1–1.7)
Tunisia, 2007	8.3 (6.6–10.4)	15.1 (12.3–18.4)	1.6 (0.8–3.1)	1.0 (0.5–2.3)	2.1 (1.0–4.5)	0.0
United Arab Emirates, 2005	8.0 (6.6–9.7)	12.1 (10.3–14.1)	3.6 (2.9–4.4)	1.3 (1.0–1.8)	2.0 (1.6–2.5)	0.3 (0.2–0.6)
West Bank, 2008[c]	21.7 (15.1–30.2)	32.8 (27.0–39.1)	12.3 (9.1–16.4)	3.9 (1.8–8.1)	6.6 (4.3–10.0)	0.7 (0.2–2.8)
Yemen, 2008	3.9 (2.5–6.2)	4.2 (2.3–7.5)	1.6 (0.8–3.1)	0.5 (0.3–0.8)	0.4 (0.1–2.7)	0.4 (0.1–2.8)
Europe	8.4 (8.1 – 8.7)	11.0 (10.5 – 11.4)	4.2 (4.0 – 4.5)	1.9 (1.8 – 2.1)	2.6 (2.4 – 2.8)	1.4 (1.3 – 1.6)
Albania, 2004	8.5 (6.8–10.5)	11.9 (9.0–15.5)	5.8 (4.5–7.5)	0.6 (0.3–1.0)	1.1 (0.6–2.1)	0.2 (0.0–0.9)
Armenia, 2004	5.0 (3.9–6.6)	10.3 (7.7–13.5)	0.9 (0.4–2.2)	1.4 (0.7–2.9)	3.3 (1.6–6.6)	0.0
Belarus, 2004	26.5 (24.0–29.1)	31.2 (27.7–35.0)	21.7 (19.0–24.8)	8.3 (6.9–10.0)	10.8 (8.4–13.6)	5.9 (4.8–7.3)
Bosnia and Herzegovina, 2008	11.7 (9.9–13.9)	14.3 (12.3–16.6)	9.4 (7.3–12.0)	3.2 (2.3–4.5)	4.4 (3.2–6.0)	2.2 (1.4–3.4)
Bulgaria, 2008	28.2 (24.1–32.7)	24.4 (20.2–29.2)	31.6 (25.9–37.9)	14.3 (12.0–17.0)	11.7 (9.6–14.2)	16.8 (13.3–21.0)
Croatia, 2007	24.1 (19.9–28.7)	21.7 (17.9–26.0)	25.6 (20.6–31.2)	8.9 (7.0–11.4)	7.8 (6.1–10.0)	9.2 (6.5–12.9)

Table 3.1.64 Continued

WHO region and WHO member state, territory, or special administrative region, and year	% Smoked cigarettes on ≥1 days of the past 30 days (current smokers)			% Smoked cigarettes on ≥20 days of the past 30 days		
	Total % (95% CI)	Males % (95% CI)	Females % (95% CI)	Total % (95% CI)	Males % (95% CI)	Females % (95% CI)
Cyprus, 2005	10.3 (9.7–10.8)	12.3 (11.5–13.2)	8.2 (7.5–8.9)	3.8 (3.5–4.1)	5.2 (4.7–5.8)	2.3 (1.9–2.7)
Czech Republic, 2007	31.1 (27.2–35.3)	29.8 (25.1–35.0)	32.7 (27.6–38.1)	9.0 (6.8–11.9)	7.9 (5.3–11.5)	10.4 (7.4–14.5)
Estonia, 2007	27.2 (23.5–31.2)	28.2 (23.5–33.3)	26.2 (21.6–31.4)	10.4 (8.6–12.4)	11.6 (8.8–15.0)	9.2 (6.8–12.3)
Georgia, 2008	8.6 (5.5–13.2)	15.2 (9.9–22.8)	2.8 (1.0–7.8)	1.5 (0.8–2.9)	3.0 (1.7–5.2)	0.3 (0.0–2.1)
Greece, 2005	10.4 (8.8–12.4)	11.3 (9.4–13.6)	9.0 (7.2–11.3)	3.1 (2.3–4.2)	3.3 (2.3–4.6)	2.5 (1.7–3.6)
Hungary, 2008	23.2 (19.2–27.7)	21.5 (16.6–27.4)	23.6 (19.4–28.3)	8.6 (6.3–11.7)	8.5 (6.1–11.6)	7.7 (5.5–10.9)
Kazakhstan, 2004	9.4 (7.7–11.4)	12.7 (10.5–15.3)	6.6 (5.1–8.5)	2.6 (1.8–3.8)	3.5 (2.4–5.1)	1.9 (1.2–2.9)
Kosovo, 2004[d]	6.5 (5.3–8.0)	7.7 (5.6–10.4)	5.4 (4.1–7.2)	1.1 (0.6–1.9)	1.0 (0.6–1.7)	1.2 (0.5–2.5)
Kyrgyzstan, 2008	4.4 (3.3–5.7)	6.8 (5.0–9.4)	2.2 (1.4–3.6)	0.6 (0.4–1.1)	0.8 (0.4–1.7)	0.5 (0.2–1.1)
Latvia, 2007	32.9 (27.2–39.0)	36.3 (30.9–42.1)	30.2 (24.1–37.0)	13.8 (10.1–18.5)	16.6 (13.0–20.9)	11.5 (7.5–17.2)
Lithuania, 2005	29.6 (26.5–32.8)	33.8 (29.4–38.6)	25.9 (21.2–31.2)	10.4 (8.3–13.0)	13.9 (10.7–17.9)	7.5 (5.0–11.1)
Macedonia, former Yugoslav Republic of, 2008	9.8 (7.4–12.7)	9.7 (7.3–12.9)	9.8 (7.2–13.1)	3.7 (2.6–5.2)	4.0 (2.7–6.1)	3.4 (2.4–4.8)
Moldova, Republic of, 2008	11.3 (9.3–13.7)	18.5 (15.0–22.6)	5.6 (4.3–7.2)	3.1 (2.3–4.1)	5.6 (4.0–7.8)	0.9 (0.6–1.4)
Montenegro, 2008	5.1 (4.0–6.4)	5.7 (4.3–7.6)	4.4 (3.1–6.1)	1.0 (0.6–1.6)	1.3 (0.7–2.2)	0.7 (0.2–2.1)
Poland, 2003	18.6 (15.7–22.0)	19.6 (15.1–25.1)	17.1 (14.1–20.5)	6.8 (5.2–8.7)	8.5 (6.2–11.7)	5.3 (3.9–7.2)
Romania, 2004	17.6 (14.0–21.9)	21.5 (16.1–28.0)	14.3 (11.4–17.7)	3.8 (2.6–5.5)	4.9 (3.1–7.7)	2.8 (1.7–4.8)

Table 3.1.64 Continued

WHO region and WHO member state, territory, or special administrative region, and year	% Smoked cigarettes on ≥1 days of the past 30 days (current smokers)			% Smoked cigarettes on ≥20 days of the past 30 days		
	Total % (95% CI)	Males % (95% CI)	Females % (95% CI)	Total % (95% CI)	Males % (95% CI)	Females % (95% CI)
Russian Federation, 2004	25.4 (23.2–27.8)	26.9 (23.5–30.6)	23.9 (20.6–27.4)	10.5 (8.9–12.4)	11.5 (8.6–15.2)	9.5 (7.2–12.4)
Serbia, 2008	9.3 (6.9–12.5)	9.3 (6.3–13.4)	8.9 (6.6–11.9)	1.9 (1.1–3.2)	2.7 (1.5–4.7)	1.3 (0.7–2.3)
Slovakia, 2007	25.0 (22.6–27.6)	26.5 (23.2–29.9)	23.4 (20.7–26.4)	8.0 (6.4–10.1)	9.9 (7.7–12.7)	6.2 (4.7–8.2)
Slovenia, 2007	20.3 (16.3–24.9)	15.2 (10.7–21.2)	23.0 (18.7–27.9)	7.7 (5.5–10.8)	5.5 (3.2–9.5)	9.0 (6.3–12.7)
Tajikistan, 2004	1.1 (0.7–1.7)	1.5 (0.9–2.5)	0.5 (0.3–0.9)	0.1 (0.0–0.4)	0.1 (0.0–0.6)	0.1 (0.0–0.9)
Turkey, 2003	6.9 (6.1–7.9)	9.4 (8.2–10.9)	3.5 (2.9–4.3)	1.5 (1.2–1.8)	2.2 (1.7–2.7)	0.5 (0.3–0.8)
Ukraine, 2005	24.0 (21.0–27.3)	27.6 (24.0–31.5)	20.6 (16.9–24.8)	7.7 (6.4–9.3)	10.4 (8.2–13.2)	5.1 (3.9–6.7)
Uzbekistan, 2008 (Tashkent)	1.8 (0.6–5.1)	2.4 (0.7–7.3)	1.2 (0.3–4.3)	0.6 (0.2–2.1)	0.7 (0.2–3.3)	0.5 (0.1–2.5)
South East Asia	4.7 (4.2 – 5.2)	4.7 (4.1 – 5.4)	2.2 (1.7 – 2.7)	0.8 (0.5 – 1.0)	1.5 (1.1 – 1.9)	0.4 (0.1 – 0.8)
Bangladesh, 2007	2.0 (1.1–3.6)	2.9 (1.7–5.0)	1.1 (0.3–3.2)	0.3 (0.1–1.0)	0.5 (0.1–2.4)	0.2 (0.0–0.8)
Bhutan, 2006	12.1 (9.6–15.2)	18.3 (13.8–23.8)	6.3 (4.1–9.6)	0.6 (0.3–1.3)	1.0 (0.3–3.0)	0.2 (0.0–2.0)
East Timor, 2006	32.4 (25.5–40.2)	50.6 (41.6–59.6)	17.3 (10.7–26.8)	6.8 (4.3–10.5)	9.7 (5.8–15.9)	3.7 (1.9–6.8)
India, 2006	3.8 (3.1–4.7)	5.4 (4.3–6.7)	1.6 (1.0–2.6)	NA	NA	NA
Indonesia, 2006	11.8 (9.5–14.5)	23.9 (18.5–30.3)	1.9 (1.2–2.8)	1.5 (1.0–2.2)	3.3 (2.2–4.9)	0.0
Maldives, 2007	3.8 (2.7–5.3)	0.9 (0.4–2.0)	6.6 (4.6–9.6)	0.9 (0.6–1.5)	0.6 (0.2–1.6)	1.4 (0.8–2.5)
Myanmar, 2007	4.9 (3.6–6.5)	8.5 (6.2–11.6)	1.3 (0.6–2.6)	0.4 (0.2–0.9)	0.7 (0.3–1.6)	0.1 (0.0–0.7)

Table 3.1.64 Continued

WHO region and WHO member state, territory, or special administrative region, and year	% Smoked cigarettes on ≥1 days of the past 30 days (current smokers)			% Smoked cigarettes on ≥20 days of the past 30 days		
	Total % (95% CI)	Males % (95% CI)	Females % (95% CI)	Total % (95% CI)	Males % (95% CI)	Females % (95% CI)
Nepal, 2007	3.9 (2.7–5.6)	5.7 (3.9–8.3)	1.9 (1.0–3.5)	0.2 (0.0–0.9)	0.4 (0.1–1.6)	0.0
Sri Lanka, 2007	1.2 (0.5–2.9)	1.6 (0.7–3.7)	0.9 (0.2–3.5)	0.4 (0.1–2.1)	0.2 (0.0–1.7)	0.6 (0.1–2.7)
Thailand, 2005	11.7 (10.0–13.7)	17.4 (15.2–20.0)	4.8 (3.6–6.4)	1.7 (1.3–2.4)	2.7 (2.1–3.4)	0.7 (0.4–1.4)
Western Pacific	13.7 (13.2 – 14.1)	18.3 (17.6 – 19.1)	6.4 (6.0 – 6.8)	1.7 (1.5 – 1.8)	2.1 (1.9 – 2.4)	0.7 (0.6 – 0.9)
American Samoa, 2005[b]	16.7 (13.9–19.9)	18.3 (14.6–22.8)	15.1 (11.7–19.3)	2.9 (1.9–4.4)	3.4 (2.1–5.6)	2.3 (1.3–4.2)
Cambodia, 2003	2.5 (1.3–4.6)	4.6 (2.4–8.6)	0.2 (0.0–1.6)	0.7 (0.3–1.4)	1.3 (0.6–2.6)	0.0
China, 2005 (Macau)[e]	10.4 (8.1–13.4)	11.0 (8.1–14.8)	9.8 (7.0–13.6)	2.7 (1.6–4.5)	2.7 (1.5–4.7)	2.7 (1.5–4.8)
China, 2005 (Shanghai)	1.7 (1.0–3.0)	2.7 (1.4–5.2)	0.8 (0.3–1.8)	0.2 (0.1–0.8)	0.5 (0.1–1.5)	0.0 (0.0–0.3)
Cook Islands, 2008	30.0 (28.9–31.2)	28.2 (26.5–29.9)	31.5 (29.9–33.1)	2.0 (1.7–2.3)	2.6 (2.1–3.2)	1.4 (1.1–1.9)
Fiji, 2005	5.0 (2.9–8.5)	6.7 (3.8–11.6)	3.1 (1.6–6.0)	0.2 (0.1–0.8)	0.2 (0.1–0.8)	0.1 (0.0–0.7)
Guam, 2002[b]	22.6 (19.9–25.5)	25.2 (21.7–29.2)	19.7 (16.3–23.5)	9.2 (7.3–11.5)	10.4 (7.7–13.8)	7.7 (5.5–10.8)
Lao People's Democratic Republic, 2007 (Vientiane Capital)	3.0 (1.9–4.6)	4.9 (2.7–8.6)	1.3 (0.7–2.5)	0.2 (0.1–0.8)	0.6 (0.2–1.7)	0.0
Malaysia, 2003	20.2 (16.6–24.3)	36.3 (30.6–42.5)	4.2 (3.0–5.9)	3.7 (2.7–5.0)	7.2 (5.5–9.5)	0.2 (0.1–0.6)
Micronesia, 2007	28.3 (23.9–33.2)	36.9 (29.9–44.5)	19.8 (15.9–24.5)	3.7 (2.7–5.0)	4.4 (2.7–7.1)	2.4 (1.6–3.7)
Mongolia, 2007	6.9 (4.4–10.5)	11.0 (7.6–15.6)	3.3 (1.4–7.3)	1.6 (0.9–2.8)	2.9 (1.5–5.4)	0.5 (0.2–1.7)
New Zealand, 2008	17.6 (12.1–24.8)	14.5 (8.6–23.4)	20.6 (15.5–26.9)	8.0 (4.3–14.4)	8.1 (3.0–20.2)	7.8 (5.4–11.2)

Table 3.1.64 Continued

WHO region and WHO member state, territory, or special administrative region, and year	% Smoked cigarettes on ≥1 days of the past 30 days (current smokers)			% Smoked cigarettes on ≥20 days of the past 30 days		
	Total % (95% CI)	Males % (95% CI)	Females % (95% CI)	Total % (95% CI)	Males % (95% CI)	Females % (95% CI)
Northern Mariana Islands, 2004[f]	29.1 (26.6–31.7)	26.6 (23.6–29.9)	31.5 (28.2–34.9)	4.8 (3.8–6.1)	4.4 (3.4–5.9)	5.2 (3.8–7.2)
Palau, 2005	26.7 (23.3–30.3)	31.0 (26.9–35.5)	22.6 (18.1–27.8)	4.1 (3.0–5.7)	5.3 (3.4–8.1)	3.1 (1.8–5.0)
Papua New Guinea, 2007	43.8 (39.4–48.2)	52.1 (47.3–56.8)	35.8 (30.0–42.0)	7.0 (5.3–9.0)	11.8 (9.0–15.4)	2.1 (1.5–3.0)
Philippines, 2007	17.5 (14.7–20.6)	23.4 (19.7–27.7)	12.0 (9.4–15.1)	1.8 (1.3–2.5)	2.5 (1.8–3.5)	1.0 (0.3–3.0)
Republic of Korea (South), 2008	8.8 (7.3–10.5)	10.8 (8.8–13.2)	6.3 (4.9–7.9)	2.8 (2.0–4.0)	3.9 (2.8–5.4)	1.5 (0.9–2.6)
Samoa, 2007	15.2 (11.5–19.8)	16.0 (10.3–24.0)	12.7 (8.2–19.2)	2.4 (1.3–4.7)	3.5 (1.6–7.5)	1.1 (0.3–3.4)
Singapore, 2000	9.1 (8.1–10.3)	10.5 (8.8–12.4)	7.5 (6.2–9.1)	2.4 (2.0–2.9)	3.0 (2.4–3.8)	1.7 (1.3–2.3)
Solomon Islands, 2008	24.2 (18.1–31.6)	24.3 (17.2–33.3)	23.4 (16.3–32.3)	3.1 (1.4–6.7)	4.3 (2.1–8.3)	2.5 (0.9–7.0)
Tuvalu, 2006	26.6 (26.4–26.8)	33.2 (32.9–33.6)	22.1 (21.9–22.4)	1.3 (1.3–1.4)	3.4 (3.3–3.6)	0.0
Vanuatu, 2007	18.2 (17.0–19.4)	28.2 (26.1–30.3)	11.4 (10.1–12.7)	1.3 (1.0–1.7)	2.2 (1.6–2.9)	0.8 (0.5–1.2)
Viet Nam, 2007 (Hanoi)	3.0 (1.7–5.2)	5.0 (2.8–8.9)	1.0 (0.5–1.9)	1.0 (0.5–1.9)	1.7 (1.0–2.8)	0.4 (0.1–1.4)

Source: CDC 2010b.
Note: **CI** = confidence interval; **NA** = question not asked; **WHO** = World Health Organization.
[a]Territory of United Kingdom
[b]Territory of United States
[c]United Nations Relief and Works Agency
[d]United Nations Administered Province
[e]Special Administrative Region of China
[f]Commonwealth in political union with the United States

Table 3.1.65 Percentage of youth 13–15 years of age who currently smoke and always have or feel like having a cigarette first thing in the morning, who want to stop smoking, and who have tried to stop smoking during the past year, by gender; Global Youth Tobacco Survey 1999–2009; worldwide

	% Always have or feel like having a cigarette first thing in the morning			% Want to stop smoking			% Tried to stop smoking during the past year		
WHO region and WHO member state, territory, or special administrative region, and year	**Total % (95% CI)**	**Males % (95% CI)**	**Females % (95% CI)**	**Total % (95% CI)**	**Males % (95% CI)**	**Females % (95% CI)**	**Total % (95% CI)**	**Males % (95% CI)**	**Females % (95% CI)**
Africa	9.6 (7.9–11.2)	9.1 (6.7–11.5)	13.1 (9.4–16.7)	82.9 (81.5–84.3)	89.9 (88.6–91.3)	75.2 (71.8–78.6)	77.9 (76.3–79.4)	77.3 (75.3–79.3)	73.2 (69.8–76.6)
Algeria, 2007 (Constantine)	18.5 (9.9–31.7)	18.6 (10.2–31.5)	NR	80.9 (71.1–87.9)	81.6 (71.0–89.0)	NR	64.5 (47.5–78.4)	66.3 (50.3–79.3)	NR
Benin, 2003 (Atlantique Littoral)	NR	NR	NR	79.6 (51.8–93.4)	83.4 (52.1–95.9)	NR	67.8 (52.0–80.3)	NR	NR
Botswana, 2008	14.8 (9.9–21.5)	16.1 (9.3–26.5)	11.0 (6.1–19.2)	78.0 (67.7–85.7)	78.1 (64.8–87.4)	83.0 (70.1–91.1)	72.6 (61.7–81.4)	74.5 (56.5–86.8)	72.0 (55.7–84.0)
Burkina Faso, 2006 (Ouagadougou)	14.7 (7.3–27.2)	NR	NR	95.5 (82.9–98.9)	97.0 (81.5–99.6)	NR	89.9 (80.1–95.1)	87.5 (75.1–94.2)	NR
Burundi, 2008	NR	NR	NR	NR	NR	NR	NR	NR	NR
Cameroon, 2008 (Yaoude)	17.5 (8.7–31.9)	NR	NR	73.2 (49.1–88.6)	NR	NR	72.9 (48.9–88.3)	NR	NR
Cape Verde, 2007	NR	NR	NR	NR	NR	NR	NR	NR	NR
Central African Republic, 2008 (Bangui)	7.0 (2.0–21.4)	NR	NR	84.9 (66.8–94.0)	NR	NR	90.3 (75.2–96.6)	NR	NR
Comoros, 2007	NR	NR	NR	NR	NR	NR	NR	NR	NR
Congo, 2006	12.5 (4.9–28.5)	15.7 (5.3–38.3)	NR	77.1 (61.9–87.4)	84.3 (71.2–92.1)	NR	84.1 (69.3–92.5)	78.3 (65.8–87.1)	NR
Côte D'Ivoire, 2003 (Abidjan)	3.6 (1.3–9.3)	3.8 (1.3–10.3)	NR	92.7 (84.6–96.7)	96.2 (88.7–98.8)	NR	87.5 (78.0–93.2)	88.0 (76.3–94.4)	NR
Democratic Republic of the Congo, 2008 (Kinshasa)	2.1 (0.2–18.3)	2.8 (0.3–22.0)	NR	76.0 (57.9–87.9)	75.0 (55.9–87.6)	NR	77.3 (58.0–89.4)	74.0 (52.9–87.8)	NR
Equatorial Guinea, 2008	NR	NR	NR	NR	NR	NR	NR	NR	NR

Table 3.1.65 Continued

WHO region and WHO member state, territory, or special administrative region, and year	% Always have or feel like having a cigarette first thing in the morning			% Want to stop smoking			% Tried to stop smoking during the past year		
	Total % (95% CI)	Males % (95% CI)	Females % (95% CI)	Total % (95% CI)	Males % (95% CI)	Females % (95% CI)	Total % (95% CI)	Males % (95% CI)	Females % (95% CI)
Eritrea, 2006	13.5 (4.6–33.6)	NR	NR	80.7 (65.3–90.3)	76.2 (52.8–90.1)	NR	84.6 (66.6–93.7)	NR	NR
Ethiopia, 2003 (Addis Ababa)	NR	NR	NR	NR	NR	NR	NR	NR	NR
Gambia, 2008 (Banjul)	26.9 (20.2–34.8)	22.2 (13.8–33.6)	31.3 (17.8–48.8)	60.4 (40.3–77.6)	NR	NR	63.2 (47.1–76.7)	NR	NR
Ghana, 2006	16.4 (8.3–29.8)	6.0 (2.6–13.5)	25.6 (12.2–46.0)	80.2 (72.2–86.3)	87.4 (72.2–94.9)	78.7 (65.5–87.8)	61.2 (46.6–74.1)	73.9 (54.9–86.8)	45.2 (24.2–68.1)
Guinea, 2008	NR	NR	NR	85.5 (75.5–91.8)	84.1 (73.4–91.1)	NR	80.4 (66.1–89.6)	NR	NR
Guinea-Bissau, 2008 (Bissau)	4.7 (1.1–18.3)	NR	NR	81.0 (65.3–90.6)	NR	NR	87.2 (74.7–94.1)	84.3 (71.6–92.0)	NR
Kenya, 2007	14.7 (9.3–22.4)	16.7 (9.6–27.4)	14.3 (8.1–24.1)	85.3 (71.4–93.1)	90.3 (72.8–97.0)	76.9 (59.0–88.5)	75.9 (67.3–82.8)	76.3 (64.2–85.3)	NR
Lesotho, 2008	12.7 (5.1–28.4)	13.0 (2.2–49.5)	10.9 (4.0–26.2)	82.0 (72.9–88.5)	81.7 (58.5–93.4)	82.2 (67.4–91.1)	66.8 (48.3–81.2)	59.4 (35.9–79.3)	76.2 (49.6–91.2)
Liberia, 2008 (Monrovia)	NR	NR	NR	NR	NR	NR	NR	NR	NR
Madagascar, 2008	1.8 (0.4–8.4)	2.5 (0.5–11.2)	NR	87.8 (53.9–97.8)	84.9 (44.0–97.6)	NR	72.7 (50.4–87.4)	70.5 (46.3–86.9)	NR
Malawi, 2005	17.5 (5.9–41.7)	NR	NR	68.0 (46.8–83.6)	NR	NR	61.4 (38.9–79.9)	NR	NR
Mali, 2008	29.4 (13.4–53.0)	22.7 (9.7–44.6)	NR	62.8 (35.5–83.8)	64.9 (35.9–85.9)	NR	60.4 (33.9–82.0)	58.2 (34.3–78.8)	NR
Mauritania, 2006	16.8 (10.7–25.6)	13.8 (7.2–24.8)	20.7 (11.3–34.6)	73.7 (61.9–82.9)	76.3 (61.1–86.8)	70.2 (54.5–82.3)	78.1 (68.3–85.5)	72.9 (59.7–83.1)	83.0 (71.6–90.5)
Mauritius, 2008	12.1 (6.6–21.4)	14.4 (7.3–26.5)	5.4 (1.8–15.3)	62.3 (46.0–76.2)	70.3 (52.2–83.7)	44.3 (22.6–68.4)	58.5 (45.5–70.4)	66.1 (53.1–77.0)	48.0 (32.1–64.3)
Mozambique, 2007 (Maputo City)	NR	NR	NR	NR	NR	NR	NR	NR	NR
Namibia, 2004	13.6 (9.8–18.4)	11.7 (6.7–19.9)	15.9 (9.0–26.6)	73.4 (65.4–80.1)	79.3 (66.7–88.0)	67.6 (57.6–76.3)	73.8 (67.5–79.3)	76.7 (67.5–83.9)	71.2 (58.1–81.6)

Table 3.1.65 Continued

WHO region and WHO member state, territory, or special administrative region, and year	% Always have or feel like having a cigarette first thing in the morning			% Want to stop smoking			% Tried to stop smoking during the past year		
	Total % (95% CI)	Males % (95% CI)	Females % (95% CI)	Total % (95% CI)	Males % (95% CI)	Females % (95% CI)	Total % (95% CI)	Males % (95% CI)	Females % (95% CI)
Niger, 2006	6.0 (1.5–20.6)	6.5 (1.7–21.9)	NR	73.1 (54.1–86.2)	74.8 (55.0–87.8)	NR	61.7 (41.6–78.4)	63.9 (42.1–81.1)	NR
Nigeria, 2008 (Cross River State)	NR	NR	NR	NR	NR	NR	NR	NR	NR
Rwanda, 2008	NR	NR	NR	NR	NR	NR	NR	NR	NR
Senegal, 2007	4.6 (1.3–15.2)	7.5 (2.3–21.8)	NR	77.4 (45.6–93.3)	87.3 (62.3–96.6)	NR	71.2 (42.2–89.3)	79.2 (56.8–91.7)	NR
Seychelles, 2007	0.0	0.0	0.0	73.4 (63.2–81.5)	NR	NR	74.1 (64.2–82.0)	76.3 (62.6–86.1)	70.9 (51.9–84.6)
Sierra Leone, 2008 (Western Area)	11.3 (3.3–32.1)	NR	NR	74.9 (52.6–89.0)	NR	NR	79.6 (60.9–90.8)	NR	NR
South Africa, 2008	11.8 (7.6–17.8)	13.3 (7.3–23.0)	9.6 (5.0–17.7)	77.0 (68.8–83.6)	78.6 (68.1–86.4)	75.2 (62.5–84.7)	79.6 (73.5–84.6)	80.9 (72.4–87.2)	78.1 (68.6–85.4)
Swaziland, 2005	0.5 (0.1–4.2)	0.9 (0.1–7.1)	0.0	72.2 (63.5–79.5)	74.5 (62.0–83.9)	66.1 (53.0–77.1)	69.9 (63.7–75.4)	72.6 (64.7–79.3)	66.4 (56.6–74.9)
Togo, 2007	0.0	0.0	NR	78.5 (69.8–85.2)	81.1 (70.7–88.5)	NR	60.7 (50.1–70.4)	60.8 (50.5–70.3)	NR
Uganda, 2007	24.0 (12.1–41.8)	14.5 (6.1–30.5)	NR	70.3 (57.1–80.8)	81.1 (59.2–92.7)	NR	76.6 (63.0–86.3)	79.0 (61.2–90.0)	NR
United Republic of Tanzania, 2008 (Arusha)	NR	NR	NR	NR	NR	NR	NR	NR	NR
Zambia, 2007 (Lusaka)	13.3 (5.3–29.7)	NR	NR	71.8 (49.8–86.7)	NR	NR	65.6 (45.9–81.1)	NR	NR
Zimbabwe, 2008 (Harare)	NR	NR	NR	NR	NR	NR	NR	NR	NR
The Americas	4.6 (3.6–5.6)	4.3 (2.9–5.7)	1.1 (0.4–1.8)	80.1 (79.0–81.2)	79.8 (78.2–81.5)	54.0 (51.7–56.3)	65.0 (63.5–66.4)	67.2 (65.2–69.1)	62.2 (60.2–64.3)
Antigua & Barbuda, 2004	NR	NR	NR	NR	NR	NR	NR	NR	NR
Argentina, 2007	9.7 (7.0–13.2)	10.7 (6.1–17.9)	8.4 (5.2–13.5)	50.2 (44.1–56.2)	47.3 (38.0–56.9)	52.3 (45.7–58.9)	62.5 (57.0–67.7)	63.2 (54.6–71.0)	62.5 (56.8–67.9)

Table 3.1.65 Continued

WHO region and WHO member state, territory, or special administrative region, and year	% Always have or feel like having a cigarette first thing in the morning			% Want to stop smoking			% Tried to stop smoking during the past year		
	Total % (95% CI)	Males % (95% CI)	Females % (95% CI)	Total % (95% CI)	Males % (95% CI)	Females % (95% CI)	Total % (95% CI)	Males % (95% CI)	Females % (95% CI)
Bahamas, 2004	NR	NR	NR	NR	NR	NR	NR	NR	NR
Barbados, 2007	6.7 (2.3–17.9)	9.0 (2.5–27.1)	NR	54.7 (39.3–69.3)	52.7 (36.7–68.2)	NR	57.2 (44.3–69.2)	53.4 (41.1–65.4)	NR
Belize, 2008	3.2 (0.8–12.6)	NR	NR	74.7 (55.5–87.5)	NR	NR	65.0 (52.4–75.9)	58.9 (43.0–73.2)	NR
Bolivia, 2003 (La Paz)	3.0 (1.4–6.5)	2.9 (1.1–7.5)	3.3 (1.0–10.7)	60.7 (51.0–69.6)	65.5 (54.8–74.8)	50.9 (41.8–60.0)	72.5 (67.6–76.8)	75.3 (68.8–80.8)	66.7 (58.0–74.5)
Brazil, 2005 (Rio de Janeiro)	5.8 (2.5–12.7)	2.7 (1.3–5.6)	6.1 (2.0–17.1)	39.2 (27.0–52.9)	NR	40.4 (30.4–51.4)	51.8 (36.0–67.1)	55.8 (39.0–71.3)	48.7 (30.8–67.0)
British Virgin Islands, 2001[a]	NR	NR	NR	NR	NR	NR	NR	NR	NR
Chile, 2008 (Santiago)	3.7 (2.2–6.2)	4.3 (2.5–7.4)	3.5 (1.8–6.5)	49.7 (45.8–53.5)	48.5 (41.9–55.2)	49.3 (44.7–54.0)	59.3 (54.1–64.3)	60.9 (51.3–69.7)	57.9 (53.4–62.3)
Colombia, 2007 (Bogota)	0.0	0.0	0.0	64.7 (56.5–72.1)	65.5 (54.2–75.3)	63.1 (49.9–74.6)	63.5 (56.9–69.6)	63.6 (55.1–71.2)	63.8 (54.3–72.4)
Costa Rica, 2008	6.1 (2.9–12.6)	5.9 (1.9–17.0)	6.5 (2.9–13.7)	57.5 (49.4–65.2)	55.2 (43.3–66.5)	59.7 (47.3–71.0)	55.7 (47.5–63.6)	57.2 (44.8–68.7)	54.5 (42.6–65.9)
Cuba, 2004 (Havana)	3.8 (1.5–9.5)	2.1 (0.3–13.4)	5.6 (1.6–17.5)	56.8 (47.1–66.0)	65.8 (55.0–75.1)	46.3 (30.5–62.9)	54.5 (42.5–65.9)	68.8 (51.5–82.1)	37.9 (27.6–49.3)
Dominica, 2004	12.1 (5.8–23.5)	NR	NR	58.6 (44.7–71.2)	NR	NR	50.8 (38.6–63.0)	NR	NR
Dominican Republic, 2004	1.9 (0.5–7.6)	1.7 (0.2–12.1)	2.0 (0.3–13.9)	50.9 (31.6–69.9)	NR	54.0 (27.4–78.5)	55.1 (36.4–72.4)	57.7 (41.8–72.2)	52.5 (27.1–76.6)
Ecuador, 2007 (Quito)	0.0	0.0	0.0	59.2 (48.9–68.8)	64.5 (53.2–74.4)	54.1 (36.9–70.4)	62.4 (56.0–68.5)	66.9 (56.2–76.0)	57.3 (45.4–68.4)
El Salvador, 2003	1.1 (0.2–5.3)	2.2 (0.5–10.1)	0.0	97.7 (93.9–99.2)	96.2 (90.3–98.5)	NR	78.2 (68.8–85.4)	77.2 (63.1–87.0)	80.3 (65.0–90.0)
Grenada, 2004	12.3 (6.2–22.7)	NR	NR	64.8 (51.5–76.2)	NR	61.0 (40.7–78.1)	57.2 (44.0–69.4)	55.8 (37.0–73.1)	NR
Guatemala, 2008	5.7 (3.0–10.5)	4.9 (2.0–11.2)	5.7 (1.8–17.2)	60.1 (51.9–67.9)	65.6 (55.9–74.1)	53.4 (40.6–65.7)	72.1 (66.3–77.2)	75.4 (65.1–83.5)	66.9 (59.2–73.7)

Table 3.1.65 Continued

WHO region and WHO member state, territory, or special administrative region, and year	% Always have or feel like having a cigarette first thing in the morning			% Want to stop smoking			% Tried to stop smoking during the past year		
	Total % (95% CI)	Males % (95% CI)	Females % (95% CI)	Total % (95% CI)	Males % (95% CI)	Females % (95% CI)	Total % (95% CI)	Males % (95% CI)	Females % (95% CI)
Guyana, 2004	NR	NR	NR	NR	NR	NR	NR	NR	NR
Haiti, 2005 (Port au Prince)	13.9 (5.8–29.8)	6.6 (3.0–13.9)	18.7 (5.3–48.6)	72.6 (56.6–84.4)	NR	77.0 (54.0–90.6)	65.6 (49.8–78.6)	52.4 (38.9–65.5)	77.4 (54.6–90.8)
Honduras, 2003 (Tegucigalpa)	6.4 (2.8–14.1)	4.2 (0.8–19.9)	8.2 (3.3–18.8)	58.8 (44.5–71.7)	70.2 (44.6–87.3)	50.2 (38.4–61.9)	64.7 (55.5–72.9)	72.7 (60.2–82.5)	57.7 (40.3–73.3)
Jamaica, 2006	5.9 (2.3–14.5)	9.3 (3.0–25.5)	1.6 (0.2–13.5)	73.3 (58.4–84.2)	75.6 (57.3–87.8)	69.6 (51.8–83.0)	60.5 (47.9–71.9)	61.3 (47.2–73.7)	60.4 (40.3–77.6)
Mexico, 2006 (Mexico City)	4.2 (2.3–7.5)	4.3 (2.0–9.0)	4.6 (1.7–11.8)	42.2 (36.3–48.4)	42.5 (34.9–50.4)	45.7 (37.8–53.8)	53.3 (46.1–60.4)	52.8 (43.6–61.7)	53.0 (42.2–63.5)
Montserrat, 2000[a]	NR	NR	NR	88.0	82.6	92.5	NR	NR	NR
Nicaragua, 2003 (Centro Managua)	3.1 (1.2–7.8)	3.8 (1.2–11.5)	2.1 (0.2–15.9)	60.4 (44.5–74.3)	65.0 (43.9–81.6)	53.0 (31.2–73.7)	69.4 (59.0–78.1)	67.6 (55.6–77.6)	73.8 (57.6–85.3)
Panama, 2008	5.3 (2.1–12.7)	4.5 (1.2–15.3)	NR	65.9 (47.8–80.3)	69.7 (51.3–83.5)	NR	75.9 (63.3–85.2)	81.2 (67.8–89.9)	NR
Paraguay, 2008	2.2 (0.7–6.9)	3.2 (1.0–10.4)	0.4 (0.1–1.8)	59.0 (42.2–74.0)	57.2 (36.7–75.6)	63.4 (46.0–77.9)	69.0 (55.1–80.1)	67.1 (48.7–81.5)	72.7 (56.7–84.4)
Peru, 2007 (Lima)	0.9 (0.1–6.9)	1.8 (0.2–12.9)	0.0	69.1 (59.7–77.1)	67.3 (50.8–80.4)	69.2 (57.1–79.2)	64.7 (56.4–72.2)	71.7 (59.9–81.2)	NR
Puerto Rico, 2004[b]	NA	NA	NA	NR	NR	NR	NR	NR	NR
Saint Kitts & Nevis, 2002	NR	NR	NR	NR	NR	NR	NR	NR	NR
Saint Lucia, 2007	3.9 (0.9–14.9)	NR	NR	57.8 (41.0–72.9)	NR	NR	60.5 (41.7–76.7)	NR	NR
Saint Vincent & The Grenadines, 2007	3.4 (0.7–14.8)	NR	NR	67.5 (46.9–83.0)	NR	NR	72.4 (57.6–83.5)	NR	NR
Suriname, 2004	0.0	NR	NR	NR	NR	NR	NR	NR	NR
Trinidad & Tobago, 2007	3.0 (0.9–9.1)	3.8 (0.9–14.4)	0.2 (0.0–1.2)	83.4 (76.2–88.7)	88.4 (73.5–95.5)	NR	79.7 (68.2–87.7)	81.1 (68.2–89.6)	77.0 (52.5–91.0)

Table 3.1.65 Continued

WHO region and WHO member state, territory, or special administrative region, and year	% Always have or feel like having a cigarette first thing in the morning			% Want to stop smoking			% Tried to stop smoking during the past year		
	Total % (95% CI)	Males % (95% CI)	Females % (95% CI)	Total % (95% CI)	Males % (95% CI)	Females % (95% CI)	Total % (95% CI)	Males % (95% CI)	Females % (95% CI)
U.S. Virgin Islands, 2004[b]	NA	NA	NA	NR	NR	NR	NR	NR	NR
Uruguay, 2007	5.4 (3.4–8.4)	10.7 (5.5–19.9)	2.4 (1.2–4.9)	46.3 (39.1–53.7)	45.8 (32.4–59.9)	46.7 (38.0–55.6)	56.1 (50.0–62.1)	57.7 (48.6–66.3)	55.2 (47.2–62.9)
Venezuela, 1999	7.8 (4.0–14.8)	12.0 (6.2–21.8)	5.6 (1.6–17.3)	69.8 (57.7–79.6)	NR	74.2 (56.8–86.3)	68.4 (56.5–78.3)	63.2 (45.0–78.3)	71.4 (56.6–82.7)
Eastern Mediterranean	10.5 (8.5–12.5)	9.5 (7.1–11.9)	7.2 (2.4–12.1)	68.9 (66.7–71.1)	73.1 (70.8–75.4)	50.7 (44.8–56.6)	65.0 (62.7–67.4)	66.6 (64.0–69.1)	56.0 (50.1–62.0)
Afghanistan, 2004 (Kabul)	NR	NR	NR	NR	NR	NR	NR	NR	NR
Bahrain, 2002	NA	NA	NA	64.3 (53.4–73.8)	68.5 (57.1–77.9)	NR	62.9 (53.6–71.3)	67.0 (58.9–74.1)	NR
Djibouti, 2003	29.9 (16.4–48.1)	29.9 (15.7–49.4)	NR	70.8 (52.1–84.3)	NR	NR	NR	NR	NR
Egypt, 2005	2.0 (0.4–8.3)	1.8 (0.2–11.8)	NR	78.7 (68.1–86.5)	86.7 (73.6–93.8)	NR	68.1 (57.2–77.4)	71.6 (52.9–84.9)	NR
Gaza Strip, 2008[c]	NR	NR	NR	NR	NR	NR	NR	NR	NR
Iran, 2007	NR	NR	NR	NR	NR	NR	NR	NR	NR
Iraq, 2008 (Baghdad)	NR	NR	NR	NR	NR	NR	NR	NR	NR
Jordan, 2008[c]	8.0 (3.9–15.9)	6.1 (1.5–21.5)	NR	74.2 (63.6–82.6)	76.7 (65.5–85.1)	NR	74.9 (65.3–82.5)	75.2 (61.8–85.0)	NR
Kuwait, 2005	0.0	0.0	NR	65.7 (57.3–73.3)	68.3 (58.6–76.7)	49.3 (35.1–63.6)	65.0 (57.0–72.2)	64.1 (53.8–73.3)	62.2 (48.4–74.4)
Lebanon, 2008[c]	9.8 (4.2–21.3)	10.8 (4.2–25.0)	NR	60.4 (46.8–72.6)	61.6 (49.4–72.5)	NR	64.9 (51.5–76.4)	65.6 (53.1–76.2)	NR
Libya, 2007	10.6 (4.1–24.6)	NR	NR	NR	NR	NR	NR	NR	NR
Morocco, 2006	12.9 (6.3–24.4)	NR	NR	NR	NR	NR	NR	NR	NR

Table 3.1.65 Continued

WHO region and WHO member state, territory, or special administrative region, and year	% Always have or feel like having a cigarette first thing in the morning			% Want to stop smoking			% Tried to stop smoking during the past year		
	Total % (95% CI)	Males % (95% CI)	Females % (95% CI)	Total % (95% CI)	Males % (95% CI)	Females % (95% CI)	Total % (95% CI)	Males % (95% CI)	Females % (95% CI)
Oman, 2007	NR	NR	NR	NR	NR	NR	NR	NR	NR
Pakistan, 2003 (Islamabad)	NR	NR	NR	NR	NR	NR	NR	NR	NR
Qatar, 2007	NR	NR	NR	59.6 (37.4–78.5)	NR	NR	55.4 (38.7–71.0)	NR	NR
Saudi Arabia, 2007	15.5 (9.8–23.5)	16.7 (9.2–28.3)	NR	71.7 (61.7–80.0)	75.9 (62.4–85.7)	NR	62.3 (51.2–72.3)	66.9 (56.7–75.7)	NR
Somalia, 2007 (Somaliland)	NR	NR	NR	NR	NR	NR	NR	NR	NR
Sudan, 2005	3.6 (1.0–12.0)	2.2 (0.7–6.9)	NR	66.4 (49.9–79.7)	72.9 (55.9–85.1)	NR	60.9 (36.6–80.8)	65.6 (38.2–85.5)	NR
Syrian Arab Republic, 2008[c]	5.1 (1.7–14.5)	4.8 (1.5–14.2)	NR	73.1 (63.6–80.8)	76.0 (67.7–82.8)	NR	71.3 (60.0–80.5)	74.7 (63.7–83.2)	NR
Tunisia, 2007	2.0 (0.5–7.9)	2.2 (0.5–8.8)	NR	84.0 (71.0–91.8)	82.3 (69.0–90.7)	NR	71.4 (56.1–83.0)	68.0 (50.9–81.3)	NR
United Arab Emirates, 2005	14.5 (11.0–18.8)	16.4 (12.0–21.9)	7.9 (4.0–14.7)	60.5 (54.8–66.0)	62.3 (55.6–68.5)	52.3 (43.2–61.2)	62.2 (55.6–68.4)	62.7 (55.8–69.2)	58.7 (48.2–68.4)
West Bank, 2008[c]	12.2 (6.1–23.0)	11.7 (5.2–24.4)	5.9 (1.4–22.2)	56.1 (44.0–67.5)	58.3 (44.9–70.6)	48.3 (28.9–68.3)	62.6 (50.3–73.4)	66.3 (55.1–75.9)	49.5 (28.8–70.5)
Yemen, 2008	NR	NR	NR	NR	NR	NR	NR	NR	NR
Europe	10.2 (9.4–11.1)	11.7 (10.5–12.9)	9.0 (7.7–10.3)	61.1 (60.1–62.1)	66.2 (64.8–67.5)	62.6 (61.1–64.1)	71.7 (70.8–72.6)	70.7 (69.6–71.8)	73.8 (71.3–82.9)
Albania, 2004	1.1 (0.2–4.7)	2.0 (0.4–8.9)	0.0	68.0 (57.8–76.8)	71.9 (60.1–81.3)	60.9 (43.8–75.8)	80.4 (73.2–86.1)	78.6 (70.8–84.7)	84.6 (65.3–94.1)
Armenia, 2004	13.8 (5.5–30.4)	14.5 (5.8–31.7)	NR	80.3 (65.8–89.6)	81.4 (66.2–90.7)	NR	71.3 (54.5–83.7)	72.1 (55.3–84.4)	NR
Belarus, 2004	6.0 (4.2–8.4)	7.0 (4.5–10.6)	4.6 (2.7–7.8)	72.1 (67.8–76.1)	72.8 (66.4–78.4)	71.2 (63.7–77.6)	77.4 (72.8–81.4)	74.7 (69.0–79.6)	81.5 (75.1–86.6)
Bosnia and Herzegovina, 2008	NA	NA	NA	52.4 (48.1–56.7)	55.8 (50.4–61.2)	48.6 (42.3–55.0)	68.9 (65.7–71.8)	67.0 (62.3–71.3)	71.9 (66.2–76.9)

Table 3.1.65 Continued

WHO region and WHO member state, territory, or special administrative region, and year	% Always have or feel like having a cigarette first thing in the morning			% Want to stop smoking			% Tried to stop smoking during the past year		
	Total % (95% CI)	Males % (95% CI)	Females % (95% CI)	Total % (95% CI)	Males % (95% CI)	Females % (95% CI)	Total % (95% CI)	Males % (95% CI)	Females % (95% CI)
Bulgaria, 2008	15.6 (10.6–22.3)	17.3 (9.3–29.9)	14.4 (9.1–21.9)	49.1 (42.5–55.8)	48.8 (40.9–56.7)	48.8 (38.0–59.7)	57.8 (52.5–63.0)	53.5 (45.3–61.5)	60.0 (53.5–66.2)
Croatia, 2007	11.1 (7.2–16.7)	12.7 (7.1–21.5)	8.9 (5.6–13.9)	41.2 (37.6–44.9)	43.6 (33.9–53.9)	38.5 (32.5–44.7)	66.4 (61.9–70.7)	66.9 (58.4–74.4)	66.1 (61.7–70.3)
Cyprus, 2005	23.3 (20.6–26.3)	26.8 (23.1–31.0)	17.8 (14.2–22.1)	48.6 (44.9–52.2)	49.8 (44.9–54.7)	46.0 (40.5–51.6)	61.4 (58.0–64.6)	57.6 (53.0–62.1)	66.0 (61.1–70.6)
Czech Republic, 2007	11.5 (7.5–17.2)	11.0 (6.4–18.3)	11.9 (7.1–19.2)	52.6 (47.7–57.5)	57.3 (49.5–64.8)	48.4 (41.7–55.1)	77.1 (74.1–79.8)	73.1 (69.6–76.3)	80.7 (75.7–84.9)
Estonia, 2007	10.1 (6.1–16.1)	12.4 (6.9–21.4)	7.1 (3.2–15.1)	69.8 (61.1–77.3)	70.4 (62.5–77.2)	69.6 (56.1–80.4)	69.0 (64.4–73.3)	70.5 (64.3–76.1)	67.1 (61.4–72.4)
Georgia, 2008	0.0	0.0	NR	67.0 (47.5–81.9)	NR	NR	73.6 (54.6–86.6)	74.8 (50.0–89.9)	NR
Greece, 2005	10.5 (7.2–15.1)	8.8 (4.5–16.5)	10.9 (5.9–19.2)	37.6 (31.3–44.4)	37.5 (28.0–48.0)	37.2 (29.1–46.1)	57.9 (50.6–64.9)	56.9 (48.4–65.0)	60.6 (49.7–70.5)
Hungary, 2008	17.4 (12.0–24.5)	15.3 (9.7–23.3)	15.5 (9.9–23.4)	41.0 (34.7–47.7)	39.5 (29.8–50.1)	40.7 (30.1–52.3)	66.3 (59.4–72.6)	64.3 (54.0–73.5)	68.6 (58.2–77.5)
Kazakhstan, 2004	7.9 (5.1–12.1)	7.9 (4.6–13.0)	8.0 (3.0–19.5)	75.7 (70.8–79.9)	74.0 (67.6–79.5)	79.1 (72.6–84.4)	69.7 (61.7–76.7)	68.7 (60.7–75.8)	71.7 (60.9–80.4)
Kosovo, 2004[d]	10.6 (4.4–23.2)	16.3 (5.4–39.6)	4.6 (0.9–19.7)	76.3 (61.2–86.8)	77.5 (55.3–90.6)	74.5 (56.6–86.8)	73.2 (59.3–83.6)	71.2 (57.6–81.8)	76.1 (48.1–91.6)
Kyrgyzstan, 2008	14.0 (5.7–30.4)	17.7 (6.4–40.2)	5.9 (1.6–19.6)	86.2 (72.0–93.8)	83.3 (63.9–93.4)	92.1 (80.2–97.1)	48.2 (25.7–71.4)	51.1 (26.2–75.5)	NR
Latvia, 2007	9.4 (7.3–11.9)	9.0 (6.6–12.3)	9.3 (5.7–14.8)	71.5 (66.7–75.8)	72.7 (66.8–77.9)	69.7 (64.0–74.8)	75.8 (70.6–80.3)	76.0 (68.3–82.4)	75.3 (65.0–83.4)
Lithuania, 2005	6.2 (3.4–11.0)	9.0 (4.7–16.8)	3.4 (1.3–9.0)	70.9 (63.4–77.5)	75.2 (66.1–82.4)	66.0 (55.9–74.9)	63.5 (57.3–69.3)	63.9 (59.3–68.2)	61.7 (50.6–71.8)
Macedonia, former Yugoslav Republic of, 2008	16.5 (12.7–21.1)	18.0 (13.0–24.4)	15.0 (9.1–23.7)	66.2 (58.4–73.,1)	65.7 (57.0–73.4)	66.7 (55.3–76.4)	77.5 (70.4–83.3)	79.2 (70.4–85.9)	75.6 (64.3–84.2)
Moldova, Republic of, 2008	9.0 (5.0–15.7)	10.9 (5.6–20.1)	4.9 (1.3–16.7)	79.7 (74.1–84.4)	84.7 (79.2–88.9)	66.8 (48.5–81.1)	79.6 (69.5–87.0)	78.1 (67.8–85.7)	81.8 (63.0–92.3)
Montenegro, 2008	7.9 (3.7–16.0)	12.0 (5.0–25.9)	2.1 (0.2–16.1)	41.2 (30.9–52.3)	39.9 (26.2–55.5)	NR	75.6 (62.3–85.2)	70.7 (53.7–83.5)	NR

Table 3.1.65 Continued

WHO region and WHO member state, territory, or special administrative region, and year	% Always have or feel like having a cigarette first thing in the morning			% Want to stop smoking			% Tried to stop smoking during the past year		
	Total % (95% CI)	Males % (95% CI)	Females % (95% CI)	Total % (95% CI)	Males % (95% CI)	Females % (95% CI)	Total % (95% CI)	Males % (95% CI)	Females % (95% CI)
Poland, 2003	10.8 (6.3–17.9)	12.4 (7.2–20.6)	7.5 (3.2–16.4)	51.3 (42.5–60.0)	50.3 (38.6–62.0)	52.7 (40.9–64.3)	61.5 (55.8–66.9)	61.3 (53.0–69.0)	62.3 (53.3–70.6)
Romania, 2004	4.7 (2.5–8.8)	6.1 (2.5–14.1)	3.3 (1.1–9.5)	55.4 (44.8–65.5)	46.5 (33.2–60.2)	66.0 (53.1–76.9)	76.3 (67.9–83.1)	72.9 (64.6–79.8)	80.8 (61.7–91.6)
Russian Federation, 2004	10.6 (6.7–16.3)	13.4 (7.2–23.7)	7.4 (4.6–11.8)	65.5 (59.0–71.5)	65.9 (59.5–71.8)	65.0 (57.2–72.1)	78.1 (73.2–82.3)	74.1 (70.8–77.1)	82.4 (73.7–88.7)
Serbia, 2008	11.9 (7.0–19.6)	13.2 (5.7–27.7)	12.0 (5.1–26.0)	47.5 (37.3–57.9)	51.7 (36.4–66.6)	44.1 (30.0–59.3)	52.5 (41.2–63.5)	40.4 (29.7–52.2)	68.9 (54.0–80.7)
Slovakia, 2007	16.6 (13.7–20.0)	19.0 (15.1–23.5)	13.4 (9.4–18.7)	64.8 (61.0–68.4)	63.3 (58.0–68.4)	67.3 (61.4–72.6)	78.2 (75.3–80.9)	76.5 (71.5–80.8)	80.7 (76.9–84.0)
Slovenia, 2007	11.6 (7.3–18.0)	12.8 (7.0–22.4)	11.3 (5.3–22.7)	39.7 (34.6–45.0)	49.5 (38.5–60.5)	34.2 (26.9–42.4)	67.0 (58.1–74.8)	66.3 (49.3–79.9)	70.8 (60.1–79.6)
Tajikistan, 2004	NR	NR	NR	NR	NR	NR	NR	NR	NR
Turkey, 2003	13.1 (9.6–17.6)	12.8 (9.0–17.8)	13.6 (7.2–24.3)	65.3 (60.4–69.9)	68.9 (63.0–74.3)	60.2 (50.6–69.1)	61.4 (55.7–66.8)	66.9 (60.5–72.7)	44.8 (31.9–58.4)
Ukraine, 2005	7.5 (5.8–9.6)	8.0 (5.8–10.9)	6.7 (3.6–12.2)	74.5 (70.2–78.4)	75.4 (68.2–81.5)	73.8 (66.3–80.2)	82.1 (77.5–86.0)	80.6 (75.9–84.6)	84.3 (76.9–89.7)
Uzbekistan, 2008 (Tashkent)	NR	NR	NR	NR	NR	NR	NR	NR	NR
South East Asia	5.2 (3.5–6.9)	7.5 (5.0–10.0)	4.9 (1.5–8.3)	82.2 (79.8–84.7)	79.7 (76.9–82.5)	70.8 (62.4–79.3)	85.1 (83.1–87.2)	84.7 (82.4–87.0)	77.1 (71.3–82.9)
Bangladesh, 2007	1.0 (0.3–3.9)	NR	NR	70.7 (45.4–87.5)	89.5 (63.3–97.7)	NR	85.0 (57.2–96.0)	92.6 (73.4–98.2)	NR
Bhutan, 2006	7.5 (2.7–19.4)	6.4 (1.3–26.0)	NR	91.7 (81.0–96.7)	89.1 (76.6–95.3)	NR	85.4 (72.4–92.9)	82.7 (70.2–90.7)	NR
East Timor, 2006	13.0 (8.9–18.8)	14.2 (9.3–21.2)	8.7 (3.1–22.0)	73.7 (63.9–81.5)	73.0 (62.0–81.8)	NR	73.6 (58.8–84.5)	72.1 (55.4–84.4)	NR
India, 2006	8.7 (5.8–12.8)	8.1 (5.3–12.4)	11.1 (4.7–23.9)	70.3 (61.6–77.8)	70.0 (60.6–77.9)	72.2 (49.7–87.3)	55.5 (44.0–66.4)	57.0 (44.0–69.1)	48.3 (29.5–67.6)
Indonesia, 2006	2.1 (0.7–6.1)	2.0 (0.6–6.5)	NR	78.1 (68.5–85.4)	80.2 (70.4–87.4)	NR	85.6 (75.1–92.1)	86.6 (75.2–93.2)	NR

Table 3.1.65 Continued

WHO region and WHO member state, territory, or special administrative region, and year	% Always have or feel like having a cigarette first thing in the morning			% Want to stop smoking			% Tried to stop smoking during the past year		
	Total % (95% CI)	Males % (95% CI)	Females % (95% CI)	Total % (95% CI)	Males % (95% CI)	Females % (95% CI)	Total % (95% CI)	Males % (95% CI)	Females % (95% CI)
Maldives, 2007	23.8 (12.8–39.9)	NR	22.6 (9.3–45.3)	65.0 (46.9–79.6)	NR	69.1 (46.1–85.4)	54.4 (32.4–74.8)	NR	54.1 (32.5–74.3)
Myanmar, 2007	5.8 (1.6–18.7)	6.8 (1.9–21.7)	NR	83.0 (66.8–92.2)	NR	NR	88.1 (78.8–93.6)	86.3 (75.7–92.7)	NR
Nepal, 2007	NR	NR	NR	92.0 (77.5–97.4)	NR	NR	93.8 (80.8–98.2)	NR	NR
Sri Lanka, 2007	NR	NR	NR	NR	NR	NR	NR	NR	NR
Thailand, 2005	7.8 (5.1–11.8)	11.3 (7.2–17.3)	3.6 (1.7–7.3)	72.3 (63.2–79.9)	75.5 (69.4–80.7)	70.9 (53.2–84.0)	83.3 (78.8–86.9)	84.3 (79.9–87.9)	82.6 (73.6–89.0)
Western Pacific	6.5 (5.5–7.4)	6.3 (4.9–7.7)	4.3 (3.0–5.6)	81.6 (80.7–82.6)	85.4 (84.2–86.6)	81.2 (79.7–82.7)	80.9 (79.8–81.9)	80.8 (79.5–82.1)	82.6 (81.2–84.0)
American Samoa, 2005[b]	NA	NA	NA	83.6 (77.4–88.4)	85.2 (75.9–91.3)	81.8 (72.9–88.2)	80.3 (73.3–85.9)	79.0 (67.8–87.1)	82.0 (71.3–89.3)
Cambodia, 2003	NR	NR	NR	NR	NR	NR	NR	NR	NR
China, 2005[e] (Macau)	NR	NR	NR	NR	NR	NR	NR	NR	NR
China, 2005 (Shanghai)	2.6 (0.8–8.1)	4.9 (1.4–15.2)	0.0	42.1 (32.9–51.9)	38.4 (27.7–50.3)	46.7 (31.0–63.1)	55.2 (45.3–64.6)	52.1 (38.3–65.7)	58.9 (47.7–69.2)
Cook Islands, 2008	6.4 (5.2–7.9)	6.1 (4.4–8.5)	6.8 (5.1–8.9)	78.2 (75.6–80.6)	88.1 (84.8–90.8)	71.1 (67.4–74.5)	82.6 (80.3–84.6)	77.9 (74.0–81.3)	85.4 (82.6–87.9)
Fiji, 2005	7.8 (2.8–20.1)	6.4 (1.7–21.7)	NR	88.2 (80.0–93.3)	89.5 (82.8–93.8)	NR	83.1 (71.8–90.5)	85.4 (71.0–93.4)	NR
Guam, 2002[b]	NA	NA	NA	75.7 (69.6–80.8)	74.2 (64.7–81.8)	77.5 (69.9–83.6)	74.7 (68.3–80.3)	69.1 (60.1–76.8)	82.5 (74.8–88.1)
Lao People's Democratic Republic, 2007 (Vientiane Capital)	NR	NR	NR	NR	NR	NR	NR	NR	NR
Malaysia, 2003	9.0 (6.0–13.2)	9.0 (5.8–13.9)	8.5 (3.7–18.4)	80.2 (75.0–84.5)	79.5 (74.0–84.1)	NR	88.3 (84.6–91.2)	87.8 (83.3–91.3)	92.1 (78.0–97.5)
Micronesia, 2007	8.4 (5.1–13.5)	10.0 (5.1–18.9)	6.8 (3.4–13.3)	86.5 (82.8–89.4)	86.4 (78.8–91.6)	91.7 (85.1–95.5)	83.2 (75.0–89.1)	79.3 (67.2–87.7)	91.9 (83.3–96.3)

Table 3.1.65 Continued

WHO region and WHO member state, territory, or special administrative region, and year	% Always have or feel like having a cigarette first thing in the morning			% Want to stop smoking			% Tried to stop smoking during the past year		
	Total % (95% CI)	Males % (95% CI)	Females % (95% CI)	Total % (95% CI)	Males % (95% CI)	Females % (95% CI)	Total % (95% CI)	Males % (95% CI)	Females % (95% CI)
Mongolia, 2007	2.4 (0.8–7.4)	3.5 (1.2–9.9)	NR	88.6 (74.7–95.3)	90.0 (79.3–95.5)	NR	84.4 (76.2–90.2)	89.6 (82.3–94.1)	NR
New Zealand, 2008	NA	NA	NA	42.6 (34.1–51.6)	26.7 (10.9–52.1)	54.2 (34.9–72.3)	52.0 (35.7–68.0)	37.4 (17.2–63.3)	62.0 (47.3–74.8)
Northern Mariana Islands, 2004[f]	NA	NA	NA	79.4 (75.1–83.2)	81.4 (75.2–86.3)	77.8 (71.3–83.1)	78.2 (73.8 -82.1)	77.9 (72.1–82.8)	78.8 (72.6–83.9)
Palau, 2005	NA	NA	NA	78.1 (70.3–84.3)	72.9 (62.5–81.3)	86.3 (73.8–93.4)	NA	NA	NA
Papua New Guinea, 2007	8.8 (6.5–11.9)	11.1 (7.6–15.9)	5.6 (2.9–10.7)	82.3 (77.9–86.1)	82.6 (75.8–87.9)	81.4 (75.5–86.1)	84.7 (81.8–87.3)	85.3 (80.4–89.2)	83.6 (78.4–87.7)
Philippines, 2007	3.0 (1.1–7.6)	3.2 (0.9–11.1)	0.3 (0.0–2.4)	88.1 (83.0–91.7)	88.0 (81.3–92.5)	89.3 (80.3–94.5)	86.0 (79.7–90.6)	88.2 (82.2–92.4)	82.9 (67.8–91.8)
Republic of Korea (South), 2008	14.4 (9.6–21.0)	17.1 (11.0–25.5)	7.4 (3.3–16.1)	66.1 (60.8–71.1)	70.7 (64.0–76.6)	59.5 (46.8–71.1)	77.1 (70.5–82.6)	79.2 (72.0–84.9)	74.7 (60.8–84.9)
Samoa, 2007	4.6 (1.4–14.0)	NR	NR	66.2 (50.0–79.4)	NR	NR	70.1 (50.4–84.5)	NR	NR
Singapore, 2000	NA	NA	NA	NA	NA	NA	61.9 (56.7–66.9)	62.0 (55.7–67.9)	61.3 (54.3–67.9)
Solomon Islands, 2008	9.4 (4.6–18.3)	13.4 (5.4–29.5)	5.7 (0.9–29.4)	90.8 (85.8–94.2)	95.9 (81.4–99.2)	85.4 (73.1–92.6)	85.4 (74.1–92.3)	84.5 (64.0–94.4)	87.6 (67.2–96.1)
Tuvalu, 2006	2.9 (2.8–3.1)	NR	NR	98.7 (98.6–98.8)	NR	NR	93.0 (92.7–93.2)	91.5 (91.1–91.9)	NR
Vanuatu, 2007	5.4 (3.8–7.6)	3.8 (2.2–6.3)	7.0 (4.1–11.5)	84.5 (81.3–87.2)	83.8 (79.7–87.3)	85.4 (79.9–89.6)	72.1 (68.3–75.7)	72.9 (68.1–77.3)	NR
Viet Nam, 2007 (Hanoi)	17.6 (6.4–40.2)	NR	NR	51.9 (24.8–77.9)	NR	NR	67.9 (44.4–84.9)	NR	NR

Source: CDC 2010b.
Note: **CI** = confidence interval; **NA** = question not asked; **NR** = cell size less than 35; **WHO** = World Health Organization.
[a]Territory of United Kingdom
[b]Territory of United States
[c]United Nations Relief and Works Agency
[d]United Nations Administered Province
[e]Special Administrative Region of China
[f]Commonwealth in political union with the United States

Table 3.1.66 Percentage of youth 13–15 years of age who have used any form of tobacco during the past 30 days and who have used any form of tobacco other than cigarettes during the past 30 days, by gender; Global Youth Tobacco Survey (GYTS) 1999–2009; worldwide

	% Used any form of tobacco in the past 30 days			% Used any form of tobacco other than cigarettes in the past 30 days		
WHO region and WHO member state, territory, or special administrative region, and year	**Total % (95% CI)**	**Males % (95% CI)**	**Females % (95% CI)**	**Total % (95% CI)**	**Males % (95% CI)**	**Females % (95% CI)**
Africa	14.1 (13.6–14.6)	17.5 (16.8–18.1)	10.5 (10.0–11.1)	9.0 (8.6–9.4)	10.0 (9.5–10.5)	7.9 (7.4–8.4)
Algeria, 2007 (Constantine)	13.8 (11.3–16.8)	25.5 (21.9–29.5)	5.7 (3.8–8.5)	8.0 (6.4–10.0)	12.7 (10.2–15.6)	4.8 (3.2–7.2)
Benin, 2003 (Atlantique Littoral)	11.0 (8.8–13.6)	14.6 (11.4–18.5)	5.8 (3.9–8.7)	5.6 (4.3–7.3)	6.7 (5.0–9.0)	4.2 (2.5–6.9)
Botswana, 2008	23.6 (20.2–27.3)	27.0 (21.7–33.0)	20.5 (17.1–24.5)	15.2 (12.8–18.0)	16.3 (13.0–20.2)	14.3 (11.7–17.5)
Burkina Faso, 2006 (Ouagadougou)	13.6 (11.3–16.3)	19.9 (16.1–24.3)	6.7 (5.0–9.0)	7.2 (5.6–9.1)	9.3 (7.1–12.1)	4.8 (3.0–7.5)
Burundi, 2008	19.3 (13.2–27.3)	20.7 (13.2–30.9)	16.8 (10.6–25.6)	16.1 (10.2–24.4)	17.1 (10.8–26.0)	14.3 (8.0–24.2)
Cameroon, 2008 (Yaoude)	10.9 (8.1–14.4)	14.0 (10.1–19.2)	8.2 (5.6–11.8)	7.3 (5.5–9.8)	8.7 (5.9–12.6)	6.0 (4.1–8.6)
Cape Verde, 2007	13.4 (11.9–15.1)	14.7 (12.3–17.5)	11.7 (9.5–14.4)	10.6 (9.1–12.4)	11.6 (8.8–15.2)	9.3 (7.6–11.2)
Central African Republic, 2008 (Bangui)	32.4 (18.0–51.1)	29.5 (23.4–36.4)	34.5 (12.8–65.4)	28.2 (13.8–49.0)	24.0 (18.2–30.9)	31.3 (10.0–65.1)
Comoros, 2007	18.1 (14.4–22.5)	21.8 (15.1–30.4)	14.8 (10.6–20.5)	11.4 (8.5–15.1)	12.5 (8.3–18.4)	9.9 (6.5–14.8)
Congo, 2006	23.8 (18.4–30.2)	26.1 (19.8–33.5)	21.9 (16.9–27.9)	16.7 (12.7–21.6)	15.6 (12.1–19.9)	17.7 (12.5–24.4)
Côte D'Ivoire, 2003 (Abidjan)	16.5 (14.7–18.5)	21.7 (19.1–24.5)	10.3 (8.0–13.3)	5.1 (4.3–6.1)	5.6 (4.6–6.9)	4.4 (3.4–5.6)
Democratic Republic of the Congo, 2008 (Kinshasa)	33.6 (26.5–41.6)	36.2 (26.1–47.8)	29.5 (22.0–38.4)	29.0 (22.2–36.8)	29.3 (19.6–41.3)	27.8 (20.2–36.9)
Equatorial Guinea, 2008	22.1 (16.5–28.9)	25.1 (18.1–33.7)	17.3 (12.6–23.2)	17.8 (12.5–24.7)	19.5 (13.2–27.9)	14.8 (10.4–20.8)
Eritrea, 2006	6.6 (5.5–7.9)	7.8 (6.4–9.6)	4.6 (3.4–6.1)	5.5 (4.4–6.9)	6.4 (5.0–8.2)	4.2 (3.0–5.8)
Ethiopia, 2003 (Addis Ababa)	7.9 (4.9–12.5)	9.9 (6.3–15.4)	4.9 (3.1–7.7)	6.6 (4.1–10.6)	8.4 (4.8–14.3)	4.4 (2.6–7.4)
Gambia, 2008 (Banjul)	36.1 (29.8–42.9)	34.0 (28.5–40.0)	36.6 (28.9–44.9)	32.7 (26.3–39.7)	29.5 (23.6–36.1)	34.3 (26.8–42.7)
Ghana, 2006	11.7 (8.9–15.2)	11.6 (8.5–15.5)	10.9 (8.2–14.4)	10.4 (7.8–13.7)	10.1 (7.3–13.8)	10.1 (7.6–13.2)
Guinea, 2008	26.1 (18.2–35.9)	30.8 (22.2–41.1)	20.0 (12.5–30.4)	21.6 (13.7–32.3)	23.4 (14.6–35.4)	18.9 (11.4–29.7)
Guinea-Bissau, 2008 (Bissau)	10.9 (9.1–13.0)	11.5 (8.7–15.0)	10.3 (7.5–13.9)	6.1 (4.4–8.6)	4.5 (2.9–6.9)	7.8 (5.0–12.1)

Table 3.1.66 Continued

WHO region and WHO member state, territory, or special administrative region, and year	% Used any form of tobacco in the past 30 days			% Used any form of tobacco other than cigarettes in the past 30 days		
	Total % (95% CI)	Males % (95% CI)	Females % (95% CI)	Total % (95% CI)	Males % (95% CI)	Females % (95% CI)
Kenya, 2007	15.1 (11.3–19.8)	14.9 (12.8–17.2)	14.5 (8.0–24.9)	10.1 (6.5–15.4)	8.2 (6.1–11.0)	11.4 (5.2–23.2)
Lesotho, 2008	24.8 (19.9–30.5)	26.4 (19.9–34.2)	21.7 (17.2–27.0)	19.5 (16.1–23.4)	20.4 (15.2–26.9)	17.9 (14.6–21.8)
Liberia, 2008 (Monrovia)	13.6 (8.9–20.1)	14.2 (6.9–27.1)	11.8 (7.7–17.6)	13.3 (8.6–20.0)	14.1 (6.7–27.1)	11.5 (7.6–17.3)
Madagascar, 2008	22.8 (16.4–30.7)	33.2 (24.0–43.8)	14.3 (8.3–23.4)	7.0 (3.2–14.6)	8.5 (4.5–15.6)	5.8 (1.8–16.6)
Malawi, 2005	18.4 (14.3–23.4)	19.1 (15.9–22.7)	17.9 (11.6–26.5)	17.1 (13.0–22.2)	17.1 (14.0–20.8)	17.1 (10.8–25.9)
Mali, 2008	16.6 (12.3–22.0)	23.1 (16.6–31.2)	8.8 (6.4–12.0)	9.0 (6.0–13.4)	10.7 (6.4–17.5)	7.2 (5.1–10.1)
Mauritania, 2006	30.7 (26.7–35.1)	31.5 (26.8–36.7)	29.5 (23.8–36.0)	18.0 (14.4–22.2)	18.4 (14.3–23.4)	17.3 (12.1–24.1)
Mauritius, 2008	13.7 (9.3–19.8)	20.3 (13.9–28.6)	7.7 (4.1–14.0)	NA	NA	NA
Mozambique, 2007 (Maputo City)	10.0 (7.5–13.1)	12.7 (9.4–16.9)	7.4 (4.7–11.4)	8.2 (6.2–10.7)	9.6 (6.8–13.3)	6.8 (4.3–10.4)
Namibia, 2004	25.8 (23.4–28.3)	28.6 (25.6–31.8)	22.9 (20.2–26.0)	15.0 (12.6–17.6)	15.1 (12.3–18.4)	14.0 (11.5–16.9)
Niger, 2006	11.7 (8.4–16.0)	15.2 (10.9–20.9)	8.0 (5.1–12.5)	6.6 (4.4–9.6)	6.1 (3.8–9.5)	7.0 (4.6–10.5)
Nigeria, 2008 (Cross River State)	26.1 (18.2–36.0)	29.6 (20.0–41.6)	18.6 (10.3–31.2)	23.3 (16.6–31.6)	23.9 (16.2–33.9)	17.5 (9.9–29.0)
Rwanda, 2008	11.5 (8.8–15.0)	13.3 (8.5–20.1)	9.5 (6.5–13.6)	10.5 (7.9–13.9)	12.0 (7.4–19.0)	8.7 (6.1–12.1)
Senegal, 2007	14.9 (9.9–21.8)	20.4 (14.7–27.8)	9.6 (4.5–19.2)	9.3 (5.5–15.3)	11.7 (8.4–15.9)	7.7 (3.0–18.0)
Seychelles, 2007	26.6 (21.7–32.1)	27.1 (20.6–34.7)	25.3 (20.4–30.9)	10.5 (7.7–14.1)	10.6 (6.9–16.0)	9.2 (6.4–13.0)
Sierra Leone, 2008 (Western Area)	23.5 (19.3–28.3)	20.3 (14.5–27.8)	24.1 (19.9–28.8)	20.7 (16.4–25.8)	16.7 (11.6–23.5)	21.8 (17.2–27.4)
South Africa, 2008	24.0 (21.6–26.6)	29.3 (26.6–32.1)	20.1 (17.2–23.4)	14.6 (12.9–16.5)	16.9 (14.8–19.3)	12.8 (10.9–15.0)
Swaziland, 2005	11.3 (10.2–12.6)	14.7 (13.0–16.5)	9.0 (7.8–10.3)	7.5 (6.5–8.7)	8.5 (7.1–10.1)	6.9 (5.8–8.2)
Togo, 2007	14.0 (11.2–17.2)	17.7 (13.3–23.1)	7.9 (5.5–11.1)	10.4 (8.5–12.8)	12.1 (9.3–15.7)	7.4 (5.2–10.4)
Uganda, 2007	16.6 (14.4–19.2)	17.3 (14.7–20.2)	15.3 (12.8–18.2)	13.9 (11.9–16.2)	13.8 (11.5–16.4)	13.5 (11.0–16.5)

Table 3.1.66 Continued

WHO region and WHO member state, territory, or special administrative region, and year	% Used any form of tobacco in the past 30 days			% Used any form of tobacco other than cigarettes in the past 30 days		
	Total % (95% CI)	Males % (95% CI)	Females % (95% CI)	Total % (95% CI)	Males % (95% CI)	Females % (95% CI)
United Republic of Tanzania, 2008 (Arusha)	10.6 (8.1–13.8)	12.4 (9.0–16.7)	8.8 (5.8–13.2)	9.5 (7.2–12.4)	10.8 (8.1–14.3)	8.2 (5.5–12.1)
Zambia, 2007 (Lusaka)	25.6 (20.0–32.2)	25.7 (19.5–33.1)	25.6 (19.6–32.7)	22.8 (17.3–29.4)	22.8 (16.7–30.2)	22.8 (16.9–30.1)
Zimbabwe, 2008 (Harare)	12.0 (9.0–15.7)	14.9 (10.9–20.1)	8.2 (5.4–12.2)	9.6 (6.9–13.3)	10.9 (7.7–15.1)	7.5 (4.8–11.6)
The Americas	17.0 (16.5–17.5)	19.7 (19.1–20.3)	14.7 (14.1–15.3)	8.1 (7.8–8.4)	9.9 (9.5–10.4)	6.5 (6.1–6.8)
Antigua & Barbuda, 2004	14.1 (11.4–17.2)	15.1 (12.1–18.8)	12.5 (9.2–16.8)	12.4 (9.9–15.4)	13.4 (10.1–17.5)	10.9 (8.0–14.7)
Argentina, 2007	28.0 (25.9–30.3)	26.1 (23.6–28.8)	29.7 (25.7–34.0)	8.9 (7.4–10.5)	11.6 (9.6–13.9)	6.5 (4.9–8.5)
Bahamas, 2004	11.9 (10.1–13.8)	12.9 (10.3–16.1)	10.2 (7.6–13.5)	8.4 (6.9–10.3)	9.4 (7.4–11.8)	7.4 (5.5–9.9)
Barbados, 2007	28.6 (25.2–32.2)	34.5 (30.1–39.3)	23.2 (19.4–27.5)	24.2 (21.3–27.3)	30.2 (26.1–34.6)	18.7 (15.6–22.1)
Belize, 2008	18.3 (15.6–21.5)	21.8 (18.2–26.0)	15.3 (12.1–19.0)	13.3 (10.5–16.7)	14.5 (10.7–19.5)	12.1 (9.8–15.0)
Bolivia, 2003 (La Paz)	20.8 (18.0–23.8)	24.7 (20.6–29.3)	16.6 (14.3–19.1)	8.2 (7.0–9.7)	9.5 (7.8–11.5)	6.9 (5.7–8.3)
Brazil, 2005 (Rio de Janeiro)	17.2 (14.6–20.2)	17.2 (14.0–21.0)	15.7 (12.3–19.8)	6.1 (4.8–7.7)	10.0 (7.0–14.0)	3.3 (2.2–5.0)
British Virgin Islands, 2001[a]	10.5 (7.4–14.7)	11.3 (6.7–18.3)	10.1 (6.8–14.7)	8.2 (5.5–12.0)	8.3 (4.5–15.0)	8.4 (5.5–12.8)
Chile, 2008 (Santiago)	35.1 (32.4–37.9)	29.8 (26.2–33.7)	39.8 (35.8–43.8)	9.2 (8.1–10.4)	9.5 (8.1–11.1)	8.8 (7.0–11.0)
Colombia, 2007 (Bogota)	27.6 (23.7–31.8)	27.0 (22.7–31.7)	27.8 (22.2–34.1)	5.0 (3.7–6.8)	6.7 (4.7–9.7)	3.6 (2.4–5.4)
Costa Rica, 2008	14.6 (13.1–16.2)	15.9 (14.0–17.9)	13.1 (11.2–15.3)	7.7 (6.6–8.9)	9.3 (8.1–10.8)	5.9 (4.5–7.7)
Cuba, 2004 (Havana)	14.6 (11.2–18.9)	15.7 (11.8–20.6)	13.6 (10.1–18.2)	5.8 (3.3–10.0)	6.0 (3.0–11.8)	5.7 (3.3–9.7)
Dominica, 2004	17.2 (14.1–20.9)	19.3 (14.8–24.8)	13.5 (10.4–17.3)	9.3 (7.6–11.4)	12.0 (9.0–15.9)	6.3 (4.5–8.9)
Dominican Republic, 2004	14.9 (13.3–16.8)	18.4 (15.9–21.1)	11.9 (9.8–14.3)	10.0 (8.5–11.8)	12.9 (10.6–15.8)	7.4 (6.0–9.0)
Ecuador, 2007 (Quito)	28.6 (23.8–33.9)	31.2 (27.9–34.8)	26.1 (18.9–34.8)	15.3 (12.7–18.3)	15.9 (12.9–19.5)	14.6 (11.1–19.0)
El Salvador, 2003	19.0 (14.7–24.3)	24.4 (19.2–30.4)	15.4 (11.2–20.7)	8.4 (6.4–10.9)	10.5 (8.4–13.0)	7.0 (5.0–9.9)

Table 3.1.66 Continued

WHO region and WHO member state, territory, or special administrative region, and year	% Used any form of tobacco in the past 30 days			% Used any form of tobacco other than cigarettes in the past 30 days		
	Total % (95% CI)	Males % (95% CI)	Females % (95% CI)	Total % (95% CI)	Males % (95% CI)	Females % (95% CI)
Grenada, 2004	16.7 (14.1–19.6)	17.6 (14.0–21.9)	15.7 (12.9–19.1)	10.5 (8.5–12.9)	11.6 (9.0–14.8)	9.3 (7.1–12.1)
Guatemala, 2008	16.6 (14.5–18.9)	19.7 (16.8–22.9)	13.3 (11.0–16.1)	7.9 (7.1–8.9)	9.5 (8.0–11.3)	6.2 (5.3–7.2)
Guyana, 2004	14.9 (11.0–19.9)	17.6 (12.9–23.5)	12.2 (8.1–18.0)	8.3 (6.4–10.7)	9.1 (6.3–12.9)	7.7 (4.9–11.9)
Haiti, 2005 (Port au Prince)	23.2 (19.7–27.1)	21.7 (17.0–27.2)	23.9 (19.2–29.3)	10.4 (8.3–13.1)	9.0 (6.5–12.3)	11.1 (7.4–16.3)
Honduras, 2003 (Tegucigalpa)	20.4 (16.9–24.4)	22.8 (19.3–26.7)	18.2 (13.8–23.7)	9.9 (8.2–11.9)	12.1 (9.3–15.6)	8.0 (5.8–10.9)
Jamaica, 2006	19.5 (14.2–26.3)	24.0 (17.8–31.6)	15.3 (10.6–21.6)	8.9 (6.5–11.9)	10.2 (7.1–14.5)	7.2 (4.8–10.8)
Mexico, 2006 (Mexico City)	28.6 (25.2–32.2)	27.8 (23.6–32.4)	28.5 (25.2–32.0)	4.8 (3.6–6.4)	5.5 (3.3–9.0)	4.0 (3.0–5.3)
Montserrat, 2000[a]	12.5	10.2	13.6	9.4	10.2	7.7
Nicaragua, 2003 (Centro Managua)	25.1 (21.1–29.6)	30.4 (26.3–34.9)	20.5 (15.6–26.4)	9.6 (7.0–12.9)	12.8 (9.8–16.5)	6.7 (3.9–11.3)
Panama, 2008	8.4 (6.4–11.0)	10.5 (7.7–14.1)	6.5 (4.8–8.7)	5.8 (4.5–7.3)	7.1 (5.3–9.5)	4.5 (3.3–6.0)
Paraguay, 2008	16.7 (15.3–18.1)	20.8 (18.9–22.7)	12.9 (11.3–14.6)	10.3 (8.9–12.0)	12.4 (10.3–14.8)	8.4 (7.0–10.0)
Peru, 2007 (Lima)	19.6 (15.5–24.5)	19.9 (15.5–25.1)	18.2 (13.5–24.0)	3.4 (2.4–4.9)	3.8 (2.3–6.4)	3.1 (1.8–5.4)
Puerto Rico, 2004[b]	11.9 (7.9–17.7)	12.8 (8.7–18.6)	10.9 (6.5–17.6)	7.7 (4.9–11.9)	9.6 (5.9–15.4)	5.5 (2.8–10.6)
Saint Kitts & Nevis, 2002	16.6 (13.4–20.4)	18.2 (13.5–24.2)	13.6 (10.9–17.0)	13.7 (11.2–16.5)	14.6 (10.5–20.0)	12.1 (9.6–15.2)
Saint Lucia, 2007	17.9 (14.8–21.4)	22.4 (16.9–29.2)	14.5 (11.3–18.4)	10.2 (7.2–14.3)	13.0 (8.4–19.6)	8.4 (5.7–12.2)
Saint Vincent & The Grenadines, 2007	19.1 (15.5–23.4)	22.0 (16.8–28.2)	16.6 (13.1–20.9)	10.3 (8.2–13.0)	11.2 (8.2–15.2)	9.6 (7.1–12.9)
Suriname, 2004	10.5 (8.7–12.6)	12.6 (9.3–16.9)	8.6 (6.1–11.8)	4.4 (3.3–6.0)	4.4 (2.7–7.1)	4.4 (3.2–6.2)
Trinidad & Tobago, 2007	19.9 (16.1–24.4)	20.8 (16.2–26.4)	17.8 (12.8–24.1)	8.9 (6.8–11.5)	8.9 (6.2–12.6)	8.7 (6.1–12.1)
U.S. Virgin Islands, 2004[b]	7.8 (6.4–9.5)	9.9 (7.6–12.7)	5.7 (4.1–7.9)	6.2 (4.9–7.8)	9.0 (6.9–11.5)	3.7 (2.3–5.7)
Uruguay, 2007	23.2 (21.0–25.5)	21.4 (18.1–25.1)	24.5 (21.8–27.4)	7.9 (6.6–9.4)	10.3 (8.1–13.0)	6.1 (4.6–8.0)
Venezuela, 1999	14.8 (12.6–17.2)	15.3 (12.3–18.8)	13.9 (11.8–16.4)	8.7 (7.3–10.4)	10.5 (8.3–13.3)	6.8 (5.5–8.3)

Table 3.1.66 Continued

WHO region and WHO member state, territory, or special administrative region, and year	% Used any form of tobacco in the past 30 days			% Used any form of tobacco other than cigarettes in the past 30 days		
	Total % (95% CI)	Males % (95% CI)	Females % (95% CI)	Total % (95% CI)	Males % (95% CI)	Females % (95% CI)
Eastern Mediterranean	18.5 (17.9–19.1)	25.7 (24.9–26.5)	13.6 (13.0–14.2)	16.5 (16.0–17.1)	19.9 (19.3–20.5)	12.2 (11.6–12.8)
Afghanistan, 2004 (Kabul)	9.8 (6.7–14.0)	13.1 (9.2–18.3)	3.2 (1.6–6.3)	5.9 (3.6–9.5)	7.0 (3.8–12.3)	3.2 (1.6–6.4)
Bahrain, 2002	19.9 (16.5–23.8)	28.0 (23.5–32.9)	11.7 (8.6–15.8)	15.3 (12.6–18.3)	19.9 (16.3–24.0)	10.5 (8.0–13.8)
Djibouti, 2003	14.9 (11.6–18.9)	17.9 (13.4–23.5)	10.7 (7.1–15.9)	11.1 (8.8–14.0)	12.3 (9.4–16.0)	9.6 (6.4–14.3)
Egypt, 2005	12.6 (10.1–15.5)	16.0 (13.0–19.6)	7.6 (6.1–9.3)	10.1 (8.1–12.4)	12.3 (9.5–15.8)	6.7 (5.1–8.6)
Gaza Strip, 2008[c]	23.6 (20.3–27.2)	26.3 (21.1–32.2)	19.2 (13.7–26.2)	21.9 (18.3–26.0)	23.8 (17.9–30.9)	18.3 (13.0–25.2)
Iran, 2007	26.6 (20.9–33.1)	32.9 (25.3–41.4)	19.5 (15.6–24.2)	26.1 (20.6–32.4)	31.9 (24.4–40.4)	19.5 (15.6–24.2)
Iraq, 2008 (Baghdad)	17.2 (15.1–19.5)	17.7 (15.4–20.3)	15.2 (12.1–18.9)	15.3 (13.2–17.6)	15.7 (13.8–17.9)	13.6 (10.7–17.2)
Jordan, 2008[c]	32.5 (26.0–39.7)	39.7 (34.7–45.0)	23.0 (20.1–26.1)	28.5 (23.2–34.4)	33.7 (29.1–38.5)	21.3 (18.6–24.2)
Kuwait, 2005	20.9 (17.3–25.1)	28.0 (24.3–32.1)	14.3 (12.3–16.7)	14.5 (12.3–16.9)	17.4 (15.0–20.1)	11.7 (9.9–13.9)
Lebanon, 2008[c]	41.4 (36.0–47.1)	48.2 (43.2–53.3)	35.8 (28.6–43.7)	38.9 (33.7–44.4)	44.1 (39.3–49.0)	34.6 (27.2–42.9)
Libya, 2007	11.1 (8.9–13.7)	15.5 (11.5–20.5)	6.1 (4.5–8.3)	7.2 (5.4–9.5)	8.6 (5.2–14.0)	5.6 (4.1–7.7)
Morocco, 2006	11.0 (9.3–13.0)	12.5 (9.6–16.1)	8.2 (6.5–10.3)	9.0 (7.5–10.8)	10.3 (7.8–13.5)	6.9 (5.5–8.7)
Oman, 2007	15.2 (11.9–19.2)	17.8 (13.4–23.3)	11.3 (8.6–14.7)	14.4 (11.4–18.0)	16.9 (12.8–22.0)	10.6 (8.1–13.7)
Pakistan, 2003 (Islamabad)	10.1 (8.0–12.8)	12.4 (9.2–16.5)	7.5 (5.4–10.2)	9.5 (7.4–12.1)	11.2 (7.9–15.6)	7.3 (5.3–10.1)
Qatar, 2007	17.9 (14.9–21.5)	25.2 (19.8–31.4)	13.1 (9.6–17.7)	15.6 (13.1–18.6)	19.4 (15.7–23.8)	12.6 (9.3–16.8)
Saudi Arabia, 2007	15.9 (13.8–18.3)	20.2 (17.7–22.8)	10.7 (7.9–14.4)	11.9 (10.3–13.8)	13.3 (12.2–14.4)	9.4 (6.8–12.9)
Somalia, 2007 (Somaliland)	15.6 (13.4–18.2)	15.5 (12.7–18.7)	12.3 (6.7–21.3)	12.5 (10.1–15.4)	12.7 (10.2–15.8)	9.8 (5.2–17.6)
Sudan, 2005	14.0 (10.8–17.9)	18.0 (13.4–23.7)	10.1 (8.0–12.8)	10.2 (8.0–12.9)	11.0 (7.8–15.4)	9.3 (7.0–12.2)
Syrian Arab Republic, 2008[c]	42.4 (37.4–47.6)	49.6 (44.7–54.5)	33.8 (27.5–40.7)	37.7 (34.0–41.7)	42.7 (37.6–47.9)	31.3 (25.3–38.1)
Tunisia, 2007	18.3 (15.8–21.2)	27.8 (23.5–32.4)	8.8 (6.6–11.7)	13.9 (11.6–16.5)	19.9 (16.1–24.3)	7.8 (5.8–10.4)

Table 3.1.66 Continued

WHO region and WHO member state, territory, or special administrative region, and year	% Used any form of tobacco in the past 30 days			% Used any form of tobacco other than cigarettes in the past 30 days		
	Total % (95% CI)	Males % (95% CI)	Females % (95% CI)	Total % (95% CI)	Males % (95% CI)	Females % (95% CI)
United Arab Emirates, 2005	19.5 (17.5–21.6)	25.2 (23.2–27.4)	13.2 (11.6–15.0)	28.8 (26.7–30.9)	32.7 (30.4–35.1)	24.7 (21.9–27.7)
West Bank, 2008[c]	45.6 (38.1–53.3)	57.6 (53.9–61.1)	35.3 (30.8–40.0)	39.4 (32.9–46.3)	49.6 (46.9–52.2)	30.6 (26.3–35.4)
Yemen, 2008	14.1 (9.8–19.8)	14.5 (8.5–23.6)	10.5 (6.1–17.6)	12.4 (8.7–17.4)	12.1 (7.2–19.6)	10.1 (5.5–18.0)
Europe	12.5 (12.1–12.8)	15.8 (15.3–16.3)	9.2 (8.8–9.6)	4.9 (4.7–5.1)	7.1 (6.8–7.5)	3.1 (2.9–3.4)
Albania, 2004	13.0 (11.0–15.3)	17.3 (13.6–21.8)	9.4 (7.8–11.3)	8.9 (7.3–10.7)	11.5 (9.0–14.6)	6.7 (5.4–8.2)
Armenia, 2004	7.3 (5.8–9.0)	13.0 (9.5–17.5)	2.7 (1.5–4.7)	5.6 (4.4–7.0)	10.0 (6.9–14.4)	1.9 (0.9–4.3)
Belarus, 2004	26.9 (24.6–29.4)	31.6 (28.3–35.0)	22.2 (19.6–25.0)	12.9 (11.3–14.6)	15.2 (13.1–17.6)	10.4 (8.7–12.4)
Bosnia and Herzegovina, 2008	13.3 (11.5–15.5)	16.3 (14.1–18.7)	10.5 (8.4–13.1)	7.5 (6.4–8.8)	9.3 (7.9–10.8)	5.8 (4.4–7.6)
Bulgaria, 2008	29.3 (25.3–33.6)	26.4 (21.9–31.5)	31.8 (26.6–37.6)	8.8 (7.0–10.9)	10.5 (7.8–13.9)	6.8 (5.6–8.3)
Croatia, 2007	24.9 (21.0–29.2)	23.3 (19.8–27.1)	25.6 (20.9–30.9)	13.9 (11.9–16.2)	14.6 (13.1–16.2)	13.0 (10.0–16.9)
Cyprus, 2005	10.9 (10.3–11.4)	13.2 (12.4–14.1)	8.4 (7.7–9.1)	3.3 (3.0–3.6)	5.2 (4.7–5.8)	1.3 (1.1–1.7)
Czech Republic, 2007	35.0 (31.9–38.2)	35.8 (31.8–39.9)	34.1 (29.3–39.2)	14.5 (12.0–17.3)	17.2 (14.3–20.7)	11.2 (8.4–15.0)
Estonia, 2007	30.8 (27.2–34.5)	33.8 (29.6–38.2)	27.8 (23.2–33.0)	21.1 (18.5–23.9)	25.4 (21.6–29.7)	16.7 (13.6–20.4)
Georgia, 2008	8.6 (5.5–13.2)	15.2 (9.9–22.8)	2.8 (1.0–7.8)	NA	NA	NA
Greece, 2005	16.2 (14.3–18.4)	17.1 (15.0–19.4)	14.4 (12.1–16.9)	10.9 (9.4–12.5)	11.8 (10.1–13.8)	8.9 (7.2–11.0)
Hungary, 2008	27.8 (24.6–31.2)	27.9 (23.6–32.6)	26.7 (23.4–30.2)	13.8 (11.4–16.5)	16.8 (13.2–21.0)	10.4 (8.0–13.3)
Kazakhstan, 2004	11.4 (9.6–13.4)	15.2 (13.0–17.7)	8.1 (6.4–10.1)	6.6 (5.5–7.9)	9.3 (7.8–11.0)	4.2 (3.2–5.6)
Kosovo, 2004[d]	10.3 (8.6–12.2)	12.7 (10.1–15.8)	7.9 (6.2–10.0)	7.0 (5.7–8.6)	9.4 (7.2–12.2)	4.6 (3.5–5.9)
Kyrgyzstan, 2008	7.2 (5.4–9.5)	10.3 (7.8–13.6)	4.4 (2.9–6.6)	5.5 (3.9–7.7)	7.3 (5.1–10.4)	3.8 (2.5–5.8)
Latvia, 2007	37.6 (32.3–43.2)	41.8 (36.3–47.5)	33.9 (28.4–39.8)	37.5 (32.8–42.5)	42.0 (36.1–48.1)	33.6 (29.2–38.4)

Table 3.1.66 Continued

WHO region and WHO member state, territory, or special administrative region, and year	% Used any form of tobacco in the past 30 days			% Used any form of tobacco other than cigarettes in the past 30 days		
	Total % (95% CI)	Males % (95% CI)	Females % (95% CI)	Total % (95% CI)	Males % (95% CI)	Females % (95% CI)
Lithuania, 2005	32.1 (29.6–34.8)	36.8 (32.6–41.2)	28.1 (24.0–32.7)	9.1 (7.1–11.6)	13.2 (9.9–17.2)	5.7 (3.7–8.7)
Macedonia, former Yugoslav Republic of, 2008	11.8 (9.7–14.4)	11.9 (9.6–14.7)	11.7 (9.2–14.9)	4.9 (4.0–6.0)	5.2 (4.0–6.7)	4.6 (3.4–6.1)
Moldova, Republic of, 2008	13.4 (11.3–15.7)	20.8 (17.3–24.7)	7.1 (5.6–9.0)	8.2 (6.6–10.1)	11.6 (9.0–14.8)	5.1 (3.7–7.0)
Montenegro, 2008	6.3 (5.2–7.5)	6.6 (5.1–8.5)	5.9 (4.6–7.5)	3.6 (2.9–4.5)	3.7 (2.6–5.2)	3.5 (2.6–4.8)
Poland, 2003	19.5 (16.5–22.9)	21.4 (16.6–27.0)	17.3 (14.5–20.6)	7.0 (5.6–8.7)	9.0 (6.6–12.2)	4.8 (3.6–6.5)
Romania, 2004	18.3 (14.7–22.6)	22.2 (17.0–28.4)	14.8 (12.0–18.2)	5.9 (4.5–7.6)	7.7 (5.4–10.8)	4.3 (3.4–5.3)
Russian Federation, 2004	27.3 (25.0–29.8)	30.1 (26.6–33.8)	24.4 (21.5–27.6)	14.7 (13.3–16.2)	18.1 (16.0–20.4)	11.1 (9.1–13.5)
Serbia, 2008	10.4 (8.0–13.4)	10.8 (7.7–15.0)	9.6 (7.6–12.2)	5.8 (4.7–7.2)	5.5 (3.8–8.0)	5.8 (4.4–7.6)
Slovakia, 2007	26.6 (24.3–28.9)	28.5 (25.8–31.4)	24.5 (21.7–27.5)	12.9 (11.6–14.4)	15.1 (13.5–16.9)	10.6 (9.1–12.3)
Slovenia, 2007	21.8 (17.6–26.6)	16.9 (12.2–23.0)	24.2 (19.4–29.8)	8.4 (5.8–12.0)	8.3 (5.3–12.7)	7.4 (5.0–10.7)
Tajikistan, 2004	5.1 (3.1–8.3)	6.8 (3.9–11.6)	2.8 (1.4–5.7)	6.0 (3.9–9.2)	8.0 (4.9–12.9)	3.4 (1.8–6.3)
Turkey, 2003	8.4 (7.5–9.4)	11.1 (9.8–12.5)	4.4 (3.7–5.3)	3.4 (3.0–3.9)	4.4 (3.8–5.1)	1.5 (1.1–1.9)
Ukraine, 2005	26.0 (22.0–30.4)	29.8 (25.0–35.1)	22.2 (18.3–26.6)	12.9 (9.6–17.3)	15.2 (10.8–20.9)	10.5 (8.0–13.8)
Uzbekistan, 2008 (Tashkent)	2.2 (0.9–5.4)	2.7 (0.9–7.5)	1.6 (0.6–4.4)	0.6 (0.3–1.5)	0.3 (0.1–1.6)	0.8 (0.3–2.6)
South East Asia	12.2 (11.3–13.1)	13.6 (12.5–14.6)	6.9 (6.0–7.7)	7.4 (6.7–8.0)	9.1 (8.2–10.0)	4.9 (4.2–5.6)
Bangladesh, 2007	6.9 (4.7–10.1)	9.1 (6.7–12.1)	5.1 (2.5–10.3)	6.0 (4.0–8.9)	8.0 (5.9–10.8)	4.2 (1.9–9.1)
Bhutan, 2006	20.2 (17.3–23.4)	28.6 (23.2–34.7)	12.4 (9.6–15.8)	14.2 (11.7–17.0)	19.7 (14.7–25.8)	9.1 (6.7–12.3)
East Timor, 2006	41.0 (33.8–48.6)	54.5 (46.4–62.3)	29.8 (21.3–40.1)	24.1 (18.9–30.1)	29.0 (22.6–36.4)	20.2 (14.4–27.6)
India, 2006	13.7 (11.6–16.3)	16.8 (14.2–19.9)	9.4 (7.1–12.5)	11.9 (9.8–14.3)	14.3 (11.8–17.2)	8.5 (6.4–11.3)
Indonesia, 2006	13.5 (11.0–16.4)	24.1 (19.0–30.1)	4.0 (3.0–5.4)	3.8 (2.8–5.1)	5.3 (3.6–7.7)	2.4 (1.5–3.7)

Table 3.1.66 Continued

WHO region and WHO member state, territory, or special administrative region, and year	% Used any form of tobacco in the past 30 days			% Used any form of tobacco other than cigarettes in the past 30 days		
	Total % (95% CI)	Males % (95% CI)	Females % (95% CI)	Total % (95% CI)	Males % (95% CI)	Females % (95% CI)
Maldives, 2007	5.9 (4.4–7.9)	3.4 (2.1–5.3)	8.5 (6.0–11.8)	3.5 (2.2–5.5)	2.7 (1.6–4.7)	4.3 (2.5–7.4)
Myanmar, 2007	15.3 (12.4–18.7)	22.5 (18.1–27.4)	8.2 (5.9–11.3)	14.1 (11.4–17.3)	20.3 (16.3–25.0)	7.9 (5.7–10.9)
Nepal, 2007	9.4 (7.2–12.2)	13.0 (9.8–16.9)	5.3 (3.0–9.1)	8.0 (6.2–10.2)	11.1 (8.5–14.4)	4.4 (2.5–7.7)
Sri Lanka, 2007	9.1 (6.8–12.2)	12.4 (8.7–17.5)	5.8 (3.6–9.4)	8.6 (6.4–11.5)	11.6 (8.0–16.6)	5.6 (3.5–8.7)
Thailand, 2005	15.7 (13.8–17.7)	21.7 (19.4–24.2)	8.4 (6.9–10.2)	7.7 (6.6–9.0)	10.4 (8.7–12.3)	4.9 (3.9–6.0)
Western Pacific	15.2 (14.9–15.3)	19.0 (18.7–19.3)	11.3 (11.1–11.5)	7.3 (7.0–7.6)	8.5 (8.1–9.0)	7.3 (6.9–7.7)
American Samoa, 2005[b]	20.3 (17.3–23.8)	23.8 (19.5–28.7)	16.6 (13.0–21.0)	9.1 (7.3–11.4)	12.1 (9.3–15.7)	5.8 (4.0–8.3)
Cambodia, 2003	5.1 (3.6–7.4)	7.2 (4.7–10.8)	3.0 (1.5–5.9)	3.1 (2.0–4.8)	3.3 (1.9–5.6)	3.0 (1.5–5.9)
China, 2005 (Macau)[e]	11.9 (9.6–14.7)	12.8 (10.0–16.2)	11.0 (8.2–14.7)	2.1 (1.4–3.0)	2.4 (1.5–3.9)	1.7 (0.9–3.1)
China, 2005 (Shanghai)	5.5 (4.1–7.4)	7.1 (5.2–9.4)	4.1 (2.3–7.0)	3.9 (2.9–5.4)	4.5 (3.4–5.9)	3.4 (1.7–6.5)
Cook Islands, 2008	35.1 (34.0–36.3)	33.7 (32.1–35.4)	36.3 (34.7–37.9)	15.3 (14.4–16.2)	17.1 (15.8–18.5)	13.8 (12.7–15.0)
Fiji, 2005	11.5 (7.4–17.6)	11.6 (7.0–18.8)	10.2 (6.4–16.0)	7.7 (4.8–12.2)	6.7 (3.8–11.4)	7.6 (4.6–12.3)
Guam, 2002[b]	27.8 (24.6–31.2)	31.5 (27.4–35.9)	23.8 (20.2–27.9)	14.1 (11.9–16.6)	17.6 (14.2–21.7)	10.1 (8.0–12.7)
Lao People's Democratic Republic, 2007 (Vientiane Capital)	5.7 (4.6–7.2)	7.8 (5.4–11.3)	3.9 (2.6–5.9)	3.1 (2.2–4.2)	3.3 (2.1–4.9)	2.7 (1.9–4.0)
Malaysia, 2003	25.8 (21.9–30.1)	40.0 (34.6–45.7)	11.5 (9.4–13.9)	8.1 (6.6–10.1)	8.8 (6.8–11.3)	7.5 (6.1–9.2)
Micronesia, 2007	46.2 (41.1–51.5)	51.9 (43.8–59.9)	39.8 (34.7–45.1)	37.0 (32.2–42.1)	41.8 (34.6–49.3)	32.1 (27.3–37.4)
Mongolia, 2007	20.7 (13.1–31.1)	25.7 (19.2–33.4)	16.0 (7.5–31.1)	15.4 (7.3–29.5)	17.9 (10.3–29.3)	12.9 (4.6–31.6)
New Zealand, 2008	20.1 (13.4–29.2)	18.7 (9.9–32.4)	21.5 (16.8–27.2)	7.7 (4.4–13.1)	10.1 (4.3–22.1)	5.1 (3.8–6.9)
Northern Mariana Islands, 2004[f]	53.4 (50.3–56.5)	57.1 (53.4–60.7)	49.8 (45.6–53.9)	45.3 (42.4–48.3)	52.3 (48.8–55.9)	38.3 (34.7–42.1)
Palau, 2005	33.1 (29.7–36.6)	38.0 (33.3–42.9)	28.4 (24.1–33.1)	20.5 (17.6–23.9)	25.0 (20.6–29.9)	16.3 (13.2–20.0)

Table 3.1.66 Continued

WHO region and WHO member state, territory, or special administrative region, and year	% Used any form of tobacco in the past 30 days			% Used any form of tobacco other than cigarettes in the past 30 days		
	Total % (95% CI)	Males % (95% CI)	Females % (95% CI)	Total % (95% CI)	Males % (95% CI)	Females % (95% CI)
Papua New Guinea, 2007	47.7 (43.7–51.7)	55.4 (51.0–59.7)	40.3 (34.9–45.9)	15.9 (13.2–18.9)	21.1 (17.3–25.6)	11.1 (9.1–13.5)
Philippines, 2007	22.7 (19.8–25.8)	28.3 (24.5–32.4)	17.5 (14.6–20.7)	7.7 (6.2–9.5)	8.2 (6.1–10.9)	7.2 (5.6–9.2)
Republic of Korea (South), 2008	13.0 (11.4–14.7)	14.9 (12.5–17.6)	10.6 (9.4–11.9)	6.2 (5.4–7.1)	7.2 (6.1–8.6)	5.0 (4.2–6.0)
Samoa, 2007	23.5 (19.0–28.7)	25.8 (19.0–33.9)	20.4 (16.1–25.5)	16.1 (12.4–20.6)	19.5 (13.6–27.1)	13.5 (9.5–19.0)
Singapore, 2000	9.1 (8.1–10.3)	10.5 (8.8–12.4)	7.5 (6.2–9.1)	NA	NA	NA
Solomon Islands, 2008	40.2 (34.1–46.6)	43.9 (34.5–53.8)	37.0 (28.0–46.9)	23.4 (18.2–29.5)	27.7 (17.4–40.9)	19.9 (15.1–25.8)
Tuvalu, 2006	36.4 (36.2–36.7)	41.6 (41.2–41.9)	32.7 (32.4–32.9)	27.1 (26.9–27.3)	33.3 (33.0–33.7)	22.4 (22.1–22.6)
Vanuatu, 2007	25.6 (24.4–26.9)	34.1 (32.0–36.3)	19.6 (18.1–21.2)	13.8 (12.8–14.8)	17.5 (15.8–19.2)	11.3 (10.2–12.6)
Viet Nam, 2007 (Hanoi)	3.3 (1.9–5.7)	5.5 (3.1–9.6)	1.1 (0.5–2.2)	1.2 (0.8–1.9)	2.0 (1.3–3.1)	0.5 (0.1–2.1)

Source: WHO 2009.
Note: These data are based on GYTS questions: (1) During the past 30 days (one month), on how many days did you smoke cigarettes? and (2) During the past 30 days (one month) have you ever used any form of tobacco products other than cigarettes (e.g., chewing tobacco, snuff, dip, cigars, cigarillos, little cigars, pipe)? **CI** = confidence interval; **NA** = question not asked; **WHO** = World Health Organization.
[a]Territory of United Kingdom
[b]Territory of United States
[c]United Nations Relief and Works Agency
[d]United Nations Administered Province
[e]Special Administrative Region of China
[f]Commonwealth in political union with the United States

Table 3.1.67 Percentage of youth 16 years of age who have smoked 40 or more cigarettes in their lifetime and who currently smoke cigarettes, overall and by gender; European School Survey Project on Alcohol and other Drugs (ESPAD) 2007; Europe

	Lifetime ≥ 40 cigarettes			Last 30 days (current smoker)		
Country	**Males %**	**Females %**	**Average %**	**Males %**	**Females %**	**Average %**
Armenia	10	0	4	17	1	7
Austria	33	38	35	42	48	45
Belgium (Flanders)	17	16	17	24	23	23
Bulgaria	26	32	29	36	44	40
Croatia	30	27	28	38	38	38
Cyprus	21	12	17	29	17	23
Czech Republic	32	37	34	36	45	41
Denmark[a]	24	27	26	30	34	32
Estonia	32	22	27	32	27	29
Faroe Islands	33	33	33	31	34	33
Finland	27	25	26	29	31	30
France	20	20	20	29	31	30
Germany[b]	27	28	27	31	35	33
Greece	16	13	14	23	21	22
Greenland	NA	NA	NA	NA	NA	NA
Hungary	24	24	24	31	34	33
Iceland	13	15	14	15	18	16
Ireland	13	18	16	19	27	23
Isle of Man	16	21	18	19	28	24
Italy	24	24	24	34	39	37
Latvia	37	28	32	44	39	41
Lithuania	31	20	26	39	29	34
Malta	16	15	15	26	26	26
Monaco	11	26	18	16	35	25
Netherlands	22	26	24	27	33	30
Norway	12	16	14	17	22	19
Poland	18	15	16	22	20	21
Portugal	15	10	12	20	18	19
Romania	18	14	16	26	23	25
Russia	37	22	29	41	29	35
Slovak Republic	30	28	29	35	38	37
Slovenia	21	23	22	28	31	29
Spain[c]	17	23	20	23	29	26
Sweden	17	18	17	19	24	21
Switzerland	20	15	18	30	29	29
Turkey	NA	NA	NA	NA	NA	NA

Table 3.1.67 Continued

	Lifetime ≥ 40 cigarettes			Last 30 days (current smoker)		
Country	**Males %**	**Females %**	**Average %**	**Males %**	**Females %**	**Average %**
Ukraine	27	15	21	38	24	31
United Kingdom	13	18	15	17	25	22

Source: Adapted from Hibell et al. 2009 with permission from the Swedish Council for Information on Alcohol and Other Drugs, © 2009.
Note: **NA** = not applicable.
[a]For methodological reasons, data may not be completely comparable with other ESPAD countries.
[b]Data are included from seven bundesländer (federated states).
[c]Spain is not an ESPAD country, and data may not be completely comparable with the ESPAD countries.

Figure 3.1.1 Percentage who currently smoke cigarettes, by age group and state; National Survey on Drug Use and Health (NSDUH) 2006–2010; United States

A. 12–17 years of age

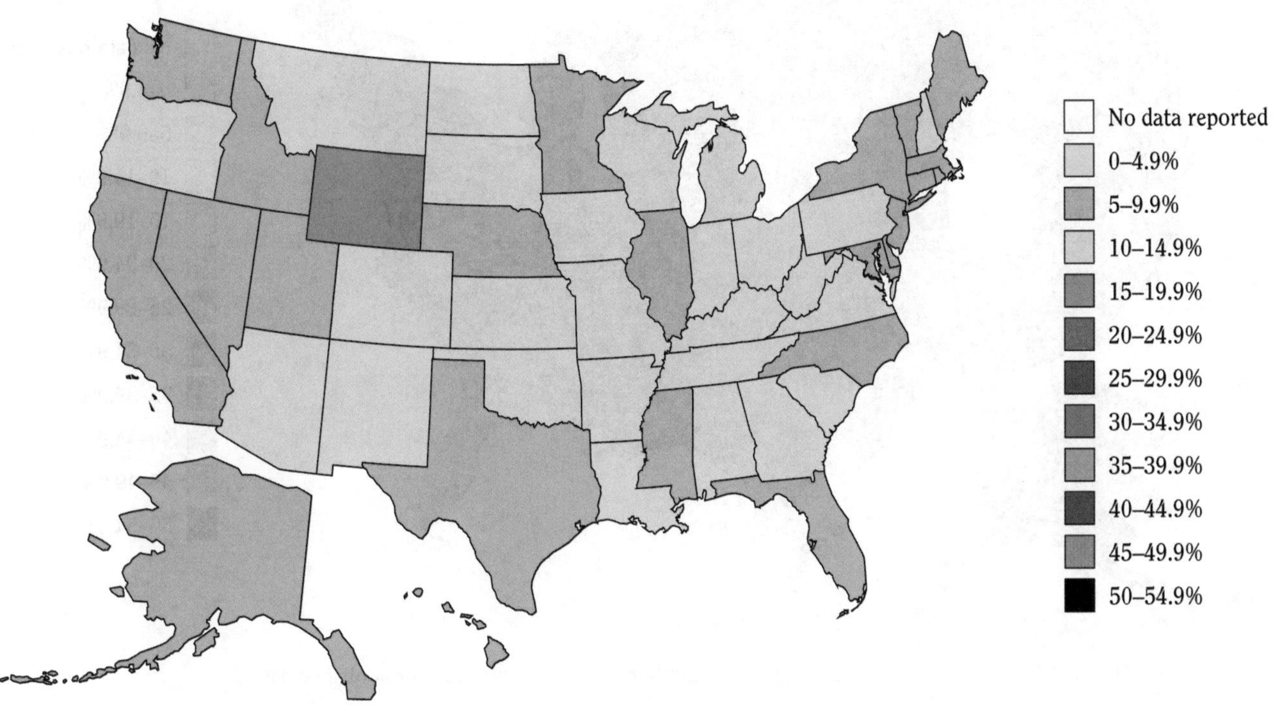

B. 18–25 years of age

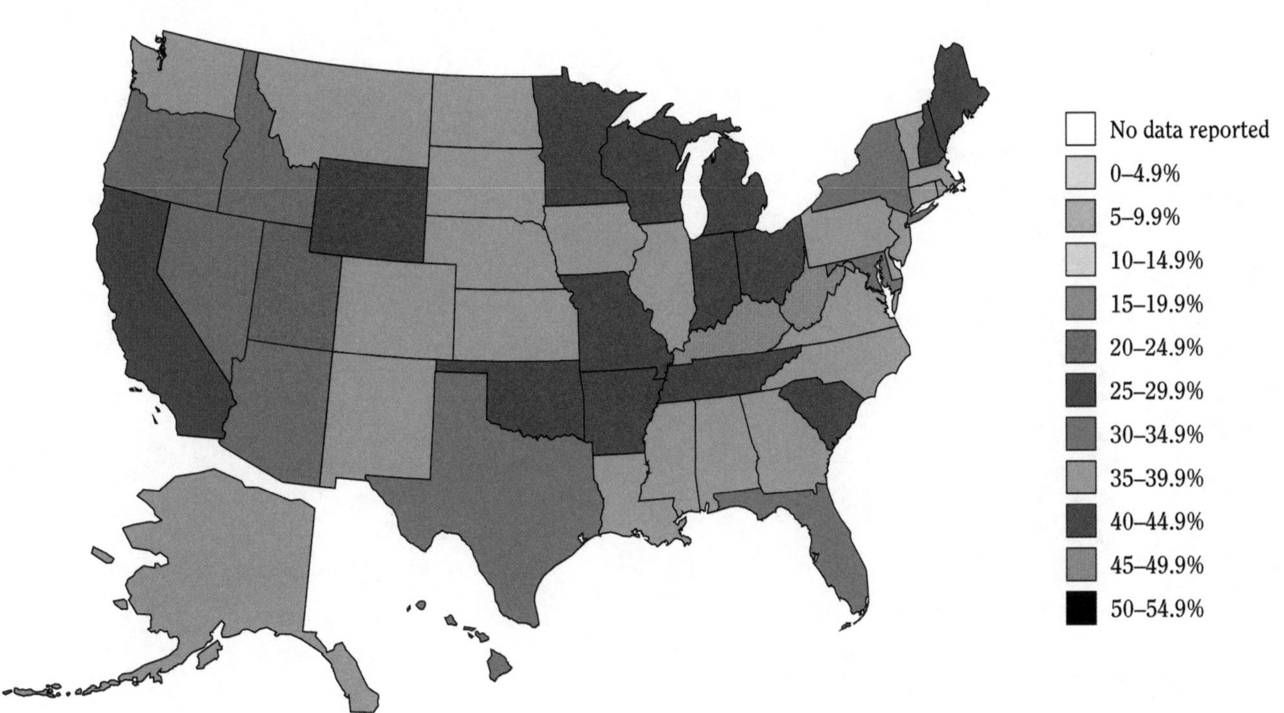

C. 26 years of age or older

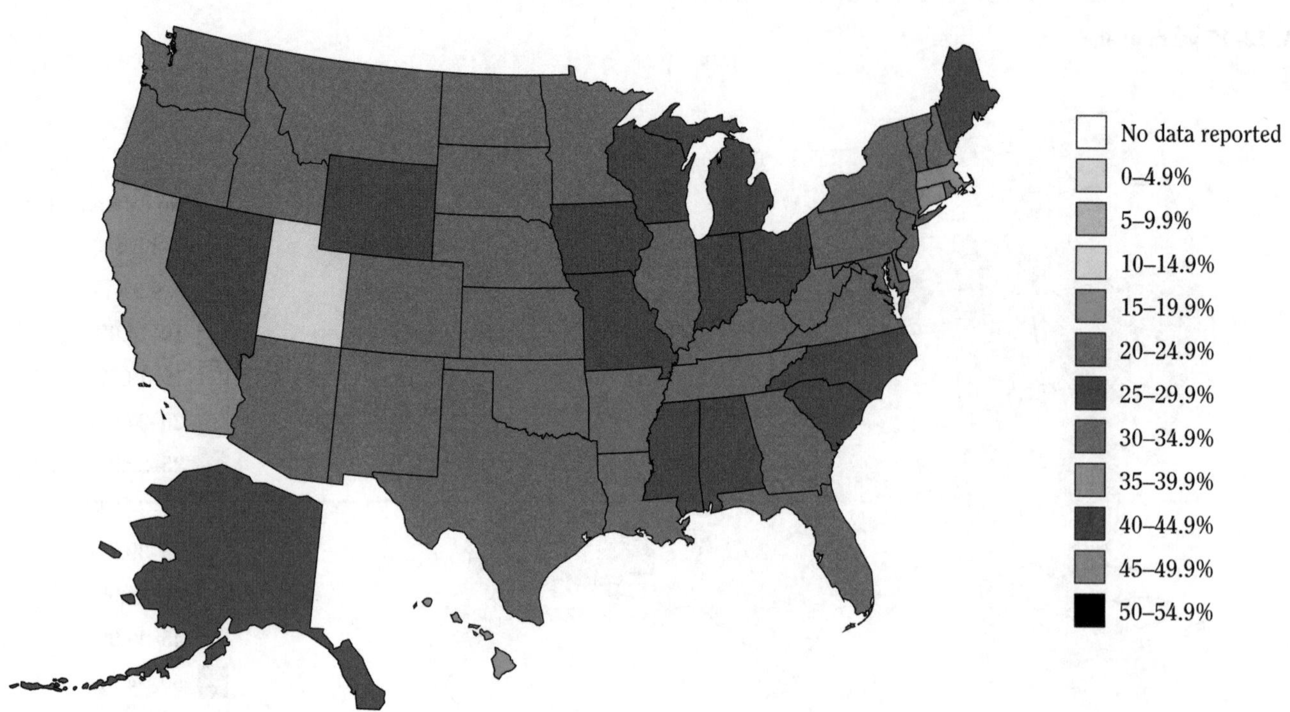

Source: 2006–2010 NSDUH: Substance Abuse and Mental Health Services Administration (unpublished data).

Figure 3.1.2 Percentage who currently smoke cigarettes, by age group, state and gender; National Survey on Drug Use and Health (NSDUH) 2006–2010; United States

A. 12–17 years of age, males

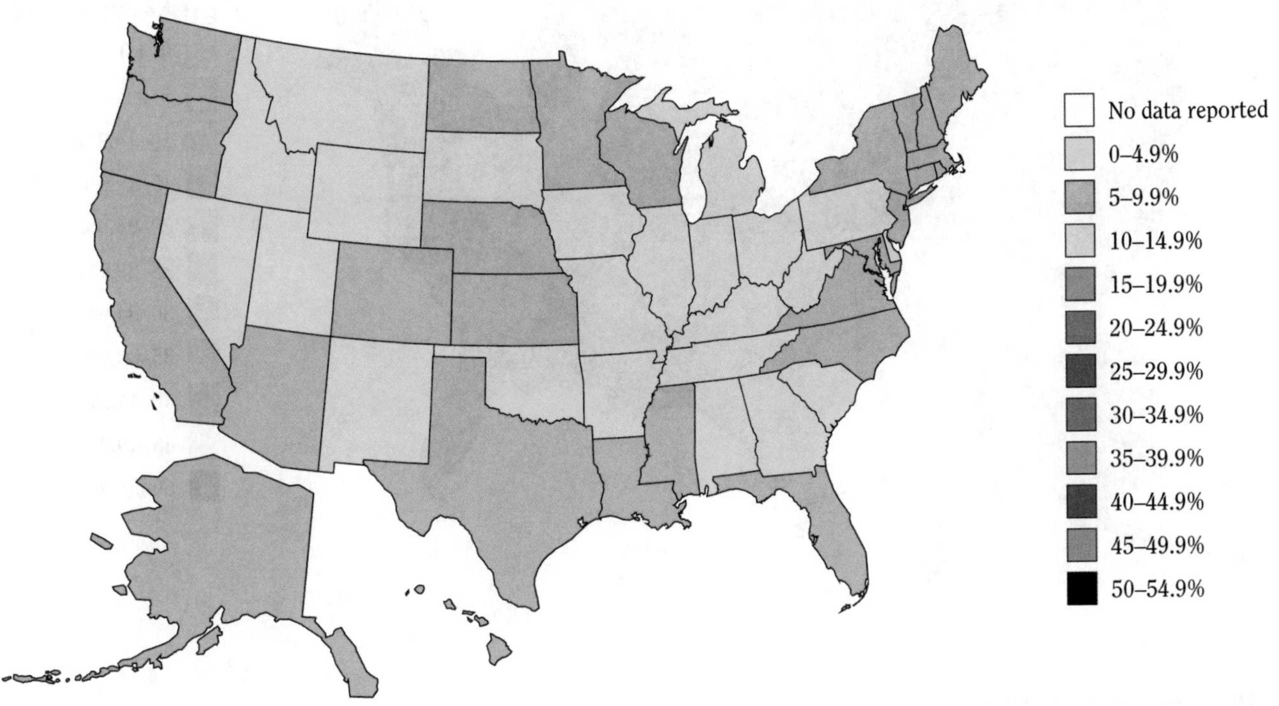

B. 12–17 years of age, females

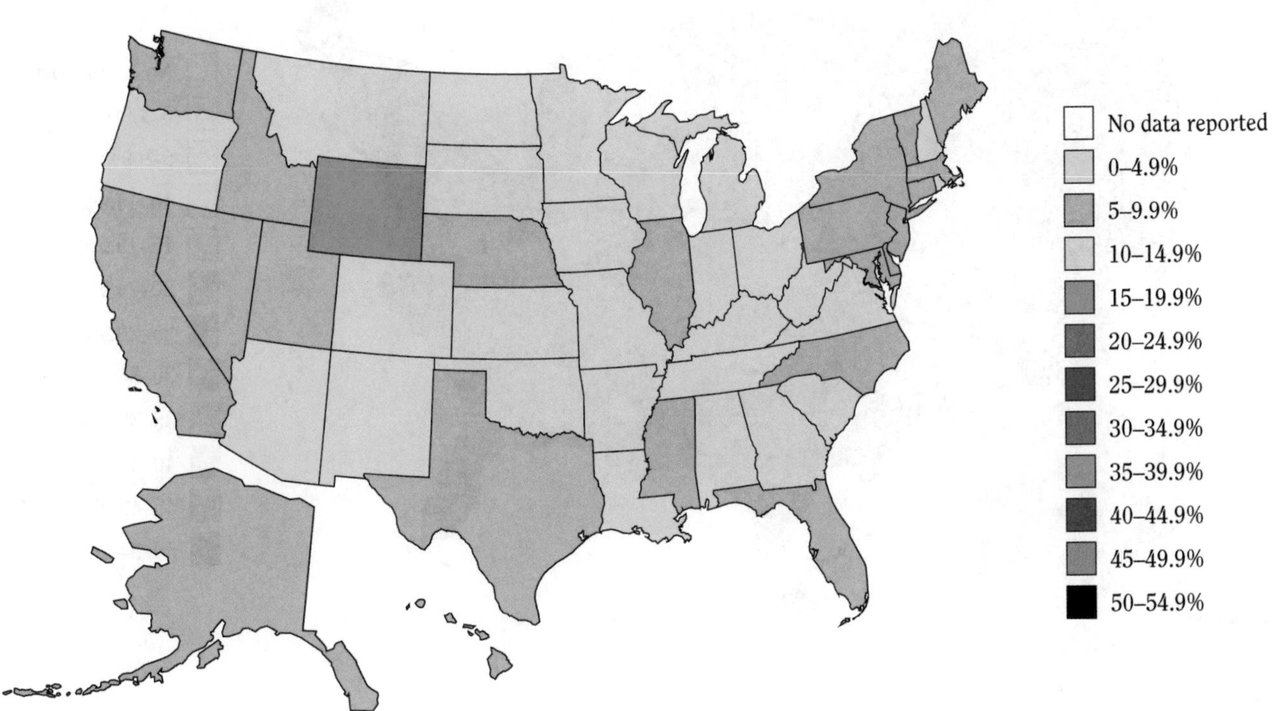

C. 18–25 years of age, males

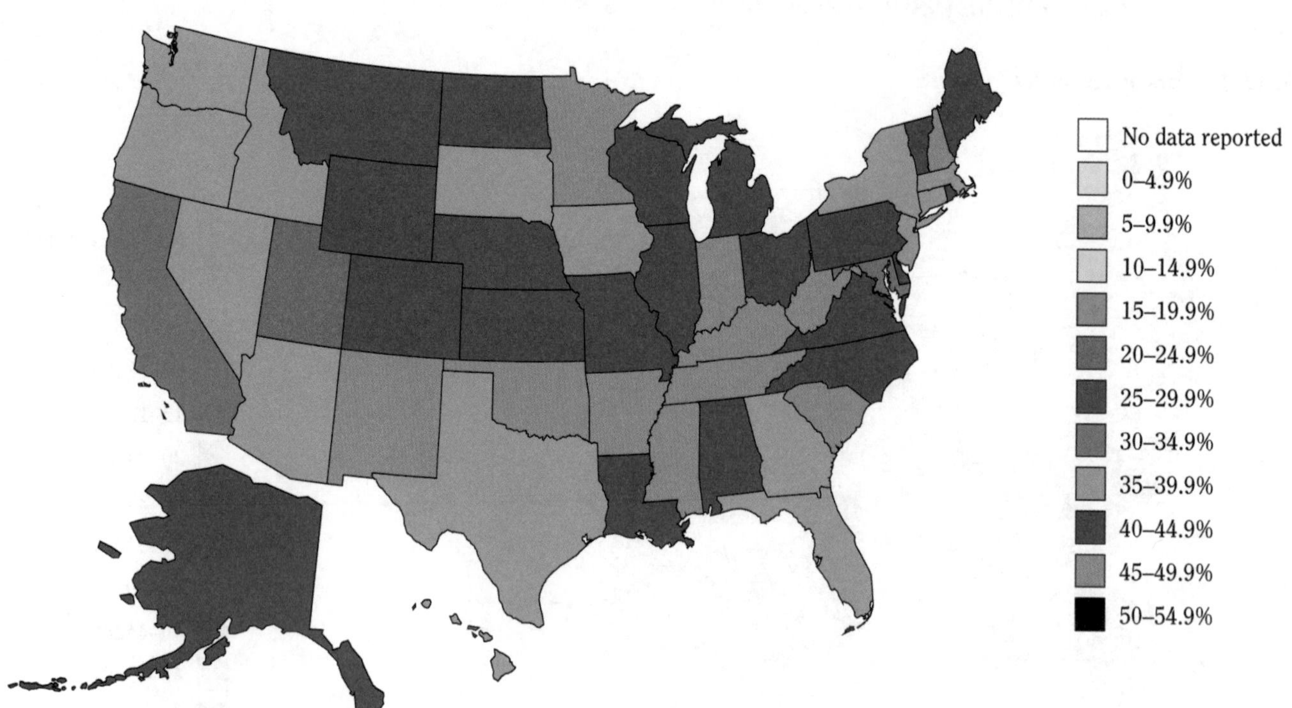

D. 18–25 years of age, females

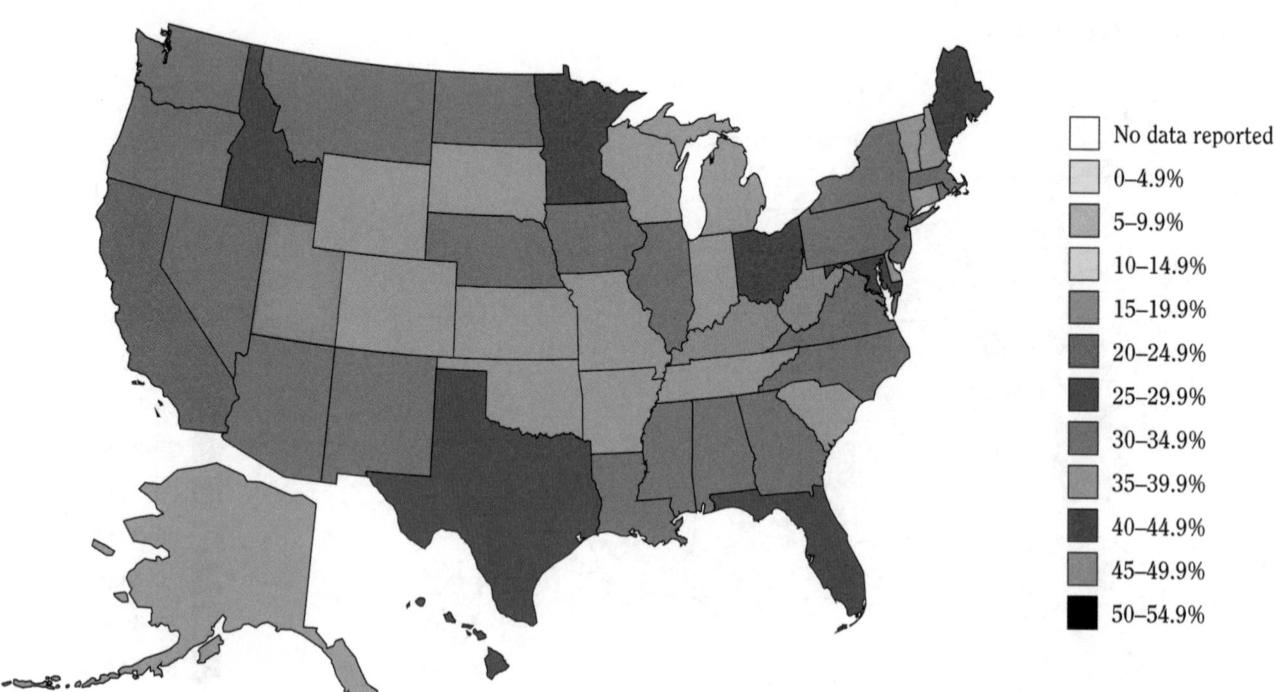

E. 26 years of age or older, males

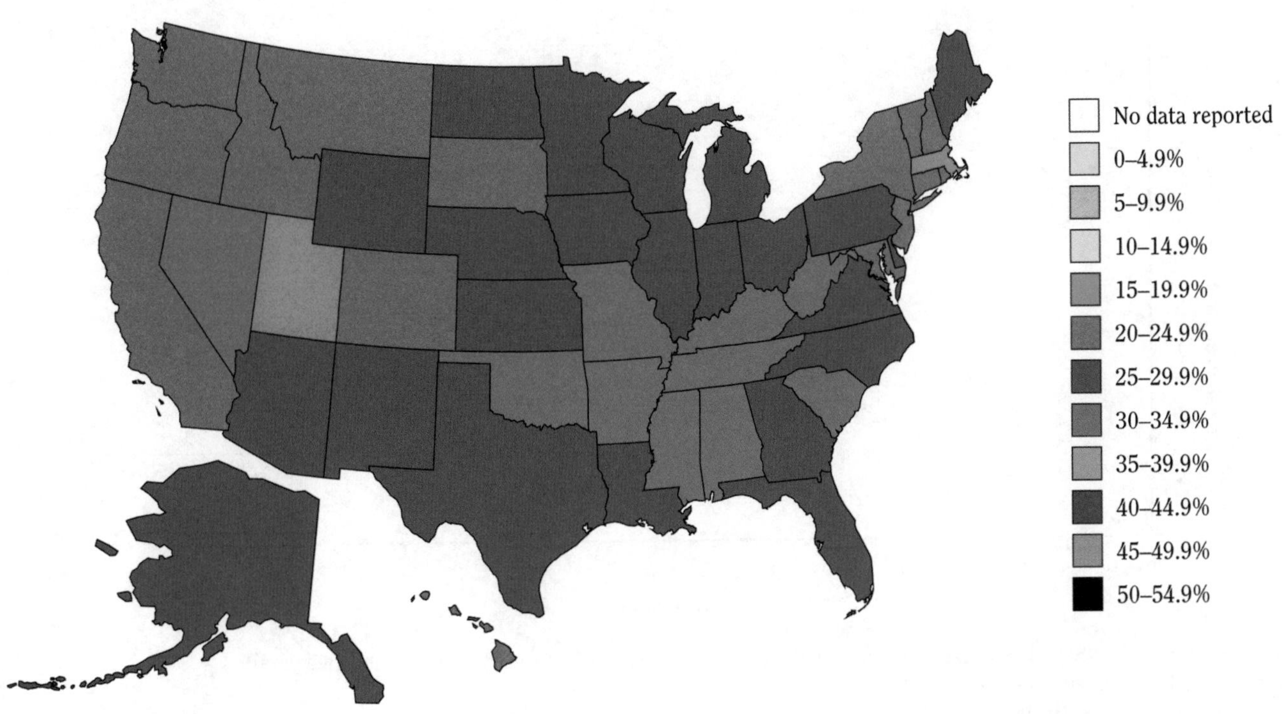

F. 26 years of age or older, females

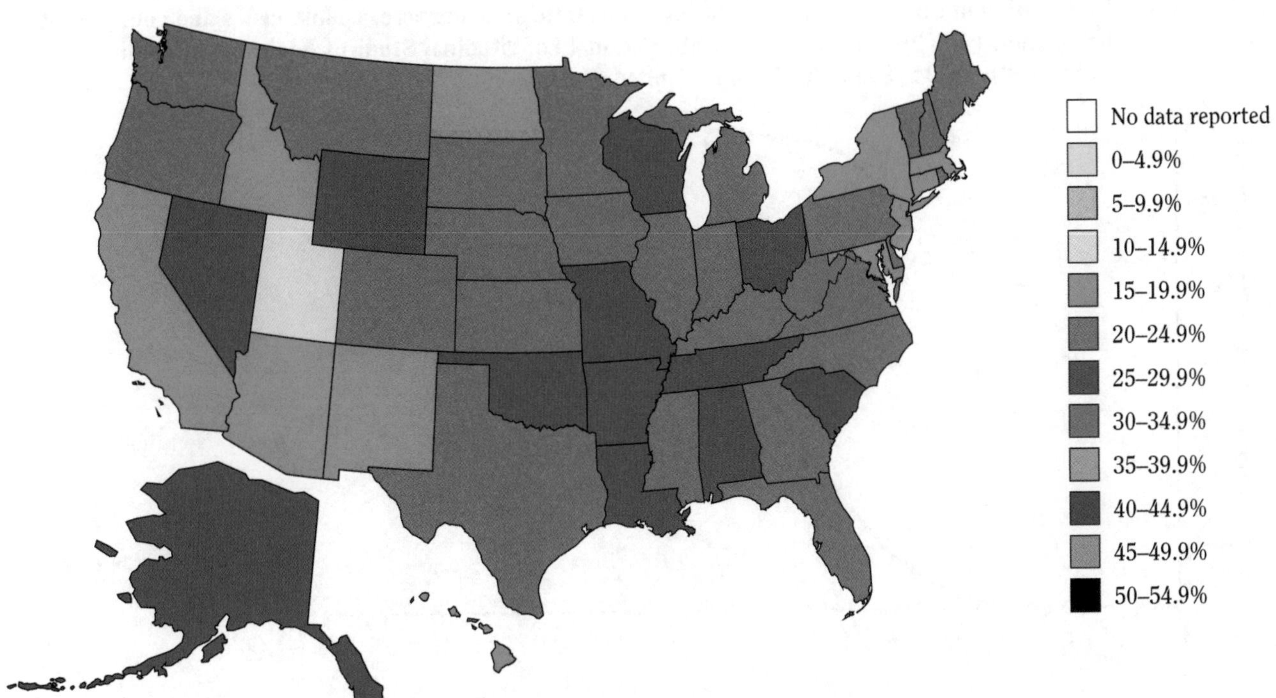

Source: 2006–2010 NSDUH: Substance Abuse and Mental Health Services Administration (unpublished data).

Figure 3.1.3 Prevalence of current cigarette smoking[a] among 12- to 17-year-olds and those 26 years of age or older, by state; National Survey on Drug Use and Health (NSDUH) 2008–2010; United States

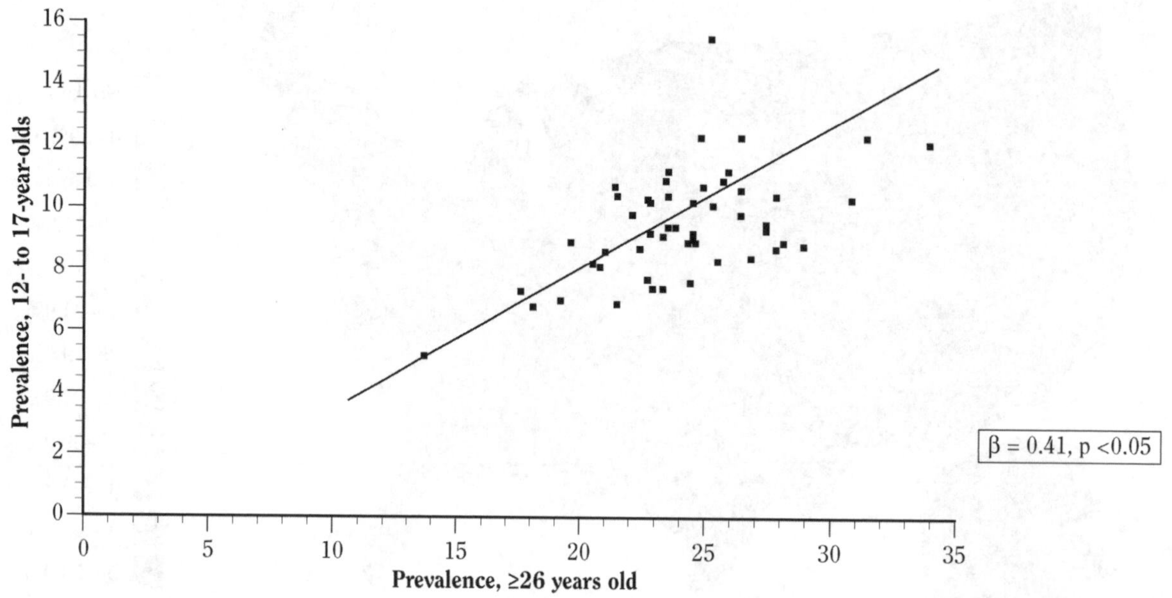

Source: 2008–2010 NSDUH: Substance Abuse and Mental Health Services Administration (unpublished data).
Note: Each dot represents a state.
[a]Based on responses to the question, "During the past 30 days, have you smoked part or all of a cigarette?" Respondents who chose "Yes" were classified as current cigarette smokers.

Figure 3.1.4 Distribution of developmental trajectories of cigarette smoking across adolescence and young adulthood, from 11 to 26 years of age, overall; National Longitudinal Study of Adolescent Health (Add Health) 1994–1996, 2001–2002; United States

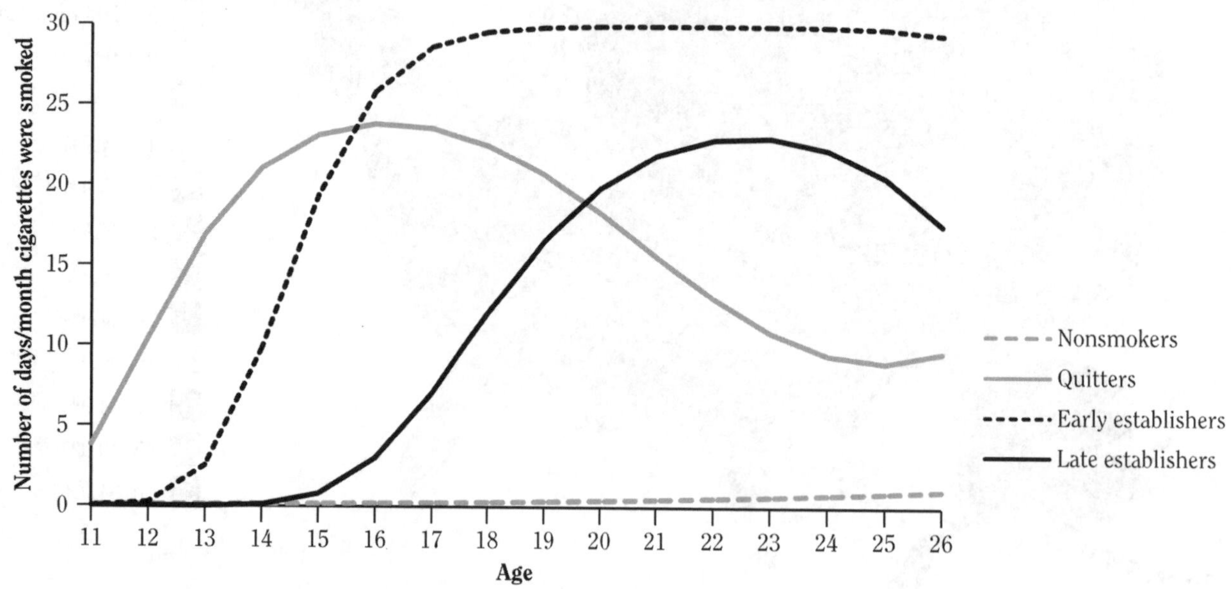

Source: 1994–1996, 2001–2002 Add Health: public use data sets.
Note: Quitters are so named because their intensity of cigarette smoking increases early in adolescence, then declines rapidly and consistently later in adolescence and early adulthood.

Figure 3.1.5 **Trends in prevalence (%) of ever smoking among young people over time, by grade level and gender; Monitoring the Future (MTF) 1975–2010; United States**

A. 8th, 10th, and 12th grades, 1975–2010

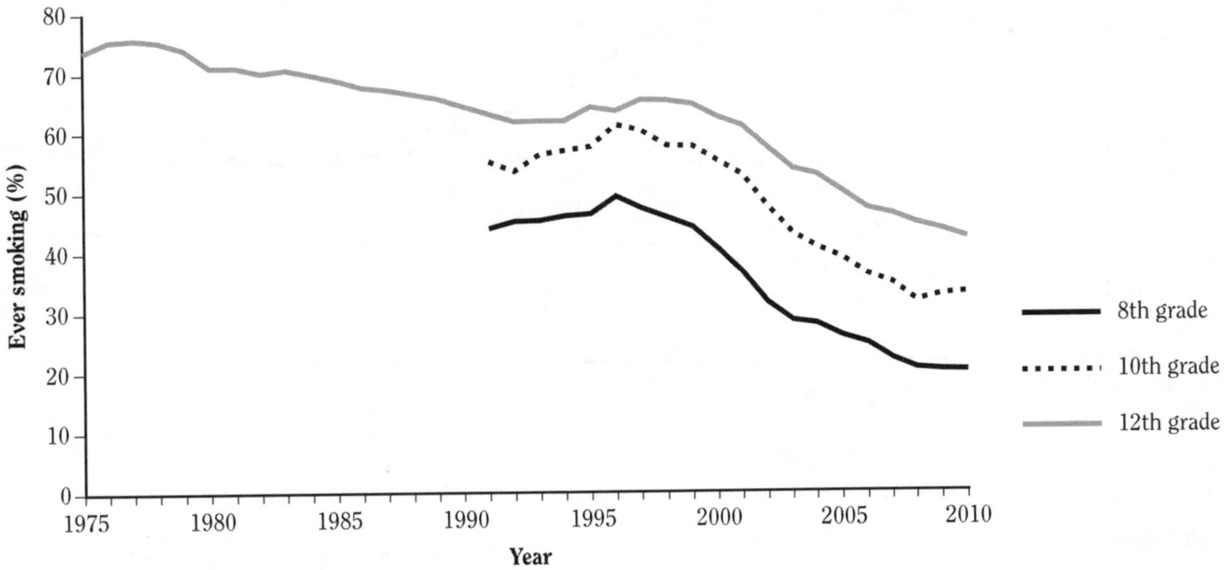

B. 8th grade, 1991–2010

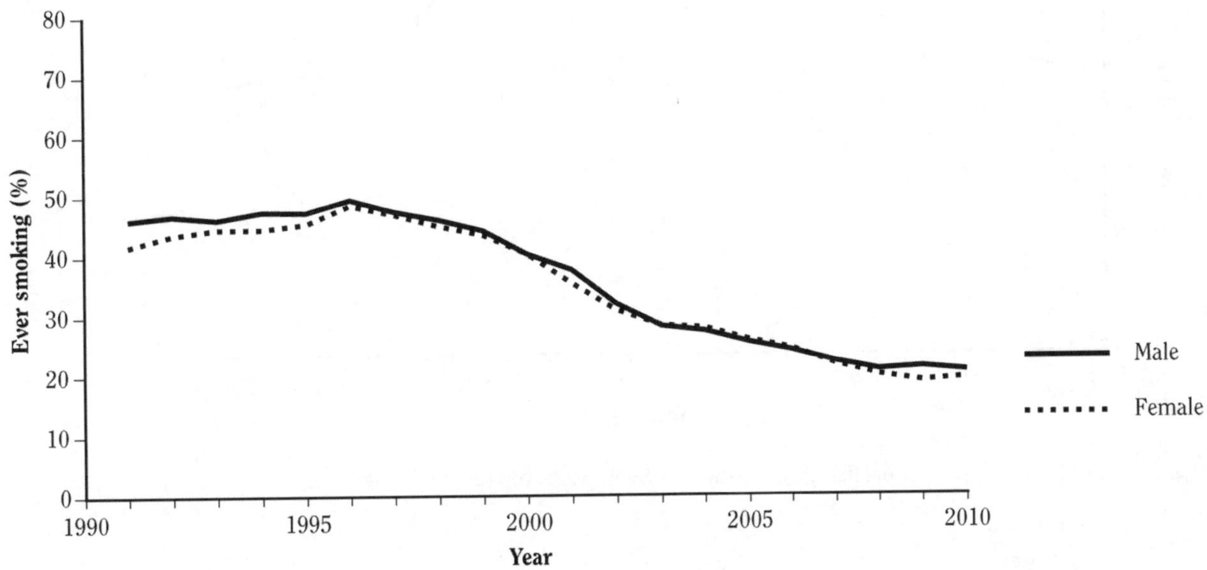

C. 10th grade, 1991–2010

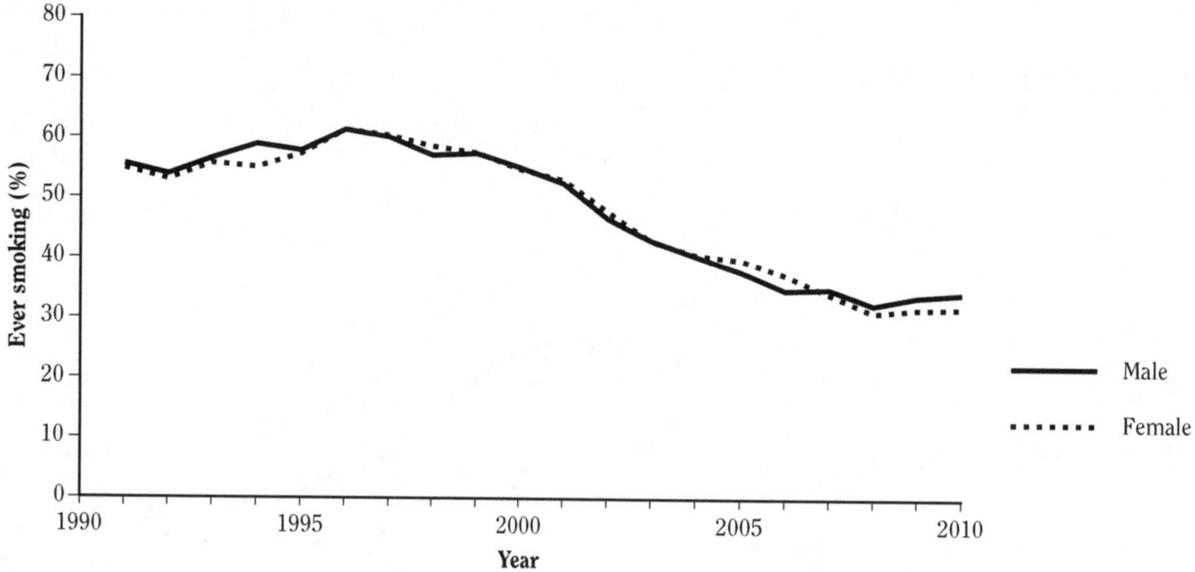

D. 12th grade, 1976–2010

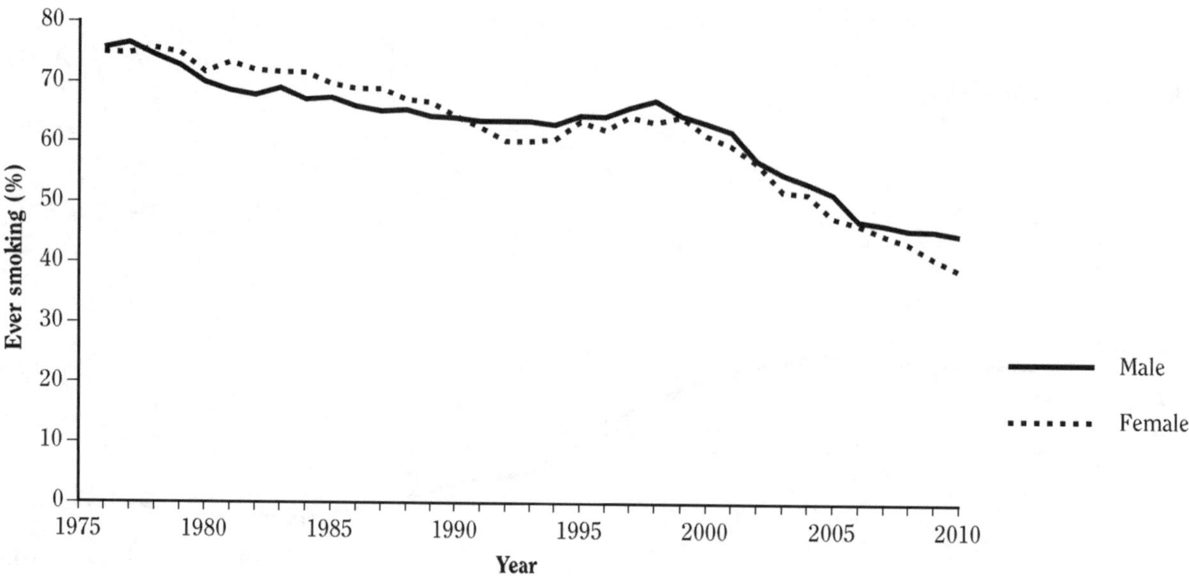

Source: 1975–2010 MTF: University of Michigan, Institute for Social Research (unpublished data).

Figure 3.1.6 Trends in prevalence (%) of ever smoking among young people, by grade level and race/ethnicity; Monitoring the Future (MTF) 1976–2010, and National Youth Risk Behavior Survey (YRBS) 1991–2009; United States

A. 8th grade, MTF, 1991–2010

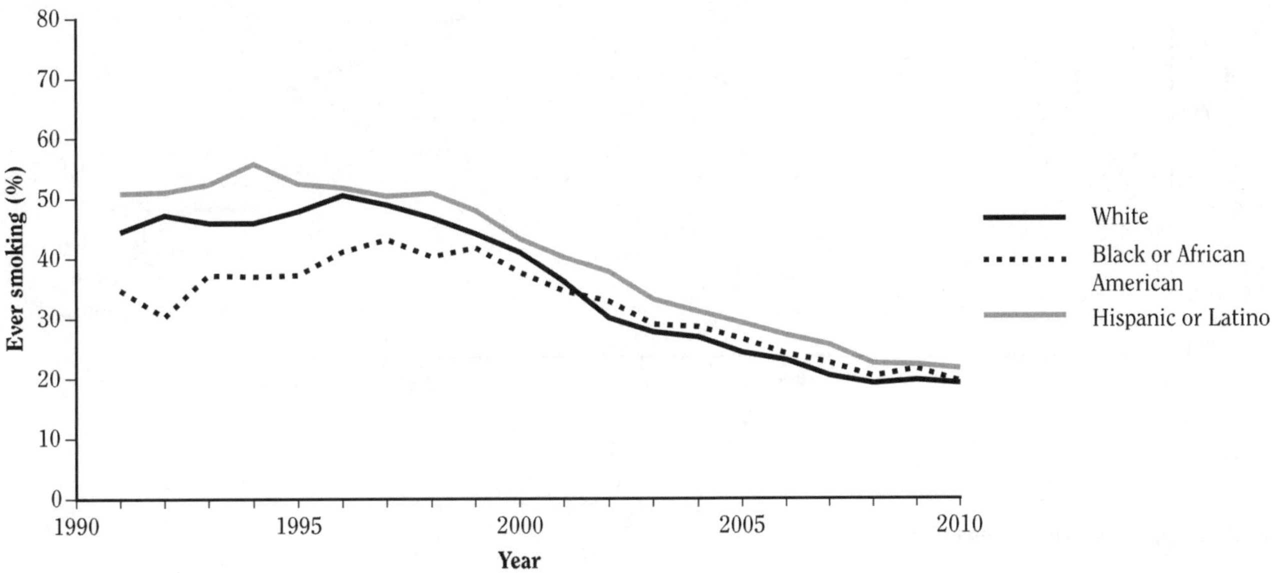

B. 10th grade, MTF, 1991–2010

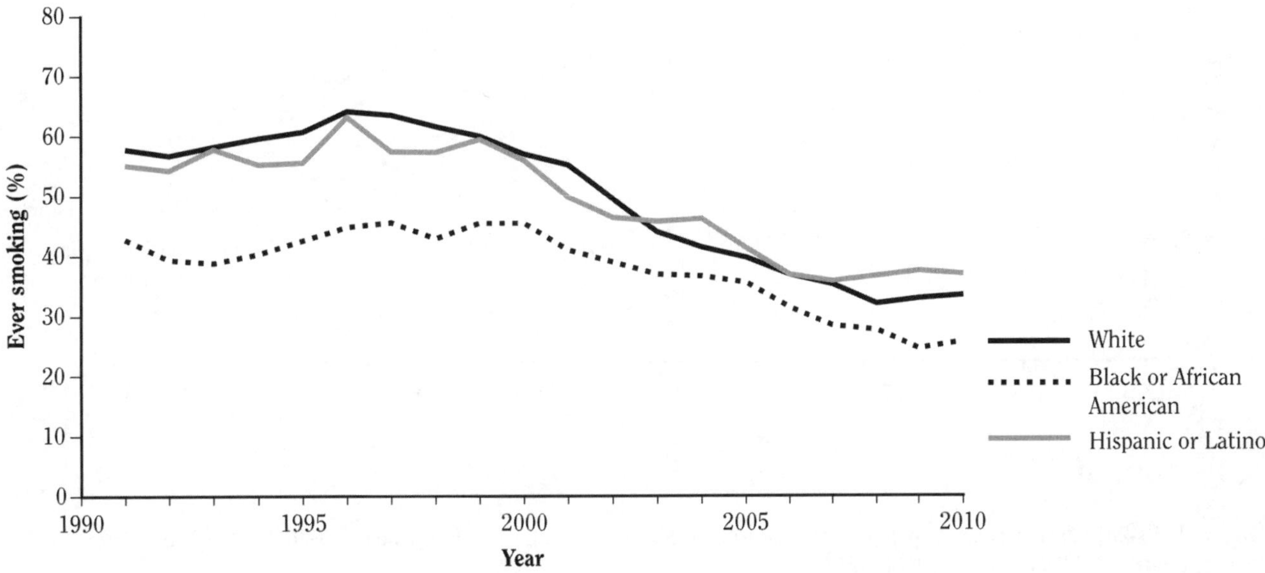

C. 12th grade, MTF, 1976–2010

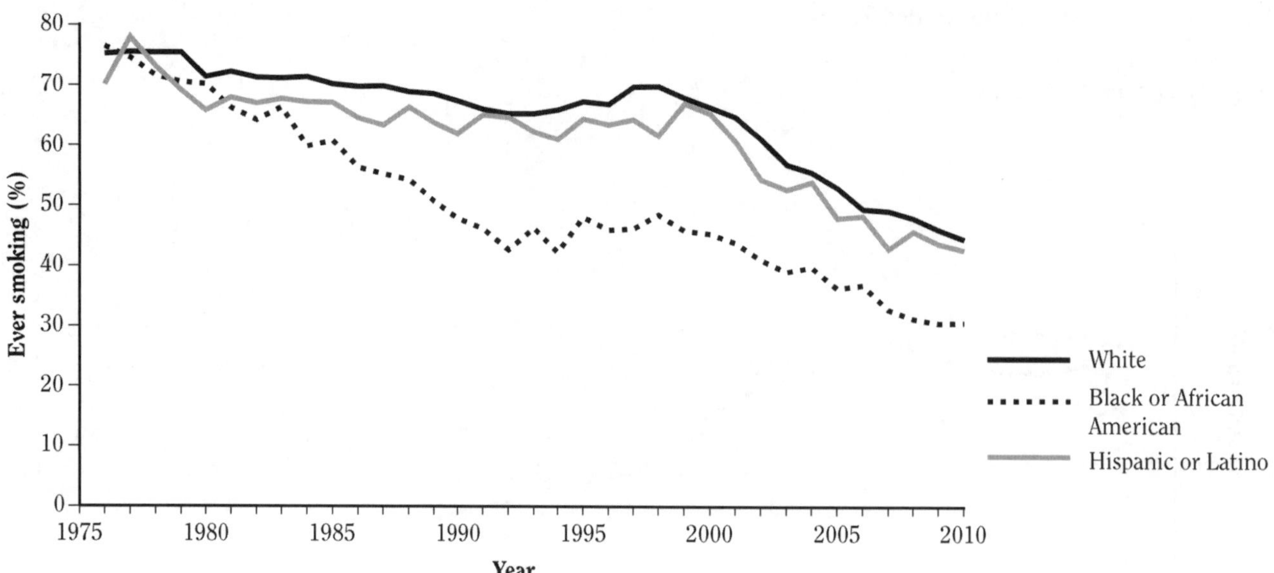

D. 9th–12th grade, YRBS, 1991–2009

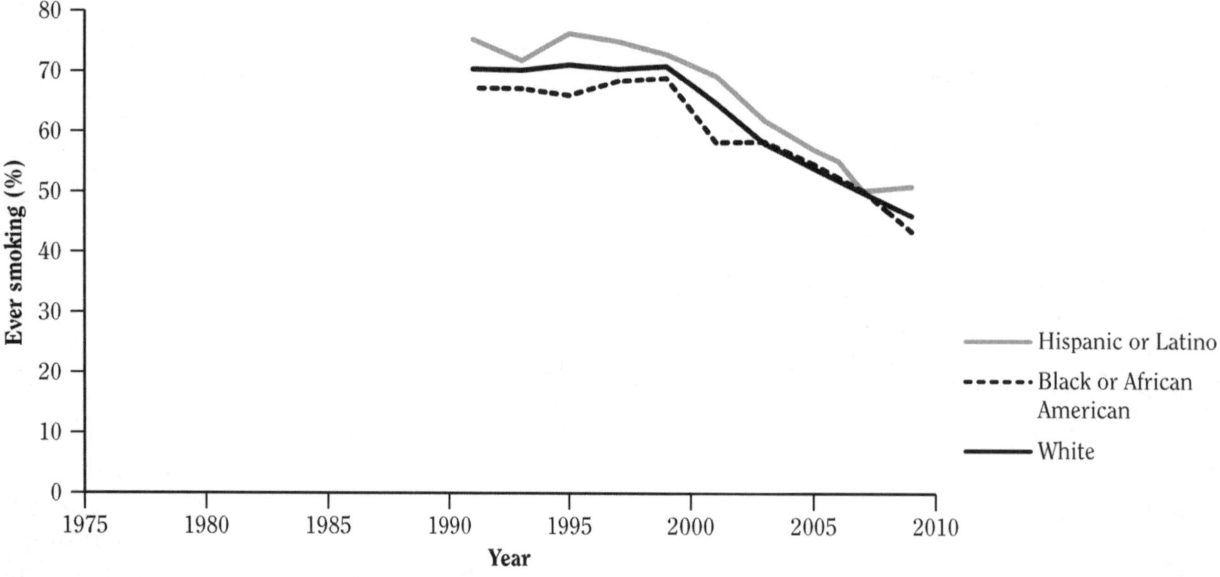

Source: 1976–2010 MTF: University of Michigan, Institute for Social Research (unpublished data); 1991–2009 YRBS: Centers for Disease Control and Prevention (CDC 2011a).

Figure 3.1.7 Trends in prevalence (%) of ever smoking and current smoking among 9th–12th grade students, by gender; National Youth Risk Behavior Survey (YRBS) 1991–2009; United States

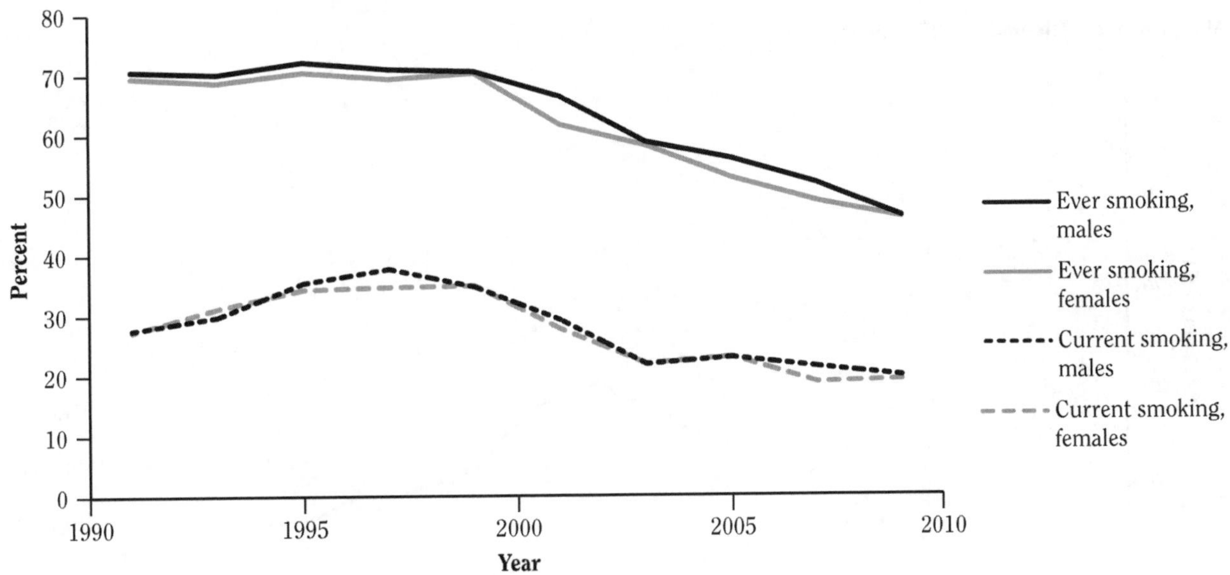

Source: 1991–2009 YRBS: Centers for Disease Control and Prevention (CDC 2011a).

Figure 3.1.8 **Trends in prevalence (%) of current smoking among young people over time, by grade level; Monitoring the Future (MTF) 1975–2010; United States**

A. 8th, 10th, and 12th grades, 1975–2010

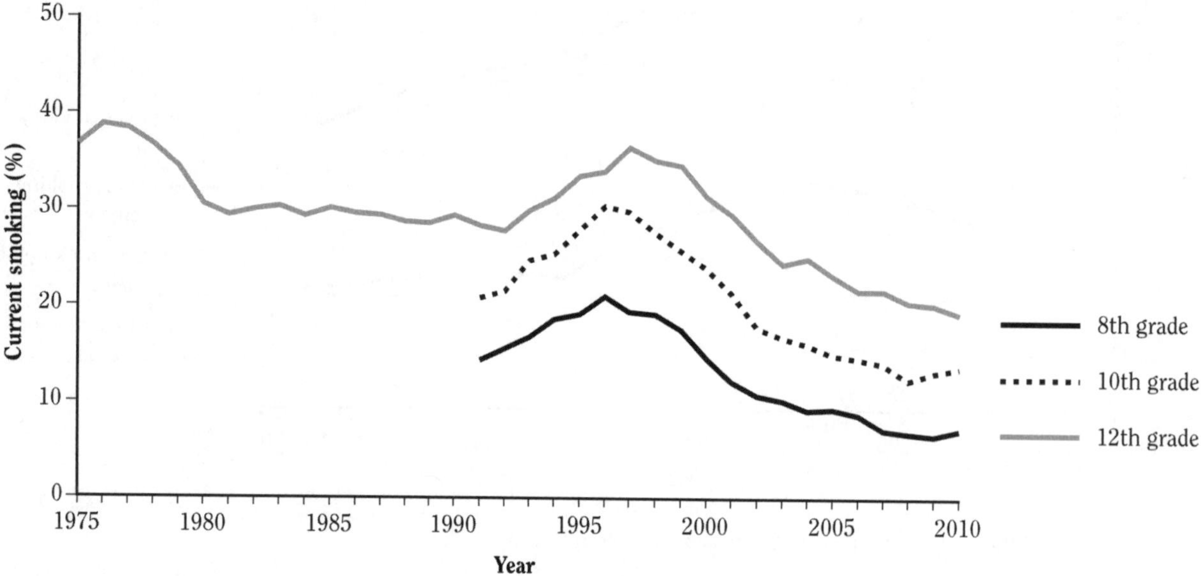

B. 8th grade, 1991–2010

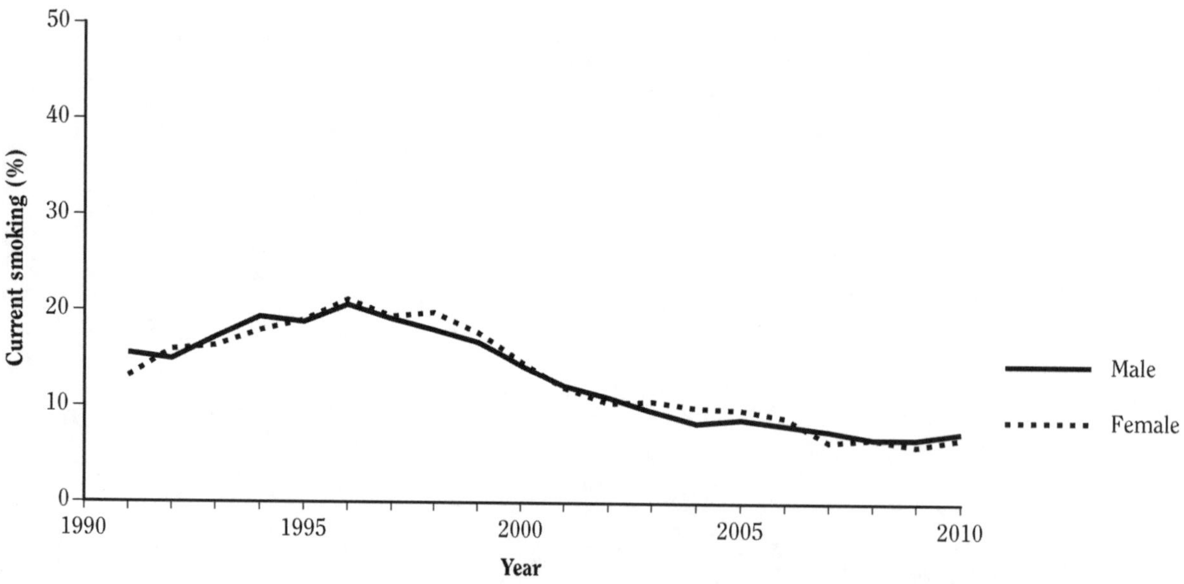

C. 10th grade, 1991–2010

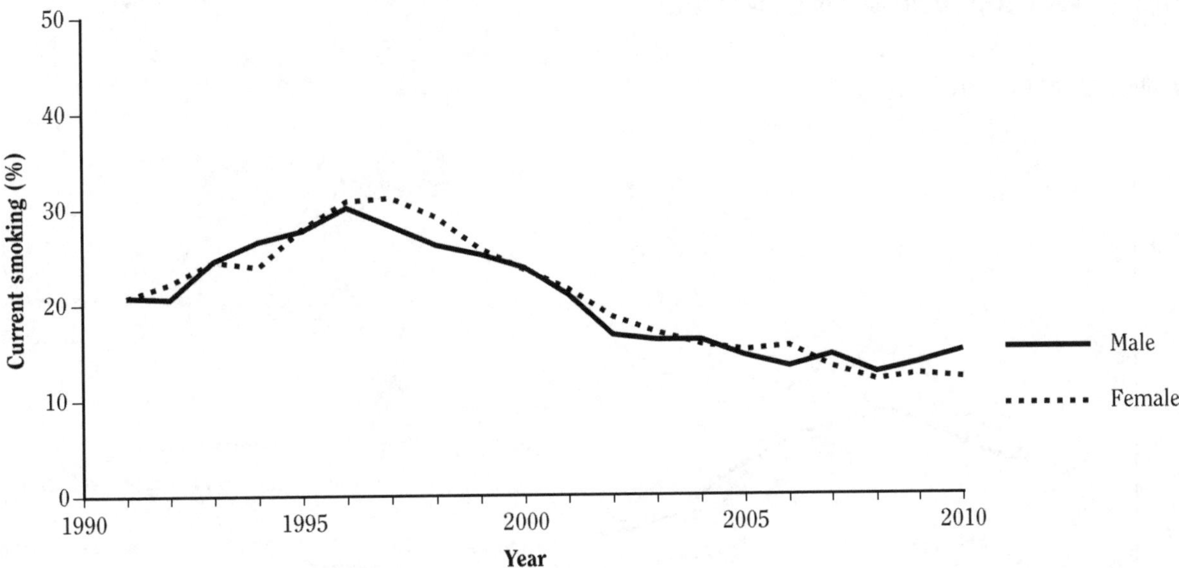

D. 12th grade, 1976–2010

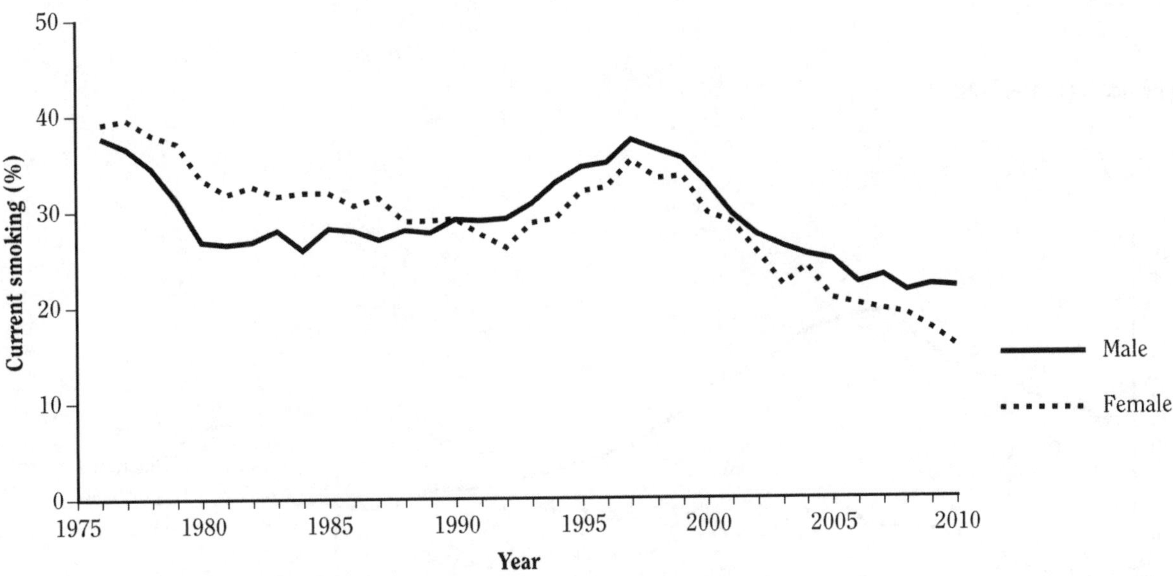

Source: 1975–2010 MTF: University of Michigan, Institute for Social Research (unpublished data).

Figure 3.1.9 **Trends in prevalence (%) of current cigarette smoking among young people over time, by grade level and race/ethnicity; Monitoring the Future (MTF) 1976–2010, and National Youth Risk Behavior Survey (YRBS) 1991–2009; United States**

A. 8th grade, MTF, 1991–2010

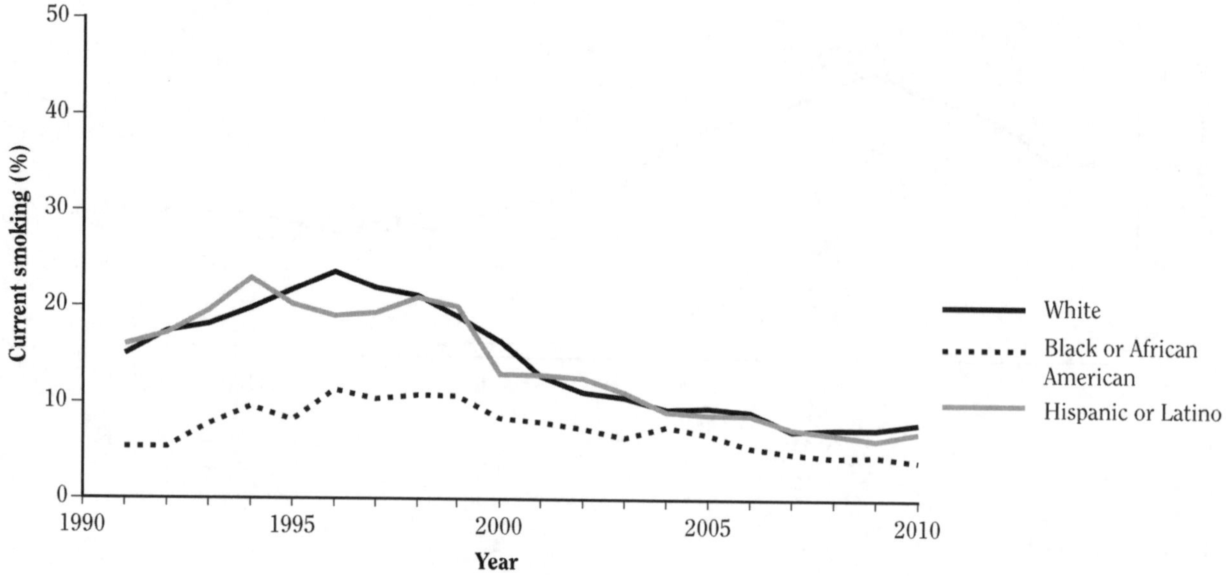

B. 10th grade, MTF, 1991–2010

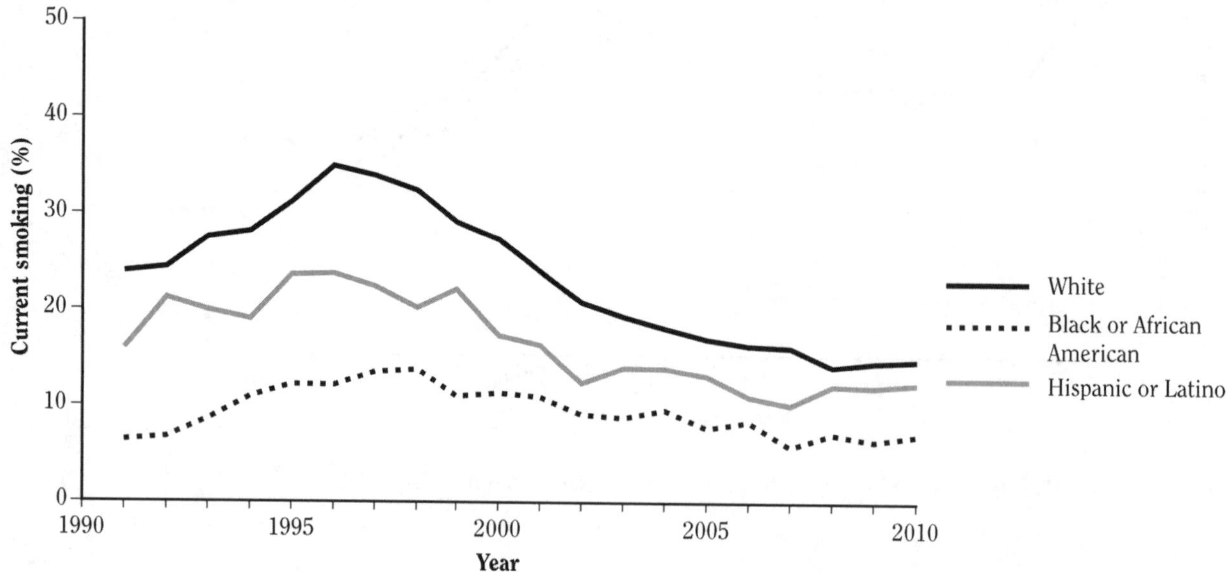

C. 12th grade, MTF, 1976–2010

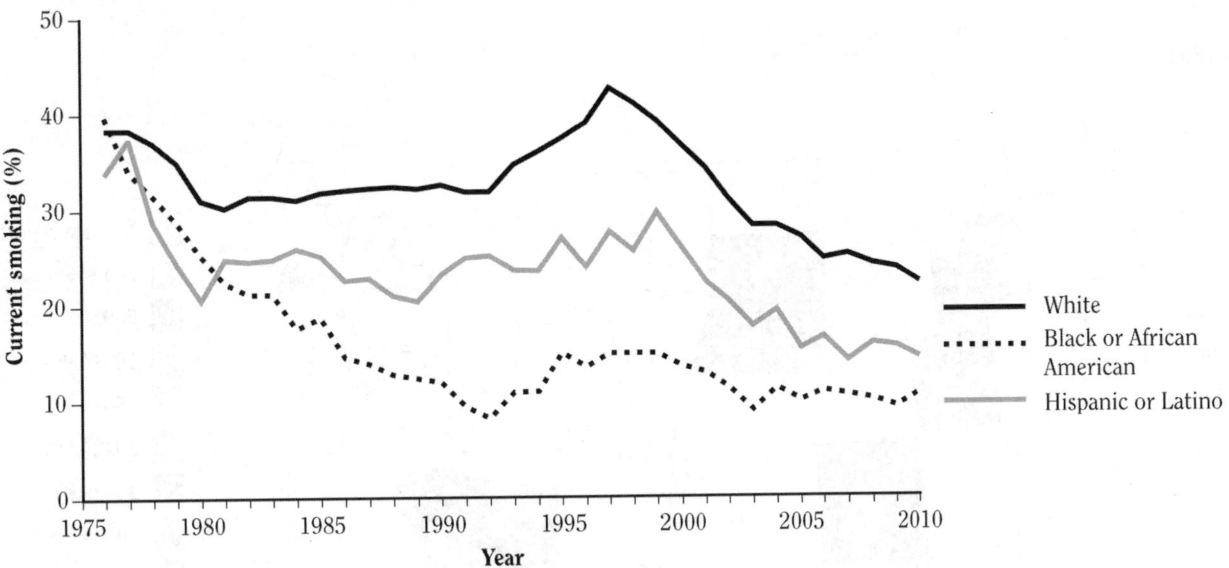

D. 9th–12th grade, YRBS, 1991–2009

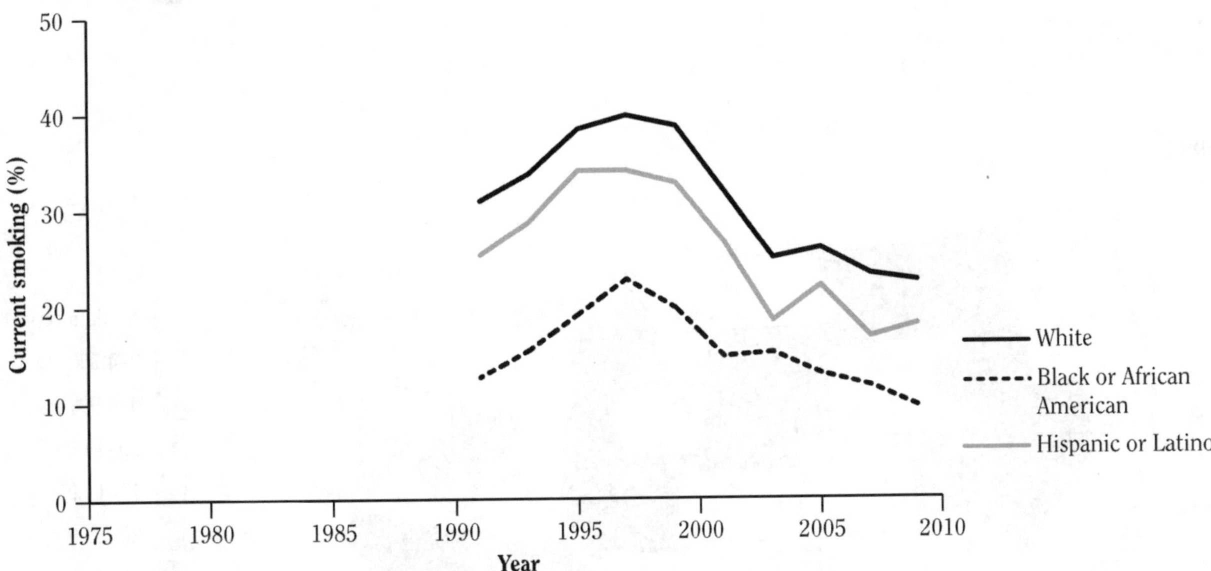

Source: 1976–2010 MTF: University of Michigan, Institute for Social Research (unpublished data); 1991–2009 YRBS: Centers for Disease Control and Prevention (CDC 2011a.)

Figure 3.1.10 Trends in the prevalence (%) of current smoking among 9th- to 12th-grade students, by state; Youth Risk Behavior Survey (YRBS) 1991–2009; United States

A. 1991

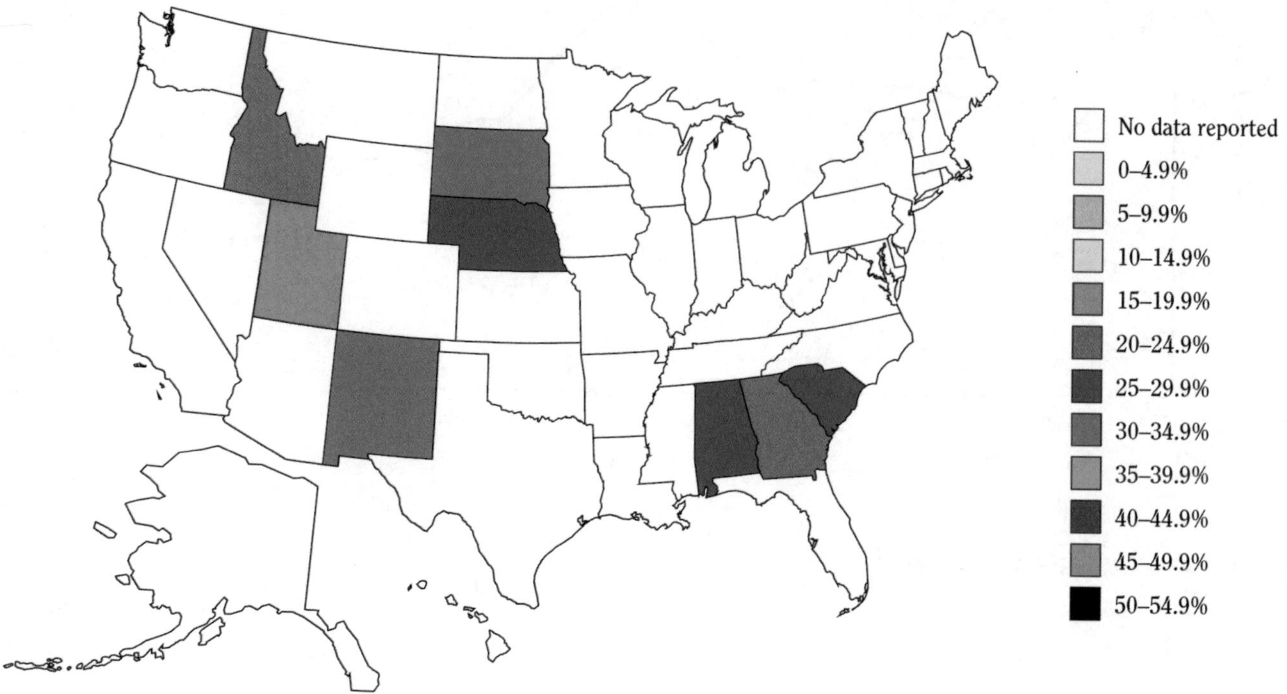

B. 1993

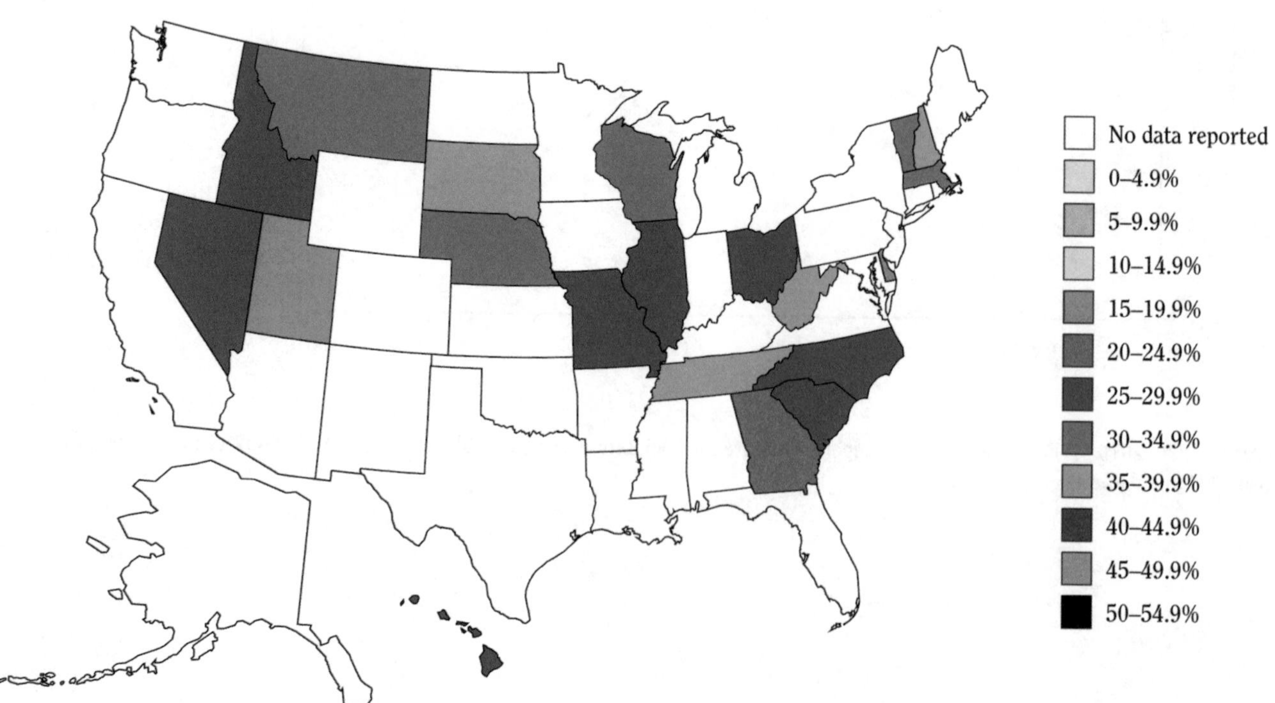

C. 1995

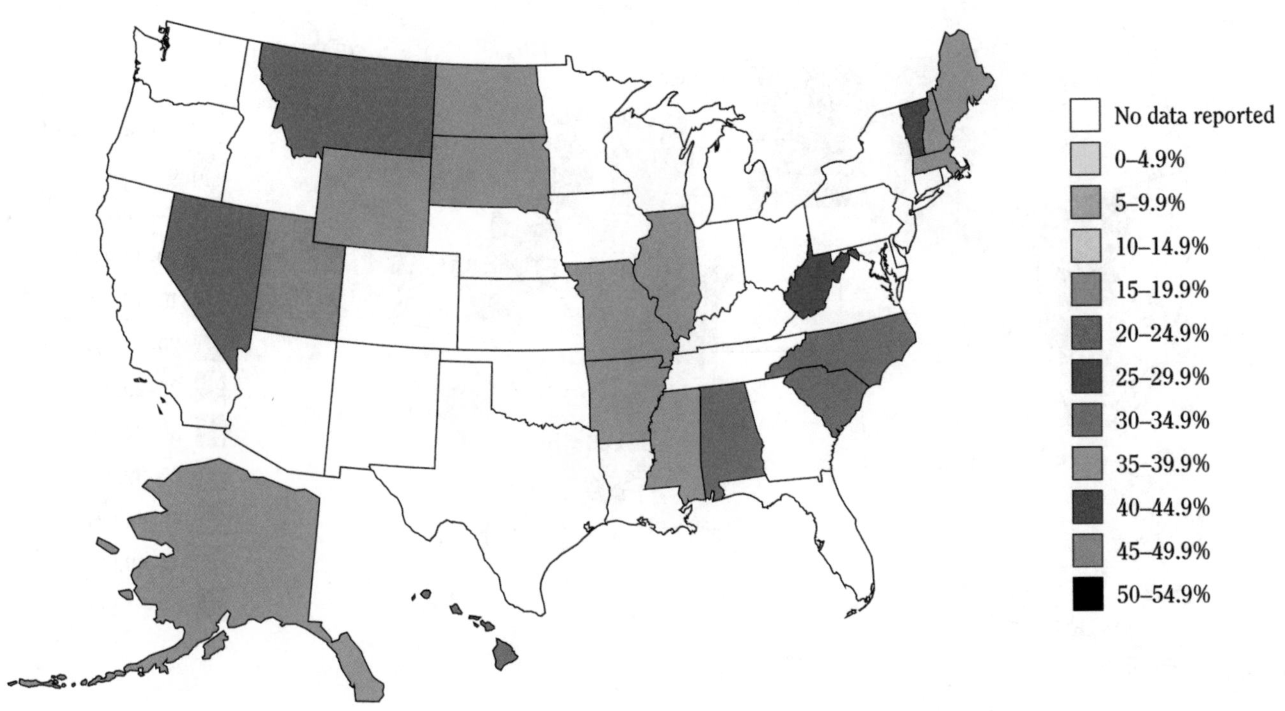
No data reported
0–4.9%
5–9.9%
10–14.9%
15–19.9%
20–24.9%
25–29.9%
30–34.9%
35–39.9%
40–44.9%
45–49.9%
50–54.9%

D. 1997

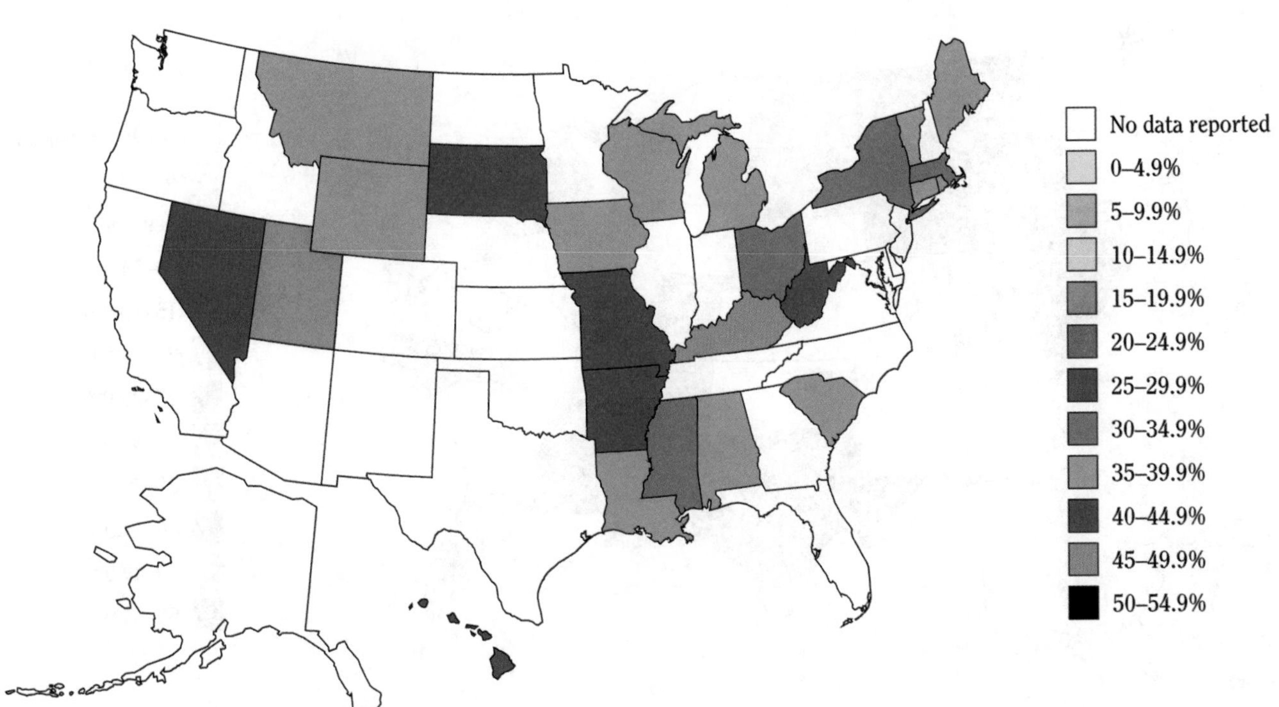
No data reported
0–4.9%
5–9.9%
10–14.9%
15–19.9%
20–24.9%
25–29.9%
30–34.9%
35–39.9%
40–44.9%
45–49.9%
50–54.9%

E. 1999

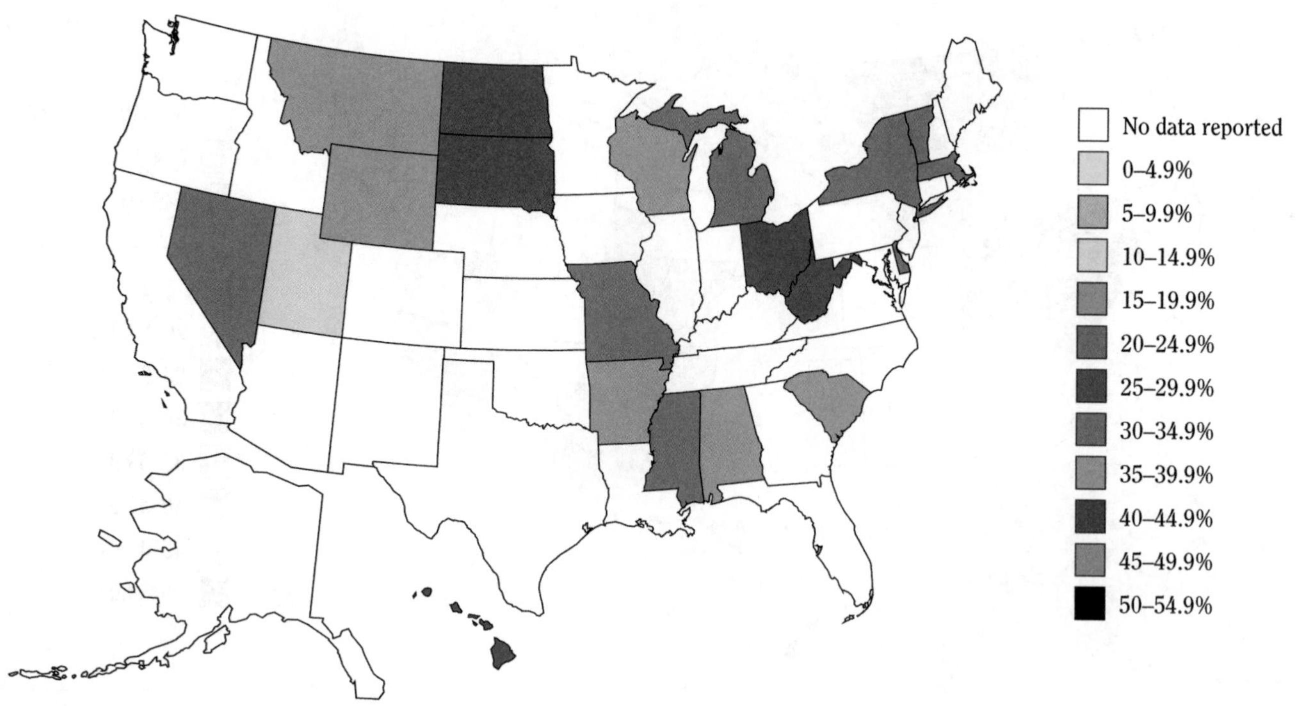
No data reported
0–4.9%
5–9.9%
10–14.9%
15–19.9%
20–24.9%
25–29.9%
30–34.9%
35–39.9%
40–44.9%
45–49.9%
50–54.9%

F. 2001

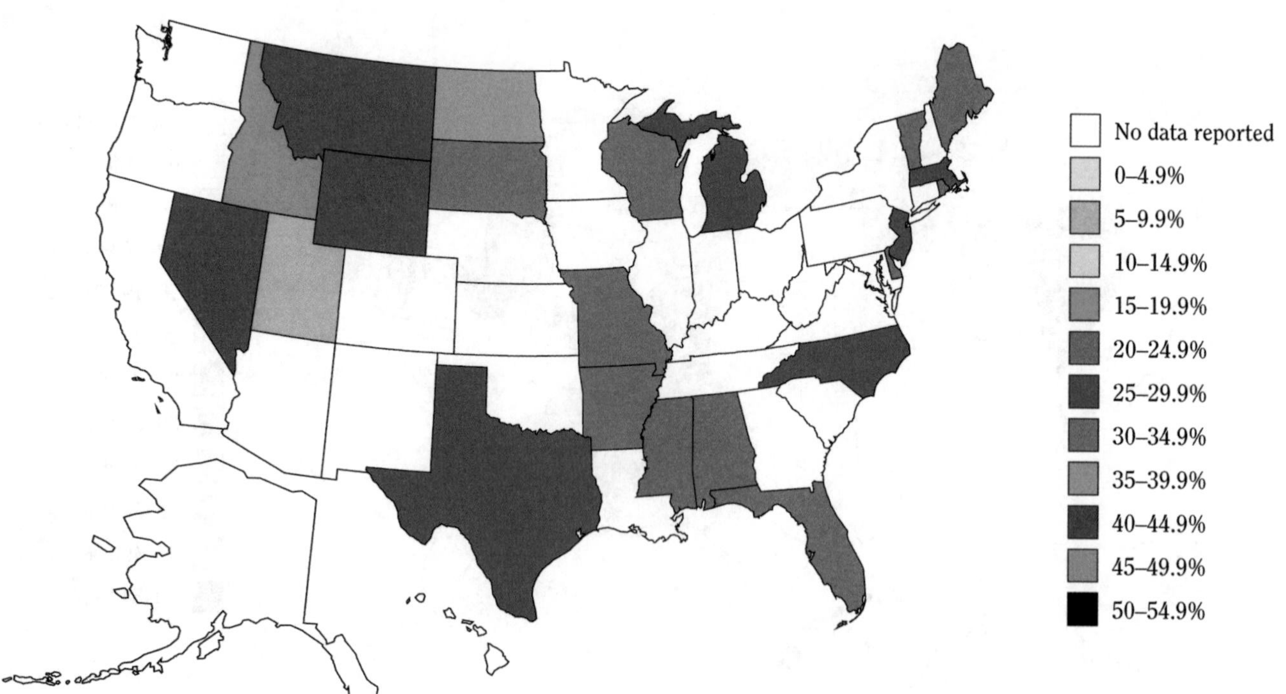
No data reported
0–4.9%
5–9.9%
10–14.9%
15–19.9%
20–24.9%
25–29.9%
30–34.9%
35–39.9%
40–44.9%
45–49.9%
50–54.9%

G. 2003

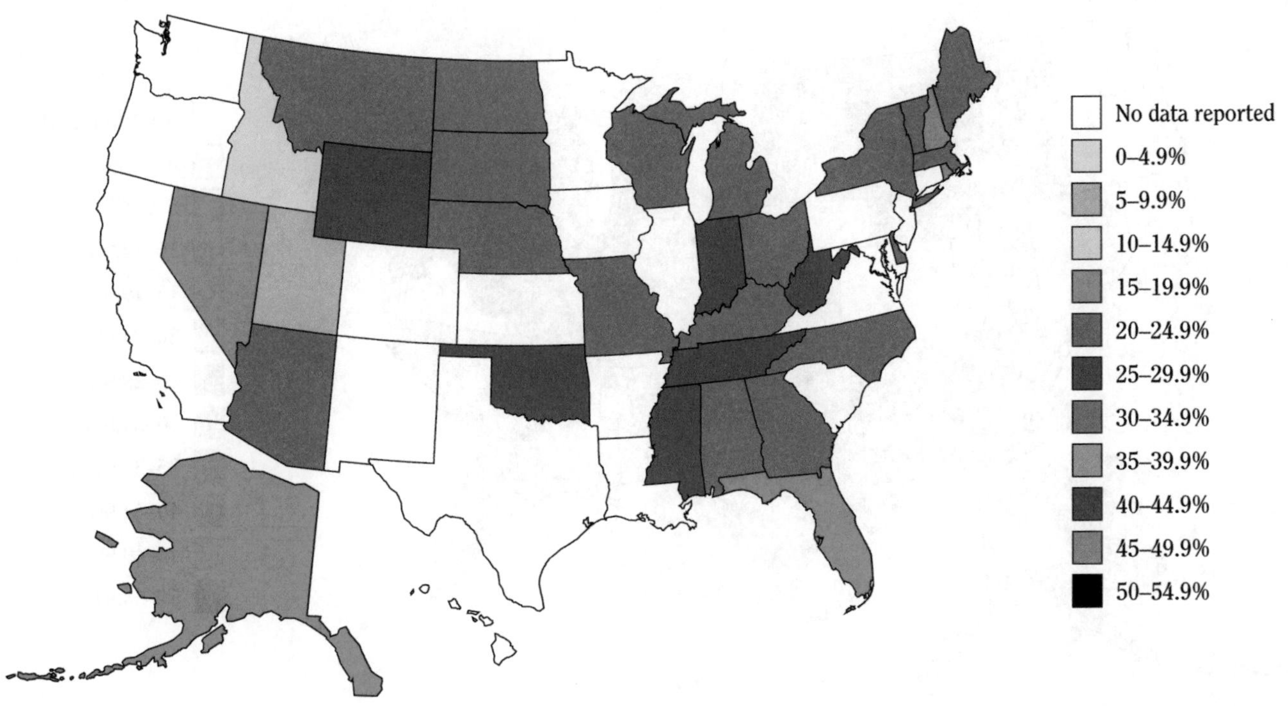
No data reported
0–4.9%
5–9.9%
10–14.9%
15–19.9%
20–24.9%
25–29.9%
30–34.9%
35–39.9%
40–44.9%
45–49.9%
50–54.9%

H. 2005

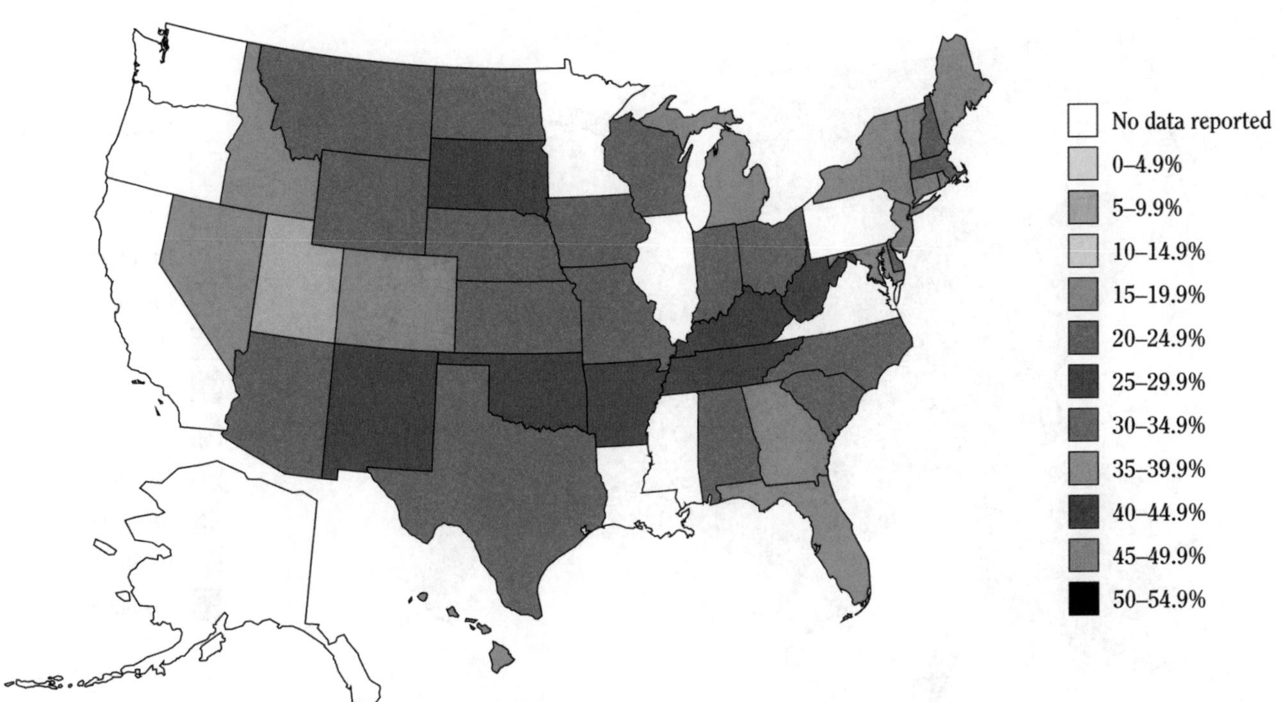
No data reported
0–4.9%
5–9.9%
10–14.9%
15–19.9%
20–24.9%
25–29.9%
30–34.9%
35–39.9%
40–44.9%
45–49.9%
50–54.9%

I. 2007

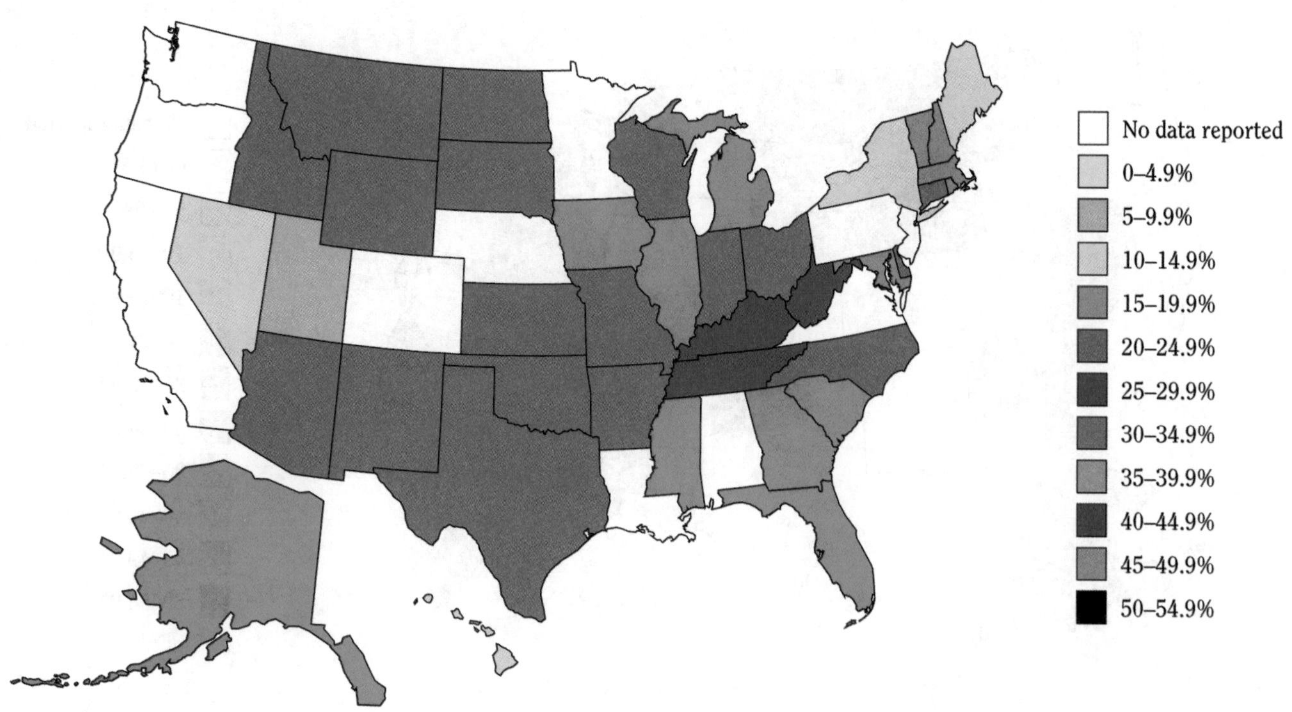

J. 2009

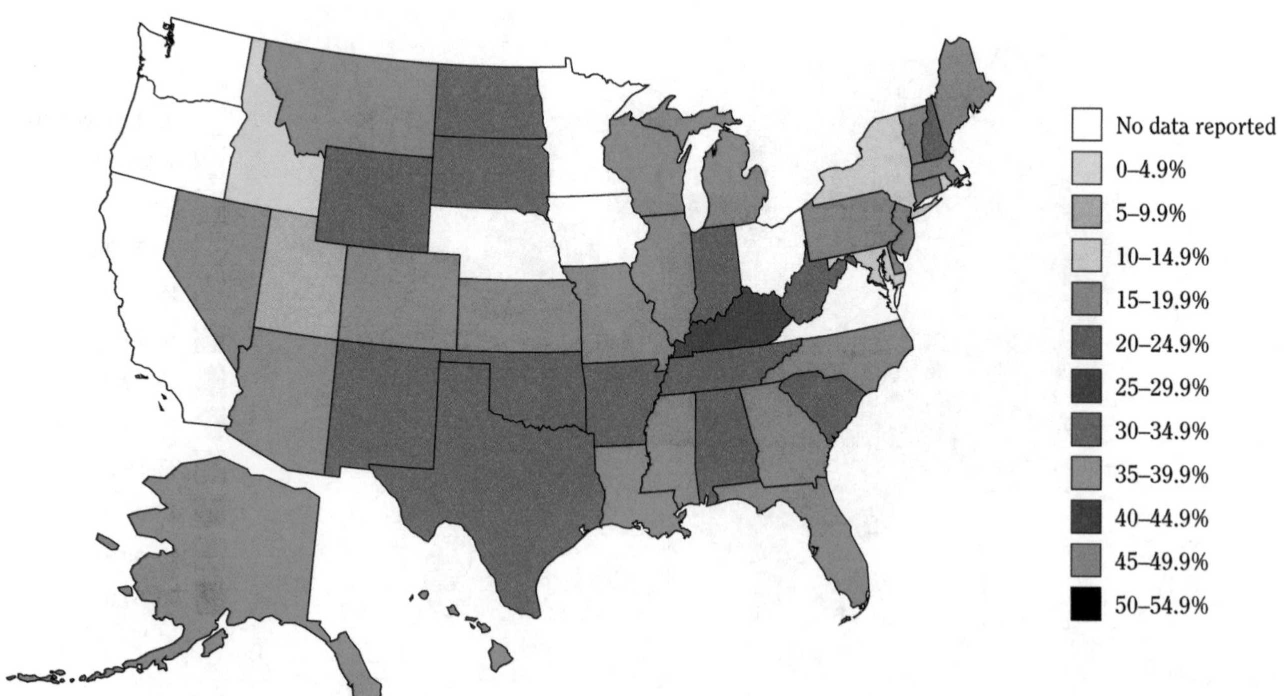

Source: 1991–2009 YRBS: Centers for Disease Control and Prevention, Division of Adolescent and School Health (CDC 2011a).

Figure 3.1.11 Trends in prevalence (%) of cigarette smoking among Hispanics, Blacks, and Whites, by age group; National Health Interview Survey (NHIS) 1978–2009; United States

A. 20–24 years of age

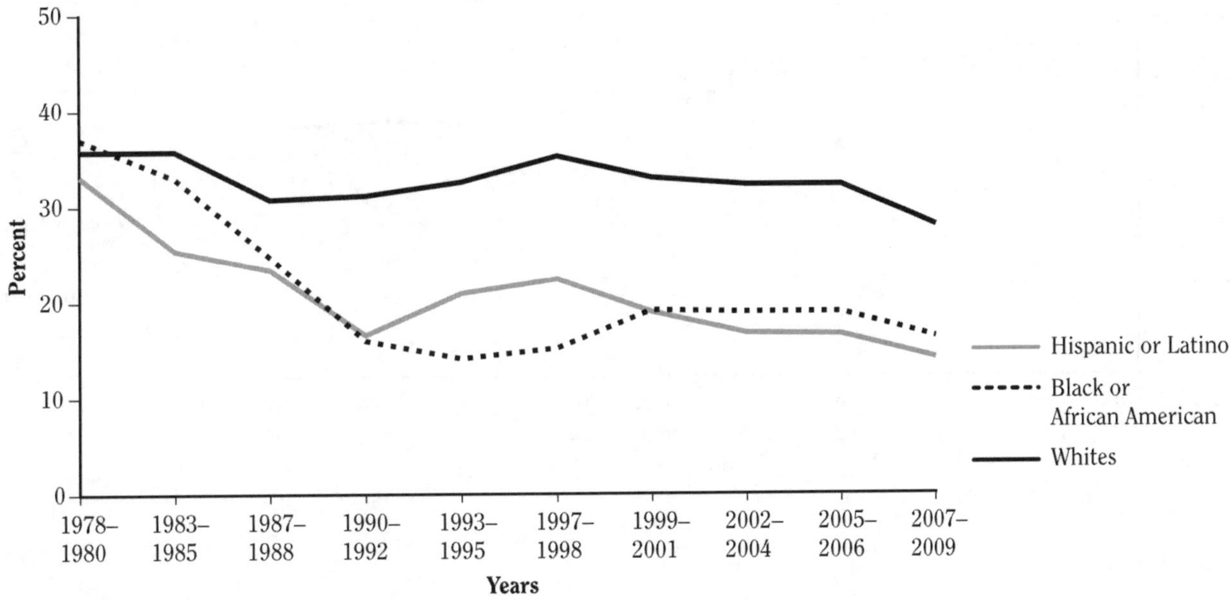

B. 25–29 years of age

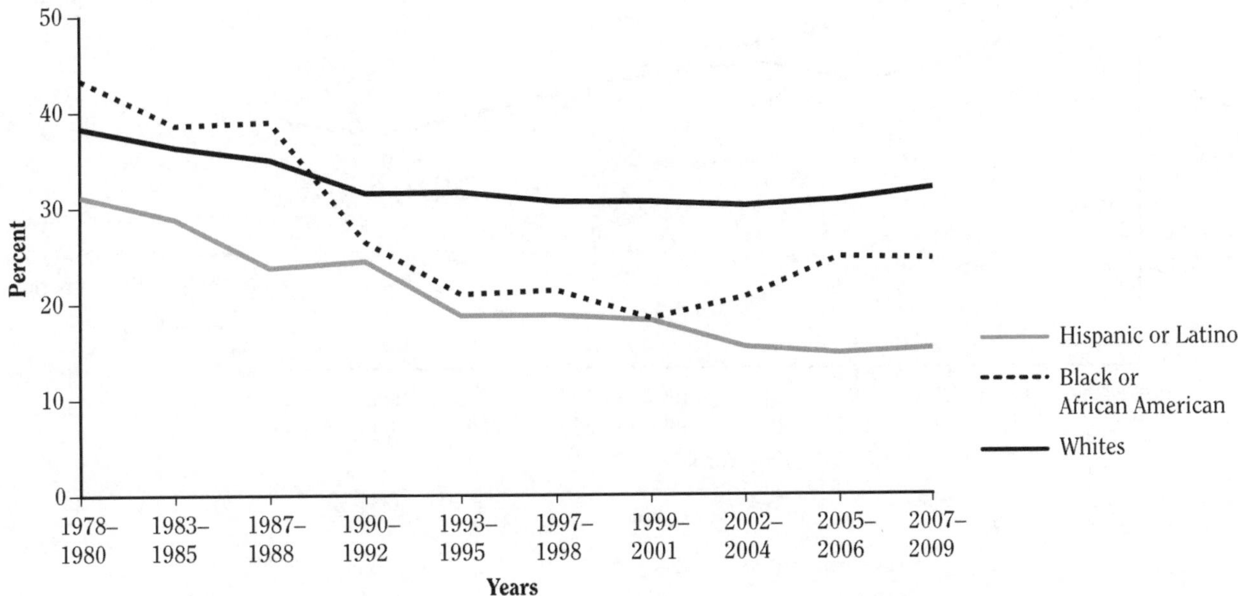

C. 30–34 years of age

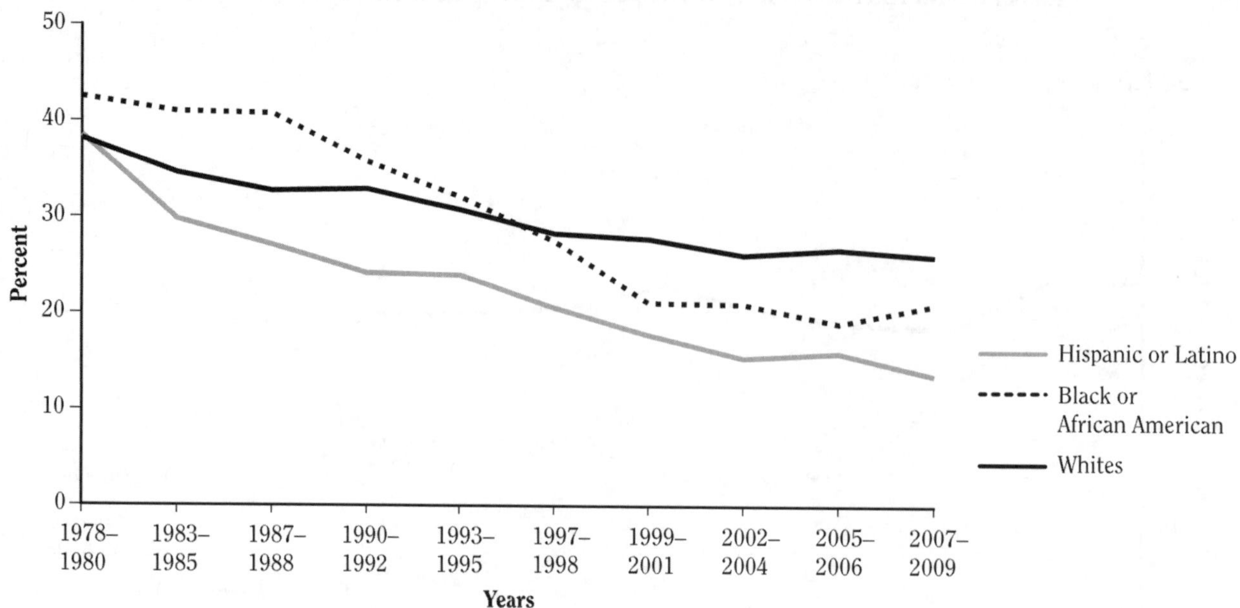

D. 35–39 years of age

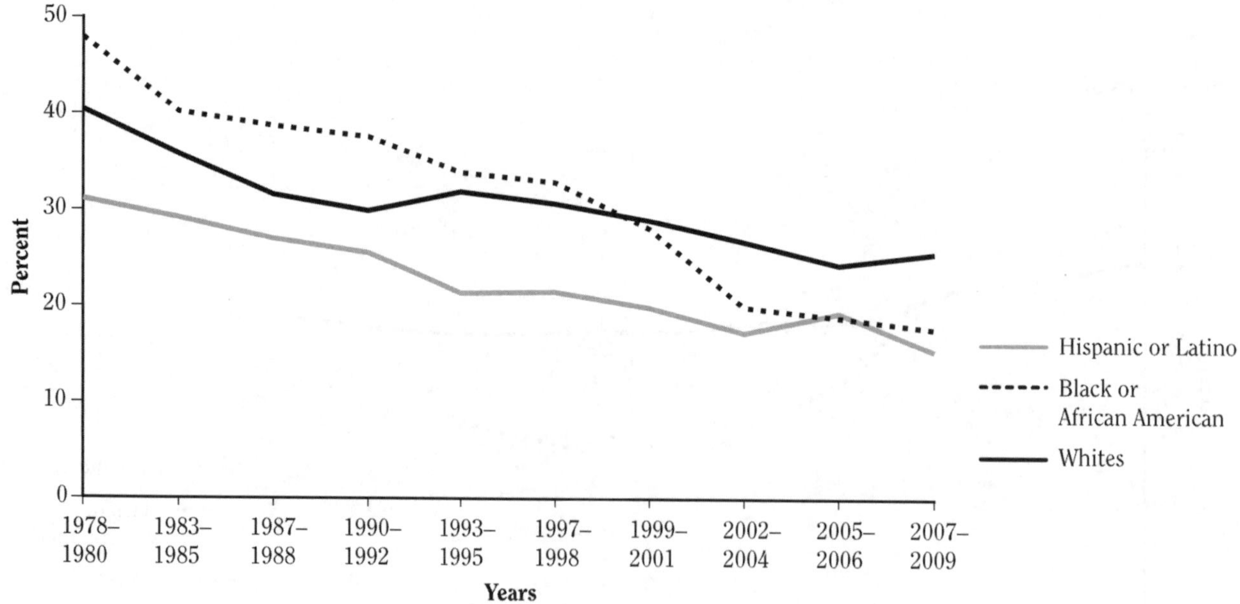

E. 40–44 years of age

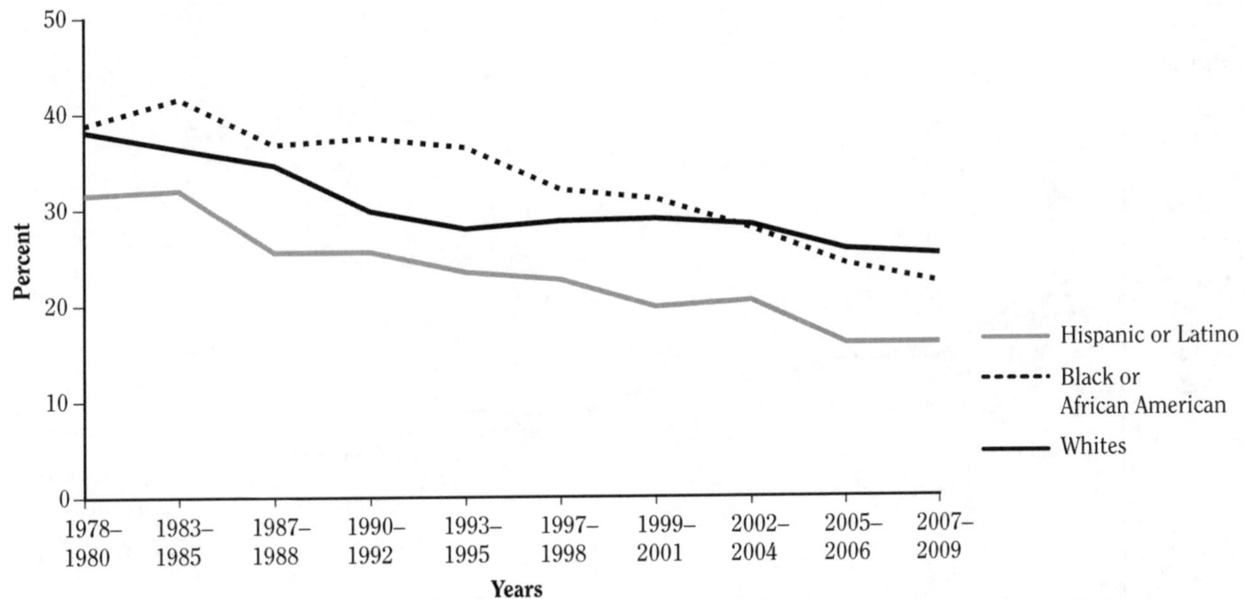

Source: 1978–2009 NHIS: Centers for Disease Control and Prevention, National Center for Health Statistics (unpublished data).

Figure 3.1.12 Trends in prevalence (%) of cigarette smoking among persons 20 years of age or older, by age group and race/ethnicity; National Health Interview Survey (NHIS) 1978–2009; United States

A. Hispanics

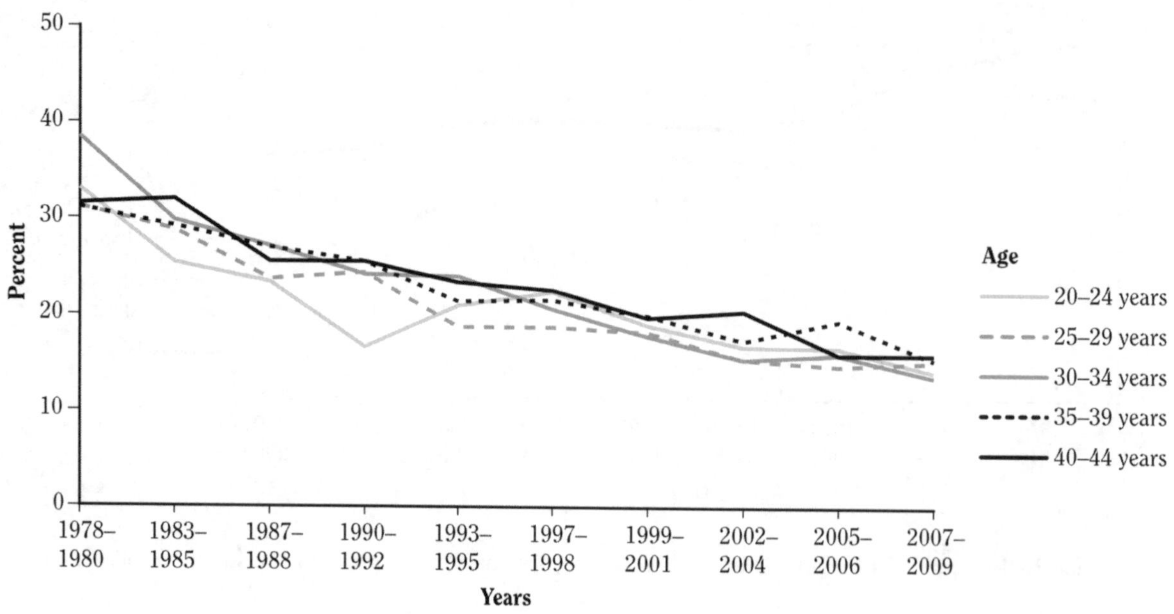

B. Blacks

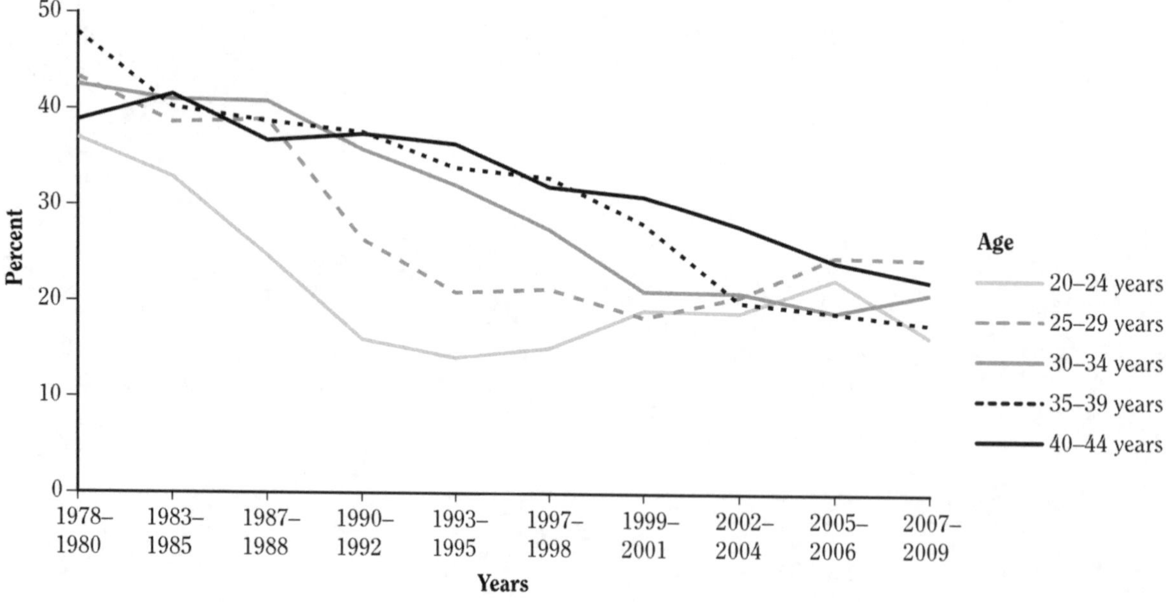

C. Whites

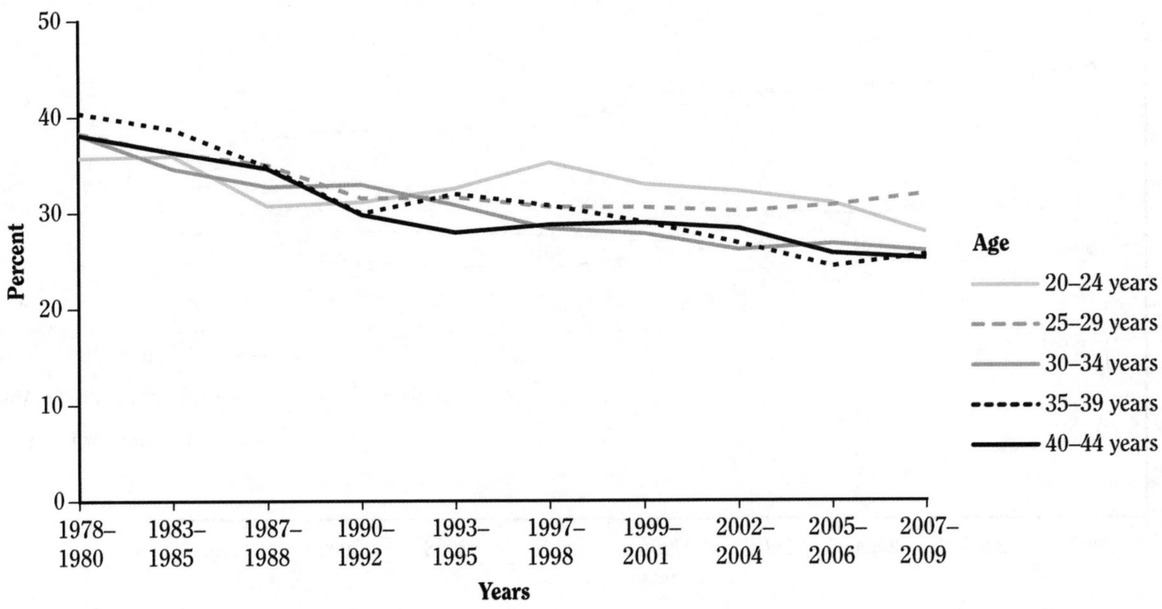

Source: 1978–2009 NHIS: Center for Disease Control and Preventon, National Center for Health Statistics (unpublished data).

Figure 3.1.13 Past-month cigarette use among young adults (18–25 years of age), by gender; National Survey on Drug Use and Health (NSDUH) 2002–2010; United States

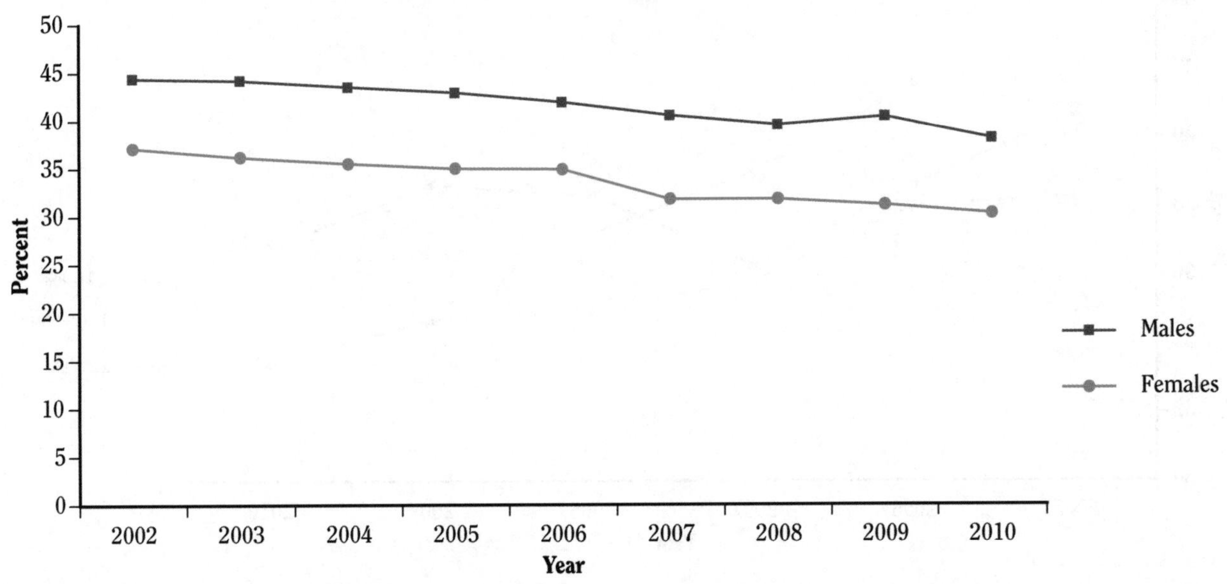

Source: 2002–2010 NSDUH: Substance Abuse and Mental Health Services Administration (unpublished data).

Figure 3.1.14 Past-month cigarette use among young adults (18–25 years of age), by race/ethnicity; National Survey on Drug Use and Health (NSDUH) 2002–2010; United States

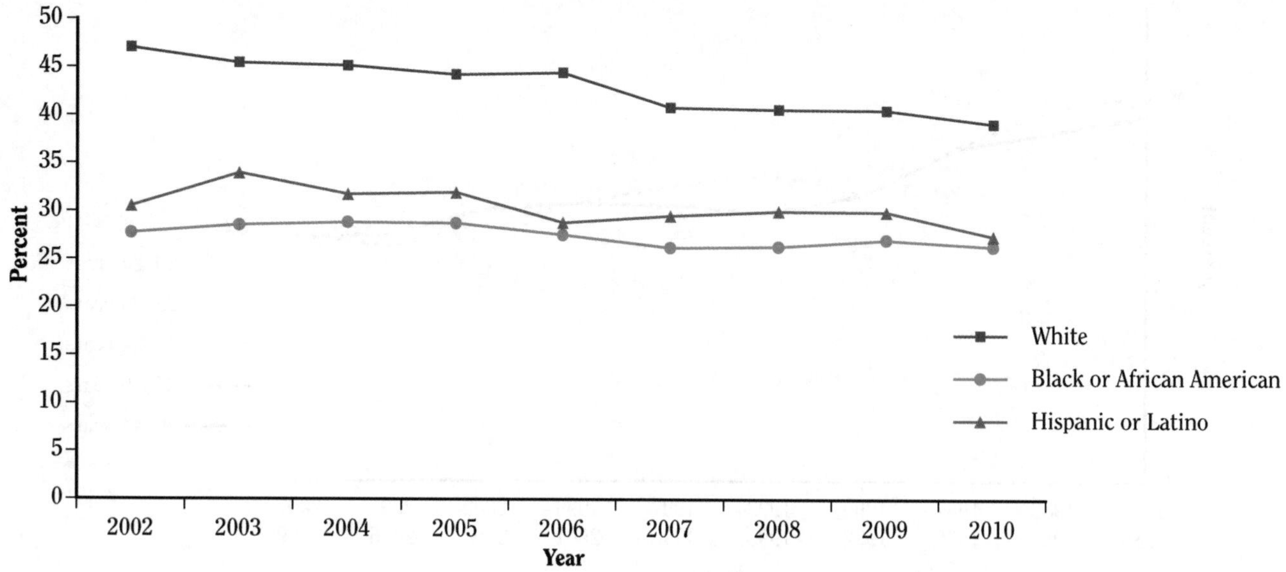

Source: 2002–2010 NSDUH: Substance Abuse and Mental Health Services Administration (detailed reports).

Figure 3.1.15 Past-month cigarette use among young adults (18–25 years of age), by poverty level; National Survey on Drug Use and Health (NSDUH) 2005–2010; United States

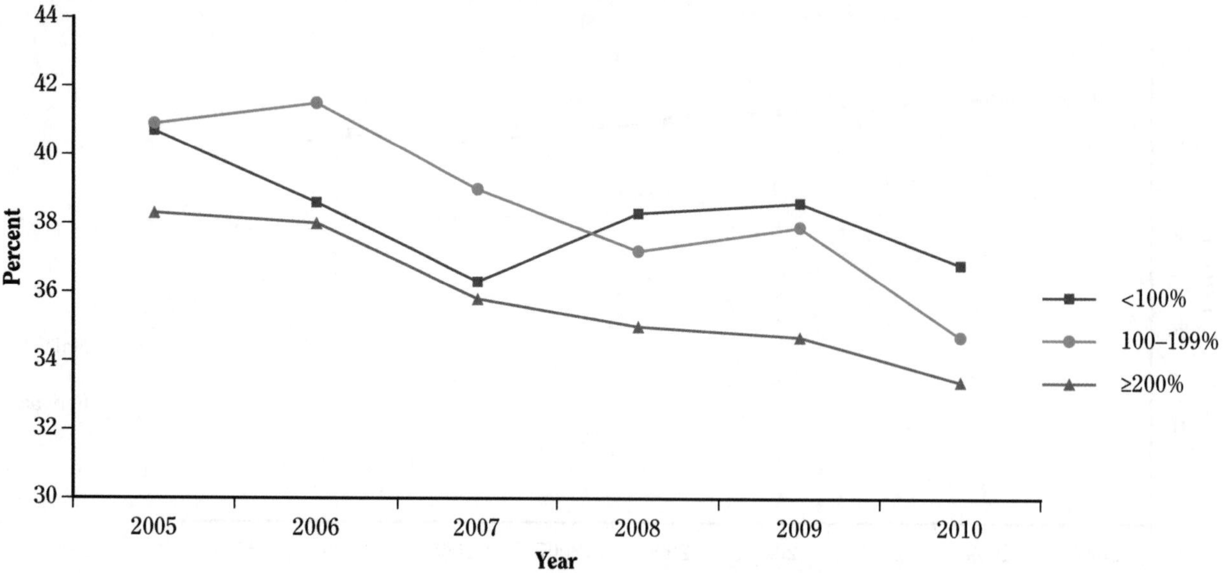

Source: 2005–2010 NSDUH: Substance Abuse and Mental Health Services Administration (unpublished data).

Figure 3.1.16 Trends in the intensity of smoking among high school seniors; Monitoring the Future (MTF) 1976–2010; United States

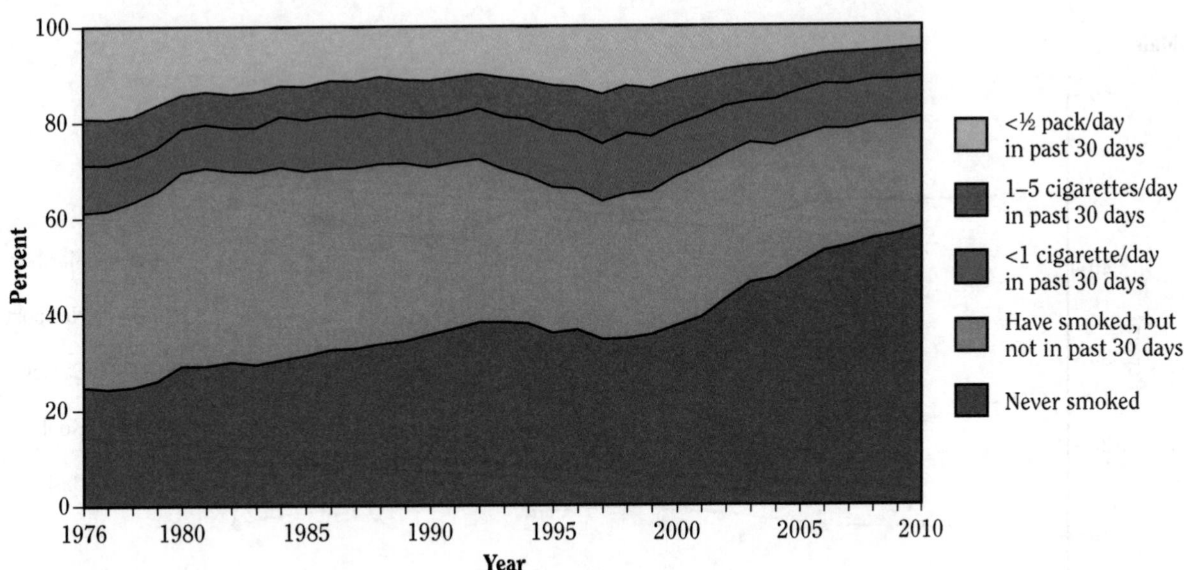

Source: 1976–2010 MTF: University of Michigan, Institute for Social Research (unpublished data).

Figure 3.1.17 Trends in cigarette brand preference for the top five cigarette brands among 12- to 17-year-olds who are current smokers, by gender; National Survey on Drug Use and Health (NSDUH) 2002–2010; United States

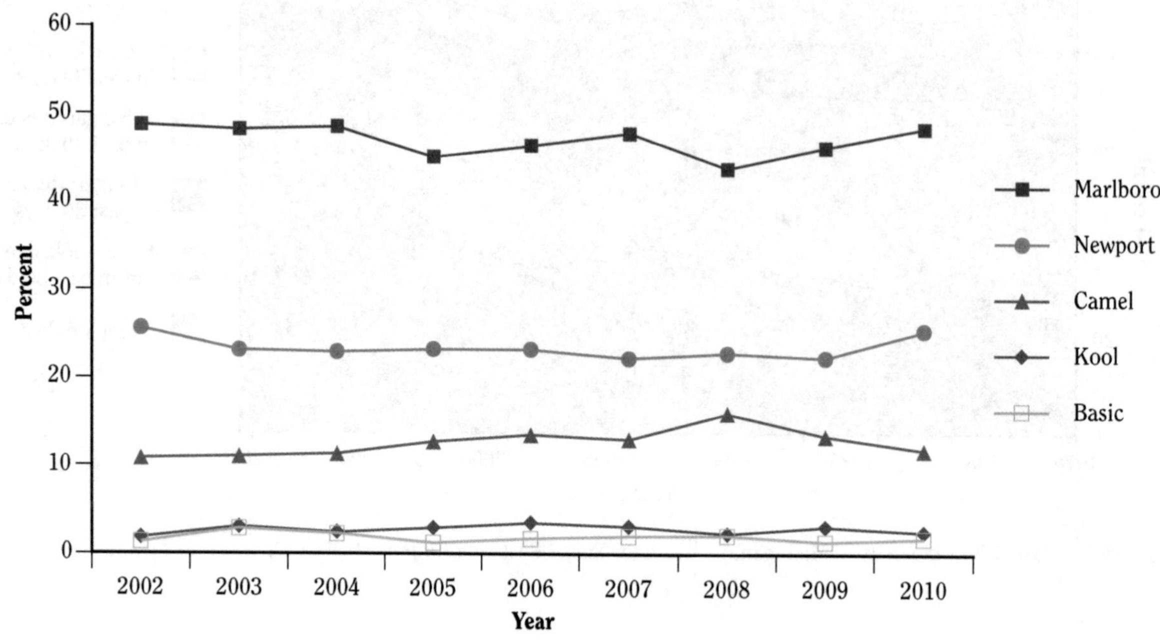

B. Females

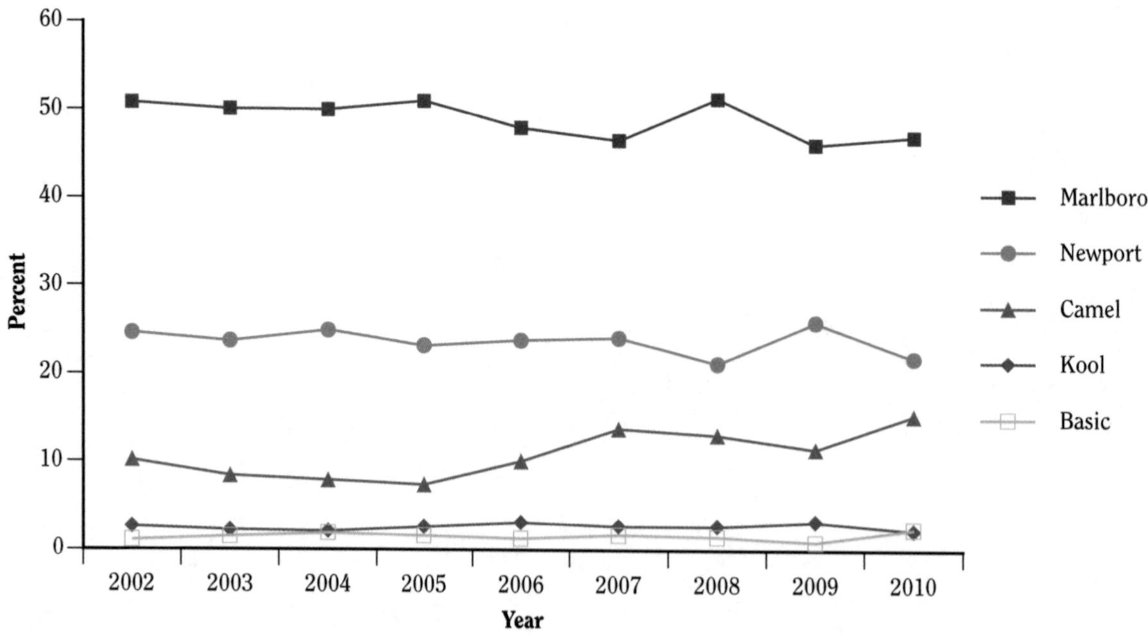

Source: 2002–2010 NSDUH: Substance Abuse and Mental Health Services Administration (unpublished data).

Figure 3.1.18 Trends in cigarette brand preference for the top five cigarette brands among 18- to 25-year-olds who are current smokers, by gender; National Survey on Drug Use and Health (NSDUH) 2002–2010; United States

A. Males

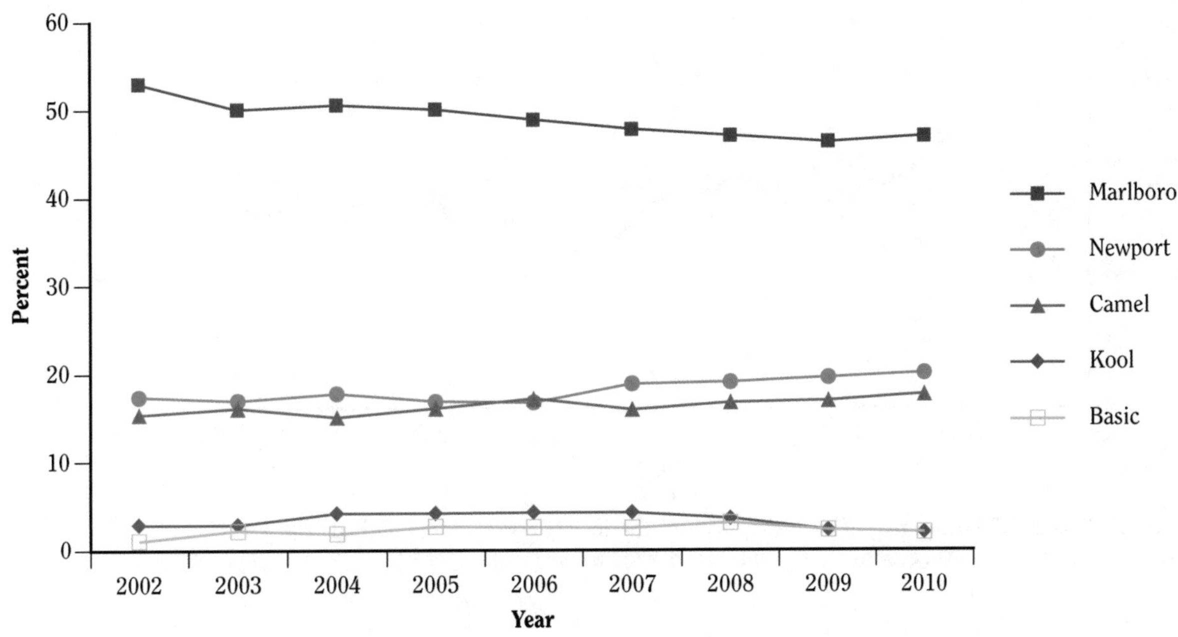

B. Females

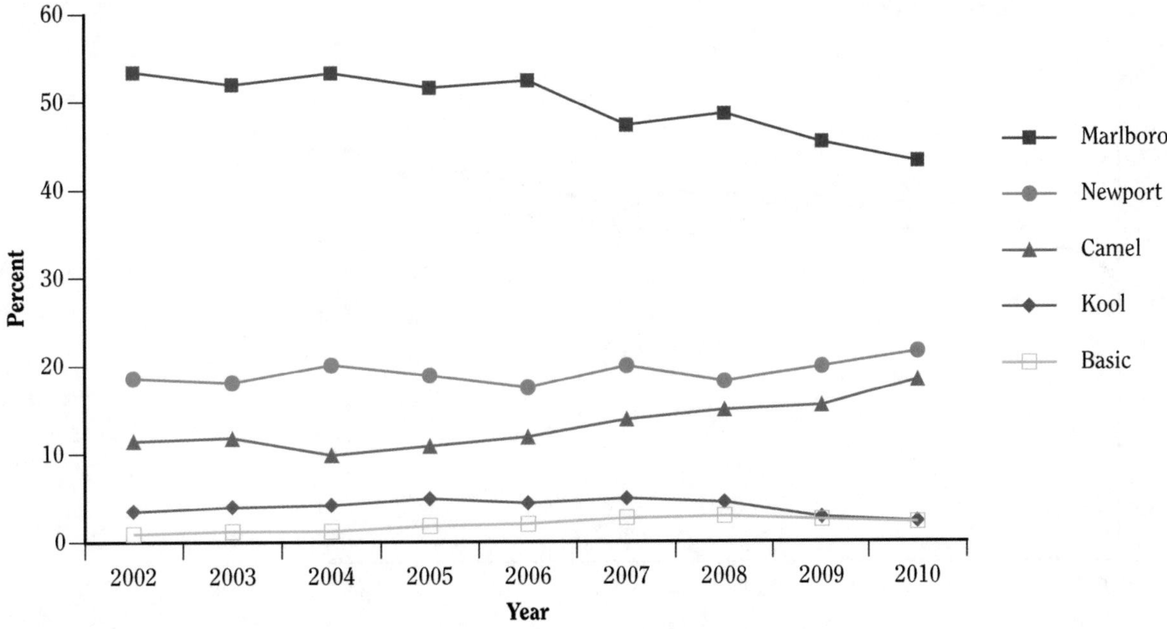

Source: 2002–2010 NSDUH: Substance Abuse and Mental Health Services Administration (unpublished data).

Figure 3.1.19 Trends in the percentage of former smokers among ever regular smokers[a] who are high school seniors, over time, by gender; Monitoring the Future (MTF) 1976–2010; United States

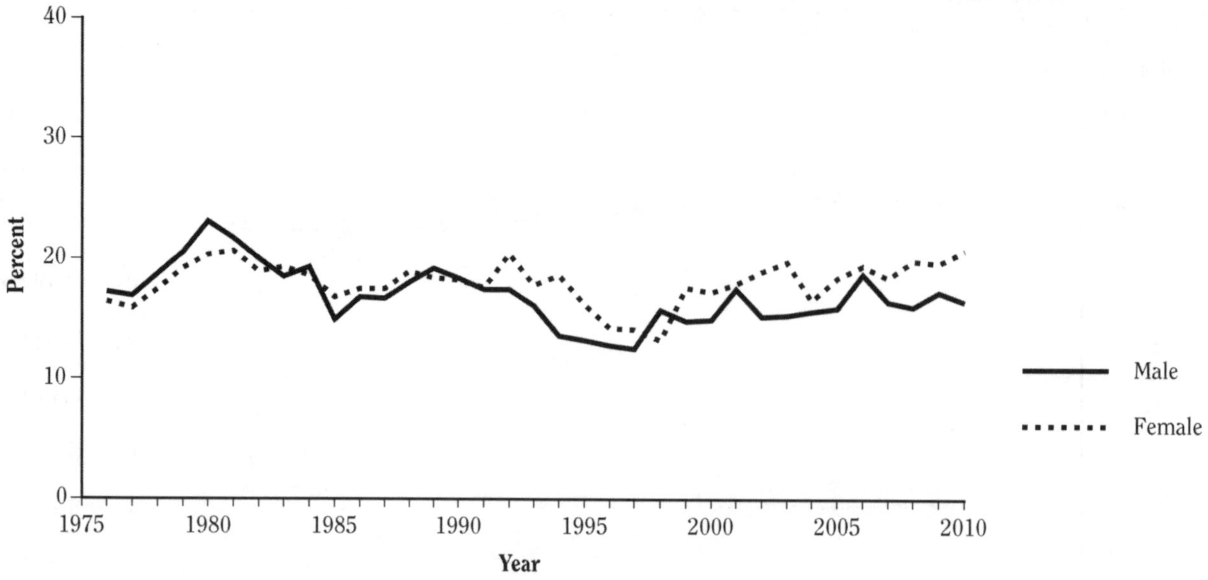

Source: 1976–2010 MTF: University of Michigan, Institute for Social Research (unpublished data).
[a]Percentage of those who had ever smoked regularly and who had not smoked during the previous 30 days.

Figure 3.1.20 Trends in the percentage of high school seniors who believe that smoking is a serious health risk and percentage of high school seniors who have ever smoked; Monitoring the Future (MTF) 1975–2010; United States

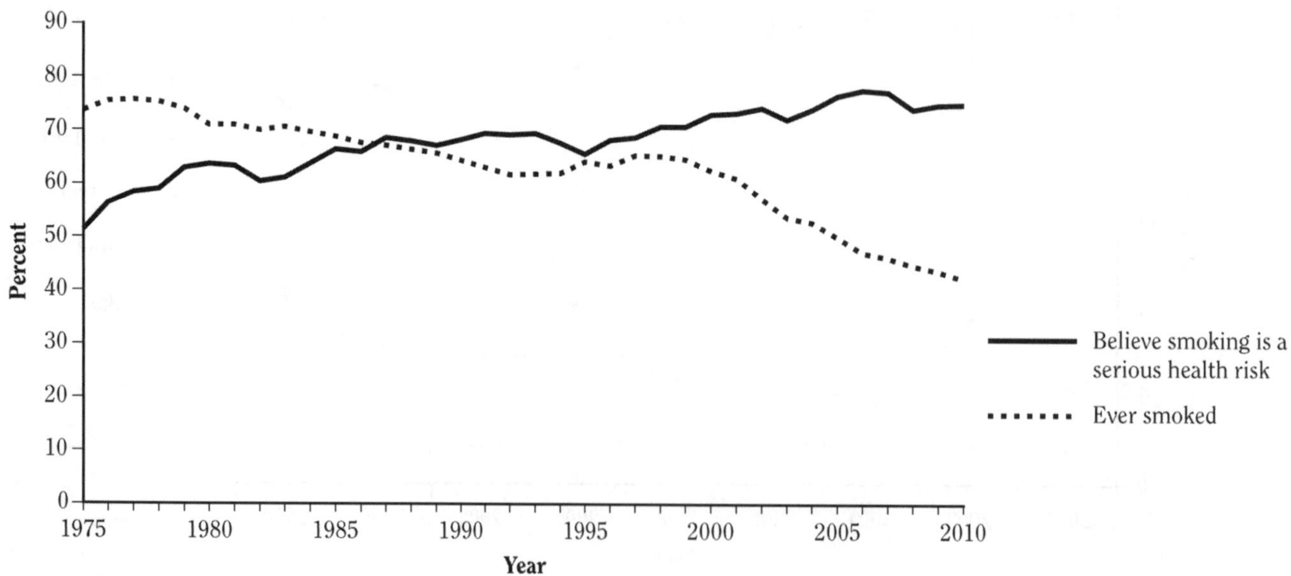

Source: 1975–2010 MTF: University of Michigan, Institute for Social Research (unpublished data).

Figure 3.1.21 Trends in the percentage of young people who believe smoking is a "dirty habit," by grade level; Monitoring the Future (MTF) 1991–2010; United States

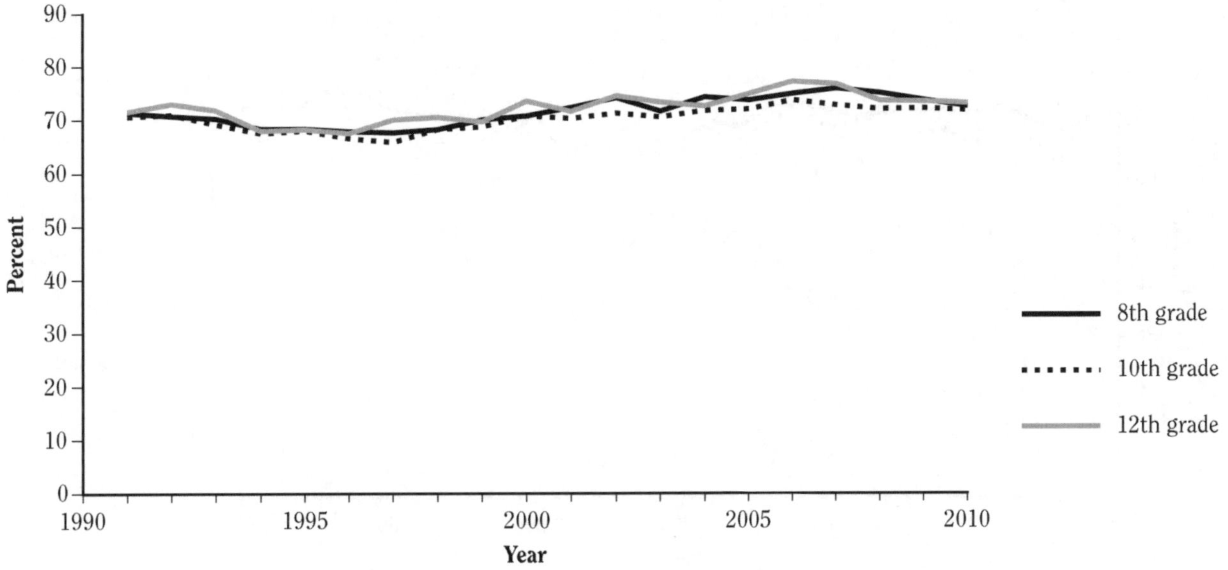

Source: 1991–2010 MTF: University of Michigan, Institute for Social Research (unpublished data).

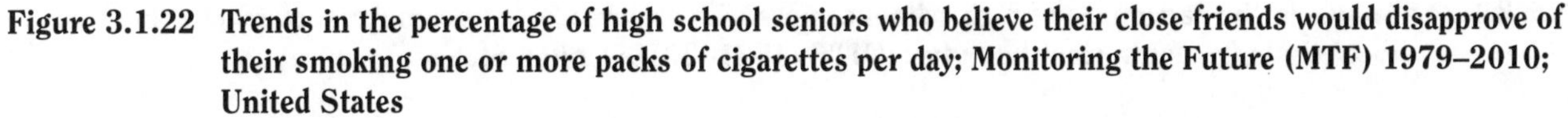

Figure 3.1.22 Trends in the percentage of high school seniors who believe their close friends would disapprove of their smoking one or more packs of cigarettes per day; Monitoring the Future (MTF) 1979–2010; United States

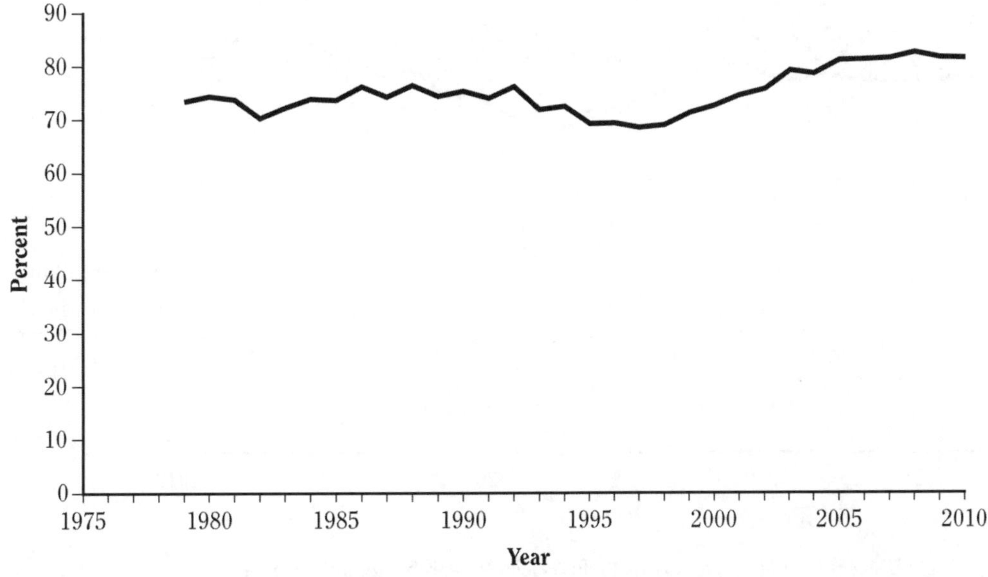

Source: 1979–2010 MTF: University of Michigan, Institute for Social Research (unpublished data).

Figure 3.1.23 Trends in the percentage of high school seniors who prefer to date nonsmokers, over time, by gender; Monitoring the Future (MTF) 1981–2010; United States

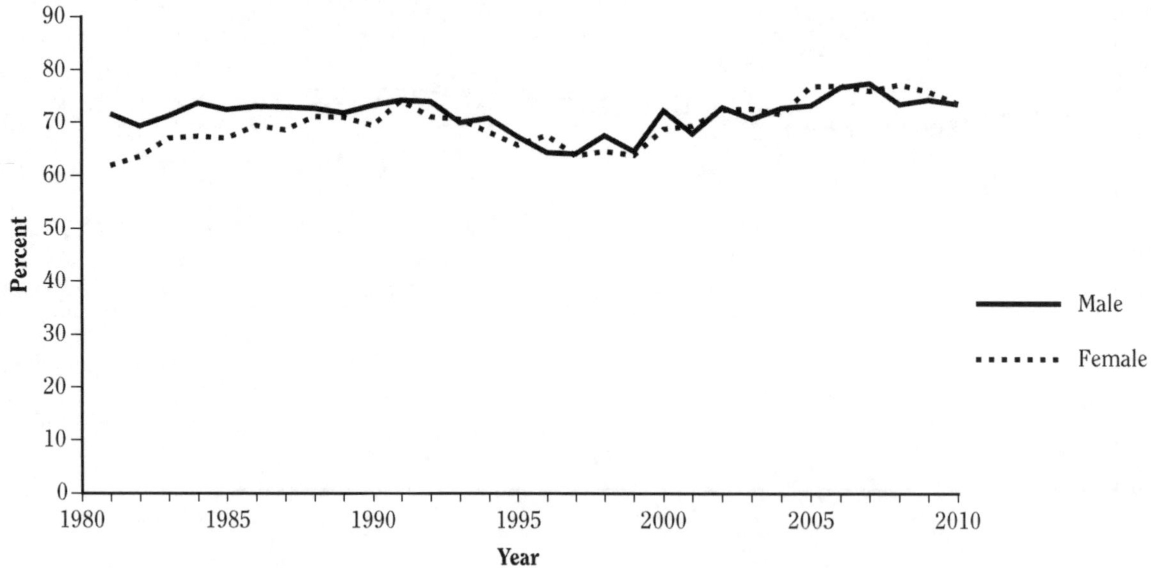

Source: 1981–2010 MTF: University of Michigan, Institute for Social Research (unpublished data).

Figure 3.1.24 Trends in the percentage of high school seniors who prefer to date nonsmokers, over time, by race/ethnicity; Monitoring the Future (MTF) 1981–2010; United States

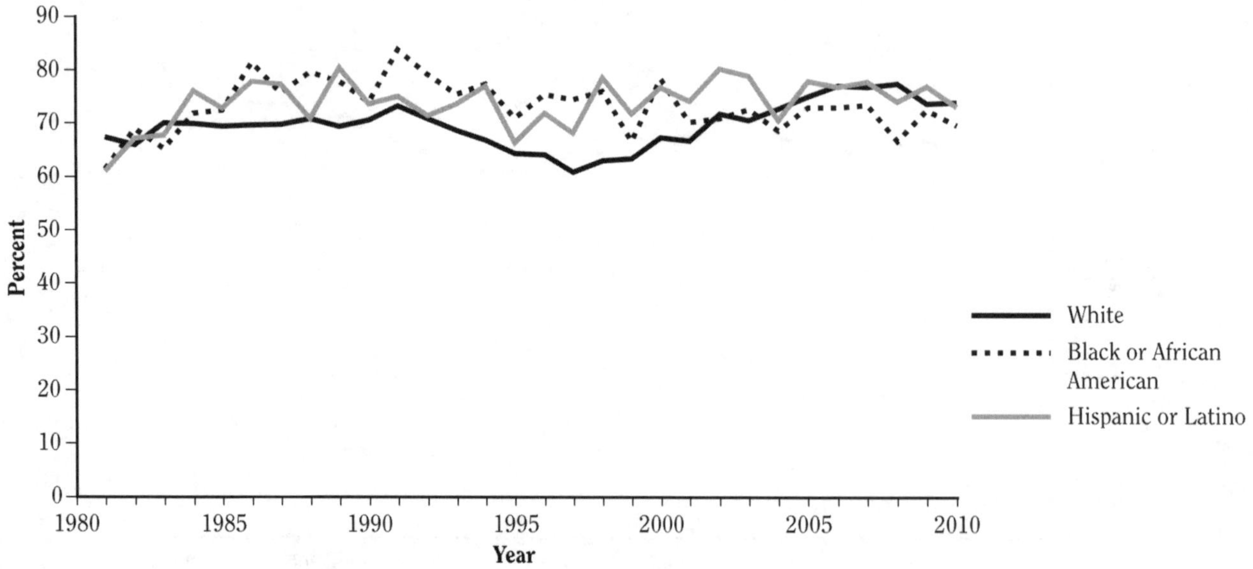

Source: 1981–2010 MTF: University of Michigan, Institute for Social Research (unpublished data).

Figure 3.1.25 Trends in the percentage of young people who do not mind being around people who smoke, by grade level; Monitoring the Future (MTF) 1991–2010; United States

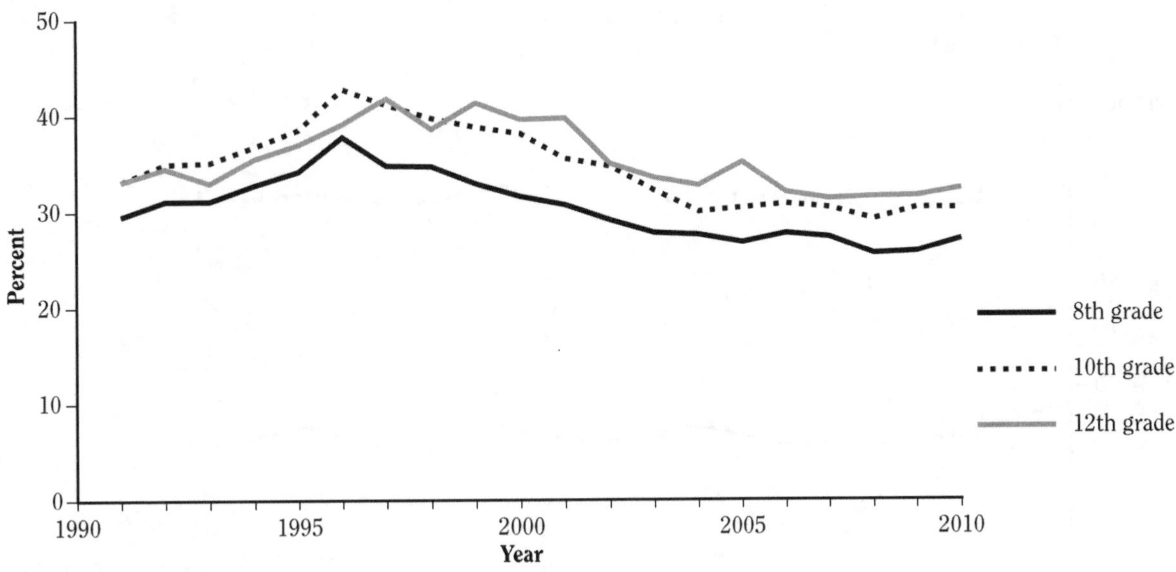

Source: 1991–2010 MTF: University of Michigan, Institute for Social Research (unpublished data).

Figure 3.1.26 Grade in which high school seniors had first tried cigarettes, smokeless tobacco, alcohol, marijuana, and cocaine among respondents who had ever used these substances by 12th grade; Monitoring the Future (MTF) 2002–2007; United States

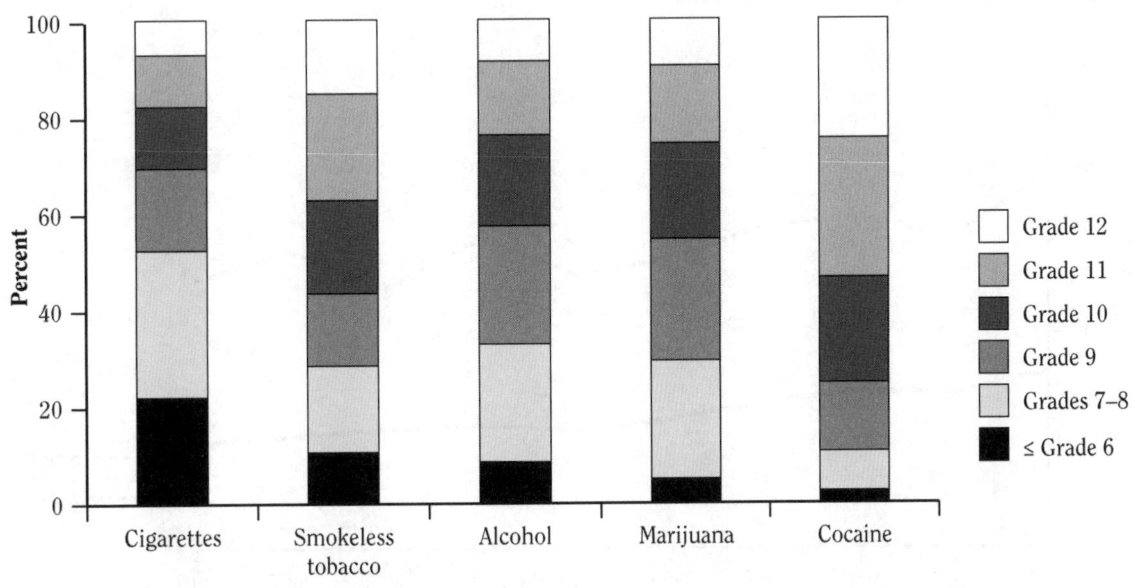

Source: 2002–2007 MTF: University of Michigan, Institute for Social Research (unpublished data).

Figure 3.1.27 Trends in health risk outcomes and behaviors among high school senior cigarette smokers and nonsmokers; National Youth Risk Behavior Survey (YRBS) 1991–2009; United States

Behaviors related to other drug use

A. Current alcohol use

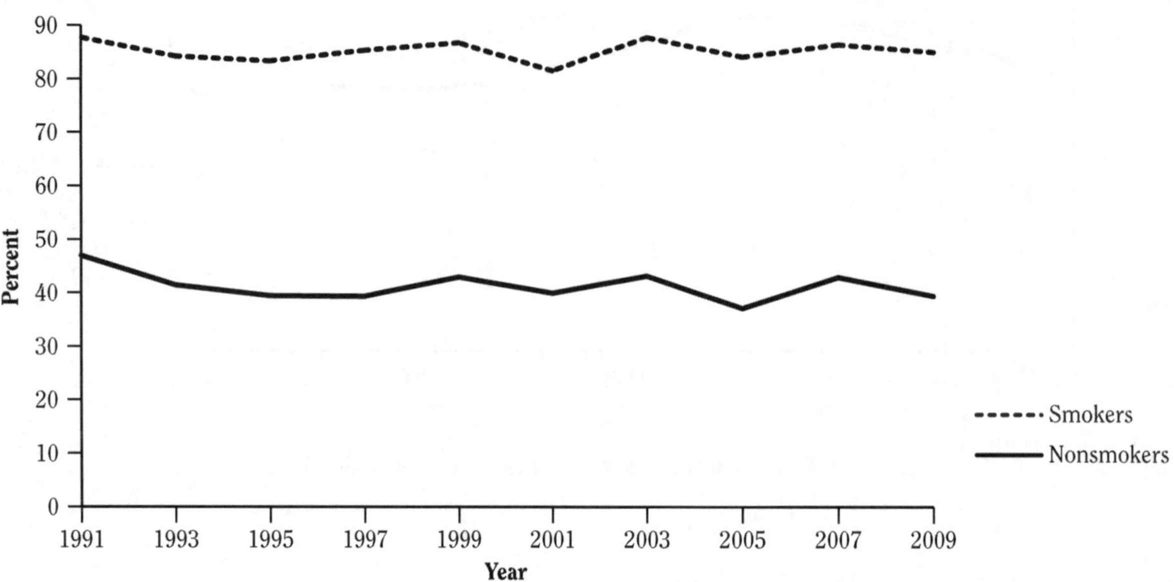

B. Rode with a driver using alcohol in the past 30 days

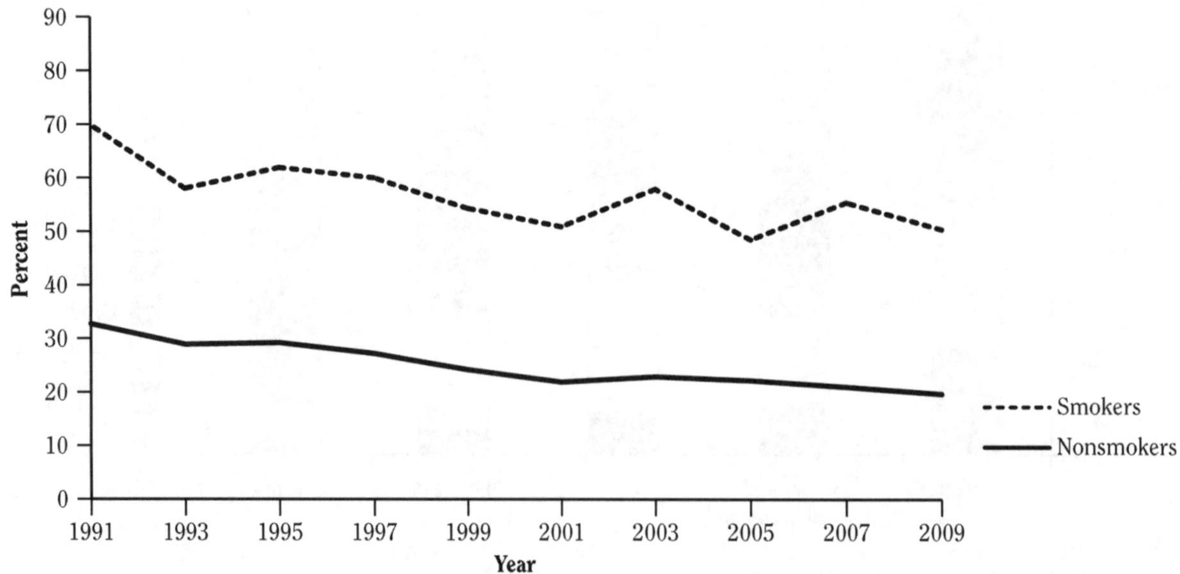

C. Current marijuana use

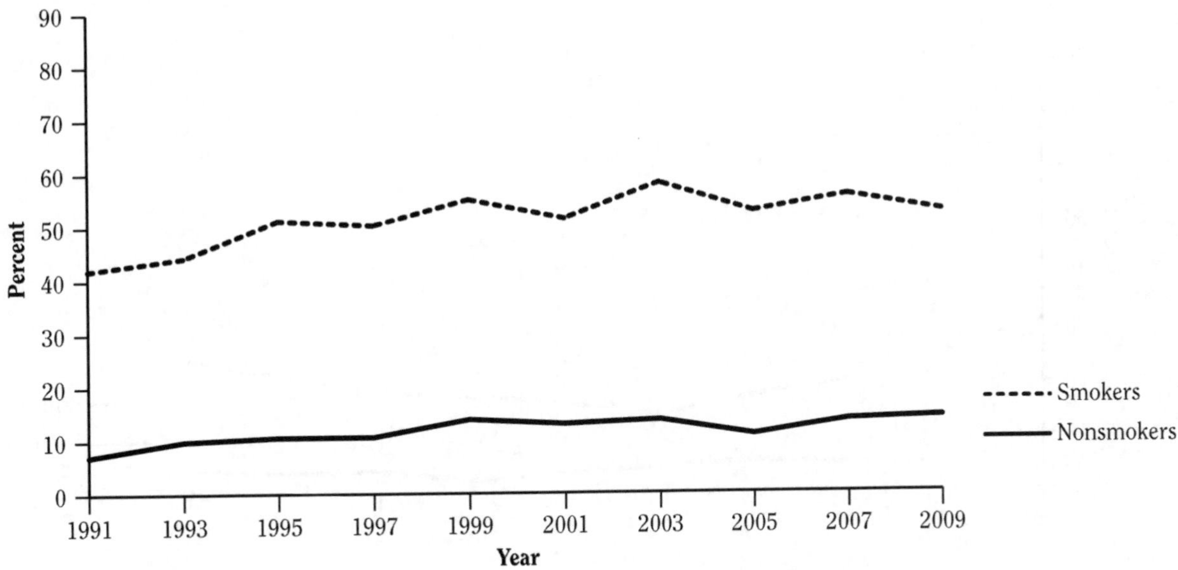

D. Current cocaine use

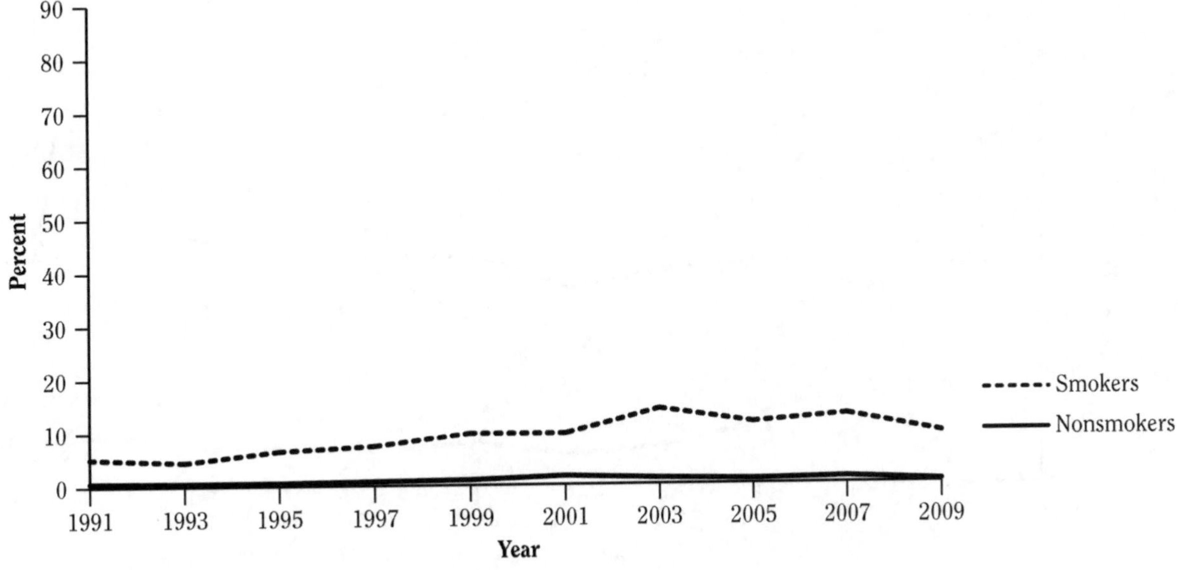

E. Current smokeless tobacco use

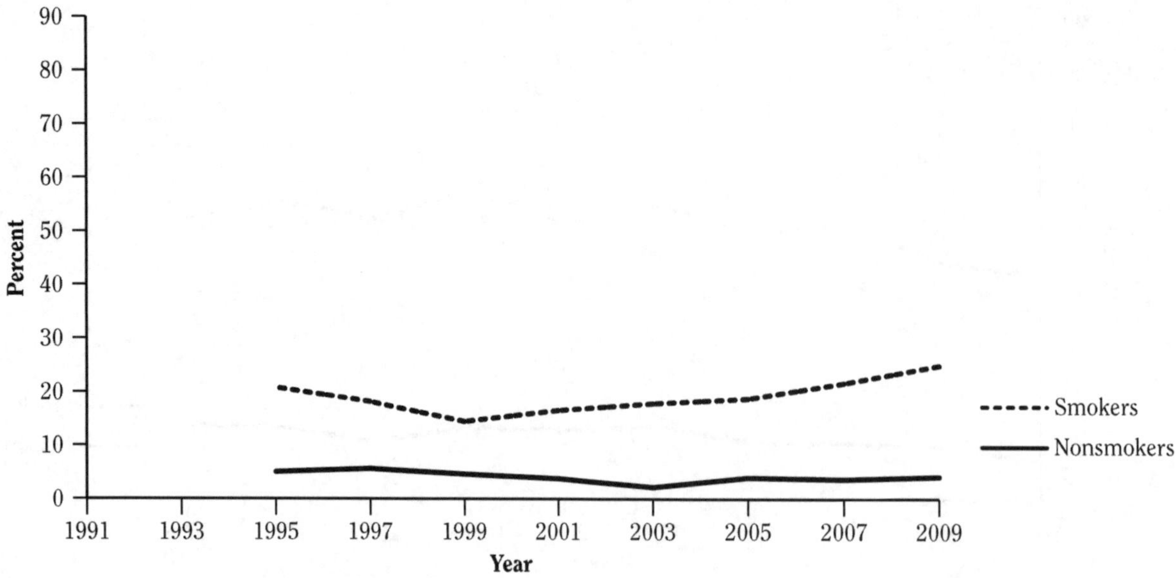

F. Current cigar use

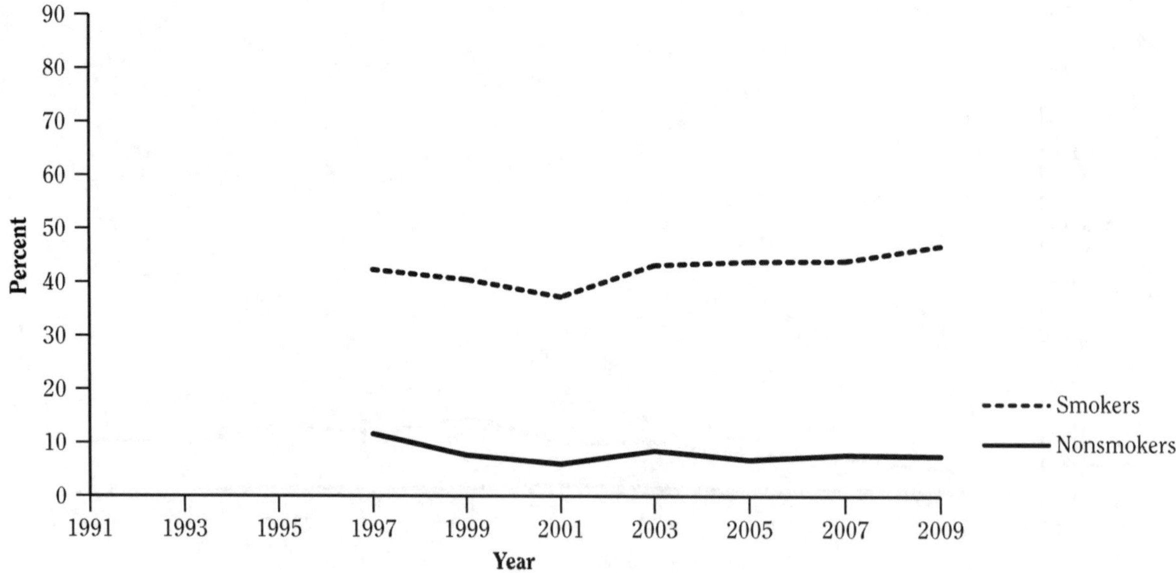

Behaviors related to sexual activity

G. Ever had sexual intercourse

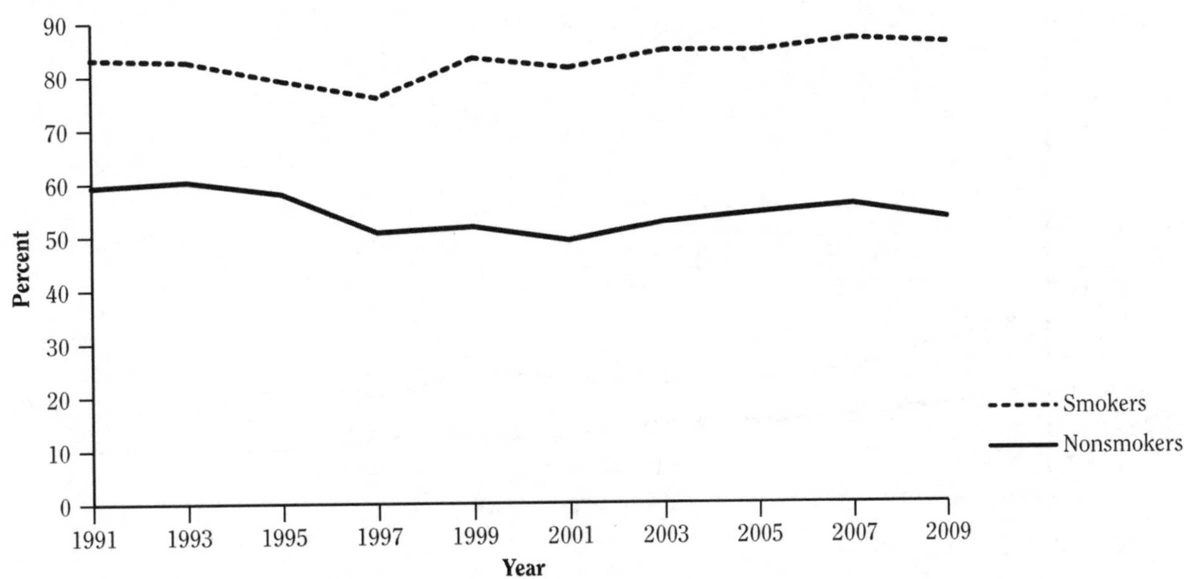

H. Used condom at last sexual intercourse

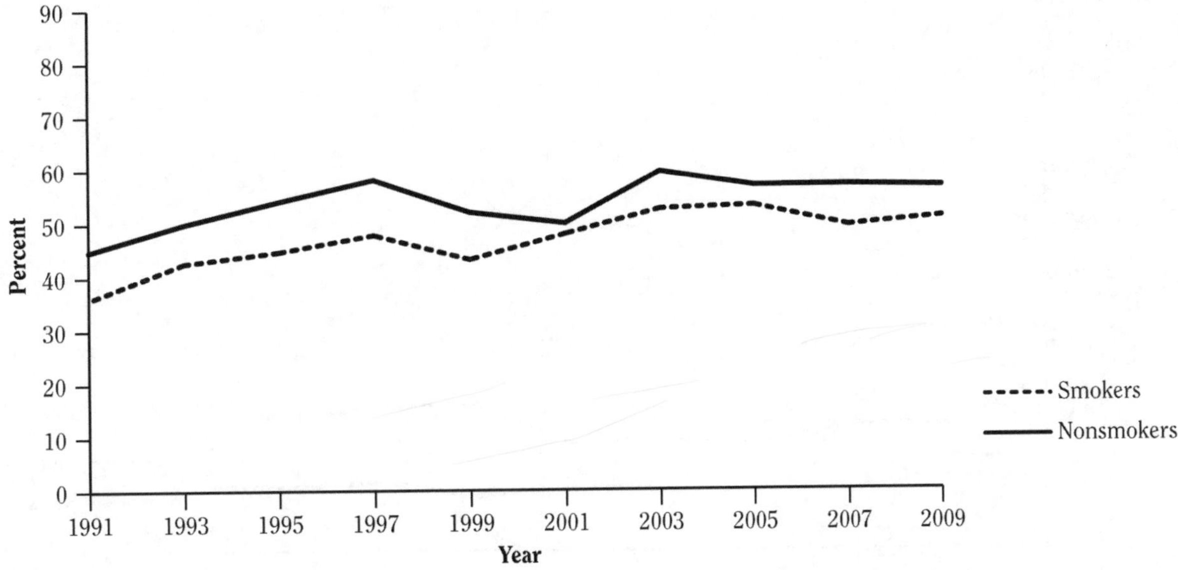

Behaviors related to suicide

I. Seriously contemplating suicide

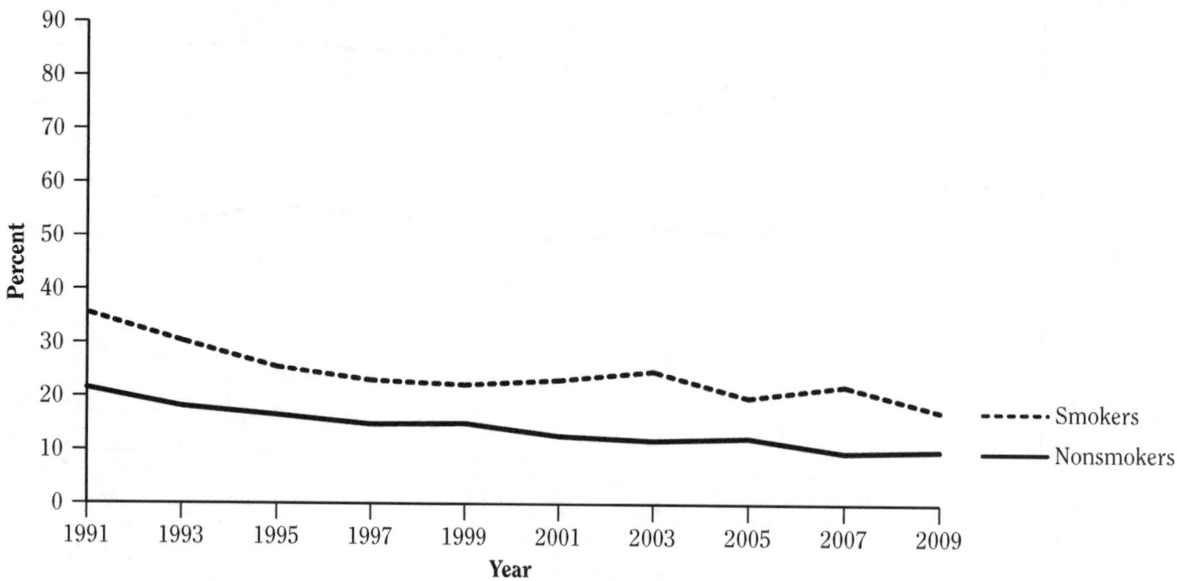

Behaviors that contribute to violence

J. Carried a weapon

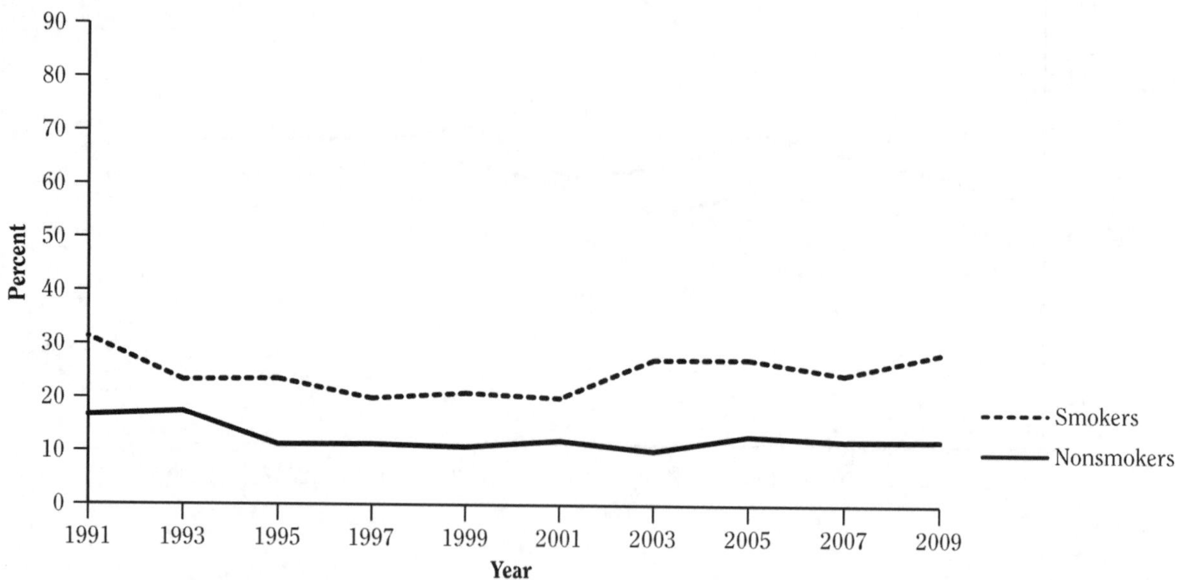

K. In a physical fight

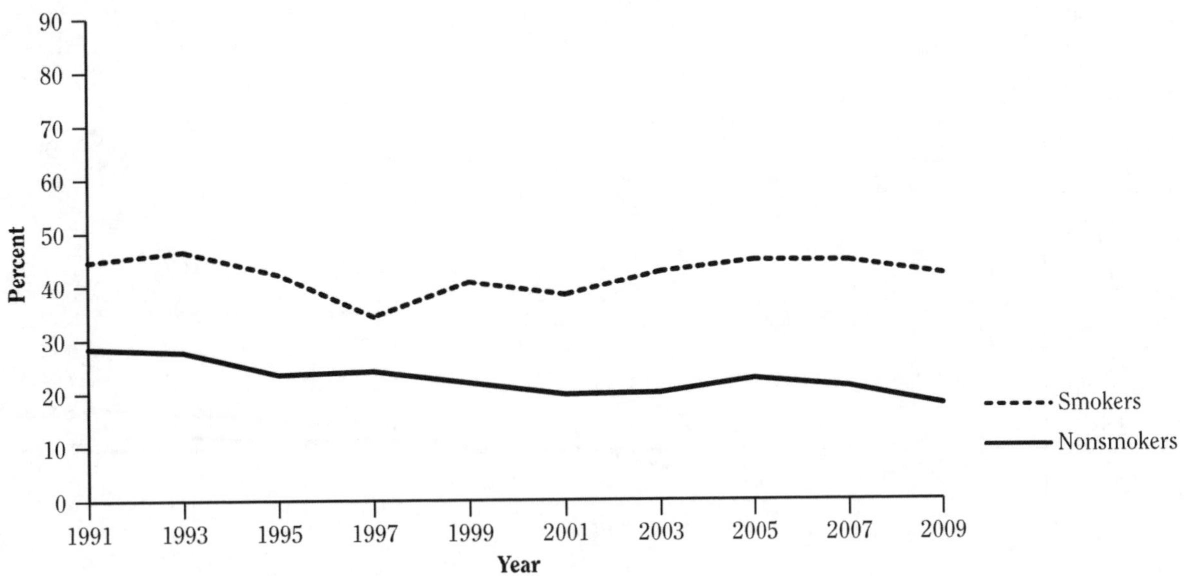

Outcomes and behaviors related to weight and weight management

L. Overweight

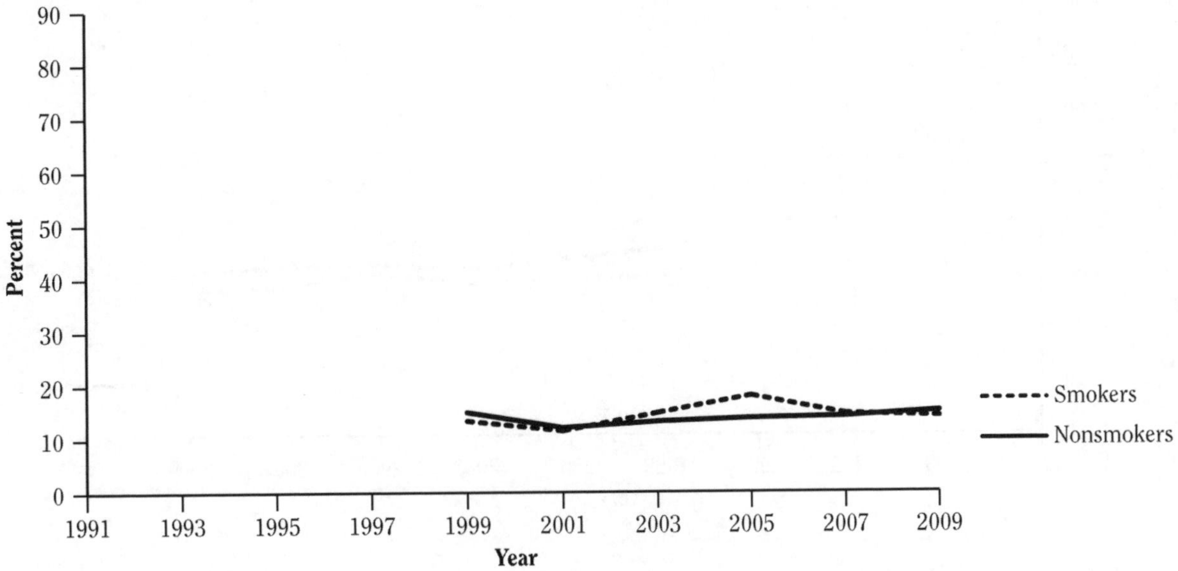

M. Obese

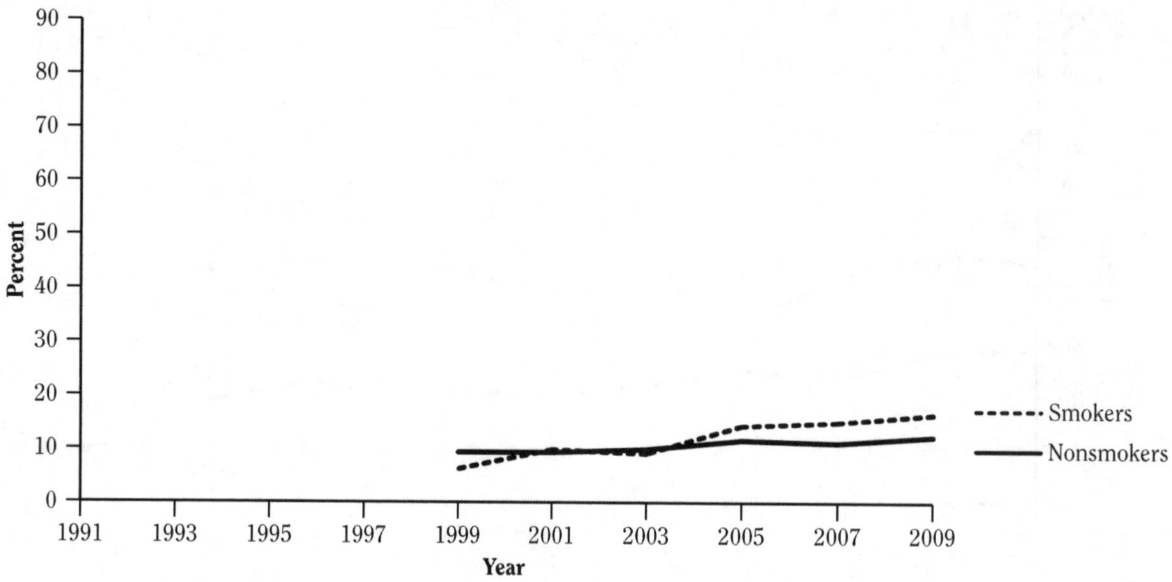

N. Television viewing for 3 or more hours per day

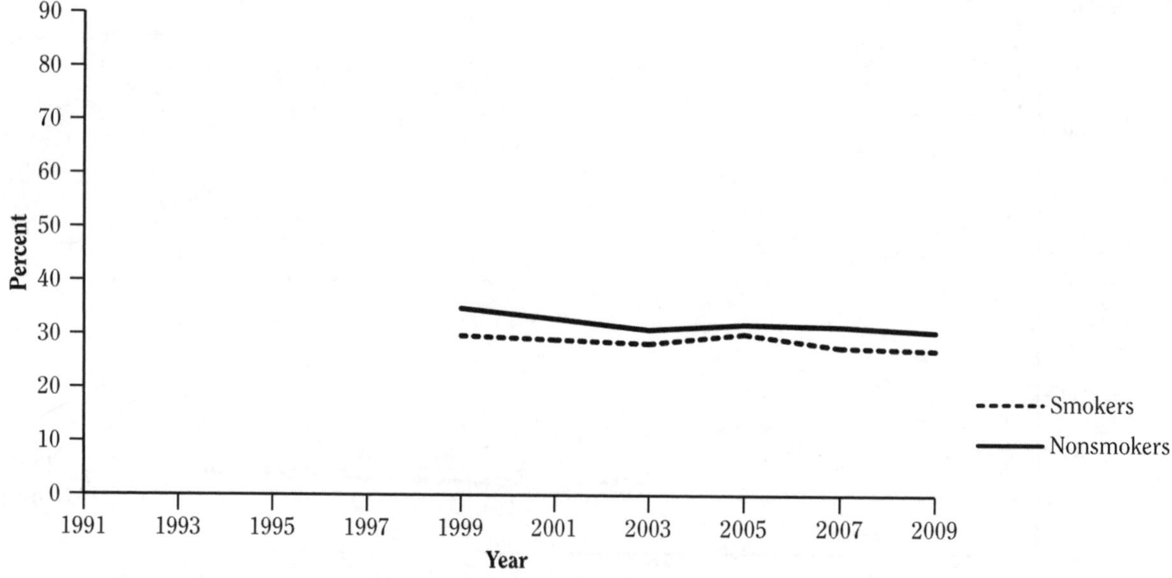

O. No moderate or vigorous physical activity participation in last 7 days

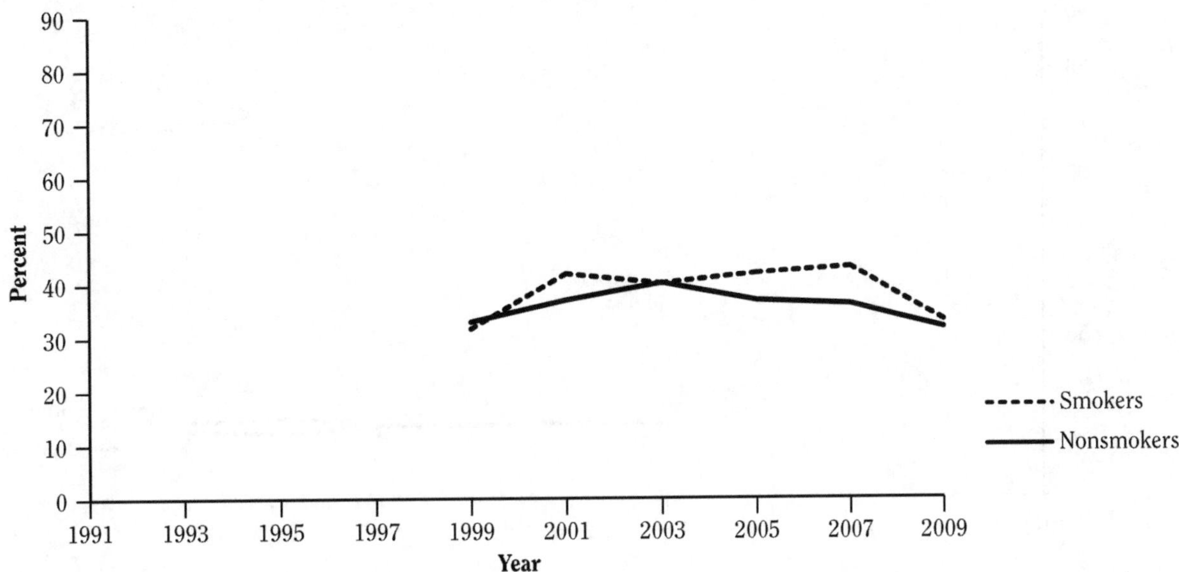

P. Fruit and vegetable intake five or more times per day

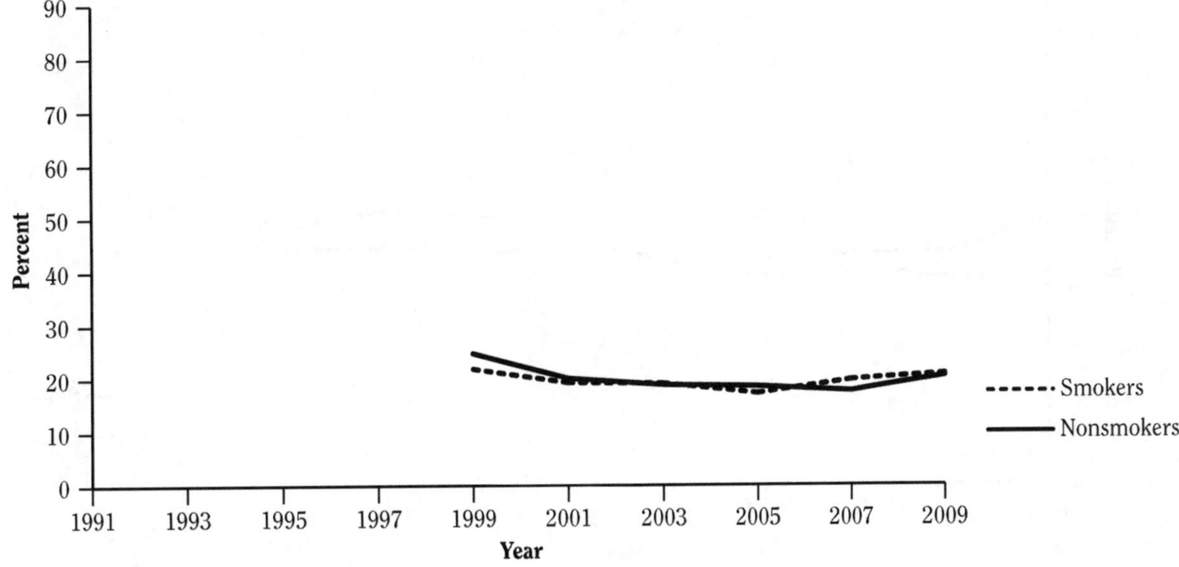

Q. Milk consumption of three or more glasses per day

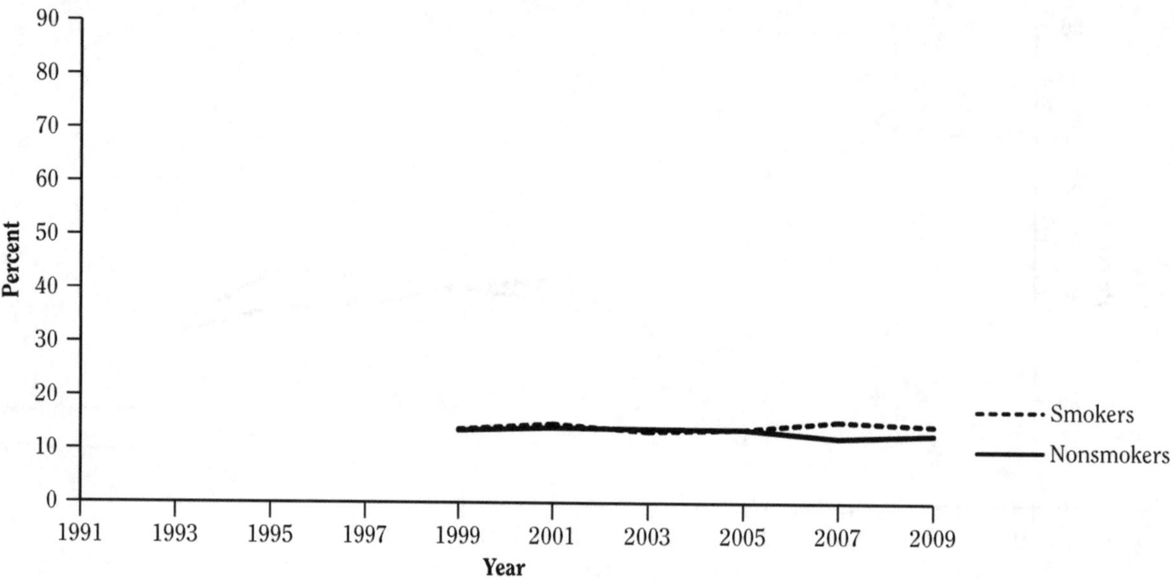

R. Trying to lose weight

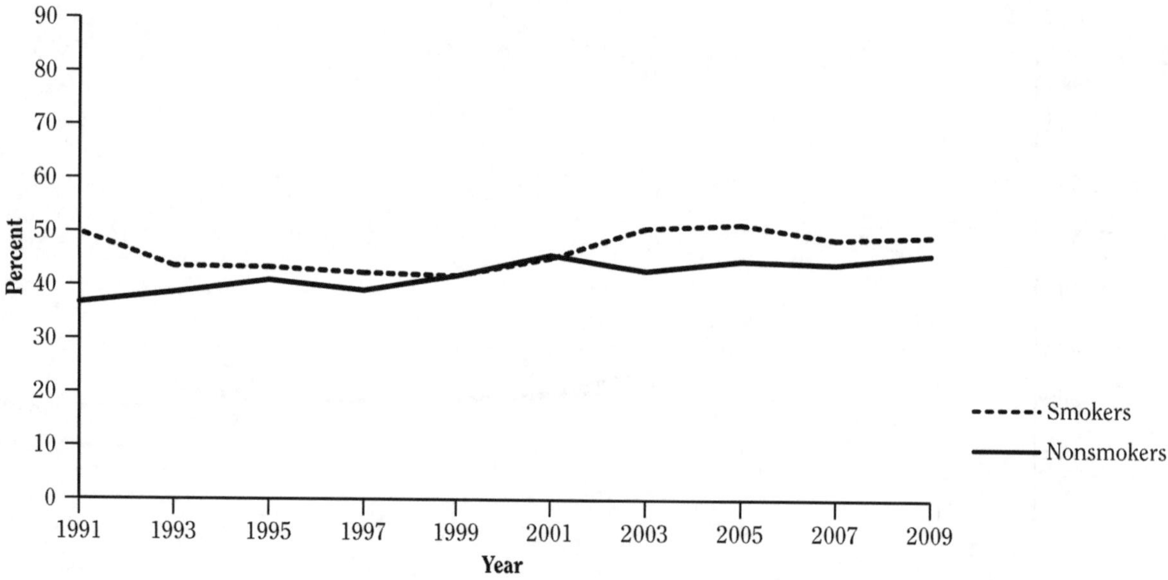

S. Engaged in unhealthy weight control behavior

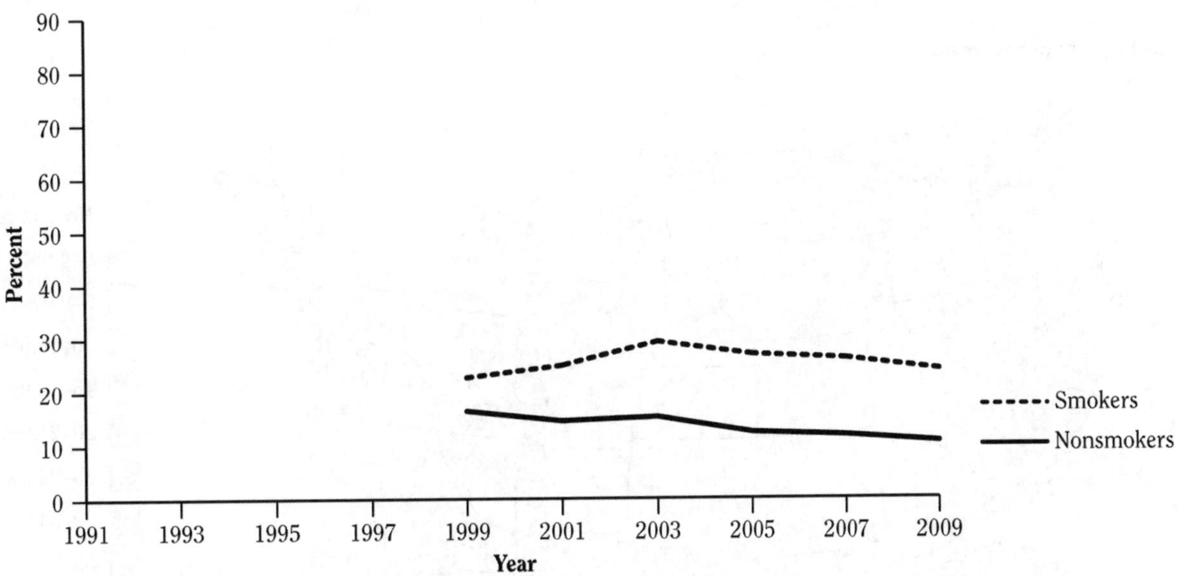

Source: 1991–2009 YRBS: Centers for Disease Control and Prevention, Division of Adolescent and School Health (unpublished data).
Note: "Overweight" and "obese" figures are based on self-reported data (figures 3.1.27L and 3.1.27M), that is, based on self-reported weight and height.

Figure 3.1.28 Percentage who currently use smokeless tobacco, by age group and state; National Survey on Drug Use and Health (NSDUH) 2006–2010; United States

A. 12–17 years of age, males

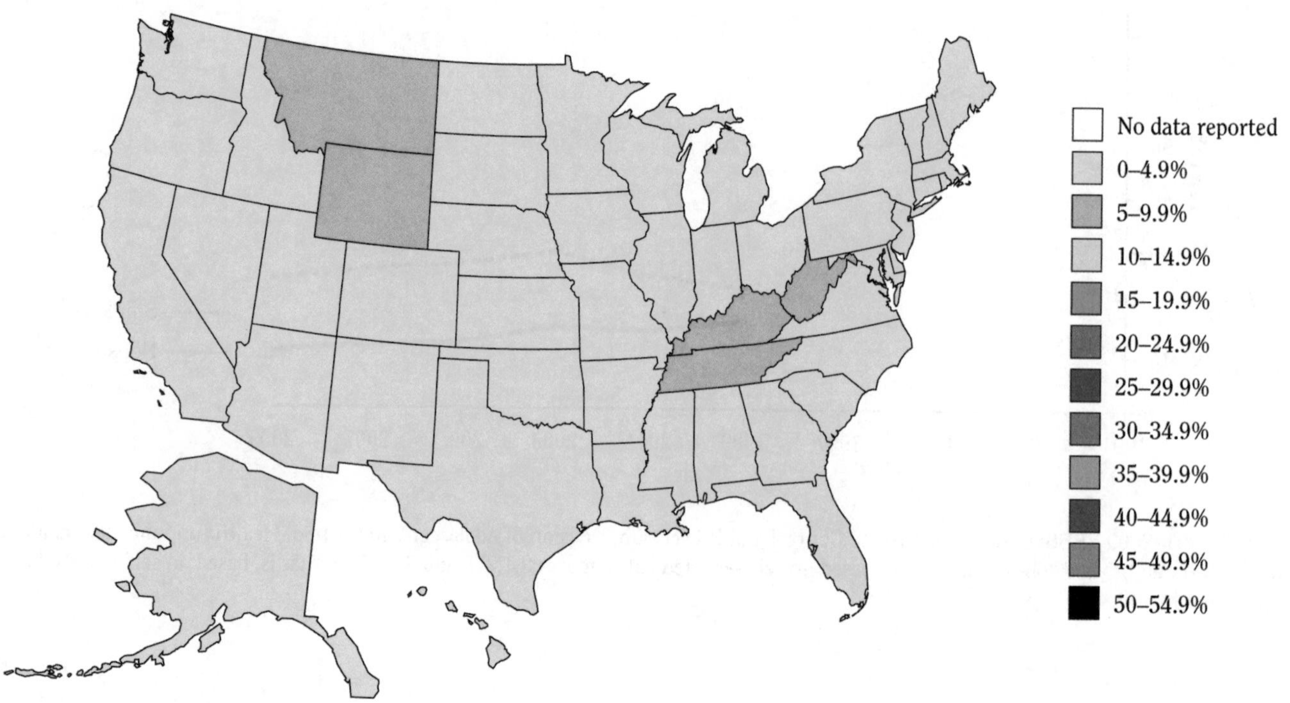

B. 18–25 years of age, male

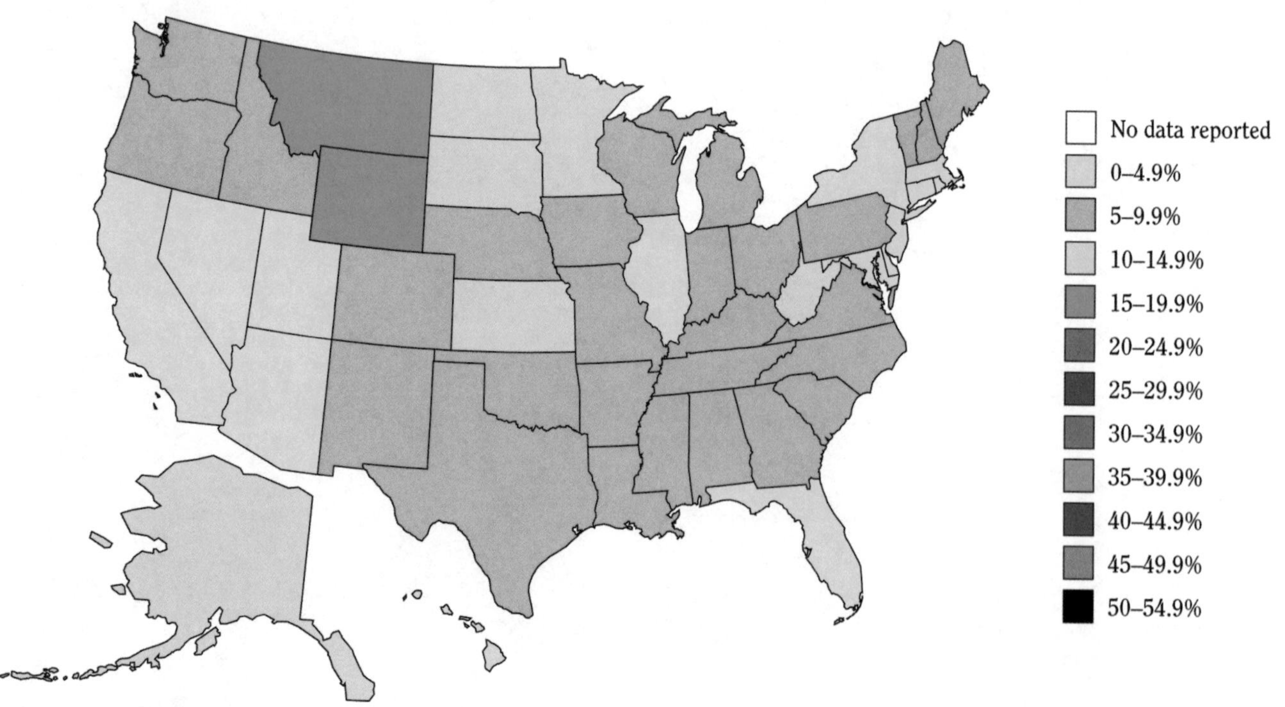

C. 26 years of age or older, male

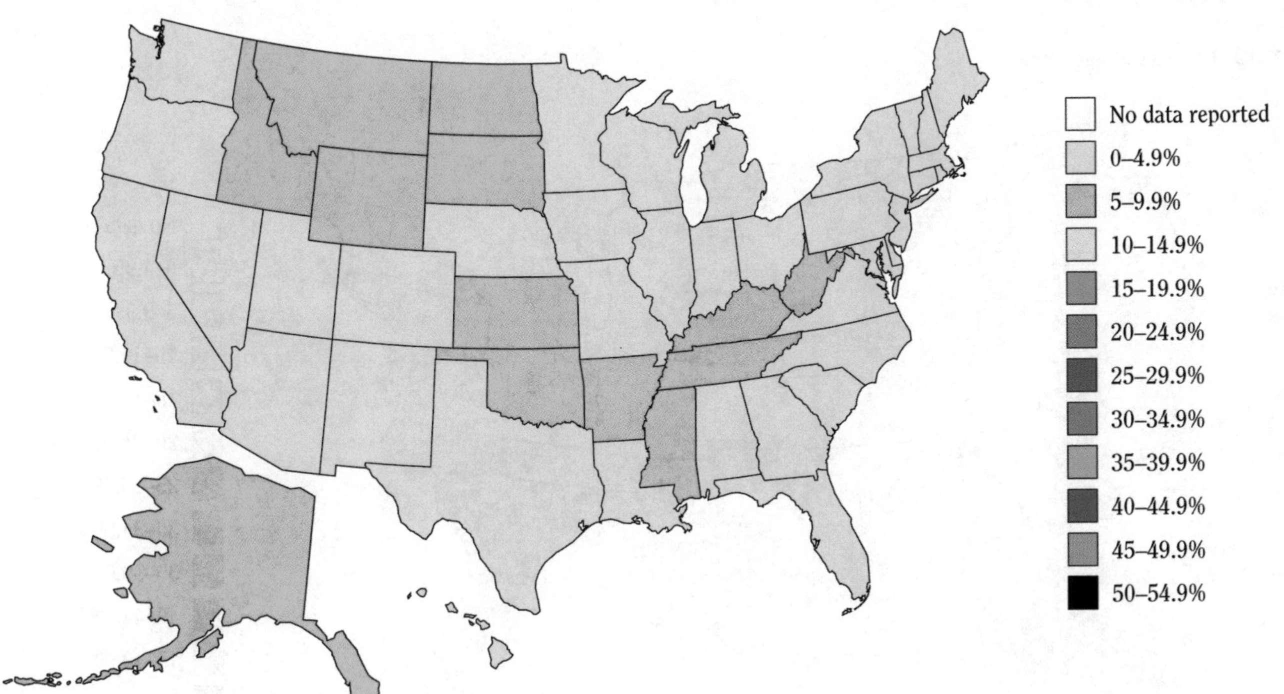

Source: 2006–2010 NSDUH: Substance Abuse and Mental Health Services Administration (unpublished data).

Figure 3.1.29 Percentage who currently use smokeless tobacco, by age group, state, and gender; National Survey on Drug Use and Health (NSDUH) 2006–2010; United States

A. 12–17 years of age, males

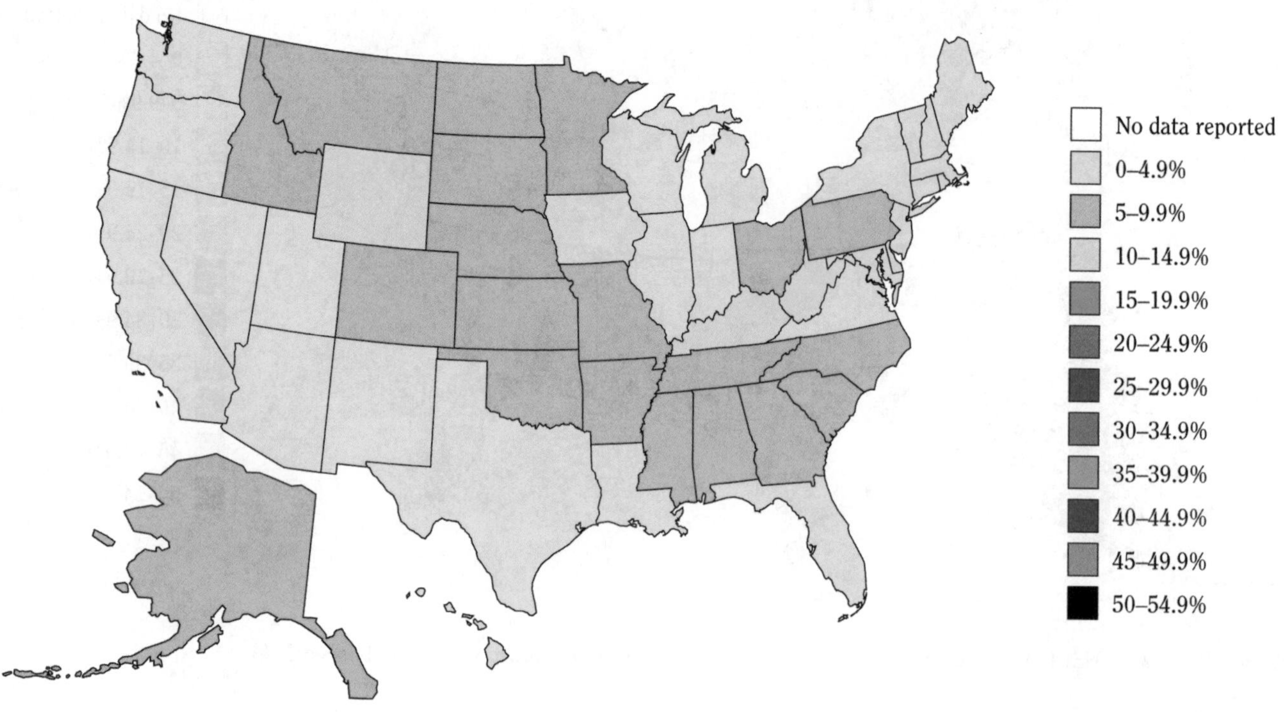

B. 12–17 years of age, females

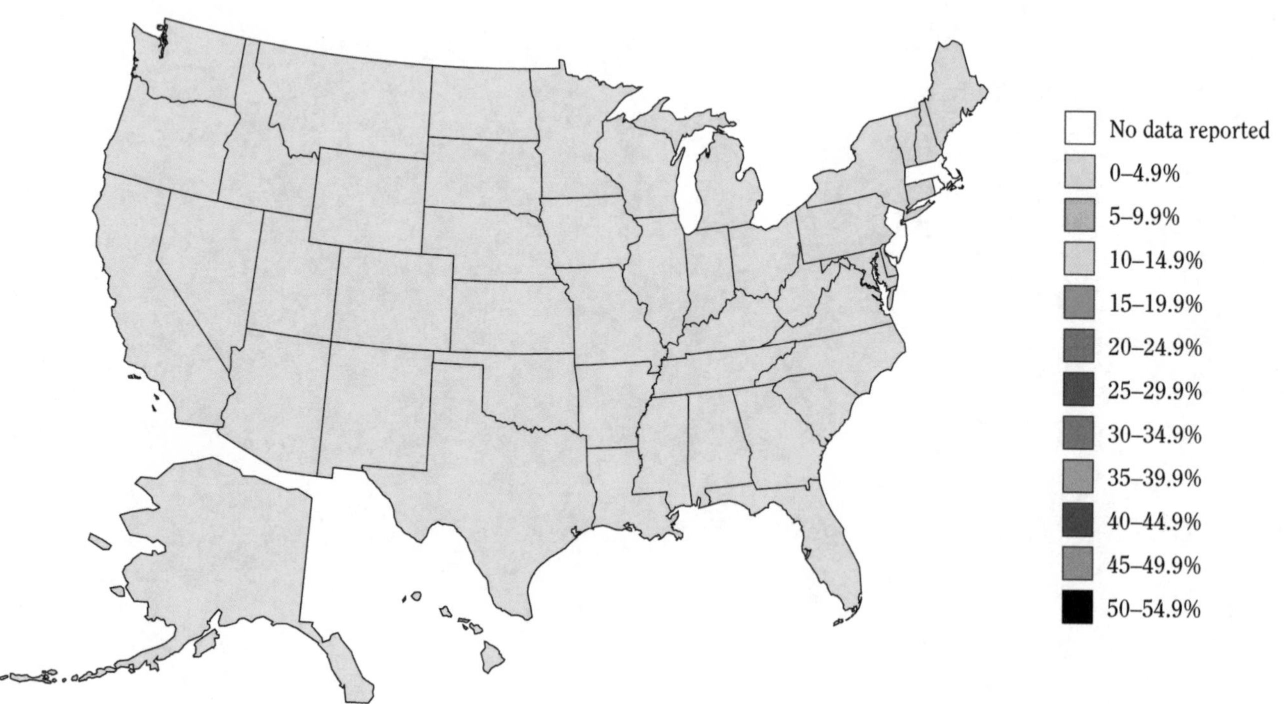

C. 18–25 years of age, males

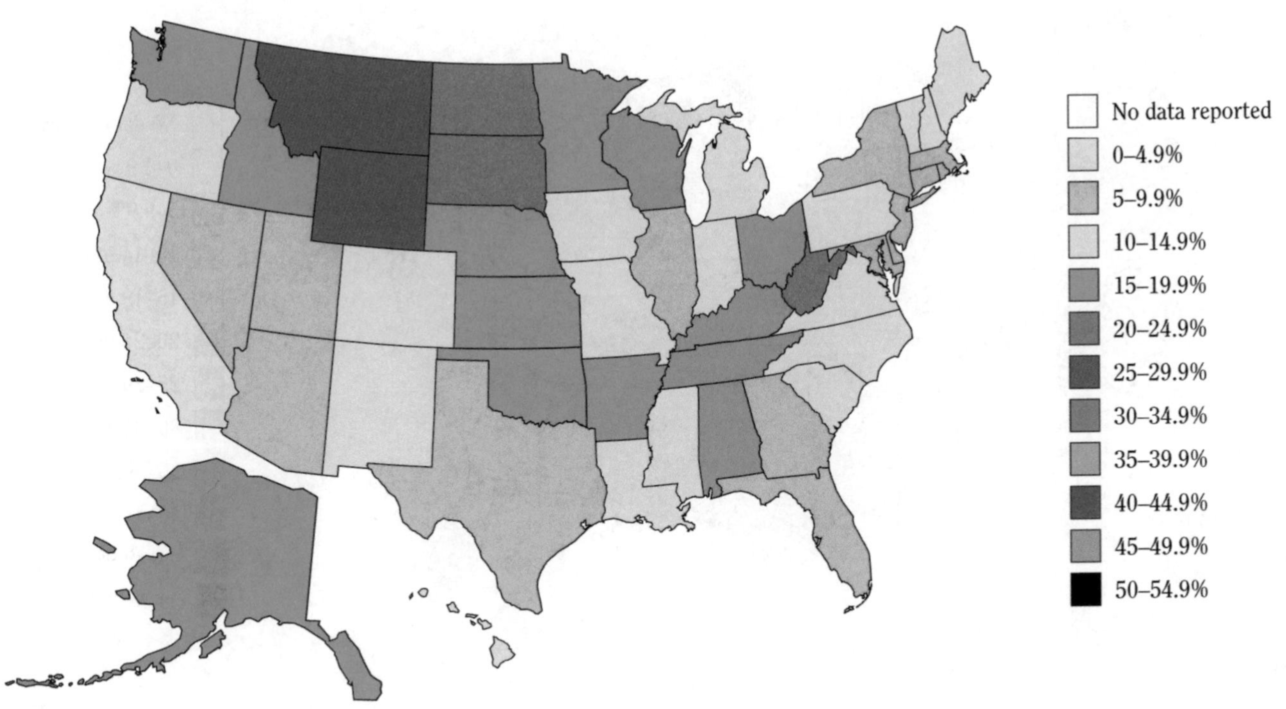

D. 18–25 years of age, females

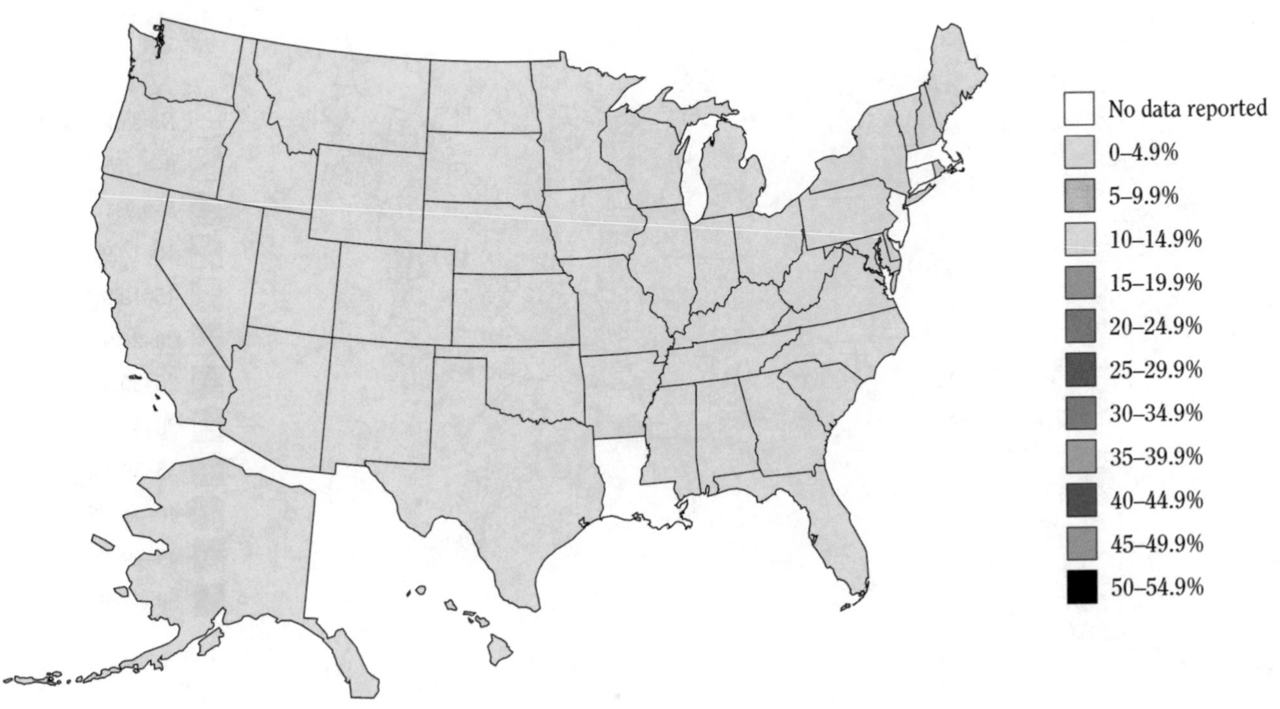

E. 26 years of age or older, males

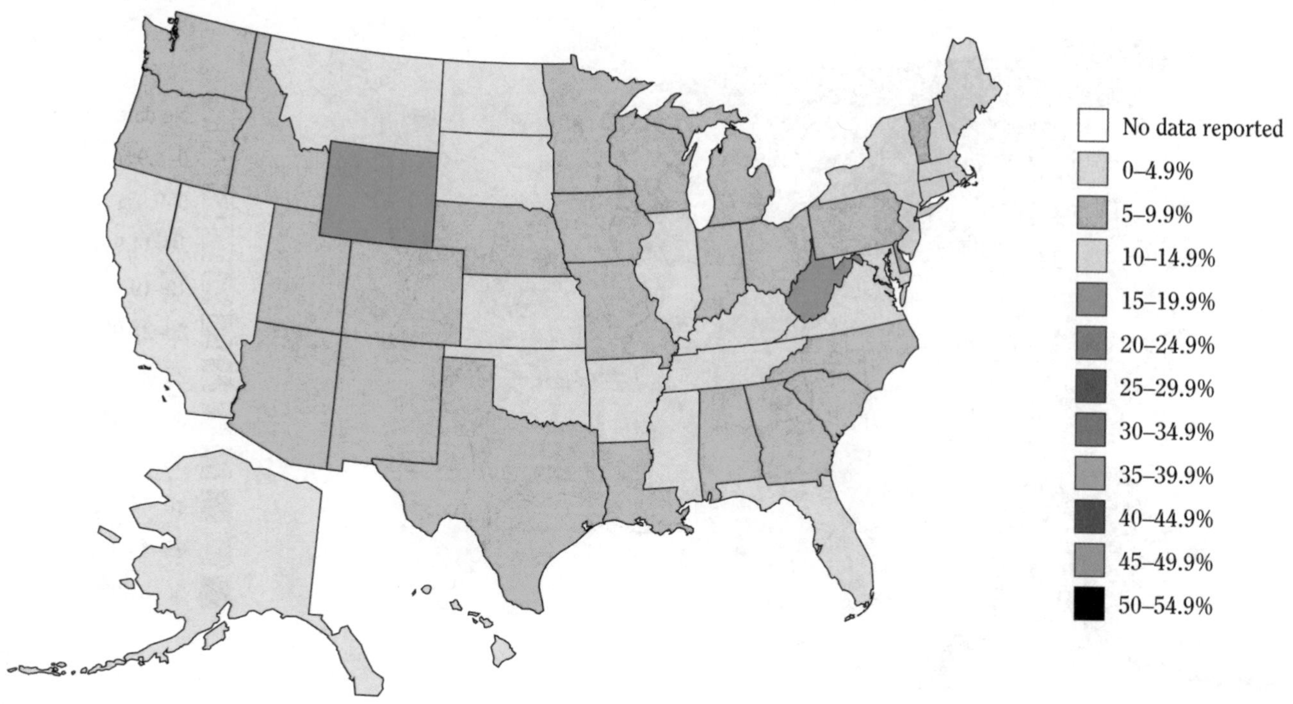

F. 26 years of age or older, females

Source: 2006–2010 NSDUH: Substance Abuse and Mental Health Services Administration (unpublished data).

Figure 3.1.30 Past-month smokeless tobacco use among young adults (18–25 years of age), by gender; National Survey on Drug Use & Health (NSDUH) 2002–2010; United States

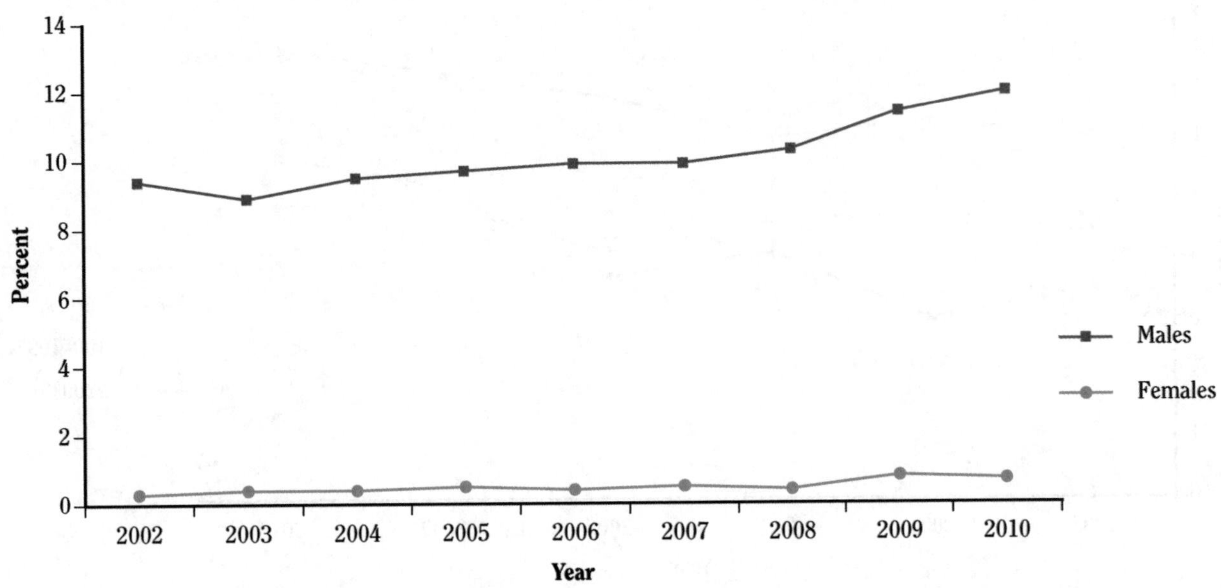

Source: 2002–2010 NSDUH: Substance Abuse and Mental Health Services Administration (unpublished data).

Figure 3.1.31 Past-month smokeless tobacco use among young adults (18–25 years of age), by race/ethnicity; National Survey on Drug Use and Health (NSDUH) 2002–2010; United States

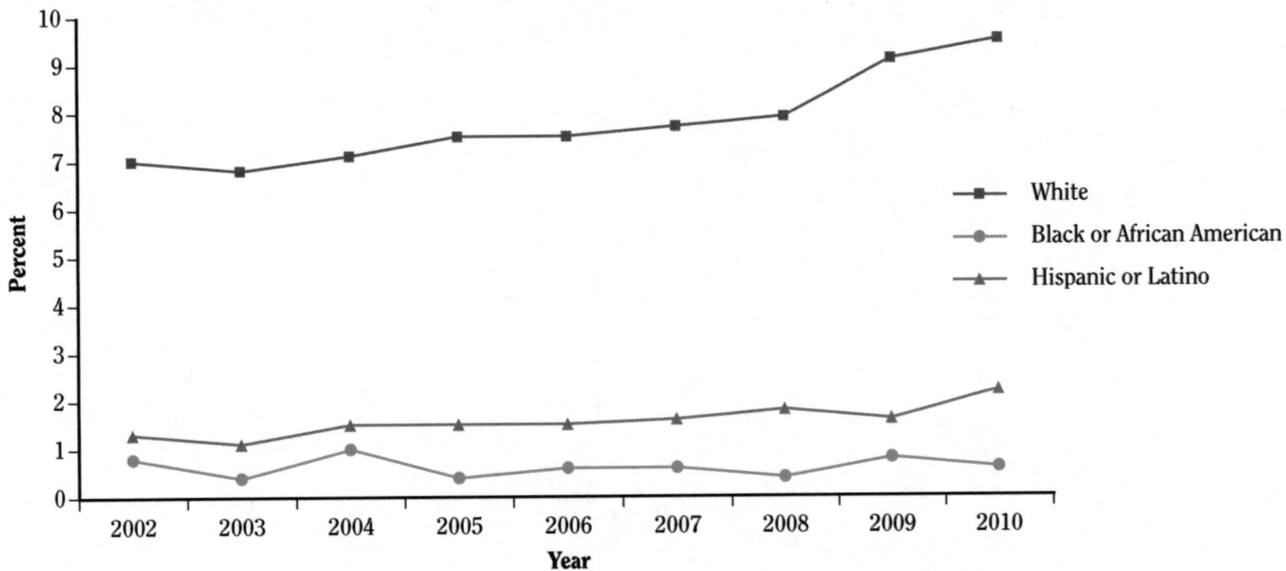

Source: 2002–2010 NSDUH: Substance Abuse and Mental Health Services Administration (detailed reports).

Figure 3.1.32 Past-month smokeless tobacco use among young adults (18–25 years of age), by poverty level; National Survey on Drug Use and Health (NSDUH) 2005–2010; United States

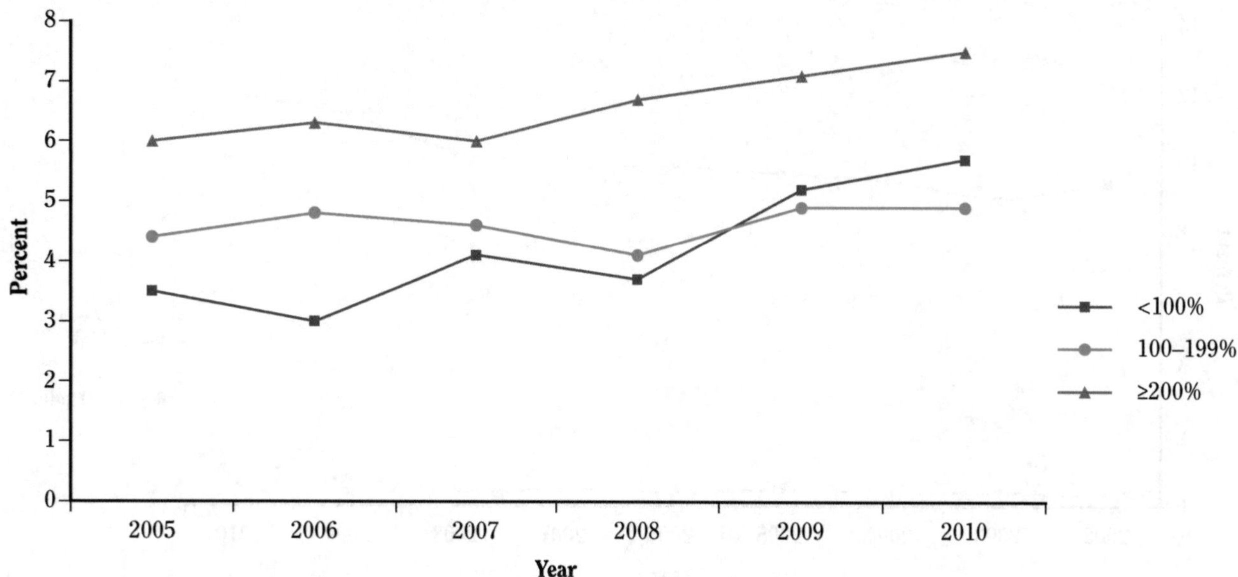

Source: 2005–2010 NSDUH: Substance Abuse and Mental Health Services Administration (unpublished data).

Figure 3.1.33 Trends in prevalence (%) of current smokeless tobacco use among young people, by grade level; Monitoring the Future (MTF) 1986–2010 and National Youth Risk Behavior Survey (YRBS) 1995–2009; United States

A. Males, 8th, 10th, and 12th grades, MTF

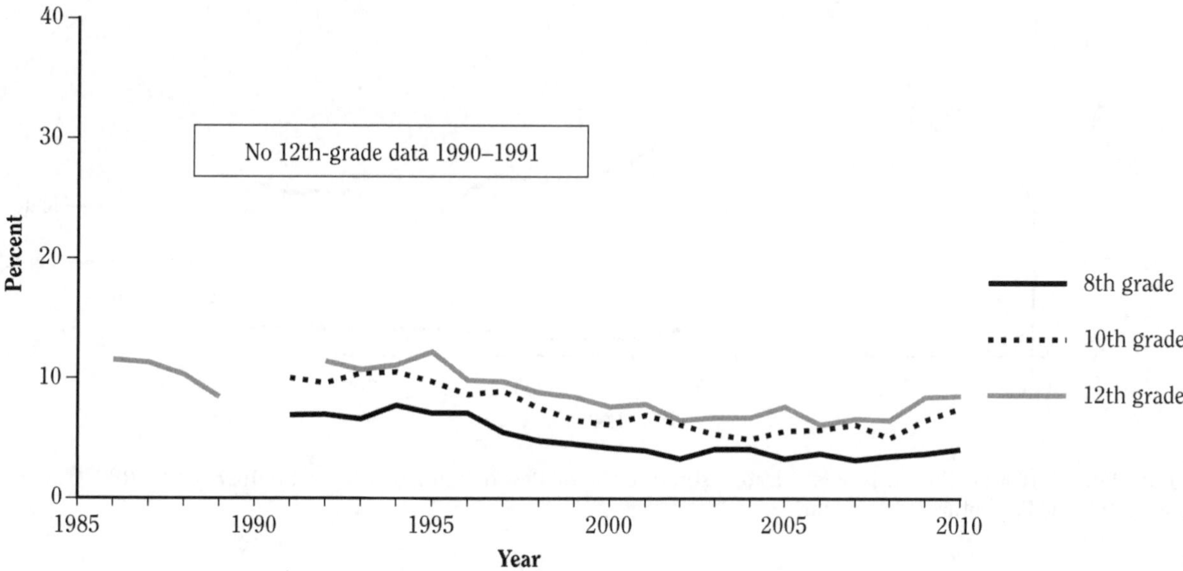

B. Males and females, 12th grade, MTF

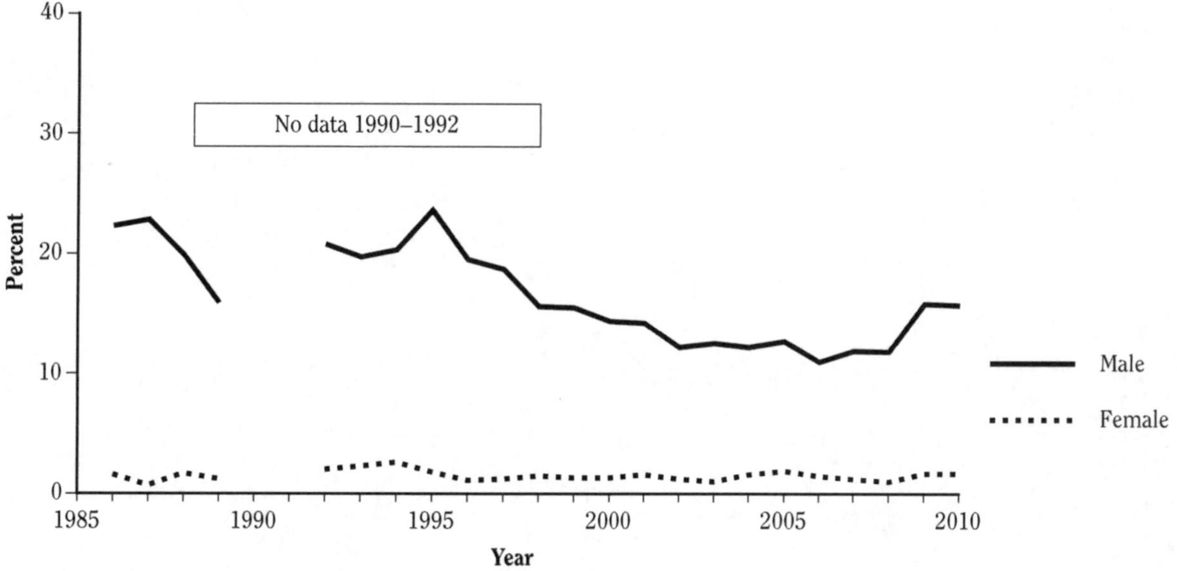

C. Males and females, 9th–12th grades, YRBS

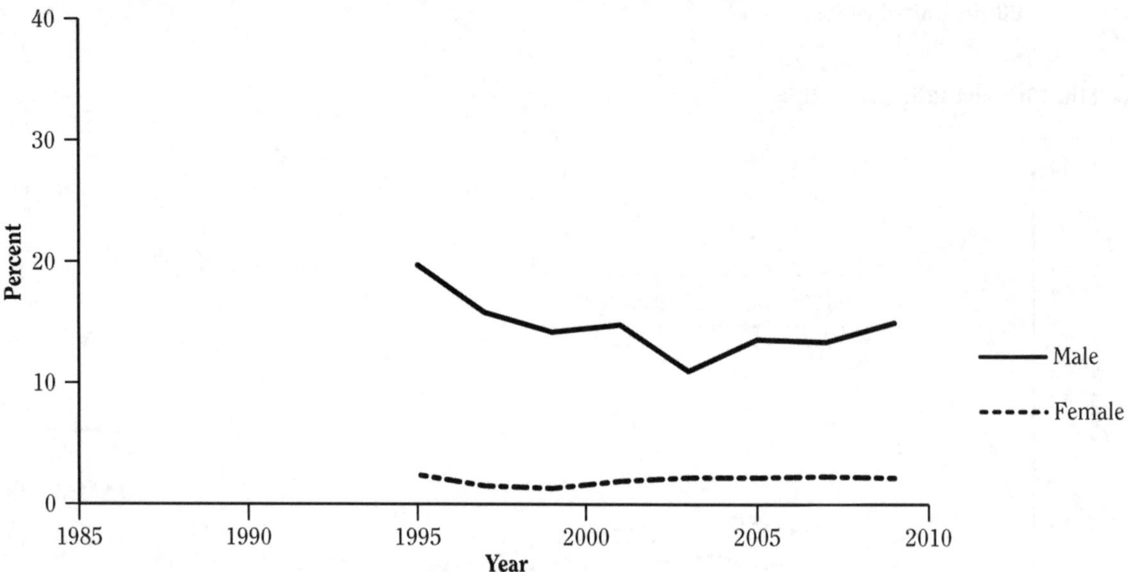

Source: 1986–2010 MTF: University of Michigan, Institute for Social Research (unpublished data); 1995–2009 YRBS: Centers for Disease Control and Prevention (CDC 2011a).

Figure 3.1.34 Trends in prevalence (%) of current smokeless tobacco use[a] among males, by grade level and race/ethnicity; Monitoring the Future (MTF) 1987–2010; United States

A. 8th grade, 1992–2010

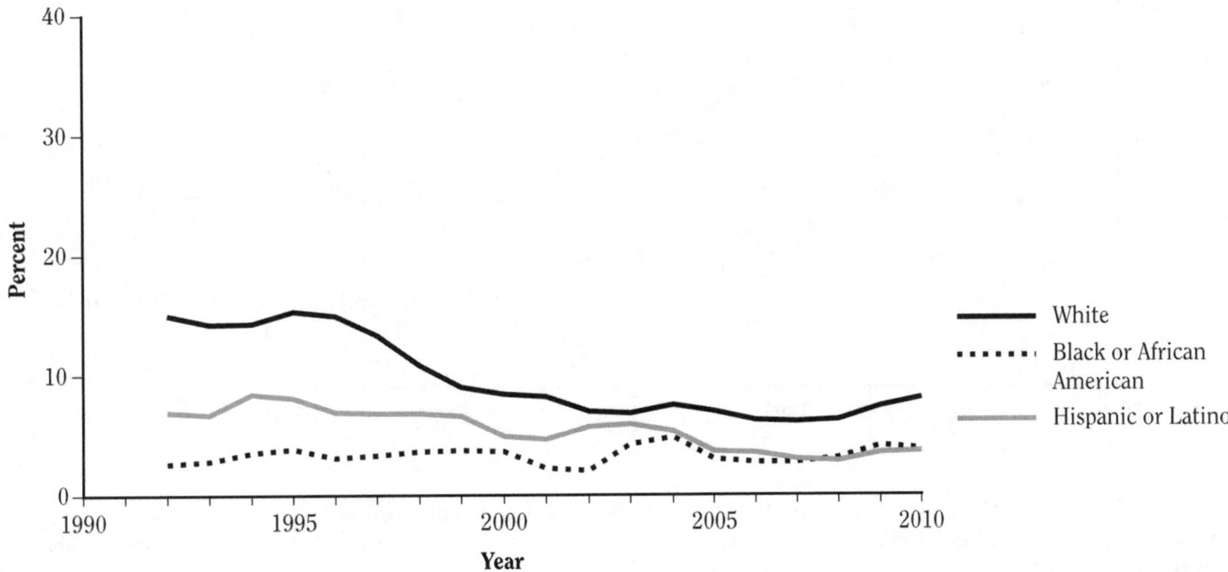

B. 10th grade, 1992–2010

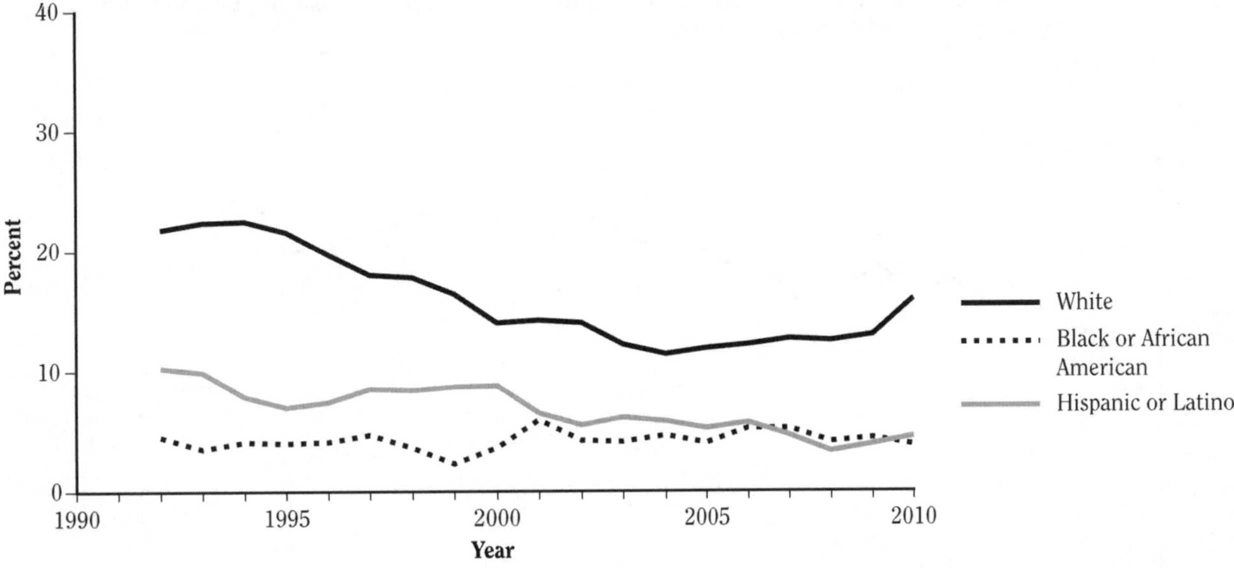

C. 12th grade, 1987–2010

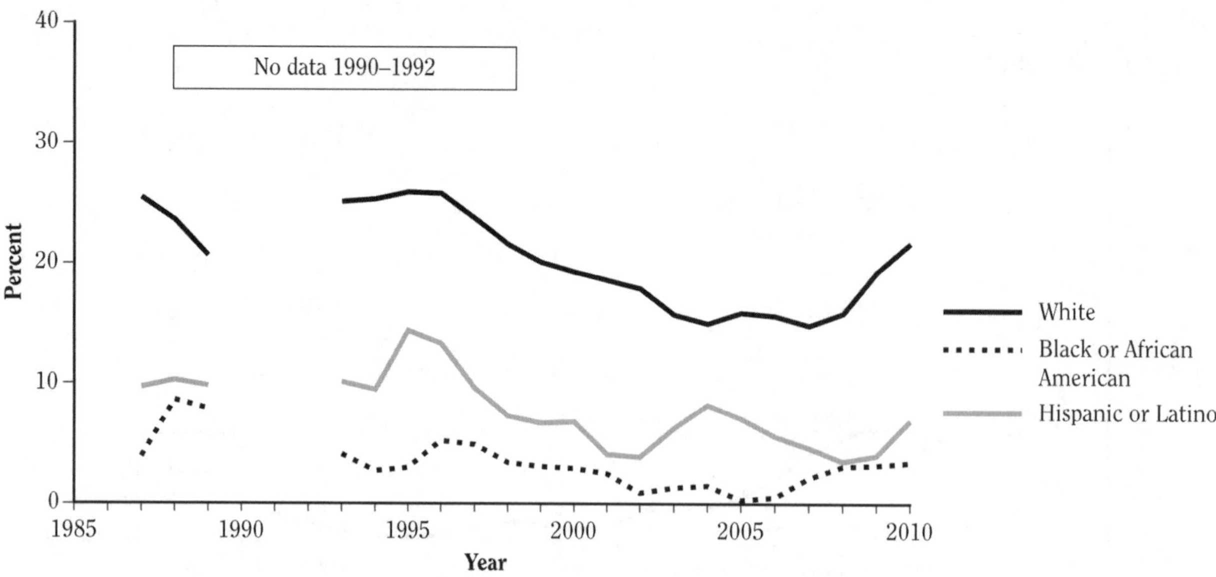

Source: 1987–2010 MTF: University of Michigan, Institute for Social Research (unpublished data).
[a]Data presented here represent current year and previous year combined (e.g., data from 1994 and 1995 are presented as data from 1995).

Figure 3.1.35 Trends in the percentage of young people who believe that smokeless tobacco is a serious health risk and in the percentage of high school seniors who have ever used smokeless tobacco; Monitoring the Future (MTF) 1986–2010; United States

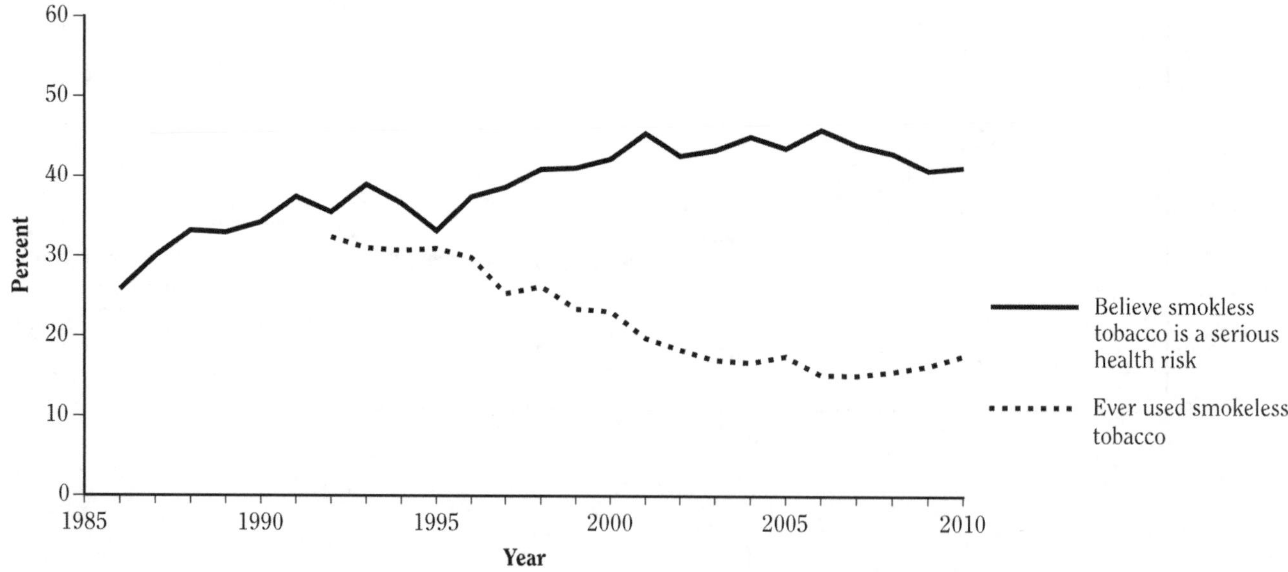

Source: 1986–2010 MTF: University of Michigan, Institute for Social Research (unpublished data).

Figure 3.1.36 Percentage who currently smoke cigars, by age group and state; National Survey on Drug Use and Health (NSDUH) 2006–2010; United States

A. 12–17 years of age

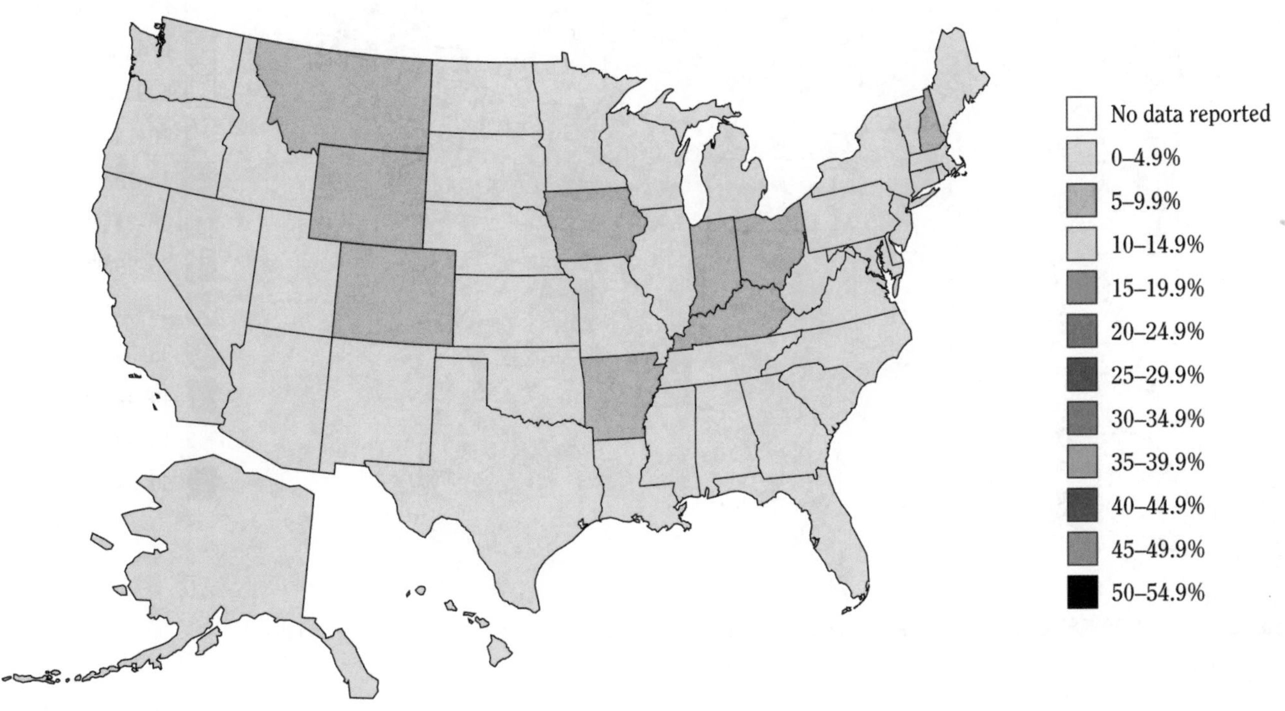

B. 18–25 years of age

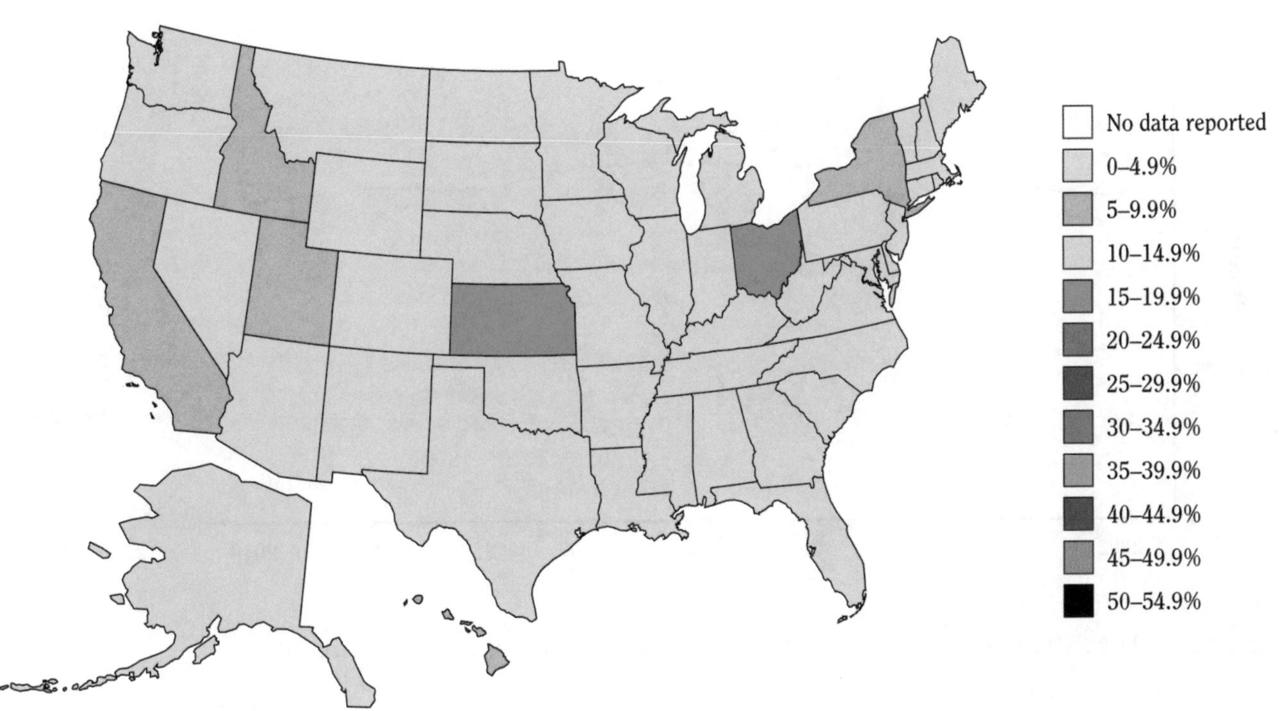

C. 26 years of age or older

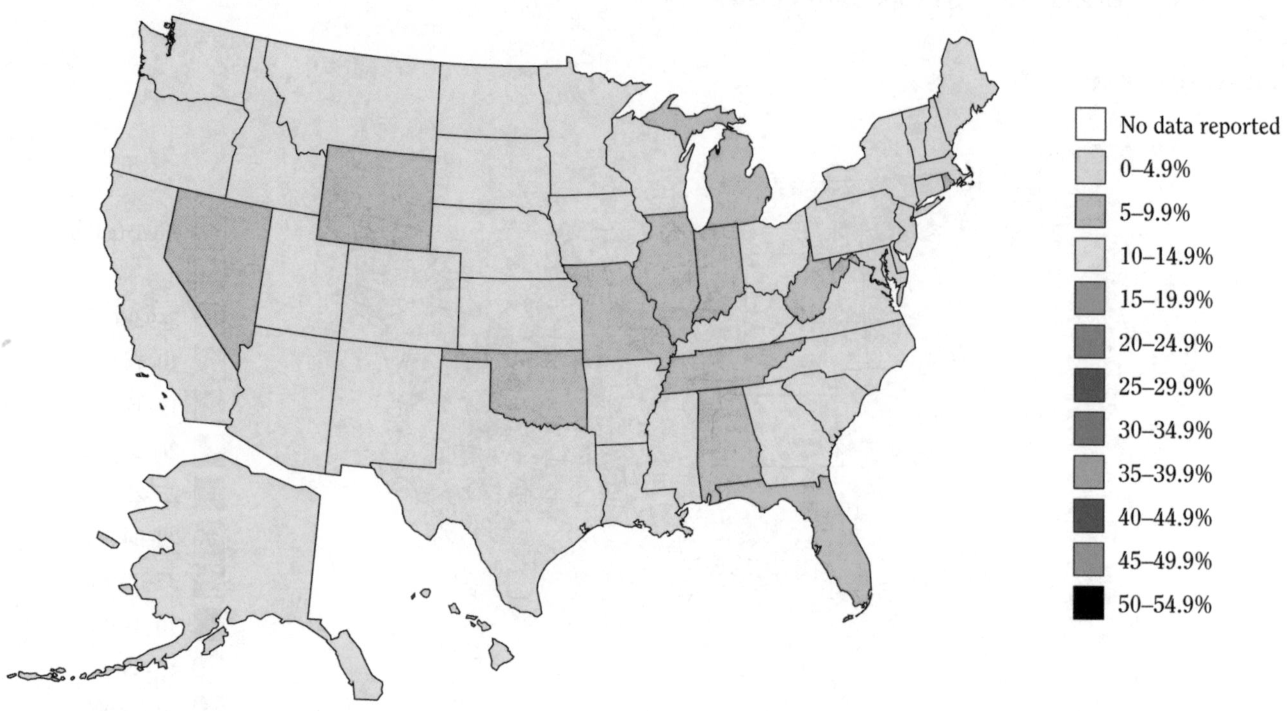

Source: 2006–2010 NSDUH: Substance Abuse and Mental Health Services Administration (unpublished data).

Figure 3.1.37 Past-month cigar use among young adults (18–25 years of age), by gender; National Survey on Drug Use and Health (NSDUH) 2002–2010; United States

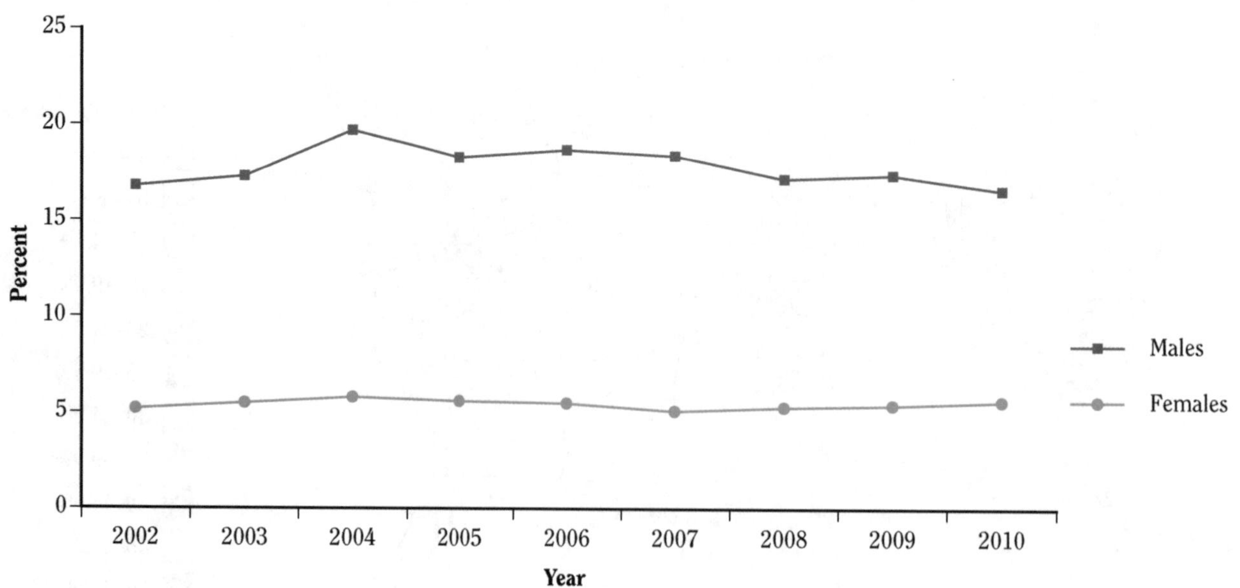

Source: 2002–2010 NSDUH: Substance Abuse and Mental Health Services Administration (unpublished data).

Figure 3.1.38 Past-month cigar use among young adults (18–25 years of age), by race/ethnicity; National Survey on Drug Use and Health (NSDUH) 2002–2010; United States

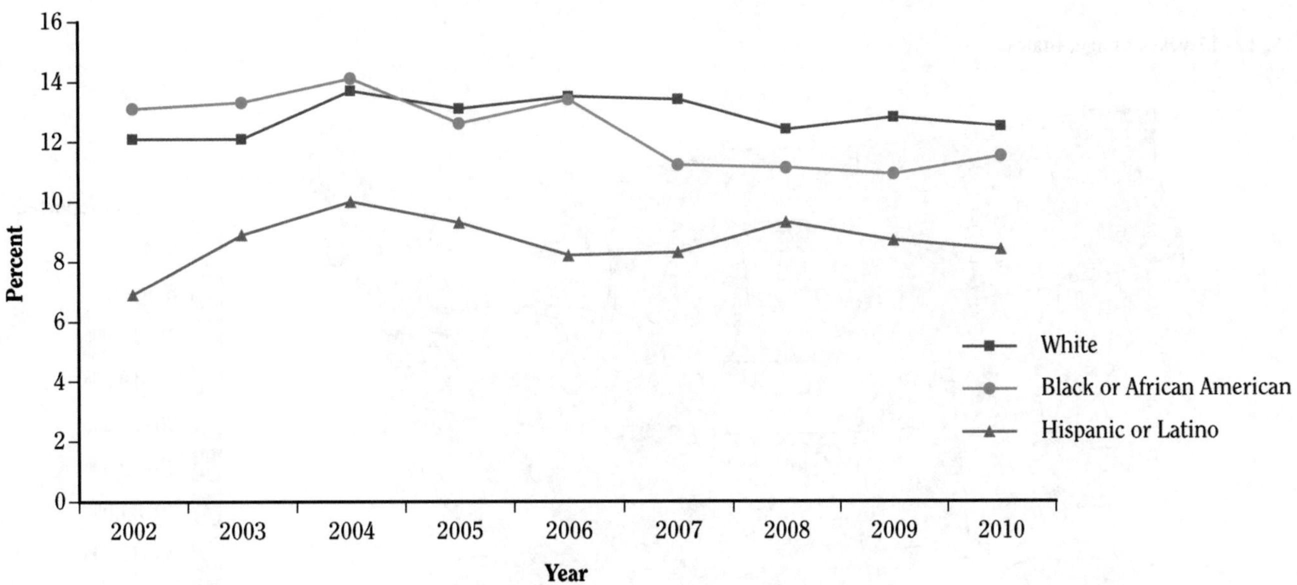

Source: 2002–2010 NSDUH: Substance Abuse and Mental Health Services Administration (detailed reports).

Figure 3.1.39 Past-month cigar use among young adults (18–25 years of age), by poverty level; National Survey on Drug Use and Health (NSDUH) 2005–2010; United States

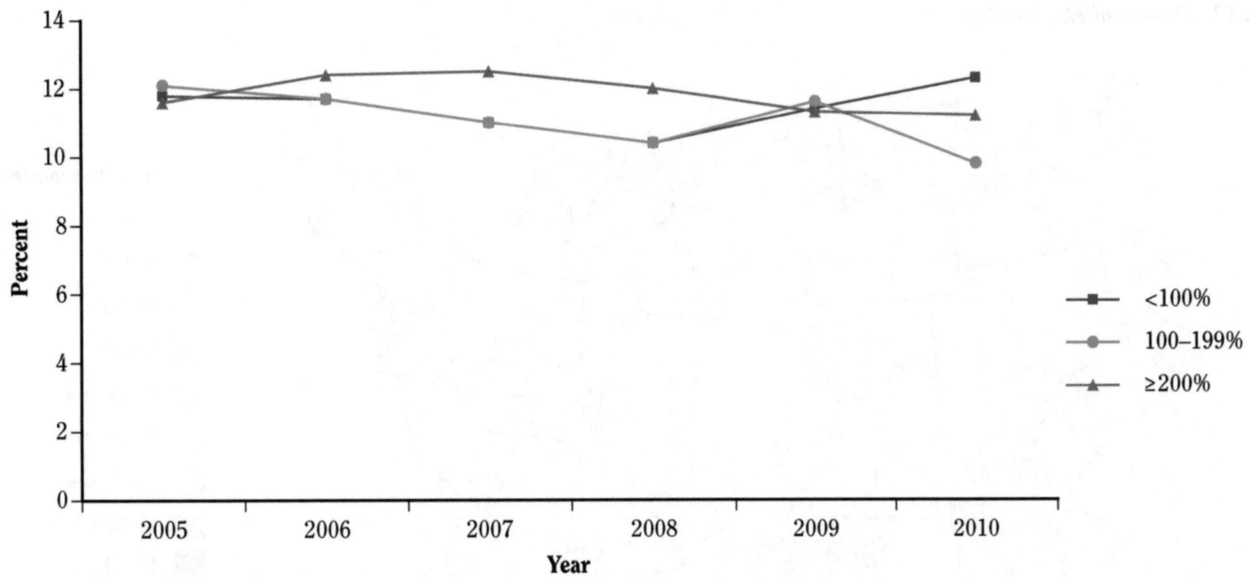

Source: 2005–2010 NSDUH: Substance Abuse and Mental Health Services Administration (unpublished data).

Figure 3.1.40 Percentage who currently smoke cigars, by age group, state, and gender; National Survey on Drug Use and Health (NSDUH) 2006–2010; United States

A. 12–17 years of age, males

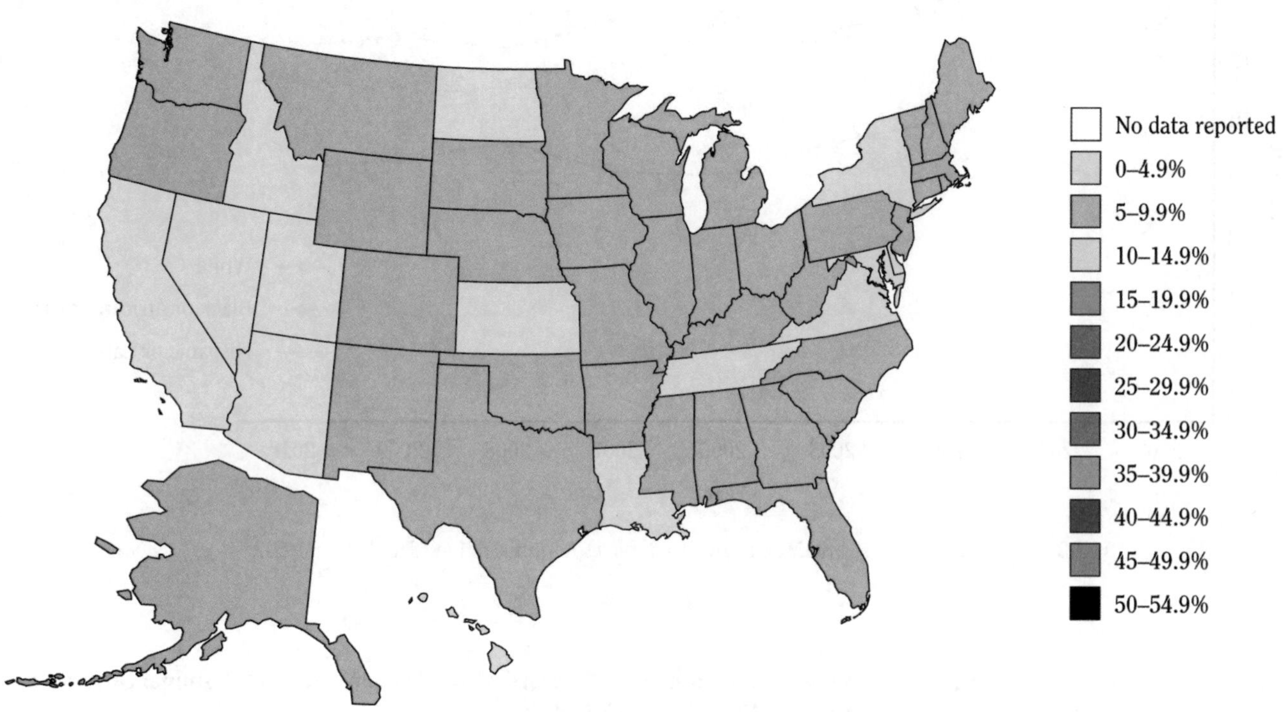

B. 12–17 years of age, females

C. 18–25 years of age, males

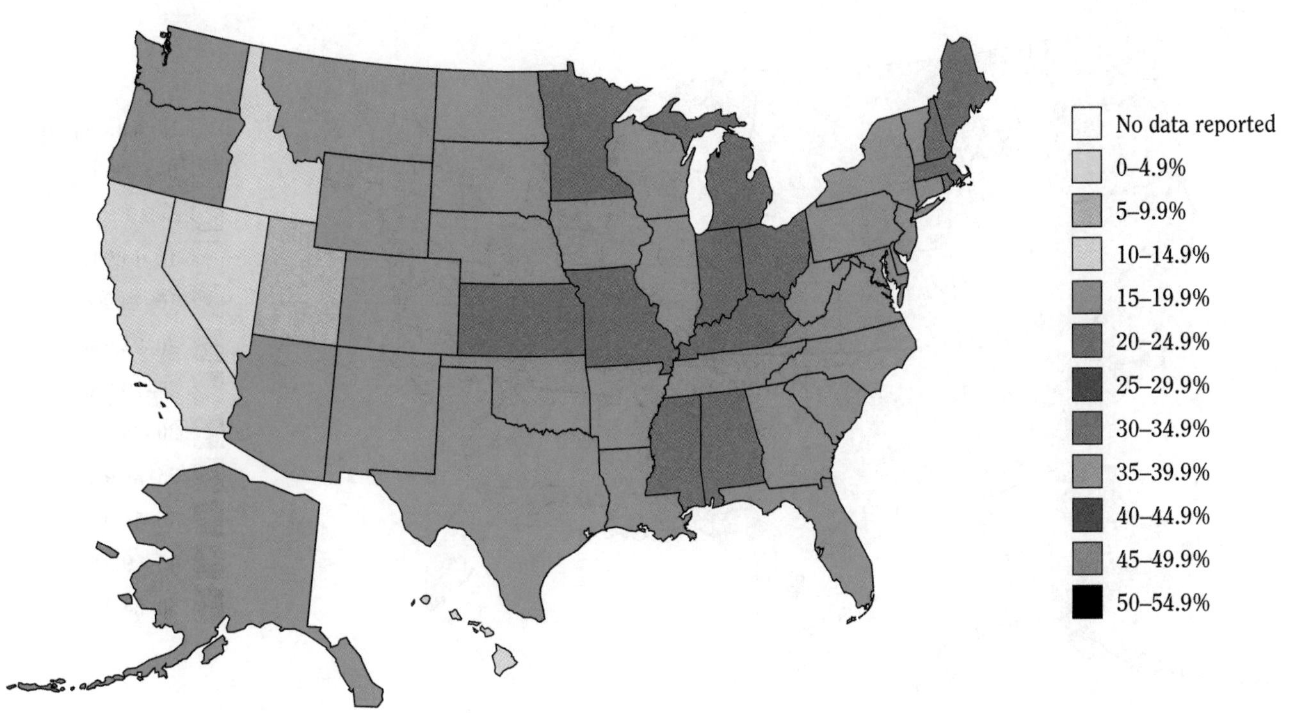

D. 18–25 years of age, females

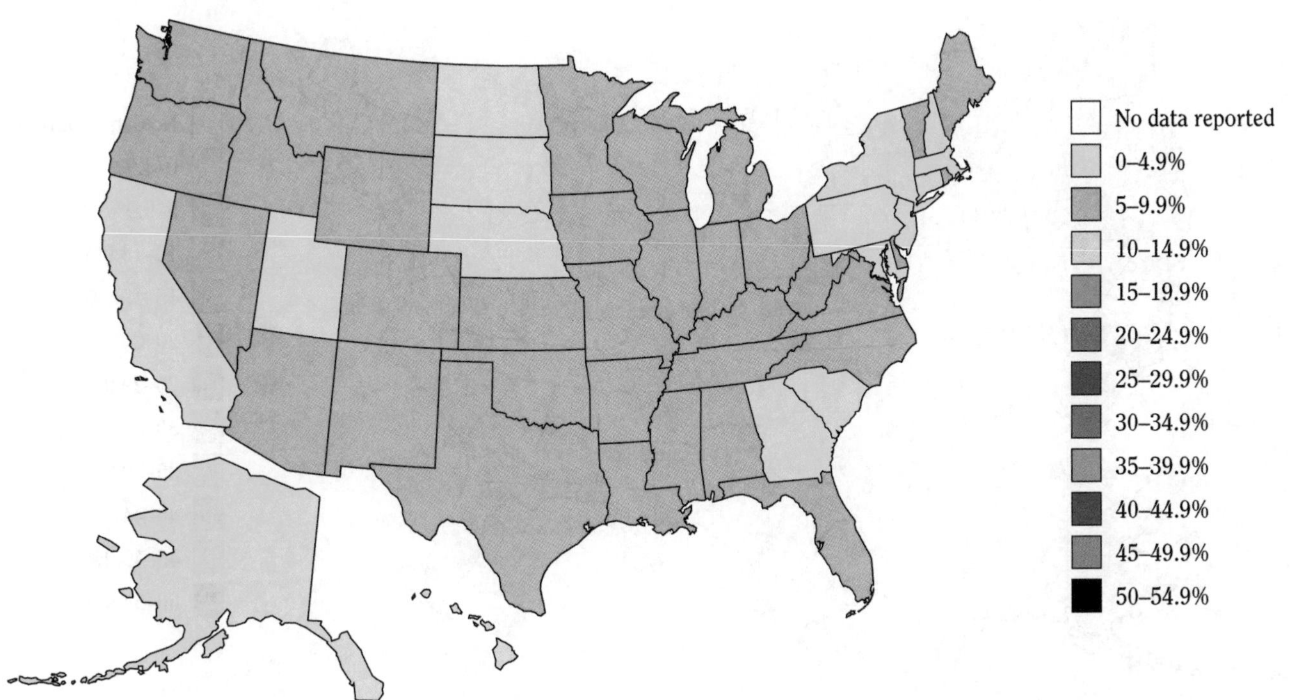

E. 26 years of age or older, males

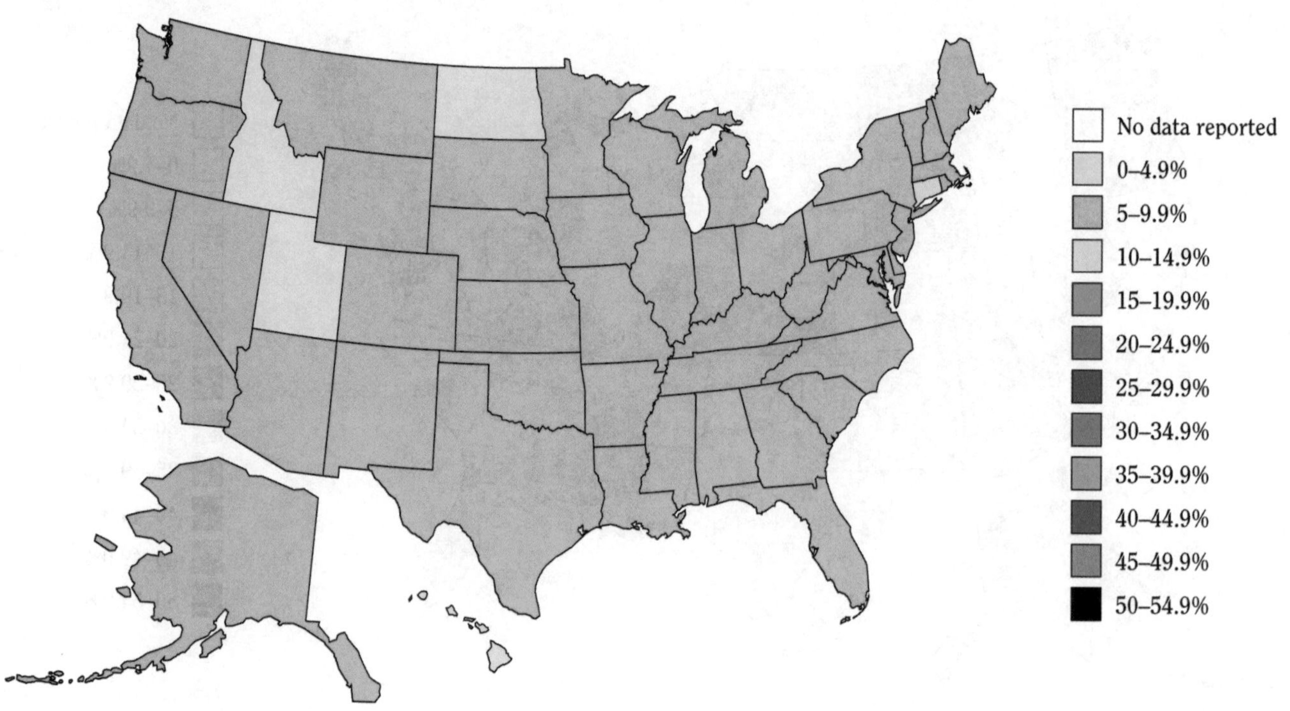

F. 26 years of age or older, females

Source: 2005–2009 NSDUH: Substance Abuse and Mental Health Services Administration (unpublished data).

Figure 3.1.41 Trends in prevalence (%) of cigar use among young people, by gender and by race/ethnicity; National Youth Risk Behavior Survey (YRBS) 1997–2009; United States

A. Gender

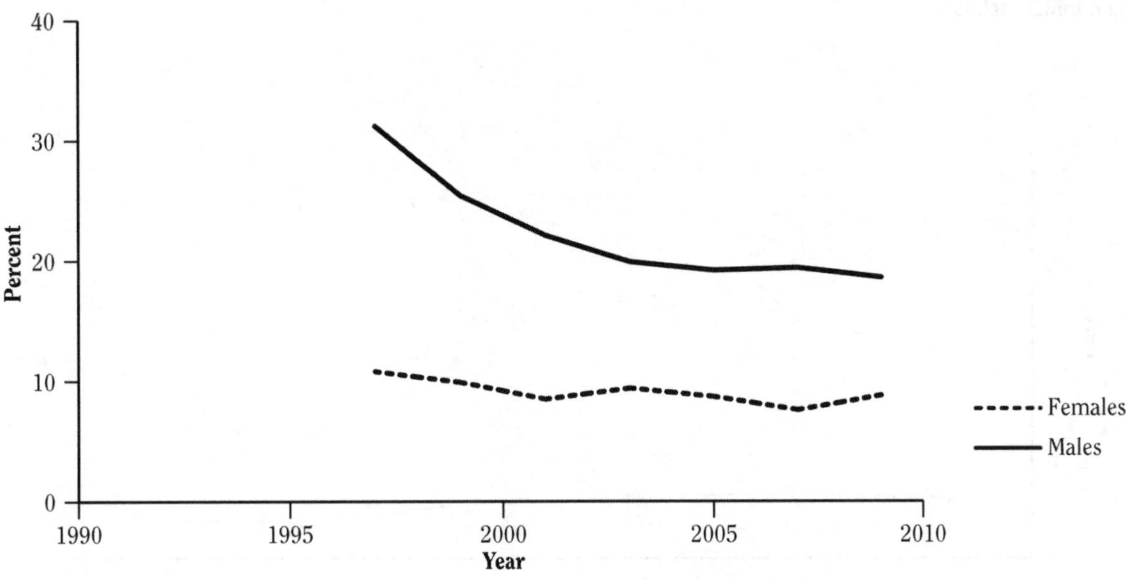

B. Race/ethnicity

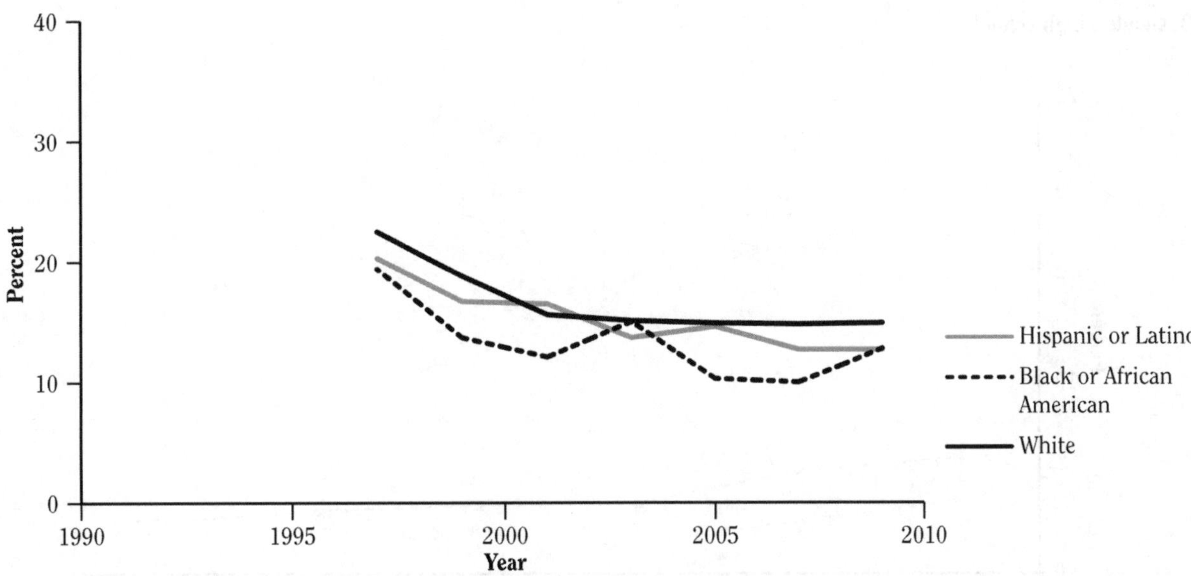

Source: 1997–2009 YRBS: Centers for Disease Control and Prevention, Division of Adolescent and School Health (unpublished data).

Figure 3.1.42 **Trends in current use of bidis and kreteks among young people, by gender and by race/ethnicity; National Youth Tobacco Survey (NYTS) for 1999, 2000, 2002, 2004, 2006, and 2009; United States**

Bidi use

A. Gender, middle school

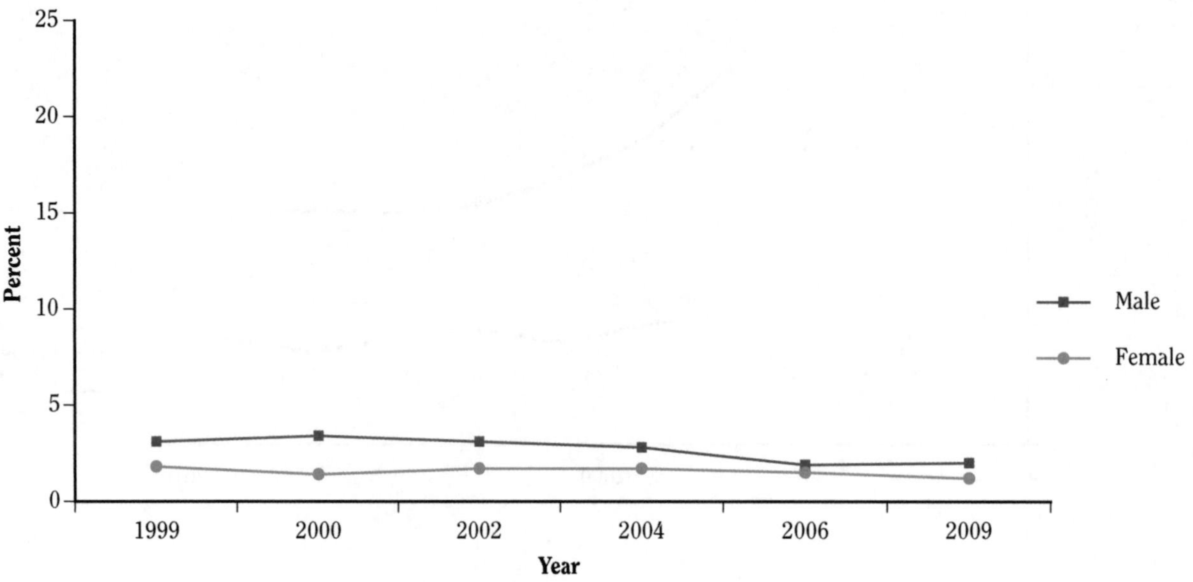

B. Gender, high school

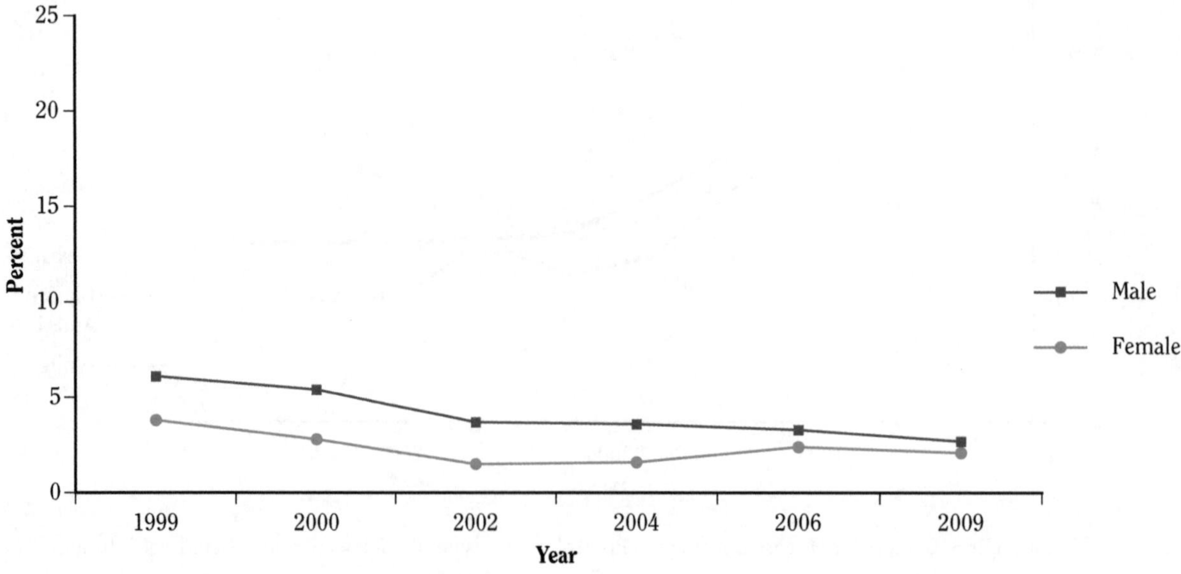

C. Race/ethnicity, middle school

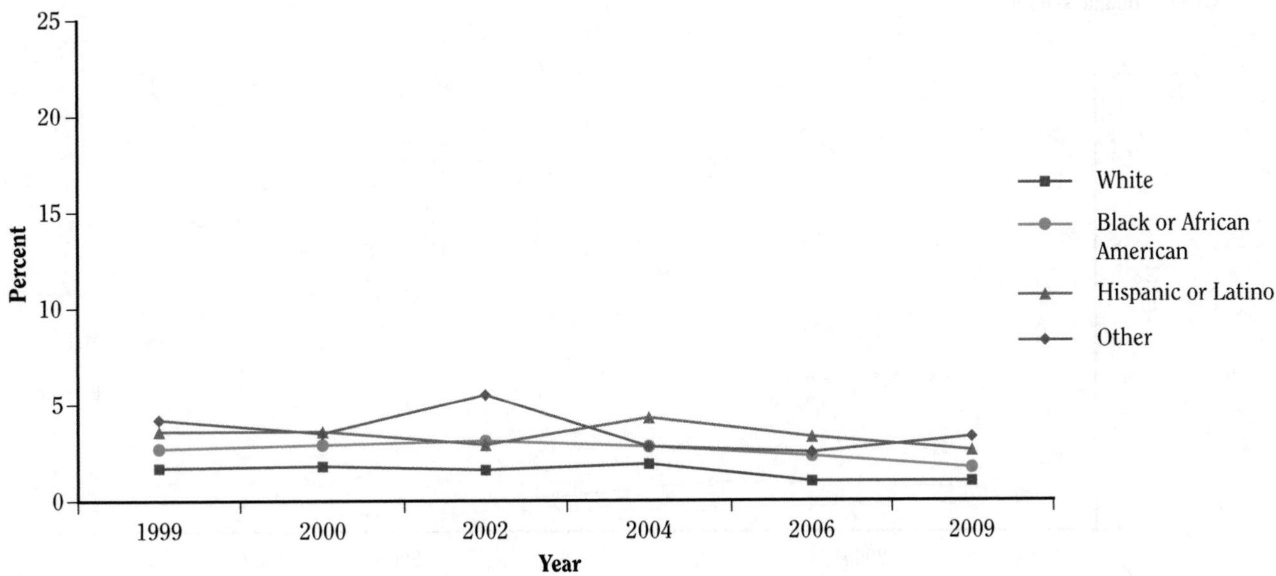

D. Race/ethnicity, high school

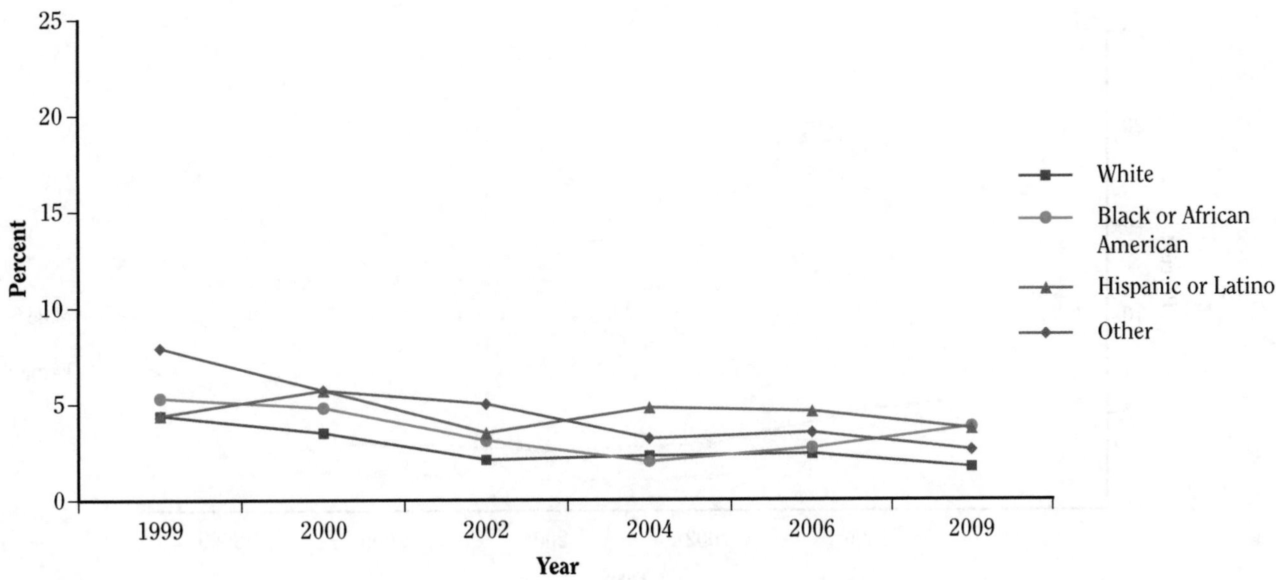

Kretek use

E. Gender, middle school

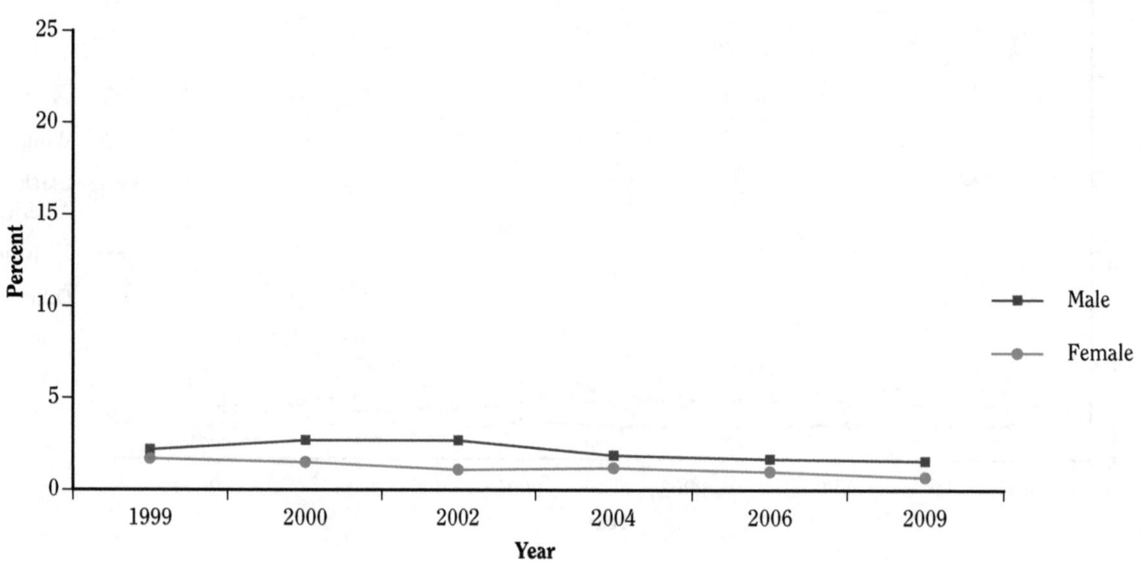

F. Gender, high school

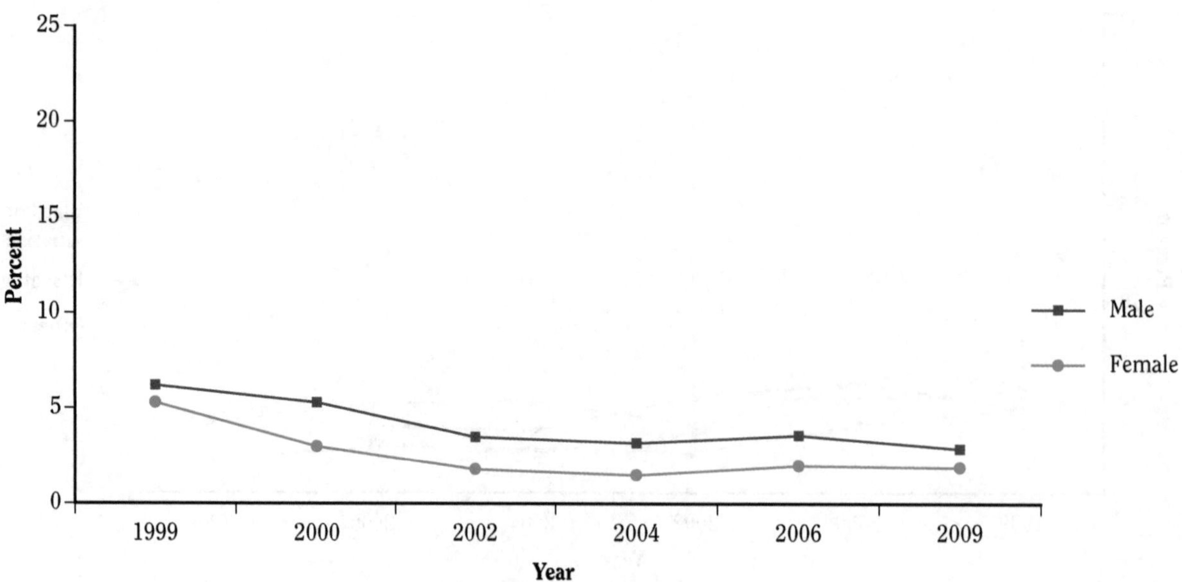

G. Race/ethnicity, middle school

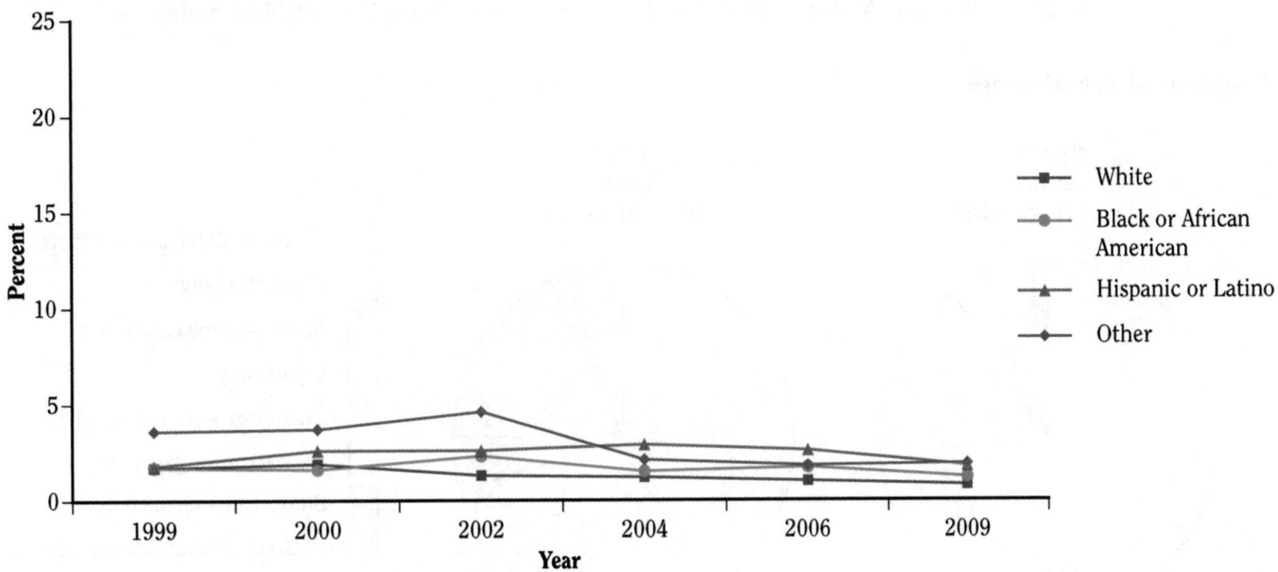

H. Race/ethnicity, high school

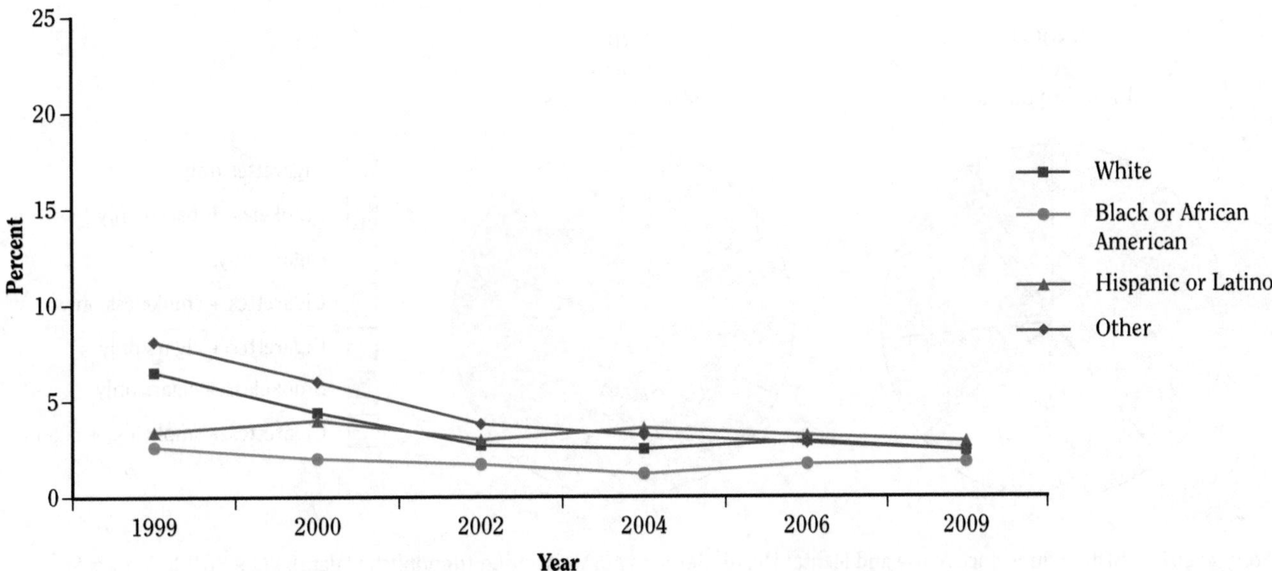

Source: 1999–2009 NYTS: Centers for Disease Control and Prevention, Division of Adolescent and School Health (unpublished data).

Figure 3.1.43 Prevalence of current use of multiple tobacco products among all males of high school age and only those males of high school age who report using tobacco; National Survey on Drug Use and Health (NSDUH) 2010 and National Youth Risk Behavior Survey (YRBS) 2009; United States

A. All males of high school age

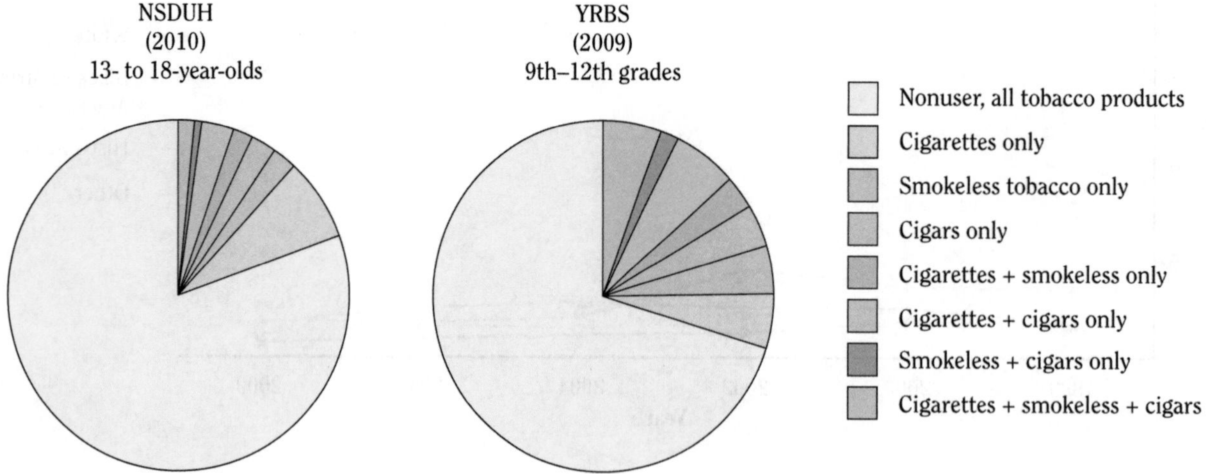

B. Males of high school age who report using tobacco

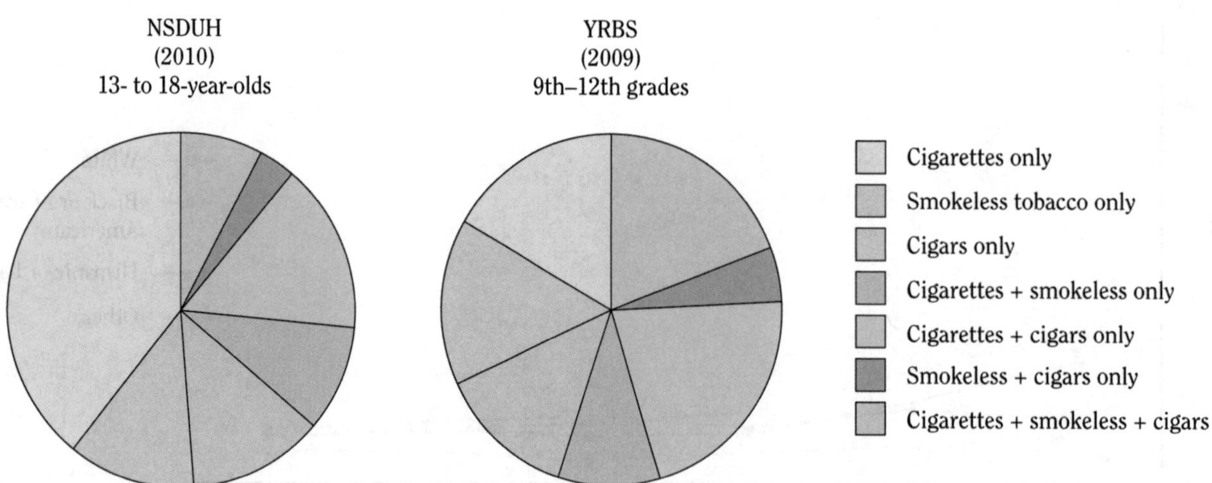

Source: 2010 NSDUH: Substance Abuse and Mental Health Services Administration (unpublished data); 2009 YRBS: Centers for Disease Control and Prevention, Division of Adolescent and School Health (unpublished data).

Figure 3.1.44 Trends in prevalence (%) of current use of two or more different tobacco products among students reporting any tobacco use, by gender and by race/ethnicity; National Youth Risk Behavior Survey (YRBS) 1997–2009; United States

A. Gender

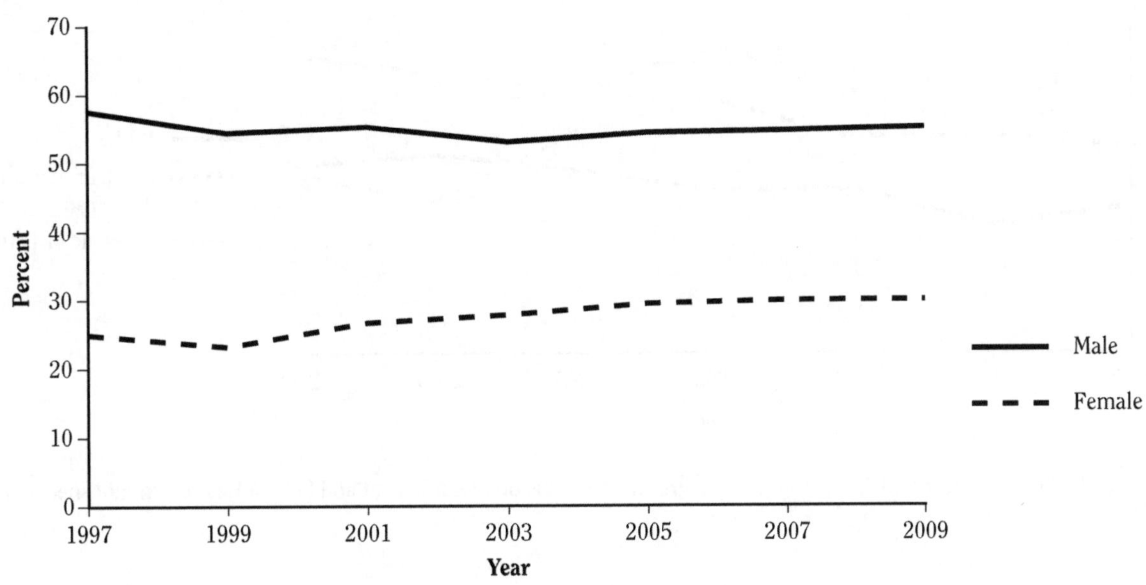

B. Males, by race/ethnicity

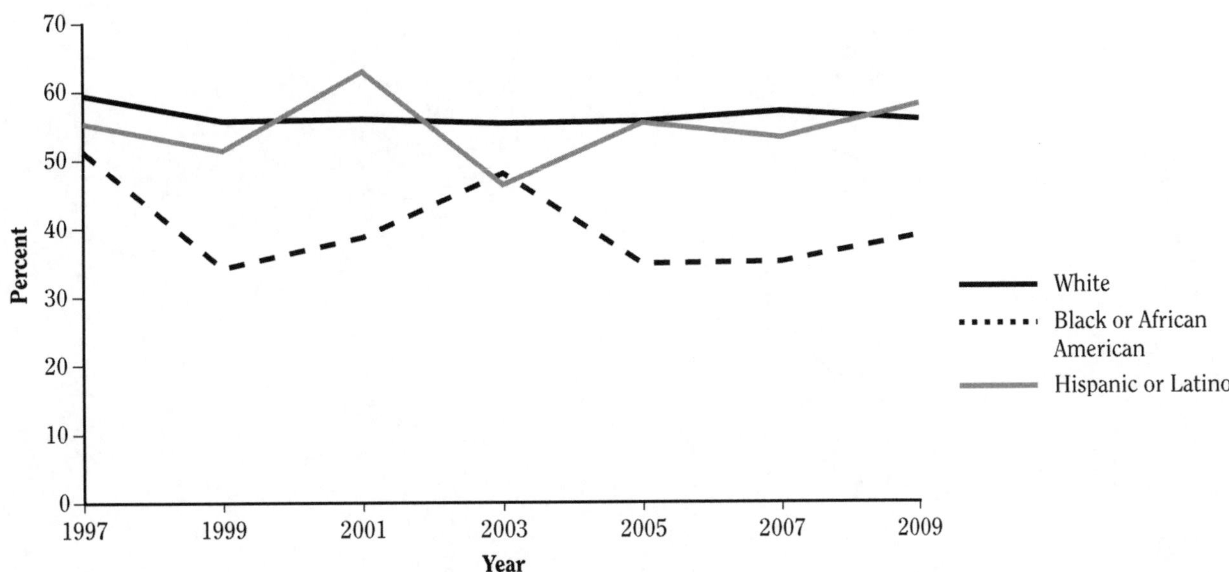

C. Females, by race/ethnicity

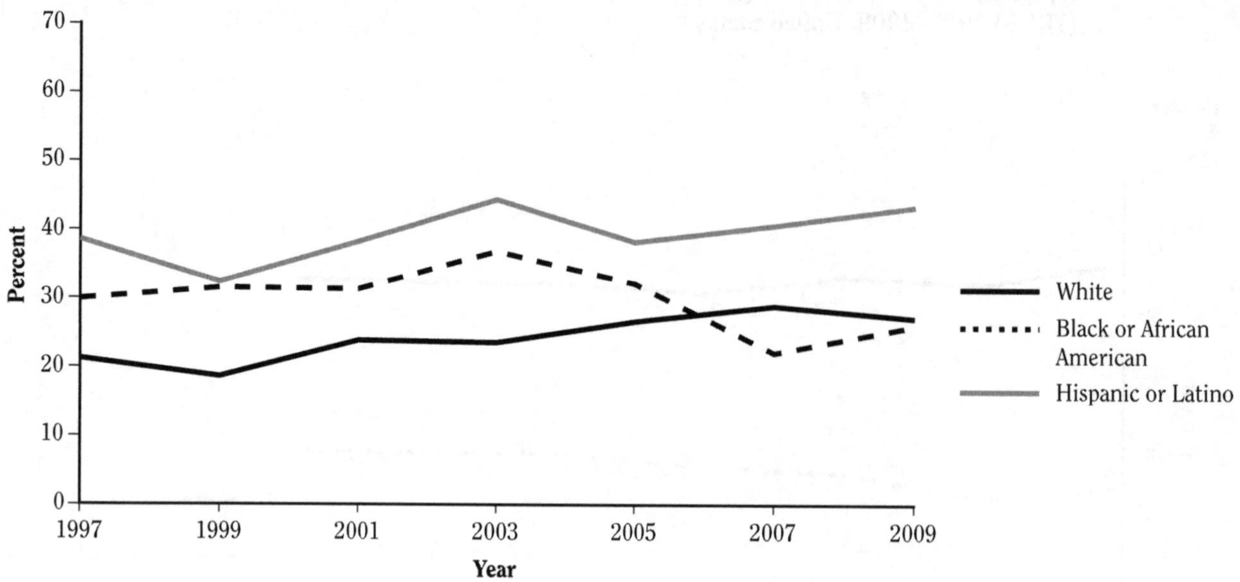

Source: 1997–2009 YRBS: Centers for Disease Control and Prevention, Division of Adolescent and School Health (unpublished data).

Figure 3.1.45 Percentage of 13- to 15-year-olds who have ever smoked cigarettes, by gender; Global Youth Tobacco Survey 1999–2007; worldwide

A. Boys

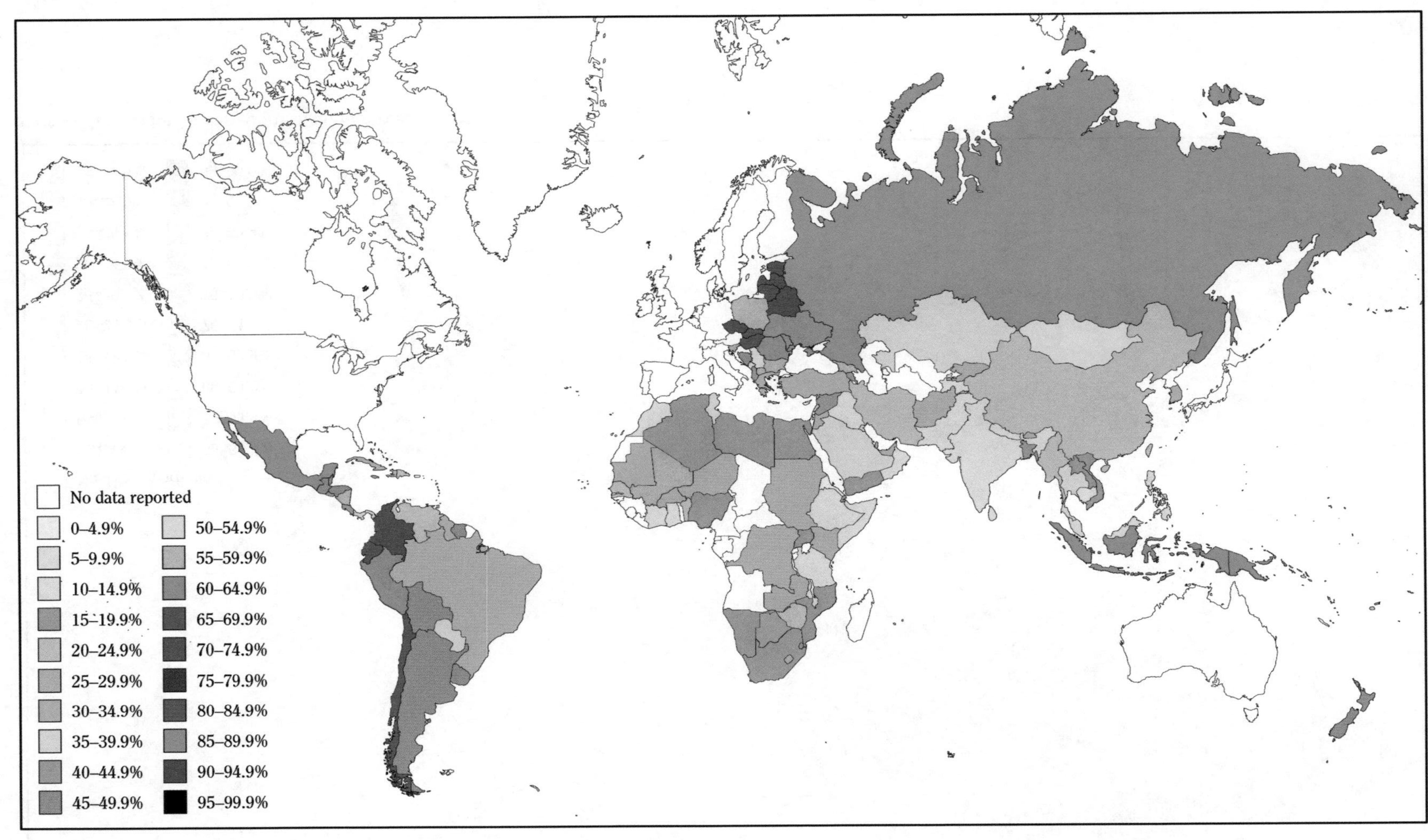

B. Girls

Source: Centers for Disease Control and Prevention 2010b.

Figure 3.1.46 Percentage of 13- to 15-year-olds who currently smoke cigarettes, by gender; Global Youth Tobacco Survey 1999–2007; worldwide

A. Boys

B. Girls

Source: Centers for Disease Control and Prevention 2010b.

Figure 3.1.47 Percentage of 13- to 15-year-olds who currently smoke and want to stop smoking, by gender; Global Youth Tobacco Survey 1999–2007; worldwide

A. Boys

B. Girls

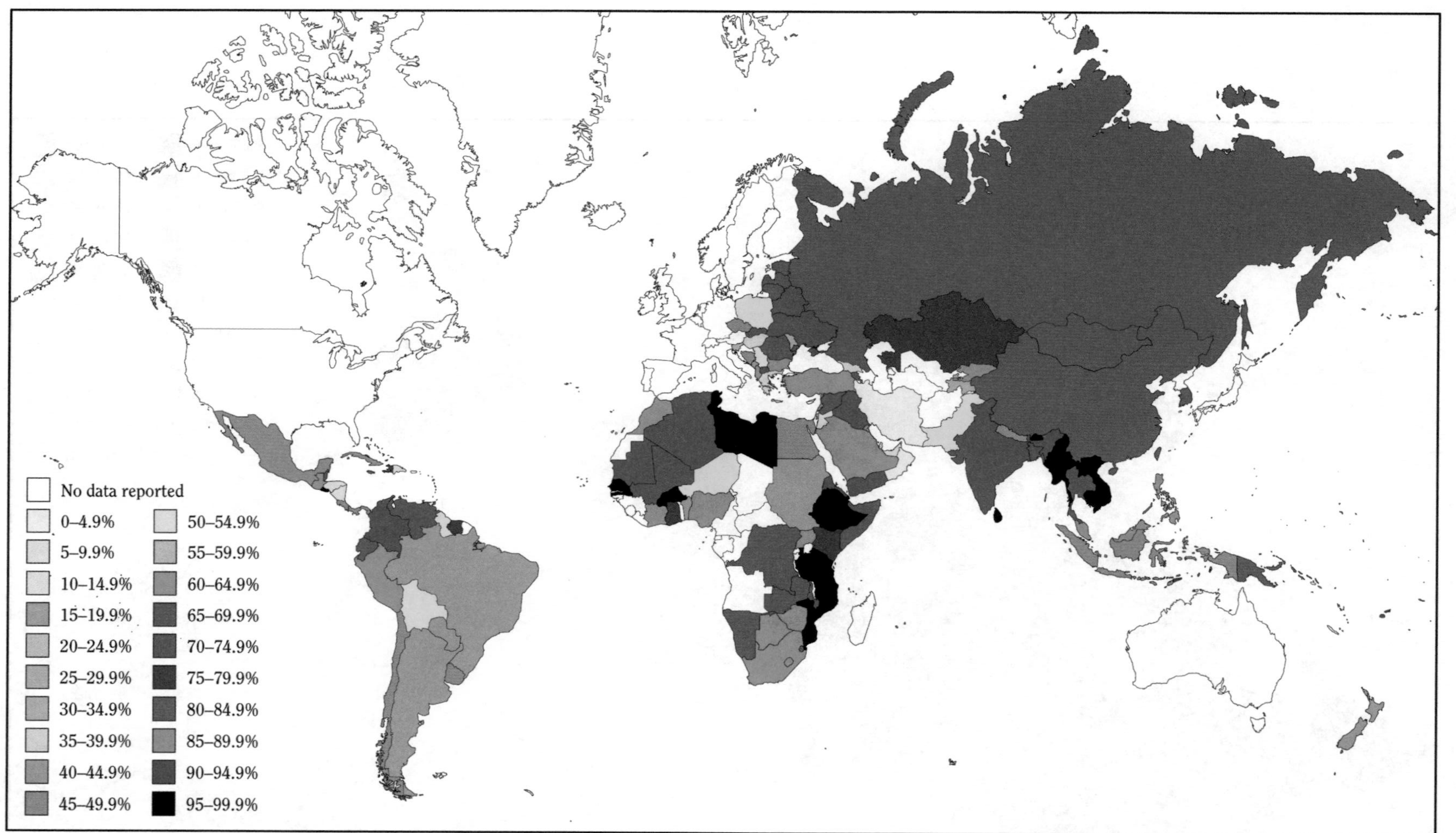

Source: Centers for Disease Control and Prevention 2010b.

Figure 3.1.48 Percentage of 13- to 15-year-olds who currently use other forms of tobacco than cigarettes, by gender; Global Youth Tobacco Survey 1999–2007; worldwide

A. Boys

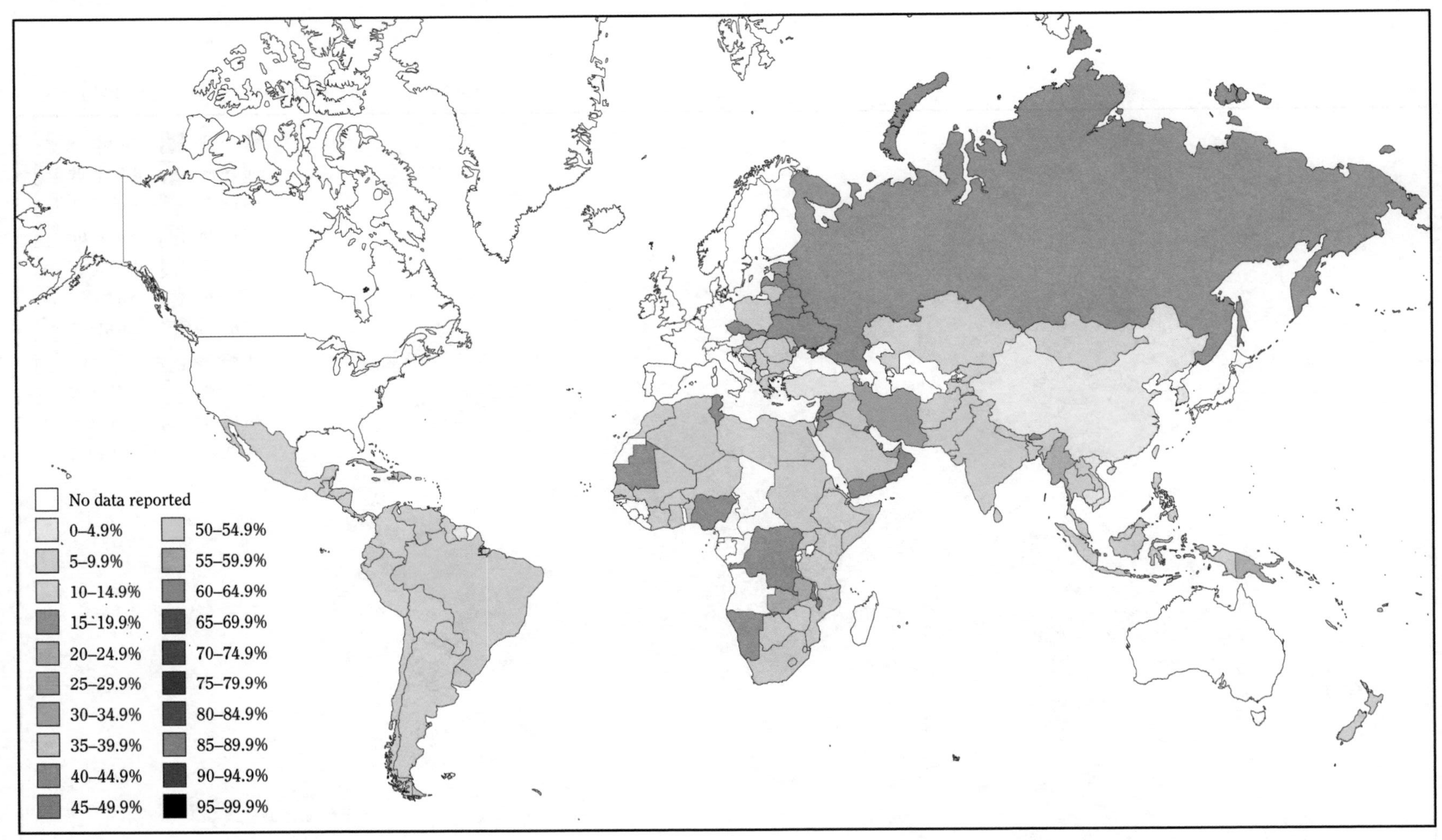

B. Girls

Source: Centers for Disease Control and Prevention 2010b.

Table 3.2.1 **Measures of tobacco use, by source, 2008 and 2009 questionnaires; United States and worldwide**

Outcome measured and source	Question	Response options	Definition of outcome
Ever smoking			
NSDUH	Have you ever smoked part or all of a cigarette?	1. Yes 2. No	Ever smoker: chose Yes
MTF	Have you ever smoked cigarettes? (Forms 1–6)	1. Never 2. Once or twice 3. Occasionally but not regularly 4. Regularly in the past 5. Regularly now	Ever smoker: chose one of options 2–5
YRBS	Have you ever tried cigarette smoking, even one or two puffs?	A. Yes B. No	Ever smoker: chose Yes
NYTS	Have you ever tried cigarette smoking, even one or two puffs?	A. Yes B. No	Ever smoker: chose Yes
Current smoking			
NSDUH	During the past 30 days, have you smoked part or all of a cigarette?	1. Yes 2. No	Current smoker: chose Yes
GYTS	During the past 30 days (one month), on how many days did you smoke cigarettes?	A. 0 days B. 1 or 2 days C. 3–5 days D. 6–9 days E. 10–19 days F. 20–29 days G. All 30 days	Current smoker: smoked cigarettes on 1 or more of the past 30 days
MTF	How frequently have you smoked cigarettes during the past 30 days?	1. Not at all 2. Less than 1 cigarette per day 3. 1–5 cigarettes per day 4. About 1/2 pack per day 5. About 1 pack per day 6. About 1 1/2 packs per day 7. 2 packs or more per day	Current smoker: chose one of options 2–7
YRBS	During the past 30 days, on how many days did you smoke cigarettes?	A. 0 days B. 1 or 2 days C. 3–5 days D. 6–9 days E. 10–19 days F. 20–29 days G. All 30 days	Current smoker: chose one of options B–G
NYTS	During the past 30 days, on how many days did you smoke cigarettes?	A. 0 days B. 1 or 2 days C. 3 to 5 days D. 6 to 9 days E. 10 to 19 days F. 20 to 29 days G. All 30 days	Current smoker: chose one of options B–G

Table 3.2.1 Continued

Outcome measured and source	Question	Response options	Definition of outcome
Intensity of smoking			
NSDUH	During the past 30 days .... that is, since __, on how many days did you smoke part or all of a cigarette?	(Enter number of days.)	Frequent smoker: entered ≥20 days
NSDUH	On the days you smoked cigarettes during the past 30 days, how many cigarettes did you smoke per day, on average?	1. Less than 1 cigarette per day 2. 1 cigarette per day 3. 2–5 cigarettes per day 4. 6–15 cigarettes per day (about 1/2 pack) 5. 16–25 cigarettes per day (about 1 pack) 6. 26–35 cigarettes per day (about 1 1/2 packs) 7. More than 35 cigarettes per day (about 2 packs or more)	Heavy smoker: chose one of options 4–7
MTF	How frequently have you smoked cigarettes during the past 30 days?	1. Not at all 2. Less than 1 cigarette per day 3. 1–5 cigarettes per day 4. About 1/2 pack per day 5. About 1 pack per day 6. About 1 1/2 packs per day 7. 2 packs or more per day	Heavy smoker: chose one of options 4–7
YRBS	During the past 30 days, on how many days did you smoke cigarettes?	A. 0 days B. 1 or 2 days C. 3–5 days D. 6–9 days E. 10–19 days F. 20–29 days G. All 30 days	Frequent smoker: chose option F or G
	During the past 30 days, on the days you smoked, how many cigarettes did you smoke per day?	A. I did not smoke cigarettes during the past 30 days B. Less than 1 cigarette per day C. 1 cigarette per day D. 2–5 cigarettes per day E. 6–10 cigarettes per day F. 11–20 cigarettes per day G. More than 20 cigarettes per day	Frequent smoker: chose option F or G
NYTS	During the past 30 days, on how many days did you smoke cigarettes?	A. 0 days B . 1 or 2 days C. 3 to 5 days D. 6 to 9 days E. 10 to 19 days F. 20 to 29 days G. All 30 days	Frequent smoker: chose option F or G

Table 3.2.1 Continued

Outcome measured and source	Question	Response options	Definition of outcome
	During the past 30 days, on the days you smoked, how many cigarettes did you smoke per day	A. I did not smoke cigarettes during the past 30 days B. Less than 1 cigarette per day C. 1 cigarette per day D. 2 to 5 cigarettes per day E. 6 to 10 cigarettes per day F. 11 to 20 cigarettes per day G. More than 20 cigarettes per day	Heavy smoker: chose option F or G
Initiation of smoking			
NSDUH	How old were you the first time you smoked part or all of a cigarette?	(Enter age)	Age of initiation
	How old were you when you first started smoking cigarettes every day?	(Enter age)	Age of initiation
MTF	When (if ever) did you FIRST do each of the following things?		
	B101M: Smoke your first cigarette?	8. Never 1. Grade 6 or below 2. Grade 7 3. Grade 8 4. Grade 9 (Freshman) 5. Grade 10 (Sophomore) 6. Grade 11 (Junior) 7. Grade 12 (Senior)	Grade
	B101A: Smoke cigarettes on a daily basis?	8. Never 1. Grade 6 or below 2. Grade 7 3. Grade 8 4. Grade 9 (Freshman) 5. Grade 10 (Sophomore) 6. Grade 11 (Junior) 7. Grade 12 (Senior)	Grade
YRBS	How old were you when you smoked a whole cigarette for the first time?	A. I have never smoked a whole cigarette B. 8 years old or younger C. 9 or 10 years old D. 11 or 12 years old E. 13 or 14 years old F. 15 or 16 years old G. 17 years old or older	Age
NHIS	How old were you when you FIRST started to smoke fairly regularly?	1. Enter age if between 6 and 84 2. Enter 6 if less than 6 years old 3. Enter 85 if 85 years old or older 4. Enter 95 if 95 years old or older 5. Never smoked regularly 6. Refused 7. Don't know	Age

Table 3.2.1 Continued

Outcome measured and source	Question	Response options	Definition of outcome
NYTS	How old were you when you smoked a whole cigarette for the first time?	A. I have never smoked a whole cigarette B. 8 years old or younger C. 9 D. 10 E. 11 F. 12 G. 13 H. 14 I. 15 J. 16 K. 17 years old or older	Age
Brand preference: cigarettes			
NSDUH	During the past 30 days, what brand of cigarettes did you smoke most often?	1. American Spirit 2. Basic 3. Benson & Hedges 4. Camel 5. Capri 6. Carlton 7. Doral 8. GPC 9. Kent 10. Kool 11. Liggett Select 12. Marlboro 13. Merit 14. Misty 15. Monarch 16. More 17. Newport 18. Pall Mall 19. Parliament 20. Salem 21. USA Gold 22. Vantage 23. Viceroy 24. Virginia Slims 25. Winston 26. A brand not on this list	Brand
	During the past 30 days, what type of cigarettes did you smoke most often?	1. Lights 2. Ultra lights 3. Mediums 4. Full flavor	Type
	Were the cigarettes you smoked during the past 30 days menthol?	1. Yes 2. No	Type

Table 3.2.1 Continued

Outcome measured and source	Question	Response options	Definition of outcome
Attempts to quit smoking			
MTF	Have you ever tried to stop smoking and found you could not?	1. Yes 2. No	Yes
	How many times (if any) have you tried to stop smoking?	1. None 2. Once 3. Twice 4. 3 to 5 times 5. 6 to 9 times 6. 10 or more times	Once or more
YRBS	During the past 12 months, did you ever try to quit smoking cigarettes?	A. I did not smoke during the past 12 months B. Yes C. No	Yes
Ever use of smokeless tobacco			
NSDUH	Have you ever used snuff, even once?	1. Yes 2. No	Ever use of smokeless tobacco: chose Yes
	Have you ever used chewing tobacco, even once?	1. Yes 2. No	Ever use of smokeless tobacco: chose Yes
MTF	Have you ever taken or used smokeless tobacco (snuff, plug, dipping tobacco, chewing tobacco)?	1. Never 2. Once or twice 3. Occasionally but not regularly 4. Regularly in the past 5. Regularly now	Ever use of smokeless tobacco: chose one of options 2–5
NYTS	Have you ever used chewing tobacco, snuff, or dip, such as Redman, Levi Garrett, Beechnut, Skoal, Skoal Bandits, or Copenhagen?	A. Yes B. No	Ever use of smokeless tobacco: chose Yes
Current use of smokeless tobacco			
NSDUH	During the past 30 days, have you used snuff, even once?	1. Yes 2. No	Current use of smokeless tobacco: chose Yes
MTF	How frequently have you taken smokeless tobacco during the past 30 days?	1. Not at all 2. Once or twice 3. Once or twice per week 4. Three to five times per week 5. About once a day 6. More than once a day	Current use of smokeless tobacco: use: chose one of options 2–6
YRBS	During the past 30 days, on how many days did you use chewing tobacco, snuff, or dip…?	A. 0 days B. 1 or 2 days C. 3 to 5 days D. 6 to 9 days E. 10 to 19 days F. 20 to 29 days G. All 30 days	Current use of smokeless tobacco: chose one of options B–G

Table 3.2.1 Continued

Outcome measured and source	Question	Response options	Definition of outcome
NYTS	During the past 30 days, on how many days did yhou use chewing tobacco, snuff, or dip?	A. 0 days B. 1 or 2 days C. 3 to 5 days D. 6 to 9 days E. 10 to 19 days F. 20 to 29 days G. All 30 days	Current smokeless tobacco use: chose one of options B–G
Initiation of smokeless tobacco			
NSDUH	How old were you the first time you used snuff?	(Enter age)	Age
	How old were you the first time you used chewing tobacco?	(Enter age)	Age
MTF	When (if ever) did you FIRST do each of the following things: try smokeless tobacco (snuff, plug, or chewing tobacco)? Don't count anything you took because a doctor told you to.	8. Never 1. Grade 6 or below 2. Grade 7 3. Grade 8 4. Grade 9 (Freshman) 5. Grade 10 (Sophomore) 6. Grade 11 (Junior) 7. Grade 12 (Senior)	Grade
GYTS	How old were you when you used chewing tobacco, snuff, or dip for the first time?	a. I have never used chewing tobacco, snuff, or dip b. 7 years old or younger c. 8 or 9 years old d. 10 or 11 years old e. 12 or 13 years old f. 14 or 15 years old g. 16 years old or older	Age
NYTS	How old were you when you used chewing tobacco, snuff, or dip for the first time?	A. I have never used chewing tobacco, snuff, or dip B. 8 years old or younger C. 9 D. 10 E. 11 F. 12 G. 13 H. 14 I. 15 J. 16 K. 17 years old or older	Age

Table 3.2.1 Continued

Outcome measured and source	Question	Response options	Definition of outcome
Brand preference: smokeless tobacco			
NSDUH	During the past 30 days, what brand of snuff did you use most often?	1. Copenhagen 2. Cougar 3. Gold River 4. Grizzly 5. Happy Days 6. Hawken 7. Kodiak 8. Red Seal 9. Redwood 10. Rooster 11. Silver Creek 12. Skoal 13. Timber Wolf 14. A brand not on this list	Brand
	During the past 30 days, what brand of chewing tobacco did you use most often?	1. Beech-Nut 2. Chattanooga Chew 3. Day's Work 4. Granger 5. H.B. Scott 6. Levi Garrett 7. Red Fox 8. Redman 9. Taylor's Pride 10. Totems 11. Work Horse 12. A brand not on this list	Type
Ever use of a cigar			
NSDUH	Have you ever smoked part or all of a cigar? By cigars we mean any kind, including big cigars, cigarillos, and even little cigars that look like cigarettes	1. Yes 2. No	Ever use of a cigar: chose Yes
NYTS	Have you ever tried smoking cigars, cigarillos, or little cigars, even one or two puffs?	A. Yes B. No	Ever cigar use: chose Yes
Current cigar use			
NSDUH	During the past 30 days, have you smoked part or all of any type of cigar?	1. Yes 2. No	Current cigar use: chose Yes
YRBS	During the past 30 days, on how many days did you smoke cigars, cigarillos, or little cigars?	A. 0 days B. 1 or 2 days C. 3 to 5 days D. 6 to 9 days E. 10 to 19 days F. 20 to 29 days G. All 30 days	Current cigar use: chose one of options B–G

Table 3.2.1 Continued

Outcome measured and source	Question	Response options	Definition of outcome
NYTS	During the past 30 days, on how many days did you smoke cigars, cigarillos, or little cigars?	A. 0 days B. 1 or 2 days C. 3 to 5 days D. 6 to 9 days E. 10 to 19 days F. 20 to 29 days G. All 30 days	Current cigar use: chose one of options B–G
Initiation of cigar use			
GYTS	How old were you when you smoked a whole cigar, cigarillo, or little cigar for the first time?	a. I have never smoked a cigar, cigarillo, or little cigar b. 7 years old or younger c. 8 or 9 years old d. 10 or 11 years old e. 12 or 13 years old f. 14 or 15 years old g. 16 years old or older	Age
NSDUH	How old were you the first time you smoked part or all of any type of cigar?	(Enter age.)	Age
YRBS	During the past 30 days, on how many days did you smoke cigars, cigarillos, or little cigars?	A. 0 days B. 1 or 2 days C. 3 to 5 days D. 6 to 9 days E. 10 to 19 days F. 20 to 29 days G. All 30 days	Current cigar use: chose one of options B–G
NYTS	How old were you when you smoked a cigar, cigarillo, or little cigar for the first time?	A. I have never smoked a cigar, cigarillo, or little cigar B. 8 years old or younger C. 9 D. 10 E. 11 F. 12 G. 13 H. 14 I. 15 J. 16 K. 17 years old or older	Age

Table 3.2.1 Continued

Outcome measured and source	Question	Response options	Definition of outcome
Brand preference: cigars			
NSDUH	During the past 30 days, what brand of cigar did you smoke most often?	1. Al Capone 2. Antonio y Cleopatra 3. Arturo Fuente 4. Backwoods 5. Black & Mild 6. Blackstone 7. Captain Black 8. Cohiba 9. Cuesta-Rey 10. Dutch Masters 11. El Producto 12. Garcia y Vega 13. Havatampa 14. King Edward 15. La Corona 16. Little Nippers 17. Macanudos 18. Montecristo 19. Muriel 20. Partagas 21. Phillies 22. Punch 23. Romeo y Julieta 24. Swisher Sweets 25. Thompson 26. Tijuana Smalls 27. White Owl 28. Winchester 29. A brand not on this list	Brand
Ever bidi use			
NYTS	Have you ever tried smoking any of the following:	A. Bidis B. Kreteks C. I have tried both bidis and kreteks D. I have never smoked bidis or kreteks	Ever bidi use: chose one of options A or C
Current bidi use			
NYTS	During the past 30 days, on how many days did you smoke bidis?	a. 0 days b. 1 or 2 days c. 3 to 5 days d. 6 to 9 days e. 10 to 19 days f. 20 to 29 days g. All 30 days	Current bidi use: chose one of options b–g
Ever kretek use			
NYTS	Have you ever tried smoking any of the following:	A. Bidis B. Kreteks C. I have tried both bidis and kreteks D. I have never smoked bidis or kreteks	Ever kretek use: chose one of options B or C

Table 3.2.1 Continued

Outcome measured and source	Question	Response options	Definition of outcome
Current kretek use			
NYTS	During the past 30 days, on how many days did you smoke kreteks?	a. 0 days b. 1 or 2 days c. 3 to 5 days d. 6 to 9 days e. 10 to 19 days f. 20 to 29 days g. All 30 days	Current kretek use: chose one of options b–g

Source: CDC 2008c, 2009c,d; Johnston et al. 2010; RTI International 2009.
Note: This table is compiled from the 2008 GYTS questionnaire and the 2009 questionnaires of the MTF, NHIS, NSDUH, NYTS, and YRBS. **GYTS** = Global Youth Tobacco Survey; **MTF** = Monitoring the Future; **NHIS** = National Health Interview Survey; **NSDUH** = National Survey on Drug Use & Health; **NYTS** = National Youth Tobacco Survey; **YRBS** = Youth Risk Behavior Survey.

Chapter 4
Social, Environmental, Cognitive, and Genetic Influences on the Use of Tobacco Among Youth

Introduction

This chapter addresses the important question of why young people begin to use tobacco. The immediate and long-term health consequences of use have been extensively documented over the past 50 years. Why anyone would begin to smoke or use smokeless products may therefore not seem "rational." This chapter (and Chapter 5, "The Tobacco Industry's Influences on the Use of Tobacco Among Youth") examines, within a theory-driven context, the risk factors associated with the onset and development of tobacco use over the course of adolescence and young adulthood. These particular stages of development within the life course are perhaps the only times in life when tobacco use might be appealing and even perceived as functional to individuals (Perry 1999). By definition, adolescence and young adulthood represent the social transition to adulthood, with accompanying risk-taking associated with trying and acquiring adult behaviors. Yet brain development is not complete, and there is immaturity in consequential thinking, impulsivity, and decision-making skills before adulthood. Notably, peer group influences emerge as powerful motivators of behavior change. These changes create a unique window of vulnerability for tobacco use onset in adolescence and young adulthood. As was shown in Chapter 3 ("The Epidemiology of Tobacco Use Among Young People in the United States and Worldwide"), by 26 years of age, nearly all people who are going to use tobacco have already begun, so the focus of primary prevention with young people really spans the ages of 12 to 25 years. This chapter provides important information on these developmental processes, examining large social and physical environments that support or discourage tobacco use, small social groups, cognitive and affective processes, and neurobiological and genetic factors.

The 1994 Surgeon General's report on preventing tobacco use among young people discussed psychosocial risk factors for initiating tobacco use (U.S. Department of Health and Human Services [USDHHS] 1994). That report, which described the developmental stages of tobacco use from onset to regular use, set forth several sets of factors that influence the initiation of tobacco use:

- Sociodemographic factors (socioeconomic status [SES], developmental challenges of adolescence, gender, and race/ethnicity);
- Environmental factors (acceptability and availability of tobacco products, interpersonal variables, perceived environmental variables);
- Behavioral factors (academic achievement, problem behaviors, influence of peer groups, participation in activities, and behavioral skills);
- Personal factors (knowledge of the long-term health consequences of using tobacco, functional meanings of tobacco use, subjective expected utility of tobacco use, variables related to self-esteem, and personality); and
- Current behavior relative to tobacco use (intentions to smoke and smoking status).

The chapter concluded that the following factors promote the initiation and use of tobacco products of some type:

- Relatively low SES,
- Relatively high accessibility and availability of tobacco products,
- Perceptions by adolescents that tobacco use is normative, that is, usual or acceptable behavior,
- Use of tobacco by significant others and approval of tobacco use among those persons,
- Lack of parental support,
- Low levels of academic achievement and school involvement,
- Lack of skills required to resist influences to use tobacco,
- Relatively low self-efficacy for refusal,
- Previous tobacco use and intention to use tobacco in the future,
- Relatively low self-image, and
- Belief that tobacco use is functional or serves a purpose.

The same factors were also found to predict two specific behaviors: cigarette smoking and the use of smokeless tobacco. In addition, having insufficient knowledge about the health consequences of using smokeless tobacco was found to predict initiation of that behavior. The report noted that use of smokeless tobacco tended to be specific to males, and both parents and youth perceived the use of smokeless tobacco to be relatively safe and acceptable when compared with cigarette smoking (USDHHS 1994).

This chapter, which updates Chapter 4 of the 1994 report, is not meant to be an all-encompassing review. Instead, it focuses on highlighting information gleaned from research conducted after the 1994 report was written. Literature was collected in a theory-guided way, using the Theory of Triadic Influences, to emphasize findings deemed important by the scientific panel convened to write this chapter. To reflect the findings of researchers during the last decade and a half, the description of etiologic factors differs substantially from the earlier report. The chapter investigates the predictors of initiation and progression of tobacco use for two groups: adolescents (girls and boys aged 12–17 years) and young adults (women and men aged 18–25 years). The time from 12–25 years of age constitutes an extended developmental period in which independence in lifestyle is gradually achieved (note that in the United States, youth cannot buy tobacco legally until at least 18 years of age).

Cigarette smoking among adolescents and young adults is a multidetermined behavior, influenced by the unique and overlapping combinations of biological, psychosocial, and environmental factors. These factors can function as either risk or protective factors. Risk factors increase the probability of smoking initiation and the likelihood of continued use, characterized by increases in frequency and intensity. Conversely, protective factors decrease the probability of smoking initiation, as well as reduce the likelihood that experimental use will progress to regular use. An individual's overall risk profile is determined by the interrelations of these various risk and protective factors.

Age-related processes also play a central role in determining smoking risk. Adolescence is a sensitive developmental period, characterized by extraordinary brain changes and high levels of emotionality, impulsivity, and risk-taking. The plasticity of the adolescent brain, together with the relatively immature neurobehavioral systems necessary for self-control and affect regulation, confer a heightened vulnerability for the development of smoking behavior (Steinberg 2007). Similarly, the period following early and middle adolescence (aged 18–25 years) has particular developmental significance with regard to smoking behavior. Many risk behaviors peak during this period of life, including rates of substance use, smoking, risky driving, and unsafe sex (Arnett 2000). It is also during this time period that young people may attend college or begin to take on more conventional adult roles, such as marriage, children, and occupational responsibilities. These life transitions are often associated with concomitant decreases in risky behavior (Bachman et al. 2001; Flora and Chassin 2005) and may represent a turning point in which an individual either permanently adopts smoking behavior or rejects it in favor of a nonsmoking lifestyle.

The development of youth smoking is a dynamic process in which youth progress from early cigarette trials, to intermittent use, to regular use and dependence. Understanding the factors that either interrupt progress along this trajectory or potentiate continued use is critical to intervening with smoking behavior. Importantly, the factors that influence early trials with cigarettes may be distinct from those that influence progression and persistence. Modern conceptualizations of smoking development emphasize a social ecological perspective which considers the broader social and environmental context in which youth tobacco use occurs (Cook 2003; Wilcox 2003; Wen et al. 2009; Ennett et al. 2010). This perspective recognizes that youth and young adults do not exist in isolation. Rather, they inhabit a complex system of layered social and environmental contexts, wherein they learn, socialize, and conduct their daily activities. Theoretical models that consider these multiple levels of neurobiological, sociocontextual, and environmental influence can be labeled "integrated biopsychosocial-ecological models" (Sussman and Ames 2008). In these models, intrapersonal predictors of tobacco use are "nested" within larger social and environmental structures. For example, a person's neurobiological variables function within a set of complex cognitive-related responses and, in turn, operate within a larger context of small social groups (e.g., families, peer groups), that ultimately function within a larger socio-environmental context (e.g., schools, neighborhoods). Large-scale environmental factors might be either social or physical (e.g., communications in the mass media, access of youth to sales of tobacco products), while environmental factors on a smaller scale could include, for example, a youth's social groups. Intrapersonal factors (e.g., cognitive processes, genetics, and brain systems and structures) could be based on biological or psychological/cognitive variables. These two kinds of predictors, environmental and intrapersonal, may affect each other. For example, a person who shows a lack of self-control related to an imbalance in neurotransmission (an intrapersonal neurobiological variable) and intends to smoke cigarettes in the future (an intrapersonal cognitive variable) would be constrained from smoking in groups of nonsmoking peers at a worksite where smoking was prohibited; here, two kinds of environmental variables would be at play: social (small groups) and physical (prohibition of smoking). Multilevel modeling techniques are commonly used to examine how factors such as intrapersonal characteristics, families, peer groups, schools, and communities, interact together to jointly influence adolescent tobacco outcomes.

The Theory of Triadic Influence (TTI) (Flay and Petraitis 1994; Petraitis et al. 1995) classifies the elements of 14 different theories about human behavior in three substantive domains. This "meta-theory" is grounded in the major behavioral theories that have been applied to tobacco use with young people. The theories, grouped by categories (in parentheses), are as follows:

- Reasoned action, planned behavior (cognitive affective);
- Social learning, social cognitive/learning (social learning);
- Social control, social development (commitment and social attachment);
- Social ecology, self-derogation, multistage social learning, family interaction (intrapersonal); and
- Problem behavior, peer cluster, vulnerability, domain (relatively comprehensive theories).

The three substantive domains are the following:

- Social/normative,
- Cultural/environmental, and
- Intrapersonal.

These three domains have different "distances" from actual tobacco use and so can be characterized as ultimate, distal, or proximal. For example, a person is affected by her or his culture (ultimate), social and physical environments (distal), and personal perceptions of those environments (proximal) that influence subsequent tobacco use (Petraitis et al. 1995; Turner et al. 2004; Sussman and Ames 2008).

This chapter divides the etiologies of tobacco use into four categories of predictors that overlap with those used by TTI and reflect how research has been undertaken in this area: large social and physical environments, small social groups, intrapersonal cognitive processes, and intrapersonal genetic and neurobiological processes.

By considering these four categories, each of which contains sets of variables, within a broad theoretical context, the etiology of tobacco use may be more completely understood, and new options for the primary prevention or cessation of tobacco use may be suggested. (Figure 5.1 in Chapter 5 provides a visual illustration of TTI.)

Developmental Stages of Tobacco Use

As presented in the 1994 report from the Surgeon General, the uptake of tobacco use can be described as proceeding in stages from nonuse to lower to higher levels of use (USDHHS 1994). Generally, initiation is defined as having ever tried tobacco, experimental use as occasional use, and regular use as an increase in the frequency and quantity of use (USDHHS 1994; Mayhew et al. 2000). In adolescence, regular use is often marked by a pattern of monthly or weekly use and may include psychological and physical dependence on tobacco (Sussman et al. 1995). Not all experimenters become regular users, and different predictors may be important at different points along the course of a person's tobacco use, which underscores the usefulness of conceptualizing the stages of use (Leventhal and Cleary 1980; Flay et al. 1983; USDHHS 1994; Sussman et al. 1995; Mayhew et al. 2000). Social and environmental factors are likely to be more influential in low-level or early tobacco use (and thus are more appropriate targets for intervention during these stages), while intrapersonal factors tend to be strong predictors of later and higher levels of use, when addiction to nicotine is more strongly involved (Tucker et al. 2003; Sussman and Ames 2008). However, a review of 11 cross-sectional and 33 prospective studies suggested that social, environmental, and intrapersonal factors predict both the onset of adolescent smoking and subsequent increases in the frequency and quantity of use (Mayhew et al. 2000). Mayhew and colleagues (2000) found that tolerance for deviance (an intrapersonal variable) appeared uniquely related to the onset of smoking in some of the prospective studies they reviewed, although previous smoking intensity, normative beliefs, estimates of the prevalence of smoking among peers, and perceived lack of parental involvement and support appeared uniquely related to higher levels of smoking onset in other studies.

The stage model is a useful heuristic device (USDHHS 1994) and, as is true with other integrative models, helps to stimulate new research and guide efforts in prevention. In reality, however, it is a simplistic presentation of the development of smoking. In fact, substantial heterogeneity exists in the uptake and progression of smoking behavior. As newer data analytic techniques have become available (e.g., latent variable growth mixture modeling), researchers have been able to empirically identify developmental trajectories of tobacco use that more clearly capture this heterogeneity (Chassin et al. 2000; Mayhew et al. 2000; Bernat et al. 2008). Several studies have identified three to six discrete smoking trajectories (e.g., Bernat et al. 2008). One of these trajectories typically captures about 10% of adolescents who progress rapidly to persistent, heavy cigarette smoking (Chassin et al. 2000; Colder et al. 2001; Soldz and Cui 2002; Orlando et al. 2004; Stanton et al. 2004; White et al. 2004; Karp et al. 2005; Brook et al. 2006; Bernat et al. 2008; Lessov-Schlaggar et al. 2008). Adolescents in this group may exhibit symptoms of dependence shortly after their first experimentation with cigarettes (Gervais et al. 2006; DiFranza et al. 2007), and they do not appear to go through a generic stage model (i.e., a series of stages) of the uptake of tobacco use. An important focus of research in this area is to identify factors that discriminate among trajectories, especially those factors associated with patterns of early and rapid escalation in smoking, since this group may be at greatest risk for lifelong nicotine dependence (Dierker and Mermelstein 2010). See Chapters 2 ("The Health Consequences of Tobacco Use Among Young People") and 3 for additional discussion of smoking trajectories.

Some studies have extended the stages of tobacco use to describe what a young person might experience before initiating use. For example, Pallonen and colleagues (1998) studied four stages of smoking acquisition: precontemplation (not intending to smoke in the future), contemplation (intending to smoke in the future), preparation (intending to smoke in the immediate future), and recent acquisition (experimenting with smoking). Another schema, the susceptibility model (Pierce et al. 1996, 1998), differentiates never smokers who are open to the possibility of smoking from those who are firmly committed to not smoking. In this model, "nonsusceptible" is the first stage. During this period, the adolescent has yet to consider the possibility of smoking. In the second stage (susceptible), the adolescent becomes open to the idea of smoking a cigarette in the future. The third stage (experimentation) is marked by the first puff of a cigarette. Experimentation continues with occasional smoking episodes until the adolescent has smoked 100 cigarettes. The lifetime smoking of that many cigarettes is a milestone used as a general estimate of the onset of nicotine dependence (stage four). Adolescents who reach the 100-cigarette point but discontinue smoking are classified as former smokers and, in this model, return to the nonsusceptible stage.

The original model of susceptibility, as proposed by Pierce and colleagues (1996), allowed adolescents who had already tried smoking to be classified as nonsusceptible if they expressed a firm commitment not to smoke in the future. Other models (Unger et al. 1997; Filice et al. 2003; Gritz et al. 2003; Sun et al. 2005) used the susceptibility concept to refer primarily to never smokers (who were classified as nonsusceptible), although youth who had already smoked were automatically classified as susceptible. Gilpin and colleagues (2001) added more intermediate stages to this model for adolescents, including puffers (have puffed on a cigarette but have not smoked a whole one), noncurrent experimenters (have smoked between 1 and 100 cigarettes but have not smoked during the past month), and noncurrent established smokers (have smoked more than 100 cigarettes but have not smoked during the past month). Other classifications and measures have been proposed (e.g., Kremers et al. 2001; Prokhorov et al. 2002) in attempts to predict which youth are more likely to become regular smokers as adults. The discussion later in this chapter will focus on specific variables within different levels of influence pertaining to adolescents and young adults but will not specifically incorporate the concept of stages, as these variables have generally not been examined relative to staging.

Considering Different Types of Tobacco Use

Most studies on the etiology of tobacco use have focused on cigarette smoking. Where available, information will be presented in this chapter on smokeless tobacco products (chewing tobacco and snuff), cigars, pipes, and other types of smoked tobacco (e.g., narghile [water pipe] smoking). Despite some differences in the social images associated with different types of tobacco products (e.g., smokeless tobacco is more strongly associated with playing sports, such as baseball, than is cigarette smoking) (Sussman et al. 1989), one could assume that the effects of the different predictors are reasonably similar across different types of tobacco products (e.g., risk taking is associated with use of both cigarettes and smokeless tobacco) (Sussman et al. 1989; Gilpin and Pierce 2003). This chapter examines the four levels of predictive factors of tobacco use and their associations with the onset of these different types of tobacco use and increased levels of use among youth.

Large Social and Physical Environments

The large social and physical environments include influences outside the individual, family, and immediate peer group that may either promote or restrict the use of tobacco. In general, these are more distal influences, including demographic factors that in some way affect a person's subjective perception about the acceptability of smoking, her or his beliefs about the social image that smoking conveys to others, and the availability of tobacco and places to smoke (Petraitis et al. 1995). Examples of these influences are described in detail below.

Large Social Environment

The large social environment defines the norms within a society about whether, when, and for whom smoking is acceptable. Social norms about smoking have changed substantially since the Surgeon General's report of 1964 (U.S. Department of Health, Education and Welfare 1964); in that year, 50% of the U.S. adult male population smoked (Garfinkel 1997), and smoking was becoming increasingly prevalent among women and youth (Cummings et al. 2002). Smoking was also acceptable in nearly all locations, such as worksites, movie theaters, hospitals, and airplanes (Americans for Nonsmokers' Rights 2005). Cigarettes were advertised in many different kinds of media and their use was tied to glamour, wealth, sex appeal, popularity, power, and good health (USDHHS 1994). Now, in the early twenty-first century, however, Americans, especially the better educated and more affluent, are much less likely to smoke (Morgan et al. 2007; Stuber et al. 2008) than in the middle of the twentieth century. According to the Centers for Disease Control and Prevention (CDC 2011), in 2010, 19.3% of adults in the United States were current smokers: 21.5% of men and 17.3% of women.

Religious and Cultural Influences

Religion

Religious doctrines can create social norms that constrain smoking behavior. However, the texts of most of the world's major religions were written before tobacco use became prevalent worldwide. Religious scholars have interpreted the texts and have issued official statements about whether tobacco use is consistent with the doctrines that have emanated from these texts (Simpson 2005). Christianity, Judaism, Buddhism, Hinduism, and Baha'i, for example, do not specifically forbid smoking but indicate that the practice is inconsistent with the teaching and writings of these varied religions, including not deliberately harming one's body, and religious leaders often suggest avoiding intoxicating and addictive substances that can impair judgment (World Health Organization [WHO] 1999). The Mormon religion forbids smoking and refuses smokers entry into the temple (Church of Jesus Christ of Latter-Day Saints 2006). In response to increasing evidence about the physical, social, and cultural effects of tobacco use, Islamic leaders have forbidden tobacco use in several countries (WHO, Eastern Mediterranean Regional Office 2001). In some religions, abstaining from tobacco use is viewed as a sign of the strength essential for religious piety (Bradby 2007).

In contrast, American Indian religions have used tobacco for healing and ceremonies but, in general, do not condone everyday smoking outside of spiritual contexts (Pego et al. 1995). A challenge for tobacco control in American Indian communities is to acknowledge that the sacred use of tobacco is culturally important while preventing recreational use and nicotine dependence. In some instances, tobacco control organizations have partnered with American Indian tribes to develop health education messages that distinguish the sacred use of tobacco from the habitual use of commercial tobacco products (American Indian Tobacco Education Network 2000). For other groups, religious beliefs and practices can create opportunities for smoking cessation during specific occasions such as Ramadan or Lent (Afifi 1997).

Across religious traditions, smoking tends to be less prevalent among those more likely to participate in religious activities. This association has been documented among Jews in Israel (Shmueli and Tamir 2007), Christians in the United States (Nasim et al. 2006; Mann et al. 2007; Turner-Musa and Lipscomb 2007), and adolescents who belong to various religious groups in the United States (Scott et al. 2006; Rostosky et al. 2007). Participation in religious or faith-based activities also appears to exert a uniquely protective effect against smoking escalation among adolescents who have already experimented with cigarettes (Choi et al. 2002; Van den Bree et al. 2004; Metzger et al. 2011). Some studies have distinguished between private religiosity (e.g., frequency of prayer, importance of religion) and public religiosity (e.g., frequency of attendance at religious services, frequency of youth group attendance) (Nonnemaker et al. 2003, 2006).

These studies found that both domains were protective but that private religiosity was more protective against smoking onset while public religiosity was more important for smoking escalation. By encouraging the bonding of adolescents to conventional social institutions and norms, religious involvement may discourage young people from affiliating with irreligious peers, who might introduce them to smoking. Furthermore, adolescents in observant families may be relatively more likely to be monitored closely by their parents, have more adult role models, and be more apt to participate in conventional community activities (Whooley et al. 2002; Bartkowski and Xu 2007).

Race, Ethnicity, and Culture

Chapter 3 of this report describes the epidemiology of smoking across racial and ethnic groups. This section focuses on people's subjective reactions to their racial, ethnic, and cultural identity, including perceived discrimination, the development of ethnic identity, and ethnic pride, in the context of tobacco use.

Research has identified multiple pathways through which race, ethnicity, and culture may influence youth smoking. Among other factors, patterns of youth smoking across racial and ethnic groups have been linked to processes of acculturation, racial/ethnic discrimination, ethnic identity, and cultural norms. Across several immigrant groups in the United States, tobacco use among adolescents increases as the groups acculturate to U.S. ways of living (Epstein et al. 1998; Chen et al. 1999a,b; Unger et al. 2000; Kaplan et al. 2001; Bethel and Schenker 2005; Weiss and Garbanati 2006; Choi et al. 2008). Compared with adolescents who are more oriented toward their families' culture of origin, adolescents who speak English, embrace the individualistic culture of the United States, and prefer U.S. media and customs are more likely to use tobacco (Lara et al. 2005). Among several ethnic minority groups, perceptions of discrimination are associated with an increased risk of smoking (Landrine and Klonoff 2000; Harris et al. 2006; Borrell et al. 2007; Chae et al. 2008; Horton and Loukas in press), perhaps because people are attempting to reduce the resulting emotional stress through self-medication. Conversely, ethnic pride was found to protect against smoking among African American youth (Wills et al. 2007), and a strong ethnic identity was found to be associated with a lower risk of tobacco use among youth in several ethnic/racial minority groups, including African Americans and Hispanics (Brook et al. 2007).

A person's subjective experiences of cultural identity and corresponding place in society may also be associated with whether and how often they use tobacco. Cultural norms against youth smoking within the African American community are thought to contribute to lower rates of youth smoking in this subgroup (Mermelstein 1999; Ellickson et al. 2004; Skinner et al. 2009; Oredein and Foulds 2011). For example, Clark and colleagues (1999) found that antitobacco socialization practices were more common in African American families than in White families. Relative to White households, African American households were more likely to set clear ground rules about smoking and to have had discussions with their children about these rules. Furthermore, Xue and colleagues (2007) found that African American youth living in predominantly African American neighborhoods were less likely to smoke than those living in predominantly White neighborhoods, suggesting that cultural norms in the African American community may operate to constrain youth smoking. Unfortunately, the adolescent advantage seen among African American youth with regard to smoking behavior is not carried into adulthood (Gardiner 2001).

As noted in Chapter 3, African Americans are more likely to smoke menthol cigarette brands than other major subgroups. The reasons probably include several factors (Allen and Unger 2007; Tobacco Products Scientific Advisory Committee 2011). First, the tobacco industry has advertised menthol cigarettes directly to African Americans by associating them with attractive or popular African American role models, including jazz and rap musicians (Gardiner 2004). Second, some African Americans may associate the taste and smell of menthol with folk remedies (e.g., menthol rubs and treatments for sore throat) that are popular in the southern United States. This association between menthol and folk medicine may cause some African Americans to believe, erroneously, that menthol cigarettes are less harmful than nonmenthol cigarettes (Castro 2004). Tobacco advertising perpetuates this belief by labeling menthol cigarettes as "cool" and "smooth." Third, because smoking menthol cigarettes has become normative among African Americans, some members of this minority group may smoke mentholated brands simply because their parents or older siblings smoked them or because they are readily available at home and from friends. The result perpetuates the stereotype that menthol cigarette brands are for African Americans, even among those who are several generations removed from the culture in which menthol was used medicinally.

Among youth in the United States, American Indians and Alaska Natives have the highest prevalence of tobacco use among all racial/ethnic subgroups (see Chapter 3), with usage rates comparable to those of adult American Indians and Alaska Natives (Hodge 2001). Traditionally,

American Indians have used tobacco in ceremonial practices to protect and heal sick individuals and, as a ceremonial tool, it is important in ritualistic exchanges used for social and peaceful purposes. This population also uses tobacco as an educational tool and often links it with storytelling (Hodge 2001). Strong social norms within these communities may support tobacco use, which can be even more of a problem when these communities, or individuals within them, are relocated to urban environments (Hodge and Nandy 2011). However, unlike the studies noted above for other populations, ethnic pride may not protect against tobacco use in this subgroup (LeMaster et al. 2002; Yu et al. 2005). It is also important to note that in epidemiologic and etiologic studies of tobacco use among American Indian and Alaska Native youth, "recreational" use of tobacco is typically not separated from ceremonial use in the design of the research study. Rather, the outcome variable in these studies is simply current (i.e., in the past 30 days) use of tobacco products (LeMaster et al. 2002; Yu et al. 2005; Osilla et al. 2007; Beebe et al. 2008; Yu 2011), and may overlook important differences in the etiology of tobacco use for these groups.

Cultural norms influence smoking in numerous other cultures as well. For example, in China, cigarettes are typically offered to guests as gifts, and refusing cigarettes is viewed as impolite. In that country, men and adolescent boys smoke together after meals as a way of cementing social bonds (Pan 2004; Chen et al. 2006; Grenard et al. 2006; Weiss et al. 2006). In addition, Westernization of developing countries, such as India, has been associated with more tobacco use (Stigler et al. 2010).

Gender

As discussed in Chapter 3, among adolescents there are only small differences by gender in the prevalence of cigarette smoking. In contrast, far larger differences are seen for two other forms of tobacco use. Boys are 4 to 10 times as likely as girls to have used smokeless tobacco in the past month (depending on age), and they are twice as likely as girls to have smoked cigars in the past month (Substance Abuse and Mental Health Services Administration [SAMHSA] 2009; Eaton et al. 2010; Johnston et al. 2011a). Differences between the genders in the prevalence of tobacco use also exist worldwide, but the magnitude of the disparities varies across countries (Warren et al. 2008). According to the 2000–2007 Global Youth Tobacco Surveys (GYTS), the prevalence of cigarette smoking was significantly higher among boys (than girls) in Africa, the Eastern Mediterranean, Southeast Asia, and the Western Pacific but not in the Americas and Europe. Among 151 GYTS sites, 87 showed no differences in cigarette smoking between the genders, 59 demonstrated a higher prevalence among boys, and 5 revealed a higher prevalence among girls. Boys were significantly more likely than girls to report using other tobacco products—pipes, water pipes, smokeless tobacco, and bidis—in the Americas, Europe, and Southeast Asia, but differences between the genders in the use of other tobacco products were not significant in other regions.

Qualitative and quantitative studies conducted in several cultural groups—including Indonesian adolescent boys (Ng et al. 2007), Korean American men (Kim et al. 2005), and Vietnamese young adults (Morrow et al. 2002)—indicate that smoking is viewed as a sign of manhood while being seen as inappropriate for females. In Europe, a study of three generations of women residing in Scotland found that those born in the 1950s associated smoking with femininity, but women born in the 1930s and 1970s did not (Hunt et al. 2004). This suggests generational fluctuations in gender-related norms, but other interpretations are possible.

As immigrant groups acculturate to the United States, gender-related differences in smoking prevalence for these groups may begin to diminish, often because increases are observed among females but not among males. For example, some research has found that acculturation is associated with an increase in smoking among Hispanic girls but not among boys (Epstein et al. 1998), and increases have been observed among Asian American girls but not among boys (Weiss and Garbanati 2006; Choi et al. 2008; Zhang and Wang 2008).

Socioeconomic Status

The SES of youth is derived from such measures as parental income or occupation, parental education, and access to resources. Population-based studies typically use indicators of SES (e.g., education or income) or self-reported measures (e.g., perceived social class or wealth relative to others), or both, to measure SES. Some studies also use measures of neighborhood- or school-level SES as the basis for individual SES.

Numerous studies worldwide have assessed the association between SES and smoking among adults and youth. Low SES has been associated with a high prevalence of smoking in population-based studies in France (Baumann et al. 2007), Germany (Haustein 2006), India (Neufeld et al. 2005; Thankappan and Thresia 2007; Mathur et al. 2008), and the United States (Flint and Novotny 1997). Moreover, even after controlling for individual-level sociodemographic factors, several studies found that the prevalence of smoking was highest in low-income neighborhoods in the the Czech Republic (Dragano et al. 2007), Germany (Dragano et al. 2007), New Zealand (Barnett 2000), the United Kingdom (Kleinschmidt et al. 1995;

Shohaimi et al. 2003), and United States (Cubbin et al. 2001; Tseng et al. 2001; Chuang et al. 2005a,b; Datta et al. 2006; Stimpson et al. 2007).

A growing body of evidence suggests that social and organizational characteristics of disadvantaged neighborhoods may contribute independently to higher rates of smoking, above and beyond the aggregate demographic profile of the community's residents. The "area effect" of smoking has been documented in both national and international studies (Kleinschmidt et al. 1995; Reijneveld 1998; Duncan et al. 1999). However, few studies have directly examined area effects in relation to youth and young adults. Some studies have found that low SES at the neighborhood level (based on income level by U.S./Canada Census block group) or school level was associated with an increased risk of adolescent smoking (Scarinci et al. 2002; Scragg et al. 2002; Matheson et al. 2011). Another study (Lee and Cubbin 2002) found that individual-level, but not neighborhood-level, SES was inversely associated with the prevalence of adolescent smoking. In contrast, one study (Chuang et al. 2005b) found that adolescents in low-SES neighborhoods had a low prevalence of smoking because they received more parental monitoring. Neighborhood characteristics such as social capital (i.e., community cohesion, civic engagement, social ties) have also been examined in relation to smoking. Evans and Kutcher (2010) examined the role of social capital in buffering the effects of neighborhood deprivation on youth smoking outcomes. They found that youth living in low-income communities with high levels of social capital had no excess risk of smoking compared to their more affluent counterparts. Conversely, Matheson and colleagues (2011) found that the effect of neighborhood-level deprivation on youth smoking risk was more pronounced among youth with a strong sense of community belonging, suggesting that in some cases community norms in disadvantaged neighborhoods may function to promote smoking behavior.

The association between SES and adolescent smoking may be moderated by racial, ethnic, and cultural factors. For example, in the National Longitudinal Study of Adolescent Health, neighborhood poverty was a risk factor for smoking among White, but not Black, adolescents (Nowlin and Colder 2007). In a similar analysis of data from the National Longitudinal Study of Adolescent Health, Goodman and Huang (2002) found that low SES was a risk factor for smoking among White adolescents but that high SES was a risk factor for smoking among non-White adolescents. In a study of adolescents in Ontario, Canada (Georgiades et al. 2006), low SES at the family level was a risk factor for smoking among adolescents, but this association was limited to native-born Canadians.

Although one assumes that low SES increases smoking rates, the relationship may actually be bidirectional, with early smoking leading to the attainment of low SES. For example, in a longitudinal study in Finland (Paavola et al. 2004), parents' SES was not a risk factor for adolescents' smoking behavior at age 13 years, but early smoking was a risk factor for adolescents' own low SES in the future (at ages 21 and 28 years). Early smoking also appeared to predict educational attainment later in life. For example, persons who smoked by age 13 years showed lower educational attainment by the age of 28 years.

Several studies have associated adolescents' access to spending money with their risk of smoking (e.g., Darling et al. 2006; Wong et al. 2007). A study of adolescents in Ontario, Canada (Wong et al. 2007), found that compared with students who had less than $10 in spending money per week, students with more than $20 per week were significantly more likely to be experimental smokers, students with more than $30 per week were significantly more likely to be current smokers, and students with more than $60 per week smoked significantly more cigarettes per day. In a New Zealand study (Scragg et al. 2002), students in low-SES schools reported receiving more spending money than students in high-SES schools, and their possession of spending money was a risk factor for smoking. In addition, adolescents who held jobs while going to school were found to have an increased risk of smoking (Wu et al. 2003), possibly because they had money to buy cigarettes or were influenced by their coworkers to smoke, or both.

Economic stress within a family may also be a risk factor for smoking. Unger and colleagues (2004) found that job loss by a parent predicted subsequent smoking among adolescents during a 1-year period. Other studies have found that unemployment (Haustein 2006) and self-reported financial stress in the household (Siahpush et al. 2003) were risk factors for smoking among adult family members, which might then affect children in the household. Employment status also represents a key risk factor for smoking among young adults. Young adults who are unemployed are more likely to be current, daily, and heavy smokers (Novo et al. 2000; Merline et al. 2004; Lawrence et al. 2007).

Educational and Academic Achievement

Among children and adolescents, low academic achievement is associated with smoking. Several studies have found that middle and high school students who smoked had lower grades than those who did not smoke (Dewey 1999; Sutherland and Shepherd 2001; Diego et al. 2003; Scal et al. 2003; Cox et al. 2007; Forrester et al. 2007; Tucker et al. 2008). In one study, this association appeared to be bidirectional, with poor grades preceding the onset of smoking and smoking preceding poor grades (Tucker et al. 2008). Youth who experience difficulties in school may also feel less connected to their school than do their high-achieving peers, putting them at greater risk for smoking. Connectedness with school (e.g., commitment to school, good relationships with teachers, and a feeling of belonging in school) (Libbey 2004) has been consistently associated with a reduced risk of smoking in the literature (Battistich and Hom 1997; Dornbusch et al. 2001; Scal et al. 2003; Dierker et al. 2004; Rasmussen et al. 2005; Bond et al. 2007).

Among young adults, college students have a lower prevalence of smoking than their peers who do not attend college. For example, in the 2003 Tobacco Use Supplement to the Current Population Survey (Green et al. 2007), current smoking prevalence among 18- to 24-year-olds who were enrolled in college or had college degrees was 14%, compared with 30% among those who did not attend college. In addition, those who did not go to college initiated smoking at younger ages and were less likely to have made quit attempts. According to the 2010 Monitoring the Future study (Johnston et al. 2011b), only 3.9% of college students reported smoking one-half pack or more of cigarettes per day, compared with 15.0% of their peers not in college. The disparity in smoking rates between college students and those not in college appears to precede actual college attendance. In their report, Johnston and colleagues (2011a) also found that the prevalence of smoking one-half pack of cigarettes or more per day was three times as high among high school seniors who were not planning to attend college (12%) as it was among seniors planning to attend college (3.1%). Table 4.1 demonstrates a strong relationship between educational attainment and smoking, with 57.0% of school dropouts aged 16–19 years estimated to be current smokers versus an estimate of 18.6% for those who remained in school (data are from 2006–2010).

School Environment

Youth spend approximately one-third of their time in the school environment (Hofferth and Sandberg 2001). The school setting is frequently used to educate youth about the risks of tobacco use and to implement antitobacco policies. See Chapter 6 ("Efforts to Prevent and Reduce Tobacco Use Among Young People") for a comprehensive discussion of school-based prevention programming. The current discussion is limited to features of the school environment that either promote or protect against youth smoking behavior. One such feature is the tolerance of smoking activity among students or teachers anywhere on the school grounds (Sussman et al. 1995; Ennett et al. 1997; Poulson et al. 2002). Youth who witness adolescents or adults smoking in public (e.g., school) are more likely to perceive smoking as a socially acceptable behavior (Alesci et al. 2003). In this regard, perceptions of prevalent tobacco use on school grounds may promote social norms that encourage smoking uptake and persistence. Studies comparing schools with high versus low smoking rates have found that attending a school with a relatively high smoking rate increases susceptibility to smoking among nonsmoking students (Leatherdale et al. 2006) and increases the odds of ever smoking and current smoking (Ennett et al. 1997; Leatherdale and Manske 2005; Leatherdale et al. 2005). School-based antitobacco policies provide school officials with a mechanism to create a tobacco-free school environment and reduce perceived acceptability of smoking (USDHHS 1994). A growing body of evidence suggests that school smoking restrictions can curb youth smoking behavior, both on and off school premises, when strictly enforced (Evans-Whipp et al. 2004). Studies have shown that consistent enforcement of school tobacco policies results in fewer observations of smoking on school grounds, as well as lower rates of ever smoking and current smoking (Wakefield et al. 2000; Griesbach et al. 2002; Piontek et al. 2008; Adams et al. 2009; Lipperman-Kreda et al. 2009; Lovato et al. 2010). Importantly, Leatherdale and colleagues (2005; Leatherdale and Manske 2005) noted that social influences (e.g., peer smoking, parental smoking) and school factors (e.g., school smoking prevalence) make independent contributions to youth smoking behavior and thus recommend that interventions target both at-risk schools and at-risk students.

Schools are regulated by laws and policies at national, state, district, and school levels. Thus, a district may have more stringent or specific policies than the state in which it resides. Further, individual schools may implement policies beyond those required by the state or district. CDC's School Health Policies and Programs Study, which collects data on school policies from all states and representative samples of school districts and schools every 6 years, shows that the majority of states (90.2%) and districts (99.4%) prohibited cigarette smoking by students in school buildings in 2006 (Jones et al. 2007). However, fewer prohibited cigarette smoking by faculty and staff in school buildings (74.5% of states and 94.3% of districts). Further, the prevalence of restrictions on smoking in other settings and smokeless tobacco use was lower. Only 38.0% of states and 55.4% of sampled districts prohibited all tobacco use during any school-related activity. Similarly, 63.6% of schools (elementary, middle, and high schools) prohibited all tobacco use during school-related activities in 2006.

Table 4.1 Prevalence of smoking in previous month among adolescents aged 16–19 years who have not completed 12th grade, by enrollment status in school; National Survey on Drug Use and Health (NSDUH) 2006–2010; United States

	Enrolled in school but have not completed 12th grade % (95% CI)	Not currently enrolled in school and have not completed 12th grade % (95% CI)
Overall	18.6 (18.1–19.1)	57.0 (54.9–59.2)
Gender		
Male	19.6 (18.9–20.4)	60.1 (57.2–62.9)
Female	17.4 (16.7–18.1)	52.6 (49.4–55.7)
Age (in years)		
16	14.1 (13.5–14.8)	46.0 (37.7–54.5)
17	18.9 (18.1–19.7)	52.3 (47.9–56.7)
18	26.1 (24.7–27.6)	58.9 (55.2–62.4)
19	38.4 (34.1–42.9)	58.5 (55.3–61.6)
Race/ethnicity		
White	22.0 (21.4–22.7)	71.1 (68.5–73.6)
Male	22.5 (21.6–23.5)	72.1 (68.5–75.4)
Female	21.5 (20.6–22.4)	69.8 (66.1–73.3)
Black or African American	11.1 (10.1–12.2)	48.3 (43.2–53.4)
Male	13.5 (12.0–15.2)	53.9 (46.9–60.8)
Female	8.5 (7.3–9.9)	38.8 (31.5–46.6)
Hispanic or Latino	15.1 (14.0–16.3)	38.2 (34.3–42.2)
Male	17.2 (15.5–19.0)	44.9 (39.7–50.3)
Female	12.8 (11.3–14.5)	27.1 (21.7–33.2)
Other[a]	15.1 (13.4–17.1)	65.2 (55.1–74.1)
Male	15.4 (13.1–18.0)	NR
Female	14.8 (12.4–17.6)	NR
Last grade completed		
9th or lower	17.1 (16.1–18.2)	52.3 (48.6–55.9)
10th	16.4 (15.7–17.2)	57.2 (53.5–60.9)
11th	21.2 (20.4–22.1)	61.5 (58.1–64.9)

Source: 2006–2010 NSDUH: Substance Abuse and Mental Health Services Administration (unpublished data).
Note: **CI** = confidence interval; **NR** = low precision, no estimate reported.
[a]Includes Asians, American Indians or Alaska Natives, Native Hawaiians or Other Pacific Islanders, and persons of two or more races/ethnicities.

In addition to school characteristics, increasing attention is being paid to the role of contextual factors within the school neighborhood. Density of tobacco outlets in proximity to schools has been investigated as a possible risk factor for youth smoking. Henriksen and colleagues (2008) found that the prevalence of smoking was 3.2 percentage points higher among students in schools with the highest density of surrounding tobacco retailers compared with students in schools without any tobacco retail outlets. Chan and Leatherdale (2011) found that the number of tobacco retailers surrounding a school increased students' susceptibility to future smoking. Leatherdale and Strath (2007) found a positive association between the density of tobacco retailers surrounding a school and the likelihood that underage minors would purchase their own cigarettes. Between-school variability in smoking prevalence has also been associated with exposure to tobacco industry promotional and advertising activities in school neighborhoods. Tobacco retail outlets located near schools with higher smoking prevalence had significantly lower cigarettes prices, fewer government-sponsored health warnings, and more in-store tobacco promotions, relative to those located near schools with lower smoking prevalence (Lovato et al. 2007).

Extracurricular and Organized Activities

Adolescents' normative development often includes participation in a wide range of organized group activities (e.g., athletics, school clubs, extracurricular) (Dye and Johnson 2006; Mahoney et al. 2006). Empirical studies have been conducted to examine the effects of different organized activities on adolescents' involvement in substance use, including cigarette smoking. Overall, participation in organized group activities appears to be protective against youth tobacco use (Elder et al. 2000). In particular, team sports involvement has been linked to lower levels of adolescent cigarette smoking (Page et al. 1998; Melnick et al. 2001), with consistent sports involvement (involvement over consecutive years) having a greater influence on smoking behavior than does intermittent participation (Rodriguez and McGovern 2004). In one of the only prospective studies of activity involvement using multiple waves of data (baseline, 15 months, and 24 months), Metzger and colleagues (2011) examined the relation between involvement in organized activities, problem peer associations, and smoking escalation among a sample of experimenting smokers. Participation in team sports directly reduced smoking behavior among current users for boys but not for girls. Among girls, participation in school clubs indirectly reduced smoking behavior via reduced exposure to problem peers.

Large Physical Environment

The large physical environment, or built environment, involves features of public and private spaces that may make tobacco use more or less tolerated or enjoyable. Features of the environment that promote smoking include the tolerance of this activity in public spaces; proximity to entertainment, recreation, and social interaction; and locations that are relatively unlikely to be monitored by adults. In contrast, two of the major goals of antismoking policies (beyond the protection of nonsmokers from exposure to secondhand smoke) are to establish antismoking social norms and to discourage smoking by forcing smokers to refrain from smoking in indoor public places, including indoor workplaces and public housing (Epstein et al. 1999; Levy and Friend 2001; Winickoff et al. 2010). Thus, increases in smoke-free indoor-air policies have logically helped to recast smoking as an activity that can be performed only in specific areas that are typically segregated from entertainment and business locations (Gilpin et al. 2004). Restrictions may create perceptions of social disapproval among both adults and youth, and structuring the physical environment to make it inconvenient for youth to smoke may influence them to not take up tobacco use (Alamar and Glantz 2006).

Another important aspect of the physical environment is the relative accessibility of tobacco products. Strict enforcement of policies that ban retail sales of cigarettes to minors, sales of cigarettes using vending machines, and other means by which youth can gain access to tobacco in the commercial setting can limit their opportunities to obtain these products (Jason et al. 1996, 2008; Rigotti et al. 1997; Stead and Lancaster 2000). The influence of tobacco industry practices is considered in great detail in Chapter 5. Here, tobacco advertising is considered only briefly. The Master Settlement Agreement from 1998 severely restricted cigarette and smokeless tobacco advertising in several venues, including billboards and print media, that have substantial youth readership (Ruel et al. 2004), but tobacco advertising is still ubiquitous in many other venues, such as convenience stores, grocery stores, and bars, and in magazines (Pierce 2007; National Cancer Institute [NCI] 2008). In addition to signs that advertise specific cigarette brands, tobacco advertising can appear on functional items that are distributed to store owners, such as trash cans or change trays near cash registers, napkins and decorations in bars, and logos on race cars or sports uniforms (CDC 2008). (While still subject to a legal challenge, the FDA rule prohibits the distribution of cigarette or smokeless tobacco branded functional items, and it prohibits brand name sponsorship of athletic events or teams [*Federal Register* 1996; 2010]). Thus, even after the Master Settlement Agreement, opportunities for exposure to tobacco brand names and images are widespread. Numerous studies have found that youth who recall more exposure to tobacco advertising are more likely to experiment with smoking or to hold favorable attitudes toward it (DiFranza et al. 2006). Furthermore, a meta-analysis of 51 studies (Wellman et al. 2006) found that exposure to protobacco marketing and media significantly increased the odds among youth of holding positive attitudes toward tobacco use (odds ratio [OR] = 1.51; 95% confidence interval [CI], 1.08–2.13) as well as the odds of initiating tobacco use (OR = 2.23; 95% CI, 1.79–2.77).

Youth are also exposed to tobacco imagery through product placements in movies, television shows, and video games. Exposure to fictional characters who smoke can create an exaggerated social norm about the prevalence and acceptability of smoking (Sargent et al. 2000). Indeed, longitudinal studies have found that adolescents whose favorite movie stars smoke on screen or who are exposed to a large number of movies portraying smokers are at a high risk of smoking initiation (Sargent et al. 2000; Distefan et al. 2004). For example, among 10- to 14-year-old adolescents, those in the highest quartile of exposure to smoking in movies were 2.6 times as likely to initiate smoking as were those in the lowest quartile (Sargent et al. 2005). Tobacco is also promoted to youth on the Internet through social media and online tobacco retailers and the informal Web sites and chat rooms that glamorize the smoking lifestyle and culture (Ribisl et al. 2003).

Research on the effects of tobacco advertising on smoking behavior is methodologically challenging, although recent approaches have provided more valid and reliable data than were available in earlier years. Still, survey measures of exposure to tobacco advertising may be inaccurate. Their validity requires the respondent to see an ad, recognize it as a tobacco ad, encode the image in memory, and retrieve the image from memory when prompted by a survey question (Unger et al. 2001). Moreover, tobacco advertising may affect tobacco-related attitudes and behaviors without the respondent's conscious awareness or recall. To avoid this problem, some studies have assessed attitudes about tobacco after having placed, and randomly assigned, study participants in artificial laboratory settings to view either tobacco advertisements or neutral stimuli (e.g., Shadel et al. 2008). These studies have internal validity but lack external validity. Another approach is to use time-series data to examine the effects of bans on tobacco advertising on the subsequent prevalence of smoking. A review of 24 such studies (Quentin et al. 2007) concluded that, overall, bans on tobacco advertising produce modest decreases in tobacco consumption, even though the changes found by the authors were not statistically significant for all of the studies. More information about the effects of tobacco advertising, promotional activities, and bans on advertising is presented in Chapters 5 and 6.

Summary

The large social environment incorporates numerous macrolevel social processes that affect tobacco use by influencing social norms relating to gender role, religion, and culture as well as norms for specific segments of the population, such as those with low SES or modest educational attainment. For most of the twentieth century, tobacco use was more socially acceptable for men than for women in the United States. In recent decades, however, such differences between the genders have greatly narrowed, although in most ethnic groups, boys and young men are still more likely than girls and young women to use certain forms of tobacco (smokeless tobacco, cigars, and pipes).

In general, religious participation protects against tobacco use. Some religions have specific prohibitions against tobacco use, while others encourage certain social behaviors to prevent youth from experimenting with substance use and rebellious actions. American Indians use tobacco as a sacred substance, but many tribes attempt to maintain a distinction between the sacred use of traditional homegrown tobacco and the use of commercially produced tobacco.

Other chapters in this report present detailed information about variations in tobacco use among different racial/ethnic groups. The present chapter points out the consistent finding that racial/ethnic pride and a strong ethnic identity generally protect against tobacco use, but perceptions of racial/ethnic discrimination are a risk factor for such use. Additional research is needed to understand the psychological and cognitive mechanisms through which perceptions of racial/ethnic identity influence decisions about tobacco use.

The differences in tobacco use between the genders are more pronounced in many other countries than they are in the United States (Warren et al. 2008). Immigrants from such countries bring their norms for gender roles with them when they move to the United States, and thus, many immigrant groups show a higher prevalence of smoking among males than among females. As immigrants acculturate, these gender-based differences narrow, generally because tobacco use among females often increases. Therefore, immigrant girls and young women who acculturate to the United States represent a higher-risk group for tobacco use.

Mainstream U.S. culture has increasingly embraced an antitobacco norm. As a result, only about one in five American adults now use tobacco, but use is far more common among those of low SES or low educational achievement. Among adolescents, poor school achievement is associated with both low SES and tobacco use. However, the association between educational achievement and tobacco use may be bidirectional, or another variable, such as risk taking, may influence educational attainment while also being tied to smoking. Furthermore, neighborhood-level risk factors may contribute to the probability of youth smoking, in excess of the risk conferred by individual-level influences. The large physical environment contains features that facilitate or impede tobacco use, including the availability of comfortable and convenient places to smoke, the availability of or access to tobacco products, and cues from the media to use tobacco. In general, the available evidence suggests that (1) nonsmoking policies create antismoking social norms and decrease smoking behavior, and (2) exposure to protobacco media messages, particularly in movies or advertising, increases perceptions of the acceptability of smoking and thus increases smoking behavior. More details about the effects of changes in the larger social and physical environments are provided in Chapter 6.

Small Social Groups

The family and peer groups are the two most important small social groups in the development of young people and their use of tobacco. This section focuses on the influence of these social groups on youth and, when research is available, on young adults.

Homogeneity of Tobacco Use Among Adolescents and Friends

Multiple cross-sectional and longitudinal studies have shown that peer factors—in particular, friends' smoking behavior and adolescents' perceptions of their friends' smoking behavior—are associated with adolescents' own smoking (Conrad et al. 1992; USDHHS 1994; Jackson 1997; Tyas and Pederson 1998; Alesci et al. 2003; Kobus 2003; Ali and Dwyer 2009; McVicar 2011; Villanti et al. 2011). The similarity, or homogeneity, of smoking patterns for adolescents and their friends has led many researchers to infer that peers influence adolescent smoking (Bauman and Ennett 1996; Kobus 2003; Arnett 2007). The mechanism of influence most often postulated is social learning (Bandura 1977b; Petraitis et al. 1995), whereby adolescents learn about tobacco use by observing peers who use tobacco and are reinforced for using tobacco by perceiving apparent advantages, such as gaining acceptance by peers or establishing a particular social identity. Other mechanisms of transmission from peers are direct pressure to smoke and offers of cigarettes and other tobacco products. However, direct peer pressure is infrequently documented as a risk factor for smoking (Urberg et al. 1990; Sussman et al. 1993; Hoving et al. 2007). Adolescents are more likely, however, to obtain cigarettes from peers than from adults or through commercial transactions (Harrison et al. 2000; Forster et al. 2003; White et al. 2005; Robinson et al. 2006a), and youth who reported receiving offers of cigarettes from friends were more likely to initiate smoking and progress to experimentation (Flay et al. 1998).

Cross-sectional studies cannot reveal whether youth are influenced to smoke by their friends or whether they choose friends on the basis of their smoking status (Bauman and Ennet 1996; Kobus 2003; Arnett 2007). Longitudinal studies, however, demonstrate that having friends who smoke is a consistent predictor of tobacco use: youth who report having more friends who smoke (than friends who do not smoke) are more likely to have initiated or to subsequently initiate smoking (Flay et al. 1994; Jackson et al. 1998; Scal et al. 2003) or to progress to higher levels of smoking (Wang 2001; Dierker et al. 2004; Audrain-McGovern et al. 2006a–c). Also, perceptions of friends' smoking predict developmental trajectories of smoking (Chassin et al. 2000; Audrain-McGovern et al. 2004; Abroms et al. 2005), and according to both cross-sectional (Boyle et al. 1997) and longitudinal (Tomar and Giovino 1998) studies, youth who perceive that their peers use smokeless tobacco are at increased risk of using that product.

Two studies (Killen et al. 1997; Urberg et al. 1997) found that having friends who smoke influences the initiation of smoking among both adolescent boys and girls, and two other studies (Hu et al. 1995; Flay et al. 1998) found the effects of friends' smoking to be stronger for girls than for boys. In addition, friends' smoking may be more salient for White than for Black youth (Headen et al. 1991; Landrine et al. 1994; Robinson et al. 2006b), although several studies observed common effects of friends' smoking on White and minority youth (Flay et al. 1994; Gritz et al. 2003; Kandel et al. 2004).

According to two studies (Chassin et al. 1986; Bauman et al. 2001), the influence of friends' smoking on progression of smoking stage remains constant throughout adolescence, although some studies suggest that peer influence may decrease as the levels of prior smoking by the adolescent increase (Hu et al. 1995), with transitions in smoking stage (Flay et al. 1998; Bricker et al. 2006b), and during later stages of adolescence (Chassin et al. 2000; Tucker et al. 2003).

Furthermore, several studies have suggested that the influence of friends' smoking fails to predict initiation of smoking in young adulthood (Ellickson et al. 2001; Choi et al. 2003; Tercyak et al. 2007; White et al. 2007), but the findings of these studies have been inconsistent. Several other studies observed no influence of friends' smoking on various measures of smoking in young adults (Oygard et al. 1995; Brook et al. 1997; Wetter et al. 2004; Patton et al. 2006), but other studies did observe such an influence (West et al. 1999; Andrews et al. 2002; Hu et al. 2006; Pederson et al. 2007; Tucker et al. 2008). Explanations for the mixed findings may rest on differences in the smoking measures examined (e.g., current smoking, daily smoking, nicotine dependence) and the timeframe for measuring the influence of friends' smoking, whether adolescence or closer to young adulthood. West and colleagues (1999), for example, found that friends' smoking at 18 years of age, but not at 15 years of age, predicted smoking among young adults between the ages of 18 and 21 years. Overall, however, studies suggest that friends' smoking may be less relevant to the initiation and progression of smoking during young adulthood than during adolescence.

Disapproval among one's peers is one of the few peer factors, other than friends' smoking, that longitudinal studies have examined in both adolescents and young adults. In general, adolescents who perceive that their friends disapprove of smoking are less likely than their peers (who perceive that their friends approve of smoking) to initiate smoking (Chassin et al. 1986; Wang et al. 1999; Gritz et al. 2003). However, some studies have found no effects of peer disapproval on initiation (Flay et al. 1994; Carvajal and Granillo 2006). A longitudinal study of college students found that peer disapproval predicted decreased progression in smoking but not its initiation (Choi et al. 2003). Another study, however, found no effects of peer disapproval of smoking on transition to regular smoking between grade 12 and 23 years of age (Tucker et al. 2003).

Most longitudinal studies of tobacco use among youth have not measured changes in friendships or tobacco use by friends. Clearly, these data are needed to assess the contribution of selection of friends to the homogeneity of tobacco use among adolescents and their friends. Evidence dating from the late 1970s and 1980s suggests that adolescents are influenced to smoke by their friends and to select friends with similar tobacco use (Cohen 1977; Fisher and Bauman 1988). Fisher and Bauman (1988) examined the contributions of selection of friends and socialization (influence by friends) to homogeneity of cigarette smoking in adolescent friendship pairs; the authors collected linked information about the identity of friends and daily smoking from seventh and ninth graders at two time points 1 year apart. Selection effects, with smokers acquiring friends who smoked and nonsmokers acquiring friends who did not, were stronger than the effects of socialization as reflected by smokers influencing nonsmoking friends to smoke.

In a cohort of students assessed five times from grades six to nine, Simons-Morton and colleagues (2004) used growth modeling methods to examine relationships between the progression of smoking stage and affiliation with friends who smoked. Findings were consistent with the idea of selection effects but not with socialization effects; that is, adolescents with higher initial levels of smoking acquired over time more friends who smoked, but having friends who smoked did not predict progression in smoking. Similarly, in a cohort of 6,527 adolescents surveyed at the ages of 13, 16, 18, and 23 years, Tucker and colleagues (2008) estimated adolescents' and their friends' cigarette smoking (as well as parental smoking and approval of smoking). The study found reciprocal associations between smoking by youth and smoking by their peers. In support of the concept of selective affiliation, having friends who smoked was predicted at all ages by prior smoking of the adolescent, but smoking by peers (socialization) predicted smoking among young people only when adolescents reached 23 years of age.

Other longitudinal studies on similarities in cigarette smoking within friendship groups or among friends have found evidence for both selection and socialization processes, with the two processes contributing about equally (Ennett and Bauman 1994; Mercken et al. 2007; Go et al. 2010), or with stronger evidence for selection than for socialization effects (Engels et al. 1997, 1999, 2004; Wang et al. 2000; de Vries et al. 2006; Hoffman et al. 2007; Mercken et al. 2009, 2010). In one of the few studies of selection and socialization processes among college students, McCabe and colleagues (2005) found that current cigarette use was higher among fraternity and sorority members than among students who did not belong to these organizations but that the difference could be attributed to selection effects rather than to the influence of membership.

For adolescents, both selection (of friends) and socialization likely contribute to the homogeneity of tobacco use among friends. For example, Hall and Valente (2007), using social network methods to explore peer influence (socialization) and peer selection simultaneously, demonstrated effects of the selection of friends (i.e., choosing relatively more friends who smoked) in sixth grade on smoking behavior in seventh grade. At the same time, processes of influence (in this case being selected as a friend by relatively more smokers) in the sixth grade shaped the peer environment in the seventh grade and increased susceptibility to smoking in that grade.

An important implication of the findings on the contribution of selection of friends to the homogeneity of tobacco use among peers is that when adolescents' inclination to select friends similar to themselves with regard to smoking is not considered, whether in cross-sectional or longitudinal studies, the effects of peer influence through selection may be overstated. At the same time, when the role of peer influence through selection is inflated, explanatory variables in the social environment other than selection of friends (e.g., characteristics of one's family as well as tobacco advertising and other attributes of the media) may be inappropriately discounted (Bauman and Ennett 1996; Kobus 2003; de Vries et al. 2006; Arnett 2007).

Aside from the selection and socialization processes, external factors may account for some similarities in tobacco use among adolescent friends. Adolescent friendships align along demographic, behavioral, and attitudinal characteristics, with the background characteristics of race/ethnicity, gender, and age or grade in school forming the largest divides (Kandel 1978; Shrum and Creek 1987; McPherson et al. 2001). Eiser and colleagues (1991) found that youth between the ages of 11 and 16 years strongly resembled their three matched friends on smoking behavior, background attributes, and a range of other attitudinal and behavioral characteristics. Future studies should continue to use analytic models that control for background and other shared characteristics to accurately assess the contributions of peers to tobacco use.

Interaction-Based Versus Identity-Based Peer Groups

Assessing the role of peers in tobacco use has become increasingly complicated because adolescents interact (network) within multiple peer groups and these multiple interactions may generate different personal perceptions within each group network (Brown 2004). Investigating interaction-based social networks is a relatively recent but growing area of inquiry in adolescent tobacco use and is accomplished by analyzing friendship linkages (Kobus 2003; Valente et al. 2004; Ennett et al. 2006). In contrast, studies of peer group identification have a long history in research on tobacco use among youth and demonstrate that adolescents' perceptions of their peers' and their own social identity are related to tobacco use (Sussman et al. 2007). Both social network and peer group identification studies are concerned with relating attributes of the larger peer group, typically all same-school peers, to adolescent tobacco use. When the larger peer network is the focus, investigating adolescent social position, social standing, reputation, and perceived norms becomes a salient consideration.

Peer Social Networks

Most social network studies of tobacco use among youth measure social networks within schools because most friendships are anchored at the school and the school is the easiest location in which to measure whole groups (Blyth et al. 1982). Youth networks, however, also exist outside of schools—in neighborhoods, sports leagues, clubs, faith organizations, cyberspace, and other places. A social network can be described as the entire set of relationships identified by adolescents' naming of other youth as friends or best friends. Researchers map these nominations by youth to discover nonrandom relational patterns of direct and indirect links between adolescents and reciprocated (mutual friendship) and absent (no friendship) linkages. Studies of social networks assume that relational patterns have implications for behavior (Wasserman and Faust 1994), and social network analysis is a set of techniques with specific mathematical algorithms and associated software (Valente et al. 2004). The techniques are used to identify and measure the characteristics of relational patterns, such as the social position of each adolescent in the network or the density of relationships in the network (Wasserman and Faust 1994; Valente et al. 2004).

An advantage of data obtained on social networks is that measures of the friends' tobacco use can be based on the friends' own reports rather than on adolescents' perceptions of their friends' use. Adolescents tend to project their own tobacco use behavior onto their friends, thereby spuriously inflating the similarity in tobacco use between adolescents and their friends (Sherman et al. 1983; Bauman and Fisher 1986; Urberg et al. 1990; Bauman and Ennett 1996). By using social network data, investigators can avoid such bias.

From the pattern of friendship links in a social network, adolescents can be categorized into three mutually exclusive social positions (Shrum and Creek 1987; Brown 2004): group members; liaisons or peripherals (those who have friendships with adolescents in different groups while not belonging to any group); and relative outsiders or isolates. Analyses of social networks have shown groups to be generally homogeneous in smoking behavior, whether characterized as predominantly smoking or nonsmoking (Ennett et al. 1994; Urberg et al. 1997; Pearson and Michell 2000). However, several studies have found that, with some qualifications, adolescents who are group members or liaisons are less likely to smoke than adolescents who are relative isolates (Ennett and Bauman 1993; Pearson and Michell 2000; Abel et al. 2002; Fang et al. 2003; Pearson et al. 2006). Forming relationships with peers may indicate social competence in navigating the school social environment and in one study appeared to be protective against smoking when compared with social marginalization (Ennett et al. 2008). In support of this possibility, multiple studies that did not use social network methods have suggested that higher social and personal competencies protect against smoking (e.g., Botvin et al. 1993; Jackson et al. 1994; Epstein et al. 2000; Finkelstein et al. 2006).

Other studies, however, found that liaisons had higher rates of smoking than did relative isolates or group members (Henry and Kobus 2007) and that liaisons (Ennett and Bauman 1994) and group peripherals (Pearson and Michell 2000) with links to smoking groups had an increased likelihood of smoking (versus those with links to nonsmoking groups). Pollard and colleagues (2010) used a multimethod analytic approach to determine whether adolescents' friendship network position (i.e., group member, liaison, or isolate) predicted membership in one of six developmental smoking trajectories. Belonging to a smoking group, or having ties to a smoking group, predicted membership in higher use smoking trajectory groups over a 6-year period. Importantly, network position accounted for variance in smoking trajectory group above and beyond that which could be explained simply by the number of smoking friends. Using a different measurement approach, Aloise-Young and colleagues (1994) found that group outsiders with a best-friend smoker were significantly more likely to become smokers 1 year later than group members with a best-friend smoker. Dishion and colleagues (1999) found that youth with fewer social skills may gravitate to peers and groups characterized by smoking and initiate smoking as a way of fitting in. Indeed, several studies point to adolescents' desire for gaining acceptance or approval by their peers as a reason for smoking (Barton et al. 1982; Perry et al. 1987; NCI 2008).

Social networks are the point of reference for an adolescent's social standing, as indicated by the youth's popularity or centrality. Results of the few social network studies that have examined whether elevated standing in the social network is associated with smoking have been inconsistent, with findings that have found greater popularity to be predictive of smoking initiation (Valente et al. 2005), no relationship to increases in cigarette smoking (Ennett et al. 2006), and a dependence on other attributes of the school environment (Alexander et al. 2001; Pearson et al. 2006) for its effect on smoking. For example, Alexander and colleagues (2001) found that the level of smoking in the school moderated the association between popularity and current smoking, such that greater popularity was associated with lower risk of smoking in schools with a lower prevalence of smoking but with a higher risk of smoking in schools with a higher prevalence of smoking.

Similar to the findings of social network studies, studies of sociometric status suggest that smoking is influenced by social marginalization and by social impact. In studies of sociometric status, youth name the peers they like the most and the least, and researchers use the choices to classify or rate individuals as popular (well liked and not often disliked), rejected (disliked and not often liked), neglected (rarely mentioned as liked or disliked), controversial (frequently mentioned as liked and disliked), or average (Brown 2004). In a longitudinal sample of 7th, 8th, and 9th graders, youth classified as rejected and controversial were more likely than average youth to report lifetime smoking in 7th grade and to begin smoking 1 year later, while popular youth were marginally less likely than average youth to report ever smoking (Aloise-Young and Kaeppner 2005). Similar results were reported in a long-term study of boys in which the onset of smoking was more common in 5th through 10th grades among those who, in 4th grade, received more "disliking" than "liking" nominations (Dishion et al. 1999) and were classified as rejected and isolated (Dishion et al. 1995). Moreover, in a long-term longitudinal study of Swedish youth, students rated by teachers as unpopular in school were more likely to smoke at 16 years of age, and being unpopular during adolescence had an indirect effect on smoking in young adulthood (Novak et al. 2007).

Identification with a Peer Group

Adolescents use such factors as perceived popularity, academic inclination, participation in athletics, substance use, and other behaviors to place themselves and their peers into peer groups or "peer crowds" (Brown 2004; Sussman et al. 2007). Identifying youth with a particular type of peer group, such as "nerds" or "jocks," makes a statement about that individual's identity within youth culture, although it may not reflect direct interactions among adolescents in the group.

In an early study of peer group identity, Mosbach and Leventhal (1988) found that higher percentages of current smoking were reported by seventh and eighth graders self-identified as "dirts," who were mainly boys who smoked cigarettes, used other drugs, were poor students, and engaged in a variety of problem behaviors (62.5% prevalence of smoking among this group), and "hotshots," who were popular and academically successful students (27.8%), than by "regulars," who did not belong to any group and were typical of junior high students (9.2%), and "jocks," those with a strong interest in organized sports (4.3%). Findings from a review of identification research in peer groups mirrored these results (Sussman et al. 2007). This review collapsed group names across studies into five general categories of peer groups: elites, athletes, academics, deviants, and others. Among the 14 studies that investigated cigarette smoking, 13 found that youth in the "deviants" group were most likely to smoke; in the remaining study, in which a deviant group was not identified, students in the "elites" group were most likely to smoke. In another analysis of the same 14 studies, "elites" were also very likely to smoke, but were not as likely to do so as deviants (Sussman et al. 2007). A concern with the studies on peer group identity is the possible redundancy in measurement of drug use or smoking stemming from the fact that adolescents may use drug behaviors to identify and differentiate peer groups. Indeed, in several studies, "druggies" were one of the peer groups included under the "deviant" classification (Sussman et al. 2007). Clearly, if smoking contributes to peer group identity, the correlation between peer group identity and smoking will be inflated. This issue can be reduced in importance, however, in longitudinal studies that control for adolescents' prior smoking behavior when predicting smoking from peer group identity.

Only two of the studies, one from 1994 and the other from 2000, that were reviewed by Sussman and colleagues were longitudinal. After adjusting for prior smoking, one study found that identification as a member of a deviant group predicted cigarette smoking 1 year later (Sussman et al. 1994), but no effects were found in the other study (Sussman et al. 2000). However, the likelihood of detecting effects on smoking among those self-identified in the deviant group may have been compromised by the restriction of the sample to youth already identified as high risk. Thus, this sample may have had less variability in deviance across peer groups than other samples of youth have had.

Normative Expectations of Peers

A large peer group, typically peers at school, is generally the reference group that adolescents use to estimate the prevalence of smoking among their peers, and this is used as an indication of their normative expectations about smoking (Sherman et al. 1983; Sussman et al. 1988; Botvin et al. 1992b). As with their estimates of smoking by close friends, adolescents' estimates of the prevalence of peer smoking reflect to some degree a projection of their own behavior in a phenomenon known as the "false consensus effect" (i.e., assuming in error that others do the same thing as one does) (Sherman et al. 1983; Bauman et al. 1992; Botvin et al. 1992b). Regardless of their own smoking status, adolescents tend to overestimate actual smoking rates among their peers, and overestimation of these rates has predicted the initiation of smoking (Botvin et al. 1992a; Simons-Morton 2002; Forrester et al. 2007), experimentation (Flay et al. 1998), and progression in smoking stage (Simons-Morton and Haynie 2003). Cunningham and Selby (2007) found that young adult smokers exhibited the same tendency to overestimate the prevalence of smoking among their peers. Earlier, Ellickson and colleagues (2003) conducted a rare study that investigated both the actual and perceived school-level prevalence of smoking. The study adjusted for individual smoking at baseline and reports of close friends' smoking. The findings indicated that the seventh graders' perceived prevalence of smoking, but not the actual prevalence of smoking among their peers, predicted smoking 1 year later among the seventh graders in this study. The results suggest that adolescents' perceptions of their peers' smoking matter more to their own smoking behaviors than what their peers are actually doing.

Family Context

The family is a source of social, genetic, and biological factors (see "Genetic Factors and Neurobiological and Neurodevelopmental Processes" later in this chapter), and its effects must be assessed as well. As with the peer context, the content and quality of interactions between youth and their family members, rather than the actions of parents alone, contribute to tobacco use among youth. Studies of the family context have focused primarily on four factors: smoking by parents and older siblings, dimensions of parenting behavior, family relationships, and parental reactions to smoking by their children (Conrad et al. 1992; Tyas and Pederson 1998; Avenevoli and Merikangas 2003).

Smoking by parents is the most frequently assessed parental risk factor for smoking by youth, given the central role that parents serve in young people's lives, but this factor has been assessed much less often in studies of young adults. Many studies have found that exposure to parental smoking is predictive of the onset, progression, and developmental trajectories of smoking by youth (e.g., Biglan et al. 1995; den Exter Blokland et al. 2004; Hill et al. 2005; Brook et al. 2006; Peterson et al. 2006; Chassin et al. 2008; Gilman et al. 2009), but other studies have failed to find any such effects (e.g., Cohen et al. 1994; Flay et al. 1994; Distefan et al. 1998). In addition, several studies suggest that the influence of exposure to parental smoking persists into young adulthood (Oygard et al. 1995; Chassin et al. 1996, 2000; Brook et al. 1997; Hu et al. 2006; Patton et al. 2006; Otten et al. 2011), but other studies have found it does not (West et al. 1999; Pederson et al. 2007). The inconsistent findings in studies of smoking among youth may be attributable to differences in the extent to which such studies have included other parenting variables, peer-smoking variables, or perhaps other variables (Tyas and Pederson 1998; Avenevoli and

Merikangas 2003). Notably, a recent meta-analysis concluded that parental smoking is strongly associated with smoking among youth (Leonardi-Bee et al. 2011). The effects of parental smoking on smoking among youth can be seen in both boys and girls (Andrews et al. 1997), but the effects may be stronger for girls (Hu et al. 1995). Findings by race/ethnicity are mixed, with several studies suggesting that parental smoking may be more salient for White than for African American/Black youth (Landrine et al. 1994; Hu et al. 1995; Griesler et al. 1998), but Gritz and colleagues (2003) drew a different conclusion, that African American youth were susceptible to smoking if anyone in their household smoked. In addition, Hu and colleagues (2006) found that parental smoking may be more important for young adults than for youth, and two studies found that such smoking may be relatively more important for Hispanic youth (Landrine et al. 1994; Griesler and Kandel 1998), but Hu and associates (1995) and Gritz and coworkers (2003) obtained contrasting results (that demonstrated the importance of household smoking and youth smoking among Hispanic youth). One study found that parental smoking predicted transition to daily smoking for three racial/ethnic groups: White, Black, and Hispanic adolescents (Kandel et al. 2004). The effects of parental smoking on smoking by adolescents appear to remain constant over the adolescent period (Chassin et al. 1986; Hu et al. 1995; Bauman et al. 2001) or may even increase (Bricker et al. 2007) throughout this time.

Longitudinal studies of effects on smoking among youth have looked at older siblings less often than they have looked at parents. Studies have found that smoking by older siblings influences smoking among youth more consistently than does smoking by parents (Conrad et al. 1992; Tyas and Pederson 1998; Avenevoli and Merikangas 2003), and this includes effects on the behaviors of initiation (e.g., Rajan et al. 2003; Forrester et al. 2007) as well as progression to higher levels of tobacco use (e.g., Hill et al. 2005; Bricker et al. 2006a). Bricker and colleagues (2006a), who followed 4,576 youth from 3rd through 12th grades, found that after controlling for smoking by parents and close friends, smoking by older siblings—measured in early childhood—predicted daily smoking by adolescents 9 years later. In fact, the effects of siblings' smoking were as strong as the effects of smoking by close friends. In contrast, some studies of smoking by young adults suggest that siblings' smoking may not be an important risk factor for the initiation or persistence of smoking in this older group (Oygard et al. 1995; West et al. 1999; White et al. 2002; Pederson et al. 2007).

Multiple studies of youth indicate that a higher quality of parent-adolescent relationships—variously defined by such indicators as closeness, supportiveness, and involvement—protects youth against smoking (e.g., Doherty and Allen 1994; Scal et al. 2003; Kandel et al. 2004; Mahabee-Gittens et al. 2011). In addition, several studies suggest that parental monitoring of their child's activities, whereabouts, and friends may reduce the likelihood of smoking (e.g., Biglan et al. 1995; Dishion et al. 1999; Simons-Morton 2002). Conversely, other studies find that some family supervisory practices (e.g., disciplinary practices) are not likely to deter youth from smoking (Chassin et al. 1986; Côté et al. 2004; Hill et al. 2005). Some studies have considered dimensions of both parental support and behavioral control by combining selected variables to define parenting styles: authoritative (high support, high control), authoritarian (low support, high control), indulgent (high support, low control), and disengaged (low support, low control) (Baumrind 1985). Jackson and colleagues (1994) observed that adolescents with authoritative parents were less likely to initiate smoking, while Chassin and coworkers (2005) found that adolescents with disengaged parents were more likely to smoke, even after controlling for parental smoking.

Two studies found that family conflict may increase the risk of smoking among youth (Duncan et al. 1998; Flay et al. 1998). Earlier, Biglan and colleagues found an indirect effect of family conflict on smoking by youth (Biglan et al. 1995). In addition, smoking-specific parental attitudes and practices appear to influence youth smoking: youth who perceive that their parents disapprove of smoking have been found to be less likely to smoke (Sargent and Dalton 2001; Miller and Volk 2002; Simons-Morton and Haynie 2003), but some studies found no such effects (Hill et al. 2005; Carvajal and Granillo 2006) or effects at only particular stages of smoking (Distefan et al. 1998) or at certain ages (Tucker et al. 2008), with effects less likely in young adulthood (Ellickson et al. 2001; Tucker et al. 2003). Similarly, studies have found parent-child communication about smoking to be a protective factor (Huver et al. 2006), but this may be the case only in nonsmoking families (Chassin et al. 2005) or at certain stages of smoking (Distefan et al. 1998). Ennett and colleagues (2001) found that multiple dimensions of parent-child communication about tobacco use had no effects on initiation of smoking among youth but that harsher parent-child communication on the rules about smoking and discipline for smoking had detrimental effects (i.e., it escalated smoking).

Additional insights into how parents influence adolescent smoking have come from complex longitudinal models that included both parental and peer factors. For example, in a longitudinal sample of 14- to 17-year-olds, Biglan and colleagues (1995) observed that family conflict led to poor parental monitoring that, in turn, led to an increased risk of smoking. Several studies found that parental smoking indirectly influenced adolescents' smoking through their selection of friends who smoked (Chassin et al. 1998; Engels et al. 1999, 2004; Tucker et al. 2003; Simons-Morton et al. 2004) and through cognitive factors, such as adolescents' expectations of the outcomes of smoking, perceptions of whether their parents approved of smoking, and intentions to smoke (Flay et al. 1994). Other studies have observed that the effects of affiliating with friends who smoked were diminished when parents were perceived to disapprove of smoking (Sargent and Dalton 2001). In general, studies suggest that parental risk factors tend to become less important relative to peer risk factors along with increasing age (Flay et al. 1994).

Summary

The literature on the contributions of small social groups to tobacco use among youth, and to a lesser extent to tobacco use among young adults, points to the importance of peers and family in the initiation of tobacco use as well as its continuation and progressive use, particularly of cigarettes. How peers and family actually affect and potentially support or deter tobacco use among youth is a complex question that is not reducible to single causal factors. Instead, the literature suggests that the entire social context (i.e., the interrelations and attributes within and between peers and family and adolescents' perceptions of their own social environment) helps to shape smoking behavior among youth.

Understanding the influence of friends' smoking is an important component of understanding the complex etiology of smoking among youth. As noted earlier in this chapter, one can expect findings on the effects of friends' tobacco use to be inflated when studies do not account for selective affiliation (i.e., the tendency for adolescents to choose friends who are similar to themselves) or for adolescents' perceptions of their friends' tobacco use, which may or may not reflect actual use. Moreover, because the effects of friends' tobacco use may be stronger for females than for males and for White than for minority youth, estimates of friends' tobacco use may be misleading if these specific effects are not considered. Indeed, assessing the causal role of friends' smoking is incomplete without these and other considerations, such as adolescents' relationships with peers.

To conclude that there is a causal linkage between parental smoking and smoking among youth, more longitudinal research is needed, perhaps focusing on varying trajectories of smoking over time in parents and their offspring, since the data to date have not been consistent or conclusive (Chassin et al. 2008). And yet, because some studies have shown that parental variables may indirectly affect adolescents' choices of friends or their thoughts about smoking, parental smoking and other family effects may be both directly and indirectly important, again suggesting the need for more sophisticated research in this area.

This review did not find sufficient evidence to implicate parental factors as being causal agents in the use of tobacco among young adults, but the evidence is suggestive of a potential causal role for parental smoking and a causal role for peer group influences.

Cognitive and Affective Processes

Mood and Affect

Affective processes appear to play an important role in the uptake, progression, and persistence of adolescent smoking. Numerous investigators have examined the role of negative affective states and affect regulation in the initiation and development of cigarette smoking behavior. In cross-sectional studies, regular and experimental smoking among youth is associated with higher levels of negative affect compared with nonsmoking peers (Mitic et al. 1985; Coogan et al. 1998; Escobedo et al. 1998; McKenzie et al. 2010). Longitudinal studies in this area demonstrate that higher levels of negative affect are not only characteristic of adolescent tobacco users but also are likely related to smoking initiation and transitions along a trajectory of use. Patton and colleagues (1998) prospectively examined the association between depression, anxiety, and smoking initiation among youth and determined that depression and anxiety predicted initiation of experimental smoking. This association was mediated by the presence or absence of smoking peers. Wills and associates (2002) showed that high levels of negative affect and life stress in a sample of adolescents predicted increases in tobacco use over a 3-year period. Siqueira and colleagues (2000) found that when teenage smokers were directly asked about the reasons for their progression from experimental to regular tobacco use, stress was identified as a primary catalyst, with endorsement by 72% of the sample. Audrain-McGovern and colleagues (2009) followed a large cohort of students (n = 1,093) from 9th grade until 12th grade to examine the temporal relationship between smoking and depression. Students were assessed annually for smoking, depression, smoking among their peers, and other potential covariates. The authors found that increased depression symptoms predicted elevated smoking levels and progression in smoking. Interestingly, greater smoking at baseline predicted a deceleration in the number of smoking peers across time, which predicted a deceleration in depression symptoms. The comorbidity of depression and smoking can possibly be explained through peer influences, since the number of smoking peers mediated the relationships between smoking and depression.

Mood benefits derived from smoking may be an important driver of smoking behavior among youth. Like adults, many youth report smoking for reasons related to affect regulation (e.g., tension reduction, negative affect relief) (Scales et al. 2009). A growing body of evidence suggests that cigarette smoking can produce immediate, reinforcing changes in both positive and negative moods among adolescents (Kassel et al. 2003, 2007; Hedeker et al. 2008, 2009). Kassel and colleagues (2007) used a matched case-comparison study design of 15- to 18-year-old smokers (n = 45) and nonsmokers (n = 27) to determine the effects that nicotine has on both positive and negative affect. Smokers in this study experienced reductions in both their positive and negative affect scores after smoking a cigarette; these reductions were moderated by nicotine dependence, the nicotine content of the cigarette (high yield vs. denicotinized), and cigarette craving. In addition, smoking expectancy moderated negative but not positive affect. Nonsmokers had no reduction in either positive or negative affect over a 10-minute interval (Kassel et al. 2007). Importantly, adolescents who expect to receive greater mood benefits from smoking experience it as more reinforcing, compared with those without strong mood-related expectancies. Colvin and Mermelstein (2010) sought to determine whether expectancies of negative affect influenced mood expectancies directly after smoking. Using handheld computers for a week to assess changes in mood throughout the day, the participating adolescents (n = 461) were given surveys to measure smoking expectancies, nicotine dependence, number of biological parents who were ever smokers, and current smoking behaviors (Colvin and Mermelstein 2010). Increased amounts of negative-affect expectancies were related to a greater decrease in negative mood and an increase in positive mood immediately following smoking.

Evidence is also accumulating to suggest that adolescents who experience greater subjective mood benefits of smoking are more likely to progress in their smoking. In a prospective study of adolescent smokers, Mermelstein and colleagues (2007) found that subjective mood benefits of smoking predicted escalation in a cohort of adolescents. Adolescents who progressed in their smoking were those who reported substantial in-the-moment mood benefits following smoking; adolescents who tried smoking but stopped did not report any subjective mood benefits following smoking. Further evidence that mood-stabilizing effects may reinforce and maintain smoking among youth comes from Weinstein and colleagues (2008), who examined variability in negative moods as it related to smoking patterns among adolescents. Students in 8th and 10th grades (n = 517) were assessed at baseline, 6 months, and 12 months on cigarette use; for 1 week, students used palmtop computers to provide momentary assessments of negative moods. Increased variability in negative mood at baseline was significantly associated with subsequent escalation of smoking compared with students who did not progress beyond experimentation.

Smoking-related expectancies are associated with many aspects of smoking motivation and behavior (Brandon and et al. 1999). Studies of adolescent smokers have demonstrated a strong relation between positive expectancies for smoking (e.g., relaxation, mood enhancement) and smoking status, such that more experienced smokers appear to have more positive expectancies for smoking (Gordon 1986; Covington and Omelich 1988). Heinz and colleagues (2010) followed a group of 568 adolescents for 2 years at four time points to determine the influence that negative affect relief expectancies (NAREs) have on smoking behavior and nicotine dependence; both were measured at the four assessments. When controlled for anxiety and depression symptoms, NAREs predicted both the progression of smoking and nicotine dependence (Heinz et al. 2010). The NAREs were measured as a subscale of 10 items (e.g., "smoking helps calm me down when I'm nervous"); responses were recorded on a 4-point scale ranging from 1 = disagree to 4 = agree. Taken together, the evidence suggests that adolescents who hold more favorable positive expectancies for smoking are more likely to begin smoking and to smoke more cigarettes.

In addition to the substantial body of evidence implicating negative affect in the etiology and progression of youth smoking, a number of studies have shown that smoking during adolescence may increase the risk for subsequent development of mood disorders. For example, Jamal and colleagues (2011) examined the relationship between age at smoking initiation and subsequent onset of mood disorders in a sample of 1,055 current and former smokers. Only smokers who were nondepressed or nonanxious when they started smoking were included in the study. Relative to late-onset smokers, early-onset smokers experienced onset of depression and/or anxiety disorders 5 years earlier, suggesting that a young age at smoking onset increases vulnerability for the subsequent development of psychopathology. Furthermore, a growing body of evidence provides support for a bidirectional relationship between smoking and negative affect. Windle and Windle (2001) used a large four-wave panel design to examine the temporal relationship between depressive symptoms and cigarette smoking in a large sample of 10th and 11th graders (n = 1,218). Students completed surveys about their depressive symptoms and smoking behavior at baseline and every 6 months thereafter, for a total of 1.5 years. Symptoms of depression predicted increases in cigarette smoking over time. Over the same study period, heavy and persistent smoking prospectively predicted increases in depressive symptoms. Similarly, Orlando and colleagues (2001) tested the hypothesis that smoking was dynamically related to emotional distress in a cohort of 2,961 adolescents. The authors examined concomitant changes in smoking behavior and emotional distress over time and found that baseline emotional distress in grade 10 predicted increased smoking in grade 12; this increase in smoking was, in turn, associated with increased emotional distress in young adulthood.

The observed bidirectional influences described above support the plausibility of shared etiologies between negative affect and smoking behavior. However, it is also possible that unique causal mechanisms are operating in each direction. For example, self-medication of depressed mood could be influencing smoking progression, whereas the effects of nicotine on neurotransmitter systems linked to depression could be driving the association with negative affect. More research is needed to explain these mechanisms.

Cognitive Processes

Two kinds of cognitive processes play roles in the development of regular smoking among youth: (1) those that are conscious, explicit, and planned and (2) those that are unconscious, implicit, and relatively automatic. These processes can act independently or interact as dual-process models; a fuller discussion follows below.

Explicit or Controlled Cognitive Factors and the Deliberate Processing of Information

The role of cognition in tobacco use can be understood more fully by examining social learning theory and cognitive-behavioral principles of learning (Brandon et al. 2004). Investigations into the etiology of tobacco use have studied three key cognitive constructs: expectancy (Goldman et al. 1999), self-efficacy (Bandura 1977a), and coping (Wills and Filer 1996). Expectancy refers to the perceived outcomes of tobacco use, and positive outcome expectancy is related to the theory of positive reinforcement of addiction. Self-efficacy is related to an individual's confidence in achieving goals through personal efforts, such as the ability to resist smoking or to remain smoke-free after quitting. Coping theories view tobacco use as a mechanism to deal with stress and other negative states; such theories include the self-medication and performance-enhancement models.

The Smoking Consequences Questionnaire (Brandon and Baker 1991), a well-known instrument for measuring expectancies, has been adapted for use among adolescents and young adults (Myers et al. 2003; Lewis-Esquerre et al. 2005; Wahl et al. 2005). This instrument measures several positive outcome expectancies about smoking, including:

- pleasant taste
- relief from boredom
- reduction in negative affect
- weight regulation
- positive social consequences
- favorable outcomes related to the health hazards of smoking

Various studies have associated these outcomes with increased intention of smoking, initiation of smoking, escalation in smoking behavior, regular smoking, and/or current smoking (Flay et al. 1998; Ausems et al. 2003; Myers et al. 2003; Lewis-Esquerre et al. 2005; Wahl et al. 2005).

Two studies linked low self-efficacy early in adolescence with smoking behavior later during the adolescent period. In one, Flay and colleagues (1998) associated low self-efficacy in skills for refusal of cigarettes from peers in 7th grade with smoking experimentation (versus never smoking) in 12th grade. Later, Ausems and colleagues (2003) found that low self-efficacy in refusal skills among 11- and 12-year-olds led to a higher likelihood of experimentation with smoking (compared with never smoking) and regular smoking (compared with experimentation).

In a multivariate analysis, Lewis-Esquerre and associates (2005) found that perceptions that both the sensory and motor aspects of smoking were pleasant constituted a significant risk factor for smoking in 7th- to 12th-grade youth and that a belief in the negative social consequences of smoking was strongly protective for this group. Among students in the 2nd through 5th grades, Hampson and colleagues (2007) found an association between a more positive social image of cigarette smoking (i.e., youth who smoke are "liked by other youth," are "exciting," and are "cool or neat") with increased intentions to smoke. Using the same sample, an analysis by Andrews and colleagues (2008) found that a positive social image of smoking was related to willingness to smoke that, in turn, predicted smoking rather than simply intention to smoke.

Among sixth- and seventh-grade urban youth, poor decision-making and lower self-efficacy were found to be related to perceived social benefits of smoking in the seventh and eighth grades, which, in turn, were positively associated with smoking 1 year later (Epstein et al. 2000). However, there was no direct relationship between decision-making skills or self-efficacy in the sixth and seventh grades and smoking 2 years later (Epstein et al. 2000). These results suggest an important role for the perceived social aspects of smoking in mediating whether smoking will be taken up.

Belief in the negative health consequences of smoking was found to be a robust protective factor against the risk that youth would smoke (Rodriguez et al. 2007). Even in 16-year-old tobacco users, Myers and coworkers (2003) found that belief in the negative health consequences of smoking was associated with lower smoking frequency, lower scores on tobacco dependence, and more quit attempts.

Velicer and colleagues (2007) identified four clusters of ninth graders on the basis of their beliefs about the negative and positive consequences of smoking and their self-efficacy for resisting the temptations of smoking. At 3-year follow-up, the cluster with the most-negative and least-positive beliefs, which also demonstrated low levels of smoking temptations, had the lowest prevalence of smoking initiation (13.2%). A second cluster, characterized by high levels of smoking temptation, and a third cluster, characterized by the least-negative outlook on the consequences of smoking, had the highest proportions of smoking initiators at follow-up (26.5% and 28.7%, respectively). The same three constructs—low self-efficacy for resistance, belief in the positive consequences of cigarette smoking, and lack of belief in the negative consequences of that behavior—have been associated with onset of smoking or rapid escalation to regular smoking following experimentation (Chassin et al. 2000; Orlando et al. 2004; Bernat et al. 2008).

Executive function, which involves such tasks as reasoning, processing speed, and the ability to inhibit a reflexive response, is another explicit cognitive factor that may affect adolescent smoking. Fried and colleagues (2006) found that slower processing speed and worse performance on tasks requiring sustained attention and abstract reasoning at 9–12 years of age were associated with smoking (≥9 cigarettes per day) at 17–21 years of age. In this study, however, performance on these tasks did not distinguish between eventual groups of lighter smokers (1–8 cigarettes per day), former smokers, and those who never became regular smokers. In addition, performance on vocabulary, memory, and tasks requiring spatial ability did not distinguish between any of the smoking groups. Elsewhere, from cross-sectional data describing 14-year-olds, Lawlor and colleagues (2005) found a higher prevalence of smoking at lower levels of nonverbal reasoning and reading abilities. These two studies suggest that specific deficits in executive function may be related to an increased risk of smoking, but neither study focused explicitly on the relationship between performance on cognitive tasks and smoking, and so adjustments for covariates could not be made in the comparisons cited.

Automatic/Implicit Cognitive Processes

Research in social cognition indicates that the acquisition of automatic behaviors (i.e., behaviors that are not consciously mediated) develops through frequent and consistent experiences with a particular social behavior that, in turn, affects the likelihood of engaging in that behavior. Conscious choice drops out as it becomes a superfluous step in the process (Bargh and Chartrand 1999).

Currently, there is a research focus on the evaluation of implicit or spontaneously activated cognitions on behaviors, such as regular tobacco use and other behaviors involving addictions (for a review, see Wiers and Stacy 2006). Implicit cognitions result from information processing of associations involving tobacco-related outcomes, such as feeling good because of dopamine-dependent associations, tobacco-relevant stimuli (e.g., cigarette advertising, cigarette packages, lighters, ashtrays), or tobacco-related situations or environmental contexts (e.g., smoking with friends at a party). These types of associations are strengthened in memory through repetitive experiences (Stacy 1995, 1997) and come to influence or guide behavior through a relatively spontaneous process that circumvents rational decision-making (Stacy 1997; Wiers and Stacy 2006). Implicit cognitive processes can influence thought processes and the interpretations of situations, contexts, and other stimuli, and they can also either make more accessible or inhibit the memory of behavioral alternatives (e.g., healthy behavioral options).

Numerous studies have evaluated the influence of implicit cognitive processes on smoking behavior among adolescents. Although a variety of cross-sectional studies on implicit associations have had robust outcomes, only a few prospective studies have evaluated the influence of such associations on subsequent smoking while controlling for potential confounders (Stacy 1997; Kelly et al. 2005, 2008; Thush et al. 2007). In a prospective study, Kelly and colleagues (2008) used the Memory Association Test (Kelly et al. 2005) to evaluate the effects of implicit tobacco-related memory associations on smoking in adolescents; this test is a variation of an indirect cue-association paradigm (Stacy et al. 1994, 1996) that contains no explicit reference to the behavior being assessed. Among high school youth, the study found that tobacco-related memory associations assessed at baseline were predictive of smoking 6 months later when they were controlled for within-subject variability in smoking and other variables. These findings suggest that youth with strong memory associations related to tobacco use may be at increased risk for subsequent smoking.

In an extensive review of the literature involving the influence of nonconsciously mediated processes on smoking dependence and cessation, Waters and Sayette (2006) found across a range of cross-sectional studies that smoking status among young adults (college students) was frequently associated with indirect tests of association, such as the Implicit Association Test (IAT).

The IAT is a categorization task that provides a method of indirectly assessing the relative strength of memory associations among different concepts (Greenwald et al. 1998). The basic assumption is that past learning (e.g., experience with smoking) is represented by facilitated information processing of associated concepts as measured by reaction time on the task. During the task, participants sort stimuli into two categories of attributes (e.g., positive vs. negative and approach vs. avoid) and two target categories (e.g., tobacco-related objects and non-tobacco-related objects). Faster responses to observed paired stimuli (e.g., a cigarette and feels bad) are interpreted to mean that the two stimuli are more strongly associated in memory than are other pairs of stimuli. Stronger implicit associations between a behavior and a variety of cues or outcomes (e.g., smoking a cigarette and being social or feeling good) are potentially significant in promoting the behavior (for reviews, see Ames et al. 2006; Waters and Sayette 2006; Wiers et al. 2006).

Several studies of adults who completed the IAT indicate that both smokers and nonsmokers have some negative implicit attitudes toward smoking when asked to categorize smoking and nonsmoking stimuli with positive and negative attributes, but smokers have relatively fewer negative attitudes toward smoking than do nonsmokers (Swanson et al. 2001; Sherman et al. 2003; Huijding et al. 2005; DeHouwer et al. 2006). In addition, DeHouwer and colleagues (2006) found that smokers reacted faster when categorizing smoking stimuli with an "I like" label, and nonsmokers reacted faster when categorizing smoking stimuli with an "I dislike" label. Such results, however, may be more reflective of individual differences in implicit attitudes and less sensitive to societal influences or attitudes toward smoking (Olson and Fazio 2004). More research with the IAT is needed to support previous findings. With an approach-avoid IAT, DeHouwer and colleagues (2006) further found that smokers associated smoking with more "approach words" than "avoid words" and that nonsmokers associated smoking with more "avoid words" than "approach words."

Sherman and colleagues (2003) found that heavier smokers had significantly more positive implicit associations toward smoking than did lighter smokers and less negative implicit associations toward that activity than did nonsmokers. Perugini (2005) reported similar findings when comparing smokers with nonsmokers on an IAT; that is, smokers' implicit attitudes toward smoking were significantly more positive than those of nonsmokers, and their explicit attitudes, also measured, were significantly more positive as well. McCarthy and Thompsen (2006) reported similar findings with a tobacco-related IAT: they found correlations between positive implicit associations and self-reported smoking behavior but no significant relationship between negative implicit associations and smoking behavior. Using a single-target IAT, Huijding and de Jong (2006) found that smokers had positive implicit affective associations toward smoking, but nonsmokers had negative (implicit) affective associations. In addition, self-reported craving correlated with negative implicit affective associations but not with self-reported attitudes. In a subsequent IAT study among smokers only, Waters and colleagues (2007) found that implicit attitudes toward smoking were robustly and positively related to self-reported craving and nicotine dependence.

Chassin and colleagues (2002) included an IAT in a study with both implicit and explicit attitudes when they evaluated the influence of parental smoking/cessation on adolescent smoking. These authors found that mothers with positive implicit attitudes toward smoking were more likely to have children who smoked. In addition, the IAT differentiated between smoking and nonsmoking/formerly smoking mothers, with mothers who smoked having more positive implicit attitudes toward the behavior. However, implicit attitudes toward smoking among youth in the study failed to correlate with parental smoking, and implicit attitudes of both fathers and youth did not correlate with the youth's smoking behavior, even though there was a correlation between mothers' attitudes and smoking by their children. Although more studies are needed on the influence on youth of the implicit attitudes of parents toward smoking, findings suggest that in conjunction with prevention efforts among youth, programs might want to target parental (particularly maternal) implicit attitudes toward smoking to help efforts to prevent this behavior.

The Go/No-go Association Test (GNAT), an indirect test of association developed by Nosek and Banaji (2001), assesses implicit associations with a single target category, thus eliminating competing or contrasting categories as in the IAT. Using a portable version of the GNAT, Bassett and Dabbs (2005) differentiated implicit attitudes of smokers from nonsmokers among 39 adults in a university environment. Smokers reacted faster to "smoking words" that were paired with "good words," and nonsmokers responded faster to "smoking words" that were paired with "bad words."

In summary, findings from IAT studies and others that have focused on implicit cognitive processes appear to reflect some differences between smokers and nonsmokers in tobacco-related implicit associations. The differences found may suggest differences in neurobiology, early-life experiences, or exposure to tobacco use. Refinement of methodologies may help further elucidate the influence of implicit associations on smoking behavior among youth. These contributions will be important to the literature and future studies of nonconsciously mediated influences on behavior (Waters and Sayette 2006; Wiers and de Jong 2006).

Dual-Process Models

Dual-process models of behavior acknowledge that goal-directed behaviors, such as tobacco use, are influenced by a range of cognitive processes, including both implicit or automatic processes and more controlled, deliberate, or executive processes (Tiffany 1990; Stanovich and West 2000; Evans 2003; Kahneman 2003; for dual-process approaches to addiction, see Wiers and Stacy 2006). In general, researchers on addiction have accepted this dual-process approach to cognition and have acknowledged the influence of both implicit and explicit processes in the development and maintenance of addictive behaviors (Bechara and Damasio 2002; Wiers and Stacy 2006). Furthermore, many studies have shown the additive and independent predictive ability of implicit and explicit processes in usage models for tobacco and other drugs (Stacy 1995, 1997; Chassin et al. 2002; Wiers et al. 2002; Sherman et al. 2003; Huijding et al. 2005; Perugini 2005; Ames et al. 2007; Thush et al. 2008). In one study, Grenard and associates (2008) found possible tobacco-related associations to be stronger predictors of smoking among youth with lower-capacity working memories than among those with a higher capacity. Ongoing research about dual-process models of addiction will help to elucidate the influence of explicit and implicit processes on goal-directed behaviors as well as explain how certain cognitive functions may inhibit behavioral tendencies that arise from more spontaneously activated implicit associations.

Summary

A robust association between youth smoking and negative affect has been demonstrated in the literature. Prospective studies suggest that this association may be bidirectional. Negative affect has been shown to be an influential factor for the onset and continuation of youth smoking. At the same time, smoking during adolescence has been found to prospectively predict subsequent negative affect and depressive symptoms. It can be concluded that smoking and mood are related to one another, but more research is needed to understand the temporal relationship. A key question regarding the association between negative affect and youth smoking is whether it reflects a direct causal influence, in one or both directions.

The cognitive processes that influence the initiation of tobacco use, continued use, and dependence include executive, or more explicit, processes and implicit processes (those that are more automatically associative). Executive processes are relevant to inhibitory control over behaviors and to counteracting the influence of more spontaneous (or implicit) cognitive processes. Evidence suggests that executive processes moderate behavior (e.g., the capacity of working memory) during decision making in complex situations (Finn and Hall 2004; Payne 2005; Grenard et al. 2008). For example, complex social situations involving cues to use tobacco or ambiguous contexts are likely to tax aspects of executive functioning for many youth, reducing their ability to inhibit intentions to resist smoking. For most youth, tobacco use is unlikely to be motivated solely by rational decision-making processes. The influence of implicit cognitive processes on behavior has been demonstrated in numerous studies across a variety of drugs and populations (for reviews, see Ames et al. 2006 for drugs; Waters and Sayette 2006 for tobacco; and Wiers et al. 2006 for alcohol). Implicit associations, or more spontaneously activated cognitions, may help to explain why some people engage in apparently irrational behaviors, such as smoking, while clearly knowing that the behavior can have negative consequences.

Both automatic and controlled cognitive processes (incorporated in dual-process models) influence behavior and, therefore, both should be considered potential targets of interventions (Wiers and Stacy 2006). However, more research is needed to evaluate the ability of dual-process models to predict the use of tobacco and other substances, the interaction between the two processes, and individual variations in these processes. Future research should focus on increasing the understanding of the role of cognitive mediators in complex social behaviors, such as the use of tobacco and other drugs, and the decision making behind engaging or not engaging in the particular behavior.

Genetic Factors and Neurobiological and Neurodevelopmental Processes

This section considers the role of genetic factors and their interaction with measured environmental factors; neurobiological processes, including addiction to nicotine; and neurodevelopmental processes (USDHHS 2010). The term "genetics" refers to a person's biological coding scheme, which may become a phenotype (expression) that at times depends on context and previous experience and exposures. The term "neurodevelopmental processes" refers to the influences of environmental experiences and maturation processes on cognitive function and, in this case, the likelihood that a person may yield to perceived social influences or curiosity and use tobacco products. Neurobiological processes are neurologic transmissions across brain structures that may predispose a person to seek out the use of tobacco or other drugs or that may be affected by tobacco or other drug use. Importantly, adolescence is a time of considerable neurodevelopmental plasticity and change (Steinberg 2007; Windle et al. 2008; Giedd and Rapoport 2010). Brain development in regions associated with impulsivity, motivation, and addiction continues well into young adulthood (Lebel and Beaulieu 2011). Maturational changes that occur during adolescence may contribute to neurologic factors that underlie vulnerability to addiction, such as increases in novelty seeking and impulsivity (Chambers et al. 2003). Some individual traits such as sensation-seeking and temperament might predispose young people toward certain problem behaviors in particular social contexts (Wills et al. 2000; Bisol et al. 2010).

Genetic Influence on Smoking Behaviors

Genetic influences have been documented at each stage in the continuum of smoking, from initiation to dependence, in twin and family studies. This broad topic was covered in depth in the 2010 Surgeon General's report on how tobacco smoke causes disease, with the conclusion that inherited genetic variation contributes to differing patterns of smoking behavior and cessation (USDHHS 2010). Some of the supporting evidence is also summarized in Chapter 2 of this report and in the present section.

This evidence in support of the heritability of smoking behavior has prompted researchers to identify specific genes and biological mechanisms that play a role in smoking behavior and nicotine dependence using a variety of genetic study designs.

Until recently, research has focused many of the genetic efforts on candidate gene and linkage studies rather than on more powerful genomewide association studies or sequencing. Some of these candidate gene studies have been fruitful, mainly because the genetics of addiction benefits from a vast knowledge of a given drug's mechanism of action; consequently, many genes are plausible candidates, and some associations have been reported. However, the more recent high-throughput approaches have provided consistent and compelling results that have advanced the science base on genetics and smoking behavior. Although incomplete, the overview below provides a picture of the approaches and findings to date.

Genetic Linkage Analyses

Genetic linkage analyses seek to identify genetic variants associated with an outcome of interest by testing genetic markers across the genome. Regions of the genome that appear strongly linked to the outcome have a higher likelihood of containing influential genetic regions or genes. Several large family-based genetic linkage analyses have been conducted to identify the chromosomal regions associated with different smoking outcomes, including smoking status, tobacco dependence, and even cigarettes smoked per day. The results of these studies have been somewhat inconsistent, however, pointing to different regions on a number of chromosomes (Munafó and Johnstone 2008; Uhl et al. 2008). Even so, the implicated regions likely contain susceptibility loci and several candidate genes whose genetic variation may explain differences in phenotypes. For example, a region on chromosome 9q22 has been linked to tobacco dependence (Li et al. 2003), a finding corroborated by three other independent studies (Bergen et al. 1999; Bierut et al. 2004; Gelertner et al. 2004). In addition, a location on chromosome 5q (D5S1354) has been strongly linked to smoking behavior in at least two studies (Bergen et al. 1999; Duggirala et al. 1999). Research has also found associations between the gamma amino butyric acid receptor subunit B2 (*GABA-B2*) and neurotrophic tyrosine kinase receptor type 2 (*NTRK2*) genes and tobacco dependence (Beuten et al. 2005, 2007). Unfortunately, only a few studies go on to identify the specific genetic variants located on the chromosomes implicated in genetic linkage analyses (Munafó and Johnstone 2008).

Candidate Gene Studies

Candidate gene studies, on the other hand, compare the prevalence of specific genetic variants by using a case-control design. The variants are selected on the basis of evidence from earlier studies that are related to the outcome of interest. Most candidate gene studies on tobacco use have evaluated the influence of genes that operate in neurotransmitter pathways (e.g., the dopamine and serotonin pathways), nicotine metabolism, and nicotinic receptors (Munafó and Johnstone 2008). The majority have focused on genes involved in the dopamine pathway, particularly the dopamine receptor D2 (*DRD2*) gene. The *DRD2 Taq1A* polymorphism has been implicated in the majority of studies, while others have found no such association (Munafó et al. 2004). Two meta-analyses have shown that the *Taq1* A1 allele is significantly more likely to be found among smokers than among nonsmokers. Other genes in the dopaminergic reward system have been investigated in the context of tobacco use and dependence, such as the dopamine transporter (*DAT*), other dopamine receptors (*DRD1, DRD4, DRD5*), catechol-*O*-methyltransferase (*COMT*), monoamine oxidases A and B, and tyrosine hydroxylase (*TH*), although none of these variants has shown a strong relationship with smoking behaviors (Munafó and Johnstone 2008). In the serotonin pathway, most studies investigating the *5-HTTLPR5* polymorphism within the *SLC6A4* gene, including one meta-analysis, found a relationship with smoking behavior (Munafó et al. 2004).

Candidate gene studies have also looked at genes in the nicotine metabolism pathway; variants in these genes might be expected to cause individual differences in susceptibility to different doses of nicotine. The most commonly studied gene in this category is the *CYP2A6* gene; there is evidence to suggest that *CYP2A6* variants that reduce nicotine metabolism are associated with reduced smoking quantity (Malaiyandi et al. 2006) and increased likelihood of cessation (Munafó et al. 2004).

Several nicotinic receptor genes have been examined, with some studies finding that *CHRNA4* plays a role in tobacco dependence. In addition, a large case-control study found several other nicotinic receptor genes to be associated with tobacco dependence, including *CHRNA5* and *CHRNB3* (Saccone et al. 2009). Replication of these findings is a necessary step toward validating the roles of these genetic variants (see below). The region on chromosome 15 that includes a group of nicotinic receptor genes has been associated in multiple populations with the quantity smoked and the risk of becoming nicotine dependent (Bierut 2010), thereby demonstrating the importance of this region.

Findings in both genetic linkage analyses and candidate gene studies demonstrate great heterogeneity, indicating that genetic influence on tobacco use and nicotine dependence is complex and likely involves multiple genes.

Genomewide Association Studies and Sequencing

Over the last decade, the science of genetics has made important progress through conceptual insights and technological breakthroughs. In 1999, the idea of evaluating hundreds to thousands of genetic variants—namely, single nucleotide polymorphisms (SNPs)—at once was beginning to take shape. One key turning point was the understanding that the genome is built by many sets of correlated SNPs, called haplotypes, which meant that rather than screening the entire SNP collection, a subset of "proxy" SNPs, or TagSNPs, could be screened without loss of information, using the so-called genomewide association study (GWAS) design. GWAS is powerful for honing in on relevant areas of the genome related to the phenotype in an unbiased way. Once a "hit" is discovered through a GWAS scan, it needs to be replicated and evaluated further to determine if it contributes to the phenotypic outcome. Therefore, GWAS provides the first step in identifying key regions for deep sequencing and functional characterization. This approach resulted in one of the most replicated findings in addiction genetics—the A5/A3/B4 nicotinic cholinergic receptor subunit cluster on chromosome 15 associated with tobacco dependence across populations (Saccone et al. 2009, 2010; Liu et al.

2010; The Tobacco and Genetics Consortium 2010; Thorgeirsson et al. 2010).

Science and genetics technologies continue to evolve at a rapid pace, and it is now possible to conduct whole-genome sequencing (complete sequence of an individual's genome) and "deep" sequencing (sequencing specific regions of a genome) of targeted regions in many people. In either approach, sequencing allows for a single-base examination of the genetic architecture within the target region, and it also allows for a higher order view of the genomic structure (e.g., copy number variation, structural variations such as deletions, insertions, inversions, and epigenetic targets).

The whole-genome sequencing and deep sequencing approaches are starting to be used to uncover additional rare genetic variants that also contribute to smoking-related phenotypes (Wessel et al. 2010). The GWAS evidence and subsequent replications showing association with tobacco dependence phenotypes with the nicotinic subunit receptor cluster on chromosome 15 (CHRNA5/A3/B4) supports the next steps of deep sequencing and functional analyses to understand the relationships and mechanisms of how those genetic variants contribute to the smoking phenotype; this work is ongoing and shows that the genetic changes in this gene cluster have effects on receptor function (Wang et al. 2009, Hong et al. 2010; Fowler et al. 2011; Smith et al. 2011).

Genetic Factors in Tobacco Use Among Youth

Studies of Twins

From data obtained from pairs of twins reared together, latent genetic and environmental contributions to phenotypic variation can be estimated. Twin models compare the correlations of twin pairs across zygosity groups. If the resemblance of twin pairs is determined by additive genetic effects transmitted from parents to their offspring, then the correlation in monozygotic (MZ) twin pairs is predicted to be twice that of dizygotic (DZ) twin pairs because MZ twins share 100% of their genes, while DZ twins share, on average, 50% of their genes and are no more similar than are any other pair of full siblings. If the resemblance of twin pairs is determined by shared environmental influences, or factors common to family members, such as home or school environment, then equal MZ and DZ correlations are expected, because both MZ and DZ twin pairs are assumed to share 100% of the shared environmental factors. If the MZ correlation is greater than, but less than twice, the DZ correlation, then both genetic and shared environmental influences contribute to phenotypic variation. Residual variation not accounted for by genetic or shared environmental factors is termed a nonshared or individual-specific environmental variance. Residual variation contributes to the dissimilarity of twin pairs and includes measurement error.

In 12- to 19-year-old adolescents, heritability for initiation of smoking (defined as having ever smoked) has been estimated to be between 36% and 56% across different samples, and the effect of shared environmental factors on initiation has been estimated to be between 30% and 44% (Han et al. 1999; McGue et al. 2000; Rhee et al. 2003). Estimates of heritability for regular cigarette smoking (defined by the frequency of smoking in the past month) range from 27% to 52%, and the range of estimates for the effect of shared environmental factors (7–43%) is wider than that for the initiation of smoking (Rende et al. 2005; Slomkowski et al. 2005; Young et al. 2006). Similar estimates have been found for dependent smoking (i.e., smoking in which the smoker is dependent on nicotine) in adolescents (heritability, 44–49%; shared environmental factors, 15–37%) (McGue et al. 2000; Young et al. 2006). Slomkowski and colleagues (2005), who looked at regular smoking, reported the lowest heritability (23%) and the highest estimate for shared environmental factors (43%) in 15-year-olds, with a shift in the relative values at 1-year follow-up (43% for heritability and 34% for shared environmental factors). In a study of 13- to 16-year-olds, questions about cigarette and other tobacco products were combined into one item of "ever consuming more than 1 cigarette or other tobacco products per day" (Maes et al. 1999, p. 295); this definition of "ever use" produced an estimate for heritability of 65% (Maes et al. 1999) and may capture daily smoking at a later stage of smoking than initiation. Overall, these results support the idea that the relative contribution of genetic influences increases from earlier (initiation) to later (regular/daily or dependent smoking) stages of tobacco use. The results also suggest that the same behavioral measure (frequency of smoking in the past month) may index different types of risk at different ages.

In a sample of 12- to 24-year-olds, heritability for smoking initiation was 39%, and the estimate for shared environmental factors was 53% (Boomsma et al. 1994; Koopmans et al. 1999). Across age groups, however, significant differences in the relative contribution of genetic and environmental factors to the initiation of smoking were not found (Boomsma et al. 1994). A substantial genetic influence was found on quantity smoked in two studies: 86% in a study by Koopmans and colleagues (1999) and 52% in a sample of young adults (aged 18–24 years) in a study by Haberstick and colleagues (2007). Neither study contained evidence for a significant influence of shared environmental factors on the quantity smoked.

Traditionally, the number of cigarettes smoked per day has been used as an indicator of tobacco dependence, the final stage of tobacco use. Latency (time) to first cigarette after waking, another indicator of dependence, was significantly heritable in young adults (55%) in the study by Haberstick and coworkers, with no significant shared environmental factors for this marker (Haberstick et al. 2007). The Heaviness of Smoking Index (HSI), which combines scores on quantity and latency measures, was strongly heritable (61%) in the Haberstick study, with no significant shared environmental factors (Haberstick et al. 2007). In contrast, the Fagerström Test for Nicotine Dependence (FTND) score, which is comprised of the two HSI items and four other items, was modestly heritable (17%) in that study, with a relatively large contribution from shared environmental factors (25%). This is not surprising in that the four additional FTND items showed no evidence for genetic influences (Haberstick et al. 2007).

Taken together, these studies suggest that the prominent role played by shared environmental factors at earlier stages of cigarette smoking, such as initiation, disappears at later stages of regular or dependent use, when genetic influences predominate. For example, Kendler and colleagues (2008) specifically examined the interplay of genetic and environmental factors over time through the use of retrospective life history data (from calendars) among 13- to 35-year-olds and found that genetic influences for number of cigarettes smoked per day first appeared around 16 years of age (about 10% heritability) and increased to about 60% by 35 years of age. In contrast, the contribution of shared environmental factors decreased from about 50% at 13–17 years of age to 0% by 35 years of age.

Studies in adults have shown that the age of smoking initiation is significantly heritable (Heath et al. 1999; Broms et al. 2006), but genetic influence on the age of initiation is independent of the genetic influence on such variables as the quantity smoked and quitting smoking (Broms et al. 2006). Furthermore, Pergadia and colleagues (2006) found similar genetic and environmental influences for regular smoking and dependence measures in adult twin pairs who first tried smoking cigarettes on the same occasion in a comparison with pairs who first tried smoking at different times or ages. These results suggest that varying ages for initiation do not appear to bias genetic and environmental estimates on later stages of smoking, perhaps because initiation and later-stage smoking may not share common genes (Broms et al. 2006).

Schmitt and associates (2005) examined the contribution of genetic and environmental factors to the use of tobacco products other than cigarettes among 20- to 58-year-olds. The relative contributions of genetic and shared environmental factors were, respectively, 43% and 28% for regular use of dip (moist snuff), 19% and 21% for use of chewing tobacco, 0% and 32% for pipe use, and 0% and 26% for cigar use. These results suggest substantial variation in the genetic contribution to regular use of different forms of tobacco.

Interaction Effects Between Genetic and Environmental Factors

The previous section summarized the evidence that genetics plays an important role in smoking behavior, particularly at later stages of smoking. Although genetic risk for cigarette smoking may be a vulnerability with which persons are born, it is not a static and obligatory influence on smoking behavior (for review, see Lynskey et al. 2010). In fact, the expression of genetic risk depends on certain environmental circumstances. For example, smoking by one's peers is a robust predictor of current smoking, regular smoking, and the transition to regular smoking and has a strong influence in adolescence, but it is also significant in adulthood even after controlling for genetic risk for smoking (Vink et al. 2003a,b). Thus, smoking by peers may inhibit the expression of genetic influences on smoking behavior. In a study by White and colleagues (2003), a heritability estimate of 15% for regular (past week) smoking by 13- to 18-year-olds was reduced to 0% after accounting for peer smoking. Two waves of follow-up assessments, about 3 years apart, showed a progressive increase in the heritability estimate for regular smoking to 20% at the second wave (sample aged 16–21 years) and 35% at the third wave (sample aged 20–25 years). In contrast, smoking by peers showed a decreasing influence across waves, explaining 37% of the variance in heritability at the second wave and 12% at the third wave. In another study, Harden and colleagues (2008) found that genetic risk for tobacco and alcohol use in adolescents correlated with best-friend's substance use, a case of gene-environment correlation, and that adolescents at high genetic risk for tobacco and alcohol use also appeared to be more sensitive to adverse peer influences, a case of gene-environment interaction.

Aside from peer influences, parental behavior may affect the expression of genetic risks for smoking. In a sample of 14-year-olds (with 67% shared environmental factors), Dick and colleagues (2007b) estimated a 21% heritability for lifetime quantity smoked, but this estimate decreased to 15% under conditions of high levels of perceived parental monitoring and increased to 60% with perceptions that parental monitoring was low. These results suggest that less perceived parental monitoring may provide conditions that are conducive for the expression of genetic risk for the smoking phenotype. In the study of 14-year-olds, the moderating effect of parental monitoring was not influenced by whether the parents were smokers (Dick et al. 2007b).

Shared time with parents, another parental variable, may affect the expression of genetic risk on lifetime quantity smoked but in an unexpected direction. Among 14-year-olds, spending more time with parents was associated with 50% heritability for lifetime quantity smoked, but spending less time with parents was associated with almost no heritable effects (Dick et al. 2007a). The authors surmised that "spending more time with biologically related relatives may engender the expression of genetic predispositions" and that "for some children, spending time with parents may be beneficial, but for other children, it may not, depending on the behavior and predispositions of the parents" (Dick et al. 2007a, p. 323). Current smoking by parents also moderated the effects of genetic predispositions.

The school environment may also moderate genetic risk for smoking behavior in adolescents. Boardman and colleagues (2008) examined the effects of the social and demographic composition of 7th- to 12th-grade students (mother's education, student's race/ethnicity), school smoking norms (smoking status of popular students), institutional control of smoking (teachers not allowed to smoke on campus, penalties for smoking infractions), and the prevalence of student smoking, on the heritability of ever smoking (heritability estimate, 51%) and daily smoking (58%). They found no effects of these school characteristics on the heritability of ever smoking, but the heritability of daily smoking was significantly lower in schools with higher proportions of White (versus non-White) students and was significantly higher in schools in which the popular students were smokers.

A further layer of detail can be achieved by investigating the interaction between measured genetic and measured environmental factors. In a study of 9th- to 12th-grade students by Audrain-McGovern and colleagues (2006c), risk genotype was not related to smoking progression among those who had had at least one puff of a cigarette but was positively related to physical activity that, in turn, was negatively related to the progression of smoking. However, the relationships between risk genotype and physical activity and between physical activity and the progression of smoking were significant only in adolescents who participated in one or more team sports. Audrain-McGovern and associates (2006c) speculated that the type of physical activity or the social aspects of participation in team sports, or both, may be particularly rewarding in adolescents with risk genotypes, which would tend to decrease the rewarding value of cigarette smoking.

Peer influences, parental behaviors, school characteristics, and school-related activities, such as participation in team sports, are likely to be shared between twins and siblings and are, therefore, likely to be included in the overall estimate of shared environmental variance for smoking behavior unless their effects on genetic risk are explicitly tested. Considering the larger importance of shared environmental factors in the early stages of smoking behavior, it is important to understand the dynamics of measured and latent genetic risk and measured shared environmental factors on smoking behavior. Overall, the interactions of genetic and shared environmental factors are quite complex and call for continued research and careful analyses. More specifically, understanding how genes affect smoking behavior will necessitate identifying key specific factors or sets of factors in the adolescent environment that dynamically interact with genetic vulnerability to affect smoking or nonsmoking.

Neurotransmission and Brain Function in Tobacco Use

Overview of the Effects of Nicotine on the Brain

Upon inhalation of cigarette smoke, nicotine quickly crosses the blood-brain barrier and binds to nicotinic acetylcholine receptors (nAChRs) in the brain (Dani and Heinemann 1996). Activation of nAChRs stimulates the mesocorticolimbic dopamine system (a reward pathway) to produce the primary reinforcing effects of nicotine (Di Chiara 2000). Stimulation of dopamine neurons in the ventral tegmental area (VTA) by nicotine via high-affinity $\alpha4\beta2$ nAChRs (and by all drugs of abuse via specific receptor targets) causes increased firing in terminal dopaminergic fields, such as the nucleus accumbens, amygdala, and the prefrontal cortex (specifically the dorsolateral prefrontal cortex and orbitofrontal cortex). Activation of dopaminergic VTA neurons is also mediated by excitatory glutamatergic neurons projecting primarily from the prefrontal cortex (Taber et al. 1995), and presynaptic $\alpha7$ nAChRs located on glutamatergic projections enhance excitatory input (Mansvelder and McGehee 2000). The GABA interneurons in the VTA, which also express nAChRs and GABA-ergic projections from the nucleus accumbens to the VTA (Walaas and Fonnum 1980; Kalivas et al. 1993), mediate inhibitory and control processes of dopamine stimulation. Thus, the overall effect of nicotine in the VTA stems from the interactions of upstream and downstream effects (Mansvelder et al. 2003). Repeated exposure to nicotine in conjunction with environmental cues (Chaudhri et al. 2007) causes lasting changes in dopaminergic function that contribute to maintenance of smoking and the experience of withdrawal symptoms upon its cessation (Miyata and Yanagita 2001; Balfour 2002).

Studies by Fowler and colleagues (2008) and Salas and colleagues (2003) showed that withdrawal in mice after nicotine intake is linked to the medial habenula and $\alpha2$ and $\alpha5$ nicotine subunits. Mice lacking these receptors show a decrease in withdrawal symptoms. Also, mice lacking these receptors demonstrate increased intake of nicotine, possibly due to a difference in the inhibitory signals (i.e., diminished input) from the habenula in response to nicotine. Thus, some individuals (either through genetics or predisposition) may be more vulnerable to nicotine addiction.

Research Using Imaging in Children and Adolescents

Reward and cognitive control neural networks are implicated in the maintenance of addictive behaviors, including the use of nicotine (Kalivas and Volkow 2005; Brody 2006). Several studies have found that 9- to 19-year-old children and adolescents are at increased risk for smoking by virtue of a family history of drug use or personal history of psychiatric illness (e.g., attention-deficit hyperactivity disorder, conduct disorder). The same youth show blunted activation of the reward system (ventral striatum and frontal cortex) and relatively less activation in a distributed network of primarily frontal and cingulate cortex. They also show relatively less activation of temporal and parietal cortical regions that subserve decision making, performance monitoring, and cognitive control (Schweinsburg et al. 2004; Tamm et al. 2004; Sterzer et al. 2005; Scheres et al. 2007; McNamee et al. 2008; Rubia et al. 2008). Decreased activation may indicate deficits in impulse control coupled with dysregulation of reward sensitivity, which may help explain the etiology of psychiatric conditions.

Blunted activation of the brain to reward and challenges to cognitive control are observed in children who have not previously taken drugs. These conditions are also observed in adolescents at heightened risk for drug use relative to age-matched controls without psychopathology or a family history of drug use. This suggests that differences in reward and control processing may exist before exposure to drugs. These differences may contribute to comorbidity involving substance use and psychopathology and may explain why, in vulnerable persons, even a low level of exposure can tip the balance toward an addicted state (Gervais et al. 2006; DiFranza et al. 2007; Scragg et al. 2008).

Tobacco Dependence in Adolescence

Research demonstrates considerable variation in the length of time that youth report it takes to become addicted to using tobacco. The Hooked on Nicotine Checklist (HONC) was developed and validated specifically for assessing adolescents' dependence on tobacco; endorsement of any 1 of the 10 "yes/no" items indicates dependence (DiFranza et al. 2000, 2002):

- Have you ever tried to quit but couldn't?
- Do you smoke *now* because it is really hard to quit?
- Have you ever felt like you were addicted to tobacco?
- Do you ever have strong cravings to smoke?
- Have you ever felt like you really needed a cigarette?
- Is it hard to keep from smoking in places where you are not supposed to, like in school?
- When you tried to stop smoking (or when you have not used tobacco for a while):
  - Did you find it hard to concentrate because you couldn't smoke?
  - Did you feel more irritable because you could not smoke?
  - Did you feel a strong need or urge to smoke?
  - Did you feel nervous, restless, or anxious because you could not smoke?

In a study by DiFranza and colleagues (2007), approximately 10% of middle school adolescents endorsed one or more HONC symptoms within 2 days after having inhaled from a cigarette for the first time. In another study by Scragg and colleagues (2008), 25% of 14- and 15-year-olds endorsed at least one HONC symptom after having smoked just one cigarette in their lives.

Using longitudinal data, one study computed the length of time taken by 25% of a sample of 12- to 13-year-olds to transition from first cigarette puff to several milestones for cigarette use (Gervais et al. 2006). Reports of feeling "mentally addicted to smoking cigarettes" and smoking one entire cigarette were made 2 to 3 months after the first puff, cravings for cigarettes about 4 to 5 months later (than the first puff), and feeling "physically addicted to smoking cigarettes" about 5 to 6 months after the initial puff. Notably, these behaviors preceded monthly smoking, which was reported about 10 months after the first puff, and preceded having smoked 100 cigarettes, which was reached 20 months after the first puff.

These studies show that symptoms of tobacco dependence are seen in some adolescents well in advance of regular smoking. Thus, at least for a subgroup of adolescents, the conceptualization of a stagewise progression toward tobacco dependence may not be appropriate because these youth are immediately or rapidly reinforced for initial smoking. In brief, these adolescents appear to transition rapidly from a tobacco-naive state to a tobacco-dependent state. Early-emerging symptoms of nicotine dependence during adolescence, however, have been found to be a poor prognostic indicator for chronicity of smoking in adulthood (Dierker and Mermelstein 2010).

Still, biological evidence is accumulating to suggest that the adolescent brain may be particularly susceptible to the addictive properties of nicotine (Chambers et al. 2003). Human and animal studies of the adolescent brain have demonstrated heightened neuronal sensitivity to nicotine and other constituents of cigarettes (Belluzzi et al. 2004, 2005; Cao et al. 2007). In addition, exposing the developing brain to nicotine has been shown to alter its structure and function in a way that introduces long-lasting vulnerability for addiction to nicotine and other substances of abuse (Leslie et al. 2004; Debry and Tiffany 2008; Dao et al. 2011).

Developmental Processes: Prenatal Exposure to Nicotine

More than 15% of pregnant women in the United States smoke (SAMHSA 2010) despite the significant perinatal and postnatal risks of this behavior to their offspring (Salihu and Wilson 2007). Of note is that more than 20% of pregnant adolescents 15–17 years of age smoke (SAMHSA 2010). Use of smokeless tobacco is common in Western Alaska Native pregnant women (58%), though less so over the entire state (17.8%), but still alarming rates in light of the prevalence in the general population of U.S. women of one-half of 1% (Renner et al. 2005; Kim et al. 2010). Use of smokeless tobacco is also prevalent (34%) among pregnant women in certain parts of India (Bloch et al. 2008). Nicotine (in tobacco smoke or in smokeless tobacco products) can have direct effects on nAChRs, which are already present in the brain and spinal cord of fetuses at 4 weeks of gestation (Hellström-Lindahl et al. 1998), suggesting that nAChRs play an important role in the development of the nervous system. Researchers performing animal studies (Slotkin 1998; Slikker et al. 2005) have surmised that prenatal exposure to nicotine affects neural development. Maternal smoking during pregnancy has been associated with increased risks for the offspring of ever smoking, regular (or current) smoking, and dependence on tobacco as preadolescents, adolescents, and young adults (Kandel et al. 1994; Kandel and Udry 1999; Cornelius et al. 2000; Buka et al. 2003; Al Mamun et al. 2006). However, some studies have not found such associations (Kandel et al. 1994; Silberg et al. 2003; Cornelius et al. 2005; Knopik et al. 2005; Roberts et al. 2005; O'Callaghan et al. 2006), and so there is need for further investigation.

Prenatal exposure to nicotine affects outcomes among offspring through established deleterious influences on fetal growth or as part of a maternal profile of substance use or comorbid psychopathology (Cornelius et al. 2011). This kind of prenatal exposure may also alter the sensitivity of the offspring to later environmental influences (Abreu-Villaça et al. 2004), which could predispose the offspring to a given behavioral trajectory. Thus, the environmental influences would become the salient proximal risk factors for behavior and might mask, in statistical analysis, the changes in sensitivity initially conferred by prenatal exposure to nicotine.

Summary

Future research should explore the influence of specific neural mechanisms at all stages of tobacco use and the relationships of such mechanisms with the underlying genetic architecture. Future work should also explore how the brain integrates information from large social and physical environments, small social groups, and cognitive factors to influence tobacco use behaviors in a measurable way.

At this time, research on neurobiological mechanisms that contributes to our knowledge of the etiology of tobacco use in humans lags significantly behind research on the other important influences on tobacco use summarized in this chapter. So far, the evidence from the literature on animals and adult humans indicates that nicotine activates brain reward pathways (Stein et al. 1998; Di Chiara 2000; Rose et al. 2003), the literature on adult humans indicates that smoking history is related to changes in the processing of reward and cognitive control (Anokhin et al. 2000; Martin-Sölch et al. 2001; Neuhaus et al. 2006; Musso et al. 2007), and the literature on adolescents indicates that the same changes in system responsiveness seen in adult smokers (vs. nonsmokers) are seen in tobacco-naive adolescents at risk for smoking (because of psychiatric history or familial substance use) relative to controls (Schweinsburg et al. 2004; Tamm et al. 2004; Sterzer et al. 2005; Scheres et al. 2007; McNamee et al. 2008; Rubia et al. 2008). These latter results suggest that differences in brain processing observed between adult smokers and nonsmokers may result from preexisting differences in brain processing between these groups. Some smokers' use of tobacco might be considered as part of a general profile of psychopathology and high-risk behavior and may not be a direct effect of brain processing on tobacco use. Although evidence from neuroimaging is consistent in that observed group differences occur in the same direction as lower or higher neural activation and in overlapping brain regions, the evidence is inconclusive as to whether neural processing is related to or causes tobacco use specifically. The evidence that genes play an important role in tobacco use behaviors is increasing in the literature and consistent across samples, age groups, and age cohorts. However, the presence of genetic risk alone is not sufficient for the expression of a tobacco use behavior. Environmental factors can modify the expression of genetic risk, making it impossible to conclude that genetic variation causes a specific tobacco use behavior. Rather, genetic predisposition likely interacts in complex ways with a number of environmental factors across the large social and physical environments and among small social groups.

Evidence Summary

This chapter covered four general levels of predictors related to the etiology of tobacco use among youth. Risk factors at each of these levels are particularly potent for adolescents and young adults as they transition from childhood to adulthood. The changes in social expectations for these age groups, the further expansion of brain functioning, and the influence of peers provide a changing and challenging context with added vulnerability to tobacco use from 12 to 25 years of age.

Large Social and Physical Environments

Factors found in large social and physical environments may establish norms that affect tobacco use. For example, youth who participate in religious activity are less likely to smoke. The expression of other cultural values, such as using cigarettes as gifts, may, conversely, stimulate tobacco use. Educational attainment and academic achievement are consistently (and negatively) associated with tobacco use from early adolescence to young adulthood. In addition, persons of lower SES may be more likely to smoke because of differential norms or as a reaction to pressures, such as discrimination, or targeted marketing (see Chapter 5). Particularly in the developing world, women, who traditionally use tobacco products less often than men, have apparently been using tobacco more in recent years, perhaps as a reaction to increased marketing appeals directed at them. Physical environments favorable to tobacco use—as might be demonstrated by the availability of ashtrays or smoking areas or the presence of advertising displays—may also influence tobacco use through implicit norms that favor use.

Small Social Groups

Social influences are among the most robust and consistent predictors of adolescent smoking. Peer influences seem to be especially salient, perhaps because adolescence is a time during which school and peer group affiliations take on particular importance. Adolescents tend to overestimate the prevalence of smoking among their peers, and perceptions that one's peers smoke consistently predict use of tobacco. Another well-established finding is that adolescents are more likely to smoke if they have friends who smoke. Young smokers tend to affiliate with other young smokers, and both selection (of friends) and socialization (influences of friends) likely contribute to homogeneity in tobacco use among groups of friends. These processes that lead to homogeneity are not separate from, and are likely nested within, a similarity in factors in large social and physical environments, such as religion, social stratification, and ethnicity. In short, youth might be guided by those closest to them and by perceived social norms and then select and be influenced by peers to use or not use tobacco products.

Social network analyses have demonstrated that peer group structure uniquely contributes to the prediction of youth smoking behavior. Youth who are able to mix successfully within small social groups are relatively less likely to conform to the tobacco use behavior of others than are isolates, who perhaps have fewer social skills or experience a sense of being lower in social status within a group. The fact that popular youth are relatively more likely to smoke in schools that have relatively greater concentrations of smokers suggests that smoking behavior among peer networks is also contingent on school-level norms and attempts to be liked by others in the group.

Research on group identification indicates that youth who self-identify as belonging to deviant groups are most likely to be smokers. In addition to these peer-related effects, smoking by parents and older siblings and the quality of family relationships and parenting practices are generally predictive of all levels of smoking among adolescents. However, parental disapproval of smoking is inconsistently related to smoking by their children, and the effects of parental smoking may be mediated by such variables as the degree of monitoring and supervision provided by parents. Evidence from studies of young adults indicates there may be a continuing influence of parental smoking on the initiation and progression of smoking, although the studies are few and the findings are not sufficient for a definitive conclusion.

Intrapersonal Cognitive Processes

Beliefs about the consequences of tobacco use, decision-making capabilities, and the ability to regulate or monitor one's behavior, all of which reflect deliberate or controlled cognitive processes, are predictive of tobacco use. For example, beliefs that tobacco use leads to positive social outcomes and is relatively safe, along with poor decision-making skills and difficulties in self-monitoring, are predictive of later tobacco use. These cognitive factors may be moderated by family-level protective factors or sociocultural factors, such as relatively high SES. Alternatively, these cognitive factors may moderate the influence of sociocultural influences on the initiation of smoking. In addition, implicit attitudes (e.g., liking smoking) tend to be more positive among smokers, and measures of tobacco-related memory/implicit associations are predictive of subsequent tobacco use. Thus, both deliberate and implicit cognitive processes may predict later tobacco use among youth. However, tobacco-related implicit associations are also potent predictors of smoking among youth whose working memory has a relatively lower capacity. Cognitive processes clearly play a key role in whether a person engages in risky behaviors, but more research is needed to clarify the interplay of controlled and automatic cognitive processes.

Genetic Factors and Neurobiological and Neurodevelopmental Processes

Heritability for tobacco use is more strongly associated with regular use and dependence than with the early stages of tobacco use, suggesting that addiction to tobacco may have a relatively strong genetic component. However, the expression of genetic risk for smoking is moderated by small-group factors (e.g., peer smoking, parental monitoring, and engagement in team sports) and larger social environmental factors (e.g., school-level norms, the prevalence of smoking among popular kids). Youth at relatively greater risk for tobacco use show relatively less activation in brain structures associated with decision making and impulse control coupled with impairment in sensitivity to reward. Thus, neurobiological input into cognitive-level factors may be associated with tobacco use. More research is needed, but some evidence suggests that some youth become dependent on nicotine shortly after trying tobacco. In addition, although available studies show mixed results, some evidence indicates that a mother's smoking during pregnancy may increase the likelihood that her offspring will become regular smokers. All of these neurobiological factors are moderated by other environmental factors, although they may affect the operation of these other factors as well.

Multilevel Influences on Tobacco Use

This chapter has focused on four primary levels of influence related to the etiology of tobacco use among adolescents and young adults. There are increasing numbers of studies that consider interactions between multiple levels of influence. Innovations in statistical techniques now allow for more sophisticated models that are helping to disentangle the relative contributions of nested factors important in the onset and progression of tobacco use among youth. Multilevel models, for example, are now being used to examine the relative influence of community-level, school-level, and individual-level risk and protective factors for tobacco use (Ali and Dwyer 2009; Mayberry et al. 2009; Wen et al. 2009; Ennett et al. 2010; Kelly et al. 2010; McVicar 2011). These studies suggest that proximal social influences (e.g., individual, peer and parental influences) are particularly potent predictors of tobacco use among young people, having a stronger, more direct, and more immediate influence than do macro-level factors (e.g., the school climate, community norms). However, these macrolevel factors are also powerful predictors, since they are pervasive in society and because they strongly affect the proximal social influences. These studies underscore corresponding findings from recent reviews on peer (Simons-Morton and Farhart 2010) and parental influences on youth tobacco use (Emory et al. 2010; Leonardi-Bee et al. 2011).

Summary

Adolescence represents a critical period of vulnerability for the onset and progression of smoking. Understanding the etiology of tobacco use in youth and young adults can be complex. The determinants of adolescent and young adult smoking are many and interrelated. Smoking uptake and progression is determined by the concurrent and joint contributions of the biological, psychosocial, and environmental factors identified in this chapter. The identified influences may exert small to large effects across adolescents' transitions from initiation to experimentation to regular use. Similarly, these factors may be more or less influential across developmental periods. For example, parental risk factors tend to become less important relative to peer risk factors with increasing age. New areas of research about the etiology of smoking among young people have been developing rapidly since the publication of the last Surgeon General's report on youth (USDHHS 1994) and have been summarized in this chapter. Much more remains to be learned, especially in the area of cognitions and the neurobiology of smoking risk and the development of tobacco dependence.

Conclusions

1. Given their developmental stage, adolescents and young adults are uniquely susceptible to social and environmental influences to use tobacco.

2. Socioeconomic factors and educational attainment influence the development of youth smoking behavior. The adolescents most likely to begin to use tobacco and progress to regular use are those who have lower academic achievement.

3. The evidence is sufficient to conclude that there is a causal relationship between peer group social influences and the initiation and maintenance of smoking behaviors during adolescence.

4. Affective processes play an important role in youth smoking behavior, with a strong association between youth smoking and negative affect.

5. The evidence is suggestive that tobacco use is a heritable trait, more so for regular use than for onset. The expression of genetic risk for smoking among young people may be moderated by small-group and larger social-environmental factors.

References

Abel G, Plumridge L, Graham P. Peers, networks or relationships: strategies for understanding social dynamics as determinants of smoking behavior. *Drugs: Education, Prevention and Policy* 2002;9(4):325–38.

Abreu-Villaça Y, Seidler FJ, Slotkin TA. Does prenatal nicotine exposure sensitize the brain to nicotine-induced neurotoxicity in adolescence? *Neuropsychopharmacology* 2004;29(8):1440–50.

Abroms L, Simons-Morton B, Haynie DL, Chen R. Psychosocial predictors of smoking trajectories during middle and high school. *Addiction* 2005;100(6):852–61.

Adams ML, Jason LA, Pokorny S, Hunt Y. The relationship between school policies and youth tobacco use. *Journal of School Health* 2009;79(1):17–23.

Afifi ZE. Daily practices, study performance and health during the Ramadan fast. *Journal of the Royal Society for the Promotion of Health* 1997;117(4):231–45.

Al Mamun A, O'Callaghan FV, Alati R, O'Callaghan M, Najman JM, Williams GM, Bor W. Does maternal smoking during pregnancy predict the smoking patterns of young adult offspring: a birth cohort study. *Tobacco Control* 2006;15(6):452–7.

Alamar B, Glantz SA. Effect of increased social unacceptability of cigarette smoking on reduction in cigarette consumption. *American Journal of Public Health* 2006; 96(8):1359–63.

Alesci NL, Forster JL, Blaine T. Smoking visibility, perceived acceptability, and frequency in various locations among youth and adults. *Preventive Medicine* 2003;36(3):272–81.

Alexander C, Piazza M, Mekos D, Valente T. Peers, schools, and adolescent cigarette smoking. *Journal of Adolescent Health* 2001:29(1):22–30.

Allen B Jr, Unger JB. Sociocultural correlates of menthol cigarette smoking among adult African Americans in Los Angeles. *Nicotine & Tobacco Research* 2007;9(4):447–51.

Ali MM, Dwyer DS. Estimating peer effects in adolescent smoking behavior: a longitudinal analysis. *Journal of Adolescent Health* 2009;45(4):402–8.

Aloise-Young PA, Graham JW, Hansen WB. Peer influence on smoking initiation during early adolescence: a comparison of group members and group outsiders. *Journal of Applied Psychology* 1994;79(2):281–7.

Aloise-Young PA, Kaeppner CJ. Sociometric status as a predictor of onset and progression in adolescent cigarette smoking. *Nicotine & Tobacco Research* 2005;7(2): 199–206.

American Indian Tobacco Education Network. *American Indian Tobacco Education Network, 2000: Campaign Reports Addressing the Areas of: Cessation Services, Countering Pro-Tobacco Influences, Social Source Access to Commercial Tobacco, and Environmental Tobacco Smoke*. Sacramento (CA): American Indian Tobacco Education Network, 2000.

Americans for Nonsmokers' Rights. Smokefree Transportation Chronology. 2005; <http://no-smoke.org/document.php?id=334>; accessed: May 1, 2009.

Ames SL, Franken IHA, Coronges K. Implicit cognition and drugs of abuse. In: Wiers RW, Stacy AW, editors. *Handbook of Implicit Cognition and Addiction*. Thousand Oaks (CA): Sage Publications, 2006:363–78.

Ames SL, Grenard JL, Thush C, Sussman S, Wiers RW, Stacy AW. Comparison of indirect assessments of association as predictors of marijuana use among at-risk adolescents. *Experimental and Clinical Psychopharmacology* 2007;15(2):204–18.

Andrews JA, Hampson SE, Barckley M, Gerrard M, Gibbons FX. The effect of early cognitions on cigarette and alcohol use during adolescence. *Psychology of Addictive Behaviors* 2008;22(1):96–106.

Andrews JA, Hops H, Duncan SC. Adolescent modeling of parent substance use: the moderating effect of the relationship with the parent. *Journal of Family Psychology* 1997;11(3):259–70.

Andrews JA, Tildesley E, Hops H, Li F. The influence of peers on young adult substance use. *Health Psychology* 2002;21(4):349–57.

Anokhin AP, Vedeniapin AB, Sirevaag EJ, Bauer LO, O'Connor SJ, Kuperman S, Porjesz B, Reich T, Begleiter H, Polich J, et al. The P300 brain potential is reduced in smokers. *Psychopharmacology* 2000;149(4):409–13.

Arnett JJ. Emerging adulthood: a theory of development from the late teens through the twenties. *American Psychologist* 2000;55(5):469–80.

Arnett JJ. The myth of peer influence in adolescent smoking initiation. *Health Education & Behavior* 2007; 34(4):594–607.

Audrain-McGovern J, Rodriguez D, Kassel JD. Adolescent smoking and depression: evidence for self-medication and peer smoking mediation. *Addiction* 2009;104(10):1743–56.

Audrain-McGovern J, Rodriguez D, Patel V, Faith MS, Rodgers K, Cuevas J. How do psychological factors influence adolescent smoking progression: the evidence for indirect effects through tobacco advertising receptivity. *Pediatrics* 2006a;117(4):1216–25.

Audrain-McGovern J, Rodriguez D, Tercyak KP, Cuevas J, Rodgers K, Patterson F. Identifying and characterizing adolescent smoking trajectories. *Cancer Epidemiology, Biomarkers & Prevention* 2004;13(12):2023–34.

Audrain-McGovern J, Rodriguez D, Tercyak KP, Neuner G, Moss HB. The impact of self-control indices on peer smoking and adolescent smoking progression. *Journal of Pediatric Psychology* 2006b;31(2):139–51.

Audrain-McGovern J, Rodriguez D, Wileyto EP, Schmitz KH, Shields PG. Effect of team sport participation on genetic predisposition to adolescent smoking progression. *Archives of General Psychiatry* 2006c;63(4):433–41.

Ausems M, Mesters I, van Breukelen G, de Vries H. Do Dutch 11-12 years olds who never smoke, smoke experimentally or smoke regularly have different demographic backgrounds and perceptions of smoking? *European Journal of Public Health* 2003;13(2):160–7.

Avenevoli S, Merikangas KR. Familial influences on adolescent smoking. *Addiction* 2003;98(Suppl 1):S1–S20.

Bachman JG, O'Malley PM, Schulenberg JE, Johnston LD, Bryant AL, Merlin AC. *The Decline of Substance Use in Young Adulthood: Changes in Social Activities, Roles, and Beliefs*. Mahwah (NJ): Lawrence Erlbaum Associates, 2001.

Balfour DJ. Neuroplasticity within the mesoaccumbens dopamine system and its role in tobacco dependence. *Current Drug Targets, CNS and Neurological Disorders* 2002;1(4):413–21.

Bandura A. Self-efficacy: toward a unifying theory of behavior change. *Psychological Review* 1977a;84(2):191–215.

Bandura A. *Social Learning Theory*. Englewood Cliffs (NJ): Prentice Hall, 1977b.

Bargh JA, Chartrand TL. The unbearable automaticity of being. *American Psychologist* 1999;54(7):462–79.

Barnett JR. Does place of residence matter: contextual effects and smoking in Christchurch. *New Zealand Medical Journal* 2000;113(1120):433–5.

Bartkowski JP, Xu X. Religiosity and teen drug use reconsidered: a social capital perspective. *American Journal of Preventive Medicine* 2007;32(6 Suppl):S182–S194.

Barton JL, Chassin L, Presson CC, Sherman SJ. Social image factors as motivators of smoking initiation in early and middle adolescence. *Child Development* 1982;53(6):1499–511.

Bassett JF, Dabbs JM Jr. A portable version of the go/no-go association task (GNAT). *Behavior Research Methods* 2005;37(3):506–12.

Battistich V, Hom A. The relationship between students' sense of their school as a community and their involvement in problem behaviors. *American Journal of Public Health* 1997;87(12):1997–2001.

Bauman KE, Botvin GJ, Botvin EM, Baker E. Normative expectations and the behavior of significant others: an integration of traditions in research on adolescents' cigarette smoking. *Psychological Reports* 1992; 71(2):568–70.

Bauman KE, Carver K, Gleiter K. Trends in parent and friend influence during adolescence: the case of adolescent cigarette smoking. *Addictive Behaviors* 2001;26(3):349–61.

Bauman KE, Ennett ST. On the importance of peer influence for adolescent drug use: commonly neglected considerations. *Addiction* 1996;91(2):185–98.

Bauman KE, Fisher LA. On the measurement of friend behavior in research on friend influence and selection: findings from longitudinal studies of adolescent smoking and drinking. *Journal of Youth and Adolescence* 1986;15(4):345–53.

Baumann M, Spitz E, Guillemin F, Ravaud J-F, Choquet M, Falissard B, Chau N, Lorhandicap Group. Associations of social and material deprivation with tobacco, alcohol, and psychotropic drug use, and gender: a population-based study. *International Journal of Health Geographics* 2007;6:50.

Baumrind D. Familial antecedents of adolescent drug use: a developmental perspective. *NIDA Research Monograph* 1985;56:13–44.

Bechara A, Damasio H. Decision-making and addiction (part I): impaired activation of somatic states in substance dependent individuals when pondering decisions with negative future consequences. *Neuropsychologia* 2002;40(10):1675–89.

Beebe LA, Vesely SK, Oman RF, Tolma E, Aspy CB, Rodine S. Protective assets for non-use of alcohol, tobacco and other drugs among urban American Indian youth in Oklahoma. *Maternal and Child Health Journal* 2008;12(Suppl 1):82–90.

Belluzzi JD, Lee AG, Oliff HS, Leslie FM. Age-dependent effects of nicotine on locomotor activity and conditioned place preference in rats. *Psychopharmacology* 2004;174(3):389–95.

Belluzzi JD, Wang R, Leslie FM. Acetaldehyde enhances acquisition of nicotine self-administration in adolescent rats. *Neuropsychopharmacology* 2005;30(4):705–12.

Bergen AW, Korczak JF, Weissbecker KA, Goldstein AM. A genome-wide search for loci contributing to smoking and alcoholism. *Genetic Epidemiology* 1999;17(Suppl 1):S55–S60.

Bernat DH, Erickson DJ, Widome R, Perry CL, Forster JL. Adolescent smoking trajectories: results from a population-based cohort study. *Journal of Adolescent Health* 2008;43(4):334–40.

Bethel JW, Schenker MB. Acculturation and smoking patterns among Hispanics: a review. *American Journal of Preventive Medicine* 2005;29(2):143–8.

Beuten J, Ma JZ, Payne TJ, Dupont RT, Cres KM, Somes G, Williams NU, Elston RC, Li MD. Single- and multilocus allelic variants within the GABAB receptor subunit 2 (*GABAB2*) gene are significantly associated with nicotine dependence. *American Journal of Human Genetics* 2005;76(5):859–64.

Beuten J, Ma JZ, Payne TJ, Dupont RT, Lou XY, Crews KM, Elston RC, Li MD. Association of specific haplotypes of Neurotrophic Tyrosine Kinase Receptor 2 gene (NTKR2) with vulnerability to nicotine dependence in African-Americans and European-Americans. *Biological Psychiatry* 2007;61(1):48–55.

Bierut LJ. Convergence of genetic findings for nicotine dependence and smoking related diseases with chromosome 15q24-25. *Trends in Pharmacological Sciences* 2010;31(1):46–51.

Bierut LJ, Rice JP, Goate A, Hinrichs AL, Saccone NL, Foroud T, Edenberg HJ, Cloninger CR, Begleiter H, Conneally PM, et al. A genomic scan for habitual smoking in families of alcoholics: common and specific genetic factors in substance dependence. *American Journal of Medical Genetics Part A* 2004;124A(1):19–27.

Biglan A, Duncan TE, Ary DV, Smolkowski K. Peer and parental influences on adolescent tobacco use. *Journal of Behavioral Medicine* 1995;18(4):315–30.

Bisol LW, Soldado F, Albuquerque C, Lorenzi TM, Lara DR. Emotional and affective temperaments and cigarette smoking in a large sample. *Journal of Affective Disorders* 2010;127(1-3):89–95.

Bloch M, Althabe F, Onyamboko M, Kaseba-Sata C, Castilla EE, Freire S, Garces AL, Parida S, Goudar SS, Kadir MM, et al. Tobacco use and secondhand smoke exposure during pregnancy: an investigative survey of women in 9 developing nations. *American Journal of Public Health* 2008;98(10):1833–40.

Blyth DA, Hill JP, Thiel KS. Early adolescents' significant others: grade and gender differences in perceived relationships with familial and nonfamilial adults and young people. *Journal of Youth and Adolescence* 1982;11(6):425–50.

Boardman JD, Saint Onge JM, Haberstick BC, Timberlake DS, Hewitt JK. Do schools moderate the genetic determinants of smoking? *Behavior Genetics* 2008; 38(3):234–46.

Bond L, Butler H, Thomas L, Carlin J, Glover S, Bowes G, Patton G. Social and school connectedness in early secondary school as predictors of late teenage substance use, mental health, and academic outcomes. *Journal of Adolescent Health* 2007;40(4):357.e9–357.e18.

Boomsma DI, Koopmans JR, Van Doornen LJ, Orlebeke JF. Genetic and social influences on starting to smoke: a study of Dutch adolescent twins and their parents. *Addiction* 1994;89(2):219–26.

Borrell LN, Jacobs DR Jr, Williams DR, Pletcher MJ, Houston TK, Kiefe CI. Self-reported racial discrimination and substance use in the Coronary Artery Risk Development in Adults Study. *American Journal of Epidemiology* 2007;166(9):1068–79.

Botvin GJ, Baker E, Botvin EM, Dusenbury L, Cardwell J, Diaz T. Factors promoting cigarette smoking among black youth: a causal modeling approach. *Addictive Behaviors* 1993;18(4):397–405.

Botvin GJ, Baker E, Goldberg CJ, Dusenbury L, Botvin EM. Correlates and predictors of smoking among black adolescents. *Addictive Behaviors* 1992a;17(2):97–103.

Botvin GJ, Botvin EM, Baker E, Dusenbury L, Goldberg CJ. The false consensus effect: predicting adolescents' tobacco use from normative expectations. *Psychological Reports* 1992b;70(1):171–8.

Boyle RG, Claxton AJ, Forster JL. The role of social influences and tobacco availability on adolescent smokeless tobacco use. *Journal of Adolescent Health* 1997; 20(4):279–85.

Bradby H. Watch out for the aunties: young British Asians' accounts of identity and substance use. *Sociology of Health & Illness* 2007;29(5):656–72.

Brandon TH, Baker TB. The Smoking Consequences Questionnaire: the subjective expected utility of smoking in college students. *Psychological Assessment* 1991; 3(3):484–91.

Brandon TH, Herzog TA, Irvin JE, Gwaltney CJ. Cognitive and social learning models of drug dependence: implications for the assessment of tobacco dependence in adolescents. *Addiction* 2004;99(Suppl 1):S51–S77.

Brandon TH, Juliano LM, Copeland AL. Expectancies for tobacco smoking. In: Kirsh I, editor. *How Expectancies Shape Experience*. Washington: American Psychological Association, 1999.

Bricker JB, Peterson AV Jr, Andersen MR, Leroux BG, Bharat Rajan K, Sarason IG. Close friends', parents', and older siblings' smoking: reevaluating their influence on children's smoking. *Nicotine & Tobacco Research* 2006a;8(2):217–26.

Bricker JB, Peterson AV Jr, Leroux BG, Andersen MR, Rajan KB, Sarason IG. Prospective prediction of children's smoking transitions: role of parents' and older siblings' smoking. *Addiction* 2006b;101(1):128–36.

Bricker JB, Peterson AV Jr, Sarason IG, Andersen MR, Rajan KB. Changes in the influence of parents' and close friends' smoking on adolescent smoking transitions. *Addictive Behaviors* 2007;32(4):740–57.

Brody AL. Functional brain imaging of tobacco use and dependence. *Journal of Psychiatric Research* 2006; 40(5):404–18.

Broms U, Silventoinen K, Madden PA, Heath AC, Kaprio J. Genetic architecture of smoking behavior: a study of Finnish adult twins. *Twin Research and Human Genetics* 2006;9(1):64–72.

Brook JS, Duan T, Brook DW, Ning Y. Pathways to nicotine dependence in African American and Puerto Rican young adults. *American Journal on Addictions* 2007;16(6):450–6.

Brook JS, Pahl K, Ning Y. Peer and parental influences on longitudinal trajectories of smoking among African Americans and Puerto Ricans. *Nicotine & Tobacco Research* 2006;8(5):639–51.

Brook JS, Whiteman M, Czeisler LJ, Shapiro J, Cohen P. Cigarette smoking in young adults: childhood and adolescent personality, familial, and peer antecedents. *Journal of Genetic Psychology* 1997;158(2):172–88.

Brown BB. Adolescents' relationships with peers. In: Lerner RM, Steinberg L, editors. *Handbook of Adolescent Psychology*. 2nd ed. Hoboken (NJ): John Wiley & Sons, 2004:363–94.

Buka SL, Shenassa ED, Niaura R. Elevated risk of tobacco dependence among offspring of mothers who smoked during pregnancy: a 30-year prospective study. *American Journal of Psychiatry* 2003;160(11):1978–84.

Cao J, Belluzzi JD, Loughlin SE, Keyler DE, Pentel PR, Leslie FM. Acetaldehyde, a major constituent of tobacco smoke, enhances behavioral, endocrine, and neuronal responses to nicotine in adolescent and adult rats. *Neuropsychopharmacology* 2007;32(9):2025–35.

Carvajal SC, Granillo TM. A prospective test of distal and proximal determinants of smoking initiation in early adolescents. *Addictive Behaviors* 2006;31(4):649–60.

Castro FG. Physiological, psychological, social, and cultural influences on the use of menthol cigarettes among blacks and Hispanics. *Nicotine & Tobacco Research* 2004;6(Suppl 1):S29–S41.

Centers for Disease Control and Prevention. State smoking restrictions for private-sector worksites, restaurants, and bars—United States, 2004 and 2007. *Morbidity and Mortality Weekly Report* 2008;57(20):549–2.

Centers for Disease Control and Prevention. Vital signs: current cigarette smoking among adults aged ≥18 years—United States, 2005–2010. *Morbidity and Mortality Weekly Report* 2011;66(35):1207–12.

Chae DH, Takeuchi DT, Barbeau EM, Bennett GG, Lindsey J, Krieger N. Unfair treatment, racial/ethnic discrimination, ethnic identification, and smoking among Asian Americans in the National Latino and Asian American study. *American Journal of Public Health* 2008;98(3):485–92.

Chambers RA, Taylor JR, Potenza MN. Developmental neurocircuitry of motivation in adolescence: a critical period of addiction vulnerability. *American Journal of Psychiatry* 2003;160(6):1041–52.

Chan WC, Leatherdale ST. Tobacco retailer density surrounding schools and youth smoking behaviour: a multi-level analysis. *Tobacco Induced Diseases* 2011; 9(1):9.

Chassin L, Presson CC, Pitts SC, Sherman SJ. The natural history of cigarette smoking from adolescence to adulthood in a midwestern community sample: multiple trajectories and their psychosocial correlates. *Health Psychology* 2000;19(3):223–31.

Chassin L, Presson CC, Rose JS, Sherman SJ. The natural history of cigarette smoking from adolescence to adulthood: demographic predictors of continuity and change. *Health Psychology* 1996;15(6):478–84.

Chassin L, Presson CC, Rose J, Sherman SJ, Davis M, Gonzalez JL. Parenting style and smoking-specific parenting practices as predictors of adolescent smoking onset. *Journal of Pediatric Psychology* 2005;30(4):333–44.

Chassin L, Presson CC, Rose J, Sherman SJ, Prost J. Parental smoking cessation and adolescent smoking. *Journal of Pediatric Psychology* 2002;27(6):485–96.

Chassin L, Presson C, Seo D-C, Sherman SJ, Macy J, Wirth RJ, Curran P. Multiple trajectories of cigarette smoking and the intergenerational transmission of smoking: a multigenerational, longitudinal study of a Midwestern community sample. *Health Psychology* 2008;27(6):819–28.

Chassin L, Presson CC, Sherman SJ, Montello D, McGrew J. Changes in peer and parent influence during adolescence: longitudinal versus cross-sectional perspectives on smoking initiation. *Developmental Psychology* 1986;22(3):327–34.

Chassin L, Presson CC, Todd M, Rose JS, Sherman SJ. Maternal socialization of adolescent smoking: the intergenerational transmission of parenting and smoking. *Developmental Psychology* 1998;34(6):1189–201.

Chaudhri N, Caggiula AR, Donny EC, Booth S, Gharib M, Craven L, Palmatier MI, Liu X, Sved AF. Self-administered and noncontingent nicotine enhance reinforced operant responding in rats: impact of nicotine dose and reinforcement schedule. *Psychopharmacology* 2007;190(3):353–62.

Chen X, Stanton B, Fang X, Li X, Lin D, Zhang J, Liu H, Yang H. Perceived smoking norms, socioenvironmental factors, personal attitudes and adolescent smoking in China: a mediation analysis with longitudinal data. *Journal of Adolescent Health* 2006;38(4):359–68.

Chen X, Unger JB, Cruz TB, Johnson CA. Smoking patterns of Asian-American youth in California and their relationship with acculturation. *Journal of Adolescent Health* 1999a;24(5):321–8.

Chen X, Unger JB, Johnson CA. Is acculturation a risk factor for early smoking initiation among Chinese American minors: a comparative perspective. *Tobacco Control* 1999b;8(4):402–10.

Choi S, Rankin S, Stewart A, Oka R. Effects of acculturation on smoking behavior in Asian Americans: a meta-analysis. *Journal of Cardiovascular Nursing* 2008; 23(1):67–73.

Choi WS, Ahluwalia JS, Harris KJ, Okuyemi K. Progression to established smoking: the influence of tobacco marketing. *American Journal of Preventive Medicine* 2002;22(4):228–33.

Choi WS, Harris KJ, Okuyemi K, Ahluwalia JS. Predictors of smoking initiation among college-bound high school students. *Annals of Behavioral Medicine* 2003; 26(1):69–74.

Chuang YC, Cubbin C, Ahn D, Winkleby MA. Effects of neighborhood socioeconomic status and convenience store concentration on individual level smoking. *Journal of Epidemiology and Community Health* 2005a;59(7):568–73.

Chuang YC, Ennett ST, Bauman KE, Foshee VA. Neighborhood influences on adolescent cigarette and alcohol use: mediating effects through parent and peer behaviors. *Journal of Health and Social Behavior* 2005b;46(2):187–204.

Church of Jesus Christ of Latter-Day Saints. Doctrine and covenants of the Church of Jesus Christ of Latter-Day Saints, Section 89, 2006; <http://scriptures.lds.org/dc/89>; accessed: May 1, 2009.

Clark PI, Scarisbrick-Hauser A, Gautam SP, Wirk SJ. Antitobacco socialization in homes of African-American and white parents, and smoking and nonsmoking parents. *Journal of Adolescent Health* 1999;24(5):329–39.

Cohen JM. Sources of peer group homogeneity. *Sociology of Education* 1977;50(4):227–41.

Cohen DA, Richardson J, LaBree L. Parenting behaviors and the onset of smoking and alcohol use: a longitudinal study. *Pediatrics* 1994;94(3):368–75.

Colder CR, Mehta P, Balanda K, Campbell RT, Mayhew KP, Stanton WR, Pentz MA, Flay BR. Identifying trajectories of adolescent smoking: an application of latent growth mixture modeling. *Health Psychology* 2001;20(2):127–35.

Colvin PJ, Mermelstein RJ. Adolescents' smoking outcome expectancies and acute emotional responses following smoking. *Nicotine & Tobacco Research* 2010; 12(12):1203–10.

Conrad KM, Flay BR, Hill D. Why children start smoking cigarettes: predictors of onset. *British Journal of Addiction* 1992;87(12):1711–24.

Coogan PF, Adams M, Geller AC, Brooks D, Miller DR, Lew RA, Koh HK. Factors associated with smoking among children and adolescents in Connecticut. *American Journal of Preventive Medicine* 1998;15(1):17–24.

Cook TD. The case for studying multiple contexts simultaneously. *Addiction* 2003;98(Suppl1):151–5.

Cornelius MD, De Genna NM, Leech SL, Willford JA, Goldschmidt L, Day NL. Effects of prenatal cigarette smoke exposure on neurobehavioral outcomes in 10-year-old children of adolescent mothers. *Neurotoxicology and Teratology* 2011;33(1):137–44.

Cornelius MD, Leech SL, Goldschmidt L, Day NL. Prenatal tobacco exposure: is it a risk factor for early tobacco experimentation? *Nicotine & Tobacco Research* 2000; 2(1):45–52.

Cornelius MD, Leech SL, Goldschmidt L, Day NL. Is prenatal tobacco exposure a risk factor for early adolescent smoking: a follow-up study. *Neurotoxicology and Teratology* 2005;27(4):667–76.

Côté F, Godin G, Gagné C. Identification of factors promoting abstinence from smoking in a cohort of elementary schoolchildren. *Preventive Medicine* 2004;39(4): 695–703.

Covington MV, Omelich CL. I can resist anything but temptation: adolescent expectations for smoking cigarettes. *Journal of Applied Social Psychology* 1988;18(3): 203–27.

Cox RG, Zhang L, Johnson WD, Bender DR. Academic performance and substance use: findings from a state survey of public high school students. *Journal of School Health* 2007;77(3):109–15.

Cubbin C, Hadden WC, Winkleby MA. Neighborhood context and cardiovascular disease risk factors: the contribution of material deprivation. *Ethnicity & Disease* 2001;11(4):687–700.

Cummings KM, Morley CP, Horan JK, Steger C, Leavell N-R. Marketing to America's youth: evidence from corporate documents. *Tobacco Control* 2002;11(Suppl 1):i5–i17.

Cunningham JA, Selby PL. Implications of the normative fallacy in young adult smokers aged 19–24 years. *American Journal of Public Health* 2007;97(8):1399–400.

Dani JA, Heinemann S. Molecular and cellular aspects of nicotine abuse. *Neuron* 1996;16(5):905–8.

Dao JM, McQuown SC, Loughlin SE, Belluzzi JD, Leslie FM. Nicotine alters limbic function in adolescent rat by a 5-HT1A receptor mechanism. *Neuropsychopharmacology* 2011;36(7):1319–31.

Darling H, Reeder AI, McGee R, Williams S. Brief report: disposable income, and spending on fast food, alcohol, cigarettes, and gambling by New Zealand secondary school students. *Journal of Adolescence* 2006;29(5):837–43.

Datta GD, Subramanian SV, Colditz GA, Kawachi I, Palmer JR, Rosenberg L. Individual, neighborhood, and state-level predictors of smoking among US Black women: a multilevel analysis. *Social Science & Medicine* 2006; 63(4):1034–44.

De Houwer J, Custers R, De Clercq A. Do smokers have a negative implicit attitude toward smoking? *Cognition & Emotion* 2006;20(8):1274–84.

de Vries H, Candel M, Engels R, Mercken L. Challenges to the peer influence paradigm: results for 12–13 year olds from six European countries from the European Smoking Prevention Framework Approach study. *Tobacco Control* 2006;15(2):83–9.

DeBry SC, Tiffany ST. Tobacco-induced neurotoxicity of adolescent cognitive development (TINACD): a proposed model for the development of impulsivity in nicotine dependence. *Nicotine & Tobacco Research* 2008;10(1):11–25.

den Exter Blokland EA, Engels RC, Hale WW 3rd, Meeus W, Willemsen MC. Lifetime parental smoking history and cessation and early adolescent smoking behavior. *Preventive Medicine* 2004;38(3):359–68.

Dewey JD. Reviewing the relationship between school factors and substance use for elementary, middle, and high school students. *Journal of Primary Prevention* 1999;19(3):177–225.

Di Chiara G. Role of dopamine in the behavioural actions of nicotine related to addiction. *European Journal of Pharmacology* 2000;393(1–3):295–314.

Dick DM, Pagan JL, Viken R, Purcell S, Kaprio J, Pulkkinen L, Rose RJ. Changing environmental influences on substance use across development. *Twin Research and Human Genetics* 2007a;10(2):315–26.

Dick DM, Viken R, Purcell S, Kaprio J, Pulkkinen L, Rose RJ. Parental monitoring moderates the importance of genetic and environmental influences on adolescent smoking. *Journal of Abnormal Psychology* 2007b;116(1):213–8.

Diego MA, Field TM, Sanders CE. Academic performance, popularity, and depression predict adolescent substance use. *Adolescence* 2003;38(149):35–42.

Dierker L, Mermelstein R. Early emerging nicotine-dependence symptoms: a signal of propensity for chronic smoking behavior in adolescents. *Journal of Pediatrics* 2010;156(5):818–22.

Dierker LC, Avenevoli S, Goldberg A, Glantz M. Defining subgroups of adolescents at risk for experimental and regular smoking. *Prevention Science* 2004;5(3): 169–83.

DiFranza JR, Rigotti NA, McNeill AD, Ockene JK, Savageau JA, St Cyr D, Coleman M. Initial symptoms of nicotine dependence in adolescents. *Tobacco Control* 2000;9(3):313–9.

DiFranza JR, Savageau JA, Fletcher K, Ockene JK, Rigotti NA, McNeill AD, Coleman M, Wood C. Measuring the loss of autonomy over nicotine use in adolescents: the DANDY (Development and Assessment of Nicotine Dependence in Youths) study. *Archives of Pediatrics & Adolescent Medicine* 2002;156(4):397–403.

DiFranza JR, Savageau JA, Fletcher K, O'Loughlin J, Pbert L, Ockene JK, McNeill AD, Hazelton J, Friedman K, Dussault G, et al. Symptoms of tobacco dependence after brief intermittent use: the Development and Assessment of Nicotine Dependence in Youth-2 study. *Archives of Pediatrics & Adolescent Medicine* 2007;161(7):704–10.

DiFranza JR, Wellman RJ, Sargent JD, Weitzman M, Hipple BJ, Winickoff JP, Tobacco Consortium, Center for Child Health Research of the American Academy of Pediatrics. Tobacco promotion and the initiation of tobacco use: assessing the evidence for causality. *Pediatrics* 2006;117(6):e1237–e1248.

Dishion TJ, Capaldi D, Spracklen KM, Li F. Peer ecology of male adolescent drug use. *Development and Psychopathology* 1995;7(4):803–24.

Dishion TJ, Capaldi DM, Yoerger K. Middle childhood antecedents to progressions in male adolescent substance use: an ecological analysis of risk and protection. *Journal of Adolescent Research* 1999;14(2):175–205.

Distefan JM, Gilpin EA, Choi WS, Pierce JP. Parental influences predict adolescent smoking in the United States, 1989–1993. *Journal of Adolescent Health* 1998; 22(6):466–74.

Distefan JM, Pierce JP, Gilpin EA. Do favorite movie stars influence adolescent smoking initiation? *American Journal of Public Health* 2004;94(7):1239–44.

Doherty WJ, Allen W. Family functioning and parental smoking as predictors of adolescent cigarette use: a six-year prospective study. *Journal of Family Psychology* 1994;8(3):347–53.

Dornbusch SM, Erickson KG, Laird J, Wong, CA. The relation of family and school attachment to adolescent deviance in diverse groups and communities. *Journal of Adolescent Research* 2001;16(4):396–422.

Dragano N, Bobak M, Wege N, Peasey A, Verde PE, Kubinova R, Weyers S, Moebus S, Möhlenkamp S, Stang A, et al. Neighbourhood socioeconomic status and cardiovascular risk factors: a multilevel analysis of nine cities in the Czech Republic and Germany. *BMC Public Health* 2007;7:255.

Duggirala R, Almasy L, Blangero J. Smoking behavior is under the influence of a major quantitative trait locus on human chromosome 5q. *Genetic Epidemiology* 1999;17(Suppl 1):S139–S144.

Duncan C, Jones K, Moon G. Smoking and deprivation: are there neighbourhood effects? *Social Science & Medicine* 1999;48(4):497–505.

Duncan SC, Duncan TE, Biglan A, Ary D. Contributions of the social context to the development of adolescent substance use: a multivariate latent growth modeling approach. *Drug and Alcohol Dependence* 1998;50(1):57–71.

Dye JL, Johnson TD. *A Child's Day: 2003 (Selected Indicators of Child Well-Being)*. Current Population Reports, P70–109. Washington: U.S. Census Bureau, 2006.

Eaton DK, Kann L, Kinchen S, Shanklin S, Ross J, Hawkins J, Harris WA, Lowry R, McManus T, Chyen D, et al. Youth risk behavior surveillance—United States, 2009. *Morbidity and Mortality Weekly Report* 2010;59(SS-5):1–142.

Eiser JR, Morgan M, Gammage P, Brooks N, Kirby R. Adolescent health behaviour and similarity-attraction: friends share smoking habits (really), but much else besides. *British Journal of Social Psychology* 1991;30(Pt 4):339–48.

Elder C, Leaver-Dunn D, Wang MQ, Nagy S, Green L. Organized group activity as a protective factor against adolescent substance use. *American Journal of Health Behavior* 2000;24(2):108–13.

Ellickson PL, Bird CE, Orlando M, Klein DJ, McCaffrey DF. Social context and adolescent health behavior: does school-level smoking prevalence affect students' subsequent smoking behavior? *Journal of Health and Social Behavior* 2003;44(4):525–35.

Ellickson PL, McGuigan KA, Klein DJ. Predictors of late-onset smoking and cessation over 10 years. *Journal of Adolescent Health* 2001;29(2):101–8.

Ellickson PL, Orlando M, Tucker JS, Klein DJ. From adolescence to young adulthood: racial/ethnic disparities in smoking. *American Journal of Public Health* 2004;94(2):293–9.

Emory K, Saquib N, Gilpin EA, Pierce JP. The association between home smoking restrictions and youth smoking behaviour: a review. *Tobacco Control* 2010;19(6): 495–506.

Engels RC, Knibbe RA, de Vries H, Drop MJ, Van Breukelen GJ. Influences of parental and best friends' smoking and drinking on adolescent use: a longitudinal study. *Journal of Applied Social Psychology* 1999;29(2): 337–61.

Engels RC, Knibbe RA, Drop MJ, de Haan YT. Homogeneity of cigarette smoking within peer groups: influence or selection? *Health Education & Behavior* 1997; 24(6):801–11.

Engels RC, Vitaro F, Blokland ED, de Kemp R, Scholte RH. Influence and selection processes in friendships and adolescent smoking behaviour: the role of parental smoking. *Journal of Adolescence* 2004;27(5):531–44.

Ennett ST, Bauman KE. Peer group structure and adolescent cigarette smoking: a social network analysis. *Journal of Health and Social Behavior* 1993;34(3):226–36.

Ennett ST, Bauman KE. The contribution of influence and selection to adolescent peer group homogeneity: the case of adolescent cigarette smoking. *Journal of Personality and Social Psychology* 1994;67(4):653–63.

Ennett ST, Bauman KE, Foshee VA, Pemberton M, Hicks KA. Parent-child communication about adolescent tobacco and alcohol use: what do parents say and does it affect youth behavior? *Journal of Marriage and the Family* 2001;63(1):48–62.

Ennett ST, Bauman KE, Hussong A, Faris R, Foshee VA, Cai L, Du Rant RH. The peer context of adolescent substance use: findings from social network analysis. *Journal of Research on Adolescence* 2006;16(2):159–86.

Ennett ST, Bauman KE, Koch GG. Variability in cigarette smoking within and between adolescent friendship cliques. *Addictive Behaviors* 1994;19(3):295–305.

Ennett ST, Faris R, Hipp J, Foshee VA, Bauman KE, Hussong A, Cai L. Peer smoking, other peer attributes, and adolescent cigarette smoking: a social network analysis. *Prevention Science* 2008;9(2):88–98.

Ennett ST, Flewelling RL, Lindrooth RC, Norton EC. School and neighborhood characteristics associated with school rates of alcohol, cigarette, and marijuana use. *Journal of Health and Social Behavior* 1997; 38(1):55–71.

Ennett ST, Foshee VA, Bauman KE, Hussong A, Faris R, Hipp JR, Cai L. A social contextual analysis of youth cigarette smoking development. *Nicotine & Tobacco Research* 2010;12(9):950–62.

Epstein JA, Botvin GJ, Diaz T. Linguistic acculturation and gender effects on smoking among Hispanic youth. *Preventive Medicine* 1998;27(4):583–9.

Epstein JA, Griffin KW, Botvin GJ. A model of smoking among inner-city adolescents: the role of personal competence and perceived social benefits of smoking. *Preventive Medicine* 2000;31(2 Pt 1):107–14.

Epstein JA, Williams C, Botvin GJ, Diaz T, Ifill-Williams M. Psychosocial predictors of cigarette smoking among adolescents living in public housing developments. *Tobacco Control* 1999;8(1):45–52.

Escobedo LG, Reddy M, Giovino GA. The relationship between depressive symptoms and cigarette smoking in US adolescents. *Addiction* 1998;93(3):433–40.

Evans GW, Kutcher R. Loosening the link between childhood poverty and adolescent smoking and obesity: the protective effects of social capital. *Psychological Science* 2010;22(1):3–7.

Evans JS. In two minds: dual-process accounts of reasoning. *Trends in Cognitive Sciences* 2003;7(10):454–9.

Evans-Whipp T, Beyers JM, Lloyd S, Lafazia AN, Toumbourou JW, Arthur MW, Catalano RF. A review of school drug policies and their impact on youth substance use. *Health Promotion International* 2004;19(2):227–34.

Fang X, Li X, Stanton B, Dong Q. Social network positions and smoking experimentation among Chinese adolescents. *American Journal of Health Behavior* 2003;27(3):257–67.

Federal Register. U.S. Department of Health and Human Services, Food and Drug Administration. Regulations restricting the sale and distribution of cigarettes and smokeless tobacco to protect children and adolescents; final rule (21 CFR Parts 801, 803, 804, 807, 820, and 897), 61 *Fed. Reg.* 44396–618 (1996).

Federal Register. U.S. Department of Health and Human Services, Food and Drug Administration. Regulations restricting the sale and distribution of cigarettes and smokeless tobacco to protect children and adolescents; final rule (21 CFR Part 1140), 75 *Fed. Reg.* 13225–32 (2010).

Filice GA, Hannan PJ, Lando HA, Joseph AM. A period of increased susceptibility to cigarette smoking among high school students. *Journal of School Health* 2003; 73(7):272–8.

Finkelstein DM, Kubzansky LD, Goodman E. Social status, stress, and adolescent smoking. *Journal of Adolescent Health* 2006;39(5):678–85.

Finn PR, Hall J. Cognitive ability and risk for alcoholism: short-term memory capacity and intelligence moderate personality risk for alcohol problems. *Journal of Abnormal Psychology* 2004;113(4):569–81.

Fisher LA, Bauman KE. Influence and selection in friend-adolescent relationships: findings from studies of adolescent smoking and drinking. *Journal of Applied Psychology* 1988;18(4):289–314.

Flay BR, d'Avemas JR, Best J, Kersell MW, Ryan KB. Cigarette smoking: why young people do it and ways of preventing it. In: McGrath PJ, Firestone P, editors. *Pediatric and Adolescent Behavioral Medicine: Issues in Treatment.* Vol. 10. New York: Springer, 1983: 132–83.

Flay BR, Hu FB, Richardson J. Psychosocial predictors of different stages of cigarette smoking among high school students. *Preventive Medicine* 1998;27(5 Pt 3):9–18.

Flay BR, Hu FB, Siddiqui O, Day LE, Hedeker D, Petraitis J, Richardson J, Sussman S. Differential influence of parental smoking and friends' smoking on adolescent initiation and escalation of smoking. *Journal of Health and Social Behavior* 1994;35(3):248–65.

Flay BR, Petraitis J. The theory of triadic influence: a new theory of health behavior with implications for preventive interventions. In: Albrecht GL, editor. *Advances in Medical Sociology: A Reconsideration of Health Behavior Change Models.* Vol. 4. Greenwich (CT): JAI Press, 1994:19–44.

Flint AJ, Novotny TE. Poverty status and cigarette smoking prevalence and cessation in the United States, 1983–1993: the independent risk of being poor. *Tobacco Control* 1997;6(1):14–18.

Flora DB, Chassin L. Changes in drug use during young adulthood: the effects of parent alcoholism and transition into marriage. *Psychology of Addictive Behaviors* 2005;19(4):352–62.

Forrester K, Biglan A, Severson HH, Smolkowski K. Predictors of smoking onset over two years. *Nicotine & Tobacco Research* 2007;9(12):1259–67.

Forster J, Chen V, Blaine T, Perry C, Toomey T. Social exchange of cigarettes by youth. *Tobacco Control* 2003; 12(2):148–54.

Fowler CD, Arends MA, Kenny PJ. Subtypes of nicotinic acetylcholine receptors in nicotine reward, dependence, and withdrawal: evidence from genetically modified mice. *Behavioural Pharmacology* 2008;19(5-6):461–84.

Fowler CD, Lu Q, Johnson PM, Marks MJ, Kenny PJ. Habenular α5 nicotinic receptor subunit signaling controls nicotine intake. *Nature* 2011;471(7340):597–601.

Fried PA, Watkinson B, Gray R. Neurocognitive consequences of cigarette smoking in young adults—a comparison with pre-drug performance. *Neurotoxicology and Teratology* 2006;28(4):517–25.

Gardiner P. The African Americanization of menthol cigarette use in the United States. *Nicotine & Tobacco Research* 2004;6(Suppl 1):S55–S65.

Garfinkel L. Trends in cigarette smoking in the United States. *Preventive Medicine* 1997;26(4):447–50.

Gelernter J, Liu X, Hesselbrock V, Page GP, Goddard A, Zhang H. Results of a genomewide linkage scan: support for chromosomes 9 and 11 loci increasing risk for cigarette smoking. *American Journal of Medical Genetics Part B Neuropsychiatric Genetics* 2004;128B(1): 94–101.

Georgiades K, Boyle MH, Duku E, Racine Y. Tobacco use among immigrant and nonimmigrant adolescents: individual and family level influences. *Journal of Adolescent Health* 2006;38(4):443.e1–443.e7.

Gervais A, O'Loughlin J, Meshefedjian G, Bancej C, Tremblay M. Milestones in the natural course of onset of cigarette use among adolescents. *Canadian Medical Association Journal* 2006;175(3):255–61.

Giedd JN, Rapoport JL. Structural MRI of pediatric brain development: what have we learned and where are we going? *Neuron* 2010;67(5):728–34.

Gilman SE, Rende R, Boergers J, Abrams DB, Buka SL, Clark MA, Colby SM, Hitsman B, Kazura AN, Lipsitt LP, et al. Parental smoking and adolescent smoking initiation: an intergenerational perspective on tobacco control. *Pediatrics* 2009;123(2):e274–e281.

Gilpin EA, Emery SL, Farkas AJ, Distefan JM, White MM, Pierce JP. *The California Tobacco Control Program: A Decade of Progress, Results from the California Tobacco Surveys, 1990–1998*. La Jolla (CA): University of California, San Diego, 2001.

Gilpin EA, Lee L, Pierce JP. Changes in population attitudes about where smoking should not be allowed: California versus the rest of the USA. *Tobacco Control* 2004;13(1):38–44.

Gilpin EA, Pierce JP. Concurrent use of tobacco products by California adolescents. *Preventive Medicine* 2003;36(5):575–84.

Go M-H, Green HD Jr, Kennedy DP, Pollard M, Tucker JS. Peer influence and selection effects on adolescent smoking. *Drug and Alcohol Dependence* 2010;109(1–3):239–42.

Goldman MS, Del Boca FK, Darkes J. Alcohol expectancy theory: the application of cognitive neuroscience. In: Leonard KE, Blane HT, editors. *Psychological Theories of Drinking and Alcoholism.* 2nd ed. New York: Guilford Press, 1999:203–46.

Goodman E, Huang B. Socioeconomic status, depressive symptoms, and adolescent substance use. *Archives of Pediatrics & Adolescent Medicine* 2002;156(5):448–53.

Gordon NP. Never smokers, triers and current smokers: three distinct target groups for school-based antismoking programs. *Health Education Quarterly* 1986;13(2):163–80.

Green MP, McCausland KL, Xiao H, Duke JC, Vallone DM, Healton CG. A closer look at smoking among young adults: where tobacco control should focus its attention. *American Journal of Public Health* 2007; 97(8):1427–33.

Greenwald AG, McGhee DE, Schwartz JL. Measuring individual differences in implicit cognition: the implicit association test. *Journal of Personality and Social Psychology* 1998;74(6):1464–80.

Grenard JL, Ames SL, Wiers RW, Thush C, Sussman S, Stacy AW. Working memory capacity moderates the predictive effects of drug-related associations on substance use. *Psychology of Addictive Behaviors* 2008; 22(3):426–32.

Grenard JL, Guo Q, Jasuja GK, Unger JB, Chou CP, Gallaher PE, Sun P, Palmer P, Anderson Johnson C. Influences affecting adolescent smoking behavior in China. *Nicotine & Tobacco Research* 2006;8(2):245–55.

Griesbach D, Inchley J, Currie C. More than words: the status and impact of smoking policies in Scottish schools. *Health Promotion International* 2002;17(1):31–41.

Griesler PC, Kandel DB. Ethnic differences in correlates of adolescent cigarette smoking. *Journal of Adolescent Health* 1998;23(3):167–80.

Griesler PC, Kandel DB, Davies M. Maternal smoking in pregnancy, child behavior problems, and adolescent smoking. *Journal of Research on Adolescence* 1998; 8(2):159–85.

Gritz ER, Prokhorov AV, Hudmon KS, Mullin Jones M, Rosenblum C, Chang CC, Chamberlain RM, Taylor WC, Johnston D, de Moor C. Predictors of susceptibility to smoking and ever smoking: a longitudinal study in a triethnic sample of adolescents. *Nicotine & Tobacco Research* 2003;5(4):493–506.

Haberstick BC, Timberlake D, Ehringer MA, Lessem JM, Hopfer CJ, Smolen A, Hewitt JK. Genes, time to first cigarette and nicotine dependence in a general population sample of young adults. *Addiction* 2007;102(4):655–65.

Hall JA, Valente TW. Adolescent smoking networks: the effects of influence and selection on future smoking. *Addictive Behaviors* 2007;32(12):3054–9.

Hampson SE, Andrews JA, Barckley M. Predictors of the development of elementary-school children's intentions to smoke cigarettes: hostility, prototypes, and subjective norms. *Nicotine & Tobacco Research* 2007; 9(7):751–60.

Han C, McGue MK, Iacono WG. Lifetime tobacco, alcohol and other substance use in adolescent Minnesota twins: univariate and multivariate behavioral genetic analyses. *Addiction* 1999;94(7):981–93.

Harden KP, Hill JE, Turkheimer E, Emery RE. Gene-environment correlation and interaction in peer effects on adolescent alcohol and tobacco use. *Behavior Genetics* 2008;38(4):339–47.

Harris R, Tobias M, Jeffreys M, Waldegrave K, Karlsen S, Nazroo J. Racism and health: the relationship between experience of racial discrimination and health in New Zealand. *Social Science & Medicine* 2006;63(6): 1428–41.

Harrison PA, Fulkerson JA, Park E. The relative importance of social versus commercial sources in youth access to tobacco, alcohol, and other drugs. *Preventive Medicine* 2000;31(1):39–48.

Haustein KO. Smoking and poverty. *European Journal of Cardiovascular Prevention and Rehabilitation* 2006;13(3):312–8.

Headen SW, Bauman KE, Deane GD, Koch GG. Are the correlates of cigarette smoking initiation different for black and white adolescents? *American Journal of Public Health* 1991;81(7):854–8.

Heath AC, Kirk KM, Meyer JM, Martin NG. Genetic and social determinants of initiation and age at onset of smoking in Australian twins. *Behavior Genetics* 1999; 29(6):395–407.

Hedeker D, Mermelstein RJ, Berbaum ML, Campbell RT. Modeling mood variation associated with smoking: an application of a heterogeneous mixed-effects model for analysis of ecological momentary assessment (EMA) data. *Addiction* 2009;104(2):297–307.

Hedeker D, Mermelstein RJ, Demirtas H. An application of a mixed-effects location scale model for analysis of ecological momentary assessment (EMA) data. *Biometrics* 2008;64(2):627–34.

Heinz AJ, Kassel JD, Berbaum M, Mermelstein R. Adolescents' expectancies for smoking to regulate affect predict smoking behavior and nicotine dependence over time. *Drug and Alcohol Dependence* 2010;111(1-2):128–35.

Hellström-Lindahl E, Gorbounova O, Seiger A, Mousavi M, Nordberg A. Regional distribution of nicotinic receptors during prenatal development of human brain and spinal cord. *Brain Research* 1998;108(1–2):147–60.

Henriksen L, Feighery EC, Schleicher NC, Cowling DW, Kline RS, Fortmann SP. Is adolescent smoking related to the density and proximity of tobacco outlets and retail cigarette advertising near schools? *Preventive Medicine* 2008;47(2):210–4.

Henry DB, Kobus K. Early adolescent social networks and substance use. *Journal of Early Adolescence* 2007; 27(3):346–62.

Hill KG, Hawkins JD, Catalano RF, Abbott RD, Guo J. Family influences on the risk of daily smoking initiation. *Journal of Adolescent Health* 2005;37(3):202–10.

Hodge FS. American Indian and Alaska Native teen cigarette smoking: a review. In: *Changing Adolescent Smoking Prevalence.* Smoking and Tobacco Control Monograph No. 14. Bethesda (MD): U. S. Department of Health and Human Services, Public Health Service, National Institutes of Health, National Cancer Institute, 2001. NIH Publication No. 02-5086.

Hodge F, Nandy K. Factors associated with American Indian cigarette smoking in rural settings. *International Journal of Environmental Research and Public Health* 2011;8(4):944–54.

Hofferth SL, Sandberg JF. How American children spend their time. *Journal of Marriage and Family* 2001;63(2):295–308.

Hoffman BR, Monge PR, Chou CP, Valente TW. Perceived peer influence and peer selection on adolescent smoking. *Addictive Behaviors* 2007;32(8):1546–54.

Hong LE, Hodgkinson CA, Yang Y, Sampath H, Ross TJ, Buchholz B, Salmeron BJ, Srivastatava V, Thaker GK, Goldman D, et al. A genetically modulated, intrinsic cingulate circuit supports human nicotine addiction. *Proceedings of the National Academy of Sciences* 2010;107(30):13509–14.

Horton K, Loukas A. Discrimination, religious coping, and tobacco use among white, African American, and Mexican American vocational school students. *Journal of Religion and Health.* In press.

Hoving C, Reubsaet A, de Vries H. Predictors of smoking stage transitions for adolescent boys and girls. *Preventive Medicine* 2007;44(6):485–9.

Hu FB, Flay BR, Hedeker D, Siddiqui O, Day LE. The influences of friends' and parental smoking on adolescent smoking behavior: the effects of time and prior smoking. *Journal of Applied Social Psychology* 1995;25(22):2018–47.

Hu MC, Davies M, Kandel DB. Epidemiology and correlates of daily smoking and nicotine dependence among young adults in the United States. *American Journal of Public Health* 2006;96(2):299–308.

Huijding J, de Jong PJ. Automatic associations with the sensory aspects of smoking: positive in habitual smokers but negative in non-smokers. *Addictive Behaviors* 2006;31(1):182–6.

Huijding J, de Jong PJ, Wiers RW, Verkooijen K. Implicit and explicit attitudes toward smoking in a smoking and a nonsmoking setting. *Addictive Behaviors* 2005; 30(5):949–61.

Hunt K, Hannah MK, West P. Contextualizing smoking: masculinity, femininity and class differences in smoking in men and women from three generations in the west of Scotland. *Health Education Research* 2004;19(3):239–49.

Huver RM, Engels RC, de Vries H. Are anti-smoking parenting practices related to adolescent smoking cognitions and behavior? *Health Education Research* 2006;21(1):66–77.

Jackson C. Initial and experimental stages of tobacco and alcohol use during late childhood: relation to peer, parent, and personal risk factors. *Addictive Behaviors* 1997;22(5):685–98.

Jackson C, Bee-Gates DJ, Henriksen L. Authoritative parenting, child competencies, and initiation of cigarette smoking. *Health Education Quarterly* 1994;21(1): 103–16.

Jackson C, Henriksen L, Dickinson D, Messer L, Robertson SB. A longitudinal study predicting patterns of cigarette smoking in late childhood. *Health Education & Behavior* 1998;25(4):436–47.

Jamal M, Does AJ, Penninx BW, Cuijpers P. Age at smoking onset and the onset of depression and anxiety disorders. *Nicotine & Tobacco Research* 2011;13(9):809–19.

Jason L, Billows W, Schnopp-Wyatt D, King C. Reducing the illegal sales of cigarettes to minors: analysis of alternative enforcement schedules. *Journal of Applied Behavior Analysis* 1996;29(3):333–44.

Jason LA, Pokorny SB, Adams M. A randomized trial evaluating tobacco possession-use-purchase laws in the USA. *Social Science & Medicine* 2008;67(11):1700–7.

Johnston LD, O'Malley PM, Bachman JG, Schulenberg JE. *Monitoring the Future National Survey Results on Drug Use, 1975–2010: Volume I, Secondary School Students*. Bethesda (MD): U.S. Department of Health and Human Services, National Institutes of Health, National Institute on Drug Abuse, 2011a. NIH Publication No. 07-6205.

Johnston LD, O'Malley PM, Bachman JG, Schulenberg JE. *Monitoring the Future National Survey Results on Drug Use, 1975–2010: Volume II, College Students and Adults Ages 19–50*. Ann Arbor: Institute for Social Research, The University of Michigan, 2011b.

Jones SE, Alexrad R, Wattigney WA. Healthy and safe school environment, part II, physical school environment: results from the School Health Policies and Programs Study 2006. *Journal of School Health* 2007;77(8)544–56.

Kahneman D. A perspective on judgment and choice: mapping bounded rationality. *American Psychologist* 2003;58(9):697–720.

Kalivas PW, Churchill L, Klitenick MA. GABA and enkephalin projection from the nucleus accumbens and ventral pallidum to the ventral tegmental area. *Neuroscience*1993;57(4):1047–60.

Kalivas PW, Volkow ND. The neural basis of addiction: a pathology of motivation and choice. *American Journal of Psychiatry* 2005;162(8):1403–13.

Kandel DB. Similarity in real-life adolescent friendship pairs. *Journal of Personality and Social Psychology* 1978;36(3):306–12.

Kandel DB, Kiros GE, Schaffran C, Hu MC. Racial/ethnic differences in cigarette smoking initiation and progression to daily smoking: a multilevel analysis. *American Journal of Public Health* 2004;94(1):128–35.

Kandel DB, Udry JR. Prenatal effects of maternal smoking on daughters' smoking: nicotine or testosterone exposure? *American Journal of Public Health* 1999; 89(9):1377–83.

Kandel DB, Wu P, Davies M. Maternal smoking during pregnancy and smoking by adolescent daughters. *American Journal of Public Health* 1994;84(9): 1407–13.

Kaplan CP, Nápoles-Springer A, Stewart SL, Pérez-Stable EJ. Smoking acquisition among adolescents and young Latinas: the role of socioenvironmental and personal factors. *Addictive Behaviors* 2001;26(4):531–50.

Karp I, O'Loughlin J, Paradis G, Hanley J, DiFranza J. Smoking trajectories of adolescent novice smokers in a longitudinal study of tobacco use. *Annals of Epidemiology* 2005;15(6):445–52.

Kassel JD, Evatt DP, Greenstein JE, Wardle MC, Yates MC, Veilleux JC. The acute effects of nicotine on positive and negative affect in adolescent smokers. *Journal of Abnormal Psychology* 2007;116(3):543–53.

Kassel JD, Stroud LR, Paronis CA. Smoking, stress, and negative affect: correlation, causation, and context across stages of smoking. *Psychological Bulletin* 2003;129(2):270–304.

Kelly AB, Haynes MA, Marlatt GA. The impact of adolescent tobacco-related associative memory on smoking trajectory: an application of negative binomial regression to highly skewed longitudinal data. *Addictive Behaviors* 2008;33(5):640–50.

Kelly AB, Masterman PW, Marlatt GA. Alcohol-related associative strength and drinking behaviours: concurrent and prospective relationships. *Drug and Alcohol Review* 2005;24(6):489–98.

Kelly AB, O'Flaherty M, Connor JP, Homel R, Toumbourou JW, Patton GC, Williams J. The influence of parents, siblings and peers on pre- and early-teen smoking: a multilevel model. *Drug and Alcohol Review* 2010; 30(4):381–7.

Kendler KS, Schmitt E, Aggen SH, Prescott CA. Genetic and environmental influences on alcohol, caffeine, cannabis, and nicotine use from early adolescence to middle adulthood. *Archives of General Psychiatry* 2008;65(6):674–82.

Killen JD, Robinson TN, Haydel KF, Hayward C, Wilson DM, Hammer LD, Litt IF, Taylor CB. Prospective study of risk factors for the initiation of cigarette smoking. *Journal of Consulting and Clinical Psychology* 1997;65(6):1011–6.

Kim SS, Son H, Nam KA. The sociocultural context of Korean American men's smoking behavior. *Western Journal of Nursing Research* 2005;27(5):604–23.

Kim SY, England L, Dietz PM, Morrow B, Perham-Hester KA. Patterns of cigarette and smokeless tobacco use before, during, and after pregnancy among Alaska native and white women in Alaska, 2000–2003. *Maternal and Child Health* Journal 2010;14(3):365–72.

Kleinschmidt I, Hills M, Elliott P. Smoking behaviour can be predicted by neighbourhood deprivation measures. *Journal of Epidemiology and Community Health* 1995;49(Suppl 2):S72–S77.

Knopik VS, Sparrow EP, Madden PA, Bucholz KK, Hudziak JJ, Reich W, Slutske WS, Grant JD, McLaughlin TL, Todorov A, et al. Contributions of parental alcoholism, prenatal substance exposure, and genetic transmission to child ADHD risk: a female twin study. *Psychological Medicine* 2005;35(5):625–35.

Kobus K. Peers and adolescent smoking. *Addiction* 2003; 98(Suppl 1):S37–S55.

Koopmans JR, Slutske WS, Heath AC, Neale MC, Boomsma DI. The genetics of smoking initiation and quantity smoked in Dutch adolescent and young adult twins. *Behavior Genetics* 1999;29(6):383–93.

Kremers SPJ, Mudde AN, de Vries H. "Kicking the initiation": do adolescent ex-smokers differ from other groups within the initiation continuum? *Preventive Medicine* 2001;33(5):392–401.

Landrine H, Klonoff EA. Racial discrimination and cigarette smoking among blacks: findings from two studies. *Ethnicity & Disease* 2000;10(2):195–202.

Landrine H, Richardson JL, Klonoff EA, Flay B. Cultural diversity in the predictors of adolescent cigarette smoking: the relative influence of peers. *Journal of Behavioral Medicine* 1994;17(3):331–46.

Lara M, Gamboa C, Kahramanian MI, Morales LS, Hayes Bautista DE. Acculturation and Latino health in the United States: a review of the literature and its sociopolitical context. *Annual Review of Public Health* 2005;26:367–97.

Lawlor DA, O'Callaghan MJ, Mamun AA, Williams GM, Bor W, Najman JM. Early life predictors of adolescent smoking: findings from the Mater-University study of pregnancy and its outcomes. *Paediatric and Perinatal Epidemiology* 2005;19(5):377–87.

Lawrence D, Fagan P, Backinger CL, Gibson JT, Hartman A. Cigarette smoking patterns among young adults aged 18–24 years in the United States. *Nicotine & Tobacco Research* 2007;9(6):687–97.

Leatherdale ST, Manske S. The relationship between student smoking in the school environment and smoking onset in elementary school students. *Cancer Epidemiology, Biomarkers & Prevention* 2005;14(7):1762–5.

Leatherdale ST, McDonald PW, Cameron R, Brown KS. A multilevel analysis examining the relationship between social influences for smoking and smoking onset. *American Journal of Health Behavior* 2005;29(6): 520–30.

Leatherdale ST, McDonald PW, Cameron R, Jolin MA, Brown KS. A multi-level analysis examining how smoking friends, parents, and older students in the school environment are risk factors for susceptibility to smoking among non-smoking elementary school youth. *Prevention Science* 2006;7(4):397–402.

Leatherdale ST, Strath JM. Tobacco retailer density surrounding schools and cigarette access behaviors among underage smoking students. *Annals of Behavioral Medicine* 2007;33(1):105–11.

Lebel C, Beaulieu C. Longitudinal development of human brain wiring continues from childhood into adulthood. *Journal of Neuroscience* 2011;31(30):10937–47.

Lee RE, Cubbin C. Neighborhood context and youth cardiovascular health behaviors. *American Journal of Public Health* 2002;92(3):428–36.

LeMaster PL, Connell CM, Mitchell CM, Manson SM. Tobacco use among American Indian adolescents: protective and risk factors. *Journal of Adolescent Health* 2002;30(6):426–32.

Leonardi-Bee J, Jere ML, Britton J. Exposure to parental and sibling smoking and the risk of smoking uptake in childhood and adolescence: a systematic review and meta-analysis. *Thorax* 2011;66(10):847–55.

Leslie FM, Loughlin SE, Wang R, Perez L, Lotfipour S, Belluzzi JD. Adolescent development of forebrain stimulant responsiveness: insights from animal studies. *Annals of the New York Academy of Sciences* 2004; 1021:148–59.

Lessov-Schlaggar CN, Hops H, Brigham J, Hudmon KS, Andrews JA, Tildesley E, McBride D, Jack LM, Javitz HS, Swan GE. Adolescent smoking trajectories and nicotine dependence. *Nicotine & Tobacco Research* 2008;10(2):341–51.

Leventhal H, Cleary PD. The smoking problem: a review of the research and theory in behavioral risk modification. *Psychological Bulletin* 1980;88(2):370–405.

Levy DT, Friend K. A framework for evaluating and improving clean indoor air laws. *Journal of Public Health Management and Practice* 2001;7(5):87–96.

Lewis-Esquerre JM, Rodrigue JR, Kahler CW. Development and validation of an adolescent smoking consequences questionnaire. *Nicotine & Tobacco Research* 2005;7(1):81–90.

Li MD, Ma JZ, Cheng R, Dupont RT, Williams NJ, Crews KM, Payne TJ, Elston RC, Framingham Heart Study. A genome-wide scan to identify loci for smoking rate in the Framingham Heart Study population. *BMC Genetics* 2003;4(Suppl 1):S103.

Libbey HP. Measuring student relationships to school: attachment, bonding, connectedness, and engagement. *Journal of School Health* 2004;74(7):274–83.

Lipperman-Kreda S, Paschall MJ, Grube JW. Perceived enforcement of school tobacco policy and adolescents' cigarette smoking. *Preventive Medicine* 2009; 48(6):562–6.

Liu JZ, Tozzi F, Waterworth DM, Pillai SG, Muglia P, Middleton L, Berrettini W, Knouff CW, Yuan X, Waeber G, et al. Meta-analysis and imputation refines the association of 15q25 with smoking quantity. *Nature Genetics* 2010;42(5):436–40.

Lovato CY, Hsu HCH, Sabiston CM, Hadd V, Nykiforuk CIJ. Tobacco point-of-purchase marketing in school neighbourhoods and school smoking prevalence: a descriptive study. *Canadian Journal of Public Health* 2007;98(4):265–70.

Lovato CY, Zeisser C, Campbell HS, Watts AW, Halpin P, Thompson M, Eyles J, Adlaf E, Brown KS. Adolescent smoking: effect of school and community characteristics. *American Journal of Preventive Medicine* 2010;39(6):507–14.

Lynskey MT, Agrawal A, Heath AC. Genetically informative research on adolescent substance use: methods, findings, and challenges. *Journal of the American Academy of Child & Adolescent Psychiatry* 2010;49(12):1202–14.

Maes HH, Woodard CE, Murrelle L, Meyer JM, Silberg JL, Hewitt JK, Rutter M, Simonoff E, Pickles A, Carbonneau R, et al. Tobacco, alcohol and drug use in eight- to sixteen-year-old twins: the Virginia Twin Study of Adolescent Behavioral Development. *Journal of Studies on Alcohol* 1999;60(3):293–305.

Mahabee-Gittens EM, Khoury JC, Huang B, Dorn LD, Ammerman RT, Gordon JS. The protective influence of family bonding on smoking initiation by racial/ethnic and age subgroups. *Journal of Child & Adolescent Substance Abuse* 2011;20(3):270–87.

Mahoney JL, Harris AL, Eccles JS. Organized activity participation, positive youth development, and the over-scheduling hypothesis. *Social Policy Report* 2006;20(4):3–15.

Malaiyandi V, Goodz SD, Sellers EM, Tyndale RF. CYP2A6 genotype, phenotype, and the use of nicotine metabolites as biomarkers during ad libitum smoking. *Cancer Epidemiology, Biomarkers & Prevention* 2006;15(10):1812–9.

Mann JR, McKeown RE, Bacon J, Vesselinov R, Bush F. Religiosity, spirituality, and depressive symptoms in pregnant women. *International Journal of Psychiatry in Medicine* 2007;37(3):301–13.

Mansvelder HD, De Rover M, McGehee DS, Brussaard AB. Cholinergic modulation of dopaminergic reward areas: upstream and downstream targets of nicotine addiction. *European Journal of Pharmacology* 2003;480(1–3):117–23.

Mansvelder HD, McGehee DS. Long-term potentiation of excitatory inputs to brain reward areas by nicotine. *Neuron* 2000;27(2):349–57.

Martin-Sölch C, Magyar S, Künig G, Missimer J, Schultz W, Leenders KL. Changes in brain activation associated with reward processing in smokers and nonsmokers: a positron emission tomography study. *Experimental Brain Research* 2001;139(3):278–86.

Matheson FI, LaFreniere MC, White HL, Moineddin R, Dunn JR, Glazier RH. Influence of neighborhood deprivation, gender and ethno-racial origin on smoking behavior of Canadian youth. *Preventive Medicine* 2011;52(5):376–80.

Mathur C, Stigler MH, Perry CL, Arora M, Reddy KS. Differences in prevalence of tobacco use among Indian urban youth: the role of socioeconomic status. *Nicotine & Tobacco Research* 2008;10(1):109–16.

Mayhew KP, Flay BR, Mott JA. Stages in the development of adolescent smoking. *Drug and Alcohol Dependence* 2000;59(Suppl 1):S61–S81.

Mayberry ML, Espelage DL, Koenig B. Multilevel modeling of direct effects and interactions of peers, parents, school, and community influences on adolescent substance use. *Journal of Youth and Adolescence* 2009; 38(8):1038–49.

McCabe SE, Schulenberg JE, Johnston LD, O'Malley PM, Bachman JG, Kloska DD. Selection and socialization effects of fraternities and sororities on US college student substance use: a multi-cohort national longitudinal study. *Addiction* 2005;100(4):512–24.

McCarthy DM, Thompsen DM. Implicit and explicit measures of alcohol and smoking cognitions. *Psychology of Addictive Behaviors* 2006;20(4):436–44.

McGue M, Elkins I, Iacono WG. Genetic and environmental influences on adolescent substance use and abuse. *American Journal of Medical Genetics* 2000;96(5): 671–7.

McKenzie M, Olsson CA, Jorm AF, Romaniuk H, Patton GC. Association of adolescent symptoms of depression and anxiety with daily smoking and nicotine dependence in young adulthood: findings from a 10-year longitudinal study. *Addiction* 2010;105(9):1652–9.

McNamee RL, Dunfee KL, Luna B, Clark DB, Eddy WF, Tarter RE. Brain activation, response inhibition, and increased risk for substance use disorder. *Alcoholism, Clinical and Experimental Research* 2008;32(3): 405–13.

McPherson M, Smith-Lovin L, Cook JM. Birds of a feather: homophily in social networks. *Annual Review of Sociology* 2001;27(1):415–44.

McVicar D. Estimates of peer effects in adolescent smoking across twenty six European countries. *Social Science & Medicine* 2011;73(8):1186–93.

Melnick MJ, Miller KE, Sabo DF, Farrell MP, Barnes GM. Tobacco use among high school athletes and non athletes: results of the 1997 Youth Risk Behavior Survey. *Adolescence* 2001;36(144):727–47.

Mercken L, Candel M, Willems P, de Vries H. Disentangling social selection and social influence effects on adolescent smoking: the importance of reciprocity in friendships. *Addiction* 2007;102(9):1483–92.

Mercken L, Snijders TAB, Steglich C, de Vries H. Dynamics of adolescent friendship networks and smoking behavior: social network analyses in six European countries. *Social Science & Medicine* 2009;69(10):1506–14.

Mercken L, Snijders TAB, Steglich C, Vartiainen E, deVries H. Dynamics of adolescent friendship networks and smoking behavior. *Social Networks* 2010; 32(1):72–81.

Merline AC, O'Malley PM, Schulenberg JE, Bachman JG, Johnston LD. Substance use among adults 35 years of age: prevalence, adulthood predictors, and impact of adolescent substance use. *American Journal of Public Health* 2004;94(1):96–102.

Mermelstein R. Explanations of ethnic and gender differences in youth smoking: A multi-site, qualitative investigation. *Nicotine & Tobacco Research* 1999;1(Suppl 1):S91–S98.

Mermelstein R, Hedeker D, Flay B, Shiffman S. Real-time data capture and adolescent cigarette smoking: moods and smoking. In: Stone A, Shiffman S, Atienza A, Nebeling L, editors. *The Science of Real-Time Data Capture: Self-report in Health Research.* New York: Oxford University Press, 2007:117–35.

Metzger A, Dawes N, Mermelstein R, Wakschlag L. Longitudinal modeling of adolescents' activity involvement, problem peer associations, and youth smoking. *Journal of Applied Developmental Psychology* 2011;32(1):1–9.

Miller TQ, Volk RJ. Family relationships and adolescent cigarette smoking: results from a national longitudinal survey. *Journal of Drug Issues* 2002;32(3):945–72.

Mitic WR, McGuire DP, Neumann B. Perceived stress and adolescents' cigarette use. *Psychological Reports* 1985;57(3 Pt 2):1043–8.

Miyata H, Yanagita T. Neurobiological mechanisms of nicotine craving. *Alcohol* 2001;24(2):87–93.

Morgan GD, Backinger CL, Leischow SJ. The future of tobacco-control research. *Cancer Epidemiology, Biomarkers & Prevention* 2007;16(6):1077–80.

Morrow M, Ngoc DH, Hoang TT, Trinh TH. Smoking and young women in Vietnam: the influence of normative gender roles. *Social Science & Medicine* 2002;55(4):681–90.

Mosbach P, Leventhal H. Peer group identification and smoking: implications for intervention. *Journal of Abnormal Psychology* 1988;97(2):238–45.

Munafò MR, Clark TG, Johnstone EC, Murphy MFG, Walton RT. The genetic basis for smoking behavior: a systematic review and meta-analysis. *Nicotine & Tobacco Research* 2004;6(4):583–97.

Munafò MR, Johnstone ED. Genes and cigarette smoking. *Addiction* 2008;103(6):893–904.

Musso F, Bettermann F, Vucurevic G, Stoeter P, Konrad A, Winterer G. Smoking impacts on prefrontal attentional network function in young adult brains. *Psychopharmacology* 2007;191(1):159–69.

Myers MG, McCarthy DM, MacPherson L, Brown SA. Constructing a short form of the Smoking Consequences Questionnaire with adolescents and young adults. *Psychological Assessment* 2003;15(2):163–72.

Nasim A, Utsey SO, Corona R, Belgrave FZ. Religiosity, refusal efficacy, and substance use among African-American adolescents and young adults. *Journal of Ethnicity in Substance Abuse* 2006;5(3):29–49.

National Cancer Institute. *The Role of the Media in Promoting and Reducing Tobacco Use.* Tobacco Control Monograph No. 19. Bethesda (MD): U.S. Department of Health and Human Services, National Institutes of Health, National Cancer Institute, 2008. NIH Publication No. 07-6242.

Neufeld KJ, Peters DH, Rani M, Bonu S, Brooner RK. Regular use of alcohol and tobacco in India and its association with age, gender, and poverty. *Drug and Alcohol Dependence* 2005;77(3):283–91.

Neuhaus A, Bajbouj M, Kienast T, Kalus P, von Haebler D, Winterer G, Galliant J. Persistent dysfunctional frontal lobe activation in former smokers. *Psychopharmacology* 2006;186(2):191–200.

Ng N, Weinehall L, Ohman A. 'If I don't smoke, I'm not a real man'—Indonesian teenage boys' views about smoking. *Health Education Research* 2007;22(6): 794–804.

Nonnemaker JM, McNeely CA, Blum RW. Public and private domains of religiosity and adolescent health risk behaviors: evidence from the National Longitudinal Study of Adolescent Health. *Social Science & Medicine* 2003;57(11):2049–54.

Nonnemaker J, McNeely CA, Blum RW. Public and private domains of religiosity and adolescent smoking transitions. *Social Science & Medicine* 2006;62(12):3084–95.

Nosek BA, Banaji MR. The go/no-go association task. *Social Cognition* 2001;19(6):625–66.

Novak M, Ahlgren C, Hammarstrom A. Inequalities in smoking: influence of social chain of risks from adolescence to young adulthood: a prospective population-based cohort study. *International Journal of Behavioral Medicine* 2007;14(3):181–7.

Novo M, Hammarström A, Janlert U. Smoking habits—a question of trend or unemployment: a comparison of young men and women between boom and recession. *Public Health* 2000;114(6):460–3.

Nowlin PR, Colder CR. The role of ethnicity and neighborhood poverty on the relationship between parenting and adolescent cigarette use. *Nicotine & Tobacco Research* 2007;9(5):545–56.

O'Callaghan FV, O'Callaghan M, Najman JM, Williams GM, Bor W, Alati R. Prediction of adolescent smoking from family and social risk factors at 5 years, and maternal smoking in pregnancy and at 5 and 14 years. *Addiction* 2006;101(2):282–90.

Olson MA, Fazio RH. Reducing the influence of extrapersonal associations on the Implicit Association Test: Personalizing the IAT. *Journal of Personality and Social Psychology* 2004;86(5):653–67.

Oredein T, Foulds J. Causes of the decline in cigarette smoking among African American youths from the 1970s to the 1990s. *American Journal of Public Health* 2011;101(10):e4–e14.

Orlando M, Tucker JS, Ellickson PL, Klein DJ. Developmental trajectories of cigarette smoking and their correlates from early adolescence to young adulthood. *Journal of Consulting and Clinical Psychology* 2004;72(3):400–10.

Orlando M, Ellickson PL, Jinnett K. The temporal relationship between emotional distress and cigarette smoking during adolescence and young adulthood. *Journal of Consulting and Clinical Psychology* 2001;69(6): 959–70.

Osilla KC, Lonczak HS, Mail PD, Larimer ME, Marlatt GA. Regular tobacco use among American Indian and Alaska native adolescents: an examination of protective mechanisms. *Journal of Ethnicity in Substance Abuse* 2007;6(3-4):143–53.

Otten R, Bricker JB, Liu J, Comstock BA, Peterson AV. Adolescent psychological and social predictors of young adult smoking acquisition and cessation: A 10-year longitudinal study. *Health Psychology* 2011;30(2):163–70.

Oygard L, Klepp KI, Tell GS, Vellar OD. Parental and peer influences on smoking among young adults: ten-year follow-up of the Oslo youth study participants. *Addiction* 1995;90(4):561–9.

Paavola M, Vartiainen E, Haukkala A. Smoking from adolescence to adulthood: the effects of parental and own socioeconomic status. *European Journal of Public Health* 2004;14(4):417–21.

Page RM, Hammermeister J, Scanlan A, Gilbert L. Is school sports participation a protective factor against adolescent health risk behaviors? *Journal of Health Education* 1998;29(3):186–92.

Pallonen UE, Prochaska JO, Velicer WF, Prokhorov AV, Smith NF. Stages of acquisition and cessation for adolescent smoking: an empirical integration. *Addictive Behaviors* 1998;23(3):303–24.

Pan Z. Socioeconomic predictors of smoking and smoking frequency in urban China: evidence of smoking as a social function. *Health Promotion International* 2004;19(3):309–15.

Patton GC, Carlin JB, Coffey C, Wolfe R, Hibbert M, Bowes G. Depression, anxiety, and smoking initiation: a prospective study over 3 years. *American Journal of Public Health* 1998;88(10):1518–22.

Patton GC, Coffey C, Carlin JB, Sawyer SM, Wakefield M. Teen smokers reach their mid twenties. *Journal of Adolescent Health* 2006;39(2):214–20.

Payne BK. Conceptualizing control in social cognition: how executive functioning modulates the expression of automatic stereotyping. *Journal of Personality and Social Psychology* 2005;89(4):488–503.

Pearson M, Michell L. Smoke rings: social network analysis of friendship groups, smoking and drug-taking. *Drugs: Education, Prevention and Policy* 2000;7(1):21–37.

Pearson M, Sweeting H, West P, Young R, Gordon J, Turner K. Adolescent substance use in different social and peer contexts: a social network analysis. *Drugs: Education, Prevention and Policy* 2006;13(6):519–36.

Pederson LL, Koval JJ, Chan SS, Zhang X. Variables related to tobacco use among young adults: are there differences between males and females? *Addictive Behaviors* 2007;32(2):398–403.

Pego CM, Hill RF, Solomon GW, Chisholm RM, Ivey SE. Tobacco, culture, and health among American Indians: a historical review. *American Indian Culture and Research Journal* 1995;19(2):143–64.

Pergadia ML, Heath AC, Agrawal A, Bucholz KK, Martin NG, Madden PA. The implications of simultaneous smoking initiation for inferences about the genetics of smoking behavior from twin data. *Behavior Genetics* 2006;36(4):567–76.

Perry CL. The tobacco industry and underage teen smoking: tobacco industry documents from the Minnesota litigation. *Archives of Pediatrics & Adolescent Medicine* 1999;153(9):935–41.

Perry CL, Murray DM, Klepp KL. Predictors of adolescent cigarette smoking and implications for prevention. *Morbidity and Mortality Weekly Report* 1987;36(Suppl 4):41S–45S.

Perugini M. Predictive models of implicit and explicit attitudes. *British Journal of Social Psychology* 2005;44(1):29–45.

Peterson AV Jr, Leroux BG, Bricker J, Kealey KA, Marek PM, Sarason IG, Andersen MR. Nine-year prediction of adolescent smoking by number of smoking parents. *Addictive Behaviors* 2006;31(5):788–801.

Petraitis J, Flay BR, Miller TQ. Reviewing theories of adolescent substance use: organizing pieces in the puzzle. *Psychological Bulletin* 1995;117(1):67–86.

Pierce JP. Tobacco industry marketing, population-based tobacco control, and smoking behavior. *American Journal of Preventive Medicine* 2007;33(6 Suppl):S327–S334.

Pierce JP, Choi WS, Gilpin EA, Farkas AJ, Merritt RK. Validation of susceptibility as a predictor of which adolescents take up smoking in the United States. *Health Psychology* 1996;15(5):355–61.

Pierce JP, Gilpin EA, Emery SL, Farkas AJ, Zhu SH, Choi WS, Berry CC, Distefan JM, White MM, Sorokos S, et al. *Tobacco Control in California: Who's Winning the War? An Evaluation of the Tobacco Control Program, 1989–1996*. La Jolla (CA): University of California, San Diego, 1998:12–18.

Piontek D, Buehler A, Rudolph U, Metz K, Kroeger C, Gradl S, Floeter S, Donath C. Social contexts in adolescent smoking: does school policy matter? *Health Education Research* 2008;23(6):1029–38.

Pollard MS, Tucker JS, Green HD, Kennedy D, Go M-H. Friendship networks and trajectories of adolescent tobacco use. *Addictive Behaviors* 2010;35(7):678–85.

Poulsen LH, Osler M, Roberts C, Due P, Damsgaard MT, Holstein BE. Exposure to teachers smoking and adolescent smoking behaviour: analysis of cross sectional data from Denmark. *Tobacco Control* 2002;11(3):246–51.

Prokhorov AV, de Moor CA, Hudmon KS, Hu S, Kelder SH, Gritz ER. Predicting initiation of smoking in adolescents: evidence for integrating the stages of change and susceptibility to smoking constructs. *Addictive Behaviors* 2002;27(5):697–712.

Quentin W, Neubauer S, Leidl R, König HH. Advertising bans as a means of tobacco control policy: a systematic literature review of time-series analyses. *International Journal of Public Health* 2007;52(5):295–307.

Rajan KB, Leroux BG, Peterson AV Jr, Bricker JB, Andersen MR, Kealey KA, Sarason IG. Nine-year prospective association between older siblings' smoking and children's daily smoking. *Journal of Adolescent Health* 2003;33(1):25–30.

Rasmussen M, Damsgaard MT, Holstein BE, Poulsen LH, Due P. School connectedness and daily smoking among boys and girls: the influence of parental smoking norms. *The European Journal of Public Health* 2005;15(6):607–12.

Reijneveld SA. The impact of individual and area characteristics on urban socioeconomic differences in health and smoking. *International Journal of Epidemiology* 1998;27(1):33–40.

Rende R, Slomkowski C, McCaffery J, Lloyd-Richardson EE, Niaura R. A twin-sibling study of tobacco use in adolescence: etiology of individual differences and extreme scores. *Nicotine & Tobacco Research* 2005;7(3):413–9.

Renner CC, Patten CA, Day GE, Enoch CC, Schroeder DR, Offord KP, Hurt RD, Gasheen A, Gill L. Tobacco use during pregnancy among Alaska Natives in western Alaska. *Alaska Medicine* 2005;47(1):12–6.

Rhee SH, Hewitt JK, Young SE, Corley RP, Crowley TJ, Stallings MC. Genetic and environmental influences on substance initiation, use, and problem use in adolescents. *Archives of General Psychiatry* 2003;60(12):1256–64.

Ribisl KM, Lee RE, Henriksen L, Haladjian HH. A content analysis of Web sites promoting smoking culture and lifestyle. *Health Education & Behavior* 2003;30(1):64–78.

Rigotti NA, DiFranza JR, Chang YC, Tisdale T, Kemp B, Singer DE. The effect of enforcing tobacco-sales laws on adolescents' access to tobacco and smoking behavior. *New England Journal of Medicine* 1997;337(15):1044–51.

Roberts KH, Munafò MR, Rodriguez D, Drury M, Murphy MF, Neale RE, Nettle D. Longitudinal analysis of the effect of prenatal nicotine exposure on subsequent smoking behavior of offspring. *Nicotine & Tobacco Research* 2005;7(5):801–8.

Robinson LA, Dalton WT 3rd, Nicholson LM. Changes in adolescents' sources of cigarettes. *Journal of Adolescent Health* 2006a;39(6):861–7.

Robinson LA, Murray DM, Alfano CM, Zbikowski SM, Blitstein JL, Klesges RC. Ethnic differences in predictors of adolescent smoking onset and escalation: a longitudinal study from 7th to 12th grade. *Nicotine & Tobacco Research* 2006b;8(2):297–307.

Rodriguez D, McGovern JA. Team sport participation and smoking: analysis with general growth mixture modeling. *Journal of Pediatric Psychology* 2004;29(4):299–308.

Rodriguez D, Romer D, Audrain-McGovern J. Beliefs about the risks of smoking mediate the relationship between exposure to smoking and smoking. *Psychosomatic Medicine* 2007;69(1):106–13.

Rose JE, Behm FM, Westman EC, Mathew RJ, London ED, Hawk TC, Turkington TG, Coleman RE. PET studies of the influences of nicotine on neural systems in cigarette smokers. *American Journal of Psychiatry* 2003;160(2):323–33.

Rostosky SS, Danner F, Riggle ED. Is religiosity a protective factor against substance use in young adulthood: only if you're straight! *Journal of Adolescent Health* 2007;40(5):440–7.

Rubia K, Halari R, Smith AB, Mohammed M, Scott S, Giampietro V, Taylor E, Brammer EJ. Dissociated functional brain abnormalities of inhibition in boys with pure conduct disorder and in boys with pure attention deficit hyperactivity disorder. *American Journal of Psychiatry* 2008;165(7):889–97.

Ruel E, Mani N, Sandoval A, Terry-McElrath Y, Slater SJ, Tworek C, Chaloupka FJ. After the Master Settlement Agreement: trends in the American tobacco retail environment from 1999 to 2002. *Health Promotion Practice* 2004;5(3 Suppl):99S–110S.

Saccone NL, Culverhouse RC, Schwantes-An TH, Cannon DS, Chen X, Cichon S, Giegling I, Han S, Han Y, Keskitalo-Vuokko K, et al. Multiple independent loci at chromosome 15q25.1 affect smoking quantity: a meta-analysis and comparison with lung cancer and COPD. *PLoS Genetics* 2010;6(8). pii:e1001053.

Saccone NL, Wang JC, Breslau N, Johnson EO, Hatsukami D, Saccone SF, Grucza RA, Sun L, Duan W, Budde J, et al. The *CHRNA5-CHRNA3-CHRNB4* nicotinic receptor subunit gene cluster affects risk for nicotine dependence in African-American and European-Americans. *Cancer Research* 2009;69(17):6848–56.

Saccone SF, Hinrichs AL, Saccone NL, Chase GA, Konvicka K, Madden PA, Breslau N, Johnson EO, Hatsukami D, Pomerleau O, et al. Cholinergic nicotinic receptor genes implicated in a nicotine dependence association study targeting 348 candidate genes with 3713 SNPs. *Human Molecular Genetics* 2007;16(1):36–49.

Salas R, Orr-Urtreger A, Broide RS, Beaudet A, Paylor R, De Biasi M. The nicotinic acetylcholine receptor subunit α5 mediates short-term effects of nicotine in vivo. *Molecular Pharmacology* 2003;63(5):1059–66.

Salihu HM, Wilson RE. Epidemiology of prenatal smoking and perinatal outcomes. *Early Human Development* 2007;83(11):713–20.

Sargent JD, Beach ML, Adachi-Mejia AM, Gibson JJ, Titus-Ernstoff LT, Carusi CP, Swain SD, Heatherton TF, Dalton MA. Exposure to movie smoking: its relation to smoking initiation among US adolescents. *Pediatrics* 2005;116(5):1183–91.

Sargent JD, Dalton M. Does parental disapproval of smoking prevent adolescents from becoming established smokers? *Pediatrics* 2001;108(6):1256–62.

Sargent JD, Dalton M, Beach M, Bernhardt A, Heatherton T, Stevens M. Effect of cigarette promotions on smoking uptake among adolescents. *Preventive Medicine* 2000;30(4):320–7.

Scal P, Ireland M, Borowsky IW. Smoking among American adolescents: a risk and protective factor analysis. *Journal of Community Health* 2003;28(2):79–97.

Scales MB, Monahan JL, Rhodes N, Roskos-Ewoldsen D, Johnson-Turbes A. Adolescents' perceptions of smoking and stress reduction. *Health Education & Behavior* 2009;36(4):746–58.

Scarinci IC, Robinson LA, Alfano CM, Zbikowski SM, Klesges RC. The relationship between socioeconomic status, ethnicity, and cigarette smoking in urban adolescents. *Preventive Medicine* 2002;34(2):171–8.

Scheres A, Milham MP, Knutson B, Castellanos FX. Ventral striatal hyporesponsiveness during reward anticipation in attention-deficit/hyperactivity disorder. *Biological Psychiatry* 2007;61(5):720–4.

Schmitt JE, Prescott CA, Gardner CO, Neale MC, Kendler KS. The differential heritability of regular tobacco use based on method of administration. *Twin Research and Human Genetics* 2005;8(1):60–2.

Schweinsburg AD, Paulus MP, Barlett VC, Killeen LA, Caldwell LC, Pulido C, Brown SA, Tapert SF. An FMRI study of response inhibition in youths with a family history of alcoholism. *Annals of the New York Academy of Sciences* 2004;1021:391–4.

Scott LD Jr, Munson MR, McMillen JC, Ollie MT. Religious involvement and its association to risk behaviors among older youth in foster care. *American Journal of Community Psychology* 2006;38(3–4):223–36.

Scragg R, Laugesen M, Robinson E. Cigarette smoking, pocket money and socioeconomic status: results from a national survey of 4th form students in 2000. *New Zealand Medical Journal* 2002;115(1158):U108.

Scragg R, Wellman RJ, Laugesen M, DiFranza JR. Diminished autonomy over tobacco can appear with the first cigarettes. *Addictive Behaviors* 2008;33(5):689–98.

Shadel WG, Tharp-Taylor S, Fryer CS. Exposure to cigarette advertising and adolescents' intentions to smoke: the moderating role of the developing self-concept. *Journal of Pediatric Psychology* 2008;33(7):751–60.

Sherman SJ, Presson CC, Chassin L, Corty E, Olshavsky R. The false consensus effect in estimates of smoking prevalence: underlying mechanisms. *Personality and Social Psychology Bulletin* 1983;9(2):197–207.

Sherman SJ, Rose JS, Koch K, Presson CC, Chassin L. Implicit and explicit attitudes toward cigarette smoking: the effects of context and motivation. *Journal of Social and Clinical Psychology* 2003;22(1):13–39.

Shmueli A, Tamir D. Health behavior and religiosity among Israeli Jews. *Israel Medical Association Journal* 2007;9(10):703–7.

Shohaimi S, Luben R, Wareham N, Day N, Bingham S, Welch A, Oakes S, Khan KT. Residential area deprivation predicts smoking habit independently of individual educational level and occupational social class: a cross sectional study in the Norfolk cohort of the European Investigation into Cancer (EPIC-Norfolk). *Journal of Epidemiology and Community Health* 2003;57(4):270–6.

Shrum W, Cheek NH Jr. Social structure during the school years: onset of the degrouping process. *American Sociological Review* 1987;52(2):218–23.

Siahpush M, Borland R, Scollo M. Smoking and financial stress. *Tobacco Control* 2003;12(1):60–6.

Silberg JL, Parr T, Neale MC, Rutter M, Angold A, Eaves LJ. Maternal smoking during pregnancy and risk to boys' conduct disturbance: an examination of the causal hypothesis. *Biological Psychiatry* 2003;53(2):130–5.

Simons-Morton BG. Prospective analysis of peer and parent influences on smoking initiation among early adolescents. *Prevention Science* 2002;3(4):275–83.

Simons-Morton B, Chen R, Abroms L, Haynie DL. Latent growth curve analyses of peer and parent influences on smoking progression among early adolescents. *Health Psychology* 2004;23(6):612–21.

Simons-Morton BG, Farhat T. Recent findings on peer group influences on adolescent smoking. *Journal of Primary Prevention* 2010;31(4):191–208.

Simons-Morton BG, Haynie DL. Psychosocial predictors of increased smoking stage among sixth graders. *American Journal of Health Behavior* 2003;27(6):592–602.

Simpson D. Italy: holy smoke! Pope swerves off track for Marlboro. *Tobacco Control* 2005;14(2):78.

Siqueira L, Diab M, Bodian C, Rolnitzky L. Adolescents becoming smokers: the roles of stress and coping methods. *Journal of Adolescent Health* 2000;27(6):399–408.

Skinner ML, Haggerty KP, Catalano RF. Parental and peer influences on teen smoking: Are white and black families different? *Nicotine & Tobacco Research* 2009; 11(5):558–63.

Slikker W Jr, Xu ZA, Levin ED, Slotkin TA. Mode of action: disruption of brain cell replication, second messenger, and neurotransmitter systems during development leading to cognitive dysfunction—developmental neurotoxicity of nicotine. *Critical Reviews in Toxicology* 2005;35(8–9):703–11.

Slomkowski C, Rende R, Novak S, Lloyd-Richardson E, Niaura R. Sibling effects on smoking in adolescence: evidence for social influence from a genetically informative design. *Addiction* 2005;100(4):430–8.

Slotkin TA. Fetal nicotine or cocaine exposure: which one is worse? *Journal of Pharmacology and Experimental Therapeutics* 1998;285(3):931–45.

Smith RM, Alachkar H, Papp AC, Wang D, Mash DC, Wang J-C, Bierut LJ, Sadee W. Nicotinic α5 receptor subunit mRNA expression is associated with distant 5' upstream polymorphisms. *European Journal of Human Genetics* 2011;19(1):76–83.

Soldz S, Cui X. Pathways through adolescent smoking: a 7-year longitudinal grouping analysis. *Health Psychology* 2002;21(5):495–504.

Stacy AW. Memory association and ambiguous cues in models of alcohol and marijuana use. *Experimental and Clinical Psychopharmacology* 1995;3(2):183–94.

Stacy AW. Memory activation and expectancy as prospective predictors of alcohol and marijuana use. *Journal of Abnormal Psychology* 1997;106(1):61–73.

Stacy AW, Ames SL, Sussman S, Dent CW. Implicit cognition in adolescent drug use. *Psychology of Addictive Behaviors* 1996;10(3):190–203.

Stacy AW, Leigh BC, Weingardt KR. Memory accessibility and association of alcohol use and its positive outcomes. *Experimental and Clinical Psychopharmacology* 1994;2(3):269–82.

Stanovich KE, West RF. Individual differences in reasoning: implications for the rationality debate? *Behavioral and Brain Sciences* 2000;23(5):645–65.

Stanton WR, Flay BR, Colder CR, Mehta P. Identifying and predicting adolescent smokers' developmental trajectories. *Nicotine & Tobacco Research* 2004;6(5):843–52.

Stead LF, Lancaster T. A systematic review of interventions for preventing tobacco sales to minors. *Tobacco Control* 2000;9(2):169–76.

Stein EA, Pankiewicz J, Harsch HH, Cho JK, Fuller SA, Hoffmann RG, Hawkins M, Rao SM, Bandetti PA, Bloom AS. Nicotine-induced limbic cortical activation in the human brain: a functional MRI study. *American Journal of Psychiatry* 1998;155(8):1009–15.

Steinberg L. Risk taking in adolescence: new perspectives from brain and behavioral science. *Current Directions in Psychological Science* 2007;16(2):55–9.

Sterzer P, Stadler C, Krebs A, Kleinschmidt A, Poustka F. Abnormal neural responses to emotional visual stimuli in adolescents with conduct disorder. *Biological Psychiatry* 2005;57(1):7–15.

Stigler M, Dhavan P, Van Dusen D, Arora M, Reddy KS, Perry CL. Westernization and tobacco use among young people in Delhi, India. *Social Science & Medicine* 2010;71(5):891-7.

Stimpson JP, Ju H, Raji MA, Eschbach K. Neighborhood deprivation and health risk behaviors in NHANES III. *American Journal of Health Behavior* 2007;31(2): 215–22.

Stuber J, Galea S, Link BG. Smoking and the emergence of a stigmatized social status. *Social Science & Medicine* 2008;67(3):420–30.

Substance Abuse and Mental Health Services Administration. *Results from the 2008 National Survey on Drug Use and Health: National Findings*. NSDUH Series H-36. Rockville (MD): U.S. Department of Health and Human Services, Substance Abuse and Mental Health Services Administration, Office of Applied Studies, 2009. DHHS Publication No. SMA 09-4434.

Substance Abuse and Mental Health Services Administration. *Results from the 2009 National Survey on Drug Use and Health: Volume I, Summary of National*

Findings. NSDUH Series H-38A. Rockville (MD): U.S. Department of Health and Human Services, Substance Abuse and Mental Health Services Administration, Office of Applied Studies, 2010. DHHS Publication No. SMA 10-4856.

Sun P, Unger JB, Sussman S. A new measure of smoking initiation and progression among adolescents. *American Journal of Health Behavior* 2005;29(1):3–11.

Sussman S, Ames SL. *Drug Abuse: Concepts, Prevention, and Cessation.* New York: Cambridge University Press, 2008.

Sussman S, Dent CW, Burton D, Stacy AW, Flay BR. *Developing School-Based Tobacco Use Prevention and Cessation Programs.* Thousand Oaks (CA): Sage Publications, 1995.

Sussman S, Dent CW, McAdams LA, Stacy AW, Burton D, Flay BR. Group self-identification and adolescent cigarette smoking: a 1-year prospective study. *Journal of Abnormal Psychology* 1994;103(3):576–80.

Sussman S, Dent CW, McCullar WJ. Group self-identification as a prospective predictor of drug use and violence in high-risk youth. *Psychology of Addictive Behaviors* 2000;14(2):192–6.

Sussman S, Dent CW, Mestel-Rauch J, Johnson CA, Hanson WB, Flay BR. Adolescent nonsmokers, triers, and regular smokers' estimates of cigarette smoking prevalence: when do overestimations occur and by whom? *Journal of Applied Social Psychology* 1988;18(7 Pt 1):537–51.

Sussman S, Hahn G, Dent CW, Stacy AW, Burton D, Flay BR. Naturalistic observation of adolescent tobacco use. *International Journal of the Addictions* 1993; 28(9):803–11.

Sussman S, Holt L, Dent CW, Flay BR, Graham JW, Hansen WB, Johnson CA. Activity involvement, risk-taking, demographic variables, and other drug use: prediction of trying smokeless tobacco. *NCI Monographs* 1989;8(8):57–62.

Sussman S, Pokhrel P, Ashmore RD, Brown BB. Adolescent peer group identification and characteristics: a review of the literature. *Addictive Behaviors* 2007;32(8): 1602–27.

Sutherland I, Shepherd JP. Social dimensions of adolescent substance use. *Addiction* 2001;96(3):445–58.

Swanson JE, Swanson E, Greenwald AG. Using the implicit association test to investigate attitude-behaviour consistency for stigmatised behaviour. *Cognition & Emotion* 2001;15(2):207–30.

Taber MT, Das S, Fibiger HC. Cortical regulation of subcortical dopamine release: mediation via the ventral tegmental area. *Journal of Neurochemistry* 1995; 65(3):1407–10.

Tamm L, Menon V, Ringel J, Reiss AL. Event-related FMRI evidence of frontotemporal involvement in aberrant response inhibition and task switching in attention-deficit/hyperactivity disorder. *Journal of the American Academy of Child and Adolescent Psychiatry* 2004;43(11):1430–40.

Tercyak KP, Rodriguez D, Audrain-McGovern J. High school seniors' smoking initiation and progression 1 year after graduation. *American Journal of Public Health* 2007;97(8):1397–8.

Thankappan KR, Thresia CU. Tobacco use and social status in Kerala. *Indian Journal of Medical Research* 2007;126(4):300–8.

Thorgeirsson TE, Gudbjartsson DF, Surakka I, Vink JM, Amin N, Geller F, Sulem P, Rafnar T, Esko T, Walter S, et al. Sequence variants at *CHRNB3-CHRNA6* and *CYP2A6* affect smoking behavior. *Nature Genetics* 2010;42(5):448–53.

Thush C, Wiers RW, Ames SL, Grenard JL, Sussman S, Stacy AW. Apples and oranges: comparing indirect measures of alcohol-related cognition predicting alcohol use in at-risk adolescents. *Psychology of Addictive Behaviors* 2007;21(4):587–91.

Thush C, Wiers RW, Ames SL, Grenard JL, Sussman S, Stacy AW. Interactions between implicit and explicit cognition and working memory capacity in the prediction of alcohol use in at-risk adolescents. *Drug and Alcohol Dependence* 2008;94(1–3):116–24.

Tiffany ST. A cognitive model of drug urges and drug-use behavior: role of automatic and nonautomatic processes. *Psychological Review* 1990;97(2):147–68.

Tobacco and Genetics Consortium. Genome-wide meta-analyses identify multiple loci associated with smoking behavior. *Nature Genetics* 2010;42(5):441–7.

Tobacco Products Scientific Advisory Committee. Menthol cigarettes and public health: Review of the scientific evidence and recommendations, 2011; http://www.fda.gov/downloads/AdvisoryCommittees/Committees-MeetingMaterials/TobaccoProductsScientificAdvisory-Committee/UCM247689.pdf>; accessed: November 28, 2011.

Tomar SL, Giovino GA. Incidence and predictors of smokeless tobacco use among US youth. *American Journal of Public Health* 1998;88(1):20–6.

Tseng M, Yeatts K, Millikan R, Newman B. Area-level characteristics and smoking in women. *American Journal of Public Health* 2001;91(11):1847–50.

Tucker JS, Ellickson PL, Klein DJ. Predictors of the transition to regular smoking during adolescence and young adulthood. *Journal of Adolescent Health* 2003;32(4):314–24.

Tucker JS, Martínez JF, Ellickson PL, Edelen MO. Temporal associations of cigarette smoking with social influences, academic performance, and delinquency: a four-wave longitudinal study from ages 13–23. *Psychology of Addictive Behaviors* 2008;22(1):1–11.

Turner L, Mermelstein R, Flay B. Individual and contextual influences on adolescent smoking. *Annals of the New York Academy of Sciences* 2004;1021:175–97.

Turner-Musa J, Lipscomb L. Spirituality and social support on health behaviors of African American undergraduates. *American Journal of Health Behavior* 2007; 31(5):495–501.

Tyas SL, Pederson LL. Psychosocial factors related to adolescent smoking: a critical review of the literature. *Tobacco Control* 1998;7(4):409–20.

Uhl GR, Drgon T, Johnson C, Fatusin OO, Liu QR, Buck K, Crabbe J. "Higher order" addiction molecular genetics: convergent data from genome-wide association in humans and mice. *Biochemical Pharmacology* 2008;75(1):98–111.

Unger JB, Cruz TB, Rohrbach LA, Ribisl KM, Baezconde-Garbanati L, Chen X, Trinidad DR, Johnson CA. English language use as a risk factor for smoking initiation among Hispanic and Asian American adolescents: evidence for mediation by tobacco-related beliefs and social norms. *Health Psychology* 2000;19(5):403–10.

Unger JB, Cruz TB, Schuster D, Flora JA, Johnson CA. Measuring exposure to pro- and antitobacco marketing among adolescents: intercorrelations among measures and associations with smoking status. *Journal of Health Communication* 2001;6(1):11–29.

Unger JB, Hamilton JE, Sussman S. A family member's job loss as a risk factor for smoking among adolescents. *Health Psychology* 2004;23(3):308–13.

Unger JB, Johnson CA, Stoddard JL, Nezami E, Chou CP. Identification of adolescents at risk for smoking initiation: validation of a measure of susceptibility. *Addictive Behaviors* 1997;22(1):81–91.

Urberg KA, Değirmencioğlu SM, Pilgrim C. Close friend and group influence on adolescent cigarette smoking and alcohol use. *Developmental Psychology* 1997; 33(5):834–44.

Urberg KA, Shyu SJ, Liang J. Peer influence in adolescent cigarette smoking. *Addictive Behaviors* 1990;15(3):247–55.

U.S. Department of Health and Human Services. *Preventing Tobacco Use Among Young People. A Report of the Surgeon General.* Atlanta (GA): U.S. Department of Health and Human Services, Public Health Service, Centers for Disease Control and Prevention, National Center for Chronic Disease Prevention and Health Promotion, Office on Smoking and Health, 1994.

U.S. Department of Health and Human Services. *How Tobacco Smoke Causes Disease—The Biology and Behavioral Basis for Tobacco-Attributable Disease: A Report of the Surgeon General*. Atlanta: U.S. Department of Health and Human Services, Centers for Disease Control and Prevention, National Center for Chronic Disease Prevention and Health Promotion, Office on Smoking and Health, 2010.

U.S. Department of Health, Education, and Welfare. *Smoking and Health: Report of the Advisory Committee to the Surgeon General of the Public Health Service*. Washington: U.S. Department of Health, Education, and Welfare, Public Health Service, Center for Disease Control, 1964. PHS Publication No. 1103.

Valente TW, Gallaher P, Mouttapa M. Using social networks to understand and prevent substance use: a transdisciplinary perspective. *Substance Use & Misuse* 2004;39(10–12):1685–712.

Valente TW, Unger JB, Johnson CA. Do popular students smoke: the association between popularity and smoking among middle school students. *Journal of Adolescent Health* 2005;37(4):323–29.

van den Bree MB, Whitmer MD, Pickworth WB. Predictors of smoking development in a population-based sample of adolescents: a prospective study. *Journal of Adolescent Health* 2004;35(3):172–81.

Velicer WF, Redding CA, Anatchkova MD, Fava JL, Prochaska JO. Identifying cluster subtypes for the prevention of adolescent smoking acquisition. *Addictive Behaviors* 2007;32(2):228–47.

Villanti A, Boulay M, Juon H-S. Peer, parent and media influences on adolescent smoking by developmental stage. *Addictive Behaviors* 2011;36(1–2):133–6.

Vink JM, Willemsen G, Boomsma DI. The association of current smoking behavior with the smoking behavior of parents, siblings, friends and spouses. *Addiction* 2003a;98(7):923–31.

Vink JM, Willemsen G, Engels RC, Boomsma DI. Smoking status of parents, siblings and friends: predictors of regular smoking: findings from a longitudinal twin-family study. *Twin Research* 2003b;6(3):209–17.

Wahl SK, Turner LR, Mermelstein RJ, Flay BR. Adolescents' smoking expectancies: psychometric properties and prediction of behavior change. *Nicotine & Tobacco Research* 2005;7(4):613–23.

Wakefield MA, Chaloupka FJ, Kaufman NJ, Orleans CT, Barker DC, Ruel EE. Effect of restrictions on smoking at home, at school, and in public places on teenage smoking: cross sectional study. *BMJ (British Medical Journal)* 2000;321(7257):333–7.

Walaas I, Fonnum F. Biochemical evidence for γ-aminobutyrate containing fibres from the nucleus accumbens to the substantia nigra and ventral tegmental area in the rat. *Neuroscience* 1980;5(1):63–72.

Wang MQ. Social environmental influences on adolescents' smoking progression. *American Journal of Health Behavior* 2001;25(4):418–25.

Wang JC, Cruchaga C, Saccone NL, Bertelsen S, Liu P, Budde JP, Duan W, Fox L, Grucza RA, Kern J, et al. Risk for nicotine dependence and lung cancer is conferred by mRNA expression levels and amino acid change in *CHRNA5*. *Human Molecular Genetics* 2009;18(16):3125–35.

Wang MQ, Eddy JM, Fitzhugh EC. Smoking acquisition: peer influence and self-selection. *Psychological Reports* 2000;86(3 Pt 2):1241–6.

Wang MQ, Fitzhugh EC, Green BL, Turner LW, Eddy JM, Westerfield RC. Prospective social-psychological factors of adolescent smoking progression. *Journal of Adolescent Health* 1999;24(1):2–9.

Warren CW, Jones NR, Peruga A, Chauvin J, Baptiste JP, Costa de Silva V, El Awa F, Tsouros A, Rahman K, Fishburn B, et al. Global youth tobacco surveillance, 2000–2007. *Morbidity and Mortality Weekly Report* 2008;57(SS-1):1–28.

Wasserman S, Faust K. *Social Network Analysis: Methods and Applications*. Cambridge: Cambridge University Press, 1994.

Waters AJ, Carter BL, Robinson JD, Wetter DW, Lam CY, Cinciripini PM. Implicit attitudes to smoking are associated with craving and dependence. *Drug and Alcohol Dependence* 2007;91(2–3):178–86.

Waters AJ, Sayette MA. Implicit cognition and tobacco addiction. In: Wiers RW, Stacy AW, editors. *Handbook of Implicit Cognition and Addiction*. Thousand Oaks (CA): Sage Publications, 2006:309–38.

Weinstein SM, Mermelstein R, Shiffman S, Flay B. Mood variability and cigarette smoking escalation among adolescents. *Psychology of Addictive Behaviors* 2008; 22(4):504–13.

Weiss JW, Garbanati JA. Effects of acculturation and social norms on adolescent smoking among Asian-American subgroups. *Journal of Ethnicity in Substance Abuse* 2006;5(2):75–90.

Weiss JW, Spruijt-Metz D, Palmer PH, Chou CP, Johnson CA, China Seven Cities Study Research Team. Smoking among adolescents in China: an analysis based upon the meanings of smoking theory. *American Journal of Health Promotion* 2006;20(3):171–8.

Wellman RJ, Sugarman DB, DiFranza JR, Winickoff JP. The extent to which tobacco marketing and tobacco use in films contribute to children's use of tobacco: a meta-analysis. *Archives of Pediatrics & Adolescent Medicine* 2006;160(12):1285–96.

Wen M, Van Duker H, Olson LM. Social contexts of regular smoking in adolescence: towards a multidimensional ecological model. *Journal of Adolescence* 2009;32(3):671–92.

Wessel J, McDonald SM, Hinds DA, Stokowski RP, Javitz HS, Kennemer M, Krasnow R, Dirks W, Hardin J, Pitts SJ, et al. Resequencing of nicotinic acetylcholine receptor genes and association of common and rare variants with the Fagerstrom Test for Nicotine Dependence. *Neuropsychopharmacology* 2010;35(12):2392–402.

West P, Sweeting H, Ecob R. Family and friends' influences on the uptake of regular smoking from mid-adolescence to early adulthood. *Addiction* 1999;94(9):1397–411.

Wetter DW, Kenford SL, Welsch SK, Smith SS, Fouladi RT, Fiore MC, Baker TB. Prevalence and predictors of transitions in smoking behavior among college students. *Health Psychology* 2004;23(2):168–77.

White HR, Nagin D, Replogle E, Stouthamer-Loeber M. Racial differences in trajectories of cigarette use. *Drug and Alcohol Dependence* 2004;76(3):219–27.

White HR, Pandina RJ, Chen PH. Developmental trajectories of cigarette use from early adolescence into young adulthood. *Drug and Alcohol Dependence* 2002; 65(2):167–78.

White HR, Violette NM, Metzger L, Stouthamer-Loeber M. Adolescent risk factors for late-onset smoking among African American young men. *Nicotine & Tobacco Research* 2007;9(1):153–61.

White MM, Gilpin EA, Emery SL, Pierce JP. Facilitating adolescent smoking: who provides the cigarettes? *American Journal of Health Promotion* 2005;19(5):355–60.

White VM, Hopper JL, Wearing AJ, Hill DJ. The role of genes in tobacco smoking during adolescence and young adulthood: a multivariate behaviour genetic investigation. *Addiction* 2003;98(8):1087–100.

Whooley MA, Boyd AL, Gardin JM, Williams DR. Religious involvement and cigarette smoking in young adults: the CARDIA Study. *Archives of Internal Medicine* 2002;162(14):1604–10.

Wiers RW, de Jong PJ. Implicit and explicit alcohol, smoking, and drug-related cognitions and emotions. In: Arlsdale JZ, editor. *Advances in Social Psychology Research*. Hauppauge (NY): Nova Science Publishers, 2006:1–35.

Wiers RW, Houben K, Smulders FTY, Conrod PJ, Jones BT. To drink or not to drink: the role of automatic and controlled cognitive processes in the etiology of alcohol-related problems. In: Wiers RW, Stacy AW, editors. *Handbook of Implicit Cognition and Addiction*. Thousand Oaks (CA): Sage Publications, 2006:339–61.

Wiers RW, Stacy AW, editors. *Handbook of Implicit Cognition and Addiction.* Thousand Oaks (CA): Sage Publications, 2006.

Wiers RW, van Woerden N, Smulders FT, de Jong PJ. Implicit and explicit alcohol-related cognitions in heavy and light drinkers. *Journal of Abnormal Psychology* 2002;111(4):648–58.

Wilcox P. An ecological approach to understanding youth smoking trajectories: problems and prospects. *Addiction* 2003;98(Suppl 1):57–77.

Wills TA, Filer M. Stress–coping model of adolescent substance use. In: Ollendick TH, Prinz RJ, editors. *Advances in Clinical Child Psychology.* Vol. 18. New York: Plenum Press, 1996:91–132.

Wills TA, Murry VM, Brody GH, Gibbons FX, Gerrard M, Walker C, Ainette MG. Ethnic pride and self-control related to protective and risk factors: test of the theoretical model for the strong African American families program. *Health Psychology* 2007;26(1):50–9.

Wills TA, Sandy JM, Yaeger AM. Temperament and adolescent substance use: an epigenetic approach to risk and protection. *Journal of Personality* 2000;68(6):1127–51.

Wills TA, Sandy JM, Yaeger AM. Stress and smoking in adolescence: a test of directional hypotheses. *Health Psychology* 2002;21(2):122–30.

Windle M, Spear LP, Fuligni AJ, Angold A, Brown JD, Pine D, Smith GT, Giedd J, Dahl RE. Transitions into underage and problem drinking: developmental processes and mechanisms between 10 and 15 years of age. *Pediatrics* 2008;121(Suppl 4):S273–S289.

Windle M, Windle RC. Depressive symptoms and cigarette smoking among middle adolescents: prospective associations and intrapersonal and interpersonal influences. *Journal of Consulting and Clinical Psychology* 2001;69(2):215–26.

Winickoff JP, Gottlieb M, Mello MM. Regulation of smoking in public housing. *New England Journal of Medicine* 2010;362(24):2319–25.

Wong G, Glover M, Nosa V, Freeman B, Paynter J, Scragg R. Young people, money, and access to tobacco. *New Zealand Medical Journal* 2007;120(1267):U2864.

World Health Organization. *Tobacco Free Initiative Meeting on Tobacco and Religion, 3 May 1999, Geneva, Switzerland.* Geneva: World Health Organization; 1999. WHO Report WHO/NCD/TFI/99.12.

World Health Organization, Eastern Mediterranean Regional Office. Distribution of the Islamic Ruling on Smoking in 53,000 Mosques within Egypt. 2001. <http://www.emro.who.int/TFI/wntd2001/islamicrulings.Htm>; accessed: May 4, 2009.

Wu L-T, Schlenger WE, Galvin DM. The relationship between employment and substance use among students aged 12 to 17. *Journal of Adolescent Health* 2003; 32(1):5–15.

Xue Y, Zimmerman MA, Caldwell CH. Neighborhood residence and cigarette smoking among urban youths: the protective role of prosocial activities. *American Journal of Public Health* 2007;97(10):1865–72.

Young SE, Rhee SH, Stallings MC, Corley RP, Hewitt JK. Genetic and environmental vulnerabilities underlying adolescent substance use and problem use: general or specific? *Behavior Genetics* 2006;36(4):603–15.

Yu M. Tobacco use among American Indian or Alaska Native middle- and high-school students in the United States. *Nicotine & Tobacco Research* 2011;13(3): 173–81.

Yu M, Stiffman AR, Freedenthal S. Factors affecting American Indian adolescent tobacco use. *Addictive Behaviors* 2005;30(5):889–904.

Zhang J, Wang Z. Factors associated with smoking in Asian American adults: a systematic review. *Nicotine & Tobacco Research* 2008;10(5):791–801.

Chapter 5
The Tobacco Industry's Influences on the Use of Tobacco Among Youth

Introduction

In most developed countries, businesses use a broad variety of marketing techniques to increase their sales, gain market share, attract new users, and retain existing customers. These techniques include product design, packaging, pricing, distribution, product placement, advertising, and a variety of promotional activities. Tobacco companies were among the earliest companies to identify and implement effective, integrated marketing strategies, and cigarettes and other tobacco products have long been among the most heavily marketed consumer products in the United States (Brandt 2007). In the late nineteenth century, James Buchanan Duke used the cost advantages he gained from his adoption of James Bonsack's mechanized cigarette rolling machine to aggressively market his cigarette brands (Chaloupka 2007). Duke's marketing practices included setting relatively low prices, providing sophisticated packaging, carrying out promotions such as including picture cards in cigarette packs and sponsoring various public events, and paying distributors and retailers to promote his brands (Kluger 1996). These strategies contributed to the growth of Duke's American Tobacco Company, which came to dominate U.S. tobacco markets in the early twentieth century before antitrust actions dissolved the trust in 1911. Despite the breakup of the trust, U.S. markets for tobacco products have remained highly concentrated, with little price competition. Even so, variations of many of the marketing practices used by Duke continue to be important marketing tools for today's tobacco companies, as discussed in this chapter.

Tobacco companies have long argued that their marketing efforts do not increase the overall demand for tobacco products and have no impact on the initiation of tobacco use among young people; rather, they argue, they are competing with other companies for market share. In contrast, the weight of the evidence from extensive and increasingly sophisticated research conducted over the past few decades shows that the industry's marketing activities have been a key factor in leading young people to take up tobacco, keeping some users from quitting, and achieving greater consumption among users (National Cancer Institute [NCI] 2008). This growing evidence has helped to spur a variety of policy interventions aimed at reducing the influence of marketing on tobacco initiation and consumption by the tobacco companies, from the 1971 ban on broadcast advertising to the constraints contained in the 1998 Master Settlement Agreement (National Association of Attorneys General [NAAG] 1998a) and Smokeless Tobacco Master Settlement Agreement (NAAG 1998b).

As research evidence has accumulated over time, the relationships between the marketing activities of tobacco companies and the use of tobacco, including use among young people, have become clear. Correspondingly, the growing strength of the evidence in this area has been reflected by the increasingly strong conclusions drawn in comprehensive reviews of this evidence, including those in previous Surgeon General's reports on smoking and health (notably the 1989, 1994, 1998, and 2000 reports [U.S. Department of Health and Human Services (USDHHS) 1989, 1994, 1998, 2000]) and other comprehensive reviews (e.g., Lynch and Bonnie 1994; *Federal Register* 1996; Lovato et al. 2003; NCI 2008).

The present chapter provides an updated and extended review of the evidence on the impact of the tobacco companies' marketing activities on tobacco use. The chapter begins by reviewing trends in marketing expenditures made by the tobacco companies and changes in the focus of these expenditures over time. This review then presents a conceptual framework that relates advertising and promotion by tobacco companies to tobacco use among young people. The section on the framework is followed by a review of the evidence on the effects of advertising and promotion on tobacco use among young people, drawing from and updating existing comprehensive reviews. Next is a discussion of the role of marketing techniques that have been given relatively little attention in most previous reviews: pricing strategies, packaging and design, marketing at the point of sale, and emerging digital marketing techniques. This is followed by a section that describes programs sponsored by tobacco companies with the stated purpose of preventing tobacco use among young people and the evidence of their impact on this population. Following this section is a review of the impact of exposure to tobacco use in the movies. The chapter closes with major conclusions about the role of marketing by the tobacco companies and depictions of smoking in movies influencing tobacco use among young people.

Marketing Expenditures of the Tobacco Companies

Cigarettes

Each year, tobacco companies are required to report detailed information on their domestic cigarette sales and marketing expenditures to the Federal Trade Commission (FTC 2011a). The publicly available data do not include the level of detail reported by tobacco companies (i.e., by company, brand, and type of activity) but are instead presented in the aggregate in FTC's regular reports on the marketing expenditures of cigarette companies. Over time, however, FTC's reports on these data have become increasingly detailed, with expenditures now reported in numerous categories. In recent years, spending has been reported for separate categories, as defined in Table 5.1.

In earlier years, FTC reported expenditures in several of the current categories as part of an aggregated category (e.g., coupons and retail value-added as one category, promotional allowances including price discounts as another). Similarly, in earlier years, expenditures on other types of marketing activities that are no longer allowed or used were reported, including expenditures on television and radio advertising and on endorsements and testimonials.

In 2008, the most recent year reported, expenditures on price discounts accounted for the largest single category—nearly three-fourths of total expenditures (Table 5.2; FTC 2011a). When other price-related discounts are included (coupons and free cigarettes from either sampling or retail-value-added promotions), spending on marketing practices that reduced cigarette prices accounted for about $6.00 of every $7.00 (about 84%) spent on cigarette marketing in 2008. In contrast, traditional advertising (including that in newspapers and magazines, outdoors, and at the point of sale) accounted for less than 2.0% of total spending on marketing (FTC 2011a).

In 2008, $9.94 billion was spent on marketing cigarettes in the United States (down from a high of $15.1 billion in 2003) by the five major U.S. cigarette companies: Altria Group, Inc. (ultimate parent company for Philip Morris USA); Commonwealth Brands, Inc.; Lorillard, Inc. (ultimate parent company for Lorillard Tobacco Company); Reynolds American, Inc. (ultimate parent company for R.J. Reynolds Tobacco Company [RJR] and Santa Fe Natural Tobacco Company, Inc.; Reynolds American Inc. acquired Brown & Williamson (B&W) Tobacco Corporation in 2004); and Vector Group Ltd. (ultimate parent company for Liggett Group, LLC, and Vector Tobacco Inc.) (Tables 5.2 and 5.3; FTC 2011a). In 2008, this amounted to 62 cents per pack of cigarettes sold (just over 18% of the average price per pack), down from a high of 84 cents per pack (almost 24% of average price) in 2003. In 2006, cigarette companies spent an estimated 28.9% of their revenues (net of state and federal cigarette excise taxes) on their marketing efforts, up somewhat from an estimated 25.4% in 2003 (FTC 2011a).

In addition to the marketing activities covered in the FTC reports, cigarette companies engage in various marketing-related activities for which data are not publicly available. For example, companies invest considerable funds in the development of new brands, brand extensions (i.e., extensions of existing brands), or new products that may help them gain market share from other companies and/or attract new consumers. The cigarette pack itself is a form of marketing, with companies developing packaging designed to attract attention, appeal to specific consumers, reinforce brand identity, or suggest specific product qualities (Wakefield et al. 2002a).

In inflation-adjusted (real) terms, marketing expenditures by the cigarette companies have generally increased over time since 1963 (Table 5.3). Real expenditures for marketing fell in the early 1970s, however, as a ban on broadcast cigarette advertising went into effect in 1971. Indeed, real spending fell by nearly one-quarter from 1970 to 1971. By 1975, spending had surpassed the level seen in the last year before the ban, as cigarette companies increased spending on other marketing activities. Real spending increased nearly every year from 1975 through 1993 before dropping 26.8% in 1994. The decline in spending from 1993 to 1994 largely resulted from industry-wide price cuts that made permanent the price reductions initially implemented through various price promotions initiated by Philip Morris USA for Marlboros on April 2, 1993 (which became known as "Marlboro Friday"), and subsequently matched by other companies on their leading brands (Chen et al. 2009). After a few years of relative stability, marketing expenditures rose sharply beginning in 1997, with total real expenditures rising by 243% from 1996 to 2003 before falling from 2004 to 2008.

The relative emphasis on different cigarette marketing activities has changed dramatically over the past four decades (Tables 5.3 and 5.4). In the 1960s and early 1970s, about 90% of total marketing expenditures were on print, broadcast, and outdoor (including transit) advertising ("Advertising" in Table 5.3). By 1980, spending on advertising (including point of sale) was down to 70% of the total, and by 1998, it was just 13.9%. The November 1998 Master Settlement Agreement contained a number of provisions that limited cigarette advertising, including a ban

Table 5.1 Cigarette company marketing activities reported to the Federal Trade Commission

Newspapers	Newspaper advertising; but excluding expenditures in connection with sampling, specialty item distribution, public entertainment, endorsements, sponsorships, coupons, and retail value added.
Magazines	Magazine advertising; but excluding expenditures in connection with sampling, specialty item distribution, public entertainment, endorsements, sponsorships, coupons, and retail value added.
Outdoor	Billboards; signs and placards in arenas, stadiums, and shopping malls, whether they are open air or enclosed; and any other advertisements placed outdoors, regardless of their size, including those on cigarette retailer property; but excluding expenditures in connection with sampling, specialty item distribution, public entertainment, endorsements, sponsorships, coupons, and retail value added.
Audiovisual	Audiovisual or video advertising on any medium of electronic communication not subject to the Federal Communications Commission's jurisdiction, including screens at motion picture theaters, video cassettes or DVDs, and television screens or monitors in stores; but excluding expenditures in connection with Internet advertising.
Transit	Advertising on or within private or public vehicles and all advertisements placed at, on or within any bus stop, taxi stand, transportation waiting area, train station, airport, or any other transportation facility; but excluding expenditures in connection with sampling, specialty item distribution, public entertainment, endorsements, sponsorships, coupons, and retail value added.
Point of sale	Point-of-sale advertisements; but excluding expenditures in connection with outdoor advertising, sampling, specialty item distribution, public entertainment, endorsements, sponsorships, coupons, and retail value added.
Price discounts	Price discounts paid to cigarette retailers or wholesalers in order to reduce the price of cigarettes to consumers, including off-invoice discounts, buy downs, voluntary price reductions, and trade programs; but excluding retail-value-added expenditures for promotions involving free cigarettes and expenditures involving coupons.
Promotional allowances—retail	Promotional allowances paid to cigarette retailers in order to facilitate the sale or placement of any cigarette, including payments for stocking, shelving, displaying and merchandising brands, volume rebates, incentive payments, and the cost of cigarettes given to retailers for free for subsequent sale to consumers; but excluding expenditures in connection with newspapers, magazines, outdoor, audiovisual, transit, direct mail, point of sale, and price discounts.
Promotional allowances—wholesale	Promotional allowances paid to cigarette wholesalers in order to facilitate the sale or placement of any cigarette, including payments for volume rebates, incentive payments, value added services, promotional execution and satisfaction of reporting requirements; but excluding expenditures in connection with newspapers, magazines, outdoor, audiovisual, transit, direct mail, point of sale, price discounts, and retail promotional allowances.
Promotional allowances—other	Promotional allowances paid to any persons other than retailers, wholesalers, and full-time company employees who are involved in the cigarette distribution and sales process in order to facilitate the sale or placement of any cigarette; but excluding expenditures in connection with newspapers, magazines, outdoor, audiovisual, transit, direct mail, point of sale, price discounts, and retail and wholesale promotional allowances.
Sampling	Sampling of cigarettes, including the cost of the cigarettes, all associated excise taxes and increased costs under the Master Settlement Agreement, and the cost of organizing, promoting, and conducting sampling. Sampling includes the distribution of cigarettes for consumer testing or evaluation when consumers are able to smoke the cigarettes outside of a facility operated by the company, but not the cost of actual clinical testing or market research associated with such cigarette distributions. Sampling also includes the distribution of coupons for free cigarettes, when no purchase or payment is required to obtain the coupons or cigarettes.

Table 5.1 Continued

Specialty item distribution—branded	All costs of distributing any item (other than cigarettes, items the sole function of which is to advertise or promote cigarettes, or written or electronic publications), whether distributed by sale, redemption of coupons, or otherwise, that bears the name, logo, or an image of any portion of the package of any brand or variety of cigarettes, including the cost of the items distributed but subtracting any payments received for the item. The costs associated with distributing noncigarette items in connection with sampling or retail-value-added programs are reported in those categories, not as specialty item distribution.
Specialty item distribution—nonbranded	All costs of distributing any item (other than cigarettes, items the sole function of which is to advertise or promote cigarettes, or written or electronic publications), whether distributed by sale, redemption of coupons, or otherwise, that does not bear the name, logo, or an image of any portion of the package of any brand or variety of cigarette, including the cost of the items distributed but subtracting any payments received for the item. The costs associated with distributing noncigarette items in connection with sampling or retail-value-added programs are reported in those categories, not as specialty item distribution.
Direct mail	Direct mail advertising; but excluding expenditures in connection with sampling, specialty item distribution, public entertainment, endorsements, sponsorships, coupons, retail value added, and Internet advertising.
Public entertainment—adult only	Public entertainment events bearing or otherwise displaying the name or logo or an image of any portion of the package of any of a company's cigarettes or otherwise referring or relating to cigarettes, which take place in an adult-only facility, including all expenditures made by the company in promoting and/or sponsoring such events.
Public entertainment—general audience	Public entertainment events bearing or otherwise displaying the name or logo or an image of any portion of the package of any of a company's cigarettes or otherwise referring or relating to cigarettes, which do not take place in an adult-only facility, including all expenditures made by the company in promoting and/or sponsoring such events.
Retail value added—bonus cigarettes	Retail-value-added expenditures for promotions involving free cigarettes (e.g., buy two packs, get one free), whether or not the free cigarettes are physically bundled together with the purchased cigarettes, including all expenditures and costs associated with the value added to the purchase of cigarettes (e.g., excise taxes paid for the free cigarettes and increased costs under the Master Settlement Agreement).
Retail value added—noncigarette bonus	Retail-value-added expenditures for promotions involving free noncigarette items (e.g., buy two packs, get a cigarette lighter), including all expenditures and costs associated with the value added to the purchase of cigarettes.
Coupons	All costs associated with coupons for the reduction of the retail cost of cigarettes, whether redeemed at the point of sale or by mail, including all costs associated with advertising or promotion, design, printing, distribution, and redemption. However, when coupons are distributed for free cigarettes and no purchase or payment is required to obtain the coupons or the cigarettes, these activities are considered to be sampling and not couponing.
Sponsorships	Sponsorships of sports teams or individual athletes, but excluding endorsements.
Endorsements and testimonials	Endorsements, testimonials, and product placement.
Company Web site	All expenditures associated with advertising on any company Internet Web site.
Internet—other	Internet advertising other than on the company's own Internet Web site, including on the World Wide Web, on commercial online services, and through electronic mail messages.

Table 5.1 Continued

Telephone	Telephone advertising, including costs associated with the placement of telemarketing calls or the operation of incoming telephone lines that allow consumers to participate in any promotion or hear prerecorded product messages; but excluding costs associated with having customer service representatives available for responding to consumer complaints or questions.
Other	Advertising and promotional expenditures not covered by another category.

Source: Federal Trade Commission (FTC) 2011a.
Note: Comparable definitions apply to various smokeless tobacco marketing efforts reported on by FTC.

on billboard and transit advertising. Since 1998, marketing expenditures for traditional cigarette advertising have fallen further, accounting for just 1.9% of total spending in 2008, with more than three-fourths of this accounted for by point-of-sale advertising.

In March 2010, the U.S. Food and Drug Administration (FDA) reissued the "1996 rule," which further restricts marketing activities that are likely to appeal to youth. Restrictions include, for example, a ban on the distribution of non-tobacco items with brand names, logos, or selling messages; a broad ban on brand name sponsorship of athletic, musical, artistic, or other social or cultural events; and teams or entries in these events (*Federal Register* 2010).

Although traditional cigarette advertising was becoming a less important component of the cigarette companies' marketing strategies, other activities were increasing. Companies began spending more on sponsorships and other public entertainment activities, but these efforts never accounted for more than 4% of overall expenditures. Spending on specialty item distribution and noncigarette retail-value-added promotions became more important in the 1980s through the mid-1990s, with programs such as "Marlboro Miles" and "Camel Cash," as well as other promotional giveaways. The Master Settlement Agreement's ban on the distribution of branded merchandise, however, put an end to many of these activities, with spending on merchandise-related promotions accounting for less than 2% of the total in recent years (Table 5.4; FTC 2011a). Expenditures on product placement at the point of sale (promotional allowances, such as those paid for through programs like Philip Morris' Retail Leaders and Wholesale Leaders trade programs) grew throughout much of the 1990s, peaking at about one-seventh of total spending (14.3%) in 2002. This spending fell to a low of about 6.5% of total spending in 2005 but has climbed steadily since, reaching 9.4% in 2008 (Table 5.4; FTC 2011a).

The largest shift, however, has taken place in marketing efforts that lower the price of cigarettes: coupons, cigarette giveaways (sampling and retail-value-added promotions), and reductions from payments to retailers and wholesalers that are passed on to smokers. Price discounts are estimated to have accounted for about one-fifth of overall marketing expenditures by cigarette companies in the late 1970s; by 1988, they were estimated to account for just over one-half of overall expenditures (Table 5.4). Since the Master Settlement Agreement, however, spending on price discounts that reduce the price of cigarettes more than doubled, from $3.5 billion in 1997 to $8.3 billion in 2008 (Table 5.5), accounting for 84% of total expenditures in that year.

Smokeless Tobacco Products

Companies that sell smokeless tobacco engage in many of the same marketing practices used by cigarette companies. In 2008, total marketing expenditures for smokeless tobacco products were $547 million (Table 5.6; FTC 2011b), just under 14% of total revenues from the sale of smokeless tobacco products. Traditional advertising is relatively more important for smokeless tobacco products than for cigarettes, accounting for between 10.6% and 21% of total marketing expenditures in recent years, with print and point-of-sale advertising accounting for nearly all of this (Tables 5.6 and 5.7). As with cigarettes, spending on price discounts accounts for the single largest share of marketing expenditures, at 59.3% in 2008 (Table 5.6; FTC 2011b). When other price-reducing marketing expenditures are added (including coupons, sampling distribution, and retail-value-added bonus products), a little less than $3.00 of every $4.00 (72.1%) currently spent on the marketing of smokeless tobacco products goes to reducing their price to consumers (Tables 5.8 and 5.9).

In addition, the traditional division of products, brand identities, and marketing between cigarette and smokeless tobacco companies has all but become nonexistent in recent years as major U.S. cigarette companies, including RJR and Altria, have acquired smokeless tobacco

Table 5.2 Detailed expenditures for cigarette marketing, in thousands of dollars, 2002–2008

	2002		2003		2004		2005	
	Expenditures ($)	As % of total	Expenditures ($)	As % of total	Expenditures ($)	As % of total	Expenditures ($)	As % of total
Newspapers	25,538	0.2	8,251	0.1	4,913	0.0	1,589	0.0
Magazines	106,852	0.9	156,394	1.0	95,700	0.7	44,777	0.3
Outdoor	24,192	0.2	32,599	0.2	17,135	0.1	9,821	0.1
Transit	0	0.0	0	0.0	0	0.0	0	0.0
Point of sale	260,902	2.1	165,573	1.1	163,621	1.2	182,193	1.4
Price discounts	7,873,835	63.2	10,808,239	71.4	10,932,199	77.3	9,776,069	74.6
Promotional allowances—retail	1,333,097	10.7	1,229,327	8.1	542,213	3.8	435,830	3.3
Promotional allowances—wholesale	446,327	3.6	683,067	4.5	387,758	2.7	410,363	3.1
Promotional allowances—other	2,767	0.0	2,786	0.0	1,323	0.0	1,493	0.0
Sampling	28,777	0.2	17,853	0.1	11,649	0.1	17,211	0.1
Specialty item distribution—branded	49,423	0.4	9,195	0.1	8,011	0.1	5,255	0.0
Specialty item distribution—nonbranded	174,201	1.4	254,956	1.7	216,577	1.5	225,279	1.7
Public entertainment—adult only	219,016	1.8	150,889	1.0	140,137	1.0	214,075	1.6
Public entertainment—general audience	34,089	0.3	32,849	0.2	115	0.0	152	0.0
Sponsorship	54,247	0.4	31,371	0.2	28,231	0.2	30,575	0.2
Direct mail	111,319	0.9	92,978	0.6	93,836	0.7	51,844	0.4
Coupons	522,246	4.2	650,653	4.3	751,761	5.3	870,137	6.6
Retail value added—bonus cigarettes	1,060,304	8.5	677,308	4.5	636,221	4.5	725,010	5.5

Table 5.2 Continued

	2002		2003		2004		2005	
	Expenditures ($)	As % of total	Expenditures ($)	As % of total	Expenditures ($)	As % of total	Expenditures ($)	As % of total
Retail value added—noncigarette bonus	24,727	0.2	20,535	0.1	14,343	0.1	7,526	0.1
Company Web site	940	0.0	2,851	0.0	1,401	0.0	2,675	0.0
Telephone	679	0.0	760	0.0	346	0.0	59	0.0
All other	112,879	0.9	117,563	0.8	102,369	0.7	99,025	0.8
FTC total	12,466,358		15,145,998		14,149,859		13,110,958	

	2006		2007		2008	
	Expenditures ($)	As % of total	Expenditures ($)	As % of total	Expenditures ($)	As % of total
Newspapers	NA	—	NA	—	169	0.0
Magazines	50,293	0.4	47,203	0.4	25,478	0.3
Outdoor	935	0.0	3,041	0.0	2,045	0.0
Transit	0	0.0	0	0.0	0	0.0
Point of sale	242,625	1.9	198,861	1.8	163,709	1.0
Price discounts	9,205,106	73.7	7,699,362	70.9	7,171,092	72.1
Promotional allowances—retail	434,239	3.5	454,139	4.2	481,500	4.8
Promotional allowances—wholesale	471,204	3.8	479,032	4.4	448,461	4.2
Promotional allowances—other	—	—	NA	—	1,245	0.0
Sampling	29,431	0.2	48,719	0.4	54,261	0.5
Specialty item distribution—branded	5,546	0.0	8,070	0.0	7,188	0.1
Specialty item distribution—nonbranded	163,761	1.3	160,047	1.5	93,798	0.9

Table 5.2 Continued

	2006		2007		2008	
	Expenditures ($)	**As % of total**	**Expenditures ($)**	**As % of total**	**Expenditures ($)**	**As % of total**
Public entertainment—adult only	168,098	1.3	160,104	1.5	154,749	1.5
Public entertainment—general audience	NA	NA	NA	—	NA	—
Sponsorship	NA	NA	NA	—	NA	—
Direct mail	102,353	0.8	81,929	0.8	89,920	0.9
Coupons	625,777	5.0	366,779	3.4	359,793	3.6
Retail value added—bonus cigarettes	817,792	6.5	981,566	9.0	721,818	7.3
Retail value added—noncigarette bonus	14,642	0.1	17,720	0.1	10,983	0.1
Company Web site	6,497	0.1	2,351	0.0	13,172	0.1
Telephone	—	—	NA	—	NA	—
All other	151,392	1.2	155,843	1.4	143,688	1.4
FTC total	12,489,692		10,864,767		9,943,068	

Source: Federal Trade Commission (FTC) 2011a.
Note: FTC reported zero expenditures in all years in three categories, which were omitted from this table: transit, endorsements and testimonials, and Internet—other. Because of rounding, in any year the sum of the individual expenditures may not equal total expenditures and the sum of percentages may not equal 100. The "all other" category includes expenditures on audiovisual to avoid disclosure of individual company data. Expenditures denoted as "NA" are included in the "all other" category to avoid disclosure of individual company data. "—" = not available.

Table 5.3 Cigarette company marketing expenditures, by major category, in millions of dollars, 1963–2008

Year	Advertising ($)	Promotion and other ($)	Total ($)	Per pack ($)	Advertising as % of total	Total, 8/11 ($)	Per pack, 8/11 ($)
1963	228.9	20.6	249.5	0.01	91.7	1,847.2	0.07
1964	240.9	20.4	261.3	0.01	92.2	1,909.6	0.08
1965	242.3	20.7	263.0	0.01	92.1	1,891.5	0.07
1966	272.7	24.8	297.5	0.01	91.7	2,080.2	0.08
1967	285.6	26.3	311.9	0.01	91.6	2,115.6	0.08
1968	283.1	27.6	310.7	0.01	91.1	2,022.6	0.07
1969	283.6	22.3	305.9	0.01	92.7	1,888.3	0.07
1970	293.3	21.4	314.7	0.01	93.2	1,837.5	0.07
1971	220.4	31.2	251.6	0.01	87.6	1,407.4	0.05
1972	226.7	30.9	257.6	0.01	88.0	1,396.1	0.05
1973	220.9	26.6	247.5	0.01	89.3	1,262.8	0.04
1974	266.5	40.3	306.8	0.01	86.9	1,409.8	0.05
1975	366.2	*125.1*	491.3	0.02	74.5	2,068.6	0.07
1976	470.0	*169.1*	639.1	0.02	73.5	2,544.6	0.08
1977	552.1	*227.4*	779.5	0.03	70.8	2,913.9	0.10
1978	600.5	*274.5*	875.0	0.03	68.6	3,040.2	0.10
1979	748.9	*334.5*	1,083.4	0.03	69.1	3,380.8	0.11
1980	869.9	*372.4*	1,242.3	0.04	70.0	3,415.5	0.11
1981	998.3	*549.4*	1,547.7	0.05	64.5	3,857.1	0.12
1982	1,040.1	*753.7*	1,793.8	0.06	58.0	4,211.2	0.13
1983	1,080.9	*819.9*	1,900.8	0.06	56.9	4,323.4	0.14
1984	1,097.5	*997.7*	2,095.2	0.07	52.4	4,568.4	0.15
1985	1,074.9	*1,401.5*	2,476.4	0.08	43.4	5,214.0	0.17
1986	931.9	*1,450.5*	2,382.4	0.08	39.1	4,924.4	0.17
1987	872.7	*1,707.9*	2,580.5	0.09	33.8	5,146.1	0.18
1988	1,046.8	*2,228.1*	3,274.9	0.12	32.0	6,271.5	0.22
1989	1,110.1	*2,506.9*	3,617.0	0.14	30.7	6,608.2	0.25
1990	1,139.0	*2,853.0*	3,992.1	0.15	28.5	6,919.6	0.26
1991	1,117.2	*3,532.9*	4,650.1	0.18	24.0	7,734.7	0.30
1992	987.5	*4,244.4*	5,231.9	0.21	18.9	8,448.1	0.33

Table 5.3 Continued

Year	Advertising ($)	Promotion and other ($)	Total ($)	Per pack ($)	Advertising as % of total	Total, 8/11 ($)	Per pack, 8/11 ($)
1993	943.0	*5,092.4*	6,035.4	0.26	15.6	9,462.3	0.41
1994	887.8	*3,945.7*	4,833.5	0.20	18.4	7,388.7	0.30
1995	823.2	*4,072.0*	4,895.2	0.20	16.8	7,276.8	0.30
1996	830.9	*4,276.8*	5,107.7	0.21	16.3	7,374.9	0.30
1997	881.0	*4,779.0*	5,660.0	0.24	15.6	7,989.1	0.33
1998	936.4	*5,796.8*	6,733.2	0.29	13.9	9,358.1	0.41
1999	817.1	*7,420.5*	8,237.6	0.40	9.9	11,201.6	0.54
2000	702.9	*8,889.8*	9,592.6	0.46	7.3	12,620.0	0.61
2001	497.1	*10,719.1*	11,216.2	0.56	4.4	14,347.7	0.72
2002	417.5	*12,048.9*	12,466.4	0.66	3.3	15,698.7	0.83
2003	362.8	*14,783.2*	15,146.0	0.84	2.4	18,648.1	1.03
2004	281.4	*13,868.5*	14,149.9	0.78	2.0	16,969.7	0.94
2005	238.4	*12,872.6*	13,111.0	0.75	1.8	15,208.5	0.87
2006	293.9	12,195.8	12,489.7	0.73	2.4	14,035.1	0.82
2007	249.1	10,615.7	10,864.8	0.64	2.3	11,871.0	0.70
2008	191.4	9,751.7	9,943.1	0.62	1.9	10,462.2	0.65

Source: Federal Trade Commission (FTC) 2011a. Adjusted to 2011 dollars using the Consumer Price Index (Bureau of Labor Statistics 2011).
Note: Italicized figures represent estimated expenditures in these categories/years. "Advertising" includes expenditures on TV and radio (banned beginning January 1971), newspapers and magazines, outdoor and transit (reported separately beginning in 1970), and point of sale (reported separately beginning in 1975). "Promotion and other" includes expenditures on all other categories reported by FTC, including promotional allowances, retail value added, price discounts, specialty item distribution, sampling distribution, public entertainment, direct mail, endorsements and testimonials, Internet, and other; new categories have been added and others disaggregated over time. "Per pack" expenditures are based on cigarette sales reported by manufacturers to FTC (number of individual cigarettes divided by 20).

Table 5.4 Cigarette company marketing expenditures, percentage of total by major category, in millions of dollars, 1975–2008

Year	Advertising (%)	Public entertainment (%)	Placement (%)	Price discounts (%)	Merchandise (%)	Other (%)	Total, 8/11 ($)	Total per pack ($)
1975	74.5	1.7	*2.7*	*18.7*	*2.1*	*0.3*	491.3	0.02
1976	73.5	1.2	*2.4*	*19.3*	*3.2*	*0.3*	639.1	0.02
1977	70.8	1.2	*2.6*	*20.3*	*4.6*	*0.4*	779.5	0.03
1978	68.6	1.3	*2.6*	*21.2*	*5.6*	*0.6*	875.0	0.03
1979	69.1	1.0	*2.3*	*21.1*	*5.8*	*0.7*	1,083.4	0.03
1980	70.0	1.4	*2.7*	*19.8*	*5.6*	*0.6*	1,242.3	0.04
1981	64.5	2.4	*2.7*	*22.2*	*7.5*	*0.7*	1,547.7	0.05
1982	58.0	3.5	*2.8*	*29.0*	*5.4*	*1.2*	1,793.8	0.06
1983	56.9	4.0	*3.6*	*28.0*	*6.8*	*0.8*	1,900.8	0.06
1984	52.4	2.9	*3.2*	*33.0*	*6.9*	*1.7*	2,095.2	0.07
1985	43.4	2.3	*4.1*	*39.2*	*8.8*	*2.2*	2,476.4	0.08
1986	39.1	3.0	*4.9*	*41.7*	*9.1*	*2.2*	2,382.4	0.08
1987	33.8	2.8	*5.0*	*40.7*	*15.4*	*2.3*	2,580.5	0.09
1988	32.0	2.7	*5.0*	*50.5*	*6.2*	*3.7*	3,274.9	0.12
1989	30.7	2.5	*5.1*	*50.3*	*7.6*	*3.7*	3,617.0	0.14
1990	28.5	3.1	*4.7*	*52.6*	*8.1*	*2.9*	3,992.1	0.15
1991	24.0	2.6	*4.6*	*61.4*	*4.6*	*2.9*	4,650.1	0.18
1992	18.9	1.7	*5.3*	*65.5*	*7.1*	*1.5*	5,231.9	0.21
1993	15.6	1.4	*4.8*	*63.5*	*13.1*	*1.6*	6,035.4	0.26
1994	18.4	1.7	*6.4*	*53.9*	*18.0*	*1.6*	4,833.5	0.20
1995	16.8	2.3	*7.0*	*58.5*	*14.0*	*1.4*	4,895.2	0.20
1996	16.3	3.4	*7.8*	*59.9*	*11.0*	*1.7*	5,107.7	0.21
1997	15.6	3.4	*8.0*	*62.0*	*9.4*	*1.6*	5,660.0	0.24
1998	13.9	3.7	*7.9*	*66.9*	*5.8*	*1.8*	6,733.2	0.29
1999	9.9	3.2	*7.9*	*72.3*	*4.8*	*1.8*	8,237.6	0.40
2000	7.3	3.2	*7.5*	*76.0*	*4.2*	*1.6*	9,592.6	0.46
2001	4.4	2.8	*7.3*	*79.4*	*3.9*	*2.1*	11,216.2	0.56
2002	3.3	2.5	14.3	76.1	2.0	1.8	12,466.4	0.66
2003	2.4	1.4	12.6	80.2	1.9	1.4	15,146.0	0.84
2004	2.0	1.2	6.6	87.2	1.7	1.4	14,149.9	0.78

Table 5.4 Continued

Year	Advertising (%)	Public entertainment (%)	Placement (%)	Price discounts (%)	Merchandise (%)	Other (%)	Total, 8/11 ($)	Total per pack ($)
2005	1.8	1.9	6.5	86.9	1.8	1.2	13,111.0	0.75
2006	2.4	1.3	7.2	85.5	1.5	2.1	12,489.7	0.73
2007	2.3	1.5	8.6	83.7	1.7	2.2	10,864.8	0.64
2008	1.9	1.6	9.4	83.5	1.1	2.5	9,943.1	0.62

Source: Federal Trade Commission (FTC) 2011a; author's calculations.
Note: Percentages are based on the actual and estimated expenditures reported in Table 5.3. Italicized figures represent estimated percentages in these categories/years. Expenditure categories are as defined in the note to Table 5.3. Per pack expenditures are based on cigarette sales reported by manufacturers to FTC (number of individual cigarettes divided by 20).

Table 5.5 Cigarette company marketing expenditures, by major category, in millions of dollars, 1975–2008

Year	Advertising ($)	Public entertainment ($)	Placement ($)	Price discounts ($)	Merchandise ($)	Other ($)	Total ($)	Total per pack ($)	Price per pack ($)	FTC sales ($)
1975	366.2	8.5	*13.3*	*91.8*	*10.2*	*1.3*	491.3	0.02	0.00	603.2
1976	470.0	7.9	*15.2*	*123.4*	*20.3*	*2.2*	639.1	0.02	0.00	609.9
1977	552.1	9.5	*20.0*	*158.6*	*36.1*	*3.2*	779.5	0.03	0.01	612.6
1978	600.5	11.6	*23.1*	*185.9*	*48.8*	*5.1*	875.0	0.03	0.01	615.3
1979	748.9	10.8	*25.3*	*228.3*	*62.8*	*7.3*	1,083.4	0.03	0.01	621.8
1980	869.9	16.9	*33.1*	*245.6*	*70.0*	*6.9*	1,242.3	0.04	0.01	628.2
1981	998.3	37.4	*42.3*	*343.0*	*116.2*	*10.5*	1,547.7	0.05	0.01	636.5
1982	1,040.1	63.2	*50.3*	*520.6*	*97.6*	*22.1*	1,793.8	0.06	0.02	632.5
1983	1,080.9	76.6	*67.6*	*531.8*	*128.8*	*15.1*	1,900.8	0.06	0.02	603.6
1984	1,097.5	60.0	*67.0*	*691.8*	*144.1*	*34.8*	2,095.2	0.07	0.02	608.4
1985	1,074.9	57.6	*101.3*	*971.6*	*217.1*	*53.9*	2,476.4	0.08	0.03	599.3
1986	931.9	71.4	*116.3*	*993.5*	*215.7*	*53.6*	2,382.4	0.08	0.03	586.4
1987	872.7	71.4	*129.6*	*1,049.9*	*397.6*	*59.4*	2,580.5	0.09	0.04	575.4
1988	1,046.8	88.1	*162.4*	*1,653.3*	*202.7*	*121.7*	3,274.9	0.12	0.06	560.7
1989	1,110.1	92.1	*184.5*	*1,819.1*	*276.4*	*134.8*	3,617.0	0.14	0.07	525.6
1990	1,139.0	125.1	*188.5*	*2,100.4*	*324.2*	*114.8*	3,992.1	0.15	0.08	523.7
1991	1,117.2	118.6	*213.4*	*2,855.4*	*211.7*	*133.8*	4,650.1	0.18	0.11	510.9
1992	987.5	89.7	*279.4*	*3,427.7*	*371.6*	*76.0*	5,231.9	0.21	0.14	506.4
1993	943.0	84.3	*287.5*	*3,832.6*	*792.9*	*95.1*	6,035.4	0.26	0.17	461.4
1994	887.8	81.3	*309.9*	*2,606.8*	*868.9*	*78.9*	4,833.5	0.20	0.11	490.2
1995	823.2	110.7	*344.3*	*2,864.0*	*684.8*	*68.3*	4,895.2	0.20	0.12	482.3
1996	830.9	171.2	*397.0*	*3,059.5*	*563.3*	*85.8*	5,107.7	0.21	0.13	484.1
1997	881.0	195.2	*450.1*	*3,511.3*	*534.7*	*87.7*	5,660.0	0.24	0.15	478.6
1998	936.4	248.5	*531.4*	*4,506.1*	*391.3*	*119.5*	6,733.2	0.29	0.20	458.6
1999	817.1	267.4	*653.9*	*5,955.3*	*394.0*	*149.9*	8,237.6	0.40	0.29	411.3
2000	702.9	309.6	*722.4*	*7,294.0*	*406.5*	*157.2*	9,592.6	0.46	0.35	413.9
2001	497.1	312.4	*821.8*	*8,903.4*	*441.9*	*239.6*	11,216.2	0.56	0.45	398.3
2002	417.5	307.4	1,782.2	9,485.2	248.4	225.8	12,466.4	0.66	0.50	376.4
2003	362.8	215.1	1,915.2	12,154.1	284.7	214.2	15,146.0	0.84	0.67	360.5
2004	281.4	168.5	931.3	12,331.8	238.9	198.0	14,149.9	0.78	0.68	361.3

Table 5.5 Continued

Year	Advertising ($)	Public entertainment ($)	Placement ($)	Price discounts ($)	Merchandise ($)	Other ($)	Total ($)	Total per pack ($)	Price per pack ($)	FTC sales ($)
2005	238.4	244.8	847.7	11,388.4	238.1	153.6	13,111.0	0.75	0.65	351.6
2006	293.9	168.1	905.4	10,678.1	183.9	260.2	12,489.7	0.73	0.62	343.3
2007	249.1	160.1	933.2	9,096.4	185.8	240.1	10,864.8	0.64	0.54	337.7
2008	191.4	154.7	931.2	8,307.0	112.0	246.8	9,943.1	0.62	0.52	320

Source: Federal Trade Commission (FTC) 2011a; author's calculations.
Note: Italicized figures represent estimated expenditures in these categories/years. "Advertising" includes newspapers and magazines, outdoor and transit, and point of sale (reported separately beginning in 1975). "Public entertainment" includes general audience and adult-only public entertainment, reported in a single category in earlier years and reported separately beginning in 2002. "Placement" includes promotional allowances paid to retailers, wholesalers, and others, reported separately beginning in 2002 and estimated for earlier years from the percentage of the combined promotional allowances category accounted for by these categories in 2002. "Price discounts" include price discounts and retail-value-added bonus cigarettes (reported separately beginning in 2002), coupons (reported separately beginning in 1997), and sampling distribution. Estimates for earlier years are based on shares in the previously aggregated categories that included those in the first year's data and are reported for disaggregated categories. "Merchandise" includes branded and nonbranded specialty item distribution (reported as a single category before 2002 and separately beginning in 2002) and retail-value-added noncigarette bonus (reported separately in 2002 and estimated for earlier years from the share of combined retail value added as reported in 2002). "Other" includes all other categories reported by FTC, including direct mail, telephone, Internet (company Web sites and other), and other; in earlier years, a portion of the FTC-reported other and direct mail expenditures is allocated to other categories (e.g., coupons and retail value added) on the basis of shares of expenditures in the first year that expenditures in more disaggregated categories are reported. Per pack expenditures are based on cigarette sales reported by manufacturers to FTC (number of individual cigarettes divided by 20).

Table 5.6 Detailed expenditures for smokeless tobacco marketing, in thousands of dollars, 2002–2008

	2002		2003		2004		2005	
	Expenditures ($)	As % of total	Expenditures ($)	As % of total	Expenditures ($)	As % of total	Expenditures ($)	As % of total
Newspapers	722	0.3	262	0.1	285	0.1	453	0.2
Magazines	23,142	9.9	22,838	9.4	25,002	10.8	20,996	8.4
Outdoor	117	0.0	101	0.0	184	0.1	207	0.1
Audiovisual	7	0.0	139	0.1	7	0.0	119	0.0
Direct mail	7,073	3.0	5,982	2.5	5,670	2.5	8,237	3.3
Point of sale	16,894	7.2	20,874	8.6	23,120	10.0	20,748	8.3
Price discounts	99,000	42.2	106,531	43.9	86,977	37.6	99,699	39.8
Promotional allowances—retail	3,245	1.4	5,103	2.1	4,285	1.9	3,406	1.4
Promotional allowances—wholesale	16,755	7.1	12,632	5.2	11,222	4.9	12,550	5.0
Promotional allowances—other	41	0.0	29	0.0	9	0.0	29	0.0
Sampling	25,754	11.0	22,483	9.3	25,156	10.9	28,180	11.2
Specialty item distribution—branded	419	0.2	45	0.0	22	0.0	119	0.0
Specialty item distribution—nonbranded	0	0.0	0	0.0	0	0.0	36	0.0
Public entertainment—adult only	0	0.0	0	0.0	7	0.0	73	0.0
Public entertainment—general audience	1,453	0.6	1,640	0.7	1,349	0.6	215	0.1
Endorsements and testimonials	130	0.1	355	0.1	355	0.2	355	0.1
Sponsorship	8,864	3.8	8,170	3.4	9,018	3.9	4,192	1.7
Coupons	12,156	5.2	11,524	4.8	10,686	4.6	28,622	11.4

Table 5.6 Continued

	2002		2003		2004		2005	
	Expenditures ($)	As % of total	Expenditures ($)	As % of total	Expenditures ($)	As % of total	Expenditures ($)	As % of total
Retail value added—bonus smokeless tobacco	13,686	5.8	16,004	6.6	14,950	6.5	9,310	3.7
Retail value added—nonsmokeless tobacco bonus	466	0.2	556	0.2	2,650	1.1	4,430	1.8
Company Web site	18	0.0	15	0.0	877	0.4	272	0.1
Internet—other	54	0.0	25	0.0	16	0.0	413	0.2
Telephone	169	0.1	374	0.2	231	0.1	120	0.0
Other	4,480	1.9	6,832	2.8	9,006	3.9	8,011	3.2
FTC total	234,645		242,514		231,084		250,792	

	2006		2007		2008	
	Expenditures ($)	As % of total	Expenditures ($)	As % of total	Expenditures ($)	As % of total
Newspapers	NA	—	NA	—	NA	—
Magazines	16,591	4.7	13,913	3.4	17,122	3.1
Outdoor	166	0.0	334	0.1	219	0.0
Audiovisual	NA	—	NA	—	NA	—
Direct mail	9,575	2.7	12,205	3.0	7,579	1.4
Point of sale	20,824	5.9	29,318	7.1	55,295	10.1
Price discounts	203,692	57.5	249,510	60.7	324,647	59.3
Promotional allowances—retail	3,731	1.1	5,349	1.3	6,416	1.2
Promotional allowances—wholesale	9,047	2.6	12,383	3.0	18,578	3.4
Promotional allowances—other	NA	—	NA	—	NA	—

Table 5.6 Continued

	2006		2007		2008	
	Expenditures ($)	**As % of total**	**Expenditures ($)**	**As % of total**	**Expenditures ($)**	**As % of total**
Sampling	41,979	11.9	35,113	8.5	29,936	5.5
Specialty item distribution—branded	NA	—	NA	—	509	0.1
Specialty item distribution—nonbranded	34	0.0	NA	—	3,079	0.6
Public entertainment—adult only	0	0.0	NA	—	14,300	2.6
Public entertainment—general audience	144	0.0	NA	—	NA	—
Endorsements and testimonials	NA	—	NA	—	NA	—
Sponsorship	NA	—	10,462	2.5	9,319	1.7
Coupons	16,133	4.6	15,452	3.8	29,474	5.4
Retail value added—bonus smokeless tobacco	12,047	3.4	8,497	2.1	10,464	1.9
Retail value added—nonsmokeless tobacco bonus	1,406	0.4	626	0.2	4,514	0.8
Company Web site	891	0.3	3,110	0.8	2,085	0.4
Internet—other	944	0.3	2,050	0.5	2,538	0.5
Telephone	NA	—	NA	—	NA	—
Other	16,920	4.8	12,917	3.1	11,802	2.2
FTC total	354,123		411,239		547,873	

Source: Federal Trade Commission (FTC) 2011b.
Note: Because FTC reported zero expenditures in all years in the transit category, it was omitted from this table. Because of rounding, in any year the sum of the individual expenditures may not equal total expenditures and the sum of percentages may not equal 100. Expenditures denoted "NA" are included in the "other" category to avoid potential disclosure of individual company data. "—" = not available.

Table 5.7 Smokeless tobacco company marketing expenditures, by major category, in millions of dollars, 1988–2008

Year	Advertising ($)	Promotion and other ($)	Total ($)	Per unit ($)	Advertising as % of total	Total, 8/11 ($)	Per unit, 8/11 ($)
1988	19.0	49.3	68.2	0.07	27.8	130.6	0.13
1989	19.5	*61.7*	81.2	0.08	24.0	148.4	0.14
1990	24.1	*66.0*	90.1	0.09	26.7	156.2	0.15
1991	23.2	*80.8*	104.0	0.10	22.3	173.0	0.16
1992	22.4	*93.0*	115.3	0.11	19.4	186.3	0.17
1993	22.6	*96.6*	119.2	0.11	19.0	186.9	0.17
1994	25.1	*100.9*	126.0	0.12	19.9	192.6	0.18
1995	28.3	*99.0*	127.3	0.12	22.2	189.3	0.17
1996	30.7	*93.2*	123.9	0.11	24.8	178.9	0.16
1997	33.2	*117.2*	150.4	0.14	22.1	212.3	0.19
1998	48.6	*96.9*	145.5	0.14	33.4	202.2	0.19
1999	47.8	*122.4*	170.2	0.16	28.1	231.5	0.22
2000	31.5	*193.1*	224.6	0.20	14.0	295.5	0.27
2001	41.2	*195.5*	236.7	0.21	17.4	302.8	0.27
2002	40.9	193.8	234.6	0.21	17.4	295.5	0.26
2003	44.1	198.4	242.5	0.21	18.2	298.6	0.26
2004	48.6	182.5	231.1	0.20	21.0	277.1	0.24
2005	42.4	208.4	250.8	0.21	16.9	290.9	0.24
2006	37.6	316.5	354.1	0.29	10.6	397.9	0.33
2007	43.6	367.7	411.2	0.34	10.6	449.3	0.37
2008	72.6	475.2	547.9	0.43	13.3	576.5	0.45

Source: Federal Trade Commission (FTC) 2011b. Adjusted to 2011 dollars using the Consumer Price Index (U.S. Bureau of Labor Statistics 2011).

Note: Italicized figures represent estimated expenditures in these categories/years. "Advertising" includes expenditures on newspapers, magazines, outdoor, transit, and point of sale. "Promotion and other" includes expenditures on all other categories reported by FTC, including promotional allowances, retail value added, price discounts, specialty item distribution, sampling, public entertainment, direct mail, endorsements and testimonials, Internet, and other; new categories have been added and others disaggregated over time. Expenditures per unit are obtained using annual data on units sold for 2002 through 2008, with unit data for earlier years estimated from pounds sold and the trend in the weight of the average unit for 2002–2008.

Table 5.8 Smokeless tobacco company marketing expenditures, by major category, in millions of dollars, 1988–2008

Year	Advertising ($)	Public entertainment ($)	Placement ($)	Price discounts ($)	Merchandise ($)	Other ($)	Total ($)
1988	19.0	*17.5*	*1.1*	*20.8*	*4.2*	5.7	68.2
1989	19.5	*19.6*	*1.4*	*26.9*	*4.8*	9.0	81.2
1990	24.1	*20.3*	*1.7*	*29.1*	*3.1*	11.9	90.1
1991	23.2	*21.1*	*2.5*	*36.2*	*4.2*	16.9	104.0
1992	22.4	*21.5*	*1.9*	*40.7*	*3.1*	25.8	115.3
1993	22.6	*22.9*	*2.2*	*41.6*	*4.7*	25.2	119.2
1994	25.1	*25.4*	*1.7*	*38.2*	*10.8*	24.8	126.0
1995	28.3	*26.7*	*1.4*	*37.1*	*10.3*	23.4	127.3
1996	30.7	*22.7*	*2.1*	*48.3*	*12.5*	4.9	123.9
1997	33.2	*28.9*	*2.5*	*60.6*	*19.2*	6.0	150.4
1998	48.6	*25.4*	*2.5*	*51.7*	*4.1*	13.1	145.5
1999	47.8	*22.1*	*5.2*	*78.5*	*3.5*	13.1	170.2
2000	31.5	*11.2*	*7.6*	*149.0*	*2.5*	22.7	224.6
2001	41.2	*18.1*	*10.2*	*141.8*	*1.7*	23.6	236.7
2002	40.9	*10.3*	*20.0*	*150.6*	*0.9*	11.9	234.6
2003	44.1	*9.8*	*17.8*	*156.5*	*0.6*	13.7	242.5
2004	48.6	*10.4*	*15.5*	*137.8*	*2.7*	16.2	231.1
2005	42.4	*4.5*	*16.0*	*165.8*	*4.6*	17.5	250.8
2006	37.6	0.1	12.8	273.9	1.4	28.3	354.1
2007	43.6	10.5	17.7	308.6	0.6	30.3	411.2
2008	72.6	23.6	25.0	394.5	8.1	24.0	547.9

Source: Federal Trade Commission (FTC) 2011b; author's calculations.
Note: Italicized figures represent estimated expenditures in these categories/years. "Advertising" includes newspapers, magazines, outdoor, transit, and point of sale. "Public entertainment" includes general audience and adult-only public entertainment and sponsorships reported in a single category in earlier years and reported separately beginning in 2002. "Placement" includes promotional allowances paid to retailers, wholesalers, and others, reported separately beginning in 2002 and estimated for earlier years from the percentage of the combined promotional allowances category accounted for by these categories in 2002. "Price discounts" include price discounts and retail-value-added bonus smokeless tobacco products (reported separately beginning in 2002), coupons (reported separately beginning in 1996), and sampling. Estimates for earlier years are based on shares in the previously aggregated categories that included those in the first year's data that are reported for disaggregated categories. "Merchandise" includes branded and nonbranded specialty item distribution (reported as a single category before 2002 and separately beginning in 2002), and nonsmokeless tobacco bonus (reported separately in 2002 and estimated for earlier years from the share of combined retail value added as reported in 2002). "Other" includes all other categories reported by FTC, including direct mail, telephone, Internet (company Web sites and other), and other.

Table 5.9 Smokeless tobacco company marketing expenditures, percentage of total by major category, in millions of dollars, 1988–2008

Year	Advertising (%)	Public entertainment (%)	Placement (%)	Price discounts (%)	Merchandise (%)	Other (%)	Total ($)
1988	27.8	*25.7*	*1.6*	*30.5*	*6.1*	8.4	68.2
1989	24.0	*24.2*	*1.7*	*33.2*	*5.9*	11.1	81.2
1990	26.7	*22.5*	*1.9*	*32.3*	*3.4*	13.2	90.1
1991	22.3	*20.3*	*2.4*	*34.8*	*4.0*	16.2	104.0
1992	19.4	*18.6*	*1.7*	*35.3*	*2.7*	22.4	115.3
1993	19.0	*19.2*	*1.8*	*34.9*	*3.9*	21.1	119.2
1994	19.9	*20.2*	*1.4*	*30.3*	*8.6*	19.7	126.0
1995	22.2	*21.0*	*1.1*	*29.1*	*8.1*	18.4	127.3
1996	25.3	*18.8*	*1.8*	*39.9*	*10.3*	4.0	123.9
1997	22.1	*19.2*	*1.6*	*40.3*	*12.7*	4.0	150.4
1998	33.4	*17.5*	*1.7*	*35.5*	*2.8*	9.0	145.5
1999	28.1	*13.0*	*3.0*	*46.1*	*2.1*	7.7	170.2
2000	14.0	*5.0*	*3.4*	*66.3*	*1.1*	10.1	224.6
2001	17.4	*7.6*	*4.3*	*59.9*	*0.7*	10.0	236.7
2002	17.4	*4.4*	*8.5*	*64.2*	*0.4*	5.1	234.6
2003	18.2	*4.0*	*7.3*	*64.5*	*0.2*	5.7	242.5
2004	21.0	*4.5*	*6.7*	*59.6*	*1.2*	7.0	231.1
2005	16.9	*1.8*	*6.4*	*66.1*	*1.8*	7.0	250.8
2006	10.6	0.0	3.6	77.3	0.4	8.0	354.1
2007	10.6	2.5	4.3	75.0	0.2	7.4	411.2
2008	13.3	4.3	4.6	72.0	1.5	4.4	547.9

Source: Federal Trade Commission 2011b; author's calculations.
Note: Italicized figures represent estimated expenditures in these categories/years. Percentages are based on the actual and estimated expenditures reported in Table 5.8. Italicized figures represent estimated percentages in these categories/years. Expenditure categories are as defined in the notes to Table 5.8.

companies and have developed new smokeless tobacco products. These include snus, a dry, spitless snuff product in a sachet, and dissolvable products containing nicotine, such as sticks, strips, and orbs. Between 2006 and 2007, the major U.S. cigarette companies began marketing new smokeless tobacco products with popular cigarette brand names, such as Camel Snus and Marlboro Snus, in nationwide test markets. These products have been promoted as a temporary way to deal with smoke-free policies in public places (Carpenter et al. 2009; Mejia and Ling 2010; Mejia et al. 2010). In 2009, RJR introduced dissolvables with the Camel cigarette brand name. In 2011, Altria introduced Marlboro and Skoal sticks.

For many years, public entertainment (e.g., sponsorships) was a key technique for marketing smokeless tobacco products, accounting for about one-fifth of overall spending in the 1990s. In recent years, however, this percentage has fallen sharply, given the restrictions on sponsorships included in the Smokeless Tobacco Master Settlement Agreement in 1998, although this decline seems to have leveled off and recently increased. As with cigarette marketing after the Master Settlement Agreement, the constraints on marketing contained in the smokeless tobacco agreement appear to have shifted most marketing of smokeless tobacco into efforts to reduce prices and gain more favorable placement for these products at the point of sale (Tables 5.8 and 5.9).

Brand Choices and Brand-Specific Marketing

In Chapter 3, "The Epidemiology of Tobacco Use Among Young People in the United States and Worldwide," of this Surgeon General's report (see Appendix 3.1, Tables 3.1.9 and 3.1.10), Marlboro, Newport, and Camel are the top three cigarette brands for each age group presented. Among young people, these three brands account for more than 80% of the choices of favorite brand; for older smokers (26 years and above), they account for just over one-half.

Although the cigarette companies report expenditures on marketing activities to FTC by brand, the fact that these data are not reported publicly makes it difficult to relate brand-level marketing to the specific consumption choices of youth, young adults, and adults. However, Pollay and colleagues (1996), using brand-based data, found that responsiveness to cigarette advertising was three times higher for adolescents than for adults. Limited data on advertising expenditures by brand are reported by NCI (2008); the available data suggest that advertising expenditures for Marlboro are well above those for other brands, with expenditures for Newport generally second, followed by Camel. As discussed in a later section, research has demonstrated the association between brand-specific advertising and brand choices, confirming the relationship suggested by these data.

Summary

Manufacturers of cigarettes and smokeless tobacco products spend a great deal of money to market their products in the United States. Efforts to constrain marketing by tobacco companies, such as the ban on broadcast advertising of cigarettes in 1971, the comparable ban on broadcast advertising of smokeless tobacco in 1986, and the bans and restrictions contained in the 1998 Master Settlement Agreement and Smokeless Tobacco Master Settlement Agreement, appear to have had the opposite effect: total expenditures on marketing for both cigarettes and smokeless tobacco rose in the years following the implementation of these constraints as companies changed their strategies in response. The impact of these restrictions on the tobacco companies' marketing activities and on tobacco use among youth is discussed more fully in Chapter 6, "Efforts to Prevent and Reduce Tobacco Use Among Young People," of this report. The remainder of the present chapter focuses on the effects of the marketing activities of tobacco companies and depictions of smoking in movies on the use of tobacco among young people.

Advertising and Other Promotional Activities Used by the Tobacco Companies to Promote Tobacco Use Among Young People

Introduction

There is strong, consistent evidence that advertising and promotion influence the factors that lead directly to tobacco use by adolescents, including the initiation of cigarette smoking as well as its continuation (USDHHS 1989, 1994, 1998, 2000; Lynch and Bonnie 1994; *Federal Register* 1996; Lovato et al. 2003; NCI 2008). The effects of tobacco advertising on tobacco use have been addressed by reports of the Surgeon General (USDHHS 2000, 2001) and an NCI monograph (NCI 2008). As documented in these reports, promotion and advertising by the tobacco industry *causes* tobacco use, including its initiation among youth. This conclusion has been buttressed by a multitude of scientific and governmental reports, and the strength of the evidence for causality continues to grow.

Tobacco companies recruit new smokers, and their advertising campaigns appeal to the aspirations of adolescents (most smokers start as adolescents or even earlier) (Perry 1999; Lovato et al. 2003; *United States v. Philip Morris USA*, 449 F. Supp. 2d 1, 980 [D.D.C. 2006]; NCI 2008). There is strong empirical evidence that tobacco companies' advertising and promotions affect awareness of smoking and of particular brands, the recognition and recall of cigarette advertising, attitudes about smoking, intentions to smoke, and actual smoking behavior. In fact, children appear to be even more responsive to advertising appeals than are adults (Pollay et al. 1996). As with all advertising, tobacco advertising frequently relies on imagery to appeal to an individual's aspirations and conveys very little, if any, factual information about the characteristics of the product. Advertising fulfills many of the aspirations of adolescents and children by effectively using themes of independence, liberation, attractiveness, adventurousness, sophistication, glamour, athleticism, social acceptability and inclusion, sexual attractiveness, thinness, popularity, rebelliousness, and being "cool" (NCI 2008). A 2003 systematic review of the published longitudinal studies on the impact of advertising concluded "that tobacco advertising and promotion increases the likelihood that adolescents will start to smoke" (Lovato et al. 2003, p. 2). Both the industry's own internal documents and its testimony in court proceedings, as well as widely accepted principles of advertising and marketing, also support the conclusion that tobacco advertising recruits new users during their youth (Perry 1999).

In the 1998 Master Settlement Agreement, the major cigarette companies agreed to some limitations on advertising and promotions targeted directly at youth, yet the industry has continued to market tobacco heavily through traditional advertising and promotion with an increased emphasis on one-on-one approaches, such as direct mailings and online marketing. Although youth are no longer exposed to some forms of advertising, such as advertising on television or on outdoor billboards, they are still exposed to some direct marketing efforts (King and Siegel 2001; Siegel 2001). In addition, industry marketing efforts directed at young adults, which are permitted under the agreement, have indirect spillover effects on youth through young adults who are aspirational role models for youth (Kastenbaum et al. 1972; Montepare and Lachman 1989; Zollo 1995). Marketing efforts directed at young adults may also have an impact on tobacco initiation rates within this population, in that the campaigns have been shown to encourage regular smoking and increase levels of consumption (Ling and Glantz 2002). There is also evidence that from 2002–2009 increasing numbers of young adults are initiating smoking though that increase leveled off in 2010 (Substance Abuse and Mental Health Services Administration [SAMHSA], unpublished data, 2005–2010; see also Chapter 3, Appendix 3.1, Table 3.1.31).

In her landmark 2006 ruling that the tobacco industry violated the *Racketeer Influenced and Corrupt Organizations (RICO) Act* (1970), Judge Gladys Kessler concluded that cigarette marketing recruits youth to smoke and that the major cigarette companies know it:

> Cigarette marketing, which includes both advertising and promotion, is designed to play a key role in the process of recruiting young, new smokers by exposing young people to massive amounts of imagery associating positive qualities with cigarette smoking. Research in psychology and cognitive neuroscience demonstrates how powerful such imagery can be, particularly for young people, in suppressing perception of risk and encouraging behavior. Slovic WD, 53:22-63:11. Defendants' own statistics demonstrate how successful they have been in marketing their three main youth brands: Philip Morris's

Marlboro, RJR's Camel, and Lorillard's Newport (*United States v. Philip Morris USA*, 449 F. Supp. 2d 1, 980 [D.C. 2006]).

In reviewing the evidence that explains how tobacco industry marketing affects adolescent smoking behaviors, this section will rely on the Theory of Triadic Influence (TTI) (Figure 5.1), which was introduced in Chapter 4, "Social, Environmental, Cognitive, and Genetic Influences on the Use of Tobacco Among Youth," and will also be used in Chapter 6, "Efforts to Prevent and Reduce Tobacco Use Among Young People." The TTI provides an organizing structure that allows assessment of the impact of marketing and advertising in conjunction with other important risk factors, such as peer and parental influence (including smoking or nonsmoking behavior), emotions, and cognitive processes. In brief, the industry uses marketing and advertising, which overtly shape sociocognitive factors, to influence tobacco use behavior.

Conceptual Framework

The processes by which tobacco marketing affects tobacco use among youth are complex and dynamic but can be conceptualized according to existing theories of health behavior (Figure 5.1). The TTI assumes that health and risk behaviors are direct products of intentions. Behaviors such as experimentation with smoking and initiation, in turn, underlie the process to begin to smoke or not smoke. This assumption is consistent with concomitant theories such as the Theory of Reasoned Action and the Theory of Planned Behavior that demonstrate a strong link between intentions and behavior (Ajzen 1991; Armitage and Conner 2001).

Factors that promote or deter smoking, as well as other health behaviors, generally can be organized into three interacting but distinct streams: intrapersonal, social-contextual, and cultural-environmental. The intrapersonal stream involves biological and personality-related factors that serve as risk or protective factors for adolescent smoking. These factors can include propensity to take risks, self-concept, and self-esteem. The social-contextual stream starts with social situations, which provide context for dynamic interactions with other people, their actions, and their beliefs, and ends with adolescents' social normative beliefs that directly influence their behavioral intentions. The cultural-environmental stream encompasses macrolevel factors and processes, including cultural convention, societal practices, and public policy. These macrolevel factors then influence adolescents' attitudes and perceptions about tobacco use.

One example of the interaction of streams of influence is seen in the suggestion from the literature that congruence (or incongruence) between an adolescent's self-image and her or his stereotype of a smoker predicts whether that young person will become a smoker (Aloise-Young and Hennigan 1996). Here, stereotypes of a smoker, which come from the social and environmental streams of influence, interact with the intrapersonal stream to influence adolescent tobacco use.

Variables or factors that might influence smoking can be said to be at three distances from actual smoking behaviors: ultimate, distal, and proximal. Ultimate factors represent the underlying causes of health and risk behaviors, including smoking. Distal factors include those that predispose youth to smoking, including peer influence, self-esteem, and cultural norms. Proximate factors are components of the process that more immediately precede behavioral change, including attitudes, beliefs, and intentions.

Much of the tobacco industry's efforts to promote smoking, including advertising and direct marketing as well as industry-sponsored youth smoking prevention advertisements (Landman et al. 2002; Wakefield et al. 2006c), act at multiple levels and points within this triadic framework. Tobacco promotion can directly influence both social-contextual and cultural-environmental streams. In addition, promotion can have an influence very early in the development of adolescents' tobacco use when they are forming attitudes and beliefs about tobacco. At this level, the influence of tobacco advertising and promotion is through mediated pathways. Advertising, promotion, industry-sponsored antismoking ads, and smoking in movies all directly influence distal-level factors, such as exposure to other smokers, peer attitudes, cultural practices, and beliefs about smoking consequences (both positive and negative). As a consequence, studies that treat peer and family smoking as independent variables understate the effects of advertising. These distal-level factors carry the influence of the tobacco industry all the way down to actual intentions and behavior. These pathways of influence are consistent with Flay's (1993) five stages of the initiation and continuation of smoking among adolescents as described in the 1994 Surgeon General's report (USDHHS 1994).

Industry marketing activities can also act as a moderator of processes at lower levels in the conceptual framework. Specifically, repeated exposures to advertising, promotion, and smoking in the movies can amplify the effects of the industry's influences on the social-contextual and cultural-environmental streams of influence. For example, some industry-sponsored antismoking ads seem to influence adolescents' perceptions and attitudes about smoking (proximal factors) in ways that

Figure 5.1 Structure supporting the effect of marketing on youth smoking based on the Theory of Triadic Influence

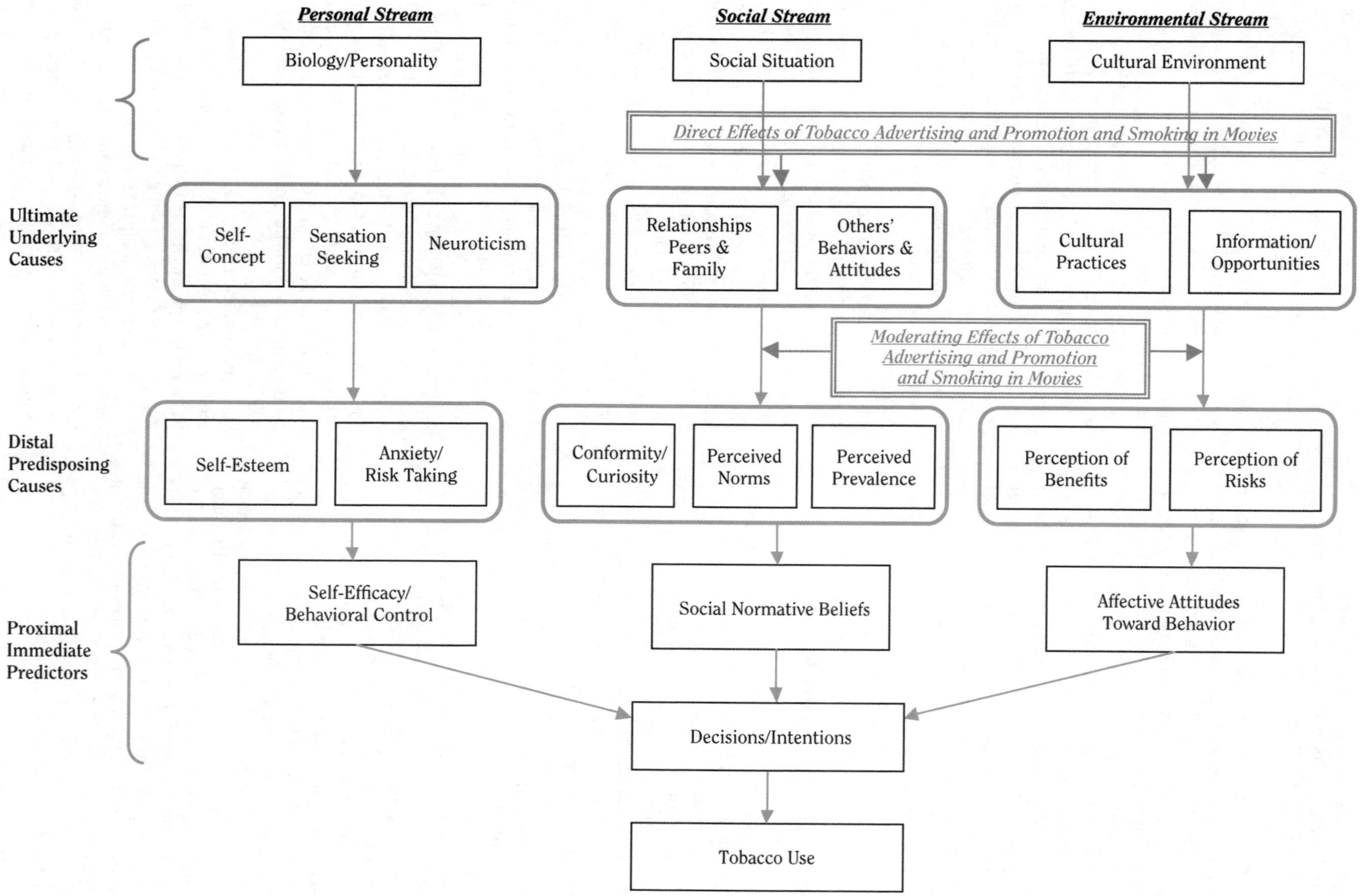

Personal Stream
Social Stream
Environmental Stream

Ultimate Underlying Causes
Biology/Personality
Social Situation
Cultural Environment
Direct Effects of Tobacco Advertising and Promotion and Smoking in Movies
Self-Concept
Sensation Seeking
Neuroticism
Relationships Peers & Family
Others' Behaviors & Attitudes
Cultural Practices
Information/ Opportunities
Moderating Effects of Tobacco Advertising and Promotion and Smoking in Movies

Distal Predisposing Causes
Self-Esteem
Anxiety/ Risk Taking
Conformity/ Curiosity
Perceived Norms
Perceived Prevalence
Perception of Benefits
Perception of Risks

Proximal Immediate Predictors
Self-Efficacy/ Behavioral Control
Social Normative Beliefs
Affective Attitudes Toward Behavior
Decisions/Intentions
Tobacco Use

Source: Adapted from Flay et al. 2009 with permission from John Wiley & Sons, Inc., © 2009.

encourage smoking; this is an example of influencing the cultural-environmental stream. Smoking in the movies can influence both social-contextual and cultural-environmental streams. (Industry-sponsored youth smoking prevention advertisements and smoking in the movies are discussed in later sections of this chapter.) In all three cases, the relationship between industry marketing, depictions of smoking in movies, and youth smoking are moderated mediation pathways: the influences of advertising, promotion, and smoking in the movies are mediated by distal factors (e.g., peer influence, family, culture), and that mediation effect on proximate factors is moderated by more exposure to the influence of the tobacco industry and depictions of smoking (Muller et al. 2005). The effectiveness of antitobacco media campaigns (discussed in detail in Chapter 6) also supports this model for the effectiveness of protobacco advertising and promotion, as antitobacco media operate through the same channels. Anti-industry messages in particular tend to blunt the tobacco industry's ability to shift attitudes toward smoking and tobacco use, and they create momentum against tobacco use. Evaluation of all components of this framework are essential, particularly the monitoring of tobacco companies' activities and efforts to prevent young people's tobacco use (Cruz 2009; Farrelly 2009).

Awareness of Smoking and the Recognition of Brands

Many studies from the early 1990s found that young children were frequently familiar with cigarette logos. For example, Fischer and coworkers (1991) reported that 30% of 3-year-olds and nearly all (91%) 6-year-old children could correctly match a picture of Joe Camel with a picture of a cigarette. The latter percentage equaled the percentage of 6-year-olds who associated Mickey Mouse with the Disney Channel (Fischer et al. 1991). (This equivalent awareness was all the more remarkable because, unlike Mickey Mouse, Joe Camel did not appear on television, which the average child spends viewing many hours each day.) The study of Fischer and colleagues did not claim to assert a relationship between children's familiarity with cigarette brand logos and their subsequent smoking behavior; it did, however, establish that marketing efforts were reaching very young children and that these children were aware that the Joe Camel cartoon character was associated with cigarette smoking. Earlier studies of 11- to 14-year-olds in Australia found that adolescents who smoked were much more likely to correctly identify advertisements for cigarettes that had words missing and to be able to complete cigarette slogans than were nonsmoking adolescents (Chapman and Fitzgerald 1982). These findings document the association between awareness of cigarette marketing campaigns and smoking behavior. Similar findings were reported in 1985 in Scotland and in 1987 and 2005 in the United States (Aitken et al. 1985; Goldstein et al. 1987; Dalton et al. 2005).

Many studies demonstrate that those young people who are more familiar with tobacco advertising can identify specific advertisements, have a favorite tobacco advertisement, or possess cigarette promotional items are more likely to begin smoking than those who do not have these characteristics (Arnett and Terhanian 1998; Feighery et al. 1998; NCI 2008). For example, Pierce and coworkers (1998) found that among a group of confirmed never smokers (aged 12–17 years) who were assessed in 1993 and followed up in 1996, those who had a favorite cigarette advertisement or who owned or were willing to own a brand promotion item were more likely to have experimented with cigarettes or to intend to smoke than those who did not have a favorite ad or possess promotional items. This continued to be observed at the 5-year follow-up (Pierce et al. 2010).

The 2000 Surgeon General's report on reducing tobacco use stated that "indirect evidence of the importance of advertising and promotion to the tobacco industry is provided by surveys that suggest that most adolescents can recall certain tobacco advertisements, logos, or brand insignia; these surveys correlate such recall with smoking intent, initiation, or level of consumption" (USDHHS 2000, p. 162).

Even earlier, research by Botvin and colleagues (1991) that asked adolescents to identify the brands in cigarette print ads that were stripped of brand information found that those who smoked and those who had experimented with cigarettes were more likely to name the brand associated with the ads than were nonsmoking adolescents. Much later, Hanewinkel and colleagues (2010a) used a similar approach to assess brand recognition and smoking behaviors among German adolescents. In their sample, 55% of adolescents (included both smokers and nonsmokers) were able to recognize Lucky Strike ads, and 34% recognized Marlboro.

The evidence shows that advertising and promotion by the tobacco industry are effective in raising awareness of smoking, increasing brand recognition, and creating favorable beliefs regarding tobacco use. This relationship has been shown not only for adults but also for youth. For example, a 1998 study of students in grades 6–12 concerning cigarette advertisements in seven states found that 95% of the students had seen at least one advertisement featuring Joe Camel or the Marlboro Man, and fully one-half had seen these advertisements six or more times

(Arnett and Terhanian 1998). More than one-half of the students believed that Joe Camel made smoking more appealing, and 40% of the students had the same belief about the Marlboro Man. In another study, adolescents who responded positively to Camel and Marlboro ads also believed the ads made smoking more appealing (Arnett 2001).

This evidence demonstrates how advertisements may influence adolescents at the emotional level (e.g., by producing a positive impression upon exposure to advertisements) and the cognitive level (e.g., making smoking more appealing). Moreover, at the individual level this influence can translate to the proliferation of smoking attitudes and behaviors via the social-contextual and cultural-environmental streams of the TTI model (Figure 5.1).

Advertising and the Desire to Smoke

There is extensive scientific data showing (1) adolescents are regularly exposed to cigarette advertising, (2) they find many of these advertisements appealing, (3) advertisements tend to make smoking appealing, and (4) advertisements serve to increase adolescents' desire to smoke (NCI 2008). The 2001 Surgeon General's report on women and smoking concluded, "Whatever children's view of smoking may be, as they approach the middle-school years, they become increasingly concerned with self-image, and messages contained in tobacco advertising and promotions likely play a role in changing their attitudes and behaviors" (USDHHS 2001, p. 504).

A study among California middle school students found that most students were at least moderately receptive to tobacco marketing materials, and those who were more receptive were also more susceptible to initiating smoking (Feighery et al. 1998). Moreover, susceptibility increased when a parent or friends smoked, but susceptibility also increased as a function of receptivity to promotional items, even when controlling for smoking by friends or parents. Elsewhere, in a randomized study, adolescents given magazines with tobacco advertisements reported more favorable attitudes toward smoking than those who were provided with magazines free of tobacco advertising (Turco 1997). In another experimental study, seventh-grade students who were randomly assigned to view cigarette advertisements were more likely to have positive attitudes about smokers than those who viewed antismoking advertisements or advertisements unrelated to smoking (Pechmann and Ratneshwar 1994).

Influences on Intentions to Smoke

According to many theoretical models of behavior, including the TTI, behavioral intentions are immediate precursors to behavior and are one of the strongest predictors of future behavior. Systematic reviews have determined that behavioral intentions (along with perceived behavioral control, attitudes, and subjective norms) are strong and robust predictors of behavior (Armitage and Connor 2001; Sheeran 2002). Furthermore, research demonstrates that advertising and promotion have affected behavioral intentions toward smoking in a way that leads to increases in the susceptibility of adolescents to the initiation of smoking and progression to established smoking. In a 2002 study, ninth-grade students exposed to cigarette ads were found to have significantly more positive beliefs about smokers as well as more positive intentions to smoke in the future than did those not exposed to such advertisements (Pechmann and Knight 2002). A study from Norway found that even in the presence of bans on advertising, limited exposure to tobacco marketing predicted both current smoking and intention to smoke in the future (Braverman and Aarø 2004). Surveys were conducted among 13- to 15-year-old adolescents in Norway in 1990 and 1995 and, despite an advertising ban, 50% of the adolescents in each cohort reported exposure to other kinds of tobacco marketing in the form of tobacco-related paraphernalia, imported newspapers, and broadcasts on television from other countries. After controlling for possible confounding factors, adolescents exposed to tobacco marketing were significantly more likely to be smokers or to expect to smoke by 20 years of age than those not exposed. This study establishes a clear association between early exposure and current and future smoking status, even when most forms of advertising are limited. These delayed effects help explain why limited restrictions on marketing so often have limited effects. A 1991 study of 640 children in Glasgow, Scotland, found that children aware of cigarette advertising at baseline were more likely to report increasing intention to smoke over the course of a year than were children less aware of or less interested in the ads. The latter group reported decreasing intention to smoke (Aitken et al. 1991).

Behavioral intentions can also predict continued nonsmoking. Lack of a firm commitment to abstain from smoking is considered to be a cognitive susceptibility to smoking (Spelman et al. 2009). In a longitudinal study of 637 California adolescents, participants who did not express a firm commitment to not smoke were two to three times as likely to smoke at a 2-year follow-up (Unger et al. 1997). A longitudinal study using Monitoring the Future (MTF) data has illustrated the importance of intentions not to smoke and the need for young people to develop and sustain firm future intentions not to smoke (Wakefield et al. 2004). After analyzing the data, Wakefield and colleagues (2004) concluded that "having a firm intention not to smoke in 5 year's (*sic*) time exerts a generally protective effect upon the likelihood of future established smoking" (p. 918, 921) that "has a protective effect, regardless of the level of current smoking experience" (p. 921). Even so, there is also evidence from the MTF data suggesting that intentions do not predict future quit behaviors. In two MTF-based studies, a large proportion of students who smoked believed they would not be smoking in 3 years, but approximately two-thirds were still smoking 5–9 years later (Lynch and Bonnie 1994; Johnston et al. 2002). These last two studies demonstrate that, like most adults, adolescents underestimate the risk of addiction (Slovic 2001; Halpern-Felsher et al. 2004). As a rule, adolescents do not expect to smoke in the future and discount the power of nicotine addiction when projecting their future smoking status. Moreover, these studies demonstrate that even slight shifts away from firm commitments to abstain from tobacco use increase the risk of adolescent smoking. In this regard, tobacco advertisements can exert an indirect influence on actual smoking behaviors by decreasing adolescents' intentions to abstain from tobacco.

Influence on Actual Smoking Behavior

There is strong and consistent evidence that marketing influences adolescent smoking behavior, including selection of brands, initiation of smoking, and overall consumption of cigarettes (Lovato et al. 2003; DiFranza et al. 2006; Goldberg 2008; NCI 2008). This section reviews the empirical data from econometric studies, studies of brand preference, and studies on changes in the initiation of smoking among adolescents and their consumption of cigarettes. Some studies have looked at the association between expenditures for advertising and promotion and overall cigarette consumption, while others have looked at the relationship between such expenditures and brand preference. Still others have looked at the effect of marketing on children's and adolescents' smoking behavior.

Evidence from Econometric Studies

Econometric analyses can be used to examine the relationship between the independent variable of marketing expenditures and the dependent variable of overall cigarette consumption over time, controlling for possible confounding or extraneous variables. In a 1992 econometric analysis, the Economics and Operational Research Division of the United Kingdom Department of Health issued what became known as the Smee Report (Department of Health 1992), which analyzed the results of 19 time-series studies of cigarette advertising from the United States, the United Kingdom, New Zealand, and Australia. This report concluded that "the great majority of results [of aggregate statistical studies] point in the same direction – towards a positive impact [on tobacco consumption]. The balance of evidence thus supports the conclusion that advertising does have a positive effect on consumption" (p. 22).

There are several limitations to econometric analysis, however, that make it difficult to quantify the relationship between advertising and use of tobacco. Because econometric analyses typically rely on aggregate marketing expenditures as a measure of the effect of marketing, the qualitative aspects of advertising, particularly the use of imagery, are not captured. In addition, econometric analyses have limited value when marketing expenditures are extremely large, in substantial measure because the marginal effect of additional dollars is difficult to assess. Some economists suggest that disaggregated data would have more variance and would more likely allow for assessing the relationship between changes in specific marketing expenditures and changes in cigarette consumption (Saffer and Chaloupka 2000). For studies of adolescent smoking, a specific problem with using econometric analyses is that the studies use overall cigarette consumption (all ages) as the outcome variable, and adolescents consume a very small proportion of cigarettes sold. Indeed, adolescents likely smoke less than 5% of the cigarettes consumed in the United States, in part because they smoke fewer cigarettes during the stages before or at the beginning of the period when they become addicted (than they do later) (DiFranza and Librett 1999).

A study (Keelor et al. 2004) on the combined effect of advertising and price on cigarette consumption following the Master Settlement Agreement in 1998 analyzed the effect of increases in cigarette prices and relatively large changes in advertising in the years around the settlement and concluded that the increase in advertising and marketing expenditures that occurred immediately before and following the settlement blunted the reduction in consumption that would otherwise have been observed as a result of the price increase. In other words, this analysis documented a simultaneous bolstering of cigarette consumption (2.7–4.7%) as a result of increased marketing expenditures and a relatively greater downward movement in consumption that was driven by price (-8.3%). The authors state:

> Results show that the increase in cigarette prices stemming from the Settlement reduced per capita cigarette consumption in the USA by 8.3%. However, the cigarette companies also increased advertising in the years immediately preceding and following the Settlement. This study estimates that this increased advertising partially offsets the effects of the higher prices, increasing cigarette consumption by 2.7 to 4.7%, and hence blunting the effects of the price increase by 33–57% (Keelor et al. 2004, p. 1623).

Lewit and colleagues (1981) were able to avoid some of the limitations in econometric analyses of the impact of advertising on youth smoking in their study of the link between cigarette advertising on television in the late 1960s (such advertising ended on January 2, 1971) and the level of adolescent smoking. These authors analyzed a series of annual surveys with 12- to 17-year-olds from 1966 to 1970, when television was the dominant medium for tobacco advertisers, and found a significant relationship between the level of exposure to tobacco advertising on television for the 12 months before each measurement of tobacco usage and the likelihood of being a current smoker at the measurement point. Holding all other factors constant, for every 10 hours per week the adolescent watched television (and so, tobacco advertising) in the previous year, he or she was 11% more likely to be a current smoker. This study is valuable because, once adult smoking is established as a result of nicotine addiction, it is unlikely that one would see large changes in smoking behavior as a function of year-to-year changes in the level of advertising. Smoking patterns were more changeable, in contrast, in the adolescents Lewit and colleagues studied (Goldberg 2008).

Another way to evaluate the effect of advertising on overall cigarette consumption is to use econometric or time-series techniques to investigate whether bans on advertising and promotion lead to a reduction in cigarette consumption. The studies in this area have generally found that partial bans have a much smaller impact on cigarette consumption, primarily because marketing dollars flow to other outlets for advertising and promotion that are not regulated or banned. Total bans on advertising and promotion, in contrast, have been associated with a reduction in cigarette consumption. An econometric analysis of 22 Organisation for Economic Co-Operation and Development (OECD) countries by Saffer and Chaloupka (2000) reported a potential 7.4% reduction in cigarette consumption if all OECD countries had enacted a comprehensive ban on advertising and promotion. The findings of Braverman and Aarø (2004) reinforce the conclusions of Saffer and Chaloupka and the importance of a comprehensive ban on all tobacco marketing. More recently, Blecher (2008) evaluated the impact of bans on tobacco advertising in developing countries and concluded that both partial and complete advertising restrictions are effective in reducing tobacco consumption, with complete bans being more effective, and that bans in developing countries may be even more effective in reducing tobacco use than are bans in developed countries.

A few studies, however, have concluded that there is no evidence that advertising bans affect cigarette consumption or the prevalence of smoking among youth. For example, Lancaster and Lancaster (2003) concluded that there is no evidence of an effect of bans directed at marketing expenditures and advertising on the consumption of cigarettes. Nelson (2003a) has even suggested that advertising may reduce the consumption of cigarettes because of (1) the addition of the cost of advertising to the price of a pack of cigarettes and (2) the communication through advertising of mandatory health warnings on the cigarette packs; he states, "[a]dvertising...increases the cost of cigarettes and many advertisements contain mandated health warnings. Thus, a ban of advertising could increase consumption by reducing prices or reducing awareness of health risks" (p. 1). In contrast to Nelson's assertion, there is some evidence (Tremblay and Tremblay 1999) that advertising bans raise the market power of existing firms by creating entry barriers; as a result, competition is reduced and prices are higher. Elsewhere, Nelson (2003b) reported no relationship between restrictions on advertising and the prevalence of adolescent smoking by using prevalence of smoking at a single point in time rather than from multiple points over time, which is more typical of econometric or time-series analyses.

In addition to methodologic issues, the validity of these studies has been questioned because some were sponsored by the tobacco industry. Industry efforts to undermine the existing science on the health effects of smoking and exposure to secondhand smoke is well-documented (e.g., see Warner 1991; Bero et al. 1993, 1994, 1995, 2001, 2005; Bero and Glantz 1993; Barnes et al., 1995; Glantz et al. 1996; Barnes and Bero 1997, 1998; Kennedy and Bero 1999; Hirschhorn 2000; Ong and Glantz 2000, 2001; Bialous and Yach 2001; Drope and Chapman 2001; Hirschhorn et al. 2001; Muggli et al. 2001; Gunja et al. 2002; Hong and Bero 2002, 2006; Tong and Glantz 2004; Bitton et al. 2005; Garne et al. 2005; Landman et al. 2008).

In conclusion, econometric studies are not the most sensitive way to assess the influence of tobacco advertising on adolescent smoking. However, these studies generally provide support for a finding that the marketing of tobacco promotes its use by adolescents.

Changes in the Initiation of Smoking and Consumption of Cigarettes Among Adolescents

The previous section presented data from econometric analyses to evaluate the impact of advertising and promotion on overall consumption (i.e., all ages, children and adults combined) as well as their effects on youth. Other literature has examined whether advertising and promotion are associated with increased cigarette consumption among adolescents in both cross-sectional and longitudinal studies. As shown below, both lines of inquiry demonstrate the influence of tobacco marketing.

Cross-sectional studies have associated adolescent smoking with awareness of cigarette advertisements and promotions, recognition and approval of such ads, and exposure and receptivity to them (Armstrong et al. 1990; Aitken et al. 1991; Evans et al. 1995; Schooler et al. 1996; Gilpin et al. 1997). These studies also found among adolescents a relationship between receipt or ownership of a promotional cigarette item and (1) a feeling that cigarette advertising may make them want to smoke a cigarette and (2) actual smoking status.

Several longitudinal studies have examined the relationship between exposure to cigarette marketing and subsequent changes in adolescent smoking behavior while controlling for possible confounding factors. In one, a prospective study by Pierce and colleagues (1998) of California adolescents who had never smoked, the authors found that those who had a favorite cigarette advertisement, or who possessed or were willing to use a cigarette promotional item, were significantly more likely to progress toward smoking as marked by increased susceptibility and greater intention to smoke than were those with neither of these characteristics. Pierce and associates (1998) estimated that, in 1993, 34% of experimentation with smoking by adolescents in California could be attributed to tobacco advertising and marketing.

A few years later, Choi and colleagues (2002) studied the smoking status in 1996 of nearly 1,000 California adolescents who had experimented with smoking in 1993. As in the previous studies, this study found that exposure to marketing increased the likelihood that adolescents would progress to established smoking. Although having peers who smoked and poor relationships with family members were both associated with progression to established smoking, the strongest predictor was related to the effects of cigarette marketing. Specifically, the authors found that adolescents who were willing to use a promotional item and who believed they could quit at any time progressed to established smoking at a higher rate (52%) than adolescents who did not believe they could quit smoking at any time and were minimally or moderately receptive to advertising (20–25%).

Additional longitudinal studies on adolescents outside of California have produced similar results. For example, Biener and Siegel (2000), who surveyed Massachusetts adolescents in 1993 and resurveyed them in 1997, found a significant relationship between the combination of owning a promotional tobacco item and having a favorite cigarette advertisement and subsequent smoking. In this study, the odds of becoming an established smoker were more than twice as great for those with both characteristics as they were for those with neither. Also in New England, a longitudinal study of a cohort of rural Vermont students that collected baseline data in 1996 and conducted follow-up in 1997 and 1998 revealed that being receptive to cigarette advertising (as indicated by owning or being willing to own an item promoting cigarettes) at baseline was associated with higher smoking rates 18 months later (Sargent et al. 2000). After controlling for possible confounders, the authors found the probability of initiating smoking was nearly double for those adolescents who were receptive to advertising compared with those who were not receptive (odds ratio [OR] = 1.9; 95% confidence interval [CI], 1.3–2.9).

In a longitudinal investigation conducted in California after the 1998 Master Settlement Agreement, Gilpin and colleagues (2007) compared two cohorts of 12- to 15-year-old adolescents, one measured in 1993 and the other in 1996. Both cohorts were reassessed 3 and 6 years later as young adults. Although there were more young adult established smokers in the 1993 cohort than in the 1996 group, the two groups exhibited the same relationship between receptivity to tobacco advertising and smoking. In both, having a favorite cigarette advertisement and owning or being willing to use a tobacco promotional item increased the adjusted odds of future young adult smoking (OR = 1.46; 95% CI, 1.1–1.9; OR = 1.84; 95% CI, 1.2–2.9, respectively).

Pierce and colleagues (2010) also assessed whether cigarette advertising campaigns conducted after the 1998 settlement continued to influence smoking among adolescents. The authors used a national longitudinal cohort of boys and girls who were 10–13 years old when they were enrolled in 2003 and asked the brand of their "favorite" cigarette advertisement (if they had one). The fifth interview with this cohort was conducted after the start of RJR's "Camel No. 9" advertising campaign in 2007. Youth who reported any favorite cigarette ad at baseline (mean age = 11.7 years) were 50% more likely to have smoked by 2008 (adjusted OR = 1.5; 95% CI, 1.0–2.3). For boys, the proportion with a favorite ad was stable over all five interviews, as it was for girls across the first four surveys, which were conducted before the start of the "Camel No. 9" campaign. After the start of that campaign, the proportion of girls who reported a favorite ad increased by

10 percentage points, to 44%. The Camel brand appears to have accounted for almost all of this increase. (The proportion of each gender that nominated the Marlboro brand remained stable.) These findings suggest that after the Master Settlement Agreement, cigarette advertising continues to reach adolescents, that adolescents continue to be responsive to cigarette advertising, and that those who are responsive are more likely to initiate smoking.

In summary, the literature on tobacco marketing and the initiation of smoking by adolescents demonstrates the continued presence of this marketing and its effect on adolescent smoking at the individual level. It is important to note that, in the TTI framework, influence at the individual level also translates to distal-level factors (Figure 5.1). Specifically, as more individuals use tobacco, they continue to influence social groups and the cultural norms for nonsmoking adolescents.

Changes in Brand Preference

In 1991, DiFranza and colleagues published the first wide-coverage study of brand recognition among youth (DiFranza et al. 1991). As discussed in more detail in the next section, having a favorite brand provides another measure of receptivity to advertising that predicts smoking behavior among youth.

In 1999, researchers in Massachusetts who studied the relationship among adolescents (aged 12–15 at baseline), between the magnitude of brand-specific cigarette advertising in magazines in 1993 and brand-specific smoking behavior 4 years later among the same group found strong, significant correlations between exposure to brand-specific advertising and the brand these young people started smoking and the brand they currently smoked (Pucci and Siegel 1999).

Elsewhere, analyses of brand-specific advertising patterns in magazines revealed that those brands disproportionately preferred by adolescents were more likely to be advertised in magazines with a higher proportion of youth readers (King et al. 1998). Similarly, in these magazines, the tobacco companies were more likely to advertise cigarette brands most popular among youth than to advertise the range of adult brands (King et al. 1998).

Tobacco companies are very interested in initial brand preference because they know it is highly associated with subsequent brand selection. The tobacco companies know that youth are very brand loyal, and once they have chosen a brand, most will continue with it. For example, a previously confidential Philip Morris document states as its "underlying premise" that "The smokers you have are the smokers you are most likely to keep" (Peters 1999, Bates No. 2070648930/8964, p. 25).

Among the other tobacco industry documents confirming the importance of brand loyalty among youth is a 1984 RJR Secret Strategic Research Report subtitled "Younger Adult Smokers: Strategies and Opportunities" that observed:

> Once a brand becomes well-developed among younger adult smokers, aging and brand loyalty will eventually transmit that strength to older age brackets....Thus, even if a brand falls from favor among younger adult smokers, the younger adults it attracted in earlier years and their increasing consumption can carry the brand's market share for years, significantly extending its overall life cycle (Burrows 1984, Bates No. 501928462/8550, p. 11, 13).

The success of Philip Morris' Marlboro brand was the major catalyst for the creation by its rival, RJR, of the Camel campaign. Specifically, RJR's marketing plan showed that it sought to "build preference by leveraging Camel's appeal among adult smokers 18-34 years of age, particularly those with an 'irreverent, less serious' mind set, gradually breaking down the pervasive peer acceptance of Marlboro" (Young & Rubicam 1990, Bates No. 508827386/7401, p.5). According to RJR's 1991 communication, the strategy was to catch Marlboro smokers' attention through the Joe Camel persona:

> Joe is the hero in all of CAMEL's communications. But he's not a spokesman, a salesman, or a shill. He is the larger-than-life personification of all that we, in our moments of playful fantasy, aspire to be. Always the winner, on top of the situation, beating the system, and covering the scene, whatever he does he does with a style and joie de vivre all his own. The twinkle in his eye and that 'cat that ate the canary' expression on his face say it all (Young & Rubicam 1990, Bates No. 508827386/7401, p. 11).

Companies continue to profile their customers and compare them with their competitors' customers, particularly their younger ones (Ling and Glantz 2002; *United States v. Philip Morris USA*, 449 F. Supp. 2d 1, 1006 [D.D.C. 2006]).

Systematic Reviews

The Cochrane Database of Systematic Reviews is the largest and most comprehensive assessment of the scientific evidence in medicine and public health. In 2003, it published its first systematic review of the impact of tobacco marketing on smoking behaviors among adolescents. Because the review found that experimental studies on the effect of marketing on adolescent smoking behavior could not ethically or practically be conducted, the authors relied on longitudinal studies, nine of which met their acceptance criteria. These studies were conducted in Australia, England, Spain, and the United States between 1983 and 2000. The authors concluded:

> Longitudinal studies consistently suggest that exposure to tobacco advertising and promotion is associated with the likelihood that adolescents will start to smoke. Based on the strength of this association, the consistency of findings across numerous observational studies, temporality of exposure and smoking behaviours observed, as well as the theoretical plausibility regarding the impact of advertising, we conclude that tobacco advertising and promotion increases the likelihood that adolescents will start to smoke (Lovato et al. 2003, p. 2).

The authors also noted that the cross-sectional studies that were considered (they viewed longitudinal studies as being stronger) also supported the conclusion that advertising influences adolescents to begin smoking (Lovato et al. 2003).

In another systematic review of the existing literature on tobacco industry marketing and smoking by adolescents, DiFranza and colleagues (2006) arrived at several major conclusions that support the conclusion that marketing by the tobacco industry causes adolescents to smoke. First, there is a dose-response relationship between exposure to tobacco marketing and initiation of tobacco use by adolescents. Second, exposure to tobacco marketing precedes initiation of tobacco use. Third, across a wide variety of promotion types, populations, and research designs, the evidence clearly points to a causal relationship between promotion by the tobacco industry and adolescent tobacco use. Finally, the scientific literature provides an understanding of the mechanisms by which tobacco marketing influences tobacco use among adolescents.

NCI's tobacco control monograph, *The Role of the Media in Promoting and Reducing Tobacco Use* (NCI 2008), also examined the evidence on how tobacco marketing efforts affect tobacco use among adolescents. Using numerous studies and tobacco industry documents, the report concluded that even brief exposure to tobacco advertising influences attitudes and perceptions about smoking and adolescents' intentions to smoke. In addition, the evidence showed that exposure to cigarette advertising influences nonsmoking adolescents to begin smoking and move toward regular smoking.

The Position and Behavior of the Tobacco Industry

The tobacco companies have consistently denied that their marketing efforts have had any effect on the smoking behavior of adolescents and contend instead that the sole purpose of marketing by individual companies has been to influence existing adult smokers to smoke the company's brands of cigarettes rather than those of a competitor. In addition, the industry has claimed that there is no evidence that cigarette marketing affects the smoking behavior of youth and that the definitive study on this matter has not yet been conducted. This section reviews the evidence on the industry's position regarding the purpose of marketing and the industry's actual behavior in using imagery to appeal to youth.

The Tobacco Industry's Position on the Purpose of Marketing: Switching of Brands by Adults

Tobacco companies have consistently stated that the purpose of spending billions of dollars on cigarette marketing is to attract and hold current adult smokers to their brands of cigarettes (Tye et al. 1987). In addition, the companies deny that marketing campaigns are intended to increase demand for cigarettes among existing smokers or to encourage young people to initiate smoking (Cummings et al. 2002). The economic value of the amount of brand switching that occurs, however, does not justify the magnitude of marketing expenditures (Tye et al. 1987; Siegel et al. 1994). Indeed, because most brands are owned by a few tobacco companies, most switching of brands would not have a substantial impact on any one company's profits. The most plausible justification for advertising expenditures at the levels that have been observed would be to attract new customers to generate a long-term cash flow for the companies (Tye et al. 1987). In addition, the nature of the imagery used in the advertisements clearly appeals to the aspirations of adolescents, suggesting that they are a target (Perry 1999).

Across industries, marketing is intended to sell existing products and to facilitate the introduction of new ones into the marketplace. In 1986, Emerson Foote, former chief executive officer (CEO) and founder of McCann-Erickson, a global advertising agency, said,

> The cigarette industry has been artfully maintaining that cigarette advertising has nothing

> to do with total sales. This is complete and utter nonsense. The industry knows it is nonsense.... I am always amused by the suggestion that advertising, a function that has been shown to increase consumption of virtually every other product, somehow miraculously fails to work for tobacco products (Foote 1981, p. 1668).

The tobacco industry aggressively pursues marketing strategies to build national and global brands geared toward young adults (Cohen 2000; Hafez and Ling 2005). RJR based Joe Camel on a popular French campaign depicting a stylized French cartoon camel (Cohen 2000) that was appealing to a younger audience. Philip Morris' strategy for Marlboro encompassed three principal foci: psychographic segmentation, brand studies, and advertising/communication (Hafez and Ling 2005). The company's strategy now appears to be translated into a standardized global strategy.

Despite the industry's arguments about brand loyalty and inducing existing smokers to switch brands, there are times when cigarette company executives themselves have acknowledged that marketing reaches and influences underage adolescents. For example, in 1997, Bennett S. LeBow, CEO of the holding company that owns Liggett, stated: "Liggett acknowledges that the tobacco industry markets to 'youth', which means those under 18 years of age, and not just those 18–24 years of age" (LeBow 1997b, Bates No. VDOJ31357/1375, p. 6).

Later that year, in litigation in Minnesota, Mr. LeBow further testified that cigarette companies targeted young people "to try to keep people smoking, keep their business going" (LeBow 1997a, Bates No. LG0312696/3542, p. 343). Draper Daniels, who first created the Marlboro man for Philip Morris, wrote in his 1974 book entitled *GIANTS, pigmies, AND OTHER ADVERTISING PEOPLE*,

> ...successful cigarette advertising involves showing the kind of people most people would like to be, doing the kind of thing most people would like to do, and smoking up a storm. I don't know any way of doing this that doesn't tempt young people to smoke, and in view of present knowledge, this is something I prefer not to do (Daniels 1974, p. 245).

After Harley-Davidson USA, a manufacturer of motorcycles, had licensed its name to Lorillard Tobacco Company for a cigarette brand to be called Harley-Davidson, the company expressed its concern about cigarette advertising to Lorillard in a letter dated August 17, 1993. Timothy K. Hoelter, vice president and general counsel for Harley-Davidson, wrote to Ronald S. Goldbrenner, associate general counsel of Lorillard, stating, "The recent California and FTC attacks on the Joe Camel advertising campaign are alarming and compel us to be sure that our Property will not be used to recruit underage smokers, intentionally or otherwise (Hoelter 1993, Bates No. 91058719/8720, p. 1). Mr. Hoelter went on to state: "We need to know what ads will be used, in what publications and on what billboards. This will help us assess the likelihood that children may be targets or so close to the intended targets as to be 'in harm's way'" (Bates No. 91058719/8720, p. 2).

Following correspondence from Lorillard, Harley-Davidson commissioned a firm with expertise in child behavior to conduct an independent study of the likely appeal of Lorillard's promotional campaign to children. The research firm conducted focus groups, group discussions, individual interviews, and telephone surveys and concluded that "Lorillard's intended promotional campaign for Harley-Davidson cigarettes would appeal to... children who are below the legal age to buy or smoke cigarettes" (Harley-Davidson 1993, Bates No. 93791722/1760, p. 30, 33). In addition, in legal filings Harley-Davidson noted that "Lorillard continued to refuse to reveal its test data and analysis about the likely effects of its promotional campaign, and Harley-Davidson inferred that the withheld data and analysis would have suggested possible or likely recruitment of underage persons" (Harley-Davidson 1993, Bates No. 93791722/1760, p. 34). As a result, the Harley-Davidson campaign was not developed.

In a 1983 confidential report, RJR emphasized the importance of "younger adults" to the industry as a whole:

> Why, then, are younger adult smokers important to RJR? Younger adults are the only source of replacement smokers. Repeated government studies (Appendix B) have shown that:
>
> - Less than one-third of smokers (31%) start after age 18.
> - Only 5% of smokers start after age 24.
>
> Thus, today's younger adult smoking behavior will largely determine the trend of Industry volume over the next several decades. If younger adults turn away from smoking, the Industry must decline, just as a population which does not give birth will eventually dwindle. In such an environment, a positive RJR sales trend would require disproportionate share gains and/or steep price increases (which could depress volume) (RJR 1983b, Bates No. 503473660/3665, p. 1).

Imagery

As is the case with all advertising, a substantial portion of tobacco advertising consists of imagery that conveys little factual information about the characteristics of the product. In effect, tobacco advertising fulfills many of the aspirations of young people by effectively using themes of independence, liberation, attractiveness, adventurousness, sophistication, glamour, athleticism, social acceptability and inclusion, sexual attractiveness, thinness, popularity, rebelliousness, and being "cool" (*United States v. Philip Morris USA*, 449F. Supp. 2d 1, 980 [D.D.C. 2006]; NCI 2008).

The use of Joe Camel is an exemplar for understanding the importance of imagery to reposition a brand for a younger age group. RJR conducted extensive studies on initiation of smoking by adolescents and factors behind the choice of their first brand (Cohen 2000). This research was geared toward repositioning Camel for a younger market, or as is said in the RJR documents, "youthening" the brand (Carpenter 1985, Bates No. 506768857, p. 1).

In fact, RJR's documents are replete with references to the importance of imagery in reaching the Camel target market, including comments such as the following:

> In order to stimulate [younger adult smokers] to think about brand alternatives, the advertising and brand personality must 'jolt' the target consumer. Since CAMEL does not have a demonstrably different or unique product (rational) benefit to sell, this jolt needs to be based on an emotional response and is unlikely to be accomplished with advertising which looks conventional or traditional. Studies have shown that the so-called 'hot buttons' for younger adults include some of the following themes: Escape into imagination.... Excitement/fun is success: Younger adults center their lives on having fun in every way possible and at every time possible. Their definition of success is 'enjoying today' which differentiates them from older smokers (RJR 1986a, Bates No. 506768775/8784, p. 9).

A 1988 Lorillard study entitled "Newport Image Study" concluded that "in all areas Newport smokers were viewed as party-goers, those that do their own thing and [are] fun-loving" and "in all areas Newport smokers were viewed younger and more fun-loving than Kool and Salem smokers" (Lorillard 1988, Bates No. 92272605/2665, p. 48). A 1991 Lorillard "Newport 1992 Strategic Marketing Plan" discussed the importance of the "Alive with Pleasure" advertising campaign, coupled with price promotions, to "generate interest and trial among entry level smokers" (Lorillard 1991, Bates No. 92011118/1156, p. 20). In addition, the industry capitalized on themes of rebellion to attract younger customers. For example, a report for an RJR Canadian subsidiary described young male smokers as "going through a stage where they are seeking to express their independence and individuality [smoking] (Pollay 1989, p. 240). In another document, it was noted that "Export A ... appeals to their rebellious nature..." (Ness Motley 1982, Bates No. 800057286/7321, p. 14). Moreover, a 1978 B&W document stated, "Imagery will continue to be important in brand selection for teenagers" (B&W 1978, Bates No. 667007711/7714, p. 1). These efforts to encourage brand loyalty by building brand image are particularly relevant for youth and young adults. Tobacco lifestyle-oriented marketing messages targeting young males have served to connect tobacco brand image with the user's self image and simultaneously portray risk-taking behavior as a normal part of masculinity (Cortese and Ling 2011). As previously discussed, the "Camel No. 9" campaign theme is geared to young women (Pierce et al. 2010). In addition, RJR employed a campaign geared toward young adult social trendsetters, who are commonly referred to as "hipsters" (Hendlin et al. 2010).

The Interplay Between Cigarette Marketing and Peer Pressure

The relationships between social relationships and youth smoking are well established through previous research and reviews, including the 1994 Surgeon General's report on preventing tobacco use among young people (USDHHS 1994). That report summarized the particularly strong association between smoking by siblings and peers and initiation of smoking among youth. The relationship between adolescents' perceptions and their use of tobacco is also well documented. As demonstrated in both cross-sectional and prospective longitudinal studies, the perceptions of youth about their social environment, including peer norms, perceived cultural norms, and perceived parental expectations, strongly predict smoking in this age group (Chassin et al. 1986; Conrad et al. 1992; USDHHS 1994).

Peer and parental influences are both associated with the decision of an adolescent to begin smoking, but it is important to understand the relationship between initiation of smoking and peer influence. Peer influence is a factor that has been consistently demonstrated to affect the onset and maintenance of smoking. As discussed earlier and in Chapter 4, it is also important to consider that, to the extent that tobacco industry marketing and promotional activities stimulate peers and parents to smoke, these influences contribute to smoking by adolescents (USDHHS 1994). Therefore, peer and parental influences are acting as mediating variables between advertising and adolescent smoking. Thus, including peer influence only as an independent variable in studies that examine the direct effect of cigarette advertising on adolescent smoking will lead to an underestimate of the total (direct and indirect, mediated by peer smoking) effect of cigarette advertising and other protobacco media influences, such as exposure to on-screen smoking in movies (Wills et al. 2007, 2008; Ling et al. 2009).

Young people want to be popular, to be seen as individuals by their friends, and to resemble those they most admire. Cigarette advertising exploits these adolescent desires, using imagery to create the impression of popularity, individuality, and kinship. There is substantial evidence that advertising of tobacco affects adolescents' perceptions of the attractiveness and pervasiveness of smoking, and the weight of the evidence suggests that cigarette marketing, particularly image-based advertising, and peer influence have additive effects on adolescent smoking (USDHHS 1994). A study by Evans and colleagues (1995) in California that examined the relationship between exposure of adolescents to tobacco marketing and susceptibility to smoking also examined such factors as smoking by peers and family and perceived school performance. In this study, tobacco marketing increased the susceptibility of adolescents to smoking in a way that was independent of exposure to friends or family who smoked. When combined, minimal exposure to tobacco marketing and exposure to other smokers increased the likelihood of susceptibility to smoking fourfold (Evans et al. 1995).

Additional research has examined the intricate relationships between tobacco marketing, peer relationships, and adolescent smoking behavior. Specifically, tobacco marketing may affect the selection of peer groups, which, in turn, influence smoking behavior among adolescents. Pechmann and Knight (2002) reported the results of a randomized experiment that compared two conditions: exposure to cigarette ads (vs. noncigarette ads) and exposure to peers who smoked (vs. peers who did not smoke). Both exposure to cigarette ads and peers who smoked had main effects on adolescents' positive stereotypes of smokers and intentions to smoke. When considered concurrently, however, the data revealed a mediation relationship for cigarette ads. Specifically, the significant influence of cigarette advertising on intentions to smoke became nonsignificant when positive stereotypic beliefs about smokers were considered, suggesting that cigarette ads increase favorable attitudes about smokers, which increase an adolescent's intention and susceptibility to smoke. These results also provide support for the idea that tobacco advertising affects adolescent smoking across multiple levels of influence (Deighton 1984; Pechmann 2001; Pechmann and Knight 2002). Advertising primes positive attitudes and beliefs about smokers; as Leventhal and Keeshan (1993) observed, adolescents may then be drawn to peers who smoke and who mirror those positive attitudes primed by advertisements. The idea that adolescents choose their peer group on the basis of their attitudes about smoking and their smoking behavior has been supported by numerous studies that aim to explain the homogeneity of peer groups (Ennett and Bauman 1994; Engels et al. 1997; Kobus 2003; de Vries et al. 2006; Mercken et al. 2007).

The preceding studies demonstrate the importance of two processes underlying the role that peers play in adolescent smoking: socialization and selection. Peers who smoke socialize the nonsmoking members of a social network by increasing perceptions of the prevalence of smoking, by modeling the behavior, and through the process of peer acceptance. Adolescents who believe smoking to be prevalent are more likely to smoke (Chassin et al. 1984; Sussman et al. 1988; Botvin et al. 1993). Moreover, adolescents who hold positive beliefs about smokers or who smoke themselves choose peers who affirm those beliefs and attitudes that were primed by tobacco marketing. In this regard, tobacco marketing, socialization, and the selection of friends contribute to a dynamic system that serves to increase adolescent smoking social networks (Kobus 2003). From internal industry documents, depositions, and trial testimony, it is clear that the tobacco industry understands the need to be accepted, particularly among youth, and has attempted to exploit this need through its marketing efforts. For example, in a 1984 report, a Philip Morris scientist stated that

> ...we need not try to understand why young people have a herd instinct. From their choices of food, clothes, transportation, entertainment, heroes, friends, hangouts, etc., it is clear that they do. More important to us (and probably to many other product categories) is why they make certain choices instead of others (Tindall 1984, Bates No. 2001265000/5045, p. 28).

In a deposition for the U.S. Department of Justice case, Nancy B. Lund, a Philip Morris executive, testified "...at least what we know about young adult smokers, for some of them, the fact that Marlboro is a popular brand may be a factor in why they choose Marlboro" (Philip Morris USA 2004a, Bates No. 5001054172/4245, p. 35). A 1998 confidential document of Leo Burnett (Philip Morris' advertising agency that developed the Marlboro Man) recommended adding camaraderie (peer appeal) to the core values of Marlboro Country (Philip Morris USA 1998). As recently as 1999, a Philip Morris "National Market Structure Study" reported, "The attributes associated with brand choices are very different from those stated to be important – popularity is key" (Philip Morris USA 1999b, Bates No. 2702700028B/0028BP, p. 12). Plans by Philip Morris to market its Parliament cigarettes to 18- to 24-year-olds in 1987 included the following statement:

> This younger age group is more likely to make decisions based on peer pressure. To convey the idea that everyone is smoking Parliament, the brand should have continuous high levels of visibility in as many pack outlets as possible (Philip Morris USA 1987, Bates No. 2045287048/7092, p. 16).

Heavy exposure leads to overestimates of smoking prevalence among adolescents, and this is understood to be a significant risk factor in leading adolescents to smoke (Botvin et al. 1993).

Philip Morris was not the only company to understand the importance of peer pressure and its relevance to marketing campaigns. RJR studied the success of Marlboro and attributed some of that success to peer acceptance. A 1986 RJR document stated, "Marlboro's key strength relates to peer acceptability and belonging.... Marlboro is perceived by younger adult smokers as a brand which provides a sense of belonging to the peer group" (RJR 1986a, Bates No. 505938058/8063, p. 7). In a 1986 RJR document about the Joe Camel campaign, vice president for marketing R.T. Caufield stated:

> Overall, CAMEL advertising will be directed toward using peer acceptance/influence to provide the motivation for target smokers to select CAMEL (Caufield 1986, Bates No. 503969238/9242, p. 1).

In another example, this one from 1984, in developing marketing materials for its upcoming Tempo brand, RJR characterized the target group as

> ...extremely influenced by their peer group... influenced by the brand choice of their friends. Third Family (the code name for Tempo) will differentiate itself from competitive brands by major usage of imagery which portrays the positive social appeal of peer group acceptance. Third Family imagery portrays relaxing and enjoyable social interaction where acceptance by the group provides a sense of belonging and security (J. Walter Thompson 1984, Bates No. TCA13320/3333, p. 5).

Pollay observed in an article published in 2000: "Put briefly, it seems that TEMPO's advertising was too trendy and heavy handed in its style and deployment, becoming transparently interested in a youthful market. This backfired because adolescents are decidedly disinterested in symbols of adolescence, wanting symbols of the adulthood they aspire to" (Pollay 2000, p. 143).

Evidence of the industry's understanding in the 1970s, 1980s, and 1990s of the importance of peer approval for adolescent smoking behavior is widespread and well documented. Proceeding from this understanding, marketing campaigns tried to emphasize the popularity of brands, hoping this would translate to their being perceived as more popular among peers. Two passages from the RJR Secret Strategic Research Report subtitled "Younger Adult Smokers: Strategies and Opportunities" are illustrative: "Marlboro's key imagery was not masculinity, it was younger adult identity/belonging" and "This could mean as social pressures tend to isolate younger adult smokers from their nonsmoking peers, they have an increased need to identify with their smoking peers, to smoke the 'belonging' brand" (Burrows 1984, Bates No. 501928462/8550, p. 28).

Lorillard considered Newport to be its "peer brand" among young adult smokers (Brooks 1993; Lorillard 1993b), and a 1999 creative strategy it used with the intention of increasing volume and gaining long-term growth was to

> Develop creative executions that continue to strengthen and refresh Newport's advantage as the peer brand of choice among younger adult smokers by reinforcing the perception that Newport delivers smoking pleasure in social settings relative to their lifestyles. Continue to leverage the Pleasure campaign equity to reinforce the brand's fun, spontaneous, upbeat image through a variety of settings portraying social interaction, spontaneous fun, refreshment and smoking situations (Lorillard 1999, Bates No. 98196920/6942, p. 8).

Judge Kessler concluded that

> According to Shari Teitelbaum, Philip Morris Director of Marketing and Sales Decision Support, Philip Morris has used the term "herd smoker" to refer to smokers of the most popular cigarette brands, like Marlboro, Camel, and Newport, because these brands attract the largest share of young adult smokers. Herd brands are "the most popular, it's for smokers that would be likely to kind of follow the herd, kind of more of a group mentality type of thing" (*United States*

v. Philip Morris USA, 449F. Supp. 2d 1, 1026 [D.D.C. 2006].

Tobacco companies pursued promotions aimed at young adults in bars and nightclubs increasingly through the 1990s (Sepe et al. 2002; Biener et al. 2004; Rigotti et al. 2005), in part because these young adults were viewed as trendsetters who were highly likely to influence the behaviors of their peers (Katz and Lavack 2002; Sepe et al. 2002). A study of young adults in California reported approximately 33% of all young adults go to bars and clubs at least sometimes, and bar and club goers had over three times greater odds to be daily smokers and over three times the odds to be social smokers (Gilpin et al. 2005).

Marketing to young adult trendsetters remains important. In a relevant study, Hendlin and colleagues (2010) used tobacco industry documents and analysis of industry marketing materials to understand why and how RJR and other tobacco companies have marketed tobacco products to young adult consumers who are social trendsetters ("hipsters") to recruit other trendsetters and average consumers, as well as youth who look to hipsters as role models, to smoke. These authors found that since 1995, when RJR developed its marketing campaigns to better suit the lifestyle, image identity, and attitudes of hip trendsetters, Camel's brand identity had actively shifted to more closely convey the hipster persona. Camel emphasized events such as promotional music tours to link the brand and smoking to activities and symbols appealing to hipsters and their emulating masses.

In sum, far from being a completely independent determinant of youth smoking, peer influence is yet another channel for communication on which the industry can capitalize to promote smoking by youth. It is important to note that the tobacco industry routinely attributes smoking to peer pressure, but it does not acknowledge the relationship between advertising and peer influence or the effects of advertising on normative behavior and perceptions of popularity and peer acceptance. Tobacco companies have consistently stated that the purpose of cigarette marketing is to attract and hold current adult smokers to their brands of cigarette, but the evidence reviewed shows that these efforts also affect peer influence to smoke and encourage smoking among young people.

Summary

The continuously accumulating evidence from the studies that have addressed the effect of advertising on smoking is consistent with a dose-dependent causal relationship. Most smokers start as adolescents: cigarette companies need to recruit new smokers from among youth, and their advertising campaigns appeal to the aspirations of adolescents. There is strong empirical evidence that advertising and promotions affect awareness of smoking and of particular brands, the recognition and recall of cigarette advertising, attitudes about smoking, intentions to smoke, and actual smoking behavior. Because youth are brand loyal, attracting them to a particular brand pays off for tobacco companies in the long term. In fact, youth appear to be even more responsive to advertising appeals than are adults (Lovato et al. 2003). The industry's own internal correspondence and testimony in court, as well as widely accepted principles of advertising and marketing, also support the conclusion that tobacco advertising recruits new users as youth and reinforces continued use among young adults.

Taking together the epidemiology of adolescent tobacco use, internal tobacco company documents describing the importance of new smokers, analysis of the design of marketing campaigns, the actual imagery communicated in the $10-billion-a-year marketing effort, the conclusions of official government reports, and the weight of the scientific evidence, it is concluded that advertising and promotion has caused youth to start smoking and continue to smoke.

The Tobacco Industry's Pricing Practices and Use of Tobacco Among Young People

In recent years, the pricing of tobacco products has become a key marketing strategy in the tobacco industry. Historically, markets for tobacco products were characterized by relatively stable prices, with changes in prices for one firm typically matched by changes by other firms (Chaloupka 2007). Moreover, price changes in the industry were infrequent and generally modest, with some exceptions. In recent years, however, price-reducing promotions have been the primary means of price competition among manufacturers, with some evidence that these promotions have been targeted to specific brands or venues that are more important for young people. These promotions also mitigate the impact of tax increases. This section briefly reviews pricing strategies in the industry and the relatively limited research that has examined the relationships between these strategies (particularly price-reducing promotions) and tobacco use among youth. Given the importance of local, state, and federal taxes in determining price, the more extensive research that examines the impact of taxes and prices on tobacco use among youth will be covered in Chapter 6. As described more fully in that chapter, one key finding demonstrates that youth respond more than adults to price changes in terms of their use of tobacco. This finding is of particular relevance to pricing strategies in the industry and helps to explain some of the changes in price and price-related marketing over the past 15–20 years.

Pricing Strategies in the Industry

Historically, advertising, product design, and other marketing efforts have been the focus of the tobacco industry's competitive activities, with competition by price being relatively limited (Chaloupka 2007). The limited price competition was largely the result of the highly concentrated nature of the markets, with relatively few manufacturers accounting for nearly all production. Price competition was seen in the offering of the "10-cent brands" of the 1930s and the emergence and growth of discount brands in the 1980s, but such competition has been rare (Chaloupka 2007).

Price Leadership

For most of the past century, the pricing of tobacco products has been characterized by price leadership, with one firm (typically the dominant firm) initiating an increase or decrease in price and the others almost immediately matching the change (Chaloupka et al. 2002; Chaloupka 2007). This practice is described in a 1976 report from the Business Planning & Analysis Department of Philip Morris entitled *Pricing Policy* (Philip Morris 1976). The report starts by describing the industry's pricing behavior on the basis of an economic model of organizational behavior in an oligopolistic (highly concentrated) market in which firms are likely to match price cuts of other firms, but not to match price increases:

> The cigarette industry is characterized by economists as a 'kinky oligopoly'.... This charming term implies that the general price level is determined by a small number of firms (price leaders); that no economic advantage can be obtained by any one firm pricing below the general price level; and that major disadvantages accrue to a firm which attempts a price above the general level. In short, the general price level results from some sparring among the potential price leaders, after which the rest of the industry accepts the resulting price structure (Philip Morris 1976, Bates No. 2023769635/9655, p. 4).

The report also describes how Philip Morris had long been one of the followers in the industry, matching the prices set by the American Tobacco Company and RJR, and then goes on to note how its role had changed by the 1970s. In addition to citing the relatively high inflation that emerged in that decade, the report notes that

> The second change which has occurred is the emergence of Philip Morris among the price leaders in the cigarette industry. We no longer follow the market: whether we initiate a price increase or not, our decision is a key factor in establishing a new industry price level, and we must examine any price move in the light of our own judgment of the appropriate level (Philip Morris 1976, Bates No. 2023769635/9655, p. 4).

The report goes on to discuss Philip Morris' pricing strategies in the 1970s as well as the trade-offs between pricing and marketing. For example, the report notes that the relative lack of price competition in the industry provided earnings that could have been invested in other marketing efforts to help gain market share. Similarly, it describes how market prices were below the level that would maximize industry profits but that any attempt to significantly increase prices would "destroy the resiliency of the system" (Philip Morris 1976, Bates No. 2023769635/9655, p. 6) (likely by creating opportunities for new entrants to compete on price) rather than result in higher long-run prices. As Chaloupka and colleagues (2002) discussed, this may have shown the industry's awareness of the greater price sensitivity of young people: if prices were set higher to maximize short-run profits (given the relatively limited price sensitivity of current addicted smokers), the resultant reductions in youth smoking would significantly reduce the number of smokers in the long run, leading to reduced future profits.

Discount Brands and "Marlboro Friday"

One exception to the limited price competition in cigarette markets was seen during the 1980s and early 1990s: The doubling of the federal excise tax in 1983 along with numerous increases in state cigarette taxes reversed the downward trend in inflation-adjusted cigarette prices that existed for much of the 1970s and early 1980s. The rising inflation-adjusted prices combined with falling incomes during the recession of the early 1980s made cigarettes much less affordable than they had been in many years (Chaloupka et al. 2002); these forces led cigarette companies to rethink their pricing strategies. For example, a 1983 report from RJR stated:

> The outlook for the future suggests that the price-sensitive environment will continue and perhaps worsen. State taxes are likely to increase. Another F.E.T. (federal excise tax) increase is possible. Contrary to our previous efforts and experience, discounted, branded cigarettes may well be successfully introduced and a multi-tiered retail price structure normally associated with "price segregation" may result. There would be heavy competitive activity and differing margins associated with the multi-tier structure (RJR 1983a, Bates No. 501927671/7685, p. 1).

During the same period, early research on differences in the price sensitivity of youth, young adult, and adult smokers began to appear in the academic literature (e.g., Lewit et al. 1981; Lewit and Coate 1982). The industry took note of these findings, which confirmed its own internal research showing that smoking among youth was more responsive to price than was smoking among adults (Chaloupka et al. 2002). This evidence appears to have influenced subsequent pricing strategies in the industry. For example, an RJR 1984 Strategic Research Report discussed the importance of pricing, combined with other marketing efforts, particularly for younger smokers:

> Pricing is a key issue in the industry. Some evidence suggests that younger adult smokers are interested in price, but unlikely to adopt a brand whose only "hook" is price. To maximize the possible pricing opportunity among younger adult smokers, several alternatives should be considered (Burrows 1984, Bates No. 501928462/8550, p. 45).

The report went on to describe the importance of branding in addition to pricing:

> A price/value brand would need a conspicuous second "hook" to reduce possible conflict between younger adults' value wants and imagery wants. The most saleable "hooks" are likely to be based on product quality, since these provide easy-to-explain public reasons for switching. Suitable imagery should also be used (Burrows 1984, Bates No. 501928462/8550, p. 46).

As Chaloupka and colleagues (2002) noted, the combined branding/pricing strategy was adopted by tobacco companies in developing the "branded generics" that came to dominate the discount cigarette markets in subsequent years. All the tobacco companies either developed new brands or repositioned old brands in the discount markets. A three-tiered price structure soon emerged, which included a relatively small number of deep-discount brands, many mid-price discount brands (including several repositioned premium brands), and many higher-priced premium brands.

By early 1993, discount brands accounted for almost 40% of cigarette consumption, with the availability of the lower-priced brands contributing to a slowing of the declines in smoking observed through the 1980s and early 1990s (Kluger 1996; Cummings et al. 1997). The price differences between deep-discount, discount, and premium brands were significant, with list prices as low as $0.65, $0.98, and $1.40 per pack ($1.02, $1.53, and $2.23 in 2011 dollars), respectively, in January 1993 (Tobacco Reporter 2000).

Philip Morris was perhaps most affected by the emergence of the discount brands. Although still the clear market leader in early 1993, the company had seen its overall market share decline despite its efforts to introduce its own discount brands. Perhaps more troubling to Philip Morris was the drop in market share for its Marlboro brand, which had been the industry's leading brand for many years and which had an even larger share of the youth market. In an effort to reverse these trends and to halt the growth in discount brands, on April 2, 1993 ("Marlboro Friday"), Philip Morris announced a variety of price-reducing promotions that reduced Marlboro prices by 40 cents per pack (Chen et al. 2009). Given the potential loss of market share, other companies soon followed with comparable reductions, and the price cuts by Philip Morris were eventually made more permanent through a reduction in its wholesale prices in August 1993.

For Philip Morris, this strategy was particularly effective in that it reversed the decline in its overall market share (its share rose by several points by the end of 1994) and in the share of its Marlboro brand (which rose by more than one-third, to 30% of the market, by the end of 1994). At the same time, sales for discount and deep-discount brands across the industry declined, with combined market share for this sector falling by about one-third over the next few years.

The combination of the price cuts for Marlboro and reductions in price for many other cigarettes all but stopped the decline in overall U.S. cigarette sales (Figure 5.2), at least for a few years, while simultaneously contributing to a sharp rise in smoking among youth during the mid-1990s (Figure 5.3) (Grossman and Chaloupka 1997; Gruber and Zinman 2001). Gruber and Zinman (2001), for example, estimated that the "Marlboro Friday" price reductions explained more than one-quarter of the rise in prevalence of smoking among youth observed in the mid-1990s.

The Master Settlement Agreement and Discount Brands

A second wave of price competition followed the industry's settlement of individual lawsuits with Florida, Minnesota, Mississippi, and Texas in 1997 and 1998, and the adoption of the Master Settlement Agreement in November 1998. The settlements with the individual states and the Master Settlement Agreement promoted a sharp rise in cigarette prices between July 1997 and November 1998; these increases were designed to cover the costs of the settlements for the "original participating manufacturers" (OPMs)—Philip Morris, RJR, B&W, and Lorillard—the four leading manufacturers at the time, and the "subsequent participating manufacturers" (SPMs), the other cigarette companies that signed on to the Master Settlement Agreement over time. There are some differences in how OPM and SPM payments are calculated that give SPMs a slight cost advantage, which has helped them gain market share in the years since the agreement was adopted, but the resulting price differences are modest (Chaloupka 2007).

The same has not been true for the price differences between the OPMs/SPMs and the cigarette companies that did not sign on to the agreement—the "non-participating manufacturers" (NPMs). The NPMs are subject to different obligations that have evolved since the agreement was adopted and that have, at least in some states at some times, given them a considerable price advantage over the OPMs and SPMs. The agreement did include provisions to help prevent this, most notably those in Exhibit T, a Model Statute, which called for the settling states to adopt legislation requiring the NPMs to pay an amount equivalent to

Figure 5.2 Cigarette prices and cigarette sales, United States, 1970–2011

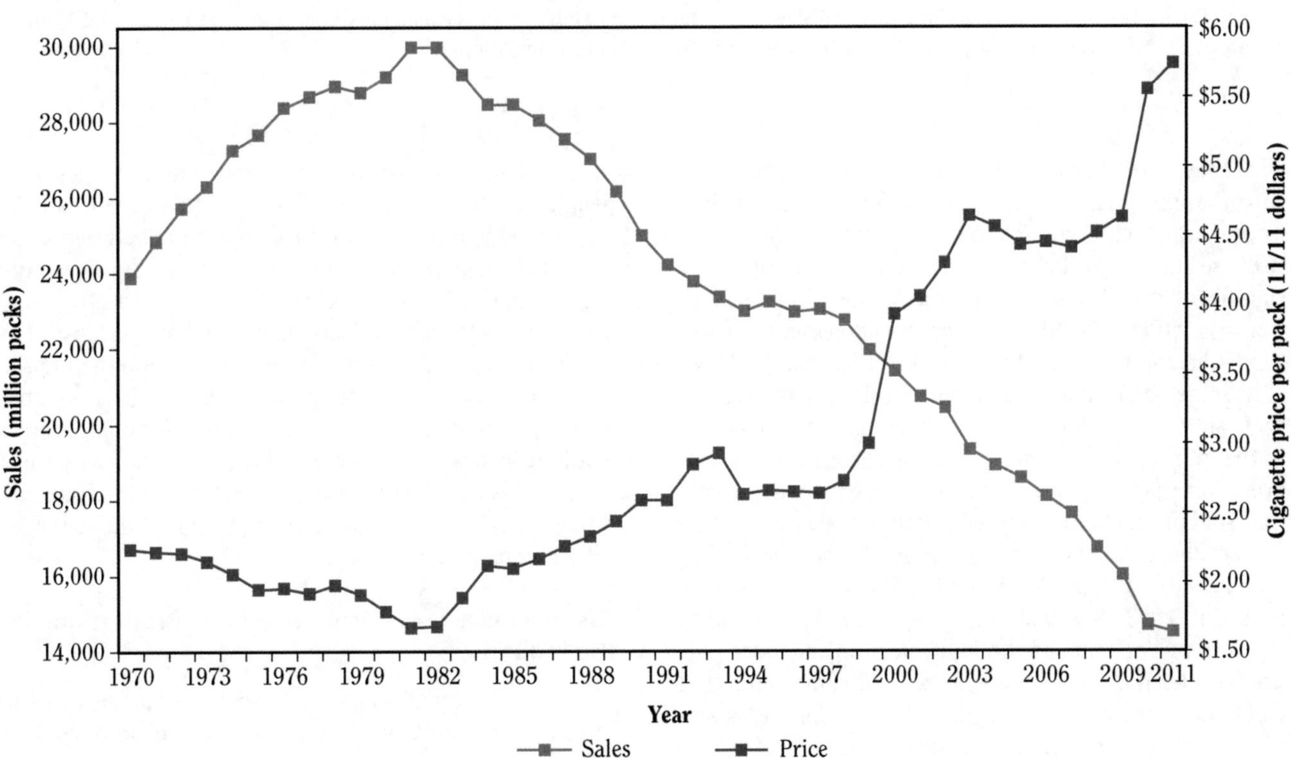

Source: Data from Orzechowski and Walker 2011; author's calculations.

Figure 5.3 Cigarette prices and prevalence of youth smoking by grade in school, United States, 1991–2011

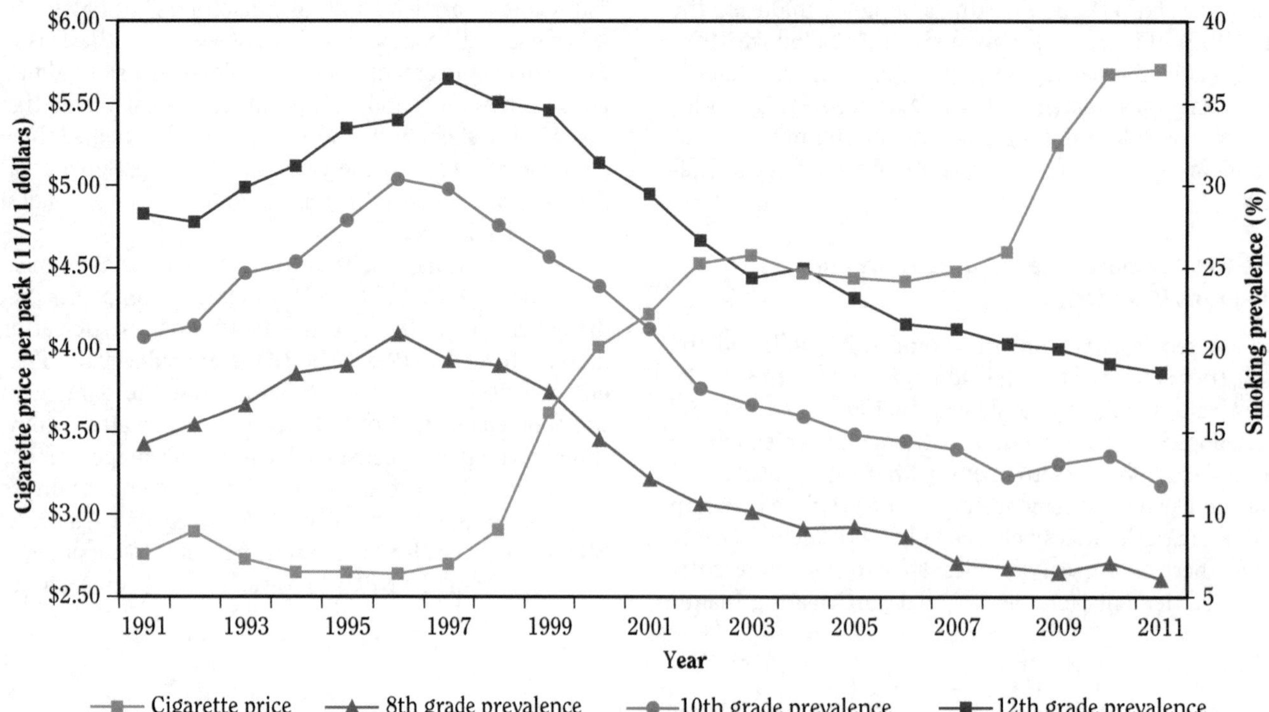

Source: Cigarette prices from Orzechowski and Walker 2011; 30-day smoking prevalence data for students in grades 8, 10, and 12 from Monitoring the Future, University of Michigan News Service 2011; author's calculations.

what they would have paid had they joined the agreement, with these payments held in escrow for 25 years against future health care cost claims made against the NPMs. Because states that did not adopt the model statute faced significant reductions in the payments they would receive from the OPMs and SPMs under the agreement, all settling states quickly adopted this model legislation. However, some NPMs may have taken advantage of the lag and their significantly lower costs, as well as some loopholes in the model statute (notably the "allocable share release" provision that returned most escrow payments to NPMs that sold products in a limited number of states), to gain market share at the expense of the OPMs and SPMs (Chaloupka 2007). The market share for NPMs appears to have peaked in 2003 at almost 10%, however, before declining in more recent years as the loopholes in the model statute have been closed, state enforcement efforts targeting NPMs have been strengthened, and prices for OPMs and SPMs have remained relatively stable (Chaloupka 2007).

In contrast to the increased smoking among youth that followed the "Marlboro Friday" price cuts, the more recent price competition led by the NPM brands appears to have had a limited impact on smoking among young people. As shown in Figure 5.3, the prevalence of smoking among youth has continued to decline between 2002 and 2007, despite the leveling off of cigarette prices during this period. However, given the evidence on the price sensitivity of tobacco use among youth that is discussed in detail in Chapter 6, along with the evidence on the impact of tax increases on prices discussed below, it is possible that the observed reductions in smoking among youth would have been even larger had the price increases from state and federal taxes not been offset at least partially by discounting and other price-related promotions by cigarette companies.

Tax Increases and Pricing and Price Promotions in the Industry

An important element of pricing strategies in the industry, particularly with respect to tobacco control efforts, relates to how prices are raised in response to increases in excise taxes on tobacco products. These strategies have changed over time, in part in response to the negative impact of price increases on smoking among young people. This is underscored by a series of internal documents from the 1980s written by Myron Johnston (a marketing researcher at Philip Morris who focused on smoking among youth) that discuss the doubling of the federal cigarette excise tax in 1983 and an anticipated increase in that tax later that decade. In 1987, in anticipation of a federal tax increase, Johnston recalled the industry's pricing strategy regarding the 1983 doubling of the tax:

> Last time, of course, we increased prices five times between February of 1982 and January of 1983. In less than a year, the price went from $20.20 to $26.90 per thousand ($2.70 more than the tax), and this fact was not lost on consumers, who could legitimately blame the manufacturers for the price increases. While price increases of this magnitude might have been tolerated during the rapid escalation in the overall inflation rate between 1977 and 1981, the increase in the price of cigarettes in 1982–83 was made even more dramatic by the fact that the overall rate of inflation was slowing considerably (Johnston 1987, Bates No. 2022216179/6180, p. 1).

Johnston cited the work by Lewit and colleagues (Lewit et al. 1981; Lewit and Coate 1982) that demonstrated the greater price sensitivity of youth and young adults regarding smoking in concluding that this strategy had a disproportionately negative impact on Philip Morris, given Marlboro brand's large share among young smokers. In anticipation of another increase, Johnston went on to say, "We don't need this to happen again" (Johnston 1987, Bates No. 2022216179/6180, p. 1) and laid out the following strategy:

> I have been asked for my views as to how we should pass on the price increase in the event of an increase in the excise tax. My choice is to do what I suggested to Wally McDowell in 1982: Pass on the increase in one fell swoop and make it clear to smokers that the government is solely responsible for the price increase, advertise to that effect, suggest that people stock up to avoid the price increase, and recommend that they refrigerate their cigarettes 'to preserve their freshness'. ...Then when people exhaust their supply and go to the store to buy more, they will be less likely to remember what they last paid and will be less likely to suffer from "sticker shock." As a result, they should be less likely to use the price increase as an incentive to stop smoking or reduce their consumption (Johnston 1987, Bates No. 2022216179/6180, p. 1).

Although the anticipated late-1980s increase in the federal tax never materialized, the tax was increased incrementally several times in the 1990s and early 2000s. Changes in wholesale prices by Philip Morris (as the industry leader) and other companies (which followed) appear to reflect the adoption of the strategy laid out by Johnston, with prices typically increasing by the amount of the tax increase, with some increases (notably the 5-cent increase in 2002) absorbed by the industry. In general, research demonstrates that state and federal tax increases result in comparable or larger increases in the retail prices for cigarettes (USDHHS 2000).

When retail prices rise following tax increases, companies engage in a variety of price-related marketing efforts that appear to be aimed at softening the impact of the increased prices. According to Chaloupka and colleagues (2002), from their review of internal industry documents, these efforts have included increased distribution of coupons (through print ads, point-of-sale promotions, and direct mailings) and multipack discounts, often coupled with efforts to encourage smokers to express their opposition to an additional tax increase through mail or telephone campaigns targeting state and federal legislators.

A combination of these strategies continues to be used in recent years. For example, in response to the large April 2009 increase (almost 62 cents per pack) in the federal cigarette excise tax, Philip Morris increased prices on leading brands (including Marlboro) by 71 cents per pack while raising prices on other brands by 78 cents per pack. At the same time, it reached out to smokers (at least via e-mail and likely through other channels) with the following message:

> On February 4th, 2009, the Federal Government enacted legislation to fund the expansion of the State Children's Health Insurance Program (SCHIP) that increases excise taxes on cigarettes by 158%. As a result, you will see the price of all cigarettes, including ours, increase in retail stores. We know times are tough, so we'd like to help. We invite you to register at *Marlboro.com* to become eligible for cigarette coupons and special offers using this code: MAR1558 (Auerbach 2009).

Tobacco Control Policies and Programs Versus Pricing and Price Promotions in the Industry

There is some evidence that the industry uses its pricing promotion strategies to respond to tobacco control efforts other than tax increases. For example, in their analysis of annual data from all states for the period from 1960 through 1990, Keeler and colleagues (1996) concluded that the industry engaged in a form of what economists call "price discrimination." Specifically, they found that cigarette prices were lower in states with stronger state and local tobacco control policies, after accounting for differences in taxes, at least in part to offset the impact of these policies on tobacco use. Other researchers have used observational and scanner-based data to describe the increased use of price-reducing promotions following the price increases and marketing limitations resulting from the Master Settlement Agreement in 1998 (Ruel et al. 2004; Loomis et al. 2006); these findings are consistent with the trends in the data on expenditures for cigarette marketing reported by FTC that were described above. Both Slater and colleagues (2001) and Loomis and colleagues (2006) found that the prevalence of price-reducing promotions was greater in states with higher spending on comprehensive tobacco control programs. Similarly, Feighery and colleagues (2008) have documented the increased use of point-of-sale advertising to highlight price-reducing promotions, while Henriksen and colleagues (2004b) have shown more point-of-sale marketing in stores that are frequented more by youth. Given the greater price sensitivity of smoking among young people, this pattern of marketing suggests that the industry's targeted pricing and price-reducing promotion strategies will have their greatest impact on youth and young adults.

Prices, Price Promotions, and Tobacco Use Among Young People

As will be described in more detail in Chapter 6, a growing and increasingly sophisticated body of research has clearly demonstrated that tobacco use among young people is responsive to changes in the prices of tobacco products. Most of these studies have found that usage levels among young people change more in response to price changes than do usage levels among adults. This research includes studies that have looked at the consumption of cigarettes and smokeless tobacco products as well as various stages of cigarette smoking among youth and young adults. Studies that have considered initiation, progression, and/or intensity of use have generally found that price has its greatest impact on youth who are further along in the uptake process, which is consistent with the transition from relying more on social sources for cigarettes to buying one's own cigarettes.

To date, however, few studies have examined the impact of price-reducing promotions on tobacco use among young people, in large part because of the lack of high-quality, geographically disaggregated data on the prevalence and intensity of these promotions over time. Only two studies have considered this issue: one was based on an analysis of internal tobacco company documents (Chaloupka et al. 2002), and the other was based on a combination of observational data on point-of-sale marketing practices and repeated cross-sectional survey data on smoking among youth (Slater et al. 2007).

From their analysis of internal documents, Chaloupka and colleagues (2002) concluded that cigarette companies employ various price-reducing promotions, often in combination with other marketing efforts and with knowledge of the greater price responsiveness of young people, to increase the use of their products. As the authors noted, this strategy was effective for RJR's efforts to promote its Camel brand among young people (particularly young males) during the mid-1980s and early 1990s. For example, one 1986 RJR document states that

> The major factor contributing to CAMEL's dramatic growth among Mid-West 18–24 year old males appears to be the increased level of Mid-West promotional support, and in particular, CAMEL's targeted promotions (which were implemented the same time as the boost in CAMEL's share and completed just prior to the downward trend) (Creighton 1986, Bates No. 505727418/7431, p. 1).

The promotions referred to included "buy three, get three free" ("six pack") discounts, coupons, the "Camel Cash" program, and other retail-value-added strategies. A subsequent report noted that these promotions were necessary to maintain the increase in Camel's market share, describing how Camel's market share among young adult smokers fell by almost 2 percentage points in the more than 1-year period, when this type of promotional support for Camel was reduced. The report stated:

> While "Old Joe" might be able to generate growth by imagery alone, the above patterns suggest that retail pack programs play an important role in maintaining loyalty among the brand's YAS [young adult smokers] franchise during this key stage in brand choice, as well as in generating trial [*sic*] which could stimulate further growth momentum. Thus, reducing CAMEL's pack presence would likely jeopardize the brand's ability to sustain the rate of YAS growth achieved in 1988 (RJR 1989, Bates No. 507533523/3535, p. 6).

This report suggests that the combination of imagery (Joe Camel) and price reductions contributed significantly to the growth in Camel's market share among adolescents and young adults in the late 1980s and early 1990s.

More recently, Slater and colleagues (2007) combined novel data on point-of-sale cigarette marketing collected in the Bridging the Gap project with MTF data on smoking among youth to assess the impact of price-reducing promotions and advertising at the point of sale on uptake of smoking among youth. Data on point-of-sale marketing practices were collected from 17,746 stores in 966 communities from 1999 to 2003; these communities reflected the location of the student population for the second-year half-sample of the 8th-, 10th-, and 12th-grade schools participating in the MTF study during these years. Data on cigarette marketing practices included in-store, exterior, and parking lot measures of advertising; the presence of low-height advertising and functional objects (defined as branded objects that have some use, such as clocks, trash cans, and grocery baskets); the presence of price-reducing and other promotions (cents-off specials, on-pack coupons, multipack discounts, and noncigarette retail-value-added promotions) for the Marlboro and Newport brands; prices for Marlboros and Newports; and product placement (self-service vs. clerk assisted). Marlboro and Newport were selected because of their popularity among young people. Indices reflecting the extent of advertising and promotion in stores located in communities near an MTF survey school were constructed from the store-level data. The measure on smoking initiation was constructed from MTF survey data on current and past smoking behavior and future smoking intentions, as described and validated by Wakefield and colleagues (2004). To fit the available data, this measure was constructed for 26,301 students and reflected six stages of uptake: never smoker; puffer (someone who has smoked once or twice, but not regularly); nonrecent experimenter (someone who has smoked occasionally but not in the 30 days before the survey); former established smoker (someone who has smoked regularly but not in the 30 days before the survey); recent experimenter (someone who has smoked occasionally, but not regularly, in the 30 days before the survey); and current established smoker (someone who has smoked regularly in the 30 days before the survey).

Using statistical methods on models that controlled for students' demographic and socioeconomic characteristics, other tobacco control policies, and other factors, and that accounted for clustering at the community level, Slater and colleagues (2007) found that cigarette marketing has a significant impact on the initiation of smoking among youth. Specifically, they found that an increased prevalence of point-of-sale advertising was associated with a significant increase in the likelihood of progressing from never smoking to experimentation (puffing), with the magnitude of the association falling and becoming insignificant for later stages of intake. In addition, and in contrast to this previous finding, they found a significant association between the prevalence of price-reducing and other promotions and later stages of smoking progression, with the magnitude of the effect and its significance increasing at these later stages. Similarly, Slater and associates (2007) found a significant inverse association between cigarette prices and smoking initiation among youth, with the size and significance of the effect consistent across the different stages of uptake (with the exception that the association for the transition from never smoking to experimentation was not significant). The findings that price and price-reducing promotions have a greater impact as youth progress to established smoking are consistent with those described in more detail in Chapter 6. Given these estimates, Slater and colleagues (2007) performed various simulations to assess quantitatively the impact of point-of-sale advertising and promotions on uptake among youth. They estimated that if none of the stores they observed had cigarette advertising, the prevalence of never smoking in their sample would have been about 9% higher. Similarly, they estimated that if no stores had cigarette promotions, the prevalence of current established smoking in their sample would have been more than 13% lower.

Summary

Tobacco companies have several options for altering the prices of their products, ranging from directly changing the wholesale prices to engaging in a variety of price-reducing promotions such as couponing, multipack discounts, and price discounts. A company that directly changes its prices will have a relatively broad impact, affecting a range of brands, and typically will be matched by other companies (particularly when the price change is made by the industry leader). In contrast, the use of price-reducing promotions can be more targeted, with promotions limited to particular brands, geographic regions, venues, or populations.

Historically, price changes in the industry have usually reflected changes in costs, including increases in federal taxes and costs associated with litigation-related decisions and settlements, resulting in relatively limited price competition. In contrast, there has been a considerable increase over time in the industry's use of price-reducing promotions. As Chaloupka (2004) described, the increased use of price-reducing promotions appears to have followed the early econometric research demonstrating that smoking among young people is more responsive to price than is smoking among adults, and this strategy accelerated following the Master Settlement Agreement's constraints on other marketing activities. Internal industry documents show clearly that cigarette companies were paying close attention to the early econometric studies, that the findings from these studies were consistent with the industry's internal research, and that this knowledge informed their use of price-reducing promotions (Chaloupka et al. 2002). In considering the numerous studies demonstrating that tobacco use among young people is responsive to changes in the prices of tobacco products, it can be concluded that the industry's extensive use of price-reducing promotions has led to higher rates of tobacco use among young people than would have occurred in the absence of these promotions.

Influence of the Tobacco Industry on Tobacco Use Among Youth: The Packaging of Tobacco Products

Background

Packaging is an integral component of the overall marketing strategy for consumer goods (Slade 1997; Underwood and Ozanne 1998; Shapiro et al. 1999; Palmer 2000; Pollay 2001; Wakefield et al. 2002a; Dewhirst 2004; FTC 2011a). It is particularly important for products such as cigarettes, which have a high degree of social visibility. Unlike many other consumer products, cigarettes are contained in packages that are displayed each time the product is used and are often left in public view between uses (Pollay 2001; Wakefield et al. 2002a). Cigarette packages also serve as a "badge" product. As John Digianni, a former designer of cigarette packages, noted, "A cigarette package is unique because the consumer carries it around with him all day.... It's a part of a smoker's clothing, and when he saunters into a bar and plunks it down, he makes a statement about himself" (Koten 1980, p. 22).

Tobacco Packaging and Brand Appeal

Tobacco packaging seeks to achieve the same general objective as other forms of marketing: to establish brand identity and to promote brand appeal. Research conducted by the tobacco industry consistently demonstrates that the brand imagery portrayed on packages is particularly influential during youth and young adulthood—the period in which smoking behavior and brand preferences develop (DiFranza et al. 1994; Pollay 2000, 2001; Wakefield et al. 2002a). In many cases, initial brand preferences are based less on the sensory properties of using the product than on perceptions of the package and brand: "one of every two smokers is not able to distinguish in blind (masked) tests between similar cigarettes....for most smokers and for the decisive group of new, younger smokers, the consumer's choice is dictated more by psychological, image factors than by relatively minor differences in smoking characteristics" (British American Tobacco [BAT], n.d., Bates No. 500062147/2159, p. 5). The brand imagery on cigarette packages is effective to the point that large majorities of youth—including nonsmoking youth—demonstrate high levels of recall for leading package designs (Goldberg et al. 1995; Pierce et al. 2010).

Historically, a package's color has also helped to segment brands and establish brand identity. For example, silver and gold colors can be used to convey status and prestige, particularly for "premium" brands (Pollay 2001). Red packages and logos can convey excitement, strength, wealth, and power (Gordon et al. 1994; Kindra et al. 1994), while pastel colors are associated with freshness, innocence, and relaxation and are more common among brands that appeal to females (see example above) (Gordon et al. 1994; Kindra et al. 1994).

Brand descriptors—words that appear on packs and are often incorporated into the brand name—can also promote brand appeal among target groups. For example, "slims" descriptors on packs promote beliefs about smoking and weight control—an important factor in smoking behavior among young women (USDHHS 2001; Carpenter et al. 2005a). In Canada, research conducted among young women and published in 2010 demonstrated that "slims" brand descriptors are associated with increased brand appeal and stronger beliefs that smoking is associated with thinness (Doxey and Hammond 2010). Other brand names also capitalize on desirable associations with female fashion and sophistication, including names such as Glamour and Vogue.

Similarly, packaging of smokeless tobacco products can communicate the strength of the product or its brand identity. Internal research conducted for U.S. Smokeless Tobacco revealed that smokeless tobacco users widely associated plastic containers with fruit flavors and youthful beginners. The cardboard/pasteboard and metal can packaging was associated with experienced users. Plastic packaging would have solved some of the problems with the smokeless product (retaining moisture, and freshness), but it was not a viable option for experienced Copenhagen users because the "beginner" perception relating to plastic packaging was so strong (B&W 1984).

Packaging and the Perception of Risk

Tobacco companies have made extensive use of cigarette packages to influence consumer perceptions about the potential risks of their products. A central feature of this strategy has been to use misleading brand descriptors. Words such as "light" and "mild" were ostensibly used in the past to denote flavor and taste, but "light" and "mild" brands were promoted in advertisements as "less harmful" (Pollay and Dewhirst 2001; Wakefield et al. 2002a). "Light" and "mild" descriptors were also applied to brands with higher levels of filter ventilation—small holes in cigarette filters (NCI 2001). Not only does filter ventilation dilute cigarette smoke to produce deceptively low tar and nicotine numbers under machine testing (NCI 2001; Kozlowski and O'Connor 2002), but it also produces "lighter tasting" smoke, which reinforces the misleading descriptors on packages. As a result, considerable proportions of adult smokers believed that "light," "mild," and "low tar" cigarette brands lowered health risk and were less addictive than "regular" or "full flavor" brands (Pollay and Dewhirst 2001). Indeed, many health-concerned smokers reported switching to these brands as an alternative to quitting (Gilpin et al. 2002). "Light" and "mild" descriptors may have also promoted the initiation of smoking among youth; one study found that U.S. youth believed that "light" and "mild" brands had lower health risks and lower levels of addiction than "regular" brand varieties, beliefs similar to those of adults (Kropp and Halpern-Felsher 2004). Similar findings were produced from an Australian study conducted in 2005 with secondary school students aged 13–15 years of age (Hoek et al. 2006). In the study, an estimated 50% of the students agreed that "light" cigarettes contain less tar than regular cigarettes, 40% believed that "light" cigarettes were less harmful, and approximately 30% believed that "light" cigarettes are easier to quit than regular cigarettes. Overall, the synergistic but subtle effect of brand descriptors, lower emission numbers, and "lighter" tasting smoke have undermined perceptions of health risk among smokers.

The *Family Smoking Prevention and Tobacco Control Act* (2009) now prohibit the descriptors "light," "mild," or "low" or similar descriptors in tobacco product label, labeling, or advertising unless an FDA order is in effect under the modified risk provisions of the statute. This restriction follows a U.S. Federal District Court ruling in 2006 that the terms "low tar," "light," "ultra light" and "mild" are deceptive (*United States. v. Philip Morris USA*, 449 F. Supp. 2d 1, 32 [D.D.C. 2006]). To date, more than 50 other countries have prohibited the terms "light," "mild," and "low tar" as part of prohibitions on misleading packaging under Article 11 of the World Health Organization (WHO) Framework Convention on Tobacco Control (FCTC) (Hammond 2009b). However, recent research conducted in Australia, Canada, and the United Kingdom, suggests that prohibiting "light" and "mild" terms may be insufficient to significantly reduce false beliefs about the risks of different cigarette brands (Borland et al. 2008). Indeed, recent evidence suggests that significant proportions of adult smokers and youth in countries such as the United Kingdom continue to report false beliefs about the relative risk of leading cigarette brands (Hammond et al. 2009).

One potential explanation for these findings is the wide range of other descriptors that remain in use, including words such as "smooth" and color descriptors such as "silver" and "blue" (Hammond 2009a). Studies conducted in Canada and the United Kingdom after the removal of "light" and "mild" descriptors suggest that replacement words such as "smooth" have the same misleading effect as "light" and "mild"; as many as one-half of adults and youth in these studies reported that a brand labeled "smooth" would have lower risk than its "regular" counterpart (Hammond and Parkinson 2009; Hammond et al. 2009). In the United States, the names of colors are among the most common replacement descriptors for the terms "light" and "mild." For example, major brands, such as Marlboro, have used "gold" and "silver" to replace "light" and "ultralight," respectively. This same approach has been used by manufacturers in Canada, the European Union, and in other jurisdictions that have prohibited "light" and "mild" descriptors. From three recent studies that examined consumers' perceptions of color descriptors in Canada, the United Kingdom, and the United States (Hammond and Parkinson 2009; Hammond et al. 2009; Bansal-Travers and Hammond 2010), it appears that consumers perceive the color descriptors in the same way as the "light" and "mild" descriptors they replaced. For example, in one study more than three-quarters of U.S. adults surveyed indicated that a brand labeled as "silver" would have lower levels of tar and less health risk than a "full flavor" brand (Bansal-Travers and Hammond 2010).

The persistence of false beliefs regarding level of risk may also be due to brand imagery and the color of packs (Pollay 2001; Wakefield et al. 2002a). Tobacco industry documents describe this phenomenon: "Lower delivery products tend to be featured in blue packs. Indeed, as one moves down the delivery sector, then the closer to white a pack tends to become. This is because white is generally held to convey a clean healthy association" (Miller 1986, Bates No. 105364841/4951, p. 2). Changing the shade of the same color and adjusting the proportion of white space on the package are commonly used to influence perceptions of a product's strength and potential risk. Indeed, a number of industry studies have shown that the color and design of the package actually influence sensory perceptions from smoking a cigarette, a process known as "sensory transfer" (Wakefield et al. 2002a). For example, when consumers smoke cigarettes placed in lighter-colored packs, they may perceive these cigarettes to taste "lighter" and less harsh than the identical cigarettes placed in darker-colored packs.

The colors of the packages and the brand descriptors they carry have also been closely integrated with the design of the cigarette. Although terms such as "light" and "mild" may have been arbitrary, they were typically applied to brands with greater filter ventilation. Package descriptors and the designs of the cigarettes reinforce the "lighter" taste of these brands and the lower tar numbers in ways that promote the belief that they are less harmful, despite evidence to the contrary (NCI 2001).

Plain (or Standardized) Packaging

Research on the removal of brand imagery on packages—so-called plain packaging—provides another source of evidence on the impact of brand appeal among youth (Freeman et al. 2007). Under a requirement for plain packaging, the appearance of cigarette packages would be standardized through the removal of all brand imagery, including corporate logos and trademarks (see example at right). Packages would display a standard background color, and manufacturers would be permitted to print only the brand name in a mandated size, font, and position. Other government-mandated information, such as health warnings, would remain.

Plain packaging has several potential effects. First, it enhances the effectiveness of health warnings by increasing their noticeability, recall, and believability (Beede and Lawson 1992; Goldberg et al. 1995, 1999; Hammond 2009a; Hammond et al. 2009). For example, in one study, New Zealand youth were significantly more likely to recall health warnings on plain packs than warnings on "normal" branded packages (Beede and Lawson 1992).

Second, plain packaging has the potential to reduce the level of false beliefs about the harmfulness of different brands. Recent research suggests that substantial proportions of youth and adults hold false beliefs that one brand is less harmful or easier to quit than another (Hammond and Parkinson 2009; Hammond et al. 2009). A 2009 study conducted among adult smokers and youth (both smokers and nonsmokers) in the United Kingdom found that when asked to compare varieties of cigarettes from eight different brands, 75% of participants falsely reported differences in risk between at least two of the varieties (Hammond et al. 2009). Removing the color and brand imagery from packages significantly reduced these beliefs. Plain packaging has also been shown to reduce beliefs about the link between smoking and weight control. In a 2010 study conducted among young women in Canada, women who viewed eight female-oriented packs with colors, such as pink, were significantly more likely to report that smoking "helps people stay slim" than women who viewed "plain" versions of the same packs (Doxey and Hammond 2010).

Third, plain packaging makes smoking less appealing. Research to date suggests that plain packages are less attractive and engaging than normal "branded" packs and may reduce the appeal of smoking among both youth and adults (Trachtenberg 1987; Northrup and Pollard 1995; Rootman and Flay 1995; Hammond et al. 2009; Germain et al. 2010). For example, a survey of Canadian youth found that strong majorities "liked" regular packages better than plain packages and indicated that plain packages are "boring" and "uglier" than regular packages (Northrup and Pollard 1995). About one-third of respondents also reported that people their age would be less likely to start smoking if all cigarettes were sold in plain packages. A similar study of Canadian and U.S. youth found that plain packages reduced positive associations with packages and were associated with more negative associations, such as "boring" (Rootman and Flay 1995). More recent research conducted with adult smokers in Australia found that

> cardboard brown packs with the number of enclosed cigarettes displayed on the front of the pack and featuring only the brand name in small standard font at the bottom of the pack face were rated as significantly less attractive and popular than original branded packs. Smokers of these plain packs were rated as significantly less trendy/stylish, less sociable/outgoing, and less mature than smokers of the original pack (Wakefield et al. 2008, p. 416).

Similar results have emerged from a study of youth and adults in the United Kingdom (Hammond et al. 2009). Marketing research conducted on behalf of the tobacco industry with adult smokers also suggests that plain packaging reduces some of the appeal of smoking, as the following quote indicates:

> ...when we offered them Marlboros at half price—in generic brown boxes—only 21% were interested, even though we assured them that each package was fresh, had been sealed at the factory and was identical (except for the different packaging) to what they normally bought at their local tobacconist or cigarette machine. How to account for the difference? Simple. Smokers put their cigarettes in and out of their pockets 20 to 25 times a day. The package makes a statement. The consumer is expressing how he wants to be seen by others (Trachtenberg 1987, Bates No. TA985253/5256, p. 3).

Together, these findings suggest that removing the color and brand imagery from packages reduces the appeal of cigarettes and may reduce their consumption. The position of tobacco companies on regulatory proposals to remove brand imagery also speaks to the importance of brand imagery. In 2008, Citi Investment Research noted,

> In the medium-term, we think plain packaging would go a long way to undermine the power of tobacco brands and it is the brands that make the industry so profitable. In our view, in cigarettes, the pack is the brand. Smokers handle their cigarette packs probably 20 times a day. Consumers pay a premium for certain brands for several reasons, but most would be undermined by plain packaging (Citi Investment Research 2008, p. 2).

Package Shape and Size

An additional component of mandated plain packaging could include regulations to standardize the shape and size of packages. Tobacco manufacturers have released numerous "special edition" packages, many of which have novel shapes and can open in different ways (Neuber 2009). Novel shapes and sizes may increase the appeal of cigarette brands and might be particularly engaging to youth. In particular, "slim" packages used to market female brands—such as the "purse" pack shown at right—may promote the widespread belief that smoking is an effective way to stay thin and control weight, an important predictor of tobacco use among girls (USDHHS 2001; Carpenter et al. 2005a; Doxey and Hammond 2010). Different shapes and sizes also have the potential to undermine the health warnings on packages. In some cases, the packages are so small and narrow that they either warp the pictures delivering the health warnings or render the text so small as to be unreadable.

Packaging shape may also be a useful marketing tool for smokeless products. The traditional smokeless product has been associated with a round can, but new smokeless tobacco products aimed at expanding the market beyond traditional users have been packaged in containers featuring a wide variety of shapes and sizes. Ariva, Revel, and the snus products have all used different packaging, perhaps to signal that they are not traditional tobacco products and that they are for different users (more urban, female, etc.) (Mejia and Ling 2010).

Tobacco Packaging and Other Forms of Marketing

Cigarette packages serve as both a form of advertising and a link to other forms of tobacco marketing (Wakefield and Letcher 2002). As described elsewhere in this chapter, packages play a central role in point-of-sale marketing (Donovan et al. 2002; Wakefield et al. 2002b). Displays of packages in retail outlets, commonly referred to as "powerwalls," have high visibility among youth and help to establish brand imagery and social norms at an early age (Wakefield et al. 2002b; Dewhirst 2004, 2009; Pollay 2007). Packages can also be used to increase the reach of "below the line" marketing activities by incorporating references to specific promotional activities through limited-edition packs and plastic overwrapping. Recent examples include packages that promote the Formula 1 racing series, advertise Benson & Hedges Kool MIXX music promotions, and promote various events at nightclubs—all of which have considerable appeal among youth and young adults (Sepe et al. 2002; Carter 2003a; Hafez and Ling 2006) (see examples at right and below). In some cases, this information is printed directly on packs; in others, it is included as an "insert" or "onsert," both of which extend the surface area of the pack. On the basis of evidence in his study, Pollay noted, "The package is the last and most critical link in an integrated chain of promotional communications" (2001, p. 3). Since the *Family Smoking Prevention and Tobacco Control Act* became law in 2009, manufacturers, distributors, and retailers are in most instances prohibited from sponsoring any athletic event, musical, artistic, or other social or cultural events, using the brand name, logo, symbol, mottos, selling message, recognizable color, or pattern of colors of any brand cigarettes or smokeless tobacco. However, firms are permitted to sponsor such events in the name of their corporation, which manufactures the tobacco product (*21 CFR 1140.34(c)*).

Clearly, the package assumes even greater importance when other forms of cigarette marketing are restricted. Package displays in retail outlets typically become more prominent following advertising bans as part of a general increase in point-of-sale marketing (Celebucki and Diskin 2002; Wakefield et al. 2002c; Hammond 2006; Canadian Cancer Society 2008). Indeed, advertising bans have prompted many companies to redesign their packages to maximize their impact at the point of sale. Research on pack design conducted in 1994 for BAT stated, "... given the consequences of a total ban on advertising, a pack should be designed to give the product visual impact as well as brand imagery.... The pack itself can be designed so that it achieves more visual impact in the point of sale environment than its competitors" (Miller 1986, Bates No. 105364841/4951, p. 18). Packages are poised to play an even greater role with the advent of point-of-sale marketing bans, already implemented in countries such as Canada, Iceland, and Thailand. In the 1990s, Philip Morris executives remarked upon this eventuality: "Our final communication vehicle with our smoker is the pack itself. In the absence of any other Marketing messages, our packaging...is the sole communicator of our brand essence. Put another way -- when you don't have anything else -- our packaging is our marketing" (Hulit 1994, Bates No. 2504015017/5042, p. 22).

Packaging strategies can also be used to offset the impact of other tobacco control measures, such as increases in price and taxation. For example, internal tobacco industry documents indicate that packaging cigarettes into smaller, more affordable units (such as 10 cigarettes per package rather than 20) is an effective strategy for targeting price-sensitive youth (Cummings et al. 2002). Legislation in many countries, including the United States, now prohibits the sale of cigarettes in units less than 20; however, innovations in the physical shape and construction of packages (see example)—such as BAT's "wallet packs," which open like a book and can be separated into two smaller packages—have been criticized as an attempt to circumvent these prohibitions.

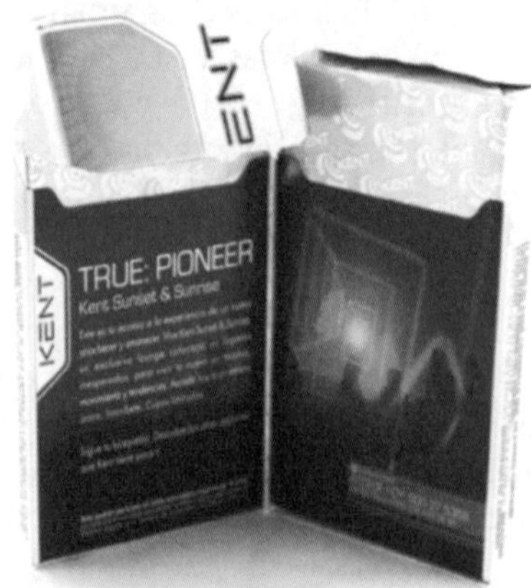

BAT's wallet packs were banned in Australia after the federal court in that country upheld an injunction against their sale (see picture previous page) (Chapman 2007). Tobacco companies have also explored packaging strategies to minimize the impact of health warnings, including changes in package design to make warnings less distinctive as well as the sale of alternate cases and covers that obscure warnings (Pollay 2001; Wilson et al. 2006). According to later research, further innovation in tobacco packaging is on the horizon: "Advances in printing technology have enabled printing of on-pack imagery on the inner frame card, outer film and tear tape, and the incorporation of holograms, collectable art, metallic finishes, multi-fold stickers, photographs, and images in pack design" (Freeman et al. 2007, p. 10).

Summary

Tobacco packaging provides a direct link to consumers as well as a highly visible form of marketing. In addition to establishing brand identity and appeal, packaging helps to shape perceptions of risk and the sensory experience of smoking. Packaging is influential during youth and young adulthood, the period in which smoking behavior and brand preferences develop. Packaging strategies will continue to evolve in response to restrictions on advertising and promotion as well as the issuance of labeling regulations that mandate larger health warnings and prohibit information deemed to be misleading or deceptive. As the exposure of youth to other forms of marketing becomes increasingly restricted, packaging will assume greater importance as a promotional tool.

The Influence of the Design of Tobacco Products on the Use of Tobacco by Young People

Designing Cigarettes for the Youth Market

Tobacco manufacturers have long recognized through their market research that certain brand features of cigarettes have greater appeal to beginning smokers than to established smokers (Cummings et al. 2002). An analysis of successful first-brand (the brand that is usually or mostly smoked by new smokers) strategies with young, presumably youth smokers, conducted by RJR, attributed Pall Mall's success in the 1940s and 1950s to the brand's promise of mildness that was conveyed by its longer length (Burrows 1984). Similarly, the success of Winston cigarettes with young smokers in the 1950s and 1960s was attributed to increasing awareness of the health effects of smoking, which helped create the demand for filtered cigarettes (Burrows 1984). In the late 1950s, cigarette manufacturers recognized that brands featuring filters were the most popular among young beginning smokers, as illustrated by internal company documents and shifting patterns in the cigarette brands popular with youth smokers between the 1953 and 1964 surveys (Danker 1959; Sugg 1959, 1964; William Esty Company 1964; Burrows 1984). A 1959 Philip Morris market research analysis concluded that "people want mildness....We also should win more young nonsmokers with mildness" (Danker 1959, Bates No. 1001755243/5244, p. 1).

Creating a Product That Eases Initiation from Harsh Smoke and Nicotine Exposure

Nicotine is one of the harshest chemicals in tobacco smoke and the most important factor in tobacco dependence (Star Scientific, Inc. 2011a). Nicotine is usually highly aversive for first-time users, yet gradual exposure to the drug is the basis for developing dependence. Through trial, experimentation, and finally conversion to regular smoking, tolerance for nicotine develops (Carchman and Southwick 1990; Philip Morris USA 2002; Monell Chemical Senses Center 2003; Kreslake et al. 2008b; Connolly et al. 2011). To enhance initiation, it is important that a product balances the innate harshness of smoke with masking agents that allow inhalation. This can be done by affecting perceptions of potential harm via the stimulation of chemosensory neurons in the head and neck—features that affect the tactile, olfactory, and gustatory perceptions in a first-time user (Perfetti et al. 1984; Harji and Irwin 1992). Such receptors can be affected by stimulating cold receptors via menthol flavoring via the maillard browning process (a form of nonenzymatic browning similar to carmelization), and design features such as increased ventilation (Aulbach et al. 1991; NCI 2001; Peier et al. 2002). Since the first truly blended American cigarette emerged in 1917 with the Camel brand, the cigarette has gone through a continued evolution to enhance the ability to optimize nicotine dosing both for initiation and maintenance of smoking (Carchman and Southwick 1990; RJR 1991).

In the 1960s, Philip Morris' Marlboro brand began to attract an increasing share of smokers, especially young males. A review of internal documents of the tobacco industry by Stevenson and Proctor (2008) recounts how Philip Morris scientists began experimenting with additives in their brands, including ammonia, diammonium phosphate, and various ethanolamines and carbonates, to improve the flavor of the smoke and enhance its smoothness.

By the mid-1970s, the Marlboro brand had become the dominant youth cigarette, and the other tobacco companies began to focus efforts on competing directly with Marlboro for market share (RJR 1974; Monahan 1977; BAT 1985). One of the strengths of Marlboro over Winston among young smokers was the perception that Marlboro was both smoother than Winston and less strong (Crayton 1971; Teague 1973b; Bernasek and Nystrom 1982; Burrows 1984; Stevenson and Proctor 2008).

In 1971, Philip Morris introduced Marlboro Lights with a ventilated filter to appeal to female smokers who desired a Marlboro blended cigarette that was perceived as less strong (Tindall 1984). By the early 1980s, Marlboro Lights had become the preferred brand among younger female smokers and had gained an increasing share of male smokers. As of 2005, it was the best-selling brand overall in the U.S. market and especially popular among adolescents (O'Connor 2005).

The success of Marlboro did not go unnoticed by competitors. For example, in 1981, RJR stated that Philip Morris had begun routinely using ammoniated reconstituted tobacco sheet in its cigarette brands in 1965, a time that corresponded to an increase in sales for Philip Morris brands, especially Marlboro (Philip Morris 1965; RJR 1981). The RJR report noted that its own market studies had shown better consumer response to brands using ammoniated tobacco sheet in the tobacco blend (Teague 1973a). The ammoniated products produced smoke perceived by consumers as being milder and smoother tasting, with positive flavor characteristics and a stronger physiological impact (Teague 1973b). Reynolds' scientists speculated that ammonia might improve the flavor of tobacco smoke by reacting with sugars to produce potentially flavorful compounds such as pyrazines (Rodgman 1982).

Internal documents reveal that the Marlboro cigarette's smoke, in comparison with RJR's own Winston brand, had a higher pH (higher alkalinity) and hence increased amounts of free nicotine in the smoke and a higher immediate nicotine kick, less irritation of the mouth, less of a "stemmy" taste and less Turkish and flue-cured flavor, and increased burley flavor and character (Crayton 1971; Teague 1973a). Reynolds' scientists noted that competitors' cigarette brands with rising sales, namely Kool and Marlboro, were using reconstituted tobacco sheet in their tobacco blend (Crayton 1971; Moore 1973; RJR 1973, 1981; Casey and Perfetti 1980; Bernasek and Nystrom 1982).

The steady growth of Marlboro, which came largely at the expense of declining sales for Winston, was cause for great concern within RJR management (RJR 1974; Monahan 1977). A 1973 report authored by RJR scientist Claude E. Teague, Jr., noted the importance of product features in successfully capturing a share of the youth smoking market:

> "...if our Company is to survive and prosper, over the long term, we must get our share of the youth market. In my opinion this will require new brands tailored to the youth market; I believe it unrealistic to expect that existing brands identified with an over-thirty 'establishment' market can ever become the 'in' products.... Thus we need new brands designed to be particularly attractive to the young smoker, while ideally at the same time being appealing to all smokers" (Teague 1973b, Bates No. 502987357/7368, p. 2).

Teague identified the following specific characteristics to be used in developing new brands tailored to the youth market: (1) nicotine level of 1.0–1.3 milligrams (mg) per cigarette, (2) pH level of the smoke delivered at a level (5.8 to 6.0) to ensure slow absorption of nicotine, (3) tar content of 12–14 mg per cigarette to achieve the desired taste and visible smoke, (4) bland smoke to address the low tolerance of the beginning smoker for irritation from the smoke, (5) 100-millimeter (mm) length to facilitate lighting, and (6) a reasonably firm rod (the barrel of the cigarette) (Teague 1973b).

A summary of a 1974 meeting of RJR senior scientists discussed cigarettes for beginning smokers, noting that such a cigarette should be "low in irritation and possibly contain added flavors to make it easier for those who never smoked before to acquire the taste for it more quickly" (Donati 1974, Bates No. 508454171/4174, p. 1). In that year, RJR began using ammoniated sheet material in its Camel Filter cigarettes; this material was added to Winston Kings in 1979. Later internal documents from RJR noted increased sales performance for both of these brands associated with the use of ammoniated reconstituted tobacco sheet (Casey and Perfetti 1980; RJR 1981; Bernasek and Nystrom 1982).

According to internal industry documents, Camel's success among young smokers in the late 1980s and 1990s was, in addition to marketing methods, the result of changes in product design to make the brand as attractive as Marlboro by creating a smoother and less harsh cigarette (Cohen 1984; Wayne and Connolly 2002). According to Wayne and Connolly (2002), RJR scientists experimented by using different blends in the front and the end of the cigarette; a puffed tobacco filler (involves a process of puffing leaves); new reconstituted tobacco blends using diammonium phosphate; new humectants (Hystar) to replace glycerin; new flavor additives combining chocolate, vanillin, and licorice at levels below what is traditionally viewed as characterization for food; changes in the circumference and density of tobacco in the rod; and the use of carbowax in the filters to alter sensations in the mouth and the perception of harshness. First-time young adult male smokers were the target group, and the term "smooth" became the main advertising theme for the brand. The use of a cartoon character of a camel called the "Smooth Character" emphasized "smoking pleasure," "smooth taste," and "less harshness." In this case, the design of the cigarette was intentional and interrelated to its marketing (Wayne and Connolly 2002).

Menthol and Other Flavor Additives

The demand for cigarettes that could provide a less harsh taste contributed to the growth of menthol cigarettes in the 1960s and 1970s (Kreslake et al. 2008a,b). By 1974, two menthol brands, Kool and Salem, were the second and third most popular brands among youth smokers (Cummings et al. 2005). Another menthol brand, Newport, was repositioned by Lorillard in the early 1970s by intentionally lowering menthol levels, which smoothed the smoke through action on thermal receptors and did not create aversive effects for new smokers from the high levels that would stimulate pain or nociceptors (Kreslake et al. 2008a).

As a milder, hipper version of Kool cigarettes, by the mid-1980s, Newport had captured a large share of the youth market (Achey 1978; Lorillard 1993a). Since then, Newport has continued to be the preferred brand of cigarettes smoked by African American youth and, overall, is the second most popular brand among adolescent smokers today (O'Connor 2005). When RJR introduced the Uptown brand in Philadelphia in the late 1980s targeting young Blacks, it provided lower levels of menthol similar to Newport (Dagnoli 1989).

Tobacco companies have long known of menthol's ability to mask harshness associated with cigarette smoke, increase the ease of smoking, and provide a cooling sensation that appeals to many smokers, particularly new smokers (Garten and Falkner 2003; Wayne and Connolly 2004; Klausner 2011; Lee and Glantz 2011). First created in 1925, menthol cigarettes were not developed specifically to appeal to youth, but by the mid-1970s tobacco industry market research began to find that they were popular among young smokers because they were perceived as less harsh and easier to smoke (Kreslake et al. 2008a; Klausner 2011; Lee and Glantz 2011). Beginning in the 1970s, tobacco companies investigated the effects of adding different amounts of menthol to cigarettes (Klausner 2011). Kreslake and colleagues (2008a) and Klausner (2011) have shown that the industry adjusted the level of menthol in cigarettes to appeal to younger smokers. For example, in 1986 an RJR document observed:

> ...once a smoker adapts to smoking a menthol product, the desire for menthol increases over time. A brand which has a strategy of maximizing franchise acceptance will invariably increase its menthol level. Thus, once a brand becomes successful, its product will evolve in a manner that is not optimal for younger adult nonmenthol smokers/switchers (RJR 1986b, Bates No. 505938058/8063, p. 2).

In 1987, a B&W document noted:

> Switching data ... clearly show that KOOL KS [king size] and 100 are not attracting their fair share of starters. Newport, on the other hand, is performing above its fair share. ...one basic product difference exists which can possibly explain part of the reason for KOOL's disparity among *starters*. Basically, it is that KOOL's menthol level is too high for *starters* [emphasis added] (Cantrell 1987, Bates No. 621079918/9921, p. 1).

By the late 1980s, all the cigarette manufacturers with major menthol cigarette brands had introduced low-level menthol varieties (Kreslake et al. 2008b). By the 1990s, Lorillard's Newport was the most successful menthol brand and was marketed with a youthful and fun campaign that often depicted young adults engaging in childlike, silly activities (Sutton and Robinson 2004). Again following Newport's successful lead in the youth and young adult markets, other companies, including RJR with its Salem menthol brand, copied the depiction of young people in their marketing materials (Klausner 2011). In 2008, Reynolds American introduced Camel Crush, a flavored extension of the Camel line. Packaged in a visually striking black and blue box, Camel Crush is a regular Camel cigarette (formerly marketed as Camel Light) with a tiny blue capsule inside its filter (Figure 5.4).

Figure 5.4 Camel crush package and filter flavor pellet

Source: Tobacco Labelling Resource Centre 2011a,b. Reprinted with permission from David Hammond.

When smokers squeeze and snap the capsule, it releases menthol. Other cigarette companies, such as Japan Tobacco, have experimented with the "crush" concept.

National survey findings on youth in the United States confirm that menthol cigarette use is disproportionately common among younger and newer teen smokers (Hersey et al. 2006, 2010; Rock et al. 2010). The latest data from the National Survey on Drug Use and Health (NSDUH) find that the rate of past month menthol cigarette use among persons aged 12 years and older has increased significantly from 7.7% in 2004 to 8.2% in 2010 (SAMHSA 2011). The survey found that the use of menthol cigarettes among young smokers aged 18–25 years increased significantly from 13.4% to 15.9% and remained stable among smokers aged 12–17 years, while nonmenthol cigarette use during this same time period in each of these age groups decreased.

Older industry marketing documents openly discuss the use of flavoring agents in cigarettes to attract the interest of young smokers (Teague 1954, 1969, 1973a; Philip Morris 1965; Crayton 1971; Marketing Innovations 1972; Ritchy 1972; Colby 1973; RJR 1973; Donati 1974; Achey 1978; Cohen 1984; Slone and Bonhomme 1993). For example, in 1972, B&W, in a review of new concepts for a youth cigarette, including cola and apple flavors as well as a sweet flavor, stated, "It's a well known fact that teenagers like sweet products. Honey might be considered" (Marketing Innovations 1972, Bates No. 170042014, p. 1). In the same year, RJR was speculating about a product that could target competitor brands (i.e., Marlboro and Kool) that had "exhibited exceptional strength in the under 35 age group, especially in the 14–20 group" (Ritchy 1972, Bates No. 501283430/3431, p. 2). One suggestion included an apple wine cigarette, an idea attributed to the growing popularity of fruit wines among young adults aged 18–25 years (Ritchy 1972).

Even after tobacco manufacturers agreed as part of the 1998 Master Settlement Agreement to discontinue any marketing that might appeal to adolescents, RJR introduced a new line of Camel cigarettes promoting unique flavors; these cigarettes had names such as Crema, Mandarin Mint, Aegean Spice, Mandalay Lime, Warm Winter Toffee, and Kauai Kolada (Sugg 1964; Connolly 2004; Carpenter et al. 2005b; Lewis and Wackowski 2006). In 2003, RJR introduced Salem Silver with flavored varieties such as Dark Currents and Cool Myst, and in the same year, B&W introduced Kool Smooth Fusions, which included flavored cigarettes such as Midnight Berry and Mocha Taboo (Sugg 1964; Connolly 2004; Carpenter et al. 2005b; Lewis and Wackowski 2006). In 2004, RJR and B&W merged to form Reynolds American, bringing all of these flavored brands under a single manufacturer. In 2005, Reynolds American introduced yet another line of Camel cigarettes, this time under the theme "High Roller High Ball," with varieties such as BlackJack Gin, SnakeEyes Scotch, and ScrewDriver Slots (Ashare et al. 2007). In 2006, however, Reynolds American voluntarily stopped selling 28 kinds of Camel, Kool, and Salem cigarettes that featured certain flavors as part of a settlement with state attorneys general who claimed that the marketing of flavored cigarettes violated the Master Settlement Agreement (Campaign for Tobacco-Free Kids 2006).

Cigarette manufacturers have consistently maintained that their flavored cigarette varieties were intended solely for adult smokers and were introduced to capitalize on consumer demand for special flavorings in products such as coffee and liquor (Finucane 2004). And yet, data from two nationally representative surveys conducted in 2004 found that younger smokers were more likely to have tried a flavored cigarette than were older smokers (Klein et al. 2008). In one of these surveys, overall use of any flavored brands in the past 30 days was 11.9% among smokers aged 17–26 years and 6.7% among smokers aged 25 years and older.

A study of college students who were shown different advertisements for flavored and nonflavored cigarette brands found that they consistently rated the flavored brands more positively regardless of their smoking status (Ashare et al. 2007). Moreover, positive expectancies of a brand were correlated with an increased intention to try the brand, independent of the subjects' smoking status. Thus, the addition of special flavorings, such as those in Camel cigarettes, most likely allowed the manufacturer to make the brand itself (in this case Camel) more attractive to starter smokers.

Under Food Law, "flavor" is defined narrowly as an entity with characterizing or recognizable gustatory effects (Food and Drugs, 21 *CFR* §101.22 [2010]). In the case of menthol, Philip Morris tested an analogue of menthol called W14, developed by Wilkerson Sword Company, that removed the gustatory effects of menthol but retained its thermoreceptor effects (Seligman 1975). In the case of cigarettes, where the flavor may be combusted or combined with other flavors (as is the case with the maillard browning process), much more than gustatory effects play a role in the influence of the flavor on initiation and maintenance of smoking (Wayne and Connolly 2002). These would include olfactory, tactile, and other chemosensory responses. The tobacco industry has long argued that flavors are safe in cigarettes based on ingestion models. However, ingestion models are not necessarily applicable because a combusted flavor that is inhaled into the lungs may be far more dangerous than one ingested orally by the body.

The *Family Smoking Prevention and Tobacco Control Act*, enacted in the United States in 2009, prohibited a cigarette or any of its component parts from containing, as a constituent or additive, certain characterizing flavors (except menthol). The act also mandated the Tobacco Product Scientific Advisory Committee (TPSAC) to produce a report and recommendations on the public health impact of menthol cigarettes, including its use among children and racial and ethnic minorities (USFDA 2011b). The TPSAC concluded that "the availability of menthol cigarettes have an adverse impact on public health in the United States by increasing the number of smokers with resulting premature death and avoidable mortality." Consequently TPSAC made the following recommendation to FDA: (USFDA 2011b, p. 225) "Removal of menthol cigarettes from the maketplace would benefit public health in the United States." However, TPSAC did not recommend any particular action by FDA, noting that there were a variety of actions that FDA might take related to menthol cigarettes. The tobacco companies submitted their industry perspective document to the FDA in March 2011, and argued that menthol cigarettes had no disproportionate impact on public health (Non-voting Industry Representatives of the TPSAC Committee 2011).

The Design of Other Tobacco Products

Cigarettes are not the only type of tobacco product used by youth; indeed, an increasing percentage of youth report using cigars and smokeless tobacco (Connolly 1995, 2004; Delnevo et al. 2003; Soldz et al. 2003; Carpenter et al. 2009; see Chapter 3). Since 1998, overall sales (all ages) of small cigars and moist snuff have increased, while cigarette sales have declined slightly (see Chapter 3). Much of the growing popularity of small cigars and smokeless tobacco is among younger adult consumers (aged <30 years) and appears to be linked to the marketing of flavored tobacco products that, like cigarettes, might be expected to be attractive to youth (Soldz et al. 2003).

Tobacco companies have long used wintergreen in the development of smokeless tobacco products, and more recently, multiple flavors. By the 1980s, U.S. Tobacco knew that new smokeless users preferred flavors (Connolly 1995) and that pH modifiers could alter pH, thus potentially affecting the level of free nicotine in the product (Manning 1981). In addition, U.S. Tobacco used mint and cherry flavored smokeless products as part of a "graduation strategy" with low free nicotine content to encourage new users to start with particular products and progress to others with higher levels of free nicotine (Figure 5.5; U.S. Smokeless Tobacco 1984). The effectiveness of such manipulations of free nicotine was confirmed in a National Institute on Drug Abuse study that demonstrated higher nicotine blood levels and stronger addictive effects in products with greater free nicotine levels (Fant et al. 1999). This integration of product design with marketing helped to reverse the mid-twentieth century decline in smokeless tobacco use and spurred a rapid increase in smokeless tobacco use by adolescents and young adult males (USDHHS 1986; Connolly 1995; Slade 1995; Tomar et al. 1995).

In 2007, Philip Morris purchased John Middleton Co., maker of the popular and inexpensive Black & Mild flavored cigars, and introduced a new line of flavored smokeless tobacco products using the Marlboro brand name (Carpenter et al. 2009). In 2005, Reynolds American purchased Conwood Tobacco Company (now American Snuff

Figure 5.5 **Graduation strategy designed to encourage new smokeless tobacco users to start with products with low free nicotine content and progress to others with higher levels of free nicotine**

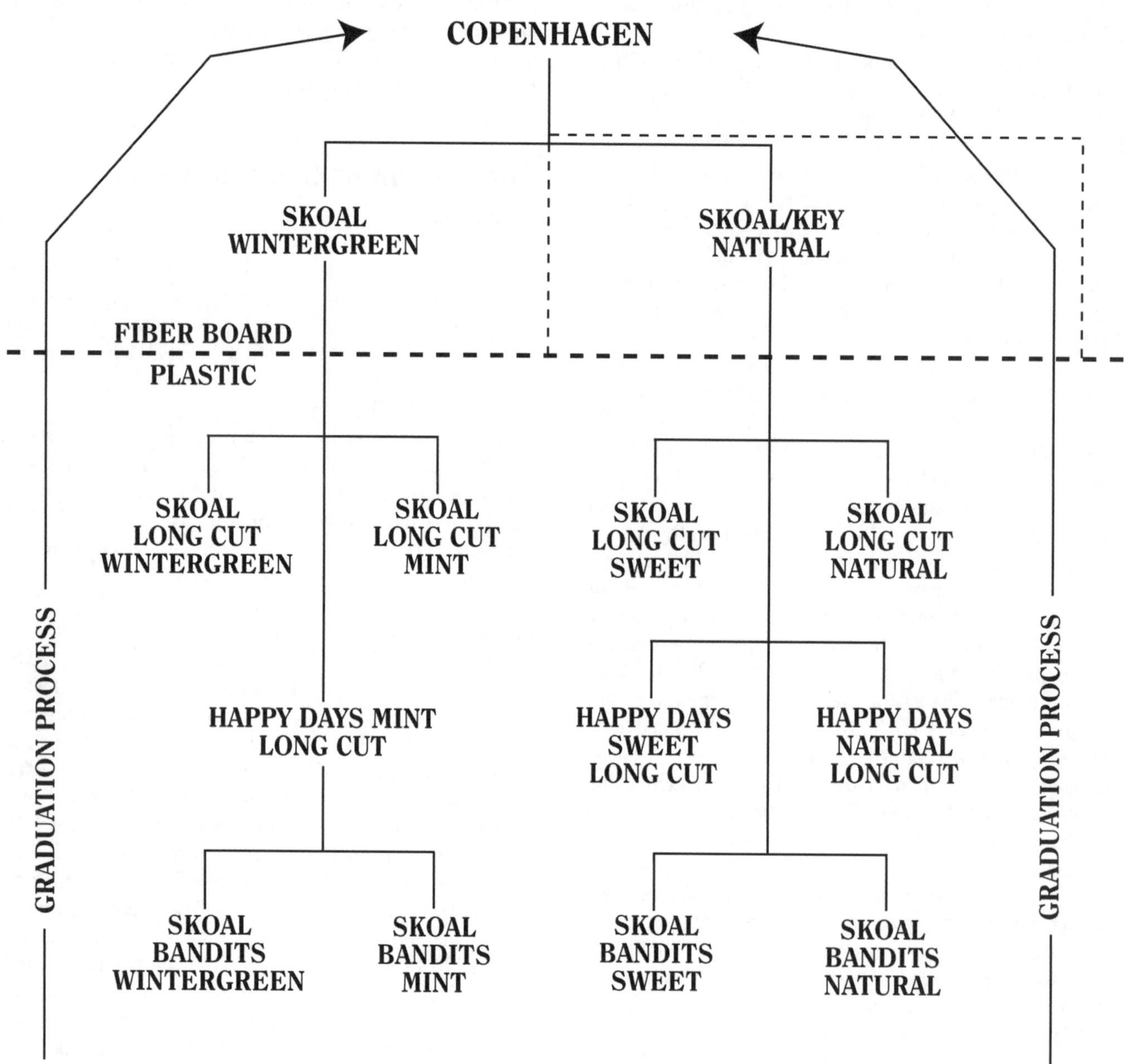

Source: U.S. Smokeless Tobacco 1984; Connolly 1995.

Company), which manufactures a wide range of tobacco products, including Kodiak and Grizzly moist snuff and Captain Black little cigars, all of which come in a range of flavors. In 2006, Reynolds American began test-marketing Camel Snus, a smokeless tobacco product in three flavors: spice, frost, and original (Carpenter et al. 2009; Mejia and Ling 2010), and began test-marketing Camel dissolvable smokeless products in 2010 (RJR 2010a). Packaging portions of smokeless tobacco in teabag-like porous pouches was also viewed as a product innovation that might ease adoption of smokeless tobacco products among novices (Beetham 1985). This prevented floating of the tobacco in the mouth and the subsequent rapid release of nicotine. The new snus products on the market in 2011 use both the portion pouch and flavored tobacco strategies. Internal industry documents as well as product testing revealed that, much as they did for cigarettes, manufacturers of smokeless tobacco altered the pH levels of their products to lower free-nicotine delivery in "starter products" that were widely distributed as free samples and were advertised as much less harsh (Connolly 1995; Djordjevic et al. 1995). Once the new user had adapted to low dose products, they were encouraged through marketing to progress to higher free-nicotine brands as dependence ensued. In addition, a recent paper by Carpenter and colleagues (2009) reveals that cigarette manufacturers are promoting smokeless tobacco products as a way for smokers to cope with restrictions on indoor smoking (also see Mejia and Ling 2010; Mejia et al. 2010). The strategy is to provide current smokers with an acceptable alternative they can use to satisfy nicotine cravings in places where smoking is not permitted.

Summary

Tobacco companies have always claimed that they do not want adolescents to use their products (Cummings et al. 2002, 2005). However, for a tobacco company to be profitable over the long term, it must compete successfully for a share of the youth market. As stated succinctly in one of RJR's marketing research documents, "Young adult smokers have been the critical factor in the growth and decline of every major brand and company over the last 50 years" (Burrows 1984, Bates No. 501928462/8550, p. 4). Internal documents and marketing practices from the industry reveal that in the past, manufacturers modified product design to enhance product appeal to novice users, including adolescents and young adults (i.e., 18- to 24-year-olds), a practice the industry has continued (U.S. Department of Justice n.d.).

Until the *Family Smoking and Prevention and Tobacco Control Act* (2009), the design and packaging of products was almost completely devoid of regulatory controls with the exception that package labels bear small text warning statements. (Henningfield et al. 2004). As a result, over the years tobacco manufacturers have relied on altering aspects of the product and its packaging as a way of attracting consumers, including new users. Policy options related to product design that have been suggested for reducing youth initiation include: (1) regulating aspects of product packaging, such as the quantity (e.g., mandating cartons only), (2) child proofing the package, (3) changing the look of the package (e.g., no color or images), and (4) modifying product design so the product itself becomes nonaddictive (e.g., limits on nicotine) and/or less palatable (e.g., no filter vents, no flavors). There are also methods that could be employed so the ingredients allow a smoker to continue but create aversion among a nonuser (Henningfield et al. 2004; Cummings et al. 2005, 2006). Making tobacco products nonaddictive, at least for youth, would have the positive effect of halting initiation quickly and permitting regular tobacco users to quit over time, which most would do (Teague 1972).

Tobacco Product Marketing at the Point of Sale

Introduction

Tobacco companies use the retail environment extensively to advertise and stimulate sales of their products (FTC 2011a). This section reviews the tobacco industry's point-of-sale strategies, the quantity and nature of retail tobacco marketing, young people's exposure to the industry's marketing messages and its impact on their smoking behavior, and policy options for affecting tobacco marketing in this environment.

The signing of the Master Settlement Agreement stimulated a dramatic shift of the industry to point-of-sale marketing, one of the few venues not affected by advertising restrictions. However, industry executives have recognized the importance of using displays and advertising at the point of sale for decades (Carter 2003b; Lavack and Toth 2006; Pollay 2007). Marketing expenditures reported by cigarette companies to FTC indicate that in 2008 tobacco companies spent approximately 84% of their marketing dollars in stores, including point-of-sale advertising, price discounts, retail promotional allowances, and retail-value-added items (see Table 5.1 for definitions and Table 5.2 for line item amounts; FTC 2011a).

Cigarette companies reach both current and future customers by advertising and promoting their products in stores (Carter 2003b; Lavack and Toth 2006); consumers, regardless of age, can be exposed to prosmoking messages in stores (Rogers et al. 1995). Most cigarettes and ads are strategically placed around checkout counters to ensure maximum exposure and stimulate impulse purchases (Pollay 2007). Like other companies in the retail sector, tobacco companies advertise, offer special sales, and try to motivate retailers to sell their products by offering volume discounts, in-store branded displays, and payments for prime shelf space; these strategies are designed to move products off the shelves quickly (Belch and Belch 1995). When tobacco products are displayed and featured with a price cut, sales increase by up to 30% (Liljenwall and Maskulka 2001).

Point-of-Sale and Industry-Sponsored Programs That Influence Product Location

Industry documents confirm that tobacco companies have sought to make their products easily visible and readily accessible to customers to stimulate impulse purchases (Pollay 2007). To reach customers, tobacco companies often engage retailers in contractual agreements (Dewhirst 2004). These contracts secure the placement of packs and cartons in highly visible locations around the counter where consumers will notice them; in return, the companies provide volume discounts and other financial incentives to retailers so their products can be offered at lower prices than those of their competitors.

Cigarette companies exert substantial control over product location, advertising, and pricing in return for the financial incentives they provide to retailers. A Philip Morris contract for its Retail Leaders included several options for retailers to select their level of participation (Philip Morris USA 2004b); the options varied by the amount and type of financial incentives offered to the retailer and the amount of control over retail space that the retailer relinquished to the company (Bloom 2001). Financial incentives include volume discounts, special sales on the companies' current inventory, and multipack discounts. In return, the retailer is required to advertise sales and promotions, accept merchandising fixtures (branded shelving units and displays), follow a detailed marketing plan that includes allocation of shelf space and brand location on shelves, and agree to inspections, reviews of inventory, and audits by the tobacco company.

In one study, a majority of tobacco retailers from small retail outlets (62.4%) in California reported receiving financial incentives from one or more tobacco companies; the comparable figures for soda companies and snack food companies in similar outlets were 16% and 6.9% (Feighery et al. 1999). On average, in 1997 stores received $3,157 from tobacco companies. A nationally representative sample of retailers reported similar results: in 2001, approximately 65% of the retailers participated in at least one cigarette company incentive program, and nearly 80% reported control by the cigarette company over location of marketing materials in their stores. Furthermore, stores that reported receiving more than $3,000 from incentive programs in the previous 3 months engaged in significantly more advertising than did those receiving no money (Feighery et al. 2004). Earlier, Bloom reported substantially higher annual benefits of up to $20,000 paid to convenience stores for fully complying with the marketing programs of tobacco companies (Bloom 2001). This finding may indicate that convenience stores receive greater financial incentives because they sell more cigarettes than any other type of store (Center for Tobacco Policy & Organizing 2008).

The Store Environment: Point-of-Sale Marketing and Product Location

Marketing expenditures and promotional strategies can shape the retail environment in significant ways. A national study of more than 1,500 stores selling cigarettes in 2000 found that 95% had at least 1 branded cigarette marketing item, with an average of 13 (Clark et al. 2002). In another study, significant increases in the amount of externally visible advertising were observed between 1998 (before the Master Settlement Agreement) and 2000 (after implementation of the agreement) (Celebucki and Diskin 2002). In a longitudinal study of tobacco retailers in California, the mean number of cigarette marketing materials per store increased from 19.1 in 2000 to 26.1 in 2004, then decreased to 17.6 in 2008. The percentage of stores with at least one ad for a sales promotion (price reduction or multipack discount) increased from 68% in 2000 to 78% in 2008 (Roeseler et al. 2010).

Tobacco Marketing in Low-Income and Ethnically/Racially Diverse Neighborhoods

Documents from the tobacco industry reveal that cigarette manufacturers have used advertising to appeal to racial and ethnic minorities (Muggli et al. 2002; Balbach et al. 2003; Hafez and Ling 2006) and children (Perry 1999). Tobacco companies implemented marketing strategies specifically developed for small stores in inner cities and used zip codes to identify and incentivize retailers to reach the target population for menthol cigarettes—that is, "young, black, relatively low income and education" (Hudson 1979, Bates No. 666015851/5864, p. 2). Studies of stores that sell tobacco have confirmed that tobacco industry marketing differentially appeals to people with the lowest income and education through point-of-sale advertising and that there is more in-store tobacco advertising in predominantly racially diverse and low-income neighborhoods (Wildey et al. 1992; Barbeau et al. 2005; John et al. 2009). A study of neighborhoods in eastern Massachusetts found that 19.4% of retail environments in a low-income neighborhood sold tobacco products, in contrast to only 3.7% of stores in an affluent neighborhood (Laws et al. 2002). In a study conducted in Ontario, Canada, stores in neighborhoods with lower median income contained more tobacco marketing and promotions than those in other neighborhoods (Cohen et al. 2008). In California, the amount of cigarette advertising and the proportion that included a sales promotion rose more rapidly over a 3-year period in stores situated in neighborhoods in which the proportion of African Americans was higher than the statewide average (Feighery et al. 2008). Similarly, menthol cigarettes were more likely to be marketed in stores near schools with higher proportions of African American students (Henriksen et al., in press).

Tobacco Marketing Strategies in Convenience Stores

More cigarettes are sold in convenience stores than in any other type of store (Dipasquale 2002). In 2006, cigarette sales generated nearly $400,000 in revenue per convenience store; these sales accounted for one-third of all sales inside a convenience store (Center for Tobacco Policy & Organizing 2008). About one-third of adolescents shop in convenience stores two or three times a week, and 70% shop in them at least weekly (Chanil 2001; Clickin Research 2005). Convenience stores have more tobacco advertising and promotions than other types of stores, which increases the likelihood of exposing youth to prosmoking messages while they are shopping and which can affect initiation rates among those exposed, particularly if stores are near schools (Centers for Disease Control and Prevention [CDC] 2002; Feighery et al. 2008; Henriksen et al. 2008, 2010). In fact, almost two-thirds of adolescents in the United States report seeing tobacco advertising all or most of the time when they visit convenience stores that do or do not sell gas (CDC National Youth Tobacco Survey [NYTS] public use data sets 2004; Duke et al. 2009).

The effect of tobacco advertising in stores is no doubt accentuated by its location. In most stores, the prime advertising space is around the checkout counter, where impulse buying is encouraged. In California, about 85% of stores were found to have marketing materials for tobacco products within 4 feet of the counter (Feighery et al. 2001). Nationally, a high proportion of tobacco shelving units (85%) and displays (93%) were located in the counter zone (Clark et al. 2002). The concentration of these types of merchandizing fixtures around the counter area suggests the important role played by packs and product displays in promoting sales (Wakefield et al. 2002a).

Another common practice is strategically locating tobacco-related marketing materials where young children will be exposed to them. Tobacco industry executives acknowledge that products and advertising should be placed at eye level (Pollay 2007), but in California, 48% of stores had at least one cigarette marketing item at or below 3 feet from the floor (Feighery et al. 2001). Furthermore, almost 25% had cigarette displays next to candy. In addition, a national study found that about one-third of the stores had low-height interior tobacco ads (Ruel et al. 2004).

Although self-service cigarette displays are prohibited under the 2009 act, that legislation does not prohibit product displays at the counter area. Following bans on counter displays in California, stores in some communities in that state put out contained transparent units with encased cigarette packs that preserved the display of products and brand imagery (Lee et al. 2001). Thus, access to the product may be restricted by the elimination of self-service displays, but exposure to the brand imagery may continue (Clark et al. 2002). Two studies conducted in countries that ban cigarette advertising at the point of sale confirm that exposure of adolescents to pack displays is associated with increased intentions to smoke among youth (Wakefield et al. 2006a; Paynter and Edwards 2009).

Tobacco marketing in stores close to schools is of particular concern because of the increased likelihood of exposure to prosmoking messages as students pass by or shop at these stores. In a study of retail outlets in 163 school catchment areas in the United States, more than 90% had some form of tobacco marketing materials; liquor and convenience stores contained more marketing materials for tobacco products than other types of stores (CDC 2002; Wakefield et al. 2002c). Stores close to schools were found to have more exterior tobacco advertising than stores further away (Rogers et al. 1995; Pucci et al. 1998), and stores where adolescents shop frequently have been found to have more cigarette marketing than other stores in the same community (Henriksen et al. 2004b). In Ontario, Canada, higher amounts of tobacco marketing and promotions were found in stores that were close to schools than in other stores (Cohen et al. 2008).

Immediately following implementation of the Master Settlement Agreement in 1998, significant increases in the prevalence of tobacco advertising and promotions (multipack discounts, gifts with purchase, and special sales) were reported in annual surveys of approximately

3,000 tobacco retailers in 175 school catchment areas (Wakefield et al. 2002c). More specifically, the proportion of stores with tobacco sales promotions increased from 45% in 1999 to 47% in 2002, and stores with interior tobacco advertising increased from 76% to 89% during the same time period (Ruel et al. 2004).

Retail Tobacco Marketing and Adolescent Tobacco Use

There is a growing body of evidence concerning the effects of exposing youth to tobacco marketing in stores. In one study, adolescents who reported frequent exposure to retail tobacco marketing were found to be more likely to attribute positive imagery to users of specific brands (Donovan et al. 2002). Elsewhere, in two experimental studies, students who saw photos of stores with tobacco displays and advertising were more likely to overestimate the percentage of adolescents and adults who smoke and to believe that tobacco is easier to buy than were those who saw photos without retail tobacco materials (Henriksen et al. 2002; Wakefield et al. 2006a). In another study, youth smokers preferred the brand most heavily advertised and promoted in the convenience store closest to school (Wakefield et al. 2002b).

Several cross-sectional studies have found relationships between exposure to retail tobacco marketing and experimentation with smoking (Schooler et al. 1996; Redmond 1999). Furthermore, in California, self-reported frequent exposure to retail cigarette marketing was independently associated with a significant increase in the odds of ever smoking (Henriksen et al. 2004a; Feighery et al. 2006). In New Zealand, where retail tobacco advertising is banned, a national cross-sectional study found that greater frequency of visits to stores selling tobacco was related to increased odds of susceptibility to smoking and experimentation among 14- to 15-year-olds (Paynter et al. 2009). In Canada, higher levels of advertised cigarette promotions and lower prices in stores situated in school neighborhoods were related to higher prevalence of smoking in those schools (Lovato et al. 2007). In the United States, a multiyear cross-sectional study of 8th-, 10th-, and 12th-grade students found a correlation between the amount of tobacco advertising and promotions in convenience stores near their schools; more specifically, higher levels of advertising, lower cigarette prices, and greater availability of cigarette promotions in stores all predicted smoking uptake among youth, and the availability of sales promotions increased the likelihood that youth would move from experimentation to regular use (Slater et al. 2007).

In a study that relied on a longitudinal survey of sixth graders in California, perceived exposure to cigarette advertising in stores and to actors smoking on television were both associated with greater susceptibility to smoking at follow-up, but this study did not examine the independent effect of retail cigarette advertising on smoking behavior (Weiss et al. 2006). Significantly, a later longitudinal study of more than 1,600 adolescents aged 11–14 years found that the odds of initiating smoking more than doubled for adolescents reporting that they visited the types of stores that contain the most cigarette advertising (convenience stores, liquor stores, and small grocery stores) two or more times a week. Although this study was limited by being conducted in a single California community, it was the first longitudinal study to document that exposure to retail cigarette advertising is a risk factor for initiation of smoking, after controlling for risk factors typically associated with uptake of smoking such as smoking by family and friends (Henriksen et al. 2010).

A systematic review of eight cross-sectional studies on the impact of tobacco promotion at the point of sale consistently found significant associations between exposure to point-of-sale tobacco promotions and initiation of smoking or susceptibility to that behavior. The authors concluded that the addictiveness of tobacco, the severity of the health hazards posed by smoking, the evidence that tobacco marketing and promotion encourages children to start smoking, and the consistency of the evidence that it influences children's smoking justify banning advertising and displays of tobacco products at the point of sale (Paynter and Edwards 2009).

Density of Retail Outlets and Tobacco Use by Adolescents

In addition to the amount and placement of in-store tobacco advertising and promotions, the number and location of stores that sell cigarettes must be considered (Ashe et al. 2003; Bonnie et al. 2007). Local zoning laws may be used to limit the total number of tobacco outlets as a way of reducing the availability of cigarettes and the visibility of cigarette ads; these laws may also require that tobacco outlets be located away from areas frequented by children (Ashe et al. 2003). Studies that have linked the density of alcohol outlets around college campuses to higher rates of drinking (Weitzman et al. 2003) and higher levels of adolescent drinking and driving (Treno et al. 2003) have set a precedent for the use of zoning laws to reduce adolescent smoking.

Neighborhoods that are more densely populated with stores selling tobacco may promote adolescent smoking not only by increasing access but also by increasing environmental cues to smoke. Two studies found that the density of tobacco outlets in high school neighborhoods was related to experimental smoking but not to established smoking among high school (Leatherdale and Strath 2007; McCarthy et al. 2009) and middle school (Pokorny et al. 2003) students. In Chicago, Illinois, youth in areas with the highest density of retail tobacco outlets were 13% more likely to have smoked in the past month than those living in areas with the lowest density of outlets (Novak et al. 2006). In a California study, the prevalence of current smoking was higher in high schools with the highest density of tobacco outlets in their neighborhoods than in high schools in neighborhoods without any outlets; the density of retail cigarette advertising in school neighborhoods was also associated with smoking prevalence (Henriksen et al. 2008). The associations found between density of cigarette retail outlets and advertising and adolescent smoking, supported by studies linking the density of retail alcohol outlets and youth's alcohol use, support the recommendation of the Institute of Medicine to restrict the number and location of retail outlets for cigarettes in communities (Bonnie et al. 2007).

Summary

Research supports the policy option of regulatory control over the retail tobaco environment. Studies show that tobacco use is associated with both exposure to retail advertising, and relatively easy access to tobacco products. Because tobacco companies use powerful financial incentives to influence the retail environment, voluntary strategies may prove ineffective in reducing youth and young adult exposure to retail tobacco marketing. However, venues such as supermarkets, which derive a relatively small portion of their overall profits from tobacco sales, may be receptive to eliminating tobacco sales from their stores. In 2008, Wegmans, a regional food chain in the United States, voluntarily eliminated tobacco sales in its stores, attributing the company's decision to the deleterious effects of smoking on health (Wegmans 2008).

Pharmacies may also be receptive to eliminating tobacco sales because of the incongruity between their primary role in health care and the negative effects of tobacco products on health. A majority of pharmacists are against tobacco sales in pharmacies (Hudmon et al. 2006), but chain community pharmacies are generally opposed to restrictions on tobacco sales in this venue. Indeed, Walgreens, a chain drugstore, has challenged a San Francisco, California, law prohibiting tobacco sales in drugstores (Egelko 2010).

Unfortunately, voluntary, partial efforts to modify retail tobacco marketing will most likely do little to reduce youth smoking. Comprehensive restrictions on advertising and sales promotion have been found to significantly reduce cigarette consumption, but partial bans are often circumvented (Saffer and Chaloupka 2000). A wide variety of product displays, which are an important communication device, can be used as advertising (Chapman 1994; Fraser 1998; Barnsley and Jacobs 2000; Wakefield et al. 2002a). Thus, Article 13 of the FCTC calls for comprehensive bans on tobacco advertising and promotions (WHO 2003).

The growing body of evidence linking exposure to tobacco marketing at the point of sale to youth smoking behavior has created pressures to regulate tobacco marketing in this environment (Bonnie et al. 2007; NCI 2008; Paynter and Edwards 2009). Efforts to restrict the exposure of U.S. children to the marketing of tobacco products have been uneven, however, and narrowly focused on specific contexts and venues, such as those described in the Master Settlement Agreement (Kunkel 2007). Comprehensive bans on tobacco advertising and product displays at the point of sale, such as those in Iceland, Ireland, Thailand, and several Canadian provinces, are notable examples of a stronger approach (Hammond 2006; Lavack and Toth 2006).

The landmark *Family Smoking Prevention and Tobacco Control Act* (2009) granted authority to FDA to regulate the manufacturing, marketing, and distribution of tobacco products; this authority establishes a number of restrictions on tobacco marketing and sales to youth.

Chapman and Freeman (2009) have argued for examining the regulatory controls that are used for pharmaceutical sales in terms of their applicability to the tobacco retail environment. Such controls could involve restricting the number and location of tobacco retail outlets, the banning of tobacco retail displays, minimum price controls, and nontransferable retail licenses that could be revoked for noncompliance with laws. Other possibilities include banning price reduction strategies, eliminating tobacco sales from specific types of stores such as pharmacies, restricting times during which tobacco may be sold, and making mandatory the posting of antitobacco signage with quitline information (Ribisl 2010).

In conclusion, tobacco marketing at the point of sale is associated with the use of tobacco by youth. Because point-of-sale marketing is an important channel for the tobacco companies, with very few restrictions, consumers, including children, are unavoidably exposed to prosmoking messages when they shop or when they are simply passing by stores. Policy options include limiting the use of the retail environment by tobacco companies to reach youth, including both potential and current users of its products.

Digital Tobacco Marketing

Introduction: The New Digital Marketing Landscape

Although traditional tobacco marketing remains a potent force, the rapid growth of the Internet and the proliferation of digital media are fundamentally transforming how corporations do business with consumers—particularly young people—in the twenty-first century. Digital marketing has established a new paradigm that is transforming advertising and marketing as we know it (Chester and Montgomery 2007). Marketers reach across platforms, from mobile devices to personal computers, with highly interactive techniques such as viral video, "gamevertising," polls, contests, and the creation of "avatars," or electronic alter egos, which travel in online digital worlds (Moore 2006).

The key objective of digital marketing is to keep the user engaged and interacting with the brand. According to Montgomery and Chester (2009), the six key features of digital marketing are ubiquitous connectivity, personalization, peer-to-peer networking, engagement, immersion, and content creation. Each feature enables marketers to keep viewers in contact with the brand to a heretofore unprecedented degree and, in many cases, makes marketing and personal communications indistinguishable.

The techniques of digital marketing are part of sophisticated behavioral targeting in which the marketer collects data on the users' every move (e.g., every click of the mouse, sign-up for a contest, forwarding to a friend) to enable ever more precisely targeted marketing. Social media applications, in particular, are desirable for marketers who gain access not only to detailed profiles about users but also to those of their friends. Marketers seek to create "brand ambassadors," who promote the product in the context of their online communications, whether or not such promotions are recognized by the users or receivers as marketing. The effect is to blur the distinction between marketing communications and market research (Dewhirst 2009). The next section describes how tobacco companies have entered the digital media world.

The Tobacco Industry Online

In 2008, tobacco companies reported spending $13.2 million on their Web sites, but the FTC report outlining industry marketing and promotion expenditures did not identify additional spending on any other Internet advertising for cigarettes, such as banner ads or direct mail advertising to e-mail accounts (FTC 2011a). Internet advertising is relatively inexpensive compared to traditional forms of marketing, in part because companies garner brand exposures at no cost when, for example, site users forward links to friends. In the case of digital marketing, exposures may be a better measure than expenditures.

Numerous researchers and tobacco control advocacy organizations closely track industry marketing efforts. The tobacco companies' corporate Web sites tend to be neutral in tone and provide factual content such as public education and information for shareholders (Cruz 2009; Ribisl et al. 2009). For example, the RJR official Web site features career opportunities and news updates, and the Web site of Philip Morris USA carries information on company highlights, recent developments in tobacco legislation and regulation, and a section on smoking cessation.

Web sites that promote specific brands and engage in electronic mail marketing could potentially have greater appeal to youth than do the companies' corporate Web sites. In 2004, B&W launched its Kool MIXX hip-hop ad campaign and included a Web component for that campaign (Hafez and Ling 2006; Ribisl et al. 2009). The Web site, called the House of Menthol, provided information about a national disk jockey battle, free software demonstrations, the history of hip-hop, and lists of retail stores where smokers could purchase the special-edition Kool MIXX cigarette packs. B&W voluntarily pulled the Kool MIXX ad campaign, including the Web site, after several state attorneys general threatened to sue, claiming that the campaign violated the Master Settlement Agreement because it targeted youth.

RJR has established Web sites at which smokers can participate in online surveys and be entered into sweepstakes as an incentive for their participation (Lewis et al. 2004). For example, RJR successfully used the Internet to elicit consumer feedback in the redesign of its Camel brand and Camel Signature Blends (Freeman and Chapman 2009). The Camel Web site (RJR 2010d) reportedly boasted that more than 5 million smokers were invited to participate in this process (Freeman and Chapman 2009). Although Camel relied on password-protected sites for consumer input, researchers Freeman and Chapman reported that they obtained passwords to the site without ever having to provide proof of age or identity. In addition, Camel's Web site has featured lifestyle content for young adults and spotlighted brand-sponsored events (Cortese et al. 2009).

In 2011, the branded Web sites for Marlboro and Camel promoted both cigarettes and the cigarette-branded smokeless tobacco products (Philip Morris USA 2011; RJR 2011). This practice could increase with the rising number of alternative tobacco products, including snus, dissolvables, and other smokeless products, which some advocates fear could be attractive to youth (Campaign for Tobacco-Free Kids 2010a). In addition, features on brand Web sites for tobacco products in 2011 included "instant win" sweepstakes, interactive games, participatory activities, blogs, message boards, and coupons (Philip Morris USA 2011; RJR 2011).

So far, however, the tobacco industry's overt presence on the Web seems to be less than that of the alcoholic beverage industry (Center on Alcohol Marketing and Youth at Georgetown University 2007; Mart et al. 2009; Chester et al. 2010) or the food industry (Chester and Montgomery 2007; Montgomery and Chester 2009). In addition, federal law prohibits the advertising of cigarettes or smokeless tobacco on "any medium of electronic communication subject to the jurisdiction of the Federal Communications Commission" (FCC) *Public Health Cigarette Smoking Act of 1969* (1970). Moreover, with the 2009 legislation granting FDA regulatory authority over tobacco products, the cigarette manufacturers may be cautious about raising their Internet profile to avoid potential imposition of restrictions on Internet marketing.

Three basic categories of tobacco-related Web sites are discussed below: those that sell tobacco, the industry-sponsored brand name or corporate image sites, and the loosely defined social networking sites (including personal Facebook pages that mention tobacco, discussion groups, and YouTube videos).

Online Sales of Tobacco

Typing "discount cigarettes" into a Google search in late 2011 yielded more than one-half million Web sites (Google 2011). Selling cheap tobacco over the Internet is both a big business and a significant challenge to those wishing to promote public health.

The tobacco-for-sale sites are used to advertise or market cigarettes as well as to sell tobacco products at discount prices that increase demand among both youth and adults; these prices generally reflect successful attempts to avoid taxes. Indeed, cigarette prices on the Internet rarely include state excise or local sales taxes and frequently do not include the applicable federal and local excise taxes (Connolly 2001). Online retailers usually purchase huge quantities of cigarettes in states with low excise taxes or from American Indian reservations or foreign countries (about one-half of the cigarette-sales Web sites are based outside the United States) and then sell at a significantly lower rate than consumers would pay at brick-and-mortar retail outlets.

Most Web sites carry some warning that sales to people under the age of 18 years are not allowed, but there is generally little if any enforcement (Ribisl et al. 2001). Moreover, Malone and Bero (2000), in examining 141 Web sites that marketed cigars, found that those sites offered low prices, and 32% accepted payment methods accessible to youth such as money orders or cashier's checks; nearly 30% featured elements with youth appeal, such as cartoons, music, or moving images.

Ribisl and colleagues (2001, 2009) identified 88 Internet cigarette vendors (ICVs) in January 2000 and about eight times that number (775) in 2004. Researchers have found that most online tobacco vendors have sold to consumers without verifying their age. In a 2001 survey of purchases, for example, youth aged 11–15 years were successful in 76 of 83 attempts (92%) in purchasing cigarettes from 55 Internet vendors (Ribisl 2003). In addition, Jensen and colleagues (2004) found that 96.7% of minors aged 15–16 years were able to find an Internet cigarette vendor and place an order in less than 25 minutes, with most completing the order in 7 minutes or less. In that study, 77% of youth successfully received their orders, with 91% of the packages delivered without requests for proof of age.

Several epidemiologic studies have examined the prevalence of buying cigarettes online among youth who smoke. According to one such study, in 1999–2000, 2% of 1,689 current smokers under 18 years of age in California reported attempting to purchase cigarettes online (Unger et al. 2001). Those who attempted online purchases were younger, smoked more frequently, and reported greater perceived difficulty in obtaining cigarettes from commercial and social sources than those who did not try online purchases. A 2001 study of 1,323 ninth-grade smokers in three western New York counties obtained similar results, finding that more than 2% of these youth reported having ever purchased cigarettes online (Abrams et al. 2003). Those who had been refused cigarette sales at retail outlets in the previous month were more than three times as likely to purchase cigarettes online as youth who had successfully purchased cigarettes at a retail outlet in that period. In a follow-up survey, the proportion of ninth-grade smokers reporting ever having purchased cigarettes online rose to 6.5%, with more than 5.2% having purchased online in the past 30 days (Fix et al. 2006).

The legislation that granted regulatory authority over tobacco products to FDA requires that agency to issue new regulations regarding the sale and distribution of tobacco products that occur through means other than a direct face-to-face exchange; it also mandates the issuing of regulations to address the promotion and marketing of tobacco products distributed through means other than a face-to-face exchange (*Family Smoking Prevention and Tobacco Control Act* 2009). The total number of cigarettes sold over the Internet is unknown; similarly, it is not known exactly how many of these sales are to youth, but the ease with which underage buyers can get cigarettes online suggests that the number could be substantial. As of late 2011, it did not appear that online sales sites are owned, directly or indirectly, by tobacco companies.

In March 2005, major credit card companies and PayPal banned the processing of sales for ICVs and, later that year, private carriers such as UPS and FedEx agreed not to deliver products from ICVs. Ribisl and colleagues (2011), who sought to determine the effect on ICVs of shipping and credit card bans implemented in 2005, visited ICV Web sites in 2003, 2005, 2006, and 2007. The authors found that after the shipping and credit card bans, the proportion of vendors accepting credit card payments decreased from 99.6% to 37.4%, but they found that the proportion of ICVs accepting checks or money orders increased from 29.6% in 2004 to 78.3% in 2006. Similarly, the proportion of vendors shipping via UPS, FedEx, or DHL decreased from 27.0% in 2004 to 5.6% in 2006; the proportion of vendors shipping via the United States Postal Service (USPS) increased from 69.4% to 92.7% in the same timeframe. In addition to the changes in payment and shipping methods, the authors found that visitor traffic for the 50 most popular ICVs decreased at a 16% monthly rate from March 2005 until October 2005; from October 2005 until January 2007, these same ICVs experienced a 2.5% monthly rate of decline.

Despite the relative ease with which youth can purchase tobacco from Internet sites, there is little evidence that these commercial sites are being actively marketed to youth (Jenssen et al. 2009). The new trend in advertising and marketing to youth is through other methods, such as social media (Idaho Department of Health and Welfare 2011). The *Prevent All Cigarette Trafficking Act of 2009* (2010), effective as of June 29, 2010, which is designed to reduce tax evasion from online sales, as well as online sales to youth, may also hinder online marketing to youth (Campaign for Tobacco-Free Kids 2010b). Research is needed to understand the actual effects of the new law (Ribisl et al. 2011).

Tobacco Industry Corporate and Brand Web Sites

In addition to the corporate Web sites of the tobacco companies, some Web sites are dedicated to particular brands. For example, the top-selling Marlboro brand has its own site (Philip Morris USA 2011), but accessing the site is difficult (Freeman and Chapman 2009). Some consumers are invited to register on the site via information collected from other promotions, such as coupons or face-to-face giveaways, and these people are given a special code for signing in. However, others must register separately and go through a cumbersome process to verify that they are 21 years of age or older. Other companies take a similar approach (see, e.g., RJR's "tobacco pleasure" site) (RJR 2010c).

There are also many Web sites for specific brands of smokeless tobacco (see, e.g., Web sites for Copenhagen and Skoal [U.S. Smokeless Tobacco Co. 2010a,b], Red Man [Pinkerton Tobacco Co. 2010], snus [RJR 2011], and other tobacco products—including dissolvables [RJR 2010a; Smokers Only 2010]). All of the sites now require registration; most include videos, games, contests, and message boards that could appeal to youth and young adults.

The creativity of the companies and their marketing advisors pose challenges to efforts to prevent youth's tobacco use. In 2008, two industry informants provided Australian tobacco control researchers a copy of a marketing presentation by a brand management company that had assisted RJR in developing an open source marketing campaign for its Camel cigarette brand (Freeman and Chapman 2009). "Open source marketing" is a term that evolved from the early development of computer software by volunteers who helped develop and then publicize new, free software applications. In marketing, however, the term refers to the blurring of market research and marketing itself. In this case, consumers were solicited online to take an active part in developing new packaging designs for RJR's Camel cigarettes. The project eventually gathered input from 30,000 participants and led to four new variations in packaging for Camels. Because of potential problems arising from the packages' cartoon-like designs, however, RJR's new Camel packages were never used.

This sort of campaign strategy is used regularly by other major marketers (Montgomery and Chester 2009; Chester et al. 2010). For example, PepsiCo's DEWmocracy campaign, an aggressive social media marketing campaign for Mountain Dew, encouraged its youth target market to become brand cocreators with a video contest to select flavors, names, colors, and other marketing details (BevReview 2008; Chester et al. 2010). The fan-created flavor sold 11 million cases (Burns 2009). The tobacco industry was an early pioneer in developing interactive customer involvement marketing (Anderson and Ling 2008).

Corporate-Sponsored Pages: RJR's "My Smokers' Rights"

The site for RJR's smokers' rights group (RJR 2010b), established in 2003, aims to be a clearinghouse for tracking efforts in tobacco control policy throughout the country at the state and local levels. The site features a U.S. map on which users can click to see the status of tobacco control policy efforts in their state.

The site requires users to fill out a fairly detailed registration form that asks for their name, birth date, e-mail address, home address, and telephone number and their opinion on current tobacco control issues (e.g., whether tobacco taxes unfairly target a minority of the population and whether efforts to curtail public smoking have gone too far). Once the form is filled out, confirmation is sent via e-mail, and the company has contact information for its database.

The site encourages interaction and extended engagement. Once people are members, a personal page with the user's state and federal legislators is established. Users are then asked to contact the appropriate legislators to voice their opinion about pending tobacco control policies. Letting their state senator know that they oppose an increase in excise taxes on tobacco, for example, requires just the click of a button.

The focus of the site appears to be encouraging opposition to tobacco control policies; there is no information about RJR's brands or off-topic diversions such as games or other links. The site is consistent with the tobacco companies' well-documented efforts to foster political activism that has the appearance of being independent of the industry (Traynor et al. 1993; Smith and Malone 2007).

Internet Marketing of Cigars and Smokeless Tobacco

To date, there is still little information regarding Internet marketing and the sales of cigars and other tobacco products beyond cigarettes. A 1998 study conducted by Malone and Bero (2000) examined Web sites used to market cigars and found that only about one-fourth prohibited sales to minors and that almost one-third of the sites featured cartoon characters or employed other marketing techniques that appeal to youth; very few sites (3.5%) explained the health effects of cigar use (Malone and Bero 2000). Last, Wackowski and colleagues (2011) analyzed the Camel Snus message boards and found that this product appealed to both current smokers and users of other smokeless products. These researchers also found that users of the message boards shared their experiences with Camel Snus and urged a national release of the product. Wackowski and colleagues (2011) determined that the message boards provided beneficial marketing research to RJR for its new Camel Snus product.

E-Cigarettes

Ads for electronic cigarettes (e-cigarettes), which are not currently sold under existing cigarette brands, are prevalent on the Web. Information about e-cigarettes is disseminated widely through Internet ads, blogs (e.g., Electronic Cigarette Tavern [2010] and Electronic Cigarette Magazine [2010]), and commercialists (e.g., Electronic Cigarettes, Inc. [2010] and SmokingEverywhere [2011]). Electronic cigarettes are battery-powered devices that heat a liquid nicotine solution inside a cigarette-shaped tube that users draw on to inhale a nicotine-filled vapor. They have been sold primarily over the Internet through commercial Web sites (Noel et al. 2011) and, to a lesser extent, through mall kiosks and tobacco stores. Web-based searches using the terms "electronic cigarette," "e-cigarette," and "e-cig" retrieve hundreds of sites that sell and/or promote electronic cigarettes, including retail marketing sites, electronic cigarette advocacy sites, blogs, advertorials, press releases, and sponsored articles. Commercial electronic cigarette Web sites include a variety of messages to promote the products, including that they are a safer, and/or healthier, alternative to smoking tobacco cigarettes (Blucigs 2011; Direct E-cig 2011; Smoking Everywhere 2011). Other messages are that electronic cigarettes are a new or modern way to smoke (Smoking Everywhere 2011), and can be used in places where tobacco smoking is not allowed (Gamucci 2011; Smoking Everywhere 2011). Many sites include instructional how-to videos (Blucigs 2011; Greensmoke 2011), testimonials about the benefits of using electronic cigarettes (Blucigs 2011; Gamucci 2011), and imagery of people using the products in venues that are covered by smoke-free laws (Blucigs 2011). Some of the sites also use social networking features, such as Facebook and Twitter, to encourage visitors to support, or "like," their products or to connect with other users (Blucigs 2011). The products are offered in various flavors, including tobacco, menthol, coffee, fruit, and candy-like flavors such as Turkish delight (Henningfield and Zaatari 2010). The U.S. Court of Appeals for the District of Columbia ruled that these products could not be regulated as drug delivery devices unless they are marketed for therapeutic purposes (USFDA 2011a).

Tobacco Social Networking Web Sites

The Internet makes it easy to find a group, blog, or individual page with a positive message about the use of tobacco. These messages might include expressions of individual appreciation and support of a favorite brand, advocacy against restrictions on smoking, or assertions that someone is sexually attracted to smoking and smokers. The origin of this content is often unknown, and it could simply reflect the actions of independent individuals or be content that is disseminated by tobacco companies or their allies (Ribisl 2003; Freeman and Chapman 2009). At the same time, the content and structure of the sites further tobacco industry interests in the same manner as smokers' rights magazines or campaigns promulgated by the Tobacco Institute did in the past (Cardador et al. 1995; Smith and Malone 2003, 2007; Lopipero and Bero 2006).

At least some of these sites could be considered appealing to youth; many are well maintained, regularly updated, and followed by very large numbers of people. Ribisl (2003) reviewed 30 Web sites on smoking; in all, 35% of the sites promoted cigarette brands, and 95% of the photographs featured people who were modeling smoking behavior. These sites also highlighted smoking scenes in popular movies and smoking by celebrities. Elsewhere, Hong and Cody (2002) conducted a content analysis of 318 protobacco Web sites and found that only 11% featured any type of health warning. Smoking was frequently associated with "glamorous" and "alternative" lifestyles, and the sites contained numerous images of young male and young, thin, attractive female smokers.

Smoking Promotion Web Sites

Yahoo!, Facebook, and Google all host smoker's groups for youth on their Web sites. A July 2010 search on Yahoo! Groups using the term "smoking" produced more than 5,000 results, including many cessation sites but also some that linked to groups that take a positive view toward tobacco. These include clubs with names such as HappySmokers and Smokerhouse1, which provide commentary on the virtues of smoking and often depict youth enjoying cigarettes. Other groups, such as Male Celebrities Smoking 3, glamorize smoking in the media and include photos of celebrities smoking, many of whom are popular with youth audiences.

A few of the prosmoking blogs are described below:

- The Smoker's Club (2010), a clearinghouse for protobacco information, includes clippings from newsletters, forums, chat rooms, and advice for opposing advocates for tobacco control.

- RJR's My Smokers' Rights page (described earlier in this section) (2010b) provides state-by-state as well as federal and local information on current efforts in tobacco control policy and suggestions for opposing these efforts.

- Smoking Lobby (2010) is a forum where people can discuss how to oppose smoking bans, identify places where people are still allowed to smoke in public, and obtain information on discount cigarettes online. In addition, visitors to the site can purchase merchandise, such as smokers' rights t-shirts.

There are countless group pages on Facebook, MySpace, Yahoo!, and similar sites that range from efforts to organize local prosmoking supporters (Yahoo! Groups 2010a,b) to pages simply dedicated to an individual's appreciation for smoking (Facebook 2010a). A very basic search of any social networking site quickly reveals hundreds or thousands of similar sites. Many are either clearly the product of individual consumers or attempts to share information about tobacco prices and/or policy. The tobacco social networking sites do not appear to feature the elaborate integrated marketing campaigns that appear on sites for other consumer products, such as alcoholic beverages (Mart et al. 2009; Chester et al. 2010), or on sites designed for children (Moore 2006). However, public health practitioners and researchers should continue to monitor social networking sites because integrated marketing of tobacco products to youth could go undetected.

Smokers' Rights Web Sites

RJR's site for its smokers' rights group is not the only Web site that focuses on this topic. Many of the Web sites that can be found with a search for "cigarettes" or "smoking" appear to have been created by individuals seeking a venue to complain about the treatment of smokers in society and serve as a place for these persons to proudly and unapologetically identify themselves as smokers. The tobacco companies' involvement with these Web sites has not been documented. However, the companies played an important role in getting smokers' rights groups, including the American Smokers Alliance and National Smokers Alliance, organized in the 1980s and 1990s as part of efforts to oppose local and state smoking restrictions and tobacco taxes (Samuels and Glantz 1991; Traynor et al. 1993; Cardador et al. 1995; Stauber and Rampton 2002). The industry also has played an active role in creating the smokers' rights movement, but it has often worked to hide its involvement (Samuels and Glantz 1991; Traynor et al. 1993; Cardador et al. 1995; Stauber and Rampton 2002). Other than the RJR Web site, whether or not tobacco companies play a role in current smokers' rights Web sites is not known.

Similar to the procigarette Web sites, there are several Web sites devoted to policy and advocacy related to electronic cigarettes (CASAA 2011; Electronic Cigarette

Ban 2011; Vapors Network 2011). These Web sites include opportunities for membership, lists of policies related to electronic cigarettes (e.g., whether their sale or import is banned, whether they are included in smoke-free policies), and suggested actions to oppose restricting the sale or use of electronic cigarettes.

There are thousands of Web pages that deal with smokers' rights, but few seem to have garnered a large audience. Although these sites seek to gain demographic and political information from their users, they do not appear to be designed to share information on brands or to nurture brand loyalty among adults or children. Many may be visited or even maintained by minors, but they do not seem to be especially appealing to youth as they lack the games, videos, and interactivity that are common on sites more overtly designed for youth.

The global Facebook Smokers' Rights (2010b) page, which was created in 2007, had only 300 members as of January 2010, but was one of the more popular pages of this type on the Web (based on a Web search, July 2010); in contrast, a generic Facebook page titled "Smoking" (2010c) but not linked specifically to smokers' rights had 101,888 people who "liked" it ("liked" is a Facebook term for page approval, with links back to a Facebook member's page). The 300-member smokers' rights group that developed through Facebook was founded with the objective of defending and looking after the "rights of smokers all around the globe" and has as its slogan, "It is not my cigarettes that might kill you, Please go search for other reasons and I am sure that there are many" (Facebook 2010b). The site features photographs, comments from visitors, and two videos: an old television commercial for Winston cigarettes featuring characters from "The Flintstones" and a comedy routine decrying the eroding rights of smokers. Other than its subject matter, this site is similar to other individual Web pages in that it is low tech and features no interactive or special features common to commercial sites. There is no information about specific tobacco brands on the site and, apart from a few comments from individuals, no call for advocacy to support smokers' rights.

At this time, the sheer number of individual Web pages that mention tobacco makes it very difficult to track them comprehensively. Verifying that none of them has been established by tobacco companies is extremely difficult. In a 2009 study that tracked a random group of 346 adolescents for 30 days, the authors found that of the approximately 1.2 million pages these youth viewed, 8,702, or less than 1%, contained smoking or tobacco content (Jenssen et al. 2009). Even though these pages constituted a small minority of total pages viewed and included antitobacco as well as protobacco messages, there is an obvious incentive for companies to participate in these virtual communities; interest in the products offered by the tobacco industry is evidenced by the number of hits returned by a search.

Exposure of Youth to the Marketing of Tobacco on the Internet

The studies examining the exposure of youth to online tobacco marketing have included surveillance surveys based on self-reports and content analysis of the archival Internet content typically viewed by youth. The 2004 NYTS conducted by CDC found that 34.1% of middle school students and 39.2% of high school students reported seeing advertisements for tobacco products on the Internet (CDC 2005). Using NYTS data, the exposure of youth to protobacco messages in various channels was compared between 2000 and 2004: exposure to protobacco messages declined in all channels studied (e.g., point of sale, newspapers, and magazines), except for the Internet, where 33% reported seeing tobacco advertisements in 2004 versus 22% in 2000 (Duke et al. 2009).

In the study by Jenssen and colleagues (2009) referenced above, in the 8,702 pages viewed by the adolescents about one-half of the tobacco-related content derived from social networking sites. Forty-three percent of the adolescents in this study were exposed to prosmoking imagery, with a median of three pages of exposure per month for this group. Tobacco products were sold on 50 of the pages viewed, and 242 pages contained links to Internet tobacco vendors. Forty-five percent of the adolescents were exposed to antismoking messages (Jenssen et al. 2009).

Although Cohen and colleagues (2001) have called for studies to determine the effects of Internet-based tobacco advertising on tobacco-related knowledge, attitudes, and behaviors, no research has been published to date on the impact of such exposure. Ribisl and colleagues (2007) have noted that given the engaging and interactive nature of Internet content, research is needed to understand how its impact compares with print marketing and exposure to smoking in movies. In addition, because interactive digital marketing encourages users to become "brand ambassadors" by sharing information among themselves, those concerned about tobacco marketing should track exposures as well as expenditures.

Summary

New media channels provide both promise and challenges for preventing youth tobacco use. Monitoring and countering the tobacco industry's uses of new media will be an ongoing challenge for researchers and regulators, but must become an essential element of tobacco control. The tobacco-related content that currently exists on the Web—thousands of pages with some kind of prosmoking or protobacco sentiment—potentially exposes huge numbers of youth and young adults to tobacco at little expense to tobacco companies. Interest in the tobacco companies' products and brands is already there, with a consumer base that is actively using the Internet to share information and extol its favorite brands to the wide world of the Web. These consumers act as "brand ambassadors," as marketers have dubbed them. But unlike the brand ambassadors a tobacco company may send out in person to promote cigarettes in bars or clubs, virtual brand ambassadors cost nothing. In fact, with or without support from the tobacco companies, the industry has achieved a prized goal in digital marketing: consumer-to-consumer chat, recommendations, and brand promotions, all at very little or no expense. Online tobacco marketing is almost completely "viral," or spread by consumers themselves as they use the social networking features of various Web sites.

Other Tobacco Company Activities and Tobacco Use Among Youth

Introduction

This section summarizes those tobacco industry programs with the stated purpose of preventing smoking among youth; those programs began emerging in the 1980s. A review of industry documents made public under the terms of legal settlements shows that the focus of these programs and their timing has been in response to mounting public concern about the industry's marketing practices and an attempt to forestall legislation or regulation that would restrict its activities (Landman et al. 2002; Mandel et al. 2006; Sebrié and Glantz 2007; Apollonio and Malone 2010). For example, a confidential presentation by the Tobacco Institute (which was dissolved in 1998 as a result of state litigation against the tobacco industry) that Landman and colleagues (2002) surmised was written around 1982–1983 indicates that the Tobacco Institute considered

> "the potential positive outcomes of adopting programs of this nature [youth smoking prevention] may be … a more sophisticated understanding by government regulators of the needs/behaviors of our industry. For example, a program to discourage adolescents from smoking (an adult decision) might prevent or delay further regulation of the tobacco industry" (Tobacco Institute, n.d., Bates No. TIMN0018970/8979, p. 7).

Sussman (2002) has provided a useful chronology of the industry's youth smoking prevention programs, which reports that these efforts have tended to focus on parental and peer influences on youth smoking, general decision making and life skills, and issues concerning youth access to tobacco, especially the notion that underage smoking is illegal. It is notable, according to Sussman, that the prevention activities and educational programs developed and supported by the industry ignore the influence of tobacco advertising and promotion on the uptake of youth smoking, the importance of parents not smoking or quitting to provide nonsmoking role models for their children, and an explanation about addiction to tobacco and the problem of serious smoking-related illnesses. In brief, the industry's youth smoking prevention activities fall broadly into five main categories: (1) family involvement self-help booklets, (2) school-based smoking prevention programs, (3) programs to prevent youth from accessing tobacco, (4) mass media campaigns advocating that youth not smoke, and (5) community-based programs for youth. These activities rarely, if ever, include more effective messages that concentrate on the industry's behavior (Figure 5.6; Mandel et al. 2006) and, consistent with industry advertising themes that present smoking as a way to join the adult world, stress that smoking is an "adult choice" or "adult decision."

Self-Help Booklets for Families

In 1984, the Tobacco Institute formed an alliance with the National Association of State Boards of Education (NASBE) to disseminate its *Helping Youth Decide* booklet, which described a program emphasizing the importance of parent-child communication and responsible decision making (USDHHS 1994, pp. 237–8). Although it acknowledged that young people should not smoke, the program offered no specific advice on preventing tobacco use (Coulson 1985). In 1987, a new version of the program focused more clearly on tobacco use, although family communication and decision making were retained as key skills

Figure 5.6 Tobacco industry paradigm shift

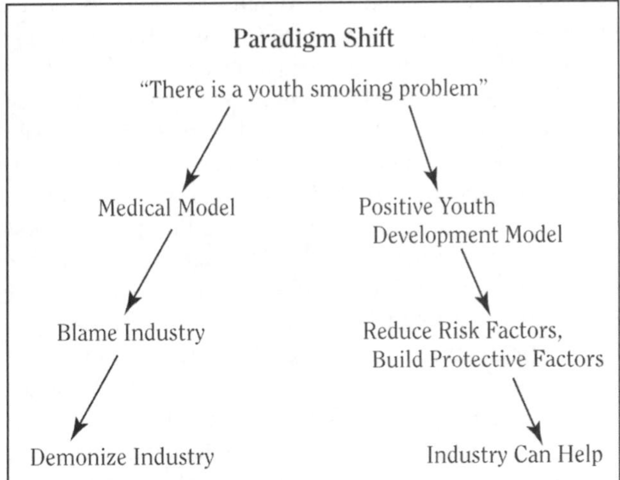

Source: Figure A (a tobacco document reproduced as Figure 1 in Mandel et al. 2006).
Note: This slide, from a 1999 Philip Morris (PM) "Key Initiative Update," describes how it hoped to use its youth smoking prevention strategy as it sought a "paradigm shift" (Philip Morris USA 1999a) away from the "medical model," such as the California Tobacco Control Program (California Department of Health Services/Tobacco Control Section 1998), which highlights the industry's deceptive behavior, to a "positive youth development model" that permits the industry to be viewed as a partner in reducing youth smoking. PM selected Life Skills Training (LST) because it believed that LST supported this objective.

required to prevent tobacco use (USDHHS 1994). In 1988, NASBE withdrew its sponsorship of the Tobacco Institute's programs after a growing conflict between the two organizations about content (Landman et al. 2002). The Tobacco Institute then created its own foundation, the Family C.O.U.R.S.E. Consortium (Communication through Open minds, Understanding, Respect and Self Esteem), which was showcased as a "not-for-profit organization comprised of educators, youth organization professionals and other interested parties" (Sparber and Blaunstein 1991, Bates No. TIMN 0188142, p. 1). No evaluation of the "Helping Youth Decide" program or Family C.O.U.R.S.E. is available to the public (USDHHS 1994).

Other parent-based booklets have been created by RJR (*Right Decisions, Right Now*), B&W (on its Web site for preventing smoking among youth), and Lorillard (*Take 10*), with the materials in those booklets similar to *Helping Youth Decide* (Sussman 2002). As of June 2008, Lorillard's program for parents available through its Web site was called "Real Parents. Real Answers" (Lorillard 2010a). The company offered a brochure, digital video discs (DVDs), and podcasts for parents as well as testimonials from parents about talking to kids and resources for organizations to use with parents. Philip Morris went even further with this kind of approach by developing a televised mass media campaign to encourage parents to talk with their children about tobacco that aired between 1999 and 2006 (see "Industry-Sponsored School-Based Prevention Programs" below). From 2007, Philip Morris has relied on information provided through its Web site, including a brochure entitled *Raising Kids Who Don't Smoke* (Philip Morris USA 2010).

Nearly two decades ago, DiFranza and McAfee (1992) expressed concern that by emphasizing smoking as an adult choice and excluding consideration of health consequences and addiction, brochures such as the Tobacco Institute's *Tobacco: Helping Youth Say No* might have adverse consequences by portraying tobacco as a "forbidden fruit" and thereby "help youth to say 'yes' to tobacco." Aside from these concerns about the possible rebound effects of the industry-preferred type of messages, a study of perceptions among youth of the brochure's content found it was rated poorly compared with similar brochures from tobacco control sources.

Somewhat more recently, DeBon and Klesges (1996) compared the Tobacco Institute's *Tobacco: Helping Youth Say No* brochure with one produced by the American Lung Association (ALA). Both brochures stressed the importance of communication, and both discussed peer pressure and responsible decision making. Unlike the Tobacco Institute brochure, however, the ALA brochure also discussed parents as role models for youth (by not smoking, or quitting) and the health consequences and other costs of smoking, and provided tips for quitting. The Tobacco Institute brochure, but not the ALA brochure, discussed smoking as an illegal act for youth. In the study by DeBon and Klesges (1996), seventh-grade students from six schools in Memphis, Tennessee, were presented with "strategy vignettes" covering all of the program components within the two brochures and were asked to rate the effectiveness of the Tobacco Institute and ALA approaches within each of seven program components. The ALA's approach was rated as more effective by students on six of the components (peer pressure, parents as role models, the health consequences of smoking, the costs of smoking, tips for quitting, and responsible decision making), and the Tobacco Institute's was rated as more effective on one (not smoking because it is illegal). Notably, the kind of approach adopted by the Tobacco Institute did not meet the recommended criteria established by NCI (USDHHS 1994) for effective smoking prevention or currently recommended criteria (see Chapter 6).

Industry-Sponsored School-Based Prevention Programs

During 1998, Philip Morris and B&W jointly decided to promote the LifeSkills Training (LST) program in schools throughout the United States (Mandel et al. 2006). This program had been found in National Instute of Health-funded research to prevent the uptake of smoking and also to reduce the use of alcohol and marijuana (Botvin and Griffiths 2002). The school-based curriculum focuses on social risk factors, including media influence and peer pressure, and personal risk factors such as anxiety and low self-esteem (B&W 1997). Three of the 12 LST units (Smoking: Myths and Realities; Smoking and Biofeedback; and Advertising) focus primarily on tobacco—including increasing awareness of the immediate and long-term health consequences of using tobacco and techniques employed by advertisers to influence consumer behavior (the lessons included in the program do not mention tobacco marketing specifically but refer to more general strategies).

An evaluation of the program by Interactive, Inc. (Ashland, Virginia) for the tobacco companies used a cohort design to assess change over time in knowledge, attitudes, and behavior relative to tobacco, alcohol, and other drugs within three groups of sixth-grade students: 1,985 students from a "national treatment sample" of 24 states implementing LST as a result of promotional efforts by APCO Worldwide, a public relations company headquartered in Washington, D.C., that does extensive public relations for tobacco companies (Mandel et al. 2006); 2,452 students from West Virginia, which had implemented the program on a statewide basis; and 547 students in a national control group (Interactive 2000). The study found that, compared to control students, those receiving LST showed improvements in their knowledge about the physiological effects of smoking but registered no change in their attitudes on the social acceptability of smoking and showed reductions in decision-making skills (Interactive 2000). Increases in 30-day smoking were observed in both the LST and control samples. Although it would have been possible to compare the LST and control groups to test whether LST slowed the rate of smoking uptake, this analysis was not done (Mandel et al. 2006). Interactive's explanation was that the control group had characteristics that differed from those of the LST students, and so the comparison could not be done.

A follow-up of these cohorts in year 2 showed increases in knowledge of the physiological effects of smoking in the national sample but decreases on the same measure in the West Virginia sample (Interactive 2001). Both of these LST cohorts showed significant declines in refusal and decision-making skills and significant increases in 30-day smoking. Again, no comparison was made with the control group on these variables (Interactive 2001). Overall, the evaluation did not show positive changes from the LST program and did show some negative changes in relation to youth smoking. No report on year 3 was made public or was located in the tobacco industry documents, but despite the poor results in terms of actual reductions in youth smoking, Philip Morris and B&W continued to disseminate LST (Mandel et al. 2006).

Mandel and colleagues (2006) provide evidence that one goal of the tobacco industry in promoting LST was to encourage states to expend state Master Settlement Agreement funds for the LST program. Companies sought matching state grants to implement the program (Mandel et al. 2006), and Philip Morris publicized how many schools were involved in LST. For example, as of June 27, 2008, the Philip Morris Web site reported that between 1999 and 2007, "we provided more than $37 million to schools and school districts in 24 states for the implementation of LifeSkills Training. With our support, more than one million middle-school students have participated in this program" (Philip Morris USA 2008a).

In 2000, 2 years after its joint decision with B&W to promote the LST program in U.S. schools, Philip Morris provided schools throughout the country with covers for school books with the message "Think. Don't Smoke" that included the company name of Philip Morris (Clegg Smith and Wakefield 2001). Some schools, however, criticized the book covers for delivering an underlying procigarette message, because the book covers were clearly identified as coming from a tobacco company. In a review of transcripts from testimony of tobacco industry witnesses in tobacco litigation cases from 1992 to 2002, Wakefield and colleagues (2006b) presented industry responses to this issue. Ellen Merlo, vice president of corporate affairs at Philip Morris, reported that even though the company had changed, it would "think long and hard, because maybe people are not yet ready for us to supply something like a book cover" (Merlo 2001).

A substantial body of research has demonstrated that antitobacco-industry attitudes reduce the likelihood of future initiation of smoking among youth and young adults (Sly et al. 2000, 2001; Farrelly et al. 2002, 2005, 2009; Hersey et al. 2003, 2005a,b; Thrasher et al. 2004, 2006; Ling et al. 2007, 2009; Davis et al. 2009). At the same time, book covers provided to students by the tobacco industry, as well as other industry-sponsored efforts with the stated purpose of preventing youth tobacco use, could create favorable impressions of the sponsoring tobacco companies among young people, their parents, or others in the community.

Industry/Community Partnerships on Tobacco Use Among Youth

The tobacco industry has also invested in other community-based programs aimed at youth, such as the national 4-H program ("Head, Heart, Hands, and Health"). 4-H is the youth education branch of the U.S. Department of Agriculture's Cooperative Extension System and a respected organization that emphasizes "learning by doing" (Landman et al. 2002). In March 1999, the National 4-H Council announced a new partnership with Philip Morris as a result of receiving a $1.7 million grant to design and implement a youth smoking prevention initiative (Landman et al. 2002). Despite protests from the public health community and the refusal of 27 of the 50 state 4-H organizations to participate, the national 4-H organization continued its partnership that led to the "Health Rocks" program (National 4-H Council 2010). This program, which includes a Web site, emphasizes general life skills and making healthy choices. Although a longitudinal evaluation of this program in collaboration with Tufts University was discussed in a Philip Morris document in 2001 (Philip Morris USA 2001), no reports were found in the publically available tobacco industry documents on the effects of this program. Philip Morris has also sponsored two programs offered by the Boys & Girls Clubs of America, "Upward Bound" and "SMART (Skills Mastery and Resistance Training) Moves" (Boys & Girls Clubs of America 2010), that had been previously evaluated (U.S. Department of Education 1997; Harvard Family Research Project 2010).

In addition to these programs, tobacco companies have historically given funds to a wide variety of youth-serving organizations (Landman et al. 2002). This practice continued through at least 2010, with grants given by the Altria companies (Philip Morris USA, John Middleton Co., and U.S. Smokeless Tobacco). The 2010 report from Altria stated that its companies gave more than $21 million to positive youth development that year; recipients included the University of Colorado at Boulder, America's Promise Alliance, Corporate Voices for Working Families, The Finance Project, the Forum for Youth Investment, Responsible Retailing Forum, Search Institute, Big Brothers/Big Sisters of America, Caron Foundation, and the University of Virginia (Altria 2011).

Industry-Sponsored Programs to Prevent Youth from Accessing Tobacco

The tobacco industry has aligned itself with efforts to prevent youth from purchasing tobacco since the late 1980s when laws to prevent sales to minors became popular in the United States. The industry has conducted a range of educational programs for tobacco retailers, and it has used the networks developed through its programs to affect legislation it perceived would harm tobacco sales (Landman et al. 2002).

Tobacco Industry Programs in Retailer Education

"It's the Law," a program introduced by the Tobacco Institute in 1990 (Tobacco Institute 1990), was an educational campaign with a primary message that it is illegal for minors to purchase tobacco (Forster and Wolfson 1998); included in the campaign were a series of decals, buttons, and educational materials for retailers. B&W launched a similar program in 1992, called "Support the Law…It Works!," partnering with the United States Junior Chamber (Sussman 2002). The program included store signage as well as a videotape and brochure to train store personnel. In a February 1992 letter to state governors, the president of the Tobacco Institute, Samuel D. Chilcote, Jr., stated that "over one million pieces of program materials have been distributed to thousands of retail outlets across the country" (Chilcote 1992, Bates No. TI41816030/6031, p. 2). In 1992, B&W reported that more than 70,000 stores received its program material on reducing youth access (Sussman 2002).

A far less optimistic view of program implementation and effectiveness was found in a 1991 study of youth aged 13–16 years and 156 retailers in Massachusetts (DiFranza and Brown 1992). This study found that only 7 of the 156 retailers were participating in "It's the Law." Furthermore, six of the seven (86%) participating retailers were found to be willing to sell tobacco to minors (based on successful attempts by youth), and 88% (131 of 149) of the nonparticipating retailers were willing to make such sales (again based on the investigation). Another study compared outcomes of 480 attempted tobacco purchases by youth aged 12–17 years in 40 selected stores participating in "It's the Law" or similar programs with data from 40 stores not participating in these programs (DiFranza et al. 1996). The study found that stores involved in "It's the Law" were as likely to make illegal cigarette sales to these youth as were nonparticipating stores.

Philip Morris took over management of "It's the Law" in 1994 (Landman et al. 2002) and made it part of its "Action Against Access" program in 1995. This program promised to end the distribution of samples, deny slotting fees (fees paid to retailers by tobacco companies to place a tobacco product on retail shelves) to retailers found to be selling tobacco to minors, require cigarettes to be in sight of sales clerks, encourage "reasonable" licensure laws, and require proof-of-age signage (Forster and Wolfson 1998). In 1995, another campaign, "We Card," was launched by the tobacco-industry-created Coalition for Responsible Tobacco Retailing, Inc., and was supported by multiple tobacco companies, including B&W, U.S. Tobacco, and RJR. The campaign included age calendars, employee training videos, and purchase attempts by youth to assess compliance (Forster and Wolfson 1998). This campaign, at least in some states, was accompanied by extensive regional training meetings with retailers.

As in other studies of industry-sponsored youth access programs, the results of evaluations found limited evidence of substantial program implementation or effectiveness. One study found that retail stores selling tobacco products and displaying the tobacco industry's "We Card" signs had average rates of sales to youth roughly equal to those of stores without signs and that the stores with the signs were significantly more likely to make illegal sales to minors than were outlets with government-sponsored signs about not selling to youth (Cowling and Robbins 2000). Tobacco industry documents show that "We Card" was undertaken for two primary purposes: to improve the tobacco industry's image, and to undermine and co-opt retailer compliance programs run by law enforcement and state public health departments (Apollonio and Malone 2010). Apollonio and Malone reported that the tobacco industry and retailers anticipated from the program's inception that "We Card" could be used to block stronger policies restricting youth access to tobacco. Furthermore, industry surveys in 1996 found that retailers considered the blocking of stronger policies to be an excellent use of the program (Sederholm Public Affairs 1996). However, Tobacco Institute lobbyists viewed the program as primarily political, noting in a 1997 report: "Once again, work by the WE CARD Coalition has been instrumental in state efforts to enact reasonable youth access laws" (Chilcote 1997, Bates No. 98876422/6426, p. 3)—that is, state laws preempting stronger local legislation. An audit of "Action Against Access" by former U.S. Senator Warren B. Rudman found that the program was not fully implemented and that retailers did not take it seriously (Campaign for Tobacco-Free Kids 2005). Two years after the program had been put in place, Philip Morris had penalized only 16 tobacco retailers out of the hundreds of thousands illegally selling to youth (Advocacy Institute 1998). In addition, despite Philip Morris' promise to withhold slotting fees from retailers who had been convicted of illegal sales to minors, the company did not respond to the lists of convicted retailers furnished to them by at least four states (Forster and Wolfson 1998).

The Influences of the Tobacco Industry's Youth Access Program on State and Local Tobacco Control Policies

By investing in retailer education programs for compliance with youth access laws, the tobacco industry further leveraged its relationships with groups of retailers, often with results that were detrimental to tobacco control. In a review of the policies and politics of youth access, for example, Forster and Wolfson (1998) found that the tobacco industry used sham citizen groups or its networks of retailers to support bills that would serve to undermine aspects of proposed laws on youth access. This finding is illustrated well by DiFranza and Godshall (1996), who reviewed bills on youth access that were introduced in 12 states by state legislators supportive of the tobacco industry. Provisions of these industry-supported bills included: (1) preemption clauses that prohibited units of local government from passing stricter laws than those passed by the state or federal government; (2) provisions restricting enforcement authority to a single state agency that was ill-equipped to carry out such enforcement (such as a department of agriculture or revenue); (3) provisions that made successful prosecution difficult or impossible (e.g., a requirement that violations of age-of-sale laws involve intent on the part of the merchant to sell tobacco products to a minor); (4) prohibition of compliance checks by individuals or organizations other than law enforcement, such as public health officials, citizen activists, or the press; and (5) prohibition of the purchase of tobacco products by minors, which would halt age-of-sale compliance operations that use youth to attempt to make purchases (DiFranza and Godshall 1996). Other studies indicate the extent to which the industry has been an active proponent of preemption laws to prohibit local government from passing stricter laws than those passed by the state (Siegel et al. 1997).

The tobacco industry has also actively supported laws to penalize youth for possessing, using, and purchasing tobacco—laws that have been criticized because they ignore the responsibilities of the industry and retailers (Wakefield and Giovino 2003). Forster and Wolfson (1998) concluded that the tobacco manufacturers' and retailer organizations' voluntary efforts to educate and train retailers were essentially aimed at exonerating them from any responsibility for smoking by youth and to focus blame on the minors who attempt to purchase tobacco and the clerks who sell it to them.

In a study of internal documents from tobacco companies, Landman and colleagues (2002) found that the industry used its programs on youth access to undermine tobacco control efforts. For example, a series of e-mails in 1996 between high-level Philip Morris executives revealed that Philip Morris placed ads for "Action Against Access" in locations where legislators would be sure to see them (Merlo 1996), and the company used the presence of programs such as this to argue against the need for government funding of further tobacco control efforts (Slavitt 1992). Furthermore, the tobacco industry used its network of retailers to disseminate information about proposed local ordinances on tobacco control in an effort to rally retailers to oppose them. A confidential 1992 report from the Tobacco Institute stated, "For monitoring purposes, we fund our allies in the convenience store group to regularly report on ordinance introductions and assist in campaigns to stop unreasonable measures.... Promotion of The Institute's 'It's the Law' program and other industry programs play a helpful role as well" (Malmgren 1992, Bates No. 2023959567/9579, p. 5).

Industry documents also reveal that it used its network of retailers to detect and oppose measures related to restrictions on advertising and laws requiring clean indoor air (Ohio Licensed Beverage Association 1995; Riskind and Bradshaw 1995; Hannah Report 1996; Philip Morris USA 1996; Welsh-Huggins 2001). A 1996 Tobacco Institute press release argued that the 1994 FDA proposal to end tobacco advertisements within 1,000 feet of schools, eliminate self-service tobacco displays, and require "tombstone" advertising (advertisements that consist only of black print on a white background, without pictures) for tobacco products was unnecessary because the industry's "We Card" program was "now making a measurable difference" (Tobacco Institute 1996, Bates No. 106018947/8948, p. 2). Philip Morris also used "Action Against Access" as part of its argument that FDA's proposal was unnecessary (Parrish 1995). Apollonio and Malone (2010) concluded that industry programs such as

> "We Card ... are designed to suggest that tobacco companies are part of the solution to the problem of youth tobacco use. In doing so, they also serve to reify youth tobacco use as the prevailing definition of the tobacco policy problem, distracting the public and policymakers from the fact that cigarettes remain the single most deadly consumer product ever made" (p. 1196).

Industry-Sponsored Antismoking Campaigns in the Mass Media

In 1996, Philip Morris launched a $10 million advertising campaign to promote youth smoking prevention (SCARC Action Alert 1996), a campaign that included newspaper and magazine advertisements and highlighted the company's initiatives on restricting youth access. This campaign and others emerged at a time when the company was facing a number of legal challenges alleging corporate misconduct (Wakefield et al. 2006b).

In the late 1990s, two tobacco companies launched televised mass-media campaigns focused on the prevention of youth smoking in the United States. A Philip Morris youth smoking prevention campaign consisting of several television and magazine advertisements carrying the slogan "Think. Don't Smoke" ran from 1998 to 2002 (Sussman 2002); according to the company, the target audience was youth aged 10–14 years (Sussman 2002). In 1999, a second Philip Morris campaign, "Talk. They'll Listen," made its debut on television; this campaign focused on parents talking to their children about smoking and ran until late 2006. Tobacco companies portrayed their allocations of funding as evidence that they were serious about reducing youth smoking. During testimony in the U.S. Department of Justice lawsuit in 2005, Philip Morris indicated that "our budget has fluctuated somewhat from year to year, but on average, we have spent $100 million a year over the last 6 years in the department. The expenditures from 1998 through 2004 total $657 million" (Willard 2005, p. 9). Philip Morris USA Senior Director of Communications, Peggy Roberts, indicated the company had spent "more than $1 billion on youth smoking prevention efforts" (Ascribe 2006).

Between 1999 and 2004, Lorillard's "Tobacco Is Whacko if You're a Teen" campaign appeared widely in youth magazines and on popular cable television, including ESPN, MTV, and Warner Bros. stations (Landman et al. 2002). Eventually, Lorillard replaced its youth campaign with advertisements targeting parents. Formerly known as "*Take 10*," the Lorillard prevention campaign adopted the slogan "Parents. The Best Thing Between Kids and Cigarettes." In 2010, the Lorillard Web site indicated it had spent more than $80 million on efforts to prevent youth smoking (Lorillard 2010b).

The monies invested in these campaigns helped to ensure widespread exposure to the industry's efforts among youth and adults. According to Nielsen media monitoring data from 1999 to 2003, the exposure of adolescents to Philip Morris' and Lorillard's youth prevention ads matched those for antitobacco advertising from all state and national tobacco control programs (Wakefield et al. 2005b). However, exposure to youth prevention advertisements sponsored by tobacco companies was found to be greatest across adult audience segments and relatively lower among adolescents (Wakefield et al. 2005b). Despite these high exposure levels, the effectiveness of these campaigns in reducing youth smoking is questionable.

Studies of the efficacy of tobacco-company-sponsored advertising have most often used individual ratings of industry sponsored ads, which are compared with ratings of antitobacco ads sponsored by public health organizations or other corporate advertising in a forced-exposure setting. In these studies, youth are exposed individually or in a group setting to a series of ads and then asked to rate each ad immediately after viewing it (e.g., Henriksen and Fortmann 2002; Niederdeppe et al. 2005; Wakefield et al. 2005a; Donovan et al. 2006). Some studies have also required youth to select the ad they perceived to be the most effective or to indicate measures of smoking-related beliefs, attitudes, and intentions following exposure (e.g., Henriksen et al. 2006; Pechmann and Reibling 2006). Others have added follow-up measures of recall and cognitive processing of the ads (e.g., Terry-McElrath et al. 2005). Of the seven studies summarized in Table 5.10, all demonstrate that tobacco-company-sponsored youth prevention ads performed poorly in terms of increased knowledge, perceived effectiveness, and influence on intention to smoke as compared with antitobacco ads sponsored by public health organizations (the seventh study had alcohol-related ads as controls). The studies generally indicate that the ads' low efficacy is due to their message strategy; consistent with other industry youth smoking prevention efforts, both Philip Morris and Lorillard have focused their messages on social themes, such as making a choice about smoking among peers and within the family or presenting the short-term benefits of not smoking. Ads with these kinds of messages generally perform poorly in comparison with ads that feature the serious health effects of smoking and the marketing and promotion practices of the industry (Farrelly et al. 2002, 2005; NCI 2008).

Studies of ninth-graders in schools in California (Pechmann and Reibling 2006) and of Western Australia youth intercepted in shopping malls (Donovan et al. 2006) found that ads with social themes generally did not lower the intention of youth to smoke in the future, but ads focusing on the serious health consequences of smoking (Pechmann and Reibling 2006) or the disgusting aspects of smoking (Donovan et al. 2006) did so. In analyses from the NCI-funded Youth Smoking and the Media study, ads from tobacco companies were found to elicit positive emotions in youth and to be of less interest to that age group than ads sponsored by tobacco control agencies (Wakefield et al. 2005a). In addition, ads that elicited negative emotions such as those with a personal testimonial or negative visceral element were more likely to be recalled, discussed, and thought about by youth at a 1-week follow-up, but ads with these kinds of features were never developed by tobacco companies (Terry-McElrath et al. 2005).

In a study of California adolescents aged 14–17 years, exposure to industry ads engendered more favorable attitudes toward tobacco companies than seeing "truth" ads from the American Legacy Foundation or control ads about drunken driving (Henriksen et al. 2006). Sympathy with the industry was measured by agreement with statements such as "cigarette companies get too much blame for young people smoking" and "cigarette companies should have the same right to sell cigarettes as other companies have to sell their products" (Henriksen et al. 2006, p. 15). In addition, in the study of Western Australia youth described above, which included both smokers and nonsmokers, industry-sponsored ads were rated as highly believable (Donovan et al. 2006). These corporate ads served to increase the credibility of the industry's message that, although unlikely to change attitudes about smoking per se, may increase positive attitudes toward the tobacco industry and, in turn, reduce criticism from youth advocacy groups in the community (Donovan et al. 2006).

Examining the effects of advertising by using forced-exposure designs can be useful for assessing immediate reactions to individual ads and their short-term influences on smoking-related beliefs and intentions, but available studies do not reflect the usual television-viewing environment with its contextual distractions of television programs, competing advertising, and variable viewer attention. Moreover, forced-exposure studies cannot assess the effects of cumulative exposure to campaign messages over time. By comparison, some study designs have relied on naturalistic exposure in the usual viewing environment and attempted to do so with samples of participants more representative of the population. In these studies, exposure to advertising has usually been measured by asking whether participants can recall seeing any antitobacco ads in a specified period and, if so, having them describe the ads they recall to generate a measure of confirmed recall (Biener 2002; Farrelly et al. 2002, 2009; Davis et al. 2007). Some studies, in contrast, have employed gross rating points (an advertising industry measure that involves multiplying the estimated audience reached by the frequency of the message) as a measure of exposure to advertising (Farrelly et al. 2005; Wakefield et al. 2006c).

Three types of naturalistic exposure studies have examined the effects of industry-sponsored media campaigns in the United States (Table 5.11). In the first type, carried out by Biener (2002), respondents were asked to assess the effectiveness of ads. The author found that adolescents aged 14–17 years rated ads that did not focus

Table 5.10 Controlled-exposure studies examining televised messages in the tobacco industry's campaign to prevent youth smoking

Study	Study design/population	Advertisement comparisons	Findings
Teenage Research Unlimited 1999	20 focus groups 7th–10th graders (N = 120) who were susceptible[a] to using tobacco Youth viewed each of 10 ads, rated them, and discussed them as a group Arizona, California, Massachusetts	10 ads produced by state tobacco control programs in Arizona, California, Florida, and Massachusetts, and by Philip Morris	• Youth reported that the Philip Morris ads, which were focused on social influences, provided no new information • Without the negative effects of smoking being mentioned, the Philip Morris ads made little sense to youth and were considered "scripted"
Henriksen and Fortmann 2002	218 18- to 25-year-old undergraduate students Youth were randomly assigned to view 4 ads; they completed baseline ratings of various companies, viewed and made ratings of each ad, and made an overall rating about various companies California	4 Philip Morris Youth Smoking Prevention (YSP) ads, 4 Philip Morris ads about charitable works, or 4 Anheuser-Busch Company ads about preventing underage drinking (the control group)	• Philip Morris YSP and charitable works ads were rated less favorably by those who knew Philip Morris was a tobacco company than by those who were unaware of that • Ads about Philip Morris' charitable works received more favorable ratings than did Philip Morris YSP ads
Niederdeppe et al. 2005	820 13- to 18-year-olds Youth completed an Internet-delivered baseline questionnaire assessing susceptibility to smoking and sensation seeking, viewed 5 randomly ordered antitobacco ads, and completed 6 individual ratings of each ad, which were summed to provide composite ratings of ad evaluations United States	3 ads from American Legacy Foundation (Legacy) "truth" campaign ("Body Bags," "Daily Dose," and "Shredder"), 1 ad from Philip Morris ("My Reasons"), and 1 ad from a state tobacco control program (result not reported)	• Participants in all smoking risk categories rated Legacy's "Body Bags" and "Daily Dose" more highly than Philip Morris' "My Reasons" and Legacy's "Shredder" • Compared with the 2 highest-ranking Legacy ads, the Philip Morris ad received favorable ratings among 13- to 15-year-olds at lowest risk for future smoking, but 16- to 18-year-olds at elevated risk of future smoking responded significantly less favorably
Youth Smoking and the Media Terry-McElrath et al. 2005; Wakefield et al. 2005a	268 8th-, 10th-, and 12th-grade susceptible nonsmokers or experimenters in Boston, Massachusetts, and Chicago, Illinois; the study was replicated in Australia and Britain for a total of 615 8th-, 10th-, and 12th-grade students in all countries combined Youth completed immediate ratings after viewing each of 10 ads in late 2000–early 2001, selected highest "stop and think" ad at end of each session; 1-week telephone follow-up to establish recall, thinking about the ads, and discussion of ads viewed	8 tobacco company YSP ads produced by Philip Morris and Lorillard, 37 public-health-sponsored antitobacco ads, and 5 pharmaceutical company ads for nicotine replacement therapy and bupropion	• Compared with public-health-sponsored antitobacco ads, tobacco company ads were more likely to elicit positive emotions and less likely to elicit negative emotions and be of interest to youth • Tobacco company ads were more likely to feature smoking not being "cool," parental advice not to smoke, and the short-term benefits of not smoking, while public-health-sponsored ads more often featured the serious health effects of smoking or secondhand smoke and deception by the tobacco industry • Tobacco control ads that employed negative visceral elements or personal testimonials were rated more highly by youth; none of the tobacco industry ads used these formats

Table 5.10 Continued

Study	Study design/population	Advertisement comparisons	Findings
Donovan et al. 2006	257 14- to 18-year-olds Youth recruited through interception of shoppers were exposed to a tobacco industry YSP ad or a tobacco control ad, after which they completed ratings of the impact of the ad on their smoking Australia	3 tobacco industry YSP ads produced and adapted for MTV in Australia, 2 youth-directed tobacco control ads featuring smoking not being "cool" or short-term harms of smoking (shown to 14- to 15-year-olds only), and several tobacco control ads portraying smoking as disgusting	• Among 14- to 15-year-olds, tobacco industry ads generally scored lower than the tobacco control ads that portrayed smoking as disgusting but were rated similarly to the other youth-focused tobacco control ads • Among 16- to 18-year-olds, the tobacco industry ads were rated as having less impact than the disgust-oriented tobacco control ads in terms of not wanting to smoke and, among smokers, in thinking about quitting
Henriksen et al. 2006	832 high school students Aged 14–17 years Youth were randomly exposed to view 5 ads; measures included ad perception, intention to smoke, and attitudes toward tobacco companies measured immediately after exposure California	5 tobacco company YSP ads (Philip Morris or Lorillard), 5 Legacy "truth" antitobacco ads, or 5 ads about preventing drunk driving	• Participants rated tobacco company YSP ads less favorably than Legacy "truth" ads • Exposure to tobacco company YSP ads engendered more favorable attitudes toward tobacco companies
Pechmann and Reibling 2006	1,725 9th graders Youth were randomly assigned to view a television program in 2002 in which particular themed ads or control ads were embedded At baseline, personality traits were measured and, after exposure, students were asked about smoking intentions, feelings and beliefs, and appraisal of the ads California	10 ad themes (3 ads of each theme); ads produced by public-health-sponsored agencies featured health effects and manipulation by tobacco industry, while all tobacco industry ads featured social themes	• Ads with social themes, including those produced by tobacco companies, did not significantly lower participants' smoking intentions • By comparison, ads focusing on young victims suffering from serious smoking-related diseases elicited disgust, enhanced anti-industry attitudes, and reduced intentions to smoke • Youth with conduct disorders, who are more likely to smoke, were not influenced by any of the ads

[a]According to criteria developed by Choi and colleagues 2001.

on tobacco-related illness as significantly less effective than ads from the state program that featured the serious health consequences of smoking (Biener 2002). These effects were more pronounced among youth aged 16–17 years than those aged 14–15 years.

The second type of study has involved comparisons of "truth" ads from the American Legacy Foundation in which nationally representative samples of U.S. adolescents aged 12–17 years have been surveyed to determine awareness of the ads, receptivity to them, and tobacco-related knowledge, attitudes, beliefs, and behavior. In the first paper from these studies, reporting a survey conducted 10 months after the launch of the national "truth" campaign, youth who recalled the "Think. Don't Smoke" ads of Philip Morris were significantly more likely than their unexposed peers to have intentions to smoke in the future; in contrast, confirmed recall of the "truth" campaign was associated with lower intentions to smoke (Farrelly et al. 2002). In addition, youth who recalled the "Think. Don't Smoke" campaign were less likely to agree with statements such as "cigarette companies deny that cigarettes cause cancer and other harmful diseases," and "I would like to see cigarette companies go out of business" (Farrelly et al. 2002, p. 904). In subsequent studies using eight cross-sectional telephone surveys, exposure to additional Philip Morris advertisements reinforced these attitudes (Farrelly et al. 2009). Unlike exposure to "truth" ads, which were associated with lower perceptions of the prevalence of smoking, recall of "Think. Don't Smoke" was unrelated to perceived smoking prevalence (Davis et al. 2007). Because the data from this second group of studies were cross-sectional, part of the explanation for the findings may be that adolescents who already held more favorable opinions about cigarette companies and expressed stronger intentions to smoke in the future were more attentive to Philip Morris ads and therefore more likely to recall them.

The third type of study featured population-based survey data linked to naturalistic data on exposure to media. Here, Wakefield and colleagues (2006c) used data from more than 100,000 students (8th-, 10th-, and 12th-grade students) who had completed the MTF school-based surveys from 1999 to 2002, where beliefs about smoking, intentions to smoke, and smoking behavior comprised the study outcomes (Wakefield et al. 2006c). This study measured exposure to advertising using gross rating points for each type of advertising campaign in the 4 months preceding the surveys in the media markets in which the schools were located. The industry-sponsored advertising included the youth prevention campaigns "Think. Don't Smoke" and "Tobacco Is Whacko if You're a Teen" and the Philip Morris parent-directed campaign "Talk. They'll Listen."

Multivariable models examined the relationship between level of exposure to advertising and attitude (beliefs), intentions to smoke, and tobacco use behavior while controlling for demographic and other personal data, region, the real price of cigarettes, an index of smoke-free air, and media utilization. The study found that greater exposure to industry-sponsored youth-directed advertising was associated with stronger intentions to smoke among 8th-grade students, but not with other outcomes for 8th-grade students or with any outcome for those in the 10th and 12th grades. Exposure to the tobacco industry's parent-directed campaign was associated with several undesirable outcomes for 10th- and 12th-grade students, including lower perceived harm from smoking, stronger approval of smoking, stronger intentions to smoke in the future, and a higher likelihood of smoking in the past month.

Wakefield and colleagues (2006c) explained these findings as follows: as adolescents mature, they consider themselves more independent and less reliant on their parents. Thus, messages aimed at parents as authority figures may invite rejection by older adolescents. Despite the sophisticated naturalistic exposure studies available in the literature that have assessed the effectiveness of the industry's advertising campaigns, the substantial investment of industry in these campaigns, and its insistence on the seriousness of its efforts, the tobacco companies have used very weak methods of program evaluation. For example, in court testimonies from 1992 to 2003, company witnesses focused on advertising reach as a measure of effectiveness (e.g., 90% of 10- to 14-year-olds had seen the advertisements) and on qualitative data, rather than on outcomes involving attitudes, intentions, and behaviors (Merlo 2000).

Although Philip Morris withdrew its television advertising campaign directed at parents after the study by Wakefield and colleagues (2006c) was published, it still cites its own weak evaluation data to suggest that its "Talk. They'll Listen" campaign had beneficial effects (Philip Morris USA 2008a). Philip Morris also decreased its "Think. Don't Smoke" campaign from 2002 following the publication of Farrelly and colleagues' (2002) population-based study indicating that exposure to the campaign was associated with increased intentions to smoke among youth. The lack of substantive studies emerging from the tobacco industry on the actual effects of programs (dollars spent and number of youth contacted, rather than changes in smoking behavior) contrasts sharply with the very detailed evaluations used for the company's other marketing efforts, as was revealed during litigation. Furthermore, neither Philip Morris, nor any of the other tobacco companies, has released any data on the effects of

Table 5.11 Naturalistic studies examining the effect of televised campaigns of the tobacco industry on preventing youth smoking

Study	Study design/population	Advertisement comparisons	Findings
Biener 2002	733 youth aged 14–17 years Youth were asked in a telephone survey whether they had seen any antitobacco ads on television in the previous month. If they had, they were asked to describe them in detail and to rate their effectiveness on a 10-point scale Massachusetts	The most prominent antitobacco ads produced by the Massachusetts (MA) Tobacco Control Program and those produced by Philip Morris; 4 categories: illness, outrage, other MA, Philip Morris	• Philip Morris ads ($p < .001$) and MA ads that did not discuss illness ($p < .001$) were rated as significantly less effective by youth than were MA ads featuring the serious health consequences of smoking
Evaluation of national "truth" campaign Farrelly et al. 2002, 2009; Davis et al. 2007	12- to 17-year-olds Nationally representative cross-sectional telephone surveys of youth before launch (N = 6,897) and 10 months after launch of national American Legacy Foundation (Legacy) "truth" campaign (N = 6,233); 2 later studies used data from 35,074 youth in 8 nationally representative cross-sectional telephone surveys from 1999 to 2003; measures included confirmed ad recall, smoking attitudes and beliefs, perceived smoking prevalence, and intention to smoke in next year United States	Legacy "truth" ads featuring manipulation messages of the tobacco industry compared with youth smoking prevention ads by Philip Morris asking youth to "Think. Don't Smoke"	• After 10 months, confirmed exposure to Philip Morris ads was associated with more positive attitudes toward the tobacco industry (generally $p < .05$) and increased intentions to smoke in the future ($p < .05$), while confirmed exposure to "truth" ads was associated with attitudes against the tobacco industry (generally $p < .05$) • After 3 years, perceived smoking prevalence was unrelated to confirmed exposure to the Philip Morris campaign, but it was reduced among those who had confirmed recall of the "truth" campaign (generally $p < .05$) • After 3 years, confirmed exposure to the Philip Morris campaign was associated with more favorable beliefs and attitudes toward tobacco companies and a trend for weaker intentions not to smoke, while "truth" exposure was associated with stronger antitobacco attitudes and intentions not to smoke in the future ($p < .001$)
Wakefield et al. 2006c	103,172 8th, 10th, and 12th graders Data from the 1999–2002 Monitoring the Future school-based surveys were merged by media market on 12- to 17-year-olds' gross rating points for antitobacco ads during the 4 months before survey completion; outcome measures included smoking attitudes and beliefs, intentions to smoke, and smoking in the past 30 days United States	Tobacco company youth-directed youth smoking prevention (YSP) ad campaigns and parent-directed YSP ad campaigns as well as public-health-sponsored antitobacco ad campaigns	• Among 8th graders, greater exposure to industry youth-directed YSP ads was associated with increased intention to smoke (OR = 1.04 [95% CI = 1.01–1.08]), but exposure was unrelated to other outcomes for this age group or for 10th and 12th graders • Among 10th–12th graders, greater exposure to parent-directed YSP ads was associated with lower perceived harm from smoking (OR = 0.93 [0.88–0.98]), stronger approval of smoking (OR = 1.11 [1.03–1.12]), stronger intentions to smoke in future (OR = 1.12 [1.04–1.21]), and greater likelihood of having smoked in the past 30 days (OR = 1.12 [1.04–1.19])

Note: **CI** = confidence interval; **OR** = odds ratio.

these programs on the sales of tobacco products, including the large Philip Morris/B&W funded study that demonstrated that LST was followed by increased smoking by youth (Mandel et al. 2006).

One study has examined the responses of youth to the industry's public relations messages about its corporate responsibility. Henriksen and Fortmann (2002) conducted a controlled-exposure study of 18- to 25-year-old undergraduates in California to determine their perceptions. The authors found that youth who had viewed four ads produced by Philip Morris that contained information on the company's charitable works had improved perceptions of that company's corporate image as compared with a control group. The improvement in perceptions was greatest among those who were unaware that Philip Morris was a tobacco company (Henriksen and Fortmann 2002).

A review of media campaigns on prevention of smoking among youth conducted for WHO concluded that industry-sponsored campaigns do not contain message features found to be effective in reducing smoking behavior among youth (Angus et al. 2008). Further, the review noted that these campaigns tend to increase favorable industry-related attitudes among youth, which is consistent with the industry's broader goal of improving their image and reputation of tobacco companies (Angus et al. 2008). The report concluded that these campaigns may serve to undermine the effectiveness of efforts that seek to increase anti-industry attitudes to deter youth from smoking (Farrelly et al. 2002; Thrasher et al. 2006; Ling et al. 2007, 2009) and pose a risk for youth as they age into adulthood in terms of retaining "an objective and critical perspective on tobacco" (Angus et al. 2008, p. 20).

Summary

The tobacco industry's youth smoking prevention activities and programs have not provided evidence that they are effective at reducing youth smoking. Indeed, unpublished internal industry documents available to the public because of litigation, and published academic studies, indicate that they are ineffective or serve to promote smoking among youth. Because older adolescents rebel against the programmatic message that tobacco is for adults only, these efforts can lead to a greater likelihood of uptake among youth (Donovan et al. 2006; Henriksen et al. 2006; Wakefield et al. 2006c).

Focusing programs on issues such as parenting, decision making by youth, life skills, and reducing youth access helps to focus the responsibility for smoking on the young people themselves and on their family environment and diverts attention from the tobacco industry's marketing efforts and the addictiveness of tobacco products. The industry's approach also positions tobacco as "forbidden fruit," with tobacco use being portrayed as an "adult only" practice (DiFranza and McAfee 1992), a message consistent with industry marketing messages that present smoking as a way to be "adult." The WHO Tobacco-Free Initiative recommends that both governmental and nongovernmental organizations avoid partnering with the industry's youth prevention programs because the programs have been proven to be ineffective and are used to persuade policymakers to opt for weaker legislation (WHO 2004).

The tobacco industry receives five benefits from its youth smoking prevention initiatives:

1. The industry uses these efforts to convey to the public, policymakers, judges, and the members of juries that it is doing something substantial about the issue of youth's tobacco use. In this way, the programs serve to promote positive attitudes about the tobacco industry. Such positive attitudes could help to limit the industry's legal liability and make it easier for its views to be heard on legislative issues.

2. More favorable impressions of tobacco companies among youth and young adults can help to maintain the potential for youth to initiate tobacco use in their young adult years (Thrasher et al. 2006; Wakefield et al. 2006c; Ling et al. 2007, 2009).

3. The industry has been able to use the relationships it has forged through its youth prevention programs to learn of proposed tobacco control legislation and to lobby against that legislation (Forster and Wolfson 1998; Landman et al. 2002; Apollonio and Malone 2010).

4. The industry is able to use its efforts to prevent smoking by youth to argue that there is less need for public-health-funded tobacco control strategies (Mandel et al. 2006).

5. Investment in these programs provides a venue for the industry to conduct research on determinants of smoking among youth for the stated purpose of developing its prevention programs. However, this information could inform the companies' tobacco marketing efforts to youth (Mandel et al. 2006). Tobacco industry research on youth has included Philip Morris' "Teenage Attitudes and Behaviors Study," which tracked the smoking behavior and motivations of approximately 20,000

11–17-year-olds annually, with a total of 180,000 teens being surveyed between 1999 and 2007 (Philip Morris USA 2008b). Although tobacco companies assert that there is a "firewall" between the research done for the department concerned with preventing smoking by youth and their cigarette marketing efforts, Philip Morris has acknowledged that it rotates employees through both departments (Tobacco on Trial 2005).

Images of Smoking in the Entertainment Media and the Development of Identity

This section addresses the impact of images of smoking in the entertainment media—primarily movies—which have been the focus of most of the research in this area. Much of that research involves the impact of depictions of smoking in movies on the uptake of tobacco by adolescents. As described below, from the 1920s to 1989 the tobacco industry entered into a variety of financial arrangements to tie smoking to movies (Mekemson and Glantz 2002). Movies receive greater First Amendment protection than commercial speech such as advertising and promotional materials. Indeed, some argue that tobacco control initiatives should not meddle with moviemakers' intentions to depict the realities of life, including smoking (Chapman 2009). Others argue that the movies to which adolescents are drawn often have nothing to do with reality (e.g., *Avatar*) and that movies are not simply art: they are products created by the entertainment industry to be sold to specific audiences. The rating of the film is part of the marketing effort for the film and the desired rating is generally decided before the film is made so overall content, language, sexual content, and violence can be calibrated to secure the desired rating. Nearly one-half (44%) of top-grossing films in the United States between 2005 and 2010 were rated PG-13, making them easily accessible to youth over the age of 13 years (Nash Information Service LLC 2011). The decision to include smoking in movies ultimately rests with the people who create the movies and the studios that pay for their production and distribution; any effort to affect when smoking is portrayed in movies and other entertainment media is logically focused on the production studios rather than on the tobacco industry.

Images of smoking in the entertainment media are a potentially powerful socializing force among adolescents, in part because they are communicated by people who are identified by youth as media stars (Bandura 1977, 1986). Adolescents actively rely on external information as they seek to shape their own identities, often looking to media stars as models of what to wear and what to do. Adolescents today are highly exposed to entertainment media, which—because they present smoking in the context of a story rather than as a commercial presentation—tend to dispel the skepticism that would attend a commercial presentation. The suspension of disbelief that occurs in viewing entertainment media, and the fact that the message is conveyed by an influential figure, provides a theoretical underpinning for an effect of entertainment media on smoking during adolescence a strong one (Bandura 1977, 1986). More important, because some image advertising has been curtailed by the Master Settlement Agreement, entertainment media are among the few remaining channels for transmission of aspirational images of smoking to large audiences (Kline 2000).

The next section builds on the work of the 2008 NCI monograph, *The Role of the Media in Promoting and Discouraging Tobacco Use* (NCI 2008). Chapter 10 of that work summarizes research (up to 2006) that links depictions of smoking in movies with adolescent smoking.

Images of Smoking in Movies and Adolescent Smoking

Historical Links Between the Tobacco Companies and the Movie Industry

It is generally assumed that smoking was common in early movies, but in fact few content analyses exist for that era. One published study assessed 20 silent movies for episodes of tobacco use and found they occurred at a mean rate of 23.3 per hour (St. Romain et al. 2007). Indeed, the movie industry was viewed as an opportunity for advertising as far back as the nickelodeon era, when movies were silent, cost only a nickel, and ad slides played between reels. By the late 1920s, the tobacco industry considered the male market for cigarettes to be mature and began to position cigarettes in advertising as a way for a man to strike up a conversation with a woman and as a method of weight control for women (e.g., the "Reach for a Lucky Instead of a Sweet" campaign); research has correlated the emergence of these ads with the dramatic rise in smoking among women during the 1930s and 1940s (Pierce and Gilpin 1995). Edward L. Bernays, the architect of many of these marketing campaigns, recognized the "power of film to shape consumer expectations" (Brandt 2007, p. 86). In the 1930s and 1940s, movies frequently showed a lead male actor using cigarettes to engage a lead female actress in conversation (Figure 5.7A, a still from *To Have and Have Not*). Note the similarity between the Humphrey Bogart/Lauren Bacall scene and Figure 5.7B, a cigarette ad from that period. Lum and colleagues (2008) found evidence of commercial relationships between the tobacco and movie industries in tobacco documents dating from as early as 1929. FTC investigations in 1930 ended this practice, and the tobacco and motion picture industries turned to cross-promotion arrangements (termed "tie-ins"), in which endorsements of cigarette brands by movie stars were used to advertise those brands and garner publicity for newly released movies. Figure 5.8 shows a tie-in ad in which film star Spencer Tracy endorses Lucky Strikes and pitches the MGM production *Test Pilot*.

Figure 5.7 Actor engaging an actress with a cigarette

A. Humphrey Bogart lighting a cigarette for Lauren Bacall in *To Have and Have Not*

B. Print advertisement showing Humphrey Bogart and Lauren Bacall engaged over tobacco

Source: Figure 5.7A. mptvimages.com 2011. Reprinted with permission from mptvimages. Figure 5.7B. *Life* September 1951.

Placement of products in movies, including tobacco, became an integral part of film production with the advent

Figure 5.8 "SHOUT, Mr. Tracy!": actor enjoying a cigarette

Source: American Tobacco Company 1938.

of product placement agencies in the late 1970s (Mekemsom and Glantz 2002; Segrave 2004). For example, a 1987 sales pitch by Liggett & Myers promoted the movie *Eight Men Out* as follows: "... based on its story, cast and subject matter, this film will appeal to young audiences.... Billboard sponsorship provides an opportunity to deliver subtle but powerful institutional and product messages to a young group, still in its stages of forming purchasing habits" (Breidenbach 1987, Bates No. 91753669/3670, p. 1).

Evidence from tobacco company documents has provided confirmation of a commercial relationship between the tobacco industry and film studios that began in the 1920s and lasted until it waned in the 1950s, the era when advertising dollars began flowing away from movies and into television (Lum et al. 2008). There was a resurgence of tobacco product placement in the movies during the 1970s after cigarette advertising was banned on television (Mekemson and Glantz 2002). Some evidence suggests that some companies sought to provide financial backing to movies as "trademark diversification" but with the demonstrated intent of incentivizing tobacco use in movies (LeGresley et al. 2006).

Evidence for the Presence of Tobacco Use in Movies: Content Analysis

Content analysis is the process by which information about a certain topic is systematically coded by watching or listening to the media source. Typically, the content is determined through a set of rules. The best analyses employ two or more coders and examine interrater reliability for an overlapping subset of content to validate the process. Over the years, there have been many content analyses of depictions of smoking in movies. A review conducted by NCI (2008), which summarized the results of 14 content-coding studies, concluded that cigarette and cigar smoking is pervasive in movies but use of smokeless tobacco is not, and it found that identifiable cigarette brands appeared in about one-third of movies released during the 1990s. It also concluded that (1) the prevalence of smoking among contemporary movie characters is approximately 25%, about twice that of movies of the 1970s and 1980s; (2) smokers in movies differ from smokers in the general population, the former being more likely to be affluent and White; (3) the health consequences of smoking are rarely depicted in movies; and (4) smoking in the movies is not related to box office success. Studies of trends in movie content published since 2005 (summarized in Table 5.12) show declines in depictions of movie smoking since the Master Settlement Agreement.

Tobacco Use in Movies

Product Placement

In a section titled "Prohibition on Payments Related to Tobacco Products and Media," the Master Settlement Agreement prohibits payments for branded product placement in motion pictures, television shows, theatrical productions, music performances, and video games (NAAG 1998a). This agreement is binding only on the domestic cigarette companies that signed the agreement, not on their international counterparts or companies outside the United States or nonparticipating domestic tobacco companies.

Figure 5.9 Proportion of movies containing tobacco brand appearances in the top 100 box office hits released each year, 1996–2008

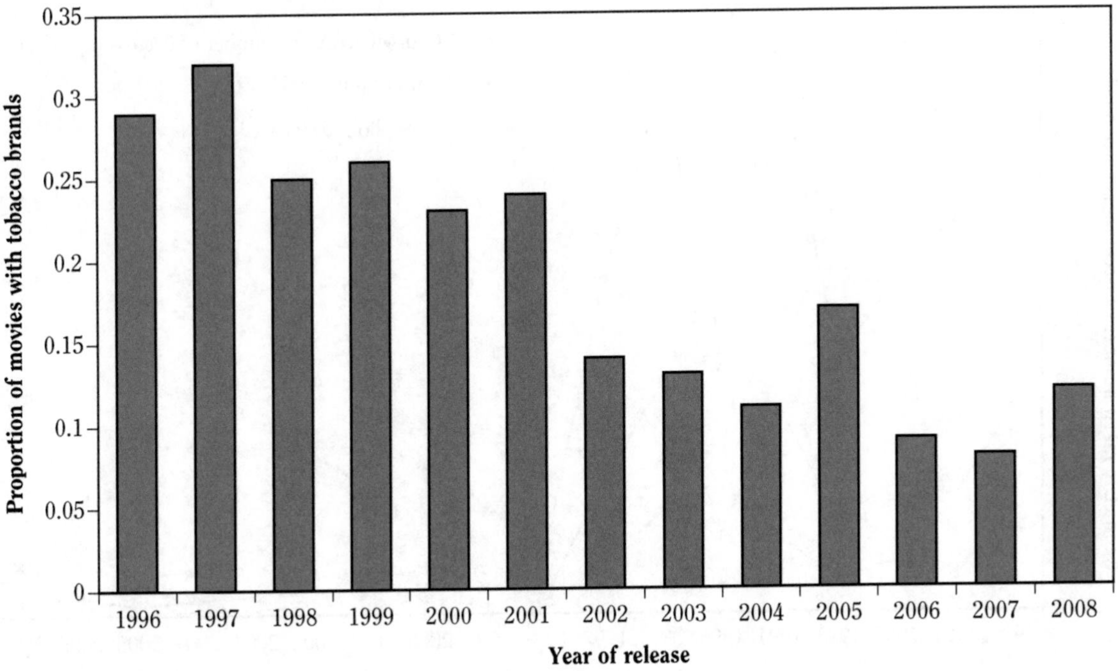

Source: Adapted from Worth et al. 2007.

Individual state attorneys general are responsible for enforcing these and other provisions of the agreement. The agreement is ambiguous, however, on whether the rules apply only to brand placement or to all product placement, including unbranded placements; the attorneys general have sought to enforce only branded placements. Other summaries (Appendix 10C of Chapter 10, NCI Monograph 19; NCI [2008]) have documented enforcement activity, in the form of letters sent from NAAG attorneys to lawyers representing tobacco corporations, asking them to confirm that no exchange of money occurred in return for a particular brand placement. Corporate attorneys representing the tobacco and movie studios have confirmed that no exchange took place. Recent trend studies suggest that enforcement has had the intended dampening effect on the placing of cigarette brands in movies.

Since the signing of the agreement, studies have reported declines in the placement of tobacco products in films (Adachi-Mejia et al. 2005; Worth et al. 2007; CDC 2010, 2011). Figure 5.9 shows the proportion of the top 100 box office hits containing an appearance of a tobacco brand for each year from 1996 through 2008; brands were present in almost 30% of movies at the beginning of the period (Sargent et al. 2001b) and in less than 10% in 2007, followed by a rise to about 12% in 2008. In 2010, the number of on-screen tobacco incidents in youth-rated (G, PG, or PG-13) movies continued a downward trend (CDC 2011).

Depictions of Smoking

Short-Term Contemporary Trends

Recent studies have examined trends for the unbranded depiction of smoking in the period surrounding the Master Settlement Agreement; these studies examined smoking grouped by movie and by movie character.

The prevalence of smoking in movies. Three recent studies of trends in movie smoking have found overall declines in that activity. Sargent and Heatherton (2009) compared trends for smoking in the top 25 box office hits each year from 1990 to 2007 with trends in youth smoking derived from the MTF survey. Figure 5.10, which is based on their work, illustrates parallel downward trends for movie smoking and adolescent smoking among eighth graders after 1996. The authors stated, "Movie smoking represents only one of several factors that contribute to youth smoking trends.... Nonetheless, the downward

Figure 5.10 **(A) Occurrences of smoking in highest-grossing movies, 1990–2007, and (B) smoking among eighth graders, 1991–2007, in the United States**

A. Top 25 box office hits per year

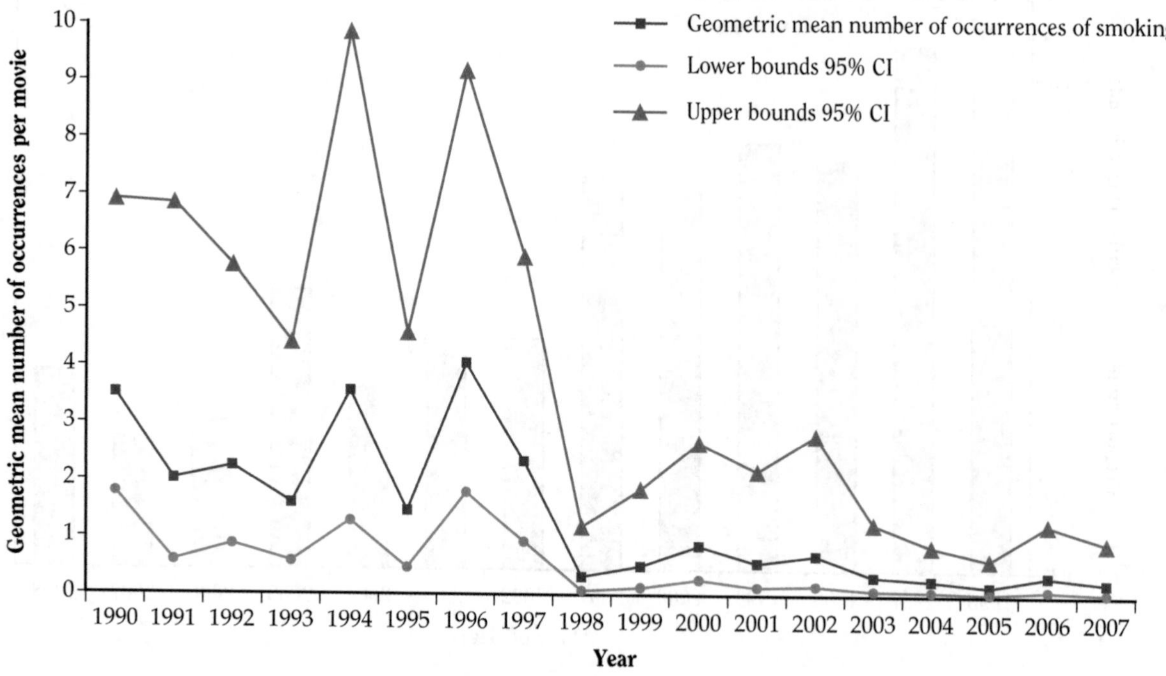

B. 99% confidence limits: 30-day prevalence of cigarette use, eighth graders, 1991–2007, MTF

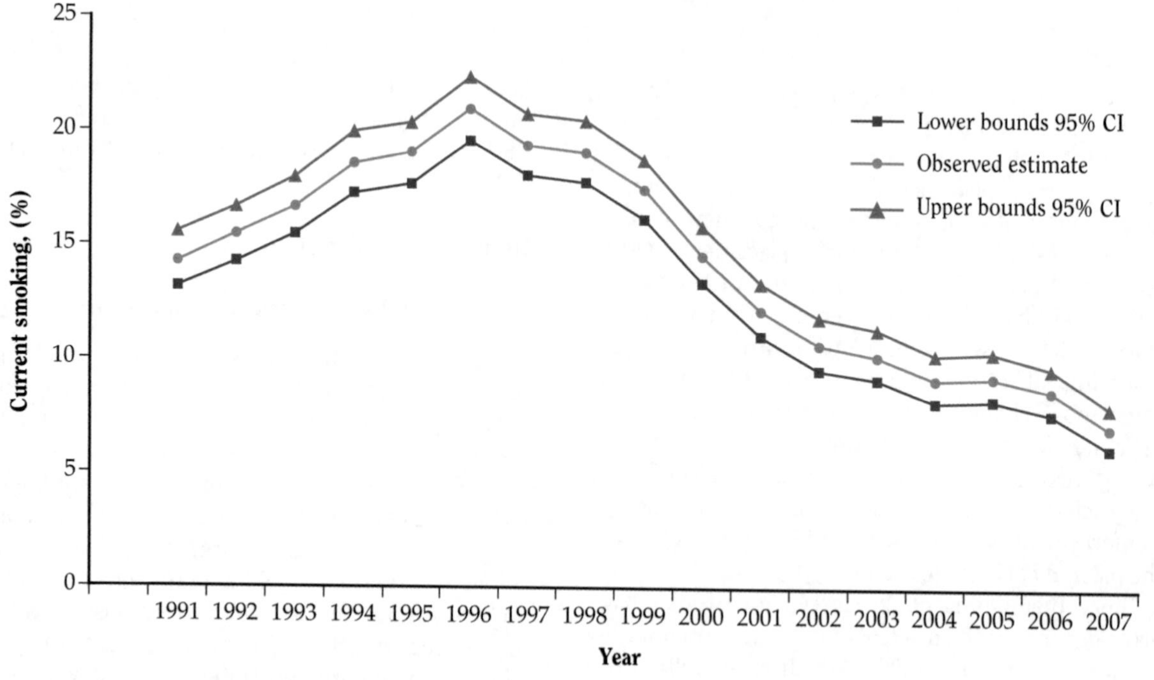

Source: Adapted from Sargent and Heatherton 2009 with permission from the American Medical Association, © 2009.
Note: Trends for the geometric mean for the number of smoking occurrences in the 25 movies with the highest U.S. box office gross revenues released each year between 1990 and 2007 (lines below and above the middle line indicate 95% CI) and current (past 30-day) smoking among eighth graders from the MTF for each year between 1991 and 2007 (lines below and above the middle line indicate 95% CI). **CI** = confidence interval; **MTF** = Monitoring the Future.

trend in movie smoking is consistent with an influence on downward trends in adolescent smoking" (p. 2212). A second content analysis examined trends by motion picture rating (Worth et al. 2007), which is important because adolescents get more exposure to movies that are rated for youth (Sargent et al. 2007b). Overall, the percentage of the top 100 box office hits that depicted smoking declined from 91% in 1996 to 63% in 2005. Despite this observed decline of almost one-third among the top 100 hits, the number of "tobacco episodes" in youth-rated movies actually increased by 27% over the period because a larger percentage of the movies were youth rated toward the end of the period (due to "ratings creep"). A third analysis looked at trends for smoking in the top 15 United Kingdom box office hits (Lyons et al. 2010) from 1989 through 2008, a sample that contained a greater number of films produced in the United Kingdom than in the United States samples, resulting in an overall downward trend from a mean of six 5-minute intervals per hour that contained smoking images to less than one per hour in 2008.

The prevalence of smoking at the level of the character. Using the level of the movie character for content analysis allows for a comparison with the prevalence of smoking in the population. Four studies have found the prevalence of smoking among characters in movies to be similar to population prevalence (Dalton et al. 2002b; McIntosh et al. 2005; Omidvari et al. 2005; Worth et al. 2006). Worth and colleagues (2006) found that the prevalence of smoking declined significantly among adult characters in the top 100 box office hits over a 9-year period, from 1996 through 2004, and that the prevalence of smoking was equivalent to that among U.S. adults over that time period.

The sociodemographics of smokers in movies have been examined by many researchers; studies show that smokers tend to be White, male, and affluent and thus not representative of smokers in society (Hazan et al. 1994; Dalton et al. 2002b; Worth et al. 2007). The result is that the images of smoking in movies are more similar to the images in cigarette advertising—wealth and power—than to the realities of smoking, which is increasingly associated with lower socioeconomic status and powerlessness. This phenomenon is due to the demographics of movie characters overall, not a biased selection of who smokes in movies. The most conspicuous example of this type of bias is in gender: the majority of "character smokers" in movies are male because 70% of movie characters are male.

Long-Term Trends

Several studies regarding trends in the portrayal of tobacco use in U.S. films since 1950 are inconsistent. Two studies (Stockwell and Glantz 1997; Glantz et al. 2004) found that the number of smoking incidents per hour declined from 10.7% in the 1950s to 4.9% in the early 1980s, but increased to a high of 10.9% in 2002. Several other studies found little or no change in the frequency of tobacco movie portrayal in the 1980s and 1990s (Hazan et al. 1994; Everett et al. 1998; Dalton et al. 2002b; Titus et al. 2009). Other studies reported downward trends in the number of smoking incidents in movies during the 1990s (Mekemson et al. 2004; Worth et al. 2006; Sargent and Heatherton 2009). One study (Jamieson and Romer 2010) sought to overcome these inconsistencies by using a common sampling frame and methodology. The authors performed a content analysis of 15 movies randomly selected from the top 30 box office hits each year from 1950 through 2006 (n = 855 movies) and coded each film in 5-minute segments to determine total tobacco-related content and main character tobacco use. The results showed a steady and considerable decline in tobacco content of movies since 1950, with total tobacco-related content peaking around 1961. The study also concluded that the decline in tobacco use by main characters was already under way in 1950 and continued to decline.

CDC published two long-term content analyses of smoking in the movies (CDC 2010, 2011) in which the sampling frame was all motion pictures that were in the top 10 films for box office receipts for at least 1 week. This was done in cooperation with the Thumbs Up! Thumbs Down! (TUTD) Project of Breathe California-Sacramento Emigrant Trails. This sample counted all tobacco incidents among the 10 top-grossing movies in any calendar week. During 2002–2008, U.S. movies that ranked in the top 10 for at least 1 week accounted for 83% of all movies exhibited in the United States and 96% of ticket sales. For this analysis, TUTD defined a tobacco incident as the use or implied use of a tobacco product by an actor. The number of movies without tobacco incidents was divided by the total number of movies to calculate the percentage of movies with no incidents, and the average number of tobacco incidents per movie was calculated for each motion picture company.

Figure 5.11 shows the results of this analysis by film rating. Using this approach, the total number of tobacco incidents in all top-grossing films has been declining since 2005. Despite this decline, there is still a substantial amount of smoking in youth-rated (G, PG, PG-13) movies. Thus, while there are some differences in results among studies using different approaches for measuring the level of onscreen smoking in films, all available studies show a decline in the level of exposure since at least 2005.

Figure 5.11 Comparison of the trend for proportion of 5-minute movie segments with tobacco (means for 15 of the top 30 box office hits from 1950 to 2005) and per capita cigarette consumption among adults, 1950–2005, in the United States

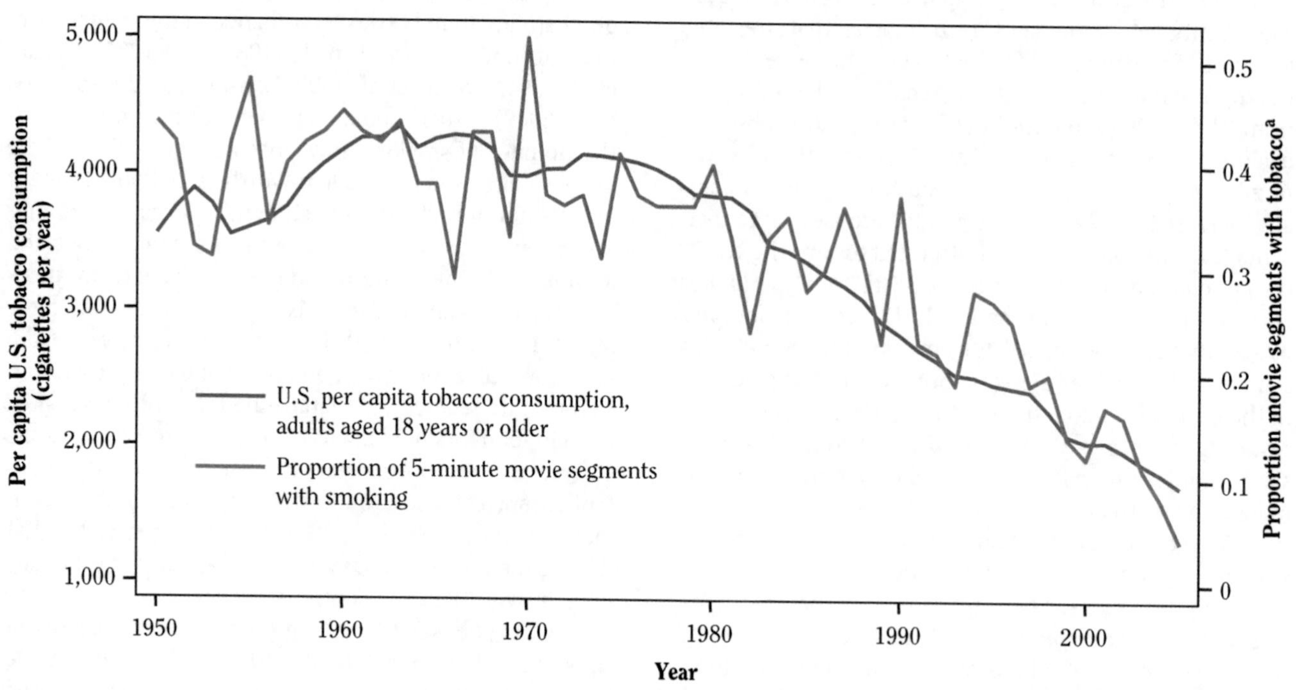

Source: Adapted from Jamieson et al. 2008 by permission of Oxford University Press, Fig. 4.4, p. 113 of *The Changing Portrayal of Adolescents in the Media Since 1950.*
Note: Mean for the percentage of film segments containing tobacco use in the top 30 U.S. films (right axis) and U.S. per capita consumption of tobacco for adults aged 18 years or older (left axis).
[a]Mean for the proportion of 5-minute movie segments that contain tobacco.

Varying Responses by Media Company

Beginning in 2004, three motion picture companies adopted and began to enforce written policies designed to reduce the amount of smoking in their films: Disney in October 2004, Time Warner in July 2005 (updated in July 2007), and Universal (then part of General Electric and since purchased by Comcast) in April 2007. These policies provided for review of scripts, story boards, daily footage, rough cuts, and the final edited film by managers in each studio with the authority to implement the policies. Although these companies have almost entirely eliminated depictions of tobacco use from their G, PG, and PG-13 movies, as of June 2011 none of the three companies had zero depictions of smoking or other tobacco imagery in the youth-rated films that they produced or distributed.

From 2005 to 2010, among these three major motion picture companies (one-half of the six members of the Motion Picture Association of America [MPAA]), the number of tobacco incidents per youth-rated movie decreased 95.8% from an average of 23.1 incidents per movie to an average of 1.0 incidents (CDC 2010). For independent companies that are not MPAA members and the three MPAA members with no antitobacco policies, tobacco incidents decreased 41.7%, from an average of 17.9 incidents per youth-rated movie in 2005 to 10.4 incidents in 2010. Among the three companies with antitobacco policies, 88.2% of their top-grossing youth-rated movies were free of tobacco incidents, compared with 57.4% of youth-rated movies among companies without policies (Viacom, News Corp, Sony, and the independent producers) (CDC 2011).

While the policies voluntarily adopted during 2004–2007 by the three major motion picture companies (Disney, Time Warner, Universal) have excluded nearly all tobacco incidents from their top-grossing youth-rated movies, none of the three company policies completely banned smoking or other tobacco imagery in the youth-rated films they produced or distributed (CDC 2011). Given the continuing varying performance among motion picture companies in reducing tobacco imagery in youth-rated films, WHO (2009) and numerous public health and health professional organizations have recommended giving movies with tobacco incidents an R rating, with exceptions: those that portray a historical figure who smoked and those that portray the negative effects of tobacco use (CDC 2011).

Tobacco Use in Movie Trailers

Depictions of smoking in movie trailers have important implications for exposure as the trailers are aired on television and may be seen by a wider audience than the movie itself. One study combined a content analysis of trailers with Nielsen data measuring media exposure among 12- to 17-year-olds (Healton et al. 2006); of all 216 movie trailers shown on television in a single year (2001–2002), 14.4% included images of tobacco use. Nielsen data indicated that during that year 95% of all U.S. youth aged 12–17 years saw at least one movie trailer on television depicting the use of tobacco, and 88.8% saw at least one of these trailers three or more times. Over the course of that year, movie trailers showing tobacco use were seen 270 million times by youth aged 12–17 years. One experimental study found that smoking by a character in a film trailer was associated with increased perceptions of that character's attractiveness among adolescent smokers (Hanewinkel 2009).

It has been noted that even if stronger policies were adopted banning smoking or other tobacco imagery in youth-rated movies, such policies would not affect youth exposures to older movies that have already been released and are available as downloads, rentals, and on television (CDC 2011). Also, evidence indicates that youth view some R-rated movies (Sargent 2007b). Therefore, antitobacco ads have been recommended for showing before movies that depict smoking (USDHHS 2010).

Summary

Recent content analyses of tobacco use in movies have documented a general decline in the appearance of tobacco brands and in depictions of tobacco use overall, especially since 2005 (Table 5.12). These trends suggest that the movie industry is responding to research and heightened attention to the issue applied by the public health community and the state attorneys general.

While these declines demonstrate the practicality of enacting policies to reduce tobacco incidents in youth-rated movies, it has been recommended that expanding the R rating to include movies with smoking could further reduce exposures of young persons to onscreen tobacco incidents (CDC 2011).

Exposure to Tobacco Use in Movies

Assessment of Exposure

Assessment of exposure to components of movies is challenging in ways similar to assessment of exposure to advertising. A recent article (Sargent et al. 2008) contrasts various methods and lists their advantages and disadvantages. The recall method (Goldberg and Baumgartner 2002) involves simply asking subjects how often they watch movies or how much they notice smoking in movies. This method is subject to recall bias; for example, a subject who smokes may pay more attention to smoking scenes. A second method involves assessing the relation between the smoking status of an adolescent's favorite movie star and the youth's own smoking status (Distefan et al. 1999). In this approach, adolescents are asked to name their favorite male and female movie stars. The smoking status of these stars is then assessed within a contemporary sample frame of movies, and this information is compared with the smoking status of the adolescent. This method has the advantage of assessing exposure to movie smoking in a way that is highly relevant to the individual, but it does not take into account that adolescents observe smoking by actors other than their favorites.

A third method determines which movies adolescents have watched and assesses these movies for tobacco exposures. This method requires adolescents to recognize a movie title when it is presented and recall whether they have seen the movie. Positive responses from participants are combined with content analysis to estimate exposure to portrayals of movie smoking. Clearly, it is not possible to ask every respondent about all available movies, and researchers have addressed this limitation in two ways. Some researchers choose a list of 40 or 50 contemporary movies with varying amounts of smoking and survey all respondents about all those specific films (Thrasher et al. 2008). This approach is easy to implement, but the conclusions apply only to the set of movies surveyed. A different approach, using the Beach method (Sargent et al. 2008), analyzes a large sample (500–600) of box office hits and then surveys each respondent about a randomly selected subsample of titles. The random subsample allows researchers to estimate exposure of the population to a relatively large sample of hits rather than limiting estimates to a specific subset of movies.

Table 5.12 Content analyses of movies in studies published since 2005

Study	Movie sample frame	Interrater reliability	Unit of analysis	Outcome variable	Results	Comments
Adachi-Mejia et al. 2005	Top 100 box office hits per year 1996–2003	Not reported	Movie	Number with appearances of tobacco brands, by year OR for appearance of a tobacco brand before vs. after Master Settlement Agreement	Brand appearances dropped from 20.8% of movies before Master Settlement Agreement to 10.5% afterward, OR = 0.45 (95% CI = 0.29–0.68)	Interrater reliabilities on this content analysis available through authors
Healton et al. 2006	All movie trailers shown on television August 1, 2001, to July 31, 2002	All smoking verified by two coders and differences resolved	Movie trailer (N = 216)	Percentage of trailers containing smoking Gross impressions for smoking in trailers among youth aged 12–17 years	Tobacco appeared in 14.4% (31) of trailers 270 million gross impressions were delivered to youth by the trailers	
Worth et al. 2006	Top 100 box office hits per year 1996–2004	Agreement = 99.6% for character smoking status	Major character smoking status	Smoking prevalence among adult major smoking characters	Smoking prevalence declined from 25.7% in 1996 to 18.4% in 2004, equivalent to declines in smoking among U.S. adults	
Worth et al. 2007	Top 100 box office hits per year 1996–2005	Mean κ for coder agreement on whether character tobacco use was occurring in 1-second intervals = 0.86 (SD = 0.17)	Tobacco episodes (handling or use of tobacco by a movie character) analyzed at the level of the movie and at the aggregate level for the top 100 box office hits each year	Percentage of movies with smoking, by movie rating Number of tobacco episodes for top 100 box office hits, by year and rating	Percentage of movies with smoking declined from 91% to 63% over study period Overall, the number of tobacco episodes declined from 650 to 400 There was an increase in tobacco episodes delivered by youth-rated movies (because a larger share of movies received youth ratings)	
Jamieson et al. 2008; Jamieson and Romer 2010	15 of the 30 top box office hits (random selection), each year 1950–2004	Krippendorff's alpha = 0.78 for tobacco	Unit of coding was the 5-minute interval (any tobacco present? yes vs. no) The unit of analysis was the percentage of 5-minute intervals containing any reference to tobacco	The outcome reported was the mean for the percentage of intervals containing any tobacco for all movies in each 5-year window	There was a continuous decline in the proportion of 5-minute intervals that contained smoking over the entire time period	

Table 5.12 Continued

Study	Movie sample frame	Interrater reliability	Unit of analysis	Outcome variable	Results	Comments
Sargent and Heatherton 2009	Top 25 box office hits 1990–2007	Interrater correlation = 0.96	A smoking occurrence was counted whenever a movie character handled or used tobacco or when tobacco use was depicted in the background Only tobacco use was coded (>90% was cigarette or cigar smoking)	Geometric mean, number of episodes per movie, by year of release	Geometric mean for movie smoking occurrences was 3.5 (95% CI = 1.8–6.9) in 1990 and 0.23 (95% CI = 0.06–0.93) in 2007 Trend analysis indicated that geometric mean for movie smoking declined by an average of 0.84 smoking occurrences (95% CI = 0.80–0.89) per year between 1990 and 2007	Downward trend in smoking among 8th graders also documented during this period
Lyons et al. 2010	Top 15 most commercially successful films United Kingdom 1989–2008	No interrater reliability reported	Unit of coding was the 5-minute interval (following categories counted separately: consumption of any tobacco product by any character, tobacco paraphernalia, inferred tobacco use, and brand appearances)	Proportion of movies with smoking, by rating Mean number of 5-minute intervals per hour	The mean rate of occurrence of tobacco intervals fell substantially and significantly ($p < 0.05$) for all categories of tobacco use between 1989 and 2008, from 3.5 to 0.6 per hour; similar trends occurred for all categories of tobacco interval	The proportion of U.K. films with brand appearances (0.36) was much higher than the rate overall (0.09) and for U.S. films (0.20)

Note: **CI** = confidence interval; **OR** = odds ratio; **SD** = standard deviation; **U.K.** = United Kingdom; **U.S.** = United States.

Total Exposures to Smoking in Movies

The exposure studies described in this section document the fact that movies overall deliver billions of smoking impressions to adolescents and conclude that how movies are rated affects these exposures. Three research groups have independently developed estimates for the exposure of adolescents to smoking contained in movies themselves, with convergent results. (Note that all three studies underestimated total exposure because they did not account for multiple DVD viewings of a given film.) Sargent and colleagues (2007b) surveyed 6,522 nationally representative U.S. adolescents aged 10–14 years in 2003; using the Beach method, they analyzed the content of 534 contemporary box office hits for smoking and assigned each movie to a random subsample of adolescents (on average, 613 adolescents per movie) who were asked whether they had seen it. Using survey weights, the authors estimated the total number of U.S. adolescents who had seen each movie and then multiplied that figure by the number of depictions of smoking in each to obtain total smoking exposures seen by adolescents. ("Gross impressions" are the total number of exposures delivered by a media schedule, such as all showings of a given film.) As of the date of the survey in 2003, the 534 movies had delivered 13.9 billion gross smoking impressions, an average of 665 per U.S. adolescent aged 10–14 years. Most of the 534 movies were rated either PG-13 (41%) or R (40%), and 74% contained smoking (3,830 total occurrences of smoking). On average, a movie was seen by 25% of the adolescents surveyed, but viewership was significantly lower for R-rated movies. Although this sample's youth-rated movies (G, PG, and PG-13) contained only 40% of smoking occurrences, they delivered 61% of smoking impressions to the targeted age group because of that group's higher viewership of those movies. Most of the gross impressions of smoking delivered by youth-rated movies came from PG-13 movies. The Sargent study also grouped gross smoking impressions by movie and by actor. Some 30 popular movies each delivered more than 100 million gross smoking impressions, and 30 actors each delivered more than 50 million smoking impressions, such that just 1.5% of the 1,961 actors who played characters in these movies delivered one-quarter of all character smoking to the adolescent sample. Some popular actors did not smoke in any of the movies.

In the second study, Polansky and Glantz (2007) examined how many gross smoking impressions were delivered to adolescents from 1,306 movies (1998–2006) that earned $500,000 or more at the box office. The estimated number of smoking occurrences was based on each movie's MPAA rating and its tobacco rating (Screenit[2012], where parents rate movie smoking). Overall, the 1,306 movies delivered an estimated 44.5 billion gross smoking impressions to audiences of all ages from 1999 to 2006, including 2.4 billion to children aged 6–11 years and 8.8 billion to youth aged 12–17 years. The study estimated that about one-half of impressions overall were delivered by youth-rated movies.

In the third study, Anderson and colleagues (2010) used a similar methodology to assess the exposure of British adolescents to smoking from 572 top-grossing films in the United Kingdom. They found higher exposure among British (than U.S.) adolescents resulting from higher exposure to movies with smoking that would have been rated R in the United States, but were rated as appropriate for youth in the United Kingdom. Because of the difference, British youth were exposed to 28% more movie smoking than were U.S. youth. These studies underline the large impact that decisions by ratings boards can make on the exposure of youth to smoking in movies; because fewer youth see adult-rated movies, a mandate by the ratings board to give movies with smoking an adult rating would greatly reduce the exposure of youth to smoking in those movies.

Further, it has been noted that almost all states offer movie producers subsidies in the form of tax credits or cash rebates to attract movie production to their states, totaling approximately $1 billion annually (CDC 2011). Millet and associates (2011) have reported that the 15 states subsidizing top-grossing movies with tobacco incidents spent more on these productions in 2010 ($288 million) than they budgeted for their state tobacco control programs in 2011 ($280 million).

The conclusion of Chapter 5 of the 1994 Surgeon General's report on smoking in young people emphasized the importance of the advertising of images in making use of cigarettes attractive to youth: "Cigarette advertising uses images rather than information to portray the attractiveness and function of smoking. Human models and cartoon characters in cigarette advertising convey independence, healthfulness, adventure-seeking, and youthful activities—themes correlated with psychosocial factors that appeal to young people" (USDHHS 1994, p. 195). Today, the delivery of billions of glamorized images of smoking by movie and television stars offers a stark contrast to the current landscape for tobacco advertising. Because some image-based tobacco advertising has been eliminated by the Master Settlement Agreement, images of smoking in movies and television may today be some of the more potent media-delivered smoking images seen by U.S. children and adolescents. The effect is compounded by the fact that many U.S. films are eventually released on television, DVD, or online, where they can reach an international audience. Thus, they have the potential to expose adolescents around the world to role models who smoke.

Population-Based Research Linking Movie Smoking to Adolescent Smoking

Cross-Sectional Studies Assessing Exposure to Movie Smoking and Smoking Among Young People

A number of cross-sectional studies have examined the association between movie smoking and adolescent smoking using a variety of approaches (Table 5.13) to assess measures of exposure: direct recall (Goldberg and Baumgartner 2002; Goldberg 2003; Henriksen et al. 2004b; McCool et al. 2005; Laugesen et al. 2007; Thompson and Gunther 2007); smoking status of favorite movie star (Distefan et al. 1999; Tickle et al. 2001; Dixon 2003); and cued recall (Sargent et al. 2001a, 2002, 2005; Hanewinkel and Sargent 2007; Thrasher et al. 2008). These cross-sectional studies assessed adolescents in Asia, Europe, Latin America, and the United States.

In these studies, the use of general recall measures resulted in weaker associations than did assessments of smoking by favorite movie star or methods that used cued recall of titles to assess exposure. The studies by Henriksen and colleagues (2004b) and Thompson and Gunther (2007) suggest that recall measures that assess the extent to which participants notice smoking in movies are unlikely to show a multivariate association with smoking. Figure 5.12 illustrates the strength and consistency of the results of cross-sectional studies of smoking onset that (1) employed cued recall of movie titles (results 1–4), (2) found adjusted ORs between 2 and 3 for high versus low exposure to movie smoking, and (3) achieved statistical significance for all estimates after controlling for a variety of potential confounders. Studies that used the participants' favorite movie stars showed significant associations between the star's smoking status and smoking among the youth who named a favorite movie star (Table 5.13). In summary, the results from cross-sectional studies are consistent with an association between exposure to smoking in movies and youth smoking.

Longitudinal Studies Assessing Exposure to Movies

A literature search identified eight published longitudinal samples, six involving U.S. adolescents, one from Germany, and one from Mexico, that were used to assess exposure to smoking in movies (Table 5.13).

The first published study was a follow-up of a sample of northern New England adolescents in which Dalton and colleagues (2003) contacted 2,603 baseline never smokers by telephone and determined that exposure to smoking in movies at baseline had a significant multivariate relationship with trying smoking over the 1- to 2-year follow-up period. When this sample was resurveyed as young adults, exposure to movie smoking during middle school was statistically associated with established smoking (>100 cigarettes lifetime). Another analysis of the same sample (Adachi-Mejia et al. 2009) found that the effect of movie smoking on established smoking was significantly stronger among those adolescents who were generally at lower risk for smoking because of their participation in team sports.

A 1-year follow-up study of never smokers in California (Distefan et al. 2004) found that adolescent girls choosing as a favorite movie star someone who had smoked in more than one movie in the 3 years preceding the survey were significantly more likely to try smoking in the follow-up period. In North Carolina, a school-based longitudinal study of a racially mixed sample of youth (Jackson et al. 2007) found that exposure to R-rated movies was associated with significantly elevated risk for trying smoking during the follow-up period for White but not Black adolescents. Having a television in the adolescent's bedroom was also a significant predictor, over and above the association with R-rated movies.

Sargent and colleagues (2007a) followed a nationally representative sample of 10- to 14-year-old adolescents at 8-month intervals for 24 months (four survey waves) and found that exposure to movie smoking at baseline predicted time to onset of established (>100 cigarettes lifetime) smoking in this cohort. In the same cohort, Tanski and colleagues (2009) found that exposure to movie smoking predicted onset of smoking among those who were never smokers at baseline and that smoking by movie characters predicted the onset of youth smoking regardless of whether the character was positively or negatively portrayed in the film.

Hanewinkel and Sargent (2008) followed 2,711 adolescents in Germany who had never smoked; after 1 year there was a significant association between exposure to movie smoking at baseline and onset of smoking. In addition, the authors reported a dose-response curve for the relation between a continuous measure of exposure to movie smoking and onset of smoking that was similar in shape to the dose-response curve for the Dalton cohort (Figure 5.13; Dalton et al. 2003). Both dose-response curves were curvilinear, with a flattening of the curves above the 75th percentile of exposure, indicating that the largest marginal effects occur at low, rather than high, levels of exposure.

Titus-Ernstoff and coworkers (2008) studied 2,627 New England fourth- and fifth-grade students and followed them up annually for 2 years; the authors assessed exposure to smoking in movies at baseline and in movies

Table 5.13 Population-based studies assessing the relation between exposure to movie smoking and smoking among young people

Study	Design	Measure of exposure	Categories of covariates used in adjustment[a]	Outcome (prevalence)	Exposure comparison categories	Measure of association, association (95% CI)[b]	Comments
				Cross-sectional			
Distefan et al. 1999	Multiethnic Aged 12–17 years Cross-sectional random-digit-dialing survey N = 6,252 (analysis performed on 3,510 never smokers) United States (California) 1996	Identified favorite movie stars of ever smokers (vs. never smokers)	S, P, SCH, SI, M	Susceptibility to smoking among never smokers (42%)	Adolescent never smokers choosing a favorite star typical of ever smokers vs. choosing a favorite star typical of other never smokers	AOR 1.35 (1.12–1.62)	Favorite actors and actresses were defined by the nominations of the subjects; study examined commonly chosen actors/actresses; 52% of adolescents were excluded because they nominated a star chosen by fewer than 5 respondents

Table 5.13 Continued

Study	Design	Measure of exposure	Categories of covariates used in adjustment[a]	Outcome (prevalence)	Exposure comparison categories	Measure of association, association (95% CI)[b]	Comments
Sargent et al. 2001a, 2002, 2009a; Tickle et al. 2006	White Aged 10–15 years Cross-sectional school-based survey N = 4,919 (3,766 never smokers) United States (Northeast) 1999	Movie title recognition—Beach method 50 titles/survey 601 U.S. box office releases, 1989–1999	S, P, SCH, PS, SI, M	Tried smoking (17%)	Quartile of exposure to movie smoking: 1 2 3 4	AOR Reference 1.9 (1.3–2.7) 2.6 (1.8–3.7) 2.5 (1.7–3.5)	A cross-sectional structural equation model (Tickle et al. 2006) identified indirect paths from exposure to movie smoking to intentions to smoke through positive expectancies and identification as a smoker, but not through normative beliefs
				Lifetime smoking level among triers (n = 794): puffers (57%), 1–19 cigarettes (19%), 20–100 cigarettes (9.7%), >100 cigarettes (13.8%)		No association between exposure to movie smoking and higher levels of lifetime smoking	
				Among never smokers: susceptibility to smoking (20%)	Quartile of exposure to movie smoking: 1 2 3 4	AOR Reference 1.2 (0.9–1.5) 1.5 (1.1–1.9) 1.6 (1.2–2.1)	
				Positive expectancies (61% endorsed no positive expectancies)	Quartile of exposure to movie smoking: 1 2 3 4	APOR Reference 1.2 (1.0–1.5) 1.3 (1.1–1.6) 1.4 (1.1–1.7)	
				Views adult smoking as normative (55%)	Quartile of exposure to movie smoking: 1 2 3 4	AOR Reference 1.2 (0.9–1.4) 1.3 (1.1–1.6) 1.4 (1.1–1.7)	

Table 5.13 Continued

Study	Design	Measure of exposure	Categories of covariates used in adjustment[a]	Outcome (prevalence)	Exposure comparison categories	Measure of association, association (95% CI)[b]	Comments
Tickle et al. 2001	White, low-income communities Aged 10–19 years Cross-sectional school-based survey N = 632 (281 never smokers) United States (New Hampshire, Vermont)	Movie character smoking status of favorite star averaged for films released up to 3 years before survey	S, SCH, SI, M	Smoking index: 0 = nonsusceptible never smoker (37%), 1 = susceptible never smoker (7%), 2 = 1–99 lifetime cigarettes smoked, but not a current (30 days) smoker (26%), 3 = 1–99 lifetime cigarettes smoked and a current smoker (9%), 4 = ≥100 cigarettes lifetime (20%) Susceptibility among never smokers (17%)	Character smoking by favorite star averaged over 3 years: None 1 2 ≥3 None 1 2 ≥3	 APOR Reference 0.78 (NS) 1.53 (1.01–2.32) 3.09 (1.34–7.12) AOR Reference 2.16 (0.86–5.45) 4.78 (1.60–14.2) 16.2 (2.33–112)	Study examined commonly chosen actors/actresses; 51% of adolescents were excluded because they nominated a star chosen by fewer than 5 respondents
Goldberg and Baumgartner 2002	Asian Aged 14–17 years Cross-sectional school-based N = 1,338 Thailand 1998	Recall measure—how many American movies have you seen in the past 2 months in theater or on video (0–1 vs. 2–3 vs. ≥4)?	None	Intent to smoke in the future Tried smoking Smoked at least 1 cigarette	0–1 movies (15%), 2–3 (14%), ≥4 (15%) 0-1 movies (24%), 2–3 (29%), ≥4 (32%) 0–1 movies (19%), 2–3 (24%), ≥4 (27%)	NS $p < 0.05$ $p < 0.05$	Results shown for exposure to American movies on video; results similar for exposure to American movies in theater
Dixon 2003	White Aged 12–18 years Cross-sectional school-based N = 2,610 participants, 1,858 experimental smokers Australia 1999	Movie character smoking status of favorite male and female star (mean smoking scenes per movie)	S, SCH, SI	Smoking uptake index: 0 nonsmokers (67%), 1 occasional smoker (12%), 2 light smokers (8%), 3 heavy smokers (5%), 4 chain smokers (1%) Null findings for negative health effects of smoking, endorsement of smokers as more popular, intent to smoke in future		APOR male actors: 1.16, $p = 0.04$ APOR female actors: NS	Stronger evidence for association among girls than in boys; study examined commonly chosen actors/actresses; 31% of adolescents were excluded because they nominated a star chosen by fewer than 5 respondents

Table 5.13 Continued

Study	Design	Measure of exposure	Categories of covariates used in adjustment[a]	Outcome (prevalence)	Exposure comparison categories	Measure of association, association (95% CI)[b]	Comments
Goldberg 2003	Asian Aged 14–17 years Cross-sectional school-based N = 1,762 Hong Kong 1998	Recall measure—how many American movies have you seen in the past 2 months (0–1 vs. 2–3 vs. ≥4)?	No covariate adjustment	Intent to smoke in the future (27%)	0–1 movies (21%), 2–3 (26%), ≥4 (30%)	p <0.01	
				Tried smoking (40%)	0–1 movies (34%), 2–3 (41%), ≥4 (47%)	p <0.01	
				Current (7 days) smoking (30%)	0–1 movies (18%), 2–3 (21%), ≥4 (22%)	NS	
Henriksen et al. 2004b	Multiethnic 6th–8th grades Cross-sectional school-based N = 2,125 California 2003	Recall measure—how often have you seen smoking in the movies or on television in the past week (never vs. sometimes/often)?	M, P, PS, S, SI, SCH	Tried smoking (prevalence not described, current [30 days] smoking 2.6–7.6%, depending on grade in school)	Past-week viewing of smoking in movies or television: Never vs. sometimes/often	AOR Reference NS (OR estimate did not survive stepwise regression)	Unadjusted OR was statistically significant = 2.2 (95% CI = 1.7–2.8)
McCool et al. 2005	Multiethnic Aged 12 or 16 years Cross-sectional school-based survey N = 3,041 New Zealand	Recall measure—3 items (How often do you see a film at the cinema?), α = 0.65 Positive smoker stereotypes (smokers in films are stylish, smart, sexy, healthy, intelligent), α = 0.79	S	Intent to smoke in the future Mediators Imagery pervasiveness ("smoking in films is common"), 3 items, α = 0.61 Nonchalance ("smoking in films is not important to me"), 3 items, α = 0.67	Continuous structural equation model; the relation between exposure to smoking in movies mediated through image pervasiveness and nonchalance Positive smoker stereotypes had a direct relation with intent to smoke in the future but were not predicted by higher exposure		

Table 5.13 Continued

Study	Design	Measure of exposure	Categories of covariates used in adjustment[a]	Outcome (prevalence)	Exposure comparison categories	Measure of association, association (95% CI)[b]	Comments
Sargent et al. 2005	Multiethnic national sample N = 6,522 Aged 10–14 years Cross-sectional random-digit-dialed survey United States 2003	Movie title recognition—Beach method 50 titles/survey 532 U.S. box office hits released from 1998 to 2003	S, P, SCH, PS, SI, SINC, ACH, EA	Tried smoking (10%)	Quartile of exposure to movie smoking: 1 2 3 4 AAF	AOR Reference 1.7 (1.1–2.6) 1.8 (1.2–2.8) 2.6 (1.7–4.1) 0.38 (0.20–0.56)	
Hanewinkel and Sargent 2007	White Aged 10–17 years Cross-sectional school-based survey N = 5,586 Germany (Schleswig-Holstein) 2005	Movie title recognition—Beach method 50 titles/survey 398 internationally distributed movies that were German box office hits and released from 1994 to 2004	S, P, SCH, PS, SI, M	Tried smoking (41%)	Quartile of exposure to movie smoking: 1 2 3 4	AOR Reference 1.7 (1.4–2.1) 1.8 (1.5–2.3) 2.2 (1.8–2.8)	
				Current (30 days) smoking (12%)	Quartile of exposure to movie smoking: 1 2 3 4	AOR Reference 1.4 (0.9–2.2) 1.7 (1.1–2.6) 2.0 (1.3–3.1)	
Laugesen et al. 2007	Annual school-based surveys 10th graders N = 96,156 New Zealand 2002–2004	How often do you watch R-rated movies? (3 venues: cinema, video, TV) Never <1/month Once/month 2–3/month ≥ once/week	S (sensitivity analysis adjusted also for SI, SINC, and PS did not change the conclusion)	Tried smoking among not current smokers	ARR Watched R-rated movies: Never 2–3 times/month Once/month Weekly	Reference 1.20 (1.12–1.28) 1.67 (1.55–1.80) 2.04 (1.90–2.18) 2.28 (2.12–2.45)	
				Current (30 days) smoking	Watched R-rated movies: Never 2–3 times/month Once/month Weekly	Reference 0.80 (0.73–0.88) 1.15 (1.05–1.26) 1.59 (1.44–1.75) 2.31 (2.10–2.54)	

Table 5.13 Continued

Study	Design	Measure of exposure	Categories of covariates used in adjustment[a]	Outcome (prevalence)	Exposure comparison categories	Measure of association, association (95% CI)[b]	Comments
Song et al. 2007	Multiethnic Aged 18–25 years Cross-sectional Web-based survey N = 1,528 United States	Movie title recognition—Beach method 60 titles/survey 500 top-grossing movies released from 2000 to 2004	S, P, SRA, SI, M, PPS	Current (30 days) smoking (31%)	AOR with exposure to movie smoking divided into quartiles and entered as a continuous variable	1.21 (1.05–1.38) for each quartile increase in exposure	For the established smoking analysis, a mediational model that showed significant paths from movie smoking to established smoking through friend smoking and positive expectancies
				Established smoking (>100 cigarettes lifetime) (25%)	AOR, same analytic approach as above	1.08 (0.93–1.25)	

Table 5.13 Continued

Study	Design	Measure of exposure	Categories of covariates used in adjustment[a]	Outcome (prevalence)	Exposure comparison categories	Measure of association, association (95% CI)[b]	Comments
Thrasher et al. 2008	Hispanic Aged 10–14 years Cross-sectional school-based survey N = 3,874 Mexico (Cuernavaca and Zacatecas) 2005	Movie title recognition—fixed list of 42 box office hits (2002–2006) with >1 minute of smoking, 15 Mexican, 23 U.S., 4 other foreign	S, P, SI, BOF	Current (30 days) smoking (12%)	Quartile of exposure to movie smoking: 1 2 3 4	AOR Reference 1.4 (0.9–2.4) 1.8 (1.0–3.2) 2.7 (1.5–4.7)	Significant multivariate association not found for perceived prevalence among adults
				Ever smoked (41%)	Quartile of exposure to movie smoking: 1 2 3 4	AOR Reference 1.3 (0.9–1.6) 1.8 (1.4–2.4) 2.3 (1.5–3.6)	
				Among never smokers susceptible to smoking (40%)	Quartile of exposure to movie smoking: 1 2 3 4	AOR Reference 1.5 (1.1–2.0) 1.8 (1.2–2.5) 1.6 (1.1–2.3)	
				Attitudes toward smoking (good or bad; pleasant or unpleasant; safe or dangerous)	Quartile of exposure to movie smoking: 1 2 3 4	UAβ Reference 0.17 (0.03–0.31) 0.18 (0.02–0.34) 0.41 (0.23–0.57)	
				Perceived prevalence among adults and youth	Quartile of exposure to movie smoking: 1 2 3 4	UAβ Reference 0.21 (0.03–0.39) 0.30 (0.16–0.44) 0.34 (0.18–0.50)	

Table 5.13 Continued

Study	Design	Measure of exposure	Categories of covariates used in adjustment[a]	Outcome (prevalence)	Exposure comparison categories	Measure of association, association (95% CI)[b]	Comments
Hunt et al. 2009	White Aged 19 years Cross-sectional N = 948 Scotland (Glasgow) 2002–2004	Movie title recognition—Beach method 50 titles/survey 532 U.S. box office hits released from 1998 to 2003	S, P, SCH, SI	Ever smoked (63%)	No bivariate or multivariate association with movie smoking	AOR Not significant	None of the associations between exposure categories was significant
				Current smoker (33%)			
				Occasional social smoker + regular smoker vs. never smoker + trier + former smoker	No bivariate or multivariate association with movie smoking		

Table 5.13 Continued

Study	Design	Measure of exposure	Categories of covariates used in adjustment[a]	Outcome (prevalence)	Exposure comparison categories	Measure of association, association (95% CI)[b]	Comments
				Longitudinal			
Dalton et al. 2003, 2009; Tickle et al. 2006; Wills et al. 2007; Adachi-Mejia et al. 2009; Sargent et al. 2009a	Longitudinal school-based survey with telephone follow-up, baseline = 1,999 N = 2,603 baseline never smokers followed up at 18 months, 1,791 at 7 years United States (New Hampshire, Vermont) Follow-up at 18 months, 5 years White Aged 10–14 years at baseline Baseline smoking status: never smoker	Movie title recognition—Beach method 50 titles/survey 601 U.S. box office releases, 1989–1999	S, P, SCH, PS, SI, M	18-month endpoint Incidence of tried smoking (10%)	Quartile of exposure to movie smoking: 1 2 3 4	ARR Reference 2.02 (1.27–3.20) 2.16 (1.38–3.40) 2.71 (1.73–4.25)	Dalton et al. (2003) also found a significant moderation effect on parental smoking (higher movie effects among adolescents whose parents did not smoke); Tickle et al. (2006) found significant indirect paths to intentions to smoke through positive expectancies and identification as a smoker; there was also a pathway to smoking behavior at 18 months through smoking status of favorite star; Wills et al. (2007) found that change in friend smoking status from time 1 to time 2 partially mediated the effect of movie exposure on smoking at 18 months; Adachi-Mejia et al. (2009) found a moderation effect for the 7-year endpoint, with stronger effect for adolescent team sports participants
				7-year endpoint		AAF 0.52 (0.30–0.67)	
			S, P, SCH, PS, SI, M	Established smoking incidence (≥100 cigarettes lifetime at survey point) (27.8%)	Quartile of exposure to movie smoking: 1 2 3 4	ARR Reference 1.36 (0.95–1.94) 1.68 (1.15–2.44) 1.98 (1.35–2.90)	

Table 5.13 Continued

Study	Design	Measure of exposure	Categories of covariates used in adjustment[a]	Outcome (prevalence)	Exposure comparison categories	Measure of association, association (95% CI)[b]	Comments
Distefan et al. 2004	Longitudinal random-digit-dial survey N = 2,084 never smokers at baseline Follow-up 3 years Multiethnic Aged 12–15 years Baseline smoking status: never smoker United States (California)	Movie character smoking status of favorite star Nonsmoker star smoked in <2 movies in preceding 3 years Smoker star smoked in ≥2 movies in the preceding 3 years	S, SCH, PS, SI, M	Tried smoking (not given, approximately 30%) Among females	Nonsmoker star Smoker star Nonsmoker star Smoker star	Reference 1.36 (1.02–1.82) Reference 1.86 (1.26–2.73)	Significantly stronger effect was found for females, with no effect for males
Jackson et al. 2007	Longitudinal school-based survey, 2001–2002 N = 735 Follow-up at 2 years White and Black Mean age 13.6 years Baseline smoking status: never smoker United States (North Carolina)	Title recognition measure—93 film titles released 2001–2002 7 (G-rated), 14 (PG-rated), 49 (PG-13 rated), 23 (R-rated)	S, SI, PS, SCH, P	Tried smoking (30%)	No movie effect for Black adolescents Among White adolescents, tercile of exposure to R-rated movies: 1 2 3	 AOR Reference 1.57 (0.73–3.35) 2.67 (1.07–6.55)	Television in the bedroom also found to be related to smoking; after controlling for this variable, the AOR for tercile 3 among White adolescents = 2.69 (1.25–5.77)

Table 5.13 Continued

Study	Design	Measure of exposure	Categories of covariates used in adjustment[a]	Outcome (prevalence)	Exposure comparison categories	Measure of association, association (95% CI)[b]	Comments
Sargent et al. 2007a; Wills et al. 2008; Tanski et al. 2009	Longitudinal random-digit-dial survey N = 6,522 baseline (5,829 never smokers) National sample Follow-up at 8 months (5,503), 16 months (5,019), 24 months (4,574) Multiethnic Aged 10–14 years at baseline Baseline smoking status: never smoker for outcome of tried smoking, not established smoker for outcome of established smoking United States 2003	Movie title recognition—Beach method 50 titles/survey Baseline pool: 532 U.S. box office hits released from 1998 to 2003 Follow-up pools: movies released to box office or DVD during interim periods (approximately 150 titles for each follow-up survey wave)	S, SI, P, PS, EA, SCH	Tried smoking (15.9% by 24 months)	Continuous measure windsorized and scaled so 0 = 5th percentile and 1 = 95th percentile, assessed by character type: Mixed Negative Positive	 AHR 1.39 (1.04–1.85) 1.46 (1.07–1.98) 1.39 (0.99–1.96)	Interaction effect for negative character smoking: AHR = 2.55 (1.50–4.32) for adolescents low in sensation seeking; Wills et al. (2008) found that the relation of movie exposure and onset of smoking was partially mediated through positive expectancies and change in the smoking status of friends; interaction effect for established smoking: AHR = 12.7 (2.0–80.6) for adolescents low in sensation seeking
			S, SI, P, PS, EA, SCH	Established smoking (≥100 cigarettes lifetime)	Continuous measure windsorized and scaled so 0 = 5th percentile and 1 = 95th percentile	AHR 2.04 (1.01–4.12)	

Table 5.13 Continued

Study	Design	Measure of exposure	Categories of covariates used in adjustment[a]	Outcome (prevalence)	Exposure comparison categories	Measure of association, association (95% CI)[b]	Comments
Hanewinkel and Sargent 2008; Sargent and Hanewinkel 2009	Longitudinal school-based survey N = 2,711 Follow-up at 1 year White Aged 10–16 years at baseline Baseline smoking status: never smoker Germany (Schleswig-Holstein) 2005	Movie title recognition—Beach method 50 titles/survey 398 internationally distributed movies that were German box office hits and released from 1994 to 2004	S, P, SCH, PS, SI, M	Tried smoking (19%)	Quartile of exposure to movie smoking: 1 2 3 4	ARR Reference 1.37 (1.09–1.68) 1.78 (1.39–2.29) 1.96 (1.55–2.47)	Hanewinkel and Sargent (2008) also found a significant moderation effect on parental smoking (higher movie effects among adolescents whose parents did not smoke); this and the dose-response curve were similar to Dalton et al. (2003)
				Smoking index (composed of lifetime smoking and current smoking items, α = 0.87)	Continuous measure windsorized and scaled so 0 = 5th percentile and 1 = 95th percentile, assessed by character type	APOR among baseline never smokers: 2.85 (1.90–4.26) Among baseline ever smokers, the interaction term was 0.55 (0.34–0.92), indicating a significantly lower response in this category of baseline smoker	

Table 5.13 Continued

Study	Design	Measure of exposure	Categories of covariates used in adjustment[a]	Outcome (prevalence)	Exposure comparison categories	Measure of association, association (95% CI)[b]	Comments
Titus-Ernstoff et al. 2008	Longitudinal, school-based, elementary schools, telephone N = 2,627 (2,499 baseline never smokers) United States (New Hampshire, Vermont) 2002–2003 Follow-up at 1 year (2,354) and 2 years (2,255) White Aged 9–12 years at baseline Baseline smoking status: never smoker	Movie title recognition—Beach method 50 titles/survey 550 popular contemporary movies, top 100 releases for each of the 5.5 years preceding baseline survey Follow-up movie pools selected on rolling basis from top 100 box office hits plus top 100 video rentals for the 12 months preceding survey		Tried smoking (9.6% by 24 months)	Exposure entered as continuous measure, with each 1-point increase equivalent to a 1-decile increase in exposure: Baseline (B) exposure 12-month exposure 24-month exposure B + 12-month exposure B + 12-month + 24-month exposure	ARR for trying smoking at 24 months 1.09 (1.03–1.15) 1.09 (1.03–1.16) 1.07 (1.00–1.14) 1.11 (1.04–1.17) 1.09 (1.02–1.16)	AAF = 0.35 (0.16–0.53); majority of movie smoking exposure was from youth-rated movies
					Using <25th percentile as reference	AAF 0.35 (0.16–0.53)	
					Using <10th percentile as reference	AAF 0.46 (0.11–0.70)	
Thrasher et al. 2009	Longitudinal school-based survey N = 3,874 baseline (2,093 never smokers) Mexico (Cuernavaca and Zacatecas) 2005 Follow-up at 1 year (1,741) Hispanic Aged 10–14 years Baseline smoking status: never smoker	Movie title recognition—fixed list of 42 box office hits (2002–2006) with >1 minute of smoking, 15 Mexican, 23 U.S., 4 other foreign	BOF, M, P, PI, S, SI	Tried smoking (36%)	Quartile of exposure to movie smoking: 1 2 3 4	ARR Reference 1.01 (0.64–1.60) 1.54 (1.01–2.64) 1.41 (0.95–2.10)	
				Current (30 days) smoking (8%)	Quartile of exposure to movie smoking: 1 2 3 4	ARR Reference 1.22 (0.59–2.51) 2.44 (1.31–4.55) 2.23 (1.19–4.17)	

Table 5.13 Continued

Study	Design	Measure of exposure	Categories of covariates used in adjustment[a]	Outcome (prevalence)	Exposure comparison categories	Measure of association, association (95% CI)[b]	Comments
Wilkinson et al. 2009	Longitudinal household survey N = 1,328 Follow-up at 6, 12, 18, and 24 months (1,286) Hispanic Aged 11–13 years Baseline smoking status: never smoker for new experimentation United States (Texas)	Movie title recognition—Beach method 50 titles/survey 250 popular contemporary movies, top 50 releases each year 1999–2004	P, S, SCH, SI	Ever tried cigarettes (n = 1,286)	Continuous measure windsorized and scaled so 0 = 5th percentile and 1 = 95th percentile	AOR 1.27 (1.10–1.39)	Interaction effect found for country of birth, with Mexican-born adolescents having a stronger response to smoking in movies, AOR = 1.52 (1.14–2.05), than did U.S. born, AOR = 1.04 (0.86–1.27)
				New experimentation with cigarettes (n = 1,129)	Continuous measure windsorized and scaled so 0 = 5th percentile and 1 = 95th percentile	AOR 1.19 (1.01–1.40)	

Note: Multiple citations within one cell are for multiple reports on the same sample. **U.S.** = United States.
[a]Covariates: **ACH** = access to cigarettes in household; **BOF** = reported seeing bogus title; **EA** = extracurricular activities; **M** = other media/advertising influences; **P** = personality characteristics; **PPS** = perceived prevalence of smoking; **PS** = parenting style/parental oversight of smoking behavior; **S** = sociodemographics; **SCH** = school attachment and function; **SI** = other social influences (friend and family smoking); **SINC** = weekly spendable income; **SRA** = smoking-related attitudes/cognitions.
[b]Measures of association: **AAF** = adjusted attributable fraction; **AHR** = adjusted hazard ratio; **AOR** = adjusted odds ratio; **APOR** = adjusted proportional odds ratio; **ARR** = adjusted relative risk; **CI** = confidence interval; **NS** = not significant; **OR** = odds ratio; **UAβ** = unstandardized beta coefficient.

Figure 5.12 Summary and meta-analysis of studies on the association between exposure to movie smoking and smoking among adolescents and young adults

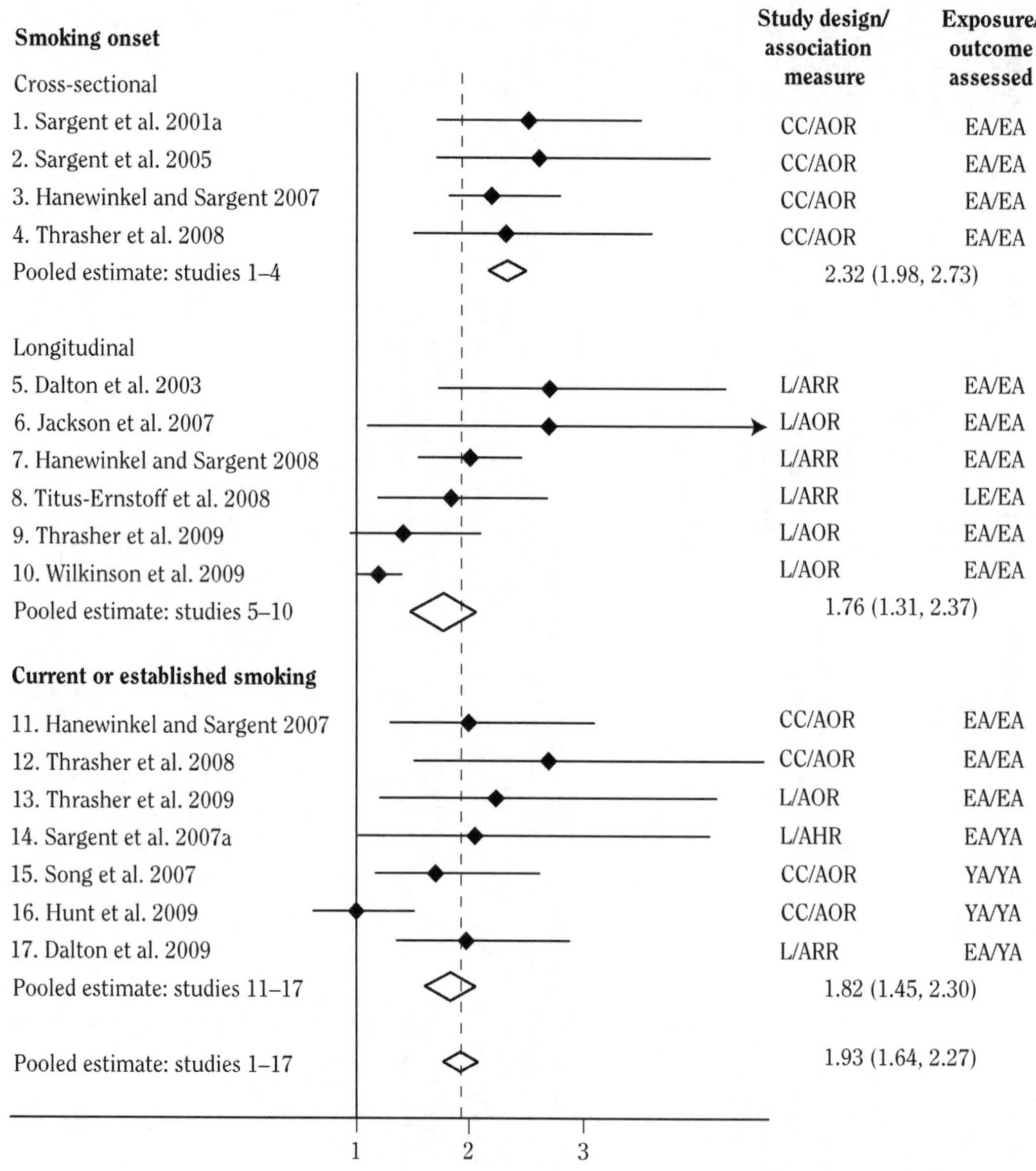

Note: Only studies that used some form of a movie title recognition method of assessing exposure are summarized; in most cases, the high category was highest quartile of exposure compared with lowest quartile. For each study, the point estimate and 95% confidence intervals are illustrated. Pooled estimates were obtained through random effects meta-analysis using Stata 10 (College Station, Texas). **AHR** = adjusted hazard ratio; **AOR** = adjusted odds ratio; **ARR** = adjusted relative risk; **CC** = cross-sectional; **EA** = early adolescents (aged 11–15 years); **L** = longitudinal; **LE** = late elementary school (aged 7–10 years); **YA** = young adults (aged 18–25 years).

Figure 5.13 Shape of the crude dose-response relation between exposure to movie smoking and smoking onset for German and U.S. samples of adolescents

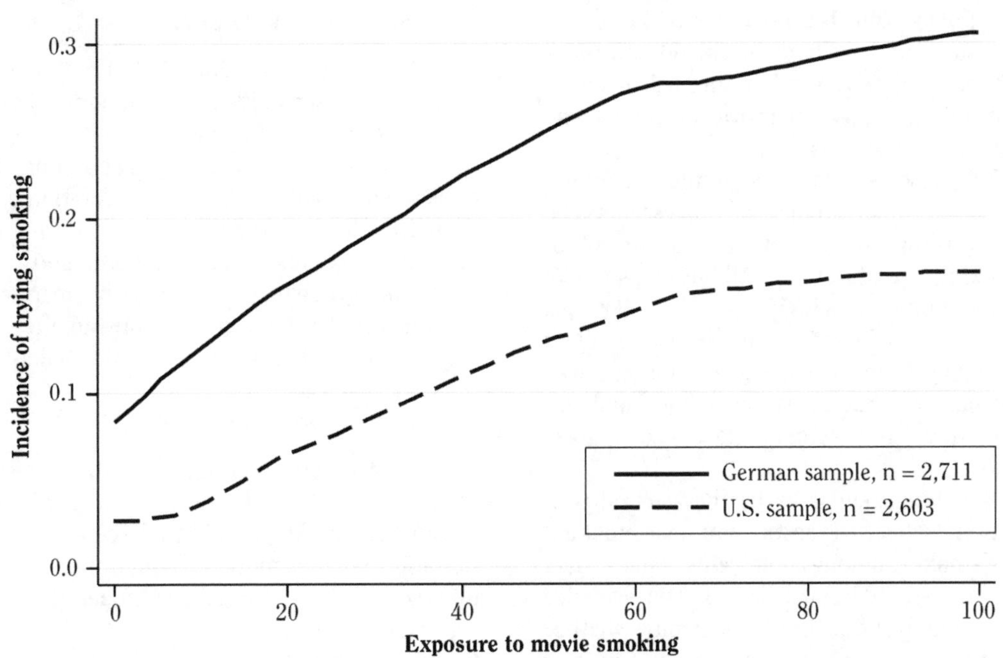

Source: Hanewinkel and Sargent 2008. Reprinted with permission from the American Academy of Pediatrics, © 2008.
Note: For the German sample, exposure was to 398 internationally distributed box office hits in the German market; for the U.S. sample, exposure was to 601 box office hits in the North American market. Because the sample of movies for the U.S. study was larger, those individuals had higher average levels of exposure to movie smoking. To compare the dose-response curves, exposure was standardized for the two studies so the lowest value was 0 and the highest was 100, with both distributions trimmed at the 95th percentile. For the German sample, the median (interquartile range) was 23 (7–48), and for the U.S. sample it was 32 (18–56).

that had been released after each previous survey. Most of the exposure (79%) in this age group came from youth-rated movies, and almost one-half of the onset of smoking in this cohort was explained by exposure to smoking in movies consistent with the results of Dalton and colleagues (2003).

Two longitudinal studies have addressed the relation between exposure to movie smoking and adolescent smoking among Latino adolescents. A study of Mexican adolescents 1 year after they were exposed to movie smoking (Thrasher et al. 2009) reported no association with trying smoking among never smokers at baseline, but significant associations with current (past 30 days) smoking among this group. The second study (Wilkinson et al. 2009) followed up a Texas-based sample of 1,328 Mexican American adolescents and reported that those who had been born in Mexico were more strongly affected by the exposure to movie smoking than were U.S.-born youths.

Figure 5.12 summarizes the results for longitudinal studies of the onset of smoking among adolescents that used cued-recall measures of movie exposure (results 5–10). Four studies of White adolescents (Dalton et al. 2003; Jackson et al. 2007; Hanewinkel and Sargent 2008; Titus-Ernstoff et al. 2008) from the United States and Germany yielded consistent results with multivariate estimates of relative risk (RR) in the 2–3 range. Smaller measures of risk were found among U.S. Latinos (Wilkinson et al. 2009), and findings were null for Mexican adolescents (Thrasher et al. 2009). Noting that marketing restrictions were strongest at the time of their study in the United States, intermediate in Germany, and weakest in Mexico, Thrasher and colleagues (2009) suggested that the strength of the association between movie smoking and adolescent smoking may depend on marketing regulations, with larger effects in countries with stronger tobacco control programs.

One study of Black adolescents using exposure to R-rated movies did not find a relationship between exposure and smoking behavior (Jackson et al. 2007). Another study found that there was a dose-response between the number of episodes of smoking by Black actors and smoking initiation among Black adolescents (Tanski et al. 2011). However, Black adolescents did not appear to be affected by smoking by White actors, unlike White adolescents who were susceptible to both Black and non-Black movie characters. Further research is needed to better understand the relation between movie exposures and smoking among minority adolescents.

Figure 5.12 also summarizes results of cross-sectional and longitudinal studies of adolescents and young adults regarding an association with current or established smoking (results 11–17). All but one study of adolescents found multivariate RRs/ORs in the 2–3 range. A cross-sectional study of young adults in experimental phases of smoking by Song and colleagues (2007) showed a significant association, but the study by Hunt and colleagues (2009) (involving young established regular smokers) did not.

In summary, longitudinal studies have found consistent associations between exposure to movie smoking and the onset of smoking among adolescents (early vs. late smoking outcomes are addressed below). The evidence base is not large enough at this time to determine whether these general results apply specifically to young adults or to racial and ethnic subgroups.

Replicated Moderation Effects

Moderation, or effect modification, is found when the association is significantly stronger or weaker in a certain subgroup. Moderation effects are often reported but rarely replicated; replication of a moderation effect would make one more certain of an underlying causal relation responsible for both the association and the moderation effect.

Early Versus Late Outcomes

It has been common to model the uptake of smoking as one continuous variable, but recent publications have raised the possibility that different risk factors could play different roles for early outcomes (e.g., the onset of smoking) versus intermediate outcomes (progression of early experimentation) versus late outcomes (daily smoking) (Robinson et al. 2006). In one study, Sargent and coworkers (2009a) found that the association between exposure to movie smoking and adolescent smoking was confined to trying smoking; the authors found no significant association between exposure to movie smoking and higher levels of lifetime smoking among the experimental smokers. A study by DiFranza and colleagues (2002) found that some adolescents move quickly from the onset of smoking to symptoms of dependence and established smoking (>100 cigarettes lifetime) and that movies have more important effects on the early phases of this process (Pomerleau 1995; DiFranza et al. 2007).

Smoking by Parents

Dalton and colleagues (2003) reported that parental smoking status modified the relationship between exposure to movie smoking and smoking among adolescents; the effect was significantly stronger among adolescents in nonsmoking households. This moderation effect was replicated in the longitudinal study of German adolescents by Hanewinkel and Sargent (2008). Thus, the stimulus for smoking behavior that smoking in movies provides appears stronger for youth in nonsmoking homes, where parents do not provide smoking role models.

Sensation Seeking

Sargent and colleagues (2007a) reported a moderation effect for sensation seeking in their study of established smoking, with adolescents who were low in sensation seeking more strongly influenced by exposure to movie smoking. This type of moderation effect was also present for trying smoking, with adolescents low in sensation seeking being more strongly affected by negative-balanced smoking (smoking by bad guys) in movies (Tanski et al. 2009).

In conclusion, the moderation effects reported to date suggest that the effects of movies are stronger for adolescents at lower risk for taking up smoking (parents do not smoke, the youth are low-sensation seekers).

Mediation Through Hypothesized Endogenous Variables

Analyses of mediation are important in behavioral science because they test whether hypothesized attitudes, cognitions, and intentions lie along the causal pathway from an exposure to a behavior. These variables are considered endogenous, part of the mental mechanism through which the exposure to media exerts its influence. Demonstrating such a mediational pathway is an important part of empirically testing the plausibility of the theory underlying the causal association.

For example, using cross-sectional and longitudinal structural models, both Tickle and colleagues (2006) and Wills and colleagues (2007) assessed whether exposure to movies affected the onset of smoking indirectly though changes in some variable for peers regarding smoking. The Wills study found that change in friends' smoking status between baseline and follow-up partially mediated the effect of exposure to movies on the adolescent's own uptake of smoking. The Tickle study found that the pathway from exposure to movie smoking to young people's intentions to smoke was mediated by positive expectancies about smoking and identification as a smoker. Finally, in a cross-sectional study of young adults, Song and colleagues (2007) found pathways from exposure to movie smoking to current smoking through friend smoking and positive expectancies about smoking. In summary, mediational analyses conducted on three samples suggest that exposure to smoking in movies affects adolescent smoking both directly and indirectly through peers and positive expectancies.

Parental Control Over Media Exposure

Although policies to reduce smoking in youth-rated movies might limit adolescents' exposure to movie smoking, about 40% of the exposure to this risk factor comes through adolescents watching movies rated for adults. Thus, an additional approach to limiting risk would be to encourage parents to control the exposure of their children to adult-rated movies. Observational studies, summarized in Table 5.14, suggest that this strategy could be complementary to policies aimed at eliminating smoking from youth-rated movies (Dalton et al. 2002a, 2006; Sargent et al. 2004; Thompson and Gunther 2007; Hanewinkel et al. 2008). Most of these studies used a form of the question "How often do your parents allow you to watch R-rated movies? (*never, once in a while, sometimes, all the time*)." Typically, only a minority of young adolescents reported complete restriction from viewing R-rated movies, and yet parental restrictions were associated with seeing fewer R-rated movies (Dalton et al. 2002a; Sargent et al. 2004; Hanewinkel et al. 2008). Most of the studies controlled for a variety of confounding influences, including some measure of authoritative parenting style. As illustrated in Figure 5.14, all the studies found that fewer parental restrictions on movie viewing were associated with higher risk of trying smoking.

The evidence that parental restrictions on the viewing of R-rated movies translates into lower risk for the onset of their children's smoking has two important implications for policy. First, it is evidence that active intervention to lower the level of exposure to on-screen smoking (the "dose") leads to lower risk of smoking (the "response"), and that intervention to move down the dose-response relationship between exposure to smoking in movies and youth smoking is possible. Second, because youth still receive a substantial amount of their exposure to on-screen smoking from youth-rated (mostly PG-13) films (Figure 5.11), even children of parents who vigorously enforce the R rating will receive substantial exposure to on-screen smoking. This remaining exposure is very important in view of the evidence that the marginal effect of exposure at lower levels is greater than at higher levels (Figures 5.12 and 5.13) and the effects of exposure to on-screen smoking are greater in youth at lower risk of smoking.

Summary of Population-Based Studies

A random effects meta-analysis of the four cross-sectional studies of smoking onset among early adolescents summarized in Figure 5.12 produced a pooled OR of 2.32 (95% CI; 1.98–2.73) for adolescent smoking in the top quartile of exposure to movie smoking compared with the bottom quartile of exposure. Similarly, a random effects meta-analysis of the six longitudinal studies in Figure 5.12 produced a pooled RR of 1.76 (95% CI; 1.31–2.37) for the same comparison. A random effects meta-analysis of the seven studies that addressed later stages of smoking yielded a pooled OR of 1.82 (95% CI; 1.45–2.30). Considering the OR to be an approximation of the RR, a random effects meta-analysis of all 17 studies provided an overall estimate of the risk of smoking as a function of high exposure to movie smoking to be 1.93 (95% CI; 1.64–2.27). In addition, the population-attributable risks for the four studies that provided such estimates (Dalton et al. 2003, 2009; Sargent et al. 2005; Titus-Ernstoff et al. 2008) yielded an overall population-attributable risk fraction of 0.44 for adolescent smoking due to exposure to smoking in movies (Millett and Glantz 2010). Because of the very widespread exposure to smoking in movies, and because movie exposures are not viewed with the same skepticism as marketing messages, some authors suggest that movie smoking may account for a larger fraction of the onset of youth smoking than does traditional cigarette advertising (Glantz 2003; Sargent and Hanewinkel 2009; Sargent et al. 2009a).

Studies Published Since the Meta-Analysis Was Completed

Since the meta-analysis discussed above was prepared, several additional epidemiological studies on the links between on-screen smoking and adolescent smoking have been completed that reinforce the conclusions of earlier work. Cross-sectional surveys with extensive controls for confounding have been published from Europe (Hunt et al. 2011; Morgenstern et al. 2011; Waylen et al. 2011). In one, approximately 16,000 adolescents were surveyed from six European Union nations, and in each country there was an association between seeing smoking in movies and youth smoking, net confounding (Hunt et al. 2011). One survey of adolescents in the U.S. Midwest

Table 5.14 Population-based studies assessing the relation between parental restrictions on viewing R-rated movies and smoking among adolescents

Study	Design	Measure of exposure	Categories of covariates used in adjustment[a]	Outcome	Exposure comparison categories	Measure of association, association (95% CI)[b]	Comments
Cross-sectional							
Dalton et al. 2002a	Cross-sectional school-based survey N = 4,544 White Aged 10–15 years United States (Northeast) 1999	"How often do your parents let you watch movies or videos that are rated R?" (p. 3) (Never, once in a while, sometimes, all the time)	M, P, PS, S, SCH, SI	Prevalence of tried smoking (18%)	Allowed to watch R-rated movies: Never (16%) Once in a while/ sometimes (53%) All the time (31%)	ARR 0.29 (0.19–0.45) 0.74 (0.65–0.85) Reference	Parental restrictions associated with lower viewership of R and PG-13 movies and lower rates of drinking alcohol
Dalton et al. 2006	School-based survey N = 2,606 Aged 9–12 years United States (Northeast)	Parental restrictions on R-rated movie viewing combined with whether they co-viewed the movies	PS, S, SI	Susceptibility to smoking (12.5%)	Permits watching, no parent Permits watching, co-views Prohibits child from watching	ARR Reference 0.72 (0.54–0.96) 0.54 (0.41–0.70)	When assessing other movie-monitoring habits (requiring child to ask before seeing, going into video store, overseeing movie viewing at friends), it appeared that these behaviors partially ameliorated the effects of seeing R-rated movies
Thompson and Gunther 2007	School-based survey of 1,687 6th–8th graders N = 1,687 United States (Wisconsin)	"How often do your parents let you watch movies or videos that are rated R?" ([1] never to [5] all the time)	PS, S, SI	Smoking susceptibility among never smokers (24%)	R-rated movie restriction: Full Partial None	AOR Reference 2.1 (1.5–2.8) 3.3 (2.3–4.6)	
				Tried smoking prevalence (29%)	R-rated movie restriction: Full Partial None	Reference 1.5 (1.0–2.8) 2.5 (1.7–3.7)	

Table 5.14 Continued

Study	Design	Measure of exposure	Categories of covariates used in adjustment[a]	Outcome	Exposure comparison categories	Measure of association, association (95% CI)[b]	Comments
				Longitudinal			
Sargent et al. 2004	Longitudinal school-based survey with telephone follow-up, baseline survey N = 2,596 baseline never smokers Follow-up at 18 months White Aged 10–14 years at baseline Baseline smoking status: never smoker United States (New Hampshire, Vermont) 1999	"How often do your parents allow you to watch movies or videos that are rated R?" (Never, once in a while, sometimes, all the time)	EA, P, PS, S, SCH, SI	Incidence of tried smoking (15.9% by 18 months)	Allowed to watch R-rated movies: Never (19%) Once in a while (29%) Sometimes/all the time (52%)	ARR Reference 1.8 (1.1–3.1) 2.8 (1.6–4.7)	Statistically significant interaction with stronger results for adolescents living in nonsmoking households; relaxation of R-rated restrictions over time resulted in greater risk of smoking; strengthening of restrictions over time resulted in lower risk
Hanewinkel et al. 2008	Longitudinal, school-based survey N = 2,110 Follow-up at 1 year White Aged 10–15 years at baseline Baseline smoking status: never smoker Germany (Schleswig-Holstein) 2005	"How often do your parents allow you to watch movies that are rated for 16-year-olds?" (Never, once in a while, sometimes, all the time)	P, PS, S, SCH, SI	Tried smoking incidence (16%) Smoking and binge drinking (5%)	Never (41%) Once in a while (28%) Sometimes (22%) All the time (9%) Never Once in a while Sometimes All the time	Reference 1.19 (0.85–1.67) 1.71 (1.33–2.20) 1.85 (1.27–2.69) Reference 1.64 (1.05–2.58) 2.30 (1.53–3.45) 2.92 (1.83–4.67)	German rating categories refer to the age below which the restriction applies; they are FSK-0 (family), FSK-6, FSK-12, FSK-16, FSK-18; lower exposure to movies in all rating categories for adolescents reporting restrictions; mediational analysis shows indirect pathway from FSK restriction through lower movie substance-use exposure to behavior

[a]Covariates: **EA** = extracurricular activities; **M** = other media/advertising influences; **P** = personality characteristics; **PS** = parenting style/parental oversight of smoking behavior; **S** = sociodemographics; **SCH** = school attachment and function; **SI** = other social influences (friend and family smoking).
[b]Measures of association: **AOR** = adjusted odds ratio; **ARR** = adjusted relative risk.

Figure 5.14 Summary of results for studies on the association between parental movie restrictions and smoking among early adolescents

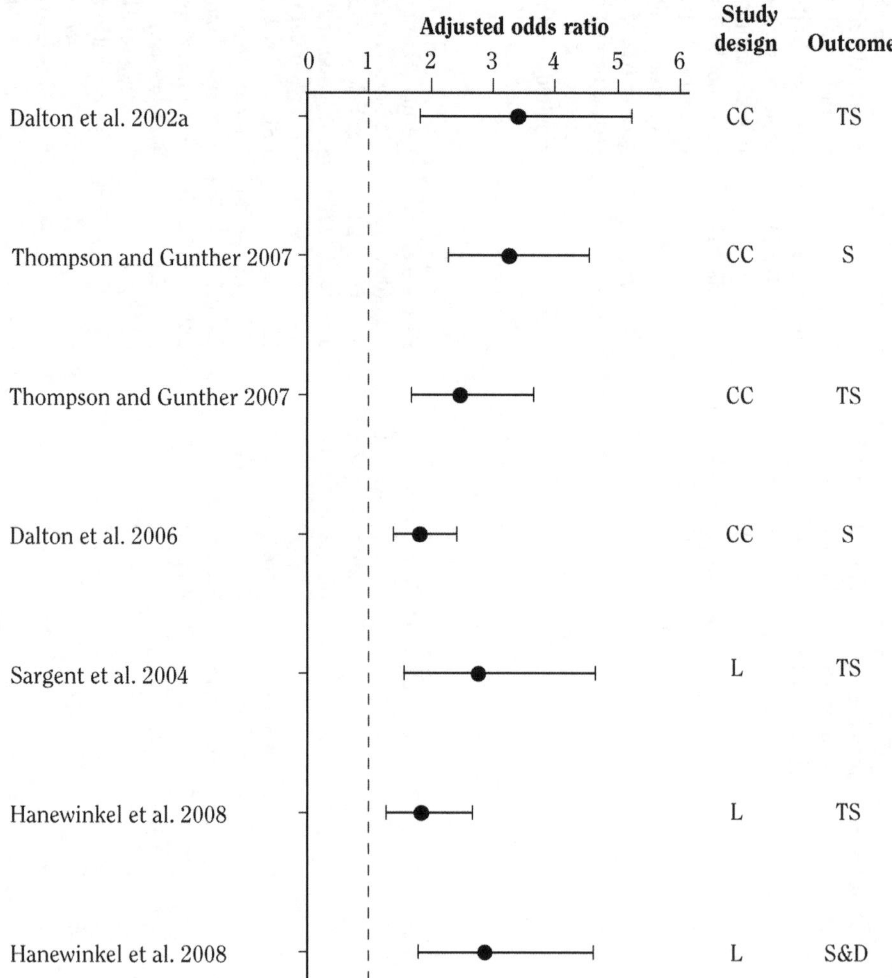

Note: The point estimate is for the comparison between being allowed to watch R-rated movies "all the time" vs. "never"; for each study, the point estimate and 95% confidence intervals are illustrated. **CC** = cross-sectional; **L** = longitudinal; **S** = susceptibility to smoking among never smokers; **S&D** = tried smoking and binge drinking; **TS** = tried smoking.

found an association between repeated measures of adolescents' own assessment of smoking in movies they saw and changes in their smoking behavior (Choi et al. 2011, in press). In that study, there was no reciprocal relationship; that is, there was no prospective association between higher levels of smoking and larger increases in perception of smoking in movies. A survey of Indian adolescents assessed their exposure to smoking in 60 Bollywood movies and found a relationship with smoking that was the same order of magnitude found in studies of youths in Western countries (Arora et al., in press). de Leeuw and colleagues (2011) found that parental restrictions on viewing R-rated movies affected smoking by decreasing growth in sensation seeking over time. Finally, a study by Wills and colleagues (2010) found that higher levels of self-control were associated with a blunted response to smoking in movies.

Experimental Research

Experimental studies have used either quasi-experimental or randomized designs to better control for risk factors and influences that could confound the effect of movie images on behavior. A recent review (NCI 2008) summarized the results from eight experimental studies that explored the effects of movie smoking on viewers' beliefs about smoking or their reactions to movies. According to that review, the results suggest that (1) viewing smoking in movies enhances viewers' perceptions of how socially acceptable smoking is (Pechmann and Shih 1999; Gibson and Maurer 2000), (2) adolescents who view adult characters smoking on screen perceive the real-world prevalence of smoking among adults to be higher than do adolescents viewing nonsmoking movie characters, and (3) exposure to smoking by characters affects personal intentions to smoke among adolescents (Pechmann and Shih 1999), but not among young adults (Gibson and Maurer 2000). The results also suggest that showing youth an antismoking advertisement before viewing a movie depicting smoking blunts the favorable attitudinal response among adolescents (Pechmann and Shih 1999). Finally, one study reported no relationship between the presence of smoking in a movie and box office success (Dalton et al. 2002b).

Recent Experimental Studies

Nine relevant experimental studies have been published since the NCI (2008) review. In one, Dal Cin and colleagues (2007) found that greater self-identification with the smoking protagonist may make smokers more likely to continue smoking and make nonsmokers more favorably disposed toward smoking.

Lochbuehler and colleagues (2009) studied reactivity to cues in movie smoking among young adults in The Netherlands and found that, although individual pictures of movie smoking prompted craving in a traditional pictorial study of reactivity to cues, a 30-minute movie segment with multiple cues to smoke did not have an effect on urge to smoke after the movie.

Golmier and colleagues (2007) evaluated the capacity of a graphic warning label to decrease the effect of movie smoking and found a significant main effect for warning labels on susceptibility to smoking. Harakeh and associates (2010) found that among young adult Dutch smokers, viewing an antismoking ad resulted in a moderate decline in all measures of smoking used, with a dose-response effect (more antismoking ads led to less smoking).

Shmueli and associates (2010) randomly assigned young adult smokers to watch an 8-minute film montage comprised of clips that either did or did not contain smoking. After watching, participants were asked to leave the room for 10 minutes while the experimenter prepared the next phase of the study. Smokers who watched the montage with smoking scenes were more likely to smoke during the break than those who watched the smoke-free montage. In addition, participants who saw the smoking films were more likely to smoke a cigarette within 30 minutes after completion of the experiment than were those who watched the smoke-free montage.

An interaction analysis suggested an enhanced effect on smoking of smoking in movies when the film included horror scenes (Sargent et al. 2009b). Another interaction effect was reported by Hanewinkel and colleagues (2010b) who replicated the findings that showing an antismoking ad before some films was associated with higher awareness of smoking in the movies and with lower levels of approval of smoking in the movie and smoking in general. These effects occurred at all ages but were stronger in youth than among adults.

Wagner and colleagues (2011) compared functional magnetic resonance imaging responses to smoking scenes in movies in a group of smokers and nonsmokers who were naive to the focus on smoking. The study assessed brain responses to movie smoking segments and compared them with responses to segments that contained no smoking. The smokers had larger responses in reward circuits and also larger responses in motor planning areas for the right hand, suggesting that the smoking scenes prompted planning for smoking. Lochbuehler and colleagues (2011) found that smokers preferentially looked at the cigarette when viewing on-screen smoking images and, in another study, that smokers smoked more when viewing movie smoking but only if they were not transported into the story (Lochbuehler et al. 2010). Finally, Shadel and colleagues (2010) showed middle-school adolescents movie clips that depicted smoking in the context of rebelliousness, relaxation, and no motive and found greater desire to smoke after adolescents viewed clips in which smoking conveyed relaxation.

Summary of Experimental Research

Experimental studies to date offer further evidence for an effect of movie images on behavior. In addition, there is a strong concordance of results for the beneficial effect of an antismoking advertisement shown before movies with smoking: more conscious awareness of movie smoking, higher disapproval of movie smoking, less intent to smoke among nonsmoking adolescents, and less actual smoking among young adult smokers. With respect to the effect of smoking in movies on urge to smoke, the results are mixed, with one quasi-experimental study showing an effect size similar to other cue reactivity studies and randomized experiments showing little or no effect. For observed smoking behavior—not urges alone—however, there is some evidence that exposure to smoking scenes increases smoking intensity. The differences in findings among some of the experimental studies may be due to differences in the type of movie. The strongest design was used by Shmueli and colleagues (2010) who randomly assigned subjects to cues from five different movies. If subjects react more strongly to smoking presented in certain contexts than others, the null results for some experiments may be explained by the choice of the particular movie or movie segment used for the prompt; this is an important area for further research.

Summary

A 2008 NCI monograph that reviewed influences of the media on tobacco use offered a summary of research on the portrayal of tobacco use in media channels, including movies, television, music, magazines, and the Internet (NCI 2008). Chapter 10 of that report concluded that exposure to smoking in movies causes tobacco use among adolescents, stating: "The total weight of evidence from cross-sectional, longitudinal, and experimental studies indicates a causal relationship between exposure to movie smoking depictions and youth smoking initiation" (p. 357). This statement was also incorporated into that report's six major conclusions (p. 12). Since this statement was issued, population-based cross-sectional studies have shown that movies deliver billions of images of smoking to young audiences. Furthermore, cross-sectional and longitudinal population studies have demonstrated an association between seeing smoking in movies and smoking among youth in samples of U.S. White and Mexican American adolescents and among adolescents in Germany. Other studies have linked higher exposure to R-rated movies with smoking among adolescents in Wisconsin and New Zealand. In no case was the estimate of risk either zero or in the negative direction. Population-based studies support a mechanism whereby movie effects are mediated through cognitions, and experimental studies demonstrate a short-term effect of movies on the attitudes and behavior of adolescents who watch them. Population studies also provide support for an association between exposure to movie smoking and later stages of adolescent smoking; it is unclear whether this effect results from movies prompting adolescents to start smoking, promoting the continuation of experimentation, or both. An MPAA policy to give films with smoking an R (adult) rating, as recommended by WHO (2009), CDC (2011), and other authorities, could eliminate youth-rated films as sources of exposure to on-screen smoking imagery and reduce the exposure of youth to smoking in movies. The adoption of such policies would contribute to a reduction in adolescent smoking behavior. Some U.S. film studios have begun to respond to public pressure through the development of internal mechanisms to limit the depiction of smoking in movies.

Experimental studies provide strong and consistent support for the idea that an antismoking adverstisement shown before a movie that contains smoking scenes influences how moviegoers view smoking and react to it; several studios have already adopted this practice.

Finally, population-based studies provide evidence to support the idea that parental restrictions on viewing R-rated movies reduces exposure to such movies and the risk of early onset of smoking when restrictions are applied during late childhood and early adolescence. Moreover, practices of restricting and monitoring media appear to work independently of more traditional types of parenting factors, such as authoritative parenting. However, parental restrictions would not address the substantial exposure of youth to smoking imagery in movies rated G, PG, and PG-13.

Evidence Summary

There is strong empirical evidence, along with the tobacco industry's own internal documents and trial testimony, as well as widely accepted principles of advertising and marketing that support the conclusion that tobacco manufacturers' advertising, marketing, and promotions recruit new users as youth and continue to reinforce use among young adults. Hence, despite claims from cigarette manufacturers that marketing and promotion of their products are intended to increase market share and promote brand loyalty among adult consumers, the evidence presented in this chapter is sufficient to conclude that marketing efforts and promotion by tobacco companies show a consistent dose-response relationship in the initiation and progression of tobacco use among young people. As has been true for many decades, today, the majority of smokers begin to use tobacco products as adolescents. Among adults who become daily smokers, nearly all (88%) first use of cigarettes occurs by 18 years of age, with 99% of first use by the age of 26 years (see Chapter 3 of this report; SAMHSA 2009). Constraints on tobacco product marketing, including the ban on broadcast advertising, have had little impact on overall industry expenditures in this area (FTC 2011a,b). Although spending for advertising and promotion of cigarettes has declined every year since 2004, the industry spent $9.94 billion on these activities in 2008 and $574 million to market smokeless tobacco products in 2008, the latest year for which data are available (FTC 2011a,b). Approximately 84% of these expenditures were for discounts, price promotions, coupons, and other activities that resulted in lower retail prices of cigarettes. Tobacco companies have several options for altering the prices of their products, ranging from changing wholesale prices to launching and promoting discount brands to engaging in a variety of price-reducing promotions. Evidence in this chapter also outlines industry actions to attract price-sensitive populations such as youth to their products, as well as to soften the price impact on consumers of increases in federal and state tobacco excise taxes (Chaloupka et al. 2002). Because there is strong evidence that as the price of tobacco products increases, tobacco use decreases, especially among young people, then any actions that mitigate the impact of increased price and thus reduce the purchase price of tobacco can increase the initiation and level of use of tobacco products among young people.

In addition to pricing policies, tobacco manufacturers have employed a wide range of advertising, marketing, and promotional initiatives that evidence shows have been key factors in the initiation and progression of tobacco use among youth and young adults (Perry 1999; King and Siegel 2001; Siegel 2001; NCI 2008). Existing theories of health behavior, including TTI, explain the processes by which tobacco marketing affects tobacco use among youth. TTI, which is consistent with other health behavior frameworks such as the Theory of Planned Behavior and the Social Cognitive Theory, organizes factors that promote or deter health behaviors such as smoking into three interacting streams: intrapersonal, social-contextual, and cultural-environmental (Flay et al. 2009). Variables that might influence smoking can be found at ultimate, distal, and proximate distances from actual smoking behaviors, and much industry marketing acts at multiple levels and points within this triadic framework, through moderated mediation pathways. Behavioral intentions are immediate precursors to behavior and are strong predictors of future behavior. Research demonstrates that tobacco marketing affects intentions toward smoking in a way that leads to increased susceptibility to smoking among adolescents exposed to the marketing. Many econometric studies analyzed in this chapter offer additional evidence that the marketing of tobacco promotes its use by adolescents.

There is strong evidence that tobacco advertising and promotion, particularly those initiatives containing imagery that associates positive qualities with tobacco use, are successful at affecting awareness of smoking, recognition of specific brands, attitudes about smoking, intentions to smoke, and actual smoking behavior among youth (Armstrong et al. 1990; Aitken et al. 1991; Evans et al. 1995; Schooler et al. 1996; Gilpin et al. 1997). Such imagery has also been proven to be effective at reducing perception of risk among young people (Pollay 2001; Wakefield et al. 2002a). Tobacco advertising has consistently contained images that evoke characteristics such as independence, adventurousness, sophistication, athleticism, social acceptability, sexual attractiveness, thinness, popularity, and rebelliousness—common aspirational themes among youth and young adults (see Chapter 3 of this report; SAMHSA 2009). Studies cited in this chapter demonstrate that young people who are more familiar with tobacco advertising can identify specific advertisements, have a favorite tobacco advertisement, or possess cigarette promotional items are more likely to begin smoking than their peers who do not have these characteristics (Arnett and Terhanian 1998; Feighery et al. 1998). Additional longitudinal studies have found increased odds of progression from initiation of smoking to established smoking among adolescents who both owned cigarette promotional items and had a favorite cigarette advertisement (Pierce et al. 1998). Although tobacco companies reported spending relatively small proportions of their marketing and advertising dollars on their Web sites in 2008, Web sites that promoted specific brands of tobacco products and engaged in electronic mail marketing were found to include features such as music, cartoons, and moving images.

A number of studies have examined the relationship between tobacco marketing, peer relationships, and adolescent smoking behavior. Adolescents who believe smoking to be prevalent are more likely to smoke, and peers who smoke increase perceptions of the prevalence of smoking (Kobus 2003). Significant research has supported the idea that adolescents choose their peer group on the basis of their attitudes about smoking and their smoking behavior (Ennett and Bauman 1994; Engels et al. 1997; Kobus 2003; de Vries et al. 2006; Mercken et al. 2007). Industry documents cited in this chapter illustrate how tobacco companies employ peer appeal in marketing campaigns and emphasize the popularity of specific brands to encourage brand loyalty as an extension of a sense of belonging (Tindall 1984; RJR 1986a; Philip Morris USA 2004a). Other research concluded that tobacco companies market their products to young adult trendsetters through promotions in bars and nightclubs because these young adults were highly likely to influence the behaviors of their peers (Hendlin et al. 2010).

In addition to advertising and promotions, the tobacco industry has invested heavily in packaging design to establish brand identity and promote brand appeal (Pollay 2001; Wakefield et al. 2002a). Research conducted by the tobacco industry and cited in this chapter has consistently demonstrated that brand imagery on packages is especially influential during adolescence and young adulthood, when smoking behavior and brand preferences are being developed (DiFranza et al. 1994; Pollay 2000, 2001). Color, words, and images on cigarette packs, as well as container shape and packaging material of smokeless tobacco products, have all been found to suggest specific product characteristics and reduce the perception of risk (Pollay 2001; Pollay and Dewhirst 2001; Wakefield et al. 2002a; Kropp and Halpern-Felsher 2004; Hammond 2009a; Hammond and Parkinson 2009; Bansal-Travers and Hammond 2010). Recent research suggests that even when terms such as "light" and "mild" are prohibited in tobacco packaging and advertising, a significant proportion of adult and youth smokers continue to report false beliefs about the relative risk of cigarette brands (Hammond et al. 2009). Studies suggest that the use of lighter colors on cigarette packs to imply lightness, as well as replacement words such as "smooth," have the same misleading effect as "light" and "mild" labels (Pollay 2001; Wakefield et al. 2002a; Hammond 2009a). The efficacy of package design as an element of tobacco marketing has been supported by research into plain packaging, which removes color and brand imagery from packaging. In addition to enhancing the effectiveness of health warnings by increasing their noticeability, plain packaging has been shown to make smoking less appealing and has the potential to reduce the level of false beliefs about the risks of different brands (Freeman et al. 2008). Plain packaging, then, has the potential to reduce youth smoking.

The evidence reviewed in this chapter strongly suggests that tobacco companies have changed the packaging and design of their products to increase their appeal to adolescents and young adults. Further, as a complementary tactic to support the effects of packaging design on brand identity, tobacco manufacturers have used product design features to appeal to specific market segments. Reviews of internal industry documents show that cigarette length, chemical additives to improve the flavor of the smoke and reduce harshness, ventilated filters, and other product modifications were all used by cigarette companies to attract beginning smokers (Burrows 1984; Tindall 1984; Stevenson and Proctor 2008). Menthol and other flavor additives including fruit and candy flavoring were used as marketing tools to attract young smokers, and national survey findings confirm that menthol cigarette use is disproportionately common among younger and newer adolescent smokers. Flavoring agents other than menthol have been banned in cigarettes but are still used in some cigars, smokeless tobacco products, and new tobacco products such as orbs, sticks, and strips. The evidence also shows that tobacco companies have used menthol and other flavor additives to increase the appeal of smokeless tobacco products to young people. Evidence presented in this chapter indicates that smokeless products have been designed on the basis of a "graduation strategy" to encourage new users to start with particular products and progress to others with higher levels of free nicotine (Figure 5.5; U.S. Smokeless Tobacco 1984). This integration of product design with marketing helped to reverse the decline in smokeless tobacco use among adolescents and young adults (Slade 1995; Tomar et al. 1995; USDHHS 1986). More recent evidence suggests that similar integration of product design with marketing to increase appeal to adolescents and young adults has continued in cigarettes and new smokeless tobacco products such as orbs, sticks, and strips (Mejia and Ling 2010).

Although some tobacco advertising and promotion activities are prohibited by the Master Settlement Agreement and the *Family Smoking Prevention and Tobacco Control Act,* consumers, regardless of age, are exposed to prosmoking messages in stores, and tobacco companies have offered retailers price promotions, volume discounts, in-store branded displays, and payment for prime shelf space. Research confirms that tobacco companies have sought to make their products easily visible and readily accessible to customers to stimulate impulse purchases and have entered into contractual agreements with retailers to secure placement of their products in highly visible locations around sales counters (Pollay 2007). Studies of stores that sell tobacco have confirmed that there is more in-store tobacco advertising in predominantly ethnic and low-income neighborhoods and that tobacco industry point-of-sale marketing differentially appeals to people with lower income and education levels (Wildey et al. 1992; Barbeau et al. 2005; John et al. 2009). Further, more cigarettes are sold in convenience stores than in any other type of store, and 70% of adolescents shop in convenience stores at least weekly. Studies have shown that tobacco advertising is more prevalent in stores located near schools and where adolescents are more likely to shop. The presence of heavy cigarette advertising in these stores has been shown to increase the likelihood of exposing youth to prosmoking messages, which can increase initiation rates among those exposed, particularly if stores are near schools. Several cross-sectional studies have identified relationships between exposure to tobacco marketing in a retail environment and experimentation with smoking; a multiyear cross-sectional study of 8th-, 10th-, and 12th-grade students found that higher levels of advertising, lower cigarette prices, and greater availability of cigarette promotions at point of sale all predicted smoking uptake among youth (Slater et al. 2007). Finally, research on the location of retail outlets selling cigarettes indicated that experimental smoking among youth was related to the density of tobacco outlets both in high school neighborhoods and in neighborhoods where youth live.

In addition to traditional advertising and point-of-sale marketing, tobacco companies have engaged in a variety of public relations strategies to position themselves as responsible corporations and to enhance their public image. Tobacco industry documents demonstrate that these strategies were undertaken in response to public concern about the industry's marketing practices and with the goal of forestalling legislation on regulation that would restrict industry activities. These strategies have included sponsorship of school-based youth smoking prevention programs, retailer education programs on enforcement of legal restrictions on youth access to tobacco products, antismoking campaigns in the mass media, and sponsorship of community-based programs aimed at youth such as the national 4-H program (SCARC Action Alert 1996; Landman et al. 2002; Mandel et al. 2006). Studies cited in this chapter show that the tobacco industry's youth smoking prevention activities have not provided evidence that they are effective at reducing youth smoking. Some studies, as well as industry documents, indicate that these programs can lead to a greater likelihood of uptake among youth by positioning smoking as an "adult only" activity, a concept that may appeal to youth. Further evidence has shown that the messages in these programs divert attention from industry marketing efforts, as well as from messages on the addictiveness of the product. At the same time, advertisements about tobacco company charitable works were shown to improve perceptions of the company's corporate image among 18–25-year-old undergraduates.

An NCI monograph that reviewed influences of the media on tobacco use by youth concluded that exposure to depictions of smoking in movies causes tobacco use among adolescents (NCI 2008). Since that report was issued, multiple population-based cross-sectional studies have provided consistent evidence supporting a causal relationship between exposure to smoking images in movies and smoking among youth in the United States. Although the incidence of on-screen smoking in movies has declined steadily since 2005 and one-half of MPAA member movie studios have adopted policies designed to reduce smoking images in their films, movies overall continue to deliver billions of these images to adolescents. Cross-sectional and longitudinal population studies have demonstrated an association between exposure to smoking in movies and smoking among youth in samples of U.S. White and Mexican American adolescents. Research cited in this chapter has shown that the association between exposure to smoking images in movies and youth smoking has a more important effect on the early phases of smoking initiation than on the transition to addiction. Experimental studies have suggested that an antismoking advertisement shown before a movie that contains smoking scenes can influence how moviegoers view smoking. Evidence indicates that parental restrictions on viewing R-rated movies reduces exposure to such movies and the risk of early onset of smoking when restrictions are applied during late childhood and early adolescence. Finally, recent evidence supports expanding the R rating to include movies with smoking in order to further reduce exposures of young persons to onscreen tobacco incidents, making smoking initiation less likely.

In summary, the tobacco industry's own internal documents and trial testimony indicate that the industry needs to recruit new smokers from among youth. The evidence provided in this chapter shows multiple strategies by which the tobacco industry continues to pursue this objective to increase the rate of initiation and use of tobacco products among young people. Cumulative research indicates that cigarette advertising and promotional activities and depictions of smoking in movies have caused young people to smoke (Lovato et al. 2011).

Conclusions

1. In 2008, tobacco companies spent $9.94 billion on the marketing of cigarettes and $547 million on the marketing of smokeless tobacco. Spending on cigarette marketing is 48% higher than in 1998, the year of the Master Settlement Agreement. Expenditures for marketing smokeless tobacco are 277% higher than in 1998.
2. Tobacco company expenditures have become increasingly concentrated on marketing efforts that reduce the prices of targeted tobacco products. Such expenditures accounted for approximately 84% of cigarette marketing and more than 77% of the marketing of smokeless tobacco products in 2008.

3. The evidence is sufficient to conclude that there is a causal relationship between advertising and promotional efforts of the tobacco companies and the initiation and progression of tobacco use among young people.

4. The evidence is suggestive but not sufficient to conclude that tobacco companies have changed the packaging and design of their products in ways that have increased these products' appeal to adolescents and young adults.

5. The tobacco companies' activities and programs for the prevention of youth smoking have not demonstrated an impact on the initiation or prevalence of smoking among young people.

6. The evidence is sufficient to conclude that there is a causal relationship between depictions of smoking in the movies and the initiation of smoking among young people.

References

Abrams SM, Hyland A, Cummings KM. Internet cigarette purchasing among ninth-grade students in Western New York. *Preventive Medicine* 2003;36(6):731–3.

Achey TL. Product information. 1978. Lorillard Collection. Bates No. 03537131/7132. <http://legacy.library.ucsf.edu/tid/tqn61e00>.

Adachi-Mejia AM, Dalton MA, Gibson JJ, Beach ML, Titus-Ernstoff LT, Heatherton TF, Sargent JD. Tobacco brand appearances in movies before and after the master settlement agreement [letter]. *JAMA: the Journal of the American Medical Association* 2005;293(19):2341–2.

Adachi-Mejia AM, Primack BA, Beach ML, Titus-Ernstoff L, Longacre MR, Weiss JE, Dalton MA. Influence of movie smoking exposure and team sports participation on established smoking. *Archives of Pediatrics & Adolescent Medicine* 2009;163(7):638–43.

Advocacy Institute. *Smoke & Mirrors: How the Tobacco Industry Buys & Lies Its Way to Power & Profits*. Washington: Advocacy Institute, 1998.

Aitken PP, Eadie DR, Hastings GB, Haywood AJ. Predisposing effects of cigarette advertising on children's intentions to smoke when older. *British Journal of Addiction* 1991;86(4):383–90.

Aitken PP, Leathar DS, O'Hagan FJ. Children's perceptions of advertising for cigarettes. *Social Science & Medicine* 1985;21(7):785–97.

Ajzen I. The theory of planned behavior. *Organizational Behavior and Human Decision Processes* 1991; 50(2):179–211.

Aloise-Young PA, Hennigan KM. Self-image, the smoker stereotype and cigarette smoking: development patterns from fifth through eighth grade. *Journal of Adolescence* 1996;19(2):163–77.

Altria Group, Inc. *2010 Annual Report*. Altria Group, Inc: Richmond (VA): 2011.

American Tobacco Company. SHOUT, Mr. Tracy!, 1938; <http://tobaccodocuments.org/pollay_ads/Luck03.08.html>; accessed: September 23, 2010.

Anderson SJ, Ling PM. "And they told two friends…and so on": RJ Reynolds' viral marketing of Eclipse and its potential to mislead the public. *Tobacco Control* 2008;17(4):222–9.

Anderson SJ, Millett C, Polansky JR, Glantz SA. Exposure to smoking in movies among British adolescents 2001–2006. *Tobacco Control* 2010;19(3):197–200.

Angus K. Brown A, Hastings G. The effect of tobacco control mass media campaigns, counter-advertising, and other related community interventions on youth tobacco use. Background paper for the WHO Tobacco Free Initiative Global Consultation on Effective Youth Tobacco Control Policy Interventions. Stirling (Scotland): University of Stirling, Institute for Social Marketing, Centre for Tobacco Control Research, 2008.

Apollonio DE, Malone RE. The "We Card" program: tobacco industry youth smoking prevention as industry self-preservation. *American Journal of Public Health* 2010;100(7):1188–201.

Armitage CJ, Connor M. Efficacy of the theory of planned behaviour: a meta-analytic review. *British Journal of Social Psychology* 2001;40(4):471–99.

Armstrong BK, de Klerk NH, Shean RE, Dunn DA, Dolin PJ. Influence of education and advertising on the uptake of smoking by children. *Medical Journal of Australia* 1990;152(3):117–24.

Arnett JJ. Adolescents' responses to cigarette advertisements for five "youth brands" and one "adult brand." *Journal of Research on Adolescence* 2001;11(4): 425–43.

Arnett JJ, Terhanian G. Adolescents' responses to cigarette advertisements: links between exposure, liking, and the appeal of smoking. *Tobacco Control* 1998;7(2):129–33.

Arora M, Mathur N, Gupta VK, Nazar GP, Reddy KS, Sargent JD. Tobacco use in Bollywood movies, tobacco promotional activities and their association with tobacco use among Indian adolescents. *Tobacco Control*. In press.

Ascribe. Philip Morris USA's cigarette brand advertising decreases by 94 percent from 1998 to 2003, June 27, 2006; <http://newswire.ascribe.org/cgi-bin/behold.pl?ascribeid=20060627.155649&time=Nov%2020%20PST&year=2009&public=1>; accessed: September 22, 2010.

Ashare RL, Hawk LW Jr, Cummings KM, O'Connor RJ, Fix BV, Schmidt WC. Smoking expectancies for flavored and non-flavored cigarettes among college students. *Addictive Behaviors* 2007:32(6):1252–61.

Ashe M, Jernigan D, Kline R, Galaz R. Land use planning and the control of alcohol, tobacco, firearms, and fast food restaurants. *American Journal of Public Health* 2003;93(9):1404–8.

Auerbach P. A reprehensible message from Philip Morris USA, 2009; <http://www.healthline.com/blogs/outdoor_health/2009/04/reprehensible-message-from-philip.html>; accessed: March 1, 2010.

Aulbach PL, Black RR, Chakraborty BB, Diesing AC, Gonterman RA, Johnson RR, Scholten DL. *Root Technology: A Handbook for Leaf Blenders and Product Developers*. 1991. Philip Morris Collection. Bates No.

2060538953/8991. <http://legacy.library.ucsf.edu/tid/hnj13e00>.

Balbach ED, Gasior RJ, Barbeau EM. R.J. Reynolds' targeting of African Americans: 1988–2000. *American Journal of Public Health* 2003;93(5):822–7.

Bandura A. *Social Learning Theory*. Englewood Cliffs (NJ): Prentice Hall, 1977.

Bandura A. *Social Foundations of Thought and Action: A Social Cognitive Theory*. Englewood Cliffs (NJ): Prentice-Hall, 1986.

Bansal-Travers M, Hammond D. Study to evaluate the influence of cigarette pack design on U.S. adults. Paper presented at the Society for Research on Nicotine & Tobacco Conference; February 28, 2010; Baltimore.

Barbeau EM, Wolin KY, Naumova EN, Balbach E. Tobacco advertising in communities: associations with race and class. *Preventive Medicine* 2005;40(1):16–22.

Barnes DE, Bero LA. Scientific quality of original research articles on environmental tobacco smoke. *Tobacco Control* 1997;6(1):19–26.

Barnes DE, Bero LA. Why review articles on the health effects of passive smoking reach different conclusions. *JAMA: the Journal of the American Medical Association* 1998;279(19):1566–70.

Barnes DE, Hanauer P, Slade J, Bero LA, Glantz SA. Environmental tobacco smoke: the Brown and Williamson documents. *JAMA: the Journal of the American Medical Association* 1995;274(3):248–53.

Barnsley K, Jacobs M. Tobacco advertising and display of tobacco products at point of sale: Tasmania, Australia. *Tobacco Control* 2000;9(2):230–2.

Beede P, Lawson R. The effect of plain packages on the perception of cigarette health warnings. *Public Health* 1992;106(4):315–22.

Beetham SW. Research project on graduation-based strategy. 1985. US Smokeless Tobacco Collection. Bates No. USTC1300123/0125. <http://legacy.library.ucsf.edu/tid/usf21b00>.

Belch GE, Belch MA. *Introduction to Advertising and Promotion: An Integrated Marketing Communications Perspective*. Chicago: Irwin, 1995.

Bernasek E, Nystrom CW. Ammonia. 1982. RJ Reynolds Collection. Bates No. 504438506/8512. <http://legacy.library.ucsf.edu/tid/gfx65d00>.

Bero L, Barnes DE, Hanauer P, Slade J, Glantz S. Lawyer control of the tobacco industry's external research program: the Brown and Williamson documents. *JAMA: the Journal of the American Medical Association* 1995;274(3):241–7.

Bero LA, Galbraith A, Rennie D. The publication of sponsored symposiums in medical journals. *New England Journal of Medicine* 1993;327(16):1135–40.

Bero LA, Galbraith A, Rennie D. Sponsored symposia on environmental tobacco smoke. *JAMA: the Journal of the American Medical Association* 1994;271(8):612–7.

Bero LA, Glantz SA. Tobacco industry response to a risk assessment of environmental tobacco smoke. *Tobacco Control* 1993;2(2):103–13.

Bero LA, Glantz S, Hong M-K. The limits of competing interest disclosures. *Tobacco Control* 2005;14(2):118–26.

Bero LA, Montini T, Bryan-Jones K, Mangurian C. Science in regulatory policy making: case studies in the development of workplace smoking regulations. *Tobacco Control* 2001;10(4):329–36.

BevReview.com. Commentary: DEWmocracy and Mountain Dew's Online Marketing, February 27, 2008; <http://www.bevreview.com/2008/02/27/commentary-dewmocracy-and-mountain-dews-online-marketing/>; accessed: September 29, 2010.

Bialous SA, Yach D. Whose standard is it anyway: how the tobacco industry determines the International Organization for Standardization (ISO) standards for tobacco and tobacco products. *Tobacco Control* 2001;10(2):96–104.

Biener L. Anti-tobacco advertisements by Massachusetts and Philip Morris: what teenagers think. *Tobacco Control* 2002;11(Suppl 2):ii43–ii46.

Biener L, Nyman AL, Kline RL, Albers AB. Adults only: the prevalence of tobacco promotions in bars and clubs in the Boston area. *Tobacco Control* 2004;13(4):403–8.

Biener L, Siegel M. Tobacco marketing and adolescent smoking: more support for a causal inference. *American Journal of Public Health* 2000;90(3):407–11.

Biener L, Nyman AL, Kline RL, Albers AB. Adults only: the prevalence of tobacco promotions in bars and clubs in the Boston area. *Tobacco Control* 2004;13(4):403–8.

Bitton A, Neuman MD, Barnoya J, Glantz SA. The *p53* tumour suppressor gene and the tobacco industry: research, debate, and conflict of interest. *Lancet* 2005;365(9458):531–40.

Blecher E. The impact of tobacco advertising bans on consumption in developing countries. *Journal of Health Economics* 2008;27(4):930–42.

Bloom PN. Role of slotting fees and trade promotions in shaping how tobacco is marketed in retail stores. *Tobacco Control* 2001;10(4):340–4.

Bluecigs.Electroniccigarette,2011;<http://bluecigs.com>; accessed: November 18, 2011.

Bonnie RT, Stratton K, Wallace RB, editors. *Ending the Tobacco Problem: A Blueprint for the Nation*. Washington: National Academies Press, 2007.

Borland R, Fong GT, Yong HH, Cummings KM, Hammond D, King B, Siahpush M, McNeill A, Hastings G,

O'Connor RJ, et al. What happened to smokers' beliefs about light cigarettes when "light/mild" brand descriptors were banned in the UK: findings from the International Tobacco Control (ITC) Four Country Survey. *Tobacco Control* 2008;17(4):256–62.

Botvin EM, Botvin GJ, Michela JL, Baker E, Filazzola AD. Adolescent smoking behavior and the recognition of cigarette advertisements. *Journal of Applied Social Psychology* 1991;21(11):919–32.

Botvin GJ, Goldberg CJ, Botvin EM, Dusenbury L. Smoking behavior of adolescents exposed to cigarette advertising. *Public Health Reports* 1993;108(2): 217–24.

Botvin GJ, Griffiths KW. Life skills training as a primary prevention approach for adolescent drug abuse and other problem behaviors. *International Journal of Emergency Mental Health* 2002;4(1):41–7.

Boys & Girls Clubs of America. Our partners, 2010; <http://www.bgca.org/partners/youthsmokingprev.asp>; accessed: March 2, 2010.

Brandt AM. *The Cigarette Century: The Rise, Fall, and Deadly Persistence of the Product That Defined America*. New York: Basic Books, 2007.

Braverman MT, Aarø LE. Adolescent smoking and exposure to tobacco marketing under a tobacco advertising ban: findings from 2 Norwegian national samples. *American Journal of Public Health* 2004;94(7):1230–8.

Breidenbach K. [Letter from Kelly Breidenbach of Baldwin Varela to Walter McDonald of Liggett & Meyers]. 1987. Lorillard Collection. Bates No. 91753669/3670. <http://legacy.library.ucsf.edu/tid/xpy90e00>.

British American Tobacco. The current group R&D projects. 1985. Research Collection. Bates No. 109870521/0561. <http://legacy.library.ucsf.edu/tid/vim66b00>.

British American Tobacco. The vanishing media. n.d. British American Tobacco Collection. Bates No. 500062147/2159. <http://legacy.library.ucsf.edu/tid/jlf17a99>.

Brooks M. Newport promotional concepts. 1993. U.S. Department of Justice Collection. Bates No. USX217108/7133. <http://legacy.library.ucsf.edu/tid/zcw36b00>.

Brown & Williamson. B&W Session #3. Implications for cigarette industry. 1978. Brown & Williamson Collection. Bates No. 667007711/7714. <http://legacy.library.ucsf.edu/tid/ebz20f00>.

Brown & Williamson. Exploratory research moist snuff tobacco. 1984. Brown & Williamson Collection. Bates No. 598000202/0224. <http://legacy.library.ucsf.edu/tid/hzi41f00>.

Brown & Williamson. *Life Skills Training Curriculum Fact Sheet*. 1997. Brown & Williamson Collection. Bates No. 208002405/2406. <http://legacy.library.ucsf.edu/tid/xud11c00>.

Brown & Williamson. *Fourth National Synar Technical Assistance Workshop (March 29-31, 1999)*. 1999. Brown & Williamson Collection. Bates No.106006959/6985. <http://legacy.library.ucsf.edu/tid/kxz11c00>.

Burns E. Mountain Dew Plugs Into Online Campaign for New Drink, January 22, 2009; <http://www.clickz.com/3632466>; accessed: April 10, 2010.

Burrows DS. Younger adult smokers: strategies and opportunities. 1984. RJ Reynolds Collection. Bates No. 501928462/8550. <http://legacy.library.ucsf.edu/tid/fet29d00>.

California Department of Health Services/Tobacco Control Section. *A Model for Change: The California Experience in Tobacco Control*. Sacramento (CA): California Department of Health Services/Tobacco Control Section, 1998.

Campaign for Tobacco-Free Kids. Cigarette company youth access initiatives: fake and ineffective [fact sheet], October 5, 2005; <http://www.tobaccofreekids.org/research/factsheets/pdf/0285.pdf>; accessed: January 9, 2012.

Campaign for Tobacco-Free Kids. State Action to Stop RJR from Marketing Candy-Flavored Cigarettes is Major Step, But More Must Be Done to Stop Tobacco Marketing to Kids [press release]. Washington: October 11, 2006; <http://www.tobaccofreekids.org/press_releases/post/id_0945>.

Campaign for Tobacco-Free Kids. The danger from dissolvable tobacco and other smokeless tobacco products, 2010a; <http://www.tobaccofreekids.org/research/factsheets/pdf/0363.pdf>; accessed: October 5, 2010.

Campaign for Tobacco-Free Kids. THE PACT ACT Preventing Illegal Internet Sales of Cigarettes & Smokeless Tobacco, 2010b; <http://www.tobaccofreekids.org/research/factsheets/pdf/0361.pdf>; accessed: October 5, 2010.

Canadian Cancer Society. Tobacco manufactures payments to retailers to display tobacco: products and signs, Canada, 2001–2007. Toronto (Canada): Canadian Cancer Society, Cancer Information Service, 2008.

Cantrell DV. Kool isn't getting the starters/236. 1987. Brown & Williamson Collection. Bates No. 621079918/9921. <http://legacy.library.ucsf.edu/tid/gas01f00>.

Carchman RA, Southwick MA. Chemical senses research. 1990. Philip Morris Collection, Bates No. 2024847429/7627. <http://legacy.library.ucsf.edu/tid/asz71f00>.

Cardador MT, Hazan AR, Glantz SA. Tobacco industry smokers' rights publications: a content analysis. *American Journal of Public Health* 1995;85(9):1212–7.

Carpenter JS. "Funny" French Camel Design. 1985. RJ Reynolds Collection. Bates No. 506768857. <http://legacy.library.ucsf.edu/tid/yjr44d00>.

Carpenter CM, Connolly GN, Ayo-Yusuf O, Wayne GF. Developing smokeless tobacco products for smokers: an examination of tobacco industry documents. *Tobacco Control* 2009;18(1):54–9.

Carpenter CM, Wayne GF, Connolly GN. Designing cigarettes for women: new findings from the tobacco industry documents. *Addiction* 2005a;100(6):837–51.

Carpenter CM, Wayne GF, Pauly JL, Koh HK, Connolly GN. New cigarette brands with flavors that appeal to youth: tobacco marketing strategies. *Health Affairs (Millwood)* 2005b;24(6):1601–10.

Carter SM. Going below the line: creating transportable brands for Australia's dark market. *Tobacco Control* 2003a;12(Suppl 3):iii87–iii94.

Carter SM. New frontier, new power: the retail environment in Australia's dark market. *Tobacco Control* 2003b;12(Suppl 3):95iii–101iii.

Casey WJ, Perfetti P. Method to improve quality of tobacco via sugar-ammonia reactions. 1980. RJ Reynolds Collection. Bates No. 504168866/8868. <http://legacy.library.ucsf.edu/tid/yrt58d00>.

CASAA. The Consumer Advocates for Smoke-free Alternatives Association, 2011; <http://casaa.org>; accessed: November 18, 2011.

Caufield RT. Camel new advertising campaign development. 1986. RJ Reynolds Collection. Bates No. 503969238/9242. <http://legacy.library.ucsf.edu/tid/pil75d00>.

Celebucki CC, Diskin K. A longitudinal study of externally visible cigarette advertising on retail storefronts in Massachusetts before and after the Master Settlement Agreement. *Tobacco Control* 2002;11(Suppl 2):ii47–ii53.

Center on Alcohol Marketing and Youth at Georgetown University. Alcohol Marketing and Youth. April 2007; <http://camy.org/factsheets/index.php?FactsheetID=1>; viewed: September 22, 2009.

Center for Tobacco Policy & Organizing. Cigarettes generate big revenue for convenience stores: analysis of 2007 state of the industry report, 2008. <http://www.center4tobaccopolicy.org/_files/_files/5376_Cigarettes_Generate_Big%20Revenue.pdf>; retrieved: September 27, 2010.

Centers for Disease Control and Prevention. Point-of-purchase tobacco environments and variation by store type—United States, 1999. *Morbidity and Mortality Weekly Report* 2002;51(9):184–7.

Centers for Disease Control and Prevention. Tobacco use, access, and exposure to tobacco in media among middle and high school students—United States, 2004. *Morbidity and Mortality Weekly Report* 2005;54(12):297–301.

Centers for Disease Control and Prevention. Smoking in top-grossing movies—United States, 1991–2009. *Morbidity and Mortality Weekly Report* 2010;59(32):1014–17.

Centers for Disease Control and Prevention. Smoking in top-grossing movies—United States, 2010. *Morbidity and Mortality Weekly Report* 2011;60(27):909–13.

Chaloupka FJ. Written Direct Examination of Frank J. Chaloupka, Ph.D., 2004; <http://www.justice.gov/civil/cases/tobacco2/Chaloupka%20Direct%20-%20final.pdf>; accessed: September 27, 2010.

Chaloupka FJ. Cigarettes: old firms facing new challenges. In: Tremblay VJ, Tremblay CH, editors. *Industry and Firm Studies,* 4th ed. Armonk (NY): ME Sharpe, 2007:80–118.

Chaloupka FJ, Cummings KM, Morley CP, Horan JK. Tax, price and cigarette smoking: evidence from the tobacco documents and implications for tobacco company marketing strategies. *Tobacco Control* 2002;11 (Suppl 1):i62–i72.

Chanil D. Profile of the convenience store customer, February 12, 2001; <http://www.allbusiness.com/retail-trade/food-stores/4492306-7.html>; accessed: October 12, 2010.

Chapman S. How astute a tobacco marketer are you? *Tobacco Control* 1994;3(1):74–5.

Chapman S. Australia: British American Tobacco "addresses" youth smoking. *Tobacco Control* 2007; 16(1):2–3.

Chapman S. With youth smoking at historic lows, how influential is movie smoking on uptake? [Commentary]. *Addiction* 2009;104(5):824–5.

Chapman S, Fitzgerald B. Brand preference and advertising recall in adolescent smokers: some implications for health promotion. *American Journal of Public Health* 1982;72(5):491–4.

Chapman S, Freeman B. Regulating the tobacco retail environment: beyond reducing sales to minors. *Tobacco Control* 2009;18(6):496–501.

Chassin L, Presson CC, Sherman SJ. Cognitive and social influence factors in adolescent smoking cessation. *Addictive Behaviors* 1984;9(4):383–90.

Chassin L, Presson CC, Sherman SJ, Montello D, McGrew J. Changes in peer and parent influence during adolescence: longitudinal versus cross-sectional perspectives on smoking initiation. *Developmental Psychology* 1986;22(3):327–34.

Chen T, Sun B, Singh V. An empirical investigation of the dynamic effect of Marlboro's permanent pricing shift. *Marketing Science* 2009;28(4):740–58.

Chester J, Montgomery K. *Interactive Food & Beverage Marketing: Targeting Children and Youth in the Digital Age*. Berkeley (CA): Berkeley Media Studies Group, 2007.

Chester J, Montgomery K, Dorfman L. *Alcohol Marketing in the Digital Age*. Berkeley (CA): Berkeley Media Studies Group, May 2010. <http://digitalads.org/alcohol.php>; accessed: July 31, 2010.

Chilcote SD Jr. More than a year ago, The Tobacco Institute announced.... 1992. Tobacco Institute Collection. Bates No. TI41816030/6031. <http://legacy.library.ucsf.edu/tid/cap78b00>.

Chilcote SD Jr. The Tobacco Institute: Memorandum (We Card). 1997. Lorillard Collection. Bates No.98876422/6426. <http://legacy.library.ucsf.edu/tid/ztn84c00>.

Choi WS, Ahluwalia JS, Harris KJ, Okuyemi K. Progression to established smoking: the influence of tobacco marketing. *American Journal of Preventive Medicine* 2002;22(4):228–33.

Choi K, Forster JL, Erickson DJ, Lazovich D, Southwell BG. Prevalence of smoking in movies as perceived by teenagers: longitudinal trends and predictors. *American Journal of Preventive Medicine* 2011;41(2):167–73.

Choi WS, Gilpin EA, Farkas AJ, Pierce JP. Determining the probability of future smoking among adolescents. Addiction 2001;96(2):313–23.

Choi K, Forster J, Erickson D, Lazovich D, Southwell BG. The reciprocal relationships between changes in adolescent perceived prevalence of smoking in movies and progression of smoking status. *Tobacco Control*. In press.

Cigarettes and Smokeless Tobacco, 21 *CFR* 1140.34(c) (2011).

Citi Investment Research. Imperial Tobacco Group PLC (IMT.L). Material new risk appears: UK govt suggests plain packaging. In: *Company Flash*. London: Citigroup Global Markets, Citi Investment Research, 2008:2.

Clark PI, Schmitt CL, Feighery EC, Ribisl KM, Myllyluoma J, Barker D. How to evaluate the changing tobacco retail outlet. Paper presented at the 2002 National Conference on Tobacco or Health; November 20, 2002; San Francisco.

Clegg Smith K, Wakefield M. USA: the name of Philip Morris to sit on 28 million school desks. *Tobacco Control* 2001;10(1):8.

Clickin Research. Convenience teens, building loyalty with the next generation. Austin (TX): Clickin Research, 2005.

Cohen JB. Playing to win: marketing and public policy at odds over Joe Camel. *Journal of Public Policy & Marketing* 2000;19(2):155–67.

Cohen PS. New brands and strategic research report: project XG qualitative exploratory III MDD topline perspective. 1984. RJ Reynolds Collection. Bates No. 502034890/4895. <http://legacy.library.ucsf.edu/tid/dnj29d00>.

Cohen JE, Planinac LC, Griffin K, Robinson DJ, O'Connor SC, Lavack A, Thompson FE, Di Nardo J. Tobacco promotions at point-of-sale: the last hurrah. *Canadian Journal of Public Health* 2008;99(3):166–71.

Cohen JE, Sarabia V, Ashley MJ. Tobacco commerce on the internet: a threat to comprehensive tobacco control. *Tobacco Control* 2001;10(4):364–7.

Colby FG. Cigarette concept to assure RJR a larger segment of the youth market. 1973. RJ Reynolds Collection. Bates No. 501166152/6153. <http://legacy.library.ucsf.edu/tid/viz49d00>.

Connolly GN. The marketing of nicotine addiction by one oral snuff manufacturer. *Tobacco Control* 1995;4(1):73–9.

Connolly GN. Smokes and cyberspace: a public health disaster in the making [editorial]. *Tobacco Control* 2001;10(4):299.

Connolly GN. Sweet and spicy flavours: new brands for minorities and youth. *Tobacco Control* 2004;13(3):211–2.

Connolly GN, Behm I, Osaki Y, Wayne GF. The impact of menthol cigarettes on smoking initiation among nonsmoking young females in Japan. *International Journal of Environmental Research and Public Health* 2011;8(1):1–14.

Conrad KM, Flay BR, Hill D. Why children start smoking cigarettes: predictors of onset. *British Journal of Addiction* 1992;87(12):1711–24.

Cortese DK, Lewis MJ, Ling PM. Tobacco industry lifestyle magazines targeted to young adults. *Journal of Adolescent Health* 2009;45(3):268–80.

Cortese DK, Ling PM. Enticing the new lad: masculinity as a product of consumption in tobacco industry-developed lifestyle magazines. *Men and Masculinities* 2011:14(1):4–30.

Coulson WR. Helping youth decide: when the fox preaches, beware the geese. *New York State Journal of Medicine* 1985;85(7):357–8.

Cowling DW, Robbins DM. Rates of illegal tobacco sales to minors varies by sign type in California [letter]. *American Journal of Public Health* 2000;90(11):1792–3.

Crayton FH. 2305 flavor development effects of ammonia - odor and smoke. 1971. Philip Morris Collection. Bates No. 2028660823/0831. <http://legacy.library.ucsf.edu/tid/cuq74e00>.

Creighton FV. Camel growth among males 18–24 years old in the Mid-west. 1986. RJ Reynolds Collection.

Bates No. 505727418/7431. <http://legacy.library.ucsf.edu/tid/vdx05d00>.

Cruz TB. Monitoring the tobacco use epidemic IV. The vector: tobacco industry data sources and recommendations for research and evaluation. *Preventive Medicine* 2009;48(1 Suppl):S24–S34.

Cummings KM, Brown A, Douglas CE. Consumer acceptable risk: how cigarette companies have responded to accusations that their products are defective. *Tobacco Control* 2006;15(Suppl 4):iv84–iv89.

Cummings KM, Brown A, Steger C. Youth marketing. In: Goodman J, editor in chief. *Tobacco in History and Culture: An Encyclopedia.* Vol. 2. Farmington Hills (MI): Charles Scribner's Sons, 2005:689–93.

Cummings KM, Hyland A, Lewit E, Shopland D. Discrepancies in cigarette brand sales and adult market share: are new teen smokers filling the gap? *Tobacco Control* 1997;6(Suppl 1):S38–S43.

Cummings KM, Morley CP, Horan JK, Steger C, Leavell NR. Marketing to America's youth: evidence from corporate documents. *Tobacco Control* 2002;11 (Suppl 1):i5–i17.

Dagnoli J. RJR's Uptown targets blacks. 1989. Philip Morris Collection. Bates No. 2060376070. <http://legacy.library.ucsf.edu/tid/ymn79a00>.

Dal Cin S, Gibson B, Zanna MP, Shumate R, Fong GT. Smoking in movies, implicit associations of smoking with the self, and intentions to smoke. *Psychological Science* 2007;18(7):559–63.

Dalton MA, Adachi-Mejia AM, Longacre MR, Titus-Ernstoff LT, Gibson JJ, Martin SK, Sargent JD, Beach ML. Parental rules and monitoring of children's movie viewing associated with children's risk for smoking and drinking. *Pediatrics* 2006;118(5):1932–42.

Dalton MA, Ahrens MB, Sargent JD, Mott LA, Beach ML, Tickle JJ, Heatherton TF. Relation between parental restrictions on movies and adolescent use of tobacco and alcohol. *Effective Clinical Practice* 2002a;5(1): 1–10.

Dalton MA, Beach ML, Adachi-Mejia AM, Longacre MR, Matzkin AL, Sargent JD, Heatherton TF, Titus-Ernstoff L. Early exposure to movie smoking predicts established smoking by older teens and young adults. *Pediatrics* 2009;123(4):e551–e558.

Dalton MA, Bernhardt AM, Gibson JJ, Sargent JD, Beach ML, Adachi-Mejia AM, Titus-Ernstoff LT, Heatherton TF. Use of cigarettes and alcohol by preschoolers while role-playing as adults: "Honey, have some smokes." *Archives of Pediatrics & Adolescent Medicine* 2005;159(9):854–9.

Dalton MA, Sargent JD, Beach ML, Titus-Ernstoff L, Gibson JJ, Ahrens MB, Tickle JJ, Heatherton TF. Effect of viewing smoking in movies on adolescent smoking initiation: a cohort study. *Lancet* 2003;362(9380):281–5.

Dalton MA, Tickle JJ, Sargent JD, Beach ML, Ahrens MB, Heatherton TF. The incidence and context of tobacco use in popular movies from 1988 to 1997. *Preventive Medicine* 2002b;34(5):516–23.

Daniels D. *GIANTS, pigmies AND OTHER ADVERTISING PEOPLE.* Chicago (IL): Crane Communications, 1974. <http://legacy.library.ucsf.edu/tid/tym76b00>.

Danker WH. Roper attitude study of January 1959. 1959. Philip Morris Collection. Bates No. 1001755243/5244. <http://legacy.library.ucsf.edu/tid/ccv74e00>.

Davis KC, Farrelly MC, Messeri P, Duke J. The impact of national smoking prevention campaigns on tobacco-related beliefs, intentions to smoke and smoking initiation: results from a longitudinal survey of youth in the United States. *International Journal of Environmental Research and Public Health* 2009;6(2):722–40.

Davis KC, Nonnemaker JM, Farrelly MC. Association between national smoking prevention campaigns and perceived smoking prevalence among youth in the United States. *Journal of Adolescent Health* 2007; 41(5):430–6.

de Leeuw RN, Sargent JD, Stoolmiller M, Scholte RH, Engels RC, Tanski SE. Association of smoking onset with R-rated movie restrictions and adolescent sensation seeking. *Pediatrics* 2011;127(1):e96–e105.

de Vries H, Candel M, Engels R, Mercken L. Challenges to the peer influence paradigm: results for 12–13 year olds from six European countries from the European Smoking Prevention Framework Approach study. *Tobacco Control* 2006;15(2):83–9.

DeBon M, Klesges RC. Adolescents' perceptions about smoking prevention strategies: a comparison of the programmes of the American Lung Association and the Tobacco Institute. *Tobacco Control* 1996;5(1):19–25.

Deighton J. The interaction of advertising and evidence. *Journal of Consumer Research* 1984;11:763–70.

Delnevo C, Hrywna M, Lewis MJ, Yulis S. Voodoo cigarillos: bidis in disguise? *Tobacco Control* 2003;12(1):109–10.

Department of Health (UK). *Effect of Tobacco Advertising on Tobacco Sponsorship: A Discussion Document Reviewing the Evidence.* London: Department of Health, Economics & Operational Research Division, 1992. <http://legacy.library.ucsf.edu/tid/pum46e00>.

Dewhirst T. POP goes the power wall: taking aim at tobacco promotional strategies utilised at retail. *Tobacco Control* 2004;13(3):209–10.

Dewhirst T. New directions in tobacco promotion and brand communication. *Tobacco Control* 2009;18(3):161–2.

DiFranza JR, Brown LJ. The Tobacco Institute's "It's the Law" campaign: has it halted illegal sales of tobacco to children? *American Journal of Public Health* 1992;82(9):1271–3.

DiFranza JR, Eddy JJ, Brown LF, Ryan JL, Bogojavlensky A. Tobacco acquisition and cigarette brand selection among the youth. *Tobacco Control* 1994;3(4):334–8.

DiFranza JR, Godshall WT. Tobacco industry efforts hindering enforcement of the ban on tobacco sales to minors: actions speak louder than words. *Tobacco Control* 1996;5(2):127–31.

DiFranza JR, Librett JJ. State and federal revenues from tobacco consumed by minors. *American Journal of Public Health* 1999;89(7):1106–8.

DiFranza JR, McAfee T. The Tobacco Institute: helping youth say "yes" to tobacco. *Journal of Family Practice* 1992;34(6):694–6.

DiFranza JR, Richards JW, Paulman PM, Wolf-Gillespie N, Fletcher C, Jaffe RD, Murray D. RJR Nabisco's cartoon camel promotes camel cigarettes to children. *JAMA: the Journal of the American Medical Association* 1991; 266(22):3149–53.

DiFranza JR, Savageau JA, Aisquith BF. Youth access to tobacco: the effects of age, gender, vending machine locks and "it's the law" programs. *American Journal of Public Health* 1996;86(2):221–4.

DiFranza JR, Savageau JA, Fletcher K, O'Loughlin J, Pbert L, Ockene JK, McNeill AD, Hazelton J, Friedman K, Dussault G, et al. Symptoms of tobacco dependence after brief intermittent use: the Development and Assessment of Nicotine Dependence in Youth-2 study. *Archives of Pediatrics & Adolescent Medicine* 2007;161(7):704–10.

DiFranza JR, Savageau JA, Rigotti NA, Fletcher K, Ockene JK, McNeill AD, Coleman M, Wood C. Development of symptoms of tobacco dependence in youths: 30 month follow up data from the DANDY study. *Tobacco Control* 2002;11(3):228–35.

DiFranza JR, Wellman RJ, Sargent JD, Weitzman M, Hipple BJ, Winickoff JP, Tobacco Consortium, Center for Child Health Research of the American Academy of Pediatrics. Tobacco promotion and the initiation of tobacco use: assessing the evidence for causality. *Pediatrics* 2006;117(6):e1237–e1248.

Dipasquale CB. Store wars. *Advertising Age* 2002;73(2):4.

Direct E-cig. Home page, 2011; <http://directecig.com>; accessed: November 18, 2011.

Distefan JM, Gilpin EA, Sargent JD, Pierce JP. Do movie stars encourage adolescents to start smoking: evidence from California. *Preventive Medicine* 1999;28(1):1–11.

Distefan JM, Pierce JP, Gilpin EA. Do favorite movie stars influence adolescent smoking initiation? *American Journal of Public Health* 2004;94(7):1239–44.

Dixon HG. Portrayal of tobacco use in popular films: an investigation of audience impact [thesis]. Melbourne (Australia): University of Melbourne, 2003.

Djordjevic MV, Hoffmann D, Glynn T, Connolly GN. US commercial brands of moist snuff, 1994. I: assessment of nicotine, moisture, and PH. *Tobacco Control* 1995;4(1):62–6.

Donati J. Conference report #23. 1974. RJ Reynolds Collection. Bates No. 508454171/4174. <http://legacy.library.ucsf.edu/tid/vxn93d00>.

Donovan RJ, Jalleh G, Carter OBJ. Tobacco industry smoking prevention advertisements' impact on youth motivation for smoking in the future. *Social Marketing Quarterly* 2006;12(2):3–13.

Donovan RJ, Jancey J, Jones S. Tobacco point of sale advertising increases positive brand user imagery. *Tobacco Control* 2002;11(3):191–4.

Doxey J, Hammond D. Deadly in pink: the impact of female oriented packaging among young women. Society for Research on Nicotine & Tobacco Conference; 2010; Baltimore, p. 15.

Drope J, Chapman S. Tobacco industry efforts at discrediting scientific knowledge of environmental tobacco smoke: a review of internal industry documents. *Journal of Epidemiology and Community Health* 2001; 55(8):588–94.

Duke JC, Allen JA, Pederson LL, Mowery PD, Xiao H, Sargent JD. Reported exposure to pro-tobacco messages in the media: trends among youth in the United States, 2000–2004. *American Journal of Health Promotion* 2009;23(3):195–202.

Egelko B. Court backs Walgreen's objection to tobacco ban. San Francisco, 2010. <http://articles.sfgate.com/2010-06-09/bay-area/21902425_1_tobacco-products-drug-stores-appeals-court>; retrieved: June 20, 2010.

Electronic Cigarette Ban. Home page, 2011; <http://electroniccigaretteban.org>; accessed: November 18, 2011.

Electronic Cigarette Magazine. ESM – The Electronic Cigarette Magazine, 2010; <http://esmokersmag.com/>; accessed: March 2, 2010.

Electronic Cigarette Tavern. Electronic Cigarette and Stop Smoking Help Portal, 2010; <http://www.electroniccigarettetavern.com/>; accessed: March 2, 2010.

Electronic Cigarettes, Inc. Welcome to Electronic Cigarettes, Inc., 2010; <http://wwwelectroniccigarettesinc.com/>; accessed: September 16, 2010.

Engels RC, Knibbe RA, Drop MJ, de Haan YT. Homogeneity of cigarette smoking within peer groups: influence or selection? *Health Education & Behavior* 1997;24(6):801–11.

Ennett ST, Bauman KE. The contribution of influence and selection to adolescent peer group homogeneity: the case of adolescent cigarette smoking. *Journal of Personality and Social Psychology* 1994;67(4):653–63.

Evans N, Farkas A, Gilpin E, Berry C, Pierce JP. Influence of tobacco marketing and exposure to smokers on adolescent susceptibility to smoking. *Journal of the National Cancer Institute* 1995;87(20):1538–45.

Everett SA, Schnuth RL, Tribble JL. Tobacco and alcohol use in top-grossing American films. *Journal of Community Health* 1998;23(4):317–24.

Facebook. Pro-smoking, 2010a; <http://www.facebook.com/pages/Pro-Smoking/30275692045>; accessed: March 2, 2010.

Facebook. Smokers rights, 2010b; <http://www.facebook.com/group.php?gid=6295027435&ref=search&sid=100000196581876.2466401364.1>; accessed: March 1, 2010.

Facebook. Smoking, 2010c; <http://www.facebook.com/pages/Smoking/112423418770356?v=stream&ref=ts>; accessed: September 16, 2010.

Family Smoking Prevention and Tobacco Control Act, Public Law 111–31, 123 Stat. 1776 (2009).

Fant RV, Henningfield JE, Nelson RA, Pickworth WB. Pharmacokinetics and pharmacodynamics of moist snuff in humans. *Tobacco Control* 1999;8(4):387–92.

Farrelly MC. Monitoring the tobacco use epidemic V. The environment: factors that influence tobacco use. *Preventive Medicine* 2009;48(1 Suppl):S35–S43.

Farrelly MC, Davis KC, Haviland ML, Messeri P, Healton CG. Evidence of a dose-response relationship between "truth" antismoking ads and youth smoking prevalence. *American Journal of Public Health* 2005;95(3):425–31.

Farrelly MC, Davis KC, Duke J, Messeri P. Sustaining "truth": changes in youth tobacco attitudes and smoking intentions after 3 years of a national antismoking campaign. *Health Education Research* 2009;24(1):42–8.

Farrelly MC, Healton CG, Davis KC, Messeri P, Hersey JC, Haviland ML. Getting to the truth: evaluating national tobacco countermarketing campaigns. *American Journal of Public Health* 2002;92(6):901–7.

Federal Register. U.S. Department of Health and Human Services, Food and Drug Administration. Regulations restricting the sale and distribution of cigarettes and smokeless tobacco to protect children and adolescents; final rule (21 CFR Parts 801, 803, 804, 807, 820, and 897), 61 *Fed. Reg*. 44396–618 (1996).

Federal Register. U.S. Department of Health and Human Services, Food and Drug Administration. Regulations restricting the sale and distribution of cigarettes and smokeless tobacco to protect children and adolescents; final rule (21 CFR Part 1140), 75 *Fed. Reg*. 13225–32 (2010).

Federal Trade Commission. *Federal Trade Commission Cigarette Report for 2007 and 2008*. Washington: U.S. Federal Trade Commission, 2011a; <http://www.ftc.gov/os/2011/07/110729cigarettereport.pdf>; accessed: September 20, 2011.

Federal Trade Commission. *Federal Trade Commission Smokeless Tobacco Report for 2007 and 2008*. Washington: U.S. Federal Trade Commission, 2011b; <http://www.ftc.gov/os/2011/07/110729smokelesstobaccoreport.pdf>; accessed: September 20, 2011.

Feighery E, Borzekowski DL, Schooler C, Flora J. Seeing, wanting, owning: the relationship between receptivity to tobacco marketing and smoking susceptibility in young people. *Tobacco Control* 1998;7(2):123–8.

Feighery E, Henriksen L, Wang Y, Schleicher NC, Fortmann SP. An evaluation of four measures of adolescents' exposure to cigarette marketing in stores. *Nicotine & Tobacco Research* 2006;8(6):751–9.

Feighery EC, Ribisl KM, Achabal DD, Tyebjee T. Retail trade incentives; how tobacco industry practices compare with those of other industries. *American Journal of Public Health* 1999;89(10):1564–6.

Feighery EC, Ribisl KM, Schleicher NC, Clark PI. Retailer participation in cigarette company incentive programs is related to increased levels of cigarette advertising and cheaper cigarette prices in stores. *Preventive Medicine* 2004;38(6):876–84.

Feighery EC, Ribisl KM, Schleicher N, Lee RE, Halvorson S. Cigarette advertising and promotional strategies in retail outlets: results of a statewide survey in California. *Tobacco Control* 2001;10(2):184–8.

Feighery EC, Schleicher NC, Boley Cruz T, Unger JB. An examination of trends in amount and type of cigarette advertising and sales promotions in California stores, 2002–2005. *Tobacco Control* 2008;17(2):93–8.

Finucane M. State health officials target sales of flavored cigarettes. *Providence Journal* May 21, 2004;Sect C:04.

Fischer PM, Schwartz MP, Richards JW Jr, Goldstein AO, Rojas TH. Brand logo recognition by children aged 3 to 6 years: Mickey Mouse and Old Joe the Camel. *JAMA: the Journal of the American Medical Association* 1991;266(22):3145–8.

Fix BV, Zambon M, Higbee C, Cummings KM, Alford T, Hyland A. Internet cigarette purchasing among 9th grade students in western New York: 2000–2001 vs. 2004–2005. *Preventive Medicine* 2006;43(3):191–5.

Flay BR. Youth tobacco use: risks, patterns, and control. In: Orleans CT, Slade J, editors. *Nicotine Addiction: Principles and Management*. New York: Oxford University Press, 1993:365–84.

Flay BR, Snyder FJ, Petraitis J. The theory of triadic influence. In: DiClemente RJ, Crosby RA, Kegler MC, editors. *Emerging Theories in Health Promotion Practice and Research*. 2nd ed. San Francisco: Jossey-Bass, 2009:451–510.

Food and Drugs, 21 *CFR* §101.22 (2010).

Foote E. Advertising and tobacco. *JAMA: the Journal of the American Medical Association* 1981;245(16):1667–8.

Forster JL, Wolfson M. Youth access to tobacco: policies and politics. *Annual Review of Public Health* 1998;19:203–35.

Fraser T. Phasing out of point-of-sale tobacco advertising in New Zealand. *Tobacco Control* 1998;7(1):82–4.

Freeman B, Chapman S, Rimmer M. The case for the plain packaging of tobacco products. *Addiction* 2008; 103(4):580–90.

Freeman B, Chapman S. Open source marketing: Camel cigarette brand marketing in the "Web 2.0" world. *Tobacco Control* 2009;18(3):212–7.

Freeman B, Chapman S, Rimmer M. The case for the plain packaging of tobacco products, 2007; <http://www.escholarship.org/uc/item/4rz0m70k?display=all>; accessed: February 3, 2011.

Gamucci. Home page, 2011; <http://gamucci.net/1/benefits.html>; accessed: November 18, 2011.

Garne D, Watson M, Chapman S, Byrne F. Environmental tobacco smoke research published in the journal Indoor and Built Environment and associations with the tobacco industry. *Lancet* 2005;365(9461):804–9.

Garten S, Falkner RV. Continual smoking of mentholated cigarettes may mask the early warning symptoms of respiratory disease. *Preventive Medicine* 2003: 37(4):291–6.

Germain D, Wakefield MA, Durkin SJ. Adolescents' perceptions of cigarette brand image: does plain packaging make a difference? *Journal of Adolescent Health* 2010;46(4):385–92.

Gibson B, Maurer J. Cigarette smoking in the movies: the influence of product placement in attitudes toward smoking and smokers. *Journal of Applied Social Psychology* 2000;30(7):1457–73.

Gilpin EA, Emery S, White MM, Pierce JP. Does tobacco industry marketing of 'light' cigarettes give smokers a rationale for postponing quitting? *Nicotine & Tobacco Research* 2002;4(Suppl 2):S147–S155.

Gilpin EA, Pierce JP, Rosbrook BS. Are adolescents receptive to current sales promotion practices of the tobacco industry? *Preventive Medicine* 1997;26(1):14–21.

Gilpin EA, White MM, Messer K, Pierce JP. Receptivity to tobacco advertising and promotions among young adolescents as a predictor of established smoking in young adulthood. *American Journal of Public Health* 2007;97(8):1489–95.

Gilpin EA, White VM, Pierce JP. How effective are tobacco industry bar and club marketing efforts in reaching young adults? *Tobacco Control* 2005;14(3):186–92.

Glantz SA. Smoking in movies: a major problem and a real solution. *Lancet* 2003;362(9380):258–9.

Glantz SA, Kacirk KW, McCulloch C. Back to the future: smoking in movies in 2002 compared with 1950 levels. *American Journal of Public Health* 2004;94(2):261–3.

Glantz SA, Slade J, Bero L, Hanauer P, Barnes D. *The Cigarette Papers*. Berkeley (CA): University of California Press, 1996.

Goldberg ME. American media and the smoking-related behaviors of Asian adolescents. *Journal of Advertising Research* 2003;43(1):2–11.

Goldberg ME. Assessing the relationship between tobacco advertising and promotion and adolescent smoking behavior: convergent evidence. In: Haugtvedt CP, Herr PM, Kardes FR, editors. *Handbook of Consumer Psychology*. New York: Taylor & Francis Group, 2008: 933–57.

Goldberg ME, Baumgartner H. Cross-country attraction as a motivation for product consumption. *Journal of Business Research* 2002;55(11):901–6.

Goldberg ME, Kindra G, Lefebvre J, Liefeld J, Madill-Marshall J, Martohardjono N, Vredenburg H. *When Packages Can't Speak: Possible Impacts of Plain and Generic Packaging of Tobacco Products*. 1995. RJ Reynolds Collection. Bates No. 521716345/6771. <http://legacy.library.ucsf.edu/tid/rce50d00>.

Goldberg ME, Liefeld J, Madill J, Vredenburg H. The effect of plain packaging on response to health warnings [letter]. *American Journal of Public Health* 1999;89(9):1434–5.

Goldstein AO, Fischer PM, Richards JW Jr, Creten D. Relationship between high school student smoking and recognition of cigarette advertisements. *Journal of Pediatrics* 1987;110(3):488–91.

Golmier I, Chebat JC, Gélinas-Chebat C. Can cigarette warnings counterbalance effects of smoking scenes in movies? *Psychological Reports* 2007;100(1):3–18.

Google. Discount cigarettes, 2011; <http://google.com>; accessed: November 18, 2011.

Gordon A, Finlay K, Watts T. The psychological effects of colour in consumer product packaging. *Canadian Journal of Marketing Research* 1994;13:3–11.

Greensmoke. Product Videos, 2011; <http://www.greensmoke.com/catalog/product-videos/info_17.html>; accessed: November 18, 2011.

Grossman M, Chaloupka FJ. Cigarette taxes: the straw to break the camel's back. *Public Health Reports* 1997;112(4):290–7.

Gruber J, Zinman J. Youth smoking in the United States: evidence and implications. In: Gruber J, editor. *Risky Behavior Among Youth: An Economic Analysis*. Chicago: University of Chicago Press, 2001:69–120.

Gunja M, Wayne GF, Landman A, Connolly G, McGuire A.

The case for fire safe cigarettes made through industry documents. *Tobacco Control* 2002;11(4):346–53.

Hafez N, Ling PM. How Philip Morris built Marlboro into a global brand for young adults: implications for international tobacco control. *Tobacco Control* 2005; 14(4):262–71.

Hafez N, Ling PM. Finding the Kool Mixx: how Brown & Williamson used music marketing to sell cigarettes. *Tobacco Control* 2006;15(5):359–66.

Halpern-Felsher BL, Biehl M, Kropp R, Rubenstein M. Perceived risks and benefits of smoking: differences among adolescents with different smoking experiences and intentions. *Preventive Medicine* 2004;39(3):559–67.

Hammond D. Canada: a new angle on packs. *Tobacco Control* 2006;15(3):150.

Hammond D. Potentially misleading information and plain packaging: new Canadian findings. World Conference on Tobacco Health; March 9, 2009a; Mumbai, India.

Hammond D. *Tobacco Labelling & Packaging Toolkit: A Guide to FCTC Article 11*. Waterloo (Canada): University of Waterloo, Department of Health Studies, 2009b. <http://www.tobaccolabels.ca/tobaccolab/iuatldtoolkit>.

Hammond D, Dockrell M, Arnott D, Lee A, McNeill A. Cigarette pack design and perceptions of risk among UK adult and youth. *European Journal of Public Health* 2009;19(6):631–7.

Hammond D, Parkinson C. The impact of cigarette package design on perceptions of risk. *Journal of Public Health (Oxford, England)* 2009;31(3):345–53.

Hanewinkel R. Cigarette smoking and perception of a movie character in a film trailer. *Archives of Pediatrics & Adolescent Medicine* 2009;163(1):15–8.

Hanewinkel R, Isensee B, Sargent JD, Morgenstern M. Cigarette advertising and adolescent smoking. *American Journal of Preventive Medicine* 2010a;38(4):359–66.

Hanewinkel R, Isensee B, Sargent JD, Morgenstern M. Effect of an antismoking advertisement on cinema patrons' perception of smoking and intention to smoke: a quasi-experimental study. *Addiction* 2010b;105(7):1269–77.

Hanewinkel R, Morgenstern M, Tanski SE, Sargent JD. Longitudinal study of parental movie restriction on teen smoking and drinking in Germany. *Addiction* 2008;103(10):1722–30.

Hanewinkel R, Sargent JD. Exposure to smoking in popular contemporary movies and youth smoking in Germany. *American Journal of Preventive Medicine* 2007;32(6):466–73.

Hanewinkel R, Sargent JD. Exposure to smoking in internationally distributed American movies and youth smoking in Germany: a cross-cultural cohort study. *Pediatrics* 2008;121(1):e108–e117.

Hannah Report. "Under 18 No Tobacco" Program Commences. 1996. Philip Morris Collection. Bates No. 2072174778/4779. <http://legacy.library.ucsf.edu/tid/zde08d00>.

Harakeh Z, Engels RCME, Vohs K, van Baaren RB, Sargent J. Exposure to movie smoking, antismoking ads and smoking intensity: an experimental study with a factorial design. *Tobacco Control* 2010;19(3):185–90.

Harji T, Irwin D. TSRT- 3rd September 1992: measurable smoking quality indicators. British American Tobacco Collection. Bates No. 303643913/3916. <http://legacy.library.ucsf.edu/tid/xje92a99>.

Harley-Davidson. *Lorillard Tobacco Company, plaintiff, vs. Harley-Davidson, Inc.* 1993. Lorillard Collection. Bates No. 93791722/1760. <http://legacy.library.ucsf.edu/tid/aov50e00>.

Harvard Family Research Project. *A Profile of the Evaluation of Boys & Girls Clubs of America—Stay SMART Program and SMART Leaders Program,* 2010; <http://www.hfrp.org/out-of-school-time/ost-database-bibliography/database/boys-girls-clubs-of-america-stay-smart-program-and-smart-leaders-program>; accessed: October 19, 2010.

Hazan AR, Lipton HL, Glantz SA. Popular films do not reflect current tobacco use. *American Journal of Public Health* 1994;84(6):998–1000.

Healton CG, Watson-Stryker ES, Allen JA, Vallone DM, Messeri PA, Graham PR, Stewart AM, Dobbins MD, Glantz SA. Televised movie trailers: undermining restrictions on advertising tobacco to youth. *Archives of Pediatrics & Adolescent Medicine* 2006;160(9): 885–8.

Hendlin Y, Anderson SJ, Glantz SA. Acceptable rebellion: marketing hipster aesthetics to sell Camel cigarettes in the U.S. *Tobacco Control* 2010;19(3):213–22.

Henningfield JE, Benowitz N, Connolly GN, Davis RM, Gray N, Myers ML, Zeller M. Reducing tobacco addiction through tobacco product regulation. *Tobacco Control* 2004;13(2):132–5.

Henningfield JE, Zaatari GS. Electronic nicotine delivery systems: emerging science foundation for policy. *Tobacco Control;* 2010,19(2):89–90.

Henriksen L, Dauphinee AL, Wang Y, Fortmann SP. Industry sponsored anti-smoking ads and adolescent reactance: test of a boomerang effect. *Tobacco Control* 2006;15(1):13–8.

Henriksen L, Feighery EC, Schleicher NC, Cowling DW, Kline RS, Fortmann SP. Is adolescent smoking related to the density and proximity of tobacco outlets and retail cigarette advertising near schools? *Preventive Medicine* 2008;47(2):210–4.

Henriksen L, Feighery EC, Schleicher NC, Haladjian HH, Fortmann SP. Reaching youth at the point of sale: cigarette marketing is more prevalent in stores where adolescents shop frequently. *Tobacco Control* 2004a;13(3):315–8.

Henriksen L, Feighery EC, Wang Y, Fortmann SP. Association of retail tobacco marketing with adolescent smoking. *American Journal of Public Health* 2004b;94(12):2081–3.

Henriksen L, Flora JA, Feighery EC, Fortmann SP. Effects on youth of exposure to retail tobacco advertising. *Journal of Applied Social Psychology* 2002;32(9):1771–91.

Henriksen L, Fortmann SP. Young adults' opinions of Philip Morris and its television advertising. *Tobacco Control* 2002;11(3):236–40.

Henriksen L, Schleicher NC, Feighery EC, Fortmann SP. A longitudinal study of exposure to retail cigarette advertising and smoking initiation. *Pediatrics* 2010;126(2):232–8.

Henriksen L, Schleicher NC, Dauphinee AL, Fortmann SP. Targeted advertising, promotion, and price for menthol cigarettes in California high school neighborhoods. *Nicotine & Tobacco Research* 2011. 2012;14(1):116–21.

Hersey JC, Niederdeppe J, Evans WD, Nonnemaker J, Blahut S, Farrelly MC, Holden D, Messeri P, Haviland ML. The effects of state counterindustry media campaigns on beliefs, attitudes, and smoking status among teens and young adults. *Preventive Medicine* 2003;37(6 Pt 1):544–52.

Hersey JC, Niederdeppe J, Evans WD, Nonnemaker J, Blahut S, Holden D, Messeri P, Haviland ML. The theory of "truth": how counterindustry campaigns affect smoking behavior among teens. *Health Psychology* 2005a;24(1):22–31.

Hersey JC, Niederdeppe J, Ng SW, Mowery P, Farrelly M, Messeri P. How state counter-industry campaigns help prime perceptions of tobacco industry practices to promote reductions in youth smoking. *Tobacco Control* 2005b;14(6):377–83.

Hersey JC, Ng SW, Nonnemaker JM, Mowery P, Thomas KY, Vilsaint MC, Allen JA, Haviland ML. Are menthol cigarettes a starter product for youth? *Nicotine & Tobacco Research* 2006;8(3):403–13.

Hersey JC, Nonnemaker JM, Homsi G. Menthol cigarettes contribute to the appeal and addiction potential of smoking for youth. *Nicotine & Tobacco Research* 2010;12(Suppl 2):S136–S146.

Hirschhorn N. Shameful science: four decades of the German tobacco industry's hidden research on smoking and health. *Tobacco Control* 2000;9(2):242–8.

Hirschhorn N, Bialous SA, Shatenstein S. Philip Morris's new scientific initiative: an analysis. *Tobacco Control* 2001;10(3):247–52.

Hoek J, Maubach N, Gendall P. Tobacco descriptors: an analysis of adolescents' beliefs and behavior. Paper presented at the Australian and New Zealand Marketing Academy Conference; December 3–5, 2006; Brisbane (Australia).

Hoelter TK. Harley-Davidson. 1993. Lorillard Collection. Bates No. 91058719/8720. <http://legacy.library.ucsf.edu/tid/elw20e00>.

Hong M-K, Bero LA. How the tobacco industry responded to an influential study of the health effects of secondhand smoke. *BMJ (British Medical Journal)* 2002;325(7377):1413–6.

Hong M-K, Bero LA. Tobacco industry sponsorship of a book and conflict of interest. *Addiction* 2006;101(8):1202–11.

Hong T, Cody MJ. Presence of pro-tobacco messages on the Web. *Journal of Health Communication* 2002;7(4):273–307.

Hudmon KS, Fenlon CM, Corell RL, Prokhorov AV, Schroeder SA. Tobacco sales in pharmacies: time to quit. *Tobacco Control* 2006;15(1): 35–8.

Hudson RC. Inner city POP program. 1979. Brown & Williamson Collection. Bates No. 666015851/5864. <http://legacy.library.ucsf.edu/tid/icb91d00>.

Hulit M. *Marketing Issues Corporate Affairs Conference, May 27, 1994 - Manila*. 1994. Philip Morris Collection. Bates No. 2504015017/5042. <http://legacy.library.ucsf.edu/tid/jga42e00>.

Hunt K, Henderson M, Wight D, Sargent JD. Exposure to smoking in films and own smoking among Scottish adolescents: a cross-sectional study. *Thorax* 2011;66(10):866–74.

Hunt K, Sweeting H, Sargent J, Lewars H, Cin SD, Worth K. An examination of the association between seeing smoking in films and tobacco use in young adults in the west of Scotland: cross-sectional study. *Health Education Research* 2009;24(1):22–31.

Interactive, Inc. *Evaluation of the Life Skills Training Program: Year One Report*. 2000. Philip Morris Collection. Bates No. 2085229685/9859. <http://legacy.library.ucsf.edu/tid/bgx12c00>.

Idaho Department of Health and Welfare. Please Filter out the Noise, September 2011; <http://www.projectfilter.org/images/stories/newsletters/tobaccoyouthsocial_media_sept2011final.pdf>.

Interactive, Inc. *Evaluation of the Life Skills Training Program: Year Two Report*. 2001. Philip Morris Collection. Bates No. 2085062398/2471. <http://legacy.library.ucsf.edu/tid/hso02c00>.

Jackson C, Brown JD, L'Engle KL. R-rated movies, bedroom televisions, and initiation of smoking by white and black adolescents. *Archives of Pediatrics & Adolescent Medicine* 2007;161(3):260–8.

Jamieson PE, More E, Lee SS, Busse P, Romer D. It matters what young people watch: health risk behaviors portrayed in top-grossing movies since 1950. In: Jamieson PE, Romer D, editors. *The Changing Portrayal of Adolescents in the Media Since 1950*. New York: Oxford University Press, 2008:105–31.

Jamieson PE, Romer D. Trends in US movie tobacco portrayal since 1950: a historical analysis. *Tobacco Control* 2010;19(3):179–84.

Jensen JA, Hickman NJ 3rd, Landrine H, Klonoff EA. Availability of tobacco to youth via the Internet [letter]. *JAMA: the Journal of the American Medical Association* 2004;291(15):1837.

Jenssen BP, Klein JD, Salazar LF, Daluga NA, DiClemente RJ. Exposure to tobacco on the Internet: content analysis of adolescents' internet use. *Pediatrics* 2009;124(2):e180–e186.

John R, Cheney M, Azad MR. Point-of-sale marketing of tobacco products: taking advantage of the socially disadvantaged? *Journal of Health Care for the Poor and Underserved* 2009;20(2):489–506.

Johnston M. Handling an excise tax increase. 1987. Philip Morris Collection. Bates No. 2022216179/6180. <http://legacy.library.ucsf.edu/tid/uvx71f00>.

Johnston LD, O'Malley PM, Bachman JG. *Monitoring the Future National Survey Results on Drug Use, 1975–2001: Volume I, Secondary School Students*. Bethesda (MD): U.S. Department of Health and Human Services, National Institutes of Health, National Institute on Drug Abuse, 2002. NIH Publication No. 02-5106.

J. Walter Thompson. Third Family Creative Direction Recommendation. 1984. Canadian Tobacco Trials Collection. Bates No. TCA13320/3333. <http://legacy.library.ucsf.edu/tid/cal70g00>.

Kastenbaum R, Derbin V, Sabatini P, Arrt S. The Ages of Me toward personal and interpersonal definitions of functional aging. *International Journal of Aging and Human Development* 1972;3(2):197–211.

Katz SK, Lavack AM. Tobacco related bar promotions: insights from tobacco industry documents. *Tobacco Control* 2002;11(Suppl 1):i92–i101.

Keeler TE, Hu TW, Barnett PG, Manning WG, Sung HY. Do cigarette producers price-discriminate by state: an empirical analysis of local cigarette pricing and taxation. *Journal of Health Economics* 1996;15(4):499–512.

Keelor TE, Hu T-W, Ong M, Sung H-Y. The US National Tobacco Settlement: the effects of advertising and price changes on cigarette consumption. *Applied Economics* 2004;36(15):1623–9.

Kennedy GE, Bero L. Print media coverage of research on passive smoking. *Tobacco Control* 1999;8(3):254–60.

Kindra GS, Laroche M, Muller TE. *Consumer Behavior: the Canadian Perspective*. 2nd ed. Scarborough (Canada): Nelson Canada, 1994.

King C III, Siegel M. The Master Settlement Agreement with the tobacco industry and cigarette advertising in magazines. *New England Journal of Medicine* 2001;345(7):504–11.

King C III, Siegel M, Celebucki C, Connolly GN. Adolescent exposure to cigarette advertising in magazines: an evaluation of brand-specific advertising in relation to youth readership. *JAMA: the Journal of the American Medical Association* 1998;279(7):516–20.

Klausner K. Menthol cigarettes and smoking initiation: a tobacco industry perspective. *Tobacco Control* 2011;20(Supp 2):ii12–ii19.

Klein SM, Giovino GA, Barker DC, Tworek C, Cummings KM, O'Connor RJ. Use of flavored cigarettes among older adolescent and adult smokers: United States, 2004–2005. *Nicotine & Tobacco Research* 2008; 10(7):1209–14.

Kline RL. Tobacco advertising after the settlement: where we are and what remains to be done. Kansas Journal of Law & Public Policy 2000;9(4):621–39.

Kluger R. *Ashes to Ashes: America's Hundred-Year Cigarette War, the Public Health, and the Unabashed Triumph of Philip Morris*. New York: Alfred A. Knopf, 1996.

Kobus K. Peers and adolescent smoking. *Addiction* 2003;98(Suppl 1):S37–S55.

Koten J. Tobacco marketers' success formula: make cigarettes in smoker's own image. *Wall Street Journal*, February 29, 1980:22.

Kozlowski LT, O'Connor RJ. Cigarette filter ventilation is a defective design because of misleading taste, bigger puffs, and blocked vents. *Tobacco Control* 2002;11(Suppl 1):i40–i50.

Kreslake JM, Wayne GF, Alpert HR, Koh HK, Connolly GN. Tobacco industry control of menthol in cigarettes and targeting of adolescents and young adults. *American Journal of Public Health* 2008a;98(9):1685–92.

Kreslake JM, Wayne GF, Connolly GN. The menthol smoker: tobacco industry research on consumer sensory perception of menthol cigarettes and its role in smoking behavior [review]. *Nicotine & Tobacco Research* 2008b;10(4):705–15.

Kropp RY, Halpern-Felsher BL. Adolescents' beliefs about the risks involved in smoking "light" cigarettes. *Pediatrics* 2004;114(4):e445–e451.

Kunkel D. Inching forward on tobacco advertising restrictions to prevent youth smoking. *Archives of Pediatrics & Adolescent Medicine* 2007;161(5):515–6.

Lancaster AR, Lancaster KM. The economics of tobacco advertising: spending, demand, and the effects of bans. *International Journal of Advertising* 2003;22(1):41–65.

Landman A, Cortese DK, Glantz S. Tobacco industry sociological programs to influence public beliefs about smoking. *Social Science & Medicine* 2008;66(4): 970–81.

Landman A, Ling PM, Glantz SA. Tobacco industry youth smoking prevention programs: protecting the industry and hurting tobacco control. *American Journal of Public Health* 2002;92(6):917–30.

Laugesen M, Scragg R, Wellman RJ, DiFranza JR. R-rated film viewing and adolescent smoking. *Preventive Medicine* 2007;45(6):454–9.

Lavack AM, Toth G. Tobacco point-of-purchase promotion: examining tobacco industry documents. *Tobacco Control* 2006;15(5):377–84.

Laws MB, Whitman J, Bowser DM, Krech L. Tobacco availability and point of sale marketing in demographically contrasting districts of Massachusetts. *Tobacco Control* 2002;11(Suppl 2):ii71–ii73.

Leatherdale ST, Strath JM. Tobacco retailer density surrounding schools and cigarette access behaviors among underage smoking students. *Annals of Behavioral Medicine* 2007;33(1):105–11.

LeBow BS. *Deposition and Exhibits of Bennett LeBow Taken in State of Minnesota v Philip Morris Inc, et al.* 1997a. Liggett & Myers Collection. Bates No. LG0312696/3542. <http://legacy.library.ucsf.edu/tid/ivo57a00>.

LeBow BS. *State of Nevada Settlement Agreement*. 1997b. Liggett & Myers Collection. Bates No. VDOJ31357/1375. <http://legacy.library.ucsf.edu/tid/tpv67a00>.

Lee RE, Feighery EC, Schleicher NC, Halvorson S. The relation between community bans of self-service tobacco displays and store environment and between tobacco accessibility and merchant incentives. *American Journal of Public Health* 2001;91(12):2019–21.

Lee YO, Glantz SA. Putting the pieces together. *Tobacco Control* 2011;20(Suppl 2):ii1–ii7.

LeGresley EM, Muggli ME, Hurt RD. Movie moguls: British American Tobacco's covert strategy to promote cigarettes in Eastern Europe. *European Journal of Public Health* 2006;16(5):505–8.

Leventhal H, Keeshan P. Promoting healthy alternatives to substance abuse. In: Millstein SG, Petersen AC, Nightingale EO, editors. *Promoting the Health of Adolescents: New Directions for the Twenty-First Century*. New York: Oxford University Press, 1993:260–84.

Lewis MJ, Wackowski O. Dealing with an innovative industry: a look at flavored cigarettes promoted by mainstream brands. *American Journal of Public Health* 2006;96(2):244–51.

Lewis MJ, Yulis SG, Delnevo C, Hrywna M. Tobacco industry direct marketing after the Master Settlement Agreement. *Health Promotion Practice* 2004;5 (3 Suppl):75S–83S.

Lewit EM, Coate D. The potential for using excise taxes to reduce smoking. *Journal of Health Economics* 1982;1(2):121–45.

Lewit EM, Coate D, Grossman M. The effects of government regulation on teenage smoking. *Journal of Law and Economics* 1981;24(3):545–69.

Life Magazine. September 1951.

Liljenwall R, Maskulka J, editors. *Marketing's Powerful Weapon: Point-of-Purchase Advertising*. Washington: Point-of-Purchase Advertising International, 2001.

Ling PM, Glantz SA. Why and how the tobacco industry sells cigarettes to young adults: evidence from industry documents. *American Journal of Public Health* 2002;92(6):908–16.

Ling PM, Neilands TB, Glantz SA. The effect of support for action against the tobacco industry on smoking among young adults. *American Journal of Public Health* 2007;97(8):1449–56.

Ling PM, Neilands TB, Glantz SA. Young adult smoking behavior: a national survey. *American Journal of Preventive Medicine* 2009;36(5):389–94.

Lochbuehler K, Engels RC, Scholte RH. Influence of smoking cues in movies on craving among smokers. *Addiction* 2009;104(12):2102–9.

Lochbuehler K, Peters M, Scholte RH, Engels RC. Effects of smoking cues in movies on immediate smoking behavior. *Nicotine & Tobacco Research* 2010;12(9)913–8.

Lochbuehler K, Voogd H, Scholte RH, Engels RC. Attentional bias in smokers: exposure to dynamic smoking cues in contemporary movies. *Journal of Psychopharmacology* 2011;25(4)514–9.

Loomis BR, Farrelly MC, Mann NH. The association of retail promotions for cigarettes with the Master Settlement Agreement, tobacco control programmes and cigarette excise taxes. *Tobacco Control* 2006;15(6):458–63.

Lopipero P, Bero LA. Tobacco interests or the public interest: 20 years of industry strategies to undermine airline smoking restrictions. *Tobacco Control* 2006;15(4): 323–32.

Lorillard. Newport image study. 1988. Lorillard Collection. Bates No. 92272605/2665. <http://legacy.library.ucsf.edu/tid/ewj60e00>.

Lorillard. Newport 1992 strategic marketing plan. 1991. Lorillard Collection. Bates No. 92011118/1156. <http://legacy.library.ucsf.edu/tid/guz20e00>.

Lorillard. Newport. 1993a. Lorillard Collection. Bates No. 92005019/5028. <http://legacy.library.ucsf.edu/tid/gjj70e00>.

Lorillard. Newport 1994 brand plan. 1993b. DATTA Collection. Bates No. USX0102227/2335. <http://legacy.library.ucsf.edu/tid/koq36b00>.

Lorillard. Newport 2000 strategic plan overview. 1999. Lorillard Collection. Bates No. 98196920/6942. <http://legacy.library.ucsf.edu/tid/hcv07a00>.

Lorillard. Real Parents; Real Answers, 2010a; <http://www.realparentsrealanswers.com/>; accessed: March 1, 2010.

Lorillard. Youth Smoking Prevention Program, 2010b; <http://www.lorillard.com/index.php?id=5>; accessed: March 1, 2010.

Lovato C, Linn G, Stead LF, Best A. Impact of tobacco advertising and promotion on increasing adolescent smoking behaviours. *Cochrane Database of Systematic Reviews* 2003, Issue 3. Art. No.: CD003439. DOI: 10.1002/14651858.CD003439.

Lovato C, Watts A, Stead LF. Impact of tobacco advertising and promotion on increasing adolescent smoking behaviours. *Cochrane Database of Systematic Reviews* 2011;(10):CD003439. DOI: 10.1002/14651858.CD003439.pub2.

Lovato CY, Hsu HC, Sabiston CM, Hadd V, Nykiforuk CI. Tobacco point-of-purchase marketing in school neighbourhoods and school smoking prevalence: a descriptive study. *Canadian Journal of Public Health* 2007;98(4):265–70.

Lum KL, Polansky JR, Jackler RK, Glantz SA. Signed, sealed and delivered: "big tobacco" in Hollywood, 1927–1951. *Tobacco Control* 2008;17(5):313–23.

Lynch BS, Bonnie RJ, editors. *Growing Up Tobacco Free: Preventing Nicotine Addiction in Children and Youths.* Washington: National Academies Press, 1994.

Lyons A, McNeill A, Chen Y, Britton J. Tobacco and tobacco branding in films most popular in the UK from 1989 to 2008. *Thorax* 2010;65(5):417–22.

Malmgren KL. Expanded local program. 1992. Philip Morris Collection. Bates No. 2023959567/9579. <http://legacy.library.ucsf.edu/tid/kdm24e00>.

Malone RE, Bero LA. Cigars, youth, and the Internet link. *American Journal of Public Health* 2000;90(5):790–2.

Mandel LL, Bialous SA, Glantz SA. Avoiding "truth": tobacco industry promotion of life skills training. *Journal of Adolescent Health* 2006;39(6):868–79.

Manning R. [Memo from Richard Manning to E Jurczenia regarding nicotine content in tobacco product]. 1981. US Smokeless Tobacco Collection. Bates No. 3730335/0336. <http://legacy.library.ucsf.edu/tid/xlc46b00>.

Marketing Innovations Inc. Project report. Youth cigarette – new concepts. 1972. Brown & Williamson Collection. Bates No. 170042014. <http://legacy.library.ucsf.edu/tid/oyq83f00>.

Mart S, Mergendoller J, Simon M. Alcohol promotion on Facebook. *The Journal of Global Drug Policy and Practice* 2009;3(3); <http://www.globaldrugpolicy.org/3/3/1.php; accessed: March 14, 2010.

McCarthy WJ, Mistry R, Lu Y, Patel M, Zheng H, Dietsch B. Density of tobacco retailers near schools: effects on tobacco use among students. *American Journal of Public Health* 2009;99(11):2006–13.

McCool JP, Cameron LD, Petrie KJ. The influence of smoking imagery on the smoking intentions of young people: testing a media interpretation model. *Journal of Adolescent Health* 2005;36(6):475–85.

McIntosh S, Ossip-Klein DJ, Hazel-Fernandez L, Spada J, McDonald PW, Klein JD. Recruitment of physician offices for an office-based adolescent smoking cessation study. *Nicotine & Tobacco Research* 2005;7(3):405–12.

Mejia AB, Ling PM. Tobacco industry consumer research on smokeless tobacco users and product development. *American Journal of Public Health* 2010;100(1):78–87.

Mejia AB, Ling PM, Glantz SA. Quantifying the effects of promoting smokeless tobacco as a harm reduction strategy in the USA. *Tobacco Control* 2010;19(4): 297–305.

Mekemson C , Glantz SA. How the tobacco industry built its relationship with Hollywood. *Tobacco Control* 2002;11(Suppl 1):i81–i91.

Mekemson C, Glik D, Titus K, Myerson A, Shaivitz A, Ang A, Mitchell S. Tobacco use in popular movies during the past decade. *Tobacco Control* 2004;13(4):400–2.

Mercken L, Candel M, Willems P, de Vries H. Disentangling social selection and social influence effects on adolescent smoking: the importance of reciprocity in friendships. *Addiction* 2007;102(9):1483–92.

Merlo E. RE: Icon ad. 1996. Philip Morris Collection. Bates No. 2046945003B. <http://legacy.library.ucsf.edu/tid/gvq65e00>.

Merlo E. *Trial Testimony of Ellen Merlo, June 23, 2000 [a.m.]. Engle v. R.J Reynolds Co.*, 2000; <http://tobaccodocuments.org/datta/MERLOE062300AM.html>; accessed: December 15, 2009.

Merlo E. *Trial Testimony of Ellen Merlo, May 2, 2001, Boeken v. Philip Morris Inc.*, 2001; <http://tobaccodocuments.org/datta/MERLOE050201.html>; accessed: December 15, 2009.

Miller L. Principles of measurement of visual standout in pack design. 1986. British American Tobacco Collection. Bates No. 105364841/4951. <http://legacy.library.ucsf.edu/tid/zlh37a99>.

Millett C, Glantz SA. Assigning an '18' rating to movies with tobacco imagery is essential to reduce youth smoking. *Thorax* 2010;65(5):377–8.

Millett C, Polansky J, Glantz S. Government inaction on ratings and government subsidies to the US film industry help promote youth smoking. PLoS Medicine 2011;8(8):e1001077.

Monahan E. Winston historical presentation. 1977. RJ Reynolds Collection. Bates No. 502634929/5122. <http://legacy.library.ucsf.edu/tid/xgk66a00>.

Monell Chemical Senses Center. *In vitro* studies of nicotine sensation: responses of cultured olfactory neurons to nicotine and effects of trigeminal stimulation on olfactory neuronal sensitivity. 2003. Philip Morris Collection. Bates No. 3001345132/5136. <http://legacy.library.ucsf.edu/tid/npl96g00>.

Montepare JM, Lachman ME. "You're only as old as you feel": self-perceptions of age, fears of aging, and life satisfaction from adolescence to old age. *Psychology and Aging* 1989;4(1):73–8.

Montgomery KC, Chester J. Interactive food and beverage marketing: targeting adolescents in the digital age. *Journal of Adolescent Health* 2009;45(3 Suppl): S18–S29.

Moore ES. *It's Child's Play: Advergaming and the Online Marketing of Food to Children*. Menlo Park (CA): Henry J. Kaiser Family Foundation, 2006.

Moore JR. Correlation of pH with share performance. 1973. RJ Reynolds Collection. Bates No. 501327013. <http://legacy.library.ucsf.edu/tid/fbn49d00>.

Morgenstern M, Poelen EA, Scholte R, Karlsdottir S, Jonsson SH, Mathis F, Faggiano F, Florek E, Sweeting H, Hunt K, et al. Smoking in movies and adolescent smoking: cross-cultural study in six European countries. *Thorax* 2011;66(10):875–83.

mptv. Home page, 2011; http://www.mptvimages.com/cgi-bin/imageFolio.cgi.

Muggli ME, Forster JL, Hurt RD, Repace JL. The smoke you don't see: uncovering tobacco industry scientific strategies aimed against environmental tobacco smoke policies. *American Journal of Public Health* 2001;91(9):1419–23.

Muggli ME, Pollay RW, Lew R, Joseph AM. Targeting of Asian Americans and Pacific Islanders by the tobacco industry: results from the Minnesota Tobacco Document Depository. *Tobacco Control* 2002;11(3):201–9.

Muller D, Judd CM, Yzerbyt VY. When moderation is mediated and mediation is moderated. *Journal of Personality and Social Psychology* 2005;89(6):852–63.

Nash Information Services LLC. US Movie Market Summary 1995 to 2011, 2011. <http://www.the-numbers.com/market/>; accessed October 21, 2011.

National Association of Attorneys General. Master Settlement Agreement, 1998a; <http://www.naag.org/backpages/naag/tobacco/msa/msa-pdf/MSA%20with%20Sig%20Pages%20and%20Exhibits.pdf/file_view>; accessed: June 9, 2011.

National Association of Attorneys General. Smokeless Tobacco Master Settlement Agreement, 1998b; <http://www.attorneygeneral.gov/uploadedFiles/Consumers/STMSA.pdf>; accessed: December 16, 2009.

National Cancer Institute. *Risks Associated with Smoking Cigarettes with Low Machine-Measured Yields of Tar and Nicotine*. Smoking and Tobacco Control Monograph 13. Bethesda (MD): U.S. Department of Health and Human Services, Public Health Service, National Institutes of Health, National Cancer Institute, 2001. NIH Publication No. 02-5047.

National Cancer Institute. *The Role of the Media in Promoting and Reducing Tobacco Use*. Tobacco Control Monograph No. 19. Bethesda (MD): U.S. Department of Health and Human Services, National Institutes of Health, National Cancer Institute, 2008. NIH Publication No. 07-6242.

National 4-H Council. Health Rocks!, 2010; <http://www.4-h.org/youth-development-programs/kids-health/preventative-health-safety/health-rocks/>; accessed: September 22, 2010.

Nelson JP. Cigarette demand, structural change, and advertising bans: international evidence, 1970–1995. *Contributions to Economic Analysis & Policy* 2003a; 2(1):Article 10. <http://www.bepress.com/bejeap/contributions/vol2/iss1/art10>.

Nelson JP. Youth smoking prevalence in developing countries: effect of advertising bans. *Applied Economics Letters* 2003b;10(13):805–11.

Ness Motley Export family strategy document, 1982. Research Collection. Bates No. 800057286/7321. <http://legacy.library.ucsf.edu/tid/yn166b00>.

Neuber D. New shapes, new feel for cigarette packs. *Tobacco Journal* 2009; July 9.

Niederdeppe J, Hersey JC, Farrelly MC, Haviland ML, Healton CG. Comparing adolescent reactions to national tobacco countermarketing advertisements using Web TV. *Social Marketing Quarterly* 2005;11(1):3–18.

Noel JK, Rees VW, Connolly GN. Electronic cigarettes: a new 'tobacco' industry [abstract]? *Tobacco Control* 2011;20(1):81.

Non-Voting Industry Representatives of the Tobacco Products Scientific Advisory Committee. Menthol Cigarettes: No Disproportionate Impact on Public Health. The Industry Menthol Report, March 23, 2011; <http://www.fda.gov/downloads/AdvisoryCommittees/CommitteesMeetingMaterials/TobaccoProductsScientificAdvisoryCommittee/UCM249320.pdf>; accessed: October 18, 2011.

Northrup D, Pollard J. Plain Packaging of Cigarettes and Other Tobacco Issues: A Survey of Grade Seven and Grade Nine Ontario Students, Fall 1995; <http://www.isr.yorku.ca/newsletter/fall95/plain.html>; accessed: September 4, 2010.

Novak SP, Reardon SF, Raudenbush JW, Buka SL. Retail tobacco outlet density and youth cigarette smoking: a propensity-modeling approach. *American Journal of Public Health* 2006;96(4):670–6.

O'Connor RJ. What brands are US smokers under 25 choosing? *Tobacco Control* 2005;14(3):213.

Ohio Licensed Beverage Association. *An Important Message About Your Board of Health*. 1995. Philip Morris Collection. Bates No. 2063417286/7294. <http://legacy.library.ucsf.edu/tid/fvv87e00>.

Omidvari K, Lessnau K, Kim J, Mercante D, Weinacker A, Mason C. Smoking in contemporary American cinema. *Chest* 2005;128(2):746–54.

Ong EK, Glantz S. Tobacco industry efforts subverting the International Agency for Research on Cancer's second-hand smoke study. *Lancet* 2000;355(9211):1253–9.

Ong EK, Glantz SA. Constructing "sound science" and "good epidemiology": tobacco, lawyers, and public relation firms. *American Journal of Public Health* 2001;91(11):1749–57.

Orzechowski and Walker. *The Tax Burden on Tobacco: Historic Compilation 2010*. Arlington (VA): Orzechowski and Walker, 2011.

Palmer A. The product. In: *Principles of Marketing*. New York: Oxford University Press, 2000:217–38.

Parrish SC. Presentation to the board: FDA issues update. 1995. Philip Morris Collection. Bates No. 2046912017/2067. <http://legacy.library.ucsf.edu/tid/iqn65e00>.

Paynter J, Edwards R. The impact of tobacco promotion at the point of sale: a systematic review. *Nicotine & Tobacco Research* 2009;11(1):25–35.

Paynter J, Edwards R, Schluter PJ, McDuff I. Point of sale tobacco displays and smoking among 14–15 year olds in New Zealand: a cross-sectional study. *Tobacco Control* 2009;18(4):268–74.

Pechmann C. A comparison of health communication models: risk learning versus stereotype priming. *Media Psychology* 2001;3(2):189–210.

Pechmann C, Knight SJ. An experimental investigation of the joint effects of advertising and peers on adolescents' beliefs and intentions about cigarette consumption. *Journal of Consumer Research* 2002;29(1):5–19.

Pechmann C, Ratneshwar S. The effects of antismoking and cigarette advertising on young adolescents' perceptions of peers who smoke. *Journal of Consumer Research* 1994;21(2):236–51.

Pechmann C, Reibling ET. Antismoking advertisements for youths: an independent evaluation of health, counter-industry, and industry approaches. *American Journal of Public Health* 2006;96(5):906–13.

Pechmann C, Shih CF. Smoking scenes in movies and antismoking advertisements before movies: effects on youth. *Journal of Marketing* 1999;63(3):1–13.

Peier AM, Moqrich A, Hergarden AC, Reeve AJ, Andersson DA, Story GM, Earley TJ, Dragoni I, McIntyre P, Bevan S, et al. A TRP channel that senses cold stimuli and menthol. *Cell* 2002;108(5):705–15.

Perfetti TA, Needs KA, Mereschak CJ, Savoca MR, Swaim MC, Hunter CS. Sensory evaluation studies with marketing and development. 1984. RJ Reynolds Collection. Bates No. 50244661/6742. <http://legacy.library.ucsf.edu/tid/piy09d00>.

Perry CL. The tobacco industry and underage youth smoking: tobacco industry documents from the Minnesota litigation. *Archives of Pediatrics & Adolescent Medicine* 1999;153(9):935–41.

Peters M. Philip Morris portfolio management discussion. 1999. Philip Morris Collection. Bates No. 2070648930/8964. <http://legacy.library.ucsf.edu/tid/tyk27a00>.

Philip Morris. The use of alkalis to improve smoke flavor. 1965. Philip Morris Collection. Bates No. 2026351158/1163. <http://legacy.library.ucsf.edu/tid/klk15e00>.

Philip Morris. Pricing policy. 1976. Philip Morris Collection. Bates No. 2023769635/9655. <http://legacy.library.ucsf.edu/tid/jtw71f00>.

Philip Morris USA. Parliament 880000 marketing plan. 1987. Philip Morris Collection. Bates No. 2045287048/7092. <http://legacy.library.ucsf.edu/tid/hoa03e00>.

Philip Morris USA. [Press release]. 1993. Philip Morris Collection. Bates No. 2070910363/0365. <http://legacy.library.ucsf.edu/tid/dts37d00>.

Philip Morris USA. Organizations in support of House Bill 299. 1996. Philip Morris Collection. Bates No. 2063422601/2602. <http://legacy.library.ucsf.edu/tid/nwv87e00>.

Philip Morris USA. U.S. Exhibit 58,941, Report, "Core Values Communication MWCRC." 1998. DATTA Collection. Bates No. USX231200/1210. <http://legacy.library.ucsf.edu/tid/zew36b00>.

Philip Morris USA. Develop and implement a YSP communication platform and strategy key initiative update. 1999a. Philip Morris Collection. Bates No. 2078044246/4255. <http://legacy.library.ucsf.edu/tid/dfw75c00 >.

Philip Morris USA. National market structure study. 1999b. Philip Morris Collection. Bates No. 2702700028B/0028BP. <http://legacy.library.ucsf.edu/tid/fpn55a00>.

Philip Morris USA. Attachment B. Research and Documentation: Longitudinal Study on the Effectiveness of Health Rocks! and the 4-H Youth Development Program in Life Skills Development. 2001. Philip Morris Collection. Bates No. 2085211380/1382. <http://legacy.library.ucsf.edu/tid/frt12c00>.

Philip Morris USA. Scientific consensus – "Addiction": smoking is a repetitive behavior mediated by many factors. 2002. Philip Morris Collection. Bates No. 3052396004/6048. <http://legacy.library.ucsf.edu/tid/yjr44d00>.

Philip Morris USA. *DOJ Supp Part 3* – pages 201–274. 2004a. Philip Morris Collection. Bates No. 5001054172/4245. <http://legacy.library.ucsf.edu/tid/evx07a00>.

Philip Morris USA. *Philip Morris USA Retail Leaders 2005 Agreement. Plan Group P.* 2004b. Philip Morris Collection. Bates No. 3002957891/7917. <http://legacy.library.ucsf.edu/tid/udu07a00>.

Philip Morris USA. Grants Programs – Philip Morris USA, May 29, 2008a; <http://web.archive.org/web/20080529232550/http://www.philipmorrisusa.com/en/cms/Responsibility/Helping_Reduce_Underage_Tobacco_Use/Our_Focus_Areas/Grant_Programs/default.aspx>; accessed: February 26, 2010.

Philip Morris USA. Teenage Attitudes & Behavior Study. Research Report #9. 2008b. Philip Morris Collection. Bates No. 5002609044/9089. <http://legacy.library.ucsf.edu/tid/vum04b00>.

Philip Morris USA. Parent Communications – Philip Morris USA, 2010; http://web.archive.org/web/20090301053934/http://philipmorrisusa.com/en/cms/Responsibility/Helping_Reduce_Underage_Tobacco_Use/Our_Focus_Areas/Parent_Communications/default.aspx?

Philip Morris USA. Marlboro; 2011; <https://www.marlboro.com/marlboro/index.action>; accessed: November 18, 2011.

Pierce JP, Choi WS, Gilpin EA, Farkas AJ, Berry CC. Tobacco industry promotion of cigarettes and adolescent smoking. *JAMA: the Journal of the American Medical Association* 1998;279(7):511–5.

Pierce JP, Gilpin EA. A historical analysis of tobacco marketing and the uptake of smoking by youth in the United States: 1890–1977. *Health Psychology* 1995; 14(6):500–8.

Pierce JP, Messer K, James LE, White MM, Kealey S, Vallone DM, Healton CG. Camel No. 9 cigarette-marketing campaign targeted young teenage girls. *Pediatrics* 2010;125(4):619–26.

Pinkerton Tobacco Co. Welcome to RedMan, 2010; <http://www.redman.com/>; accessed: September 15, 2010.

Pokorny SB, Jason LA, Schoeny ME. The relation of retail tobacco availability to initiation and continued smoking. *Journal of Clinical Child and Adolescent Psychology* 2003;32(2):193–204.

Polansky JR, Glantz S. *First-Run Smoking Presentations in U.S. Movies 1999–2006*. San Francisco: University of California, Center for Tobacco Control Research and Education, 2007.

Pollay RW. *The Functions and Management of Cigarette Advertising*. Vancouver (Canada): University of British Columbia, History of Advertising Archives, Working Paper, 1989.

Pollay RW. Targeting youth and concerned smokers: evidence from Canadian tobacco industry documents. *Tobacco Control* 2000;9(2):136–47.

Pollay RW. The Role of Packaging Seen through Industry Documents. Expert Report prepared for: JTI-Macdonald, Imperial Tobacco Canada Ltd and Rothmans, *Benson & Hedges Inc. v. Attorney General of Canada and Canadian Cancer Society* (intervenor). Supreme Court, Province of Quebec, District of Montreal. Defense Exhibit D-116, 2001; <http://www.sauder.ubc.ca/AM/Template.cfm?Section=Tobacco&Template=/CM/ContentDisplay.cfm&ContentID=36037>; accessed: December 15, 2009.

Pollay RW. More than meets the eye: on the importance of retail cigarette merchandising. *Tobacco Control* 2007;16(4):270–4.

Pollay RW, Dewhirst T. Marketing cigarettes with low machine measured yields. In: *Risks Associated with Smoking Cigarettes with Low Machine-Measured Yields of Tar and Nicotine*. Smoking and Tobacco Control Monograph 13. Bethesda (MD): U.S. Department of Health and Human Services, Public Health Service, National Institutes of Health, National Cancer Institute, 2001:199–235. NIH Publication No. 02-5047.

Pollay RW, Siddarth S, Siegel M, Haddix A, Merritt RK, Giovino G, Eriksen MP. The last straw: cigarette advertising and realized market shares among youths and adults. *Journal of Marketing* 1996;60(2):1–16.

Pomerleau O. Individual differences in sensitivity to nicotine: implications for genetic research on nicotine dependence. *Behavior Genetics* 1995;25(2):161–77.

Prevent All Cigarette Trafficking Act of 2009, Public Law 111-154, 124 *U.S. Statutes at Large* 1087 (2010).

Public Health Cigarette Smoking Act of 1969, Public Law 91-222, *U.S. Statutes at Large* 84 (1970), codified at *U.S. Code* 15 §1331.

Pucci LG, Joseph HM Jr, Siegel M. Outdoor tobacco advertising in six Boston neighborhoods: evaluating youth exposure. *American Journal of Preventive Medicine* 1998;15(2):155–9.

Pucci LG, Siegel M. Exposure to brand-specific cigarette advertising in magazines and its impact on youth smoking. *Preventive Medicine* 1999;29(5):313–20.

Racketeer Influenced and Corrupt Organizations ("RICO") *Act*, Public Law 91-452, 84 Stat. 922 (1970), codified at *U.S. Code* 18 §§ 1961-68 (1994).

Redmond WH. Effects of sales promotion on smoking among U.S. ninth graders. *Preventive Medicine* 1999;28(3):243–50.

Ribisl K. Point-of-sale regulation of tobacco sales and marketing. Presented at CDC CPPW State and Territory Initiative; June 8, 2010; Atlanta (GA).

Ribisl KM. The potential of the internet as a medium to encourage and discourage youth tobacco use. *Tobacco Control* 2003;12(Suppl 1):i48–i59.

Ribisl KM, Kim AE, Williams RS. Web sites selling cigarettes: how many are there in the USA and what are their sales practices? *Tobacco Control* 2001;10(4): 352–9.

Ribisl KM, Kim AE, Williams RS. Sales and marketing of cigarettes on the Internet: emerging threats to tobacco control and promising policy solutions. In: Bonnie RJ, Stratton K, Wallace RB, editors. *Ending the Tobacco Problem: A Blueprint for the Nation*. Washington: National Academy Press, 2007:653–78.

Ribisl KM, Kim AE, Williams RW. Internet Cigarette Sales Knowledge Asset, Web site created by the Robert Wood Johnson Foundation's Substance Abuse Policy Research Program, May 2009; <http://www.saprp.org/knowledgeassets/knowledge_detail.cfm?KAID=3>.

Ribisl KM, Williams RS, Gizlice Z, Herring AH. Effectiveness of state and federal government agreements with major credit card and shipping companies to block illegal Internet cigarette sales. PLoS ONE 2011;6(2):e16754.

Rigotti NA, Moran SE, Wechsler H. US college students' exposure to tobacco promotions: prevalence and association with tobacco use. *American Journal of Public Health* 2005;95(1):138–44.

Riskind J, Bradshaw J. Tobacco forces, foes to butt heads on smoking. *Columbus Dispatch* February 4, 1995:1C.

Ritchy AP. Apple wine cigarette project. 1972. RJ Reynolds Collection. Bates No. 501283430/3431. <http://legacy.library.ucsf.edu/tid/buq49d00>.

R.J. Reynolds Tobacco Company. Implications and activities arising from correlation of smoke pH with nicotine impact, other smoke qualities, and cigarette sales. 1973. RJ Reynolds Collection. Bates No. 509314122/4154. <http://legacy.library.ucsf.edu/tid/jbr73d00>.

R.J. Reynolds Tobacco Company. R.J. Reynolds Tobacco Company domestic operating goals. 1974. RJ Reynolds Collection. Bates No. 500796928/6934. <http://legacy.library.ucsf.edu/tid/tgh69d00>.

R.J. Reynolds Tobacco Company. Technology: ammoniation. 1981. RJ Reynolds Collection. Bates No. 509018864/8865A. <http://legacy.library.ucsf.edu/tid/kik83d00>.

R.J. Reynolds Tobacco Company. Action alternatives in a price sensitive market: management summary. 1983a. RJ Reynolds Collection. Bates No. 501927671/7685. <http://legacy.library.ucsf.edu/tid/tct29d00>.

R.J. Reynolds Tobacco Company. The importance of younger adults. 1983b. RJ Reynolds Collection. Bates No. 503473660/3665. <http://legacy.library.ucsf.edu/tid/xbf95d00>.

R.J. Reynolds Tobacco Company. Camel advertising development "White Paper." 1986a. Research Collection. Bates No. 506768775/8784. <http://legacy.library.ucsf.edu/tid/uhn76b00>.

R.J. Reynolds Tobacco Company. Low level menthol opportunity summary. 1986b. RJ Reynolds Collection. Bates No. 505938058/8063. <http://legacy.library.ucsf.edu/tid/eax18c00>.

R.J. Reynolds Tobacco Company. Volume impact of Camel YAS growth. 1989. RJ Reynolds Collection. Bates No. 507533523/3535. <http://legacy.library.ucsf.edu/tid/dol24d00>.

R.J. Reynolds Tobacco Company. Nicotine delivery expert system. 1991. RJ Reynolds Collection. Bates No. 510962740/2741. <http://legacy.library.ucsf.edu/tid/qxn53d00>.

R.J. Reynolds Tobacco Company. Camel dissolvables, 2010a; <https://dissolvables.tobaccopleasure.com/modules/security/Login.aspx>; accessed: September 15, 2010.

R.J. Reynolds Tobacco Company. My Smokers' Rights, 2010b; <https://mysmokersrights.rjrt.com/SGRHome.jsp>; accessed: March 1, 2010.

R.J. Reynolds Tobacco Company. Tobacco Pleasure, 2010c; <https://pallmall.tobaccopleasure.com/modules/security/Login.aspx?brand=PAL>; accessed: March 2, 2010.

R.J. Reynolds Tobacco Company. You're Among Friends, 2010d; <https://camel.tobaccopleasure.com/modules/Security/Login.aspx>; accessed: March 2, 2010.

R.J. Reynolds Tobacco Company. Snus, 2011; <https://snus.tobaccopleasure.com/modules/security/Login.aspx>; accessed: November 18, 2011.

Robinson LA, Murray DM, Alfano CM, Zbikowski SM, Blitstein JL, Klesges RC. Ethnic differences in predictors of adolescent smoking onset and escalation: a longitudinal study from 7th to 12th grade. *Nicotine & Tobacco Research* 2006;8(2):297–307.

Rock VJ, Davis SP, Thorne SL, Asman K, Caraballo R. Menthol cigarette use among racial and ethnic groups in the United States, 2004–2008. *Nicotine & Tobacco Research* 2010;12(Suppl 2):S117–S124.

Rodgman A. Sugar-ammonia reaction products (flavor improvement of low-quality tobacco). 1982. RJ Reynolds Collection. Bates No. 500907420/7421. <http://legacy.library.ucsf.edu/tid/fft59d00>.

Roeseler A, Feighery EC, Cruz TB. Tobacco marketing in California and implications for the future. *Tobacco Control* 2010;19(Suppl 1):i21–i29.

Rogers T, Feighery E, Tencati EM, Butler JL, Weiner L. Community mobilization to reduce point-of-purchase advertising of tobacco products. *Health Education Quarterly* 1995;22(4):427–42.

Rootman I, Flay BR. *A Study on Youth Smoking: Plain Packaging, Health Warnings, Event Marketing and Price Reductions. Key Findings*. Toronto (Canada): University of Toronto, University of Illinois at Chicago, York University, Ontario Tobacco Research Unit, Addiction Research Foundation, 1995.

Ruel E, Mani N, Sandoval A, Terry-McElrath Y, Slater SJ, Tworek C, Chaloupka FJ. After the Master Settlement Agreement: trends in the American tobacco retail environment from 1999 to 2002. *Health Promotion Practice* 2004;5(3 Suppl):99S–110S.

Saffer H, Chaloupka F. The effect of tobacco advertising bans on tobacco consumption. *Journal of Health Economics* 2000;19(6):1117–37.

Samuels B, Glantz SA. The politics of local tobacco control. *JAMA: the Journal of the American Medical Association* 1991;266(15):2110–7.

Sargent JD, Beach ML, Adachi-Mejia AM, Gibson JJ, Titus-Ernstoff LT, Carusi CP, Swain SD, Heatherton TF, Dalton MA. Exposure to movie smoking: its relation to smoking initiation among US adolescents. *Pediatrics* 2005;116(5):1183–91.

Sargent JD, Beach ML, Dalton MA, Ernstoff LT, Gibson JJ, Tickle JJ, Heatherton TF. Effect of parental R-rated movie restriction on adolescent smoking initiation: a prospective study. *Pediatrics* 2004;114(1):149–56.

Sargent JD, Beach ML, Dalton MA, Mott LA, Tickle JJ, Ahrens MB, Heatherton TF. Effect of seeing tobacco use in films on trying smoking among adolescents: cross sectional study. *BMJ (British Medical Journal)* 2001a;323(7326):1394–7.

Sargent JD, Dalton M, Beach M, Bernhardt A, Heatherton T, Stevens M. Effect of cigarette promotions on smoking uptake among adolescents. *Preventive Medicine* 2000;30(4):320–7.

Sargent JD, Dalton MA, Beach ML, Mott LA, Tickle JJ, Ahrens MB, Heatherton TF. Viewing tobacco use in movies: does it shape attitudes that mediate adolescent smoking? *American Journal of Preventive Medicine* 2002;22(3):137–45.

Sargent JD, Gibson J, Heatherton TF. Comparing the effects of entertainment media and tobacco marketing on youth smoking. *Tobacco Control* 2009a;18(1): 47–53.

Sargent JD, Hanewinkel R. Comparing the effects of entertainment media and tobacco marketing on youth smoking in Germany. *Addiction* 2009;104(5):815–23.

Sargent JD, Heatherton TF. Comparison of trends for adolescent smoking and smoking in movies, 1990–2007 [letter]. *JAMA: the Journal of the American Medical Association* 2009;301(21):2211–3.

Sargent JD, Maruska K, Morgenstern M, Isensee B, Hanewinkel R. Movie smoking, movie horror, and urge to smoke. *Przegl Lek* 2009b;66(10):545–7.

Sargent JD, Stoolmiller M, Worth KA, Dal Cin S, Wills TA, Gibbons FX, Gerrard M, Tanski S. Exposure to smoking depictions in movies: its association with established adolescent smoking. *Archives of Pediatrics & Adolescent Medicine* 2007a;161(9):849–56.

Sargent JD, Tanski SE, Gibson J. Exposure to movie smoking among US adolescents aged 10 to 14 years: a population estimate. *Pediatrics* 2007b;119(5):e1167–e1176.

Sargent JD, Tickle JJ, Beach ML, Dalton MA, Aherns MB, Heatherton TF. Brand appearances in contemporary cinema films and contribution to global marketing of cigarettes. *Lancet* 2001b;357(9249):29–32.

Sargent JD, Worth KA, Beach M, Gerrand M, Heatherton TF. Population-based assessment of exposure to risk behaviors in motion pictures. *Communications Methods and Measures* 2008;2(1–2):134–51.

SCARC Action Alert. An embattled Philip Morris Launches Advocacy Advertising Campaign, April 17, 1996; <www.tobacco.org/Misc/aaaalert.html>; accessed: December 15, 2009.

Schooler C, Feighery E, Flora JA. Seventh graders' self-reported exposure to cigarette marketing and its relationship to their smoking behavior. *American Journal of Public Health* 1996;86(9):1216–21.

Screenit. Full content movie reviews, 2012; <http://www.screenit.com/>; accessed: January 25, 2012.

Sebrié EM, Glantz SA. Attempts to undermine tobacco control: tobacco industry youth smoking prevention programs to undermine meaningful tobacco control in Latin America. *American Journal of Public Health* 2007;97(8):1357–67.

Sederholm Public Affairs. *Final Report to the National Association of Convenience Stores: Implementation of the 'We Card' Tobacco Education and Training Program Among the Largest Companies of the Convenience Store Industry*. 1996. Philip Morris Collection. Bates No.2063536249/6256. <http://legacy.library.ucsf.edu/tid/rte38d00>.

Seligman RB. Wilkinson Sword, Inc.—new idea. 1975. Philip Morris Collection. Bates No. 1003717046/7048. <http://legacy.library.ucsf.edu/tid/zgz97e00>.

Segrave K. *Product Placement in Hollywood Films: A History*. Jefferson (NC): McFarland, 2004.

Sepe E, Ling PM, Glantz SA. Smooth moves: bar and nightclub tobacco promotions that target young adults. *American Journal of Public Health* 2002;92(3):414–9.

Shadel WG, Martino SC, Haviland A, Setodji C, Primack BA. Smoking motives in movies are important for understanding adolescent smoking: a preliminary investigation. *Nicotine & Tobacco Research* 2010;12(8):850–4.

Shapiro SJ, Perreault WD, McCarthy EJ. *Basic Marketing: A Global-Managerial Approach*. Toronto (Canada): McGraw-Hill, 1999.

Sheeran P. Intention—behavior relations: a conceptual and empirical review. *European Review of Social Psychology* 2002;12:1–36.

Shmueli D, Prochaska JJ, Glantz SA. Effect of smoking scenes in films on immediate smoking: a randomized controlled study. *American Journal of Preventive Medicine* 2010;38(4):351–8.

Siegel M. Counteracting tobacco motor sports sponsorship as a promotional tool: is the tobacco settlement enough? *American Journal of Public Health* 2001;91(7):1100–6.

Siegel M, Carol J, Jordan J, Hobart R, Schoenmarklin S, DuMelle F, Fisher P. Preemption in tobacco control: review of an emerging public health problem. *JAMA: the Journal of the American Medical Association* 1997;278(10):858–63.

Siegel M, Nelson DE, Peddicord JP, Merritt RK, Giovino GA, Eriksen MP. The extent of cigarette brand switching among current smokers: data from the 1986 Adult Use-of-Tobacco Survey. *American Journal of Preventive Medicine* 1994;12(1):14–6.

Slade J. Are tobacco products drugs: evidence from US Tobacco. *Tobacco Control* 1995;4(1):1–2.

Slade J. The pack as advertisement. *Tobacco Control* 1997;6(3):169–70.

Slater S, Chaloupka FJ, Wakefield M. State variation in retail promotions and advertising for Marlboro cigarettes. *Tobacco Control* 2001;10(4):337–9.

Slater SJ, Chaloupka FJ, Wakefield M, Johnston LD, O'Malley PM. The impact of retail cigarette marketing practices on youth smoking uptake. *Archives of Pediatrics & Adolescent Medicine* 2007;161(5):440–5.

Slavitt JJ. Counter assist plan. 1992. Research Collection. Bates No. 2023916866/6867. <http://legacy.library.ucsf.edu/tid/ser76b00>.

Slone M, Bonhomme J. Flavored cigarette qualitative research. 1993. Philip Morris Collection. Bates No. 2048886618/6619. <http://legacy.library.ucsf.edu/tid/dko36e00>.

Slovic P. Cigarette smokers: rational actors or rational fools? In: Slovic P, editor. *Smoking: Risk, Perception, & Policy*. Thousand Oaks (CA): Sage Publications, 2001:97–124.

Sly DF, Heald G, Hopkins RS, Moore TW, McCloskey M, Ray S. The industry manipulation attitudes of smokers and nonsmokers. *Journal of Public Health Management Practices* 2000;6(3):49–56.

Sly DF, Hopkins RS, Trapido E, Ray S. Influence of a counteradvertising media campaign on initiation of smoking: the Florida "truth" campaign. *American Journal of Public Health* 2001;91(2):233–8.

Smith EA, Malone RE. Thinking the "unthinkable": why Philip Morris considered quitting [review]. *Tobacco Control* 2003;12(2):208–13.

Smith EA, Malone RE. 'We will speak as the smoker': the tobacco industry's smokers' rights groups[review]. *European Journal of Public Health* 2007;17(3):306–13.

Smoker's Club. Home page, 2010; <http://www.smokers-club.com/>; accessed: March 2, 2010.

Smokers Only. For smokers only, 2010; <http://www.smokersonly.org/>; accessed: September 15, 2010.

SmokingEverywhere. Home page, 2011; <http://www.smokingeverywhere.com>; accessed: November 18, 2011.

Smoking Lobby. Forum for Smokers Rights. Smoking Lobby, 2010; <http://www.smokinglobby.com/>; accessed: March 2, 2010.

Soldz S, Huyser DJ, Dorsey E. Youth preferences for cigar brands: rates of use and characteristics of users. *Tobacco Control* 2003;12(2):155–60.

Song AV, Ling PM, Neilands TB, Glantz SA. Smoking in movies and increased smoking among young adults. *American Journal of Preventive Medicine* 2007;33(5):396–403.

Sparber P, Blaunstein P. Family C.O.U.R.S.E. consortium program offering. 1991. Tobacco Institute Collection. Bates No. TIMN0188142/8145. <http://legacy.library.ucsf.edu/tid/peh82f00>.

Spelman AR, Spitz MR, Kelder SH, Prokhorov AV, Bondy ML, Frankowski RF, Wilkinson AV. Cognitive susceptibility to smoking: two paths to experimenting among Mexican origin youth. *Cancer Epidemiology, Biomarkers & Prevention* 2009;18(12):3459–67.

Star Scientific, Inc. *Materials Submitted in Connection with July 21–22, 2011 Meeting of the Tobacco Products Scientific Advisory Committee (TPSAC) on Dissolvable Tobacco*. Bethesda (MD): Star Scientific, 2011; <http://www.fda.gov/downloads/AdvisoryCommittees/Commit-

teesMeetingMaterials/TobaccoProductsScientificAdvisoryCommittee/UCM263306.pdf>; accessed: November 29, 2011.

St. Romain T, Hawley SR, Ablah E, Kabler BS, Molgaard CA. Tobacco use in silent film: precedents of modern-day substance use portrayals. *Journal of Community Health* 2007;32(6):413–8.

Stauber J, Rampton S. *Toxic Sludge is Good For You! Lies, Damn Lies and the Public Relations Industry.* Monroe (ME): Common Courage Press, 2002.

Stevenson T, Proctor RN. The secret and soul of Marlboro: Philip Morris and the origins, spread, and denial of tobacco freebasing. *American Journal of Public Health* 2008;98(7):1184–94.

Stockwell TF, Glantz SA. Tobacco use is increasing in popular films. *Tobacco Control* 1997;6(4):282–4.

Substance Abuse and Mental Health Services Administration. *Results from the 2008 National Survey on Drug Use and Health: National Findings.* NSDUH Series H-36. Rockville (MD): U.S. Department of Health and Human Services, Substance Abuse and Mental Health Services Administration, Office of Applied Studies, 2009. DHHS Publication No. SMA 09-4434.

Substance Abuse and Mental Health Services Administration. The NSDUH Report: recent trends in menthol cigarette use. Rockville (MD): U.S. Department of Health and Human Services, Substance Abuse and Mental Health Services Administration, Office of Applied Studies, 2011; <http://www.samhsa.gov/data/2k11/WEB_SR_088/WEB_SR_088.pdf>; accessed: December 20, 2011.

Sugg WA. Survey of smoking by high school and college students. 1959. RJ Reynolds Collection. Bates No. 501113722. <http://legacy.library.ucsf.edu/tid/nbd59d00>.

Sugg WA. Attached is a report of a survey of cigarette smoking as of early January, based upon returns from approximately 5,000 families and 7,500 individual smokers. 1964. RJ Reynolds Collection. Bates No. 501795141. <http://legacy.library.ucsf.edu/tid/wwd39d00>.

Sussman S. Tobacco industry youth tobacco prevention programming: a review. *Prevention Science* 2002;3(1):57–67.

Sussman S, Dent CW, Mestel-Rauch J, Johnson CA, Hansen WB, Flay BR. Adolescent nonsmokers, triers, and regular smokers' estimates of cigarette smoking prevalence: when do overestimations occur and by whom? *Journal of Applied Social Psychology* 1988;18(7):537–51.

Sutton CD, Robinson RG. The marketing of menthol cigarettes in the United States: populations, messages, and channels. *Nicotine & Tobacco Research* 2004;6(Suppl 1):S83–S91.

Tanski SE, Stoolmiller M, Dal Cin S, Worth K, Gibson J, Sargent JD. Movie character smoking and adolescent smoking: who matters more, good guys or bad guys? *Pediatrics* 2009;124(1):135–43.

Tanski SE, Stoolmiller M, Gerrard M, Sargent JD. Moderation of the association between media exposure and youth smoking onset: race/ethnicity, and parent smoking. *Prevention Science* 2011; doi 10.1007/S11121-011-0244-3.

Teague C. Research planning memorandum on the nature of the tobacco business and the crucial role of nicotine therein. 1972. Bates No. 511241932/1941. <http://legacy.library.ucsf.edu/tid/npd53d00>.

Teague C. Implications and activities arising from correlation of smoke ph with nicotine impact, other smoke qualities, and cigarette sales. 1973a. RJ Reynolds collection. Bates No. 500917506/7534. <http://legacy.library.ucsf.edu/tid/tlr59d00>.

Teague CE Jr. Modification of tobacco stem materials by treatment with ammonia and other substances. 1954. RJ Reynolds Collection. Bates No. 504175083/5084. <http://legacy.library.ucsf.edu/tid/gpt58d00>.

Teague CE Jr. Proposal of a new, consumer-oriented business strategy for RJR Tobacco Company. 1969. RJ Reynolds Collection. Bates No. 500915701/5719. <http://legacy.library.ucsf.edu/tid/drr59d00>.

Teague CE Jr. Research planning memorandum on some thoughts about new brands of cigarettes for the youth market. 1973b. RJ Reynolds Collection. Bates No. 502987357/7368. <http://legacy.library.ucsf.edu/tid/act68d00>.

Teenage Research Unlimited. Counter-Tobacco Advertising Exploratory Summary Report, January–March 1999; <http://www.tobaccofreekids.org/reports/smokescreen/study.shtml>; accessed: October 5, 2010.

Terry-McElrath Y, Wakefield M, Ruel E, Balch GI, Emery S, Szczypka G, Clegg-Smith K, Flay B. The effect of antismoking advertisement executional characteristics on youth comprehension, appraisal, recall, and engagement. *Journal of Health Communication* 2005;10(2):127–43.

Thompson EM, Gunther AC. Cigarettes and cinema: does parental restriction of R-rated movie viewing reduce adolescent smoking susceptibility? *Journal of Adolescent Health* 2007;40(2):181.e1–e6.

Thrasher JF, Jackson C, Arillo-Santillán E, Sargent JD. Exposure to smoking imagery in popular films and adolescent smoking in Mexico. *American Journal of Preventive Medicine* 2008;35(2):95–102.

Thrasher JF, Niederdeppe J, Farrelly MC, Davis KC, Ribisl KM, Haviland ML. The impact of anti-tobacco industry prevention messages in tobacco producing regions: evidence from the US truth campaign. *Tobacco Control* 2004;13(3):283–8.

Thrasher JF, Niederdeppe JD, Jackson C, Farrelly MC. Using anti-tobacco industry messages to prevent smoking among high-risk adolescents. *Health Education Research* 2006;21(3):325–37.

Thrasher JF, Sargent JD, Huang L, Arillo-Santillán E, Dorantes-Alonso A, Pérez-Hernández R. Does film smoking promote youth smoking in middle-income countries: a longitudinal study among Mexican adolescents. *Cancer Epidemiology, Biomarkers & Prevention* 2009;18(12):3444–50.

Tickle JJ, Hull JG, Sargent JD, Dalton MA, Heatherton TF. A structural equation model of social influences and exposure to media smoking on adolescent smoking. *Basic and Applied Social Psychology* 2006;28(2): 117–29.

Tickle JJ, Sargent JD, Dalton MA, Beach ML, Heatherton TF. Favourite movie stars, their tobacco use in contemporary movies, and its association with adolescent smoking. *Tobacco Control* 2001;10(1):16–22.

Tindall J. Cigarette market history and interpretation. 1984. Philip Morris Collection. Bates No. 2001265000/5045. <http://legacy.library.ucsf.edu/tid/nzb98e00>.

Titus K; Polansky JR, Glantz S. *Smoking Presentation Trends in U.S. Movies 1991–2008*. San Francisco: Breathe California of Sacramento-Emigrant Trails and University of California, San Francisco, Center for Tobacco Control Research and Education, 2009.

Titus-Ernstoff L, Dalton MA, Adachi-Mejia MA, Longacre MR, Beach ML. Longitudinal study of viewing smoking in movies and initiation of smoking by children. *Pediatrics* 2008;121(1):15–21.

Tobacco Institute. Major new initiatives to discourage youth smoking announced: efforts focus on access, marketing and education [news release]. Washington: Tobacco Institute, Dec. 11, 1990.

Tobacco Institute. FDA regulations called ineffective and illegal. Industry shares goal of reducing youth smoking, joins with others in opposition to FDA rules [published press release]. 1996. Brown & Williamson Collection. Bates No. 106018947/8948. <http://legacy.library.ucsf.edu/tid/col41d00>.

Tobacco Institute. The development of tobacco industry strategy. n.d. Tobacco Institute Collection. Bates No. TIMN0018970/8979. <http://legacy.library.ucsf.edu/tid/ddm03f00>.

Tobacco Labelling Resource Centre. Camel Crush – Flavour bead, 2011a; <http://www.tobaccolabels.ca/gallery/unitedstatespacks/camelcrushusaaug2010flavourbeadcropjpg>; accessed: January 20, 2011.

Tobacco Labelling Resource Centre. Camel Crush – Open cig, 2011b; <http://www.tobaccolabels.ca/gallery/unitedstatespacks/camelcrushusaaug2010opencigcropjpg>; accessed: January 20, 2011.

Tobacco on Trial. Blogging U.S. vs. Philip Morris, Inc., April 12, 2005; <http://www.tobacco-on-trial.com/2005/04/12/day-91-brooker-ysp-program-a-sham/>; accessed: September 22, 2010.

Tobacco Reporter. *Maxwell Tobacco Fact Book*, 2000. Raleigh (NC): Tobacco Reporter, 2000.

Tomar SL, Giovino GA, Eriksen MP. Smokeless tobacco brand preference and brand switching among US adolescents and young adults. *Tobacco Control* 1995;4(1): 67–72.

Tong EK, Glantz SA. ARTIST (Asian regional tobacco Industry scientist team): Philip Morris's attempt to exert a scientific and regulatory agenda on Asia. *Tobacco Control* 2004;13(Suppl 2):ii118–ii124.

Trachtenberg JA. Here's one tough cowboy, 1987. Canadian Tobacco Trials Collection. Bates No. TA985253/5256. <http://legacy.library.ucsf.edu/tid/gtl70g00>.

Traynor MP, Begay ME, Glantz SA. New tobacco industry strategy to prevent local tobacco control. *JAMA: the Journal of the American Medical Association* 1993;270(4):479–86.

Tremblay CH, Tremblay V. Re-interpreting the effect of an advertising ban on cigarette smoking. *International Journal of Advertising* 1999;18(1):41–9.

Treno AJ, Grube JW, Martin SE. Alcohol availabilty as a predictor of youth drinking and driving: a hierarchical analysis of survey and archival data. *Alcoholism, Clinical and Experimental Research* 2003;27(5):835–40.

Turco MR. Effects of exposure to cigarette advertisements on adolescents' attitudes toward smoking. *Journal of Applied Social Psychology* 1997;27(13):1115–30.

Tye JB, Warner KE, Glantz SA. Tobacco advertising and consumption: evidence of a causal relationship. *Journal of Public Health Policy* 1987;8(4):492–508.

Underwood RL, Ozanne JL. Is your package an effective communicator: a normative framework for increasing the communicative competence of packaging. *Journal of Marketing Communication* 1998;4(4):207–20.

Unger JB, Johnson CA, Stoddard JL, Nezami E, Chou CP. Identification of adolescents at risk for smoking initiation: validation of a measure of susceptibility. *Addictive Behaviors* 1997;22(1):81–91.

Unger JB, Rohrbach LA, Ribisl KM. Are adolescents attempting to buy cigarettes on the Internet? *Tobacco Control* 2001;10(4):360–3.

United States v. Philip Morris USA, 449 F. Supp. 2d 1 (D.D.C. 2006) (amended final opinion).

University of Michigan News Service. More good news on teen smoking; rates at or near record lows [press release]. Ann Arbor (MI): University of Michigan News Service, December 11, 2008. <http://monitoringthefuture.org/pressrelease/08cigpr_complete.pdf>.

U.S. Bureau of Labor Statistics. Consumer Price Index, 2009; <http://www.bls.gov/CPI>; accessed: February 18, 2011.

U.S. Department of Education. The National Evaluation of Upward Bound: Summary of First-year Impacts and Program Operations, 1997;<http://www2.ed.gov/offices/OUS/PES/higher/upward3.html>; accessed: September 22, 2010.

U.S. Department of Health and Human Services. *The Health Consequences of Using Smokeless Tobacco. Report of the Advisory Committee to the Surgeon General*. Rockville (MD): U.S. Department of Health and Human Services, Public Health Service, 1986. NIH Publication No. (CDC) 86-2874.

U.S. Department of Health and Human Services. *Reducing the Health Consequences of Smoking: 25 Years of Progress. A Report of the Surgeon General*. Rockville (MD): U.S. Department of Health and Human Services, Public Health Service, Centers for Disease Control, National Center for Chronic Disease Prevention and Health Promotion, Office on Smoking and Health, 1989. DHHS Publication No. (CDC) 89-8411.

U.S. Department of Health and Human Services. *Preventing Tobacco Use Among Young People. A Report of the Surgeon General*. Atlanta (GA): U.S. Department of Health and Human Services, Public Health Service, Centers for Disease Control and Prevention, National Center for Chronic Disease Prevention and Health Promotion, Office on Smoking and Health, 1994.

U.S. Department of Health and Human Services. *Tobacco Use Among U.S. Racial/Ethnic Minority Groups—African Americans, American Indians and Alaska Natives, Asian Americans and Pacific Islanders, and Hispanics. A Report of the Surgeon General.* Atlanta (GA): U.S. Department of Health and Human Services, Centers for Disease Control and Prevention, National Center for Chronic Disease Prevention and Health Promotion, Office on Smoking and Health, 1998.

U.S. Department of Health and Human Services. *Reducing Tobacco Use. A Report of the Surgeon General.* Atlanta (GA): U.S. Department of Health and Human Services, Centers for Disease Control and Prevention, National Center for Chronic Disease Prevention and Health Promotion, Office on Smoking and Health, 2000.

U.S. Department of Health and Human Services. *Women and Smoking. A Report of the Surgeon General*. Atlanta (GA): U.S. Department of Health and Human Services, Centers for Disease Control and Prevention, National Center for Chronic Disease Prevention and Health Promotion, Office on Smoking and Health, 2001.

U.S. Department of Health and Human Services. Ending the Tobacco Epidemic: A Tobacco Control Strategic Action Plan for the U.S. Department of Health and Human Services. Washington: Office of the Assistant Secretary for Health, 2010.

U.S Department of Justice. Litigation against tobacco companies, n.d.; <http://www.justice.gov/civil/cases/tobacco2/index.htm>; accessed: January 9, 2012.

U.S. Food and Drug Administration. Regulation of E-Cigarettes and Other Tobacco Products [letter], April 25, 2011a; <http://www.fda.gov/NewsEvents/PublicHealthFocus/ucm252360.htm>.

U.S. Food and Drug Administration. Tobacco Products Scientific Advisory Committee, 2011b; <http://www.fda.gov/AdvisoryCommittees/CommitteesMeetingMaterials/TobaccoProductsScientificAdvisoryCommittee/default.htm>; accessed: November 30, 2011.

U.S. Smokeless Tobacco. Graduation process: Copenhagen. 1984. US Smokeless Tobacco Collection. Bates No. 4604754. <http://legacy.library.ucsf.edu/tid/lvy71b00>.

U.S. Smokeless Tobacco Co. Copenhagen, 2010a; <https://www.freshcope.com/Default.aspx>; accessed: September 15, 2010.

U.S. Smokeless Tobacco Co. Skoal, 2010b; <https://www.skoal.com/>; accessed: September 15, 2010.

Vapors Network. About Ecigs, 2011; <http://vapersnetwork.org>; accessed: November 18, 2011.

Wackowski OA, Lewis MJ, Delnevo CD. Qualitative analysis of Camel Snus' Web site message board—users product perceptions, insights and online interactions. *Tobacco Control* 2011;20(2):e1.

Wagner DD, Dal Cin S, Sargent JD, Kelley WM, Heatherton TF. Spontaneous action representation in smokers when watching movie characters smoke. *Journal of Neuroscience* 2011;31(3):894–8.

Wakefield M, Balch GI, Ruel E, Terry-McElrath Y, Szczykpa G, Flay B, Emery S, Clegg-Smith K. Youth responses to anti-smoking advertisements from tobacco-control agencies, tobacco companies, and pharmaceutical companies. *Journal of Applied Social Psychology* 2005a;35(9):1894–1910.

Wakefield M, Germain D, Durkin SJ. How does increasingly plainer cigarette packaging influence adult smokers' perceptions about brand image: an experimental study. *Tobacco Control* 2008;17(6):416–21.

Wakefield M, Germain D, Durkin S, Henriksen L. An experimental study of effects on schoolchildren of exposure to point-of-sale cigarette advertising and pack displays. *Health Education Research* 2006a;21(3):338–47.

Wakefield M, Giovino G. Teen penalties for tobacco possession, use, and purchase: evidence and issues. *Tobacco Control* 2003;12(Suppl 1):i6–i13.

Wakefield M, Kloska DD, O'Malley PM, Johnston LD, Chaloupka F, Pierce J, Giovino G, Ruel E, Flay BR. The role of smoking intentions in predicting future smoking among youth: findings from Monitoring the Future data. *Addiction* 2004;99(7):914–22.

Wakefield M, Letcher T. My pack is cuter than your pack. *Tobacco Control* 2002;11(2):154–6.

Wakefield M, McLeod K, Perry C. Stay away from them until you're old enough to make a decision: tobacco company testimony about youth smoking initiation. *Tobacco Control* 2006b;15(Suppl 4):iv44–iv53.

Wakefield M, Morley C, Horan JK, Cummings KM. The cigarette pack as image: new evidence from tobacco industry documents. *Tobacco Control* 2002a;11(Suppl 1):i73–i80.

Wakefield M, Ruel EE, Chaloupka FJ, Slater SJ, Kaufman NJ. Association of point-of-purchase tobacco advertising and promotions with choice of usual brand among teenage smokers. *Journal of Health Communication* 2002b;7(2):113–21.

Wakefield M, Szczypka G, Terry-McElrath Y, Emery S, Flay B, Chaloupka F, Saffer H. Mixed messages on tobacco: comparative exposure to public health, tobacco company- and pharmaceutical company-sponsored tobacco-related television campaigns in the United States, 1999–2003. *Addiction* 2005b;100(12):1875–83.

Wakefield M, Terry-McElrath Y, Chaloupka FJ, Barker DC, Slater SJ, Clark PI, Giovino GA. Tobacco industry marketing at point of purchase after the 1998 MSA billboard advertising ban. *American Journal of Public Health* 2002c;92(6):937–40.

Wakefield M, Terry-McElrath Y, Emery S, Saffer H, Chaloupka FJ, Szczypka G, Flay B, O'Malley PM, Johnston L. Effect of televised, tobacco company-funded smoking prevention advertising on youth smoking-related beliefs, intentions, and behavior. *American Journal of Public Health* 2006c;96(12):2154–60.

Warner KE. Tobacco industry scientific advisors: serving society or selling cigarettes? *American Journal of Public Health* 1991;81(7):839–42.

Wayne GF, Connolly GN. How cigarette design can affect youth initiation into smoking: Camel cigarettes 1983–93. *Tobacco Control* 2002;11(Suppl 1):i32–i39.

Wayne GF, Connolly GN. Application, function, and effects of menthol in cigarettes: a survey of tobacco industry documents. *Nicotine & Tobacco Research* 2004;6(Suppl 1):S43–S54.

Waylen AE, Leary SD, Ness AR, Tanski SE, Sargent JD. Cross-sectional association between smoking depictions in films and adolescent tobacco use nested in a British cohort study. *Thorax* 2011;66(10):856–61.

Wegmans. Wegmans to stop selling cigarettes [press release]. Rochester (NY): Wegmans, January 4, 2008.

Weiss JW, Cen S, Schuster DV, Unger JB, Johnson CA, Mouttapa M, Schreiner WS, Cruz TB. Longitudinal effects of pro-tobacco and antitobacco messages on adolescent smoking susceptibility. *Nicotine & Tobacco Research* 2006;8(3):455–65.

Weitzman E, Folkman A, Folkman MP, Wechsler H. The relationship of alcohol outlet density to heavy and frequent drinking and drinking-related problems among college students at eight universities. *Health & Place* 2003;9(1):1–6.

Welsh-Huggins A. Lawmakers try again to stop health boards from banning smoking. Associated Press State and Local Wire. October 11, 2001.

Wildey MB, Young RL, Elder JP, de Moor C, Wolf KR, Fiske KE, Sharp E. Cigarette point-of-sale advertising in ethnic neighborhoods in San Diego, California. *Health Values* 1992;16(1):23–8.

Wilkinson AV, Spitz MR, Prokhorov AV, Bondy ML, Shete S, Sargent JD. Exposure to smoking imagery in the movies and experimenting with cigarettes among Mexican heritage youth. *Cancer Epidemiology, Biomarkers & Prevention* 2009;18(12):3435–43.

Willard HA III. Written trial testimony of Howard A. Willard III. 2005. DATTA Collection. Bates No. WILLARDH040405ER. <http://legacy.library.ucsf.edu/tid/qhq07a00>.

William Esty Company. National studies of trends in cigarette smoking and brand preference: base period study – January, 1964. 1964. RJ Reynolds Collection. Bates No. 500396569/6607. <http://legacy.library.ucsf.edu/tid/zot79d00>.

Wills TA, Sargent J, Stoolmiller M, Gibbons FX, Gerrard M. Movie smoking exposure and smoking onset: a longitudinal study of mediation processes in a representative sample of U.S. adolescents. *Psychology of Addictive Behaviors* 2008;22(2):269–77.

Wills TA, Sargent JD, Stoolmiller M, Gibbons FX, Worth KA, Cin SD. Movie exposure to smoking cues and adolescent smoking onset: a test for mediation through peer affiliations. *Health Psychology* 2007;26(6):769–76.

Wills TA, Gibbons FX, Sargent JD, Gerrard M, Lee HR, Dal Cin S. Good self-control moderates the effect of mass media on adolescent tobacco and alcohol use: tests with studies of children and adolescents. *Health Psychology* 2010;29(5):539–49.

Wilson N, Thomson G, Howden-Chapman P, Signal L. Regulations should ban the sale of cigarette pack covers of health warnings. *New Zealand Medical Journal* 2006;119(1243):U2251.

World Health Organization. WHO Framework Convention on Tobacco Control, World Health Assembly Resolution 56.1, 2003; <http://www.who.int/tobacco/framework/final_text/en/print.html>; accessed: December 17, 2009.

World Health Organization. *Building Blocks for Tobacco Control: A Handbook*. Geneva (Switzerland): World Health Organization, 2004.

World Health Organization. *Smoke-free Movies: From Evidence to Action*. Geneva (Switzerland): World Health Organization, 2009.

Worth KA, Cin SD, Sargent JD. Prevalence of smoking among major movie characters: 1996–2004. *Tobacco Control* 2006;15(6):442–6.

Worth KA, Duke J, Green M, Sargent JD. *Character Smoking in Top Box Office Movies*. Legacy First Look Report 18. Washington: American Legacy Foundation, 2007.

Yahoo Groups. Minnesota smokers, 2010a; <http://groups.yahoo.com/group/minnesotasmokers/>; accessed: March 2, 2010.

Yahoo Groups. Washington State smokers alliance, 2010b; http://groups.yahoo.com/group/WashStateSmokersAlliance/; accessed: March 2, 2010.

Young & Rubicam Agency. Camel advertising overview. 1990. Mangini Collection. Bates No. 508827386/7401.<http://legacy.library.ucsf.edu/tid/ejx52d00>.

Zollo P. *Wise Up to Teens: Insights into Marketing and Advertising to Teenagers*. Ithaca (NY): New Strategist Publications, 1995.

Chapter 6:
Efforts to Prevent and Reduce Tobacco Use Among Young People

Introduction

This chapter examines the history and effectiveness of efforts to prevent and reduce tobacco use among young people, with an emphasis on those under 18 years of age. The first section provides background on changes in prevention strategies since the 1994 Surgeon General's report on preventing tobacco use among young people (U.S. Department of Health and Human Services [USDHHS] 1994), including summaries of scientific evidence on strategies to reduce youth smoking, the theories underlying prevention efforts, various approaches to prevention, and the criteria for judging the evidence of the effectiveness of prevention strategies. The remaining sections, which review the evidence for the effectiveness of prevention, are divided into (1) large social environments, such as community and statewide programs and mass media campaigns; (2) regulatory and policy-driven approaches, such as the Synar Amendment to the *ADAMHA Reorganization Act* (1992), which seeks to limit the access of youth to tobacco products (Substance Abuse and Mental Health Services Administration [SAMHSA] 2011), and policies that affect product labeling, create smoke-free environments, restrict advertising, and raise tobacco taxes; (3) small social environments, such as families, clinical settings, and schools; and (4) special issues, such as preventing the use of smokeless tobacco and other tobacco products, conducting preventive efforts with vulnerable populations, and implementing cessation interventions for youth. The coordinated use of all the strategies reviewed in this chapter can help to protect youth from the psychosocial risk factors discussed in Chapter 4, "Social, Environmental, Cognitive, and Genetic Influences on the Use of Tobacco Among Youth" and the promotional efforts of the tobacco industry discussed in Chapter 5, "The Tobacco Industry's Influences on the Use of Tobacco Among Youth."

The 1994 Surgeon General's report, which reviewed the history of prevention initiatives (USDHHS 1994), concluded that early informational and affective approaches were not effective in preventing smoking among youth, and that approaches based on social-cognitive theory that focused on the teaching of social and self-management skills held the greatest promise. Since then, social-cognitive approaches have been elaborated, and some approaches focused on changing normative beliefs have also been tried. In addition, social and environmental factors are recognized as increasing risk for, or providing protection against, smoking by young people and are used as venues for prevention. For example, as documented in Chapter 4, families can have a major impact on the likelihood of smoking by young people. Thus, some research during the last 18 years has focused on involving families in educational efforts, and on changing family dynamics, to protect young people against smoking. Other ecologically driven efforts involve reducing youth access to tobacco products, increasing taxes on tobacco, enacting clean indoor air policies, and reducing images of smoking in movies.

In the United States, some researchers and practitioners have focused on individuals, while others have emphasized policies and programs operating at the societal level (Giovino 2007). Both approaches are covered in this chapter, but since 1994 the emphasis on policy and environmental approaches has increased (Warner 2007a,b). However, as will be shown in this report, the effects of nearly all kinds of preventive efforts decay over time if they are not maintained. Just as school-based programs in middle school require booster sessions in high school to maintain their effects, for example, so must mass media programs be repeated or continued to maintain their effects. Similarly, regulations are effective while they are enacted and enforced, and taxation is effective when it is enacted and adjusted for currency values.

Theories Underlying Prevention Efforts

Most prevention efforts have used the public health language of targeting risk and protective factors, sometimes buttressed by various psychological, educational, sociological, or ecological theories. Interventions attempt to change the causes of tobacco use behaviors or to take advantage of protective factors. Among the many causes of and influences on tobacco use among young people, some are proximal (such as an adolescent's attitudes toward smoking or intentions to use tobacco), others are more distal (such as the motivation of an adolescent to comply with parents or friends), and still others are broad and even more removed from use (ultimate influences, such as cultural backgrounds and personality traits).

Flay and colleagues have provided a useful model for understanding the development of adolescent behaviors by integrating and organizing these variables along two dimensions—levels of causation and streams of influence—thereby providing a metatheoretical framework:

the Theory of Triadic Influence (TTI) (Flay and Petraitis 1994; Petraitis et al. 1995, 1998; Flay 1999; Flay et al. 2009), discussed in Chapters 4 and 5. This is not the only behavioral theory that has been applied to tobacco use interventions, but it encompasses most of the primary theories in its structure.

TTI was developed with theories and variables arranged by different levels (or tiers) of causation. Some variables, such as intentions to smoke, have direct effects on behavior and are causally proximal or immediate, and some, such as motivation to comply with or please others, are mediated through other variables, such as social normative beliefs, and are more causally distal or predisposing. Additional variables, such as the style of parenting that a youth experienced during childhood or the imposition of taxes on cigarettes, are mediated by still more variables and are even more causally distal, and still others, such as ethnic culture, neighborhood poverty, and personality, represent the underlying or ultimate causes of behavior.

TTI is also based on the assumption that theories and variables can be arranged into three relatively distinct types or streams of influence (see Chapter 5, Figure 5.1), each of which acts through the multiple levels of causation:

1. The *intrapersonal* stream represents personal characteristics that contribute to self-efficacy regarding specific behaviors.

2. The *social/normative* stream represents interpersonal social influences in the social situation or context (the microenvironment) that contribute to social normative beliefs about specific behaviors.

3. The *environmental* stream represents broad cultural and environmental influences (macroenvironmental factors) that contribute to attitudes toward specific behaviors.

In the case of the onset of cigarette smoking among adolescents, for example, these influences include (1) intrapersonal (biological or personality) influences on skills, together with the will or confidence to use them (to avoid smoking) or a presumed lack of will or confidence to use them (resulting in the taking up of smoking); (2) family and school situational/contextual influences on adolescents' perceptions of social norms concerning smoking, together with these youths' motivation to comply or not to comply with them; and (3) broad societal or macroenvironmental influences on the adolescents' knowledge and values that influence their attitudes toward smoking.

TTI then proposes that the effects of ultimate and distal causes of behavior flow predominantly within each of the three streams of influence and act through a small set of proximal cognitive-affective predictors of behavior (self-efficacy, social normative beliefs, attitudes, and intentions), with multiple mediating factors between these levels. In addition, experience with a behavior feeds back and changes the original causes of that behavior; that is, influences on behavior make up a dynamic system that changes as youth develop and as they have (or do not have) experience with the behavior.

The Role of Human Development

In addition to integrating prominent theories of health behavior, TTI helps practitioners, researchers, and policymakers understand tobacco use behavior by emphasizing the three streams of influence. Meanwhile, other investigators have made it clear that the *plasticity* of biological and social development plays an important role in determining behavior (Merzenich 2001; Lerner 2006; Lerner et al. 2009): the multiple causes of behavior constitute a *dynamic system* that changes as people develop and have new experiences with particular behaviors (Lerner 1978, 2006).

The relative importance of self-efficacy (intrapersonal stream), social normative beliefs (social/normative stream), and attitudinal variables (environmental stream) changes as children develop. Attitudinal influences are most important for younger children, social and normative processes become more important during adolescence, and self-efficacy becomes more important as youth gain experience and skills in the area of social behaviors.

From a developmental perspective, three focal areas that are essential for promoting the health of adolescents are the development of personality, social development, and cognitive development. All three present challenges for healthy development with implications for prevention, however. First, adolescents begin to exert their independence from their parents, often by bonding more closely with their peers. At puberty, positive interactions between adolescents and parents may diminish (Steinberg 1991), and adolescents begin seeking independence from their parents (Montemayor and Flannery 1991). Their independence from their parents is accompanied by greater dependence on their peers, and relations with peers "become more pervasive, more intense, and carry greater psychological importance" (Foster-Clark and Blyth 1991, p. 768). Not surprisingly, adolescents are more susceptible to and compliant with social pressures than are younger children or adults (Landsbaum and Willis 1971; Berndt 1979). This is especially true of pressures to engage in substance use (Brown et al. 1986; Flay et al. 1994).

Second, during early adolescence, the search for self-identity begins, and adolescents start "trying out" adult behaviors and roles (Steinberg and Morris 2001; Tanti et al. 2011). The search is not easy, and during this time adolescents are psychologically vulnerable (Konopka 1991), self-conscious, concerned about social appearances (Elkind and Bowen 1979), and highly self-critical (Lowenthal et al. 1975; Rosenberg 1985), possibly because, for the first time, they can envision discrepancies between who they are and who they want or ought to be (Higgins 1987; Damon 1991; Tanti et al. 2011). However, the finding about being highly self-critical might be a cohort effect. Compared with earlier generations, people born after the early 1970s seem less inclined toward self-criticism and higher in self-esteem, but they often face a crisis in early adulthood when their high, but rarely tested or confirmed, self-esteem confronts reality. As a result, self-esteem is at an all-time high for young people today, but so is anxiety (Twenge 2006; Gentile et al. 2010). Risky behaviors, such as substance use, might serve as a coping mechanism as adolescents search for an identity and feel vulnerable and self-conscious during this stage of intrapersonal flux (Flammer 1991; DuBois et al. 2009).

Third, before adulthood, cognitive and affective skills are not fully developed and, to varying degrees, children and adolescents have difficulty understanding abstract information, appreciating events that might occur in the distant future (Orr and Ingersoll 1991), or reacting calmly to emotional situations (Dahl 2001, 2004; Steinberg et al. 2006). These characteristics, paired with generally good health (Brindis and Lee 1991), might contribute to adolescents' cavalier attitudes about their personal health (Levenson et al. 1984) and tendency to underestimate their own risks of health-compromising behaviors (Millstein 1991), such as tobacco use.

Overall, TTI provides a clear and organized metatheoretical framework for understanding behavior, and it also offers a guide to integrating the theoretical frameworks that interventions to prevent tobacco use have employed. Figure 6.1 demonstrates how the major approaches to preventing tobacco use can be mapped onto TTI; this framework provides a unique display of the levels and streams a specific intervention may influence. For example, the first approaches to prevention were school-based programs that focused on knowledge about the consequences of and attitudes toward smoking; they addressed only one small aspect of TTI (bottom right, Figure 6.1). Subsequent programs, particularly those based on the social influences approach, attempted to address the affective/cognitive elements of all three streams of TTI by addressing attitudes toward smoking, social normative beliefs about this behavior, and the social skills and self-efficacy needed to resist the social pressures to smoke (bluish "bricked" area of Figure 6.1). More recent school-based programs and clinic-based approaches also address a more general set of self-management and social skills. And yet, most school-based programs are still focused on the proximal causes of behavior and can be expected to have limited effects unless the programs are maintained and reinforced. In addition, school-based programs are likely to have broader and more sustainable effects if they are supplemented by school policies and family, clinic-based, or mass media programs.

Family-based interventions are more likely to target both proximal and distal influences but are usually confined to the social stream of TTI (green crosshatched area of Figure 6.1). In particular, they may alter patterns of parent-child bonding and communication and thereby change children's perceived norms and motivation to comply with (or please) their parents or peers. As for mass media, some of the early campaigns targeted information, but more recent mass media campaigns have operated in the TTI areas shown in the general cultural environment (the upper right-hand corner of Figure 6.1) and have targeted a broader array of more distal predisposing influences in the cultural environment. Mass media approaches have, in particular, influenced the informational environment (red-shaded area of Figure 6.1), and regulatory approaches have influenced the regulatory environment (orange-shaded area of Figure 6.1); these approaches have then "flowed down" the environmental stream as well as the other two streams of TTI to influence community, family, and peer group behavior. Regulatory approaches and mass media campaigns have stronger effects on a greater proportion of the population than do many other approaches because they start at such an ultimate level and then flow down and across the streams. In addition, community-based and state-level programs have the potential to provide the optimal combination of interventions to influence the complete population of a community or state (yellow-shaded area of Figure 6.1). Regardless, as will be described further below, a combination of effective evidence-based strategies can provide the most powerful approach to prevention (as opposed to a single strategy) when implemented at a level of high intensity, with integrity, and in a sustained way.

Criteria for Evidence for Prevention

This chapter will rely on the general scale used in other chapters for characterizing the evidence that an intervention approach is effective (see Chapter 1, "Introduction, Summary, and Conclusions"). However, the

Figure 6.1 Approaches to smoking prevention overlaid on the Theory of Triadic Influence

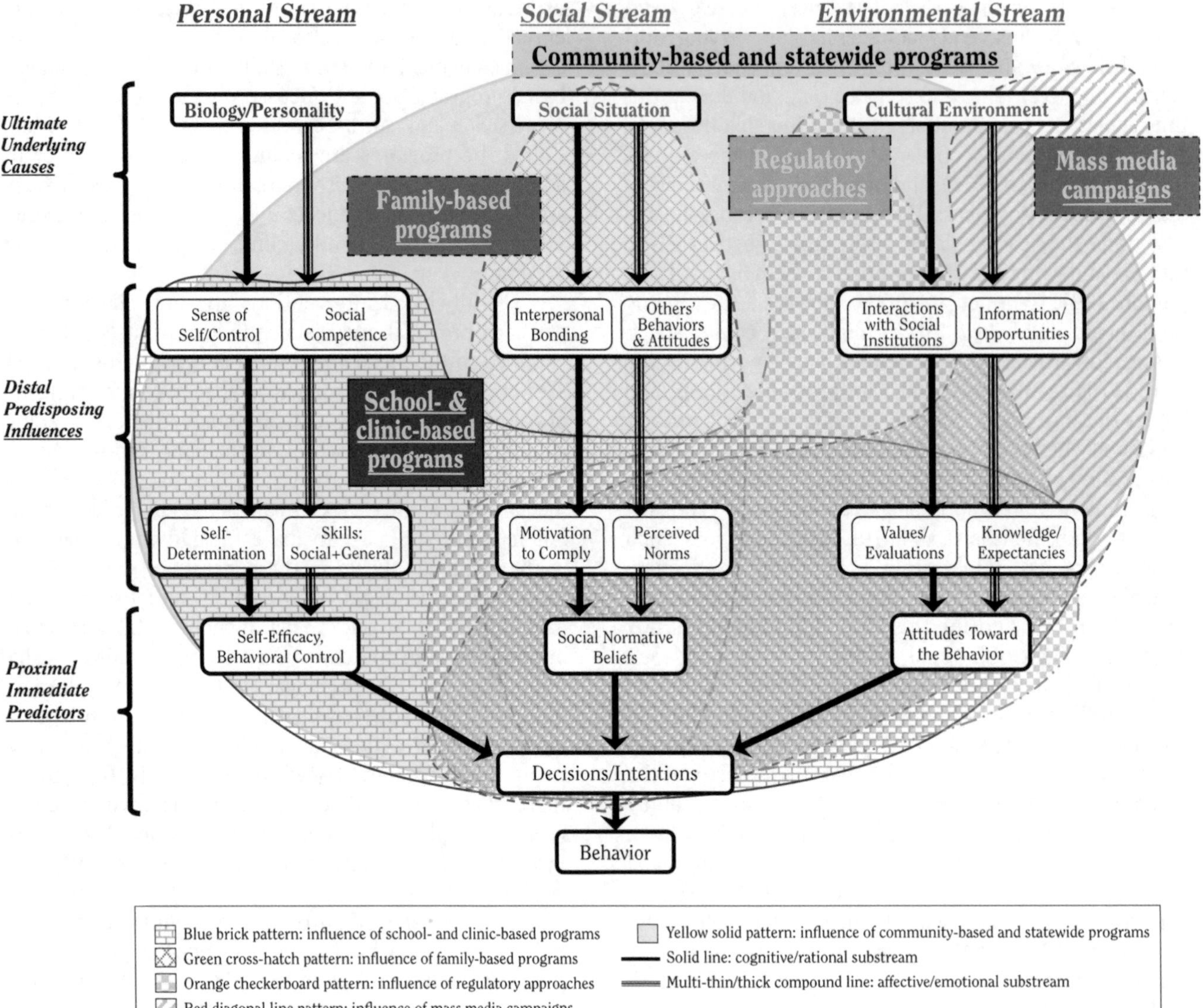

kind of evidence required to meet each of the criteria set forth in the other chapters may differ across the different approaches to prevention. For example, individually focused interventions can be tested in randomized controlled trials (RCTs), some conducted at the individual level and some in cluster- or group-based RCTs. Important examples of the latter include school-based programs, which are most often evaluated by randomly assigning schools to receive a program. For these kinds of studies, well-established standards are applied (Flay et al. 2005). For community-based programs, RCTs are also appropriate, but may be less practical or even impossible, so other evaluation designs have been used. Time-series and multiple-baseline designs meet the highest statistical standards for the evaluation of community programs (Biglan et al. 2000b).

Evidence for Prevention and Reduction of Youth Tobacco Use

The evidence for prevention approaches in this chapter is organized into sections including large social environments, regulatory or legislative approaches, and small social environments. An additional section deals with the special issues of preventing the use of smokeless and other forms of tobacco by youth, prevention for vulnerable populations, and interventions targeting tobacco cessation among youth. Because this literature is large, robust, and important for the primary prevention of tobacco use, this review does not include strategies aimed at reducing tobacco use among young adults, even though there are important emerging strategies with that age group.

Large Community Environments

This section of the report covers three kinds of initiatives: mass media campaigns, community-wide interventions, and state-level tobacco control programs.

Mass Media Campaigns

Mass media campaigns have increasingly become a key strategy in efforts to reduce smoking among youth and young adults. Able to reach large proportions of the population, mass media messages have the potential to influence not only individual behaviors but also social norms and institutional policies, which in turn can shape patterns of population-wide tobacco use (Flay 1981; Flay and Burton 1990; Hopkins et al. 2001; Hornik 2002).

The first antismoking mass media campaign was aired on U.S. television and radio soon after the 1967 Federal Communications Commission ruled that the Fairness Doctrine applied to cigarette advertising, leading to a common practice of airing one free antismoking advertisement for every three cigarette commercials (Siegel 1998). Messages in this campaign were primarily about the health consequences of smoking and continued to be aired into early 1971. Exposure to these messages was associated with reduced prevalence of smoking among both youth and adults (Lewit et al. 1981; USDHHS 1994). Between 1970 and 1971, cigarette advertising decreased substantially and, therefore, the number of antitobacco spots also decreased in that period. Antismoking ads on television and radio ceased when, effective January 2, 1971, Congress banned cigarette advertising on both of these media (Warner 1979; National Cancer Institute [NCI 2008]). Beginning in the 1980s, however, mass media campaigns on television and radio, often combined with school-based prevention programs, began using psychosocial theory-based messages in population-based prevention trials, such as in Minnesota during the 1980s (Murray et al. 1994) and in controlled field trials in various locations (e.g., Flynn et al. 1992). These campaigns focused on awareness among youth of the short-term effects of smoking (bad breath, being unfit), the highlighting of social influences, and teaching skills to resist peer pressure. In more recent times, mass media campaigns broadcast as part of state and national tobacco control programs have focused on (1) changing social norms about smoking through messages about secondhand smoke (e.g., in California beginning in 1990 [Popham et al. 1994]); (2) messages designed specifically for youth that portray the tobacco industry as deceptive and manipulative (e.g., in California from 1989 [Balbach and Glantz 1998], in Florida from 1997 [Sly et al. 2001a,b, 2002], and the American Legacy Foundation's "truth" campaign from 2000 [Farrelly et al. 2002, 2005; Thrasher et al. 2004, 2006]); and (3) campaigns targeting a general audience that emphasize the adverse health consequences of smoking through personal stories or graphic depictions of smoking-related illness (e.g., Massachusetts from 1994 [Siegel and Biener 2000]).

The tobacco industry entered the arena in 1998 with youth-targeted ads that emphasized personal choice about becoming or not becoming a smoker (Philip Morris' "Think. Don't Smoke" and Lorillard's "Tobacco Is Whacko if You're a Teen"). Philip Morris also broadcast a campaign from 1999 to 2006 about parental responsibility for their children's smoking ("Talk. They'll Listen"). These ads are reviewed in Chapter 5. Advertising by pharmaceutical companies for nicotine replacement therapy and other stop-smoking medications began in 1992 (NCI 2008). From 1999 to 2003, ratings data for television indicated that the most extensive tobacco-related advertising was for smoking cessation products from pharmaceutical companies and that tobacco company youth smoking prevention advertising was aired as much as the publicly funded national and state antitobacco broadcast campaigns (Wakefield et al. 2005b; NCI 2008). Since this period, exposure of the population to publicly funded mass media campaigns has declined as overall expenditures on tobacco control have been reduced (Campaign for Tobacco-Free Kids 2011a).

Publicly funded campaigns have used many different media channels to expose youth to antismoking messages, including television, radio, print, and billboards, and they have also employed cessation contests, media activism, and "new" interactive media (NCI 2008). Because the vast majority of the U.S. campaigns tracked by the Centers for Disease Control and Prevention's (CDC's) Media Campaign Resource Center used television (98%), radio (94%), print (89%), and/or billboards (87%) (NCI 2008), the focus of this chapter is on the effects of campaigns that include these media. A comprehensive review of the impact of new interactive media, as well as short-term cessation events, contests, and media advocacy, is available in NCI's *The Role of the Media in Promoting and Reducing Tobacco Use* (2008, pp. 441–445, 463–468).

Studies of the effects of mass media campaigns reviewed here fall into three broad categories: controlled field trials, in which unexposed communities served as a control; evaluations of the effects of campaigns funded by state or national governments; and examinations of elements and factors that may optimize the effectiveness of campaigns. This last category includes examinations of different types of messages (in terms of theme, tone, format, and executional characteristics), how messages may influence youth by personal characteristics (gender, age, race/ethnicity, socioeconomic status, and high risk), and the ideal intensity of these campaigns and duration for airing them. Conclusions on the effectiveness of mass media campaigns from authoritative reviews and new evidence since 1994 from each of these types of studies are reviewed in turn; but first, the theoretical rationale for how mass media campaigns may help to prevent youth and young adult smoking is addressed.

Theories Underlying the Strategy

An understanding of the relationship between ill health, disease, and behavioral choices led early health communication researchers to create prescriptive messages urging people to make healthier choices. Messages focused more clearly on influencing attitudes and beliefs have traditionally been more effective than messages without these types of information (Hornik 2002).

Individual-based theories of behavior change provide a rationale for how public health messages may affect behavior by influencing knowledge, attitudes, and beliefs. Early models of behavior change focused on different aspects of eliciting behavior change. The Health Belief Model focused on susceptibility, perceived severity of consequences for a behavior, cost-benefit analysis, and health motivation (Rosenstock 1974). The Theory of Reasoned Action (TRA) (Fishbein and Ajzen 1975) and the Theory of Planned Behavior (TPB) (Ajzen 1991) focused on behavioral beliefs, norms, and control beliefs and their effect on intention to engage in a behavior. Another example is the Social Cognitive Theory, which (Bandura 1986, 2004) focuses on the relationship between personal factors, environmental factors, and behavior, which is often affected by modeling. TRA and TPB have been updated in the Integrated Model of Behavior Change (IMBC). In IMBC, a number of exogenous variables, including exposure to media and health interventions, contribute to beliefs about a particular health-related topic (Bleakley et al. 2011). Behavioral beliefs lead to attitudes, intentions, and finally to behaviors. In these models, an individual's attitudes, beliefs, and environmental factors (such as perception of norms) are thought to be central to influencing intentions and ultimately behavior change.

A number of communication theories on persuasion add to this literature by providing guidance on how to change attitudes and beliefs. The Elaboration Likelihood Model of Persuasion (Petty and Cacioppo 1986) and the Heuristic-Systematic Model (Eagly and Chaiken 1993) propose two processing systems. One system involves "central" or "systematic" processing in which the message content is considered more carefully and is elaborated upon more fully. The other system is the "peripheral" or "heuristic" system that involves processing of cues such as source credibility to reject or accept the message. "Central" and "peripheral" systems can be activated individually or simultaneously at varying levels. The models suggest that lasting change and persuasion are most likely to occur when an individual has the motivation and ability to process a message centrally if the argument contained in the message is presented well. However, if the argument in the message is poor, peripheral processing may produce more desirable effects, depending on the peripheral cues.

Many theorists also emphasize the importance of emotion for message processing and behavior change (Cohen 1990; Eagly and Chaiken 1993; Forgas 1995; Escalas et al. 2004; Dillard and Nabi 2006; Lang 2006; Baumeister et al. 2007). Public health messages that activate emotion systems may increase personal perceptions of vulnerability to a health risk by producing a mental shortcut through increases in emotional associations with actions, images, or ideas (Damasio 1994; Finucane et al. 2000) that a person may use when making decisions or judgments (Slovic 2001). Emotional information may function by increasing resources allocated to processing until information overload occurs, that is, until the number of resources required to process the message becomes more than the resources allocated to processing (Lang 2006). There are two basic parts of emotional activation: arousal, which is related to how much activation is occurring unrelated to the type of emotion being experienced, and valence. Valence can be divided into appetitive (positive) and aversive (negative) activation (Cacioppo and Gardner 1999; Lang 2006) or into discrete emotions such as happiness, sadness, or hopefulness (Nabi 2010).

There has also been increasing work in health communication on using narratives and exemplars to decrease processing defensiveness and thereby increase persuasiveness of health communication messages. Dunlop and colleagues (2010) found that greater levels of transportability (which is associated with becoming absorbed in the message's narrative) were associated with greater intention to quit smoking. Furthermore, Moyer-Guse and Nabi (2010) found that narratives reduce reactance, thus increasing persuasion of messages that were high in narrativity.

Mass media messages may also exert influence through indirect interpersonal or social influences pathways (Rogers 1995b; Ball-Rokeach 1998; Yanovitzky and Stryker 2001). People obtain information about how best to respond to a health threat not only through direct exposure to campaign messages but also from social networks when the message is shared or discussed with others. For example, discussion among peers of antismoking messages is associated with increased perceptions of personal risk in adolescents (Hafstad and Aarø 1997; Morton and Duck 2001), and so, the social context in which a message is received and interpreted may influence the effects of that message (Lazarsfeld et al. 1944; Katz and Lazarsfeld 1955; McCombs and Shaw 1972).

Review Methodology

Many previous reviews have focused specifically on the effects of mass media antismoking messages on youth (USDHHS 1994; Pechmann 1997, 2001; Sowden 1998; Pechmann and Reibling 2000a; Farrelly et al. 2003a; Wakefield et al. 2003b,c). Other reviews have examined the broad impact of antismoking campaigns on both adults and youth (Flay 1987; Friend and Levy 2002; Siegel 2002; Jepson et al. 2006; Schar et al. 2006; NCI 2008) and the effects of campaigns on youth within the context of other strategies to prevent youth smoking (Lantz et al. 2000; Richardson et al. 2007).

This chapter examines the conclusions from these previous reviews and describes in Tables 6.1 and 6.2 the published studies of the effects of mass media campaigns on youth addressed in the three most recent comprehensive reviews (Richardson et al. 2007; Angus et al. 2008; NCI 2008). In addition, a systematic literature review for articles published since the latest review (NCI 2008) from May 2007 to June 2008 was conducted using the same search terms. The focus in that review, and for this section, was on studies that assessed the influence of mass media interventions (e.g., television, radio, print, and outdoor advertising) alone or in combination with other interventions (e.g., school, community, policy) (NCI 2008). These newer studies on youth are included in Tables 6.1–6.3.

Overall Effectiveness of Mass Media Campaigns in Preventing Youth Smoking

Controlled field trials. The NCI review (2008) of the media and tobacco use described above highlights the difficulty of evaluating the media components of several early quasi-experimental studies of community-based cardiovascular programs because the media elements were combined with other program elements (e.g., in the North Karelia Project and the Minnesota Heart Health Program). However, the evaluations of the overall effects of these programs indicate positive immediate and intermediate effects on smoking levels among youth (Vartiainen et al. 1986; Perry et al. 1992) and on long-term effects on initiation of smoking by youth at 8- and 15-year follow-ups (Vartiainen et al. 1990, 1998). In contrast, another cardiovascular program aimed primarily at adults, the Stanford Five-City Project, allowed for the examination of the media effects alone and did not show any differences between intervention and control communities in the prevalence of smoking that could be traced to the media component. There was evidence, however, of a strong secular trend that may have reduced the ability to detect effects (Winkleby et al. 1993).

Early reviews of the published literature focused heavily on the findings of some of the controlled field experiments on the effectiveness of community-based antismoking programs for youth. Some of these trials were able to randomize allocation to the media campaign (Bauman et al. 1991; Flay et al. 1995; Biglan et al. 2000a), and others used matched "unexposed" communities as controls (Flynn et al. 1992; Slater et al. 2006). These programs varied greatly in the length and intensity of exposure to the campaign message and the time to follow-up assessment.

Reviewing the available literature up to the early 1990s from controlled field trials and limited population-based evaluations, the 1994 Surgeon General's report on preventing tobacco use among young people emphasized that the mass media campaigns to prevent smoking by youth conducted up to that point were "meager" compared with the highly coordinated and well-funded marketing activities of the tobacco industry (USDHHS 1994). State agencies and volunteer organizations had conducted only "short-term efforts that have had limited evaluations" (USDHHS 1994, p. 150), and evaluations were completed on only a handful of the campaigns described in the report. Of the few reviewed experimental studies of different media strategies that had been conducted, only one had found a significant reduction in smoking among adolescents (Flynn et al. 1992).

Table 6.1 Summaries of controlled field trials of community-based mass media programs, by review(s)

Reviews that included the study/studies	Study	Design/population	Intervention description	Findings	Strengths, limitations, and comments
USDHHS 1994; Pechmann and Reibling 2000b; Friend and Levy 2002; Farrelly et al. 2003a; Wakefield et al. 2003b; Richardson et al. 2007; Angus et al. 2008; National Cancer Institute (NCI) 2008	Southeastern United States Study Bauman et al. 1988, 1991	Longitudinal sample of adolescents in probability sample of 12- to 14-year-olds was assessed for a number of attitudinal and smoking behavior variables at baseline and 11 and 17 months postintervention Prescreened standard metropolitan statistical areas (SMSAs) were randomly allocated (2 each) to 6 intervention (I) and 4 control (C) conditions Started in 1985 Number of subjects across SMSAs ranged from 132 to 232 (2,534 eligible)	C = no intervention I^1 = 11 radio antismoking messages I^2 = same as I^1 plus radio advertisement of a nonsmoking sweepstakes (encouraging communication with peers to discourage smoking) I^3 = same as I^2 plus television advertisement of the sweepstakes Lasted 15 months Messages reached 81% of intended audience on average 4.5 times in each of the 3- to 4-week periods	• Moderate effect of the radio campaign (I^1 and I^2) on expected consequences of smoking and friends' approval of smoking • No differences in smoking behavior detected at 11 and 17 months postintervention	Individual-level variation taken into account in analysis of SMSAs; selection of SMSAs was influenced by cost of advertising, legal restrictions (e.g., sweepstakes illegal in some areas), and need for nonoverlapping broadcast areas; salivary validation of smoking status was conducted

Table 6.1 Continued

Reviews that included the study/studies	Study	Design/population	Intervention description	Findings	Strengths, limitations, and comments
USDHHS 1994; Sowden 1998; Lantz et al. 2000; Pechmann and Reibling 2000a,b; Pechmann 2001; Farrelly et al. 2003a; Wakefield et al. 2003a,b; Schar et al. 2006; Richardson et al. 2007; Angus et al. 2008; NCI 2008	Vermont Study Worden et al. 1988, 1996 Flynn et al. 1992, 1994, 1995, 1997	Quasi-experimental 2 pairs of matched study communities assigned to intervention on the basis of available media markets Students in grades 4–6 Smoking behavior index, interpreted as the number of cigarettes smoked per week, any smoking in the past week, or smoking yesterday Longitudinal cohort of youth, randomly selected from metropolitan statistical areas, were surveyed at baseline and annually until 2 years postintervention; analyzed on both an individual and community basis Unclear whether community-level analysis accounted for individual-level variability	C = school-only antismoking educational program I = school-based education (same as C) plus television and radio antismoking media campaign Started in 1985; lasted 4 years	• At 2 years postintervention, students receiving the full intervention were significantly lower on the smoking index (41%), smoking last week (35%), and smoking yesterday (34%) than those receiving just the school curriculum • The combined program appeared particularly effective in high-risk youth	

Table 6.1 Continued

Reviews that included the study/studies	Study	Design/population	Intervention description	Findings	Strengths, limitations, and comments
USDHHS 1994; Sowden 1998; Pechmann and Reibling 2000b; Friend and Levy 2002; Wakefield et al. 2003b; Angus et al. 2008; NCI 2008	Television, School and Family Smoking Prevention and Cessation Project Flay et al. 1988, 1995; Brannon et al. 1989; Sussman et al. 1989	Schools in Los Angeles (35; 7 per condition) and San Diego (12; 6 per condition) randomly assigned to treatment conditions Started in 1986 and lasted 4 years Subjects: 12- to 14-year-olds Students assessed longitudinally, twice in grade 7 and once in each of grades 8 and 9 Smoking in the past week and ever smoking were analyzed	Los Angeles: C^1 = no treatment C^2 = basic health information curriculum only I^1 = school-based (social-resistance) education I^2 = television media intervention I^3 = school-based education plus television media intervention San Diego: C = no treatment I = school-based (social-resistance) education only (no television)	• No significant effects on smoking behavior (at 2-year follow-up) • Strong, significant effects on knowledge of smoking consequences, perceived prevalence of smoking, and efforts to resist trying cigarettes	Analysis accounted for individual variability within classrooms within schools

Table 6.1 Continued

Reviews that included the study/studies	Study	Design/population	Intervention description	Findings	Strengths, limitations, and comments
Sowden 1998; Farrelly et al. 2003a; Wakefield et al. 2003b; Jepson et al. 2006; Richardson et al. 2007; Angus et al. 2008; NCI 2008	Hafstad et al. 1996, 1997a,b; Hafstad 1997; Hafstad and Aarø 1997	Quasi-experimental One pair matched counties. Unknown basis for assignment to I or C Subjects: 14- to 15-year-old students; both males and females, but females were targeted Daily, weekly, less than weekly, occasional, or nonsmoker status analyzed with longitudinal assessment at 6–12 months and at 3 years (1 year after third campaign) Main analyses examined any current smoking with interaction effects of baseline status and gender Attrition slightly higher in C, but differential attrition not analyzed	C = no intervention I = 3 consecutive waves of mass media campaigns designed to prevent adolescent smoking (newspaper advertisements, poster, television spot, and cinema spot); each of the 3 waves had a different message focus and was broadcast for 3 weeks once a year Started in 1992 in Norway; lasted 3 years	Three-year follow-up: • Significant reduction in overall odds of being a smoker for I group compared with C group for boys and girls • Reduction in odds of smoking for baseline male and female smokers • Reduction in odds of smoking for baseline nonsmokers evident only for the girls	
Lantz et al. 2000; Pechmann and Reibling 2000b; Pechmann 2001; Farrelly et al. 2003a; Wakefield et al. 2003a,b; Angus et al. 2008; NCI 2008	Minnesota Heart Health Program (MHHP) Pentz et al. 1989b,d; Perry et al. 1992	Quasi-experimental 6th graders in all 13 grade schools in MHHP study community and matched control community in South Dakota Weekly prevalence of smoking and smoking intensity among students in all schools in each community were assessed annually (longitudinally through 3-year follow-up, and cross-sectionally) until their senior year in high school	C = no intervention I = health behavior and smoking prevention school program plus mass media focused on heart health, including smoking cessation Started in 1983; lasted 6 years	• Both 3-year longitudinal and cross-sectional results showed significantly less weekly smoking and lower smoking intensity for the students in the intervention community than in the control community; difference was present early and maintained through the senior year	Intraclass correlation considered in analyses; attrition analysis showed bias in favor of finding no effect

Table 6.1 Continued

Reviews that included the study/studies	Study	Design/population	Intervention description	Findings	Strengths, limitations, and comments
Lantz et al. 2000; Wakefield et al. 2003b; Angus et al. 2008; NCI 2008	Project Sixteen Biglan et al. 2000a	Eight matched pairs of small Oregon communities were randomly assigned to 1 of the 2 conditions Subjects: students in grades 7 and 9 Students in grade 7 and all students in grade 9 in all schools in each community were surveyed annually and cross-sectionally (preintervention, 3 times during intervention, postintervention) A composite measure of weekly smoking was evaluated	C = school intervention only I = school-plus-community intervention with paid antismoking media on radio, newspaper articles, and posters Messages based on social influences theories (health facts, refusal skills, modeling) Started in 1990; lasted 3 years	• Both at project completion and at 1-year follow-up, students in the school-plus-community intervention had significantly lower rates of past-week smoking	Analyses were nested students within communities; schools had to agree to implement prevention program and to be assessed; smoking status was validated by measuring carbon monoxide in expired air from students
Wakefield et al. 2003a,b; Angus et al. 2008; NCI 2008	North Karelia Vartiainen et al. 1986, 1990, 1998	Quasi-experimental 7th-grade students (12- to 13-year-olds) from 4 schools in North Karelia (intervention province) received school program for 2 years and were compared with 2 schools in a control province that did not receive it, starting in 1978 Schools were selected to match for various characteristics Smoking at least once or twice a month was assessed in the same cohort before and after intervention; additional follow-ups later	I^1 = peer-led social influences school program plus adult-focused mass media campaign plus community activities aimed at promoting cessation among adults I^2 = teacher-led social influences school program plus adult-focused mass media campaign plus community activities aimed at promoting cessation among adults Lasted 2 years	• At 4-year follow-up, smoking prevalence was significantly lower in both intervention groups relative to the comparison group • At 8- and 15-year follow-ups, smoking initiation rates were still lower for baseline nonsmokers in the intervention groups, with no difference in quit rates for baseline smokers	Some differences in follow-up rates not analyzed; analysis of simple proportions smoking at each follow-up

Table 6.1 Continued

Reviews that included the study/studies	Study	Design/population	Intervention description	Findings	Strengths, limitations, and comments
Wakefield et al. 2003a; Angus et al. 2008; NCI 2008	Stanford Five-City Project Fortmann et al. 1995; Winkleby et al. 1996	Quasi-experimental 2 pairs of matched communities in each condition Cross-sectional population surveys assessed prevalence of daily smoking before, during, and following the intervention Target: 12- to 24-year-olds	C = no intervention I = media advocacy and (primarily) adult-focused antismoking advertising Started in 1979; lasted 6 years	• At no time (1979–90) was there a difference in the prevalence of daily smoking between intervention and control communities	Strong secular trend was present
Richardson et al. 2007	Smith and Stutts 2006	Random assignment to conditions Over a semester, 235 Texas high school students were assigned to 1 of 9 messages x media conditions; in each condition, there were different executions of the message via TV, print, and Internet Baseline smoking behavior and self-classified smoking status (nonsmoker, smoker who quit, experimenter, or regular user) were compared with status at final follow-up	Short-term cosmetic effects, long-term health effects C = filler ads only (control) Presented in either TV, print, or Internet format All 3 ads' themes (in all 3 media) depicted 3 scenes of a boyfriend/girlfriend relationship in a high school setting in front of school lockers	• Those exposed to antismoking messages were less likely to smoke, had lower intentions to start smoking, and had greater intentions to quit than those not exposed	One of few studies to examine differential effects of different media
Angus et al. 2008	Chicago: culturally relevant program Kaufman et al. 1994	Quasi-experimental Grade 6 and 7 public school students from 3 predominantly African American inner city neighborhoods in Chicago were randomly assigned to intervention (2 schools, N = 131) or control (1 school, N = 76) Baseline and follow-up surveys at 1 week and 6 months postintervention conducted to measure the message's reach, substance use, knowledge about cigarettes, attitudes toward smoking, social support, and minor delinquency	C = media program only (newspaper curriculum, 8 radio announcements, call-in talk show, a rap contest, billboard contest) I = school-plus-media program	• Smoking rates between intervention and control were not significantly different at posttest or follow-up • Smoking rates for both intervention and control groups decreased significantly from pretest	Media intervention was not compared with a no-media control

Table 6.1 Continued

Reviews that included the study/studies	Study	Design/population	Intervention description	Findings	Strengths, limitations, and comments
NCI 2008	Multiple U.S. communities Slater et al. 2006	Randomization constrained Two schools in 8 no-media communities were randomly assigned to I^1 and I^2, and 2 schools in 8 media communities were randomly assigned to I^3 and I^4 Middle and junior high school students, mean age 12.2 years Longitudinal sample was measured pre-program, following curriculum, and twice thereafter	I^1 = no intervention I^2 = no community media, no in-school curricula I^3 = community media, no in-school media, curricula I^4 = community media, in-school media, curricula Communities were selected from all regions of the United States The 2-year media period was staggered for communities Started in 1999; ended in 2003	• Study evaluated uptake of marijuana, alcohol, and smoking. • The community-media intervention significantly reduced uptake rates for all substances • By survey 4, the lowest uptake rates were observed for condition I^4	Four-level model included time, student, school, and community

Table 6.1 Continued

Reviews that included the study/studies	Study	Design/population	Intervention description	Findings	Strengths, limitations, and comments
NCI 2008	Texas Tobacco Prevention Pilot Initiative Meshack et al. 2004	Random assignment of intervention level to communities contingent on having a unique media market The largest and most ethnically diverse school in each community was selected for evaluation; in some cases, 2 schools were selected; 11 schools evaluated altogether Subjects: students in grade 6 Eight sites selected for maximum ethnic diversity Pre-post cross-sectional school surveys evaluated student attitudes and tobacco use (any in the last 30 days) and susceptibility to smoking Preintervention survey was conducted in spring 2000 Various interventions took place during the summer and fall of 2000, with the postintervention survey of a new 6th-grade cohort in late fall 2000	C = no intervention I^1 = no program/no media I^2 = no program/low media I^3 = no program/intensive media I^4 = enhanced school/no media I^5 = enhanced school/low media I^6 = enhanced school/intensive media I^7 = multicomponent/low media I^8 = multicomponent/intensive media Started in 2000; lasted 6 months	• Combining the intensive or low media campaign with the multicomponent community program (I^7 or I^8) was most effective in suppressing positive attitudes toward smoking • Combining the intensive media campaign with the multicomponent community program (condition I^8) consistently reduced tobacco use, susceptibility to smoking, and prosmoking attitudes • Smoking was reduced more in I^2 than in I^3, but not tested against C	Analyses considered intraclass correlation within schools

Table 6.1 Continued

Reviews that included the study/studies	Study	Design/population	Intervention description	Findings	Strengths, limitations, and comments
Not previously reviewed	Solomon et al. 2009	Longitudinal analyses of exposure to campaign in 4 media markets in 4 states (Florida, South Carolina, Texas, Wisconsin), with 4 matched media markets as comparison communities Subjects: 2,030 adolescents, grades 7–10, who had smoked in the past 30 days at baseline school survey were recontacted to complete a baseline telephone survey (987 in intervention; 1,043 in control) and were surveyed annually for 3 years Measured smoking in past month, number of cigarettes smoked per day, demographic characteristics, number of other smokers in household, social norms, and intention to smoke in the next 30 days Used generalized mixed-model approach to account for similarities in response within individuals and within communities	I = radio/television campaign based on social-cognitive theory; social norms ads were developed and used Typically, 10 television and 15 radio ads were aired each year, with an estimated average of 380 gross ratings points per week over 9 months of each year C = unexposed matched comparison communities During the 3-year campaign, 68%, 62%, and 58% of those in the exposed condition reported seeing or hearing at least 1 sample ad broadcast	• Those in intervention communities had greater cessation rates (30-day point prevalence quit rate of 18.1%) than those in the control communities (14.8%) after the first year of the intervention • However, there were no further gains up to 3 years, with light and occasional smokers most likely to quit • The quit rate was 16% in the intervention community and 12.8% in the comparison group • Fewer ever smokers resumed smoking in the intervention community (59.4%) than in the control group (66.1%) • Increases in intent to smoke were similar across conditions • Social norms variables thought to mediate effects usually did not differ between groups across time • Those in the exposed group who had reported seeing at least 1 television message were less likely to have smoked in the past 30 days than those who had not seen any messages (54% vs. 62.6%) • No differences were found for those who had heard at least 1 radio message	Baseline rates of smoking in comparison group were higher at baseline, and therefore the condition effect at 3-year follow-up, in the absence of a time-by-condition interaction, may have been due to these higher baseline rates; having no effects from mediating variables provides no support for social cognitive theory; used an intent-to-treat method, assuming those who were lost at follow-up to have smoked at least 1 cigarette in the past 30 days, minimizing possible biased attrition effects; used analyses that accounted for similarities in within-individual responses and within-community responses

Note: **USDHHS** = U.S. Department of Health and Human Services.

Table 6.2 Summary of longitudinal and cross-sectional population-based studies examining the effects on youth of mass media antismoking campaigns

Reviews that included the study/studies	Study	Design/population	Description of intervention	Findings	Strengths, limitations, and comments
			Longitudinal studies		
Lantz et al. 2000; Pechmann and Reibling 2000a,b; Friend and Levy 2002; Farrelly et al. 2003a; Schar et al. 2006; Richardson et al. 2007; Angus et al. 2008; National Cancer Institute (NCI) 2008	Minnesota Murray et al. 1994	Cross-sectional pre-post surveys Minnesota youth were compared with unexposed Wisconsin youth Measured: recall, attitudes, and smoking behavior Expenditure approximately $2 million per year (NCI 2008, p. 433)	Minnesota's first stand-alone antismoking campaign Launched in 1986 and ran until 1990 Targeted youth TV, radio, print, billboard media Message aimed to increase awareness of negative social consequences of smoking and to change the social norms about smoking	• Small but statistically significant increase in exposure to antismoking messages, but no significant changes in attitudes or smoking behavior	Used a comparison group in another state; reach may have been a problem given the low campaign spending and only small increase in exposure to antismoking message

Table 6.2 Continued

Reviews that included the study/studies	Study	Design/population	Description of intervention	Findings	Strengths, limitations, and comments
Pechmann 2001; Siegel 2002; Farrelly et al. 2003a; Wakefield et al. 2003b; Schar et al. 2006; Richardson et al. 2007; Angus et al. 2008; NCI 2008	Florida Sly et al. 2001b	Longitudinal analyses 1,480 nonsmokers were followed up 5–10 months after a baseline survey, conducted within 6 months of the campaign launch Measured: exposure to any of the advertisements that had aired since the inception of the campaign, agreement with key campaign messages, attitudes, and initiation of smoking Controlled for month of the baseline survey, age, gender, whether the respondent had at least 1 friend who smoked, and whether the youth had a parent who smoked Mean monthly exposures of 12- to 17-year-olds to state antitobacco television advertising (target rating points [TRPs]): 1999 = 4.88; 2000 = 2.87; 2001 = 4.19; 2002 = 3.72; 2003 = 1.07 (NCI 2008, p. 437)	Part of Florida's antitobacco program Media campaign began in April 1998, and 12 ads were run during the first 10 months of the campaign Targeted youth who were susceptible to smoking Florida "truth" messages "attacked the [tobacco] industry and portrayed its executives as predatory, profit hungry, and manipulative" (Sly et al. 2001b, p. 233) Total media budget for first year was ~$26.5 million	• Those who scored higher on the exposure index were less likely to become smokers and established smokers	Controlled for a comprehensive set of potential baseline confounders; exposure index was a problem, as it relied on recall at follow-up; exposure index also a problem because it required agreement with a key campaign belief question that may mediate the pathway between exposure to the campaign and initiation of smoking

Table 6.2 Continued

Reviews that included the study/studies	Study	Design/population	Description of intervention	Findings	Strengths, limitations, and comments
Pechmann 2001; Farrelly et al. 2003a; Wakefield et al. 2003b; Richardson et al. 2007; Angus et al. 2008; NCI 2008	Massachusetts Siegel and Biener 2000	Longitudinal analyses 1,069 12- to 15-year-olds at baseline in October 1993–March 1994; 618 were contacted again at 4-year follow-up Measured: knowledge, attitudes, perception of youth smoking prevalence, and smoking behavior Baseline control variables: age group; gender; race; smoking status; exposure to smoking by parents, siblings, and friends; television viewing; and exposure to antismoking messages unrelated to the media campaign Mean monthly exposures of 12- to 17-year-olds to state antitobacco television advertising (TRPs): 1999 = 2.55; 2000 = 2.11; 2001 = 1.83; 2002 = 0.40; 2003 = 0.49 (NCI 2008, p. 437)	Part of Massachusetts antitobacco program that included an increase in the cigarette excise tax in January 1993 Media campaign was launched in October 1993 and ran until 2002 Messages targeted adults but consisted of television, radio spots, and billboards for the youth-focused media Messages aimed to highlight the negative consequences of smoking and positive consequences of quitting and to give advice about quitting	• Among all youth, there was no association between recall of media on 7 of the 8 knowledge and attitude outcomes • At 4-year follow-up, smoking initiation was significantly lower among those aged 12–13 years at baseline who recalled campaign messages than among those who did not • The 12- to 13-year-olds who recalled campaign messages at baseline were also more likely to have an accurate versus an inflated perception of the prevalence of youth smoking • There were no statistically significant effects for youth aged 14 or 15 years	Controlled for a comprehensive set of potential baseline confounders; baseline survey data included weights that reflected probability of each respondent's initial selection; demonstrated that recall of media messages at baseline was not associated with smoking status; analyses or weighting not used to adjust for nonresponse at follow-up; baseline assessment occurred just after the implementation of an increase in the cigarette excise tax

Table 6.2 Continued

Reviews that included the study/studies	Study	Design/population	Description of intervention	Findings	Strengths, limitations, and comments
Schar et al. 2006; Richardson et al. 2007; Angus et al. 2008; NCI 2008	Florida Sly et al. 2002	Longitudinal analyses 1,805 baseline nonsmokers who were followed up 22 months after launch Measured: self-reported exposure to any of the 11 advertisements that had aired since the inception of the campaign, agreement with key campaign messages, attitudes, and initiation of smoking Controls included age, gender, and how many of the respondent's best friends smoked (susceptibility) at baseline	As above	• The number of advertisements recalled, agreement with the key campaign message, and the industry attitude index were all associated with decreased initiation of smoking • Compared with those who recalled 0 ads, those who recalled 1 to 3 Florida "truth" ads were 23% more likely to have remained a nonsmoker and 22% less likely to become established smokers; those who recalled 4 or more ads were 71% more likely to have remained a nonsmoker and 91% less likely to have become established smokers, after controlling for influence of the message theme, tobacco attitudes/beliefs, age, gender, and susceptibility • Those with higher levels of agreement with campaign-targeted attitudes and beliefs at follow-up were 90% more likely to remain a nonsmoker and almost 4 times less likely to become established smokers than those with low levels of these attitudes	Controlled for a comprehensive set of potential baseline confounders; exposure measure was improved by separating recall from beliefs and smoking behavior; exposure index still relied on recall at follow-up; unlike the above study (Sly et al. 2001b), there was no control for parental smoking or the timing of the baseline survey

Table 6.2 Continued

Reviews that included the study/studies	Study	Design/population	Description of intervention	Findings	Strengths, limitations, and comments
Richardson et al. 2007	California Weiss et al. 2006	Longitudinal analyses Baseline and 3-year follow-up 2,292 middle school students completed self-report on exposure to protobacco and antitobacco media and smoking susceptibility	Part of California antitobacco program Media campaign launched in 1990 and still running Targeted youth and adults TV, radio, print, and billboard messages were aimed to change social norms about tobacco use and include secondhand smoke and anti-industry and cessation/prevention themes	• Increased levels of protobacco media exposure at baseline were positively associated with susceptibility, while increased levels of exposure to antitobacco media were associated with lower rates of smoking susceptibility	
Not previously reviewed	Ohio Evans et al. 2007	Longitudinal baseline and multiple postlaunch surveys of exposure to the Ohio Tobacco Use Prevention and Control Foundation's "Stand" campaign and affiliation with the "Stand" brand 1,657 11- to 17-year-old nonsmoking youth surveyed 2–6 weeks after launch (July to September 2003) and then followed up 8 and 20 months later Measured: smoking attitudes, beliefs, behavior, and affiliation with the "Stand" antitobacco brand Affiliation measures included dimensions of brand loyalty, leadership, personality, popularity, and awareness Controlled for gender, age, race/ethnicity, if 1 or more friends smoke, and smoking susceptibility	Ohio stand-alone "Stand" campaign/brand was launched in 2003 Television, radio, print, and billboard advertising as well as a Web site and Internet advertisements placed on external youth-targeted Web sites Targeted youth	• Those with greater campaign consistent attitudes and beliefs at baseline had lower levels of smoking initiation at the first 8-month follow-up and lower levels to a smaller degree at 20-month follow-up	Did not report any details of media campaign; measures were of "brand awareness"; controlled for a set of potential baseline confounders; differential attrition among older adolescents (who may be more likely to initiate smoking) vs. younger adolescents and among certain racial/ethnic groups; these attrition effects were analyzed but no adjustment was made for them in analyses or through weighting; participation rates were 74.8% for 1st follow-up and 66.7% for 2nd follow-up

Table 6.2 Continued

Reviews that included the study/studies	Study	Design/population	Description of intervention	Findings	Strengths, limitations, and comments
Cross-sectional studies: individual states					
USDHHS 1994; Lantz et al. 2000; Pechmann and Reibling 2000a; Pechmann 2001; Friend and Levy 2002; Siegel 2002; Farrelly et al. 2003a; Richardson et al. 2007; Angus et al. 2008; NCI 2008	California Popham et al. 1994	Cross-sectional pre- and postintervention surveys Grades 4–12 (N = 29,264) were surveyed in schools 3, 7, and 12 months after start of the California antitobacco program but before the media campaign, and 2, 6, and 11 months after the campaign launch Measured: self-reported exposure to campaign ads, tobacco use, smokers' intentions to quit, nonsmokers' intentions not to start, attitudes toward smoking Expenditures for campaign: 59¢ per capita 1989 to 1992–1993, 41¢ per capita 1993–1994 to 1995–1996 (NCI 2008, p. 446)	Part of California antitobacco program that also included tax increases Media campaign launched in 1990 and still running Targeted youth and adults TV, radio, print, billboard media Messages aimed to change social norms about tobacco use and included secondhand smoke, anti-industry and cessation/ prevention themes	• Positive changes in tobacco attitudes, intentions, and use from before the campaign to 2 months after the campaign launch • However, at the 12-month follow-up, there were no differences in prevalence of smoking and thinking about quitting between those exposed and those unexposed • Also, at the 12-month follow-up, comparisons of those who reported awareness of the campaign with those who did not indicated conflicting results; those exposed showed significantly more health-enhancing attitudes, but among the nonsmokers, more indicated they were thinking about starting to smoke; selective attention among nonsmokers susceptible to smoking may explain this result	Very large representative sample; no comparison group in other states; assessment used simple t-tests and did not control for potential confounding influences among those reporting and not reporting exposure; assessment occurred before the implementation of most other statewide tobacco control activities, but it followed a 25¢/pack increase in the cigarette excise tax; protobacco advertising directed at youth increased during the campaign

Table 6.2 Continued

Reviews that included the study/studies	Study	Design/population	Description of intervention	Findings	Strengths, limitations, and comments
Pechmann 2001; Siegel 2002; Farrelly et al. 2003a; Wakefield et al. 2003b; Schar et al. 2006; Richardson et al. 2007; Angus et al. 2008; NCI 2008	Florida Sly et al. 2001a	Multiple cross-sectional surveys 1,800 12- to 17-year-olds in Florida compared with 1,000 youth from the rest of the United States (excluding states that had preexisting campaigns), conducted between April 1998 and May 1999 Measured: recall, beliefs, smoking behaviors	As above 89% of youth reported seeing at least 1 of the Florida "truth" advertisements	• Florida youth had more favorable beliefs than those in the national sample by May 1999 • Current smoking declined but not significantly; however, significant decreases occurred in "ever tried" and percent open to smoking • The categories of ever trying, current smoking, and open to smoking among Florida youth compared favorably with national sample • The percentage who reported talking with friends about ads rose from 10% at baseline before the Florida "truth" campaign began, and when audience had been exposed to mild humorous public service announcements (PSAs), up to 34% after 1 year; those reporting the ads made them think increased from 28% to 61%	Control group of states without preexisting campaigns was included

Table 6.2 Continued

Reviews that included the study/studies	Study	Design/population	Description of intervention	Findings	Strengths, limitations, and comments
Friend and Levy 2002; Siegel 2002; Farrelly et al. 2003a; Wakefield et al. 2003b; Schar et al. 2006; NCI 2008	Florida Bauer et al. 2000	Cross-sectional prelaunch and postlaunch surveys More than 20,000 Florida students in more than 240 middle and high schools Surveys conducted before launch in 1998 and postlaunch in both 1999 and 2000 Measured: smoking susceptibility and behavior Mean monthly 12- to 17-year-olds' exposures (TRPs): 1999 = 4.88; 2000 = 2.87; 2001 = 4.19; 2002 = 3.72; 2003 = 1.07 (NCI 2008, p. 437)	Part of Florida's antitobacco program Media campaign began in April 1998 Targeted youth susceptible to smoking Florida "truth" messages "attacked the [tobacco] industry and portrayed its executives as predatory, profit hungry, and manipulative" (Sly et al. 2001b, p. 233)	• Over the 2-year period, both experimentation and current smoking declined markedly for both middle and high school students • Among never nonsmokers, there was a significant increase in those committed to never smoking • Among experimenters, there was a significant increase in those who said they would not smoke again	Very large representative sample used; no comparison group in other states
Richardson et al. 2007	California Unger et al. 2001	Cross-sectional survey Representative survey of 5,870 students in grade 8 Evaluated various measures of receptivity to tobacco marketing and recall and perceived effectiveness of protobacco and antitobacco marketing Sample weighted to represent California youth	As above	• Recognition and perceived persuasiveness of antitobacco marketing was highest among established smokers	

Table 6.2 Continued

Reviews that included the study/studies	Study	Design/population	Description of intervention	Findings	Strengths, limitations, and comments
Richardson et al. 2007; Angus et al. 2008; NCI 2008	Florida Niederdeppe et al. 2004	Multiple cross-sectional surveys 1,097 12- to 17-year-olds in Florida compared with 6,381 youth from the rest of the United States (excluding states with large-scale media campaigns in Arizona, California, Massachusetts, Mississippi, and Oregon), conducted between fall 2000 and spring 2001 Measured: recall, beliefs, smoking susceptibility, and smoking behavior	As above	• Florida adolescents were less likely than youth nationally to have smoked in the past 30 days, to have ever tried smoking, and to be open to smoking in the future (among never smokers) • Higher awareness of "truth" and antitobacco awareness than their national counterparts • Less favorable beliefs about cigarette companies than among youth nationally, but all other beliefs were similar	Control group of states without preexisting campaigns was included
Richardson et al. 2007	Kaiser Permanente and Group Health Northwest campaigns Seghers and Foland 1998	Cross-sectional pre- and postintervention survey ~300 students completed a written questionnaire, and ~200 students completed a telephone survey measuring recall and intention to quit	Kaiser Permanente and Group Health Northwest campaigns	• Intention to quit smoking in the next 30 days increased from 37% to 56% • Those aged less than 13 years increased their intention to quit smoking from 18% to 50% • Television ads were recalled more often than other formats	No information was provided on sampling, data analysis, and measurement methods
Richardson et al. 2007	Mississippi Reinert et al. 2004	Cross-sectional survey Representative survey of 1,151 students in grades 6–12 Structured interviews were conducted after implementation of media campaign against tobacco	Statewide antitobacco campaign in Mississippi	• Students who heard antitobacco messages from a variety of sources were less likely to use tobacco	Measures of use and intentions not clear

Table 6.2 Continued

Reviews that included the study/studies	Study	Design/population	Description of intervention	Findings	Strengths, limitations, and comments
NCI 2008	Minnesota Sly et al. 2005	Cross-sectional surveys ~1,100 12- to 17-year-olds surveyed between the summer of 2002 and winter of 2003 The last survey was conducted 5 months after the last advertisement aired Measured: self-reported awareness of campaign advertising and brand, attitudes, smoking susceptibility, intentions to smoke Mean monthly 12- to 17-year-old exposures (TRPs): 1999 = 0.02; 2000 = 1.91; 2001 = 4.62; 2002 = 2.99; 2003 = 2.70 (NCI 2008, p. 437)	Minnesota's second stand-alone campaign, "Target Market" Launched in 1999 and ran for 4 years to 2003 TV, radio, print, billboard media Targeted youth	• By the last survey, awareness of the advertising dropped from 59% to 50%, and awareness of the brand dropped from 85% to 57% • By the last survey, the 2 measures of smoking susceptibility increased, as did intentions to smoke in the next year, and scores on all 3 attitudinal scales decreased	Showed the absence of the campaign led to adverse changes; no comparison group in other states were examined
None	Not previously reviewed	Cross-sectional postintervention-only survey More than 900 12- to 18-year-olds who recalled at least 1 antismoking campaign ad were surveyed approximately 6 months after launch Control variables included age, gender, and race Also examined the effects of ever smoking and smoking by family and friends within the first step of the model	Wisconsin's first stand-alone antismoking campaign was launched in July 2001 and ran until December 2001 Television and radio Targeted middle and high school-age youth Messages: primary theme of industry deception and antismoking imagery; additional themes of addiction and "secondhand smoke kills" Cost: $6 million, or $1.21 per capita	• "Liking" the ad campaign predicted antismoking beliefs (agreement that tobacco industry is deceptive, secondhand smoke is harmful, smoking is addictive) and intentions to smoke	One postlaunch was the only survey; no comparison group in other states was used; used "liking" the campaign as predictor of beliefs and intentions

Table 6.2 Continued

Reviews that included the study/studies	Study	Design/population	Description of intervention	Findings	Strengths, limitations, and comments
Not previously reviewed	Florida Niederdeppe et al. 2008	Multiple cross-sectional surveys 5,010 12- to 18-year-olds surveyed for campaign recall, anti-industry beliefs, and nonsmoking intentions Assessed by using 5 waves of the Florida Antitobacco Media Evaluation survey from April 1998 to May 2000 Control measures included demographics, smoking in the home and degree of parental smoking, and parental monitoring Rates of change were examined by using an interrupted time-series technique before and after the Florida Tobacco Control Program budget cuts	Florida's "truth" campaign Budget cuts occurred between waves 3 and 4 of the survey (between May 1999 and September 1999)	• Upward trends in recall and nonsmoking intentions were reduced after budget cuts to the Florida "truth" campaign	This study provides evidence that reductions in tobacco control funding have immediate effects on program exposure and cognitive precursors to initiation of smoking
Not previously reviewed	Wisconsin Tangari et al. 2007	Cross-sectional surveys 901 Wisconsin 12- to 18-year-olds were asked in a telephone survey whether they recalled any of the ads in 4 antismoking campaigns aired (*Mohammed, FACT, Janet Sachman, Patrick Reynolds*) Those who recalled ads were then asked about their attitudes toward the campaign and their perceptions of the ad message's strength Controlled for race/ethnicity, age, head of household's education, gender, and trial of smoking	Targeted adolescents and adults Five ads were based on the following themes: tobacco industry's deceptive practices, addictiveness of smoking, harm of secondhand smoke $6.5 million was allocated over a 7-month period	• Attitudes toward the campaign were positively related to antismoking beliefs, with this effect stronger among those who had tried smoking • A greater number of advertisements recalled was positively associated with most antismoking beliefs • Attitude toward the campaign and number of campaign ads recalled were significantly associated with lower intentions to smoke • Perceptions of strength of the argument were not significantly associated with intentions to smoke	Controlled for demographics and smoking experience; post-intervention-only survey

Table 6.2 Continued

Reviews that included the study/studies	Study	Design/population	Description of intervention	Findings	Strengths, limitations, and comments
		Cross-sectional studies: multistate			
Richardson et al. 2007; Angus et al. 2008 NCI 2008	U.S. state campaigns Hersey et al. 2003	Cross-sectional survey Random sample of 6,875 12-to 24-year-olds from California, Florida, and Massachusetts, with enhanced representation of African Americans, Asians, Hispanics, and Latinos conducted in winter 1999–2000 Examined a theoretical model that predicted that campaign-related beliefs mediated the effects of the impact of the American Legacy Foundation (Legacy) "truth" campaign Weighted the sample to allow for comparisons across surveys. Structural equation modeling was used to examine a theoretical model that predicted that campaign-related beliefs mediated the effects of the impact of the "truth" campaign on smoking status Controlled for age, gender, and race/ethnicity	States that ran the Legacy "truth" campaign	• Adolescents from "counter-industry" states were more likely to agree with campaign-targeted beliefs that cigarette companies lie, cigarette companies try to get young people to smoke, and cigarette companies deny that cigarettes are addictive	

Table 6.2 Continued

Reviews that included the study/studies	Study	Design/population	Description of intervention	Findings	Strengths, limitations, and comments
Richardson et al. 2007; Angus et al. 2008; NCI 2008	U.S. state campaigns Emery et al. 2005	Multiple cross-sectional surveys linked exposure to state antismoking commercials Nationally representative Monitoring the Future (MTF) surveys of students in grades 8 (N = 19,043), 10 (N = 16,131), and 12 (N = 15,911) from 1999 and 2000 Used data on commercial ratings from Nielsen Media Research to calculate a measure of audience exposure to antismoking advertising across the 75 largest media markets for 1999–2000 Controlled for other tobacco-related advertisements and a comprehensive set of potential confounding influences, such as demographics, family structure, parents' education, average state cigarette prices, laws on clean indoor air, and secular trends	Various state-based campaigns Various targets	• Exposure to at least 1 state-funded antismoking advertisement in the previous 4 months was associated with lower perceived rates of friends' smoking, greater perceived harm of smoking, stronger intentions not to smoke in the future, and lower likelihood of being a smoker	Multiple large nationally representative surveys; controlled for a comprehensive set of potential confounders, including other tobacco-related advertisements, prices, laws on clean indoor air, and secular trends; could not control for preexisting correlations between levels of smoking and number and frequency of ads aired in each region; actual exposure was estimated rather than directly measured
Richardson et al. 2007; Angus et al. 2008; NCI 2008	U.S. state campaigns Hersey et al. 2005a	Cross-sectional survey National survey of 15,452 12- to 17-year-olds; survey oversampled African Americans, Asians, Hispanics, Latinos, and adolescents from states with active tobacco counter-marketing campaigns; survey was conducted 8 months and 15 months after the launch of the Legacy "truth" campaign Structural equation modeling was used to examine a theoretical model that predicted that campaign-related beliefs mediated the effects of the impact of the "truth" campaign on smoking status	States that ran the Legacy "truth" campaign	• Youth in markets with higher levels of campaign exposure were more likely to agree with beliefs and attitudes targeted by the campaign • Higher levels of cumulative exposure to the Legacy "truth" campaign were associated with less favorable beliefs about the tobacco industry that were targeted by the campaign and with lower values on a smoking status continuum	

Table 6.2 Continued

Reviews that included the study/studies	Study	Design/population	Description of intervention	Findings	Strengths, limitations, and comments
Richardson et al. 2007; Angus et al. 2008; NCI 2008	U.S. state campaigns Hersey et al. 2005b	Cross-sectional multiple surveys National survey of 12- to 17-year-olds that oversampled African Americans, Asians, Hispanics, and Latinos: N = 3,424 at phase 1 in November 1999 to January 2000 before the launch of the national Legacy "truth" campaign; N = 12,967 at phase 2 (autumn 2000–spring 2001); N = 10,855 at phase 3 (spring 2002–autumn 2002) Compared rates of decline in youth smoking between (1) states with long, well-funded counter-industry campaigns (California, Florida, Massachusetts); (2) states with more recently funded counter-industry campaigns (Indiana, Minnesota, Mississippi, New Jersey); and (3) other states Controlled for demographic (age, gender, race/ethnicity) differences between states, number of parents in home, attendance at religious services, employment status, average weekly earnings, and media-use variables (average daily television hours, average daily radio hours) as well as exposure to other elements of state tobacco control programs (taxes, laws on clean indoor air, awareness of community antitobacco groups, exposure to school antitobacco curricula) Also included controls for number of months since baseline survey, the population media market, and launch of the national "truth" campaign	States that ran the Legacy "truth" campaign	• Between 1999 and 2002, rates of current and established smoking decreased significantly faster in states with established and newly funded counterindustry campaigns (52.6%) than in other states (24.9%) after controlling for demographic differences • Over time, campaign-targeted beliefs showed an increasingly strong relationship with smoking status in campaign states	Multiple surveys; addressed missing data and response rates; accounted for confounders; reported reliability of measurement methods

Table 6.2 Continued

Reviews that included the study/studies	Study	Design/population	Description of intervention	Findings	Strengths, limitations, and comments
Richardson et al. 2007; Angus et al. 2008	U.S. state campaigns Johnston et al. 2005	Multiple cross-sectional surveys Nationally representative MTF surveys of students in grades 8 (N = 29,724), 10 (N = 24,639), and 12 (N = 12,138) from 1997 to 2001 Self-reported recall of antismoking advertising was measured, as were judged impact and perceived exaggeration of such advertising Controlled for ethnicity, gender, academic grades, parental education level, frequency of media use, and residence in states that had existing comprehensive media campaigns in effect at least 2 months before survey	Various state-based and national campaigns Various targets	• Among those who had recalled antismoking advertising, there were significant increases in perceptions that these ads made them less likely to smoke but also in perceptions that ads exaggerated the dangers or risks of smoking; both especially increased among students in grade 8 • There was no increase in judged impact for non-tobacco-control states until 2000, suggesting no significant increase associated with the Philip Morris campaign, which began in late 1998 • There were significant increases in overall exposure to antismoking advertising from 1997 to 2001 • Recall was highest in states with active campaigns at baseline and especially for grade 12 in these states; this effect diminished in 2001 once a number of new statewide and national campaigns had begun	Multiple nationally representative surveys; controlled for a comprehensive set of potential confounders, including frequency of media use and residence in states that had existing comprehensive media campaigns in effect at least 2 months before surveying; also included weights to account for multistage sampling procedures

Table 6.2 Continued

Reviews that included the study/studies	Study	Design/population	Description of intervention	Findings	Strengths, limitations, and comments
NCI 2008	U.S. state campaigns Emery et al. 2005	Cross-sectional multiple surveys linked to exposure to state antismoking commercials Nationally representative MTF surveys of students in grades 8 (N = 25,800), 10 (N = 20,800), and 12 (N = 19,927) from 1999 and 2000 Used commercial ratings data from Nielsen Media Research to calculate a measure of audience exposure to antismoking advertising across the 75 largest media markets for 1999–2000 Controlled for other tobacco-related advertisements and a comprehensive set of potential confounding influences, such as demographics, family structure, parents' education, average state cigarette prices, laws on clean indoor air, and secular trends	Various state-based campaigns Various targets	• Exposure to at least 1 state antitobacco ad within the previous 4 months, compared with lower exposure, was associated with lower odds of current smoking, decreased perceptions that friends smoke, and stronger intentions not to smoke • These findings were generally consistent across different gender and racial/ethnic groups	Multiple nationally representative surveys; controlled for a comprehensive set of potential confounders, including other tobacco-related advertisements, prices, laws on clean indoor air, and secular trends; also controlled for preexisting correlations between levels of smoking and number and frequency of ads aired in each region; actual exposure was estimated rather than directly measured

Table 6.2 Continued

Reviews that included the study/studies	Study	Design/population	Description of intervention	Findings	Strengths, limitations, and comments
Cross-sectional studies: national campaign					
Lantz et al. 2000; Schar et al. 2006; NCI 2008	Fairness Doctrine Lewit et al. 1981	Analyses of cross-sectional surveys 6,768 of 12- to 17-year-olds surveyed between March 1966 and March 1970 Measured: self-reported smoking behavior (current smoking status and number of cigarettes smoked/day) and various measures of exposure to antismoking advertisements Proxy measure of exposure to ads was estimated from the number of antismoking commercials that aired in a given year and the number of hours per day that each youth spent watching television Controlled for cigarette prices, family income, family size, employment status, family structure, parents' education, age, gender, race, and exposure to prosmoking messages	United States Fairness Doctrine requires 1 antismoking ad for every 3 tobacco industry ads Targeted a general audience Messages in this campaign were primarily about the health consequences of smoking	• Prevalence of youth smoking was between 3.0 and 3.4 percentage points lower during the Fairness Doctrine period than during the 16 months before the initiation of the doctrine • Youth who watched more television during the Fairness Doctrine era were less likely to smoke cigarettes • The proxy measure for the number of antismoking messages seen was statistically and negatively associated with a lower probability of smoking; however, the squared term for this proxy had a positive and significant effect on smoking, indicating that this impact was subject to diminishing returns • No effects were found for number of cigarettes smoked per day, but this is not surprising considering that many youth are not yet addicted smokers	Pioneered measures of potential exposure; actual exposure was estimated rather than directly measured

Table 6.2 Continued

Reviews that included the study/studies	Study	Design/population	Description of intervention	Findings	Strengths, limitations, and comments
Farrelly et al. 2003a; Schar et al. 2006; Richardson et al. 2007; Angus et al. 2008; NCI 2008	Legacy campaign Farrelly et al. 2002	Cross-sectional prelaunch and postlaunch surveys National sample of 12- to 17-year-olds (N = 3,439 survey 1; N = 6,233 survey 2) from the Legacy survey Enhanced representation of African Americans, Asians, and Hispanics Baseline before launch and a 10-month follow-up Measured: recall, attitudes, beliefs, and smoking intentions	Legacy's national "truth" campaign Launched in 2000 Targeted youth At 10 months postlaunch of Legacy survey, 75% had seen at least 1 specific campaign ad	• Increase in proportion agreeing with campaign-targeted beliefs • Significant reductions in intention to smoke in future • Awareness of ad associated with greater anti-industry attitudes and beliefs • Exposure to Philip Morris' "Think. Don't Smoke" campaign was associated with an increase in intentions to smoke	Multiple measures used
Jepson et al. 2006; Richardson et al. 2007; Angus et al. 2008; NCI 2008	Australia's national tobacco campaign White et al. 2003	Cross-sectional surveys of youth: 1 national telephone survey of 14- to 17-year-olds and 1 school-based survey of 12- to 17-year-olds Measured: campaign recognition, beliefs, smoking behavior	Australia's national tobacco campaign was launched in 1997 and ran until 1997–2003 Targeted adults aged 18–39 years of age Used fear- and disgust-evoking messages that graphically depicted the short-term consequences of smoking: "Every cigarette is doing you damage" In addition, 1 ad showed a smoker calling the quitline	• Recognition of campaign was high (90% or greater) • High agreement with campaign-related beliefs • Compared with never smokers, a higher proportion of those who had ever smoked took at least 1 action; among established smokers, 27% cut down, 26% were thinking about quitting, 18% tried to quit, but 42% did nothing	No comparison group in other states was possible; single surveys after launch of campaign

Table 6.2 Continued

Reviews that included the study/studies	Study	Design/population	Description of intervention	Findings	Strengths, limitations, and comments
Schar et al. 2006; Richardson et al. 2007; Angus et al. 2008; NCI 2008	Legacy campaign Farrelly et al. 2005	Cross-sectional survey linked to exposure to state antismoking commercials Nationally representative MTF surveys of students in grades 8, 10, and 12 (N ~50,000) conducted each spring from 1997 to 2002 Estimated the prevalence of youth smoking as a function of the "truth" campaign's intensity measured at the media market level Used commercial ratings data from Nielsen Media Research to calculate a measure of audience exposure to antismoking advertising	As above	• Significant decline in smoking prevalence • Average annual percentage decline: 1997–1999 = -3.2%; 2000–2002 = -6.8% • Prevalence of smoking among students in grades 8, 10, and 12 combined declined from 28% to 18% between 1997 and 2002 • The Legacy "truth" campaign accounted for approximately 22% of this decline • This effect strengthened over time and, as expected, had little effect in the early months after the campaign's launch • For all grades, there was a significant dose-response relationship between the exposure to the "truth" campaign and the current prevalence of youth smoking (OR = 0.78; 95% CI, 0.63–0.97, $p < 0.05$)	Examined effects of campaign intensity; controlled for a comprehensive set of potential confounders and preexisting levels of smoking in each of the U.S. media markets; relied on self-reported measures of youth smoking; note that Messeri et al. 2007 chemically validated smoking status in a school setting and found a low rate of underreporting, which was not related to recall of the "truth" campaign

Table 6.2 Continued

Reviews that included the study/studies	Study	Design/population	Description of intervention	Findings	Strengths, limitations, and comments
Angus et al. 2008	Australia's national tobacco campaign Edwards et al. 2004	Quasi-experimental 2,038 12- to 17-year-old females attending cinemas in New South Wales, Australia, were surveyed about attitudes toward smoking in movies and their intentions to smoke in the future after viewing a movie with or without a 30-second antismoking ad before the movie was shown	Australia's National Tobacco Campaign "tar" antismoking ad, which graphically demonstrates the damage smoking does by pouring a beaker of tar over a lung, was used in the exposure condition with an altered voice-over from a popular soap opera star emphasizing that she and most other actors do not smoke	• Significantly more nonsmokers exposed to the antismoking message thought that the smoking in the movie was "not OK" than those not exposed; however, there were no differences between groups in smoking intentions • For smokers, there were no differences between groups in perception that the smoking in the movie was "not OK"; however, significantly more smokers in the exposed group were unlikely to smoke in the next 12 months than in the control group	
NCI 2008	Legacy campaign Evans et al. 2004a	Cross-sectional pre- and postintervention launch surveys National sample of 12- to 17-year-olds (N = 20,058) from 3 waves of the Legacy survey from 1999 to 2001; enhanced representation of African Americans, Asians, and Hispanics Using structural equation modeling, aimed to examine relationships between exposure to "truth" campaign, differences in social images about not smoking, related measures, and smoking behavior	Legacy's national "truth" campaign Launched in 2000 Targeted youth	• Model showed satisfactory fit where social imagery and perceived tobacco independence mediated the relationship between exposure to "truth" campaign and smoking status	

Table 6.2 Continued

Reviews that included the study/studies	Study	Design/population	Description of intervention	Findings	Strengths, limitations, and comments
NCI 2008	Legacy campaign Thrasher et al. 2004	Cross-sectional precampaign and multiple postcampaign launch surveys of 12- to 17-year-olds from the nationally representative Legacy survey Examined attitudes in tobacco-producing states compared with non-tobacco-producing states with low, medium, and high funding	As above	• No significant differences in how antitobacco attitudes changed over time among the different state groups • Concluded that response to the campaign was not influenced by residence in a tobacco-producing state	
Not previously reviewed	Australia's national tobacco campaign White et al. 2008a	Triennial cross-sectional national studies of representative random samples of secondary students, 12–17 years of age, were conducted from 1987 to 2005 Numbers ranged from 19,203 in 1987 to 29,853 in 1996 Self-reported anonymous surveys assessed cigarette use in the past month, week (current smokers), and on at least 3 of the previous 7 days (committed smokers) Students' residential postcodes were collected, and the Index of Relative Socioeconomic Disadvantage associated with each postcode determined socioeconomic status (SES) quartiles	Australia's National Tobacco Campaign was launched in 1997 and ran until 2002–2003 Campaign targeted adults 18–39 years of age Campaign used fear- and disgust-evoking messages that graphically depicted the short-term consequences of smoking, "Every cigarette is doing you damage"; in addition, 1 ad showed a smoker calling the quitline	• Over the period 1987–2005, the prevalence of smoking among Australian adolescents at school increased and then decreased, with a large decrease between 1996 and 2005—a period coinciding with the third phase of tobacco control activity in Australia • No significant change occurred between 1987 and 1990 for either younger or older students • Between 1990 and 1996, the proportion of younger and older students involved with smoking increased significantly • Among younger students, the increase in monthly and weekly smoking was greater among lower-SES students (p for interactions <0.05) • Between 1996 and 2005, the prevalence of monthly and weekly smoking decreased significantly among both younger and older students, and these decreases were consistent across SES groups	Well-funded, population-based tobacco control programs can be effective in reducing smoking among students from all SES groups

Table 6.2 Continued

Reviews that included the study/studies	Study	Design/population	Description of intervention	Findings	Strengths, limitations, and comments
Not previously reviewed	Legacy campaign Thrasher et al. 2006	Used data from a nationally representative survey of 10,035 adolescents, 12 to 17 years of age, to test whether reactions to anti-industry ads, the attitudes these ads targeted, and the relationship between these attitudes and smoking differed by social bonding and sensation-seeking risk factors	As above	• Results indicated that reactions to anti-industry ads and the strength of anti-industry attitudes were comparable between adolescents with high levels of sensation seeking and those with low levels • Weakly bonded adolescents had less favorable reactions to ads and weaker anti-industry attitudes than did strongly bonded adolescents • Social bonding also moderated the influence of sensation seeking on reactions to anti-industry ads, such that sensation seeking had a positive influence among more strongly bonded adolescents and no influence among weakly bonded adolescents • Finally, the relationship between anti-industry attitudes and smoking appeared consistent across risk groups, whether risk was defined using social bonding, sensation seeking, or the interaction between the 2 factors	Overall, these results suggest that anti-industry messages are a promising strategy for preventing smoking among high- and low-risk adolescents alike

Note: **CI** = confidence interval; **OR** = odds ratio; **USDHHS** = U.S. Department of Health and Human Services.

Table 6.3 Controlled exposure and naturalistic exposure studies examining the relative effectiveness of different advertising messages for youth

Reviews that included the study/ studies	Study	Design/population	Comparison of advertisements	Findings	Strengths, limitations, and comments
Controlled exposure studies					
Lantz et al. 2000; Pechmann and Reibling 2000b; Pechmann 2001; Siegel 2002; Farrelly et al. 2003a; Wakefield et al. 2003b; Schar et al. 2006; DeCicca et al. 2008a; National Cancer Institute (NCI) 2008	Goldman and Glantz 1998	Controlled exposure Reviewed results of 186 focus groups involving >1,500 children and adults who examined 188 different advertisements and ad concepts from California, Massachusetts, and Michigan	8 themes were compared: industry manipulation, secondhand smoke, addiction, cessation, youth access, short-term effects, long-term health effects, and romantic rejection	• Industry manipulation and secondhand smoke were judged as the most effective themes to use for youth in denormalizing smoking • Addiction messages were average, but when addiction was combined with industry manipulation, it was judged as effective for youth • Short-term effects, long-term health effects, and romantic rejection were judged as not effective for youth	Study has been criticized for failing to provide transparent criteria for how "effectiveness" was determined (Worden et al. 1998; Connolly et al. 1998)
Pechmann 2001; Farrelly et al. 2003a; Schar et al. 2006; Richardson et al. 2007; NCI 2008	Pechmann et al. 2003	Controlled exposure, random assignment 1,129 students in grades 7 and 10 grouped 194 ads into 7 distinct themes 1,667 students in grades 7 and 10 were randomly assigned to view 1 message theme, after which they were asked about their feelings and thoughts in relation to the advertisements, attitudes toward smoking, and intention to smoke	56 advertisements in total were shown; each ad was categorized into 7 antitobacco advertisement themes: disease and death, endangers others, cosmetic effects, smokers' negative life circumstances, role model of refusal skills, marketing tactics, and selling disease and death	• Industry manipulation and secondhand smoke were judged as the most effective themes to use for youth in denormalizing smoking • Addiction messages were average, but when addiction was combined with industry manipulation, it was judged as effective for youth • Short-term effects, long-term health effects, and romantic rejection were judged as not effective for youth	Study has been criticized for failing to provide transparent criteria for how "effectiveness" was determined (Worden et al. 1998; Connolly et al. 1998)
Pechmann and Reibling 2000b; Siegel 2002; Wakefield et al. 2003b (includes earlier unpublished version of Pechmann and Goldberg Study)	Pechmann and Goldberg 1998			• Impact of smoking on babies and children, smoking is socially unacceptable, and nonsmoking is the norm; these topics significantly influenced youth's reported intentions to smoke • Tobacco industry marketing practices and health consequences of smoking had no effect	

Table 6.3 Continued

Reviews that included the study/ studies	Study	Design/population	Comparison of advertisements	Findings	Strengths, limitations, and comments
Pechmann and Reibling 2000b; Pechmann 2001; Siegel 2002; Wakefield et al. 2003b; Schar et al. 2006; NCI 2008	Teenage Research Unlimited 1999	Controlled exposure 20 focus groups of students in grades 7–10 (N = 120) who were susceptible to using tobacco in Arizona, California, and Massachusetts Youths viewed each of 10 ads and evaluated the main message and how much the ad would make them "stop and think" about not smoking; they discussed the ads as a group	10 ads produced by state tobacco control programs in Arizona, California, Florida, and Massachusetts and by Philip Morris Ads were categorized into 8 message themes, 2 executional styles, and by target group (youth vs. general audience)	• Advertisements portraying the serious negative consequences of smoking in either a graphically or dramatically emotional way were rated most highly • Advertisements using an industry manipulation theme were rated high in terms of "stop and think" by respondents in California only, where these themes were familiar to participants • Advertisements with a theme emphasizing that adolescents need to make a choice about whether to smoke had the lowest ratings	Used a variety of scales to measure response to ads
Schar et al. 2006; NCI 2008	Murphy 2000	Controlled exposure and focus groups 285 youth aged 11–18 years were exposed to 35 spots on primary and secondary prevention Youth ranked their top 10 ads based on attention getting and being most likely to affect intention to maintain smoke-free status or consider quitting Subsequently, 8 focus groups were conducted in Utah to examine which of the identified ads were most thought provoking and likely to result in a behavioral intention to not smoke or to quit	The top 10 ads were identified using the controlled exposure: *Voice Box*, *Cowboy*, *Bad Influence*, *Janet Sackman*, *Cattle*, *Pam Laffin*, *Smart Dog*, *Camel*, *Girlfriend*, and *Maggots*	• The testimonial ads from people who have suffered diseases and disabilities (*Voice Box*, *Cowboy*, *Pam Laffin*, *Janet Sackman*) were more thought provoking and likely to result in a behavioral intention to not smoke or to quit • *Bad Influence* was also rated highly among those who were concerned about their influence over younger siblings • The *Camel*, *Girlfriend*, and *Smart Dog* ads were rated as average and seen as not affecting viewers' behavior • The cessation theme ad *Quit* was rated low	Convenience sample; focus groups' evaluation did not use standardized validated instruments to measure comparative effectiveness

Table 6.3 Continued

Reviews that included the study/ studies	Study	Design/population	Comparison of advertisements	Findings	Strengths, limitations, and comments
Richardson et al. 2007	Devlin et al. 2007	Controlled exposure 12 focus groups of students in grades 7–9 (3 or 4 youth in each group) who were either experimenters or regular smokers from 3 regions in England Youth were exposed to 3–4 ads for each of 3 message themes chosen by the moderator from a pool of 16 ads in total Youth discussed their views, attitudes, and behaviors in response to different types of message themes	3 message themes were explored: appeals to fear, social norms, and industry manipulation	• Ads appealing to fear appeared to be effective in evoking strong emotional "shock" emotions and motivation to think about giving up; however, many distanced themselves from the type of smoker portrayed (adult, long-term smoker) • Social norms ads were most effective with those who had just started experimenting; more committed smokers were less likely to identify with images that portrayed smokers and smoking negatively—these were in contrast to their experience • Industry manipulation provided new information that led to greater interest; however, comprehension was a barrier, with many needing the ideas explained	
Richardson et al. 2007	Grandpre et al. 2003	Controlled exposure 612 students in grades 4, 7, and 10 attending 22 different schools were randomly assigned to message condition and then answered a series of evaluation questions	Students were assigned to 1 of 4 message conditions: explicit vs. implicit x antitobacco vs. protobacco messages	• More negative evaluation was given to the source of protobacco messages than the source of antismoking messages • Implicit messages resulted in more positive source evaluation than did explicit messages • Students in grade 7 had the most positive evaluations	
Richardson et al. 2007	Henriksen et al. 2006	Controlled exposure 832 school students in California, aged 14–17 years, were randomly exposed to 5 ads Measures included perception of the ads, intention to smoke, and attitudes toward tobacco companies, as measured immediately after exposure	Five tobacco company ads on preventing smoking among youth (Philip Morris or Lorillard, Inc.), 5 Legacy "truth" antitobacco ads, or 5 ads about preventing drunk driving	• Participants rated tobacco company ads on preventing smoking among youth less favorably than Legacy "truth" ads	

Table 6.3 Continued

Reviews that included the study/ studies	Study	Design/population	Comparison of advertisements	Findings	Strengths, limitations, and comments
Richardson et al. 2007	Kim 2006	Controlled exposure 142 nonsmoking male students from South Korea (mean age 16) were randomly assigned to message condition The study examined the role of regulatory focus in the effectiveness of message framing in antitobacco ads After exposure, persuasiveness was measured	2 (goal priming: promotion vs. prevention) x 2 (message frame: promotion vs. prevention), between-subjects design	• Lower intentions to smoke, lower perceived pharmacologic benefits of smoking, and lower perceived psychological benefits of smoking were found when the fit between regulatory goal and the message frame was congruent	
Richardson et al. 2007	Niederdeppe et al. 2005	Controlled exposure 820 U.S. youth aged 13–18 years completed an Internet-delivered baseline questionnaire assessing susceptibility to smoking and sensation seeking They then viewed 5 randomly ordered antitobacco ads and completed 6 individual ratings of each ad These ratings were summed to provide composite ratings of the ads	Three ads from the American Legacy Foundation (Legacy) "truth" campaign (*Body Bags*, *Daily Dose*, and *Shredder*), 1 ad from Philip Morris (*My Reasons*), and 1 ad from a state tobacco control program (result not reported) were compared	• Participants in all smoking risk categories rated Legacy's *Body Bags* and *Daily Dose* more highly than Philip Morris' *My Reasons* and Legacy's *Shredder* • Compared with the 2 highest-ranking Legacy ads, the Philip Morris ad received favorable ratings among 13- to 15-year-olds at lowest risk for future smoking, but 16- to 18-year-olds at elevated risk for future smoking responded significantly less favorably	
Richardson et al. 2007	Smith and Stutts 2006	Controlled exposure Random assignment to conditions Over a semester, 235 Texas high school students were assigned to 1 of 9 messages x media conditions In each condition, there were 3 different executions of the message Baseline self-classified smoking status (experimenter or regular user) was compared with status at final follow-up	Short-term cosmetic effects, long-term health effects, or filler ads only (control) were presented in either TV, print, or Internet format All 3 ads' themes (in all 3 media) depicted 3 scenes of a boyfriend-girlfriend relationship in a high school setting in front of school lockers	• Cosmetic ads and health ads were similarly effective in making youth less likely to smoke; however, ads about health effects were more effective in lowering intentions to start smoking and increasing intentions to quit	Random assignment to different message themes

Table 6.3 Continued

Reviews that included the study/ studies	Study	Design/population	Comparison of advertisements	Findings	Strengths, limitations, and comments
NCI 2008	Donovan et al. 2006	Controlled exposure 257 14- to 18-year-old Australian youth recruited through interception of shoppers were exposed to a tobacco industry ad on preventing smoking among youth or a tobacco control ad, after which they completed ratings of the impact of the ad on their smoking	Three tobacco industry ads on preventing smoking among youth produced and adapted for MTV in Australia, 2 youth-directed tobacco control ads featuring smoking not being cool or short-term harms of smoking (shown to 14- and 15-year-olds only), and several tobacco control ads portraying smoking as disgusting	• Among 14- and 15-year-olds, tobacco industry ads generally scored lower than the tobacco control ads that portrayed smoking as disgusting, but they were rated similarly to the other youth-focused tobacco control ads • Among 16- to 18-year-olds, the tobacco industry ads were rated as having less impact than the disgust-oriented tobacco control ads in terms of not wanting to smoke and, among smokers, in thinking about quitting	
NCI 2008	Henriksen and Fortmann 2002	Controlled exposure 218 18- to 25-year-old undergraduate students in California were randomly assigned to view 4 ads; they completed baseline ratings of various companies, viewed and rated each ad, and then made final ratings of various companies	4 Philip Morris ads on preventing smoking among youth, 4 Philip Morris ads about charitable works, or 4 Anheuser-Busch ads about preventing underage drinking (the control group), and several Pfizer and Chevron ads concerning community service	• Philip Morris' ads on preventing youth smoking and on charitable works were rated less favorably by those who knew Philip Morris was a tobacco company than by those who were unaware of that fact • Ads about Philip Morris' charitable works received more favorable ratings than did Philip Morris' ads on preventing youth smoking	

Table 6.3 Continued

Reviews that included the study/studies	Study	Design/population	Comparison of advertisements	Findings	Strengths, limitations, and comments
Richardson 2008; NCI 2008	Pechmann and Reibling 2006	Controlled exposure 1,725 9th-grade students in California were randomly assigned to view 1 of 9 videotapes containing a television program in which particular themed advertisements or control advertisements were embedded At baseline, personality traits were measured; after exposure, students were asked about smoking intentions, feelings and beliefs, and appraisal of advertisement	8 types of advertisements, including serious health effects of smoking (disease and suffering); tobacco industry manipulation; and social themes from California, Florida, Legacy, Massachusetts, and Philip Morris	• Compared with the control ad, advertisements focusing on young victims suffering from serious smoking-related disease (OR = 0.46; 95% CI, 0.28–0.75) elicited disgust, enhanced anti-industry motivation, and reduced intentions to smoke among non-conduct-disordered youth • Acceptance of nonsmokers, cosmetic effects, counterindustry, and industry marketing tactics did not have any of the above effects • Youth who had conduct disorders were not influenced by any advertisements' themes	Random assignment to different message themes

Table 6.3 Continued

Reviews that included the study/ studies	Study	Design/population	Comparison of advertisements	Findings	Strengths, limitations, and comments
Not previously reviewed	Dickinson and Holmes 2008	Controlled exposure 353 14- to 16-year-olds from Western Australia were randomly assigned to 1 of 6 message conditions or the control condition with approximately 50 respondents in each condition Study aimed to examine the utility of protection motivation theory in predicting effective appeals involving threats Survey assessed emotional response (disgust, guilt, shyness, stress and anger) and coping response using adaptations of standardized measures Theoretically, "adaptive" coping responses indicate the message is accepted as a result of rational cognitive processes, while "maladaptive" coping responses indicate avoidance of the notion of danger	6 messages were varied across 3 levels of threat plus 2 types of threat: physical consequences vs. social rejection due to smoking: • Low physical threat included a man having difficulty running • Moderate physical threat showed a man who had been hospitalized • High physical threat showed a lifeless man in a hospital bed • Low social threat depicted a disappointed look from a boyfriend • Moderate social threat depicted a boyfriend not wanting to kiss his girlfriend • High social threat showed the boyfriend having left the girl for another	• Low-level threats, followed by moderate levels of threat (especially social threats), were most effective at producing "adaptive coping responses" • Physical threats produced stronger emotional response than did social threats, with moderate level producing the strongest emotional responses, followed by high-level then low-level threats • There was no significant relationship between strong overall emotional responses and the associated coping response; however, disgust was positively related to coping response	t-tests and ANOVAs were used; i.e., no control variables were included

Table 6.3 Continued

Reviews that included the study/ studies	Study	Design/population	Comparison of advertisements	Findings	Strengths, limitations, and comments
Not previously reviewed	Flynn et al. 2007	Controlled exposure 1,255 9- to 18-year-olds from 4 public school districts in California, Florida, Texas, and the District of Columbia (in areas with household incomes below the national median) rated the appeal of messages by the degree to which they liked the antismoking social norms messages Using repeated-measures ANOVA, the authors included student characteristics (age group) and the community of residence as grouping factors, and messages as the repeating factor Additional models that added the effects of race/ethnicity and gender were subsequently conducted The analyses could not account for selection of students from particular schools, as age group was confounded with school	8 television and 5 radio messages were chosen by using a message-rating method from a pool of ads developed using formative research and based on social cognitive theory Themes included "not smoking cigarettes is advantageous," "smoking cigarettes has disadvantages," "most young people don't smoke," and "it is not difficult to avoid smoking in social situations"	• Televised messages generally received higher ratings than did radio messages • Strong differences occurred between age group ratings with younger students more likely than older students to give higher ratings of message appeal • Boys and girls generally rated messages similarly • Overall ratings were similar across race/ethnicity categories; however, there was more variability in older groups, particularly among oldest African American raters • Those at higher risk of smoking (had ever smoked and had family members who smoked) and those with lower academic achievement generally scored messages lower	It may be particularly difficult to design these types of social norms messages to be appealing to older youth, those at higher risk of smoking, and those reporting lower academic achievement

Table 6.3 Continued

Reviews that included the study/studies	Study	Design/population	Comparison of advertisements	Findings	Strengths, limitations, and comments
Not previously reviewed	Helme et al. 2007	Controlled exposure 1,272 Colorado front range area middle school students were randomly assigned to 1 of 2 message conditions (high vs. low sensation value) Responses were tracked as the students completed 3 sessions exposing them to 3 antitobacco and 3 antidrug messages, each separated by approximately 2 weeks; a postmeasure was taken approximately 2 weeks after completion of the final session Students' level of sensation seeking (high vs. low) was also measured	18 antitobacco public service announcements (PSAs) were selected for inclusion from a pool of 195 ads Coding and focus testing indicated the 9 messages with the highest sensation value and the 9 with the lowest sensation value An additional 9 antidrug messages were interspersed with the antitobacco ads	• The study found no differences between high- and low-sensation-value messages in changing antismoking attitudes, future intentions to smoke, self-efficacy not to smoke, perceived effectiveness of the message, and perceived risk for self and others • High-sensation seekers were more likely to show changes than were low-sensation seekers on changes in antismoking attitudes, intentions not to smoke, self-efficacy not to smoke, perceived effectiveness of the message, and perceived risk from smoking	No description was given of the content/story of the messages
Not previously reviewed	Zhao and Pechmann 2007	Controlled exposure Study 1: 443 students in grade 9 who were not past or current smokers were randomly exposed to 1 of 4 message conditions, plus a control condition Students' promotion or prevention focus was measured Study 2: 719 students in grade 9 who were not past or current smokers were randomly exposed to 1 of 4 message conditions exactly the same as in study 1, plus a control condition Students were primed to be promotion or prevention focused before being exposed	4 versions of the same basic social disapproval antismoking message (depicted an indoor gathering of a group of young college students) that varied along 2 dimensions (positive vs. negative frame; promotion- vs. prevention-focused message) The control message was a PSA that attempted to dissuade adolescents from dropping out of school	• All the ads had null effects on intentions to smoke compared with the control unless the student's regulatory focus (promotion vs. prevention focus) was aligned with the message's regulatory focus (promotion vs. prevention focus) and frame (positive vs. negative) • For promotion-focused adolescents, promotion-focused positively framed messages were most effective at persuading them not to smoke • For prevention-focused adolescents, prevention-focused negatively framed messages were most effective • The enhanced ad effectiveness was mediated by message accessibility and diagnosticity	

Table 6.3 Continued

Reviews that included the study/ studies	Study	Design/population	Comparison of advertisements	Findings	Strengths, limitations, and comments
Not previously reviewed	Sutfin et al. 2008	Controlled exposure 488 high school students were randomly assigned to 1 of 3 antitobacco ad conditions or a control condition Students completed a measure addressing demographics and smoking behavior before exposure and then rated ads immediately after viewing on cognitive and emotional responses and on intentions to smoke Ads were chosen from a pool of 33 ads being aired as part of state tobacco prevention programs aimed at adolescents Ads were chosen on the likely appeal of the topic to adolescents and the inclusion of actors their own age	Three ads represented 3 message themes: • Endangering others (semi-trailer with chemicals inside, compare hurricane deaths to tobacco deaths, waitress with red eyes) • Negative life circumstances (jeopardizing driver's license, running into glass door, and going outside with metal rod in a thunderstorm were related to smoking) • Industry manipulation (smoking in movies, teaching actors how to smoke, e-mail to big tobacco)	• Participants exposed to industry manipulation ads had less positive cognitive responses than did those exposed to endangering-others ads • Participants who viewed ads on negative life circumstances had stronger positive emotional responses than did those who viewed either industry manipulation ads or endangering-others ads • Participants who viewed the endangering-others ads had more negative emotions than did participants who viewed the ads on negative life circumstances • Those exposed to the ads on negative life circumstances reported lower intentions to smoke than did those exposed to control ads or industry manipulation ads	Number of smokers exposed to each condition was about 20; no smoking attitudes, intentions, or behavior were assessed
Naturalistic exposure studies					
Richardson et al. 2007; NCI 2008	Niederdeppe 2005	Naturalistic exposure 3,409 12- to 15-year-olds and 4,171 16- to 18-year-olds involved in at least 1 of the Florida Antitobacco Media Evaluation surveys The study aimed to explore the relationship between executional characteristics and message processing Message processing was measured by using "thought-listing" measures The study controlled for demographics, smoking behavior, friends, and household smoking	Ads were coded for features that increased the sensation value of the message, such as unrelated cuts, the use of suspenseful images, and second-half punch	• Together, the presence of unrelated cuts, intense images, and second-half punch were associated with increased message processing in younger and older teens • Separately, message processing in older adolescents improved when messages incorporated unrelated cuts and used suspenseful images	

Table 6.3 Continued

Reviews that included the study/studies	Study	Design/population	Comparison of advertisements	Findings	Strengths, limitations, and comments
NCI 2008	Biener 2002	Naturalistic exposure 733 youth, aged 14–17-years, were asked in a telephone survey whether they had seen any antitobacco advertisements on television in the previous month; if so, they were asked to describe the ad or ads in detail and to rate the ads' effectiveness on an 11-point scale	The most prominent antitobacco ads broadcast by the Massachusetts Tobacco Control Program and those produced by Philip Morris in 4 categories: illness, outrage, other Massachusetts ads, and Philip Morris	• Advertisements featuring serious consequences of smoking were seen as significantly more effective by youth than Massachusetts advertisements that did not discuss illness or the Philip Morris "Think. Don't Smoke" ads	
NCI 2008	Biener et al. 2004	Naturalistic longitudinal exposure 618 Massachusetts youth, aged 12–15-years, were followed from 1993 to 1997 with a telephone survey which confirmed recall of the ads and perceived effectiveness on a scale from 0 to 10	Massachusetts ads broadcast over the period leading up to 1997 4 ads featured serious illness 2 ads used humor 2 ads were about normative behavior	• Youth were more likely to recall and perceive as effective ads featuring messages about serious health consequences that had been independently rated as high in negative emotion than ads featuring messages about normative behavior or ads relying on humor • Advertising intensity was related positively to ad recall but negatively to perceived effectiveness	The measure was "perceived effectiveness," but it is unclear whether ratings of perceived effectiveness predicted future attitudes and behavior

Table 6.3 Continued

Reviews that included the study/ studies	Study	Design/population	Comparison of advertisements	Findings	Strengths, limitations, and comments
NCI 2008	Evaluation of Legacy national "truth" campaign Farrelly et al. 2002, 2009 Davis et al. 2007a	Naturalistic exposure Nationally representative cross-sectional telephone surveys of 12- to 17-year-old youth before launch (N = 6,897) and 10 months after launch of national "truth" campaign (N = 6,233) 2 later studies used data from 35,074 youth in 8 nationally representative cross-sectional telephone surveys from 1999–2003; measures included confirmed recall of ad, attitudes and beliefs about smoking, perceived prevalence of smoking, and intention to smoke in next year	Legacy "truth" ads featuring manipulation messages from the tobacco industry compared with Philip Morris' ads on preventing smoking by youth that asked young people to "Think. Don't Smoke"	• Exposure to Legacy "truth" ads was associated with increase in antitobacco attitudes and beliefs, but exposure to Philip Morris ads was not; those exposed to Philip Morris ads were more likely to be open to smoking • After 3 years, perceived prevalence of smoking was reduced among those who had confirmed recall of the "truth" campaign (generally $p < 0.05$) but was unrelated to confirmed exposure to the Philip Morris campaign • After 3 years, confirmed exposure to the "truth" campaign was associated with stronger antitobacco attitudes and intentions not to smoke in the future ($p < 0.001$), but exposure to the Philip Morris campaign was associated with more favorable beliefs and attitudes toward tobacco companies and a trend for weaker intentions not to smoke	

Table 6.3 Continued

Reviews that included the study/ studies	Study	Design/population	Comparison of advertisements	Findings	Strengths, limitations, and comments
NCI 2008	Wakefield et al. 2006	Naturalistic exposure 103,172 students in grades 8, 10, and 12 in the United States Data collected during the 1999–2002 Monitoring the Future school-based surveys were merged by media market with 12- to 17-year-olds' gross rating points for antitobacco advertisements for the 4 months before survey completion Outcome measures included smoking attitudes and beliefs, intentions, and smoking in the past 30 days	Tobacco company youth-directed advertising campaigns on preventing youth smoking and parent-directed advertising campaigns to prevent youth smoking as well as public-health-sponsored antitobacco advertising campaigns	• Among 8th-grade students, greater exposure to industry youth-directed advertising on preventing youth smoking was associated with increased intention to smoke (OR = 1.04; 95% CI, 1.01–1.08), but exposure was unrelated to other outcomes for this age group or for students in grades 10 and 12 • Among students in grades 10 and 12, greater exposure to advertising directed at parents on preventing youth smoking was associated with lower perceived harm from smoking (OR = 0.93; 95% CI, 0.88–0.98), stronger approval of smoking (OR = 1.11; 95% CI, 1.03–1.12), stronger intentions to smoke in future (OR = 1.12; 95% CI, 1.04–1.21), and greater likelihood of having smoked in the past 30 days (OR = 1.12; 95% CI, 1.04–1.19)	
Not previously reviewed	Niederdeppe et al. 2007	Naturalistic exposure 32,977 adolescents from 7 cross-sectional waves of the Legacy Media Tracking Surveys were assessed for confirmed recall of television ads from the "truth" campaign Need for sensation was also assessed Analyses controlled for a comprehensive set of ad-specific features, demographics, and market-level "truth" gross rating points	Stylistic features of 45 ads from the Legacy "truth" campaign were compared Stylistic features included edits, unrelated cuts, intense images, sound saturation, loud and fast music, "acting out" (youth or adults engaged in actions or activities that directly correspond to the ad's main theme), and second-half punch (shocking or surprising ending)	• Odds of recall increased with more frequent edits and unrelated cuts, intense imagery, sound saturation, loud and fast music, and second-half punch; however, "acting out" decreased the odds of recall • Results were nearly identical for youth with high and low needs for sensation, although the magnitude of recall was somewhat higher for youth with a high need for sensation • Greater recall was linearly related to a greater number of stylistic features within each ad	

Table 6.3 Continued

Reviews that included the study/ studies	Study	Design/population	Comparison of advertisements	Findings	Strengths, limitations, and comments
Not previously reviewed	Biener et al. 2008	Naturalistic exposure 3,332 12- to 17-year-old adolescents from the baseline survey of the UMass Tobacco Study conducted from January 2001 to June 2002 were assessed for confirmed recall of 9 specific antitobacco ads Volume of broadcast of the 9 ads was also estimated from adolescent target ratings points (TRPs) Analyses controlled for demographics, household education level, frequency of TV watching, and smoking status	Ads were given an emotional intensity score based on an ad-rating study with adolescents	• Level of the ads' emotional intensity was a significant predictor of recall • As emotional intensity increased from the lowest to the highest level, the odds of recall increased by a factor of 3.07 (95% CI, 2.86–3.30) • The volume of broadcast was also a significant predictor of recall • As the TRPs increased from the lowest to the highest level, the odds of recall increased by a factor of 2.38 (95% CI, 1.93–2.94) • TRPs were a significantly stronger predictor of recall of the 2 ads low in emotional intensity (2.68) than the 2 ads high in emotional intensity (1.36)	Indicates that for ads high in emotional intensity, less media weight was required to generate recall as compared with those low in emotional intensity; ads of low emotional intensity required more media weight to generate the same levels of recall

Note: **ANOVA** = analysis of variance; **CI** = confidence interval; **OR** = odds ratio.

In that study, Flynn and colleagues (1992) examined the effects of a media (television and radio)-plus-school intervention (refusal skills, accurate social norms, positive views of nonsmoking) and of a school intervention alone that both ran over 4 years. Assessments at the end of the 4-year intervention and then at a 2-year follow-up (Flynn et al. 1994) found that those in the media-plus-school intervention had significantly lower smoking rates than those in the school-only intervention. The 1994 Surgeon General's report (USDHHS 1994) concluded that mass media campaigns can be cost-effective but that messages should be pretested to avoid and test for unintended effects (Worden et al. 1988) and that these campaigns should be intense enough and sufficient in length to ensure impact.

A Cochrane review completed a few years later (Sowden 1998) included longer-term follow-up reports for some of the studies (Bauman et al. 1991; Flynn et al. 1994, 1997; Flay et al. 1995) reviewed in the 1994 Surgeon General's report (USDHHS 1994) as well as a new study (Hafstad and Aarø 1997; Hafstad et al. 1997a) and concluded that there was some evidence, although it was not strong, that mass media can be effective in preventing the uptake of smoking in young people. As did the 1994 Surgeon General's report (USDHHS 1994), the Cochrane review emphasized that the effective campaigns were based on theory, used formative research to develop messages, and had relatively intense and ongoing exposure of messages.

In reviews published after 2000, Pechmann (2001), Friend and Levy (2002), Farrelly and colleagues (2003a), Wakefield and colleagues (2003b,c), and the Task Force on Community Preventive Services (2005) all concluded that the findings from controlled experiments indicate that campaigns have the potential to decrease tobacco use among youth, with some evidence that campaigns are more likely to succeed when they are coordinated with school- or community-based programs. Wakefield and colleagues (2003a,c) also highlighted the idea that the effects seem to be more reliable when exposure occurs in preadolescence or early adolescence and when ads lead to emotional arousal. Consistent with theoretical models indicating that the effect of public health messages may be mediated through interpersonal communication (Flay and Burton 1990; Yanovitzky and Stryker 2001), Wakefield and colleagues (2003a,c) also suggested that the discussion of media campaigns may play an important role in either reinforcing or neutralizing the potential effects of antismoking advertising, as indicated by the findings from Hafstad and Aarø (1997).

Methodologic shortcomings highlighted by Hornik (2002) and NCI (2008) may explain some of the variation in findings from the controlled field trials. These problems have included: (1) difficulties in developing the televised components of the media exposure (Flay et al. 1988, 1995); (2) a low intensity of the media campaign or short duration of exposure to it (Bauman et al. 1991; Meshack et al. 2004); (3) insufficient control for baseline community characteristics and smoking-related risk factors and for prior and concurrent secular trends (Winkleby et al. 1993); and (4) differential attrition in longitudinal samples (Perry et al. 1992; Hafstad et al. 1997a; Vartiainen et al. 1998). Also, most analyses were not based on the primary sampling units considered as a whole that received the intervention (i.e., communities, schools). Rather, analyses were conducted on individuals within these sampling units, which can increase the chance of a Type 1 (false-positive) error due to an artificially inflated sample and failure to consider the effect on responses of shared experience within communities (see Hornik [2002] and NCI [2008] for further discussion of these issues).

In an analysis that considered the early cardiovascular programs of the 1970s and 1980s along with specific controlled field trials of youth media campaigns, NCI (2008) determined that media can "play an important role in affecting smoking behavior" (p. 508). Only one of the four reviewed studies that examined the effect of media alone found a positive effect (Hafstad et al. 1996, 1997a; Hafstad and Aarø 1997), however, the other three did not (Bauman et al. 1991; Winkleby et al. 1993; Flay et al. 1995). In comparison, five of six studies found evidence for an effect when the media was combined with a school-based intervention (Vartiainen et al. 1986; Perry et al. 1992; Flay et al. 1995; Flynn et al. 1997; Biglan et al. 2000a; Meshack et al. 2004).

Adding to this literature, a 2009 longitudinal controlled field trial by Solomon and colleagues included four matched pairs of media markets across four states randomly allocated to receive a 3-year television-and-radio intervention to increase smoking cessation and reduce smoking prevalence among adolescents. The media messages were based on social-cognitive theory. Although the authors did not find a significant time-by-condition interaction, significantly fewer participants in the intervention group were smoking in the past month at 3-year follow-up than in the control group after adjustment for baseline smoking status. Those in the intervention communities had greater cessation rates (an 18.1% 30-day point prevalence rate of quitting) than those in the control communities (14.8%) after the first year of the intervention, but no further gains were made up to 3 years, and light and occasional smokers were most likely to quit. The analyses used an intention to treat (ITT) method, assuming those who were lost at follow-up to have smoked at least one cigarette in the past 30 days, minimizing the possible effects of attrition bias. Unlike many others, this study used multilevel analytic techniques to account for similarities in reaction within individuals and similarities due to shared experience within matched media markets (Solomon et al. 2009).

Longitudinal population studies. Pechmann (2001) stated that there is limited direct evidence from controlled trials that media alone can influence youth smoking, but reported indirect evidence of the effects of stand-alone media campaigns from longitudinal population surveys of adolescents. These population surveys linked self-reported exposure to ads and reductions in smoking initiation (Siegel and Biener 2000; Sly et al. 2001b). Siegel and Biener (2000) examined the effect of the Massachusetts state campaign on smoking initiation by following 12- to 15-year-olds over 4 years and found that those who were 12 or 13 years of age and recalled campaign messages at baseline were less likely to start smoking than those who did not recall the messages. There were no effects for 14- and 15-year-olds and no effects on most knowledge and attitude measures. Similarly, Sly and colleagues (2001b, 2002) conducted longitudinal surveys to examine the effects of the Florida "truth" campaign on smoking initiation; they found that the number of advertisements recalled and campaign-related beliefs among youth at follow-up were associated with decreased smoking initiation.

Pechmann (2001) cautioned, however, that reverse causality cannot be ruled out with this type of evidence because adolescents who had strong antismoking beliefs at baseline and/or follow-up may have been more likely to pay attention to antismoking ads and also less likely to start smoking. However, Sly and associates (2001a,b) and Siegel and Biener (2000) minimized the likelihood of this possibility by controlling for baseline age, gender, prior smoking status, and the smoking status of friends and parents; Siegel and Biener (2000) also controlled for extent of television viewing. But as pointed out in the NCI review (2008) of the media and tobacco use, the studies by Sly and colleagues (2001b, 2002) measured recall at follow-up and the one by Siegel and Biener (2000) did not adjust for nonresponse at follow-up through weighting or analytic techniques. If those in the studies by Sly and colleagues who recalled the advertisements and those in the study by Siegel and Biener who completed the follow-up survey were relatively more likely to be nonsmokers, the possibility of finding an effect could well have been inflated.

Cross-sectional population studies. The 1967 ruling by the Federal Communications Commission that the Fairness Doctrine applied to cigarette advertising provided the first chance to examine the effects of antismoking messages on youth smoking. Much later, Lewit and colleagues (1981) associated various estimates of exposure to the antismoking advertisements with adolescent smoking behavior while controlling for a comprehensive range of covariates (Table 6.2). These authors found that the prevalence of smoking among youth was 3.0–3.4 percentage points lower during the Fairness Doctrine period than during the 16 months before it and that those who watched more television and were exposed to more antismoking messages were less likely to smoke. This study used measures of potential exposure based on hours of daily television watching reported by youth that were related by the authors to the number of antismoking advertisements aired during the Fairness Doctrine period in a given year. The NCI review of the media and tobacco use (2008) described this early study as making "significant strides in using more complex measures of exposure" (p. 518); more sophisticated measures than those used in the early days were not employed again until much later (Emery et al. 2005; Farrelly et al. 2005; Terry-McElrath et al. 2007), when campaign exposure was measured using gross rating points (GRPs). GRPs measure the relative reach and frequency of exposure to the campaign among the target audience within specific media markets. Emery and colleagues (2005) found that exposure to at least one U.S. state-funded antismoking advertisement in the prior 4 months was associated with lower perceived rates of friends' smoking, greater perceived harm of smoking, stronger intentions not to smoke in the future, and lower likelihood of being a smoker. The variation in campaign exposure across different media markets in this study design provided natural comparison groups for examining the effects of campaigns and different intensities of exposure. These studies all used a comprehensive set of potential confounders, but only one (Terry-McElrath et al. 2007) also controlled for preexisting prevalence of youth smoking (in this case in 1995–1996) in different media markets to account for correlations between these rates and the frequency of antismoking advertisements aired in each market.

The findings from these and other cross-sectional, population-based evaluations of state and national antismoking campaigns developed by tobacco control programs can be more fully understood by examining the reported findings from 20 relevant papers cited in the three most recent comprehensive reviews (Richardson et al. 2007; Angus et al. 2008; NCI 2008). Of the 12 studies that examined attitudes or beliefs relating to smoking (Murray et al. 1994; Popham et al. 1994; Sly et al. 2001a, 2002; Farrelly et al. 2002; Hersey et al. 2003, 2005a,b; White et al. 2003; Niederdeppe et al. 2004; Emery et al. 2005; Terry-McElrath et al. 2007), all but 1 (Murray et al. 1994) found favorable changes associated with exposure to the campaign, and all 13 studies that examined intentions to smoke found favorable effects of such exposure (Popham et al. 1994; Seghers and Foland 1998; Bauer et al. 2000; Sly et al. 2001a,b, 2005; Farrelly et al. 2002; Niederdeppe et al. 2004; Emery et al. 2005; Hersey et al. 2005a,b; Johnston et al. 2005; Terry-McElrath et al. 2007; White et al. 2003). Fourteen of 16 cross-sectional population studies that examined smoking behavior (i.e., smoking prevalence, initiation of smoking, or quitting) associated with televised antismoking campaigns found a favorable change in the behavior (Lewit et al. 1981; Popham et al. 1994; Bauer et al. 2000; Siegel and Biener 2000; Sly at al. 2001a,b; White et al. 2003; Niederdeppe et al. 2004; Emery et al. 2005; Farrelly et al. 2005; Hersey et al. 2005a,b; Johnston et al. 2005; Terry-McElrath et al. 2007).

New studies published since these reviews further support these findings, indicating that well-funded state and national antismoking campaigns can reduce smoking among youth (Davis et al. 2007a; Evans et al. 2007; Tangari et al. 2007; Niederdeppe et al. 2008; White et al. 2008b; Farrelly et al. 2009). For example, Niederdeppe and colleagues (2008) surveyed 5,010 12- to 18-year-olds for their recall of Florida's "truth" campaign ads, anti-industry beliefs, and nonsmoking intentions from April 1998 to May 2000. Rates of change were examined using interrupted time series techniques before and after budget cuts by the Florida Tobacco Control Program that took place between May 1999 and September 1999. After controlling for demographics, smoking in the home, degree of parental smoking, and parental monitoring, the study found that upward trends in recall of the Florida "truth" campaign weakened and nonsmoking intentions became relatively less prevalent following the budget cuts to the campaign.

As outlined in a number of reviews (Pechmann 2001; Jepson et al. 2006; NCI 2008), there are methodological issues with cross-sectional population studies to consider in determining the relative strength of those findings that linked media campaigns with preventing smoking among youth. Some of the cross-sectional studies used post-only (White et al. 2003) or single pre-post surveys (Seghers and Foland 1998; Bauer et al. 2000); these designs make it difficult to gauge whether any changes found were due to the media campaign or to secular trends in the exposed community and/or other events and activities unrelated to the media exposure. Use of a comparison group (Murray et al. 1994; Sly et al. 2001a; Niederdeppe et al. 2004), along with a comprehensive set of controls for preexisting demographic characteristics and levels of smoking in the community, may help to increase confidence that the observed effects are due to campaign exposure rather than preexisting baseline factors or secular trends (Farrelly et al. 2002, 2005; Emery et al. 2005; Terry-McElrath et al. 2007). Studies that provide measures at multiple baselines (e.g., Farrelly et al. 2002) can also help establish prior secular trends. Use of multiple measures during and after the campaign (Popham et al. 1994; Bauer et al. 2000; Niederdeppe et al. 2004; Emery et al. 2005; Johnston et al. 2005) and observation of changes in factors thought to be mediators of the effect of campaigns, such as certain beliefs and attitudes (Sly et al. 2002; Hersey et al. 2003, 2005a,b; Evans et al. 2004a), can also help increase confidence that any observed changes in smoking behaviors are the result of campaign activity rather than alternate trends or concurrent events.

Still, a key difficulty in attempting to assess the specific media effects of statewide and national media campaigns is the fact that most were developed and run within the context of broader tobacco control programs and activities, such as tax increases (Friend and Levy 2002; Farrelly et al. 2003a). Regardless, some authorities suggest that integrating media campaigns within a broader tobacco control program is important to their effectiveness (Schar et al. 2006; Angus et al. 2008; NCI 2008), and thus, considerations of precisely determining the effects of the media campaigns, while important, perhaps need to be seen as less compelling than meeting the goal of offering a program that produces positive changes. Schar and colleagues (2006) point to the success of mass media campaigns in Finland as well as in California, Massachusetts, and a number of other states that have implemented youth tobacco campaigns that included other program elements (see "Comprehensive State-Level Tobacco Control Programs" later in this chapter for more detail); these included such initiatives as a school curriculum, cessation programs, and policy changes that increased cigarette taxes and smoke-free environments and strengthened laws restricting youth access. Schar and colleagues (2006) conclude that "a key contributor to successful mass media campaigns is the synergy resulting from the different program elements working together to change society's prevailing attitudes about tobacco use" (p. 5). Finally, Richardson and colleagues (2007) indicate that campaigns are likely to "work best when combined with broader tobacco control initiatives produced by tobacco control bodies" (p. 4).

The consistent positive findings across a variety of study designs provide convincing evidence that antismoking media campaigns can be effective in reducing youth smoking but that certain factors and conditions are required for their success. There is broad consensus that these factors include the use of formative research in the development of messages and, for campaign messages, sufficient intensity and duration of exposure (USDHHS 1994; Sowden 1998; Pechmann and Reibling 2000b; Siegel 2002; Farrelly et al. 2003a). Recent research and reviews have begun to focus more heavily on which message characteristics work best, what the ideal level of exposure is, and which types of youth are most or least affected by mass media campaigns against smoking.

Factors That May Optimize the Effectiveness of Mass Media Campaigns

Mass media campaigns against smoking, especially those with televised components, require considerable investment, making it particularly important to understand the factors and strategies that optimize their effectiveness. This section summarizes conclusions from various reviews and new research (Pechmann 2001; Siegel 2002; Farrelly et al. 2003a; Wakefield et al. 2003b,c; Schar et al. 2006; Richardson et al. 2007; Angus et al. 2008; NCI 2008) on the effects of different types of messages, the optimum intensity and duration of exposure to messages, and how messages may influence different youth (i.e., classified by gender, age, race/ethnicity, socioeconomic status, risk status).

Theme, emotional tone, format, and characteristics of execution. Studies to assess differences in the responses of youth to various types of ads have usually used controlled exposures; less often, they have employed naturalistic exposures. In controlled-exposure studies, youth typically view a series of messages and then either discuss their reactions to them (often in focus groups) or complete an experimental study. In experimental studies youth may rate ads in terms of their emotional impact, liking, or other features thought to be associated with increased antismoking attitudes and behaviors, or are asked about these attitudes and behaviors directly. It is also possible that youth will complete cognitive processing tasks (Shen et al. 2009), have physiological data recorded such as heart rate (Leshner et al. 2011), or complete memory questions on viewed messages (Leshner et al. 2010) among many possible experimental approaches aimed at better understanding the processes behind mediated message effects for youth.

The limitations of these controlled-exposure methods are that the exposure does not mimic real-world viewing contexts and that one cannot examine the effects of multiple exposures occurring over months and years. The advantages of naturalistic studies are that the effects of different types of messages can be examined in a real-world setting: messages are viewed within a crowded media environment, often within a person's home; there are a myriad of distractions; and the effects of exposure over weeks, months, or years can be studied. The limitations of these naturalistic-exposure studies are that they rely on self-reported recall of messages, which may be correlated with smoking intentions and behaviors, and they cannot rule out other factors that may influence outcomes, such as policy changes and geographic or historic differences in exposure to different types of messages.

Pechmann's (2001) review highlighted the mixed findings from the early controlled-exposure studies that compared different ad themes (Goldman and Glantz 1998; Teenage Research Unlimited 1999). For example, one study that used 20 focus groups indicated that ads showing the serious physical consequences of smoking—portrayed either graphically, dramatically, or emotionally—performed well (Teenage Research Unlimited 1999), while another study, summarizing the findings of 186 focus groups, indicated that ads about secondhand smoke or about industry manipulation rated best (Goldman and Glantz 1998). And in a copy-test study (representative populations view ads and answer survey questions afterwards), Pechmann and colleagues (2003) found that ads depicting the impact of smoking on infants and children, those showing that smoking is socially unacceptable, and ads indicating that nonsmoking is the norm significantly decreased youth's reported intentions to smoke.

Siegel (2002) suggested that the mixed findings from early studies may be explained by the fact that the studies considered only differences in the messages' themes (Goldman and Glantz 1998; Pechmann et al. 2003) and not their emotional content. Subsequent reviews (Farrelly et al. 2003a; Wakefield et al. 2003b; Schar et al. 2006; NCI 2008) have considered both the theme and emotional tone of advertisements and have examined findings of more recent naturalistic studies as well as controlled-exposure studies. In support of theories of persuasion that emphasize emotion (Cohen 1990; Eagly and Chaiken 1993; Forgas 1995; Escalas et al. 2004; Baumeister et al. 2007), these reviews concluded that there is consistent evidence that ads eliciting strong emotional responses (such as disgust, loss, sadness, dread, and anger) through personal testimonials and visceral imagery of the health effects of smoking, or that portray deception on the part of the tobacco industry, can increase attention, generate greater recall and appeal, and affect young audiences' smoking-related beliefs and intentions to smoke. However, exposure to high levels of negative emotion may actually hinder persuasiveness and elicit undesirable negative consequences depending on the stimulus itself (Erceg-Hurn and Steed 2011). This makes message testing extremely important. Ads featuring harm to appearance, addiction, and decreased athletic performance are concluded to be less effective than those about health effects or the tobacco industry's deceptive practices (Goldman and Glantz 1998; Pechmann et al. 2003; Smith and Stutts 2006). The NCI review (2008) of the media and tobacco use noted that some themes (e.g., those on health effects) lend themselves to the elicitation of negative emotions more readily than others, while the "encouragement to quit" theme is often more upbeat and positive. Copy-test studies have shown that when the message's theme and executional style have been controlled, it is the negative emotional elements that are independently related to more encouraging appraisals of the message (Terry-McElrath et al. 2005; Wakefield et al. 2005a).

The American Legacy Foundation "truth" campaign used a mix of serious and sarcastic ads to get the overall message across to youth that tobacco companies are deceptive and misleading; the intent was to elicit outrage and spur young people to resist tobacco use. Recent population-based research on the effects of the first 3 years of the "truth" campaign (Davis et al. 2007a; Farrelly et al. 2009) indicated that confirmed exposure to the campaign was associated with stronger antitobacco attitudes and intentions not to smoke in the future. Reviews caution, however, that ads that use humor have been found to be less effective than those that evoke negative emotions (Schar et al. 2006; NCI 2008). It is not known whether "truth" ads that evoke negative emotions differ in effectiveness from those that use humorous techniques in terms of creating the observed effects. Also, reviews have suggested the need for repeated exposure over time to several different types of ads that deal with the industry's manipulations and deceptive practices to educate audiences about these topics, as the ads may be misunderstood at first (Wakefield et al. 2003b; Schar et al. 2006). The reviews also caution that research into the effectiveness of the counter-industry ads (typically those used in the "truth" campaign that highlight the deceptive practices of the industry) has been limited to the United States, and the findings may have limited transferability to countries where the tobacco industry has a lower profile. Indeed, a recent focus group conducted in the United Kingdom (Devlin et al. 2007) found that industry-manipulation ads provided new information that led to greater interest among adolescents, but comprehension was a barrier with many youth needing the ideas explained.

One review (Schar et al. 2006) summarized findings from controlled field trials, controlled-exposure studies, and focus groups and suggested that ads about the social consequences of smoking and about refusal skills can be effective (Flynn et al. 1992, 2007; Biglan et al. 2000a; Pechmann et al. 2003; Devlin et al. 2007). In addition, a recent longitudinal controlled field study conducted in four media markets within each of four states, detailed earlier in this chapter, provided some modest support for the ability of ads about social norms to influence smoking by youth (Solomon et al. 2009). A new series of controlled-exposure studies added to this literature (Zhao and Pechmann 2007) by examining four versions of the same basic social-disapproval antismoking message (depicting a gathering of young college students) that varied along two dimensions (positive vs. negative frame, promotion- vs. prevention-focused message) that were presented to adolescents categorized as either promotion focused (motivated by achievements and advancement) or prevention focused (motivated to avoid threats to security and safety). The study found that promotion-focused, positively framed messages were most effective at persuading promotion-focused adolescents not to smoke and that prevention-focused, negatively framed messages were most effective for prevention-focused adolescents. Most of these studies examining the influence of these types of themes have been conducted using controlled exposure to ads; one population-based study that specifically used these message themes found no effects on antismoking attitudes or smoking behavior (Murray et al. 1994). Therefore, the extent to which these messages would be effective at the level of a broad population-based mass media campaign is unclear.

As discussed in Chapter 5, ads developed by the tobacco industry that counsel youth not to smoke and emphasize personal choice, such as the "Think. Don't Smoke" ads developed by Phillip Morris, generally had the lowest ratings and effects on smoking intentions or behavior among all ads that were viewed (Teenage Research Unlimited 1999; Biener 2002; Niederdeppe et al. 2005; Wakefield et al. 2005a; Henriksen et al. 2006; Pechmann and Reibling 2006; Farrelly et al. 2008). Angus and colleagues (2008) reported that four of five studies reviewed found that industry campaigns performed poorly compared with tobacco control campaigns. One of these studies showed that youth who recalled the industry campaigns were significantly more likely than their unexposed peers to have intentions to smoke in the future (Farrelly et al. 2002). Another study (Wakefield et al. 2006) found that greater exposure to industry ads directed at youth was associated with stronger intentions to smoke among younger survey participants, and that exposure to industry ads directed at parents was associated with several undesirable outcomes, including stronger approval of smoking and stronger intentions to smoke, for older survey participants. Supporting this research, a new study by Farrelly and colleagues (2009) found that at 3-year follow-up, exposure to the Philip Morris campaign was associated with more favorable beliefs and attitudes toward tobacco companies and a trend for weaker intentions not to smoke.

The NCI review (2008) of the role of the media and tobacco use pointed out that structural features, such as pacing, use of loud music, and cuts or edits of advertisements, may be important in that they can increase the "message sensation value," which has been associated with greater processing of the message (Niederdeppe et. al 2007). Niederdeppe and colleagues (2007) examined 32,977 adolescents from seven cross-sectional waves of the American Legacy Foundation's Media Tracking Surveys, which assessed these youth for confirmed recall of television ads from the "truth" campaign and their need for sensation. After controlling for a comprehensive set of ad features, demographics, and "truth" campaign GRPs, the odds that the messages were recalled increased with more frequent edits and unrelated cuts, intense imagery, sound saturation, loud and fast music, and second-half punch (surprising or shocking ending).

Despite the common use of television, radio, and outdoor advertising in many state and national antismoking campaigns, few studies have examined the relative effectiveness of these different formats, although commercial information suggests that television has the broadest reach. In a cross-sectional study, Seghers and Foland (1998) found that television ads were associated with greater recall than were other formats, and in a controlled-exposure study, Flynn and colleagues (2007) found that televised messages generally received higher ratings than did radio messages. In a recent controlled field trial (Solomon et al. 2009), no differences in smoking outcomes were found by format for those in the exposed group who had heard at least one radio message, but those who had reported seeing at least one television message were less likely to have smoked in the past 30 days than were those who had not seen any messages (54% vs. 62.6%). In a longitudinal study (Siegel and Biener 2000), neither radio nor outdoor advertising was associated with reduced initiation of smoking at 4-year follow-up, but recall of a television message was associated with reduced initiation in 12- and 13-year-olds. It is unclear whether the lack of success of these radio campaigns was due to the format, the messages typically broadcast on the radio stations, or the lower population reached by radio.

In recent years, antismoking messages have increasingly been presented via antitobacco Web sites. A study of differences between design elements, persuasive strategies, and information content across the Web sites of youth antitobacco organizations (which also included the areas for prevention of youth smoking on tobacco industry Web sites) indicated that the industry sites provided the weakest persuasive messages; grassroots (costkids.org [2012]) and government sites provided the strongest messages; and medical sites provided mostly scientific information for specialists (Lin and Hullman 2005). Delivering a message through the Internet can encourage changes in smoking behavior through interactive communication; interactivity can range from quizzes, contests, and games to connecting to campaign Web sites and other users through sites such as Facebook and MySpace. Antismoking campaigns may be able to increase their reach and persuasive impact by using these social networking sites, given a survey indicating that over one-half of U.S. youth who use the Internet have accessed these sites (Lenhart and Madden 2007). For example, the American Legacy Foundation launched the truth profile pages (INFECT truth) on a range of social networking sites. Preliminary results indicate that the addition of these profile pages was associated with an estimated increase of 20,000 unique visitors a week to the truth Web site (2010) in a comparison with traffic during typical campaigns that do not involve social networking sites (Vallone 2007). The video-sharing Web site YouTube provides another modality through which youth may be exposed to both traditional and innovative antitobacco messages from antitobacco organizations and motivated individuals (e.g., "Thanks Tobacco: You Killed My Mom" posted on April 13, 2007 [YouTube 2007]). YouTube also allows viewers to post comments about videos and send links to others. Determining the impact of messages conveyed through this medium is a fertile area for new research. The effects of antismoking messages delivered via text messaging and the use of this technology as a way for smokers to seek help for quitting smoking after exposure to antismoking messages is another important area for research.

Intensity and duration. Despite the conclusion of most reviews that campaign funding and exposure need to be "sufficient" to ensure effects, there is little research as to what levels of intensity and duration might be "sufficient." Nevertheless, studies indicate that increased exposure to antismoking messages over time results in a greater likelihood of having beliefs consistent with the campaign against smoking, decreased youth smoking, a lower intent to smoke, and less initiation of smoking than in those not exposed (Emery et al. 2005; Farrelly et al. 2005; Johnston et al. 2005; Terry-McElrath et al. 2007).

Sly and colleagues (2002) found a dose-response effect of Florida's antismoking advertising in its "truth" campaign, with greater numbers of different ads recalled at follow-up (but not greater overall exposure) associated with greater odds of remaining a nonsmoker during a 22-month period. Later, Emery and colleagues (2005) reported that if the average exposure among youth was less than one state-sponsored antismoking ad over a 4-month period, there were no discernible effects. Exposure to one or more ads for the same period was associated with lower odds of being a smoker. Elsewhere, Farrelly and colleagues (2005) found dose-response effects of the American Legacy Foundation "truth" campaign for up to an average of four ads per month (average cumulative 10,000 GRPs over a 2-year period), after which there were diminishing returns. This suggests that in efforts to reduce youth smoking, there is a threshold of exposure below which antitobacco advertising may not have an influence, and effects increase with increasing exposure up to four ads per month (CDC 2007b). Terry-McElrath and colleagues (2007) used the same study design as Emery and colleagues (2005), but with more years of data from state antitobacco campaigns, and also found a dose-response effect with no point of diminishing returns. It should be noted, however, that state tobacco control campaigns that aired during the 1999–2003 period of this study may not have been broadcast at a level sufficient to detect the point of wear out (among 12- to 17-year-olds the average was just 1.08 target rating points [TRPs] per month) (Wakefield et al. 2005b). Only Arizona in 1999 and 2000, Florida in 1999, Minnesota in 2001, and Utah in 2001–2003 averaged more than four exposures per month to state antitobacco ads among 12- to 17-year-olds (Szczypka et al. 2005).

A more recent study by Biener and colleagues (2008) provides strong support for the relative utility of emotionally evocative advertising as well as an idea of how its effects relate to broadcast intensity (broadcast volume, i.e., media weight or rating points in reaching targeted audiences). The authors assessed confirmed recall of nine specific antitobacco ads in a sample of 3,332 12- to 17-year-old adolescents from January 2001 to June 2002. The intensity and duration of the broadcast of the nine ads were estimated from adolescent TRPs, and each ad was given an emotional intensity score based on a previous study of ad ratings with adolescents. The analyses controlled for demographics, household education level, TV-watching frequency, and smoking status; the findings indicated that the level of the ads' emotional intensity was a significant predictor of recall. As emotional intensity increased from the lowest to the highest level, the odds of recall rose by more than a factor of three. The authors also found that the broadcast volume (media weight) was a significant predictor of recall: as the TRPs increased from the lowest to the highest level, the odds of recall more than doubled. In addition, TRPs were a significantly stronger predictor of recall of the two ads low in emotional intensity (odds ratio [OR] = 2.68) than of the two ads high in emotional intensity (OR = 1.36). These findings indicate that for ads high in emotional intensity, less media weight is required to generate recall than for those that are low in emotional intensity.

Higher recall does not necessarily equate to the effectiveness of an ad and, ultimately, to changes in behavior. However, population-based research indicates that recall of campaign messages has been associated with reduced smoking behavior in youth (Siegel and Biener 2000; Sly et al. 2002). Other research indicates that emotionally evocative messages are perceived as more effective (Pechmann and Reibling 2006), even after controlling for recall (Biener et al. 2000; Biener 2002).

Research linking cuts in the funding for antitobacco campaigns to the halting of declines in youth smoking or even to increases in youth smoking (Sly et al. 2005; Niederdeppe et al. 2008; White et al. 2008b) indicates that optimal implementation for campaigns would involve ongoing exposure at regular intervals. This conclusion highlights the notion, widely acknowledged in advertising literature, that media campaigns influence behavior while they are on air but that their effect diminishes very quickly once they are removed from the air (Tellis 2004).

Context. There is a need not only to identify the characteristics of messages and the level of exposure most likely to change attitudes and behavior among youth about smoking, but also to understand the influence of the circumstances surrounding exposure to messages. Evidence from the broader public health and advertising domains indicates that the contexts in which ads are viewed (Goldberg and Gorn 1987; Sharma 2000) and the extent and type of discussion that ads generate (Morton and Duck 2001) can influence the processing and impact of the messages they impart. Research into the effect of these factors on the responses of adults to antismoking campaigns has shown that messages may be processed less effectively when they are aired during programs that transport viewers into the story (e.g., drama and soap operas [Durkin and Wakefield 2006, 2008]) rather than during lighter entertainment (e.g., comedy). Other research has found that engagement in ad-related discussions can enhance the impact of antismoking messages on both intentions to quit and attempts to quit by adolescents (Hafstad et al. 1996, 1997a; Hafstad and Aarø 1997) as well as adults (Durkin and Wakefield 2006; Dunlop et al. 2008). Several studies (Hafstad et al. 1996, 1997a; Hafstad and Aarø 1997) found that in adolescents the most important predictor of positive behavioral reactions was campaign-stimulated discussion with peers. In a more recent study, adults were most likely to discuss advertising that contained information about the negative health consequences of smoking presented through graphic images or simulations of bodily processes (Dunlop et al. 2008). This result is consistent with the observation that interpersonal discussion can bring antismoking messages into an immediate social environment that may lead to either the extension or reduction of a message's impact (Flay and Burton 1990; Southwell and Yzer 2008).

Audience segmentation. Tailoring the message's content to specific audience subgroups (defined, for example, by age, gender, race/ethnicity, a desire for sensation, or socioeconomic status) has the potential advantage of increasing a message's relevance and ability to persuade. However, tailoring the ad's message, settings, and actors to specific population subgroups requires funding multiple campaigns to convey a variety of messages or tailored versions of a key message rather than simply producing general campaigns to convey messages likely to resonate with all population groups. Also, given the finite resources of most public health campaigns, this type of tailoring may result in having a lower proportion of funds available to broadcast these ads, resulting in lower rates of exposure to the messages. The extent of tailoring and segmentation, therefore, needs to be weighed carefully against goals of maximizing campaign exposure.

Youth- versus adult-targeted campaigns. Although most of the reviewed studies examined campaigns that were specifically targeted to youth, it is a matter of debate whether these campaigns are the best choice for reducing youth smoking (Hill 1999). Beaudoin (2002) found that many youth-targeted campaigns presented the short-term, social consequences of smoking and used humor, while ads targeted to adults more often highlighted the long-term consequences and evoked fear. A study by Flynn and colleagues (2007) that examined ratings for a series of messages on social norms (many of which used humor) indicated that it may be particularly difficult to design messages that appeal to older youth and found strong differences in ratings between age groups. Evidence that younger youth may be more likely than older youth to decrease their intentions to smoke in response to counter industry mass media campaigns (Sly et al. 2001b; Wakefield et al. 2003b; Farrelly et al. 2005) was interpreted in one review (Schar et al. 2006) as indicating that older adolescents may be better addressed by campaigns targeted to a general audience.

Evidence from studies that compared responses from younger and older youth to a range of youth- and adult-targeted messages (e.g., on cessation, secondhand smoke, family guidance, health benefits, health effects, industry manipulation, and smoking being "uncool") found that youth responded as favorably to adult-targeted ads as to youth-targeted ads (Terry-McElrath et al. 2005; Wakefield et al. 2005a, 2006; NCI 2008). This finding is consistent with findings from adult-targeted mass media campaigns that have successfully reduced the initiation of smoking and of smoking behavior among youth (Lewit et al. 1981; Siegel and Biener 2000; White et al. 2003; Schar et al. 2006). In population studies of U.S. youth (Emery et al. 2005; Terry-McElrath et al. 2007), beneficial effects on youth smoking were found from exposure to the overall complement of state antitobacco campaign ads, not just youth-targeted campaigns, and a study by Emery and colleagues (2007) indicated that a majority of the state campaign GRPs came from adults rather than youth. The NCI review (2008) of the media and tobacco use proposed that the success of adult-targeted campaigns for adolescents may be due in part to changing the broader social norms about smoking. Further exploring this issue, Angus and colleagues (2008) suggested that using adult-focused campaigns for reducing smoking in youth may avoid the danger that "using youth targeted mass media campaigns in isolation may create the impression that, whilst children should avoid it, tobacco use is an acceptable adult behavior" (p. 16).

Gender, race/ethnicity, and socioeconomic status. The limited amount of research that has examined differences between youth subgroups in their appraisals of antitobacco ads has not yet found any systematic differences by gender, race/ethnicity, or nationality (Terry-McElrath et al. 2005, 2007; Wakefield et al. 2005a; Flynn et al. 2007). In fact, these studies indicate that the advertisement's characteristics are much more important than the characteristics of the audience. Consistent with this research and with studies of adult responses to advertising against smoking (Siahpush et al. 2007), White and colleagues (2008b) found that across socioeconomic groups, 12- to 15-year-old adolescents showed parallel reductions in smoking behavior during the period of the well-funded Australian National Tobacco Campaign, which included emotionally evocative messages about the health effects of smoking. However, during periods of low funding, when adolescents were exposed to sparse, sporadic campaigns, smoking among 12- to 15-year-olds increased, and those from the lower socioeconomic groups had the greatest monthly and weekly increases. This study suggests that when well-funded campaigns are not on the air, it is youth from lower socioeconomic groups who are most negatively affected. This is consistent with research that suggests disparities in health knowledge may widen when there are only low or moderate levels of publicity about these campaigns (Viswanath et al. 2006).

High-sensation seekers and high-risk youth. Despite early indications that media interventions may be especially effective for high-risk youth (Flynn et al. 1994, 1997), subsequent studies have provided mixed results on this issue. For example, population-based studies have shown that the impact of the American Legacy Foundation's national "truth" campaign on smoking by youth was similar among high- and low-sensation-seeking adolescents (Farrelly et al. 2005; Niederdeppe 2005; Thrasher et al. 2006). Niederdeppe and colleagues (2007) examined the structural elements of ads and found that results were nearly identical between youth with high needs to seek sensation and those with low needs, although the magnitude was somewhat higher among youth with a high need for sensation. Thrasher and colleagues (2006) also found that anti-industry attitudes were similar across sensation-seeking groups, but were lower among adolescents weakly bonded to social supports such as families, schools, and communities. However, the relationship between anti-industry attitudes and smoking was consistent across both risk groups (both sensation-seeking and weakly social-bonding risk groups).

In contrast to early predictions, Pechmann and Reibling (2006) found that youth with conduct disorders (who also are often high-sensation seekers) did not give a variety of antitobacco messages higher ratings than they gave to the control message, but for youth who did not have conduct disorders (81% of the sample), advertisements focusing on young victims suffering from serious smoking-related disease elicited disgust, enhanced anti-industry motivation, and reduced intentions to smoke. A study by Helme and colleagues (2007) randomly allocated middle school students to either a high- or low-sensation-value message. Students' level of need for sensation seeking (high vs. low) was also measured. The authors found no differences between high- and low-sensation-value messages in changing antismoking attitudes, future intentions to smoke, self-efficacy not to smoke, perceived effectiveness of the message, and perceived risk for self and others. The authors found, however, that high-sensation seekers were more likely to show changes than were low-sensation seekers in antismoking attitudes, intentions not to smoke, self-efficacy not to smoke, perceived effectiveness of the message, and perceived risk from smoking. In assessing the importance of the effects of these campaigns on high-risk youth, however, it is important that the proportion of youth who fall into these categories (of high- and low-sensation seeking) be considered. A greater population effect on the prevalence of smoking among youth is likely to be achieved by focusing on what is effective for the majority of youth, and the proportion of youth who have high needs for sensation might not be large enough in some cases to make them a specific target group for interventions to prevent smoking.

Theoretical implications. Some support for models of health behavior change is provided by studies finding that exposure to antismoking messages leads to changes in, or increased salience of, attitudes, beliefs, and intentions relative to smoking as well as reduced smoking behavior (e.g., Popham et al. 1994; Sly et al. 2001b, 2005; Farrelly et al. 2002; White et al. 2003; Meshack et al. 2004; Niederdeppe et al. 2004; Emery et al. 2005). These cross-sectional studies could not, however, examine whether the changes in attitudes and beliefs preceded the changes in intentions and behavior. Controlled and longitudinal studies are better for testing these pathways. Some longitudinal studies have found changes in smoking intentions and behavior without concurrent changes in attitudes and beliefs (Siegel and Biener 2000; Solomon et al. 2009), and others have found that changes in these proposed mediators have occurred before the change in smoking behavior. Flynn and colleagues (1992, 1994) found support for social-cognitive theory, with differences between intervention and control groups on mediating variables (such as smoking norms, attitudes toward smoking, refusal skills) occurring before differences in smoking behavior. Further support for the idea of changes in health behaviors resulting from exposure to antismoking messages is afforded by a series of cross-sectional, population-based studies that surveyed youth in states with relatively higher exposure to the American Legacy Foundation "truth" campaign and found them to have greater agreement with campaign-relevant beliefs and lower rates of smoking initiation than youth from states with relatively lower exposure (Hersey et al. 2005a). Finally, Evans and colleagues (2004a) found that the perceptions of positive social images for not smoking among nonsmokers targeted by the "truth" campaign mediated the relationship between exposure to the campaign and smoking status.

Summary of the Current Evidence Base Regarding the Use of Mass Media

The power of the mass media to influence public perceptions of tobacco was first documented in the aftermath of the 1967 Fairness Doctrine ruling, when considerable reductions in youth smoking were shown to be associated with government-sponsored antismoking television messages. Reviews of early field trials provided some support for the effectiveness of media interventions combined with school programs within communities, but since then, a host of population-based investigations on mass media campaigns have provided convincing evidence that these campaigns, by themselves, can decrease youth smoking. The NCI review (2008) of the media and tobacco use concludes that: "Evidence from controlled field experiments and population studies conducted by many investigators in many countries shows that antitobacco mass media campaigns can reduce tobacco use" (NCI 2008, p. 537). More recent studies (Davis et al. 2007a; Farrelly et al. 2009; Solomon et al. 2009) provide further support for the utility of mass media campaigns to reduce youth smoking.

In summary, the evidence is sufficient to infer a causal relationship between adequately funded antismoking media campaigns and a reduced prevalence of smoking among youth. Evidence has been consistently strong across a wide range of longitudinal-cohort and cross-sectional, population-based studies that have controlled for a variety of potential confounders, have compared effects of exposure with less or no exposure, and have shown diminishing effects when exposure is reduced.

Evidence also suggests a dose-response relationship between exposure to antismoking media messages and reduced smoking behavior among youth, which is further evidence of the effectiveness of these messages. Very few studies, however, have explored the optimum level and duration of exposure to these messages for exerting effects on youth smoking. The few studies to examine this question suggest that levels between one ad per 4-month period and four exposures of the target audience per month are needed to observe an impact, with dose-response findings indicating closer to four exposures per month are needed to be more effective and one study indicating that emotionally evocative messages need less exposure than less emotional messages.

The research reviewed in this section also provides consistent, strong evidence through controlled-exposure and population-wide studies that media ads designed for adults decrease the prevalence of smoking among youth. This effect may be the result of changing the social norms of youth about smoking by altering their perceptions of smoking prevalence among adults as well as reduced exposure to adult smoking (NCI 2008). In addition, a number of population-based and controlled-exposure studies provide evidence that the characteristics of advertising messages seem to be more influential than the characteristics of the audience in terms of the results obtained, suggesting that messages developed for specific target groups may in fact translate successfully to broader audiences and that the expense of developing and airing many different ads for specific target groups may be able to be alleviated.

It is clear that not all campaigns will be equally effective, and recent research has focused on the factors that differentiate influential campaigns and messages from those that are less successful. The research provides consistent evidence from controlled-exposure studies that ads evoking strong negative emotions (including those about the health effects of smoking and exposure to secondhand smoke as well as those about the deceptiveness of the tobacco industry) show greater recall and are rated higher on measures of appeal and smoking-related beliefs and intentions not to smoke than are ads that do not evoke these kinds of emotions.

This review, then, provides important evidence on the efficacy of antismoking mass media campaigns and considerable direction on how those campaigns should be developed in content, tone, and intensity.

Community Interventions

In the last two decades, growing recognition of the influence of social contextual factors on smoking among youth has led to the development and implementation of numerous community interventions. Schofield and colleagues (1991) have argued that the community approach to the prevention of smoking has several key elements: multidimensionality, coordination of activities to maximize the ability to reach all community members, and ongoing, widespread support for nonsmoking behavior. Interventions with multiple components, such as tobacco age-of-purchase laws, smoke-free public places, and the use of mass media and school programs, are often implemented to create community-wide initiatives to prevent the uptake of tobacco use among young people.

Prior Reviews

A Cochrane review of community-based interventions for preventing smoking in young people defined community interventions as coordinated, widespread programs in a particular geographic area or in groupings of people who share common interests or needs that support nonsmoking behavior (Sowden and Stead 2003). The review included 17 RCTs and non-RCTs published up to 2002 that assessed the effectiveness of multicomponent community interventions in comparisons with no intervention or with single-component interventions or school programs alone in young people under the age of 25 years. Four studies reported interventions aimed at preventing the uptake of smoking in the community among young people that were part of larger, community-wide programs to reduce cardiovascular disease in all age groups in specific areas: California (Winkleby et al. 1993); Minnesota (Perry et al. 1994); North Karelia, Finland (Vartiainen et al. 1998); and Rotherham, England (Baxter et al. 1997). One study evaluated an intervention targeted at cancer prevention in New South Wales, Australia (Hancock et al. 2001), and another examined a community-level intervention in Minnesota and Wisconsin that focused on deterring tobacco use via a public policy initiative (Murray et al. 1994). Five other interventions focused exclusively on preventing the uptake of smoking in young people in specific locations: Wensleydale, England (Davidson 1992); Chicago, Illinois (Kaufman et al. 1994); Cardiff, Wales (Gordon et al. 1997); Sydney, Australia (Tang et al. 1997); and Oregon (Biglan et al. 2000a). Six other interventions were aimed specifically at young people, with the focus on preventing or reducing the use of tobacco, alcohol, and drugs in certain locations: Kansas City, Kansas, and Kansas City, Missouri (Pentz et al. 1989b); Wisconsin (Piper et al. 2000); Boys & Girls Clubs of America across the United States (St. Pierre et al. 1992); New Jersey (Aguirre-Molina and Gorman 1995); California (Sussman et al. 1998); and American Indian reservations (Schinke et al. 2000).

All 17 studies in the Cochrane review used a controlled trial design, with 6 using random allocation of schools or communities. Of 12 studies that compared community interventions with no-intervention controls, 2 (both part of programs to prevent cardiovascular disease) reported a lower prevalence of smoking following the intervention (Perry et al. 1994; Vartiainen et al. 1998). Of four studies comparing community interventions with school-based programs, only one found differences in the reported prevalence of smoking (Biglan et al. 2000a), and samples of expired carbon monoxide detected no differences in smoking between groups. One study reported a lower rate of increase in the prevalence of smoking in a community receiving a multicomponent intervention than in a community exposed to a mass media campaign alone (Kaufman et al. 1994). Finally, one study reported a significantly lower prevalence of smoking among the group receiving media, school, and homework components than in the group receiving the media component only (Pentz et al. 1989b).

Overall, Sowden and Stead (2003) concluded that there was some support for the effectiveness of community interventions in preventing the uptake of smoking by young people. The reviewers found it was not possible to pool the results because the studies were heterogeneous in terms of interventions, communities, participants, and measurement of outcomes. Indeed, it could be argued that the very nature of a community intervention means that no two initiatives could ever be the same and, therefore, that their findings should not be aggregated. Furthermore, establishment of control groups in these kinds of studies is difficult and may require extensive negotiations or a "delayed" intervention condition. And because communities are assigned to intervention or control groups, the analysis of outcomes needs to be at the level of the community rather than the individual level. Furthermore, the large size of community interventions means that the measurement of their implementation can be difficult and expensive. Regardless, the studies included in the review represent the most methodologically rigorous set of studies available on the effectiveness of community interventions in influencing smoking among young people.

In their review, Sowden and Stead (2003) recommended several principles to be considered in planning future community interventions: building on the elements of existing programs shown to be effective rather than repeating methods with limited success, adapting program components to suit the community, pretesting and fine-tuning program messages and activities before full implementation, being guided by theoretical constructs of behavior change, and ensuring that activities reach the intended audience.

Newer Studies

Several studies published since the Cochrane review by Sowden and Stead (2003) also suggest modest support for community interventions. One such study involved an evaluation of the effects on youth of the NCI-funded Community Intervention Trial for Smoking Cessation (COMMIT), a multicomponent, community-based intervention designed to decrease the prevalence of smoking among adults and increase quitting among adult smokers (*Journal of the National Cancer Institute* 1991). In addition to its components for adults, COMMIT (Lichtenstein et al. 1994) included youth-oriented activities in four principal areas: school-based education programs, smoking policies in schools, legislative activities related to youth smoking, and participation by students and teachers in other COMMIT activities. The evaluation, which was reported by Bowen and colleagues (2003), involved a two-group pretest/posttest with matched communities randomly assigned to either control or intervention; the ninth-grade classroom (students 14 and 15 years of age) was the unit of assessment. Bowen and coworkers (2003) found no differences in changes in smoking over time between youth in the intervention and control communities.

Full Court Press (FCP), a multifaceted community intervention to change social norms about tobacco use, was intended to reduce the uptake of smoking among youth in Tucson, Arizona. The program included media advocacy, mobilization of youth to build a network of young people committed to reducing tobacco use and advocating for policy change, improvements in the enforcement of laws governing youth access, and development of cessation services (Ross et al. 2006). Results indicated that the prevalence of youth smoking declined 27% between 1996 and 2000 in Tucson during the FCP intervention period, which was larger than changes observed in national and statewide trends for prevalence after accounting for gender and racial/ethnic differences. A subsequent study of FCP that adjusted for other changes in the sociodemographic and economic environment (e.g., increases in cigarette prices) also found beneficial effects on the prevalence of smoking (Ross et al. 2006).

Summary Regarding Community-Level Programs

Coordinated, multicomponent community programs may be able to reduce smoking among young people, and they do so more effectively than can single strategies. Results are likely to depend upon the mix of strategies chosen and the reach of the program's efforts into communities. The most effective components should form the basis for future community interventions (Sowden and Stead 2003).

Comprehensive State-Level Tobacco Control Programs

Because comprehensive tobacco control programs in the United States evolved from community mobilization at the local or state levels, they were not funded research projects like the various community intervention trials, which had formal hypotheses and planned research designs (USDHHS 2000b). Comprehensive tobacco control programs have included a range of coordinated and complementary strategies designed to prevent the initiation of smoking among youth, promote quitting among adults and youth, eliminate exposure of youth and adults to secondhand smoke, and identify and eliminate disparities in the use of tobacco between population groups (USDHHS 2000b). Comprehensive programs include community interventions, countermarketing, program policy and regulation, and surveillance and evaluation (USDHHS 2000b). The idea that multiple education (including paid media), taxation, legislative, and regulatory approaches are needed to address the social, economic, and environmental influences on tobacco use is underpinned by established theories and principles of health promotion (Kickbusch 1989; Green and Richard 1993; Flay and Petraitis 1994; Mullan 2000; USDHHS 2000b; Flay et al. 2009).

Following the establishment of statewide programs in Minnesota in 1985 and California in 1989, comprehensive tobacco control programs began to develop during the 1990s (USDHHS 1994). NCI's American Stop Smoking Intervention Study (ASSIST) was established in 17 states in 1991 (NCI 2005), and the SmokeLess States coalitions, funded by the Robert Wood Johnson Foundation with a national program office at the American Medical Association, were established in 19 states during 1993–2004 (Gerlach and Larkin 2005; NCI 2005). In 1994, CDC funded 32 non-ASSIST states and the District of Columbia through its Initiatives to Mobilize for the Prevention and Control of Tobacco Use (IMPACT) program (USDHHS 2000b). Five years later, in 1999, CDC launched the National Tobacco Control Program, which provides financial support and technical assistance and training for tobacco control programs in all 50 states, the District of Columbia, eight U.S. territories, six national networks, and eight tribal support centers.

Some of the statewide comprehensive tobacco control programs have been funded by an increase in the excise tax on cigarettes that came from either voter initiatives or state-legislated increases in tobacco taxes. California's program was funded by voter initiatives (1989), as were programs in Massachusetts (from 1993), Arizona (from 1994), and Oregon (from 1996). In 1997, Florida began a comprehensive program paid for by a percentage of funding from the state's settlement with the tobacco industry rather than by a tax increase. Mississippi, Texas, and Minnesota used some of the money from their individual settlements with the tobacco industry for tobacco control programs, as did many of the 46 other states that signed the 1998 Master Settlement Agreement, although this was not specified in the agreement (Campaign for Tobacco-Free Kids 2011a). After 1998, many states began to invest in tobacco control, but the amount of funding fell far short of recommendations made by CDC (2007b). Table 6.4 shows the level of program funding allocated by states in fiscal year 2011 compared with the level recommended by CDC (Campaign for Tobacco-Free Kids 2011a). Analyses of factors determining the level of allocation of state master settlement funds to tobacco control indicate that tobacco-producing states tended to spend less than other states on this activity (Gross et al. 2002; Sloan et al. 2005). In addition, the analysis by Gross and colleagues (2002) indicated that the states' tobacco-related health burdens were unrelated to the proportion of master settlement funds allocated to funding tobacco control (Gross et al. 2002). State-level political factors (Sloan et al. 2005), competing claims on master settlement funds, and lobbying by the tobacco industry (Balbach and Glantz 1998; Balbach et. al 2000; Ibraham et. al 2004; Ibraham and Glantz 2006, 2007; NCI 2008) have all played a role in the extent to which tobacco taxes and master settlement funds have—or have not—been used for state efforts in tobacco control.

Prior Reviews

Several reviews have examined the effectiveness of statewide tobacco control programs on reducing smoking by youth. Wakefield and Chaloupka (2000), who reviewed published literature, reports of program evaluations, and working papers about the effects of state programs in Arizona, California, Florida, Massachusetts, and Oregon, found youth in these states to have high levels of recall of the state's mass media campaigns and generally positive improvements in tobacco-related beliefs and attitudes. In addition, the combination of program activity and increases in tobacco taxes was found to reduce cigarette consumption more than would be expected from price increases alone. Reviews of programs in California and Massachusetts documented beneficial effects on the prevalence of adolescent smoking compared with other states (Briton et al. 1997; CDC 1999a; Independent Evaluation Consortium 2002), and Florida had promising indications of reduced smoking when its program was reviewed (CDC 1999b). Siegel (2000) reviewed these three state programs, as well as those of Arizona and Oregon, commenting that the extent of the tobacco industry's attempts to undermine the programs was a good indicator of the programs'

Table 6.4 Budgeted state funding of tobacco control programs in fiscal year 2011 in relation to funding levels recommended by the Centers for Disease Control and Prevention (CDC)

Status of funding	States
States that have funded tobacco prevention programs at a level that meets CDC's minimum recommendation (2 states)	Alaska and North Dakota
States that have committed substantial funding to tobacco prevention programs (5 states); at least 50% of CDC's minimum recommendation	Delaware, Hawaii, Maine, Montana, Wyoming
States that have committed modest funding to tobacco prevention programs (10 states); 25–49% of CDC's minimum recommendation	Arizona, Arkansas, Florida, Minnesota, Mississippi, New Mexico, Oklahoma, South Dakota, Utah, Vermont
States that have committed minimal funding to tobacco prevention programs (30 states plus the District of Columbia); less than 25% of CDC's minimum recommendation	Alabama, California, Colorado, Connecticut, District of Columbia, Georgia, Idaho, Illinois, Indiana, Iowa, Kansas, Kentucky, Louisiana, Maryland, Massachusetts, Michigan, Missouri, Nebraska, New Jersey, New York, North Carolina, Oregon, Pennsylvania, Rhode Island, South Carolina, Tennessee, Texas, Virginia, Washington, West Virginia, Wisconsin
States that have committed none of their tobacco settlement money for tobacco prevention programs (3 states)	New Hampshire, Nevada, Ohio

Source: Campaign for Tobacco-Free Kids 2011a.
Note: Federal funds come from CDC's National Tobacco Control Program. Sources of state-level funds differ greatly by state. Most states use funds from one or more of the following sources: general revenues, tobacco taxes, and Master Settlement Agreement payments.

effectiveness. Responses by the tobacco industry had been aggressive, including more intensive tobacco marketing; increased lobbying at the state and local levels; attempts to limit the tobacco control programs' funding, scope, and messages (Ibraham et. al. 2004; Ibraham and Glantz 2006, 2007); promotion of preemption legislation to allow state laws to override more stringent local laws; and funding of local groups to fight against ordinances mandating clean indoor air (Siegel 2000). A later review by Pierce (2007), with the benefit of more recent data from states, rated the evidence as strong that state programs reduced tobacco use, including among youth (Sly et al. 2001a; Rigotti et al. 2002; Soldz et al. 2002; Niederdeppe et al. 2004; Pierce et al. 2005). Similarly, Bonnie and colleagues (2007) found "compelling" evidence that comprehensive state tobacco control programs can achieve substantial reductions in tobacco use. Such reductions, however, could well rely on the extent to which strategies are comprehensive and integrated. To be effective, they must also be consistent, and budget cuts in many states' tobacco control programs have threatened that consistency. Thus, a report by the Institute of Medicine recommended that all states maintain funding for their tobacco control activities at the level suggested by CDC—about $15 to $20 per capita, depending on the state's population, demography, and smoking rate (Bonnie et al. 2007). The President's Cancer Panel's report made the same recommendation in 2007 (NCI 2007).

A challenge for evaluating these state programs is that, by definition, they have multiple components, making it difficult to assess the relative contribution of each one. Still, several studies have attempted to quantify the relative amounts of effort expended by state tobacco control programs. For example, Schmitt and colleagues (2007) surveyed partners in state tobacco control—including the state health department, voluntary health agencies, and tobacco control coalitions—to assess the strength of tobacco control in various states by determining the proportion of partners working on interventions recommended by the Task Force on Community Preventive Services (2001). In addition, the community guide recommended a standardized approach, but this study found great variation between states in their overall levels of effort and in the relative degree of effort apportioned to media campaigns, tax increases, legislation on clean indoor air, supporting cessation assistance for smokers wanting to quit, and quitline services. Regardless, the strength of state-based tobacco control measures has not been the subject of studies to determine whether it is related to change in youth smoking.

Several studies, however, have focused on the overall level of tobacco control efforts within the states in an attempt to determine their impact on youth (and adult) smoking (Farrelly et al. 2003b, 2008; Tauras et al. 2005a). For example, Tauras and colleagues (2005a) related annual inflation-adjusted per capita expenditures on tobacco control to annual survey data for 8th-, 10th-, and 12th-grade students completing Monitoring the Future (MTF) surveys from 1991 to 2000. State expenditures were summed from (1) real per capita state-specific excise tax funding and other state-appropriated funds earmarked for tobacco control programs; (2) real per capita nongovernmental state-level expenditures on tobacco control; and (3) per capita tobacco control expenditures from ASSIST, IMPACT, SmokeLess States, and the National Tobacco Control Program (Tauras et al. 2005a). After adjusting for cigarette prices; the strength of laws on clean indoor air; laws on youth access; possession, use, and purchase (PUP) laws; and a range of individual characteristics associated with smoking, real per capita tobacco control expenditures had a statistically significant negative relationship with the prevalence of student smoking and the amount smoked by students. If states had spent the minimum amount of funding recommended by CDC, the relative prevalence of student smoking would have been between 3.3% and 13.5% lower than was observed over this period (Tauras et al. 2005a). Reduced prevalence was not observed in all states, however, as documented by Alesci and colleagues (2009) in Minnesota.

Fichtenberg and Glantz (2000) investigated the effects of the California Tobacco Control Program, implemented in 1989, on cigarette consumption and age-adjusted death rates from heart disease. Between 1989 and 1992, the rates of decline in per capita cigarette consumption and mortality from heart disease in California, relative to the rest of the United States, were significantly greater than the pre-1989 rates ($p < 0.001$). These rates of decline were reduced significantly when the program was cut back beginning in 1992. The researchers estimated that the program was associated with 59,000 fewer deaths from heart disease between 1989 and 1997 than would have been expected if the earlier trend in heart disease mortality had continued.

Lightwood and colleagues (2008) modeled the dynamic relationships between per capita tobacco control expenditures, per capita cigarette consumption, and health care expenditures in California, showing $86 billion in reduced personal health care expenditures between 1989 and 2004 than would have been expected absent the state's tobacco control program. Lightwood and Glantz (2011) used a similar approach to investigate the relationship between per capita tobacco control expenditures, cigarette consumption, and health care expenditures in Arizona, which employed a youth-focused tobacco control program. The state's tobacco control expenditures were associated with reduced cigarette consumption and with reductions in health care expenditures amounting to about 10 times the cost of the program through 2004.

Previous reports have reviewed the programmatic components and outcomes of state tobacco control programs, especially states that adopted these programs during the 1990s (USDHHS 1994, 2000b; Siegel 2000; Wakefield and Chaloupka 2000; Bonnie et al. 2007; NCI 2008). The next section outlines the comprehensive tobacco control program in New York state that began in 2000, with information provided as well on separate programmatic efforts in New York City from 2002, and the positive effects of these efforts on smoking among youth. Taken together, results from statewide comprehensive tobacco control programs provide strong evidence that they reduce the prevalence of smoking by youth. To maintain their effectiveness, such programs need to be funded according to CDC recommendations in a sustained manner and include policy change, such as creation of smoke-free environments that reinforce a nonsmoking norm.

Case Study: New York Statewide Program

In 2000, New York state began implementing a comprehensive tobacco control program with funds from the Master Settlement Agreement and revenue from the state's cigarette tax. The New York Tobacco Control Program (NYTCP) implements three key strategies: taking community action, producing and disseminating public health communications, and carrying out interventions to promote cessation. The program, whose components are supported by surveillance, evaluation, and statewide coordination, has attempted to reduce smoking among youth by working to change adult smoking norms and behaviors. From 2000 to 2005, funding for the program was one-half of what CDC recommended as a minimum (RTI International 2004), and in the first independent evaluation, which covered 2000–2003, NYTCP was found not to have expended all available funds in any year since the program had begun and thus did not have a fully implemented program (RTI International 2004). Bureaucratic procedures prevented NYTCP from fully implementing its strategic plan, especially a countermarketing campaign, and from establishing contracts with partners and contractors in a timely fashion (RTI International 2004). However, in 2002, New York increased its tobacco tax, and this produced reductions in smoking (RTI International 2004). Unfortunately, the program missed an opportunity to have a large impact on its intended outcomes by failing to implement media campaigns consistently with messages that elicited strong emotional responses among the target audiences and by not timing its media to coincide with the implementation of the *Clean Indoor Air Act* (2003) (RTI International 2004).

During 2004–2005, NYTCP began to broadcast more ads with high emotional impact, but there was a 6-month period when no media messages at all were broadcast. The program also established 19 centers focused on increasing the number of health care organizations with systems in place that supported smoking cessation, more actively promoted a fax-based quitline referral system to health care providers, distributed free starter kits of nicotine replacement therapy to eligible quitline callers, and implemented a new statewide initiative to combat the influence of tobacco advertising, sponsorships, and promotions. In 2004, the *Fire Safety Standards for Cigarettes Act* was implemented, requiring manufacturers to certify that all cigarettes offered for sale in New York met a specific standard for propensity to ignite. Cigarette-caused fires and deaths caused by cigarette fires both declined following implementation of the law (New York State Department of Health 2009). A 2005 evaluation by RTI International found that the program was having an impact on tobacco use and that rates of decline in New York had outpaced rates of decline in the rest of the country (RTI International 2005). However, tax evasion (i.e., purchasing cigarettes from low-tax or untaxed sources) reduced the effect of the increases in cigarette excise taxes by negatively affecting outcomes for smoking cessation (RTI International 2005).

The *Clean Indoor Air Act* (2003) noted above was associated with reductions in exposure to secondhand smoking among both youth and adults in New York state (RTI International 2005). During 2004–2005, the budget for NYTCP doubled from $44 million to $85 million (the latter around 90% of CDC's minimum recommended level), and by 2007, the program had significantly expanded its media campaign efforts, promotion of quitlines, and partnerships. In 2006, the prevalence of smoking among youth and adults declined faster in New York than in the United States as a whole, and the use of other tobacco products by youth and adults also declined (RTI International 2007). Between 2000 and 2006, smoking among middle school students in the state declined from 10.5% to 4.1% (RI = 61%); among high school students it declined from 27.1% to 16.3% (relative improvement [RI] = 40%) (RTI International 2007).

Alongside efforts at the state level, New York City began implementing its own five-point tobacco control program in 2002 with increased taxation to a level greater than the New York state tax, then continued in 2003 with the establishment of smoke-free workplaces (including restaurants and bars), education of the public and of health care providers, cessation services, and rigorous evaluation of its program. The latter included annual, cross-sectional, citywide telephone surveys using the same measures as CDC's state-based Behavioral Risk Factor Surveillance System (CDC 2007c). Starting in 2006, New York City implemented an extensive, television-based, antitobacco media campaign using graphic images of the health effects of smoking, a campaign that was aired simultaneously with the New York state antitobacco media campaign. Declines in the prevalence of adult smoking were observed during 2002–2004 (Frieden et al. 2005; CDC 2007c), coinciding with the tax increase and smoke-free laws, and in 2006 among men and Hispanics, coinciding with the first year of the city's media campaign (CDC 2007c). From 2003 to 2005, smoking among high school youth in New York City decreased substantially, from 14.8% to 11.2% (RI = 24%), while the rate nationally remained unchanged at approximately 23% (CDC 2007c).

Summary Regarding State-Level Programs

The total weight of evidence from the consistent findings of cross-sectional studies that have controlled for differences between exposed and unexposed populations, combined with high theoretical plausibility and coherence, is sufficient to infer a causal relationship between exposure to comprehensive state-level tobacco control programs and reduced prevalence of smoking among youth.

Legislative and Regulatory Approaches

This section, which examines the effectiveness of regulatory approaches to prevent tobacco use among young people, focuses in particular on the impact of various governmental interventions on reducing cigarette consumption among youth and young adults, including policies related to minors' access to tobacco products, labeling of tobacco products, clean indoor air, advertising restrictions, and taxation of tobacco. In 2009, federal legislation was passed that regulates the manufacturing, marketing, and distribution of tobacco products (*Family Smoking Prevention and Tobacco Control Act* 2009); one of the law's provisions restricts tobacco companies from using "light," "mild," or "low", or similar descriptions for their products without an order from FDA (*Family Smoking Prevention and Tobacco Control Act* 2009).

Taxation of Tobacco

In the United States, the federal government, all 50 states, the District of Columbia, and many local

Table 6.5 Federal cigarette excise taxes, selected dates, 1993–2009

Effective date	Tax per pack of 20 cigarettes (in cents)
January 1, 1993	$0.24
January 1, 2000	$0.34
January 1, 2002	$0.39
April 1, 2009	$1.01

Source: Orzechowski and Walker 2010 and U.S. Department of the Treasury 2009.

governments tax tobacco products. Although many factors affect the final price of cigarettes and other tobacco products, the most important policy-related determinants of tobacco prices are excise taxes on tobacco products.

Taxes on tobacco provide revenue to governments at a relatively low administrative cost, making these taxes especially appealing during periods of shortfalls in the budget. Moreover, taxes on tobacco have the ability to decrease its consumption and thereby improve public health. This combination of increasing revenues and improving public health has made tobacco taxation a popular policy lever in recent decades.

The sections below briefly review the current status of tobacco excise taxes at the federal, state, and local levels, focusing on the period since the publication of the last Surgeon General's report on tobacco use among youth in 1994 (USDHHS 1994). In addition, these sections examine the relationship between increases in tobacco prices and consumption of tobacco by young people, focusing on the period since the most recent comprehensive Surgeon General's review on reducing tobacco use was written in 2000 (USDHHS 2000b).

Federal Taxes

As part of the *Balanced Budget Act of 1997,* Congress passed a two-stage increase in the federal tax: the first stage increased the federal excise tax from $0.24 per pack to $0.34 per pack on January 1, 2000, and the second increased it from $0.34 to $0.39 per pack on January 1, 2002. These were the first changes to federal excise taxes on cigarettes since January 1, 1993 (Table 6.5). Moreover, the *Balanced Budget Act of 1997* increased the excise tax rates on all other tobacco products in two stages and established an excise tax rate for roll-your-own tobacco (Table 6.6). On April 1, 2009, the federal excise tax on cigarettes was increased from $0.39 to $1.01 per pack (Table 6.5), and federal excise taxes on other tobacco products were also increased. Revenue generated from the 2009 tobacco

Table 6.6 Federal tax rates on other tobacco products, selected dates, 1993–2009

Tobacco product	January 1, 1993 tax rate (in dollars)	January 1, 2000 tax rate (in dollars)	January 1, 2002 tax rate (in dollars)	April 1, 2009 tax rate (in dollars)
Snuff (per pound)	0.36	0.51	0.585	1.51
Chewing tobacco (per pound)	0.12	0.17	0.195	0.50
Pipe tobacco (per pound)	0.675	0.9567	1.0969	2.83
Roll your own (per pound)		0.9567	1.0969	24.78
Small cigars (per 1,000)	1.125	1.594	1.828	50.33
Large cigars (per 1,000)	12.75% of wholesale price (but not more than $30/1,000)	18.063% of wholesale price (but not more than $42.50/1,000)	20.719% of wholesale price (but not more than $48.75/1,000)	52.75% (but not more than $402.60/1,000)

Source: Tax data from Orzechowski and Walker 2010 and U.S. Department of the Treasury 2009.

excise tax hikes was used to fund an expansion of the Children's Health Insurance Program.

State and Local Taxes

All 50 states and the District of Columbia currently impose an excise tax on cigarettes. As of August 1, 2011, the rates ranged from $0.17 per pack in Missouri to $4.35 per pack in New York (Table 6.7). State excise taxes have increased considerably in recent years. Since January 1, 2002, 47 states, the District of Columbia, and several U.S. territories have increased their cigarette excise taxes 105 times. Even Kentucky, North Carolina, and Tennessee—tobacco-producing states that have traditionally resisted raising tobacco taxes—have increased their tax rates on cigarettes. Moreover, hundreds of municipalities impose taxes on cigarettes, but the rates are generally relatively small when compared with state taxes. However, in recent years, several cities and counties have implemented large increases. For example, in 2002, New York City increased its tax on cigarettes from $0.08 per pack to $1.50 per pack. Similarly, both the city of Chicago and Cook County, Illinois (Cook County includes Chicago as well as many other jurisdictions), raised taxes on cigarettes. Combining federal, state, and local taxes, individuals purchasing cigarettes in New York City and Anchorage, Alaska, pay the highest cigarette excise taxes in the country at $5.85 and $4.20 per pack, respectively, as of October 7, 2011 (Campaign for Tobacco-Free Kids 2011b).

Another kind of tax, the general sales tax, is also quite common. In 2010, 45 states and the District of Columbia imposed general sales taxes on cigarettes (Table 6.7; Orzechowski and Walker 2010); as of November 1, 2010, these taxes added between $0.14 and $0.43 to the price of a pack of cigarettes. In addition, 49 states currently apply excise taxes on tobacco products other than cigarettes; these taxes are predominantly ad valorem. Finally, in most states the general sales tax is applied to other tobacco products as well as to cigarettes.

Cigarette Taxes and Cigarette Prices

Increases in taxes on cigarettes and other tobacco products increase their purchase price. Excise taxes are per unit taxes, but unless they are increased regularly, the inflation-adjusted value of the tax will fall over time. Given the importance of taxes in determining the price of cigarettes, increasing them only infrequently will likely result in declines in the inflation-adjusted price for cigarettes.

The years 1997–2002 witnessed some of the most dramatic increases in the inflation-adjusted retail price of cigarettes in the United States; during this period the inflation-adjusted price increased by 71.1% (Figure 6.2). This large increase was partly the result of the two federal tax increases mentioned earlier and the numerous increases in state excise taxes, and it also reflected the significant increases in the wholesale price of cigarettes. In fact, between 1998 and 2003, wholesale prices for cigarettes increased 122% (Capehart 2004), largely as a result of increased costs associated with expenses for individual state tobacco settlements and expenses related to the Master Settlement Agreement.

Effects of Price on the Demand for Tobacco Products

One of the fundamental principles of economics is that as the real price of a good increases, consumption of that good falls (the downward slope of demand). Some researchers once believed that because of the addictive properties of nicotine, tobacco products might be an exception to this fundamental principle, but numerous econometric studies conducted over the past four decades, including several studies that explicitly modeled the addictive nature of cigarettes, have confirmed that an inverse relationship indeed exists between the prices of cigarettes and their consumption. Because increases in tobacco taxes have the potential to increase the real price of tobacco, increasing those taxes can be an effective policy lever for decreasing tobacco consumption.

Economists measure how responsive tobacco consumption is to changes in the real price of tobacco with a concept known as the "price elasticity of demand." Formally, this is the percentage change in the amount of tobacco consumed that results from a 1% increase in the price of tobacco. For example, a price elasticity of -0.4 implies that a 10% increase in price will decrease consumption by 4%.

The two most recent comprehensive reviews of the literature on the impact of price on tobacco consumption include the International Agency for Research on Cancer (IARC) *Handbooks of Cancer Prevention in Tobacco Control Volume 14* (IARC 2011) and a summary of key findings by Chaloupka and colleagues (2011). A few conclusions can be drawn from these reviews. First, increases in cigarette prices lead to substantial reductions in cigarette smoking. The consensus estimate from the two reviews is that a 10% increase in cigarette price will result in a 3–5% reduction in overall cigarettes consumed. Second, increases in cigarette prices will decrease not only the prevalence of smoking but also the average number of cigarettes smoked by smokers. Third, a majority of the previous research on cigarette consumption among youth suggests that both youth and young adults are more responsive than adults to changes in cigarette prices, with several studies finding youth and young adults to be two to three times as responsive to changes in price as adults.

Table 6.7 State cigarette excise taxes (dollars per pack) and sales tax rate applied to cigarettes

State	Excise tax, September 30, 2011 (in dollars)	Sales tax rate November 1, 2010 (%)	State	Excise tax, September 30, 2011 (in dollars)	Sales tax rate November 1, 2010 (%)
Alabama	0.425	4	Montana	1.70	0
Alaska	2.00	0	Nebraska	0.64	5.5
Arizona	2.00	6.6	Nevada	0.80	6.85
Arkansas	1.15	6	New Hampshire	1.68	0
California	0.87	7.25	New Jersey	2.70	7
Colorado	0.84	2.9	New Mexico	1.66	5.125
Connecticut	3.40	6	New York	4.35	4
Delaware	1.60	0	North Carolina	0.45	5.75
District of Columbia	2.50	6	North Dakota	0.44	5
Florida	1.339	6	Ohio	1.25	5.5
Georgia	0.37	4	Oklahoma	1.03	4.5
Hawaii	3.20	4	Oregon	1.18	0
Idaho	0.57	6	Pennsylvania	1.60	6
Illinois	0.98	6.25	Rhode Island	3.46	7
Indiana	0.995	7	South Carolina	0.57	6
Iowa	1.36	6	South Dakota	1.53	4
Kansas	0.79	6.3	Tennessee	0.62	7
Kentucky	0.60	6	Texas	1.41	6.25
Louisiana	0.36	4	Utah	1.70	4.65
Maine	2.00	5	Vermont	2.62	6
Maryland	2.00	6	Virginia	0.30	5
Massachusetts	2.51	6.25	Washington	3.025	6.5
Michigan	2.00	6	West Virginia	0.55	6
Minnesota	1.23	6.875	Wisconsin	2.52	5
Mississippi	0.68	7	Wyoming	0.60	4
Missouri	0.17	4.225			

Mean state excise tax: $1.46 — Mean sales tax rate: 5.06%

Median state excise tax: $1.25 — Median sales tax rate: 6%

Source: Sales tax data from Orzechowski and Walker 2010. Excise tax data from Centers for Disease Control and Prevention, Office on Smoking and Health, State Tobacco Activities Tracking and Evaluation (STATE) System (CDC 2011b).

Figure 6.2 Cigarette prices and prevalence of smoking among youth, 1975–2011

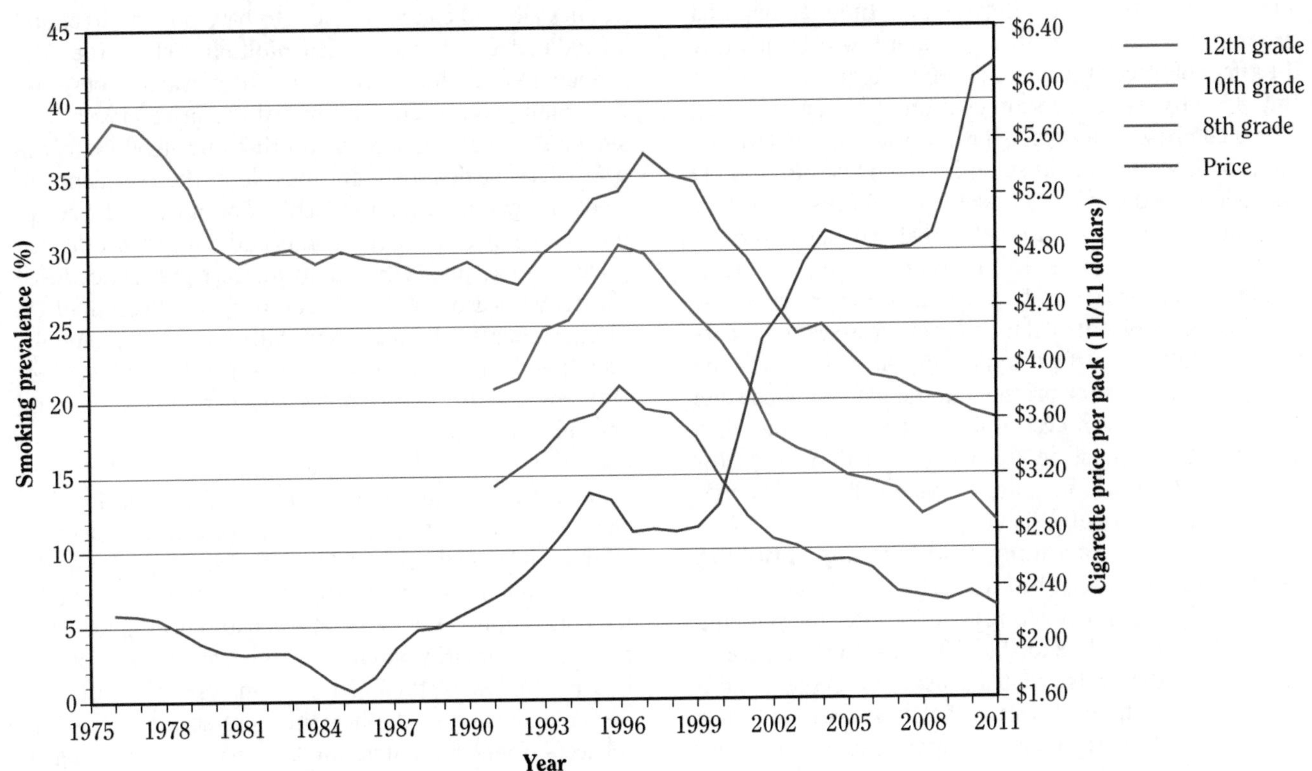

Source: Cigarette prices from Orzechowski and Walker 2011; 30-day smoking prevalence data for students in grades 8, 10, and 12 from Monitoring the Future 2011, University of Michigan News Service; author's calculations.

Finally, mixed results have been found in the relatively few studies that have examined the impact of cigarette prices on the initiation of smoking among adolescents.

Most of the research published since 2000 supports the conclusion of previous reviews that an inverse relationship exists between age and responsiveness to changes in cigarette prices. Drawing the conclusion that youth will be the most responsive to price, however, does not settle things in terms of calculating demand among younger people. For example, a central issue when estimating equations for cigarette demand among youth (or any other sector of the population) is how to account for antitobacco sentiment in different states. This is important because during a particular period it may be sentiment against tobacco that is driving both changes in cigarette smoking and changes in cigarette excise taxes. Not controlling for antitobacco sentiment may result in bias from omitting a variable, thereby producing a spurious negative relationship between price and smoking and resulting in estimated price elasticities biased away from zero. Several strategies have been suggested to account for antismoking sentiment in equations on youth smoking, including controlling for state tobacco control policies that affect primarily adults and controlling for whether the respondent resides in a tobacco-producing state. To the extent that the enactment of tobacco control policies that affect adults (and have little impact on smoking by adolescents, such as worksite restrictions on smoking) and residing in a tobacco-producing state can serve as proxies for antismoking sentiment, the inclusion of these variables in the regression model will mitigate some of the bias from omitted variables on the price estimates (Tauras et al. 2005a).

Another approach is to approximate the magnitude of antitobacco sentiment within states by using the attitudes of individuals toward smoking and beliefs about tobacco policies obtained from survey data. Still another approach is to eliminate state-level heterogeneity that is time invariant (such as types of housing) and unobserved through the use of state-level fixed effects. To the extent that sentiment toward tobacco within states is time invariant during the period under investigation, the inclusion of state-level fixed effects will eliminate the bias from an omitted variable on the price estimates. The use of state-level fixed effects relies on within-state variation in cigarette prices or taxes over time (as opposed to interstate differences in prices and taxes) to quantify the effect of price on consumption. In essence, the use of state-level fixed effects in conjunction with year-level fixed effects compares the effect of tax (or price) on smoking for individuals who reside in states in which taxes (or prices) changed with the effects of tax (or price) on smoking for individuals who reside in states that did not observe a change in tax (or price) in that year. For the state-level fixed-effects approach to be viable, researchers must use multiple years of state data; 1 year of cross-sectional data would result in perfect multicollinearity between the state-specific taxes (or prices) and the dichotomous state indicators. Moreover, even if multiple years of state data are used, there must be reasonable variation in tax (or price) over time within states to avoid collinearity issues with the tax (or price) variable.

Prevalence of smoking and average smoking among youth. As can be seen in Figure 6.2, an inverse relationship exists between prevalence rates for smoking among young people and the inflation-adjusted price of cigarettes in the United States. Most of the research conducted during the past decade that has controlled for a host of other factors thought likely to affect youth smoking, including antitobacco sentiment in the state, supports the conclusion of previous reviews that an inverse relationship exists between smoking among youth and cigarette prices.

For example, using 1 year of cross-sectional data collected in 1996 for the Study of Smoking and Tobacco Use Among Young People, Ross and Chaloupka (2003) examined the effect of cigarette prices on smoking among high school students in the United States. Although they controlled for both state-level laws on smoke-free air and youth-access laws, the authors assessed the use of several alternative measures of cigarette prices in their analysis, including average state prices and perceived prices among the students. In their preferred specifications, they estimated total price elasticities of demand of -0.67 and -1.02 when using average state prices and perceived prices among youth, respectively. The price elasticity estimates were confirmed in a subsequent analysis by Ross and Chaloupka (2004) that also explicitly controlled for compliance with youth-access laws. The estimates from these studies suggest that adolescents are considerably more responsive to price changes than are adults on the basis of the consensus estimate for the latter population (Chaloupka and Warner 2000).

Using the same cross-sectional data as Ross and Chaloupka (2003), Powell and colleagues (2005) reexamined the determinants of smoking prevalence among high school students, incorporating the importance of peer effects in their analyses. Specifically, Powell and colleagues allowed cigarette prices to have both a direct and an indirect effect, via a social multiplier effect (i.e., the influence of peer interactions), on the prevalence of smoking among youth. They estimated the price elasticity of smoking prevalence among youth to be -0.50, with the peer effect playing a significant role in the prevalence of smoking by high school students. Specifically, the aforementioned price elasticity comprised a direct-prevalence price elasticity of -0.32 and an indirect-prevalence price elasticity (measuring the social multiplier effect) of -0.18. These estimates are consistent with Ross and Chaloupka (2003) and suggest a rather large social multiplier effect with respect to price changes and participation among youth in smoking.

Katzman and associates (2007) extracted data from the 1995–2001 national Youth Risk Behavior Surveys (YRBSs) to estimate equations for cigarette demand among individuals in grades 9–12. In this study, the authors took into account the manner in which the adolescents acquired their cigarettes, distinguishing between those who primarily bought their own and those who primarily "borrowed" them. In their analyses, the researchers controlled for whether the adolescents resided in tobacco-producing states, for laws banning smoking in private worksites, and for PUP laws. Although they allowed changes in cigarette prices to affect both the probability of being a buyer and borrower and the quantity smoked, given group membership, the authors concluded that the total price elasticity of cigarette demand among adolescents ranged from -0.556 to -0.857. Again, these results imply that high school students respond more to price changes than do adults.

Earlier, Gruber and Zinman (2001) controlled for both state and year fixed effects in their analyses of smoking by youth. These researchers used three data sets from the 1990s in their analyses: MTF surveys of 8th-, 10th-, and 12th-grade students, YRBSs of 9th- to 12th-grade students, and the Vital Statistics Natality detail files of mothers during pregnancy. The authors concluded that price had a sizable and significant impact on smoking by high school seniors, with prevalence-price elasticities ranging from -0.38 in the Natality data to -1.5 in the YRBS data, with the most reliable estimate of -0.66 coming from the MTF data. Moreover, they concluded that younger adolescents are less responsive to price changes than are high school seniors.

Tauras and colleagues (2005b) investigated the impact of cigarette prices and tobacco control policies on propensity to smoke and intensity of smoking among youth and young adults during the late 1990s through the early 2000s, a period characterized by dramatic increases in cigarette prices and taxes. These investigators used the first five waves of data (1997–2001) from the National Longitudinal Survey of Youth 1997 cohort (NLSY97). Using a two-way fixed-effects technique that controls for unobserved individual-level heterogeneity and individual-invariant year-specific unobserved heterogeneity, they found a strong negative impact of cigarette prices and taxes on propensity to smoke and intensity of smoking among youth and young adults and estimated the total price elasticity of cigarette demand to be -0.827. These authors separately considered the impact of price and tax on the probability of smoking and on the average number of cigarettes smoked by smokers, estimating smoking prevalence-price elasticity of demand and the conditional price elasticity of demand to be -0.311 and -0.516, respectively. These estimates imply that a 10% increase in the real price of cigarettes would decrease the number of adolescent and young adult smokers by approximately 3.1% and reduce the average number of cigarettes smoked by adolescent and young adult smokers by 5.2%. The estimated total price elasticity was twice as large (in absolute value) as the consensus estimate for adults (0.4) and is consistent with the notion that an inverse relationship exists between age and the price elasticity of cigarette demand (USDHHS 2000b; Chaloupka and Warner 2000).

Sloan and Trogdon (2004) used Behavioral Risk Factor Surveillance data from the 1990s and early 2000s to estimate equations for smoking prevalence among young adults (18–20 years of age) and older adults (21 years of age and older). Using both state and year fixed effects, the authors concluded that propensity to smoke among young adults was the most responsive to cigarette prices, with an estimated smoking prevalence elasticity of demand of -0.27. In addition, the authors found evidence that the absolute value of the price elasticity of smoking participation declined monotonically with age until 65 years of age.

More recently, DeCicca and colleagues (2008a) developed a direct measure of state-specific antismoking sentiment with a factor analysis technique using data extracted from the Tobacco Use Supplements to the Current Population Surveys during the 1990s. Employing data from the 1992 and 2000 waves of the National Education Longitudinal Study (NELS), they found that price had a strong negative (and significant) impact on the prevalence of smoking and on average consumption for youth and young adult smokers. The estimated price elasticities of smoking prevalence and average consumption by smokers ranged from -0.59 to -0.76 and from -0.3 to -0.66, respectively. Moreover, price was found to have a strong negative influence on average smoking by youth smokers in the 2000 cross-section even after controlling for the new measure of antismoking sentiment. However, when smoking sentiment was included in equations for smoking prevalence, the price effects lost statistical significance. Using the 2000 wave of data, the authors tested models that employed the newly developed direct measure of antismoking sentiment and compared it with models using alternative approaches to dealing with such sentiment. The strong negative impact of price on average smoking was robust to all the methods of dealing with unobserved state-level sentiment toward tobacco. Moreover, in all the models except the model that included the new measure of sentiment, price was found to have a significant negative impact, reducing smoking prevalence among youth. Given the findings when the direct measure of antismoking sentiment was included in the models, DeCicca and colleagues questioned the adequacy of using proxies to control for antismoking sentiment. However, some caution should be used in interpreting models that include a direct measure of antismoking sentiment in that reverse causality is likely in this type of estimation strategy. That is, the amount of smoking within a state is likely to have an impact on the level of antismoking sentiment within that state, resulting in simultaneity bias.

Carpenter and Cook (2008) addressed the concerns of DeCicca and colleagues (2008a) in a recent paper that used national, state, and local YRBSs from 1991 to 2005; they tested three alternative methods of dealing with antismoking sentiment. First, they estimated a cross-sectional model that relied on intrastate variation in cigarette taxes to identify the impact of price on youth smoking. Second, they estimated a two-way fixed-effects model that controlled for area and year fixed effects. Finally, they employed the same direct measure of antismoking sentiment used by DeCicca and colleagues (2008a). Carpenter and Cook found consistent evidence of a significant negative effect of cigarette taxes on smoking prevalence in the cross-sectional and fixed-effects approaches. Moreover, using the new direct measure of antismoking sentiment, they found a strong negative effect of taxes on the prevalence of smoking among youth, alleviating the concerns raised by DeCicca and colleagues. Using the tax effects from the national and state samples, Carpenter and Cook estimated price elasticities for the prevalence of smoking among youth of -0.56 and -0.25, respectively.

Effects of cigarette prices on smoking transitions. Many researchers examining the influence of price on the prevalence of smoking among youth have assumed that much of the effect of price reflects its impact on the initiation of smoking, while the effects of price on young adults and adults are thought to be dominated by its effects on escalation of smoking and on cessation. Whether these judgments are true or not, several recent studies have attempted to directly quantify the impact of price on initiation among youth and the effects of price on escalation and cessation among young adults. Most of the recent studies have used longitudinal data on smoking behavior and other determinants of smoking over time.

Initiation of smoking. Tauras and colleagues (2001) were the first to examine the impact of price on initiation of smoking among youth by using longitudinal data, in this case from three cohorts of students enrolled in the 8th and 10th grades in 1991–1993 who were part of the longitudinal component of the MTF. The authors examined three alternative measures of the smoking process over time, including a transition from not smoking to smoking any amount; daily smoking, defined as smoking at least one to five cigarettes per day on average; and heavy daily smoking, defined as smoking at least one-half pack per day on average. After controlling for youth-access laws and regional fixed effects, the average price elasticity estimates for smoking cigarettes for (1) any smoking, (2) smoking at least one to five cigarettes per day on average, and (3) smoking at least one-half pack per day on average were -0.271, -0.811, and 0.955, respectively. These estimates imply that the process of smoking uptake among youth responds to changes in cigarette prices.

Cawley and associates (2004), who investigated the determinants of smoking initiation among youth by using more recent data from the first four waves (1997–2000) of NLSY97, looked at two alternative measures of smoking initiation. The first was a transition from nonsmoker to smoking any quantity of cigarettes (termed "less stringent initiation"), and the second ("more stringent initiation") was the transition from nonsmoker to frequent smoker, as measured by having smoked on at least 15 of the past 30 days. Although they controlled for smoke-free air laws, youth-access laws, and residence in tobacco-producing states, the authors concluded that initiation of smoking among male adolescents was very responsive to changes in cigarette prices, with the average price elasticities estimated to be -0.86 for less stringent initiation and -1.49 for more stringent initiation. Initiation of smoking among female adolescents was not significantly related to cigarette prices but was very responsive to concerns about body weight.

A follow-up paper on the initiation of smoking among youth by Cawley and associates (2006) found results very similar to the earlier paper by Cawley and colleagues (2004) despite the use of a longitudinal data set that spanned a longer period: the data were from 1988 to 2000 and were taken from the children's cohort of NLSY79. After controlling for smoke-free air laws and youth-access laws, researchers found cigarette prices to have a negative impact on the initiation of smoking in all the models that were estimated; however, the price coefficients differed significantly from zero in only the male equations. Specifically, the price elasticity of smoking initiation among males on the basis of any cigarettes consumed was estimated to be -1.20.

In a series of papers, DeCicca and colleagues (2000, 2008a,b) examined the influence of price and tax on the initiation of smoking among youth and young adults. In one of the papers, DeCicca and associates (2008a) used data from the 1988, 1990, 1992, and 2000 waves of NELS to examine the influence of cigarette prices on decisions about smoking among adolescents and young adults. The authors found price to have a strong and significant negative influence on initiation when state fixed effects were omitted from the model. However, when state fixed effects were included in the regression analyses, price failed to reach significance at conventional levels. These researchers concluded that unobserved state-level heterogeneity (possibly in the form of differential antismoking sentiment), not price, drives decisions to smoke among youth and young adults. In a different paper, DeCicca and colleagues (2008b) used data from the 1992 and 2000 waves of NELS to examine the influence of cigarette excise taxes on initiation of smoking among young adults (18–26 years of age). These authors used three identification strategies in their equations: First, they used intrastate variation in cigarette excise taxes to identify the impact of price on initiation of smoking. Second, they included the direct measure of antismoking sentiment developed by DeCicca and colleagues (2008a) in their equations for initiation. Finally, they used variation in cigarette taxes faced by young adults who moved across state lines between 1992 and 2000 versus young adults who remained in the same state in these two specific years.

In this paper (DeCicca et al. 2008b), cigarette taxes were found to have a significant negative impact on the initiation of smoking among young adults for only those who remained in the same state (the third identification strategy). The authors concluded that cigarette prices have little impact on the initiation of smoking, but these results should be viewed with caution. First, the study was conducted on a sample of individuals who initiated smoking later in life (they were nonsmokers in high school but smokers by a modal age of 26 years). Most adults who have ever smoked initiate smoking before the age range investigated by DeCicca and colleagues, and the decisions on initiation of an older cohort may be quite different from those of younger individuals. Second, as discussed above, antismoking sentiment may be an endogenous variable that is determined simultaneously with smoking. Third, in the models that relied solely on intrastate variation in taxes, the authors found only weak evidence of a negative effect of taxes on the prevalence of smoking (the price effect failed to reach 5% significance levels in a two-tailed test). Finally, in an earlier study, DeCicca and colleagues

(2000) examined the determinants of initiation among individuals of different races and ethnicities with data extracted from the 1988–1992 NELS. After controlling for state and year fixed effects, they found price to have a dramatic negative impact on decisions to initiate smoking among Hispanics and African Americans, but price had no influence on decisions to initiate smoking by Whites. The authors estimated that a price increase of $1.50 would decrease rates of initiation among Hispanics and African Americans to approximately 1%. However, the authors cautioned that the prediction for African Americans was based on a statistically insignificant estimate of the price coefficient. Regardless, the results of this earlier study (DeCicca et al. 2000) indicate that conclusions about the relationship between initiation and cigarette taxes may well need to consider race or ethnicity rather than being simply drawn for the population as a whole.

Dinno and Glantz (2009) used the February 2002 panel of the Tobacco Use Supplement of the Current Population Survey (54,024 individuals representing the U.S. population aged 15–80 years) to study the independent association of cigarette prices and state or local strong clean indoor air laws with current smoker status and consumption in a multilevel framework, including interactions with educational attainment, household income, and race/ethnicity. They found nonlinear relationships between price and smoking status and per smoker consumption, with no effect at higher prices. Below $3.28 per pack (in 2002), the OR for smoking, given a 10-cent increase in price, was 0.95 (95% confidence interval [CI] 0.93–0.97); this relationship ended above that price. The association of cigarette price with smoker status did not change with educational attainment, household income, or race/ethnicity. There was no interaction between clean indoor air coverage and cigarette price. There was no interaction between cigarette price (or strong clean indoor air laws) and educational attainment, household income, or race/ethnicity. Price increases (and clean indoor air laws) appear to benefit all socioeconomic and racial/ethnic groups in the study equally in terms of reducing smoking participation and consumption.

Smoking cessation. A few studies have examined the impact of price on the decisions of adolescents and young adults to quit smoking. Tauras and Chaloupka (2001) were the first to model decisions on cessation with longitudinal data that tracked individuals' smoking behavior over time. In particular, these researchers used the longitudinal component of MTF surveys and a semiparametric Cox regression to assess the probability that smokers would make a transition from smoking to nonsmoking. The authors concluded that the likelihood of making an attempt to quit among both men and women increases significantly as cigarette prices rise. Their estimated price elasticities for smoking cessation ranged between 0.27 and 0.92 for men and 0.34 to 0.71 for women, implying that a 10% increase in price raises the probability of making a cessation attempt by as much as 10% for men.

Expanding on the original study, Tauras (2004) used the longitudinal component of MTF surveys and employed a stratified Cox regression to model multiple attempts to quit among young adults. His findings confirmed a positive relationship between cigarette prices and smoking cessation, with a 10% increase in the price of cigarettes increasing successful cessation by young adults by an estimated 3.5%.

DeCicca and colleagues (2008b), in their study using data from the 1992 and 2000 waves of NELS, examined the influence of cigarette excise taxes on the decisions of young adults to quit smoking. When these authors used intrastate variation in cigarette excise taxes to identify the impact of taxes on smoking cessation, they found young adults to be very responsive to tax changes; indeed, the price elasticity of cessation was estimated to be 0.93. In a different specification, these investigators added the direct measure of antismoking sentiment developed by DeCicca and associates (2008a) and estimated the price elasticity of cessation to be 0.47, but here the parameter estimate for price was insignificant, indicating that the elasticity was substantially driven by variation in cigarette excise taxes and antismoking sentiment. Finally, as discussed within "*Initiation of smoking*" earlier in this section, they used variation in cigarette taxes faced by young adults who moved across state lines between 1992 and 2000 versus young adults who remained in the same state in 1992 and 2000. In this specification, cigarette taxes were found to have a positive impact on smoking cessation among young adults only for those who moved to a different state in those 2 years. The price elasticity of cessation among those who moved was relatively large (1.49), and the authors concluded that despite the lack of significance of price in this specification, most likely owing to the small sample (n = 321), price is likely to play a strong role in decisions to quit smoking among young adults.

Finally, using an experimental framework, Ross and colleagues (2005) examined the expected reaction to a future price increase among smokers in high school. The authors used cross-sectional data collected in 1996 for the Study of Smoking and Tobacco Use Among Young People, which contained information on individuals' current smoking status and expected smoking behavior after a hypothetical change in cigarette price. After controlling for smoke-free air laws and youth access laws, the authors found increases in cigarette prices to have a strong positive impact on decisions by youth to quit smoking: the estimated price elasticity of cessation ranged from 0.895 to 0.930.

Other smoking transitions. In a study that looked at smoking transitions other than initiation or cessation, Tauras (2005) examined the impact of cigarette prices on such transitions among youth and young adults in the United States. This author examined the transition from nondaily to daily smoking and the transitions from light smoking intensity (defined as 1–5 cigarettes per day) and moderate smoking intensity (defined as 10 cigarettes per day on average) to higher intensities. Tauras (2005) employed baseline surveys from the 1976–1993 longitudinal component of MTF data along with follow-up surveys through 1995 in the analyses and controlled for antismoking sentiment with a variety of techniques. These included having separate indicators for whether the individual resided in a tobacco-producing state or resided in Utah, using U.S. Census Bureau division fixed effects to capture differences between these divisions in smoking sentiment, and estimating the smoking progression equations on a subsample of the respondents who did not reside in either a tobacco-producing state or in Utah during the time the survey was conducted. Cigarette prices were found to have a strong negative impact on all of the estimated smoking transitions. In particular, the estimated mean price elasticities of daily uptake, moderate uptake, and heavy uptake were -0.646, -0.576, and -0.412, respectively. These results indicate that a 10% increase in cigarette prices will decrease daily uptake, moderate uptake, and heavy uptake by an estimated 6.46%, 5.76%, and 4.12%, respectively. These findings clearly indicate that increases in cigarette prices will prevent many young adults from progressing into higher intensities of smoking.

Other tobacco products. Numerous studies on the economic determinants of demand for cigarettes among youth have been published during the past decade, but very few recent econometric studies have been published on the impact of taxes on other tobacco products.

In one such study, Tauras and colleagues (2007) used data extracted from the 1995–2001 national YRBSs to examine the impact of taxes on smokeless tobacco on use of this product among male high school students. The estimates developed clearly indicate that higher taxes on smokeless tobacco would significantly reduce the number of male students who use this product and the number of days they would use it. The estimated tax elasticities of the prevalence of smokeless tobacco ranged from -0.197 to -0.121, and the estimated tax elasticities of days using smokeless tobacco ranged from -0.085 to -0.044. The study also found that cigarette prices had a significant negative impact on both the prevalence of smokeless tobacco and the number of days that male high school students used smokeless tobacco. The estimated cross-price elasticity of the prevalence of smokeless tobacco was -0.715, and the cross-price elasticity of the number of days of use of smokeless tobacco was -0.413. These estimates indicate that a 10% increase in the price of cigarettes would decrease the prevalence of smokeless tobacco by an estimated 7% and would lower the number of days using smokeless tobacco by an estimated 4% among male high school students. Thus, the estimates indicate that smokeless tobacco products and cigarettes are economic complements in consumption for young males. These findings are particularly important in light of the fact that the cigarette companies have purchased smokeless tobacco companies and are now actively promoting dual use of cigarettes and smokeless tobacco with the same branding (e.g., Marlboro Snus and Camel Snus) (Mejia et al. 2010). (More data on the use of multiple tobacco products by young males can be found in Chapter 3.)

Finally, Ringel and colleagues (2005) used data from the 1999 and 2000 waves of the National Youth Tobacco Survey to estimate the impact of cigar prices on demand for cigars among adolescents in grades 6–12. After controlling for laws on smoke-free air and on youth access, the researchers found the price of cigars to be inversely related to the prevalence of cigar use among youth. Specifically, the price elasticity of the prevalence of cigar smoking among youth was estimated to be -0.34.

Tax Avoidance

A preponderance of the aforementioned studies on the effects of price on the demand for tobacco products among adolescents used individual-level survey data and state-level price data. Aside from the problem of intrastate variation in prices, using average prices within a state does not account for an individual's opportunities to avoid taxes. For example, some individuals living near American Indian reservations or close to the border of a state with lower taxes on cigarettes will be able to pay less than the average price for cigarettes in their own state. Thus, when using individual-level data, this type of measurement error in the independent variable (i.e., price) will likely result in an underestimate of the true price elasticity of demand. There will be an underestimate of the response to price because some smokers will maintain their consumption after a tax increase by turning to cheaper (tax-avoided) cigarettes, making it look as though the tax increase had little or no impact on their consumption. Future studies on demand that account for a person's opportunities for tax avoidance are warranted.

Summary Regarding Taxation and Pricing

A few general conclusions can be drawn from recent studies on the effects of taxes and prices on tobacco consumption among youth and young adults:

1. Most of the research over the past decade has concluded that increases in cigarette prices lead to reductions in the prevalence of smoking and its intensity among youth and young adults.

2. A majority of the existing research suggests that the effects of price on smoking prevalence involve both a decrease in initiation of smoking among youth and an increase in cessation among young adults.

3. Most of the recent research has concluded that adolescents and young adults are more responsive than adults to changes in cigarette prices.

4. Limited evidence suggests that higher cigarette prices will prevent young adults from progressing into higher intensities of smoking.

5. A few recent studies have found an inverse relationship among adolescents between product-specific tobacco taxes (or prices) and the propensity to use smokeless tobacco, the intensity of its use, and the prevalence of cigar smoking.

6. The magnitude of the impact of taxes (or prices) on the demand for cigarettes seems to depend on how the model controls for antismoking sentiment.

Future research that uses a large number of waves of longitudinal data on adolescents and young adults during a period of significant changes in tobacco taxes and prices should be helpful in obtaining the most precise estimates for the impact of price on the intensity, prevalence, initiation, and cessation of smoking, smokeless tobacco use, and on other tobacco use transitions.

Policies on Clean Indoor Air

Policies on clean indoor air take the form of legislation and/or regulations at the federal, state, local, and institutional levels that prohibit smoking in specified locations, such as workplaces, public places, restaurants, bars and casinos, schools, day care centers, and health care facilities (USDHHS 1989, 2000b). Although there have been laws on clean indoor air for more than 30 years, their coverage has expanded dramatically in recent years. As of July 1, 2011, 23 states, the District of Columbia, and Puerto Rico have laws that prohibit smoking in all workplaces, including bars and restaurants (American Nonsmokers' Rights Foundation 2011b). The movement for laws on clean indoor air largely began at the local level, and many of the states without comprehensive laws have cities or counties with such laws. The American Nonsmokers' Rights Foundation estimated that as of July 1, 2011, comprehensive local and/or state laws on clean indoor air covered 48.0% of the U.S. population (American Nonsmokers' Rights Foundation 2011a). Figure 6.3 provides a map of the implementation of these laws, (American Nonsmokers' Rights Foundation [2011a]).

Many locations are smoke-free, because of their potential effects on youth. According to the CDC School Health Policies and Programs Study from 2006, in that year 70% of states as well as 95% of school districts included in a nationally representative sample prohibited smoking by students in school buildings, grounds, vehicles, and off-campus school-sponsored events (Jones et al. 2007). However, only 47% of the states but 78% of the school districts had smoke-free schools in which the same restrictions applied to staff (Jones et al. 2007). At least 466 U.S. colleges and universities are completely smoke-free, which includes having 100% smoke-free residential housing policies (American Nonsmokers' Rights Foundation 2011d). On the basis of data from the Tobacco Use Supplement of the Current Population Survey (CDC 2008c), CDC reported that in 2007 the median proportion (by state) of households with smoke-free policies for everyone living in or entering the home was 66%. Finally, smoking has been prohibited in vehicles when children are present in nine U.S. cities or counties, four states, Puerto Rico, eight Canadian provinces/territories, and five Australian states (Blumenfeld 2008; Global Advisors Smokefree Policy 2011).

To this point, little evidence is available about sociodemographic disparities in the coverage of smoke-free policies in public and private locations. In one study, Skeer and coworkers (2004) examined differences in community characteristics in relation to the strength of their local policies on clean indoor air in public places; they found that towns with higher education levels and greater per capita income were more likely to have the most restrictive policies. A recent CDC report using 1999–2004 National Health and Nutrition Examination Survey (NHANES) data found that youth were three to four times as likely as adults to be exposed to secondhand smoke in the home (CDC 2008a). In this study, Black non-Hispanic persons were the most likely and Mexican Americans the least likely to be exposed to secondhand smoke at home, and low-income families were three times as likely to be exposed as their counterparts in the highest income group.

The primary purpose of laws and policies on clean indoor air is to protect smokers and nonsmokers alike from exposure to the toxic effects of secondhand smoke. However, a growing body of evidence suggests that these policies may have the additional benefit of producing lower

Figure 6.3 Map of 100% smoke-free air laws, United States, July 1, 2011

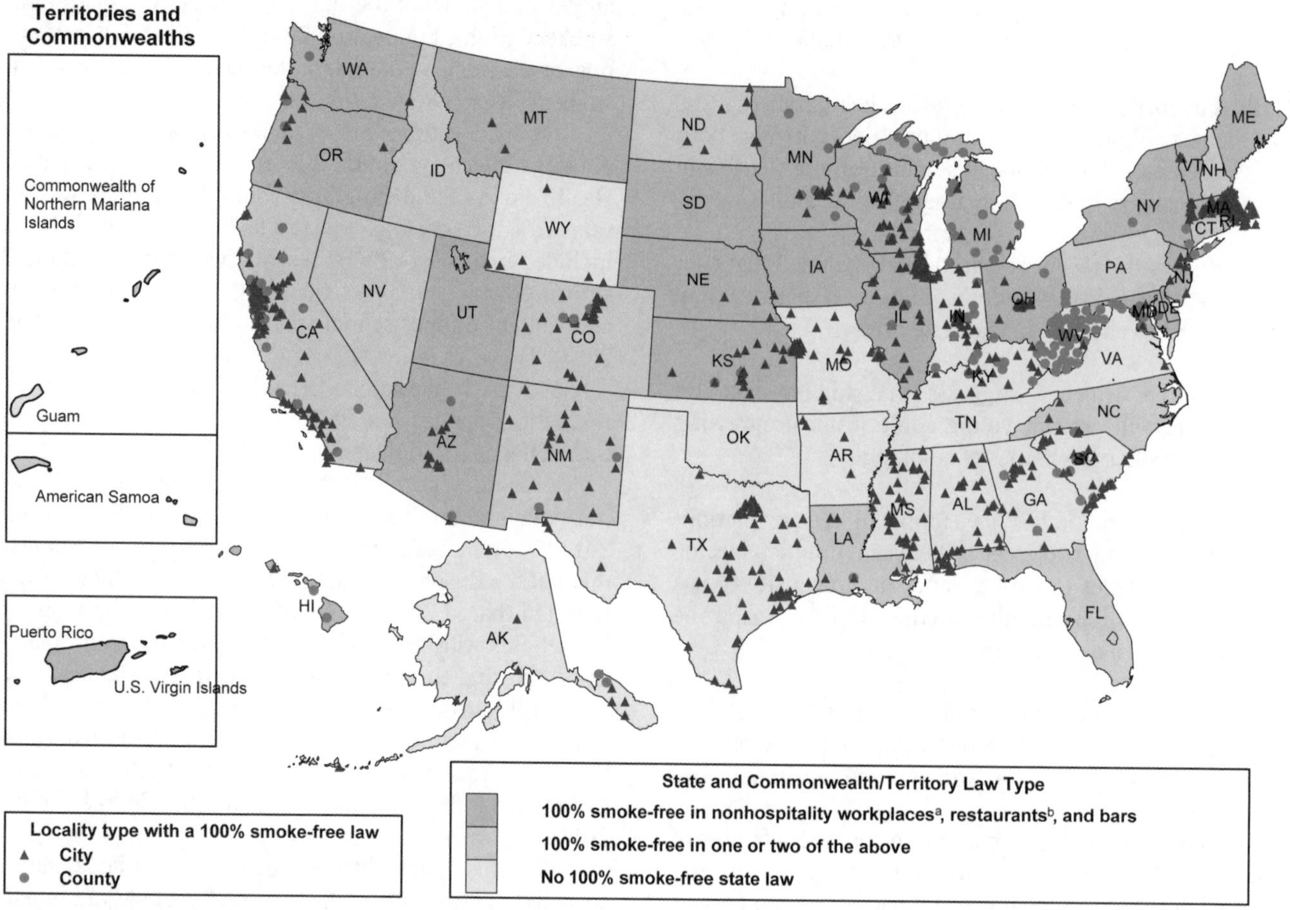

Territories and Commonwealths

Locality type with a 100% smoke-free law
- ▲ City
- ● County

State and Commonwealth/Territory Law Type
- 100% smoke-free in nonhospitality workplaces[a], restaurants[b], and bars
- 100% smoke-free in one or two of the above
- No 100% smoke-free state law

Source: American Nonsmokers' Rights Foundation 2011a.
Note: American Indian and Alaska Native sovereign tribal laws are not reflected on this map.
[a]Includes both public and private nonhospitality workplaces, including, but not limited to, offices, factories, and warehouses.
[b]Includes any attached bar in the restaurant.

smoking rates among youth and young adults. Although the mechanism for this effect is not clear, these laws could result in lower visibility of role models who smoke, fewer opportunities to smoke alone or with others, and diminished social acceptability and social advantage for smoking (Alesci et al. 2003; Eisenberg and Forster 2003; Wakefield and Forster 2005). Dinno and Glantz (2009) showed that, while smoking prevalence and cigarette consumption were higher in people with low education and income (using the 2002 Tobacco Use Supplement to the Current Population Survey), this population exhibited the same reductions in smoking associated with the presence of clean indoor air laws and tax increases on tobacco products as did people in higher education and income groups.

Effects of Clean Indoor Air Laws on Smoking by Youth

The first evidence that laws and policies on clean indoor air could reduce adolescent smoking came from cross-sectional studies. Liang and colleagues (2003), who reviewed studies on the effects of tobacco control policies, including the effects of clean indoor air laws on youth smoking rates, found that restrictive laws and workplace policies were an effective tool for reducing smoking among youth. They also reviewed the evidence concerning smoking policies in households and found several studies showing a strong inverse relationship between the presence of such policies and the chances of trying smoking as well as experimentation (Liang et al. 2003). Since that review, McMullen and colleagues (2005) used data from both the YRBS and the National Survey on Drug Use and Health (NSDUH) to examine the relationship between the prevalence of youth smoking at the state level and the "state clean indoor air law score" as reported by the State Cancer Legislative Database. For both sets of data, the strength of laws on clean indoor air was inversely related to the prevalence of smoking among youth.

Using the longitudinal data on young adults from MTF, Tauras (2004) found that stronger restrictions on smoking in private worksites and public places increased the probability of smoking cessation among young adults. Later, Siegel and colleagues (2005, 2008) published two papers from a longitudinal study of adolescents (n = 3,834) in Massachusetts; comparing baseline figures and the 2-year follow-up surveys they reported that youth who lived in a town with a strong smoke-free ordinance for local restaurants were significantly less likely to progress to regular smoking than were youth in towns where such restrictions were either weak or of medium strength (Siegel et al. 2005). These researchers reported that at the 4-year follow-up, youth in the group with a strong ordinance on smoking in restaurants had reduced odds for both overall progress to established smoking and transition from experimentation to regular smoking (Siegel et al. 2008). More recently, Klein and colleagues (2009) reported a much smaller effect in a report from the Minnesota Adolescent Community Cohort Study, which included 4,233 Minnesota youth who were 11–16 years of age at baseline. Participants were interviewed every 6 months from 2000 to 2006. The authors found a 6% lower likelihood of monthly smoking and a 13% lower likelihood of weekly smoking if youth lived in areas with a strong policy on clean indoor air. The study also found a strong association between a household smoking ban and reduction in the likelihood of smoking by youth.

Prohibitions by colleges on smoking may have characteristics of worksite, school, and household smoking bans because they can affect one or more aspects of the students' lives. As discussed in "School-Based Programs to Prevent Smoking" later in this chapter, the amount of research on the role of school policy in preventing youth smoking is surprisingly small and, similarly, there are few published reports on college policies regarding students' smoking behavior. Using data from the 1999 survey of the Harvard School of Public Health College Alcohol Study, Wechsler and associates (2001) found that current smoking prevalence was lower among students living in smoke-free campus residences than among those living in unrestricted residences. In addition, smokers who started smoking in college reported smoking fewer cigarettes if they lived in smoke-free residences. Czart and associates (2001), who used 1997 survey data from the Harvard School of Public Health College Alcohol Study, found that complete smoke-free policies lowered the intensity of smoking and strong enforcement decreased participation in smoking, but both findings were of only marginal significance statistically.

Effects of Home Smoking Policies on Youth Smoking

Restrictions in the home may be a powerful tool to reduce smoking by youth. In a report on 1996 survey data for high school students across the United States, from the Study of Smoking and Tobacco Use Among Young People, Wakefield and colleagues (2000) found that a 100% smoke-free policy for everyone in the home was associated with a reduced likelihood that youth would advance from their current smoking stage for every stage from susceptible to established smoker. In addition, in a study of youth 15–17 years of age from the Current Population Surveys of 1992–1993 and 1995–1996, those who lived in smoke-free households were only 74% as likely to be smokers as those who lived in households with unrestricted smoking (Farkas et al. 2000), independent of the smoking status of individuals in the household. Furthermore, youth already smoking were more likely to quit. However, partial restrictions showed no effect on smoking. Later, analysis of the 1998–1999 Current Population Survey produced the same results and extended them to young adults living with parents (Clark et al. 2006). In both adolescents and young adults, complete bans on smoking were associated with never having been a regular smoker, not being a current smoker, and having quit smoking. The adjusted odds of being a current smoker (using never smoking as the referent) were about 50% lower in households with strict smoking rules than in those without rules on smoking.

At this point, more information is needed on how home smoking policies vary by sociodemographic characteristics. Some information is available, however, on American Indian youth. In a recent study of a convenience sample of 336 urban youth who were American Indian, 43% reported living in a household that banned smoking for everyone (Forster et al. 2008). Lifetime nonsmokers to date were significantly more likely to live in a completely restrictive household than those who had ever smoked, and bans on smoking were associated with level of smoking among these youth. There is also a positive effect of smokefree legislation that applies to workplaces and public places on the prevalence of voluntary home smokefree policies (Cheng et al. 2011; Mills et al. 2011; Hovell et al. 2011). Cheng and colleagues (2011) found that living in a county fully covered by a 100% clean indoor air law in workplaces, restaurants, or bars is associated with an increased likelihood of having a voluntary 100% smoke-free home policy both for people living with smokers (OR = 7.76; 95% CI, 5.27–11.43) and not living with smokers (OR = 4.12; 95% CI, 3.28–5.16).

Effects of Home Smoking Policies on Exposure of Youth to Secondhand Smoke

In addition to reducing youth smoking, bans on smoking in the household have the potential to reduce youth's exposure to secondhand smoke. Youth who reside in multiunit housing are particularly at risk of exposure, even if they do not live with a smoker, as smoke can travel through walls, air ducts, windows, and ventilation systems (Wilson et al. 2011). An analysis of NHANES data from 2001 to 2006 found that young people living in an apartment in which no one smoked had significantly higher cotinine levels (a biological measure of smoke exposure) than those living in a detached home in which no one smoked (Wilson et al. 2011). In 2009, the U.S. Department of Housing and Urban Development issued a memorandum strongly encouraging public housing authorities to implement nonsmoking policies in some or all of their public housing units (Winickoff et al. 2010).

Summary Regarding Policies on Clean Indoor Air

Laws and policies on clean indoor air support multilevel efforts that can be effective in reducing exposure to secondhand smoke and potentially youth smoking. This argues for a comprehensive approach to reducing smoking among youth.

Regulations on Youth Access

One component in a comprehensive strategy to prevent smoking among youth is restricting the supply of cigarettes to minors. Youth can obtain cigarettes in two ways: commercially (from a store or vending machine) and socially (borrowing, buying, or stealing them from other youth or adults). A variety of strategies aim at restricting commercial access, and these strategies in turn can limit social access by reducing the total number of cigarettes accessible to youth.

Laws restricting youth access became widespread after the 1992 Synar Amendment (*ADAMHA Reorganization Act* [1992]) mandated that all states and territories legally prohibit the sale of tobacco to minors by the middle of 1995. Before this amendment, youth obtained cigarettes from commercial sources with relative ease (DiFranza and Brown 1992; CDC 1993, 2002; USDHHS 1994; Naum et al. 1995). In the 1994 Surgeon General's report (USDHHS 1994), the average over-the-counter success rate for purchase attempts by minors was reported to be 67% (based on 13 studies conducted between 1987 and 1993). The Synar Amendment called for the states to enforce laws on youth access through compliance checks and to report progress in this area to the Secretary of USDHHS. The annual goal as stated by the federal government is to reach the minimum percentage of sales to underage decoys in compliance checks. States noncompliant with the amendment's annual goals can have their monies from the Substance Abuse Prevention and Treatment block grant reduced (USDHHS 1995). Figure 6.4 shows that since the passage of the amendment, the noncompliance rate (as measured by the states' mandated test purchases under that law) has dropped substantially.

Local jurisdictions—including states, counties, and cities—also have several policy options that address the access of youth to retail purchases, including requiring the licensure of tobacco retailers and banning self-service sales of tobacco if the authority of these jurisdictions has not been preempted by prior legislation. Another option for local jurisdictions is penalizing youth for possession, purchase, and use of tobacco products. Possible penalties include citations, fines, and ordering the youth to attend cessation classes.

Possible Strategies

The three possible strategies for encouraging compliance to age-of-sale laws are taking appropriate steps in the retail environment, educating merchants, and actively enforcing the laws. Taking appropriate steps in the retail environment includes requiring that tobacco products be located behind the counter, posting signage informing customers that it is illegal for minors to purchase tobacco, and banning vending machines and self-service sales (Forster and Wolfson 1998). Taking these steps reduces the likelihood that youth will obtain cigarettes even if the store's clerk is inattentive. Education of merchants is an attempt to inform retailers of the laws; it is assumed that educated retailers would be less likely to sell cigarettes to minors (Rigotti 1999). "Self-enforcement" and education of merchants are not enough, however, to prevent minors from purchasing tobacco from commercial establishments (Feighery et al. 1991; DiFranza and Brown 1992; Landrine et al. 1996; Gemson et al. 1998; Altman et al. 1999; Rigotti 1999); penalties are needed. Penalties for selling tobacco to minors include revoking store licenses and fining merchants and clerks who sell to youth, both of which are usually done after a random compliance check.

Figure 6.4 Synar noncompliance rate by year: average of 50 states and the District of Columbia weighted by state population

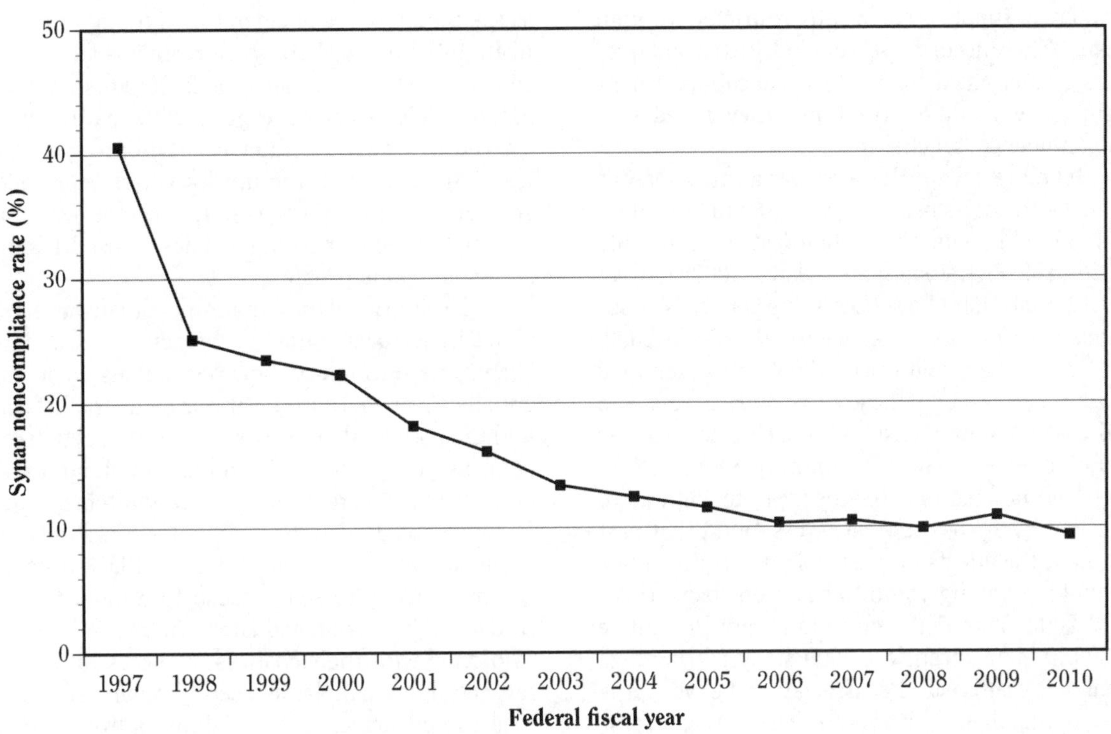

Source: Substance Abuse and Mental Health Services Administration 2011.
Note: With the Synar Amendment (Section 1926 of Alcohol, Drug Abuse, and Mental Health Administration Reorganization Act, Public Law 102-321), Congress mandated that all states and territories must legally prohibit sale of tobacco to minors by the middle of 1995. In 1997, Arkansas, Kentucky, Montana, Nevada, North Dakota, Oregon, and Texas did not report rates. In 1998, Delaware and Rhode Island did not report rates.

The 1992 Synar Amendment can be seen as a supply-side strategy for limiting and controlling the supply of cigarettes. Its premise is that if youth-access policies are well enforced, they will lead to less youth smoking. This sentiment is echoed by CDC, which includes control of youth access in its *Best Practices for Comprehensive Tobacco Control Programs Guide* (CDC 2007b) as well as in *Healthy People 2010*, which specifies policy goals on youth access (USDHHS 2000a).

Another strategy is penalizing youth for possessing, using, or purchasing tobacco. The underlying theory behind PUP strategies is that these consequences will reduce demand among youth for tobacco. One potential downside of this approach, as discussed in Chapter 5 (Wakefield and Giovino 2003), is that punitive legal measures directed at youth may distract from focusing on the role of the tobacco industry or retailers.

Criteria for Evidence of Prevention

Of the two key criteria for evidence that strategies to limit access are effective, the first is that the supply of cigarettes available to youth is actually reduced; the second is that strategies affect the prevalence, intensity, initiation, and/or cessation of youth smoking. Rigorous evaluation of available strategies presents challenges, but such evaluations are necessary to determine whether these strategies meet the goals of prevention.

Effects of Interventions to Limit Youth Access: Prior Reviews

Several English-language systematic analyses have been conducted of interventions to limit the access of youth to tobacco, with the key paper a Cochrane review conducted by Stead and Lancaster (2005). These authors concluded that policies to limit youth access and enforcement of these policies can improve the compliance of retailers, and the prevalence of smoking will be affected if the commercial supply is sufficiently restricted through these means. The authors also concluded that enforcement had a greater effect than did the education of merchants, but as with all interventions, they noted that sustained compliance is a challenge.

The second review in this area was a meta-analysis of policy on youth access based on data from nine studies; the authors found no effect on smoking at any threshold of access control (Fichtenberg and Glantz 2002; Ling et al. 2002), although there have been some concerns about the methods used in this meta-analysis (DiFranza 2002; Jason et al. 2003). Levy and Friend (2002) also examined the empirical studies of policies on youth access and concluded that a comprehensive approach that includes active enforcement of laws, community mobilization, and training of merchants is the most promising way to control access. Even so, these reviewers found that past studies showed the effects of these policies on the prevalence of smoking among youth to be inconclusive (Levy and Friend 2002; Task Force on Community Preventive Services 2005). More recently, a 2009 study by DiFranza and colleagues examined the association between the compliance of merchants with youth access laws and current daily smoking while controlling for cigarette prices, restaurant smoking bans, media campaigns, and demographic variables. The study showed that the odds of daily smoking were reduced by 2% for each 1% increase in merchant compliance (DiFranza et al. 2009).

Wakefield and Giovino (2003) reviewed the empirical evidence for PUP laws and their enforcement and concluded that these laws were associated with reduced smoking among youth only for those young people who were unlikely to initiate smoking. Notably, both the existence of PUP laws and their enforcement have become extremely common in the United States.

Effects of Interventions to Limit Youth Access: Current Evidence Base

Critics of strategies that promote policies to limit youth access have argued that even if the commercial supply of cigarettes could be successfully reduced, the social supply of cigarettes would grow to fill the gap (Ling et al. 2002). Indeed, in communities where cigarettes have become relatively difficult for underage youth to purchase from commercial sources, adolescent smokers have increasingly relied on social sources (Forster et al. 1998; Altman et al. 1999; DiFranza and Coleman 2001). But this trend from relying on commercial sources to using social sources appears to be associated with less consumption of cigarettes among youth (DiFranza et al. 2009). Another finding of interest is that among adolescents who smoke, the heavier smokers are less likely to use social sources as their only source of cigarettes, although they are more likely to be a social source for other adolescents (Wolfson et al. 1997; Harrison et al. 2000; Forster et al. 2003). Finally, Widome and colleagues (2007) have demonstrated a trend in which a greater proportion of youth become heavy smokers in communities where more adolescent smokers exclusively use commercial sources, thus reinforcing the need for strong policies to restrict commercial access for young people.

The impact of the Synar Amendment appears to have varied by sociodemographic characteristics, and there has been some research on how restrictions on access differentially affect youth from various demographic groups. In a Florida study, there was evidence that retailers in Hispanic neighborhoods in Miami (although not in the other cities studied) were more likely to sell tobacco to minors (Asumda and Jordan 2009). In contrast, stores in neighborhoods with a high percentage of Black residents were not more likely to sell tobacco to minors (Asumda and Jordan 2009). For individual youth, race/ethnicity may be associated with their chances of successfully purchasing tobacco. For example, a recently published study examined compliance checks in California from 1999 to 2003 and found more sales to Black and Asian underage decoys than to their White counterparts (Landrine et al. 2008). Earlier, Chaloupka and Pacula (1999) found that although restrictions on youth access had no impact on smoking rates among White youth, they were associated with a lower prevalence of smoking among Black youth.

Discussion Regarding Youth Access

Data on whether interventions to restrict access can lead to a reduction in the number of retailers selling tobacco to minors are mixed, although the Community Preventive Task Force concluded that community mobilization combined with additional interventions, such as stronger local laws directed at retailers, active enforcement of retailer sales laws, and retailer education with reinforcement are recommended (Task Force on Community Preventive Services 2005). A recent comprehensive review also supports the efficacy of enforced reductions in the sales of cigarettes to minors (DiFranza 2011).

Bans on Advertising

In discussing advertising it is important to clarify what it is and what it is not (see Richards and Curran 2002). Advertising is a type of marketing that uses media to create positive product imagery or positive product associations or to connect the product with desirable personal traits, activities, or outcomes (Richards and Curran 2002). Marketing can be defined as the mix of all activities designed to increase sales (including both advertising and promotional activities). Advertising, for example, could take the form of ads in print; such an ad might show attractive couples smoking cigarettes in an appealing environment. Promotional activities usually do not rely on advertising and can take a variety of forms, including reducing the price paid by consumers. Price promotion may take the form of coupons, merchandise add-ons, and free samples. Another form would be allowances paid to retailers to increase their profit margins; in return, the retailer places the tobacco products in favorable places within the store. The retailer could pass the promotional allowance on to consumers in the form of lower prices. Other types of promotion include sponsorship of events, sale or distribution of branded items, and contests that encourage user participation in exchange for prizes.

Statistical Issues in Tobacco Advertising

Many empirical studies on the effects of cigarette advertising can be found in the academic literature that have used a variety of methodologies. Some have relied on small samples of data to address a specific question; for example, some small surveys have measured smoking behavior, exposure to advertising, receptivity or attitudes to tobacco advertising, or brand awareness during a baseline period and again during follow-up. Other studies have relied on large-scale data sets developed for public use, while some studies have used aggregated data at the national or international level. Advertising studies also can be divided into those using self-reported data on advertising, such as exposure or impact, and those containing market-level data. Studies have also addressed the impact of bans on advertising.

Regardless of the type of study, each raises statistical issues that researchers must consider carefully. These issues include the problems of dealing with measurement error, of properly adjusting for the effects of time by using a weighted average of current and past-period advertising, and the needs to specify an estimation equation, address the problem of uncontrolled individual heterogeneity, and deal with endogeneity, or reverse causality.

Measurement error is common in studies that rely on expenditures for advertising or on measurements of exposure to ads. The data here are either self-reported or are market-level data purchased from a firm specializing in advertising data. Measurement error will generally result in bias toward a finding of no effect of advertising. Self-reported advertising data contain measurement error because individuals who are considering use of a product, or who are current users, will generally be more aware of advertising for that product than other individuals will be. In the case of cigarettes, for example, individuals who are considering smoking, or who smoke, will usually report awareness of more tobacco ads than will other individuals. Thus, controlling for awareness levels will likely result in underestimating the impact of those most likely to smoke. Market-level data can be interpreted erroneously because everyone in the market is assigned the same value for assumed exposure to advertising, but not everyone in the market will actually have the same exposure. Thus, market-level data should preferably be evaluated by using a probability measure of exposure, since those most exposed are likely to be more strongly influenced by advertising and using a probability measure increases variability and the ability to detect a relationship between advertising and behavior.

The second issue, dealing with the effects of time, can also be challenging. For example, advertising in the current (present) period will have a lingering although smaller effect in the next period, but how much the effect declines over time remains unclear. In the case of cigarettes, research such as that by Boyd and Seldon (1990), found that the effects of advertising depreciate fully within a year. And yet, advertising has lingering effects as noted, and knowledge of these effects is the basis for a widely used technique known as “pulsing.” A pulse is a burst of advertising, in a specific market, that lasts for only a short time; after a period of time with no or minimal advertising, the market is exposed to another pulse. These pulses create variability in the amount of actual advertising from one period to the next, but because of lingering effects, a stock of advertising is created. To account for this stock of advertising, researchers should measure advertising as a weighted average of current and past-period advertising.

The third issue, specification of the estimation equation, is important because advertising has a diminishing marginal product. In brief, increments in advertising result in ever smaller increments in sales. That there is diminishing outcomes is a well-established tenet of economics and advertising; the important implication of this principle is that the functional relationship between advertising and sales should be specified as nonlinear.

The fourth issue, addressing the problem of not controlling for individual heterogeneity, can also be a vexing one. The ideal method for estimating the effects of advertising on smoking is a randomized trial, but ethical considerations prohibit experimentation with cigarette advertising. Without random selection, all individual characteristics that might influence smoking behavior must be controlled to ensure that the variation in advertising is the factor that causes the variation in smoking. This is not easily accomplished in standard regression models, however, and thus bias induced by heterogeneity is common. Fortunately, data sets from panels of individuals can be used to control for time-invariant individual characteristics, such as gender or race/ethnicity, and reduce this type of bias.

The fifth and final issue—endogeneity, known also as reverse causality—also creates bias; this is a problem in any study of advertising. Here, for example, rather than advertising driving revenues, revenues drive amounts of advertising; this may be particularly true for mature products. Thus, if smoking decreases, there may be less sales revenue to use for advertising, and advertising may decrease. The problem in this case is that lower advertising might be misunderstood as responsible for lower sales. This may also be a problem in studying the effects of advertising bans: a high level of smoking can lead to public pressure to legislate such bans and, for example, give the impression that such high levels are associated with bans. Endogeneity can be addressed with a well-identified structural model or a natural experiment that examines already existing data.

A partial ban on advertising may not reduce the total level of advertising but should reduce the effectiveness of the remaining media that are not banned (a ban on one or more media will generally result in substitution into the remaining media). This apparently counterintuitive phenomenon should be seen because each medium is subject to diminishing marginal product; the increased use of the nonbanned media will result in a lower average product for these media. Firms may try to compensate with more advertising, or they might increase the use of other marketing techniques, such as promotional allowances to retailers. From the research perspective, because bans on particular media result in cessation of advertising in those media, there are fewer issues overall with measurement error, diminishing marginal product, or lingering effects. Heterogeneity and reverse causality could still create problems for the investigator, however, depending on the nature of the data. In addition, researchers should be aware that there must be comprehensive bans in place to avoid substitution into other media. Finally, the researcher must control for other marketing activities. Data from a single country could reduce some problems caused by reverse causality in studies on bans, and longitudinal or aggregate data could reduce problems with heterogeneity.

Effects of Advertising Bans: A Prior Review

Lancaster and Lancaster (2003) reviewed 21 studies of advertising bans and found that 10 of these reported significant negative coefficients indicating that the bans on advertising were associated with decreased smoking or consumption. Of the 199 reported coefficients, 29.1% were negative and significant, 5.5% were positive and significant, and 65.3% were insignificant. Some of the coefficients may have been nonsignificant because the bans were limited to a few media, allowing substitution into other media. None of these studies accounted for the possibility of endogeneity (reverse causality).

Effects of Advertising Bans: Current Evidence Base

In a study of bans on advertising, Saffer and Chaloupka (2000) used an international data set from 22 countries that covered 1970 to 1992. Bans were considered weak if they were nonexistent or only one or two kinds of media, such as television and radio advertising, were banned; limited, if three or four media were banned; or comprehensive, if five, six, or seven media were banned. In an analysis limited to 1984 to 1992, they found that limited bans were not effective but that comprehensive bans were effective. Their results suggest that moving from a limited to a comprehensive set of bans can have a compounding effect, which is consistent with the theory that limited bans allow substitution of other media. The problem of endogeneity was not considered.

Iwasaki and colleagues (2006) found that advertising restrictions required by the 1998 Master Settlement Agreement decreased consumption of cigarettes in the United States. These restrictions included a ban on outdoor advertising and restrictions on youth-targeted advertising; in addition, the agreement provided funds for counteradvertising. Earlier, Chung and colleagues (2002) reported that the agreement's restrictions on advertising to youth were easily avoided; they also noted that counter-advertising took a few years to initiate.

Iwasaki and associates (2006) constructed a time series data set from 1955 to 2002 for the United States in which the regression equations included interactions of advertising expenditures with dichotomous variables for four progressively more restrictive periods for advertising during the timeframe in question. These periods were 1955 to 1967, 1968 to 1971, 1971 to 1997, and 1998 to 2002. A break was seen between 1967 and 1968 because the first Surgeon General's report on smoking was in 1964 (and related news on smoking causing lung cancer began in the 1950s and had substantial impact up to 1967). The 1971 break reflects the elimination of broadcast advertising, and the 1998 break reflects the Master Settlement Agreement. The coefficients from the first three periods were insignificant, perhaps because the United States did not have enough restrictions in place to prevent the substitution of television and radio advertising with other types of advertising and marketing activities. The coefficient from the final time period was both negative and significant, indicating that the agreement had reduced smoking. Thus, these data suggest that the most restrictive rules, including the ban on outdoor advertising, reduced smoking. Endogeneity was a problem, however, because, over time, sentiment against tobacco was increasing, and this sentiment would affect cigarette use as well as the passage of the Master Settlement Agreement. On the other hand, problems with controlling for heterogeneity of the population were reduced because aggregate data were used, but it should also be noted that there was no control for other forms of marketing. Data from the U.S. Federal Trade Commission (FTC 2011) indicated that other marketing expenditures increased dramatically after the Master Settlement Agreement.

Discussion Regarding Advertising Bans

According to FTC (2011), in 2008 more than $190 million was spent on cigarette advertising in the United States, but this represented only 1.9% of total monies spent for cigarette promotion (see Chapter 5, Table 5.3). Regardless, this amount of advertising constitutes a public health problem if it increases overall smoking or encourages youth to begin to smoke. The tobacco industry and associated researchers (e.g., Heckman et al., 2008) contend that there is no definitive research showing that advertising increases smoking, but this has now been countered with longitudinal research (see Chapter 5). Also, from a cost-benefit point of view, the potential public health advantage (such as in long-term worker productivity) of banning cigarette advertising is far greater than the private costs to tobacco companies and advertisers, and so a ban on such advertising makes sense from an economic perspective. As concluded in NCI Monograph 19: "The studies of tobacco advertising bans in various countries show that comprehensive bans reduce tobacco consumption. Noncomprehensive restrictions generally induce an increase in expenditures for advertising in 'nonbanned' media and for other marketing activities, which offset the effect of the partial ban so that any net change in consumption is minimal or undetectable" (NCI 2008, p. 281).

Product Labeling

Health warnings on cigarette packages are a direct, cost-effective means of communicating information on health risks of smoking to consumers. At present, packages in most countries carry a health warning, but the position, size, and general strength of these warnings vary considerably across jurisdictions. In the United States, health warnings first appeared on cigarette packages in 1966 and in cigarette advertisements in 1972. Since 1984, U.S. cigarette packages have carried one of four government-mandated text warnings on the side panels of packages (Figure 6.5 shows the four warnings and an example). In some other countries, however, large pictorial warnings cover 50% or more of the package (Aftab et al. 1999).

Given their reach and frequency of exposure to users, tobacco packages are an excellent medium for communicating health information. A pack-a-day smoker, for example, is potentially exposed to the warnings more than 7,000 times per year in the process of getting a cigarette from the pack. These warnings are also unique among tobacco control initiatives in that they are delivered directly to smokers at both the point of sale and the time of smoking. As a result, warnings on cigarette packages are among the most prominent sources of health information for smokers in many countries. Indeed, smokers in Western countries report getting more information about the risks of smoking from packages than from any other source except television (Hammond et al. 2006). However, as the following sections discuss, the extent to which smokers, including youth, read, think about, and act upon the warnings depends heavily on the size, position, and design of these messages.

Effects on Youth of Current U.S. Health Warnings

A number of research studies indicate that the current U.S. text warnings have relatively little impact on youth smokers. Indeed, several studies of U.S. warnings suggest they are rarely noticed and suffer from low recall among youth, as illustrated by two studies that used eye-tracking equipment to examine attention paid to U.S. tobacco ads and recall of these warnings (Fischer et al. 1989; Krugman et al. 1994). The first study compared two existing U.S. health warnings in magazine ads with two "new" warnings and found that the "new" warnings were associated with more reading and attracted attention more quickly. However, relatively few respondents could accurately recall the wording or the general concepts of any of the four warnings. In the second study, adolescents were asked to view five tobacco ads that included a health warning. The average viewing time of the health warning was only 8% of the total time spent viewing the ads, and participants subsequently demonstrated a low recall of the warnings.

Brubaker and Mitby (1990), who conducted one of the few studies to examine U.S. text-based warnings on

Figure 6.5 Health warnings on cigarette packages in the United States

(1) SURGEON GENERAL'S WARNING: Smoking Causes Lung Cancer, Heart Disease, Emphysema, and May Complicate Pregnancy.
(2) SURGEON GENERAL'S WARNING: Quitting Smoking Now Greatly Reduces Serious Risks to Your Health.
(3) SURGEON GENERAL'S WARNING: Smoking By Pregnant Women May Result in Fetal Injury, Premature Birth, and Low Birth Weight.
(4) SURGEON GENERAL'S WARNING: Cigarette Smoke Contains Carbon Monoxide.

Example of warning label on U.S. cigarette package:

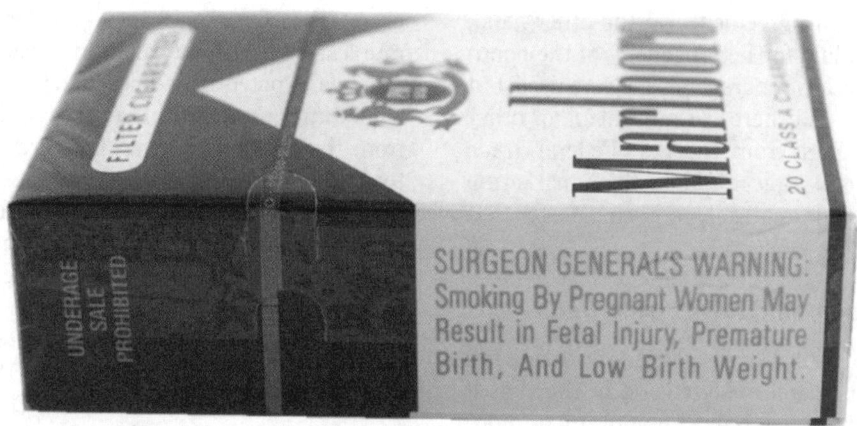

Source: Comprehensive Smoking Education Act (1984); Tobacco Labelling Resource Centre 2011b.

smokeless tobacco products, found results similar to those for Krugman and colleagues (1994): less than one-half of the persons (43%) exposed to the warnings recalled seeing them, and only one-third of those who recalled seeing them remembered the content of the message. Overall, the warning labels had no significant effect on whether adolescents would use the product.

More recent research suggests that although most youth report the U.S. cigarette health warnings to be "believable" (Cecil et al. 1996), few find them to be informative or relevant (Crawford et al. 2002). For example, in a series of focus groups conducted in 2001 among adolescents, most considered the warnings to be personally irrelevant and described the warnings as "vague," "stale," and "worn-out" (Crawford et al. 2002, p. 16).

In one of the few longitudinal studies of health warnings among youth, Robinson and Killen (1997) examined the association between adolescents' knowledge of U.S. cigarette warning labels and subsequent smoking behavior by surveying 1,747 youth. At baseline, adolescent smokers were more familiar with the health warnings than were nonsmokers. When cigarette packages serve as the medium for health warnings, however, one would expect that consumption levels at baseline would be associated with knowledge of the warning labels.

Effects on Youth of the Size and Position of Health Warnings

Several studies demonstrate that an increase in the size of text warnings increases their impact (Environics Research Group 1999). For example, in studies in which Canadian youth were asked to rate the effectiveness of different health warnings, the largest warnings were most likely to be rated as effective (Environics Research Group 1999; Les Études de Marché Créatec 2008). These findings are consistent with research conducted among adults showing that smokers were more likely to recall larger warnings and often equated the size of the warning with the magnitude of the risk (*Health Education Journal* 1985; AGB Spectrum Research 1987; Cragg Ross and Dawson 1990; Centre for Behavioural Research in Cancer 1992; Action on Smoking and Health 1998; Strahan et al. 2002). Warnings that appear on the "front" or principal display area of packages are also likely to have greater impact. In one study, Rootman and Flay (1995) compared the effectiveness of U.S. and Canadian health warnings in 1995 among a youth sample. At the time, Canadian packages carried one of eight black-and-white text warnings on the front and back of packages, covering 25% of the display area on the package. Students were shown a package for 1 minute and then asked to recall everything they could about it. The most notable finding was that 83% of Canadian students mentioned the health warning on Canadian packs, a larger percentage than those who could recall the brand name. In contrast, health warnings on U.S. packs were recalled by only 6% of the U.S. students. A survey conducted with youth in The Netherlands also suggests that more prominent text warnings on the principal display area have relatively greater impact (Teeboom 2002). In addition, recent experimental research in Canada found that increasing the size of warnings from 50% to 75%, 90%, or 100% of the principal display area enhanced their impact among youth smokers and "vulnerable" youth nonsmokers (Les Études de Marché Créatec 2008).

Effects on Youth of Pictorial Health Warnings

In 2000, Canada became the first country in the world to introduce pictorial warnings on tobacco packages (Figure 6.6 provides an example). A series of focus groups and population-based surveys conducted among Canadian youth around this time suggested that large pictorial warnings were considerably more legible and credible and more likely to be noticed than were text warnings (Environics Research Group 1999, 2000; Nilsson 1999). A survey taken in 1999 in Canada, the year before the large pictorial health warnings on cigarette packages were introduced, found that youth in that country—both smokers and nonsmokers—supported the use of pictorial health warnings on cigarette packages (Environics Research Group 1999). When shown health messages with and without pictures, 80% of youth reported that the message with the picture was more noticeable. Three years later, in a national survey of more than 19,000 Canadian youth between 11 and 15 years of age, the majority found the pictorial health warnings on cigarette packages to be believable and agreed that health-warning messages should be on cigarette packages (Chaiton et al. 2002). In a large national study conducted following implementation of the pictorial warnings, about 95% of Canadian youth reported that pictorial health warnings communicated the risks of smoking better than text-only warning labels (Bonnie et al. 2007, p. 294). Overall, the believability of the health warnings and the degree of endorsement were either similar to, or above, levels measured in 1994, 6 years before introduction of the large pictorial warnings. This research demonstrates that introducing large pictorial warnings does not decrease support or credibility among youth for messages about the health risks of cigarettes.

Figure 6.6 Pictorial warning on cigarette package in Canada

Source: Tobacco Labelling Resource Centre 2011a.

In addition, a series of 12 cross-sectional surveys were conducted with Canadian youth before and after the implementation of the large pictorial health warnings in 2000; these surveys showed significant increases in the frequency with which youth noticed, read, and thought about the health warnings after the pictorial messages were introduced. The most recent survey, in 2006, found that 86% of youth smokers reported the messages as effective in informing them about the health effects of smoking; 70% said that the messages had been effective in getting them to try to quit smoking; 66% reported that the messages had increased their desire to quit; and 56% said they smoked less around others as a result of the messages (Environics Research Group 2006).

Evidence from focus groups in Australia supports these findings. For example, although many Australian youth expressed a general lack of concern about the effects of smoking, they nevertheless reported being influenced by the health warnings (Elliott & Shanahan Research 2002). In particular, descriptive or emotive messages in the pictorial warnings had considerable impact, particularly those images portraying the external effects of smoking. Follow-up studies among Australian youth came to similar conclusions on the effectiveness of pictorial warnings (Elliott & Shanahan Research 2003; BRC Marketing & Social Research 2004). Evaluations have been conducted on pictorial warnings implemented in Australia (see Figure 6.7 for an example). A school-based study in

Figure 6.7 Pictorial warning on cigarette package in Australia

Source: Tobacco Labelling Resource Centre 2011c.

western Australia found that students were more likely to report they had read, attended to, thought about, or talked about health warnings after the pictorial warnings were implemented in 2006 (White et al. 2008a). In addition, experimental and established smokers were more likely to have thought about quitting and forgoing cigarettes, and intention to smoke was lower among those students who had talked about the warning labels and had forgone cigarettes (White et al. 2008a).

In addition to increasing perceptions of risk, pictorial health warnings have been found to undermine the brand appeal of packages (Clemenger BBDO 2004; Thrasher et al. 2007; Les Études de Marché Créatec 2008; Stark et al. 2008). In addition, more than 80% of Canadian youth in a 2006 survey indicated that large pictorial health warning messages made smoking seem less attractive (Environics Research Group 2006). Overall, findings on the effectiveness of large pictorial warnings among youth are consistent with research conducted among adults, which has found associations between larger pictorial warnings and greater health knowledge, increased motivation to quit smoking, and greater attempts to quit (Hill 1988; Tandemar Research 1996; Borland and Hill 1997a,b; Liefeld 1999; Environics Research Group 2001; Portillo and Antoñanzas 2002; Willemsen et al. 2002; Cavalcante 2003; Hammond et al. 2003, 2004, 2006, 2007; Koval et al. 2005; Willemsen 2005; O'Hegarty et al. 2006; Ramesh 2006; UK Department of Health 2006; Quit Victoria 2007; Thrasher et al. 2007).

Evidence from numerous studies of adult populations indicates that health warnings are more likely to be effective if they elicit stong emotions, are larger and more visible (CDC 2011a). Although fewer studies examining the effects of pictorial warning labels have been conducted with youth than with adults, findings across countries show that the pictorial warnings better communicate the risks of smoking to young people than do text-only warnings.

Effects of "New" and Rotating Health Messages

Health warnings that are new or periodically updated are likely to have greater impact among youth than will "older" warnings, even in the absence of changes in the size and position of the messages. Indeed, youth commonly report on the stale or ineffective nature of "old" warnings that remain unchanged for more than several years (Environics Research Group 1999, 2000; Crawford et al. 2002). According to research findings from adults, health warnings have their greatest impact shortly after implementation and decline in effectiveness over time (Borland and Hill 1997b; Hammond et al. 2007). This is consistent with the basic principles of advertising and health communications, which suggest that the salience of a communication is greatest upon initial exposure and erodes thereafter (Bornstein 1989; Blair 2000).

Discussion Regarding Warning Labels

Research conducted to date demonstrates that the effectiveness of health warnings among youth increases with their size and placement as well as with the use of pictures. Small text-only warnings located in nonprominent locations, such as the side of the package in the United States, have relatively little impact. Furthermore, pictorial warnings that cover a significant proportion (e.g., 50% or more) of the package are associated with increases in health knowledge and motivation to quit smoking. Pictorial warnings also have the potential to reduce sociodemographic disparities in health knowledge and tobacco use among youth (CRÉATEC + Market Studies 2003). The existing text warnings in the United States require a college reading level, but pictorial warnings are easily understood by those with low literacy skills, including young children, youth with lower levels of education, and youth who may be literate but not in the language of the text warnings, such as young people in some immigrant families (Malouff et al. 1992).

The significant evidence base that has been developed since several countries implemented pictorial warning labels on cigarette packs clearly demonstrates that pictorial warning labels are an important component of tobacco control (Fong et al. 2009). The 2007 Institute of Medicine Report, "Ending the tobacco problem: A blueprint for the nation," concluded that based on the available evidence, large, graphic warnings like those implemented in Canada, Brazil, and Thailand "...would promote greater public understanding of the risks of using tobacco products or reduce consumption" (Bonnie et al. 2007, p. 16). The report also recommended that FDA require pictorial and text-based warnings that cover 50% of the cigarette package (Bonnie et al. 2007). This requirement is currently subject to legal challenges. In June 2011, FDA announced it will require pictorial graphic warning labels on all packs of cigarettes sold in the United States (Figure 6.8) (USFDA 2011). One of nine pictures paired with one of nine text-based messages will be displayed on the top 50% of the front and back panels of each pack of cigarettes (USFDA 2011). These FDA requirements and related provisions of the *Family Smoking Prevention and Tobacco Act* are currently under judicial review. The evidence base is expected to increase in parallel with regulatory developments in tobacco labeling, which are rapidly progressing in response to the issuance of international standards through the World Health Organization's (WHO's) Framework Convention on Tobacco Control (FCTC) (WHO 2003). FCTC *recommends* warnings that cover 50% of the front and back panels but only *requires* warnings to cover 30%. Also, the treaty permits the use of pictures or graphics. More than 30 countries have either implemented or have committed to implementing large pictorial warnings that meet the recommended guidelines of FCTC.

Small Social Environments

The small social environments within which social or behavioral interventions can be conducted to prevent youth tobacco use or addiction include families, medical clinics, and schools. Families have an obvious influence on the likelihood that a child or adolescent will take up smoking or become a regular tobacco user, and they exert their effects from birth (even prenatally) through young adulthood. Health-service clinics, together with pedia-

Figure 6.8 Proposed pictorial warnings on cigarette packages in the United States

Source: U.S. Food and Drug Administration 2011.

tricians and family physicians, are potentially of critical importance to preventing tobacco use among youth and for providing cessation advice and treatment. In addition, because young people are exposed to other youth and adults when they attend school, peer influences and school policies have an important impact on the development of behavioral patterns, including tobacco use. For these reasons, this report reviews the application of opportunities for prevention in all three of the small social environments.

The Family

According to the responses of youth in grades 6–12 on the Pride Surveys (2006), which are local surveys of problem behaviors and associated risk factors, parental disapproval is the major reason for young people not to use tobacco and other drugs. In addition, per these surveys, almost three-fourths of parents believe that they are the most effective "anti-drug." However, parents underestimate the percentage of youth who use tobacco. For instance, the Pride Surveys indicate that less than 1% of parents of 7th graders and just 5% of parents of 12th graders believe that their kids have used tobacco in the past year, when in fact, the surveys indicate that 12.2% of 7th graders and 38.8% of 12th graders had used cigarettes in the past year (Pride Surveys 2006). In addition, according to the Pride Surveys, 18.7% of these 12th graders use tobacco at home.

Two systematic Cochrane Collaboration reviews of family interventions for preventing tobacco use in adolescents (Thomas et al. 2003; Thomas and Perera 2006; Petrie et al. 2007) suggest that family interventions implemented with high quality are likely to reduce rates of tobacco use in youth. The present report summarizes these reviews, adds an analysis of the types of family interventions likely to be most successful, and discusses the added benefit of combining family-focused and youth-only interventions.

Types of Parenting and Family-Focused Approaches

Several investigators have tried to classify the different types of family-focused approaches for prevention, but researchers in this field have not agreed on the definitions of the classifications. The review by the Center for Substance Abuse Prevention (CSAP 1998) of family-focused approaches defined eight approaches, but at that time, only four had sufficient validity to be considered evidence based: (1) cognitive-behavioral training for parents; (2) family skills training, including training of the parents, skills training of the children, and family practice time together; (3) family therapy (structural, functional, or behavioral); and (4) in-home family support or case management programs. Since the 1998 CSAP review, the very-low-cost strategy of involving parents with their children in homework assignments on the prevention of substance abuse has also shown promise as a cost-effective approach (Williams et al., 1995). In addition, cost-effective video, CD (compact disc), interactive DVD (digital video disc), and online versions of family programs have shown positive results (Gordon 2000; Schinke et al. 2000, 2004).

Theories Underlying the Strategy

The general logic of the family-based approach is that if parents learn and practice skills to become more effective at parenting and improve the parent-child relationship, learn how to be more effective in disciplining their children, and become better monitors, their children will have better developmental outcomes of all types, including those that relate to tobacco use. In addition, attention to the mechanisms of change has been identified as a crucial component for advancing theory in family-based treatment for substance use and ultimately for developing more effective prevention programs. For most family interventions, the underlying psychological theories are cognitive-behavioral, social learning, and/or family systems theory (Liddle et al. 2002). A key concept of many evidence-based programs is to reduce particular parent-child interactions that give rise to antisocial behavior and tobacco use, a process well documented by Patterson (1986) at the Oregon Social Learning Center. In general, the family systems approach uses reframing and cognitive restructuring methods to foster behavior change. Evidence-based interventions involve the whole family (rather than just the parents or the children) in processes that involve interaction, the building of skills, or behavior change rather than providing didactic educational lessons. These programs stress the importance of the engagement process and reducing barriers to attendance at program sessions, often through building relationships; extending personal invitations; providing meals, child care, and transportation; and sometimes by paying families for their time. Most begin with sessions designed to improve positive feelings in the family through positive reframing or through skills exercises that stress family strengths. Structured methods for communication and disciplinary techniques are also practiced once positive family feelings are established.

Systematic Reviews

For this Surgeon General's report, two systematic Cochrane reviews of family-focused interventions in preventing tobacco use were identified (Thomas et al. 2003, 2007; Petrie et al. 2007); these reviews suggest that such interventions are effective.

In one of the Cochrane reviews, Thomas and associates (2007) assessed 20 RCTs of family-based interventions that included children or youth (5–18 years of age) plus family members and met their criteria for inclusion. Fourteen of the RCTs were conducted in the United States, two in Norway, and one each in Australia, Finland, India, and the United Kingdom. The studies reported on smoking status of children from baseline to at least 6 months from the start of the intervention; all 20 included at least a 1-year follow-up: 8 with 1 year; 1 with 20 months; 2 studies with 24 months; 6 with 36 months; and 1 each with 7, 15, 27, and 29 years, respectively, of follow-up data.

Of the 20 RCTs identified, 6 were classified by the Cochrane criteria for assessment of bias or quality of study (selection, performance, attrition, and detection) as Category 1, or of high quality with minimal risk of biased results (Bauman et al. 2001; Spoth et al. 2001, 2002; Storr et al. 2002; Curry et al. 2003; Schinke et al. 2004), 9 as Category 2, or medium risk of bias (Biglan et al. 1987; Ary et al. 1990; Nutbeam et al. 1993; Cullen and Cullen 1996; Elder et al. 1996; Jøsendal et al. 1998; Stevens et al. 2002; Wu et al. 2003; Jackson and Dickinson 2006), and 5 as Category 3, or high risk of bias. Studies in the last group were not included in the analysis.

Overall, the review by Thomas and colleagues (2007) found statistically significant results in 50% (three of six) of the Category 1 studies (Spoth et al. 2001; Storr et al. 2002; Schinke et al. 2004). In contrast, only 33% (three of nine) of the Category 2 studies (Jøsendal et al. 1998; Wu et al. 2003; Jackson and Dickinson 2006) found significant results for the interventions. The reviewers suggested potentially positive results for the family interventions when they were implemented with high-quality training and fidelity as was found in category 1 studies. In their review, the authors did not examine differential effectiveness by the major types of family interventions; many of the family interventions tested were minimal-contact, homework-based programs.

The second Cochrane review (Petrie et al. 2007) assessed 46 articles on 20 studies that met the authors' review criteria for an RCT or were carried out as controlled before-and-after studies that focused on improving parenting skills. Although not mentioned as a criterion for inclusion, all the studies had at least 1 year of follow-up, with up to 6 years of follow-up for two studies. Of the 20 studies, 13 measured tobacco outcomes, of which 9 (representing 11 programs) resulted in significant positive reductions in tobacco use. Seven of the studies focused on the prevention of substance use in general (not tobacco specifically). Four of the nine programs found effective in this review were previously identified as effective by Thomas and colleagues (2003) in the protocol for the first Cochrane review of family-based smoking prevention programs.

The relative improvement (RI) rates calculated for the 11 effective programs are reported in the program descriptions below, and other details of the studies are shown in Table 6.8 (the programs that were not effective are discussed in Petrie et al. 2007). RI is the posttest difference between intervention (I) and control (C) groups minus the pretest difference between groups, divided by the control group posttest level: $[(I_{\% \text{ or mean}} - C_{\% \text{ or mean}})_{post} - (I_{\% \text{ or mean}} - C_{\% \text{ or mean}})_{pre}] / C_{\% \text{ or mean post}}$, expressed as a percentage. RI is similar to an effect size (ES) when the latter is defined as the posttest difference between groups divided by the pooled standard deviation (SD) at posttest: $(I_{\% \text{ or mean}} - C_{\% \text{ or mean}})_{post} / SD_{(I + C)\, post}$.

The Family-School Partnership intervention incorporated the Parents on Your Side program, which in this intervention included nine workshops for parents. In a 3-day workshop, teachers were trained to communicate better to parents. The parents also completed weekly parent-child homework assignments. Results for this family intervention (RI = 20.3%, relative risk [RR] = 0.69) were positive but almost the same as for a comparison group that received the classroom-based Good Behavior Game (RI = 22.2%, RR = 0.57) instead of the Parents on Your Side intervention (Storr et al. 2002).

Smoke-free Kids consisted of newsletters, six mailed tips on parenting, and gifts for participation. This program reduced initiation of smoking after 3 years to 11.9% of students, compared with 19.3% of minimal-contact controls, who had received five tobacco fact sheets (RI = 38%, RR = 8.4%, OR for not starting = 2.16) (Jackson and Dickinson 2003, 2006).

BE smokeFREE, a Norwegian school-based program reported by Jøsendal and associates (1998, 2005), found significant differences in number of cigarettes smoked per week (10 vs. 17 for controls, OR = 0.48, RI = 41%) at 6-month follow-up. A 3-year follow-up for 10th graders found reductions in lifetime (ever) use (31.5% vs. 41.7%, RI = 24%), weekly smoking (4.1% vs. 6.2% for controls, RI = 47%), and daily smoking (15.5% vs. 23.0%, RI = 28%) for the three-component intervention (a classroom program, involvement of parents, and teacher courses). The family component was not tested separately, but when the parenting intervention was dropped from the total intervention, the percentage of never smokers dropped 4.4 percentage points, from 41.7% to 37.3%, and RI dropped 6 percentage points, from 24% to 18%. However, the percentage of weekly smokers increased from 4.1% to 5.4%, and RI dropped 18 percentage points, from 47% to 29%. The percentage of daily smokers 3 years later among a group of 10th graders was 23% for controls, 15.5% for the

Table 6.8 Descriptions and effect sizes (expressed as relative improvements) of parenting and family interventions for preventing use of tobacco among adolescents

								Effect size as relative improvement at last follow-up			
Investigator	**Program name**	**Design**	**Number of students**	**Length of evaluation**	**Dosage/ type of intervention**	**Grade**	**Grade at follow-up**	**Life**	**Month**	**Week**	**Average ES**
Universal prevention: family-skills training, school-based programs											
Spoth et al. 2001	Iowa Strengthening Families Program (ISFP) 10–14 Project Family	R-S	283 (141 E, 142 C)	4 years	7-FST/SB	6	10	34.8			34.8
Spoth et al. 2001	Preparing for the Drug Free Years Project Family	R-S	270 (128 E, 142 C)	4 years	5-FST/SB	6	10	12.5			12.5
Spoth et al. 2002	ISFP 10–14 years + LifeSkills Training (LST)	R-S	869 (453 E, 416 C)	1 year	7-FST/SB	7	8	27.5			27.5
Means for family-skills training, school-based programs								**24.9**			**24.9**

								Effect size as relative improvement at last follow-up			
Investigator	**Program name**	**Design**	**Number of students**	**Length of evaluation**	**Dosage/ type of intervention**	**Grade**	**Grade at follow-up**	**Life**	**Month**	**Week**	**Average ES**
Universal prevention: mailing out homework assignments to the family, community-based programs											
Bauman et al. 2001, 2002	Family Matters	R-F	1,135 (531 E, 604 C)	3 months and 1 year	4-FH	6–8	7–9	7.3			7.3
Means for approach of mailing out homework assignments to the family, community-based programs								**7.3**			**7.3**

Table 6.8 Continued

Investigator	Program name	Design	Number of students	Length of evaluation	Dosage/ type of intervention	Grade	Grade at follow-up	Effect size as relative improvement at last follow-up			
								Life	Month	Week	Average ES
Universal prevention: family homework assignments plus youth groups, school based											
Pentz et al. 1989d	Midwestern Prevention Program	PR-S	15+	2 years	S+C	6–7/ 7–8	9–10		18.0		18.0
Perry et al. 1989, 1992	Minnesota Class of 89	NR-C	17+		S+C	6–10	12			39.4	39.4
Jøsendal et al. 1998, 2005	Be Smoke Free	R-S	4,215	6 months 18 months 3 years	8-YST + 2 FH + 2-day TT/SB	7	10	24 total 18 if no FH		47 total 29 if no FH	35.5
Storr et al. 2002	Parents on Your Side in Family-School Partnership	R-C	448 (229 E, 219 C)	7 years	9-FST + Weekly FH + SB	1	8	20.3			20.3
Means for family homework plus youth groups								**22.2**	**18.0**	**43.2**	**28.3**

Table 6.8 Continued

Investigator	Program name	Design	Number of students	Length of evaluation	Dosage/ type of intervention	Grade	Grade at follow-up	Effect size as relative improvement at last follow-up			
								Life	Month	Week	Average ES
Selective prevention for high-risk youth											
Jackson and Dickinson 2003, 2006	Smoke-Free Kids	R-F	776 (371 E, 405 C children of smokers)	3 years	6 FH-CB	3	6	38			38
Schinke et al. 2004	CD-ROM LST	R-F	469	3 years	10 YST + 2 FST + 1 video + 2 FH	4–6	7–9		31		31
Means for selective prevention interventions for high-risk youth								**38.0**	**31**		**32.7**
Overall means for family programs								**23.6**	**24.5**	**43.2**	**26.4**

Note: All studies took place in the United States, except Jøsendal and associates (1998, 2005), Be Smoke Free, which took place in Norway. **C** = classroom; **CB** = community-based; **E** = education group; **F** = family; **FH** = family homework assignments; **FST** = family skills training; **NR** = nonrandom; **PR** = partial random; **R** = random; **S** = school; **SB** = school based; **TT** = teacher training; **YST** = youth skills training.

model program, and 21.1% for the intervention minus the parenting component, for an RI of 13%, compared with an RI of 28% for the full intervention. Hence, the contribution of the parenting component appeared to be greater in the longer term for preventing daily smoking.

The Iowa Strengthening Families Program (ISFP) for youth aged 10–14 years (Kumpfer et al. 1996) is a seven-session family skills training program that was implemented during evenings for all sixth-grade students in randomly selected schools in an RCT in Iowa. Each session of ISFP involves parents and students in 1 hour of separate classes on parenting skills and on skills training for children followed by 1 hour of family practice time. The 4-year follow-up ITT analysis found a 32.6% rate of smoking initiation in the group receiving ISFP compared with 50% for the minimal-contact control group (RI = 34.8%) (Spoth et al. 2001).

Preparing for the Drug Free Years (PFDY), now called Guiding Good Choices, was tested in the same RCT as ISFP. PFDY is a five-session intervention that involves parents in five 1-hour parenting classes; the sixth-grade students had one session on peer-resistance skills. The same 4-year follow-up ITT analysis found a 44% rate of smoking initiation for the experimental group compared with 50% for the control group (RI = 12.5%). This comparative research suggests that ISFP was about three times as effective as PFDY in reducing the rate of initiation of cigarette use (Spoth et al. 2001).

Another study conducted in the Midwest (this time involving seventh graders) combined the seven-session ISFP and LifeSkills Training (LST), a school-based, youth-centered intervention that does not involve parents. Those who went through the combined program had a 12.1% rate for new use of cigarettes, compared with 16.7% for controls (RI = 27.5% reduction) and 13.9% for LST only (RI = 16.8% reduction) (Spoth et al. 2002). When the ISFP family program was replicated in a multicommunity RCT and combined with one of three youth-only programs (LST, All Stars, or Project ALERT), the percentage of new tobacco users dropped from 32% to 17% after 18 months (RI = 47%, Cohen's d = 0.29) (Spoth et al. 2007).

Project STAR (Students Taught Awareness and Resistance), also known as the Midwestern Prevention Project (MPP) (Pentz et al. 1989b,c; Johnson et al. 1990), included homework assignments for the parents of youth who were engaged in a comprehensive prevention program that also featured a classroom curriculum and a mass media campaign. The family component (the homework assignments) was not tested separately. The 1-year RI was 41%, and the 3-year RI was 18% for reduction in tobacco use during a 30-day period.

Family Matters consisted of four brochures on parenting that were mailed to recruited parents and followed up by a call from a health educator. This minimal intervention was found by Bauman and colleagues (2001) to reduce the percentage of smokers from 55% to 48% at one-year follow-up, but at baseline the percentage of smokers was lower in the experimental group (24.5%) than in the control group (27.5%). The RI was 7.3%; the OR of 1.30 in the original analysis became 1.27 when Petrie and colleagues (2007) corrected for the design effect, producing a nonsignificant difference from the control group (p = 0.0595). This corrected result may explain why the Cochrane review conducted by Thomas and colleagues (2007) concluded that this program was not effective.

Another program reviewed by Thomas and colleagues (2007) was the intervention reported by Schinke and associates (2004), the CD-ROM (compact disc read-only memory) Youth and Parent program, a CD-ROM version of a youth and parenting program that was tested in an RCT. This program produced an RI of 31%.

Wu and associates (2003) tested Focus on Kids (FOK), an eight-session, small-group intervention providing training in social skills that is led by two older peers, both with and without a program called Informed Parents and Children Together (ImPACT), a 2-hour video on parenting skills plus two home visits by an instructor for practice sessions. The authors compared these two conditions with a third condition of both interventions plus two booster sessions. The study involved 817 high-risk Black youth 12–16 years of age in low-income communities in Baltimore, Maryland. At the 6-month follow-up, youth in families assigned to FOK plus ImPACT reported significantly lower rates of cigarette use than youth in families assigned to FOK only (RI = 20%). The booster sessions delivered at 7 and 10 months made no significant difference.

Elsewhere, a review of the D.A.R.E. (Drug Abuse Resistance Education) and D.A.R.E. Plus (Play and Learn Under Supervision) programs found significant reductions in smoking, alcohol use, and violence among boys but not among girls or for the total population when the D.A.R.E. Plus components (parent, peer, and extracurricular activities) were added to the junior high D.A.R.E. program (Perry et al. 2003).

A combined examination of the programs included in the two Cochrane reviews shows that the most effective family-focused program for preventing tobacco use by adolescents was a selective prevention program, Smokefree Kids, that was targeted to high-risk children of smokers (RI = 38%). This program (Jackson and Dickinson 2003, 2006) was unusual in that it was a minimal-contact intervention. The next-best single intervention in terms of ES was ISFP, a purely family-focused intervention developed by Kumpfer and colleagues (1996). This program is of significantly greater dosage than others in its category because it involves the whole family in seven sessions of 2 hours of skills training (RI = 34.8%) (Spoth et al. 2001). Lowering the dosage and not including the children in the sessions seems to result in a lower ES. Generally, with higher-risk families, a higher dosage (or more time) is needed to produce effective behavioral changes. The CD-ROM version of Schinke and associates' (2004) youth and parenting program also had a large RI (31%).

As a group, the family-involved programs targeting high-risk youth and their families had the largest ES, with a mean RI of 32.7%. The limited research reported here suggests that targeted selective prevention programs are likely to produce the largest ES in reducing tobacco use among adolescents. In the same RCT that included ISFP, the five-session PFDY parenting program (youth came for one session) had an RI of only 12.5% (Spoth et al. 2001). Adding the LST program to ISFP resulted in a lower RI (27.5%) than for the ISFP alone, but participants were in seventh grade rather than sixth, making a direct comparison difficult (Spoth et al. 2002).

Another group, not specifically targeting parents, the multicomponent school-based programs that consisted primarily of training in youth life skills with the added involvement of parents in homework assignments, averaged an RI of 28.3%. The largest ES in this category was for the Minnesota Heart Health Program and Class of 1989 Study, which indicated positive immediate and intermediate effects on smoking levels for youth smoking, with a large RI of 39.4% (Vartiainen et al. 1986; Perry et al. 1992).

The least effective type of family intervention, with an RI of 7.3%, was the universal application of a minimal intervention relying on mailings to parents followed up by calls from a health educator: the Family Matters program (Bauman et al. 2001). The base rates of smoking may have been too low in this universal sample, however, for a minimal-contact intervention like this one to produce significant changes compared with the no-treatment controls.

Ineffective Adolescent Tobacco Programs That Included Family Components

According to the Cochrane reviews, ineffective programs included (1) Kickbutts (Tang et al. 1997); (2) the South Carolina COPE program (Forman et al. 1990); (3) Biglan and colleagues' (1987) training program in refusal skills; (4) Steering Clear clinical trial (Curry et al. 2003); (5) the Busselton Health Study (Cullen and Cullen 1996); and (6) one test of PFDY (Hawkins et al. 1999).

The ineffective programs were generally shorter (two to five sessions) than the effective ones, which were usually five to eight sessions plus two boosters or at least seven sessions. In their systematic review, Thomas and colleagues (2003) concluded that the ineffective programs had fewer training requirements for program delivery staff than the more effective programs. Also, fidelity to the implementation was higher in the more effective programs. Thus, it is not enough to have an effective structured intervention with good content; it is also necessary to develop an effective training and quality control system for the program's dissemination.

Thomas and colleagues' (2003) analysis looked at other questions in comparing the research, including whether family interventions were as effective as school interventions. From their analysis, family interventions seem to be as effective as school interventions: five of the RCTs that tested both a family intervention and a school intervention showed significant positive effects for both. However, these authors found that none of the six studies that compared a family program plus a school program with a school program alone showed significant positive effects from adding the family program to the school program. In the one trial that tested a more general risk-reduction intervention (not specific to tobacco) but measured tobacco outcomes, the combined parent-and-adolescent intervention resulted in less smoking than the youth-only intervention.

Limitations of the Studies Reviewed

Most of the RCT studies reviewed here relied on self-reported measures by the students or their parents. A second limitation of those programs that included family components is that for many of the school-based or community-based interventions, the family programming was merely a minimal dose added to a more substantial program for youth. The one exception was the totally family-focused ISFP (Spoth et al. 2001).

A major weakness of the studies reviewed is that few of them tested the family or parenting intervention separately from the youth intervention to determine the unique contribution of the family or parenting intervention. Another limitation is that of all the family studies, only ISFP was replicated by someone other than the program developer. This was, however, a semi-independent replication; Karol L. Kumpfer, the original developer, was a coprincipal investigator on the grant that conducted the replication.

In addition, of all the interventions, only one was either culturally adapted or gender specific, the BE smoke-FREE program designed specifically for Norwegian youth and parents (Jøsendal et al. 1998, 2005). Although cultural adaptations of evidence-based interventions are likely to improve outcomes to get to "deep" structure (Resnicow et al. 1999), even those with "surface" structure cultural adaptations have shown few improvements in outcomes over the generic versions (Botvin et al. 1995b). One exception is that the involvement of parents and families in terms of attendance and retention was found to improve results by about 40% if the evidence-based intervention was culturally adapted (based on a comparison across five studies of the 14-session ISFP in culturally adapted form with the multiethnic version) (Kumpfer et al. 2002).

It is not known whether the programs reviewed in this section are equally effective for girls and boys because analyses for subgroups are rarely reported (Kumpfer et al. 2008). One exception was the D.A.R.E. Plus program, which resulted in significant reductions in smoking, alcohol use, and violence for boys but not for girls or the total population (Perry et al. 2003).

Discussion and Recommendations

Several different programs that involve parenting or families may be effective in reducing tobacco use. Most of the tested programs were interventions added to school-based programs in which the parents were sent materials or homework assignments to complete with their children. The most effective programs in terms of ES or percentage of reduction in smokers had one or more of the following characteristics:

1. Targeted high-risk adolescents with selective interventions;

2. Combined skills training among youth with homework assignments for parents on parenting;

3. Focused specifically on the family, with skills training for the family that included more sessions or included time with the families to learn together;

4. Provided longer periods to train the staff in the intervention methods;

5. Conducted checks on the fidelity of implementation or on quality;

6. Used interventions for skills training among families that were based on behavior change theory; and

7. Stressed active parental involvement and parenting skills and developed social competencies and self-regulation among youth.

Thus, it appears that some well-executed family interventions with sufficient dosage may help to prevent smoking among adolescents, but the reports in the literature on RCTs of family interventions that were less well executed have had mostly limited results. There may, therefore, be a need for more well-designed and properly executed RCTs in the area of family-focused tobacco prevention, particularly those testing the family component separately from the youth component. Studies of disseminating effective family interventions are also needed.

Clinical Interventions: The Role of Health Care Providers in Preventing and Reducing Smoking Among Youth

Primary health care providers are potentially well positioned to help prevent tobacco use among children and adolescents; indeed, there is evidence that adolescents view physicians as a preferred source of information about smoking in general and about smoking cessation specifically (Ackard and Neumark-Sztainer 2001; Marcell and Halpern-Felsher 2007). A health care visit represents an excellent opportunity for health care professionals to provide clinical services aimed at reducing tobacco use.

Several national guidelines have been developed to guide physicians (American Medical Association [AMA] 1997; USDHHS 1998; Bonnie et al. 2007; Hagan et al. 2008); in general, they recommend that all children and adolescents have an annual visit in which they receive confidential preventive services. These services should include screening, education, and counseling in several areas, including health risk behaviors such as tobacco use. Guidelines, including those from the American Academy of Pediatrics, also recommend that pediatricians discuss substance use as part of routine health care during the prenatal visit, as part of a home assessment, and for youth seen during ambulatory visits (NCI 1994; Kulig and American Academy of Pediatrics Committee on Substance Abuse 2005).

The U.S. Preventive Services Task Force (USPSTF 2003), however, has concluded that the empirical evidence is insufficient to recommend regular screening for tobacco use among youth or interventions for those young people who smoke. An updated recommendation is being prepared by USPSTF. Guidelines from many other national groups also address the prevention of tobacco use among adolescents: these guidelines typically recommend that physicians inquire about tobacco use in general and query those youth who use tobacco about the extent of their use; the settings in which they use tobacco; and whether tobacco use has had a negative impact on their social, educational, or vocational activities (Kulig and American Academy of Pediatrics Committee on Substance

Abuse 2005). The American Academy of Pediatrics (Hagan et al. 2008) also recommends screening for the tobacco use of friends, given that smoking behavior among peers is a powerful determinant of smoking behavior for youth (Forrester et al. 2007).

The primary recommended method of delivering direct, brief, tobacco-related prevention and cessation services is known as the "5 A's" model, originally developed for use in adult populations. The model's five steps include *Asking* the patient about tobacco use; *Advising* patients who smoke to quit; *Assessing* the patient's willingness to quit; *Assisting* the patient to attempt quitting by providing brief counseling, pharmacotherapy, and appropriate referrals; and *Arranging* a follow-up visit or telephone call, preferably 1 week after an established quit date (USPSTF 2009; Prokhorov et al. 2010).

Practice guidelines also recommend that health care providers inquire about tobacco use in the child's home (including use by parents, siblings, and other family members), encourage tobacco-free homes, and provide guidance and assistance to parents and youth on tobacco cessation (USDHHS 1998; Kulig and American Academy of Pediatrics Committee on Substance Abuse 2005; Committee on Environmental Health 2009). Finally, emerging recommendations state that providers should maintain an office that supports a tobacco-free norm by employing a tobacco-free staff, displaying antitobacco messages, making educational materials readily available, terminating subscriptions to waiting-room magazines that contain tobacco advertisements, and establishing policies for routinely charting tobacco use (Feinson and Chidekel 2006).

Rates of Delivery of Tobacco Prevention Services to Youth in Health Care Settings

In 2006, 84.2% of adolescents (aged 10–17 years) and 72.0% of young adults (aged 18–24 years) had visited a doctor's office in the past year, not including hospitalizations, emergency room visits, or surgeries (Mulye et al. 2009). Female young adults were much more likely to have visited a doctor than male young adults (84.7% vs. 59.3%), but the difference by gender was less pronounced among adolescents (85.5% for females vs. 83.0% for males). White adolescents and young adults were more likely to have seen a doctor than were their Black counterparts, with Hispanics having lower rates than Blacks. The rates varied greatly by insurance status, with 87.2% of insured adolescents and 80.1% of insured young adults visiting a doctor compared with 54.9% of uninsured adolescents and 46.2% of uninsured young adults.

National guidelines support providing tobacco prevention services to youth and promote brief tobacco-screening questionnaires under the presumption that they are effective (Benuck et al. 2001). Still, delivery rates of these services have been insufficient among physicians in private practices, community-based practices, and managed care settings. Studies have shown that less than 60% of adolescents were provided guidance about smoking (Marks at al. 1990), and only 1% of office visits by adolescents included advice about smoking cessation (Igra and Millstein 1993). In a large survey of family practitioners, pediatricians, internists, and obstetrician-gynecologists, Ewing and colleagues (1999) found that less than one-half of these physicians routinely inquired about smoking. In a survey of pediatricians and family physicians, Klein and colleagues (2001b) found that these physicians asked more than 90% of their adolescent patients about smoking but discussed tobacco-related health risks with only about 75%. Inquiries about parental smoking, peer smoking, and use of smokeless tobacco were less common, ranging from 32% to 54% of patients. Although more than 80% of the physicians promoted abstinence from smoking among their nonsmoking patients and assessed motivation to quit among those who smoked, less than one-half followed up with cessation materials or referrals.

Halpern-Felsher and colleagues (2000) reported that 77% of adolescents in a managed care setting were screened for tobacco use. Among those patients who reported tobacco use, however, only three-quarters were screened further about the amount they smoked and only 84% were counseled on the risks of smoking. This same study also found that no more than 43% of the patients' parents were told about the need to monitor youths for risk behaviors, including substance use. Galuska and colleagues (2002) found that less than one-half of pediatricians counseled adolescents about tobacco use by others in the home.

In general, the provision of tobacco prevention services remain low, even for particularly vulnerable adolescent populations, such as low-income, asthmatic, or chronically ill youth (Fairbrother et al. 2005; Rand et al. 2005; Tercyak et al. 2007). In addition, physicians are more likely to ask older adolescents about their smoking status than to deliver preventive advice to preadolescents who might benefit more from prevention messages because they are less likely to have started smoking (Makni et al. 2002). A study of almost 1,000 pediatricians randomly selected from a national sample in 1998–1999 found that only 29% always counseled younger children (6–12 years of age) about tobacco use, but 69% always counseled their 13- to 18-year-old patients about using tobacco (Galuska et al. 2002).

The rates at which adolescents are screened for tobacco use and other risk behaviors vary by physicians' characteristics, including age, gender, year of graduation, practice setting, and subspecialty. Two studies found that rates of counseling for tobacco use and other preventive services were greater among female providers and among pediatricians who were able to spend relatively more time with their patients (Klein et al. 2001a,b; Galuska et al. 2002). More recently, Perry and Kenney (2007) found that pediatricians were more likely than physician subspecialists, as well as nonphysician providers, to advise patients that smoking in the home is harmful. Earlier, Ewing and colleagues (1999) found that physicians under the age of 50 years were more likely than older physicians to provide tobacco-related clinical preventive services. Still earlier, Blum and colleagues (1996) found that the provision of clinical services was lowest in nonadolescent-focused practice settings, independent of patient age or gender. Halpern-Felsher and colleagues (2000) found greater provision of clinical preventive services among female physicians, recent graduates from medical school, and physicians with a greater number of older adolescent patients. Similarly, Klein and colleagues (2001b) found that rates of delivery for tobacco-related preventive services varied by provider characteristics, with women being more likely than men to ask about smoking behaviors and smoking by parents and peers and men more likely to ask about the use of smokeless tobacco.

Relatively little is known about how to improve the rates at which services to prevent tobacco use are delivered to children and adolescents. Ozer and colleagues (2005) showed that training physicians could increase the rates at which health care providers screen and counsel youth about risk behaviors, including tobacco use. Providers' self-efficacy to provide preventive services was found to be linked to the actual delivery of services (Ozer et al. 2005) and can be enhanced through trainings (Buckelew et al. 2008). Studies from the literature on adult patients indicate that the use of paper-based, computer-generated, or computerized reminders in patient charts is particularly effective at increasing the delivery rates of smoking cessation services (Dexheimer et al. 2008). In addition, the literature on adolescents suggests that providing charting tools can improve the rates at which services are delivered to younger patients (Ozer et al. 2001, 2005). Electronic health care record systems that require documentation of service delivery may also increase the rates at which preventive services are delivered. More research is needed to determine the extent to which the implementation of provider training, electronic systems, or other charting tools increases the delivery of tobacco-related preventive services to children and youth.

Hymowitz and colleagues (2004, 2007, 2008) focused on increasing the provision of tobacco-related preventive services (and self-efficacy to deliver them) by adding a training program in tobacco to residencies in pediatrics. As Hymowitz and associates (2004) pointed out, few pediatric residents receive any training in addressing the use of tobacco by patients or their parents, and many pediatricians question the efficacy of counseling. In a randomized study, pediatric residents were assigned to either standard training or a new training, Solutions for Smoking (SOS), which used a combination of CD-ROM and Web site programming to provide information on interviewing skills, the use of the "5 A's," and behavioral and pharmacologic methods for reducing tobacco use. The researchers found that from baseline to 4 years after the program, residents in the SOS training were more likely to inquire about secondhand smoke in the home and to provide specific advice and materials to help parents stop smoking; those in the SOS program also reported feeling more efficacious for addressing tobacco issues. These studies do not, however, directly address the effects of the intervention on whether the pediatricians trained in the program had any effect on tobacco use by children or adolescents.

Rather than focus directly on health care providers, Christakis and colleagues (2006) demonstrated the effectiveness of using a Web-based intervention to encourage the parents of younger children (0–11 years of age) to discuss health topics, including tobacco use, with their pediatricians. The authors found that parents were more likely to discuss topics with their pediatrician during a well-child visit if the parents participated in an interactive Web site, thus, in turn, changing the physician's behavior in a way that produced greater levels of preventive services. Future studies are needed to test the effectiveness of this intervention with parents of older children and adolescents.

Research Support for Tobacco Prevention Strategies Involving Health Care Providers

Unfortunately, there has been little research on whether increased rates of preventive screening, counseling, and education by health care providers actually lower the rates of tobacco use among youth. Nor have studies determined the mechanisms by which these interventions might be most effective (Christakis et al. 2003; Krowchuk 2005). In fact, there is no research at all demonstrating the effectiveness of the "5 A's" in preventing tobacco use among children and adolescents, although the Prokhorov and colleagues (2010) study did involve pediatricians and demonstrated some success. It also remains unclear how many providers adhere to antitobacco policies in their offices or how effective such policies are in changing smoking norms or preventing smoking initiation among youth.

The first RCT to test the effectiveness of a program for preventing tobacco use among youth involved training orthodontists to deliver eight "prescriptions" to their patients over time (Hovell et al. 1996, 2001). These prescriptions included providing advice on eight tobacco-related topics, such as "tobacco and sports" and "nicotine and tobacco addiction." Rates of smoking initiation did not differ between the prevention and control groups over a 2-year follow-up, but higher rates of delivering the prescriptions by orthodontists predicted lower rates of smoking initiation. Later, Hollis and colleagues (2005) conducted an RCT to examine the long-term effects of brief counseling, physician advice, and computer-based intervention on prevention of smoking and on cessation among adolescents 14–17 years of age. Compared with controls participating in a dietary intervention, adolescents in the tobacco intervention were significantly less likely to report smoking 1 and 2 years after that intervention than those in the control group. These effects were even stronger for those reporting smoking at baseline. Among that group, 24% indicated at the 2-year follow-up that they had quit. However, this brief intervention had less of an effect on preventing the onset of smoking.

Three other studies that used RCTs of interventions to prevent smoking in medical settings found that preventive services had little or no effect on smoking among youth. In one, screening for smoking behavior and providing pictures of tooth discoloration at annual dental visits did not reduce the prevalence of smoking (Kentala et al. 1999). In a second, mailing age-appropriate information about the advantages of remaining a nonsmoker to primary care patients at 3-month intervals produced a significant but still small difference in smoking rates between youth in the intervention and control groups (Fidler and Lambert 2001). In the third study, Curry and colleagues (2003) implemented and evaluated an RCT of a family-based smoking prevention program in a managed care setting. The intervention included a smoking prevention kit mailed to parents, newsletters for the parents, follow-up telephone calls by health educators, materials for the children, and information placed in medical records and charts as reminders to the physician to deliver prevention messages. Although the intervention had small but significant effects on increasing parent-child communication about tobacco, no differences between the intervention and control groups were found in rates of susceptibility to smoking, experimentation with smoking, or monthly smoking rates.

Another study investigated whether implementing an office-systems approach would prevent or delay adolescents' drinking and smoking behaviors (Stevens et al. 2002). The idea of the approach in question, as expressed by Klein and Camenga (2004), is that the primary care physician provides anticipatory guidance and screening, the entire office staff endorses the prevention messages, and prevention materials are provided in the office. Stevens and associates (2002) found that despite evidence that their intervention was implemented successfully, it did not significantly affect adolescents' tobacco use. The authors suggested that their program might have been ineffective in part because it focused on increasing parent-child communication rather than on targeting adolescents' behaviors.

Ozer and colleagues (2004) presented preliminary results of a study indicating that adolescents who received clinical preventive services in managed care settings were less likely to increase the regular use of tobacco over a 1-year period, but they did not report the effects on initiation of tobacco use. More recently, Brown and associates (2007) examined the impact of a single-lesson course in tobacco cessation given to fourth and fifth graders at a health education center. The lesson focused on improving knowledge of tobacco, the identification of refusal techniques, and lowering intent to smoke. General knowledge about tobacco and refusal techniques significantly increased, but rates of intent to smoke did not decrease, perhaps because the rate was low before the intervention.

In summary, the few studies that have examined the efficacy of provider-based interventions suggest that the strategies they have employed may not be effective. However, the results must be interpreted with caution. Only a limited number of strategies have been assessed, and none of the studies on a specific prevention strategy have been replicated. This problem is complicated by the fact that most youth and many young adults are low-volume, intermittent smokers who often do not think of themselves as smokers. Furthermore, efforts directed at youth have been investigated in just a few health care settings, such as physicians' and orthodontists' offices and specialty clinics. Additionally, little is known about the impact of youth-focused efforts to prevent tobacco use that are conducted in specialty services such as asthma clinics, urgent care facilities, or emergency rooms.

Barriers to the Provision of Clinical Preventive Services to Youth

Physicians cite numerous barriers to providing clinical preventive services, including (1) having a large number of patients, which limits their time per patient; (2) competing health care demands during preventive visits; (3) insufficient education and training; (4) lack of information about how to access referral and treatment resources; (5) lack of dissemination to physicians of research that supports positive treatment outcomes and the negative effects of failure to intervene; (6) fear of alienating patients and families; and (7) inadequate reimbursement relative to the time and effort required to provide such services (Cheng et al. 1999; Kulig and American Academy of Pediatrics Committee on Substance Abuse 2005; Oscós-Sánchez et al. 2008; Sanders and Colson 2008). Research also suggests that physicians' confidence in their ability to screen and advise adolescents about tobacco use is related to how frequently they deliver preventive services (Cheng et al. 1999; Ozer et al. 2004). Education and training of health care professionals can reduce the impact of several of these barriers; indeed, studies have shown that even a few hours of training on tobacco use can significantly improve medical students' and physicians' knowledge about this behavior as well as their confidence in delivering preventive services and the likelihood that they do so (Pederson et al. 2006; Fiore et al. 2008).

Summary Regarding Clinical Interventions with Young People

As primary sources of health information and potential role models, health care providers are well suited to address the prevention of tobacco use among youth. National guidelines for the provision of preventive services recognize the pivotal role that health care providers can play in preventing tobacco use and stipulate that prevention be addressed at least once per year throughout adolescence (AMA 1997; USDHHS 1998; USPSTF 2003; Bonnie et al. 2007; Hagan et al. 2008). The available literature indicates that adherence to recommended screening and prevention activities for patients who are children or adolescents, such as implementing the "5 A's," is low (Galuska et al. 2002). Studies suggest that tobacco-training programs and paper- and computer-based reminders for health care professionals to deliver services may be viable options for increasing the rates at which services to prevent tobacco use are delivered to children and adolescents (Ozer et al. 2005; Pederson et al. 2006; Dexheimer et al. 2008). Finally, little is known about the effectiveness of tobacco prevention services delivered to children and adolescents in health care settings, although a recent meta-analysis suggests that counseling may be effective in reducing adolescent smoking (Fiore et al. 2008). As a result, there is currently no clear evidence to suggest that any prevention strategies delivered in health care settings are effective in preventing the initiation of smoking in this population, but clinicians may be important in encouraging young smokers to quit.

School-Based Programs to Prevent Smoking

During the past 30 years, numerous school-based programs to prevent tobacco use have been developed. As reviewed in the 1994 Surgeon General's report on preventing tobacco use among young people (USDHHS 1994), approaches to the prevention of smoking have gone through several phases: informational, affective/motivational, and psychosocial (normative). As early as the late 1970s, Thompson (1978), in a review of all English-language papers on smoking prevention between 1960 and 1976, concluded that most methods used up to that point (i.e., informational and affective approaches) were not effective, and this view was later echoed by Beattie (1984). Informational approaches stressed the harmful consequences of smoking; affective approaches used fear-based messages and values clarification as strategies. Many programs can effectively change knowledge, which in itself is important, but such change is not enough to alter behavior (Goodstadt 1978) and, in any case, the effects of knowledge acquisition decay quickly (Hwang et al. 2004). Sometimes, information can make behavior worse (Goodstadt 1978, 1980), as can some programs that address affective issues (Petrosino et al. 2000). During the late 1980s and early 1990s, U.S. government agencies concluded that traditional school-based approaches (informational and affective) were largely ineffective at prevention and that approaches based on social-psychological models (McGuire 1964; Evans 1976) were modestly effective across a variety of settings, times, and populations (Glynn 1989; NCI 1991; Lynch and Bonnie 1994; USDHHS 1994). For example, the 1994 Surgeon General's report (USDHHS 1994) concluded that (1) school-based programs that identified social influences on tobacco use and taught resistance skills had shown significant reductions in youth smoking, and (2) those programs were enhanced and sustained by comprehensive school health education and community-wide programs.

Multiple reviews of approaches to the control of tobacco use or preventing substance abuse published after 1990 have examined school-based smoking prevention (NCI 1991, 2001; Burns 1992; Hansen 1992; Lynch and Bonnie 1994; USDHHS 1994, 2000b; Stead et al. 1996; Pentz 1999; Sussman et al. 1999; Lantz et al. 2000; Sussman 2001; Vickers et al. 2002; Buttross and Kastner 2003; Skara and Sussman 2003; Tingle et al. 2003; Warner et al. 2003; Lober Aquilino and Lowe 2004; Krowchuk 2005; La Torre et al. 2005; Park 2006; Ranney et al. 2006; Thomas and Perera 2006; Bonnie et al. 2007; Davis et al. 2007b; Flay 2007; Dobbins et al. 2008) as well as meta-analyses on the subject (Bruvold 1993; Rooney and Murray 1996; Tobler and Stratton 1997; Black et al. 1998; Tobler et al. 2000; Tingle et al. 2003; Hwang et al. 2004; Wiehe et al. 2005). These reviews and meta-analyses have repeatedly reinforced the conclusion that informational and affective programs do not by themselves change behavior. However, the meta-analyses have established that some psychosocial programs and strategies, particularly those that are interactive (i.e., that offer chances for communication among participants and provide an opportunity for the exchange of ideas, role playing, and the practice of new social skills) and are based on the social influences approach (educating youth about social norms and influences and providing skills for resisting such influences) can be effective in preventing the onset of smoking.

Regardless, assessing findings in the field is sometimes confusing because some of the early or short psychosocial programs reported promising short-term effects that were not sustained over time (Flay et al. 1989; Murray et al. 1989b; Ellickson et al. 1993; Shean et al. 1994; Shope et al. 1998; Hawkins et al. 1999). In addition, some tested programs simply were not effective (Peterson et al. 2000). D.A.R.E. is an example of a program that seems similar to many successful programs in numerous ways and yet has been proven ineffective in multiple studies and two meta-analyses (Ennett et al. 1994a,b; West and O'Neal 2004). These mixed results for school-based programs have led some to question the overall value of such programs (Glantz and Mandel 2005). In the most recent review of school-based prevention, however, Dobbins and colleagues (2008) concluded that "there is reason for optimism regarding the effectiveness of prevention programs on smoking behavior and initiation, albeit in the short term" (p. 296).

CDC continues to recommend providing school-based prevention (CDC 2003, 2007a,b, 2008b). More specifically, CDC suggests offering a curriculum that focuses on tobacco use prevention from kindergarten to 12th grade, with increased intensity in junior high or middle school (CDC 2007a), the stage of life with the most acceleration of onset rates. The agency (2007b) suggests implementing school-based prevention in combination with mass media and other community-wide approaches.

The following sections provide a more detailed review of findings from meta-analyses and previous reviews and a systematic review of the potential for long-term effectiveness of school-based programs to prevent smoking.

Review of Meta-Analyses and a Cochrane Review

Flay (2009b) provided a review of meta-analyses and of the Cochrane review by Thomas and Perera (2006) in an effort to determine from past reviews whether school-based smoking prevention can be effective. Among the multiple meta-analyses of school-based programs was one that included 74 studies of smoking prevention among 207 studies on the prevention of substance abuse (Tobler et al. 2000), another that evaluated 65 separate programs (Hwang et al. 2004), a review of 94 randomized trials that reviewed only 23 in detail because of methodologic limitations with the remaining studies (Thomas and Perera 2006), and a review focusing on the quality of 11 evaluations but not their outcomes (Tingle et al. 2003). Reviews of the long-term effects of these programs have varied in scope: one review included 25 studies with at least 2-years of follow-up (Skara and Sussman 2003), and another found only 8 studies with outcome data for grade 12 (or 18 years of age) (Wiehe et al. 2005). The findings range from precise and substantial ESs for some types of programs (Tobler et al. 2000; Hwang et al. 2004) to conclusions that most school-based prevention programs are effective (Dobbins et al. 2008) or do not work (Glantz and Mandel 2005; Wiehe et al. 2005).

Tobler and colleagues (2000), after summarizing a series of meta-analyses, suggested that programs that used interactive learning strategies and involved same- or similar-aged peers as leaders or facilitators were most effective. In addition, Tobler and colleagues (2000) found that smoking prevention programs produced an average ES of 0.16, with interactive programs producing a significantly larger ES than did noninteractive programs (0.17 vs. 0.05). These authors also found that programs that addressed multiple substances were less effective at reducing tobacco use than were programs that targeted only tobacco (ES = 0.10 vs. 0.17), but the multiple-substance programs had the added benefit of reducing alcohol and other substance use. These researchers also found program effects to be larger in schools with predominantly special or high-risk populations (characterized by minority populations, high absenteeism or dropout rates, or poor academic records). Hwang and colleagues (2004), in a review of 65 programs, estimated an average short-term ES of 0.19 for outcomes involving smoking behaviors. These authors reported ESs of 0.22 for attitudes and skills and 0.53 for knowledge and found that all program effects were smaller at those follow-ups that did not take place immediately after the intervention. Outcomes involving behavior, however, decayed very little over 1–3 years (from the original 0.19 to 0.18) but, without further programming, they decayed by one-half (to 0.09) at follow-ups of 3 or more years. Knowledge decayed by over 60% by 1-year follow-up (to 0.19), and attitudes and skills decayed to under one-half their original effects by 1-year follow-up (to 0.10 and 0.09, respectively).

Hwang and colleagues (2004) also estimated the effects of different approaches to school-based smoking prevention: social influences, cognitive-behavioral interventions (programs that included the elements of the social influences approach plus at least two cognitive skills), and life skills. They found that social influences approaches had average ESs of 0.12 at short-term follow-up, 0.15 at 1–3 years, and 0.07 at more than 3 years; cognitive-behavioral approaches had average ESs of 0.21 at both short-term follow-up and 1–3 years; and life skills approaches had average ESs of 0.29 at short-term follow-up and 0.16 at 1–3 years. There were too few studies in their meta-analysis to provide estimates of the longer-term effects (more than 3 years) of cognitive-behavioral or life skills approaches.

Hwang and colleagues (2004) also distinguished between programs based only at a school and those in school-plus-community settings. They found that school-only programs reported average ESs of 0.22, 0.16, and 0.06 in the short term, at 1–3 years, and more than 3 years, respectively, and school-plus-community programs reported average ESs of 0.16 in the short term and 0.21 at 1–3 years. In an earlier systematic review of school and school-plus-community programs in preventing substance abuse, Flay (2000) concluded that school-plus-community programs produced about double the effect of the school-only programs when the type of school program was held constant.

Rooney and Murray's (1996) meta-analysis of 131 smoking prevention programs adjusted for studies with an error in the unit of analysis (i.e., the group analyzed was not the correct one, a common error in the relevant literature at that time), but this adjustment had little or no effect on the overall ESs. The average ES was around 0.10 at long-term follow-up, which would be about a 5% relative reduction in smoking (Rosenthal 1984). Using a modeling approach, the authors estimated that the impact of programs could be increased if they began around sixth grade as part of a multicomponent health program, gave same-age peer leaders a role in program delivery, and used booster sessions. They estimated that this might achieve a relative reduction in smoking of between 19% and 29% (or ESs in the 0.5–0.8 range).

Thomas and Perera (2006), who completed the most thorough systematic review of school-based smoking prevention studies to date (it is included in the Cochrane Database of Systematic Reviews), required a minimum of 6 months' follow-up after the completion of the intervention. They restricted their reviews to RCTs and found 94 of them. The authors rated the methodologic biases of each study and classified them as having minimal, medium, or high risk of bias; they analyzed in detail only the 23 studies they judged to be of the highest quality. They determined statistical significance from their own analysis of ORs—the odds of those who were lifetime nonsmokers at baseline starting to smoke by the posttest in the intervention group compared with the control group. When intraclass correlation coefficients (ICCs) were not reported, they assumed an ICC of 0.097, the average found in a limited set of older studies (Siddiqui et al. 1996). Another criterion imposed by Thomas and Perera (2006) was requiring a minimum of one assessment at least 6 months beyond the end of the intervention. As interventions have become more comprehensive and longer in duration, it is becoming more difficult to meet this standard; it is not clear that a study should be excluded from consideration because the last posttest was less than 6 months after the last session, especially if the bulk of the intervention took place several years earlier. The only outcome reported by Thomas and Perera (2006) was the prevalence of smoking among participants who were never smokers at pretest, and thus they did not include such possible outcomes as changes in the proportion or prevalence of ever, weekly, or monthly smokers.

In terms of program types, Thomas and Perera (2006) assigned the 94 studies to five groups: (1) information only; (2) social competence (e.g., the Good Behavior Game, the Seattle Social Development Project); (3) social influences (e.g., Project CLASP, Waterloo Smoking Prevention Project); (4) combined social competence/influences (e.g., LST, Project Towards No Tobacco Use, Child Development Project); and (5) multimodal (i.e., including family or community components). However, as Thomas and Perera (2006) acknowledged, it is extraordinarily difficult for people not intimately involved in the field to determine how to group the different interventions. In addition, over time, the programs have become more alike in principle as they incorporate ideas from each other.

Based on the above inclusion criteria, Thomas and Perera (2006) concluded the following about school-based programs to prevent smoking:

1. There is little evidence that information alone is effective.

2. Nine of 13 studies of social influences that met their criteria for inclusion demonstrated positive effects.

3. The longest-lasting test (65 lessons over 8 years) of a social influences program (Hutchinson Smoking Prevention Project) found that the program was not effective.

4. There was limited evidence for the effectiveness of social competence programs (only two studies met criteria for inclusion).

5. Of only three high-quality studies of the combination of social competence and social influences, just one showed a significant effect overall, and one

showed a significant effect only for the condition in which the program was led by a health educator (not significant for the self-instruction condition).

6. Three of the four studies of multimodal approaches that met criteria for inclusion produced positive effects.

7. There is little evidence of the long-term effectiveness of school-based programs to prevent smoking.

Assessing Short- and Long-Term Effects of Prevention Programs

Although there are multiple studies of school-based programs that have demonstrated short-term effects (at the completion of the program), there has been some concern about the maintenance of these outcomes in the long term (end of high school or beyond). Wiehe and colleagues (2005) conducted a meta-analysis of the eight studies they could locate with results reported at 12th grade or 18 years of age. Of the studies reviewed, only the LST program, an interactive program of 30 sessions (15 in 7th grade, 10 in 9th grade, and 5 in 10th grade) that incorporates the social influences approach, as well as the teaching of other general personal and social skills, was effective at long-term follow-up.

Skara and Sussman (2003) reviewed studies of 25 programs to prevent the use of tobacco or other drugs that included follow-up of at least 24 months. Eighteen of the studies reported significant short-term effects, and 15 reported significant long-term effects. Of 17 studies with both pretest and posttest data, 11 (65%) reported significant long-term effects, with an average reduction in the percentage of baseline nonusers who initiated smoking in the program (using the rate of initiation in the control group as the comparison) of 11.4% (range: 9–14.2%, ES = 0.28). Of the studies with significant short-term effects, 72% (13 of 18) had significant long-term effects. Program effects were less likely to decay when there was extended programming or booster sessions were given.

The Task Force on Community Preventive Services (Zaza et al. 2005), on behalf of the CDC, examined the effectiveness of school-based tobacco use interventions that were published from 1980 to 2001. The Task Force examined 117 studies from 154 published papers. Of these, 48 studies were excluded due to limited quality of implementation or poor study design, leaving 69 studies that were seen to provide the "best evidence" concerning the effectiveness of school-based interventions. Fifty-two studies measured changes in tobacco use prevalence among adolescents. A summary of these studies and their outcomes is shown in Table 6.9. The Task Force noted an overall median effect of nearly -1.0% in absolute difference in smoking prevalence between control and intervention groups (with a range from -10% to +4%). The Task Force concluded that school-based tobacco use interventions can be effective in the short term, but that evidence was insufficient from their review to include a recommendation of implementation at the national level, given the lack of long-term outcomes for most studies.

In a second review, the Task Force on Community Preventive Services (Zaza et al. 2005) reviewed studies of comprehensive community-wide programs that included a school-based tobacco use prevention intervention. Community-wide programs included mass media campaigns, clean indoor air legislation or ordinances, excise tax increases on tobacco products, community education efforts conducted by local groups, and interventions to restrict minors' access to tobacco products. The Task Force reviewed studies that had been published from 1980 to 2001 and identified 17 studies that (1) evaluated community or statewide multicomponent interventions that included a school-based intervention and (2) measured differences or changes in student tobacco use. Of these, one study was excluded because it did not provide measurements of differences or changes in student tobacco use behavior. A summary of the studies deemed sufficient quality for inclusion (n = 16) is found in Table 6.10. Of the 16 studies reviewed, 14 found significant reductions in student tobacco use. In particular, the combination of school-based programs, mass media campaigns, and community education demonstrated a consistent and strong reduction in adolescent tobacco use over time, with a median effect of -4.5% in absolute difference in smoking prevalence between control and intervention groups (with a range of -13% to -2%). The Task Force recommended school-based tobacco use prevention programs be implemented in combination with mass media campaigns and additional community-wide educational activities (The Community Guide 2011).

Dobbins and colleagues (2008) conducted a comprehensive review of the effectiveness of school-based tobacco use prevention programs, examining all systematic reviews and meta-analyses from 1985 to 2007. From an initial analysis of 10,163 abstracts and titles, 92 papers were potentially relevant, and 12 reviews were considered relevant with moderate or strong methodologies. Smoking behavior was reported in 11 of the 12 reviews, with 6 reviews showing a positive effect of school-based programs, 2 showing promising effects, and 3 reporting no impact on smoking outcomes. The reviewers concluded that school-based tobacco use prevention programs are effective in reducing smoking prevalence, onset, and intentions to smoke in the short term. Flay (2007) provided a review of the long-term effectiveness of school-based smoking

Table 6.9 Studies of the effectiveness of school-based interventions to reduce tobacco use

Author & year (study period) Design suitability: design Quality of execution (number of limitations) Evaluation setting	Intervention (I) and comparison (C)	Population; sample size	Effect measure	Reported baseline	Reported effect	Value used in summary	Follow-up time
Hurd et al. 1980 (NR) 8 month (m) intervention Greatest: group nonrandomized trial Fair (4 limitations) Schools (junior high schools: 7th grade)	Minneapolis-St. Paul, Minnesota School-based education 3 arms; resist social pressures; immediate harmful effects; model behavior-nonsmoking peer leaders and older role models; commitment activity; videotapes, role-playing; 5 class sessions in health and science classes Compared with usual care	All junior high schools in district: n = 4 1: control 2: monitored control 3: curriculum + monitor 4: curriculum + monitor + other activities 7th-grade students n = 1,636 (99%) n = 1,245 (76%) with pre + post data 1: 440 2: 332 3: 365 4: 389	(1) Student self-reported smoker (not an experimenter)	I-3 13.7% I-4 4.9% C-1 5.7% C-2 9.0% Consolidated I 3-4 9.2% C 1-2 7.1%	I-3 20.3% I-4 5.9% C-1 9.6% C-2 21.1% I 3-4 12.9% C 1-2 14.5%	+6.6 percentage points (pct pts) +1.0 pct pts +3.9 pct pts +12.1 pct pts -3.7 pct pts NR	6 months

Table 6.9 Continued

Author & year (study period) Design suitability: design Quality of execution (number of limitations) Evaluation setting	Intervention (I) and comparison (C)	Population; sample size	Effect measure	Reported baseline	Reported effect	Value used in summary	Follow-up time
Perry et al. 1980 (1978) Greatest: group randomized trial Fair (4 limitations) Schools (high schools; 10th grade)	Stanford area, California School-based education, smoking prevention/cessation curriculum, 4 45-minute sessions delivered by trained teachers in health class; social pressures, selling strategies, modeled counter self-verbalizations, resisting peer pressures; cessation procedures; physiological measures-health effects Compared with usual care	All high schools in 2 districts: n = 5 I: n = 3 C: n = 2 10th-grade students in study schools I: 498 C: 399	(1) Student self-reported smoking (%) (prevalence)	Day Week Month I 13.9 19.5 29.2 C 14.5 21.6 26.3	Day Week Month 9.7 16.3 23.6 21.9 30.4	Day-2.8 pct pts NS Week –3.5 pct pts Post p <0.05 Month –9.7 pct pts Post p <0.05	6 months
			(3) Student self-reported "general opinion about smoking"	I NR C NR	I 68% C 65%	+3 pct pts NS	
			(4) Student knowledge (9 survey questions)	I various C various	I various C various	Increased. 7 of 9 questions with statistically significant difference	

Table 6.9 Continued

Author & year (study period) Design suitability: design Quality of execution (number of limitations) Evaluation setting	Intervention (I) and comparison (C)	Population; sample size	Effect measure	Reported baseline	Reported effect	Value used in summary	Follow-up time
Denson and Stretch 1981 (1976–78) Greatest: group randomized trial Fair (3 limitations) Schools (elementary schools)	Saskatoon, Canada School-based education for 6th or 7th grades; 4 sessions; film, lectures, discussion; harmful effects of smoking/ addiction	Elementary schools (n = 6) Matched pairs with assignment	1) Student self-reported tobacco use—regular smoking at end of grade 8 (prevalence)	1976 I 25.7% C 27.8%	1978 I 17.5% C 26.1% p <0.01	-6.5 pct pts	2 years (post)
		8th graders in annual surveys (90% response rates)	(1) Interval self-reported uptake of smoking (Initiation between 7th and 8th grades)	I 14.1% C 10.4%	I 17.5% C 26.1%	-12.3 pct pts p <0.001	
	Compared with usual care	1976 pre 1978 post I 315 292 C 273 307	(4) Student responses (yes) "do you believe smoking is a form of drug addiction?" (knowledge)	I NR C NR	I 62% C 39%	More (post) +23 pct pts p <0.05	

Table 6.9 Continued

Author & year (study period) Design suitability: design Quality of execution (number of limitations) Evaluation setting	Intervention (I) and comparison (C)	Population; sample size	Effect measure	Reported baseline	Reported effect	Value used in summary	Follow-up time
Evans et al. 1981 (NR) Greatest: other design with a concurrent comparison group Fair (4 limitations) Schools (middle schools; 7th grade)	Houston, Texas School-based education; delivered during physical education time with graduate + undergraduate coordinators; social learning theory, immediate consequences of smoking, social pressure coping	Selected, matched junior high schools N = 13 schools assigned to 1 of 6 study conditions	(1) Student self-reported regular/ frequent tobacco use (2 or more cigarettes per day) (prevalence) E1 vs. C1 arms	I1 2.8% C1 2.4%	I1 9.5% C1 14.2% Post differences p <0.001	-5.1 pct pts	3 years (post)
			3) Student self-reported intentions to smoke-median intention scores (lower score=greater intention to smoke) (attitudes)	I1 4.91 C1 4.89	I1-2-3 4.86 C1-2-3 4.79 Post differences p=0.21	Lower intentions to smoke (not statistically significant)	
	Compared with usual care	Students (consent) participating 7th pre / 9th post I 284 / 995 C 165 / 408	(4) Student level of knowledge about smoking	I1 NR C1 NR	I1 NR C1 NR	NR (scores related to smoking intention and behavior)	

Table 6.9 Continued

Author & year (study period) Design suitability: design Quality of execution (number of limitations) Evaluation setting	Intervention (I) and comparison (C)	Population; sample size	Effect measure	Reported baseline	Reported effect	Value used in summary	Follow-up time
Pederson et al. 1981 (NR) Greatest: group nonrandomized trial Fair (4 limitations) Schools (grades 4–6)	London, Canada School-based education; 12 classroom hours; curriculum based on ALA publication Compared with usual care Note: subset of a larger study	Selected public school classrooms N = 8 classrooms I: n = 4 C: n = 4 Students in study classrooms N = 99 4th graders N = 101 6th graders	(1) Student self-reported smoking behaviors (prevalence) "Regular"	NR	NR	No significant effect	Post inter-vention
			"Experimental"	NR	NR	No significant effect	
			(3) Student self-reported attitudes (attitudes)	NR	NR	Attitudes of I group became less negative p <0.10	
			(4) Student mean knowledge scores (estimated from chart) (knowledge)	I 8.9 C 12.1	I 11.8 C 10.4	Increased 11.6%; F(1,196) = 13.67 p <0.01	
Coe et al. 1982 (NR) Greatest: group nonrandomized trial Fair (4 limitations) Schools (public middle)	St. Louis, Missouri School-based education, 8 1-hour sessions delivered by trained medical students, peer pressures, mass media advertising, class incentive awards Compared with usual care	Selected public middle schools: 2 One class in each school I: n = 2 classes C: n = 2 classes 7th or 8th graders School A/School B Pre / 1 year I 39/63 / 28/38 C 52/72 / 41/43	(1) Student self-reported smoking (at least one cigarette in past 30 days) (prevalence)	A / B I 17.9% / 2.6% C 9.8% / 9.5%	A / B I 14.3% / 10.3% C 34.1% / 18.6%	A / B -20.7 / -1.4 pct pts (NR)	1 year
			(3) Student self-reported attitude toward smoking (less favorable)	I NR / NR C NR / NR	I 22.8% / 37.0% C 31.9% / 30.0%	-9.1 / +7.0 pct pts (NR)	

Table 6.9 Continued

Author & year (study period) Design suitability: design Quality of execution (number of limitations) Evaluation setting	Intervention (I) and comparison (C)	Population; sample size	Effect measure	Reported baseline	Reported effect	Value used in summary	Follow-up time
Telch et al. 1982; McAlister et al. 1980 (1977–79) Greatest: group nonrandomized trial Fair (4 limitations) Schools: (junior high schools: 7th grade) Project CLASP (Counseling Leadership Against Smoking Pressure)	San Jose, California School-based education, (drug abuse prevention); social pressures training; 6 class sessions in year 1; 2 45-minute sessions in year 2 (smoking focus in first session); peer-led trained teams of high school students Compared with school-based education (school health curriculum project with no special resistance skills training)	Selected junior high school (2) I school matched to C school on demographics 7th-grade students Baseline 21m 33m I 353 340 82.5% C 217 186 80.2%	(1) Student self-reported smoking during the preceeding week (proxy of weekly) (prevalence)	Estimated from graph: I (2%) C (1%)	21m 33m I 7.1% 5% C 18.8% 15%	At 33 months -11 pct pts (post difference -10 pct pts $x^2 = 12.2$ p <0.001)	33 months (9th grade)

Table 6.9 Continued

Author & year (study period) Design suitability: design Quality of execution (number of limitations) Evaluation setting	Intervention (I) and comparison (C)	Population; sample size	Effect measure	Reported baseline	Reported effect	Value used in summary	Follow-up time
Alexander et al. 1983 (1979–80) Greatest: group randomized trial Fair (4 limitations) Schools (years 5-6)	New South Wales, Australia School-based education; 9 weeks x 1.5 hours/week led by class teacher (1-day training); increase knowledge, recognize pressures to smoke Compared with usual care	Schools: n = 88 Students in years 5–6 (aged 10–12 years) with complete data n = 5,616 (86%) at analysis I = 2,782 C = 2,904	(1) Self-reported smoker (any use in the last 4 weeks) Monthly Note: Recalculated totals from available data	I 10.39% C 9.12%	I 18.66% C 18.46%	-1.07 pct pts NR (NS subgroups)	6 months (post 1 year)
			(1) Self-reported initiation of tobacco use by baseline nonsmokers	14.5% in usual care group	14.3% across all intervention groups	-0.2 pct pts (initiation)	
			(2) Self-reported smoking cessation by baseline smokers at follow-up	42.8%	43.6%	+0.8 pct pts (cessation)	
			(3) Percentage of students expressing strong disapproval of tobacco use and cigarette advertising (attitudes)	Subgroup data Range: 41.3–50.1%	Subgroup data Range: 38.7–50.2%	Group differences were not significant but trend decrease	
			(4) Student tobacco knowledge scores (out of 28 responses)	Subgroup data 17.2 out of 28	Subgroup data 17.8 out of 28	+0.6 score p <0.001	

Table 6.9 Continued

Author & year (study period) Design suitability: design Quality of execution (number of limitations) Evaluation setting	Intervention (I) and comparison (C)	Population; sample size	Effect measure	Reported baseline	Reported effect	Value used in summary	Follow-up time
Shaffer et al. 1983 (1980) Greatest: group nonrandomized trial Fair (4 limitations) Schools (7th grade)	Cambridge, Massachusetts School-based education, skill acquisition and rehearsal; manual for instructors; 6 45-minute sessions; film and slideshows, skits/role-playing	Selected public schools: n = 2 Selected classrooms n = 7 I: n = 5 C: n = 2 7th-grade students n = 114	(1) Student self-reported smoking (prevalence) Daily	I 8.9% C 8.6%	I 5.1% C 9.7%	-4.9 pct pts NR (past day measure p <0.01 posttest)	3 months
			Past month	I 18% C 17%	I 10% C 22% p <0.01	-13 pct pts	
	Compared with school-based education-single session		(2) Students reporting "used to smoke but quit" (proxy cessation)	I 5.1% C 20%	I 10.1% C 6.5%	(+18.5 pct pts) Post only +3.6 pct pts NR	
Best et al. 1984 (NR) Greatest: group nonrandomized trial Fair (4 limitations) Schools (grades 6–8) Waterloo Smoking Prevention Project	Ontario, Canada School-based education, social-influences model; grade 6 with booster in grades 7 and 8. Compared with usual care (routine health education)	Participating schools in 2 districts N = 22 schools; 11 matched pairs 6th-grade students (consent) n = 654 n = 439 (67%) with complete data at 8th-grade follow-up	(1) Student self-reported smoker (prevalence compiled from stratified results regular + exp smoker=smoker vs. nonsmoker)	I 9.7% C 13.6%	I 22.6% C 34.6%	-8.1 pct pts (no overall measure of significance)	2 years (post grade 6)
			(1) Student self-reported smoker (any)-baseline nonsmokers (initiation)	I (0%) C (0%)	I 40% C 53%	-13 pct pts p <0.08	
			(2) Student self-reported quitter-baseline regular user (n = 13) (cessation)	I (100%) C (100%)	I 40% C 25%	+15 pct pts NS (very small quitter sample)	

Table 6.9 Continued

Author & year (study period) Design suitability: design Quality of execution (number of limitations) Evaluation setting	Intervention (I) and comparison (C)	Population; sample size	Effect measure	Reported baseline	Reported effect	Value used in summary	Follow-up time
Gillies and Wilcox 1984 (1980) Greatest: group nonrandomized trial Fair (4 limitations) Schools (primary schools) My Body Project	Sheffield, United Kingdom School-based education (health education); respiratory health, cardiovascular health; antismoking component Compared with usual care	Selected primary schools matched N = 6 schools Students (aged 9–11 years) Baseline 2-year follow-up I 15 136(86%) C 161 134(83)	(1) Student self-reported smoking (prevalence) Regular Never	 I 4% C 4% I 71% C 77%	 I 9% C 6% I 46% C 34%	 +3 pct pts (NR) (+) 18 pct pts in retaining never smokers (NR)	2 years
			(1) Student self-reported initiation of smoking in baseline nonsmokers (initiation)	I (0%) C (0%)	I 36% C 55%	-19 pct pts RR 2.19, 95% CI (1.2, 3.8) p <0.02	
			(4) Student knowledge scores (knowledge)	I 6.4 (SD 1.49) C 6.7 (SD 1.59)	I 8.6 (SD 1.32) C 8.5 (1.29)	No difference at 2 years t = 0.56 NS	
Connell et al. 1985 (1982–84) Moderate: retrospective cohort (exposure assessment) Fair (4 limitations) Schools (4th–6th grades) School Health Education Evaluation of School Health Curriculum Project	United States School-based education Curricula for grades 4–6 (units for each grade). Compared with usual care	4 school districts Classrooms by exposure (n = 73) Grade 4th 5th Exposed 15 27 Unexposed 10 22 Students in study classrooms (5th or 6th grade at follow-up) N = 1,397	(1) Average percentage of students self-reporting smoking activity by exposure	Exposure Two units (full) One unit (partial) No units (unexposed)	 1.6% 2.7% 6.6%	 -5 pct pts -3.9 pct pts Reference p <0.05 overall	1-2 years post exposure
			(3) Average percentage of students self-reporting intent to smoke by exposure	Exposure Two units (full) One unit (partial) No units (unexposed)	 7.3% 7.7% 14.5%	 -7.2 pct pts -6.8 pct pts Reference Overall p <0.01	

Table 6.9 Continued

Author & year (study period) Design suitability: design Quality of execution (number of limitations) Evaluation setting	Intervention (I) and comparison (C)	Population; sample size	Effect measure	Reported baseline	Reported effect	Value used in summary	Follow-up time
Dielman et al. 1985 (1981–82) Greatest: group nonrandomized trial Fair (4 limitations) Schools (elementary schools)	Michigan School-based education; 4 sessions over 8 weeks led by research staff; resisting pressures to smoke films, discussion, role-playing Compared with usual care	1 district's elementary schools n = 10 I: 4 schools Mixed: 2 schools C: 4 schools 5th and 6th graders Pre Post I 301 225 C 291 198	(1) Student self-reported smoking (prevalence)				15 months
			Past month	I 4% C 1%	I 8% C 15%	-10 pct pts p = 0.003	
			Ever	I 30% C 30%	I 50% C 49%	+1 pct point NS	
			(3) Student self-reported intention to smoke in the future (attitude)	I 9% C 6%	I 9% C 10%	-4 pct pts NS	
Schinke and Gilchrist 1985 (NR) Greatest: group randomized trial Fair (3 limitations) Schools (6th grade) Note: See Gilchrist et al. 1986, Schinke and Gilchrist 1986, Schinke et al. 1986 for similar studies. Unclear if overlapping reports	United States; NR School-based education (2 versions with overlap)-graduate student led Health information (info) curriculum: 10 1-hour weekly sessions: debates, film, homework Skills building curriculum: 10 1-hour weekly sessions; problem-solving, resisting smoking pressures Compared with usual care	Selected elementary schools (9) I-skills 3 schools I-info 3 schools C: 3 schools 6th-grade students n = 689 follow-up rates 91-94%	(1) Student self-reported tobacco use in the last week (proxy weekly) (prevalence)	I-Info 3.4% I-Skills 4% C 3.7%	I-Info 11.5% I-Skills 7.8% C 12.0%	-0.2 pct pts NS -4.5 pct pts (significant) Reference	24 months
			(3) Student intentions to smoke cigarettes in high school (attitudes)	NR	NR	I-Skills and I-Info had lower scores than did C students	24 months
			(4) Student smoking knowledge scores (knowledge)	NR	NR	I-Skills students had higher knowledge scores compared with I-Info and C	12 months

Table 6.9 Continued

Author & year (study period) Design suitability: design Quality of execution (number of limitations) Evaluation setting	Intervention (I) and comparison (C)	Population; sample size	Effect measure	Reported baseline	Reported effect	Value used in summary	Follow-up time
Gilchrist et al. 1986 (NR) Greatest: group randomized trial Fair (4 limitations) Schools (5th- and 6th-grade students)	United States; NR School-based education (2 arms)-both 8 60-minute sessions with homework; film; testimonials Self-control skills: communication and problem solving skills; role plays; videotape examples Health education: smoking effects; advertising impact Compared with usual care	Public elementary schools assigned to condition N = NR Students (5th to 6th grade) in study schools N = 741 pre N = 701 (95%) follow-up	(1) Student self-reported smoking 1 or more cigarettes in the preceding week	Skills 4% Education 3.5% C 4%	Skills 5.8% Education 9.6% C 8.3%	-2.5 pct pts +1.8 pct pts Reference: skills vs. other F(2,697) = 3.52 p <0.05	13-month follow-up (15m after pre)
			(3) Student self-reported intentions to smoke (posttest mean score)	C 0.51	Skills 0.32 Education 0.30	Skills and education arms had lower intentions to smoke p <0.05	Posttest
			(3) Skills-refusal skills score on survey items	C 2.09	Skills 3.36 Education 2.46	Refusal skill score higher in skill arm p <0.05	Posttest
			(4) Student knowledge mean score	C 7.72	Skills 10.61 Education 11.13	Skills and education arms with higher score p <0.05	Posttest
Schinke and Gilchrist 1986 (NR) Greatest: group nonrandomized trial Fair (3 limitations) Schools (grades 5 and 6)	United States; NR School-based education, I-full: education sessions and problem-solving exercises and media analysis I-info: education sessions-age relevant effects, use rates Compared with usual care	Selected public schools (n = 3) Participating students in grades 5 and 6 N = 214 N = 196 (92%) at 12-month follow-up	(1) Student self-reported smoking in the past week (proxy weekly) (prevalence)	I-Full 3.8% I-Info 2.9% C 3.4%	I-Full (3.7%) I-Info (11.5%) C (13.1%)	I-Full vs. C -9.8 pct pts F(2, 196) = 5.12 p <0.001 I-Info vs. C-Comp 1.1 pct pts (NS)	12 months
			(4) Mean differences (pre to 12 month follow-up) in student knowledge scores (knowledge)		I-Full +11.9 I-Info +7.3 C +4.4	I-Full: Increased p <0.001	

Table 6.9 Continued

Author & year (study period) Design suitability: design Quality of execution (number of limitations) Evaluation setting	Intervention (I) and comparison (C)	Population; sample size	Effect measure	Reported baseline	Reported effect	Value used in summary	Follow-up time
Schinke et al. 1986 (NR) Greatest: group randomized trial Fair (3 limitations) Schools (5th and 6th grades)	Western Washington state School-based education Tobacco use prevention (smoked and smokeless); 8 50-minute sessions led by adults delivered to 5th and 6th graders; both arms with homework Skills building arm: health effects education + communication and decision-making skills training and rehearsal; refusal skills Discussion (disc) arm: health effects education (films, testimonials, debates, games) Compared with usual care	Randomly selected elementary schools assigned to condition N = 12 5th–6th grade students n = 1,281 baseline loss to follow-up 10.8%	(1) Student self-reported smoking in the past week (prevalence) (1) Student self-reported smokeless tobacco use in the past week (prevalence)	I-Skills 4% I-Disc 3% C 4% I-Skills 3% I-Disc 3% C 2%	I-Skills 7% I-Disc 11% C 12% I-Skills 12% I-Disc 16% C 15%	-5 pct pts 0 pct pts Reference (skills vs. other p <0.05) -4 pct pts 0 pct pts Reference (skills vs. other p <0.05)	24 months 24 months

Table 6.9 Continued

Author & year (study period) Design suitability: design Quality of execution (number of limitations) Evaluation setting	Intervention (I) and comparison (C)	Population; sample size	Effect measure	Reported baseline	Reported effect	Value used in summary	Follow-up time
Biglan et al. 1987 (NR) Greatest: group randomized trial Fair (4 limitations) Schools (middle + high schools)	Lane County, Oregon School-based education Refusal skills training: 4 sessions over 2 weeks Compared with usual care	Participating schools in two districts N = 3 high schools + 6 middle schools Classrooms random assignment 7th–10th graders N = 1,730 baseline n = 1,180 (68.2%) at 1-year follow-up	(1) Student self-reported tobacco use (smoking index) (2) Student self-reported smoking-baseline regular smokers (cessation)	I NR C NR I NR C NR	I NR C NR I 22.33 (mean) C 50.35 (mean)	None of the differences were significant on x^2 (+) 28 ? ANCOVA F = 4.55 p = 0.04	1 year
Hansen et al. 1988a (1981–83) Greatest: group nonrandomized trial Fair (3 limitations) Schools (6th and 7th grades) TAPP (Tobacco and Alcohol Prevention Project)	Los Angeles, California School-based education,(drug use prevention-alcohol and tobacco); trained teachers and peer opinion leaders; 15 50-minute sessions; pressure resistance training; discussion; role-playing; student workbooks; public commitments Compared with usual care	Participating districts/ schools (assigned) 2 student cohorts Cohort 1 Los Angeles county District A: 556 District B: 605 Note: follow-up resp %: I (54%), C (49%) Cohort 2 Other District A: 1,379 District C: 328	(1) Student self-reported cigarette smoking in the previous 30 days (monthly) (prevalence)	Cohort 1 7th grade (pre) I (8%) C (9%) 6th grade District A C I NR NR C NR NR	Cohort 1 10th grade (follow-up) I 26% C 34% p=0.13 9th grade District A C I NR 8.3% C NR 20.0% NS NS	Cohort 1 Overall difference -8 pct pts (NS) No overall assessment Differences were not statistically significant	3 years

Table 6.9 Continued

Author & year (study period) Design suitability: design Quality of execution (number of limitations) Evaluation setting	Intervention (I) and comparison (C)	Population; sample size	Effect measure	Reported baseline	Reported effect	Value used in summary	Follow-up time
Hansen et al. 1988b (NR) Greatest: group randomized trial Fair (4 limitations) Schools (junior high schools; 7th grade) Project SMART (Self-Management and Resistance Training)	Los Angeles, California School-based education (drug use prevention); two curricula (social influences I-SI; affective education I-SE); trained teachers/school health staff delivered with recruited peer assistants; 1 session per week for 12 sessions Compared with usual care	Junior high schools N = 44 (70%) assigned 14 (32%) recruited and initial cohort report on 8 schools School / Class I-AE: 2 / 24 I-SI: 2 / 25 C: 4 / 35 7th-grade students n = 2,863 with pre + post data 1,374 (48%)	(1) Student self-reported tobacco use-smoking index mean (prevalence) (1) Student self-reported onset of tobacco use	I-AE NR I-SI NR C NR I-AE NR I-SI NR C NR	I-AE 1.508 I-SI 0.544 C 0.888 I-AE NR I-SI 11.8% C 17.8%	(Compared to C) Increased p <0.01 Not significantly different p = 0.3 Increased +86.4% -6.0 pct pts p <0.05	12 months

Table 6.9 Continued

Author & year (study period) Design suitability: design Quality of execution (number of limitations) Evaluation setting	Intervention (I) and comparison (C)	Population; sample size	Effect measure	Reported baseline	Reported effect	Value used in summary	Follow-up time
Killen et al. 1988 (NR) Greatest: group nonrandomized trial Fair (4 limitations) Schools (high schools)	Northern California School-based education (cardiovascular disease prevention- including one module on cigarette smoking); 3 days/week x 7 weeks delivered by 8 special full-time instructors and 1 coordinator; information, behavioral skills and resisting social influences	Selected high schools n = 4 I: 2 C: 2 All 10th graders in study schools N = 1,447 baseline N = 1,130 (78%) follow-up I: 622 C: 508	(1) Student self-reported smoking behaviors-undefined (6-level scale) (prevalence)			Overall treatment vs. comparison group differences were significant p = 0.0001	2 months
			Boys	I 3.1 (1.3) C 3.2 (1.5)	I 4.6 (2.1) C 3.3 (1.5)		
			Girls	I 3.1 (1.3) C 3.2 (1.4)	I 5.0 (1.7) C 3.6 (1.7)		
			(1) Student self-reported change in smoking status over study period (initiation)	I 0% C 0%	I 9.7%, C 14.5%	-4.8 pct pts p = 0.25	
	Compared with usual care		(2) Student baseline smoker self-reporting cessation at 2m follow-up (cessation)	I 0% C 0%	I 3.5% C 9.3% p=0.39	-5.8 pct pts NS	

Table 6.9 Continued

Author & year (study period) Design suitability: design Quality of execution (number of limitations) Evaluation setting	Intervention (I) and comparison (C)	Population; sample size	Effect measure	Reported baseline	Reported effect	Value used in summary	Follow-up time
Botvin et al. 1989 (NR) Greatest: group randomized trial Fair (3 limitations) Schools (7th grade public) LifeSkills training	New York, New York School-based education; smoking prevention and social resistance/competence enhancement; 15 sessions delivered by teachers using tailored lessons (reading level) Compared with usual care	8 schools from 6 school districts in New York, New Jersey metropolitan area Random assignment 7th-grade students in study schools Pre / Analysis I 256 / 189 (74) C 215 / 156 (73)	(1) Student self-reported smoking (prevalence)				Post (3.5 months)
			Past week	I 0.07 C 0.09	I NR C NR	NR: logistic regression (log reg) NS	
			Past month	I 0.09 C 0.12	I NR C NR	NR log reg p = 0.0618 (NS)	
			Past day	I 0.04 C 0.06	I NR C NR	NR log reg NS	
			(3) Student self-reported attitude regarding peer smoking (attitudes)	I 3.60 scale score C 3.61	I 3.51 C 4.05	Improved Posttest p <0.01	
			(4) Student knowledge-smoking prevalence (Knowledge)	I 0.59 scale score C 0.52	I 0.91 C 0.51	Improved Posttest p <0.0001	

Table 6.9 Continued

Author & year (study period) Design suitability: design Quality of execution (number of limitations) Evaluation setting	Intervention (I) and comparison (C)	Population; sample size	Effect measure	Reported baseline	Reported effect	Value used in summary	Follow-up time
Bush et al. 1989a,b (1983–85) Greatest: group randomized trial Fair (4 limitations) Schools (initiated grades 4–6 to grades 7–9) Know Your Body	Washington, D.C. School-based education + school-based health screening + parent education + parent activities (involvement in intervention) Compared with school-based health screening (parents notified of results)	Selected public elementary schools n = 9 Full I: n = 3 Partial I: n = 3 C: n = 3 Students in 4th–6th grades Baseline: 892 (72%) Follow-up: 431 (35%)	(1a) Percentage of screened students included in analysis with serum thiocyanate levels >100 umoles/L	I 5.2% C 0.0%	I 0.9% C 5.0%	-9.3 pct pts significant NR	3 years (post)
			Observed mean differences in serum thiocyantate levels over study period (3 years)-adjusted results	NA	NA	-15.74 ± 2.85 µmoles/L p = 0.000	
			(3) Mean differences in student self-reported attitudes toward cigarettes (negative)-adjusted	NA	NA	2.78 ± 1.10 p = 0.012	
Figa-Talamanca and Modolo (1989) (NR) Greatest: group nonrandomized trial Fair (4 limitations) Schools (high schools)	5 cities, Italy School-based education; health educator-led; 3 consecutive days of sessions; smoking awareness, immediate health effects; spirometry demos (I-A intervention arm used spirometry demo; I-B arm did not) Compared with usual care	Selected classes in selected high schools in each city 6 classes per school randomly assigned to arm Students baseline I-A: n = 199 I-B: n = 195 C: n = 178 Response rate at follow-up: 93%	(1) Student self-reported smoking "regularly" (prevalence)	I-A 17.7% I-B 23.9% C 15.9%	I-A 20.4% I-B 24.2% C 17.2%	+4.0 pct pts NR +1.6 pct pts NR Reference	1 year
			(2) Student self-reported smoking status as "ex-smoker" (cessation)	I-A 15.7% I-B 15.8% C 12.5%	I-A 21.2% I-B 18.9% C 9.9%	+8.1 pct pts +5.7 pct pts Reference	
			(4) Student responses on knowledge assessed as "good" (knowledge)	I-A 11.0% I-B 16.2% C 7.9%	I-A 27.6% I-B 18.6% C 7.7%	+16.8 pct pts* +2.6 pct pts Reference *p ≤0.01	

Table 6.9 Continued

Author & year (study period) Design suitability: design Quality of execution (number of limitations) Evaluation setting	Intervention (I) and comparison (C)	Population; sample size	Effect measure	Reported baseline	Reported effect	Value used in summary	Follow-up time
Flay et al. 1989 (1979–80 [with 6-year follow-up]) Greatest: group randomized trial Fair (3 limitations) Schools (grade 6) Waterloo Trial	Waterloo, Canada School-based education; social influences model; information and skills development to resist social influences and improve decision making; 6 sessions in 6th grade with 2 booster sessions at end of 6th, in 7th, and 1 booster in 8th grade; research staff delivered Compared with usual care	N = 22 matched and randomly assigned schools I: n = 11 C: n = 11 Students (consent) N = 654 (94%) pre N = 551 (81%) responding at 12th-grade follow-up	(1) Self-reported regular smokers (once per week or more) (weekly) (prevalence) (estimated from graph) Logit model for 12th-grade regular smoking	Pre (6th) Post (8th) I (3%) 7.64% C (5%) 9.13% Note: At end of 8th grade–overall difference +0.51	Follow-up (12th) I 34% C 32%	+4 pct pts OR 1.24, 95% CI (0.83, 1.86)	6 years
Walter 1989 (1979–85) Greatest: group randomized trial Fair (4 limitations) Schools (elementary; 4th grade) Know Your Body	New York School-based education (cardiovascular disease risk factor reduction); teacher-led; 2 hours per week throughout 4th grade; Curriculum continued through 9th grade Compared with usual care	Participating elementary schools Bronx West Schools 22 15 Students at analysis 1,036 593 (66%) (65%) Westchester follow-up was 6 yrs with smoking results	(1) School means of students with biochemical indications of cigarette smoking at 9th grade (prevalence)	I 0.0 C 0.0	I 3.5 ± 4.3 C 13.1 ± 5.p <0.005	-9.6 pct pts Note: No significant differences at 5 yrs	6 years

Table 6.9 Continued

Author & year (study period) Design suitability: design Quality of execution (number of limitations) Evaluation setting	Intervention (I) and comparison (C)	Population; sample size	Effect measure	Reported baseline	Reported effect	Value used in summary	Follow-up time
Armstrong et al. 1990 (1981–83) Greatest: group randomized trial Fair (4 limitations) Schools (year 7; year 9 follow-up)	Australia; NR School-based education peer-led (P); teacher-led (T): social consequences curriculum Compared with usual care	Participating schools: n = 45 Stratified by size and location then randomly assigned Students in year 7 N = 2,366 baseline 2-year follow-up 1,514 (64%) Subset analyses Baseline nonsmokers Girls Boys Ipeer 164 166 Iteacher 196 162	(1) Student self-reported smoking (subset of responders to both follow-up surveys)				2 years
			<u>Girls</u> P 215 T 275	IP 23.7% IT 28.7% C 29.9%	IP 49.3% IT 49.5% C 59.3%	-3.8 pct pts -8.6 pct pts Reference (I-both vs. C p = 0.03)	
			<u>Boys</u> P 252 T 256	IP 33.7% IT 36.7% C 36.1%	IP 52.0% IT 45.7% C 49.3%	+5.1 pct pts -4.2 pct pts Reference (I-T vs. C p = 0.009)	
			(2) Student self-reported smoking at 2-year follow-up in baseline nonsmokers (initiation) Logistic regression analyses (95% CI not reported here)				
			<u>Girls</u> P 164 T 196			IP –8.1 pct pts NS IT –6.6 pct pts NS	
			<u>Boys</u> P 166 T 162			IP +6.4 pct pts NS IT -2.8 pct pts NS	

Table 6.9 Continued

Author & year (study period) Design suitability: design Quality of execution (number of limitations) Evaluation setting	Intervention (I) and comparison (C)	Population; sample size	Effect measure	Reported baseline	Reported effect	Value used in summary	Follow-up time
Botvin et al. 1990a,b Also Botvin et al. 1984 Fair (3 limitations) Schools (junior high schools; 7th-grade baseline; 8th-grade booster and follow-up) Life skills training	New York, New York School-based education, 18 sessions (drug use prevention), teacher (T) vs. older peer delivered (P), cognitive behavioral approaches, homework, self-improvement project; refusal skills 10-session booster (B) in 8th grade delivered to 2 intervention arms Compared with usual care	Selected junior high schools (10) Peer: n = 4 Teacher: n = 4 Usual care: n = 2 7th graders Pre: 1,311 Post: 1,185 (90%) Follow-up: 998 (76%) at 1 year post pretest (8th grade)	(1) Student self-reported tobacco use Monthly/weekly/daily Post-test adjusted differences at 1 year Peer-led ± booster in 8th grade Teacher-led ± booster in 8th grade Note: 4m post result not presented here	I-P NR I-PB NR I-T NR I-TB NR C NR	Mth Wkly Day I-P 0.31 0.22 0.17 PB 0.12 0.05 0.03 I-T 0.26 0.16 0.11 TB 0.34 0.21 0.16 C 0.23 0.16 0.13	Mth Weekly Day I-P .08 .06 .04 PB* -.11 -.11 -.10 I-T .03 .00 -.02 TB .11 .05 .03 C ref ref ref *All PB difference $p < 0.05$	Post (1-year) B arms or 1-year follow-up non-B arms
			(3) Student self-reported tobacco attitudes (scale score) (attitudes)	I-P NR I-PB NR I-T NR I-TB NR C NR	Score I-P 37.84 I-PB 38.95 I-T 38.29 I-TB 37.19 C 37.29	I-P increased NS I-PB increased $p < 0.01$ I-T increased $p < 0.5$ I-TB decreased NS C reference	
			(3) Student self-reported locus of control (skills)	I-P NR I-PB NR I-T NR I-TB NR C NR	Score I-P 7.53 I-PB 6.68 I-T 7.69 I-TB 8.19 C 7.71	I-P -0.18 I-PB –1.03 $p < 0.01$ I-T -0.02 I-TB +0.43 C reference	

Table 6.9 Continued

Author & year (study period) Design suitability: design Quality of execution (number of limitations) Evaluation setting	Intervention (I) and comparison (C)	Population; sample size	Effect measure	Reported baseline	Reported effect	Value used in summary	Follow-up time
Botvin et al. 1990a,b Continued			(4) Student tobacco knowledge (scale score) (knowledge)	I-P NR I-PB NR I-T NR I-TB NR C NR	Score I-P 7.95 I-PB 8.50 I-T 7.36 I-TB 8.55 C 6.74	I-P increased p <0.0001 I-PB increased p <0.0001 I-T increased p <0.0001 I-TB increased p <0.0001 C NR	
Gatta et al. 1991 (1982–86) Greatest: group randomized trial Fair (4 limitations) Schools (year 4) Italian League Against Cancer (Milan)	Milan, Italy School-based education; tobacco prevention; health effects and consequences, 1 day of lessons, slides, films, posters, comic strips, delivered by trained teachers to students in year 4 (aged 9–10 years) Compared with usual care	Schools in Milan N = 163 of 165 schools: Random assignment I: 55 C: 56 Mixed: 52 Class (I; C) Students: Year 4 / Year 8 I 8,549 / 5,007 (58%) C 8,897 / 5,310 (60%)	(1) Student self-reported status as smoker (prevalence) post only comparison	I NR C NR	I 8.0% C 8.7%	-0.7 pct pts NS Risk ratio = 0.92 (95% CI 0.79, 1.06)	4 years

Table 6.9 Continued

Author & year (study period) Design suitability: design Quality of execution (number of limitations) Evaluation setting	Intervention (I) and comparison (C)	Population; sample size	Effect measure	Reported baseline	Reported effect	Value used in summary	Follow-up time
Hansen et al. 1991 (1987–88) Greatest: group randomized trial Fair (4 limitations) Schools (junior high schools; 7th grade)	Los Angeles and Orange counties, California School-based education (drug use prevention); social influence theory); resistance skills training or correcting normative (norm) perceptions of use; project staff delivered 9 classroom sessions in each study arm Compared with school-based education (resistance skills vs. normative arms)	Participating, selected junior high schools: n = 12 Assigned to one of 4 study arms by school 7th-grade students in study schools N = 3,011 at baseline N = 2,416 (80%) at 1-year follow-up (8th grade)	(1) Student self-reported cigarette smoking (prevalence) within 30 days Ever use Note: Data were incompletely reported for each study arm; analyses were reported for comparisons of students exposed to normative education or resistance skills training	I-Norm: NR C-Other: NR I-Norm: NR C-Other: NR	I-Norm: 4.8% C-Other: 6.5% I-Norm 8.1% C-Other 10.3%	-1.7 pct pts I-Norm: $F = 4.71$ $p < 0.05$ -2.2 pct pts	1 year

Table 6.9 Continued

Author & year (study period) Design suitability: design Quality of execution (number of limitations) Evaluation setting	Intervention (I) and comparison (C)	Population; sample size	Effect measure	Reported baseline	Reported effect	Value used in summary	Follow-up time
Severson et al. 1991 (1985–87) Greatest: group randomized trial Fair (4 limitations) Schools (middle and high schools) PATH	Lane County, Oregon School-based education + parent education; smokeless content included: 7 sessions over 2–3 weeks with social influences content and emphasis on refusal skills training; teacher led with use of same-age peers (middle schools); decision making; health consequences; videos; 3 messages mailed to parents Compared with usual care	22 recruited schools matched, stratified, and random assignment Students (MS + HS) N = 2,552 baseline N = 1,768(69%) follow-up MS HS I 610 172 C 483 503	(1) High school student self-reported tobacco use (average number per month)				1 year
			Cigarettes	Boys Girls I 9.4 5.7 C 3.2 13.9	Boys Girls 24.9 22.7 17.9	Boys: +2.8 cigs/month NS Girls: +13 cigs/month NS	
			Smokeless	Boys I 15.5 C 16.0	I 11.7 C 21.5	-9.3 chews/month p <0.05 but NS on logistic transformation	
			(1) Middle school student self-reported tobacco use (average number per month)				
			Cigarettes	Boys Girls I 0.7 1.9 C 1.3 1.1	9.1 13.6 3.4 12.4	Boys: +6.3cigs/month Girls: +0.4cigs/month	
			Smokeless	Boys I 4.8 C 2.6	I 5.1 C 7.3	-4.0 chews/month p <0.05; NS on logistic transformation	

Table 6.9 Continued

Author & year (study period) Design suitability: design Quality of execution (number of limitations) Evaluation setting	Intervention (I) and comparison (C)	Population; sample size	Effect measure	Reported baseline	Reported effect	Value used in summary	Follow-up time
Botvin et al. 1992 (NR) Greatest: group randomized trial Fair (2 limitations) Schools (7th grade; public and parochial)	New York, New York School-based education, 15 sessions by teachers (manual with lesson plans) using tailored curriculum Social resistance/ competence enhancement Compared with usual care	Schools in 4 New York City boroughs: n = 47 I C Public 6 5 Parochial 19 17 7th-grade students n = 3,518 baseline n = 3,153 (90%) at analysis I: 1,795 C: 1,358	(1) Student self-reported smoking during the past month (prevalence)	I 4.86% C 5.03%	I 5.19% C 7.15%	-1.79 pct pts F(1,41) = 4.14 p <0.05	4 months (post)
			(1) Student self-reported smoking-baseline nonsmokers (initiation)	I (0%) C (0%)	I NR C NR	NR (reduced) F(1,42) = 5.74 p <0.03	
			(1) Student self-reported current smoking	I NR C NR	I NR C NR	NR F(1,41) = 3.27 p <0.08	
			(1) Student self-reported smoking in the past day or the past week	I NR C NR	I NR C NR	NR differences NS	
			(3) Student self-reported anti-smoking attitudes (scale scores)	I 40.43 C 40.51	I 37.71 C 38.32	No significant difference	
			(4) Student smoking knowledge (various) Smoking prevalence	I 0.91 C 0.88	I 0.86 C 0.57	Higher p <0.0001	

Table 6.9 Continued

Author & year (study period) Design suitability: design Quality of execution (number of limitations) Evaluation setting	Intervention (I) and comparison (C)	Population; sample size	Effect measure	Reported baseline	Reported effect	Value used in summary	Follow-up time
Elder et al. 1993; Kellam et al. 1998 (see also Eckhardt et al. 1997) (1988–91) Greatest: group nonrandomized trial Fair (3 limitations) Schools (7th grade) Project SHOUT (Students Helping Others Understand Tobacco)	San Diego, California School-based education; 18 sessions (10 in 7th grade, 8 in 8th grade) led by trained undergrads; refusal skills training; activities, health consequences (some student activities outside of class) + mail/telephone support (9th-grade proactive follow-up with 2 calls/semester per student) Compared with usual care	Selected, participating schools n = 22 Matched + assigned I: 11 schools C: 11 schools 7th graders at baseline: n = 3,655 9th grade at follow-up: n = 2,668 (73%) I: 1,174 C: 1,494	(1) Student self-reported tobacco use in the past month (prevalence) Logistic regression analyses (1) Combined tobacco use in the past month (1) Combined tobacco use in the past week Note: At end of second year of study (school-based component), differences in student self-reported tobacco use in the past month was –1.8 (NS), so an additional follow-up intervention was implemented	I 5.7% C 6.4%	I 14.2% C 22.5%	–7.1 pct pts significance NR OR = 0.71 p <0.05 OR = 0.66 p <0.05	2 years (post)

Table 6.9 Continued

Author & year (study period) Design suitability: design Quality of execution (number of limitations) Evaluation setting	Intervention (I) and comparison (C)	Population; sample size	Effect measure	Reported baseline	Reported effect	Value used in summary	Follow-up time
Klepp et al. 1993; Tell and Vellar 1987 (1979–81 with 1989 follow-up) Greatest: group nonrandomized trial Fair (4 limitations) Schools (grades 5–7) Oslo Youth Study Smoking Prevention Program	Oslo, Norway School-based education; (cardiovascular disease risk factor reduction): social influences curriculum: training to resist social pressures; role-models; public commitment to remain nonsmoker 10 sessions (smoking prevention program); partly led by older students Compared with usual care	Selected schools N = 6 I(3) C(3) Participating students in grades 5–7 (N; participation rate) 1979 1981 1989 827 718 796 (82%) (66%) (74%) At analysis 1981: 567 (52%) 1989: 570 (53%)	(1) Student self-reported weekly smoking (prevalence)	I NR C NR	I 50.3% C 53.0%	-2.7 pct pts NS	10 years
			Subgroup analysis: male students	I NR C NR	I 43.1% C 51.7%	-8.6 pct pts NS Logistic regression OR 1.73, 95% CI (1.04, 2.89)	
			(1) Student self-reported weekly smoking at follow-up in baseline nonsmokers (initiation + prevalence) Males	I (0%) C (0%)	I 35.0% C 50.0%	-15 pct pts p <0.05 OR 2.09 (1.2, 3.6)	
			Females	I (0%) C (0%)	I 55.0% C 53.0%	+2 pct pts NS	
			(3) Student self-reported intentions to not smoke daily 5 years from now (attitude)	I 66.2% C 57.5%	I (+13.8 pct pts) C (+12.6 pct pts)	Overall difference +1.2 pct pts p <0.05	2 years (post)
			Subgroup analysis: student self-reported intentions to not smoke daily 5 years from now (attitude)-baseline nonsmokers	Boys Girls I 69.4% 72.5% C 64.6% 57.7%	Boys Girls I +18.7 +11.0 C +13.9 +17.9	Boys Girls +4.8 -6.9 (NR) (NR)	2 years
			(4) Student smoking knowledge test scores (maximum 14)	I 8.6 8.2 C 8.1 7.5	I +1.3 +1.7 C +1.2 +1.4	Overall: increased p <0.05	2 years

Table 6.9 Continued

Author & year (study period) Design suitability: design Quality of execution (number of limitations) Evaluation setting	Intervention (I) and comparison (C)	Population; sample size	Effect measure	Reported baseline	Reported effect	Value used in summary	Follow-up time
Nutbeam et al. 1993 (1988–89, 1990) Greatest: group nonrandomized trial Fair (3 limitations) Schools (secondary)	Wales and England School-based education-MN curriculum I-M program; social consequences, peer, family, media influences; skills training; 5 teacher-delivered lessons for 12- to 13-year-olds Family smoking education program I-FSE 3 hours class lessons (11- to 12-year-olds), teacher delivered; parent leaflets Compared with usual care	Selected 2 schools Arm N schools C 10 I-FSE 10 I-M 9 I-FSE+M 10 All students in first year of secondary school N = 4,538 (89%) N = 3,677 (72%) at 1-year follow-up	(1) Student self-reported current smoker (prevalence)	C 2.2% I-FES 1.8% I-M 4.4% I-FSE+M 1.7%	C 11.3% I-FES 14.4% I-M 12.0% I-FSE+M 10.1%	Reference +3.5 pct pts -1.5 pct pts -0.7 pct pts Group difference NS	1 year
			(4) Student knowledge score (maximum 12) baseline and interval change	C 5.18 I-FES 5.57 I-M 5.38 I-FSE+M 5.47	Interval change +1.04 +1.09 +0.91 +1.28	Group differences were small and not statistically significant	1 year

Table 6.9 Continued

Author & year (study period) Design suitability: design Quality of execution (number of limitations) Evaluation setting	Intervention (I) and comparison (C)	Population; sample size	Effect measure	Reported baseline	Reported effect	Value used in summary	Follow-up time
Sussman et al. 1993a,b (NR) Greatest: group randomized trial Fair (2 limitations) Schools (junior high schools) Project Towards No Tobacco Use (TNT)	Southern California School-based education, social influences (SI) theory, 4 curricula (arms: countering normative SI; countering informational SI; physical consequences of use non-SI; combined curricula), 10-day curricula presented by trained health educators; single booster session in 8th grade Compared with usual care	Recruited junior high schools N = 48 schools from 27 districts (8 schools per arm with 16 C schools) Study cohorts of 7th graders (n = 2) Cohort 1: All 7th graders in 20 schools Cross-sectional samples (3 classes x 28 schools) Baseline: 6,716 response 1-year follow-up: 7,052	(1) Student self-reported smoking-weekly cigarette use (prevalence) (1) Student self-reported trial cigarette use (ever tried) (prevalence-ever) (1) Student self-reported weekly smokeless tobacco use (prevalence-smokeless) Abbreviated results	I-norm SI NR I-info SI NR I-non SI NR I-combined NR C-usual care NR I-norm SI NR I-info SI NR I-non SI NR I-combined NR C-usual care NR NR	Change in use +0.053 +0.032 +0.026 +0.020 +0.056 reference Change in use +0.102 +0.071 +0.061 +0.073 +0.093 I-combined –0.004 C-usual care +0.005	-0.3 pct pts NS -2.4 pct pts* -3.0 pct pts* -3.6 pct pts* Reference *p <0.05 +0.9 pct pts NS -2.2 pct pts* -3.2 pct pts* -2.0 pct pts* Reference *p <0.05 -0.9 pct pts p <0.05 (all others NS)	1 year (8th grade)

Table 6.9 Continued

Author & year (study period) Design suitability: design Quality of execution (number of limitations) Evaluation setting	Intervention (I) and comparison (C)	Population; sample size	Effect measure	Reported baseline	Reported effect	Value used in summary	Follow-up time
Sussman et al. 1993a,b Continued							
Addendum Dent et al. 1995 (2nd-year follow-up results) (NR) Greatest: group randomized trial Fair (4 limitations) Schools (junior high schools; 7th-grade with 9th-grade follow-up		Students surveyed in high schools fed by study junior high schools N = 7,219 9th graders Self-reported exposure to TNT 65% (n = NR but calculated 4,692) Exposed: 4,692 Unexposed: NR (2,527; but unclear if this includes students from nonstudy schools)	(1) Student self-reported weekly cigarette use (prevalence) School as unit of analyses	I-norm SI NR I-info SI NR I-non SI NR I-combined NR C-usual care NR	Change in use +9 +12 +8 +4 +9	Differences +3 pct pts NS +0 pct pts NS -1 pct pt NS -5 pct pts p <0.05 Reference (note statistically significant vs. all others)	2 years (9th grade)
			(1) Student self-reported trial cigarette use (ever tried) (prevalence-ever)	I-norm SI NR I-info SI NR I-non SI NR I-combined NR C-usual care NR	+17 +15 +13 +16 +23	-6 pct pts* -8 pct pts* -10 pct pts* -7 pct pts* Reference (*all p <0.05 compared to reference)	
			(1) Student self-reported weekly smokeless tobacco use (prevalence-smokeless)	I-norm SI NR I-info SI NR I-non SI NR I-combined NR C-usual care NR	+2 +2 -1 -0 +1	+3 pct pts NS +3 pct pts NS -2 pct pts p <0.05 -1 pct pt (marginal) Reference	
			(1) Student self-reported trial smokeless tobacco use (prevalence-ever) (results abbreviated)	NR	I-non SI +0 C +7	-7 pct pts p <0.05 (others were NS)	

Table 6.9 Continued

Author & year (study period) Design suitability: design Quality of execution (number of limitations) Evaluation setting	Intervention (I) and comparison (C)	Population; sample size	Effect measure	Reported baseline	Reported effect	Value used in summary	Follow-up time
De Vries et al. 1994 (1986–87) Greatest: group nonrandomized trial Fair (3 limitations) Schools (8th grade) Vocational (Voc) schools High schools	The Netherlands School-based education for 8th-grade students based on social influences; 5 45-minute sessions based on peer-led program on video; peer training and peer led small group activities; manual Compared with usual care	Recruited schools Voc HS I 3 5 C 3 3 Students in study classes (9 month follow-up) Voc HS I 343 585 C 217 384	(1) Student self-reported regular smoking (daily + weekly prevalence) grade 9	Voc HS I 16.4% 3.6% C 15.8% 3.0%	Voc HS I 23.5% 7.1% C 30.0% 5.7%	Voc HS -7.1 pct pts +0.8 OR 2.24 OR 0.78 (1.3, 3.9) (0.4,1.6)	9 months (9th)
			(2) Student initiation of experimental smoking-baseline nonsmokers (initiation)	C 56.5% C 52.1%	I 64.0% I 41.6%	+7.5 NS -10.5 p <0.02	
			(3) Student cessation of smoking (baseline users) (cessation)	C 19.4% C 33.3%	I 27.4% I 28.1%	+8 NS –5.2 NS	
			(4) Student intentions to smoke (attitudes)	NR	NR	No significant differences	
			(5) Student knowledge	NR	NR	Voc HS NS change Increased p <0.01	

Table 6.9 Continued

Author & year (study period) Design suitability: design Quality of execution (number of limitations) Evaluation setting	Intervention (I) and comparison (C)	Population; sample size	Effect measure	Reported baseline	Reported effect	Value used in summary	Follow-up time
Botvin et al. 1995a,b (1985–91 [follow-up 1994]) Greatest: group randomized trial Good (1 limitation) Schools (7th–9th grades) Life skills training	3 areas of New York state School-based education; drug use prevention; teacher-delivered 7th grade (15 sessions), 8th grade (10 sessions), 9th grade (5 sessions); social influences; development of personal and social skills for coping; self-esteem Compared with usual care	Recruited schools in 3 areas of New York Schools assigned I1 18 I2 16 C22 Students in study schools N = 5,954 7th grade N = 3,597 12th-grade follow-up Group N at follow-up I1 762 I2 848 C 1,142	(1) Student self-reported cigarette smoking (prevalence) Weekly	I1 4% I2 5% C 4%	I1 23% p <0.05 I2 21% p <0.05 C 27% reference	-4 pct pts -7 pct pts Reference	6 years (3 years post at end of 12th grade)
			Monthly	I1 6% I2 8% C 7%	I1 27% p <0.05 I2 26% p <0.01 C 33% reference	-5 pct pts -10 pct pts Reference	
			Note: High-fidelity subsample demonstrated differences of greater magnitude; alcohol and marijuana data are not presented here				
			(3) Student self-reported normative expectations-adult smoking	I1 NR I2 NR C NR	I1 3.92 p <0.0001 I2 3.95 p <0.0001 C 4.22 reference	Lower (improved) Lower (improved)	3 years (post 9th grade)
			(4) Student knowledge on 10-item test (score) Smoking prevalence (actual)	I1 NR I2 NR C NR	I1 1.10 p <0.0001 I2 1.16 p <0.0001 C 0.93 reference	Higher (post) Higher (post) Reference	

Table 6.9 Continued

Author & year (study period) Design suitability: design Quality of execution (number of limitations) Evaluation setting	Intervention (I) and comparison (C)	Population; sample size	Effect measure	Reported baseline	Reported effect	Value used in summary	Follow-up time
Hawthorne et al. 1995 (NR [5 year intervention]) Greatest (other design with a concurrent comparison group) Fair (4 limitations) Schools (elementary)	Melbourne, Australia School-based education ("Life Education" drug use prevention); 5–12 years of age with new module for each class year; teacher-delivered; self-esteem, body function, drug use pressures; discussion and role-plays Compared with school-based education (usual care but equivalent hours)	Selected, stratified sample of schools in Melbourne area I: 42 C: 44 Students in year 6 (post-only) Aged 11–12 years I: 1,721 C: 1,298	(1) Student self-reported smoking (any) in the previous month (prevalence) (1) Student self-reported smoking (any) ever (prevalence)	I NR (post only) C NR I NR C NR	I 7.8% C 5.8% I 32% C 28%	+2 pct pts Logistic regression OR 1.3 (school) 95% CI (1.0, 1.9) +4 pct pts OR 1.2 (school) 95% CI (1.0, 1.4)	Post (5 school years)

Table 6.9 Continued

Author & year (study period) Design suitability: design Quality of execution (number of limitations) Evaluation setting	Intervention (I) and comparison (C)	Population; sample size	Effect measure	Reported baseline		Reported effect	Value used in summary	Follow-up time
Eckhardt et al. 1997 (see also Elder et al. 1993) (1988–91; 1992) Greatest: individual randomized trial Fair (4 limitations) Schools (7th–11th grades) Project SHOUT extension	San Diego, California As per Elder 1993: School-based education, SWAT, and mail/telephone support; tobacco use prevention; 7th–9th grades. Addition of 11th grade mailed newsletters (2) and proactive phone call (1) (2 study arms) Compared with 2 arms: usual care; no 11th-grade intervention	Students in the original grades 7–9 cohort contacted in 10th grade: n = 2,051 (76%) I grades (7–11) Lapsed grades (7–9) Delayed grade (11 only) C-usual care At analysis n = 1,545 (75%; 58% overall)	(1) Student self-reported smoking (any) in the past 30 days (prevalence) Note: Elder 1993 reported <u>combined</u> tobacco use rates	I Lapsed Delayed C Differences	NR NR NR NR NS	7%* 10.8% 9.4% 12.6% *x^2=6.33 $p < 0.05$	-5.6 pct pts -1.8 pct pts -3.2 pct pts Reference	Post (4 years) 1-year follow-up Post (4 years)

Table 6.9 Continued

Author & year (study period) Design suitability: design Quality of execution (number of limitations) Evaluation setting	Intervention (I) and comparison (C)	Population; sample size	Effect measure	Reported baseline	Reported effect	Value used in summary	Follow-up time
Jøsendal et al. 1998 (1995–97) Greatest: group nonrandomized trial Fair (4 limitations) Schools (grade 7)	Norway; nationwide sample School-based education, 8 sessions in grade 7 delivered by teachers; decision-making and social skills to resist smoking pressures; short-term consequences of use; parent education brochures and pledge; teacher training Compared with usual care	Random sample of secondary schools (99) systematically assigned to condition A: usual care B: education + parent + teacher C: education + parent D: education + teacher 7th grade students n = 4,441 eligible n = 3,820 (86%) follow-up	(1) Student self-reported smoking Weekly Note: Statistical significance was reported for comparison of nonsmoking (significant in favor of the intervention B vs. usual care	C 0.8% I-B 1.6% I-C 1.7% I-D 1.8%	C 3.0% n = 1,091 I-B 1.6% 1,060 I-C 1.1% 791 I-D 2.7% 878	Reference -2.2 pct pts -2.8 pct pts -1.3 pct pts	6 months
			Less than once/week	C 4.1% I-B 4.2% I-C 4.4% I-D 5.2%	C 5.9% I-B 4.9% I-C 5.9% I-D 6.7%	Reference -1.1 pct pts -0.3 pct pts -0.3 pct pts	
			Daily	C 2.2% I-B 1.1% I-C 2.1% I-D 3.2%	C 6.6% I-B 2.2% I-C 5.6% I-D 7.1%	Reference -2.2 pct pts -0.9 pct pts -0.5 pct pts	

Table 6.9 Continued

Author & year (study period) Design suitability: design Quality of execution (number of limitations) Evaluation setting	Intervention (I) and comparison (C)	Population; sample size	Effect measure	Reported baseline	Reported effect	Value used in summary	Follow-up time
Noland et al. 1998 (1992–93) Greatest: group randomized trial Fair (2 limitations) Schools (7th and 8th grade)	Kentucky School-based education; tobacco use prevention; social influences content: 6 45–50 minute sessions in 7th grade delivered by classroom teachers + 3 sessions in 8th grade delivered by project educators Compared with usual care	Selected schools in study areas assigned to condition (blocked on baseline tobacco use prevalence) I: n = 10 schools C: n = 9 schools 7th-grade students at baseline: n = 3,588 At 9th-grade follow-up N = 3,072 (86%)	(1) Student self-reported cigarette use (prevalence) 7-day use	I 9.7% C 11.4%	I 30.1% C 37.9% p <0.01	-6.1 pct pts	1 year (7th–9th grades)
			30-day use	I 12.9% C 16.7%	I 33.6% C 43.5% p <0.01	-6.1 pct pts	
			24-hour use	I 5.2% C 6.2%	I 21.6% C 27.9% p <0.05	-5.3 pct pts	
			Ever use	I 51.1% C 51.4%	I 72.2% C 77.0% NS	-4.5 pct pts	
Sussman et al. 1998 (1994–95) Greatest: group randomized trial Fair (2 limitations) Schools (continuation high schools)	Southern California School-based education; drug use prevention/cessation; 9 classroom sessions over 3 weeks delivered by trained project staff; health motivation, social skills, decision-making; emphasis on motivational activities; additional schoolwide activities (SAC) in one arm Compared with usual care	Selected continuation high schools (21 schools from 29 districts) Blocked random assignment Class: 7 schools Class + SAC: 7 schools Usual care: 7 schools Students (all grades) N = 2,863 available N = 1,587 consent N = 1,074 (38%) at analysis	(1) Adjusted means of student self-reported cigarette use in the past 30 days (prevalence) Adjusted for baseline use, interaction between condition and baseline level, and method of follow-up	I-Class NR I-Class + SAC NR C-Usual care NR Note	I-C 34.53 (%) I-SAC 33.08 C 30.71	+3.82 pct pts +2.37 pct pts Reference Condition effect F(2,18) = 0.16 p = 0.85 Interaction effect F(2,1049) = 0.45 p = 0.64	1 year

Table 6.9 Continued

Author & year (study period) Design suitability: design Quality of execution (number of limitations) Evaluation setting	Intervention (I) and comparison (C)	Population; sample size	Effect measure	Reported baseline	Reported effect	Value used in summary	Follow-up time
Botvin et al. 1999 (NR) Greatest: group randomized trial Fair (2 limitations) Schools (grade 7) Life skills training: girls	New York, New York School-based education; drug use prevention; life skills training: 15 classroom sessions led by regular teachers; social resistance skills training; promotion of general personal and social competence skills Compared with school-based education (5 session information only)	Selected junior high schools in New York City (inner-city, low income) N = 29 assigned 7th-grade female students in study school n = 2,690 N = 2,209 (82%) at 8th-grade follow-up I: 1,278 C: 931	(1) Student self-reported smoking in the past month (prevalence-monthly)	I 4.2% C 4.0%	I 8.8% C 12.3%	-3.7 pct pts $x^2 = 7.1$ $p < 0.005$	1 year (8th grade)
			(1) Student self-reported ever smoking (prevalence-ever)	I 19.1% C 19.2%	I 28.3% C 34.5%	-6.1 pct pts p = 0.001	1 year
			(1) Self-reported initiation of tobacco use over study period (initiation-undefined)	I (0%) C (0%)	I 19.6% C 23.9%	-4.3 pct pts p = 0.02	1 year
			(3) Student self reported intentions to smoke in the future (attitudes)	Adjusted means of scores at follow-up	I 1.68 (SE 0.03) C 1.85 (SE 0.04)	Improved p = 0.002	1 year
			(3) Student anti-smoking attitudes (attitude)	Adjusted means of scores at follow-up	I 87.23 (SE 0.51) C 86.34 (SE 0.62)	No significant difference	1 year
			(4) Student smoking knowledge score	Adjusted means of scores at follow-up	I 36.12 (SE 0.70) C 30.19 (SE 0.84)	Increased p = 0.001	1 year

Table 6.9 Continued

Author & year (study period) Design suitability: design Quality of execution (number of limitations) Evaluation setting	Intervention (I) and comparison (C)	Population; sample size	Effect measure	Reported baseline	Reported effect	Value used in summary	Follow-up time
Cameron et al. 1999 (NR [1992]) Greatest: group randomized trial Fair (2 limitations) Schools ("elementary" grades 6, 7, 8) [Canada] Waterloo Curriculum	Ontario, Canada School-based smoking prevention program; social influences; lessons in grade 6 (6), grade 7 (3), and grade 8 (6); modeling, rehearsal, discussions, audio visual aids, manuals; 4 intervention arms (training/provider comparisons) Compared with usual care	7 school districts Participating schools (n = 100) stratified on baseline risk score then randomly assigned I: 4 arms C: 1 arm Students: N = 4,466 baseline response N = 3,821 (85.6%) at post	(1) Student self-reported smoking status (experimental + regular/weekly) (prevalence) Subset analysis: students in schools with baseline high risk score Note: No significant differences as function of training method or provider	I NR (post only) C NR (post only) I NR C NR	I 17.9% C 21.0% I 16.0% C 26.9%	-3.1 pct pts NS -10.9 pct pts logistic regression $F_{1,26} = 8.99$ $p = 0.006$	Post (8th grade-3 year intervention period)

Table 6.9 Continued

Author & year (study period) Design suitability: design Quality of execution (number of limitations) Evaluation setting	Intervention (I) and comparison (C)	Population; sample size	Effect measure	Reported baseline	Reported effect	Value used in summary	Follow-up time
Chatrou et al. 1999 (1987–89) Greatest: group randomized trial Fair (4 limitations) Schools (age 12–14 years) Brabant Smoking Prevention Program	Brabant, The Netherlands 2 intervention arms of 3 class sessions over 3 weeks; video presentation; class discussions; organized by trained adults Emotional/self group (I1) smoking effects; risky behavior situations and emotional aspects Health/technical group (I2) focused on health and technical aspects of smoking Compared with usual care	Selected schools: n = 4 (vocation and high school); random allocation by classes Classes Students I1 13 284 I2 15 315 C 20 350 Follow-up at 18 months n = 794 (84%)	(1) Student self-reported smoking (monthly or greater) (prevalence)	I1 7.4% I2 15.5% C 11.0% p <0.01	I1 28.4% I2 36.9% C 34.7%	-2.7 pct pts -2.3 pct pts Reference OR = 0.91 95% CI (0.48, 1.72)	18 months
			(2) Student smoking-baseline nonsmokers (initiation)	I1 (0)% I2 (0)% C (0)%	I1 NR I2 NR C NR	NR (not significant) NR (not significant) NR	
			(3) Student self-reported "high" intentions to smoke in the future (attitudes)	I1 12.0% I2 21.6% C 18.6% p <0.01	I1 26.1% I2 39.9% C 34.1%	-1.7 pct pts +2.8 pct pts Reference OR = 1.18 95% CI (0.66, 2.09)	

Table 6.9 Continued

Author & year (study period) Design suitability: design Quality of execution (number of limitations) Evaluation setting	Intervention (I) and comparison (C)	Population; sample size	Effect measure	Reported baseline	Reported effect	Value used in summary	Follow-up time
Dijkstra et al. 1999 (1990–92) Greatest: group randomized trial Fair (4 limitations) Schools (grades 8 and 9; high school)	The Netherlands School-based education; smoking prevention; 5 45-minute lessons delivered weekly; social influences (SI) or decision-making + SI curriculum with and without 3 magazines distributed in class as boosters (B). Compared with usual care	Recruited high schools n = 52 randomly assigned to condition Students: 8th grade at baseline: n = 4,826 N = 3,104 (64%) at post (18 months) Group N post I-SI + B 526 I-SI 575 I-SI-DM+B 351 I-SI+DM 460 C 1,192	(1) Student self-reported smoking (combined daily + weekly + occasional) (prevalence)	I-SI+B 5.3% I-SI 7.3% I-SI+DM+B 7.7% I-SI+DM 13.5% C 6.4%	15.0% 21.2% 20.5% 23.9% 21.3%	-5.2 pct pts $p < 0.005$ -1 pct pt NS -2.1 pct pts NS -4.5 pct pts $p < 0.07$ Reference	Post 18 months
Hawkins et al. 1999 (1981–86 [follow-up 1993]) Greatest: group nonrandomized trial Fair (4 limitations) Schools (elementary)	Seattle, Washington School-based education (general social competence) + teacher education + parent education Compared with usual care	Elementary schools n = 18 assigned std to condition Students baseline follow-up Full 156 149 Late 267 243 C 220 206	(1) Student self-reported cigarette smoking-lifetime (ever) at follow-up (age 18) (prevalence) Heavy cigarette smoking	C 54.4% C NR	I-Full 53.7% I-Later 52.7% NR	-0.7 pct pts (-10.6, 10.4) NS -1.7 pct pts (-10.5, 8.0) NS No significant effects	6 years

Table 6.9 Continued

Author & year (study period) Design suitability: design Quality of execution (number of limitations) Evaluation setting	Intervention (I) and comparison (C)	Population; sample size	Effect measure	Reported baseline	Reported effect	Value used in summary	Follow-up time
Lynam et al. 1999 also Clayton et al. 1996 (1987–88 [follow-up 1997]) Greatest: group randomized trial Fair (4 limitations) Schools (grade 6; elementary) DARE (Drug Abuse Resistance Education)	Lexington-Fayette County, Kentucky DARE: school-based education; drug use prevention; 1 hour sessions x 17 weeks delivered by trained law enforcement officers; skills teaching social pressures; decision-making; self-esteem; drug information and alternatives Compared with school-based education (usual care)	Recruited elementary schools in county: n = 31 I: 23 schools C: 8 schools Students in study schools Baseline 5 yrs 10 yrs 2,071 1,143 (55%) 1,002 (48%) I 762 10 year C 240 follow-up	(1) Student self-reported cigarette use (variety of frequency and prevalence measures) (prevalence) Hierarchical linear models with fixed effect estimates (group mean centered) (3) Positive expectancies toward cigarettes (attitude) Fixed effect estimates	I NR C NR Frequency past month cigarette use	I NR C NR Fixed effect: 0.101 0.053	No significant differences at 5-year or 10-year follow-up NS NS	10 years and 5 years
Bergamaschi et al. 2000 (1993–94) Moderate: Retrospective cohort Fair (4 limitations) Schools (middle schools) Leave Us Clean	Italy; 3 communities in Romagna School-based education campaign; antismoking; 6 units led by regular teachers for middle school students; resist influences to start smoking Compared with exposed vs. not exposed while middle school students	2nd year high school students (aged 16 years) present on date of survey N = 2,691 Exposed 863 (32.1%) Unexposed 1,828 (67.9%)	(1) Student self-reported smoker	Exposed NR Unexposed NR	Exposed 19.1% Unexposed 23.2%	-4.1 percentage points x^2=5.54 $p < 0.05$	3 years

Table 6.9 Continued

Author & year (study period) Design suitability: design Quality of execution (number of limitations) Evaluation setting	Intervention (I) and comparison (C)	Population; sample size	Effect measure	Reported baseline	Reported effect	Value used in summary	Follow-up time
Peterson et al. 2000 (1984–99) Greatest: group randomized trial Good (0 limitations) Schools (grades 3–10) Hutchinson Smoking Prevention Project	Washington state School-based education, based on social influences; led by trained teachers with curriculum for grades 3–10; 65 classroom lessons 30–50 minute each (5–10 lessons/grade) total 46.75 hours (3.2 hours/grade); also self-help cessation materials and promotion (grades 9–12), and biannual newsletters for teachers Compared with usual care (school education was noted at 2.9 hours/grade)	Recruited school districts (40 of 41) Matched pair randomization to condition I: n = 20 districts C: n = 20 districts Students 3rd-grade baseline I 4,177 C 4,211 2 years post 12th grade follow-up I 3,919 (94%) C 3,946 (94%)	(1) Mean school district smoking prevalence-daily smoking (prevalence)	I NR (3rd grade) C NR	I 28.42% C 29.07%	-0.65 pct pts 95% CI (-2.8, +3.8) p=0.68 +1.4 pct pts p=0.38 -2.6 pct pts p=0.30	2 years post 12th grade 4 years post education intervention 11 years post baseline
			Subset Girls	NR	I 27.0% C 25.6%		
			Subset Boys	NR	I 29.9% C 32.5%		
			(1) Mean school district smoking prevalence-daily smoking (prevalence)	I NR (3rd grade) C NR	I 25.4% C 25.7%	-0.3 pct pts 95% CI (-3.5, +3.7) p=0.86	12th grade 9 years post baseline

Table 6.9 Continued

Author & year (study period) Design suitability: design Quality of execution (number of limitations) Evaluation setting	Intervention (I) and comparison (C)	Population; sample size	Effect measure	Reported baseline	Reported effect	Value used in summary	Follow-up time
Aveyard et al. 2001 (1997–98) Greatest: group randomized trial Fair (4 limitations) Schools (year 9)	West Midlands region, United Kingdom School-based education (6 sessions computer + classroom) Compared with school-based education (national health education curriculum)	Participating schools n = 53 (58%) I: 27 C: 26 Students in year 9 n = 8,352 enrolled n = 6,819 (73%) at 2-year follow-up	(1) Self-reported regular weekly smoking (prevalence years 9–11) (2) Self-reported smoking in baseline regular, daily smokers (cessation)	I 13.3% C 12.8% I (100%) C (100%)	I 23.5% C 22.4% I 76.1% C 76.6%	+0.6 pct pts overall; -1.1 pct pts (post-only) Adjusted OR 1.06 (0.86, 1.31) +0.5 pct pts (-6.8, +9.9)	2 years

Note: **CI** = confidence interval; **ALA** = American Lung Association; **ANCOVA** = analysis of covariation; **HS** = high school; **MS** = middle school; **NR** = not reported; **NS** = not significant; **OR** = odds ratio; **SD** = standard deviation; **SWAT** = Students Working Against Tobacco; **µmoles/L** = micrometer per liter.

Table 6.10 Studies of the effectiveness of multicomponent interventions that include school-based programs to reduce tobacco use

Author & year (study period) Design suitability (design) Quality of execution (number of limitations) Evaluation setting	Intervention (I) and comparison (C)	Population/sample size	Effect measure	Reported baseline	Reported effect	Value used in summary	Follow-up time
Flay 1987 (1982–1984) Greatest (group non-randomized trial) Fair (3 limitations) Community-wide	Los Angeles, California School-based education + mass media series (5 TV news segments) Compared with unexposed to school program (possible media exposure)	7th-grade students At analysis N = 1,419 I = 783 C = 636	(1) Self-reported current cigarette use Pre-post mean increase	Immediately post I = -0.56 C = -0.67	2-year follow-up I = +0.03 C = +0.08	Overall difference: -0.16 No significant difference on analyses	2 years
Johnson et al. 1990 (1984–1986) Greatest (group randomized trial) Good (1 limitation) Community-wide	Kansas City, Kansas School-based education + community education + mass media campaign Compared with usual care with potential exposure to mass media	Schools selected for evaluation N = 8 (4I + 4C) 6th- and 7th-grade students N = 1,607 baseline N = 1,122 at 2 years N = 1,105 (69%) at 3-year follow-up	(1) Self-reported cigarette smoking (any) in the last 30 days Odds ratio (intervention group) for self-reported cigarette use in the last month Adjusted net differences in the percentage of smokers (between I and C schools) in the last month	I = 9.8% C = 10.0% NR NR	I = 24.8% C = 30.5% NR NR	Overall difference -5.5 percentage points (pct pts) Multiple logistic regression p = 0.21 OR = 0.58 p <0.10 -16.0 pct pts p <0.01	3 years

Table 6.10 Continued

Author & year (study period) Design suitability (design) Quality of execution (number of limitations) Evaluation setting	Intervention (I) and comparison (C)	Population/sample size	Effect measure	Reported baseline	Reported effect	Value used in summary	Follow-up time
Perry et al. 1992 (1983–1989) Greatest (group non-randomized trial) Fair (3 limitations) Community-wide	Minnesota Mass media campaign + school-based education + community education Compared with usual care	Communities: n = 2 Schools: n = NR Students in both 1983 and 1989 surveys 6th–12th grades N = 1,080 (45% of baseline) Cross-sectional N = 1,439 in 1989	(1) Self-reported smoking status (weekly) School as unit of analysis	Cohort I = 1% C = 1% Cross-sectional I = 1.5% C = 2.5%	Cohort I = 14.6% C = 24.1% p = 0.011 Cross-sectional I = 15% C = 24.5% p = 0.007	Overall difference - 9.5 pct pts -8.5 pct pts	5 years
Winkleby et al. 1993 (1979–1990) Greatest (group non-randomized trial) Fair (4 limitations) Community-wide	4 cities in California Community education + mass media + school education (for 1 year) Compared with usual care	2 I cities 2 C cities Adolescents/young adults aged 12–24 years N = 2,605 across 4 cross-sectional surveys Aged 12–15 years: n = 651 Aged 16–19 years: n = 629	Self-reported smoking prevalence (mean of pre-post differences between treatment cities: survey periods pre-post implementation of school education) Note: Multiple logistic regression was used for comparison Comparison results were summarized as "not significant" although interval changes were noted within cities Results given here are calculations based on presented data	1981–82 survey Aged 12–15 years I1 = 3.8% I2 = 12.5% C3 = 1.7% C4 = 0.0% Aged 16–19 years I1 = 28.6% I2 = 38.5% C3 = 24.3% C4 = 10.9%	1985–86 survey Aged 12–15 years I1 = 8.2 I2 = 5.6 C3 = 4.0 C4 = 6.3 Aged 16–19 years I1 = 5.9 I2 = 24.0 C3 = 17.1 C4 = 7.0%	Mean interval change Aged 12–15 years I1&I2 -1.2 C3&C4 +4.3 Overall -5.5 Aged 16–19 years I1&I2 -18.6 C3&C4 -5.6 Overall -13 Differences were not significant	2-year follow-up of school education period

Table 6.10 Continued

Author & year (study period) Design suitability (design) Quality of execution (number of limitations) Evaluation setting	Intervention (I) and comparison (C)	Population/sample size	Effect measure	Reported baseline	Reported effect	Value used in summary	Follow-up time
Kaufman et al. 1994 (1989–1990) Greatest (group non-randomized trial) Fair (4 limitations) Community-wide	Chicago, Illinois School-based education + mass media series (contest) Compared with media only	6th- and 7th-grade students in 3 selected schools N = 276	(1) Self-reported tobacco product use Mean score on Botvin scale	I = 13.01 C = 12.29	I = 11.63 C = 10.99	Scale difference -0.08 points F(1,145) = 0.08 NS	6 months high school
Murray et al. 1994 (1986–1990) Greatest (other design with a concurrent comparison group) Fair (3 limitations) Community-wide	Minnesota (I) and Wisconsin (C) School-based education + excise tax + mass media education + community education Compared with usual care	9th-grade students Estimated 3,600 students/year	(1) Self-reported prevalence of smoking (at least one cigarette/week)	I = 12.6 C = 15.8	I = 10.3 C = 15.9	Overall difference over study period -2.4 pct pts F = 1.17 p = 0.324	5 years
Flay et al. 1995 (1986–1988) Greatest (group randomized trial) Fair (2 limitations) Community-wide	Los Angeles and San Diego, California School-based education + mass media series (17 TV news segments) Compared with school + media; media alone; school alone; usual care	7th-grade students in 47 study schools N = 6,695 baseline N = 3,155 (47%) at 2-year follow-up	(1) Self-reported tobacco use behaviors			Logistic regression analysis No significant predictors of smoking at any post-test	2 years

Table 6.10 Continued

Author & year (study period) Design suitability (design) Quality of execution (number of limitations) Evaluation setting	Intervention (I) and comparison (C)	Population/sample size	Effect measure	Reported baseline	Reported effect	Value used in summary	Follow-up time
Baxter et al. 1997 (1991–1994) Greatest (group non-randomized trial) Fair (4 limitations) Community-wide	Rotherham, United Kingdom Community education + school education (cardiovasular health promotion) Compared with usual care	7th- and 10th-grade students 1991: n = 1,327 1994: n = 1,678 Cohort 1991–1994 Cross-sectional analysis	(1) Student self-reported "active smoking" Cohort sample (aged 11–14 years)	I = <1% C = 4%	I = 21% C = 24%	0 Note: NS on cross-sectional analysis	3 years
			(2) Student self-reported "passive smoking" Cohort sample (aged 11–14 years)	I = 52% C = 57%	I = 49% C = 45%	+9 pct pts Note: NS on cross-sectional analysis	3 years
Flynn et al. 1997 (1985–1991) Greatest (group non-randomized trial) Good (1 limitation) Community-wide	Northeast United States and Montana School-based education + mass media campaign Compared with school-based education only	Students in study schools (grades 4, 5, 6 at baseline with follow-up through grades 10, 11, 12) N = 5,458 (cohort) N = 2,086 (38%) Observed in all 6 surveys	(1) Self-reported tobacco use behaviors Odds ratio for weekly smoking status Individual as the unit of analysis (Significant differences were also observed using the community as the unit of analysis)			Stepwise logistic regression Intervention OR = 0.62 95% CI (0.49, 0.78)	6 years (2 years post I)

Table 6.10 Continued

Author & year (study period) Design suitability (design) Quality of execution (number of limitations) Evaluation setting	Intervention (I) and comparison (C)	Population/sample size	Effect measure	Reported baseline	Reported effect	Value used in summary	Follow-up time
Lewit et al. 1997 (1990, 1992 surveys) Least (cross-sectional surveys) Fair (3 limitations) Community-wide	United States + Canada 21 communities Variable: cigarette price, and the presence/absence of COMMIT (community education), clean indoor air laws, school smoking policies, school education, antitobacco media exposure, protobacco media exposure, minors' access restrictions Compared with cross-sectional 1990 and 1992	Random samples of classrooms 9th-grade students n = 15,432 (88% of respondents)	Variable for cumulative school education exposure (self-reported total of grades with class instruction for grades 1-8) Mean exposure was 3.29 grades	NA	NA	Variable -0.02 p ≤0.05	NA
			Variable for school smoking policy (self-reported scale score from 0-allowed anywhere to 3-not allowed on school property) Mean of scale score was 2.58 Note: Primary outcomes reported were price elasticity estimates (not presented)	NA	NA	Variable -0.13 NS	NA
Chou et al. 1998 (1987–1990) Greatest (group randomized trial) Fair (3 limitations) Community-wide	Indianapolis, Indiana School-based education + other school (parent program, policy focus) + mass media campaign + community education Compared with usual care	Subset analysis 7th-grade students using tobacco at baseline Baseline / Follow-up N = 212 I / 53 I N = 188 C / 55 C	Subset analysis: baseline tobacco users (1) Interval decrease in self-reported tobacco use in the previous month	I = NR C = NR	I = NR C = NR	Odds ratio for decreasing use OR = 1.53 95% CI (1.05, 2.24)	3.5 years

Table 6.10 Continued

Author & year (study period) Design suitability (design) Quality of execution (number of limitations) Evaluation setting	Intervention (I) and comparison (C)	Population/sample size	Effect measure	Reported baseline	Reported effect	Value used in summary	Follow-up time
Vartiainen et al. 1998 (1978–1993) Greatest (group non-randomized trial) Fair (4 limitations) Community-wide	Finland School-based education (10 sessions or 5 sessions) + mass media campaign + community education Compared with usual care	Students in study schools Cohort follow-up N = 903 baseline N = 786 at 4-year follow-up N = 640 (71%) at 15-year follow-up	(1) Self-reported smoking status Any	I10 = 15% I5 = 13.2% C = 8.4%	I10 = 34.6% I5 = 34.3% C = 42.8%	Overall differences vs. comparison I10: -14.8 pct pts I5: -13.3 pct pts	15 years
			Daily	I10 = 3.1% I5 = 2.5%	I10 = 32.5% I5 = 32.8%	I10: -4.2 pct pts I5: -3.3 pct pts	15 years
			Individual as the unit of analysis	C = 1.1%	C = 34.7%		
			School as unit of analysis Self-reported smoking (any) Any education vs. usual care on baseline nonsmokers	NA NA	I = 30% C = 41%	-11 pct pts F = 11.7 p = 0.027	15 years
CDC 1999a,b (1998–1999) Least (before-after) Fair (4 limitations) Community-wide	Florida Mass media campaign + community education + student-directed community education Compared with before-after	Public school students Representative sample of middle school and high school students N = 43,518	(1) Student self-reported tobacco product use (1998–1999) High school students	27.4%	25.2%	-2.2 pct pts p<0.02	12 months
			Middle school students	18.5%	15.0%	-3.5 pct pts p <0.01	12 months

Table 6.10 Continued

Author & year (study period) Design suitability (design) Quality of execution (number of limitations) Evaluation setting	Intervention (I) and comparison (C)	Population/sample size	Effect measure	Reported baseline	Reported effect	Value used in summary	Follow-up time
Biglan et al. 2000a,b Also Biglan et al. 1995 and 1996 (1991–1995) Greatest (group randomized trial) Fair (3 limitations) Community-wide	16 rural communities in Oregon Community education + retailer education + school-based education Compared with school-based education only	N = 16 7th- and 9th-grade students in study school districts (approximately 2,100 students in each grade in each annual survey)	(1) Student self-reported tobacco use measured as a weekly smoking index (Link 8)	I = 10.5% C = 8.0%	I = 12.0% C = 13.9%	Reported net difference: (-)3.8 95% CI (0.2,7.3)	4 years
			(2) Student self-reported awareness of efforts to prevent illegal sales (Link 6)	NR (negative slope)	NR (positive slope)	p = 0.0026	
			(3) Parents' perceived community support for tobacco access restrictions (Link 1)	NR	NR	p = 0.006 (year 4) NS (year 5)	
CDC 2001 (1999–2000) Greatest (group non-randomized trial) Fair (3 limitations) Community-wide	Oregon Funded school-based education + mass media + excise tax + community education Compared with/ without funded school-based education	Schools surveyed in both 1999 and 2000 I = 38 C = 14 8th-grade students participating in surveys 1999: n = 3,519 2000: n = 5,556	(1) Student self-reported tobacco use (any) in the previous 30 days	I = 16.6% C = 17.0%	I = 13.0% C = 15.7%	Overall difference -2.3 pct pts No measure	12 months
			Subset analysis: (2) Student self-reported tobacco use (any) in the previous 30 days High-level implementation schools Nonfunded schools	I = 14.2% C = 17.0%	I = 8.2% C = 15.7%	-4.7 pct pts Logistic regression OR = 0.65 95% CI (0.45, 0.94)	

Table 6.10 Continued

Author & year (study period) Design suitability (design) Quality of execution (number of limitations) Evaluation setting	Intervention (I) and comparison (C)	Population/sample size	Effect measure	Reported baseline	Reported effect	Value used in summary	Follow-up time
Texas Department of Health Services 2001 (2000) Greatest (other design with a concurrent comparison group) Fair (4 limitations) Community-wide	14 counties in east Texas Mass media education + school education and/or community prevention programs Compared with usual care (no media, no school or community programs) Note: cessation measures compare high school students in high media exposure + combined program (n = 1,066) to others (n = 14,370)	Selected "sentinal schools": n = NR Students in study schools 7th–12th grades <u>Baseline</u> <u>Post</u> 32,560 35,781 Focus Middle Grades 6th 4,070 4,366 7th 628 735	(1) Student self-reported tobacco use (any product in the past month) High media exposure + school/community vs. none	I = 8% C = 14%	I = 3% C = 11%	-2 pct pts (Difference outcomes reported in study)	1 year
			(2) High school student smoker self-reporting cessation attempt in the last 6 months	I = NR C = NR	I = 66% C = 59%	+7 pct pts Post only	
			(3) High school student smoker + quit attempter self-reporting cessation	I = NR C = NR	I = 33% C = 26%	+7 pct pts Post only	

Note: **CDC** = Centers for Disease Control and Prevention; **CI** = confidence interval; **COMMIT** = Community Intervention Trial for Smoking Cessation; **NA** = not available; **NR** = not reported; **NS** = not significant; **OR** = odds ratio.

prevention for the 2007 Institute of Medicine report on tobacco control (Bonnie et al. 2007, Appendix D). From an examination of the previous reviews and meta-analyses reviewed above, Flay concluded that school-based programs to prevent smoking can have significant long-term effects if they have the following attributes: (1) They are interactive programs based on social influences or social skills; (2) 15 or more sessions are involved, including some up to at least ninth grade; and (3) substantial short-term effects are produced.

Working from these three conclusions, Flay (2009a) reviewed evaluations of programs that had included 15 or more sessions (preferably some in high school), had demonstrated effects at both short- and medium-term follow-up, and followed students to the end of high school and beyond. Only three school-based programs and three school-plus programs (i.e., plus small media, plus mass media, or plus family or community components) fulfilled these criteria. This review was not limited to randomized trials, but most of the studies reviewed by Flay (2009a) were of this type. The two groups of studies (involving school-based and school-plus programs) are labeled as Category 1. All six programs evaluated in the Category 1 studies had been included in the 25 studies with at least 2 years of follow-up reviewed by Skara and Sussman (2003), as well as in the Task Force review (2003). For Category 1, only studies that included follow-up into high school were considered. Few studies included follow-up beyond high school, but for those that did, the reported effects are of interest.

The percentage of RI was used as the indicator of ES since it was readily available for all programs, while the detailed statistics needed to calculate ES were incompletely reported. Also, RI is widely used in calculations of cost and benefit and readily understood. For randomized trials, pretest levels of smoking should be the same in both the program and control groups, and RI would be the difference between posttest control (C) and program (P) groups divided by the level in the control group: (%C – %P)/%C. However, pretest levels in the programs were not always the same (because randomization does not always result in equal pretest levels), and adjustments should be made for these differences. In cases in which pretest data were reported, RI is the posttest difference between groups minus the pretest difference between groups, divided by the control group posttest level—that is, $(\%\triangle C - \%\triangle P)/\%C_{post}$—expressed as a percentage. One may compare the ESs reported in meta-analyses and RIs by translating the ES into an RI on the basis of the area under the curve in the *Z* distribution (Rosenthal 1984). (For a convenient conversion tool, see Wilderdom [2012]). This approach translates an ES of 0.17 into a 7% relative reduction in smoking (an ES of 0.96 = an RI of 33%).

Category 1 school-based programs included the Tobacco and Alcohol Prevention Project (TAPP) (Hansen et al. 1988b), the LST program (Botvin et al. 1995a), and Project SHOUT (Students Helping Others Understand Tobacco) (Elder et al. 1993; Eckhardt et al. 1997) (see Table 6.9). On average, these three social influences/social competence programs, counting only those instances of 15 or more sessions during 2–4 years, preferably with some content in high school, had significant short-term effects (i.e., at grades seven or eight) of 21.8% (a range of 9–30%) and significant long-term effects (i.e., at grades 10–12) of 27.6% (a range of 19–44%) in terms of relative reduction in smoking. TAPP was the only one without any high school content and for which short-term effects decreased over time. Project SHOUT (Elder et al. 1993; Eckhardt et al. 1997) produced effects that may have been due to added content on activities of the tobacco industry, the teaching and encouragement of advocacy skills, and personal attention during high school. The long-term effects for the three programs suggest that a minimal personal-contact intervention of this kind in high school could increase the effects of any other program delivered in middle school. From these studies, Flay (2007) concluded that programs oriented to social influences/social competence that are of proven effectiveness and well implemented can produce long-term RIs of between 25% and 30% or ESs between 0.7 and 0.8.

The Category 1 school-plus studies included the North Karelia Project (Vartiainen et al. 1983, 1986, 1990, 1998), the Minnesota Class of 89 project (Perry et al. 1989, 1992, 1994), and MPP (Pentz et al. 1989b–e; Johnson et al. 1990). These programs produced mean short-term RIs of 40.7%, almost twice as high as the school-only programs, a finding consistent with a previous review by Flay (2000). These effects decayed over time an average of 21% to reach 32% RI. The long-term effects of school-plus-community or mass media programs were 12% better than school-only programs. It should be noted, however, that program effects were maintained at a higher level (at almost 40%, or 31% better than school-only programs) for those programs that included a high school component (North Karelia and Minnesota Class of 89), suggesting that programming in high school may reduce the decay of effects.

That the use of multiple delivery modalities increases a program's effectiveness over that obtained from school-only programs (Flay 2000) is consistent with theories about the influences on behavior that exist across multiple domains of life (Bronfenbrenner 1977, 1979, 1986; Flay and Petraitis 1994; Petraitis et al. 1995; Flay et al.

2009). Thus, it has been argued that prevention programs will be more effective if students receive consistent messages across community contexts and over time. On the basis of the Category 1 school-plus studies, Flay concluded that ongoing programs of proven short-term and intermediate-term effectiveness that combine school intervention with mass media or a community program can produce a long-term RI of between 35% and 40% or an ES between 1.0 and 1.3.

Additional School-Based Smoking Prevention Programs, 2008–2011

The systematic reviews discussed above cover the peer-reviewed literature up to 2008. Since that time, six studies have been published that provide further support for the effectiveness of school-based smoking prevention programs and comprehensive community-wide interventions that include a school-based program. The studies also point to the potential for dissemination and adaptation of programs in other countries, peer involvement, new technologies, and community-wide strategies.

Ariza and colleagues (2008) examined the effects of a school-based program (16 sessions over 3 years), smokefree policies, smoking cessation for teachers, parent education, and community-based activities, using a quasi-experimental design in schools in Barcelona, Spain. At 36 months, when the cohort was 15 and 16 years of age, 18.6% of the boys and 31.2% of the girls were regular smokers in the intervention group, compared with 21.6% of the boys and 38.3% of the girls in the control group ($p < .001$).

Campbell and associates (2008) evaluated the ASSIST intervention in a randomized trial of 59 schools in England and Wales. The intervention consisted of training influential students to act as peer supporters outside the classroom in informal interactions with their peers and to encourage their peers not to smoke. Using data from all three follow-ups, the odds of being a smoker in an intervention school compared to a control school was 0.78 (0.64–0.96), although annual data were not as compelling.

Prokhorov and colleagues (2008) examined the long-term efficacy of the computer-based ASPIRE program for culturally diverse high school students in Houston, Texas. ASPIRE is a computer-based theoretically driven program on smoking prevention and cessation for high school students. Students randomized into the ASPIRE program had significantly lower smoking initiation rates than did students in the control group (1.9% vs. 5.8%, $p < 0.05$) at the 18-month follow-up.

Perry and colleagues (2009) assessed the effectiveness of Project MYTRI, a 2 year multicomponent school-based tobacco intervention, in Delhi and Chennai, India. MYTRI, based on social cognitive theory, included peer-led activities, posters hung in the school, parental postcards, and peer activism outside of the classroom. Students in 32 schools, in sixth and eighth grades, were recruited and schools were randomized into either intervention or control groups; baseline, intermediate, and outcome data were collected for the two cohorts. At the end of the 2-year period, all students in the intervention group were significantly less likely to have smoked either bidis ($p < 0.01$) or cigarettes ($p = 0.05$) than students in the control group.

Lotrean and associates (2010) examined the effectiveness of a video and peer-led school-based smoking prevention program among students 13 and 14 years of age in Romania. Pretest and posttest data were collected 9 months apart from 1,071 students. The program was focused on increasing both self-efficacy and cigarette refusal skills. At follow-up, 4.5% of students receiving the intervention reported weekly smoking compared with 9.5% in the control group; multivariate logistic regression demonstrated that nonsmokers in the control groups were twice as likely to become smokers (OR = 2.23, $p < 0.01$) compared to nonsmokers in the intervention group.

Hawkins and colleagues (in press) evaluated the effectiveness of the Communities that Care (CTC) prevention program on levels of risk and adolescent problem behaviors, including cigarette use. Twenty-four communities were matched and randomly assigned to either the intervention or the control group; 4,407 5th-grade students, in 2004, were recruited and surveyed annually through 10th grade, in 2009. Students in the CTC communities were 21% less likely to report smoking cigarettes in the past 30 days compared to students in the control communities (adjusted OR = 0.79, $p < 0.05$).

Summary of Review of Reviews

Ultimately, the purpose of reviews of smoking prevention programs is to provide guidance to schools and communities as to what approaches might be effective. In a field such as school-based smoking prevention, which compares disparate programs with differing formats, theoretical orientations, targeted behaviors, and targeted populations and age groups, the application of meta-analysis methods can be difficult. Despite the challenges, the meta-analyses by Tobler and colleagues (2000) and Hwang and associates (2004) both provide clear directions on what types of programs are most effective. From a systematic review of reviews and individual studies of mediators, boosters, peer-directed versus adult-led programs, and community components of drug prevention programs, Cuijpers (2002) developed a useful summary of the important ingredients of effective prevention programs that can be set forth as follows:

1. They use interactive delivery methods.
2. They employ the social influences model (defined more broadly than by Hwang and colleagues [2004]).
3. They include components on norms and commitments not to use tobacco and intentions not to use this product.
4. They add community components.
5. They include the use of peer leaders rather than relying totally on adult providers.
6. They include training and practice in the use of refusal and other life skills.

In addition, meta-analyses have established that programs that have relatively more sessions and continue for multiple years are more effective. From a systematic review of the long-term effects of school-based prevention, Flay (2007) concluded that programs with demonstrated short- and intermediate-term effectiveness could have large long-term effects in the range of 35%–40% reductions in the proportion of youth who smoke.

Additional Comments on Reviews and Meta-Analyses

Evidence-based programs. In recent years, evidence-based practice and related terms have become part of the language for clinicians and health care researchers in the United States and other countries. Multiple agencies have reviewed evaluations of programs to prevent substance abuse and produced lists of scientifically proven or evidence-based programs (CDC 2009), and the University of Colorado at Boulder (2010) has provided a comparative matrix.

The stated purpose of such lists and guides is to help decision makers at both the federal and local levels choose programs supported by the best available evidence (Petrosino 2003). After the U.S. Department of Education compiled one such list (of 9 "exemplary" and 33 "promising" programs) with the help of a panel of eminent researchers in prevention, school districts using federal funds were strongly encouraged to select a program from that list (Weiss et al. 2005). These lists of programs are very useful as guides; of course, content and fit for a given community need to be considered.

Cultural sensitivity. Cultural sensitivity is believed to be important for effective prevention (Schinke et al. 1987, 1988, 1990; LaFromboise et al. 1993; Lynagh et al. 1997; Klonoff and Landrine 1999; Litrownik et al. 2000; Vélez 2001; Sussman et al. 2003; Chen 2004; Flay et al. 2004; Shelley et al. 2004; Miranda et al. 2005; Hecht and Krieger 2006; Ferketich et al. 2007). Many studies have evaluated the effectiveness of untargeted or targeted prevention curricula in White, minority, or diverse samples, but few studies have directly compared culturally relevant curricula for smoking prevention with curricula that do not address cultural issues (Johnson et al. 2005). In one study, Botvin and colleagues (1995a) found that culturally targeted and nontargeted versions of their life-skills program were more effective than a control condition in preventing smoking among African American and Hispanic adolescents. Later, another group of researchers (Gosin et al. 2003; Hecht et al. 2003, 2006; Hecht and Krieger 2006; Warren et al. 2006) compared prevention curricula targeted to the values of several cultural groups: Mexican Americans, Blacks/Whites (the study was conducted in a region with a very low prevalence of Blacks), and a multicultural group. All three curricula were more effective than a control curriculum and the Mexican American and multicultural curricula affected more outcome variables (regardless of the students' ethnic characteristics) than did the Black/White curriculum.

In a study in ethnically diverse schools (Hispanic, Asian American, and White) in Southern California, Johnson and colleagues (2005, 2007) compared two eight-session curricula based on the social influences approach. One, Project CHIPS (Choosing Healthy Influences for a Positive Self), a version of Project SMART (Self –Management and Resistance Training) (Hansen et al. 1988a), had content that emphasized "looking after yourself." The other, Project FLAVOR (Fun Learning about Vitality, Origin, and Respect), included cultural values from Hispanic and Asian cultures that emphasized group objectives, interdependence of family members, respect for ancestors, and harmonious interpersonal relations. The authors found that the multicultural curriculum (Project FLAVOR) was effective for Hispanic students in mostly Hispanic schools. In contrast, the curriculum framed for individuals (Project CHIPS) was effective only for Asian students in Asian/multicultural schools.

The results reported above suggest that caution is needed when implementing programs with different ethnic groups or in different cultures. Some programs seem to be equally effective with many different groups, but studies suggest that making programs culturally relevant might be very important. Clearly, more research is needed on this issue. In the meantime, any community or country adopting a program will need to evaluate it rigorously to determine its effectiveness in the new setting or culture.

The role of school policies. Before the 1994 Surgeon General's report (USDHHS 1994), several researchers and educators had suggested that school smoking policies could reduce smoking among youth. School policies generally include rules about tobacco use on campus by students, teachers, staff, and visitors and rules about possession of tobacco products. For example, Pentz and associates (1989a) examined the effects of school policies on adolescents in California and concluded that they were associated with reduced smoking in that group. Overall, the literature on the effectiveness of school smoking policies is surprisingly small, perhaps because such policies are now universally and widely applied to students and schools.

By the late 1980s, most school districts had some type of policy or regulation on tobacco smoking (CDC 1989), and the federal *Pro-Children Act of 1994* prompted the majority of schools to create additional tobacco-related policies. However, although research exists relative to facilitating the adoption of tobacco-free school policies (Goldstein et al. 2003), once such policies are implemented, their enforcement and application to students and staff vary considerably. Kumar and colleagues (2005) examined the association between certain variables related to school policies and smoking among middle school (8th grade) and high school (10th and 12th grades) students using the1999–2000 MTF survey to obtain smoking prevalence and relying on data about school policies provided by administrators. The authors found that permissive smoking policies for school staff were positively but not significantly associated with student smoking in middle schools and that this was the only school policy variable associated with the prevalence of smoking in high school. The level of monitoring of smoking in the school was inversely related to the prevalence of smoking among middle school but not among high school students. The severity of consequences was not related to the prevalence of smoking in either group of students, a finding consistent with previous research (Pentz et al. 1989a). This research suggests that to be successful, schools need to take a proactive approach to implementing school no-smoking policies. Similarly, in a study of nearly 5,000 Australian students, Hamilton and colleagues (2003) found that rates of smoking among students were lower in schools that provided education or counseling rather than a discipline-only approach.

Wakefield and associates (2000) examined 1996 survey data for high school students across the United States as part of the Study of Smoking and Tobacco Use Among Young People; the authors examined the effects of both the existence of a smoking ban (as reported by students) and whether the ban was enforced. They found no effect on youth smoking from the existence of a ban but found that an enforced ban was associated with a lower likelihood of progressing from a lower to a higher intensity of smoking. Later, Powell and colleagues (2005) examined the same data on students but used information from administrators on the existence of a smoking ban; they found that the effect of bans on the prevalence of smoking was attenuated by including levels of peer smoking in the statistical model, although the effect of the smoking ban remained significant.

Students' perceived enforcement of their school's smoking policy may also be an important factor in reducing the risk of smoking. Murnaghan and colleagues (2008), in a study of 10th-grade Canadian students, found that students who believed that tobacco policies were enforced were less likely to smoke. Similarly, using a random sample of schools from five Canadian provinces, Lovato and colleagues (2007) reported that students' perception of enforcement was a significant predictor of the prevalence of smoking.

The research reviewed above highlights the importance of implementing and enforcing school tobacco policies and ensuring that students perceive that the policies are enforced. Thus, to provide accurate conclusions when evaluating a policy, studies should evaluate its enforcement (Murnaghan et al. 2007).

Students' attitudes toward school policies may also have an impact on their decisions to smoke. Using data from a representative sample of 10th-grade California students, Unger and associates (1999) explored adolescents' attitudes toward no-smoking policies, including school-based policies. Attitudes toward no-smoking policies varied widely and were associated with smoking status, other psychosocial variables, and smoking-related advocacy efforts by the students. The researchers suggested that attitudes toward no-smoking policies may be either a determinant or a consequence of smoking behavior.

In summary, school policies on tobacco use have been recommended as an important component of comprehensive, multicomponent efforts to prevent use (CDC 1989; Barnett et al. 2007). Overall, research has shown that, to be effective, tobacco-related policy needs to be enforced and should foster a proactive approach by schools to prevention.

Ineffective programs. Many programs and prevention activities that have received a lot of attention have been shown to be ineffective, especially in the long term, when they were evaluated fully. Examples include one-time visiting speakers, other 1-day special events, poster competitions, lotteries, and other similar efforts. Other programs that are more similar to the multiple-session school-based prevention programs reviewed above have also been shown to be ineffective.

The D.A.R.E. program was developed by the Los Angeles Police Department and the Los Angeles Unified School District in the early 1980s. These groups essentially took the two variants of Project SMART being tested with seventh-grade students in Los Angeles schools at the time (Graham et al. 1990), combined them, and added a great deal of information about drugs (including, in some variants of the program, what they looked like, where to get them, and how they were used). Police officers were to deliver the program to students in fifth and sixth grades. The results of a randomized trial of the two Project SMART variants found that the program in resistance skills was effective but that the self-management component led to increased drug use relative to that of control group students (Hansen et al. 1988a; Graham et al. 1990). These results, combined with evidence that providing only information does not generally influence behavior change (Goodstadt 1978, 1980), and the use of police officers who are not trained to be highly skilled teachers, indicate that D.A.R.E. is most likely an ineffective program.

Although early nonrandomized studies suggested that D.A.R.E. sometimes had small effects for elementary school students, multiple randomized trials (Ennett et al. 1994a; Rosenbaum et al. 1994; Clayton et al. 1996; Dukes et al. 1996; Rosenbaum and Hanson 1998; Lynam et al. 1999) and two meta-analyses (Ennett et al. 1994b; West and O'Neal 2004) have established that D.A.R.E. has little or no impact on drug use in the short term and no impact in the long term, indicating its ineffectiveness. Even so, D.A.R.E. has been disseminated widely (Rogers 1995a; Des Jarlais et al. 2006). In response to the increasing evidence of the program's ineffectiveness, the D.A.R.E. organization has developed new programs for junior and senior high school students, but the program for junior high also has been shown to be ineffective (Perry et al. 2000, 2003), and evaluations of the high school program are not yet completed (Sloboda et al. 2009).

The Hutchinson Smoking Prevention Project (conducted at the Fred Hutchinson Cancer Research Center, University of Washington) has received much attention because the outcome evaluation was of such high quality and conducted over the long term. The project was designed to be a multiyear (grades 3–10) social influences program. A large randomized trial (20 school groups per condition) of the project produced no significant effects either by the end of grade 12 or 2 years later (Peterson et al. 2000). The findings of the trial are, however, quite difficult to interpret. The investigators did not report what its effects were at any time other than the two times noted above, including before entering high school (when most other programs report short-term and immediate-term results) or at the end of the program (grade 10). The effects of an intervention are generally measured immediately or shortly after the program ends to see the maximum impact, and the long-term measurement should serve to assess how permanent the effect was or how quickly it decayed.

Youth Empowerment and Activism

Interventions that rely on empowering youth or urging them to be activists are a relatively recent approach to preventing tobacco use. As Holden and colleagues (2004b) summarized, youth empowerment programs can be regarded as an offshoot of the second generation of community-based interventions. Initially, community-based interventions were theory driven and multicomponent, but the community's participation was limited to advisory roles and volunteer work in implementation. The second generation of community-based interventions emerged in the 1990s, with community input playing a more critical role throughout the research process. Youth empowerment programs are designed to engage youth in the planning, implementation, and evaluation stages of a program; tobacco-related prevention is a fitting venue for interventions to include youth empowerment, because experimentation and initiation with tobacco generally begin during adolescence (Haviland 2004). To date, much of the research regarding youth empowerment has been funded by the American Legacy Foundation, the creator of the "truth" campaign (this campaign is discussed in detail under "Mass Media Campaigns" earlier in this chapter). Up to this point, there are few studies on the efficacy of youth empowerment programs (Altman and Feighery 2004), and empirical evidence has only begun to emerge. The following section discusses youth empowerment programs that are not delivered through the mass media.

Because interventions to empower young people are relatively new, researchers face the task of operationalizing the concept of empowerment. One of several recent studies that sought to do this was conducted by Holden and colleagues (2004b), who reported that a panel of experts was convened at the American Legacy Foundation's YE (Youth Empowerment) Work Group to build a conceptual model establishing key components of youth empowerment and a set of operational measures. The conceptual framework had five major domains: (1) predisposing characteristics (i.e., reason for joining/motivation, demographic characteristics, history of involvement in similar groups and tobacco control, and smoking environment); (2) collective participation (duration, level, and intensity of participation; roles played by youth; and opportunities for involvement); (3) group structure (incentives provided, decision-making process, relationships to existing groups, opportunities for involvement, and available support and resources); (4) adult and institutional involvement (characteristics of adult coordinator, parental support, agency support, and support from the state program); and

(5) group climate (resiliency, cohesion, collective efficacy, and efficacy for outcomes). The attributes included in the conceptual framework were then operationalized though a set of questions. In turn, the findings were used to guide the development of an evaluation plan. In addition, Holden and colleagues (2004a) sought to determine the extent to which involvement in local efforts related to tobacco control influenced empowerment. The results suggest that involvement in local efforts is an independent component of empowerment and may influence this construct. Subsequently, using a convenience sample of youth participating in local tobacco control efforts, Holden and associates (2005) examined the attributes used to operationalize empowerment; the results provided a framework for understanding the potential outcomes of tobacco-related interventions, but empowerment is a complex phenomenon. More recently, with a sample of 112 participants in tobacco-related youth empowerment programs, Marr-Lyon and associates (2008) developed a measure of individual empowerment and discussed challenges related to evaluating empowerment among youth.

Earlier, Evans and colleagues (2004b) explored adult and group influences on the participation of youth in the Statewide Youth Movement Against Tobacco Use (SYMATU) programs. The SYMATU initiative "aims to engage youths in community action against tobacco use, to build state and local youth coalitions, and to foster meaningful youth-led tobacco prevention activities" (Hinnant et al. 2004, p. 629). Adults play several roles, which include serving as coordinators of youth groups, leaders of state tobacco control organizations, and teachers and mentors of participating youth. In addition, the adults are parents and members of the communities in which the youth reside. Results indicated that the involvement of adults did not have a significant direct effect on youth participation, but characteristics of the groups had a significant direct effect on participation by youth and mediated the relationship between adult involvement and such participation. The results emphasize the importance of group characteristics as influences on participation in youth empowerment programs.

Using case studies of five youth empowerment programs funded by the American Legacy Foundation, LeRoy and associates (2004) employed these programs as the unit of analysis to determine how organizational structures, program design features, and intraorganizational processes lead to organizational empowerment. They defined organizational empowerment as "organizational efforts that generate psychological empowerment among members and organizational effectiveness needed for goal achievement" (LeRoy et al. 2004, p. 577). These researchers reported that, on the basis of the data, there were three organizational models among the five programs: centralized, decentralized, and participatory. In the centralized model, a subcontract was given to a statewide prevention network with officials located in all of the state's counties. In the decentralized model, the state, in accordance with the belief that local organizations better understand and serve their constituents, subcontracted with regional organizations. In the participatory model, the state issued a request for proposals to all community-based organizations in the state and, after proposals were reviewed by a committee of adolescents, awarded grants. The research suggested that several intraorganizational processes are important for empowerment, including leadership and social support.

Ribisl and associates (2004) described the North Carolina Youth Empowerment Study, a 3-year participatory evaluation of tobacco prevention programs in North Carolina. The authors found that the number of groups working on tobacco-related issues in the state that included youth had grown in recent years. These groups were working on policy advocacy activities and expressed frustration with attempting to change tobacco-related policies because of the political and economic power of the tobacco industry in the state. Overall, the data suggested that youth had been influential in changing school-based policies in North Carolina. Hinnant and colleagues (2004) explored the influence of community support on the quantity and focus of group activities in youth empowerment programs. Using a convenience sample of adult coordinators of SYMATU youth groups in 17 states, they found that (1) community support variables were not related to the total number of group activities, although there was a marginally significant positive relationship between school support and the number of such activities; (2) the total number of group members, having a paid adult coordinator, and the hours an adult coordinator devoted to group supervision were all associated with the number of group activities; (3) community support was not associated with the number of educational activities performed by the group; (4) the size of a group's annual budget was related to the number of educational activities; and (5) support by youth outside the group and a group's annual budget were both significant predictors of the number of policy-related activities. Overall, adult coordinators believed that schools provided the greatest support for tobacco control issues, but these coordinators did not believe these issues received a high level of support from any other specific entity in the community.

In summary, a literature base on youth empowerment is emerging. As public health practice incorporates a more participatory research approach (Holden et al. 2004b) and emphasizes positive youth development (Kim et al. 1998; Flay 2002; Catalano et al. 2004), a more comprehensive understanding of interventions incorporating youth empowerment has been developing.

Cost-Effectiveness

It is difficult to estimate the costs and benefits of successful prevention programs and, therefore, their cost-benefit ratio (Caulkins et al. 1999; Foster et al. 2003). First, the costs and benefits for a particular program are variable; second, the long-term effectiveness of these programs has varied a great deal as well (Tengs 1996). Nevertheless, several scholars have provided estimates of cost-benefit ratios, using different techniques to do so.

One analysis estimated the cost of an effective 30-session prevention program in the United States at US$150 per student for program materials, training, teacher time, and other expenses (Caulkins et al. 1999). The estimated savings from such programs owing to the benefits of preventing significant numbers of students from initiating smoking and delaying the start date for those who later initiate smoking (and therefore the lifetime consumption) were substantial (Caulkins et al. 2004). For example, the estimated social benefits of smoking prevention alone were about US$300 per student, for a cost-benefit ratio of 2.0, and the estimated total benefits were about US$840, a cost-benefit ratio of 5.6.

The cost of an effective school-based smoking prevention program in Canada was estimated at C$67 per student (Stephens et al. 2000). Assuming a modest 4% level of long-term effectiveness, the benefits of smoking prevention were estimated to be lifetime savings for health care of C$3,400 per person and an increase in (lifetime) productivity of almost C$14,000 (Stephens et al. 2000), a cost-benefit ratio of 15.4. In other words, a moderately successful school-based smoking prevention program could produce a savings of C$15.40 for every C$1.00 spent.

Almost two decades ago, Hodgson (1992) asserted that smokers incur about US$9,379 more in lifetime health costs than do nonsmokers. Using this information, Wang and colleagues (2001) estimated the cost-effectiveness of LST to be about US$13,316 per life saved and US$8,482 per quality-adjusted life year (QALY), with the program costing US$13.29 per student. Given the large increases in unit costs for health care since 1992, these figures would have to be updated, but the results are instructive as to the cost-effectiveness of LST.

A group that looked at Project Towards No Tobacco Use (TNT) estimated its costs at US$48 per student and determined that it would cost about US$20,000 per QALY gained (Tengs et al. 2001). Although TNT was not cost saving, the authors concluded that the prevention of smoking offers gains in both survival and health-related quality of life that make it worth the cost. This latter statement is based on citizens' demonstrated "willingness to pay" for gains on the order of several hundred thousand dollars per QALY saved. In addition, an earlier analysis by Tengs and coworkers (1995) found that the median cost of 587 medical and public health interventions was US$42,000 per year of life saved and concluded that school-based smoking prevention is more efficient than most health/medical interventions.

The social benefits of even broader programs for improving behavior could be considerably greater. For example, Aos and colleagues (2004), at the Washington State Institute for Public Policy, who analyzed the cost-effectiveness of about 70 prevention programs, estimated that LST cost US$29 per student and led to benefits of US$746 (from the prevention of both smoking and drug abuse), a benefit of over US$25.61 per dollar spent, or a cost-benefit ratio of 25.61. In addition, they estimated that TNT cost US$5 per student and produced a benefit of US$279, a cost-benefit ratio of 55.84. Other programs included in both that review and in this chapter include the Good Behavior Game (cost-benefit ratio = 25.92), the MPP (ratio of 5.29), the Minnesota Smoking Prevention Program (ratio of 102.29), and a category of "other social influence/skills building substance prevention programs" (cost-benefit ratio of 70.34).

Although these cost effectiveness studies have focused on school-based prevention programs, their results support all prevention efforts. From a societal perspective, the costs of effective prevention are justified, both to the individual student and to society as a whole. In the study by Aos and colleagues (2004), cost-benefit ratios ranged from 2 to more than 100 for the prevention programs reviewed.

Summary Regarding School-Based Prevention

There are effective school-based smoking prevention programs that can be adopted, adapted, and deployed with at least short-term outcomes among adolescents. Programs can be found at the National Registry of Evidence-based Programs and Policies. Communities and school districts should invest only in the research-proven programs and avoid spending money on programs with little or no evidence of effectiveness. When implementing programs, decision makers must pay attention to maintaining program fidelity to ensure quality control.

Unfortunately, the inconsistent results and conclusions reported in the literature have caused many researchers, educators, and policymakers to conclude that school-based prevention does not work. Prior reviews have suggested that a more appropriate conclusion would be that many existing school-based programs have demonstrated effectiveness in the short term and that selected programs have demonstrated long-term effectiveness (Skara and Sussman 2003; Flay 2007, 2009a). Importantly, school-based programs produce *larger and more sustained* effects when they are implemented in combination with supplementary or complementary family-, mass media-, or community-based programs (Table 6.3). Similarly, other kinds of interventions produce larger effects when carried out in combination with other interventions (e.g., mass media plus taxation). Theories from sociology and public health (Bronfenbrenner 1977, 1979, 1986; Flay and Petraitis 1994; Flay et al. 2009) reveal that the more risk and protective factors an intervention or set of interventions addresses, the greater will be the effects. All of these data support the conclusion that a comprehensive, multicomponent approach to tobacco use prevention is more efficacious than a single strategy.

Thus, for school-based prevention to be effective, the programs should be comprehensive, interactive, start early, be sustained, incorporate an appropriate number of lessons, and be integrated into a community-wide approach (Flay 2007). Even among studies that have presented different conclusions regarding the effectiveness of school-based prevention, numerous studies (Sutton 2000; Cuijpers 2002; La Torre et al. 2005; Davis et al. 2007b; Warner 2007b) have concluded that school-based prevention works when combined with a comprehensive approach; that is, prevention efforts must address more distal, social, and community influences, too.

Smoking Cessation Among Youth

Research indicates that the prevalence of daily cigarette smoking in the United States increases from an estimated 4% among 12-year-olds to 8% among 16-year-olds, 12% among 18-year-olds, and 15% among 20-year-olds, and then levels off at 22% among 26-year-olds before dropping to 18% among older adults (Johnston et al. 2007a,b). The relatively steep curve for the prevalence of daily smoking that is evident during adolescence supports the need for cessation programming during this period of life. The need becomes even more evident when one considers that an estimated 60–85% of young tobacco users are likely to have made at least one attempt to quit and failed (Burt and Peterson 1998; Warren et al. 2000; Swart et al. 2001; Sithole 2003; Sirichotiratana et al. 2005; Sussman et al. 2006; Gervais et al. 2007; Johnston et al. 2007a,b). It appears that most youth who want to quit tobacco prefer to quit cold turkey (Mermelstein 2003), but few are successful using this approach.

Unique Aspects of Tobacco Cessation Among Youth

Cognitive differences between adolescents and adults suggest that effective interventions in the cessation of tobacco use have to be designed specifically for adolescents. Sussman (2002) has argued that adolescents are less likely than adults to structure their lives (e.g., keep careful records and schedule meetings) and to engage in higher-order thinking tasks (e.g., to take interest in analyzing their motivation for smoking). These attributes of adolescents also make it difficult to reach a large number of adolescents with an intensive face-to-face intervention. Mermelstein (2003) has recommended developmentally appropriate interventions for adolescents because they often do not have well-developed cognitive self-regulation skills (i.e., the ability to identify their own behaviors, engage in self-monitoring, and anticipate and develop practical plans for problem situations). "Simply taking strategies and presentations that are developed for adults and putting them into the jargon of adolescents or imbedding them in fun formats does not necessarily overcome the cognitive complexities of the strategies involved" (Mermelstein 2003, p. i31).

Adolescence is a time of change and experimentation, and during the initiation stage, tobacco use behaviors are highly variable. Adolescents may be experimenting with both cigarettes and smokeless tobacco as well as trying alcohol and other drugs. Because of their limited access to such products, their increased mobility as they get older, and environmental and cost restrictions on their behavior, the frequency with which adolescents use tobacco is likely to vary a great deal from day to day. Furthermore, adolescents who do not use tobacco for days or even weeks at a time may not label these times as periods of cessation. Although some measures of addiction to nicotine can occur fairly rapidly, it may take several years of experimentation and increased use before adolescents develop nicotine dependence (Biglan and Lichtenstein 1984; see Chapter 2, "The Health Consequences of Tobacco Use Among Young People"). In this age group, interventions will need to be designed to help both regular, more dependent daily users (NCI 2008) and those who are less dependent.

Review

Programming for the cessation of cigarette smoking among adolescents is defined as any type of programming in any setting that targets an age range of 12–19 years, that focuses on persons who smoke cigarettes at baseline (generally at least once in the last 30 days), and that encourages them to quit cigarette smoking. There have been nine systematic reviews of the relevant literature. In the first, Sussman and colleagues (1999) evaluated 34 trials, 17 on smoking cessation and 17 on smoking prevention, for their impact on cessation of cigarette smoking. Next, Sussman (2002) provided an enlarged review of 66 cessation trials and 17 studies of self-initiated quitting, and then McDonald and colleagues (2003) provided a review of many of the same studies (Sussman 2002). Garrison and colleagues (2003) reviewed six studies that used relatively rigorous designs, and Backinger and colleagues (2003) performed a qualitative review of prevention and cessation programs.

In the first meta-analysis of smoking cessation programs for adolescents, Sussman and colleagues (2006) included 48 studies with control groups. Shortly thereafter, Grimshaw and Stanton (2006) provided a Cochrane meta-analysis of 15 studies. The main difference in inclusion criteria between the two meta-analyses was that Grimshaw and Stanton required that studies contain follow-ups at least 6 months after the intervention (the standard used for adult cessation programs), while Sussman and colleagues did not. Both meta-analyses included RCTs, cluster RCTs, and non-RCTs. Next, Gervais and colleagues (2007) empirically reviewed 16 RCTs derived from previous reviews and data searches up to November 2006.

Sussman and Sun (2009) provided the most recent review; their literature search covered January 1970 to December 2007. This review included 64 studies, 16 more than the initial meta-analysis by Sussman and associates (2006), and included any English-language article or report with data on the contents of an adolescent smoking cessation effort, rates of quitting, and an age range of 12–19 years. Studies that included fewer than eight cigarette smokers at baseline were excluded because of the extremely small sample (fewer than five smokers per condition). Tobacco-related interventions for pregnant females were not included, and all reviewed studies included both genders. Data available through surveys of practitioners in the field were not reviewed. Finally, only studies that included a control condition were selected, and multiple-baseline, quasi-experimental, or experimental designs were permitted.

The 64 controlled trials that met the criteria for inclusion in the Sussman and Sun (2009) review were selected from an initial 130 studies; 50% of those 130 lacked control conditions (were single-group designs) and were not included in the review. An estimated one-third of the studies completed after 2000 that were in the initial group of 130 were single-group designs, suggesting some improvement in the design of these types of studies in recent years. Also, about one-third of the original 130 studies were published in 2000 or later (n = 42), an indication of increasing interest in adolescent cessation. A summary of the studies included in this review can be found in Table 6.11.

The variables examined by Sussman and Sun (2009) included program content, modalities of delivery, number of contacts, and expected rates of quitting at follow-ups. In addition, the means of recruiting and retaining smokers in the programs and suggestions on the lead time needed for a measurable effect were discussed. The results of the Sussman and Sun (2009) review were consistent with all previous reviews, except that of Garrison and colleagues (2003), which reviewed only six studies. The 64 studies in Sussman and Sun (2009) had an average reach to the recruited target audience of more than 35% and an average retention rate of approximately 75% for follow-up. The studies reviewed showed little evidence of disruption during implementation, sessions that were omitted, or restart of the intervention. However, specific documentation of the fidelity of implementation was not provided in most studies. Across the 64 studies, direct interpersonal contact of the treatment provider with potential participants and recruitment in contexts (e.g., classrooms) in which most of the members were potential participants led to relatively higher participation in the programs.

Sussman and colleagues (2006) and Sussman and Sun (2009) examined the mean estimated effects for four main predictors of outcomes (Tables 6.12–6.15) from their reviews. The five types of focus were social influences, cognitive-behavioral, motivational, medical, and other (e.g., reduction of supply and clarification of affect). The nine modalities of delivery were classified as classroom, school clinics, medical clinics, family, systemwide, computer, sensory deprivation, court diversion, and interventions in other public settings (e.g., worksite, shopping mall, and dormitory). The number of sessions varied from one to four, five to eight, to nine or more (three categories). Length of follow-up ranged from 0 to 3 months, 4 to 12 months, and more than 12 months past immediate posttest (three categories).

Most studies on adolescent cessation were underpowered statistically; in this case, the samples tended to be too small to detect significant differences between the program and control means with reasonable certainty (Cohen 1988). Also, most studies failed to use analyses that were appropriate for clustered data; in this instance when one unit, such as a cessation group, is nested within another, such as a school, the study should account for the confounding of the association between the cessation group and the school to permit a more accurate interpretation of rates of quitting. In addition, randomization generally is most effective with large sample sizes, so differences in treatment groups at baseline needed to be considered.

Table 6.11 Studies on smoking cessation among youth

Study (country)	Intervention theory, modality (number of sessions/contacts)	Design and total baseline sample size	Last follow-up (months)	Relative improvement; notes
Suedfeld et al. 1972 (United States)	Other Sensory deprivation (1)	Experimental with standard care control (SCC) n = 40	3	0%; affect oriented
Beaglehole et al. 1978 (New Zealand)	Social influences Classroom (16)	Quasi-experimental with SCC n = 128	3	0%
Greenberg and Deputat 1978 (United States)	Other School-based clinic (7)	Quasi-experimental with SCC n = 100	5	8.3%; affect oriented
Perry et al. 1980 (United States)	Social influences Classroom (4)	Quasi-experimental with SCC n = 243	4	1.7%
Jason et al. 1982 (United States)	Social influences Classroom (6)	Quasi-experimental with SCC n = 32	17	41.0%
Lotecka and McWhinney 1983 (United States)	Cognitive-behavioral School-based clinic (4)	Quasi-experimental with minimal program control (MPC) n = 49	0	0%; coping versus information only (programs equated for amount of delivery time)
Peterson and Clark 1986 (Australia)	Social influences School-based clinic (3)	Quasi-experimental with SCC n = 22	1	0%
Chan and Witherspoon 1988 (United States)	Motivation College dormitory (1)	Experimental with MPC n = 40	9	21.3%; health-risk assessment plus feedback versus health-risk assessment only
Killen et al. 1988 (United States)	Social influences Classroom (20)	Quasi-experimental with SCC n = 180	2	-5.5%
Ary et al. 1990 (United States)	Social influences Classroom (10)	Experimental with SCC n = 776	12	5.8%
Zavela et al. 1991 (United States)	Medical model School-based clinic (5)	Experimental with MPC n = 42	1	11.3%
Charlton 1992 (United Kingdom)	Cognitive-behavioral School-based clinic (6)	Quasi-experimental with MPC n = 87	6	7.8%
Baskerville et al. 1993 (Canada)	Motivation Systemwide (2)	Quasi-experimental with SCC n = 331	0; 6 months but not reported	17.9%; contingency-based reinforcement

Table 6.11 Continued

Study (country)	Intervention theory, modality (number of sessions/contacts)	Design and total baseline sample size	Last follow-up (months)	Relative improvement; notes
Diguisto 1994 (Australia)	Cognitive-behavioral School-based clinic (6)	Quasi-experimental with SCC n = 277	4	7.5%
Murray et al. 1994 (United States)	Other Systemwide (4)	Quasi-experimental with SCC n = 450	0	6.0%; supply reduction
Sussman et al. 1995 (United States)	Cognitive-behavioral School-based clinic (5)	Experimental with SCC n = 244	3	7.0%
Cinnomin and Sussman 1995 (United States)	Cognitive-behavioral School-based clinic (6)	Experimental with only program conditions n = 60	1	17.0%; programs equated for amount of delivery time
Horswell and Horton 1997 (Canada)	Social influences School-based clinic (3)	Quasi-experimental with SCC n = 36	6	6.0%
Hotte et al. 1997 (Canada)	Cognitive-behavioral School-based clinic (10)	Quasi-experimental with MPC n = 558	6	5.0%; at 1-month follow-up
Rigotti et al. 1997 (United States)	Other Systemwide (1)	Quasi-experimental with SCC n = 2,900	24	3%; supply reduction
Dino et al. 1998 (United States)	Cognitive-behavioral School-based clinic (8)	Quasi-experimental with SCC n = 29	2	22.0%
Forster et al. 1998 (United States)	Other Systemwide (4)	Experimental with SCC n = 660	36	-5.4%; supply reduction
Aveyard et al. 1999 (United Kingdom)	Motivation Computer based (6)	Experimental with MPC n = 1,090	5	0%; stages of change
Bloor et al. 1999 (United Kingdom)	Social influences Classroom (about 3)	Quasi-experimental with SCC n = 12	3	-2.3%; use of peer-nominated group leaders as teachers
Coleman-Wallace et al. 1999 (United States)	Motivation School-based clinic (8)	Quasi-experimental with SCC n = 351	0	15.0%; stages of change
Etter et al. 1999 (Switzerland)	Other Systemwide (2)	Quasi-experimental with SCC n = 582	7	0%; supply reduction
Glasgow et al. 1999 (United States)	Motivation Medical clinic (2)	Experimental with MPC n = 506	6	4.3%

Table 6.11 Continued

Study (country)	Intervention theory, modality (number of sessions/contacts)	Design and total baseline sample size	Last follow-up (months)	Relative improvement; notes
Kentala et al. 1999 (Finland)	Motivation Medical clinic (2)	Experimental with SCC n = 148	36	6.1%; dental clinic
Bauman et al. 2000 (United States)	Motivation Family (5)	Experimental with SCC n = 110	12	11.5%; home based
Cai et al. 2000 (Singapore)	Medical model Medical clinic (12)	Experimental with SCC n = 330	3	-1.3%; laser vs. sham acupuncture
Quinlan and McCaul 2000 (United States)	Motivation School-based clinic (1)	Experimental with SCC 3 conditions n = 94	1	14%; stages of change: personal match to stage of change (3%) or action-oriented stage (14%) vs. SCC (0%)
Adelman et al. 2001 (United States)	Cognitive-behavioral School-based clinic (8)	Experimental with MPC n = 74	3	9.6%
Dino et al. 2001a (United States)	Cognitive-behavioral School-based clinic (14)	Quasi-experimental with SCC n = 100	5	1.1%
Dino et al. 2001b (United States)	Cognitive-behavioral School-based clinic (12)	Quasi-experimental with MPC n = 346	5	3.2%
Hancock et al. 2001 (Australia)	Social influences Systemwide (about 3)	Experimental with SCC n = 3,800	42	5.2%
Lazovich et al. 2001 (United States)	Contingency based Court diversion (1)	Experimental with MPC n = 112	3	0%; attended court diversion class or paid a fine (the MPC)
Sussman et al. 2001 (United States)	Motivation School-based clinic (5)	Experimental with SCC n = 335	5	9.8%
Sussman et al. 2002 (United States)	Motivation School-based clinic (5)	Experimental with SCC n = 583	12	5.4%
Brown et al. 2003 (United States)	Motivation Medical clinic (2)	Experimental with MPC n = 191	12	4.4%
Lando et al. 2007 (and unpublished data) (United States)	Motivation Medical clinic (2)	Experimental with MPC n = 344	12	-4.5%

Table 6.11 Continued

Study (country)	Intervention theory, modality (number of sessions/contacts)	Design and total baseline sample size	Last follow-up (months)	Relative improvement; notes
Robinson et al. 2003 (United States)	Motivation School-based clinic (4)	Experimental with MPC n = 316	12	-1.7%; for youth caught smoking; control was the CDC "I Quit" self-help guide
Lipkus et al. 2004 (United States)	Motivation Other public setting (about 2)	Experimental with MPC n = 402	8	2.5%; shopping mall and home telephone counseling
Winkleby et al. 2004 (United States)	Social influences Classroom (5)	Experimental with MPC n = 813	6	5.0%; tobacco-focused advocacy; intervention versus modified drug abuse prevention program; programs equated for amount of delivery time
Zheng et al. 2004 (China)	Motivation School-based clinic (5)	Single-group multiple baseline within group control n = 46	4	11.3%; in the 2006 review, the immediate posttest results were used; these have not been replaced in the current paper with the 4-month follow-up results
Colby et al. 2005 (United States)	Motivation Medical clinic (2)	Experimental with MPC n = 85	6	7.1%
Hamilton et al. 2005 (Australia)	Motivation Classroom (8)	Experimental with SCC n = 2,335	24	4.5%; harm reduction
Hollis et al. 2005 (United States)	Motivation Computer based (3)	Quasi-experimental with SCC n = 448	24	10.0%; stages of change
Horn et al. 2005a (North Carolina and West Virginia, United States)	Cognitive-behavioral School-based clinic (12)	Quasi-experimental with MPC n = 250	15	2.5%
Horn et al. 2005a (Florida 1997–1998 cohort, United States)	Cognitive-behavioral School-based clinic (10)	Quasi-experimental with MPC n = 153	0	17.7%
Horn et al. 2005a (Florida 1998–1999 cohort, United States)	Cognitive-behavioral School-based clinic (10)	Quasi-experimental with MPC n = 305	0	8.9%
Horn et al. 2005a (Florida 1999–2000 cohort, United States)	Cognitive-behavioral School-based clinic (10)	Quasi-experimental with MPC n = 237	0	3.8%
Horn et al. 2005a (Florida 2000–2001 cohort, United States)	Cognitive-behavioral School-based clinic (10)	Quasi-experimental with MPC n = 186	0	-0.7%

Table 6.11 Continued

Study (country)	Intervention theory, modality (number of sessions/contacts)	Design and total baseline sample size	Last follow-up (months)	Relative improvement; notes
Horn et al. 2005a (North Carolina 2001–2002 cohort, United States)	Cognitive-behavioral School-based clinic (10)	Quasi-experimental with MPC n = 122	0	3.4%
Horn et al. 2005a (North Carolina and West Virginia 2000–2001, United States)	Cognitive-behavioral School-based clinic (10)	Quasi-experimental with MPC n = 128	0	8.4%
Horn et al. 2005b (United States)	Cognitive-behavioral School-based clinic (10)	Quasi-experimental with MPC n = 74	3	8.9%; American Indians
Myers and Brown 2005 (United States)	Motivation Medical clinic (6)	Quasi-experimental with SCC n = 54	6	6.1%
Rodgers et al. 2005 (New Zealand)	Cognitive-behavioral Computer based (about 3)	Experimental with SCC n = 617	6	2.2%; use of cell phone text messaging
Stoddard et al. 2005 (United States)	Social influences Other public setting (8)	Experimental with SCC n = 560	12	6.9%; worksites
Zack et al. 2005 (United States)	Cognitive-behavioral School-based clinic (6)	Experimental with SCC n = 125	12	10.4%
Audrey et al. 2006 (United Kingdom)	Cognitive-behavioral Classroom (about 3)	Experimental with SCC n = 424	12	3.0%; use of peer-nominated group leaders as teachers
Pbert et al. 2006 (United States)	Medical Medical clinic (4)	Experimental with SCC n = 1,148	3	20.0%; nurses as deliverers of the "5 A's" quit approach
Horn et al. 2007 (United States)	Motivation Medical clinic (4)	Experimental with SCC n = 75	6	0%; motivational interviewing in emergency room
Sussman et al. 2007 (United States)	Motivation Classroom (8)	Experimental with SCC n = 461	12	4.1%
Kohler et al. 2008 (United States)	Cognitive-behavioral School-based clinic (14)	Quasi-experimental with SCC n = 492	12	2.1%

Note: The 64 studies are controlled trials that met the criteria for the Sussman and Sun 2009 review. **CDC** = Centers for Disease Control and Prevention.

Table 6.12 Youth cessation treatment means, 2006 and 2007 analyses, stratified by duration of follow-up

Duration of follow-up	2006 estimate	2007 estimate
0–3 months (36, 38)	3.88	4.17
4–12 months (21, 29)	2.92	4.06
>12 months (5, 8)	6.62	6.78

Note: Numbers in parentheses are the sample sizes of studies in the Sussman et al. (2006) and Sussman and Sun (2009) reviews, respectively. Data were intent-to-treat (ITT) quit rates, and weighted least squares random effects models were used to pool results from study net effects (program minus control) estimates. When pooled, studies were weighted by sample size and adjusted for follow-up duration category in the overall estimate, theory, modality, and number of sessions models. The effects reported are pooled ITT net effects.

Table 6.13 Youth cessation treatment means, 2006 and 2007 analyses, stratified by theory

Theory	2006 estimate	2007 estimate
Social influence (8, 11)	3.77	4.34
Cognitive-behavioral (17, 23)	4.72	5.32
Motivation (15, 22)	3.66	3.97
Medical (1, 3)	13.16	15.86
Other (6, 6)	-0.16	-0.17

Note: Numbers in parentheses are the sample sizes of studies in the Sussman et al. (2006) and Sussman and Sun (2009) reviews, respectively. Data were intent-to-treat (ITT) quit rates, and weighted least squares random effects models were used to pool results from study net effects (program minus control) estimates. When pooled, studies were weighted by sample size and adjusted for follow-up duration category in the overall estimate, theory, modality, and number of sessions models. The effects reported are pooled ITT net effects.

Table 6.14 Youth cessation treatment means, 2006 and 2007 analyses, stratified by modality

Modality	2006 estimate	2007 estimate
Classroom (7, 11)	4.15	4.21
School clinics (25, 29)	5.62	6.30
Medical clinics (5, 9)	2.40	4.62
Family (1, 1)	21.37	19.10
Systemwide (5, 6)	-0.22	0.81
Computer (2, 3)	5.60	5.40
Other public setting (2, 5)	1.45	3.92

Note: Numbers in parentheses are the sample sizes of studies in the Sussman et al. (2006) and Sussman and Sun (2009) reviews, respectively. Data were intent-to-treat (ITT) quit rates, and weighted least squares random effects models were used to pool results from study net effects (program minus control) estimates. When pooled, studies were weighted by sample size and adjusted for follow-up duration category in the overall estimate, theory, modality, and number of sessions models. The effects reported are pooled ITT net effects.

Table 6.15 Youth cessation treatment means, 2006 and 2007 analyses, stratified by number of sessions

Number of sessions	2006 estimate	2007 estimate
1–4 (17, 26)	-0.08	3.20
5–8 (15, 20)	6.43	6.24
≥9 (15, 18)	4.47	4.20

Note: Numbers in parentheses are the sample sizes of studies in the Sussman et al. (2006) and Sussman and Sun (2009) reviews, respectively. Data were intent-to-treat (ITT) quit rates, and weighted least squares random effects models were used to pool results from study net effects (program minus control) estimates. When pooled, studies were weighted by sample size and adjusted for follow-up duration category in the overall estimate, theory, modality, and number of sessions models. The effects reported are pooled ITT net effects.

On average, almost twice as many in the treatment groups quit as in the control groups: 13.4% versus 7.4% (RI = 6.4%; $p < 0.001$). The most effective studies used programs based on social influences, cognitive-behavioral theory, or programming to enhance motivation as the theory behind their intervention design. Results also appeared promising for medical-/recovery-based programming, but the number of studies here was too small ($n = 3$) to infer consistent effects. The modalities in which programming achieved the strongest effects were classroom-based educational programs, school-based clinics, and computer-based programming.

One limitation in trying to differentiate the effects of theory from modality is that these were not independent categorizations. In the current sample, 7 of 11 classroom-based studies involved manipulations of social influences;

20 of 29 school clinic studies were cognitive-behavioral; 8 of 9 medical clinic studies were based on enhancement of motivation; 4 of 6 systemwide studies were in the "other" theory category; and 2 of 3 computer-based studies were based on enhancing motivation.

Relatively higher rates of quitting were found for programs having five or more sessions (none with fewer than five sessions produced significant findings, but those with five or more sessions showed a 5% increase in quitting compared with controls). In addition, effects for programs with five or more sessions were also maintained at short-term (1 year or less) and long-term (greater than 1 year) follow-ups. Eight studies examined follow-ups longer than 12 months, and in these studies, the short-term effects were maintained. More studies with long-term follow-ups are needed; even so, these data are promising, suggesting that adolescent cessation rates tend not to decrease much over time.

Use of Pharmacologic Adjuncts for Cessation

There is a strong interest in pharmacologic adjuncts for tobacco cessation in adolescents because these agents have been very useful among adults (Fiore et al. 2000). Pharmacologic agents have generally been used as an adjunct to other treatment programming, such as cognitive-behavioral treatment; that is, many trials have compared an active treatment alone with the active treatment plus a pharmacologic adjunct. (Studies with these types of designs were not contained in the meta-analysis by Sussman and Sun [2009] because the comparison condition was an "active" control.)

Ten studies have assessed the use of pharmacologic adjuncts for cessation with adolescents, seven of which were controlled trials (Smith et al. 1996; Hurt et al. 2000; Hanson et al. 2003; Killen et al. 2004; Niederhofer and Huber 2004; Sussman et al. 2004; Moolchan et al. 2005; Roddy et al. 2006; Muramoto et al. 2007). All of these studies included cognitive-behavioral programming (e.g., standard counseling on cessation, including instruction on coping skills).

Five of the seven controlled trials failed to show an effect for the use of nicotine replacement as an adjunct among youth. In the other two studies, the effects were not significant. The mean effect at last follow-up for nicotine gum was 2.5% (two controlled studies: 4% and 1%); for the nicotine patch it was 6% (four controlled studies: 2%, 15%, 1%, and 0%); and for bupropion it was 1% (three controlled studies: 1%, 1%, and 37%). Only Moolchan and colleagues (2005) found a significant treatment effect for nicotine gum (4%) and the nicotine patch (15%, 6-month trial, n = 120). In addition, only Niederhofer and Huber (2004) found an effect for bupropion (37% absolute difference, 3-month trial, n = 22). It is not known why the effects in these two studies differed from the rest.

Use of Electronic Technology for Smoking Cessation Among Youth

Another area of current interest is the use of electronic communications technology to assist in helping adolescents to quit smoking; here, five studies with comparison groups were identified (Rabius et al. 2004; Rodgers et al. 2005; Chen and Yeh 2006; Mermelstein and Turner 2006; Patten et al. 2006). Only two of these studies (Rabius et al. 2004; Rodgers et al. 2005) were included in the 64-study review by Sussman and Sun (2009).

Chen and Yeh (2006) compared a smoking cessation group plus instruction through an Internet-assisted program with a standard-care group in a pre-post quasi-experimental design with 77 high school adolescents in Taiwan for 6 weeks. Being in the program resulted in a higher reduction in rates of daily smoking (reduction of 21% vs. an increase of 2.5% in the control group) and a greater number of attempts to quit (an average of one more attempt during the 6-week period). The youth appeared to have been favorably disposed to including the Internet component, but data on cessation, or the means to estimate this rate, were not provided in the paper.

Mermelstein and Turner (2006) contrasted Not On Tobacco (N-O-T), a school-based cessation clinic, with a condition that included the clinic plus an Internet Web site and proactive telephone calls. In a clustered RCT (n = 351, 14- to 19-year-olds) at 29 high schools, the enhanced condition doubled rates of quitting at the 3-month follow-up in a comparison with use of the clinic alone (7-day rates of quitting: 14% vs. 7%), but the difference was only marginally significant.

Patten and associates (2006) contrasted a four-session office-based program (n = 139) that involved motivational interviewing and problem solving among 11- to 18-year-olds with a home-based Internet program (Stomp Out Smokes) in an RCT. In the Internet condition, access was provided for 24 weeks; 66% of participants stopped using the program by its third week. The 30-day ITT rate of quitting at 36 weeks favored the office-based program, 13% versus 6%, but this difference was not significant.

In a study by Rabius and associates (2004), one group received five sessions of telephone counseling while the other received only self-help booklets. This was an RCT among 18–25-year-olds (12% of the sample of 420 young adults was either 18 or 19 years of age). At 6-month follow-up, 10% versus 3% had quit (defined as no smoking in the last 48 hours); this difference was statistically significant.

The use of mobile telephones and text messaging by adolescents has potential for future intervention efforts. As of 2010, 75% of adolescents aged 12–17 years owned cell telephones, up from 45% in 2004. In addition, 72% of these adolescents were text messagers (and made up 88% of all adolescent users of cell telephones) (Lenhart et al. 2010). A recent meta-analysis of youth and adults shows some promise for at least short-term smoking cessation using text messaging (Whittaker et al. 2009), in that the authors found significant short-term increases in cessation rates. Finally, a study by Rodgers and colleagues (2005) involved an RCT of 617 adolescent smokers. One group received personalized text messaging from a cell telephone that involved a cognitive-behavioral approach for 1 week before and 4 weeks after a designated "quit day," while the control group received bimonthly general text messages to keep them involved in the study. Although the early results looked promising (14% vs. 6% quit rates based on ITT at 6 weeks; 29% vs. 19% at 12 weeks), there was essentially no difference between the test and control groups at 6-month follow-up (25% vs. 24%).

In conclusion, the use of telephone counseling appears to be promising. Use of the Internet or text messaging may be effective if programming is bolstered during a long period.

Summary Regarding Smoking Cessation Programs for Youth

Overall, several smoking cessation programs for adolescents have been found to be efficacious. Many of the findings for youth programs are consistent with those found in the literature on adults, particularly regarding the importance of using cognitive-behavioral strategies and achieving a sufficient dosage of programming (Fiore et al. 2000). For example, the N-O-T Program targeting 14–19-year-old daily smokers is based on social cognitive theory and includes 10 hour-long sessions (plus 4 boosters) covering such topics as self-management, social influences, relapse prevention, and managing nicotine withdrawal (Horn et al. 2005a). One difference is that, at present, there is little evidence of the efficacy of pharmacologic adjuncts for youth, in contrast with the strong efficacy for adults. Future work on the metabolism of pharmacologic adjuncts, patterns of tobacco use among youth, and self-reported withdrawal symptoms might help researchers and policymakers improve their understanding of the potential effectiveness of pharmacologic adjuncts among youth.

There is a strong need for more research on youth cessation that makes use of appropriate controls, uses more standard measures of cessation, and conducts longer follow-ups (12 months and perhaps longer). Research on how to effectively recruit young smokers is needed. Also, metrics such as the cost-effectiveness of treatment per QALYs gained and years of disability avoided should be examined in future studies on youth smoking cessation. The use of such metrics could demonstrate even greater cost-effectiveness for early interventions than would be found for smoking cessation programs among adults. There is also a need for evaluating whether different cessation programs are needed for different levels of use or for different kinds of tobacco products, such as smokeless tobacco.

Special Issues

This section examines special issues in both the prevention of tobacco use and in cessation for young people. In particular, it focuses on preventing the use of smokeless tobacco and on cessation programs that target smokeless tobacco use. Although most research on tobacco use among young people has focused on smoking, increasing attention is being paid to smokeless tobacco. Furthermore, since the broad adoption of smokefree ordinances, the use of smokeless tobacco may be promoted in response to restrictions on smoking. Now that cigarette companies are increasingly focusing on bringing new "spitless" smokeless tobacco products to market, these new tobacco products may be heavily marketed, and their use may be growing among young people (see Chapter 3, "The Epidemiology of Tobacco Use Among Young People in the United States and Worldwide"). The section below on preventing the use of smokeless tobacco discusses efforts to prevent the use of snuff and chew with a variety of interventions. The next section focuses on cessation of smokeless tobacco use, a subject that has received far less attention than has cessation of cigarette smoking among youth.

Community-, Family-, and Health-Care-Based Prevention of Smokeless Tobacco Use

Few studies have been conducted on the prevention of smokeless tobacco use by youth and young adults. Federal agencies, voluntary groups, and professional organizations freely offer a limited selection of booklets, videos, posters, and other written materials about the risks of smokeless tobacco, but as yet, it is not known whether they have been widely disseminated or whether they have had an impact on reducing the uptake of smokeless tobacco by young people. Most prevention programs with a smokeless tobacco component that have been evaluated have been conducted in schools, with a small number in community, family, or health care settings.

Community-based efforts incorporating a comprehensive approach to prevention that includes schools, media, family, advocacy, and public policy may be effective in preventing the use of smokeless tobacco by youth. Project SixTeen (Biglan et al. 2000a), an RCT of a community intervention to prevent adolescent tobacco use, tested whether a comprehensive community-wide effort to prevent tobacco use among adolescents would have a greater deterrent effect on tobacco use than would a school-based tobacco prevention program alone. The community intervention included a media advocacy component, a youth antitobacco module, family communication activities, and a youth-access campaign. The school-based intervention consisted of an evidence-based curriculum called Programs to Advance Teen Health. The study found a significant effect on decreasing the prevalence of smokeless tobacco use among boys after 1 year of the community intervention but no change with the school-based condition. The results suggest that a community intervention that targets multiple influences on adolescent tobacco use can be effective for reducing boys' smokeless tobacco use.

Despite the paucity of efforts to prevent the use of smokeless tobacco, studies showed an overall decline in adolescent use of this product through the late 1990s and an increase in the percentage of 8th-, 10th-, and 12th-grade students who perceived regular use of smokeless tobacco as harmful (Nelson et al. 2006). The efforts against tobacco use among youth that took place throughout the country in the 1990s, although focused primarily on cigarette smoking, may have helped to increase the perception that smokeless tobacco is harmful as well (Nelson et al. 2006). However, the use of smokeless tobacco began to increase again in 2003 and subsequently the prevalence has stalled (see Chapter 3, "The Epidemiology of Tobacco Use Among People in the United States and Worldwide"). Data from Massachusetts are suggestive here; beginning in 1993, the Massachusetts Tobacco Control Program fostered efforts to prevent smoking among youth through a statewide comprehensive approach in communities and schools and through the media. An analysis of school survey data from the Massachusetts Prevalence Study (Soldz et al. 2000) between 1993 and 1996 found a decline in the use of smokeless tobacco greater than that seen nationally, suggesting that the program was effective in preventing smokeless tobacco use (it was also effective in lowering the use of cigarettes among middle school males).

Elsewhere, in an RCT of a family-directed program designed to decrease tobacco (cigarettes and smokeless tobacco) and alcohol use among adolescents, effects were observed for smoking, but because so few adolescents reported the use of smokeless tobacco, the sample was simply too small to assess for effects of the program on the onset of its use (Bauman et al. 2001).

Interventions by health care providers also appear to offer a natural conduit to the prevention of smokeless tobacco use—in particular, interventions by oral health professionals who have a unique opportunity to see the consequences of smokeless tobacco use. Although dental settings have provided an avenue for several cessation studies (Severson et al. 1998; Andrews et al. 1999; Bauman et al. 2001; Gordon and Severson 2001), this clinical setting has not been evaluated for providing preventive interventions. A study based in pediatric primary care physicians' practices in New England attempted to prevent smokeless tobacco use as part of a comprehensive systems-based effort to influence adolescent health behaviors, but found no significant effect on the prevention of smokeless tobacco use (Stevens et al. 2002).

Tobacco control policies, including higher taxes on smokeless tobacco, higher minimum ages for the legal purchase of tobacco products, strong provisions for licensing the sale of tobacco, restrictions on the distribution of free samples, and the posting of signs for minimum age of purchase, are effective in reducing the use of smokeless tobacco among adolescent males (Chaloupka et al. 1997). By one estimate, as reported earlier in this chapter, a 10% increase in the price of smokeless tobacco products would reduce consumption of this product among male youth by about 5.9% (Chaloupka et al. 1997).

In sum, there have been few evaluations of community-, family-, or health-care-based interventions to reduce the rate at which young people take up smokeless tobacco or to prevent its use altogether in this group. The results reported by Biglan and colleagues (2000a) are encouraging, but additional research is needed to determine effective ways to educate both children and parents about the health risks of using this product. The dental health care setting offers a unique venue to provide preventive education to youth and families, but studies to date have focused on youth and adult cessation in this setting rather than youth prevention.

Interventions in the School Curriculum

The lack of effective education on smokeless tobacco in the schools is perplexing but may have many explanations. Most schools teach both males and females, but in the United States the primary users of smokeless tobacco are male; overall prevalence is somewhat lower than that of cigarette smoking; there are large regional and geographic differences restricting the issue to areas of the country with higher prevalence rates. Parents are more likely to accept their child's use of smokeless tobacco than of cigarettes, since they view smokeless tobacco as less dangerous. However, recent research showing that early use of smokeless tobacco may be a significant risk factor for subsequent smoking (Severson et al. 2007) may alter this perception. Another reason for the lack of effective education may be that most interventions for smokeless tobacco in schools are simply too broad to adequately affect those youth at high risk for use, or they may focus too little on prevention.

One study that demonstrated a preventive effect on the use of smokeless tobacco among young people was a school-based social influences program conducted by the Oregon Research Institute (Severson et al. 1991) that was delivered by regular classroom teachers and peer leaders in randomly assigned schools. This study sought to make students sensitive to both overt and covert pressures to use smokeless tobacco and cigarettes. Students practiced refusal skills, and in addition to using a structured curriculum with role-play activities, teachers used videotapes to standardize instruction and maintain student engagement. Although only two of the seven class periods in the intervention were devoted to smokeless tobacco, use among boys in both seventh, and to a lesser extent, the ninth grade, was reduced. However, parallel analyses failed to show that the intervention had any positive effect on cigarette smoking.

In another school-based program, Elder and colleagues (1993) developed Project SHOUT and evaluated it in 22 junior high schools in San Diego County, California. Based on an operant conditioning model of tobacco use (Elder and Stern 1986), the intervention was delivered in randomly assigned schools to seventh-grade students; intervention and assessment continued for 3 years through ninth grade. At the 3-year follow-up, the intervention had a significant effect on cigarette use, use of smokeless tobacco, and use of cigarettes and smokeless tobacco combined. The intervention effect was particularly strong during the ninth grade.

The school curriculum titled Project Towards No Tobacco Use (Sussman et al. 1993b; Dent et al. 1995) has also shown promising results for preventing the use of smokeless tobacco and its component on physical consequences has shown particular promise. Consistent with most social influences programs, this project had three primary components: the teaching of refusal skills, awareness of misperceptions about social values, and physical consequences. Although the combined curriculum was effective in reducing initial and weekly use of smokeless tobacco, a 2-year follow-up suggested that the curriculum on physical consequences was the only one to have a long-term impact on whether students tried that product. The results contradicted previous research that had found programming on social influences to be superior to programming focused primarily on physical consequences. However, the programming on physical consequences had several novel features that may have contributed to its effectiveness, such as correcting myths about experimentation with tobacco and addiction, role-playing that one has a disease, and presenting probabilities of consequences in ways more personally relevant to youth. In the long run, presenting information on physical consequences was deemed especially important for preventing the use of smokeless tobacco.

School- and community-based efforts have shown promising results, but by broadly targeting substance use and tobacco, many prevention programs do not emphasize use of smokeless tobacco enough and are unlikely to show a significant impact on initiation rates for this behavior. It is not known whether these programs would be effective if they were more narrowly focused; it appears that most tobacco prevention programs focus almost exclusively on smoking and pay relatively little attention to smokeless tobacco.

Special Populations

Overall, usage rates for smokeless tobacco among youth are considerably lower than those for cigarette smoking, but certain subgroups have rates notably higher than the average. Use of smokeless tobacco is much more common in males than in females (Hatsukami and Severson 1999), with the highest rates observed in American Indians and Alaska Natives, in the southern states, and in rural populations with low socioeconomic status (Hatsukami and Severson 1999). Use is also more common among young players of particular sports, such as baseball (Severson et al. 2005).

A study that focused on American Indian youth (Schinke et al. 2000) developed and tested a skills- and community-based approach to prevent substance abuse, including the use of smokeless tobacco. Intervention sessions in school involved instruction, modeling, and rehearsal in cognitive and behavioral skills associated with preventing substance abuse. The program was carefully tailored to the cultural prerogatives and everyday realities of American Indian young people in the targeted western reservations. Although cigarette use was unaffected, at follow-up, rates of smokeless tobacco use were lower for youth who received the skills intervention.

Various studies have documented that high school males frequently use smokeless tobacco when playing or watching a sport (Creath et al. 1988; Murray et al. 1988; Boyd and Glover 1989; Colborn et al. 1989; Riley et al. 1991; Gottlieb et al. 1993), and the greater their athletic involvement, the more likely they are to be users (Colborn et al. 1989). A behavioral intervention that targeted male high school baseball athletes (Walsh et al. 2003) was designed to promote cessation of smokeless tobacco use and discourage initiation. This intervention, conducted in rural high schools in California, included an interactive peer-led component and a dental component with a screening examination for oral cancer. Although the intervention was found to be effective in promoting cessation, it was ineffective in preventing initiation by nonusers. The strongest predictors of initiation to past-month smokeless tobacco use were being a current smoker, trying smokeless tobacco in the past, and perceiving high use of smokeless tobacco among teammates. These findings suggest that prevention of relapse and providing information that many leading baseball players do not use smokeless tobacco would be important components of an effective prevention program.

Summary Regarding the Prevention of Smokeless Tobacco Use

Three well-designed school-based interventions have shown positive preventive effects for the use of smokeless tobacco, but this small body of evidence pales against the extensive literature reviewed in this chapter on school-based prevention of cigarette smoking. School-based prevention programs that include special attention to the negative physical and health effects of smokeless tobacco may be helpful in reducing the likelihood that young males will start using it. There have been few community interventions, but one well-controlled trial was encouraging. Other interventions that have targeted families or used health care settings have not been adequately evaluated. Because the use of smokeless tobacco is very high among some special populations, such as high school baseball athletes and American Indians, it is encouraging that special interventions have been adapted for these groups. To date, no interventions have been evaluated with populations of Alaska Natives, although studies report their use to be very high (Angstman et al. 2007).

Cessation of Smokeless Tobacco Use Among Youth

Adolescent use of smokeless tobacco represents an important public health problem, and yet little research has focused on developing efficacious, practical cessation tools that are appealing to this age group. Most cessation programs have been aimed at college-aged or adult users, and the small number of interventions designed for youth have usually been incorporated as a secondary element of multicomponent programs to prevent tobacco use. Even if school- or community-based prevention programs have an impact on reducing initiation or use, there is still a need for programs to help young users quit using snuff and chewing tobacco.

Research on Smokeless Tobacco Cessation with Youth

Of the few publications describing programs to quit smokeless tobacco for youth (Table 6.16; Sussman et al. [2006]), most have focused on high school or college athletes who are known to have higher rates of use (Boyd and Glover 1989; Colborn et al. 1989). Some reviews of more broadly targeted programs, designed to reduce the adoption of overall tobacco use by middle school and high school youth, have examined the impact of these programs on cessation among those students who were using tobacco products at baseline. A handful of these studies have included smokeless tobacco as a part of their comprehensive focus on the tobacco problem, but none has teased out the results for smokeless tobacco in a manner that provides guidance as to which components of the intervention are most effective for quitting the use of this product, nor do they provide long-term cessation results for smokeless tobacco that serve as useful benchmarks (Mermelstein 2003; Skara and Sussman 2003; Sussman et al. 2003). One highly relevant report described results from a focus group of 27 adolescents on the acceptability and appeal of a Web-based smoking prevention program (Parlove et al. 2004) and formative data suggest that this could be a promising avenue to providing assistance with cessation for smokeless tobacco, but no outcome data were reported.

Eakin and colleagues (1989) tested a three-session, multicomponent, cognitive-behavioral intervention that included self-monitoring of smokeless tobacco use, a component designed to increase the user's awareness of health risks, behavioral coping strategies, frequent telephone contact, and training in the prevention of relapse. Biochemical (carbon monoxide and cotinine) verification of self-reports was obtained. Twenty-one of the 25 adolescents in the original study (14–18 years of age, averaging five to eight dips per day) completed treatment, 9 (36%) were abstinent at the conclusion of the program, and 4 (16%) maintained abstinence at the 3-month follow-up. Participants who did not achieve complete abstinence reported substantial reductions in use of smokeless tobacco. Of those who also were cigarette smokers, none reported an increase in cigarette consumption as a result of reducing the use of or quitting smokeless tobacco. Predictors of cessation for smokeless tobacco included lower baseline consumption levels and involvement in school athletics.

In the study of high school baseball players in rural California (Eakin et al. 1989; Walsh et al. 2000, 2003) described above, 44 high schools were randomly assigned to a treatment condition (516 participants) or a no-treatment control (568 participants). The intervention

Table 6.16 Studies on smokeless tobacco cessation for youth

Study	Intervention theory, modality, and number of sessions/contacts	Design, age, and sample size	Last follow-up	Percentage who quit	Biochemical verification of self-report
Eakin et al. 1989	Cognitive-behavioral 3 sessions/group treatment	14- to 18-year-olds Within-person replicated cognitive-behavioral design N = 25	3 months	36% at end of treatment 16% at 3-month follow-up	Yes
Chakravorty 1992	Oral substitutes to aid cessation 2 group sessions	3-group design N = 70	1 month	13% across treatment groups No difference between groups	No
Walsh et al. 1999	Psychosocial education and oral exams 2 milligrams nicotine gum 1 group session/2 phone calls	16 colleges randomized N = 171 treatment N = 189 control	1 year	35% treatment 16% control	No (bogus pipeline)
Walsh et al. 2000	Psychosocial education Group treatment with oral exam	Cluster randomized control N = 516 treatment N = 569 control	1 year	27% for treatment schools 14% for control schools	No
Fisher et al. 2001	Cognitive-behavioral Interactive computer program Individual treatment	Median age: 20 years N = 50	6 weeks	44% (intent to treat)	No
D'Onofrio et al. 2002	Social influences theory Group sessions	Random assignment N = 36 pairs (4-H club)	1 year	Cessation rates not reported	No
Stotts et al. 2003	Behavioral treatment with pharmacology adjunct Group treatment/6 weeks	14- to 19-year-olds Randomized double-blind controlled trial N = 303	1 year	Active patch: 17.3% Placebo patch: 25% Control group: 11.4% Combined active and placebo patch: 21%	Yes
Gansky et al. 2005	Diffusion of innovation and cognitive-behavioral theory Peer-led educational and oral exam 2 sessions with oral exam	Colleges matched and randomized N = 702 control N = 883 treatment	1 year	36% treatment group 37% control group	No
Gala et al. 2008	Health belief model Interactive Web site Individual treatment	No control group College baseball players N = 18	1 month	8% at 1 month No control	No
Burton et al. 2009	Cognitive-behavioral Group treatment	Randomly assigned to group within school Grades 9–12 N = 42	4 months	45% at end of treatment 14.3% intent to treat Control = 0%	Yes

included discussion of the harmful effects of using smokeless tobacco, refusal skills, a strong peer opinion leader who encouraged cessation of smokeless tobacco, a meeting with parents and coaches to obtain their support and a self-help guide for quitting, a dental exam (with advice on cessation from a dentist and behavioral counseling from a dental hygienist), and booster sessions to prevent relapse. Cessation was observed in 27% of the athletes attending the intervention schools and 14% of athletes in the control schools (RI = 17.8%). The results were based on self-reports, but the authors did take saliva samples from participants who were told that the samples could be used to confirm the veracity of the self-reports (Evans et al. 1977; Murray and Perry 1987), even though there was no intention to test all of them (this is the "bogus-pipeline" procedure). The multiple intervention components, including the use of oral health screening exams, brief counseling, and peer-led educational sessions were successful in doubling the rate of quitting over that obtained by participants in control schools. Previous studies on cessation with adults have reported that oral exams can be a significant motivator for users of smokeless tobacco to quit (Severson and Hatsukami 1999; Ebbert et al. 2007).

A study similar to the one in rural California was designed to determine the efficacy of a college-based intervention that targeted athletes at 16 of the public colleges in California (Walsh et al. 1999). Permission was sought from participating schools to assess all varsity athletes at a team meeting early in the season to seek their participation. Players completed a questionnaire assessing their tobacco use, and the 16 colleges were matched on the prevalence of smokeless tobacco use within these institutions. The intervention schools had 171 participants, and the control schools (no intervention) had 189. The groups did not differ on demographics, characteristics of tobacco use, or motivation to quit.

The intervention was based on cognitive social learning theory (Bandura 1986). A dentist examined the oral soft tissues of each team member in the intervention schools, advised users to quit, pointed out tissue changes related to smokeless tobacco, showed photographs of facial disfigurement caused by oral cancer, provided a self-help cessation guide, and offered the smokeless users a single 15- to 20-minute session of individual counseling. Players who wanted to quit were offered 2 mg of nicotine gum to mitigate their withdrawal symptoms. Dental hygienists met with nonusers in small groups to discuss the quitting process and encourage them to support the efforts of the users to quit. Two follow-up telephone calls were made to users attempting to quit. On average, the observed self-reported rates of quitting were 34.5% for intervention schools and 15.9% for control schools (RI = 28%; $p < .008$) at 1-year follow-up. In addition to doubling the rate of quitting, the intervention led to significant reductions in reported use of smokeless tobacco for participants who did not quit. The use of the nicotine gum did not appear to be related to success in quitting.

A more recent study involved the direction by athletic trainers of a smokeless tobacco cessation program for collegiate baseball players (Gansky et al. 2005), who are known to be high users of snuff (Severson et al. 2005). This study involved 52 California colleges (27 intervention colleges and 25 control schools) in a stratified cluster RCT to prevent initiation of smokeless tobacco use and promote its cessation among baseball players. Schools were stratified by tertiles on the basis of their baseline prevalence of smokeless tobacco use. The intervention included videoconference training, newsletters, a screening exam for each player, a self-help guide for quitting, and a counseling session for interested players. Players who expressed an interest in quitting received follow-up support and referral. Student athletes who were peer leaders conducted a single 60-minute educational team meeting that included video and slides. The overall program reduced the initiation of smokeless tobacco use at 1-year follow-up, but there was no effect on cessation. The authors attributed the lack of effects to a small number of dependent users who were enrolled in the study.

In an earlier study, Chakravorty (1992) assigned 83 male users of smokeless tobacco (14–18 years of age, averaging 1.5 dips per day) to one of three conditions in a school setting: use of a nontobacco product composed of crushed mint leaves (mint snuff), use of nicotine chewing gum, or attendance at a lecture-only control condition. More than 90% of study participants were reached at posttest, and 13% of the participants in both intervention conditions were found to have quit using smokeless tobacco (confirmed by biochemical validation) compared with no quitters in the control group ($p < .05$). No long-term follow-up figures were reported.

A cessation study on smokeless tobacco among younger users (10–14 years of age) was implemented in 4-H clubs throughout California (D'Onofrio et al. 2002). Seventy-two clubs were matched and then assigned to the intervention (tobacco education delivered by volunteers in five successive monthly club meetings) or a no-treatment control condition. At the 1-year follow-up, results from 1,438 club members (77.6% of eligible participants) in the intervention condition revealed significantly improved knowledge regarding the harmful effects of using smokeless tobacco. Seven of the 24 program effects (including knowledge, attitudes, and intentions) were significant at 1-year follow-up; however, no significant differences were seen in use of smokeless tobacco between intervention and control clubs at the 2-year follow-up (Lynch and Bonnie 1994; D'Onofrio et al. 2002).

In another study, Stotts and associates (2003) examined whether adolescent users of smokeless tobacco (14–19 years of age) were aided in their cessation attempts by using nicotine patches and receiving several follow-up telephone counseling sessions. Three hundred students were assigned to one of three conditions: (1) counseling only (6 weeks of 50-minute age-relevant behavioral intervention classes based on NCI materials); (2) counseling plus an active nicotine patch and telephone support; and (3) counseling plus a placebo patch and telephone calls. Following completion of the class, students who were enrolled in the counseling-only condition were contacted at 2-week and 1-year assessment points, and participants in the two groups that received a patch (active or placebo) plus telephone support received seven 15-minute telephone calls that included "stage-based counseling" and a $5 gift certificate. Analysis of the 1-year follow-up indicated no differences between the two groups receiving a patch and telephone calls, but these conditions combined were more successful in encouraging cessation of smokeless tobacco (32.8%) than was the counseling-only condition (22.9%) (RI = 14.7%). This was a highly intensive intervention, however, and it is not clear whether the telephone calls or the patch (nicotine or placebo) produced the significant effect. The lack of effects for nicotine replacement (vs. placebo) is consistent with studies evaluating the efficacy of nicotine replacement for cessation of smokeless tobacco use among adults.

Burton and colleagues (2009) reported on a school-based study that compared two models of cessation for both smokers and users of smokeless tobacco in high schools. Students were randomly assigned to one of three groups: an addiction group, a psychosocial dependency group (both were treatment groups), or a control group. Sixteen schools in California and Illinois participated, with two treatment groups per school. Each of the 32 groups met for five sessions spaced over 1 month, with follow-up completed 4 months after the end of treatment. The majority of participants were smokers, but 8% of California's participants and 17.3% of Illinois' participants used smokeless tobacco only, and an additional 8% and 9% of participants, respectively, reported both smoking and current use of smokeless tobacco. The treatment groups shared some components of the intervention, and the sessions were divided between presentation of information and group discussion. Video clips were used to elicit discussion, and users of smokeless tobacco were encouraged to use oral substitutes. All participants received incentives for participation and attendance. On the basis of an ITT analysis and according to both verbal reports and biochemical verification of these self-reports, the smokeless tobacco users were more likely to be abstinent from tobacco use at the 4-month follow-up than were smokers. The validated rate of quitting at the 4-month follow-up was 14.3% for smokeless tobacco users, while the control group had no one reporting abstinence (RI = 14.3%).

Consistent with the studies discussed above, a Cochrane review of smokeless tobacco cessation by Ebbert and colleagues (2007) concluded that pharmacotherapy has not been shown to affect long-term abstinence in young adults and adults.

Young people are using computers, smartphones, and the Internet with increasing frequency, and these channels might provide a unique opportunity to engage youth in quitting. Fisher and colleagues (2001) reported on an interactive, computer-mediated intervention designed to help adolescents quit smokeless tobacco. This small pilot study was conducted with 50 high school students who used the cessation program Chewer's Choice; the study used a baseball field as an interface, which appealed to the mostly male users. Participants were given brief instructions before using the program on their own. The authors reported that 85% of the users had made an attempt to quit, and at the 6-week follow-up, 58% reported having quit all tobacco for at least 24 hours. Neither biochemical verification of self-report nor long-term follow-up was included.

Gala and colleagues (2008) reported on a pilot study in which an Internet-based program on cessation of smokeless tobacco use was evaluated using 17 baseball athletes attending California colleges. The interactive Web site appeared to be feasible, was acceptable to users, and resulted in a 26% self-reported reduction in use of smokeless tobacco at 1-month follow-up, but only one subject reported abstinence at this point.

The use of the Internet to deliver a cessation program to young users is being more fully evaluated in a current study supported by NCI; this randomized clinical trial involves the evaluation of a Web-based cessation program (My Last Dip 2010) offered to young users of smokeless tobacco between the ages of 15 and 24 years (Severson and Danaher 2009). The study will evaluate the efficacy of two Web sites designed for this population of young chewers. One Web condition will provide a text-based site designed to offer a proven cessation program as well as information and resources on quitting smokeless tobacco; the other site will offer a tailored and more interactive site that provides video and other engaging activities in addition to the opportunity to post to blogs. One unique feature of this study is that no parental consent is required to participate; previous research has shown that requiring consent from parents can be a significant deterrent to enrolling young people in cessation or prevention studies (Severson and Ary 1983; Severson and Biglan 1989; Gala et al. 2008).

Although no data are yet available on the efficacy of this program, a previous study with adult users of smokeless tobacco demonstrated the efficacy of providing cessation support through the Internet. That study compared an interactive, tailored, Web-based intervention (enhanced condition) with a more linear text-based Web site (basic condition) in a randomized trial with 2,523 adult users (Severson et al. 2008). The point prevalence of all tobacco use (smoking and smokeless use) at 3 months, 6 months, and both 3 and 6 months was 48%, 45%, and 34%, respectively. The researchers found that participants in the enhanced condition quit at significantly higher rates than those in the basic condition. The intent-to-treat analysis indicated quit rates of 12.6% among those in the enhanced condition and 7.9% for those in the basic condition ($p < 0.001$). With the use of complete case analysis, including those with data at all time points, it was found that abstinence was 41% in the enhanced condition and 21% in the basic condition ($p < 0.001$). Program use was significantly related to the outcomes as well as to attrition. The authors concluded that a tailored, interactive, Web-based cessation program may be a promising method of helping to stop the use of smokeless tobacco. It remains to be seen whether these encouraging results can be replicated with a younger population of users, but given the high use of the Internet by young people and the reach of such a program, a program designed specifically for young users could provide a low-cost alternative for promoting cessation.

Discussion Regarding Cessation of Smokeless Tobacco Use

Although many studies have been conducted on smoking cessation for youth, few have focused on smokeless tobacco in this age group. The relative lack of research on smokeless tobacco may be due to the far lower overall prevalence of using this product (vs. cigarette smoking), particularly in females. In addition, the use of chewing tobacco and snuff varies significantly by region and is viewed as a behavior confined mostly to rural and small-town areas in some parts of the country.

Most of the interventions for smokeless tobacco cessation have been based on multicomponent cognitive-behavioral interventions used in smoking cessation (Severson and Hatsukami 1999). Although the basic elements of these interventions apply equally well to smokeless tobacco, cessation of smokeless tobacco use has some unique aspects. The most obvious is the opportunity presented by oral exams to both motivate users to quit and to show them the direct effects of regular use of smokeless tobacco products. Not all users will have observable oral lesions, but it has been reported that 73% of snuff users will have identifiable oral lesions within 3 years of regular use. The lesions' severity and ratings are directly related to the amount of tobacco used weekly and the number of years of use (Little et al. 1992). The use of oral exams has been a key element of several interventions described above and, for this reason, it has been recommended that a dentist or dental hygienist be part of the intervention team. Other modifications of the interventions focused on smokeless tobacco users involve modified measures used for assessing dependence and use (Hatsukami and Severson 1999).

There is currently a need for innovative, validated, easily delivered, and low-cost interventions to facilitate cessation in smokeless tobacco users, an underserved population. The Internet and interactive computer-based cessation may offer channels of intervention that are particularly attractive to young users, but the data on the efficacy of these interventions are limited.

Although the literature is not extensive, the outcomes of several well-controlled studies suggest that young users can be effectively helped to quit smokeless tobacco. The focus on male athletes who use smokeless tobacco is encouraging, but studies are lacking that target other high-risk or high-use groups, including Alaska Natives, American Indians, and athletes who are involved in rodeo. The prevalence of smokeless tobacco use is very high in these groups, and specialized interventions may be needed to help them to quit.

Evidence Summary

There is a large, robust, and consistent evidence base that documents known effective strategies in reducing the initiation, prevalence, and intensity of smoking among youth and young adults. This science base includes studies, analyses, and evidence reviews of multicomponent programs, as well as studies on individual strategies and theories underlying these strategies. Sustained programs combining mass media campaigns; tax increases on tobacco products; regulatory initiatives such as those that ban advertising to youth, restrict youth access to tobacco, and establish smokefree public and workplace environments; and statewide, community-wide, and school-based programs and policies are effective in reducing the initiation, prevalence, and intensity of smoking among youth and young adults.

Several health behavior theories underlie interventions designed to prevent tobacco use among young people. TTI, which is consistent with other health behavior frameworks applied to tobacco use interventions, organizes factors that promote or deter health behaviors such as smoking along two dimensions—levels of causation and streams of influence—and into three interacting streams: intrapersonal, social/normative, and environmental (Flay et al. 2009). Variables that might influence smoking can be found at ultimate, distal, and proximal distances from actual smoking behaviors. TTI's metatheoretical framework not only provides a construct for understanding behavior, but also facilitates application of behavioral theory to specific interventions for preventing youth tobacco use.

In addition to examining theoretical bases for adolescent and young adult attitudes and behavior relative to tobacco use, this chapter reviews evidence for various approaches to preventing tobacco use within these populations. Since the release in 1994 of the first Surgeon General's report on preventing tobacco use among young people, the emphasis on environmental and policy approaches to tobacco control has increased. For example, the 2007 CDC Best Practices for Comprehensive Tobacco Control Programs strongly recommended comprehensive programs that include increasing the unit price of tobacco products and implementing smoking bans through policies, regulations, and laws, as well as other coordinated efforts that establish smokefree social norms. This focus on environmental and regulatory/policy approaches has also been supported by other reviews including the National Institutes of Health's State-of-the-Science Conference (NIH State-of-the-Science Panel 2006).

Evidence indicates that mass media campaigns can be one of the most effective strategies in changing social norms and preventing youth smoking. Studies cited in this chapter find that youth exposure to antismoking messages, particularly in mass media campaigns, leads to changes in, or increased salience of, attitudes, beliefs, and intentions relative to smoking as well as reduced smoking behavior (Popham et al. 1994; Sly et al. 2001b, 2005: Farrelly et al. 2002; White et al. 2003; Meshack et al. 2004; Niederdeppe et al. 2004; Emery et al. 2005). A significant number of population-based investigations on mass media campaigns has provided convincing evidence that these campaigns, even as stand-alone initiatives, can decrease youth smoking (Davis et al. 2007a; NCI 2008; Farrelly et al. 2009; Solomon et al. 2009). Evidence also suggests a dose-response relationship between exposure to antismoking media messages and reduced smoking behavior among youth and provides strong evidence that media ads designed for adults also decrease the prevalence of smoking among youth. Influential and successful campaigns contain a number of essential elements including optimized themes, appropriate emotional tone, appealing format, clear messages, intensity, and adequate repetition (Pechmann 2001; Siegel 2002; Farrelly et al. 2003a; Wakefield et al. 2003b,c; Schar et al. 2006; Richardson et al. 2007; Angus et al. 2008; NCI 2008). Mass media campaigns lacking these elements have been shown to be less effective. Nonetheless, the evidence is sufficient to conclude that there is a causal relationship between adequately funded antismoking media campaigns and a reduced prevalence of smoking among youth.

In addition to mass media campaigns a number of high-impact legislative or regulatory strategies have been proven to reduce tobacco use (USDHHS 2000b; Task Force on Community Preventive Services 2005; NIH State-of-the-Science Panel 2006; CDC 2007a,b). There is compelling evidence from CDC, as well as the reviewed research, that increasing tobacco prices is effective at lowering both smoking prevalence and consumption levels of tobacco products, especially by youth and young adults and other price-sensitive populations (Zaza et al. 2005). Federal, state, and local taxes that raise prices on tobacco products improve public health by reducing initiation, prevalence, and intensity of smoking among young people. Comprehensive reviews of the literature on the effect of price on tobacco consumption estimate a 3–5% reduction in overall cigarettes consumed as a result of a 10% increase in cigarette prices, and youth and young adults have proven to be even more responsive than adults to higher cigarette prices (USDHHS 2000b; Chaloupka and Warner 2000). Higher cigarette prices, including those resulting from increased excise taxes, have also been shown to increase cessation among young adults; one study (Tauras 2004) confirmed a positive relationship between cigarette prices and smoking cessation, with a 10% rise in price increasing successful cessation by young adults by an estimated 3.5%.

In the past decade, there has been significant growth in the number of states enacting comprehensive smoke-free policies for public places including worksites, bars, restaurants, schools, child care centers, and other public facilities. The number of colleges, universities, and technical schools adopting smokefree policies also has grown significantly in recent years. This movement toward clean indoor air has occurred in large part as a result of strong evidence of the serious health risks associated with secondhand smoke, but this chapter also examines the impact of these policies on youth smoking. Reviewing data from YRBS and NSDUH, McMullen and colleagues (2005) determined that the strength of clean indoor air laws was inversely related to the prevalence of smoking among youth. Smoke-free policies have also been found to contribute to cessation; using the longitudinal data on young adults from MTF, Tauras (2004) found that stronger restrictions on smoking in private worksites and public places increased the probability of smoking cessation among young adults. Further, as clean air policies change social norms relative to public smoking, there has been an increase in the number of private households establishing smokefree norms, restrictions that may be a powerful tool to reduce youth smoking in the future (IARC 2009; Emory et al. 2010).

With the enactment of the *Family Smoking Prevention and Tobacco Control Act* in 2009, FDA was given regulatory authority and responsibility over the manufacture, marketing, and distribution of tobacco products. The 2009 law required that U.S. cigarette packs contain larger pictorial labels covering 50% of the front and back of the packs instead of small text-only health warning labels. This requirement, which is currently under legal review, also applies to a requirement for health warnings to cover 20% of advertising materials for tobacco products. Smokeless tobacco products are now required to have larger text warnings covering 30% of the two main surfaces (and 20% of advertising). Data in this chapter include studies examining the effects of such tobacco product labeling; these data conclude that small text-only health warning labels have limited impact on youth and young adults (Fischer et al. 1989; Brubaker and Mitby 1990; Krugman et al. 1994; Crawford et al. 2002; Bonnie et al. 2007). Larger warnings and warnings that include pictures that elicit strong emotional reactions are significantly more effective at discouraging tobacco use (Environics Research Group 1999; Nilsson 1999; Bonnie et al. 2007; Hammond 2011).

Regulations under the 2009 *Family Smoking Prevention and Tobacco Control Act* also continued a progression of legislative and regulatory initiatives that have reduced youth access to tobacco products; for example, the act bans self-service or vending machine sale of cigarettes and smokeless tobacco except in facilities that persons under 18 years of age are prohibited from entering. Other legislative initiatives have included the 1992 Synar Amendment (*ADAMHA Reorganization Act* 1992), which required states to restrict youth access to tobacco products and to enforce the restrictions through compliance checks, and state and local laws prohibiting underage possession, use, and purchase of tobacco products. Although data are mixed, a Cochrane review concluded that policies to limit youth access and enforcement of these policies can improve the compliance of retailers, and the prevalence of smoking will be affected if the commercial supply is sufficiently restricted through these means (Stead and Lancaster 2005). The Community Preventive Task Force concluded that community mobilization combined with additional interventions, such as stronger laws directed at retailers, active enforcement of retailer sales laws, and retailer education with reinforcement are recommended (Task Force on Community Preventive Services 2005). Youth are known to obtain tobacco products both through commercial means and through social means—buying, borrowing, or stealing them from other youth and adults. Accordingly, even well-enforced commercial restrictions on youth access may not adequately reduce the supply of tobacco products available to young people (Forster et al. 1998; Altman et al. 1999; DiFranza and Coleman 2001; Ling et al. 2002).

One policy initiative that has been shown to reduce youth tobacco consumption is the use of bans on tobacco product advertising targeted to youth. After the U.S. ban on TV and radio tobacco advertising went into effect in 1971, additional advertising restrictions were included in the 1998 Master Settlement Agreement, which addressed outdoor advertising and advertising that targeted youth. The *Family Smoking Prevention and Tobacco Control Act* directed FDA to promulgate rules banning a variety of other promotional activities traditionally used by the tobacco industry (e.g., sponsorship of music and sports events, sale and distribution of tobacco-branded products such as clothing and accessories, etc.) that are especially appealing to youth and young adults. Evidence cited in this chapter from a broad range of studies has concluded that bans on cigarette advertising, especially if the bans are comprehensive rather than partial, reduce youth smoking (Saffer and Chaloupka 2000; Lancaster and Lancaster 2003; Iwasaki et al. 2006; NCI 2008).

Numerous studies over many years have consistently concluded that comprehensive state tobacco control programs that include a range of coordinated and complementary strategies have been effective at not only reducing tobacco use by youth and young adults but also have resulted in overall reductions in smoking prevalence and concomitant decreases in state spending on tobacco-related health care (USDHHS 2000b; Sly et al. 2001a; Rigotti et al. 2002; Soldz et al. 2002; Niederdeppe et al. 2004; Pierce et al. 2005; Bonnie et al. 2007; Lightwood et al. 2008; NCI 2008; Lightwood and Glantz 2011). These comprehensive state tobacco control programs combine the strategies found to be most effective individually; these include mass media campaigns, increasing the price of tobacco products, establishing smokefree policies, and other programmatic and policy interventions that influence social norms, systems, and networks (CDC 2007a,b). Evidence on the efficacy of community-based tobacco control programs, which have combined a more limited range of policy and environmental strategies to reduce youth tobacco, has been less consistent. A Cochrane review of 17 studies that examined such initiatives (Sowden and Stead 2003) found only limited support for the effectiveness of these interventions in preventing the uptake of smoking by young people. Later studies have also been inconsistent, with some community programs having little or no effect on youth tobacco use (Bowen et al. 2003) and some resulting in youth smoking declines (Ross et al. 2006).

Evidence on school-based programs points to short-term results for programs based on the social influences model using interactive delivery methods, and teaching refusal skills, with some school-based prevention programs, also demonstrating longer-term outcomes. A thorough systematic review of school-based smoking prevention studies to 2006 by Thomas and Perera concluded that while information-only school programs had limited effect on smoking prevention, the majority of programs that addressed social influences on tobacco use demonstrated positive effects. However, this review also concluded that there was little evidence of the long-term effectiveness of school-based programs to prevent smoking. Two meta-analyses (Tobler et al. 2000; Hwang et al. 2004) provided clear directions on the types of programs they found most effective: those that are interactive, address social influences, include components on intentions not to use tobacco, use peer leaders, add community components, and include life skills practice. Another examination of evidence reviews and meta-analyses (Flay 2009a) concluded that school-based programs to prevent smoking can have significant long-term effects if they are interactive and are based on social influences or social skills, contain at least 15 sessions including some up to at least ninth grade, and have produced substantial short-term effects. Newer studies included in Table 6.9 and 6.10 assess the influence on youth of various tobacco control interventions including school-based programs alone and in combination with other strategies. Overall, evidence cited in this chapter shows that several existing school-based programs have demonstrated effectiveness in the short term and that selected programs have demonstrated long-term effectiveness. As is the case with other strategies to prevent and reduce youth tobacco use, school-based programs produce larger and more sustained effects when they are implemented in combination with other initiatives such as mass media campaigns, family programs, and state and community programs.

Although some specific programs, stand-alone elements, programmatic approaches, and strategies with narrower focus have been proven ineffective in addressing youth tobacco use, the preponderance of evidence suggests that there are multiple intervention strategies and approaches that are effective at preventing smoking, reducing tobacco consumption, and assisting cessation within the youth and young adult populations. Further, the evidence indicates that sustained programs combining mass media campaigns; price increases including those that result from tax increases; regulatory initiatives such as those that ban advertising to youth, restrictions on youth access to tobacco, and establishment of smokefree public and workplace environments; and statewide, community-wide, and school-based programs and policies are effective in reducing the initiation, prevalence, and intensity of smoking among youth and young adults.

Conclusions

1. The evidence is sufficient to conclude that mass media campaigns, comprehensive community programs, and comprehensive statewide tobacco control programs can prevent the initiation of tobacco use and reduce its prevalence among youth.

2. The evidence is sufficient to conclude that increases in cigarette prices reduce the initiation, prevalence, and intensity of smoking among youth and young adults.

3. The evidence is sufficient to conclude that school-based programs with evidence of effectiveness, containing specific components, can produce at least short-term effects and reduce the prevalence of tobacco use among school-aged youth.

References

Ackard DM, Neumark-Sztainer D. Health care information sources for adolescents: age and gender differences on use, concerns, and needs. *Journal of Adolescent Health* 2001;29(3):170–6.

Action on Smoking and Health. *Tobacco Product Warnings: A Survey of Effectiveness*. London: Action on Smoking and Health, 1998.

ADAMHA Reorganization Act, Public Law 102-321, 42 *U.S. Code* § 300x-26 (1992).

Adelman WP, Duggan AK, Hauptman P, Joffe A. Effectiveness of a high school smoking cessation program. *Pediatrics* 2001;107(4):E50.

Aftab M, Kolben D, Lurie P. International cigarette labeling practices. *Tobacco Control* 1999;8(4):368–72.

AGB Spectrum Research. *Testing the Positions of Health Warnings on Cigarette Packages.* Prepared for Health Promotion Programme, Department of Health, New Zealand, 1987; <http://legacy.library.ucsf.edu/tid/lel70g00>.

Aguirre-Molina M, Gorman DM. The Perth Amboy Community Partnership for Youth: assessing its effects at the environmental and individual levels of analysis. *International Quarterly of Community Health Education* 1995;15(4):363–78.

Ajzen I. The theory of planned behavior. *Organizational Behavior and Human Decision Processes* 1991; 50(2):179–211.

Alesci NL, Forster JL, Blaine T. Smoking visibility, perceived acceptability, and frequency in various locations among youth and adults. *Preventive Medicine* 2003;36(3):272–81.

Alesci NL, Forster JL, Erickson DJ. Did youth smoking behaviors change before and after the shutdown of Minnesota Youth Tobacco Prevention Initiative? *Nicotine & Tobacco Research* 2009;11(10):1196–204.

Alexander HM, Callcott R, Dobson AJ, Hardes GR, Lloyd DM, O'Connell DL, Leeder SR. Cigarette smoking and drug use in schoolchildren. IV: factors associated with changes in smoking behaviour. *International Journal of Epidemiology* 1983;12(1):59-66.

Altman DG, Feighery EC. Future directions for youth empowerment: commentary on application of youth empowerment theory to tobacco control. *Health Education & Behavior* 2004;31(5):641–7.

Altman DG, Wheelis AY, McFarlane M, Lee H, Fortmann SP. The relationship between tobacco access and use among adolescents: a four community study. *Social Science & Medicine* 1999;48(6):759–75.

American Medical Association. *Guidelines for Adolescent Preventive Services (GAPS): Recommendations Monograph*. Chicago: American Medical Association, 1997.

American Nonsmokers' Rights Foundation. Municipalities with Local 100% Smokefree Laws, 2011a; <http://www.no-smoke.org/pdf/100ordlisttabs.pdf>; accessed: July 15, 2011.

American Nonsmokers' Rights Foundation. Summary of 100% Smokefree State Laws and Population Protected by 100% US Smokefree Laws, 2011b; <http://www.no-smoke.org/pdf/SummaryUSPopList.pdf>; accessed: May 24, 2011.

American Nonsmokers' Rights Foundation. United States 100% Smokefree Air Laws, 2011c; <http://www.no-smoke.org/pdf/100Map.pdf>; accessed: July 15, 2011.

American Nonsmokers' Rights Foundation. U.S. Colleges and Universities with Smokefree Air Policies, 2011d; <http://www.no-smoke.org/pdf/smokefreecollegesuniversities.pdf>; accessed: May 24, 2011.

Andrews JA, Severson HH, Lichtenstein E, Gordon JS, Barckley MF. Evaluation of a dental office tobacco cessation program: effects on smokeless tobacco use. *Annals of Behavioral Medicine* 1999;21(1):48–53.

Angstman S, Patten CA, Renner CC, Simon A, Thomas JL, Hurt RD, Schroeder DR, Decker PA, Offord KP. Tobacco and other substance use among Alaska Native youth in western Alaska. *American Journal of Health Behavior* 2007;31(3):249–60.

Angus K, Brown A, Hastings G. The effect of tobacco control mass media campaigns, counter-advertising, and other related community interventions on youth tobacco use. Background paper for the WHO Tobacco Free Initiative Global Consultation on Effective Youth Tobacco Control Policy Interventions. Stirling (Scotland): University of Stirling, Institute for Social Marketing, Centre for Tobacco Control Research, 2008.

Aos S, Lieb R, Mayfield J, Miller M, Pennucci A. *Benefits and Costs of Prevention and Early Intervention Programs for Youth*. Olympia (WA): Washington State Institute for Public Policy, 2004.

Ariza C, Nebot M, Tomás Z, Giménez E, Valmayor S, Tarilonte V, De Vries H. Longitudinal effects of the European smoking prevention framework approach (ESFA) project in Spanish adolescents. *European Journal of Public Health* 2008;18(5):491–7.

Armstrong BK, de Klerk NH, Shean RE, Dunn DA, Dolin PJ. Influence of education and advertising on the uptake of smoking by children. *Medical Journal of Australia* 1990;152(3):117–24.

Ary DV, Biglan A, Glasgow R, Zoref L, Black C, Ochs L, Severson H, Kelly R, Weissman W, Lichtenstein E, et al. The efficacy of social-influence prevention programs versus "standard care": are new initiatives needed? *Journal of Behavioral Medicine* 1990;13(3):281–96.

Asumda F, Jordan L. Minority youth access to tobacco: a neighborhood analysis of underage tobacco sales. *Health Place* 2009;15(1):140–7.

Audrey S, Holliday J, Campbell R. It's good to talk: adolescent perspectives of an informal, peer-led intervention to reduce smoking. *Social Science & Medicine* 2006;63(2):320–34.

Aveyard P, Cheng KK, Almond J, Sherratt E, Lancashire R, Lawrence T, Griffin C, Evans O. Cluster randomised controlled trial of expert system based on the transtheoretical ("stages of change") model for smoking prevention and cessation in schools. *BMJ (British Medical Journal)* 1999;319(7215):948–53.

Aveyard P, Sherratt E, Almond J, Lawrence T, Lancashire R, Griffin C, Cheng KK. The change-in-stage and updated smoking status results from a cluster-randomized trial of smoking prevention and cessation using the transtheoretical model among British adolescents. *Preventive Medicine* 2001;33(4):313–24.

Backinger CL, Fagan P, Matthews E, Grana R. Adolescent and young adult tobacco prevention and cessation: current status and future directions. *Tobacco Control* 2003;12(Suppl 4):iv46–iv53.

Balanced Budget Act of 1997, Public Law 105-33, 111 *U.S. Statutes at Large* 251.

Balbach ED, Glantz SA. Tobacco control advocates must demand high-quality media campaigns: the California experience. *Tobacco Control* 1998;7(4):397–408.

Balbach ED, Traynor MP, Glantz SA. The implementation of California's tobacco tax initiative: the critical role of outsider strategies in protecting proposition 99. *Journal of Health Politics, Policy and Law* 2000;25(4): 689–715.

Ball-Rokeach SJ. A theory of media power and a theory of media use: different stories, questions, and ways of thinking. *Mass Communication and Society* 1998; 1(1–2):5–40.

Bandura A. *Social Foundations of Thought and Action: A Social Cognitive Theory*. Englewood Cliffs (NJ): Prentice-Hall, 1986.

Bandura A. Health promotion by social cognitive means. *Health Education & Behavior* 2004;31(2):143–64.

Barnett TA, Gauvin L, Lambert M, O'Loughlin J, Paradis G, McGrath JJ. The influence of school smoking policies on student tobacco use. *Archives of Pediatrics & Adolescent Medicine* 2007;161(9):842–8.

Baskerville B, Hotte A, Dunkley G. *Evaluation of a High School Quit and Win Smoking Cessation Program*. Ottawa (Canada): University of Ottawa, Community Health Research Unit, 1993. CHRU Publication No. M93-4.

Bauer UE, Johnson TM, Hopkins RS, Brooks RG. Changes in youth cigarette use and intentions following implementation of a tobacco control program: findings from the Florida Youth Tobacco Survey, 1998–2000. *JAMA: the Journal of the American Medical Association* 2000;284(6):723–8.

Bauman KE, Brown JD, Bryan ES, Fisher LA, Padgett CA, Sweeney JM. Three mass media campaigns to prevent adolescent cigarette smoking. *Preventive Medicine* 1988;17(5):510–30.

Bauman KE, Ennett ST, Foshee VA, Pemberton M, King TS, Koch GG. Influence of a family-directed program on adolescent cigarette and alcohol cessation. *Prevention Science* 2000;1(4):227–37.

Bauman KE, Ennett ST, Foshee VA, Pemberton M, King TS, Koch GG. Influence of a family program on adolescent smoking and drinking prevalence. *Prevention Science* 2002;3(1):35–42.

Bauman KE, Foshee VA, Ennett ST, Hicks K, Pemberton M. Family Matters: a family-directed program designed to prevent adolescent tobacco and alcohol use. *Health Promotion Practice* 2001;2(1):81–96.

Bauman KE, LaPrelle J, Brown JD, Koch GG, Padgett CA. The influence of three mass media campaigns on variables related to adolescent cigarette smoking: results of a field experiment. *American Journal of Public Health* 1991;81(5):597–604.

Baumeister RF, Vohs KD, DeWall CN, Zhang L. How emotion shapes behavior: feedback, anticipation, and reflection, rather than direct causation. *Personality and Social Psychology Review* 2007;11(2):167–203.

Baxter AP, Milner PC, Hawkins S, Leaf M, Simpson C, Wilson KV, Owen T, Higginbottom G, Nicholl J, Cooper N. The impact of heart health promotion on coronary heart disease lifestyle risk factors in schoolchildren: lessons learnt from a community-based project. *Public Health* 1997;111(4):231–7.

Beaglehole R, Brough D, Harding W, Eyles E. A controlled smoking intervention programme in secondary schools. *New Zealand Medical Journal* 1978;87(610):278–80.

Beattie A. Health education and the science teacher: invitation to a debate. *Education and Health* 1984;2(1): 9–16.

Beaudoin CE. Exploring antismoking ads: appeals, themes, and consequences. *Journal of Health Communication* 2002;7(2):123–37.

Benuck I, Gidding SS, Binns HJ. Identification of adolescent tobacco users in a pediatric practice. *Archives of Pediatrics & Adolescent Medicine* 2001;155(1):32–5.

Bergamaschi A, Gambi A, Gentilini F, Monti C, Stampi S, Zanetti F. Tobacco smoking among high school students in Romagna (Italy) and evaluation of a prevention campaign. *Substance Use & Misuse* 2000;35(9):1277–95.

Berndt TJ. Developmental changes in conformity to peers and parents. *Developmental Psychology* 1979;15(6):608–16.

Best JA, Flay BR, Towson SM, Ryan KB, Perry CL, Brown KS, Kersell MW, D'Avernas JR. Smoking prevention and the concept of risk. *Journal of Applied Social Psychology* 1984;14(3):257–73.

Biener L. Anti-tobacco advertisements by Massachusetts and Philip Morris: what teenagers think. *Tobacco Control* 2002;11(Suppl 2):ii43–ii46.

Biener L, Ji M, Gilpin EA, Albers AB. The impact of emotional tone, message, and broadcast parameters in youth anti-smoking advertisements. *Journal of Health Communication* 2004;9(3):259–74.

Biener L, McCallum-Keeler G, Nyman AL. Adults' response to Massachusetts anti-tobacco television advertisements: impact of viewer and advertisement characteristics. *Tobacco Control* 2000;9(4):401–7.

Biener L, Wakefield M, Shiner CM, Siegel M. How broadcast volume and emotional content affect youth recall of anti-tobacco advertising. *American Journal of Preventive Medicine* 2008;35(1):14–9.

Biglan A, Ary D, Koehn V, Levings D, Smith S, Wright Z, James L, Henderson J. Mobilizing positive reinforcement in communities to reduce youth access to tobacco. *American Journal of Community Psychology* 1996;24(5):625–38.

Biglan A, Ary D, Smolkowski K, Duncan T, Black C. A randomised controlled trial of a community intervention to prevent adolescent tobacco use. *Tobacco Control* 2000a;9(1):24–32.

Biglan A, Ary D, Wagenaar AC. The value of interrupted time-series experiments for community intervention research. *Prevention Science* 2000b;1(1):31–49.

Biglan A, Glasgow R, Ary D, Thompson R, Severson H, Lichtenstein E, Weissman W, Faller C, Gallison C. How generalizable are the effects of smoking prevention programs: refusal skills training and parent messages in a teacher-administered program. *Journal of Behavioral Medicine* 1987;10(6):613–28.

Biglan A, Henderson J, Humphreys D, Yasui M, Whisman R, Black C, James L. Mobilising positive reinforcement to reduce youth access to tobacco. *Tobacco Control* 1995;4(1):42–8.

Biglan A, Lichtenstein E. A behavior-analytic approach to smoking acquisition: some recent findings. *Journal of Applied Social Psychology* 1984;14(3):207–23.

Black DR, Tobler NS, Sciacca JP. Peer helping/involvement: an efficacious way to meet the challenge of reducing alcohol, tobacco, and other drug use among youth? *Journal of School Health* 1998;68(3):87–93.

Blair MH. An empirical investigation of advertising wearin and wearout. *Journal of Advertising Research* 2000;40(6):95–100.

Bleakley A, Hennessy M, Fishbein M, Jordan A. Using the integrative model to explain how exposure to sexual media content influences adolescent sexual behavior. *Health Education and Behavior* 2011;38(5):530–40.

Bloor M, Frankland J, Parry Langdon N, Robinson M, Allerston S, Catherine A, Cooper L, Gibbs L, Gibbs N, Hamilton-Kirkwood L, et al. A controlled evaluation of an intensive, peer-led, schools-based, anti-smoking programme. *Health Education Journal* 1999;58(1):17–25.

Blum RW, Beuhring T, Wunderlich M, Resnick MD. Don't ask, they won't tell: the quality of adolescent health screening in five practice settings. *American Journal of Public Health* 1996;86(12):1767–72.

Blumenfeld K. *Smoke-free Vehicles When Children are Present*. Summit (NJ): New Jersey GASP (Global Advisors on Smokefree Policy), 2008.

Bonnie RJ, Stratton K, Wallace RB, editors. *Ending the Tobacco Problem: A Blueprint for the Nation*. Washington: National Academies Press, 2007.

Borland R, Hill D. Initial impact of the new Australian tobacco health warnings on knowledge and beliefs. *Tobacco Control* 1997a;6(4):317–25.

Borland R, Hill D. The path to Australia's tobacco health warnings. *Addiction* 1997b;92(9):1151–7.

Bornstein RF. Exposure and affect: overview and meta-analysis of research, 1968–1987. *Psychological Bulletin* 1989;106(2):265–89.

Botvin GJ, Baker E, Dusenbury L, Botvin EM, Diaz T. Long-term follow-up results of a randomized drug abuse prevention trial in a white middle-class population. *JAMA: the Journal of the American Medical Association* 1995a;273(14):1106–12.

Botvin GJ, Baker E, Dusenbury L, Tortu S, Botvin EM. Preventing adolescent drug abuse through a multimodal cognitive-behavioral approach: results of a 3-year study. *Journal of Consulting and Clinical Psychology* 1990a;58(4):437–46.

Botvin GJ, Baker E, Filazzola AD, Botvin EM. A cognitive-behavioral approach to substance abuse prevention: one-year follow-up. *Addictive Behaviors* 1990b;15(1):47–63.

Botvin GJ, Baker E, Renick NL, Filazzola AD, Botvin EM. A cognitive-behavioral approach to substance-abuse prevention. *Addictive Behaviors* 1984;9(2):137–47.

Botvin GJ, Dusenbury L, Baker E, James-Ortiz S, Botvin EM. Smoking prevention among urban minority youth: assessing effects on outcome and mediating variables. *Health Psychology* 1992;11(5):290–9.

Botvin GJ, Dusenbury L, Baker E, James-Ortiz S, Kerner J. A skills training approach to smoking prevention among Hispanic youth. *Journal of Behavioral Medicine* 1989;12(3):279–96.

Botvin GJ, Griffin KW, Diaz T, Miller N, Ifill-Williams M. Smoking initiation and escalation in early adolescent girls: one-year follow-up of a school-based prevention intervention for minority youth. *Journal of the American Medical Women's Association* 1999;54(3):139–43, 152.

Botvin GJ, Schinke SP, Epstein JA, Diaz T, Botvin EM. Effectiveness of culturally focused and generic skills training approaches to alcohol and drug abuse prevention among minority adolescents: two-year follow-up results. *Psychology of Addictive Behaviors* 1995b;9(3):183–94.

Bowen DJ, Orlandi MA, Lichtenstein E, Cummings KM, Hyland A. Intervention effects on youth tobacco use in the community intervention trial (COMMIT). *Journal of Epidemiology and Community Health* 2003;57(2):159–60.

Boyd GM, Glover ED. Smokeless tobacco use by youth in the U.S. *Journal of School Health* 1989;59(5):189–94.

Boyd RG, Seldon BJ. The fleeting effect of advertising: empirical evidence from a case study. *Economics Letters* 1990;34(4):375–9.

Brannon BR, Dent CW, Flay BR, Smith G, Sussman S, Pentz MA, Johnson CA, Hansen WB. The television, school, and family project. V: the impact of curriculum delivery format on program acceptance. *Preventive Medicine* 1989;18(4):492–502.

BRC Marketing & Social Research. *Smoking Health Warnings Study: Optimising Smoking Health Warnings, Stage 2 – Text Graphics, Size and Colour Testing.* Wellington (New Zealand): BRC Marketing & Social Research, 2004.

Brindis CD, Lee PR. Illness, adolescents conceptualization. In: Lerner RM, Petersen AC, Brooks-Gunn J, editors. *Encyclopedia of Adolescence*. Vol. I. New York: Garland Publishing, 1991:534–40.

Briton NJ, Clark TW, Baker AK, Posner B, Soldz S, Krakow M. *Adolescent Tobacco Use in Massachusetts; Trends Among Public School Students 1984–1996.* Boston: Health and Addictions Research, 1997.

Bronfenbrenner U. Toward an experimental ecology of human development. *American Psychologist* 1977; 32(7):513–31.

Bronfenbrenner U. *The Ecology of Human Development: Experiments by Nature and Design*. Cambridge (MA): Harvard University Press, 1979.

Bronfenbrenner U. Ecology of the family as a context for human development: research perspectives. *Developmental Psychology* 1986;22(6):723–42.

Brown BB, Clasen DR, Eicher SA. Perceptions of peer pressure, peer conformity dispositions, and self-reported behavior among adolescents. *Developmental Psychology* 1986;22(4):521–30.

Brown RA, Ramsey SE, Strong DR, Myers MG, Kahler CW, Lejuez CW, Niaura R, Pallonen UE, Kazura AN, Goldstein MG, et al. Effects of motivational interviewing on smoking cessation in adolescents with psychiatric disorders. *Tobacco Control* 2003;12(Suppl 4):iv3–iv10.

Brown S, Birch D, Thyagaraj S, Teufel J, Phillips C. Effects of a single-lesson tobacco prevention curriculum on knowledge, skill identification and smoking intention. *Journal of Drug Education* 2007;37(1):55–69.

Brubaker RG, Mitby SK. Health-risk warning labels on smokeless tobacco products: are they effective? *Addictive Behaviors* 1990;15(2):115–8.

Bruvold WH. A meta-analysis of adolescent smoking prevention programs. *American Journal of Public Health* 1993;83(6):872–80.

Buckelew SM, Adams SH, Irwin CE Jr, Gee S, Ozer EM. Increasing clinician self-efficacy for screening and counseling adolescents for risky health behaviors: results of an intervention. *Journal of Adolescent Health* 2008;43(2):198–200.

Burns DM. Positive evidence on effectiveness of selected smoking prevention programs in the United States. *Journal of the National Cancer Institute Monographs* 1992;(12):17–20.

Burt RD, Peterson AV Jr. Smoking cessation among high school seniors. *Preventive Medicine* 1998;27(3): 319–27.

Burton D, Chakravorty B, Weeks K, Flay BR, Dent C, Stacy A, Sussman S. Outcome of a tobacco cessation randomized trial with high-school students. *Substance Use & Misuse* 2009;44(7):965–80.

Bush PJ, Zuckerman AE, Taggart VS, Theiss PK, Peleg EO, Smith SA. Cardiovascular risk factor prevention in black school children: the "Know Your Body" evaluation project. *Health Education Quarterly* 1989a;16(2): 215–27.

Bush PJ, Zuckerman AE, Theiss PK, Taggart VS, Horowitz C, Sheridan MJ, Walter HJ. Cardiovascular risk factor prevention in black schoolchildren: two-year results of the "Know Your Body" program. *American Journal of Epidemiology* 1989b;129(3):466–82.

Buttross LS, Kastner JW. A brief review of adolescents and tobacco: what we know and don't know. *American Journal of the Medical Sciences* 2003;326(4):235–7.

Cacioppo JT, Gardner WL. Emotion. *Annual Review of Psychology* 1999;50:191–214.

Cai Y, Zhao C, Wong SU, Zhang L, Lim SK. Laser acupuncture for adolescent smokers—a randomized double-blind controlled trial. *American Journal of Chinese Medicine* 2000;28(3/4):443–9.

Cameron R, Brown KS, Best JA, Pelkman CL, Madill CL, Manske SR, Payne ME. Effectiveness of a social influences smoking prevention program as a function of provider type, training method, and school risk. *American Journal of Public Health* 1999;89(12):1827–31.

Campaign for Tobacco-Free Kids. *A Broken Promise to Our Children: The 1998 State Tobacco Settlement 13 Years Later*. Washington: Campaign for Tobacco-Free Kids, American Heart Association, American Cancer Society, Cancer Action Network, American Lung Association, and Robert Wood Johnson Foundation, 2011a; http://www.tobaccofreekids.org/what_we_do/state_local/tobacco_settlement/; accessed: December 8, 2011.

Campaign for Tobacco Free Kids. Top combined state-local cigarette tax rates (state plus county plus city) [fact sheet], October 7, 2011b; <http://www.tobaccofreekids.org/research/factsheets/pdf/0267.pdf>; accessed: November 7, 2011.

Campbell R, Starkey F, Holliday J, Audrey S, Bloor M, Parry-Langdon N, Hughes R, Moore L. An informal school-based peer-led intervention for smoking prevention in adolescence (ASSIST): a cluster randomised trial. *Lancet* 2008;371(9624):1595–602.

Capehart T. The Changing Tobacco User's Dollar. Electronic Outlook Report from the Economic Research Service. Washington: U.S. Department of Agriculture, 2004; <http://www.ers.usda.gov/publications/tbs/OCT04/tbs25701/tbs25701.pdf>; accessed: June 10, 2009.

Carpenter C, Cook PJ. Cigarette taxes and youth smoking: new evidence from national, state, and local Youth Risk Behavior Surveys. *Journal of Health Economics* 2008;27(2):287–99.

Catalano RF, Berglund ML, Ryan JAM, Lonczak HS, Hawkins JD. Positive youth development in the United States: research findings on evaluations of positive youth development programs. *Annals of the American Academy of Political and Social Science* 2004; 591(1):98–124.

Caulkins JP, Pacula RL, Paddock S, Chiesa J. What we can—and cannot—expect from school-based drug prevention. *Drug and Alcohol Review* 2004;23(1):79–87.

Caulkins JP, Rydell CP, Everingham SS, Chiesa J, Bushway S. *An Ounce of Prevention, a Pound of Uncertainty: The Cost-Effectiveness of School-Based Drug Prevention Programs.* Santa Monica (CA): RAND, 1999. Publication No. MR-923-RWJ.

Cavalcante TM. *Labeling and Packaging in Brazil*. Geneva: World Health Organization, 2003.

Cawley J, Markowitz S, Tauras J. Lighting up and slimming down: the effects of body weight and cigarette prices on adolescent smoking initiation. *Journal of Health Economics* 2004;23(2):293–311.

Cawley J, Markowitz S, Tauras J. Obesity, cigarette prices, youth access laws, and adolescent smoking initiation. *Eastern Economic Journal* 2006;32(1):149–70.

Cecil H, Evans RI, Stanley MA. Perceived believability among adolescents of health warning labels on cigarette packs. *Journal of Applied Social Psychology* 1996; 26(6):502–19.

Center for Substance Abuse Prevention. *Preventing Substance Abuse Among Children and Adolescents: Family-Centered Approaches. Reference Guide.* Prevention Enhancement Protocols System Series. Washington: U.S. Government Printing Office, 1998. DHHS Publication No. (SMA) 3223-FY98.

Centers for Disease Control and Prevention. School policies and programs on smoking and health—United States, 1988. *Morbidity and Mortality Weekly Report* 1989;38(12):202–3.

Centers for Disease Control and Prevention. Minors' access to tobacco—Missouri, 1992, and Texas, 1993. *Morbidity and Mortality Weekly Report* 1993;42(7):125–8.

Centers for Disease Control and Prevention. Cigarette smoking among high school students—11 states, 1991–1997. *Morbidity and Mortality Weekly Report* 1999a;48(31):686–92.

Centers for Disease Control and Prevention. Tobacco use among middle and high school students—Florida, 1998 and 1999. *Morbidity and Mortality Weekly Report* 1999b;48(12):248–53.

Centers for Disease Control and Prevention. Effectiveness of school-based programs as a component of a statewide tobacco control initiative—Oregon 1999–2000. *Morbidity and Mortality Weekly Report* 2001;50(31):663–6.

Centers for Disease Control and Prevention. Usual sources of cigarettes for middle and high school students—Texas, 1998–1999. *Morbidity and Mortality Weekly Report* 2002;51(40):900–1.

Centers for Disease Control and Prevention. *Promising Practices in Chronic Disease Prevention and Control: A Public Health Framework for Action*. Atlanta (GA): U.S. Department of Health and Human Services, Centers for Disease Control and Prevention, National Center for Chronic Disease Prevention and Health Promotion, 2003; <http://www.hpclearinghouse.ca/downloads/Promising_Practices_cdc.pdf>; accessed: November 30, 2011.

Centers for Disease Control and Prevention. *Addressing Tobacco Use and Addiction*. Atlanta, (GA): U.S. Department of Health and Human Services, Centers for Disease Control and Prevention, Division of Adolescent and School Health, 2007a.

Centers for Disease Control and Prevention. *Best Practices for Comprehensive Tobacco Control Programs—2007.* Atlanta (GA): U.S. Department of Health and Human Services, Centers for Disease Control and Prevention, National Center for Chronic Disease Prevention and Health Promotion, Office on Smoking and Health, 2007b.

Centers for Disease Control and Prevention. Decline in smoking prevalence—New York City, 2002–2006. *Morbidity and Mortality Weekly Report* 2007c;56(4):604–8.

Centers for Disease Control and Prevention. Disparities in secondhand smoke exposure—United States, 1988–1994 and 1999–2004. *Morbidity and Mortality Weekly Report* 2008a;57(27):744–7.

Centers for Disease Control and Prevention. *Guidelines for School Health Programs to Prevent Tobacco Use: Summary*. Atlanta (GA): U.S. Department of Health and Human Services, Centers for Disease Control and Prevention, Division of Adolescent and School Health, National Center for Chronic Disease Prevention and Health Promotion, 2008b.

Centers for Disease Control and Prevention. State Tobacco Activities Tracking and Evaluation (STATE) System; 2007 Tobacco Control Highlights Minnesota. Atlanta (GA): Centers for Disease Control and Prevention, 2008c; <http://apps.nccd.cdc.gov/statesystem/statehilite.aspx>; accessed: May 7, 2009.

Centers for Disease Control and Prevention. Registries of Programs Effective in Reducing Youth Risk Behaviors, February 2009; <http://www.cdc.gov/HealthyYouth/AdolescentHealth/registries.htm>; accessed: March 16, 2010.

Centers for Disease Control and Prevention. Cigarette package health warnings and interest in quitting smoking—14 countries, 2008–2010. *Morbidity and Mortality Weekly Report* 2011a;60(20):645–51.

Centers for Disease Control and Prevention. State Tobacco Activities Tracking and Evaluation (STATE) System, 2011b; <http://apps.nccd.cdc.gov/statesystem/Default/Default.aspx>; accessed: December 29, 2011.

Centre for Behavioural Research in Cancer. *Health Warnings and Contents Labelling on Tobacco Products: Review, Research and Recommendations*. Carlton South (Australia): Centre for Behavioural Research in Cancer, 1992.

Chaiton M, Cohen J, Kaiserman MJ, Leatherdale ST. Beliefs and attitudes. In: *2002 Youth Smoking Survey Technical Report*. Ottawa (Canada): Health Canada, 2002.

Chakravorty BJ. A product substitution approach to adolescent smokeless tobacco cessation [dissertation]. Chicago: University of Illinois at Chicago, 1992.

Chaloupka FJ, Grossman M, Tauras JA. Public policy and youth smokeless tobacco use. *Southern Economic Journal* 1997;64(2):503–16.

Chaloupka FJ, Pacula RL. Sex and race differences in young people's responsiveness to price and tobacco control policies. *Tobacco Control* 1999;8(4):373–7.

Chaloupka FJ, Straif K, Leon ME, International Agency for Research on Cancer Working Group. Effectiveness of tax and price policies in tobacco control. *Tobacco Control* 2011;20(3):235–8.

Chaloupka FJ, Warner KE. The economics of smoking. In: Culyer AJ, Newhouse JP, editors. *Handbook of Health Economics*. New York: Elsevier, 2000:1539–1627.

Chan CW, Witherspoon JM. Health risk appraisal modifies cigarette smoking behavior among college students. *Journal of General Internal Medicine* 1988;3(6):555–9.

Charlton A. Smoking cessation help for young people: the process observed in two case studies. *Health Education Research* 1992;7(2):249–57.

Chatrou M, Maes S, Dusseldorp E, Seegers G. Effects of the brabant smoking prevention programme: a replication of the Wisconsin programme. *Psychology & Health* 1999;14(1):159–78.

Chen H-H, Yeh M-L. Developing and evaluating a smoking cessation program combined with an Internet-assisted instruction program for adolescents with smoking. *Patient Education and Counseling* 2006;61(3):411–8.

Chen MS Jr. Challenges in tobacco use prevention among minority youth. *Cancer Epidemiology, Biomarkers & Prevention* 2004;13(3):253s–255s.

Cheng TL, DeWitt TG, Savageau JA, O'Connor KG. Determinants of counseling in primary care pediatric practice: physician attitudes about time, money, and health issues. *Archives of Pediatrics & Adolescent Medicine* 1999;153(6):629–35.

Cheng K-W, Glantz SA, Lightwood JM. Association between smokefree laws and voluntary smokefree-home rules. *American Journal of Preventive Medicine* 2011;41(6):566–72.

Chou C-P, Montgomery S, Pentz MA, Rohrbach LA, Johnson CA, Flay BR, MacKinnon DP. Effects of a community-based prevention program on decreasing drug use in high-risk adolescents. *American Journal of Public Health* 1998;88(6):944–8.

Christakis DA, Garrison MM, Ebel BE, Wiehe SE, Rivara FP. Pediatric smoking prevention interventions delivered by care providers: a systematic review. *American Journal of Preventive Medicine* 2003;25(4):358–62.

Christakis DA, Zimmerman FJ, Rivara FP, Ebel B. Improving pediatric prevention via the Internet: a randomized controlled trial. *Pediatrics* 2006;118(3):1157–66.

Chung PJ, Garfield CF, Rathouz PJ, Lauderdale DS, Best D, Lantos J. Youth targeting by tobacco manufacturers since the Master Settlement Agreement. *Health Affairs (Millwood)* 2002;21(2):254–63.

Cinnamin D, Sussmann S. In: Sussman S, Dent CW, Burton D, Stacy AW, Flay BR, editors. *Developing School-Based Tobacco Use Prevention and Cessation Programs*. Newbury Park (CA): Sage, 1995.

Clark PI, Schooley MW, Pierce B, Schulman J, Hartman AM, Schmitt CL. Impact of home smoking rules on smoking patterns among adolescents and young adults. *Preventing Chronic Disease* 2006;3(2):A41; <http://www.cdc.gov/pcd/issues/2006/apr/05_0028.htm>; accessed: December 22, 2010.

Clayton RR, Cattarello AM, Johnstone BM. The effectiveness of Drug Abuse Resistance Education (project DARE): 5-year follow-up results. *Preventive Medicine* 1996;25(3):307–18.

Clean Indoor Air Act, N.Y. Pub. Health Law § 1399n (2003).

Clemenger BBDO. *Marketing Inputs to Assist the Development of Health Warnings for Tobacco Packaging*. Sydney (Australia): Clemenger BBDO, 2004.

Coe RM, Crouse E, Cohen JD, Fisher EB Jr. Patterns of change in adolescent smoking behavior and results of a one year follow-up of a smoking prevention program. *Journal of School Health* 1982;52(8):348–53.

Cohen J. *Statistical Power Analysis for the Behavioral Sciences*. 2nd ed. Hillsdale (NJ): Lawrence Erlbaum Associates, 1988.

Cohen J. Attitude, affect, and consumer behavior. In: Moore BS, Isen AM, editors. *Affect and Social Behavior*. New York: Cambridge University Press, 1990:152–206.

Colborn JW, Cummings KM, Michalek AM. Correlates of adolescents' use of smokeless tobacco. *Health Education & Behavior* 1989;16(1):91–100.

Colby SM, Monti PM, O'Leary Tevyaw T, Barnett NP, Spirito A, Rohsenow DJ, Riggs S, Lewander W. Brief motivational intervention for adolescent smokers in medical settings. *Addictive Behaviors* 2005;30(5):865–74.

Coleman-Wallace D, Lee JW, Montgomery S, Blix G, Wang DT. Evaluation of developmentally appropriate programs for adolescent tobacco cessation. *Journal of School Health* 1999;69(8):314–9.

Committee on Environmental Health, Committee on Substance Abuse, Committee on Adolescence, Committee on Native American Child Health. From the American Academy of Pediatrics: Policy statement—Tobacco use: a pediatric disease. *Pediatrics* 2009;124(5):1474–87.

Connell DB, Turner RR, Mason EF. Summary of findings of the School Health Education Evaluation: health promotion effectiveness, implementation, and costs. Journal of School Health 1985;55(8):316–21.

Connolly GN, Harris JE, Goldman LK, Glantz SA. Evaluating antismoking advertising campaigns [letter]. *JAMA: the Journal of the American Medical Association* 1998; 280(11):964–5.

Cost Kids. Children Opposed to Smoking Tobacco, 2010; <http://www.costkids.org/>; accessed: January 30, 2012.

Cragg Ross and Dawson. *Health Warnings on Cigarette and Tobacco Packs: Report on Research to Inform European Standardization*. London: 1990.

Crawford MA, Balch GI, Mermelstein R, Tobacco Control Network Writing Group. Responses to tobacco control policies among youth. *Tobacco Control* 2002;11(1): 14–19.

CRÉATEC + Market Studies. *Effectiveness of Health Warning Messages on Cigarette Packages in Informing Less-literate Smokers: Final Report*. Montreal (Canada): CRÉATEC + Market Studies, 2003.

Creath CJ, Shelton WO, Wright JT, Bradley DH, Feinstein RA, Wisniewski JF. The prevalence of smokeless tobacco use among adolescent male athletes. *Journal of the American Dental Association* 1988;116(1):43–8.

Cuijpers P. Effective ingredients of school-based drug prevention programs: a systematic review. *Addictive Behaviors* 2002;27(6):1009–23.

Cullen KJ, Cullen AM. Long-term follow-up of the Busselton six-year controlled trial of prevention of children's behavior disorders. *Journal of Pediatrics* 1996;129(1):136–9.

Curry SJ, Hollis J, Bush T, Polen M, Ludman EJ, Grothaus L, McAfee T. A randomized trial of a family-based smoking prevention intervention in managed care. *Preventive Medicine* 2003;37(6 Pt 1):617–26.

Czart C, Pacula RL, Chaloupka FJ, Wechsler H. The impact of prices and control policies on cigarette smoking among college students. *Contemporary Economic Policy* 2001;119(2):135–49.

Dahl RE. Affect regulation, brain development, and behavioral/emotional health in adolescence. *CNS Spectrums* 2001;6(1):60–72.

Dahl RE. Adolescent brain development: a period of vulnerabilities and opportunities. *Annals of the New York Academy of Sciences* 2004;1021:1–22.

Damasio AR. *Descartes' Error: Emotion, Reason, and the Human Brain*. New York: Penguin Group USA, 1994.

Damon W. Self-concept, adolescent. In: Lerner RM, Petersen AC, Brooks-Gunn J, editors. *Encyclopedia of Adolescence*. Vol. II. New York: Garland Publishing, 1991:987–91.

Davidson L. *Wensleydale Smokebusters: Project Report*. Northallerton (England): Northallerton Health Authority, 1992.

Davis KC, Nonnemaker JM, Farrelly MC. Association between national smoking prevention campaigns and perceived smoking prevalence among youth in the United States. *Journal of Adolescent Health* 2007a;41(5):430–6.

Davis RM, Wakefield M, Amos A, Gupta PC. The Hitchhiker's Guide to Tobacco Control: a global assessment of harms, remedies, and controversies. *Annual Review of Public Health* 2007b;28:171–94.

De Vries H, Backbier E, Dijkstra M, Van Breukelen G, Parcel G, Kok G. A Dutch social influence smoking prevention approach for vocational school students. *Health Education Research* 1994;9(3):365–74.

DeCicca P, Kenkel D, Mathios A. Racial differences in the determinants of smoking onset. *Journal of Risk and Uncertainty* 2000;21(2–3):311–40.

DeCicca P, Kenkel D, Mathios A. Cigarette taxes and the transition from youth to adult smoking: smoking initiation, cessation, and participation. *Journal of Health Economics* 2008a;27(4):904–17.

DeCicca P, Kenkel D, Mathios A, Shin YJ, Lim JY. Youth smoking, cigarette prices, and anti-smoking sentiment. *Health Economics* 2008b;17(6):733–49.

Denson R, Stretch S. Prevention of smoking in elementary schools. *Canadian Journal of Public Health* 1981;72(4):259–63.

Dent CW, Sussman S, Stacy AW, Craig S, Burton D, Flay BR. Two-year behavior outcomes of project towards no tobacco use. *Journal of Consulting and Clinical Psychology* 1995;63(4):676–7.

Des Jarlais DC, Sloboda Z, Friedman SR, Tempalski B, McKnight C, Braine N. Diffusion of the D.A.R.E. and syringe exchange programs. *American Journal of Public Health* 2006;96(8):1354–8.

Devlin E, Eadie D, Stead M, Evans K. Comparative study of young people's response to anti-smoking messages. *International Journal of Advertising* 2007;26(1): 99–128.

Dexheimer JW, Talbot TR, Sanders DL, Rosenbloom ST, Aronsky D. Prompting clinicians about preventive care measures: a systematic review of randomized controlled trials. *Journal of the American Medical Informatics Association* 2008;15(3):311–20.

Dickinson S, Holmes M. Understanding the emotional and coping responses of adolescent individuals exposed to threat appeals. *International Journal of Advertising* 2008;27(2):251–78.

Dielman TE, Lorenger AT, Leech SL, Lyons AL, Klos DM, Horvath WJ. Fifteen-month follow-up results of an elementary school based smoking prevention project: resisting pressures to smoke. *Hygie* 1985;4(4):28–35.

DiFranza JR. Is it time to abandon youth access programmes [letter]? *Tobacco Control* 2002;11(3):282.

DiFranza JR. Which interventions against the sale of tobacco for minors can be expected to reduce smoking? *Tobacco Control* 2011;Oct 12 [epub ahead of print].

DiFranza JR, Brown LJ. The Tobacco Institute's "It's the Law" campaign: has it halted illegal sales of tobacco to children? *American Journal of Public Health* 1992; 82(9):1271–3.

DiFranza JR, Coleman M. Sources of tobacco for youths in communities with strong enforcement of youth access laws. *Tobacco Control* 2001;10(4):323–8.

DiFranza JR, Savageau JA, Fletcher KE. Enforcement of underage sales laws as a predictor of daily smoking among adolescents: a national study. *BMC Public Health* 2009;9:107.

Diguisto E. Pros and cons of cessation interventions for adolescent smokers at school. In: Richmond R, editor. *Interventions for Smokers: An International Perspective*. Baltimore: Williams & Wilkins, 1994:107–36.

Dijkstra M, Mesters I, De Vries H, van Breukelen G, Parcel GS. Effectiveness of a social influence approach and boosters to smoking prevention. *Health Education Research* 1999;14(6):791–802.

Dillard JP, Nabi RL. The persuasive influence of emotion in cancer prevention and detection messages. *Journal of Communication* 2006;56(Suppl s1):S123–S139.

Dinno A, Glantz S. Tobacco control policies are egalitarian: a vulnerabilities perspective on clean indoor air laws, cigarette prices, and tobacco use disparities. *Social Science and Medicine* 2009;68(8):1439–47.

Dino G, Horn KA, Goldcamp J, Fernandes A, Kalsekar I, Massey C. A 2-year efficacy study of Not On Tobacco in Florida: an overview of program successes in changing teen smoking behavior. *Preventive Medicine* 2001a;33(6):600–5.

Dino GA, Horn KA, Goldcamp J, Maniar SD, Fernandes A, Massey CJ. Statewide demonstration of Not On Tobacco: a gender-sensitive teen smoking cessation program. *Journal of School Nursing* 2001b;17(2):90–7.

Dino GA, Horn KA, Meit H. A pilot study of Not on Tobacco: a stop smoking programme for adolescents. *Health Education* 1998;98(6):230–41.

Dobbins M, DeCorby K, Manske S, Goldblatt E. Effective practices for school-based tobacco use prevention. *Preventive Medicine* 2008;46(4):289–97.

D'Onofrio CN, Moskowitz JM, Braverman MT. Curtailing tobacco use among youth: evaluation of project 4-health. *Health Education & Behavior* 2002; 29(6):656–82.

Donovan RJ, Jalleh G, Carter OBJ. Tobacco industry smoking prevention advertisements' impact on youth motivation for smoking in the future. *Social Marketing Quarterly* 2006;12(2):3–13.

DuBois DL, Flay BR, Fagen MC. Self-esteem enhancement theory: an emerging framework for promoting health across the life-span. In: DiClemente RJ, Crosby RA, Kegler MC, editors. *Emerging Theories in Health Promotion Practice and Research.* 2nd ed. San Francisco: Jossey-Bass, 2009:97–130.

Dukes RL, Ullman JB, Stein JA. Three-year follow-up of Drug Abuse Resistance Education (D.A.R.E.). *Evaluation Review* 1996;20(1):49–66.

Dunlop SN, Wakefield M, Kashima Y. Pathways to persuasion: cognitive and experiential responses to health-promoting mass media messages. *Communication Research* 2010;37(1):133–64.

Dunlop SM, Wakefield M, Kashima Y. The contribution of anti-smoking advertising to quitting: intra- and interpersonal processes. *Journal of Health Communication* 2008;13(3):250–66.

Durkin S, Wakefield M. Maximizing the impact of emotive antitobacco advertising: effects of interpersonal discussion and program placement. *Social Marketing Quarterly* 2006;12(3):3–14.

Durkin S, Wakefield M. Interrupting a narrative transportation experience: program placement effects on responses to antismoking advertising. *Journal of Health Communication* 2008;13(7):667–80.

Eagly AH, Chaiken S. *The Psychology of Attitudes*. Fort Worth (TX): Harcourt Brace Jovanovich College Publishers, 1993.

Eakin E, Severson H, Glasgow RE. Development and evaluation of a smokeless tobacco cessation program: a pilot study. *National Cancer Institute Monographs* 1989;(8):95–100.

Ebbert JO, Montori V, Vickers KS, Erwin PC, Dale LC, Stead LF. Interventions for smokeless tobacco use cessation. *Cochrane Database of Systematic Reviews* 2007, Issue 4. Art. No.: CD004306. DOI: 10.1002/14651858.CD004306.pub3.

Eckhardt L, Woodruff SI, Elder JP. Relative effectiveness of continued, lapsed, and delayed smoking prevention intervention in senior high school students. *American Journal of Health Promotion* 1997;11(6):418–21.

Edwards CA, Harris WC, Cook DR, Bedford KF, Zuo Y. Out of the smokescreen: does an anti-smoking advertisement affect young women's perception of smoking in movies and their intentions to smoke? *Tobacco Control* 2004;13(3):277–82.

Eisenberg ME, Forster JL. Adolescent smoking behavior: measures of social norms. *American Journal of Preventive Medicine* 2003;25(2):122–8.

Elder JP, Perry CL, Stone EJ, Johnson CC, Yang M, Edmundson EW, Smyth MH, Galati T, Feldman H, Cribb P, et al. Tobacco use measurement, prediction, and intervention in elementary schools in four states: the CATCH Study. *Preventive Medicine* 1996;25(4):486–94.

Elder JP, Stern RA. The ABCs of adolescent smoking prevention: an environment and skills model. *Health Education Quarterly* 1986;13(2):181–91.

Elder JP, Wildey M, de Moor C, Sallis JF Jr, Eckhardt L, Edwards C, Erickson A, Goldbeck A, Hovell M, Johnston D, et al. The long-term prevention of tobacco use among junior high school students: classroom and telephone interventions. *American Journal of Public Health* 1993;83(9):1239–44.

Elkind D, Bowen R. Imaginary audience behavior in children and adolescents. *Developmental Psychology* 1979;15(1):38–44.

Ellickson PL, Bell RM, McGuigan K. Preventing adolescent drug use: long-term results of a junior high program. *American Journal of Public Health* 1993;83(6):856–61.

Elliott & Shanahan Research. *Developmental Research for New Australian Health Warnings on Tobacco Products—Stage 1.* Sydney (Australia): Elliott & Shanahan Research, 2002.

Elliott & Shanahan Research. *Developmental Research for New Australian Health Warnings on Tobacco Products—Stage 2.* Sydney (Australia): Elliott & Shanahan Research, 2003.

Emery S, Szczypka G, Powell LM, Chaloupka FJ. Public health obesity-related TV advertising: lessons learned from tobacco. *American Journal of Preventive Medicine* 2007;33(4 Suppl):S257–S263.

Emery S, Wakefield MA, Terry-McElrath Y, Saffer H, Szczypka G, O'Malley PM, Johnston LD, Chaloupka FJ, Flay B. Televised state-sponsored antitobacco advertising and youth smoking beliefs and behavior in the United States, 1999–2000. *Archives of Pediatrics & Adolescent Medicine* 2005;159(7):639–45.

Emory K, Saquib N, Gilpin EA, Pierce JP. The association between home smoking restrictions and youth smoking behaviour: a review. *Tobacco Control* 2010;19(6): 495–506.

Ennett ST, Rosenbaum DP, Flewelling RL, Bieler GS, Ringwalt CL, Bailey SL. Long-term evaluation of drug abuse resistance education. *Addictive Behaviors* 1994a;19(2):113–25.

Ennett ST, Tobler NS, Ringwalt CL, Flewelling RL. How effective is drug abuse resistance education: a meta-analysis of Project DARE outcome evaluations. *American Journal of Public Health* 1994b;84(9):1394–401.

Environics Research Group. *Canadian Adult and Youth Opinions on the Sizing of Health Warning Messages.* Toronto (Canada): Environics Research Group, 1999.

Environics Research Group. *Testing New Health Warning Messages for Cigarette Packages: A Summary of Three Phases of Focus Group Research—Final Report.* Toronto (Canada): Environics Research Group, 2000.

Environics Research Group. *Evaluation of New Warnings on Cigarette Packages.* Toronto (Canada): Environics Research Group, 2001.

Environics Research Group. *Wave 11: The Health Effects of Tobacco and Health Warning Messages on Cigarette Packages, Survey of Youth.* Toronto (Canada): Environics Research Group, 2006.

Escalas JE, Moore MC, Britton JE. Fishing for feelings: hooking viewers helps! *Journal of Consumer Psychology* 2004;14(1–2):105–14.

Erceg-Hurn DM, Steed LG. Does exposure to cigarette health warnings elicit psychological reactance in smokers? *Journal of Applied Psychology* 2011;41(1):219–37.

Etter JF, Ronchi A, Perneger T. Short-term impact of a university based smoke free campaign. *Journal of Epidemiology and Community Health* 1999;53(11):710–5.

Evans RI. Smoking in children: developing a social psychological strategy of deterrence. *Preventive Medicine* 1976;5(1):122–7.

Evans RI, Hansen WB, Mittelmark MB. Increasing the validity of self-reports of smoking behavior in children. *Journal of Applied Psychology* 1977;62(4):521–3.

Evans WD, Price S, Blahut S, Hersey J, Niederdeppe J, Ray S. Social imagery, tobacco independence, and the truthSM campaign. *Journal of Health Communication* 2004a;9(5):425–41.

Evans WD, Renaud J, Blitstein J, Hersey J, Ray S, Schieber B, Willett J. Prevention effects of an anti-tobacco brand on adolescent smoking initiation. *Social Marketing Quarterly* 2007;13(2):2–20.

Evans RI, Rozelle RM, Maxwell SE, Raines BE, Dill CA, Guthrie TJ. Social modeling films to deter smoking in adolescents: results of a three-year field investigation. *Journal of Applied Psychology* 1981;66(4):399–414.

Evans WD, Ulasevich A, Blahut S. Adult and group influences on participation in youth empowerment programs. *Health Education & Behavior* 2004b; 31(5):564–76.

Ewing GB, Selassie AW, Lopez CH, McCutcheon EP. Self-report of delivery of clinical preventive services by U.S. physicians: comparing specialty, gender, age, setting of practice, and area of practice. *American Journal of Preventive Medicine* 1999;17(1):62–72.

Fairbrother G, Scheinmann R, Osthimer B, Dutton MJ, Newell KA, Fuld J, Klein JD. Factors that influence adolescent reports of counseling by physicians on risky behavior. *Journal of Adolescent Health* 2005;37(6): 467–76.

Family Smoking Prevention and Tobacco Control Act, Public Law 111-13, 123 *U.S. Statutes at Large* 1776 (2009).

Farkas AJ, Gilpin EA, White MM, Pierce JP. Association between household and workplace smoking restrictions and adolescent smoking. *JAMA: the Journal of the American Medical Association* 2000;284(6):717–22.

Farrelly MC, Davis KC, Duke J, Messeri P. Sustaining 'truth': changes in youth tobacco attitudes and smoking intentions after 3 years of a national antismoking campaign. *Health Education Research* 2009;24(1): 42–8.

Farrelly MC, Davis KC, Haviland ML, Messeri P, Healton CG. Evidence of a dose-response relationship between "truth" antismoking ads and youth smoking prevalence. *American Journal of Public Health* 2005;95(3):425–31.

Farrelly MC, Healton CG, Davis KC, Messeri P, Hersey JC, Haviland ML. Getting to the truth: evaluating national tobacco countermarketing campaigns. *American Journal of Public Health* 2002;92(6):901–7.

Farrelly MC, Niederdeppe J, Yarsevich J. Youth tobacco prevention mass media campaigns: past, present, and future directions. *Tobacco Control* 2003a;12(Suppl 1):i35–i47.

Farrelly MC, Pechacek TF, Chaloupka FJ. The impact of tobacco control program expenditures on aggregate cigarette sales: 1981–2000. *Journal of Health Economics* 2003b;22(5):843–59.

Farrelly MC, Pechacek TF, Thomas KY, Nelson D. The impact of tobacco control programs on adult smoking. *American Journal of Public Health* 2008;98(2):304–9.

Federal Trade Commission. *Federal Trade Commission Cigarette Report for 2007 and 2008.* Washington: U.S. Federal Trade Commission, 2011; <http://www.ftc.gov/os/2011/07/110729cigarettereport.pdf>; accessed: September 20, 2011>.

Feighery E, Altman DG, Shaffer G. The effects of combining education and enforcement to reduce tobacco sales to minors: a study of four northern California communities. *JAMA: the Journal of the American Medical Association* 1991;266(22):3168–71.

Feinson JA, Chidekel AS. What physicians can do about the tobacco problem: best practice interventions for your practice and office. *Delaware Medical Journal* 2006;78(4):137–45.

Ferketich AK, Kwong K, Shek A, Lee M. Design and evaluation of a tobacco-prevention program targeting Chinese American youth in New York City. *Nicotine & Tobacco Research* 2007;9(2):249–56.

Fichtenberg CM, Glantz SA. Association of the California tobacco control program with declines in cigarette consumption and mortality from heart disease. *New England Journal of Medicine* 2000;343(24):1772–7.

Fichtenberg CM, Glantz SA. Youth access interventions do not affect youth smoking. *Pediatrics* 2002;109(6): 1088–92.

Fidler W, Lambert TW. A prescription for health: a primary care based intervention to maintain the non-smoking status of young people. *Tobacco Control* 2001; 10(1):23–6.

Figá-Talamanca I, Modolo MA. Evaluation of an antismoking educational programme among adolescents in Italy. *Hygie* 1989;8(3):24–8.

Finucane ML, Alhakami A, Slovic P, Johnson SM. The affect heuristic in judgments of risks and benefits. *Journal of Behavioral Decision Making* 2000;13(1):1–17.

Fiore MC, Bailey WC, Cohen SJ, Dorfman SF, Goldstein MG, Gritz ER, Heyman RB, Jaén CR, Kottke TE, Lando HA, et al. *Treating Tobacco Use and Dependence.* Clinical Practice Guideline. Rockville (MD): U.S. Department of Health and Human Services, Public Health Service, 2000.

Fiore MC, Jaén CR, Baker TB, Bailey WC, Benowitz NL, Curry SJ, Dorfman SF, Froelicher ES, Goldstein MG, Healton CG, et al. *Treating Tobacco Use and Dependence: 2008 Update*. Clinical Practice Guideline. Rockville (MD): U.S. Department of Health and Human Services, Public Health Service, 2008.

Fire Safety Standards for Cigarettes, N.Y. Comp. Codes R. & Regs. Title 19, §429.1 (2004).

Fischer PM, Richards JW Jr, Berman EJ, Krugman DM. Recall and eye tracking study of adolescents viewing tobacco advertisements. *JAMA: the Journal of the American Medical Association* 1989;261(1):84–9.

Fishbein M, Ajzen I. *Belief, Attitude, Intention and Behavior: An Introduction to Theory and Research*. Reading (MA): Addison-Wesley, 1975.

Fisher KJ, Severson HH, Christiansen S, Williams C. Using interactive technology to aid smokeless tobacco cessation: a pilot study. *American Journal of Health Education* 2001;32(6):332–40.

Flammer A. Self-regulation. In: Lerner RM, Petersen AC, Brooks-Gunn J, editors. *Encyclopedia of Adolescence*. Vol. II. New York: Garland Publishing, 1991:1001–3.

Flay BR. On improving the chances of mass media health promotion programs causing meaningful changes in behavior. In: Meyer M, editor. *Health Education by Television and Radio: Contributions to an International Conference with a Selected Bibliography.* New York: Saur, 1981:56–91.

Flay BR. Mass media and smoking cessation: a critical review. *American Journal of Public Health* 1987; 77(2):153–60.

Flay BR. Understanding environmental, situational and intrapersonal risk and protective factors for youth tobacco use: the Theory of Triadic Influence. *Nicotine & Tobacco Research* 1999;1(Suppl 2):S111–S114.

Flay BR. Approaches to substance use prevention utilizing school curriculum plus social environment change. *Addictive Behaviors* 2000;25(6):861–85.

Flay BR. Positive youth development requires comprehensive health promotion programs. *American Journal of Health Behavior* 2002;26(6):407–24.

Flay BR. The long-term promise of effective school-based smoking prevention programs. In: Bonnie RJ, Stratton K, Wallace RB, editors. *Ending the Tobacco Problem: A Blueprint for the Nation.* Washington: National Academies Press, 2007:449–77.

Flay BR. School-based smoking prevention programs with the promise of long-term effectiveness. *Tobacco Induced Diseases* 2009a;5:6.

Flay BR. The promise of long-term effectiveness of school-based smoking prevention programs: a critical review of reviews. *Tobacco Induced Diseases* 2009b;5:7.

Flay BR, Biglan A, Boruch RF, Castro FG, Gottfredson D, Kellam S, Mościcki EK, Schinke S, Valentine JC, Ji P. Standards of evidence: criteria for efficacy, effectiveness and dissemination. *Prevention Science* 2005;6(3): 151–75.

Flay BR, Brannon BR, Johnson CA, Hansen WB, Ulene AL, Whitney-Saltiel DA, Gleason LR, Sussman S, Gavin MD, Glowacz KM, et al. The television, school and family smoking prevention and cessation project. I: theoretical basis and program development. *Preventive Medicine* 1988;17(5):585–607.

Flay BR, Burton D. Effective mass media communication campaigns for public health. In: Atkin C, Wallack L, editors. *Mass Communication and Public Health.* Newberry Park (CA): Sage Publications, 1990:129–46.

Flay BR, Graumlich S, Segawa E, Burns JL, Holliday MY, Aban Aya Investigators. Effects of 2 prevention programs on high-risk behaviors among African American youth: a randomized trial. *Archives of Pediatrics & Adolescent Medicine* 2004;158(4):377–84.

Flay BR, Hu FB, Siddiqui O, Day LE, Hedeker D, Petraitis J, Richardson J, Sussman S. Differential influence of parental smoking and friends' smoking on adolescent initiation and escalation of smoking. *Journal of Health and Social Behavior* 1994;35(3):248–65.

Flay BR, Koepke D, Thomson SJ, Santi S, Best JA, Brown KS. Six-year follow-up of the first Waterloo school smoking prevention trial. *American Journal of Public Health* 1989;79(10):1371–6.

Flay BR, Miller TQ, Hedeker D, Siddiqui O, Britton CF, Brannon BR, Johnson CA, Hansen WB, Sussman S, Dent C. The television, school, and family smoking prevention and cessation project. VIII: student outcomes and mediating variables. *Preventive Medicine* 1995;24(1):29–40.

Flay BR, Petraitis J. The theory of triadic influence: a new theory of health behavior with implications for preventive interventions. In: Albrecht GI, editor. *Advances in Medical Sociology: A Reconsideration of Models of Health Behavior Change*. Vol. 4. Stamford (CT): JAI Press, 1994:19–44.

Flay BR, Snyder FJ, Petraitis J. The theory of triadic influence. In: DiClemente RJ, Kegler MC, Crosby RA, editors. *Emerging Theories in Health Promotion Practice and Research.* 2nd ed. San Francisco: Jossey-Bass, 2009:451–510.

Flynn BS, Worden JK, Bunn JY, Dorwaldt AL, Connolly SW, Ashikaga T. Youth audience segmentation strategies for smoking-prevention mass media campaigns based on message appeal. *Health Education & Behavior* 2007;34(4):578–93.

Flynn BS, Worden JK, Secker-Walker RH, Badger GJ, Geller BM. Cigarette smoking prevention effects of mass media and school interventions targeted to gender and age groups. *Journal of Health Education* 1995;26(2 Suppl):S45–S61.

Flynn BS, Worden JK, Secker-Walker RH, Badger GJ, Geller BM, Costanza MC. Prevention of cigarette smoking through mass media intervention and school programs. *American Journal of Public Health* 1992; 82(6):827–34.

Flynn BS, Worden JK, Secker-Walker RH, Pirie PL, Badger GJ, Carpenter JH. Long-term responses of higher and lower risk youths to smoking prevention interventions. *Preventive Medicine* 1997;26(3):389–94.

Flynn BS, Worden JK, Secker-Walker RH, Pirie PL, Badger GJ, Carpenter JH, Geller BM. Mass media and school interventions for cigarette smoking prevention: effects 2 years after completion. *American Journal of Public Health* 1994;84(7):1148–50.

Fong GT, Hammond D, Hitchman SC. The impact of pictures on the effectiveness of tobacco warnings. *Bulletin of the World Health Organization* 2009;87(8):640–3.

Forgas JP. Mood and judgment: the affect infusion model (AIM). *Psychological Bulletin* 1995;117(1):39–66.

Forman SG, Linney JA, Brondino MJ. Effects of coping skills training on adolescents at risk for substance abuse. *Psychology of Addictive Behaviors* 1990;4(2):67–76.

Forrester K, Biglan A, Severson HH, Smolkowski K. Predictors of smoking onset over two years. *Nicotine & Tobacco Research* 2007;9(12):1259–67.

Forster J, Chen V, Blaine T, Perry C, Toomey T. Social exchange of cigarettes by youth. *Tobacco Control* 2003;12(2):148–54.

Forster JL, Brokenleg I, Rhodes KL, Lamont GR, Poupart J. Cigarette smoking among American Indian youth in Minneapolis-St. Paul. *American Journal of Preventive Medicine* 2008;35(6 Suppl):S449–S456.

Forster JL, Murray DM, Wolfson M, Blaine TM, Wagenaar AC, Hennrikus DJ. The effects of community policies to reduce youth access to tobacco. *American Journal of Public Health* 1998;88(8):1193–8.

Forster JL, Wolfson M. Youth access to tobacco: policies and politics. *Annual Review of Public Health* 1998;19:203–35.

Fortmann SP, Flora JA, Winkleby MA, Schooler C, Taylor CB, Farquhar JW. Community intervention trials: reflections on the Stanford Five-City Project Experience. *American Journal of Epidemiology* 1995;142(6):576–86.

Foster EM, Dodge KA, Jones D. Issues in the economic evaluation of prevention programs. *Applied Developmental Science* 2003;7(2):76–86.

Foster-Clark FS, Blyth DA. Peer relations and influences. In: Lerner RM, Petersen AC, Brooks-Gunn J, editors. *Encyclopedia of Adolescence*. Vol. II. New York: Garland Publishing, 1991:767–71.

Frieden TR, Mostashari F, Kerker BD, Miller N, Hajat A, Frankel M. Adult tobacco use levels after intensive tobacco control measures: New York City, 2002–2003. *American Journal of Public Health* 2005;95(6): 1016–23.

Friend K, Levy DT. Reductions in smoking prevalence and cigarette consumption associated with mass-media campaigns. *Health Education Research* 2002;17(1): 85–98.

Gala S, Pesek F, Murray J, Kavanagh C, Graham S, Walsh M. Design and pilot evaluation of an Internet spit tobacco cessation program. *Journal of Dental Hygiene* 2008;82(1):11.

Galuska DA, Fulton JE, Powell KE, Burgeson CR, Pratt M, Elster A, Griesemer BA. Pediatrician counseling about preventive health topics: results from the Physicians' Practices Survey, 1998–1999. *Pediatrics* 2002; 109(5):e83.

Gansky SA, Ellison JA, Rudy D, Bergert N, Letendre MA, Nelson L, Kavanagh C, Walsh MM. Cluster-randomized controlled trial of an athletic trainer-directed spit (smokeless) tobacco intervention for collegiate baseball athletes: results after 1 year. *Journal of Athletic Training* 2005;40(2):76–87.

Garrison MM, Christakis DA, Ebel BE, Wiehe SE, Rivara FP. Smoking cessation interventions for adolescents: a systematic review. *American Journal of Preventive Medicine* 2003;25(4):363–7.

Gatta G, Malvezzi I, Sant M, Micheli A, Panico S, Ravasi G, Berrino F. Randomized trial of primary school education against smoking. *Tumori* 1991;77(5):367–71.

Gemson DH, Moats HL, Watkins BX, Ganz ML, Robinson S, Healton E. Laying down the law: reducing illegal tobacco sales to minors in central Harlem. *American Journal of Public Health* 1998;88(6):936–9.

Gentile B, Twenge JM, Campbell WK. Birth cohort differences in self-esteem, 1988–2008: a cross-temporal meta-analysis. *Review of General Psychology* 2010; 14(3):261–8.

Gerlach KK, Larkin MA. The SmokeLess States program. In: Isaacs SL, Knickman JR, editors. *To Improve Health and Health Care. Vol. VIII: The Robert Wood Johnson Foundation Anthology*. San Francisco: Jossey-Bass, 2005:29–46.

Gervais A, O'Loughlin J, Dugas E, Eisenberg MJ. A systematic review of randomized controlled trials of youth smoking cessation interventions. *Drugs, Health and Society* 2007;6(Suppl II):ii1–ii26.

Gilchrist LD, Schinke SP, Bobo JK, Snow WH. Self-control skills for preventing smoking. *Addictive Behaviors* 1986;11(2):169–74.

Gillies PA, Wilcox B. Reducing the risk of smoking amongst the young. *Public Health* 1984;98(1):49–54.

Giovino GA. The tobacco epidemic in the United States. *American Journal of Preventive Medicine* 2007;33(6 Suppl):S318–S326.

Glantz SA, Mandel LL. Since school-based tobacco prevention programs do not work, what should we do [editorial]? *Journal of Adolescent Health* 2005;36(3):157–9.

Glasgow RE, Strycker LA, Eakin EG, Boles SM, Whitlock EP. Concern about weight gain associated with quitting smoking: prevalence and association with outcome in a sample of young female smokers. *Journal of Consulting and Clinical Psychology* 1999;67(6):1009–11.

Global Advisors Smokefree Policy. Smoke-free vehicles when children are present [fact sheet], October 26, 2011; <http://www.njgasp.org/f_SF%20cars,kids,%20info,%20arguments.pdf >; accessed: November 7, 2011.

Glynn TJ. Essential elements of school-based smoking prevention programs. *Journal of School Health* 1989; 59(5):181–8.

Goldberg ME, Gorn GJ. Happy and sad TV programs: how they affect reactions to commercials. *Journal of Consumer Research* 1987;14(3):387–403.

Goldman LK, Glantz SA. Evaluation of antismoking advertising campaigns. *JAMA: the Journal of the American Medical Association* 1998;279(10):772–7.

Goldstein AO, Peterson AB, Ribisl KM, Steckler A, Linnan L, McGloin T, Patterson C. Passage of 100% tobacco-free school policies in 14 North Carolina school districts. *Journal of School Health* 2003;73(8):293–9.

Goodstadt MS. Alcohol and drug education: models and outcomes. *Health Education Monographs* 1978; 6(3):263–79.

Goodstadt MS. Drug education—a turn on or a turn off? *Journal of Drug Education* 1980;10(2):89–99.

Gordon DA. Parent training via CD-ROM: using technology to disseminate effective prevention practices. *Journal of Primary Prevention* 2000;21(2):227–51.

Gordon I, Whitear B, Guthrie D. Stopping them starting: evaluation of a community-based project to discourage teenage smoking in Cardiff. *Health Education Journal* 1997;56(1):42–50.

Gordon JS, Severson HH. Tobacco cessation through dental office settings. *Journal of Dental Education* 2001;65(4):354–63.

Gosin M, Marsiglia FF, Hecht ML. Keepin' it R.E.A.L.: a drug resistance curriculum tailored to the strengths and needs of pre-adolescents of the southwest. *Journal of Drug Education* 2003;33(2):119–42.

Gottlieb A, Pope SK, Rickert VI, Hardin BH. Patterns of smokeless tobacco use by young adolescents. *Pediatrics* 1993;91(1):75–8.

Graham JW, Johnson CA, Hansen WB, Flay BR, Gee M. Drug use prevention programs, gender, and ethnicity: evaluation of three seventh-grade project SMART cohorts. *Preventive Medicine* 1990;19(3):305–13.

Grandpre J, Alvaro EM, Burgoon M, Miller CH, Hall JR. Adolescent reactance and anti-smoking campaigns: a theoretical approach. *Health Communication* 2003; 15(3):349–66.

Green LW, Richard L. The need to combine health education and health promotion: the case of cardiovascular disease prevention. *Promotion & Education* 1993:11–8.

Greenberg JS, Deputat Z. Smoking intervention: comparing three methods in a high school setting. *Journal of School Health* 1978;48(8):498–502.

Grimshaw G, Stanton A. Tobacco cessation interventions for young people. *Cochrane Database of Systematic Reviews* 2006, Issue 4. Art. No.: CD003289. DOI: 10.1002/14651858.CD003289.pub4.

Gross CP, Soffer B, Bach PB, Rajkumar R, Forman HP. State expenditures for tobacco-control programs and the tobacco settlement. *New England Journal of Medicine* 2002;347(14):1080–6.

Gruber J, Zinman J. Youth smoking in the United States: evidence and implications. In: Gruber J, editor. *Risky Behavior among Youth: An Economic Analysis*. Chicago: University of Chicago Press, 2001: 69–120.

Hafstad A. Provocative anti-smoking appeals in mass-media campaigns: an intervention study on adolescent smoking [dissertation]. Oslo: University of Oslo, 1997.

Hafstad A, Aarø LE. Activating interpersonal influence through provocative appeals: evaluation of a mass media-based antismoking campaign targeting adolescents. *Health Communication* 1997;9(3):253–72.

Hafstad A, Aarø LE, Engeland A, Andersen A, Langmark F, Stray-Pedersen B. Provocative appeals in anti-smoking mass media campaigns targeting adolescents—the accumulated effect of multiple exposures. *Health Education Research* 1997a;12(2):227–36.

Hafstad A, Aarø LE, Langmark F. Evaluation of an anti-smoking mass media campaign targeting adolescents: the role of affective responses and interpersonal communication. *Health Education Research* 1996;11(1):29–38.

Hafstad A, Stray-Pedersen B, Langmark F. Use of provocative emotional appeals in a mass media campaign designed to prevent smoking among adolescents. *European Journal of Public Health* 1997b;7(2):122–7.

Hagan JF Jr, Shaw JS, Duncan P, editors. *Bright Futures: Guidelines for Health Supervision of Infants, Children, and Adolescents, Third Edition*. Elk Grove Village (IL): American Academy of Pediatrics, 2008.

Halpern-Felsher BL, Ozer EM, Millstein SG, Wibbelsman CJ, Fuster CD, Elster AB, Irwin CE Jr. Preventive services in a health maintenance organization: how well do pediatricians screen and educate adolescent patients? *Archives of Pediatrics & Adolescent Medicine* 2000;154(2):173–9.

Hamilton G, Cross D, Lower T, Resnicow K, Williams P. School policy: what helps to reduce teenage smoking? *Nicotine & Tobacco Research* 2003;5(4):507–13.

Hamilton G, Cross D, Resnicow K, Hall M. A school-based harm minimization smoking intervention trial: outcome results. *Addiction* 2005;100(5):689–700.

Hammond D. Health warning messages on tobacco products: a review. *Tobacco Control* 2011;20(5):327–37.

Hammond D, Fong GT, Borland R, Cummings KM, McNeill A, Driezen P. Text and graphic warnings on cigarette packages: findings from the International Tobacco Control Four Country Study. *American Journal of Preventive Medicine* 2007;32(3):202–9.

Hammond D, Fong GT, McDonald PW, Brown KS, Cameron R. Graphic Canadian cigarette warning labels and adverse outcomes: evidence from Canadian smokers. *American Journal of Public Health* 2004;94(8):1442–5.

Hammond D, Fong GT, McDonald PW, Cameron R, Brown KS. Impact of the graphic Canadian warning labels on adult smoking behaviour. *Tobacco Control* 2003;12(4):391–5.

Hammond D, Fong GT, McNeill A, Borland R, Cummings KM. Effectiveness of cigarette warning labels in informing smokers about the risks of smoking: findings from the International Tobacco Control (ITC) Four Country Survey. *Tobacco Control* 2006;15(Suppl 3):iii19–iii25.

Hancock L, Sanson-Fisher R, Perkins J, Girgis A, Howley P, Schofield M. The effect of a community action intervention on adolescent smoking rates in rural Australian towns: the CART Project. *Preventive Medicine* 2001;32(4):332–40.

Hansen WB. School-based substance use prevention: a review of the state of the art in curriculum, 1980–1990. *Health Education Research* 1992;7(3):403–30.

Hansen WB, Graham JW. Preventing alcohol, marijuana, and cigarette use among adolescents: peer pressure resistance training versus establishing conservative norms. *Preventive Medicine* 1991;20(3):414–30.

Hansen WB, Johnson CA, Flay BR, Graham JW, Sobel J. Affective and social influences approaches to the prevention of multiple substance abuse among seventh grade students: results from Project SMART. *Preventive Medicine* 1988a;17(2):135–54.

Hansen WB, Malotte CK, Fielding JE. Evaluation of a tobacco and alcohol abuse prevention curriculum for adolescents. *Health Education Quarterly* 1988b;15(1):93–114.

Hanson K, Allen S, Jensen S, Hatsukami D. Treatment of adolescent smokers with the nicotine patch. *Nicotine & Tobacco Research* 2003;5(4):515–26.

Harrison PA, Fulkerson JA, Park E. The relative importance of social versus commercial sources in youth access to tobacco, alcohol, and other drugs. *Preventive Medicine* 2000;31(1):39–48.

Hatsukami DK, Severson HH. Oral spit tobacco: addiction, prevention and treatment. *Nicotine & Tobacco Research* 1999;1(1):21–44.

Haviland L. Introduction. *Health Education & Behavior* 2004;31(5):546–7.

Hawkins JD, Catalano RF, Kosterman R, Abbott R, Hill KG. Preventing adolescent health-risk behaviors by strengthening protection during childhood. *Archives of Pediatric & Adolescence Medicine* 1999;153(3):226–34.

Hawkins JD, Oesterle S, Brown EC, Monahan KC, Abbott RD, Arthur MW, Catalano RF. Sustained decreases in risk exposure and youth problem behaviors after installation of the Communities That Care prevention system in a randomized trial. *Archives of Pediatrics & Adolescent Medicine*, in press.

Hawthorne G, Garrard J, Dunt D. Does Life Education's drug education programme have a public health benefit? *Addiction* 1995;90(2):205–15.

Health Education Journal. Health warnings. *Health Education Journal* 1985;44(4):218–9.

Hecht ML, Graham JW, Elek E. The drug resistance strategies intervention: program effects on substance use. *Health Communication* 2006;20(3):267–76.

Hecht ML, Krieger JLR. The principle of cultural grounding in school-based substance abuse prevention: the Drug Resistance Strategies Project. *Journal of Language and Social Psychology* 2006;25(3):301–19.

Hecht ML, Marsiglia FF, Elek E, Wagstaff DA, Kulis S, Dustman P, Miller-Day M. Culturally grounded substance use prevention: an evaluation of the keepin' it R.E.A.L. curriculum. *Prevention Science* 2003; 4(4):233–48.

Heckman JJ, Flyer F, Loughlin C. An assessment of causal inference in smoking initiation research and a framework for future research. *Economic Inquiry* 2008;46(1):37–44.

Helme DW, Donohew RL, Baier M, Zittleman L. A classroom-administered simulation of a television campaign on adolescent smoking: testing an activation model of information exposure. *Journal of Health Communication* 2007;12(4):399–415.

Henriksen L, Dauphinee AL, Wang Y, Fortmann SP. Industry sponsored anti-smoking ads and adolescent reactance: test of a boomerang effect. *Tobacco Control* 2006;15(1):13–8.

Henriksen L, Fortmann SP. Young adults' opinions of Philip Morris and its television advertising. *Tobacco Control* 2002;11(3):236–40.

Hersey JC, Niederdeppe J, Evans WD, Nonnemaker J, Blahut S, Farrelly MC, Holden D, Messeri P, Haviland ML. The effects of state counterindustry media campaigns on beliefs, attitudes, and smoking status among teens and young adults. *Preventive Medicine* 2003;37(6 Pt 1):544–52.

Hersey JC, Niederdeppe J, Evans WD, Nonnemaker J, Blahut S, Holden D, Messeri P, Haviland ML. The theory of "truth": how counterindustry campaigns affect smoking behavior among teens. *Health Psychology* 2005a;24(1):22–31.

Hersey JC, Niederdeppe J, Ng SW, Mowery P, Farrelly M, Messeri P. How state counter-industry campaigns help prime perceptions of tobacco industry practices to promote reductions in youth smoking. *Tobacco Control* 2005b;14(6):377–83.

Higgins ET. Self-discrepancy: a theory relating self and affect. *Psychological Review* 1987;94(3):319–40.

Hill D. New cigarette-packet warnings: are they getting through? *Medical Journal of Australia* 1988;148(9): 478–80.

Hill D. Why we should tackle adult smoking first. *Tobacco Control* 1999;8(3):333–5.

Hinnant LW, Nimsch C, Stone-Wiggins B. Examination of the relationship between community support and tobacco control activities as a part of youth empowerment programs. *Health Education & Behavior* 2004;31(5):629–40.

Hodgson TA. Cigarette smoking and lifetime medical expenditures. *Milbank Quarterly* 1992;70(1):81–125.

Holden DJ, Crankshaw E, Nimsch C, Hinnant LW, Hund L. Quantifying the impact of participation in local tobacco control groups on the psychological empowerment of involved youth. *Health Education & Behavior* 2004a;31(5):615–28.

Holden DJ, Evans WD, Hinnant LW, Messeri P. Modeling psychological empowerment among youth involved in local tobacco control efforts. *Health Education & Behavior* 2005;32(2):264–78.

Holden DJ, Messeri P, Evans WD, Crankshaw E, Ben-Davies M. Conceptualizing youth empowerment within tobacco control. *Health Education & Behavior* 2004b;31(5):548–63.

Hollis JF, Polen MR, Whitlock EP, Lichtenstein E, Mullooly JP, Velicer WF, Redding CA. Teen Reach: outcomes from a randomized, controlled trial of a tobacco reduction program for teens seen in primary medical care. *Pediatrics* 2005;115(4):981–9.

Hopkins DP, Briss PA, Ricard CJ, Husten CG, Carande-Kulis VG, Fielding JE, Alao MO, McKenna JW, Sharp DJ, Harris DJ, et al. Reviews of evidence regarding interventions to reduce tobacco use and exposure to environmental tobacco smoke. *American Journal of Preventive Medicine* 2001;20(2 Suppl):S16–S66.

Horn K, Dino G, Hamilton C, Noerachmanto N. Efficacy of an emergency department-based motivational teenage smoking intervention. *Preventing Chronic Disease* 2007;4(1); <http://www.cdc.gov/pcd/issues/2007/jan/ 06_0021.htm>; accessed: December 22, 2010.

Horn K, Dino G, Kalsekar I, Mody R. The impact of Not on Tobacco on teen smoking cessation: end-of-program evaluation results, 1998 to 2003. *Journal of Adolescent Research* 2005a;20(16):640–61.

Horn K, McGloin T, Dino G, Manzo K, Lowry-Chavis L, Shorty L, McCracken L, Noerachmanto N. Quit and reduction rates for a pilot study of the American Indian Not On Tobacco (N-O-T) program. *Preventing Chronic Disease* 2005b, serial online; <http://www.cdc.gov/pcd/issues/2005/oct/05_0001.htm>; accessed: June 24, 2009.

Hornik R. *Public Health Communication: Evidence for Behavior Change*. Mahwah (NJ): Lawrence Erlbaum Associates, 2002.

Horswell L, Horton SA. *Telling Our Story: "PITS" – Pack in Those Smokes—A Teen Support Group Quit Smoking Program*. Vancouver (Canada): Canadian Cancer Society, 1997.

Hotte A, McCulloch R, Welch L, Lindsay L, Bordeau D, Meloche A. *Dissemination and Evaluation of the Quit-4-Life Cessation Program in Ottawa-Carleton High Schools: Final Report.* Ottawa (Canada): Ottawa-Carleton Lung Association, University of Ottawa, Ottawa-Carleton Health Department, 1997.

Hovell MF, Jones JA, Adams MA. The feasibility and efficacy of tobacco use prevention in orthodontics. *Journal of Dental Education* 2001;65(4):348–53.

Hovell MF, Lessov-Schlaggar CN, Ding D. Smokefree community policies promote home smoking bans: unknown mechanisms and opportunities for preventive medicine. *American Journal of Preventive Medicine* 2011;41(6):650–2.

Hovell MF, Slymen DJ, Jones JA, Hofstetter CR, Burkham-Kreitner S, Conway TL, Rubin B, Noel D. An adolescent tobacco-use prevention trial in orthodontic offices. *American Journal of Public Health* 1996;86(12):1760–6.

Hurd PD, Johnson CA, Pechacek T, Bast LP, Jacobs DR, Luepker RV. Prevention of cigarette smoking in seventh grade students. *Journal of Behavioral Medicine* 1980;3(1):15–28.

Hurt RD, Croghan GA, Beede SD, Wolter TD, Croghan IT, Patten CA. Nicotine patch therapy in 101 adolescent smokers: efficacy, withdrawal symptom relief, and carbon monoxide and plasma cotinine levels. *Archives of Pediatrics & Adolescent Medicine* 2000;154(1):31–7.

Hwang MS, Yeagley KL, Petosa R. A meta-analysis of adolescent psychosocial smoking prevention programs published between 1978 and 1997 in the United States. *Health Education & Behavior* 2004;31(6):702–19.

Hymowitz N, Pyle SA, Haddock CK, Schwab JV. The Pediatric Residency Training on Tobacco Project: year-four parent outcome findings. *Preventive Medicine* 2008;47(2):221–4.

Hymowitz N, Schwab J, Haddock CK, Burd KM, Pyle S. The Pediatric Residency Training on Tobacco Project: a baseline findings from the residence tobacco survey and observed structured clinical examinations. *Preventive Medicine* 2004;39(3):507–16.

Hymowitz N, Schwab JV, Haddock CK, Pyle SA, Schwab LM. The Pediatric Residency Training on Tobacco Project: four-year resident outcome findings. *Preventive Medicine* 2007;45(6):481–90.

Ibrahim JK, Glantz SA. Tobacco industry litigation strategies to oppose tobacco control media campaigns. *Tobacco Control* 2006;15(1):50–8.

Ibrahim JK, Glantz SA. The rise and fall of tobacco control media campaigns, 1967–2006. *American Journal of Public Health* 2007;97(8):1383–96.

Ibrahim JK, Tsoukalas TH, Glantz SA. Public health foundations and the tobacco industry: lessons from Minnesota. *Tobacco Control* 2004;13(3):228–36.

Igra V, Millstein SG. Current status and approaches to improving preventive services for adolescents. *JAMA: the Journal of the American Medical Association* 1993;269(11):1408–12.

Independent Evaluation Consortium. *Final Report of the Independent Evaluation of the California Tobacco Control Prevention and Education Program: Wave 1, 2, and 3 (1996–2000)*. Rockville (MD): The Gallup Organization, 2002.

International Agency for Research on Cancer. *Evaluating the Effectiveness of Smoke-Free Policies*. IARC Handbooks of Cancer Prevention. Vol. 13. Lyon (France): International Agency for Research on Cancer, 2009.

International Agency for Research on Cancer. *Effectiveness of Tax and Price Policies for Tobacco Control*. IARC Handbooks of Cancer Prevention in Tobacco Control, Volume 14. Lyon (France): International Agency for Research on Cancer, 2011.

Iwasaki N, Tremblay CH, Tremblay VJ. Advertising restrictions and cigarette smoking: evidence from myopic and rational addiction models. *Contemporary Economic Policy* 2006;24(3):370–81.

Jackson C, Dickinson D. Can parents who smoke socialise their children against smoking: results from the Smoke-free Kids intervention trial. *Tobacco Control* 2003;12(1):52–9.

Jackson C, Dickinson D. Enabling parents who smoke to prevent their children from initiating smoking: results from a 3-year intervention evaluation. *Archives of Pediatrics & Adolescent Medicine* 2006;160(1):56–62.

Jason LA, Mollica M, Ferrone L. Evaluating an early secondary smoking prevention intervention. *Preventive Medicine* 1982;11(1):96–102.

Jason LA, Pokorny SB, Schoeny ME. It is premature to abandon youth access to tobacco programs. *Pediatrics* 2003;111(4 Pt 1):920–1.

Jepson R, Harris F, Rowa-Dewar N, MacGillivray S, Hastings G, Kearney N, Walker S, Glanville J. *A Review of the Effectiveness of Mass Media Interventions Which Both Encourage Quit Attempts and Reinforce Current and Recent Attempts to Quit Smoking.* Stirling (Scotland): University of Stirling Cancer Care Research Centre and The Centre for Social Marketing, and University of Abertay, The Alliance for Self Care Research, 2006.

Johnson CA, Cen S, Gallaher P, Palmer PH, Xiao L, Ritt-Olson A, Unger JB. Why smoking prevention programs sometimes fail: does effectiveness depend on sociocultural context and individual characteristics? *Cancer Epidemiology, Biomarkers & Prevention* 2007;16(6):1043–9.

Johnson CA, Pentz MA, Weber MD, Dwyer JH, Baer N, MacKinnon DP, Hansen WB, Flay BR. Relative effectiveness of comprehensive community programming for drug abuse prevention with high-risk and low-risk adolescents. *Journal of Consulting and Clinical Psychology* 1990;58(4):447–56.

Johnson CA, Unger JB, Ritt-Olson A, Palmer PH, Cen SY, Gallaher P, Chou CP. Smoking prevention for ethnically diverse adolescents: 2-year outcomes of a multicultural, school-based smoking prevention curriculum in Southern California. *Preventive Medicine* 2005;40(6):842–52.

Johnston LD, O'Malley PM, Bachman JG, Schulenberg JE. *Monitoring the Future National Survey Results on Drug Use, 1975–2006: Volume I, Secondary School Students*. Bethesda (MD): U.S. Department of Health and Human Services, National Institutes of Health, National Institute on Drug Abuse, 2007a. NIH Publication No. 07-6205.

Johnston LD, O'Malley PM, Bachman JG, Schulenberg JE. *Monitoring the Future National Survey Results on Drug Use, 1975–2006: Volume II, College Students and Adults Ages 19–45*. Bethesda (MD): U.S. Department of Health and Human Services, National Institutes of Health, National Institute on Drug Abuse, 2007b. NIH Publication No. 07-6206.

Johnston LD, Terry-McElrath YM, O'Malley PM, Wakefield M. Trends in recall and appraisal of anti-smoking advertising among American youth: national survey results, 1997–2001. *Prevention Science* 2005;6(1):1–19.

Jones SE, Fisher CJ, Greene BZ, Hertz MF, Pritzl J. Healthy and safe school environment, part I: results from the School Health Policies and Programs Study 2006. *Journal of School Health* 2007;77(8):522–43.

Jøsendal O, Aarø LE, Bergh IH. Effects of a school-based smoking prevention program among subgroups of adolescents. *Health Education Research* 1998;13(2): 215–24.

Jøsendal O, Aarø LE, Torsheim T, Rasbash J. Evaluation of the school-based smoking-prevention program "BE smokeFREE." *Scandinavian Journal of Psychology* 2005;46(2):189–99.

Journal of the National Cancer Institute. Community Intervention Trial for Smoking Cessation (COMMIT): summary of design and intervention, COMMIT Research Group. *Journal of the National Cancer Institute* 1991;83(22):1620–8.

Katz E, Lazarsfeld PF. *Personal Influence: The Part Played by People in the Flow of Mass Media*. Glencoe (IL): Free Press, 1955.

Katzman B, Markowitz S, McGeary KA. An empirical investigation of the social market for cigarettes. *Health Economics* 2007;16(10):1025–39.

Kaufman JS, Jason LA, Sawlski LM, Halpert JA. A comprehensive multi-media program to prevent smoking among black students. *Journal of Drug Education* 1994;24(2):95–108.

Kellam SG, Anthony JC. Targeting early antecedents to prevent tobacco smoking: findings from an epidemiologically based randomized field trial. *American Journal of Public Health* 1998;88(10):1490–5.

Kentala J, Utriainen P, Pahkala K, Mattila K. Can brief intervention through community dental care have an effect on adolescent smoking? *Preventive Medicine* 1999;29(2):107–11.

Kickbusch I. Approaches to an ecological base for public health. *Health Promotion International* 1989;4(4): 265–8.

Killen JD, Robinson TN, Ammerman S, Hayward C, Rogers J, Stone C, Samuels D, Levin SK, Green S, Schatzberg AF. Randomized clinical trial of the efficacy of bupropion combined with nicotine patch in the treatment of adolescent smokers. *Journal of Consulting and Clinical Psychology* 2004;72(4):729–35.

Killen JD, Telch MJ, Robinson TN, Maccoby N, Taylor CB, Farquhar JW. Cardiovascular disease risk reduction for tenth graders: a multiple-factor school-based approach. *JAMA: the Journal of the American Medical Association* 1988;260(12):1728–33.

Kim YJ. The role of regulatory focus in message framing in antismoking advertisements for adolescents. *Journal of Advertising* 2006;35(1):143–51.

Kim S, Crutchfield C, Williams C, Hepler N. Toward a new paradigm in substance abuse and other problem behavior prevention for youth: youth development and empowerment approach. *Journal of Drug Education* 1998;28(1):1–17.

Klein EG, Forster JL, Erickson DJ, Lytle LA, Schillo B. The relationship between local clean indoor air policies and smoking behaviours in Minnesota youth. *Tobacco Control* 2009;18(2):132–7.

Klein JD, Allan MJ, Elster AB, Stevens D, Cox C, Hedberg VA, Goodman RA. Improving adolescent preventive care in community health centers. *Pediatrics* 2001a;107(2):318–27.

Klein JD, Camenga DR. Tobacco prevention and cessation in pediatric patients. *Pediatrics in Review* 2004; 25(1):17–26.

Klein JD, Levine LJ, Allan MJ. Delivery of smoking prevention and cessation services to adolescents. *Archives of Pediatrics & Adolescent Medicine* 2001b;155(5): 597–602.

Klepp K-I, Tell GS, Vellar OD. Ten-year follow-up of the Oslo Youth Study Smoking Prevention Program. *Preventive Medicine* 1993;22(4):453–62.

Klonoff EA, Landrine H. Acculturation and cigarette smoking among African Americans: replication and implications for prevention and cessation programs. *Journal of Behavioral Medicine* 1999;22(2):195–204.

Kohler CL, Schoenberger YM, Beasley TM, Phillips MM. Effectiveness evaluation of the N-O-T smoking cessation program for adolescents. *American Journal of Health Behavior* 2008;32(4):368-79.

Konopka G. Adolescence, concept of, and requirements for a healthy development. In: Lerner RM, Petersen AC, Brooks-Gunn J, editors. *Encyclopedia of Adolescence*. Vol. I. New York: Garland Publishing, 1991:10–3.

Koval JJ, Aubut J-AL, Pederson LL, O'Hegarty M, Chan SS. The potential effectiveness of warning labels on cigarette packages: the perceptions of young adult Canadians. *Canadian Journal of Public Health* 2005; 96(5):353–6.

Krowchuk HV. Effectiveness of adolescent smoking prevention strategies. *MCN: the American Journal of Maternal Child Nursing* 2005;30(6):366–72.

Krugman DM, Fox RJ, Fletcher JE, Fischer PM, Rojas TH. Do adolescents attend to warnings in cigarette advertising: an eye-tracking approach. *Journal of Advertising Research* 1994;34(6):39–52.

Kulig JW, American Academy of Pediatrics Committee on Substance Abuse. Tobacco, alcohol, and other drugs: the role of the pediatrician in prevention, identification, and management of substance abuse. *Pediatrics* 2005;115(3):816–21.

Kumar R, O'Malley PM, Johnston LD. School tobacco control policies related to students' smoking and attitudes toward smoking: national survey results, 1999–2000. *Health Education & Behavior* 2005;32(6):780–94.

Kumpfer KL, Alvarado R, Smith P, Bellamy N. Cultural sensitivity in universal family-based prevention interventions. *Prevention Science* 2002;3(3):241–6.

Kumpfer KL, Molgaard V, Spoth R. The Strengthening Families Program for the prevention of delinquency and drug use in special populations. In: Peters RD, McMahon RJ, editors. *Preventing Childhood Disorders, Substance Abuse, and Delinquency*. Thousand Oaks (CA): Sage Publications, 1996:241–67.

Kumpfer KL, Smith P, Summerhays JF. A wake-up call to the prevention field: are prevention programs for substance use effective for girls? *Substance Use & Misuse* 2008;43(8–9):978–1001.

La Torre G, Chiaradia G, Ricciardi G. School-based smoking prevention in children and adolescents: review of the scientific literature. *Journal of Public Health* 2005;13(6):285–90.

LaFromboise T, Coleman HL, Gerton J. Psychological impact of biculturalism: evidence and theory. *Psychological Bulletin* 1993;114(3):395–412.

Lancaster AR, Lancaster KM. The economics of tobacco advertising: spending, demand, and the effects of bans. *International Journal of Advertising* 2003;22(1):41–65.

Lando HA, Hennrikus D, Boyle R, Lazovich D, Stafne E, Rindal B. Promoting tobacco abstinence among older adolescents in dental clinics. *Journal of Smoking Cessation* 2007;2(1):23–30.

Landrine H, Corral I, Klonoff EA, Jensen J, Kashima K, Hickman N, Martinez J. Ethnic disparities in youth access to tobacco: California statewide results, 1999–2003. *Health Promotion Practice* 2008, DOI: 10.1177/1524839908317230.

Landrine H, Klonoff EA, Alcaraz R. Asking age and identification may decrease minors' access to tobacco. *Preventive Medicine* 1996;25(3):301–6.

Landsbaum JB, Willis RH. Conformity in early and late adolescence. *Developmental Psychology* 1971;4(3):334–7.

Lang A. Using the limited capacity model of motivated mediated message processing to design effective cancer communication messages. *Journal of Communication* 2006;56(Suppl s1):S57–S80.

Lantz PM, Jacobson PD, Warner KE, Wasserman J, Pollack HA, Berson J, Ahlström A. Investing in youth tobacco control: a review of smoking prevention and control strategies. *Tobacco Control* 2000;9(1):47–63.

Lazarsfeld PF, Berelson B, Gaudet H. *The People's Choice: How the Voter Makes Up His Mind in a Presidential Campaign*. New York: Duell, Sloan & Pearce, 1944.

Lazovich D, Ford J, Forster J, Riley B. A pilot study to evaluate a tobacco diversion program. *American Journal of Public Health* 2001;91(11):1790–1.

Lenhart A, Madden M. Social Networking Websites and Teens: An Overview. Washington: Pew Internet & American Life Project, 2007; <http://www.pewinternet.org/media//Files/Reports/2007/PIP_SNS_Data_Memo_Jan_2007.pdf.pdf>; accessed: June 4, 2009.

Lenhart A, Ling R, Campbell S, Purcell K. Teens and Mobile Phones. Washington: Pew Internet & American Life Project, 2010; <http://pewinternet.org/Reports/2010/Teens-and-Mobile-Phones.aspx.>; accessed: June 7, 2011.

Lerner RM. Nature, nurture, and dynamic interactionism. *Human Development* 1978;21(1):1–20.

Lerner RM. Developmental science, developmental systems, and contemporary theories of human development. In: Damon W, Lerner RM, editors-in-chief. *Handbook of Child Psychology, Vol. 1: Theoretical Models of Human Development.* 6th ed. Hoboken (NJ): Wiley & Sons, 2006:1–17.

Lerner RM, Abo-Zena MM, Bebiroglu N, Brittian A, Lynch AD, Issac SS. Positive youth development: contemporary theoretical perspectives. In: DiClemente R, Santelli JS, Crosby RA, editors. *Adolescent Health: Understanding and Preventing Risk Behaviors*. San Francisco: Jossey-Bass, 2009:115–28.

LeRoy L, Benet DJ, Mason T, Austin WD, Mills S. Empowering organizations: approaches to tobacco control through youth empowerment programs. *Health Education & Behavior* 2004;31(5):577–96.

Les Études de Marché Créatec. *Quantitative Study of Canadian Youth Smokers and Vulnerable Non-Smokers: Effects of Modified Packaging Through Increasing the Size of Warnings on Cigarette Packages.* Montreal (Quebec, Canada): Les Études de Marché Créatec, 2008.

Leshner G, Bolls P, Wise K. Motivated processing of fear appeal and disgust images in televised anti-tobacco ads. *Journal of Media Psychology* 2011;23(2):77–89.

Leshner G, Vultee F, Bolls PD, Moore J. When a fear appeal isn't just a fear appeal: the effects of graphic anti-tobacco message. *Journal of Broadcasting & Electronic Media* 2010;54(3):485–507.

Levenson PM, Marrow JR Jr, Pfefferbaum BJ. Attitudes toward health and illness: a comparison of adolescent, physician, teacher, and school nurse views. *Journal of Adolescent Health Care* 1984;5(4):254–60.

Levy D, Friend KB. Strategies for reducing youth access to tobacco: a framework for understanding empirical findings on youth access policies. *Drugs: Education, Prevention and Policy* 2002;9(3):285–303.

Lewit EM, Coate D, Grossman M. The effects of government regulation on teenage smoking. *Journal of Law and Economics* 1981;24(3):545–69.

Lewit E, Hyland A, Kerrebrock N, Cummings KM. Price, public policy, and smoking in young people. *Tobacco Control* 1997; 6(Suppl 2): S17–S24.

Liang L, Chaloupka F, Nichter M, Clayton R. Prices, policies and youth smoking, May 2001. *Addiction* 2003;98(Suppl 1):S105–S122.

Lichtenstein E, Hymowitz N, Nettekoven L. Community Intervention Trial for Smoking Cessation (COMMIT): adapting a standardized protocol for diverse settings. In: Richmond R, editor. *Interventions for Smokers: An International Perspective.* Baltimore: Williams & Wilkins, 1994:259–91.

Liddle HA, Santisteban DA, Levant RF, Bray JH. *Family Psychology: Science-Based Interventions*. Washington: American Psychological Association, 2002.

Liefeld JP. *The Relative Importance of the Size, Content & Pictures on Cigarette Package Warning Messages.* Ottawa (Canada): Health Canada, 1999.

Lightwood J, Glantz S. Effect of the Arizona tobacco control program on cigarette consumption and healthcare expenditures. *Social Science & Medicine* 2011; 72(2):166–72.

Lightwood JM, Dinno A, Glantz SA. Effect of the California tobacco control program on personal health care expenditures. *PLoS Medicine* 2008;5(8):e178. DOI:10.1371.journal.pmed.0050178.

Lin CA, Hullman GA. Tobacco-prevention messages online: social marketing via the Web. *Health Communication* 2005;18(2):177–93.

Ling PM, Landman A, Glantz SA. It is time to abandon youth access tobacco programmes. *Tobacco Control* 2002;11(1):3–6.

Lipkus IM, McBride CM, Pollak KI, Schwartz-Bloom RD, Tilson E, Bloom PN. A randomized trial comparing the effects of self-help materials and proactive telephone counseling on teen smoking cessation. *Health Psychology* 2004;23(4):397–406.

Litrownik AJ, Elder JP, Campbell NR, Ayala GX, Slymen DJ, Parra-Medina D, Zavala FB, Lovato CY. Evaluation of a tobacco and alcohol use prevention program for Hispanic migrant adolescents: promoting the protective factor of parent-child communication. *Preventive Medicine* 2000;31(2 Pt 1):124–33.

Little SJ, Stevens VJ, Severson HH, Lichtenstein E. Effective smokeless tobacco intervention for dental hygiene patients. *Journal of Dental Hygiene* 1992;66(4):185–90.

Lober Aquilino M, Lowe JB. Approaches to tobacco control: the evidence base. *European Journal of Dental Education* 2004;8(Suppl 4):11–7.

Lotecka L, MacWhinney M. Enhancing decision behavior in high school "smokers." *International Journal of the Addictions* 1983;18(4):479–90.

Lotrean LM, Dijk F, Mesters I, Ionut C, De Vries H. Evaluation of a peer-led smoking prevention programme for Romanian adolescents. *Health Education Research* 2010;25(5):803–14.

Lovato CY, Sabiston CM, Hadd V, Nykiforuk CI, Campbell HS. The impact of school smoking policies and student perceptions of enforcement on school smoking prevalence and location of smoking. *Health Education Research* 2007;22(6):782–93.

Lowenthal M, Thurnher M, Chiriboga D. *Four Stages of Life*. San Francisco: Jossey-Bass, 1975.

Lynagh M, Schofield M, Sanson-Fisher R. School health promotion programs over the past decade: a review of the smoking, alcohol and solar protection literature. *Health Promotion International* 1997;12(1):43–60.

Lynam DR, Milich R, Zimmerman R, Novak SP, Logan TK, Martin C, Leukefeld C, Clayton R. Project DARE: no effects at 10-year follow-up. *Journal of Consulting and Clinical Psychology* 1999;67(4):590–3.

Lynch BS, Bonnie RJ, editors. *Growing Up Tobacco Free: Preventing Nicotine Addiction in Children and Youths*. Washington: National Academies Press, 1994.

Makni H, O'Loughlin JL, Tremblay M, Gervais A, Lacroix C, Déry V, Paradis G. Smoking prevention counseling practices of Montreal general practitioners. *Archives of Pediatrics & Adolescent Medicine* 2002;156(12): 1263–7.

Malouff J, Gabrilowitz D, Schutte N. Readability of health warnings on alcohol and tobacco products [letter]. *American Journal of Public Health* 1992;82(3):464.

Marcell AV, Halpern-Felsher BL. Adolescents' beliefs about preferred resources for help vary depending on the health issue. *Journal of Adolescent Health* 2007;41(1):61–8.

Marks A, Fisher M, Lasker S. Adolescent medicine in pediatric practice. *Journal of Adolescent Health Care* 1990;11(2):149–53.

Marr-Lyon L, Young K, Quintero G. An evaluation of youth empowerment tobacco prevention programs in the Southwest. *Journal of Drug Education* 2008;38(1): 39–53.

McAlister A, Perry C, Killen J, Slinkard LA, Maccoby N. Pilot study of smoking, alcohol and drug abuse prevention. *American Journal of Public Health* 1980;70(7):719–21.

McCombs ME, Shaw DL. The agenda-setting function of mass media. *Public Opinion Quarterly* 1972;36(2): 176–87.

McDonald P, Colwell B, Backinger CL, Husten C, Maule CO. Better practices for youth tobacco cessation: evidence of review panel. *American Journal of Health Behavior* 2003;27(Suppl 2):S144–S158.

McGuire WJ. Some contemporary approaches. *Advances in Experimental Social Psychology* 1964;1:191–229.

McMullen KM, Brownson RC, Luke D, Chriqui J. Strength of clean indoor air laws and smoking related outcomes in the USA. *Tobacco Control* 2005;14(1):43–8.

Mejia AB, Ling PM, Glantz SA. Quantifying the effects of promoting smokeless tobacco as a harm reduction strategy in the USA. *Tobacco Control* 2010;19(4): 297–305.

Mermelstein R. Teen smoking cessation. *Tobacco Control* 2003;12(Suppl 1):i25–i34.

Mermelstein R, Turner L. Web-based support as an adjunct to group-based smoking cessation for adolescents. *Nicotine & Tobacco Research* 2006;8(Suppl 1):S69–S76.

Merzenich MM. Cortical plasticity contributing to child development. In: McClelland JL, Siegler R, editors. *Mechanisms of Cognitive Development: Behavioral and Neural Perspectives*. Mahwah (NJ): Lawrence Erlbaum Associates, 2001:67–95.

Meshack AF, Hu S, Pallonen UE, McAlister AL, Gottlieb N, Huang P. Texas Tobacco Prevention Pilot Initiative: processes and effects. *Health Education Research* 2004;19(6):657–68.

Mills AL, White MM, Pierce JP, Messer K. Home smoking bans among U.S. households with children and smokers: opportunities for intervention. *American Journal of Preventive Medicine* 2011;41(6):559–65.

Millstein SG. Health beliefs. In: Lerner RM, Petersen AC, Brooks-Gunn J, editors. *Encyclopedia of Adolescence*. Vol. I. New York: Garland Publishing, 1991:445–9.

Miranda J, Bernal G, Lau A, Kohn L, Hwang WC, LaFromboise T. State of the science on psychological intervention for ethnic minorities. *Annual Review of Clinical Psychology* 2005;1:113–42.

Montemayor R, Flannery DJ. Parent-adolescent relations in middle and late adolescence. In: Lerner RM, Petersen AC, Brooks-Gunn J, editors. *Encyclopedia of Adolescence*. Vol. II. New York: Garland Publishing, 1991:729–34.

Moolchan ET, Robinson ML, Ernst M, Cadet JL, Pickworth WB, Heishman SJ, Schroeder JR. Safety and efficacy of the nicotine patch and gum for the treatment of adolescent tobacco addiction. *Pediatrics* 2005;115(4): e407–e414.

Morton TA, Duck JM. Communication and health beliefs: mass and interpersonal influences on perception of risk to self and others. *Communication Research* 2001;28(5):602–26.

Moyer-Gusé E, Nabi RL. Explaining the effects of narrative in an entertainment television program: overcoming resistance to persuasion. *Human Communication Research* 2010;36(1):26–52.

Mullan F. Don Quixote, Machiavelli, and Robin Hood: public health practice, past and present. *American Journal of Public Health* 2000;90(5):702–6.

Mulye TP, Park MJ, Nelson CD, Adams SH, Irwin CE Jr, Brindis CD. Trends in adolescent and young adult health in the United States. *Journal of Adolescent Health* 2009;45(1):8–24.

Muramoto ML, Leischow SJ, Sherrill D, Matthews E, Strayer LJ. Randomized, double-blind, placebo-controlled trial of 2 dosages of sustained-release bupropion for adolescent smoking cessation. *Archives of Pediatrics & Adolescent Medicine* 2007;161(11):1068–74.

Murnaghan DA, Leatherdale ST, Sihvonen M, Kekki P. A multilevel analysis examining the association between school-based smoking policies, prevention programs and youth smoking behavior: evaluating a provincial tobacco control strategy. *Health Education Research* 2008;23(6):1016–28.

Murnaghan DA, Sihvonen M, Leatherdale ST, Kekki P. The relationship between school-based smoking policies and prevention programs on smoking behavior among grade 12 students in Prince Edward Island: a multilevel analysis. *Preventive Medicine* 2007;44(4):317–22.

Murphy RL. Development of a low-budget tobacco prevention media campaign. *Journal of Public Health Management and Practice* 2000;6(3):45–8.

Murray DM, Perry CL. The measurement of substance use among adolescents: when is the 'bogus pipeline' method needed? *Journal of Addictive Behaviors* 1987;12(3):225–33.

Murray DM, Pirie P, Luepker RV, Pallonen U. Five- and six-year follow-up results from four seventh-grade smoking prevention strategies. *Journal of Behavioral Medicine* 1989b;12(2):207–18.

Murray DM, Prokhorov AV, Harty KC. Effects of a statewide antismoking campaign on mass media messages and smoking beliefs. *Preventive Medicine* 1994;23(1):54–60.

Murray DM, Roche LM, Goldman AI, Whitbeck J. Smokeless tobacco use among ninth graders in a north-central metropolitan population: cross-sectional and prospective associations with age, gender, race, family structure, and other drug use. *Preventive Medicine* 1988;17(4):449–60.

My Last Dip. Home page, 2010; <http://www.mylastdip.com>; accessed: March 16, 2010.

Myers MG, Brown SA. A controlled study of a cigarette smoking cessation intervention for adolescents in substance abuse treatment. *Psychology of Addictive Behaviors* 2005;19(2):230–3.

Nabi RL. The case for emphasizing discrete emotions in communication research. *Communication Monographs* 2010;77(2):153–9.

National Cancer Institute. *Strategies to Control Tobacco Use in the United States: A Blueprint for Public Health Action in the 1990's.* Smoking and Tobacco Control Monograph No. 1. Bethesda (MD): U.S. Department of Health and Human Services, National Institutes of Health, National Cancer Institute, 1991. NIH Publication No. 92-3316.

National Cancer Institute. *Tobacco and the Clinician: Interventions for Medical and Dental Practice.* Smoking and Tobacco Control Monograph No. 5. Bethesda (MD): U.S. Department of Health and Human Services, Public Health Service, National Institutes of Health, National Cancer Institute, 1994. NIH Publication No. 94-3693.

National Cancer Institute. *Changing Adolescent Smoking Prevalence*. Smoking and Tobacco Control Monograph No. 14. Bethesda (MD): U.S. Department of Health and Human Services, Public Health Service, National Institutes of Health, National Cancer Institute, 2001. NIH Publication No. 02-5086.

National Cancer Institute. *ASSIST: Shaping the Future of Tobacco Prevention and Control.* Tobacco Control Monograph No. 16. Bethesda (MD): U.S. Department of Health and Human Services, National Institutes of Health, National Cancer Institute, 2005. NIH Publication No. 05-5645.

National Cancer Institute. *Promoting Healthy Lifestyles: Policy, Program, and Personal Recommendations for Reducing Cancer Risk.* 2006–2007 Annual Report President's Cancer Panel. Bethesda (MD): U.S. Department of Health and Human Services, National Institutes of Health, National Cancer Institute, 2007.

National Cancer Institute. *The Role of the Media in Promoting and Reducing Tobacco Use.* Tobacco Control Monograph No. 19. Bethesda (MD): U.S. Department of Health and Human Services, National Institutes of Health, National Cancer Institute, 2008. NIH Publication No. 07-6242.

Naum GP 3rd, Yarian DO, McKenna JP. Cigarette availability to minors. *Journal of the American Osteopathic Association* 1995;95(11):663–5.

Nelson DE, Mowery P, Tomar S, Marcus S, Giovino G, Zhao L. Trends in smokeless tobacco use among adults and adolescents in the United States. *American Journal of Public Health* 2006;96(5):897–905.

New York State Department of Health. *Cigarette Fire Safety Act,* July 2009; <http://www.nyhealth.gov/prevention/tobacco_control/current_policies.htm>; accessed: March 16, 2010.

Niederdeppe JD. Syntactic indeterminacy, perceived message sensation value-enhancing features, and message processing in the context of anti-tobacco advertisements. *Communication Monographs* 2005;72(3):324–44.

Niederdeppe J, Davis KC, Farrelly MC, Yarsevich J. Stylistic features, need for sensation, and confirmed recall of national smoking prevention advertisements. *Journal of Communication* 2007;57(2):272–92.

Niederdeppe J, Farrelly MC, Haviland ML. Confirming "truth": more evidence of a successful tobacco countermarketing campaign in Florida. *American Journal of Public Health* 2004;94(2):255–7.

Niederdeppe J, Farrelly MC, Hersey JC, Davis KC. Consequences of dramatic reductions in state tobacco control funds: Florida, 1998–2000. *Tobacco Control* 2008;17(3):205–10.

Niederdeppe J, Hersey JC, Farrelly MC, Haviland ML, Healton CG. Comparing adolescent reactions to national tobacco countermarketing advertisements using Web TV. *Social Marketing Quarterly* 2005;11(1):3–18.

Niederhofer H, Huber M. Bupropion may support psychosocial treatment of nicotine-dependent adolescents: preliminary results. *Pharmacotherapy* 2004;24(11):1524–8.

NIH State-of-the-Science Panel. National Institutes of Health State-of-the-Science Conference Statement: Tobacco Use: Prevention, Cessation, and Control. *Annals of Internal Medicine* 2006;145(1):839–44.

Nilsson T. *Legibility and Visual Effectives of Some Proposed and Current Health Warnings on Cigarette Packages*. Charlottetown (Canada): University of Prince Edward Island, 1999.

Noland MP, Kryscio RJ, Riggs RS, Linville LH, Ford VY, Tucker TC. The effectiveness of a tobacco prevention program with adolescents living in a tobacco-producing region. *American Journal of Public Health* 1998;88(12):1862–5.

Nutbeam D, Macaskill P, Smith C, Simpson JM, Catford J. Evaluation of two school smoking education programmes under normal classroom conditions. *BMJ (British Medical Journal)* 1993;306(6870):102–7.

O'Hegarty M, Pederson LL, Nelson DE, Mowery P, Gable JM, Wortley P. Reactions of young adult smokers to warning labels on cigarette packages. *American Journal of Preventive Medicine* 2006;30(6):467–73.

Orr DP, Ingersoll G. Cognition and health. In: Lerner RM, Petersen AC, Brooks-Gunn J, editors. *Encyclopedia of Adolescence*. Vol. I. New York: Garland Publishing, 1991:130–2.

Orzechowski and Walker. *The Tax Burden on Tobacco: Historic Compilation 2010*. Arlington (VA): Orzechowski and Walker, 2010.

Oscós-Sánchez MA, White D, Bajorek E, Dahlman M, Albright T, Treviño J, Bauge SK. SAFE TEENS: facilitators of and barriers to adolescent preventive care discussions. *Family Medicine* 2008;40(2):125–31.

Ozer EM, Adams SH, Gardner LR, Mailloux DE, Wibbelsman CJ, Irwin CE Jr. Provider self-efficacy and the screening of adolescents for risky health behaviors. *Journal of Adolescent Health* 2004;35(2):101–7.

Ozer EM, Adams SH, Lustig JL, Gee S, Garber AK, Gardner LR, Rehbein M, Addison L, Irwin CE Jr. Increasing the screening and counseling of adolescents for risky health behaviors: a primary care intervention. *Pediatrics* 2005;115(4):960–8.

Ozer EM, Adams SH, Lustig JL, Millstein SG, Camfield K, El-Diwany S, Volpe S, Irwin CE Jr. Can it be done: implementing adolescent clinical preventive services. *Health Services Research* 2001;36(6 Pt 2):150–65.

Park E. School-based smoking prevention programs for adolescents in South Korea: a systematic review. *Health Education Research* 2006;21(3):407–15.

Parlove AE, Cowdery JE, Hoerauf SL. Acceptability and appeal of a Web-based smoking prevention intervention for adolescents. *International Electronic Journal of Health Education* 2004;7:1–8.

Patten CA, Croghan IT, Meis TM, Decker PA, Pingree S, Colligan RC, Dornelas EA, Offord KP, Boberg EW, Baumberger RK, et al. Randomized clinical trial of an Internet-based versus brief office intervention for adolescent smoking cessation. *Patient Education and Counseling* 2006;64(1–3):249–58.

Patterson GR. Performance models for antisocial boys. *American Psychologist* 1986;41(4):432–44.

Pbert L, Osganian SK, Gorak D, Druker S, Reed G, O'Neill KM, Sheetz A. A school nurse-delivered adolescent smoking cessation intervention: a randomized controlled trial. *Preventive Medicine* 2006;43(4):312–20.

Pechmann C. Does anti-smoking advertising combat underage smoking: a review of past practices and research. In: Goldberg ME, Fishbein M, Middlestadt SE, editors. *Social Marketing: Theoretical and Practical Perspectives*. Mahwah (NJ): Lawrence Erlbaum Associates, 1997:189–216.

Pechmann C. Changing adolescent smoking prevalence: impact of advertising interventions. In: *Changing Adolescent Smoking Prevalence*. Tobacco Control Monograph No. 14. Bethesda (MD): U.S. Department of Health and Human Services, Public Health Service, National Institutes of Health, National Cancer Institute, 2001. NIH Publication No. 02-5086.

Pechmann C, Reibling ET. Anti-smoking advertising campaigns targeting youth: case studies from USA and Canada. *Tobacco Control* 2000a;9(Suppl 2):ii18–ii31.

Pechmann C, Reibling ET. Planning an effective anti-smoking mass media campaign targeting adolescents. *Journal of Public Health Management and Practice* 2000b;6(3):80–94.

Pechmann C, Reibling ET. Antismoking advertisements for youths: an independent evaluation of health, counter-industry, and industry approaches. *American Journal of Public Health* 2006;96(5):906–13.

Pechmann C, Zhao G, Goldberg ME, Reibling ET. What to convey in antismoking advertisements for adolescents: the use of protection motivation theory to identify effective message themes. *Journal of Marketing* 2003;67(2):1–18.

Pederson LL, Baskerville JC, Lefcoe NM. Change in smoking status among school-aged youth: impact of a smoking-awareness curriculum, attitudes, knowledge and environmental factors. *American Journal of Public Health* 1981;71(12):1401–4.

Pederson LL, Blumenthal DS, Dever A, McGrady G. A Web-based smoking cessation and prevention curriculum for medical students: why, how, what, and what next. *Drug and Alcohol Review* 2006;25(1):39–47.

Pentz MA. Effective prevention programs for tobacco use. *Nicotine & Tobacco Research* 1999;1(Suppl 2):S99–S107.

Pentz MA, Brannon BR, Charlin VL, Barrett EJ, MacKinnon DP, Flay BR. The power of policy: the relationship of smoking policy to adolescent smoking. *American Journal of Public Health* 1989a;79(7):857–62.

Pentz MA, Dwyer JH, MacKinnon DP, Flay BR, Hansen WB, Wang EY, Johnson CA. A multicommunity trial for primary prevention of adolescent drug abuse: effects on drug use prevalence. *JAMA: the Journal of the American Medical Association* 1989b;261(22):3259–66.

Pentz MA, Johnson A, Dwyer JH, MacKinnon DM, Hansen WB, Flay BR. A comprehensive community approach to adolescent drug abuse prevention: effects on cardiovascular disease risk behaviors. *Annals of Medicine* 1989c;21(3):219–22.

Pentz MA, MacKinnon DP, Dwyer JH, Wang EY, Hansen WB, Flay BR, Johnson CA. Longitudinal effects of the Midwestern Prevention Project on regular and experimental smoking in adolescents. *Preventive Medicine* 1989d;18(2):304–21.

Pentz MA, MacKinnon DP, Flay BR, Hansen WB, Johnson CA, Dwyer JH. Primary prevention of chronic diseases in adolescence: effects of the Midwestern Prevention Project on tobacco use. *American Journal of Epidemiology* 1989e;130(4):713–24.

Perry C, Killen J, Telch M, Slinkard LA, Danaher BG. Modifying smoking behavior of teenagers: a school-based intervention. *American Journal of Public Health* 1980;70(7):722–5.

Perry CD, Kenney GM. Differences in pediatric preventive care counseling by provider type. *Ambulatory Pediatrics* 2007;7(5):390–5.

Perry CL, Kelder SH, Klepp KI. Community-wide cardiovascular disease prevention in young people: long-term outcomes of the Class of 1989 Study. *European Journal of Public Health* 1994;4(3):188–94.

Perry CL, Kelder SH, Murray DM, Klepp KI. Communitywide smoking prevention: long-term outcomes of the Minnesota Heart Health Program and the Class of 1989 Study. *American Journal of Public Health* 1992;82(9):1210–6.

Perry CL, Klepp KI, Sillers C. Community-wide strategies for cardiovascular health: the Minnesota Heart Health Program youth program. *Health Education Research* 1989;4(1):87–101.

Perry CL, Komro KA, Veblen-Mortenson S, Bosma LM, Farbakhsh K, Munson KA, Stigler MH, Lytle LA. A randomized controlled trial of the middle and junior high school D.A.R.E. and D.A.R.E. Plus Programs. *Archives of Pediatrics & Adolescent Medicine* 2003;157(2):178–84.

Perry CL, Komro KA, Veblen-Mortenson S, Bosma L, Munson K, Stigler M, Lytle LA, Forster JL, Welles SL. The Minnesota DARE PLUS Project: creating community partnerships to prevent drug use and violence. *Journal of School Health* 2000;70(3):84–8.

Perry CL, Stigler MH, Arora M, Reddy KS. Preventing tobacco use among young people in India: Project MYTRI. *American Journal of Public Health* 2009;99(5):899–906.

Peterson AJ, Clark AW. Using group decision to reduce adolescent girls' smoking. *Psychological Reports* 1986;58(1):179–85.

Peterson AV Jr, Kealey KA, Mann SL, Marek PM, Sarason IG. Hutchinson Smoking Prevention Project: long-term randomized trial in school-based tobacco use prevention—results on smoking. *Journal of the National Cancer Institute* 2000;92(24):1979–91.

Petraitis J, Flay BR, Miller TQ. Reviewing theories of adolescent substance use: organizing pieces in the puzzle. *Psychological Bulletin* 1995;117(1):67–86.

Petraitis J, Flay BR, Miller TQ, Torpy EJ, Greiner B. Illicit substance use among adolescents: a matrix of prospective predictors. *Substance Use & Misuse* 1998;33(13):2561–604.

Petrie J, Bunn F, Byrne G. Parenting programmes for preventing tobacco, alcohol or drugs misuse in children <18: a systematic review. *Health Education Research* 2007;22(2):177–91.

Petrosino A. Standards for evidence and evidence for standards: the case of school-based drug prevention. *Annals of the American Academy of Political and Social Science* 2003;587(1):180–207.

Petrosino A, Turpin-Petrosino C, Finckenauer JO. Well-meaning programs can have harmful effects: lessons from experiments of programs such as Scared Straight. *Crime & Delinquency* 2000;46(3):354–79.

Petty RE, Cacioppo JT. The elaboration likelihood model of persuasion. In: Berkowitz L, editor. *Advances in Experimental and Social Psychology*. Vol. 19. New York: Academic Press, 1986:123–205.

Pierce JP. Tobacco industry marketing, population-based tobacco control, and smoking behavior. *American Journal of Preventive Medicine* 2007;33(6 Suppl):S327–S334.

Pierce JP, White MM, Gilpin EA. Adolescent smoking decline during California's tobacco control programme. *Tobacco Control* 2005;14(3):207–12.

Piper DL, Moberg DP, King MJ. The Healthy for Life Project: behavioral outcomes. *Journal of Primary Prevention* 2000;21(1):47–73.

Popham WJ, Potter LD, Hetrick MA, Muthén LK, Duerr JM, Johnson MD. Effectiveness of the California 1990–1991 tobacco education media campaign. *American Journal of Preventive Medicine* 1994;10(6):319–26.

Portillo F, Antoñanzas F. Information disclosure and smoking risk perceptions: potential short-term impact on Spanish students of the new European Union directive on tobacco products. *European Journal of Public Health* 2002;12(4):295–301.

Powell LM, Tauras JA, Ross H. The importance of peer effects, cigarette prices and tobacco control policies for youth smoking behavior. *Journal of Health Economics* 2005;24(5):950–68.

Pride Surveys. Parents, kids, alcohol and drugs: a disconnect?, June 20, 2006; <www.pridesurveys.com/newsletters/archive/062006.htm>; accessed: May 15, 2009.

Pro-Children Act of 1994, Public Law 103-227, 108 *U.S. Statutes at Large* 125.

Prokhorov AV, Hudmon KS, Marani S, Foxhall L, Ford KH, Luca NS, Wetter DW, Cantor SB, Vitale F, Gritz ER. Engaging physicians and pharmacists in providing smoking cessation counseling. *Archives of Internal Medicine* 2010;170(18):1640–6.

Prokhorov AV, Kelder SH, Shegog R, Murray N, Peters R Jr, Agurcia-Parker C, Cinciripini PM, de Moor C, Conroy JL, Hudmon KS, Ford KH, et al. Impact of A Smoking Prevention Interactive Experience (ASPIRE), an interactive, multimedia smoking prevention and cessation curriculum for culturally diverse high-school students. *Nicotine & Tobacco Research* 2008;10(9):1477–85.

Quinlan KB, McCaul KD. Matched and mismatched interventions with young adult smokers: testing a stage theory. *Health Psychology* 2000;19(2):165–71.

Quit Victoria. New set of graphic health warnings on cigarettes to hit the shelves, as data shows confronting images increase Quitline calls, Feb. 28, 2007; <http://www.quit.org.au/media.asp?ContentID=19175;> accessed: May 15, 2008.

Rabius Y, McAlister AL, Geiger A, Huang P, Todd R. Telephone counseling increases cessation rates among young adult smokers. *Health Psychology* 2004; 23(5):539–41.

Ramesh S. Smokers heed graphic warnings on cigarette packs, May 17, 2006; <http://www.act.tobaccochina.net/englishnew/content.aspx?id=23879>; accessed: May 15, 2009.

Rand CM, Auinger P, Klein JD, Weitzman M. Preventive counseling at adolescent ambulatory visits. *Journal of Adolescent Health* 2005;37(2):87–93.

Ranney L, Melvin C, Lux L, McClain E, Morgan L, Lohr KN. *Tobacco Use: Prevention, Cessation, and Control.* Evidence Report/Technology Assessment No. 140. Research Triangle Park (NC): RTI International-University of North Carolina Evidence-based Practice Center, 2006. AHRQ Publication No. 06-E015.

Reinert B, Carver V, Range LM. Anti-tobacco messages from different sources make a difference with secondary school students. *Journal of Public Health Management and Practice* 2004;10(6):518–23.

Resnicow K, Baranowski T, Ahluwalia JS, Braithwaite RL. Cultural sensitivity in public health: defined and demystified. *Ethnicity & Disease* 1999;9(1):10–21.

Ribisl KM, Steckler A, Linnan L, Patterson CC, Pevzner ES, Markatos E, Goldstein AO, McGloin T, Peterson AB, North Carolina Youth Empowerment Study. The North Carolina Youth Empowerment Study (NCYES): a participatory research study examining the impact of youth empowerment for tobacco use prevention. *Health Education & Behavior* 2004;31(5):597–614.

Richards JI, Curran CM. Oracles on "advertising": searching for a definition. *Journal of Advertising* 2002; 31(2):63–77.

Richardson L, Allen P, McCullough L, Bauld L, Assanand S, Greaves L, Amos A, Hemsing N, Humphries K. *Interventions to Prevent the Uptake of Smoking in Children and Young People.* Vancouver (Canada): Centre of Excellence for Women's Health, 2007.

Rigotti NA. Youth access to tobacco. *Nicotine & Tobacco Research* 1999;1(Suppl 2):S93–S97.

Rigotti NA, DiFranza JR, Chang Y, Tisdale T, Kemp B, Singer DE. The effect of enforcing tobacco-sales laws on adolescents' access to tobacco and smoking behavior. *New England Journal of Medicine* 1997;37(15): 1044–51.

Rigotti NA, Regan S, Majchrzak NE, Knight JR, Wechsler H. Tobacco use by Massachusetts public college students: long term effect of the Massachusetts Tobacco Control Program. *Tobacco Control* 2002;11(Suppl 2):ii20–ii24.

Riley WT, Barenie JT, Mabe PA, Myers DR. The role of race and ethnic status on the psychosocial correlates of smokeless tobacco use in adolescent males. *Journal of Adolescent Health* 1991;12(1):15–21.

Ringel JS, Wasserman J, Andreyeva T. Effects of public policy on adolescents' cigar use: evidence from the National Youth Tobacco Survey. *American Journal of Public Health* 2005;95(6):995–8.

R.J. Reynolds Tobacco Co. v. U.S. Food and Drug Administration, Civil Case No. 11-1482 (D.D.C. 2011).

Robinson LA, Vander Weg MW, Riedel BW, Klesges RC, McLain-Allen B. "Start to stop": results of a randomised controlled trial of a smoking cessation programme for teens. *Tobacco Control* 2003;12(Suppl 4):iv26–iv33.

Robinson TN, Killen JD. Do cigarette warning labels reduce smoking: paradoxical effects among adolescents. *Archives of Pediatrics & Adolescent Medicine* 1997;151(3):267–72.

Roddy E, Romilly N, Challenger A, Lewis S, Britton J. Use of nicotine replacement therapy in socioeconomically deprived young smokers: a community-based pilot randomised controlled trial. *Tobacco Control* 2006;15(5):373–6.

Rodgers A, Corbett T, Bramley D, Riddell T, Wills M, Lin RB, Jones M. Do u smoke after txt: results of a randomised trial of smoking cessation using mobile phone text messaging. *Tobacco Control* 2005;14(4):255–61.

Rogers EM. Diffusion of drug abuse prevention programs: spontaneous diffusion, agenda setting, and reinvention. In: Backer TE, David SL, Saucy G, editors. *Reviewing the Behavioral Science Knowledge Base on Technology Transfer*. NIDA Research Monograph 155. Rockville (MD): U.S. Department of Health and Human Services, Public Health Service, National Institutes of Health, National Institute on Drug Abuse, 1995a:90–105. NIH Publication No. 95-4035.

Rogers EM. *Diffusion of Innovations*. 4th ed. New York: Free Press, 1995b.

Rooney BL, Murray DM. A meta-analysis of smoking prevention programs after adjustment for errors in the unit of analysis. *Health Education Quarterly* 1996;23(1):48–64.

Rootman I, Flay BR. *A Study on Youth Smoking: Plain Packaging, Health Warnings, Event Marketing and Price Reductions*. Key Findings. Toronto (Canada): University of Toronto, University of Illinois at Chicago, York University, Ontario Tobacco Research Unit, Addiction Research Foundation, 1995.

Rosenbaum DP, Flewelling RL, Bailey SL, Ringwalt CL, Wilkinson DL. Cops in the classroom: a longitudinal evaluation of Drug Abuse Resistance Education (D.A.R.E.). *Journal of Research in Crime and Delinquency* 1994;31(1):3–31.

Rosenbaum DP, Hanson GS. Assessing the effects of school-based drug education: a six-year multilevel analysis of Project D.A.R.E. *Journal of Research in Crime and Delinquency* 1998;35(4):381–412.

Rosenberg M. Self-concept and psychological well-being in adolescence. In: Leahy RL, editor. *The Development of the Self*. Orlando (FL): Academic Press, 1985:205–46.

Rosenstock IM. The health belief model and preventive health behavior. *Health Education Monographs* 1974;2(4):354–86.

Rosenthal R. *Meta-Analytic Procedures for Social Research*. Beverly Hills (CA): Sage Publications, 1984.

Ross H, Chaloupka FJ. The effect of cigarette prices on youth smoking. *Health Economics* 2003;12(3):217–30.

Ross H, Chaloupka FJ. The effect of public policies and prices on youth smoking. *Southern Economic Journal* 2004;70(4):796–815.

Ross H, Powell LM, Bauer JE, Levy DT, Peck RM, Lee HR. Community-based youth tobacco control interventions: cost effectiveness of the Full Court Press project. *Applied Health Economics and Health Policy* 2006;5(3):167–76.

Ross H, Powell LM, Tauras JA, Chaloupka FJ. New evidence on youth smoking behavior based on experimental price increases. *Contemporary Economic Policy* 2005;23(2):195–210.

RTI International. *First Annual Independent Evaluation of New York's Tobacco Control Program: Final Report*. Research Triangle Park (NC): RTI International, 2004.

RTI International. *Second Annual Independent Evaluation of New York's Tobacco Control Program: Final Report*. Research Triangle Park (NC): RTI International, 2005.

RTI International. *Fourth Annual Independent Evaluation of New York's Tobacco Control Program: Final Report*. Research Triangle Park (NC): RTI International, 2007.

Saffer H, Chaloupka F. The effect of tobacco advertising bans on tobacco consumption. *Journal of Health Economics* 2000;19(6):1117–37.

Sanders JL, Colson YL. Leveraging primary care in the fight against lung cancer. *Journal of General Internal Medicine* 2008;23(3):344–7.

Schar E, Gutierrez K, Murphy-Hoefer R, Nelson DE. *Tobacco Use Prevention Media Campaigns: Lessons Learned from Youth in Nine Countries*. Atlanta (GA): U.S. Department of Health and Human Services, Centers for Disease Control and Prevention, National Center for Chronic Disease Prevention and Health Promotion, Office on Smoking and Health, 2006.

Schinke SP, Botvin GJ, Orlandi MA, Schilling RF, Gordon AN. African-American and Hispanic-American adolescents, HIV infection and preventive intervention. *AIDS Education and Prevention* 1990;2(4):305–12.

Schinke SP, Gilchrist LD, Schilling RF II, Walker RD, Locklear VS, Bobo JK, Maxwell JS, Trimble JE, Cvetkovich GT. Preventing substance abuse among American Indian and Alaska Native youth. *Journal of Social Service Research* 1987;9(4):53–67.

Schincke SP, Gilchrist LD. Preventing substance abuse with children and adolescents. *Journal of Consulting and Clinical Psychology* 1985;53(5):596–602.

Schinke SP, Gilchrist LD. Preventing tobacco use among young people. *Health and Social Work* 1986;11(1):59–65.

Schinke SP, Gilchrist LD, Schilling RF II, Senechal VA. Smoking and smokeless tobacco use among adolescents: trends and intervention results. *Public Health Reports* 1986;101(4):373–8.

Schinke SP, Orlandi MA, Botvin GJ, Gilchrist LD, Trimble JE, Locklear VS. Preventing substance abuse among American-Indian adolescents: a bicultural competence skills approach. *Journal of Counseling Psychology* 1988;35(1):87–90.

Schinke SP, Schwinn TM, Di Noia J, Cole KC. Reducing the risks of alcohol use among urban youth: three-year effects of a computer-based intervention with and without parent involvement. *Journal of Studies on Alcohol* 2004;65(4):443–9.

Schinke SP, Tepavac L, Cole KC. Preventing substance use among Native American youth: three-year results. *Addictive Behaviors* 2000;25(3):387–97.

Schmitt CL, Malarcher AM, Clark PI, Bombard JM, Strauss W, Stillman FA. Community guide recommendations and state level tobacco control programmes: 1999–2004. *Tobacco Control* 2007;16(5):318–24.

Schofield MJ, Redman S, Sanson-Fisher RW. A community approach to smoking prevention: a review. *Behaviour Change* 1991;8(1);17–25.

Seghers T, Foland S. Anti-tobacco media campaign for young people. *Tobacco Control* 1998;7(Suppl 1): S29–S30.

Severson HH, Andrews JA, Lichtenstein E, Gordon JS, Barckley MF. Using the hygiene visit to deliver a tobacco cessation program: results of a randomized clinical trial. *Journal of the American Dental Association* 1998;129(7):993–9.

Severson HH, Ary DV. Sampling bias due to consent procedures with adolescents. *Addictive Behaviors* 1983; 8(4):433–7.

Severson HH, Biglan A. Rationale for the use of passive consent in smoking prevention research: politics, policy, and pragmatics. *Preventive Medicine* 1989; 18(2):267–79.

Severson HH, Danaher BG. An Internet-Based Smokeless Tobacco Cessation Program for Teens, October 6, 2009; <http://clinicaltrials.gov/ct2/show/NCT00680615>; accessed: March 16, 2010.

Severson HH, Forrester K, Biglan A. Use of smokeless tobacco is a risk factor for cigarette smoking. *Nicotine & Tobacco Research* 2007;9(12):1331–7.

Severson HH, Glasgow R, Wirt R, Brozovsky P, Zoref L, Black C, Biglan A, Ary D, Weissman W. Preventing the use of smokeless tobacco and cigarettes by teens: results of a classroom intervention. *Health Education Research* 1991;6(1):109–20.

Severson HH, Gordon JS, Danaher BG, Akers LA. ChewFree.com: evaluation of a Web-based cessation program for smokeless tobacco users. *Nicotine & Tobacco Research* 2008;10(2):381–91.

Severson HH, Hatsukami D. Smokeless tobacco cessation. *Primary Care* 1999;26(3):529–51.

Severson HH, Klein K, Lichtensein E, Kaufman N, Orleans CT. Smokeless tobacco use among professional baseball players: survey results, 1998 to 2003. *Tobacco Control* 2005;14(1):31–6.

Shaffer H, Beck JC, Boothroyd P. The primary prevention of smoking onset: an inoculation approach. *Journal of Psychoactive Drugs* 1983;15(3):177–84.

Sharma A. Recall of television commercials as a function of viewing context: the impact of program-commercial congruity on commercial messages. *Journal of General Psychology* 2000;127(4):383–96.

Shean RE, de Klerk NH, Armstrong BK, Walker NR. Seven-year follow-up of a smoking-prevention program for children. *Australian Journal of Public Health* 1994;18(2):205–8.

Shelley D, Fahs M, Scheinmann R, Swain S, Qu J, Burton D. Acculturation and tobacco use among Chinese Americans. *American Journal of Public Health* 2004;94(2):300–7.

Shen L, Monahan JL, Rhodes N, Roskos-Ewoldsen D. The impact of attitude accessibility and decision style on adolescents' biased processing of health-related public service announcements. *Communication Research* 2009;36(1);104–28.

Shope JT, Copeland LA, Kamp ME, Lang SW. Twelfth grade follow-up of the effectiveness of a middle school-based substance abuse prevention program. *Journal of Drug Education* 1998;28(3):185–97.

Siahpush M, Wakefield M, Spittal M, Durkin S. Antismoking television advertising and socioeconomic variations in calls to Quitline. *Journal of Epidemiology and Community Health* 2007;61(4):298–301.

Siddiqui O, Flay BR, Hu FB. Factors affecting attrition in a longitudinal smoking prevention study. *Preventive Medicine* 1996;25(5):554–60.

Siegel M. Mass media antismoking campaigns: a powerful tool for health promotion. *Annals of Internal Medicine* 1998;129(2):128–32.

Siegel M. The effectiveness of state-level tobacco control interventions: a review of program implementation and behavioral outcomes. *Annual Review of Public Health* 2000;23:45–71.

Siegel M. Antismoking advertising: figuring out what works. *Journal of Health Communication* 2002; 7(2):157–62.

Siegel M, Albers AB, Cheng DM, Biener L, Rigotti NA. Effect of local restaurant smoking regulations on progression to established smoking among youths. *Tobacco Control* 2005;14(5):300–6.

Siegel M, Albers AB, Cheng DM, Hamilton WL, Biener L. Local restaurant smoking regulations and the adolescent smoking initiation process: results of a multilevel contextual analysis among Massachusetts youth. *Archives of Pediatrics & Adolescent Medicine* 2008;162(5):477–83.

Siegel M, Biener L. The impact of an antismoking media campaign on progression to established smoking: results of a longitudinal youth study. *American Journal of Public Health* 2000;90(3):380–6.

Sirichotiratana N, Techatraisakdi C, Sujirarat D, Rahman K, Warren CW, Jones NR, Asma S, Lee J. *Linking Global Youth Tobacco Survey (GYTS) Data to the WHO Framework Convention on Tobacco Control: The Case for Thailand*. Bangkok (Thailand): Mahidol University, 2005.

Sithole EGV. *Global School–Based Health Survey Zimbabwe 2003*. Harare (Zimbabwe): Ministry of Health and Child Welfare, 2003.

Skara S, Sussman S. A review of 25 long-term adolescent tobacco and other drug use prevention program evaluations. *Preventive Medicine* 2003;37(5):451–74.

Skeer M, George S, Hamilton WL, Cheng DM, Siegel M. Town-level characteristics and smoking policy adoption in Massachusetts: are local restaurant smoking regulations fostering disparities in health protection? *American Journal of Public Health* 2004;94(2):286–92.

Slater MD, Kelly KJ, Edwards RW, Thurman PJ, Plested BA, Keefe TJ, Lawrence FR, Henry KL. Combining in-school and community-based media efforts: reducing marijuana and alcohol uptake among younger adolescents. *Health Education Research* 2006;21(1):157–67.

Sloan FA, Carlisle ES, Rattliff JR, Trogdon J. Determinants of states' allocations of the master settlement agreement payments. *Journal of Health Politics, Policy and Law* 2005;30(4):643–86.

Sloan FA, Trogdon JG. The impact of the master settlement agreement on cigarette consumption. *Journal of Policy Analysis and Management* 2004;23(4):843–55.

Sloboda Z, Stephens P, Pyakuryal A, Teasdale B, Stephens RC, Hawthorne RD, Marquette J, Williams JE. Implementation fidelity: the experience of the Adolescent Substance Abuse Prevention Study. *Health Education Research* 2009;24(3):394–406.

Slovic P. Cigarette smokers: rational actors or rational fools? In: Slovic P, editor. *Smoking: Risk, Perception & Policy*. Thousand Oaks (CA): Sage Publications, 2001:97–124.

Sly DF, Arheart K, Dietz N, Trapido EJ, Nelson D, Rodriguez R, McKenna J, Lee D. The outcome consequences of defunding the Minnesota youth tobacco-use prevention program. *Preventive Medicine* 2005;41(2):503–10.

Sly DF, Heald GR, Ray S. The Florida "truth" anti-tobacco media evaluation: design, first year results, and implications for planning future state media evaluations. *Tobacco Control* 2001a;10(1):9–15.

Sly DF, Hopkins RS, Trapido E, Ray S. Influence of a counteradvertising media campaign on initiation of smoking: the Florida "truth" campaign. *American Journal of Public Health* 2001b;91(2):233–8.

Sly DF, Trapido E, Ray S. Evidence of the dose effects of an antitobacco counteradvertising campaign. *Preventive Medicine* 2002;35(5):511–18.

Smith KH, Stutts MA. Effects of short-term cosmetic versus long-term health fear appeals in anti-smoking advertisements on the smoking behaviour of adolescents. *Journal of Consumer Behaviour* 2006;3(2):157–77.

Smith TA, House RF Jr, Croghan IT, Gauvin TR, Colligan RC, Offord KP, Gomez-Dahl LC, Hurt RD. Nicotine patch therapy in adolescent smokers. *Pediatrics* 1996;98(4 Pt 1):659–67.

Soldz S, Clark TW, Stewart E, Celebucki C, Walker DK. Decreased youth tobacco use in Massachusetts 1996 to 1999: evidence of tobacco control effectiveness. *Tobacco Control* 2002;11(Suppl 2):ii14–ii19.

Soldz S, Kreiner P, Clark TW, Krakow M. Tobacco use among Massachusetts youth: is tobacco control working? *Preventive Medicine* 2000;31(4):287–95.

Solomon LJ, Bunn JY, Flynn BS, Pirie PL, Worden JK, Ashikaga T. Mass media for smoking cessation in adolescents. *Health Education & Behavior* 2009;36(4):642–59.

Southwell BG, Yzer MC. The roles of interpersonal communication in mass media campaigns. In: Beck CS, editor. *Communication Yearbook*. New York: Lawrence Erlbaum Associates, 2008;31:420–62.

Sowden AJ. Mass media interventions for preventing smoking in young people. *Cochrane Database of Systematic Reviews* 1998, Issue 4. Art. No.: CD001006. DOI: 10.1002/14651858.CD001006.

Sowden AJ, Stead LF. Community interventions for preventing smoking in young people. *Cochrane Database of Systematic Reviews* 2003, Issue 1. Art. No.: CD001291, DOI: 10.1002/14651858.CD001291.

Spoth R, Redmond C, Shin C, Greenberg M, Clair S, Feinberg M. Substance abuse outcomes at 18 months past baseline: the PROSPER Community-University Partnership Trial. *American Journal of Preventive Medicine* 2007;32(5):395–402.

Spoth RL, Redmond C, Shin C. Randomized trial of brief family interventions for general populations: adolescent substance use outcomes 4 years following baseline. *Journal of Consulting and Clinical Psychology* 2001;69(4):627–42.

Spoth RL, Redmond C, Trudeau L, Shin C. Longitudinal substance initiation outcomes for a universal preventive intervention combining family and school programs. *Psychology of Addictive Behaviors* 2002;16(2):129–34.

St. Pierre T, Kaltreider DL, Mark MM, Aikin KJ. Drug prevention in a community setting: a longitudinal study of the relative effectiveness of a 3-year primary prevention program in Boys & Girls Clubs across the nation. *American Journal of Community Psychology* 1992;20(6):673–706.

Stark E, Kim A, Miller C, Borgida E. Effects of including a graphic warning label in advertisements for reduced-exposure products: implications for persuasion and policy. *Journal of Applied Social Psychology* 2008;38(2):281–93.

Stead LF, Lancaster T. Interventions for preventing tobacco sales to minors. *Cochrane Database of Systematic Reviews* 2005, Issue 1. Art. No.: CD001497. DOI: 10.1002/14651858.CD001497.pub2.

Stead M, Hastings G, Tudor-Smith C. Preventing adolescent smoking: a review of options. *Health Education Journal* 1996;55(1):31–54.

Steinberg L. Parent-adolescent relations. In: Lerner RM, Petersen AC, Brooks-Gunn J, editors. *Encyclopedia of Adolescence*. Vol. II. New York: Garland Publishing, 1991:724–8.

Steinberg L, Dahl R, Keating D, Kupfer DJ, Masten AS, Pine DS. The study of developmental psychopathology in adolescence: integrating affective neuroscience with the study of context. In: Cicchetti D, Cohen DJ, editors. *Developmental Psychopathology Vol. 2: Developmental Neuroscience*. 2nd ed. Hoboken (NJ): John Wiley & Sons, 2006:710–41.

Steinberg L, Morris AS. Adolescent development. *Annual Review of Psychology* 2001;52:83–110.

Stephens T, Kaiserman MJ, McCall DJ, Sutherland-Brown C. School-based smoking prevention: economic costs versus benefits. *Chronic Diseases in Canada* 2000;21(2):62–7.

Stevens MM, Olson AL, Gaffney CA, Tosteson TD, Mott LA, Starr P. A pediatric, practice-based, randomized trial of drinking and smoking prevention and bicycle helmet, gun, and seatbelt safety promotion. *Pediatrics* 2002;109(3):490–7.

Stoddard AM, Fagan P, Sorensen G, Hunt MK, Frazier L, Girod K. Reducing cigarette smoking among working adolescents: results from the SMART Study. *Cancer Causes & Control* 2005;16(10):1159–64.

Storr CL, Ialongo NS, Kellam SG, Anthony JC. A randomized controlled trial of two primary school intervention strategies to prevent early onset tobacco smoking. *Drug and Alcohol Dependence* 2002;66(1):51–60.

Stotts RC, Roberson PK, Hanna EY, Jones SK, Smith CK. A randomised clinical trial of nicotine patches for treatment of spit tobacco addiction among adolescents. *Tobacco Control* 2003;12(Suppl 4):iv11–iv15.

Strahan EJ, White K, Fong GT, Fabrigar LR, Zanna MP, Cameron R. Enhancing the effectiveness of tobacco package warning labels: a social psychological perspective. *Tobacco Control* 2002;11(3):183–90.

Substance Abuse and Mental Health Services Administration. FFY 2010 Annual Synar Reports: Youth Tobacco Sales, 2011. Rockville (MD): U.S. Department of Health and Human Services, Substance Abuse and Mental Health Services Administration. <http://store.samhsa.gov/shin/content/SYNAR-11/SYNAR-11.pdf>.

Suedfeld P, Landon PB, Pargament R, Epstein YM. An experimental attack on smoking (Attitude Manipulation in Restricted Environments, III). *Substance Use & Misuse* 1972;7(4):721–33.

Sussman S. School-based tobacco use prevention and cessation: where are we going? *American Journal of Health Behavior* 2001;25(3):191–9.

Sussman S. Effects of sixty six adolescent tobacco use cessation trials and seventeen prospective studies of self-initiated quitting. *Tobacco Induced Diseases* 2002;1(1):35–81.

Sussman S, Dent CW, Brannon BR, Glowacz K, Gleason LR, Ullery S, Hansen WB, Johnson CA, Flay BR. The television, school and family smoking prevention/cessation project. IV: Controlling for program success expectancies across experimental and control conditions. *Addictive Behaviors* 1989;14(6):601–10.

Sussman S, Dent CW, Burton D, Stacy AW, Flay BR. *Developing School-Based Tobacco Use Prevention and Cessation Programs*. Thousand Oaks (CA): Sage Publications, 1995.

Sussman S, Dent CW, Lichtman KL. Project EX: outcomes of a teen smoking cessation program. *Addictive Behaviors* 2001;26(3):425–38.

Sussman S, Dent CW, Stacy AW. Project Towards No Drug Abuse: a review of the findings and future directions. *American Journal of Health Behavior* 2002;26(5): 354–65.

Sussman S, Dent CW, Stacy AW, Craig S. One-year outcomes of Project Towards No Drug Abuse. *Preventive Medicine* 1998;27(4):632–42.

Sussman S, Dent CW, Stacy AW, Hodgson CS, Burton D, Flay BR. Project Towards No Tobacco Use: implementation, process and post-test knowledge evaluation. *Health Education Research* 1993a;8(1):109–23.

Sussman S, Dent CW, Stacy AW, Sun P, Craig S, Simon TR, Burton D, Flay BR. Project Towards No Tobacco Use: 1-year behavior outcomes. *American Journal of Public Health* 1993b;83(9):1245–50.

Sussman S, Lichtman K, Ritt A, Pallonen UE. Effects of thirty-four adolescent tobacco use cessation and prevention trials on regular users of tobacco products. *Substance Use & Misuse* 1999;34(11):1469–1503.

Sussman S, McCuller WJ, Zheng H, Pfingston YM, Miyano J, Dent CW. Project EX: a program of empirical research on adolescent tobacco use cessation. *Tobacco Induced Diseases* 2004;2(3):119–32.

Sussman S, Miyano J, Rohrbach LA, Dent CW, Sun P. Six-month and one-year effects of Project EX-4: a classroom-based smoking prevention and cessation intervention program. *Addictive Behaviors* 2007;32(12):3005–14.

Sussman S, Sun P. Youth tobacco use cessation: 2008 update. *Tobacco Induced Diseases* 2009;5:3.

Sussman S, Sun P, Dent CW. A meta-analysis of teen cigarette smoking cessation. *Health Psychology* 2006; 25(5):549–57.

Sussman S, Yang D, Baezconde-Garbanati L, Dent CW. Drug abuse prevention program development: results among Latino and non-Latino white adolescents. *Evaluation & the Health Professions* 2003;26(4):355–79.

Sutfin EL, Szykman LR, Moore MC. Adolescents' responses to anti-tobacco advertising: exploring the role of adolescents' smoking status and advertisement theme. *Journal of Health Communication* 2008;13(5):480–500.

Sutton CD. A hard road: finding ways to reduce teen tobacco use [editorial]. *Tobacco Control* 2000;9(1):1–2.

Swart D, Reddy P, Pitt B, Panday S. *The Prevalence & Determinants of Tobacco-Use Among Grade 8 – 10 Learners in South Africa*. Cape Town (South Africa): National Health Promotion Research & Development Group, Medical Research Council, 2001.

Szczypka G, Wakefield M, Emery S, Flay B, Chaloupka F, Slater S, Terry-McElrath Y, Saffer H. *Population Exposure to State Funded Televised Anti-Tobacco Advertising in the United States - 37 States and the District of Columbia, 1999–2003.* Chicago: University of Illinois at Chicago, 2005.

Tandemar Research. *Cigarette Packaging Study: The Evaluation of New Health Warning Messages*. Toronto (Canada): Tandemar Research, 1996.

Tang KC, Rissel C, Bauman A, Dawes A, Porter S, Fay J, Steven B. Evaluation of Kickbutts—a school and community-based smoking prevention program among a sample of year 7 and 8 students. *Health Promotion Journal of Australia* 1997;7(2):122–7.

Tangari AH, Burton S, Andrews JC, Netemeyer RG. How do antitobacco campaign advertising and smoking status affect beliefs and intentions: some similarities and differences between adults and adolescents. *Journal of Public Policy & Marketing* 2007;26(1):60–74.

Tanti C, Stukas A, Halloran MJ, Foddy M. Social identity change: shifts in social identity during adolescence. *Journal of Adolescence* 2011;34(3):555–67.

Task Force on Community Preventive Services. Recommendations regarding interventions to reduce tobacco use and exposure to environmental tobacco smoke. *American Journal of Preventive Medicine* 2001;20(2 Suppl):S10–S15.

Task Force on Community Preventive Services. Tobacco. In: Zaza S, Briss PA, Harris KW, editors. *Preventive Services: What Works to Promote Health?* New York: Oxford University Press, 2005:3–79. <http://www.thecommunityguide.org/tobacco/Tobacco.pdf>

Tauras JA. Public policy and smoking cessation among young adults in the United States. *Health Policy* 2004; 68(3):321–32.

Tauras JA. Can public policy deter smoking escalation among young adults? *Journal of Policy Analysis and Management* 2005;24(4):771–84.

Tauras J, Powell L, Chaloupka F, Ross H. The demand for smokeless tobacco among male high school students in the United States: the impact of taxes, prices and policies. *Applied Economics* 2007;39(1):31–41.

Tauras JA, Chaloupka FJ. Determinants of smoking cessation: an analysis of young adult men and women. In: Grossman M, Hsieh C-R, editors. *Economic Analysis of Substance Use and Abuse: The Experience of Developed Countries and Lessons for Developing Countries*. Cheltenham (England): Edward Elgar Publishing, 2001:337–64.

Tauras JA, Chaloupka FJ, Farrelly MC, Giovino GA, Wakefield M, Johnston LD, O'Malley PM, Kloska DD, Pechacek TF. State tobacco control spending and youth smoking. *American Journal of Public Health* 2005a;95(2):338–44.

Tauras JA, Markowitz S, Cawley J. Tobacco control policies and youth smoking: evidence from a new era. *Advances in Health Economics and Health Services Research* 2005b;16:277–91.

Tauras JA, O'Malley PM, Johnston LD. *Effects Of Price And Access Laws On Teenage Smoking Initiation: A National Longitudinal Analysis*. Working Paper No. 8331. Cambridge (MA): National Bureau of Economic Research, 2001.

Teeboom Y. *Waarschuwende Teksten op Sigarettenpakjes* (Warning Texts on Cigarette Packs) [Dutch]. Amsterdam: Dutch Institute for Public Opinion and Market Research, 2002.

Teenage Research Unlimited. *Counter-Tobacco Advertising Exploratory Summary Report January-March 1999*. Northbrook (IL): Teenage Research Unlimited, 1999.

Telch MJ, Killen JD, McAlister AL, Perry CL, Maccoby N. Long term follow-up of a pilot project on smoking prevention with adolescents. *Journal of Behavioral Medicine* 1982;5(1):1–8.

Tell GS, Vellar OD. Noncommunicable disease risk factor intervention in Norwegian adolescents: the Oslo Youth Study. In: Hetzel BS, Berenson GS, eds. *Cardiovascular Risk Factors in Childhood: Epidemiology and Prevention*. Amsterdam (Netherlands): Elsevier Science Publishers BV;1987:203–17.

Tellis GJ. *Effective Advertising: Understanding When, How, and Why Advertising Works*. Thousand Oaks (CA): Sage Publications, 2004.

Tengs TO. Enormous variation in the cost-effectiveness of prevention: implications for public policy. *Current Issues in Public Health* 1996;2:13–7.

Tengs TO, Adams M, Pliskin J, Safran DG, Siegel JE, Weinstein MC, Graham JD. Five-hundred life-saving interventions and their cost-effectiveness. *Risk Analysis* 1995;15(3):369–90.

Tengs TO, Osgood ND, Chen LL. The cost-effectiveness of intensive national school-based anti-tobacco education: results from the tobacco policy model. *Preventive Medicine* 2001;33(6):558–70.

Tercyak KP, Peshkin BN, Abraham A, Wine L, Walker LR. Interest in genetic counseling and testing for adolescent nicotine addiction susceptibility among a sample of adolescent medicine providers attending a scientific conference on adolescent health. *Journal of Adolescent Health* 2007;41(1):42–50.

Terry-McElrath Y, Wakefield MA, Emery S, Saffer H, Szczypka G, O'Malley P, Johnston LD, Chaloupka FJ, Flay BR. State anti-smoking advertising and smoking outcomes by gender and race/ethnicity. *Ethnicity and Health* 2007;12(4):339–62.

Terry-McElrath Y, Wakefield M, Ruel E, Balch GI, Emery S, Szczypka G, Clegg-Smith K, Flay B. The effect of antismoking advertisement executional characteristics on youth comprehension, appraisal, recall, and engagement. *Journal of Health Communication* 2005;10(2):127–43.

Texas Department of State Health Services. *Texas Tobacco Prevention Initiative: Infrastructure and Baseline Data*. Texas Department of Health, Austin(TX): 2001; <http://www.dshs.state.tx.us/tobacco/ttpireps.shtm>; accessed: November 16, 2011.

The Community Guide. Home page, 2011; <http://www.thecommunityguide.org/index.html>; accessed: December 29, 2011.

The Truth. Home page, 2010; <http://www.thetruth.com>; accessed: March 16, 2010.

Thomas RE, Baker PRA, Lorenzetti D. Family-based programmes for preventing smoking by children and adolescents (Protocol). *Cochrane Database of Systematic Reviews* 2003, Issue 4. Art. No.: CD004493. DOI: 10.1002/14651858.CD004493.

Thomas RE, Baker PRA, Lorenzetti D. Family-based programmes for preventing smoking by children and adolescents. *Cochrane Database of Systematic Reviews* 2007, Issue 1. Art. No.: CD004493. DOI: 10.1002/14651858.CD004493.pub2.

Thomas RE, Perera R. School-based programmes for preventing smoking. *Cochrane Database of Systematic Reviews* 2006, Issue 3. Art. No.: CD001293. DOI: 10.1002/14651858.CD001293.pub2.

Thompson EL. Smoking education programs 1960–1976. *American Journal of Public Health* 1978;68(3):250–7.

Thrasher JF, Hammond D, Fong GT, Arillo-Santillán E. Smokers' reactions to cigarette package warnings with graphic imagery and with only text: a comparison between Mexico and Canada. *Salud Pública de México* 2007;49(Suppl 2):S233–S240.

Thrasher JF, Niederdeppe J, Farrelly MC, Davis KC, Ribisl KM, Haviland ML. The impact of anti-tobacco industry prevention messages in tobacco producing regions: evidence from the US truth campaign. *Tobacco Control* 2004;13(3):283–8.

Thrasher JF, Niederdeppe JD, Jackson C, Farrelly MC. Using anti-tobacco industry messages to prevent smoking among high-risk adolescents. *Health Education Research* 2006;21(3):325–37.

Tingle LR, DeSimone M, Covington B. A meta-evaluation of 11 school-based smoking prevention programs. *Journal of School Health* 2003;73(2):64–7.

Tobacco Labelling Resource Centre. Camel Filters, 2011a; <http://www.tobaccolabels.ca/gallery/canadapacks/camelfilterscanadaapr2007jpg>; accessed: January 20, 2011.

Tobacco Labelling Resource Centre. Large (Marlboro package), 2011b; <http://www.tobaccolabels.ca/gallery/emission/usconsti/large>; accessed: January 20, 2011.

Tobacco Labelling Resource Centre. Original (Australian warning), 2011c; <http://www.tobaccolabels.ca/gallery/australi/aussi!~76/original>; accessed: January 20, 2011.

Tobler NS, Roona MR, Ochshorn P, Marshall DG, Streke AV, Stackpole KM. School-based adolescent drug prevention programs: 1998 meta-analysis. *Journal of Primary Prevention* 2000;20(4):275–336.

Tobler NS, Stratton HH. Effectiveness of school-based drug prevention programs: a meta-analysis of the research. *Journal of Primary Prevention* 1997;18(1):71–128.

Twenge JM. *Generation Me: Why Today's Young Americans Are More Confident, Assertive, Entitled—and More Miserable Than Ever Before*. New York: Free Press, 2006.

U.K. Department of Health. *Consultation on the Introduction of Picture Warnings on Tobacco Packs*. London: U.K. Department of Health, 2006.

Unger JB, Cruz TB, Schuster D, Flora JA, Johnson CA. Measuring exposure to pro- and anti-tobacco marketing among adolescents: intercorrelations among measures and associations with smoking status. *Journal of Health Communication* 2001;6(1):11–29.

Unger JB, Rohrbach LA, Howard KA, Cruz TB, Johnson CA, Chen X. Attitudes toward anti-tobacco policy among California youth: associations with smoking status, psychosocial variables and advocacy actions. *Health Education Research* 1999;14(6):751–63.

University of Colorado at Boulder. Program Matrix, 2010; <http://www.colorado.edu/cspv/blueprints/matrixfiles/matrix.pdf>; accessed: March 16, 2010.

U.S. Department of Health and Human Services. *Reducing the Health Consequences of Smoking: 25 Years of Progress. A Report of the Surgeon General*. Rockville (MD): U.S. Department of Health and Human Services, Public Health Service, Centers for Disease Control, National Center for Chronic Disease Prevention and Health Promotion, Office on Smoking and Health, 1989. DHHS Publication No. (CDC) 89-8411.

U.S. Department of Health and Human Services. *Preventing Tobacco Use Among Young People. A Report of the Surgeon General.* Atlanta (GA): U.S. Department of Health and Human Services, Public Health Service, Centers for Disease Control and Prevention, National Center for Chronic Disease Prevention and Health Promotion, Office on Smoking and Health, 1994.

U.S. Department of Health and Human Services. *State Oversight of Tobacco Sales to Minors*. Rockville (MD): U.S. Department of Health and Human Services, Office of the Inspector General, 1995. OEI-02-94-00270.

U.S. Department of Health and Human Services. *Put Prevention into Practice.* Clinician's Handbook of Preventive Services, 2nd ed. Washington: U.S. Government Printing Office, 1998.

U.S. Department of Health and Human Services. *Healthy People 2010: Understanding and Improving Health*. 2nd ed. Washington: U.S. Government Printing Office, 2000a.

U.S. Department of Health and Human Services. *Reducing Tobacco Use. A Report of the Surgeon General.* Atlanta (GA): U.S. Department of Health and Human Services, Centers for Disease Control and Prevention, National Center for Chronic Disease Prevention and Health Promotion, Office on Smoking and Health, 2000b.

U.S. Department of the Treasury. Federal Excise Tax Increase and Related Provisions, 2009; http://www.ttb.gov/main_pages/schip-summary.shtml; accessed: May 24, 2011.

U.S. Food and Drug Administration. Cigarette health warnings, 2011; <http://www.fda.gov/TobaccoProducts/Labeling/CigaretteWarningLabels/default.htm>; accessed: July 6, 2011.

U.S. Preventive Services Task Force. *Counseling to Prevent Tobacco Use and Tobacco-Caused Disease. Recommendation Statement.* Rockville (MD): Agency for Healthcare Research and Quality, 2003.

U.S. Preventive Services Task Force. Counseling and interventions to prevent tobacco use and tobacco-caused disease in adults and pregnant women: U.S. Preventive services Task Force reaffirmation recommendation statement. *Annals of Internal Medicine* 2009;150(8):551–5.

Vallone D. Media and social marketing: the next generation of NCI state and community tobacco control policy research and dissemination. Presentation at the Society for Research on Nicotine and Tobacco; February 23, 2007; Austin (TX).

Vartiainen E, Fallonen U, McAlister AL, Puska P. Eight-year follow-up results of an adolescent smoking prevention program: the North Karelia Youth Project. *American Journal of Public Health* 1990;80(1):78–9.

Vartiainen E, Paavola M, McAlister A, Puska P. Fifteen-year follow-up of smoking prevention effects in the North Karelia Youth Project. *American Journal of Public Health* 1998;88(1):81–5.

Vartiainen E, Pallonen U, McAlister A, Koskela K, Puska P. Effect of two years of educational intervention on adolescent smoking (the North Karelia Youth Project). *Bulletin of the World Health Organization* 1983;61(3):529–32.

Vartiainen E, Pallonen U, McAlister A, Koskela K, Puska P. Four-year follow-up results of the smoking prevention program in the North Karelia Youth Project. *Preventive Medicine* 1986;15(6):692–8.

Vélez MB. The role of public social control in urban neighborhoods: a multilevel analysis of victimization risk. *Criminology* 2001;39(4):837–64.

Vickers KS, Thomas JL, Patten CA, Mrazek DA. Prevention of tobacco use in adolescents: review of current findings and implications for healthcare providers. *Current Opinion in Pediatrics* 2002;14(6):708–12.

Viswanath K, Breen N, Meissner H, Moser RP, Hesse B, Steele WR, Rakowski W. Cancer knowledge and disparities in the information age. *Journal of Health Communication* 2006;11(Suppl 1):S1–S17.

Wakefield M, Balch GI, Ruel E, Terry-McElrath Y, Szczypka G, Flay B, Emery S, Clegg-Smith K. Youth responses to anti-smoking advertisements from tobacco control agencies, tobacco companies, and pharmaceutical companies. *Journal of Applied Social Psychology* 2005a; 35(9):1894–910.

Wakefield M, Chaloupka F. Effectiveness of comprehensive tobacco control programmes in reducing teenage smoking in the USA. *Tobacco Control* 2000;9(2):177–86.

Wakefield M, Durrant R, Terry-McElrath Y, Ruel E, Balch GI, Anderson S, Szczypka G, Emery S, Flay B. Appraisal of anti-smoking advertising by youth at risk for regular smoking: a comparative study in the United States, Australia, and Britain. *Tobacco Control* 2003a;12(Suppl 2):ii82–ii86.

Wakefield M, Flay B, Nichter M, Giovino G. Effects of anti-smoking advertising on youth smoking: a review. *Journal of Health Communication* 2003b;8(3):229–47.

Wakefield M, Flay B, Nichter M, Giovino G. Role of the media in influencing trajectories of youth smoking. *Addiction* 2003c;98(Suppl 1):S79–S103.

Wakefield M, Forster J. Growing evidence for new benefit of clean indoor air laws: reduced adolescent smoking [editorial]. *Tobacco Control* 2005;14(5):292–3.

Wakefield M, Giovino G. Teen penalties for tobacco possession, use, and purchase: evidence and issues. *Tobacco Control* 2003;12(Suppl 1):i6–i13.

Wakefield M, Szczypka G, Terry-McElrath Y, Emery S, Flay B, Chaloupka F, Saffer H. Mixed messages on tobacco: comparative exposure to public health, tobacco company- and pharmaceutical company-sponsored tobacco-related television campaigns in the United States, 1999–2003. *Addiction* 2005b;100(12):1875–83.

Wakefield M, Terry-McElrath Y, Emery S, Saffer H, Chaloupka FJ, Szczypka G, Flay B, O'Malley PM, Johnston LD. Effect of televised, tobacco company-funded smoking prevention advertising on youth smoking-related beliefs, intentions, and behavior. *American Journal of Public Health* 2006;96(12):2154–60.

Wakefield MA, Chaloupka FJ, Kaufman NJ, Orleans CT, Barker DC, Ruel EE. Effect of restrictions on smoking at home, at school, and in public places on teenage smoking: cross sectional study. *BMJ (British Medical Journal)* 2000;321(7257):333–7.

Walsh MM, Ellison J, Hilton JF, Chesney M, Ernster VL. Spit (smokeless) tobacco use by high school baseball athletes in California. *Tobacco Control* 2000;9(Suppl 2):ii32–ii39.

Walsh MM, Hilton JF, Ellison JA, Gee L, Chesney MA, Tomar SL, Ernster VL. Spit (smokeless) tobacco intervention for high school athletes: results after 1 year. *Addictive Behaviors* 2003;28(6):1095–113.

Walsh MM, Hilton JF, Masouredis CM, Gee L, Chesney MA, Ernster VL. Smokeless tobacco cessation intervention for college athletes: results after 1 year. *American Journal of Public Health* 1999;89(2):228–34.

Walter HJ. Primary prevention of chronic disease among children: the School-Based "Know Your Body" Intervention Trials. *Health Education Quarterly* 1989; 16(2):201–14.

Wang LY, Crossett LS, Lowry R, Sussman S, Dent CW. Cost-effectiveness of a school-based tobacco-use prevention program. *Archives of Pediatrics & Adolescent Medicine* 2001;155(9):1043–50.

Warner KE. Clearing the airwaves: the cigarette ad ban revisited. *Policy Analysis* 1979;5(4):435–50.

Warner KE. Charting the science of the future: where tobacco-control research must go. *American Journal of Preventive Medicine* 2007a;33(6 Suppl):S314–S317.

Warner KE. To educate or not to educate: is that the question? *Addiction* 2007b;102(9):1352–3.

Warner KE, Jacobson PD, Kaufman NJ. Innovative approaches to youth tobacco control: introduction and overview. *Tobacco Control* 2003;12(Suppl 1):i1–i15.

Warren CW, Riley L, Asma S, Eriksen MP, Green L, Blanton C, Loo C, Batchelor S, Yach D. Tobacco use by youth: a surveillance report from the Global Youth Tobacco Survey project. *Bulletin of the World Health Organization* 2000;78(7):868–76.

Warren JR, Hecht ML, Wagstaff DA, Elek E, Ndiaye K, Dustman P, Marsiglia FF. Communicating prevention: the effects of the *keepin' it REAL* classroom videotapes and televised PSAs on middle-school students' substance use. *Journal of Applied Communication Research* 2006;34(2):209–27.

Wechsler H, Kelley K, Seibring M, Kuo M, Rigotti NA. College smoking policies and smoking cessation programs: results of a survey of college health center directors. *Journal of American College Health* 2001;49(5): 205–12.

Weiss CH, Murphy-Graham E, Birkeland S. An alternate route to policy influence: how evaluations affect D.A.R.E. *American Journal of Evaluation* 2005;26(1):12–30.

Weiss JW, Cen S, Schuster DV, Unger JB, Johnson CA, Mouttapa M, Schreiner WS, Cruz TB. Longitudinal effects of protobacco and anti-tobacco messages on adolescent smoking susceptibility. *Nicotine & Tobacco Research* 2006;8(3):455–65.

West SL, O'Neal KK. Project D.A.R.E. outcome effectiveness revisited. *American Journal of Public Health* 2004;49(6):1027–9.

White V, Tan N, Wakefield M, Hill D. Do adult focused anti-smoking campaigns have an impact on adolescents? The case of the Australian National Tobacco Campaign. *Tobacco Control* 2003;12(Suppl 2):ii23–ii29.

White V, Webster B, Wakefield M. Do graphic health warning labels have an impact on adolescents' smoking-related beliefs and behaviours? *Addiction* 2008a;103(9):1562–71.

White VM, Hayman J, Hill D. Can population-based tobacco-control policies change smoking behaviors of adolescents from all socioeconomic groups: findings from Australia: 1987–2005. *Cancer Causes & Control* 2008b;19(6):631–40.

Whittaker R, Borland R, Bullen C, Lin RB, McRobbie H, Rodgers A. Mobile phone-based interventions for smoking cessation. *Cochrane Database of Systematic Reviews* 2009, Issue 4. Art. No.: CD006611. DOI: 10.1002/14651858.CD006611.pub2.

Widome R, Forster JL, Hannan PJ, Perry CL. Longitudinal patterns of youth access to cigarettes and smoking progression: Minnesota Adolescent Community Cohort (MACC) study (2000–2003). *Preventive Medicine* 2007; 45(6):442–6.

Wiehe SE, Garrison MM, Christakis DA, Ebel BE, Rivara FP. A systematic review of school-based smoking prevention trials with long-term follow-up. *Journal of Adolescent Health* 2005;36(3):162–9.

Wilderdom. ZCalc, 2012. <http://www.wilderdom.com/research/ZCalc.xls>; accessed: January 30, 2012.

Willemsen MC. The new EU cigarette health warnings benefit smokers who want to quit the habit: results from the Dutch Continuous Survey of Smoking Habits. *European Journal of Public Health* 2005;15(4):389–92.

Willemsen MC, Simons C, Zeeman G. Impact of the new EU health warnings on the Dutch quit line. *Tobacco Control* 2002;11(4):381–2.

Williams CL, Perry CL, Dudovitz B, Veblen-Mortenson S, Anstine PS, Komro KA, Toomey T. A home-based prevention program for sixth grade alcohol use: results from Project Northland. *Journal of Primary Prevention* 1995;16(2):125–47.

Wilson KM, Klein JD, Blumkin AK, Gottlieb M, Winickoff JP. Tobacco-smoke exposure in children who live in multiunit housing. *Pediatrics* 2011;127(1):85–92.

Winickoff JP, Gottlieb M, Mello MM. Regulation of smoking in public housing. *New England Journal of Medicine* 2010;362(24):2319–25.

Winkleby MA, Feighery E, Dunn M, Kole S, Ahn D, Killen JD. Effects of an advocacy intervention to reduce smoking among teenagers. *Archives of Pediatrics & Adolescent Medicine* 2004;158(3):269–75.

Winkleby MA, Fortmann SP, Rockhill B. Cigarette smoking trends in adolescents and young adults: the Stanford Five-City Project. *Preventive Medicine* 1993;22(3): 325–34.

Winkleby MA, Taylor CB, Jatulis D, Fortmann SP. The long-term effects of a cardiovascular disease prevention trial: the Stanford Five-City Project. *American Journal of Public Health* 1996;86(12):1773–9.

Wolfson M, Forster JL, Claxton AJ, Murray DM. Adolescent smokers' provision of tobacco to other adolescents. *American Journal of Public Health* 1997;87(4):649–51.

Worden JK, Flynn BS, Geller BM, Chen M, Shelton LG, Secker-Walker RH, Solomon DS, Solomon LJ, Couchey S, Constanza MC. Development of a smoking prevention mass media program using diagnostic and formative research. *Preventive Medicine* 1988;17(5):531–58.

Worden JK, Flynn BS, Secker-Walker RH, Balch GI, Rudman G, Goldman LK, Glantz SA. Antismoking advertising campaigns for youth [letter]. *JAMA: the Journal of the American Medical Association* 1998;280(4):323–4.

Worden JK, Flynn BS, Solomon LJ, Secker-Walker RH, Badger GJ, Carpenter JH. Using mass media to prevent cigarette smoking among adolescent girls. *Health Education Quarterly* 1996;23(4):453–68.

World Health Organization. WHO Framework Convention on Tobacco Control, 2003; <http://www.who.int/fctc/text_download/en/index.html>; accessed: January 31, 2012.

Wu Y, Stanton BF, Galbraith J, Kaljee L, Cottrell L, Li X, Harris CV, D'Alessandri D, Burns JM. Sustaining and broadening intervention impact: a longitudinal randomized trial of 3 adolescent risk reduction approaches. *Pediatrics* 2003;111(1):e32–e38.

Yanovitzky I, Stryker J. Mass media, social norms, and health promotion efforts: a longitudinal study of media effects on youth binge drinking. *Communication Research* 2001;28(2):208–39.

YouTube. Thanks, Tobacco: You Killed My Mom, April 13, 2007; <http://www.youtube.com/watch?v=u_8BerrJg0M>; accessed: March 16, 2010.

Zack SL, Hoffman J, Nemes S, Weil J, Hess L. Participation in a successful and multifaceted teen cessation program. Paper presented at the National Conference on Tobacco or Health; May 5, 2005; Chicago.

Zaza S, Briss PA, Harris, KW, editors. Tobacco. In: *The Guide to Community Preventive Services: What Works to Promote Health?* Atlanta (GA): Oxford University Press; 2005:3–79.

Zavela, Harrison, Owens. APHHA 119th meeting poster presentation, 1991.

Zhao G, Pechmann C. The impact of regulatory focus on adolescents' response to antismoking advertising campaigns. *Journal of Marketing Research* 2007;44(4): 671–87.

Zheng H, Sussman S, Chen X, Wang Y, Xia J, Gong J, Liu C, Shan J, Unger J, Anderson Johnson C. Project EX: a teen smoking cessation initial study in Wuhan, China. *Addictive Behaviors* 2004;29(9):1725–33.

Chapter 7
A Vision for Ending the Tobacco Epidemic

History of Tobacco Control Among Young People in the United States

For generations, public health policies and programs in the United States have attempted to prevent young people from using tobacco products. Laws prohibiting the sale of tobacco products to minors appeared in New Jersey and Washington as early as 1883, in Nebraska in 1885, and in Maryland in 1886 (U.S. Department of Health and Human Services [USDHHS] 2000). When the health consequences of cigarette smoking became well established in the middle of the twentieth century, the need to prevent youth and young adults from becoming addicted to tobacco products gained a new importance (USDHHS 1994, 2000). In 1964, the Surgeon General's Advisory Committee concluded, "Cigarette smoking is a health hazard of sufficient importance in the United States to warrant appropriate remedial action" (U.S. Department of Health, Education, and Welfare [USDHEW] 1964, p. 33). This conclusion led to a permanent change in the way this country and the world considered the marketing and sales of tobacco products. And yet, by 1979 the lack of progress in preventing smoking was discouraging. The 1979 Surgeon General's report, *Smoking and Health*, noted that since the release of the 1964 report, "... smoking among teenage boys is remaining virtually constant and among teenage girls it is actually increasing" (USDHEW 1979, p. 17–5). The 1979 report stated as well:

> Becoming a smoker may have the immediate value to some teenagers of being accepted by their peers, feeling more mature because smoking is an adult behavior forbidden to the child, providing a level of physiological stimulation and pleasure, and might even serve the function of an act of defiance to authority figures. The prevention programs reviewed rarely incorporate such concepts. Rather, they focus primarily on information relating to the long-term dangers of smoking (USDHEW 1979, p. 17–6).

Over the next 15 years, research on new prevention strategies increased, and some progress was made in reducing smoking rates among youth. By the 1990s, however, the need for greater emphasis on preventing youth from smoking was recognized. Rates of current smoking among high school seniors had declined from 38.8% in 1976 to 29.4% in 1981 but had remained almost unchanged during the 1980s at around 29–30% (see Chapter 3, "The Epidemiology of Tobacco Use Among Young People in the United States and Worldwide," Figure 3.8). However, data on smoking from the early 1990s suggested that rates among high school students were increasing again (Centers for Disease Control and Prevention [CDC] 1992, 2000, 2011b; Kann et al. 1995; Burns and Johnston 2001).

The landmark 1994 Surgeon General's report, *Preventing Tobacco Use Among Young People*, the first report to focus solely on youth, came during a time when the tobacco industry had been implementing advertising and promotional strategies to ensure that it had "replacement smokers" for the adult smokers who were quitting or dying (USDHHS 1994; Perry 1999). The "Joe Camel" campaign typified the industry's efforts at that time, a period in which the rate of initiation of smoking and the prevalence of smoking increased among youth (Pierce et al. 1998; Wayne and Connolly 2002; DiFranza et al. 2006). From 1991 to 1997, the rate of current smoking among high school students increased from 27.5% to 36.4%. Thus, 30 years after the historic 1964 Surgeon General's report, it was clear that much more needed to be done to stop the tobacco epidemic and that the young people's tobacco use needed to be addressed. The 1994 report was an important element in mobilizing nationwide action to reduce rates of smoking among youth and young adults (Lynch and Bonnie 1994; USDHHS 1994).

As reviewed in the 2000 Surgeon General's report, *Reducing Tobacco Use* (USDHHS 2000), the period of the 1990s saw many important events in tobacco control:

- Under Commissioner David Kessler, the U.S. Food and Drug Administration (FDA) asserted its intention to regulate tobacco products.

- State attorneys general began suing the tobacco industry to recover Medicaid payments made for tobacco-caused diseases.

- Four states—Florida, Minnesota, Mississippi, and Texas—settled the lawsuits brought by their attorneys general, making these states the recipients of awards that, over 25 years, will total in the billions of dollars for each of them. The settlements also yielded many restrictions on the marketing and sales of tobacco products. Major new statewide tobacco control programs were funded in Florida, Massachusetts, Minnesota, and Mississippi.

- The remaining 46 states and the District of Columbia settled the lawsuits brought by their attorneys general as well as in the Master Settlement Agreement, in which the tobacco industry agreed to pay the states approximately $206 billion over the following 25 years.

- The American Legacy Foundation was funded through the Master Settlement Agreement and took Florida's "truth" media campaign nationwide.

- Industry documents obtained during the legal discovery process of the Minnesota and state attorneys general lawsuits were made available to the public.

From 1997 into the start of the twenty-first century, rates of smoking among youth fell sharply, and it seemed that the flow of "replacement smokers" into the customer base of the tobacco industry could finally be shut off. The statewide programs and the national "truth" campaign of the American Legacy Foundation used the insights in the 1994 report to act on the evidence that almost all future smokers start and get addicted to tobacco products in adolescence and young adulthood. For example, Table 7 in the 1994 report (USDHHS 1994, p. 65) documented that of the adults who had ever smoked daily, 82% tried their first cigarette before the age of 18 years, and 98% became daily smokers before the age of 25 years. Thus, the evidence was clear: if we were able to prevent the onset of tobacco use completely until age 25, the epidemic would decline and indeed would end in the near future, as the remaining adult smokers were helped to quit. The prevention efforts mounted in this period involved a true paradigm shift, a recognition that the attractiveness of tobacco products to youth needed to be countered less by "health information" than by hard-hitting, graphic, depictions of the immediate harms of smoking, unveiling the manipulations of the tobacco industry, and presenting denormalizing themes (Farrelly et al. 2002, 2005, 2009).

Tobacco Control Among Youth and Young Adults: The Recent Disappointing Trends

Unfortunately, the rapid decline in tobacco use in the early twenty-first century has not continued at the same pace. Tobacco use among youth remains unacceptably high, and national surveys show that declines in rates of current smoking have been slower and more sporadic in recent years (see Chapter 3). At this time, almost one in four high school seniors is a current cigarette smoker. Among youth who smoke cigarettes, the concurrent use of other tobacco products—particularly cigars and smokeless tobacco—has not declined since 2001. More than one-half of White and Hispanic male cigarette smokers in high school also use tobacco products other than cigarettes, as do almost one-half of Hispanic female smokers in high school. This is worrisome as the use of multiple tobacco products may help promote and reinforce addiction, as well as lead to greater health problems. In addition, since 2005, initiation rates have actually risen among young adults, aged 18–25 years, for both smoking and use of smokeless tobacco.

Evidence reviewed in this report indicates, then, that initiation rates of tobacco use among youth and young adults should continue to cause great concern and, indeed, that the situation is similar in several ways to what was observed in the 1994 report. For example, as shown in Table 7.1, in 1991, 81.9% of adults 30–39 years of age who had ever smoked daily had first tried a cigarette before the age of 18 years; for 2010, the corresponding estimate was 88.2%. In 1991, 94.8% of such persons had begun smoking daily before 25 years of age; for 2010, the estimate was 95.6%. Also, data from the National Survey on Drug Use and Health for 2008–2010 indicate that Marlboro, Newport, and Camel, the three most heavily advertised brands and the brands of choice for established smokers among adolescents and young adults in 1994, remained the top selections for young people in 2007–2009.

This report has updated our understanding of the many factors involved in the initiation and use of tobacco products. Chapter 4, "Social, Environmental, Cognitive, and Genetic Influences on the Use of Tobacco Among Youth," reviewed the evidence that adolescents and young adults are uniquely susceptible to social and environmental influences to use tobacco. As was noted in the 1979 Surgeon General's report, adolescence through young adulthood remains the period in life when use of tobacco products can be perceived by young people as being an "acceptable rebellion" or "mild bad behavior" that they can discontinue in the future (McAlister et al. 1979). If tobacco

Table 7.1 Cumulative percentages of recalled age at which respondents first tried a cigarette and began to smoke daily among 30- to 39-year-olds who have ever smoked daily, 1991 compared with 2010

	First tried a cigarette		Began smoking daily	
Age (in years)	1991	2010	1991	2010
<12	15.6	20.9	1.9	4.7
<14	36.7	43.6	8.0	16.0
<16	62.2	72.9	24.9	40.9
<18	81.9	88.2	53.0	65.1
<20	91.3	93.2	77.0	80.2
<25	98.4	98.8	94.8	98.6

Source: 2010 National Survey on Drug Use and Health: Substance Abuse and Mental Health Services Administration (unpublished data)

use were similar to getting a tattoo or dyeing one's hair, for example, which might also be rebellious behaviors, we would not be as concerned. It is the addictiveness of tobacco use and its short- and long-term health and economic consequences that transform this "act of rebellion" into a major public health problem. Thus, the effects on personal behavior of social and environmental influences continue to make up one of the major challenges to preventing smoking among young people. This is particularly important since tobacco marketing utilizes themes that are appealing to adolescents, such as being rebellious and attractive. However, more fully using our understanding that young people often use tobacco because of these influences can help us create better and more effective prevention efforts.

The situation is unfortunately complicated by the fact that the social and environmental factors that promote tobacco use continue to evolve. Chapter 5, "The Tobacco Industry's Influences on the Use of Tobacco Among Youth," reviewed the evidence that the tobacco industry's advertising and promotional activities as well as its pricing practices are causally related to the initiation and progression of tobacco use among young people. Similarly, images of smoking in the entertainment media, particularly movies, have created a prosmoking environment that causes the initiation of smoking and its continued use. Also, there is evidence suggesting that other factors, including the packaging and design of tobacco products, the creation of new products, and other activities of the tobacco industry may have a role in increasing the appeal of tobacco products to adolescents and young adults.

The evidence reviewed in this report indicates that the practices of the tobacco industry are evolving in the areas of promotion and advertising even as it tries to minimize the role played by such activities as major causes of tobacco use among youth and young adults (see Chapter 5, Figure 5.5). For example, recent industry campaigns have attempted to reframe the use of tobacco products as an "acceptable rebellion" within a hipster aesthetic (Hendlin et al. 2010). The ways in which the industry's practices in recruiting "replacement smokers" have evolved and continue to be effective have been set forth in a review by the National Cancer Institute (NCI 2008) and are described in *United States v. Philip Morris* Final Opinion (*U.S. v. Philip Morris* No. 99-2496 [D.D.C. Aug. 17, 2006]). The evidence clearly indicates that youth and young adults remain heavily exposed to and influenced by advertising and promotional efforts aimed at increasing the use of tobacco products. These advertising and promotional activities can be considered under the four "Ps" of marketing: Product, Price, Promotion, and Placement (Cummings et al. 2002).

- *Product:* Evidence reviewed in this report suggests that tobacco products are designed to be attractive and appealing to youth and young adults. Chapter 5 provided evidence indicating how certain features of cigarettes and other tobacco products can appeal to younger smokers. In addition, there is evidence that highly addictive, smooth-tasting tobacco products (e.g., menthol cigarettes [with lower levels of menthol]) have been modified for this market, raising concerns about how changes in product design may be contributing to an increased likelihood that tobacco will be consumed by young people.

- *Price:* Chapter 5 documented how the marketing and promotional expenditures of the tobacco industry have become increasingly concentrated on efforts to reduce the prices of tobacco products. The evidence continues to grow that youth and young adults are more price sensitive than are adults.

- *Promotion:* The evidence continues to show that youth and young adults are more sensitive than adults in general to advertising and promotional campaigns. As greater restrictions have been placed on traditional advertising of tobacco products, the retail environment has become a primary location to bombard youth with brand imagery, which has made tobacco products appear attractive and broadly acceptable. Emerging evidence was provided in Chapter 5 regarding the widespread promotion of tobacco products in the new digital marketing landscape, which includes both tobacco industry corporate and brand Web sites as well as social networking sites.

- *Placement:* The evidence in Chapter 5 pointed to the industry-sponsored programs that influence product location within the retail environment as well as the concentration of these activities in low-income and racially diverse neighborhoods. This report has documented the fact that industry-sponsored programs affect point-of-sale marketing and product location in the store environment and that these initiatives are effective in reaching youth.

In addition, as was reviewed in NCI Monograph No. 19, *The Role of the Media in Promoting and Reducing Tobacco Use*, a variety of media influences continue to create social norms of acceptability of tobacco use that encourage the use of tobacco products (NCI 2008). Chapters 4 and 5 in this report build upon the NCI review and provided a conceptual framework of how these advertising, social, and media influences affect youth and young adults. Chapter 5 also provided a comprehensive review of the impact of smoking in the movies and the evidence linking exposure to images of smoking in the entertainment media to the initiation of adolescent smoking. Evidence indicates that there is a strong dose-response relationship between the number of smoking depictions viewed by nonsmoking adolescents and the rate of initiation of smoking in that group. Fortunately, there is evidence that efforts to reduce exposures to such depictions of smoking, such as parental restrictions on what their children may watch, can reduce risks of smoking initiation. More promising still is the potential for policies that will discourage depictions of smoking in movies viewed by children. Recent evidence indicates that new policies may already be leading to declines in the level of smoking imagery in youth-rated movies (CDC 2011a), but depictions of smoking in DVDs (digital video discs), cable channels, and other media remain common and continue to create a social environment that presents smoking as socially acceptable and appealing to youth.

Since 1964, the Surgeon General's reports have documented the continuing need to mobilize national efforts to prevent the initiation of tobacco use among youth. Yet, as Chapter 3 showed, almost one-fifth of high school youth today are smokers, one-tenth of high school senior males are smokeless tobacco users, and one-fifth of high school senior males are cigar smokers. Virtually all (98%) adult daily cigarette smokers initiate smoking by 25 years of age—identical to what was reported in 1994.

So why has progress in reducing smoking rates among young people been so hard to achieve? As noted above, the advertising and promotional activities of the tobacco industry and depictions of smoking in the entertainment media have continued, and they remain potent factors promoting tobacco use. Unfortunately, our national efforts to counter these influences have not kept pace in recent years, and funding for several of the boldest and most innovative statewide programs, in Florida, Massachusetts, Minnesota, Mississippi, Oregon, New York, and Washington, has been sharply reduced or virtually eliminated (Campaign for Tobacco-Free Kids 2011). Correspondingly, the overall level of investment in statewide tobacco control programs has declined since 2003 (Campaign for Tobacco-Free Kids 2011). Exposure to counteradvertising, funded by states, is now only 3.5% of recommended levels. Moreover, the annual payments by industry under the Master Settlement Agreement to the American Legacy Foundation were stopped after the initial 5-year period, substantially reducing the intensity of the foundation's national "truth" media campaign (American Legacy Foundation 2006). The U.S. Food and Drug Administration's (FDA's) attempt to assert authority over tobacco products was blocked in 2000 by a Supreme Court decision (*Food and Drug Administration v. Brown & Williamson Tobacco Corp.*, 529 U.S. 120 [2000]; 120 S. Ct. 1291), and the agency only gained this authority through legislation in 2009 (*Family Smoking Prevention and Tobacco Control Act*). Finally, as reviewed above, the tobacco industry adapted to the new post–Master Settlement Agreement environment in its marketing and promotional campaigns and is keeping its spending on marketing at a very high level—nearly $10 billion allocated to marketing to the U.S. in 2008.

Tobacco Control Among Youth and Young Adults: How to Make Progress

Chapter 6 ("Efforts to Prevent and Reduce Tobacco Use Among Young People") in this report reviewed the evidence on what the most effective strategies are to prevent and reduce tobacco use among young people. With the release of the 2000 Surgeon General's report, *Reducing Tobacco Use*, Surgeon General David Satcher stated that

> Our lack of greater progress in tobacco control is attributable more to the failure to implement proven strategies than it is to a lack of knowledge about what to do (USDHHS 2000, p. 436).

Dr. Satcher's statement clearly applies to our national efforts to prevent the initiation of tobacco use among youth and young adults. The evidence strongly supports the need for coordinated, multicomponent interventions that combine mass media campaigns, tobacco tax increases, school-based policies and programs, and statewide and community-wide changes in smoke-free policies and norms. Unfortunately, the decrease in state investments for comprehensive programs to prevent tobacco use, including media campaigns to prevent smoking (Campaign for Tobacco-Free Kids 2011), is an indicator that lack of funding has become a problem for implementing proven strategies. Chapter 6 provided clear evidence that the initiation and use of tobacco by youth and young adults could be significantly and effectively reduced by implementing mass media campaigns, comprehensive community programs, and comprehensive statewide tobacco control programs. Moreover, following the 1998 Master Settlement Agreement between 46 states and the District of Columbia and the tobacco industry, together with the independent settlements in the remaining 4 states (Florida, Minnesota, Mississippi, and Texas), state investments in comprehensive tobacco control programs increased to $821.4 million in fiscal year 2002 (CDC, in press). Sadly, the level of investments has since declined to $643.1 million in 2010, only 17.7% of the investment level recommended by CDC's *Best Practices for Comprehensive Tobacco Control Programs—2007* (CDC 2007). Evidence indicates that states that have made larger investments in comprehensive tobacco control programs have seen the prevalence of smoking among adults and youth decline faster as investments levels increased (Farrelly et al. 2008). And yet, several of the states that were demonstrating the most progress in reducing youth smoking rates (among them California and New York) had their levels of funding severely reduced (Campaign for Tobacco-Free Kids 2011).

One of the critical impacts of the reduced level of funding for statewide tobacco control programs has been a lowering of the intensity of countermarketing media campaigns. In its 2007 *Best Practices*, CDC recommended that states fund countermarketing media campaigns to prevent tobacco use at a level so that 80% of the youth in the state would on average be exposed to at least 10 prevention messages per quarter (800 total rating points [TRPs]) (CDC 2007). With the reduced funding levels in the states, CDC's 2010 *Tobacco Control State Highlights* found that the median level of exposure across states in 2008 was only 28 TRPs, or 3.5% of the recommended level (CDC 2010). The evidence reviewed in Chapter 6 supports the need to sustain countermarketing media campaigns at an intensity level similar to those recommended by CDC *Best Practices* (2007). Further, the evidence reviewed there indicates that the countermarketing messages should build upon the growing evidence base regarding the themes, emotional content, format, and characteristics of execution of the campaigns that have demonstrated the greatest efficacy. Given the continuing high level of protobacco messages to which youth and young adults are being exposed, the reduced levels of countermarketing media campaigns by the states has been identified by Ibrahim and Glantz (2007) as one of the factors that could be contributing to the slowing of progress in preventing tobacco use among youth.

Chapter 6 also reviewed the potential for additional regulatory approaches to reduce the initiation and practice of smoking among youth and young adults. The 2009 legislation giving FDA authority to regulate the manufacture, distribution, advertising, and promotion of tobacco products is no doubt the most significant advance on the regulatory scene. Some of FDA's responsibilities include reviewing premarket applications for new and modified-risk tobacco products, requiring new health warnings on cigarette packs (and smokeless tobacco products), and establishing and enforcing restrictions on advertising and promotion. FDA has additional authorities that it can exercise, including subjecting tobacco products such as cigars, dissolvables, and e-cigarettes to Chapter 9 of the Food, Drug, and Cosmetic Act. FDA could also establish product standards for nicotine yields or for the reduction or elimination of other constituents, as appropriate, for the protection of the public's health. Also, the Substance Abuse and Mental Health Services Administration has been enforcing the Synar Amendment of 1992, which requires the states, the District of Columbia, and the eight U.S. territories to enact and enforce laws prohibiting the sale of tobacco products to individuals younger than 18 years of age. FDA is now also enforcing federal law prohibiting the sale of cigarettes and smokeless tobacco to individuals younger than 18 years of age. FDA is now also enforcing federal law prohibiting the sale of cigarettes and smokeless tobacco to individuals younger than 18 years of age.

Additionally, in 2011, FDA and NIH released requests for applications, and also funded projects to study a number of research areas including epidemiology and cohort study based-studies, the basic science of addiction, the toxicology of toxic substances in tobacco products, and behavioral studies. The findings from these research studies will contribute to the evidence base that FDA will draw from as it establishes tobacco authority decision-making rules.

Internationally, there has been even stronger regulatory action. The *WHO Report on the Global Tobacco Epidemic, 2011; Warning About the Dangers of Tobacco* provides a summary of these actions (World Health Organization [WHO] 2011). Among the actions covered in the report are the use of large, pictorial warning labels on cigarette packs, the elimination of point-of-sale promotions and advertisements, and the imposition of tobacco excise taxes at levels much higher than any currently in the United States. In the United States, researchers are calling for a review of these and other policy and regulatory efforts to define potential "novel policy directions" to be considered in the future (Warner and Mendez 2010). However, as these endgame policy innovations are considered and evaluated, much more can be done now to reduce the rates of tobacco use among American youth and young adults.

In November 2010, USDHHS released a strategic action plan to end the tobacco epidemic in this country (USDHHS 2010). The evidence in the current Surgeon General's report confirms the conclusion of that action plan: we know how to end the tobacco epidemic. The USDHHS plan, *Ending the Tobacco Epidemic: A Tobacco Control Strategic Action Plan for the U.S. Department of Health and Human Services*, endorsed five strategies for ending the tobacco epidemic, as shown in Table 7.2:

- Youth targeted mass-media countermarketing campaigns
- Adoption of comprehensive smoke-free laws
- Availability of accessible, affordable tobacco cessation options
- Raising the retail price of tobacco products through excise tax increases
- Restricting advertising and promotion

Besides the five strategies shown in Table 7.2, the USDHHS *Strategic Action Plan* (2010) pointed out the need to (1) build sustainable capacity and infrastructure for comprehensive tobacco control programs, noting the 2007 CDC recommendation of investing $9–$18 per capita for optimal tobacco control outcomes and (2) regulate the manufacture, marketing, and distribution of tobacco products, noting that a number of activities in the action plan will provide key department-wide support for the new tobacco regulatory mission of FDA in implementing the 2009 *Family Smoking Prevention and Tobacco Control Act*.

In December 2010, USDHHS released *Healthy People 2020*, the nation's disease prevention and health promotion plan. The 20 tobacco objectives served as the foundation for the USDHHS *Strategic Action Plan* (2010). A complete list of the *Healthy People 2020* objectives can be found on their Web site (USDHHS 2011).

The USDHHS *Strategic Action Plan* (2010) recognized that the use of tobacco products by this nation's youth has deadly health consequences. Recent evidence has shown the impact of the failure to maintain the rate of decline in youth smoking since 2003. If high school students' smoking levels had continued to decline at the rate observed from 1997 to 2003, the prevalence of current smoking among high school students in 2009 would have been only about 8% (vs. 19.5%) (Figure 7.1). This would have resulted in approximately 3 million fewer smokers among youth and young adults by 2009. We need to regain the momentum of the 1997–2003 decline in tobacco use, and viable evidence-based, methods to do so are available.

The feasibility of this projection (Figure 7.1) of a continuing decline in smoking rates among youth is supported by the declines observed from 2003 to 2009 in New York City and in states that were maintaining funding for comprehensive tobacco prevention programs (Campaign for Tobacco-Free Kids 2011). In addition, the 2009 Youth Risk Behavior Survey reported that among Black female high school seniors, the rate of current smoking was only 4.8%. These data suggest that rates of smoking among high school students could be reduced by more than 50% over the next decade and thus could be in the single digits by 2020 if all the evidence-based strategies defined in this report were implemented.

Table 7.2 Strategic actions to end the tobacco epidemic

Youth-targeted mass-media countermarketing campaigns	Tobacco use prevalence declines when adequately funded mass-media countermarketing campaigns are combined with other strategies in multicomponent tobacco control programs. The most prominent of these efforts is the national truth® campaign (February 2000–2004), which resulted in approximately 450,000 fewer adolescents initiating smoking in the United States. During 2000–2002, the truth® campaign spent $324 million on media, research, public relations, and related expenditures. A cost-utility analysis found that the campaign recouped its costs and that just under $1.9 billion in medical costs were averted for society over the lifetimes of the youth who did not become smokers.
Adoption of comprehensive smoke-free laws	Smoke-free policies improve indoor air quality, reduce negative health outcomes among nonsmokers, decrease cigarette consumption, encourage smokers to quit, and change social norms regarding the acceptability of smoking. A 2009 IOM report, *Secondhand Smoke Exposure and Cardiovascular Effects: Making Sense of the Evidence,* confirmed a strong causal relationship between implementation of smoke-free laws and decreases in heart attacks. Elimination of secondhand smoke exposure also reduces lung cancer and other pulmonary diseases.
Availability of accessible, affordable tobacco cessation options	Tobacco dependence is a chronic disease that often requires repeated interventions and multiple quit attempts. The U.S. Public Health Service Clinical Practice Guideline, *Treating Tobacco Use and Dependence: 2008 Update,* notes that tobacco dependence treatments, such as counseling and use of medications, are effective across a broad range of populations. The combined use of medication and counseling almost doubles the smoking abstinence rate compared with either medication or counseling alone. Quitlines are among the most cost-effective clinical preventive services and can reach large numbers of smokers with proper promotion and clinical referral.
Raising the retail price of tobacco products through excise tax increases	For every 10% increase in the price of tobacco products, consumption falls by approximately 4% overall, with a greater reduction among youth. The 2009 enactment of the 62-cent federal cigarette excise tax increase to fund an expansion of the State Children's Health Insurance Program is projected to prevent initiation of smoking by nearly 2 million children. The tax increase will also have the projected benefits of causing more than 1 million adult smokers to quit, averting nearly 900,000 smoking-attributed deaths, and producing $44.5 billion in long-term health care savings by reducing tobacco-related health care costs. Similar effects are found when states raise tobacco excise taxes.
Restricting advertising and promotion	The National Cancer Institute 2008 monograph, *The Role of the Media in Promoting and Reducing Tobacco Use,* documents that tobacco advertising and promotion increase tobacco use. It concludes that countries that have implemented comprehensive tobacco advertising bans have been successful in reducing tobacco consumption by as much as 5.4%.

Source: U.S. Department of Health and Human Services 2010.

It is important to note that communities that have been the most successful at driving down youth initiation have done so in the context of comprehensive programs that also focused on decreasing adult smoking by changing the social norms and policies around smoking. As reviewed above, prior Surgeon General's reports have called for a greater mobilization of our national prevention efforts to stop the annual flow of "replacement smokers" into the deadly addiction of tobacco use. Unfortunately, although significant progress was achieved for some years following each of these reports, progress has not been sustained. Failure to stem this flow of "replacement smokers" results in millions more youth and young adults becoming addicted to tobacco products and suffering the immediate and longer-term health effects of this addiction, including premature disability and death. Chapter 2 of this report, "The Health Consequences of Tobacco Use Among Young People," documents that these health effects can be observed even sooner than prior reports had indicated. Lung cancer, heart disease, chronic obstructive pulmonary disease, and other major chronic diseases caused by smoking will continue to be leading causes of premature death until the tobacco epidemic is stopped.

Figure 7.1 Current rates of cigarette smoking among high school students and projected rates if the 1997–2003 decline had continued; Youth Risk Behavior Survey (YRBS) 1991–2009; United States

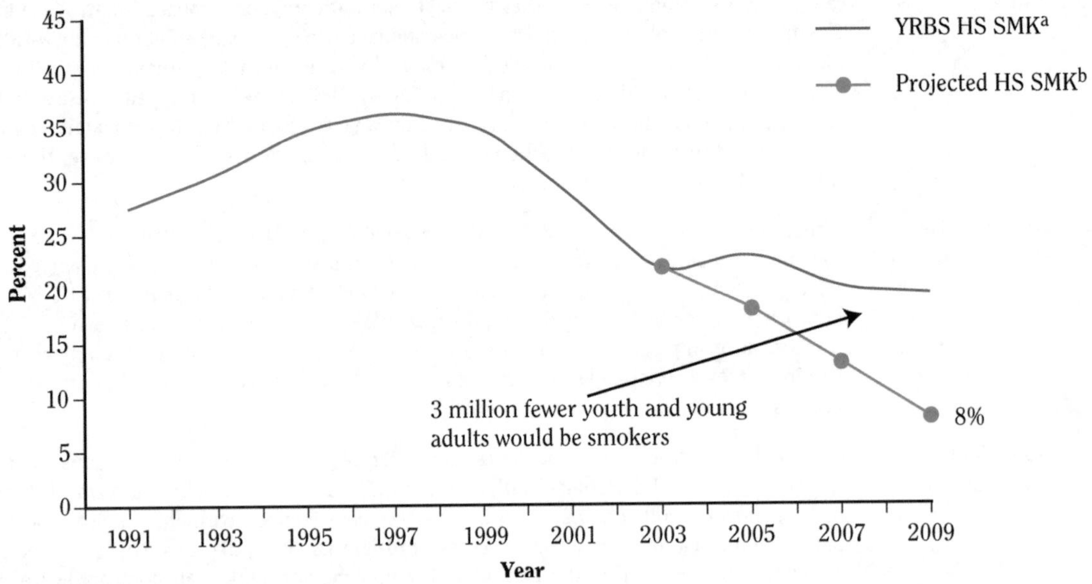

Source: 1991–2009 YRBS: Centers for Disease Control and Prevention, Division of Adolescent and School Health (unpublished data).
Note: **HS SMK** = high school smokers.
[a]High school students who smoked on 1 or more of the 30 days preceding the survey.
[b]Projected high school students who smoked on 1 or more days of the past 30 days if 1997–2003 decline had been maintained.

The USDHHS *Strategic Action Plan* (2010) recognized that dramatic action was needed to change social norms and decrease the social acceptability of tobacco use. This plan concluded that the overriding objective is

> ...to reinvigorate national momentum toward tobacco prevention and control by applying proven methods for reducing the burden of tobacco dependence. HHS will lead this transformative national endeavor by example, leveraging existing resources and expertise and making new investments to the furthest extent possible to maximize the nation's tobacco prevention and control efforts. The recommendations set forth here, when fully implemented, will markedly accelerate our nation's effort to defeat the tobacco epidemic (USDHHS 2010, p. 26).

Final Call to Action

The findings in this report and experience from 1998 to 2005 show that we have evidence-based strategies and tools that can rapidly drop youth initiation and prevalence rates down into the single digits. Key points from this report that must be considered in this effort include

- Harm from smoking begins immediately, ranging from addiction to serious damage to the heart and lungs.
- Prevention efforts must include both adolescents and young adults to encompass both initial experimentation and progression to daily use.
- Tobacco company advertising and promotional activities cause adolescent and young adult smoking initiation and are compounded by depictions of smoking in the movies.

- Tobacco use among youth declined from the late 1990s, but this decline has slowed in recent years.

- Our best strategy for creating large, rapid declines is through coordinated, adequately funded multicomponent interventions rather than a single "silver bullet" program or policy.

In addition, the FDA's new regulatory authority provides strong opportunities for further ensuring the elimination of the harms caused by tobacco use for our youth.

The evidence and findings of this Surgeon General's report require us all to work together to rekindle and increase the momentum of previous decades to create a society free from tobacco-related death and disease. The evidence is clear: we can prevent youth and young adults from ever using tobacco products. We can end the tobacco epidemic.

> If we do not act decisively today, a hundred years from now our grandchildren and their children will look back and seriously question how people claiming to be committed to public health and social justice allowed the tobacco epidemic to unfold unchecked.
>
> Former WHO Director-General
> Gro Harlem Brundtland (1999)

References

American Legacy Foundation. *2006 Annual Report: The Story of the Year.* Washington: American Legacy Foundation, 2006.

Brundtland GH. Speech to the WHO International Conference on Tobacco and Health; November 15, 1999; Kobe, Japan. <http://www.who.int/director-general/speeches/1999/english/19991115_kobe.html>; accessed: July 29, 2011.

Burns DM, Johnston LD. Overview of recent changes in adolescent smoking behavior. In: *Changing Adolescent Smoking Prevalence—Where It Is and Why.* Smoking and Tobacco Control Monograph No. 14. Bethesda (MD): U.S. Department of Health and Human Services, National Institutes of Health, National Cancer Institute, 2001. NIH Publication No. 02-5086.

Campaign for Tobacco-Free Kids. *A Broken Promise to Our Children: The 1998 State Tobacco Settlement 12 Years Later*. Washington: Campaign for Tobacco-Free Kids, American Heart Association, American Cancer Society, Cancer Action Network, American Lung Association, and Robert Wood Johnson Foundation. 2011; <http://www.tobaccofreekids.org/content/what_we_do/state_local_issues/settlement/FY2011/StateSettlementReport_FY2011_web.pdf>; accessed: December 6, 2011.

Centers for Disease Control and Prevention. Tobacco, alcohol, and other drug use among high school students—United States, 1991. *Morbidity and Mortality Weekly Report* 1992;41(37):698–703.

Centers for Disease Control and Prevention. Trends in cigarette smoking among high school students—United States, 1991–1999. *Morbidity and Mortality Weekly Report* 2000;49(33):755–8.

Centers for Disease Control and Prevention. *Best Practices for Comprehensive Tobacco Control Programs—2007.* Atlanta (GA): U.S. Department of Health and Human Services, Centers for Disease Control and Prevention, National Center for Chronic Disease Prevention and Health Promotion, Office on Smoking and Health, 2007.

Centers for Disease Control and Prevention. *Tobacco Control State Highlights, 2010.* Atlanta (GA): U.S. Department of Health and Human Services, Centers for Disease Control and Prevention, National Center for Chronic Disease Prevention and Health Promotion, Office on Smoking and Health, 2010.

Centers for Disease Control and Prevention. Smoking in top-grossing movies—United States, 2010. *Morbidity and Mortality Weekly Report* 2011a;60(27):909–13.

Centers for Disease Control and Prevention. Trends in the Prevalence of Tobacco Use: National YRBS: 1991–2009 [fact sheet]. National Center for Chronic Disease Prevention and Health Promotion, Division of Adolescent and School Health, 2011b; <http://www.cdc.gov/healthyyouth/yrbs/pdf/us_tobacco_trend_yrbs.pdf>; accessed: July 29, 2011.

Centers for Disease Control and Prevention. State tobacco control funding following state tobacco settlement agreement—United States, 1998–2010, in press.

Cummings KM, Morley CP, Horan JK, Steger C, Leavell N-R. Marketing to America's youth: evidence from corporate documents. *Tobacco Control* 2002;11(Suppl 1):i5–i17.

DiFranza JR, Wellman RJ, Sargent JD, Weitzman M, Hipple BJ, Winickoff JP, Center for Child Health Research of the American Academy of Pediatrics. Tobacco promotion and the initiation of tobacco use: assessing the evidence for causality. *Pediatrics* 2006;117(6):e1237.

Family Smoking Prevention and Tobacco Control Act, Public Law 111-13, 123 U.S. *Statutes* at Large 1776 (2009).

Farrelly MC, Davis KC, Duke J, Messeri P. Sustaining 'truth': changes in youth tobacco attitudes and smoking intentions after 3 years of a national antismoking campaign. *Health Education Research* 2009;24(1):42–8.

Farrelly MC, Davis KC, Haviland ML, Messeri P, Healton CG. Evidence of a dose-response relationship between "truth" antismoking ads and youth smoking prevalence. *American Journal of Public Health* 2005;95(3):425–31.

Farrelly MC, Healton CG, Davis KC, Messeri P, Hersey JC, Haviland ML. Getting to the truth: evaluating national tobacco countermarketing campaigns. *American Journal of Public Health* 2002;92(6):901–7.

Farrelly MC, Pechacek TF, Thomas KY, Nelson D. The impact of tobacco control programs on adult smoking. *American Journal of Public Health* 2008;98(2):304–9.

Food and Drug Administration v. Brown and Williamson, 529 U.S. 120 (2000); 120 S. Ct. 1291, available at http://ciel.org/Publications/FDA_Brown_Willamson.pdf.

Hendlin Y, Anderson SJ, Glantz SA. 'Acceptable rebellion': marketing hipster aesthetics to sell Camel cigarettes in the US. *Tobacco Control* 2010;19(3):213–22.

Ibrahim JK, Glantz SA. The rise and fall of tobacco control media campaigns, 1967–2006. *American Journal of Public Health* 2007;87(8):1383–96.

Kann L, Warren CW, Harris WA, Collins JL, Douglas KA, Collins ME, Williams BI, Ross JG, Kolbe LJ. Youth Risk Behavior Surveillance—United States, 1993. *Morbidity and Mortality Weekly Report* 1995;44(SS-1):1–55.

Lynch BS, Bonnie RJ, editors. *Growing Up Tobacco Free: Preventing Nicotine Addiction in Children and Youths.* Washington: National Academies Press, 1994.

McAlister AL, Perry C, Maccoby N. Adolescent smoking: onset and prevention. *Pediatrics* 1979;63(4):650–8.

National Cancer Institute. *The Role of the Media in Promoting and Reducing Tobacco Use.* Tobacco Control Monograph No. 19. Bethesda (MD): U.S. Department of Health and Human Services, National Institutes of Health, National Cancer Institute, 2008. NIH Publication No. 07-6242.

Perry CL. The tobacco industry and underage teen smoking: tobacco industry documents from the Minnesota litigation. *Archives of Pediatrics & Adolescent Medicine* 1999;153(9):935–41.

Pierce JP, Choi WS, Gilpin EA, Farkas AJ, Berry CC. Tobacco industry promotion of cigarettes and adolescent smoking. *JAMA: the Journal of the American Medical Association*. 1998;279(7):511–15.

U.S. Department of Health and Human Services. *Preventing Tobacco Use Among Young People. A Report of the Surgeon General.* Atlanta (GA): U.S. Department of Health and Human Services, Public Health Service, Centers for Disease Control and Prevention, National Center for Chronic Disease Prevention and Health Promotion, Office on Smoking and Health, 1994.

U.S. Department of Health and Human Services. *Reducing Tobacco Use: A Report of the Surgeon General.* Atlanta (GA): U.S. Department of Health and Human Services, Centers for Disease Control and Prevention, National Center for Chronic Disease Prevention and Health Promotion, Office on Smoking and Health, 2000.

U.S. Department of Health and Human Services. *Ending the Tobacco Epidemic: A Tobacco Control Strategic Action Plan for the U.S. Department of Health and Human Services.* Washington: Office of the Assistant Secretary for Health, 2010.

U.S. Department of Health and Human Services, Office of Disease Prevention and Health Promotion. Healthy People 2020, 2011; <http://www.healthypeople.gov/2020/default.aspx>; accessed: November 1, 2011.

U.S. Department of Health, Education, and Welfare. *Smoking and Health: Report of the Advisory Committee to the Surgeon General of the Public Health Service.* Washington: U.S. Department of Health, Education, and Welfare, Public Health Service, Center for Disease Control, 1964. PHS Publication No. 1103.

U.S. Department of Health, Education, and Welfare. *Smoking and Health. A Report of the Surgeon General.* Washington: U.S. Department of Health, Education, and Welfare, Public Health Service, Office of the Assistant Secretary for Health, Office on Smoking and Health, 1979. DHEW Publication No. (PHS) 79-50066.

U.S. v. Philip Morris, No. 99-2496 (D.D.C. Aug. 17, 2006), available at <http://www.library.ucsf.edu/sites/all/files/ucsf_assets/FinalOpinion_full_version.pdf>.

Warner KE, Mendez D. Tobacco control policy in developed countries: yesterday, today, and tomorrow. *Nicotine & Tobacco Research* 2010;12(9): 876–87.

Wayne GF, Connolly GN. How cigarette design can affect youth initiation into smoking: Camel cigarettes 1983–93. *Tobacco Control* 2002;11(Suppl 1):i32–i39.

World Health Organization. *WHO Report on the Global Tobacco Epidemic, 2011: Warning About the Dangers of Tobacco.* Geneva (Switzerland): World Health Organization, 2011.

List of Abbreviations

AAFP American Academy of Family Physicians
Add Health National Longitudinal Study of Adolescent Health
ADHD attention deficit hyperactivity disorder
AFRO WHO Africa
AHA American Heart Association
ALA American Lung Association
AMA American Medical Association
ASSIST American Stop Smoking Intervention Study
B&W Brown & Williamson Tobacco Corporation
BAT British American Tobacco
BHR bronchial hyperresponsiveness
BMI body mass index
BRFSS Behavioral Risk Factor Surveillance System
CAI computer-assisted interviewing
CARDIA Coronary Artery Risk Development in Young Adults
CDC Centers for Disease Control and Prevention
CEO chief executive officer
CHIPS Choosing Healthy Influences for a Positive Self
CI confidence interval
COMMIT Community Intervention Trial for Smoking Cessation
COPD chronic obstructive pulmonary disease
CSAP Center for Substance Abuse Prevention
CT computed tomography
D.A.R.E. Drug Abuse Resistance Education
DSM-IV *Diagnostic and Statistical Manual of Mental Disorders- 4th edition*
DVD digital video disc
DZ dizygotic
EDI Eating Disorders Inventory
ED-NOS eating disorders-not otherwise specified
EMRO WHO Eastern Mediterranean
ES effect size
ESFA European Smoking Prevention Framework Approach
ESPAD European School Survey Project on Alcohol and Other Drugs
EURO WHO Europe
FCC Federal Communications Commission
FCP Full Court Press
FCTC Framework Convention for Tobacco Control
FDA U.S. Food and Drug Administration
FEF forced expiratory flow
FEF_{25-75} FEF between 25% and 75% of forced vital capacity
FEV_1 forced expiratory volume in 1 second
FLAVOR Fun Learning about Vitality, Origin, and Respect
FOK Focus on Kids
FTC Federal Trade Commission
FTND Fagerström Test of Nicotine Dependence
FTQ Fagerström Tolerance Questionnaire
FVC forced vital capacity
g gram
GABA gamma-aminobutyric acid
GNAT Go/No-go Association Test
GRP gross rating point
GTSS Global Tobacco Surveillance System
GYTS Global Youth Tobacco Survey
HDL high-density lipoprotein
HONC Hooked on Nicotine Checklist
HSI Heaviness of Smoking Index
IARC International Agency for Research on Cancer
IAT Implicit Association Test
ICC intraclass correlation coefficient
ICV Internet cigarette vendors
IMBC Integrated Model of Behavior Change
ImPACT Informed Parents and Kids Together
IMPACT Initiatives to Mobilize for the Prevention and Control of Tobacco Use
IOM Institute of Medicine
IRR incidence rate ratio
ISAAC International Study of Asthma and Allergies in Childhood
ISFP Iowa Strengthening Families Program
ITT intent to treat
kg kilogram
L liter
LCA latent class analysis
LDL low-density lipoprotein
Legacy American Legacy Foundation
LST LifeSkills Training
LTA latent transition analysis

MDD	major depressive disorder
mFTQ	modified Fagerström Tolerance Questionnaire
mg	milligram
MI	myocardial infarction
mL	milliliter
mm	millimeter
MPAA	Motion Picture Association of America
MPP	Midwestern Prevention Project
MRI	magnetic resonance imaging
MSA	metropolitan statistical area
MSS	Minnesota Student Survey
MTF	Monitoring the Future
MVPA	moderate-to-vigorous intensity physical activity
MZ	monozygotic
NAAG	National Association of Attorneys General
nAChR	nicotinic acetylcholine receptor
NARE	negative affect relief expectancy
NASBE	National Association of State Boards of Education
NCI	National Cancer Institute
NDSS	Nicotine Dependence Syndrome Scale
NELS	National Education Longitudinal Study
NHANES	National Health and Nutrition Examination Survey
NHIS	National Health Interview Survey
NIH	National Institutes of Health
NLSY97	National Longitudinal Survey of Youth 1997 Cohort
NPM	nonparticipating manufacturer
NSDUH	National Survey on Drug Use and Health
NYTCP	New York Tobacco Control Program
NYTS	National Youth Tobacco Survey
OECD	Organisation for Economic Co-operation and Development
OPM	original participating manufacturer
OR	odds ratio
OSH	Office on Smoking and Health
PAHO	WHO Pan American Health Organization
PDAY	Pathobiological Determinants of Atherosclerosis in Youth
PEF	peak expiratory flow
PFDY	Preparing for the Drug Free Years
PSU	primary sampling unit
PUP	possession, use, and purchase
QALY	quality-adjusted life year
RCT	randomized controlled trial
RI	relative improvement
RICO	*Racketeer Influenced and Corrupt Organizations Act*
RJR	R.J. Reynolds Tobacco Company
RR	relative risk
SAMHSA	Substance Abuse and Mental Health Services Administration
SCQ	Smoking Consequences Questionnaire
SCQ-S	Smoking Consequences Questionnaire-Spanish
SD	standard deviation
SEARO	WHO South-East Asia
SES	socioeconomic status
SEU	subjective expected utility
SHOUT	Students Helping Others Understand Tobacco
SIDS	sudden infant death syndrome
SMART	Self-Management and Resistance Training
SNP	single nucleotide polymorphisms
SOS	Solutions for Smoking
SPM	subsequent participating manufacturer
SSQ	Smoking Situations Questionnaire
SYMATU	Statewide Youth Movement Against Tobacco Use
TAPP	Tobacco and Alcohol Prevention Project
TCP	tobacco prevention and control program
TNT	Project Towards No Tobacco Use
TPB	Theory of Planned Behavior
TPSAC	Tobacco Product Scientific Advisory Committee
TRA	Theory of Reasoned Action
TRP	total rating point
TTI	Theory of Triadic Influence
TUTD	Thumbs Up! Thumbs Down! Project
UCSF	University of California, San Francisco
UNC	University of North Carolina
URI-TW	upper respiratory infection-triggered wheezing
USDA	U.S. Department of Agriculture
USDHHS	U.S. Department of Health and Human Services
USDHEW	U.S. Department of Health, Education, and Welfare
USPS	United States Postal Service
USPSTF	U.S. Preventive Services Task Force
VLDL	very-low-density lipoprotein
VTA	ventral tegmental area
WCSS	Weight Control Smoking Scale
WHO	World Health Organization
WPRO	WHO Western Pacific
YRBS	Youth Risk Behavior Survey
YRBSS	Youth Risk Behavior Surveillance System

List of Tables and Figures

Chapter 1
Introduction, Summary, and Conclusions

Chapter 2
The Health Consequences of Tobacco Use Among Young People

Chapter 3
The Epidemiology of Tobacco Use Among Young People in the United States and Worldwide

Chapter 3 Appendices
The Epidemiology of Tobacco Use Among Young People in the United States and Worldwide

Chapter 4
Social, Environmental, Cognitive, and Genetic Influences on the Use of Tobacco Among Youth

Chapter 5
The Tobacco Industry's Influences on the Use of Tobacco Among Youth

Chapter 6
Efforts to Prevent and Reduce Tobacco Use Among Young People

Chapter 7
A Vision for Ending the Tobacco Epidemic

Index

A

B

C

D

E

F

G

H

I

J

K

L

M

N

O

P

Q

R

S

T

U

V

W

Y